EUROPEAN DRAMA CRITICISM

1900–1975

Compiled by
HELEN H. PALMER

Second Edition

The Shoe String Press, Inc.

Dawson

1977

78-1177

© The Shoe String Press Inc 1977
First published 1977

Archon Books, The Shoe String Press Inc
995 Sherman Avenue, Hamden, Connecticut 06514 USA
Wm Dawson & Sons Ltd, Cannon House
Folkestone, Kent, England

Library of Congress Cataloging in Publication Data

Palmer, Helen H
    European drama criticism, 1900-1975.

    Includes indexes.
    1. Drama—History   and   criticism—Bibliography.   I.
Title.
Z5781.P2   1977   [PN1721]   016.809'2   77-171
Shoe String ISBN 0-208-01589-2
Dawson   ISBN 0 7129 0792 0

Printed in the United States of America

Dedicated to
Anne

CONTENTS

Preface   vii

Critical Writings   1

List of Books Indexed   577

List of Journals Indexed   611

Author/Title Index   629

PREFACE

The main purpose of *European Drama Criticism* is to provide a source book for a selection of critical writings about representative European plays. The playwrights included are those cited in drama histories as the outstanding playwrights of their respective countries and contemporary playwrights of international renown. This second edition is a comprehensive listing of criticisms which have appeared in books and periodicals, in English and foreign languages, from 1900 to 1975.

The original volume was published in 1968 and covered 1900 to 1966. Supplement I, published in 1970, updated the basic bibliography to 1970, and added interpretations from three additional journals. Supplement II included critical articles through 1972 and added a few new playwrights as well as critical material from earlier dates not included in the earlier volumes. The second edition includes in one volume and one alphabet all the materials previously published plus new materials through 1975.

Only articles directly concerned with the play as a whole, or with a large or important part of it, are included. References to a word, line, or one or two lines have been omitted, as have criticisms of Shakespeare's plays, which have been dealt with in a number of individual bibliographies. The quality of the articles was not considered; the primary criterion has been that critical material relating to a certain play could be located in a particular book or article.

The arrangement is alphabetical by playwright, with the plays alphabetized under the author's name and the sources in alphabetical order under the plays. There are cross references from foreign to English titles where the main entries could be found. (I used the *McGraw-Hill Encyclopedia of World Drama*, 1972, for translations of foreign titles and for the dates of play production.) Cross references are also included for pseudonyms and joint authors. Dates of first production are given where obtainable. An index lists plays and authors and gives dates for the authors where known. Also included are lists of books and of journals indexed.

In this type of book it is inevitable that errors will appear, but I have endeavored to be as accurate as possible. Both the author and the publisher will be grateful if omissions and such errors as appear are drawn to their attention so that corrections can be incorporated into future editions.

I thank Don D. Moore, English Department, Louisiana State University, for his interest and recommendations, my granddaughter, Anne Ward Thomas, for her valuable assistance, and my husband, Arthur M. Palmer, for his encouragement and patience.

Helen H. Palmer

KJELD ABELL

Anna Sophie Hedvig, 1939
  Madsen, Børge Gedsø, "Leading Motifs in the Dramas of Kjeld Abell",
    Scandinavian Studies (1961), 33:127-36
  Sprinchorn, Evert, ed., *The Genius of the Scandinavian Theater.* 1964. Pp.
    466-75

Dage Paa en Sky *SEE* Days on a Cloud

Days on a Cloud, 1947
  Madsen, Børge Gedsø, "Leading Motifs in the Dramas of Kjeld Abell",
    Scandinavian Studies (1961), 33:127-36
  Sprinchorn, Evert, ed., *The Genius of the Scandinavian Theater.* 1964. Pp.
    466-75

Den Blaa Pekingeser, 1954
  Madsen, Børge Gedsø, "Leading Motifs in the Dramas of Kjeld Abell",
    Scandinavian Studies (1961), 33:127-36

Eva Aftjener Sin Barncpligt *SEE* Eva Serves Her Time as a Child

Eva Serves Her Time as a Child, 1936
  Madsen, Børge Gedsø, "Leading Motifs in the Dramas of Kjeld Abell",
    Scandinavian Studies (1961), 33:127-36
  Sørensen, Per, "Kjeld Abell, Stage Cartoonist", *Theater Arts* (1940), 24:426-30
  Sprinchorn, Evert, ed., *The Genius of the Scandinavian Theater.* 1964. Pp.
    466-75

Judith, 1940
  Madsen, Børge Gedsø, "Leading Motifs in the Dramas of Kjeld Abell",
    Scandinavian Studies (1961), 33:127-36
  Sprinchorn, Evert, ed., *The Genius of the Scandinavian Theater.* 1964. Pp.
    466-75

Kameliadamen, 1959
  Madsen, Børge Gedsø, "Leading Motifs in the Dramas of Kjeld Abell",
    Scandinavian Studies (1961), 33:127-36

Melodien, Der Blev Vaek *SEE* The Melody That Got Lost

The Melody That Got Lost, 1935
  Madsen, Børge Gedsø, "Leading Motifs in the Dramas of Kjeld Abell",
    Scandinavian Studies (1961), 33:127-36
  Sørensen, Per, "Kjeld Abell, Stage Cartoonist", *Theater Arts* (1940), 24:426-30
  Sprinchorn, Evert, ed., *The Genius of the Scandinavian Theater.* 1964. Pp.
    466-75
  Theater Arts, 20:872-77, Nov. 1936

The Scream, 1961
  Sprinchorn, Evert, ed., *The Genius of the Scandinavian Theater.* 1964. Pp.
    466-75

Silkeborg, 1946
  Madsen, Børge Gedsø, "Leading Motifs in the Dramas of Kjeld Abell",
    Scandinavian Studies (1961), 33:127-36

Vetsera Blomster Ikke for Enhver, 1950
  Madsen, Børge Gedsø, "Leading Motifs in the Dramas of Kjeld Abell",
    Scandinavian Studies (1961), 33:127-36

ABRAHAM AND ISAAC

SEE

MIRACLE, MORALITY AND MYSTERY PLAYS

ARTHUR ADAMOV

All Against All, 1953
  Lynes, Carlos, Jr., "Adamov of 'Le Sens Litteral' in the Theatre", *Yale French
    Studies* (1954-55), #14:48-56
  France Illustration, #396:704, May 16, 1953

L'Aveu, n. d.
  Dort, Bernard, *Théâtre Réel, 1967-1970*, 1971. Pp. 190-99.
  Sherrell, Richard E., "Arthur Adamov and Invaded Man", *Modern Drama*
    (1964-65), 7:399-404

The Direction of the March, 1953
  Esslin, Martin, *The Theatre of the Absurd*. 1961. Pp. 59-60

La Grande et la Petite Manouvre   *SEE*   The Great and Small Maneuver

The Great and Small Maneuver, 1950
  Esslin, Martin, *The Theatre of the Absurd*. 1961. Pp. 57-59
  Lumley, Frederick, *New Trends in Twentieth Century Drama; A Survey since
    Ibsen and Shaw*. 1967. Pp. 216-18
  Lynes, Carlos, Jr., "Adamov or 'Le Sens Litteral' in the Theatre", *Yale French
    Studies* (1954-55), #14:48-56

L'Invasion, 1950
  Esslin, Martin, The Theatre of the Absurd. 1961. Pp. 55-57
  Lynes, Carlos, Jr., "Adamov of 'Le Sens Litteral' in the Theatre", *Yale French
    Studies* (1954-55), #14:48-56
  Serreau, Genevieve, *Histoire du "Nouveau Théâtre"*. 1966. Pp. 71-72
  Sherrell, Richard E., "Arthur Adamov and Invaded Man", *Modern Drama*
    (1964-65), 7:399-404
  Sherrell, Richard, *The Human Image; Avant-Garde and Christian*. 1969. Pp.
    115-23

Off Limits, 1968
  Dort, Bernard, *Théâtre Réel, 1967-1970*. 1971. Pp. 190-99
  Gaudy, Rene. "Ou Vont les Personnages d' 'Off Limits' ", *La Nouvelle Critique*,
    (1973), #66:27-32

Paolo Paoli, 1957
  Esslin, Martin, *The Theatre of the Absurd*. 1961. Pp. 69-72
  Lumley, Frederick, *New Trends in Twentieth Century Drama; A Survey since
    Ibsen and Shaw*. 1967. Pp. 216-18
  Serreau, Genevieve, *Histoire du "Nouveau Théâtre"*. 1966. Pp. 79-80

La Parodie, 1952
  Corvin, Michel, "Approche Semiologique d'un Texte Dramatique, 'La Parodie'
    d'Arthur Adamov",, *Litterature* (1973), 9:86-100
  Esslin, Martin, *The Theatre of the Absurd.* 1961. Pp. 52-55
  Lynes, Carlos, Jr., "Adamov of 'Le Sens Litteral' in the Theatre", *Yale French
    Studies* (1954-55), #14:48-56

Ping Pong, 1956
  Corvin, Michel, *Le Théâtre Nouveau en France.* 1963. Pp. 84-89
  Dort, Bernard, *Théâtre Réel, 1967-1970.* 1971. Pp. 190-99
  Esslin, Martin, *The Theatre of the Absurd.* 1961. Pp. 65-69
  Lumley, Frederick, *New Trends in Twentieth Century Drama; A Survey since
    Ibsen and Shaw.* 1967. Pp. 216-18
  Prince, Gerald, "Le Couple dans 'Le Ping Pong'", *Romance Notes* (1970),
    12:5-10
  Serreau, Genevieve, *Histoire du "Nouveau Théâtre".* 1966. Pp. 75-79

Le Printemps 71   *SEE*   Spring 71

Le Professeur Taranne, 1953
  Esslin, Martin, *The Theatre of the Absurd.* 1961. Pp. 61-64
  Lynes, Carlos, Jr., "Adamov of 'Le Sens Litteral' in the Theatre", *Yale French
    Studies* (1954-55), #14:48-56
  Sherrell, Richard, *The Human Image; Avant-Garde and Christian.* 1969. Pp.
    123-29

Le Sens de la Marche   *SEE*   The Direction of the March

Spring 71, 1963
  Corvin, Michel, *Le Théâtre Nouveau en France.* 1963. Pp. 84-89
  Serreau, Genevieve, *Histoire du "Nouveau Théâtre".* 1966. Pp. 80-82

Tous Contre Tous   *SEE*   All Against All

AESCHYLUS

Agamemnon, 458 B. C.
  Adrados, F. R., "El Tema del Leon en el 'Agamemnon' de Esquilo" *Emerita;
    Revista de Linguistica y Filologia Classica* (1965), 33:1-6
  Agar, T. L., "Aeschylus' 'Agamemnon'", *Classical Quarterly*, 18:163-64, July
    1924
  Beerbohm, Max, *Around Theatres.* 1953. Pp. 87-91
  Bennett, James O'Donnell, *Much Loved Books; Best Sellers of the Ages.* 1927.
    Pp. 160-66
  Bergson, L., "The Hymn to Zeus in Aeschylus' 'Agamemnon'", *Eranos* (1967),
    65:12-24
  Brower, Reuben Arthur, *Mirror on Mirror; Translation, Imitation, Parody.*
    (Harvard Studies in Comparative Literature, 33). 1974. Pp. 159-80
  Campbell, A. Z., "'Agamemnon'", *Classical Quarterly*, 29:25-36, 168-70, 1935
    _____ ,"Odd Points in the 'Agamemnon'", *Classical Review*, 51:
    116-18, Sept., 1937
    _____ , "Opening Period of the 'Agamemnon'", *Classical Review*,
    50:51-54, 1936
  Chapouthier, F., "Sur 'L'Agamemnon' d'Eschyle", *Mercure de France*, 306:
    521-24, July 1949

Counts, J. Wilma, "Cassandra: An Approach to Aeschylus' 'Agamemnon'",
   English Journal (1973), 62:33-36
Diggie, J., "Notes on the 'Agamemnon' and 'Persae' of Aeschylus", *Classical
   Review*, n. s. (1968), 18:1-4
Duchemin, J., "Le Deroulement du Temps et la Composition de 'L'Agamem-
   non' d'Eschyle", *L'Information Litteraire* (1967), 19:165-72
Edwards, W. M., "Eagles and the Hare; Aeschylus' 'Agamemnon'", *Classical
   Quarterly*, 33:204-07, July, 1939
Gassner, John, *Dramatic Soundings; Evaluations and Retractions Culled
   from Thirty Years of Dramatic Criticism.* 1968. Pp. 5-7, 12-13
Greene, W. C., "Dramatic and Ethical Motives in the 'Agamemnon'", *Har-
   vard Studies in Classical Philology* (1943), 54:25-34
Harsh, Philip Whaley, *A Handbook of Classical Drama.* 1944. Pp. 63-72
Kitto, Humphrey Davy, *Form and Meaning in Drama; A Study of Six Greek
   Plays and of "Hamlet".* 1956. Pp. 1-38
Lallot, I., "Xumbola Kranai: Reflexions sur la Fonction du Symbolon dans
   'L'Agamemnon' d'Eschyle", *Cahiers Internationaux de Symbolisme* (1974),
   26:39-48
Leahy, D. M., "Representation of the Trojan War in Aeschylus' 'Agamem-
   non'", *American Journal of Philology* (1974), 95:1-23
Lesky, Albin, *Greek Tragedy.* 1967. Pp. 72-79
Oliver, J. H., "On the 'Agamemnon' of Aeschylus", *American Journal of
   Philology*, 81:311-14, July, 1960
Olson, Elder, *Tragedy and the Theory of Drama.* 1966. Pp. 171-94
Pope, M., "Merciful Heavens? A Question in Aeschylus' 'Agamemnon'",
   Journal of Hellenic Studies (1974), 94:100-13
Radt, S. L., "Zu Aischylos' 'Agamemnon'", *Mnemosyne, Bibliotheca Classica
   Batava* (1973), 26:113-26
Reeves, C. H., "The Parados of the 'Agamemnon'", *Classical Journal*, 55:
   165-71, 1960
Sedgewick, G. G., *Of Irony, Especially in Drama.* 1967. Pp. 62-72 and 75-77
Simpson, Michael, "Why Does Agamemnon Yield?", *La Parola del Passato.
   Rivista di Studi Antichi* (1971), 137:94-101
Smethurst, Mae J., "The Authority of the Elders", *Classical Philology* (1972),
   67:89-93 and 68:202-03
Smith, Ole Langwitz, "Once Again: The Guilt of Agamemnon" *Eranos. Acta
   Philologia Svecana* (1973), 71:1-11
Studies in Theatre and Drama; Essays in Honor of Hubert C. Heffner, ed. by
   Oscar G. Brockett. 1972. p. 21-47
Young, D. C. C., "Gentler Medicines in the 'Agamemnon'", *Classical Quar-
   terly* (1964), 14:1-23

Choephoroe   *SEE*   The Libation Bearers

Eumenides, 458 BC
   Dover, K. J., "The Political Aspects of Aeschuylus' 'Eumenides'", *Journal
      of the Hellenic Society* (1957), 77:230-37
   Gassner, John, *Dramatic Soundings; Evaluations and Retractions Culled
      from Thirty Years of Dramatic Criticism.* 1968. Pp. 9-13
   Harsh, Philip Whaley, *A Handbook of Classical Drama.* 1944. Pp. 81-87
   Hamburger, Käte, *From Sophocles to Sartre; Figures from Greek Tragedy,
      Classical and Modern.* 1969. Pp. 27-29

Hirst, M. E., "'Eumenides' and the 'Oedipus Tyrannus'", *Classical Review*, 48:170, 1934

Kitto, Humphrey Davy, *Form and Meaning in Drama; A Study of Six Greek Plays and of "Hamlet"*. 1956. Pp. 54-86

Lesky, Albin, *Greek Tragedy*, 1967. Pp. 82-85

Robertson, D. S., "Delphian Succession in the opening of the 'Eumenides'", *Classical Review*, 55:69-70, Sept., 1941

Hepta Epi Thebas *SEE* Seven Against Thebes

The Libation Bearers, 458 BC

Baldry, H. C., *The Greek Tragic Theatre*. 1971. Pp. 111-17

Diggie, J., "Transposition in the Choephori", *Classical Review* (Dec. 1970), n. s. 20:267-69

Dodds, E. R., "Four Notes on the 'Choephori'", *Classical Quarterly*, 32:1-4, Jan., 1938

Hamburger, Käte, *From Sophocles to Sartre; Figures from Greek Tragedy, Classical and Modern*. 1969. Pp. 22-44 and 45-68

Harsh, Philip Whaley, *A Handbook of Classical Drama*. 1944. Pp. 73-80

Kitto, Humphrey Davy, *Form and Meaning in Drama; A Study of Six Greek Plays and of "Hamlet"*. 1956. Pp. 39-53

Lesky, Albin, *Greek Tragedy*. 1967. Pp. 79-82 and 169-71

Sedgewick, G. G., *Of Irony, Especially in Drama*. 1967. Pp. 69-77 and 80-83

Tierney, M., "Three Notes on the 'Choephori'", *Classical Quarterly*, 100-04, 1936

Whallon, W., "The Serpent at the Breast", *Transactions and Proceedings of the American Philological Association*, 89:271-75, 1958

Orestia, 458 B. C.

Abel, Lionel, *Metatheatre; A New View of Dramatic Form*. 1963. Pp. 74-76

Anderson, F. M. B., "Character of Clytemnestra in the 'Choephorae' and the 'Eumenides'", *American Journal of Philology*, 53:301-19, Oct., 1932

Anderson, Quentin and Mazzeo, Joseph Anthony, eds., *The Proper Study; Essays on Western Classics*. 1962. Pp. 51-77

Arrowsmith, W., "The Criticism of Greek Tragedy", *Tulane Drama Review* (1959), 3:31-56

Barthes, Roland, *Critical Essays*. 1972. Pp. 60-66

Bennett, A., "'Orestia'", *New Statesman*, 16:670-71, March 12, 1921

Burke, K., "Form and Persecution in the 'Oresteia'", *Sewanee Review*, 60: 377-96, July, 1952

Burke, Kenneth, *Language as Symbolic Action; Essays on Life, Literature and Method*. 1966. Pp. 125-38

Burnshaw, Stanley, ed., *Varieties of Literary Experience; Eighteen Essays in World Literature*. 1962. Pp. 259-82

Coheen, R. F., "Aspects of Dramatic Symbolism; Three Studies in 'Oresteia'", *American Journal of Philology*, 76:113-37, April, 1955

Conacher, D. J., "Interaction Between Chorus and Characters in the 'Orestia'", *American Journal of Philology* (1974), 95:323-43

Cornford, F. M., "Notes on 'Oresteia'", *Classical Review*, 53:162-65, Nov., 1939

Cunningham, M. P., "Didactic Purpose in the 'Orestia'", *Classical Philology* (1950), 45:183-85

Dodds, E. P., "Morals and Politics in the 'Orestia'", *Proceedings of the Cambridge Philological Society* (1960), 6:19:31

Downs, Robert Bingham, *Famous Books, Ancient and Medieval.* 1964. Pp. 43-48

Driver, Tom Faw, *Sense of History in Greek and Shakespearean Drama.* 1960. Pp. 116-42

Dyer, R. R., "The Iconography of the 'Orestia' after Aeschylus", *American Journal of Archeology* (1967), 71:175-76

Eckert, C. W., "The Festival Structure of the Orestes-Hamlet Tradition", *Comparative Literature*, 15:321-37, 1953

Estal, G. del. "La 'Orestiada' y su genio juridico", *La Ciuded de Dios*, 76:268-318, 1960

Finley, John Huston, *Pindar and Aeschylus*, (Martin Classical Lectures, Vol. 14), 1955. Pp. 246-82

Flugel, H., "Notizen zur 'Orestie' von Aischylos", *Radius Vierteljahresschrift der Engelischen Akademikerschaft in Duetschland* (1963), 61:5-17

Forbes, P. B. R., "Law and Politics in 'The Oresteia'", *Classical Review*, 62:99-104, 1948

Friedman, J. and S. Gassel, "Orestes", *Psychoanalytic Quarterly* (1951), 20:423-33

Gassner, John, *Dramatic Soundings; Evaluations and Retractions Culled from Thirty Years of Dramatic Criticism.* 1968. Pp. 3-20

Goheen, R. F., "Aspects of Dramatic Symbolism: Three Studies in the 'Orestia'", *American Journal of Philology* (1955), 76:113-37

Goody, Jack, ed., *The Character of Kinship.* 1974. Pp. 145-59

Hamburger, Kate, *From Sophocles to Sartre; Figures from Greek Tragedy, Classical and Modern.* 1969. Pp. 17-20, 22-44 and 45-68

Hammond, N. G. L., "Personal Freedom and Its Limitations in the 'Orestia'", *Journal of Hellenic Studies* (1965), 85:42-55

Hathorn, Richmond, *Tragedy, Myth and Mystery.* 1962, Pp. 38-61

Jepson, Laura, *Ethical Aspects of Tragedy; A Comparison of Certain Tragedies by Aeschylus, Sophocles, Euripides, Seneca, and Shakespeare.* 1953. Pp. 10-26

Jones, Henry John Franklin, *On Aristotle and Greek Tragedy.* 1962. Pp. 65-137

Kernodle, George R., *Invitation to the Theatre.* 1967. Pp. 167-69

Knox, B. M. W., "The Lion in the House", *Classical Philology* (1952), 47:17-25

Kott, Jan, *The Eating of the Gods; An Interpretation of Greek Tragedy.* 1973. Pp. 240-67

Levy, Harry L., "'The Oresteia' of Aeschylus", *Drama Survey*, 4:149-58, 1965

Lloyd-Jones, H., "The Guilt of Agamemnon", *Classical Quarterly*, 12:187-99, 1962

Musurillo, Herbert S. J., "Chasse et Sacrfice dans 'l'Orestie' d' Eschyle", *La Parola del Passato. Revista di Studi Antichi* (1969), Fasc. 129:401-25

Myths, Dreams and Religion, ed. by Joseph Campbell. 1970. Pp. 26-47

Nicol, Bernard de Bear, ed., *Varieties of Dramatic Experience.* 1969. Pp. 14-19

Novick, Julius, *Beyond Broadway; The Quest for Permanent Theatres.* 1968. Pp. 323-25

Pearson, Lionel Ignacius Cusack, *Popular Ethics in Ancient Greece.* 1962 Pp. 90-135

Peradotto, J. J., "Some Patterns of Nature Imagery in the 'Oresteia'", *American Journal of Philology*, 85:378-93, Oct., 1964

Porter, T. E. *Myth and Modern American Drama*. 1969. Pp. 26-52
Pour Alain, etc., "Chasse et Sacrifice dans 'l'Orestie' d'Eschyle". *La Parola del Passato, Rivista di Studi Antichi* (1969), Fasc. 129:401-25
Reiter, Seymour, *World Theater; The Structure and Meaning of Drama*. 1973. Pp. 138-45
Rexroth, Kenneth, "The Oresteia", *Saturday Review*, 48:21, Aug. 14, 1965
Robinson, D. M., "Illustrations of Aeschylus' 'Choephoroi' and of a Satyr-Play on Hydrias by the Niobid Painter", *American Journal of Archeology*, 36:401-07, Oct., 1932
Schlesinger, A. C., "Aeschylus' Persian Trilogy", *Classical Philology*, 20:274-76, July, 1925
Schroeder, O., "Zum Zeushymnus in der Parados des 'Agamemnon' ", *Philologus*, 87 #4:467-69, 1932
Scott, W. C., "Wind Imagery in the 'Orestia' ", *Transactions and Proceedings of the American Philological Association* (1966), 97:459-71
Seidlin, Oskar, "The 'Orestia' Today; A Myth Dehumanized", *Thought* (1959), 34:434-52
Solmsen, F., "Electra and Orestes; Three Recognitions in Greek Tragedy", *Medelingen de Koninklijke Nederlanse Akademie van Wetenschappen Afd. Letterkunde* (1967), 30:3-34
Stanford, W. B., *Ambiguity in Greek Literature*. 1939. Pp. 137-62
Thomson, G., "Notes on 'Orestia' ", *Classical Quarterly*, 28:72-78, 1934, and 30:105-15, 1936
Thomson, J. A. K., *Irony*. 1926. Pp. 39-53
Van Doren, Mark, ed., *New Invitation to Learning*. 1942. Pp. 16-29
Versenyi, Laszlo, *Man's Measure; A Study of the Greek Image of Man from Homer to Sophocles*. 1974. Pp. 208-51
von Fritz, K., "Die Danaidentrilogie des Aeschylus", *Philologus*, 91 #2:121-36, and #3:249-69, 1936
Wainwright, P. *The Burning Fountain*. 1954. Pp. 232-67
Whallon, William, "Maenadism in the 'Orestia' ", *Harvard Studies in Classical Philology*, 68:317-27, 1964
Whallon, W., "The Serpent at the Breast", *Transactions and Proceedings of the American Philological Association* (1958), 89:271-75
_____ ,"Why is Artemis Angry?", *American Journal of Philology*, 82:78-88, 1961
Winnington-Ingram, R. P., "Clytemnestra and the Vote of Athens", *Journal of the Hellenic Society* (1948), 68:130-47
Winnington-Ingram, R. P., "Role of Apollo in the 'Oresteia' ", *Classical Review*, 47:97-104, July, 1933
Zeitlin, F. I., "The Motif of the Corrupted Sacrifice in Aeschylus' 'Orestia' ", *Transactions and Proceedings of the American Philological Association* (1965), 96:463-508
Zeitlin, F. I., "Postscript to Sacrificial Imagery in the 'Orestia' ", *Transactions and Proceedings of the American Philological Association* (1966), 97:645:53

Persae *SEE* The Persians

The Persians, 472 BC
Alexanderson, B., "Darius in the 'Persians' ", *Eranos* (1967), 65:1-11
Anderson, Michael, "The Imagery of 'The Persians' ", *Greece and Rome* (1972), 19:166-74

Avery, H. C., "Dramatic Devices in Aeschylus' 'Persiana'", *American Journal of Philology*, 85:173-84, April, 1964

Campbell, A. Y., "Three Restorations in Aeschylus' 'Persae'", *Classical Review*, 49:50-53, 1935

Campbell, Lewis, "Morality in Aeschylus", *Hibbert Journal*, 2:83-97, 1903 *Classical Studies in Honor of W. A. Oldfather*. 1943. Pp. 83-93

Craig, J. D., "The Interpretation of Aeschylus' 'Persae'", *Classical Review* (1924), 38:98-101

Dale, A. M. "Metrical Observations on Aeschylus' 'Persae'", *Classical Quarterly*, 31:106-10, April, 1937

Diggie, J., "Notes on the 'Agamemnon' and 'Persae' of Aeschylus", *Classical Review* n. s. (1968), 18:1-4

Driver, Tom Faw, *Sense of History in Greek and Shakespearean Drama*. 1960. Pp. 87-115

Finley, John Huston, *Pindar and Aeschylus*, (Martin Classical Lectures, v. 14). 1955. Pp. 209-19

Flugel, H., "Tragik in der Geschichte; Eine Betrachtung über 'Die Persae' des Aeschylus", *Deutsche Rundschau*, 267:117-24, June, 1941

Goodall, Thomas Dwight, *Athenian Tragedy; A Study in Popular Art*. 1969. Pp. 141-45

Haldane, Joan A., "Barbaric Cries", *Classical Quarterly* (1972), 22:42-50

Harsh, Philip Whaley, *A Handbook of Classical Drama*. 1944. Pp. 45-48

Headlam, W., "Ghost-Raising, Magic and the Underworld", *Classical Review* (1902), 16:52-61

Holtsmark, Erling B., "Ring Composition and the 'Persae' of Aeschylus", *Symbolae Osloenses* (1970), 45:5-23

Ireland, S., "Dramatic Structure in 'The Persians' and 'Prometheus' of Aeschylus", *Greece and Rome* (1973), 20:162-68

Lattimore, Richmond Alexander, *Poetry of Greek Tragedy*. 1958. Pp. 28-55

Lawson, J. C., "Evocation of Darius", *Classical Quarterly*, 28:79-89, April 1934
_____ , "Notes on Aeschylus' 'Persae'", *Classical Review*, 48:4-8 and 55-59, 1934

Lawton, W. C. "'Persians' of Aeschylus", *Atlantic Monthly*, 70:228-48, Aug., 1892

Lesky, Albin, *Greek Tragedy*. 1967. Pp. 60-63

Nevinson, Henry Woodd, *Essays in Freedom and Rebellion*. 1921. Pp. 7-12

Pearson, Lionel Ignacius Cusack, *Popular Ethics in Ancient Greece*. 1962, Pp. 90-135

Reeves, Charles H., "Love in Aeschylus; The Earlier Plays", *Theatre Annual* (1968), 24:14-19

Sartori, Franco, "Echi Political Ne 'Il Persiani' di Eschilo", *Atti dell'Istituto Veneto di Scienze, Lettere, Arti, Classe di Scienze Morali e Lettere* (1970), 128:771-97

Verrall, A. W., *The "Bacchants" of Euripides and Other Essays*. 1910. Pp. 223-308

Prometheus Bound, 479 BC

Adams, S. M., "Four Elements in the 'Prometheus Vinctus'", *Classical Philology*, 28:97-103, April, 1933

Bacon, J. R., "Three Notes on Aeschylus' 'Prometheus Vinctus'", *Classical Review*, 42:115-20, Sept., 1928

Bailey, John Cann, *Continuity of Letters.* 1923. Pp. 103-38

Cairns, Huntington and Others, *Invitation to Learning.* 1941. Pp. 183-97

Campbell, Lewis, "Morality in Aeschylus", *Hibbert Journal*, 2:83-97, 1903

Downs, Robert Bingham, *Famous Books, Ancient and Medieval.* 1964. Pp. 43-48

Duysinx, F., "Les Passages Lyriques dans le 'Promethee Enchaine' d'Eschyle", *L'Antiquite Classique* (1965), Fasc. 1:47-83

Farnell, L. R., "The Paradox of the 'Prometheus Vinctus'", *Journal of the Hellenic Society* (1933), 53:40-50

Finley, John Huston, *Pindar and Aeschylus*, (Martin Classical Lectures, v. 14). 1955. Pp. 220-33

Fitton-Brown, A. D., "Prometheus", *Journal of the Hellenic Society* (1959), 79:52-60

Fowler, B. H., "Imagery of the 'Prometheus Bound'", *American Journal of Philology*, 78:173-84, April, 1957

Garzya, A., "Le Tragique du 'Promethee Enchainee' d'Eschyle", *Mnemosyne. Bibliotheca Classica Batava* (1965), 18:113-26

Gile, F. H., "Prometheus Bound and Unbound", *Arena*, 39:430-36, April, 1908

Golden, Leon, "Zeus the Protector and Zeus the Destroyer", *Classical Philology*, 57:20-26, 1962

Grene, D., "Prometheus Bound", *Classical Philology*, 35:22-38, Jan., 1940

Harsh, Philip Whaley, *A Handbook of Classical Drama.* 1944. Pp. 52-59

Havelock, Eric Alfred, *Liberal Temper in Greek Politics.* 1957. Pp. 52-86

Herington, C. J., "Introduction to 'Prometheus Bound'", *Arion* (1973-74), n. s. 1:640-67

———————, "A Study in Prometheia", *Phoenix* (1963) 17:180-97 and 236-43

———————, "Unique Technical Feature of the 'Prometheus Bound", *Classical Review*, n. s. 13:5-7, March, 1963

Ireland, S., "Dramatic Structure in 'The Persians' and 'Prometheus' of Aeschylus", *Greece and Rome* (1973), 20:162-68

Kott, Jan, *The Eating of the Gods; An Interpretation of Greek Tragedy.* 1973. Pp. 3-42

Lattimore, Richmond Alexander, *Poetry of Greek Tragedy.* 1958. Pp. 56-80

Lesky, Albin, *Greek Tragedy.* 1967. Pp. 86-89

Long, H. S., "Notes on Aeschylus's 'Prometheus Bound'", *Proceedings of the American Philosophical Society*, 102:229-80, 1958

Mullens, H. G., "'Hercules Furens' and 'Prometheus Vinctus'", *Classical Review*, 53:165, Nov., 1939

Musurillo, Herbert S. J., "Particles in the 'Prometheus Bound'", *Classical Philology* (1970), 65:175-77

Myres, J. L., "Wanderings of Io", *Classical Review*, 60:2-4, April 1946

Pearson, Lionel Ignacius Cusack, *Popular Ethics in Ancient Greece.* 1962. Pp. 90-135

Post, L. A., "Note on Prometheus", *American Journal of Philology*, 58:342-43, July, 1937

Robertson, J. M., "Aeschylus and the Messianic Idea; A Re-Reading of 'Prometheus Bound'", *London Quarterly and Holborn Review*, 168:33-41, Jan., 1943

Rosenmeyer, Thomas Gustav, *The Masks of Tragedy; Essays on Six Greek Dramas*, 1963. Pp. 49-102

Smyth, H. W., "Commentary on Aeschylus' 'Prometheus' in the Codex Neo-politanus", *Harvard Studies in Classical Philology*, 32:1-98, 1921

Thomson, A. K., "Religious Background of the 'Prometheus Vinctus'", *Harvard Studies in Classical Philology*, 31:1-37, 1920

Thomson, G., "Notes on 'Prometheus Vinctus'", *Classical Quarterly*, 23:155-63, July, 1929

Todd, O. J., "Character of Zeus in Aeschylus' 'Prometheus Bound'", *Classical Quarterly*, 19:61-67, April, 1925

Trousson, R., "l'Elément Dramatique dans le Prométhée Enchaîné'", *Revue des Etudes Greques* (Paris), #349-350:20-24, 1961

Weaver, B., "'Prometheus Bound' and 'Prometheus Unbound'", *Modern Language Association. Publications* (PMLA), 64:115-33, 1949

Whalley, George, "Coleridge on the 'Prometheus' of Aeschylus", *Proceedings and Transactions of the Royal Society of Canada* Ser. 3 (1957) 51:Sec. 2, 13-24

Will, F., "'Prometheus' and the Question of Self-Awareness in Greek Literature", *American Journal of Philology*, 83:72-85, Jan., 1962

Septem Contra Thebas　*SEE*　Seven Against Thebes

Seven Against Thebes, 467 BC

Bacon, H. H., "The Shield of Eteocles", *Arion* (1964), 3:27-38

Burnett, Anne, "Curse and Dream in Aeschylus' 'Septem'", *Greek, Roman and Byzantine Studies* (1973), 14:343-68

Campbell, Lewis, "Morality in Aeschylus", *Hibbert Journal*, 2:83-97, 1903

Dawe, R. D., "The End of 'Seven Against Thebes", *Classical Quarterly* (1967), 17:16-28

Finley, John Huston, *Pindar and Aeschylus*, (Martin Classical Lectures, v. 14). 1955. Pp. 234-45

Fraenkel, E., "Zum Schluss der 'Sieben Gegen Theben'", *Museum Helveticum* (1964), 21:58-64

Golden, L., "Character of Eteocles and the Meaning of the Septem", *Classical Philology*, 59:79-89, April 1964

Hamilton, Edith, *The Ever-Present Past*. 1964. Pp. 111-15

Harsh, Philip Whaley, *A Handbook of Classical Drama*. 1944. Pp. 49-51

Klotz, O., "Zu Aischylos Thebanischer Tetralogie", *Rheinisches Museum für Philologie* (1917-18), 72:616-25

Lattimore, Richmond Alexander, *Poetry of Greek Tragedy*. 1958. Pp. 28-55

Lesky, Albin, "Eteokles in den 'Sieben Gegen Theben'", *Studien, Wiener. Zeitschrift fur Klassische Philologie* (1961), 74:5-17

————————, *Greek Tragedy*. 1967. Pp. 63-66

Lloyd-Jones, H., "The End of 'Seven Against Thebes'", *Classical Quarterly* (1959), 9:80-115

McCulloh, W. E., "'Metaphysical Solace' in Greek Tragedy", *Classical Journal*, 59:109-15, 1963

Mosk, J., "Die Parodos der Sieben gegen Theben", *Philologus*, 89 #4:454-59, 1934

Otis, B., "The Unity of 'Seven Against Thebes'", *Greek, Roman and Byzantine Studies in Classical Philology* (1960), 3:153-74

Patzel, H., "Die Dramatische Handlung der 'Sieben Gegen Theben'", *Harvard Studies in Classical Philology* (1958), 63:97-119

Pearson, Lionel Ignacius Cusack, *Popular Ethics in Ancient Greece*. 1962. Pp. 90-135

Podlecki, A. J., "The Character of Eteocles in Aeschylus' 'Septem'", *Transactions and Proceedings of the American Philological Association* (1964), 95:283-99

Reeves, Charles H., "Love in Aeschylus; The Earlier Plays", *Theatre Annual* (1968), 24:14-19

Regenbogen, O., "Bemerkungen zu dem 'Sieben' des Aischylos", *Hermes* (1933), 68:51-69

Rosenmeyer, Thomas Gustav, *The Masks of Tragedy; Essays on Six Greek Dramas*. 1963. Pp. 5-48

Sheppard, J. T., "The Plot of the 'Septem Contra Thebas'", *Classical Quarterly* (1913), 7:73-82

Solmsen, F., "The Erinys in Aischylos' 'Septem'", *Transactions and Proceedings of the American Philological Association* (1937), 68:197-211

Wolff, E., "Die Entscheidung Eteokles in den 'Sieben Gegen Theban'", *Harvard Studies in Classical Philology* (1958), 63:89-95

The Suppliants, 463 B. C.

Campbell, Lewis, "Morality in Aeschylus", *Hibbert Journal*, 2:83-97, 1903

Diamantopoulos, A., "The Danaid Tetralogy of Aeschylus", *Journal of the Hellenic Society* (1957), 77:220-29

Finley, John Huston, *Pindar and Aeschylus*, (Martin Classical Lectures, v. 14). 1955. Pp. 195-208

Golden, Leon, "Zeus the Protector and Zeus the Destroyer", *Classical Philology*, 57:20-26, 1962

Harsh, Philip Whaley, *A Handbook of Classical Drama*. 1944. Pp. 42-44

Lattimore, Richmond Alexander, *Poetry of Greek Tragedy*. 1958. Pp. 11-27

Lembke, J., "Aeschylus' "Suppliants': Design in a Beholder's Eye", *Arion* (1973-74), n. s. 1:627-39

Lesky, Albin, *Greek Tragedy*. 1967. Pp. 58-60, 66-72

Livingstone, Richard, "Rights of the Weak, A Modern Problem in Ancient Dress; 'The Suppliants' of Aeschylus", *Hibbert Journal*, 39:65-73, 1940

Looy, Herman van, "Tragica I: Aeschyli 'Supplices' . . . Und Ein Ende?", *L'Antiquite Classique* (1969), 38:489-96

Macurdy, Grace Harriet, "Had the Danaid Trilogy a Social Problem?", *Classical Philology*, 39:95-100, April, 1944

Murray, Robert Duff, "The Motif of Io in Aeschylus's 'Suppliants'", *Classical Journal*, 54:137-40, 1958

Pearson, Lionel Ignacius Cusack, *Popular Ethics in Ancient Greece*. 1962. Pp. 90-135

Robertson, D. S., "The End of the 'Supplices' Triology of Aeschylus", *Classical Review* (1924), 38:51-53

Schottlaender, R., "Friedenhoffnung in Tragödie und Komödie", *Das Altertum, Im Auftrage der Sektion für Altertumswissenschaft. bei der Deutschen Akademie der Wissenschaften zu Berlin*, 8:195-204 1962

Von Fritz, K., "Die Danaiden Trilogie des Aeschylus", *Philologus* (1936) 91:12-36 and 249-69

Winnington-Ingram, R. P., "The Danaid-Trilogy of Aeschylus", *Journal of the Hellenic Society* (1961), 81:141-52

LEONID ANDREEV

SEE

LEONID NIKOLAEVICH ANDREYEV

LEONID NIKOLAEVICH ANDREYEV

Anathema, 1909
  Lewisohn, Ludwig, "Anathema", *Nation*, 116:500-01, April 25, 1923
  Netick, Anne S. R., "Expressionism in the Plays of Leonid Andreyev", *Dissertation Abstracts International* (1973), 33:4428A
  Thompson, O. R. H., "Andreyev's 'Anathema' and the Faust Legend", *North American Review*, 194:882-87, Dec., 1911

The Beautiful Sabine Women, 1912
  Firkins, O. W., "Sabine Women", *Review*, 2:441-42, April 24, 1920

The Black Maskers, 1908
  Netick, Anne S. T., "Expressionism in the Plays of Leonid Andreyev", *Dissertation Abstracts International* (1973), 33:4428A
  Woodward, James B., "The Theme and Structural Significance of Leonid Andreev's "The Black Masks", *Modern Drama* (1967), 10:95-103

Chyornye Maski *SEE* Black Maskers

He Who Gets Slapped, 1915
  Catholic World, 163:168, May, 1946
  Commonweal, 44:14, April 19, 1946
  Nathan, George Jean, *Theatre Book of the Year, 1945-46.* Pp. 336-38
  Nathanson, W., "He Who Gets Slapped", *Open Court*, 39:7-20, Jan., 1925
  Nation, 162:409, April 6, 1946
  Netick, Anne S. R., "Expressionism in the Plays of Leonid Andreyev" *Dissertation Abstracts International* (1973), 33:4428A
  New Republic, 114:479, April 8, 1946
  New Yorker, 22:42, March 30, 1946
  Newsweek, 27:84, April 1, 1946
  Parker, R. A., "He Who Gets Slapped", *Independent*, 108:90-92, Jan. 28, 1922
  Saturday Review, 39:30, March 24, 1956
  Saturday Review of Literature, 29:34, April 13, 1946
  Shipp, H., "He Who Gets Slapped", *English Review*, 45:728-30, Dec., 1927
  Theatre Arts, 30:252, 264-65, May, 1946
  Time, 47:76, April 1, 1946
  Young, Stark, *Flower in Drama and Glamour; Theatre Essays and Criticism,* Scribner, 1955, p. 64-70
  ————————— , "He Who Gets Slapped", *New Republic*, 29:283-84, Feb. 1, 1922
  Zilboorg, G., "He Who Gets Slapped", *Drama*, 11:191-92, March, 1921

K Zvezdam *SEE* To the Stars

Katerina, 1913
  Commonweal, 9:571, March 20, 1929
  Dial, 86:440-2, May, 1929

London Mercury, 14:78, May, 1926
New Statesman, 26:806, April 10, 1926
Outlook (London), 57:281, April 10, 1926
Saturday Review, 141:472-73, April 10, 1926
Spectator, 136:666-67, April 10, 1926

The Life of Man, 1906
Baring, M., "Russian Mystery Play: 'Life of Man'", *Living Age*, 258:786-92, Sept. 26, 1908
Lake, K., "The Life of Man", *New Republic*, 33:176-77, Jan. 10, 1923
Netick, Anne S. T., "Expressionism in the Plays of Leonid Andreyev", *Dissertation Abstracts International* (1973), 33:4428A
Woodward, James B., "Leonid Andreyev and 'Conventionalism' in the Russian Theatre", *Modern Language Review* (Apr. 1971), 66:365-78

The Ocean, 1911
Netick, Anne S. T., "Expressionism in the Plays of Leonid Andreyev", *Dissertation Abstracts International* (1973), 33:4428A

Okean   *SEE*   The Ocean

Prekrasnye Sabinyanki   *SEE*   The Beautiful Sabine Women

Samson in Chains, 1914
Netick, Anne S. T., "Expressionism in the Plays of Leonid Andreyev", *Dissertation Abstracts International* (1973), 33:4428A

Samson v Okovakh   *SEE*   Samson in Chains

Savva (Ignis Sanat)   *SEE*   Savva; or, Fire Cures

Savva; or, Fire Cures, 1906
Netick, Anne S. T., "Expressionism in the Plays of Leonid Andreyev", *Dissertation Abstracts International* (1973), 33:4428A

To the Stars, 1906
Netick, Anne S. T., "Expressionism in the Plays of Leonid Andreyev", *Dissertation Abstracts International* (1973), 33:4428A

Tot, Kto Poluchayet Roshchechiny *SEE* He Who Gets Slapped

Tsar Golod   *SEE*   Tsar Hunger

Tsar Hunger, 1907
Netick, Anne S. T., "Expressionism in the Plays of Leonid Andreyev", *Dissertation Abstracts International* (1973), 33:4428A
Woodward, James B., "Leonid Andreyev and 'Conventionalism' in the Russian Theatre", *Modern Language Review* (Apr. 1971), 66:365-78

Zhizn' Cheloveka   *SEE*   The Life of Man

JEAN ANOUILH

L'Alouette   *SEE*   The Lark

Antigone, 1944
Baxter, K. M., *Speak What We Feel: A Christian Looks at the Contemporary Theatre*. London. 1964. Pp. 40-44 and 49-52

Belli, Angela, *Ancient Greek Myths and Modern Drama; A Study in Continuity.* 1971. Pp. 97-111

Bishop, Thomas, "Anouilh's 'Antigone' in 1970", *American Society of Legion of Honor Magazine* (1970), 41:41-53

Burdick, Dolores M., "Antigone Grows Middle-Aged; Evolution of Anouilh's Hero", *Michigan Academician* (1974), 7:137-47

Calin, William, "Patterns of Imagery in Anouilh's 'Antigone' ", *French Review* (1967), 41:76-83

Cohn, Ruby, *Currents in Contemporary Drama.* 1969. Pp. 96-100

Dickinson, Hugh, *Myth on the Modern Stage.* 1969. Pp. 260-66

Firges, Jean, "As 'Antigone'; Ein Exempel der Pathologie oder der Metaphysik?", *Die Neueren Sprachen* (1973), 22:595-607

Freedman, Morris, *The Moral Impulse; Modern Drama From Ibsen to the Present.* 1967. Pp. 118-19

Glenisson, E., "Vision du Monde du Héros d'Anouilh dans 'Eurydice', 'Antigone', et 'La Sauvage' ", *Culture*, 12:263-75, 1961

Hamburger, Kate, *From Sophocles to Sartre; Figures from Greek Tragedy, Classical and Modern.* 1969. Pp. 147-66

Heiney, Donald, "Jean Anouilh: The Revival of Tragedy", *College English*, 16:331-35, 1955

Jausz, H. R., "Racines 'Andromaque' und Anouilhs 'Antigone' ", *Die Neueren Sprachen*, #9:428-44, 1960

Joseph, E., "The Two Antigones: Sophocles and Anouilh", *Thought*, 38:578-606, 1963

Kernodle, George R., *Invitation to the Theatre.* 1967. p. 305-09

Krüger, Manfred, "Private Existenz und Offentliche Meinung", *Zeitschrift für Französische Sprache und Literatur* (1967), 77:64-89

Lenski, B. A., *Jean Anouilh; Stages in Rebellion.* 1975. Pp. 35-46

Lumley, Frederick, *New Trends in Twentieth Century Drama; A Survey Since Ibsen and Shaw.* 1967. Pp. 170-81

Merigon, C., "Deux Antigone", *Europe* (1967), 45:130-32

Moore, Harry T., *Twentieth Century French Literature to World War II.* 1966. Vol. 1. Pp. 205-07

Nazareth, Peter, "Anouilh's 'Antigone'; An Interpretation", *English Studies in Africa* (1963), 6:51-69

Pronko, Leonard Cabell, *The World of Jean Anouilh.* 1961. Pp. 24-28 and 200-07

Saisselin, Remy G., "Is Tragic Drama Possible in the Twentieth Century?", *Theatre Annual* (1960), 17:12-21

Siepmann, E. O., "The New Pessimism in France", *Nineteenth Century*, 143:275-78, 1948

Spingler, Michael, "Anouilh's Little Antigone; Tragedy, Theatricalism, and the Romantic Self", *Comparative Drama* (1974), 8:228-38

Williams, Raymond, *Drama from Ibsen to Brecht.* 1968. Pp. 227-29

Ardele, 1948

Hewes, Henry, "The Tried and the Untried", *Saturday Review* (May 10, 1969), 52:40

Lumley, Frederick, *New Trends in Twentieth Century Drama; A Survey Since Ibsen and Shaw.* 1967. Pp. 170-81

Pronko, Leonard Cabell, *The World of Jean Anouilh*, 1961, Pp. 44-45

Le Bal des Voleurs *SEE* Thieves' Carnival

Becket; or, The Honor of God, 1958
Barjon, Louis, "Becket ou L'Honneur de Dieu", *Etudes*, 303:329-40, 1959
Bunjevac, Milan, "Notes Sur le Personnage de Becket dans 'Becket, ou L'Honneur de Dieu'", *Bulletin des Jeunes Romanistes* (1967), 14:42-47
Cancel, Rafael A., "Two Studies on Theatre", *Revista de Letras* (1972), 4:257-79
Clurman, Harold, *The Naked Image; Observations on the Modern Theatre.* 1966. Pp. 27-30
Cohn, Ruby, *Currents in Contemporary Drama.* 1969. Pp. 104-06
Dierickx, J., "King and Archbishop: Henry II and Becket from Tennyson to Fry", *Revue des Langues Vivantes* (1962), 28:424-35
Gassner, John, *Dramatic Soundings; Evaluations and Retractions Culled from Thirty Years of Dramatic Criticism.* 1968. Pp. 497-99
Gatlin, J. C., "Becket and Honor: A Trim Reckoning", *Modern Drama*, 8:277-83, Dec., 1965
Groh, Marianne, "Jean Anouilh: 'Becket ou L'Honneur de Dieu'", *Die Neueren Sprachen*, 13:187-92, 1964
Hudson Review, 13:588-90, Winter, 1960-61
Jolivet, Philippe, "Le Personnage de Thomas Becket dans 'Der Heilege' de C. F. Meyer, 'Murder in the Cathedral' de T. S. Eliot, et 'Becket ou l'Honneur de Dieu' de Jean Anouilh', *Etudes Germaniques*, 16:235-41, 1961
Lenski B. A., *Jean Anouilh; Stages in Rebellion.* 1975. Pp. 35-46
Maxfield, Malinda R., "A Comparative Analysis of T. S. Eliot's 'Murder in the Cathedral' and Jean Anouilh's 'Becket' in the Light of Medieval and Contemporary Religious Drama in England and France", *Dissertation Abstracts International* (1970), 30:4458A
Pronko, Leonard Cabell, *The World of Jean Anouilh.* 1961. Pp. 56-61
Reiter, Seymour, *World Theater; The Structure and Meaning of Drama.* 1973. Pp. 13-35
Roy, Emil, "The Becket Plays: Eliot, Fry and Anouilh", *Modern Drama*, 8: 268-76, 1965
Saturday Review, 43-22, Oct. 22, 1960 and 44:26, May 27, 1961
Sewanee Review, 69:339-41, Spring, 1961
Spectator, 207:92-3, July 21, 1961
Theatre Arts, 44:9-11, Dec., 1960
Time, 76:54, Oct. 17, 1960 and 77:78, April 7, 1961

Becket; ou, L'Honneur de Dieu *SEE* Becket; or, The Honor of God

Catch as Catch Can, 1962
Lenski, B. A., *Jean Anouilh; Stages in Rebellion.* 1975. Pp. 58-66

The Cavern, 1961
Lumley, Frederick, *New Trends in Twentieth Century Drama; A Survey Since Ibsen and Shaw.* 1967. Pp. 170-81

Cher Antoine *SEE* Dear Antoine

Colombe, 1951
Bentley, Eric Russell, *Dramatic Event; An American Chronicle.* 1954. Pp. 182-85

Gassner, John, *Theatre at the Crossroads; Plays and Playwrights of the Mid-century American Stage.* 1960. Pp. 245-47

Lumley, Frederick, *New Trends in Twentieth Century Drama; A Survey Since Ibsen and Shaw.* 1967. Pp. 170-81

Pickering, J. V., "Several Worlds of Anouilh's 'Colombe'", *Drama Survey* (1966-67), 5:267-75

Pronko, Leonard Cabell, *The World of Jean Anouilh.* 1961. Pp. 47-49

Scott-James, Paule, "The Theatre of Jean Anouilh", *Contemporary Review,* 179:302-08, 1951

Spectator, 187:852, Dec. 21, 1951

Dear Antoine, 1969
New Yorker (Nov. 29, 1969), 45:96
Time (Nov. 14, 1969), 94:57

Dinner With The Family, 1937
English, 12:59-60, Summer, 1958
Illustrated London News, 231:1142, Dec. 28, 1959
New Yorker, 37:114-15, March 11, 1961
Pronko, Leonard Cabell, *The World of Jean Anouilh.* 1961. 15-16, and 185-88
Theatre Arts, 45:56, May, 1961
Time, 77:45, March 17, 1961

Don't Awaken Madame, 1970
Clurman, Harold, *The Divine Pastime; Theatre Essays.* 1974. Pp. 293-95

The Ermine, 1931
Lumley, Frederick, *New Trends in Twentieth Century Drama; A Survey Since Ibsen and Shaw.* 1967. Pp. 170-81
Pronko, Leonard Cabell, *The World of Jean Anouilh.* 1961. Pp. 4-6
Stevens, L. C., "Hybris in Anouilh's 'L'Hermine' and 'La Sauvage'", *French Review,* 37:658-63, 1964

Eurydice, 1941
Dickinson, Hugh, *Myth on the Modern Stage.* 1969. Pp. 250-60
Free, Mary G., "On the Function of the Two Waiters in Anouilh's 'Eurydice'", *Notes on Contemporary Literature* (1972), 2,ii:13-15
Glénisson, E., "Vision du Monde du Héros d'Anouilh dans 'Eurydice', 'Antigone', et 'La Sauvage'", *Culture,* 12:263-75, 1961
Heiney, Donald, "Jean Anouilh: The Revival of Tragedy", *College English,* 16:331-35, 1955
Lasso de la Vega, José S., "Una Interpretación psicológica del mito de Orfeo: 'Eurydice' de Anouilh", *Cuadernos Hispanoamericanos* (1974), 284:267-312
Lumley, Frederick, *New Trends in Twentieth Century Drama; A Survey Since Ibsen and Shaw.* 1967. Pp. 170-81
Porter, David H., "Ancient Myth and Modern Play; A Significant Counterpoint", *Classical Bulletin* (Nov. 1971), 48:1-9
Pronko, Leonard Cabell, *The World of Jean Anouilh.* 1961. Pp. 22-24, 33-36 and 195-200
Scott-James, Paule, "The Theatre of Jean Anouilh", *Contemporary Review,* 179:302-08, 1951

Fighting Cock, 1959
America, 102:538, Jan. 30, 1960

Brustein, Robert Sanford, *Seasons of Discontent; Dramatic Opinions*, 1959-1965. Pp. 101-04

Clurman, Harold, *The Naked Image; Observations on the Modern Theatre*. 1966. Pp. 25-27

Hooker, Ward, "Irony and Absurdity in the Avant-Garde Theatre", *Kenyon Review*, 22:436-54, 1960

Lenski, B. A., *Jean Anouilh; Stages in Rebellion*. 1975. Pp. 58-66

Lumley, Frederick, *New Trends in Twentieth Century Drama; A Survey Since Ibsen and Shaw*. 1967. Pp. 170-81

Nation, 189:495-96, Dec. 26, 1959

New Republic, 142:20-21, Jan. 4, 1960

New Yorker, 35:79-81, Dec. 19, 1929

Newsweek, 54:83, Dec. 21, 1959

Pronko, Leonard Cabell, *The World of Jean Anouilh*. 1961. Pp. 53-56

Saturday Review, 42:29-30, June 20, 1959 and 42:24, Dec. 26, 1959

Time, 74:34, Dec. 21, 1959

La Foire d'Empoigne *SEE* Catch as Catch Can

La Grotte *SEE* The Cavern

L'Hurluberlu *SEE* The Fighting Cock

L'Invitation au Chateau *SEE* Ring Round the Moon

Jezabel, 1932
Pronko, Leonard Cabell, *The World of Jean Anouilh*. 1961. Pp. 6-9

The Lark, 1953
America, 90:420-21, Jan. 23, 1954

Cohn, Ruby, *Currents in Contemporary Drama*. 1969. Pp. 110-12

Gassner, John, *Theatre at the Crossroads; Plays and Playwrights of the Mid-century American Stage*. 1960. Pp. 247-49

Groh, M., "Jean Anouilh: 'Jeanne ou l'Alouette'", *Die Neueren Sprachen*, #1:33-9, 1963

Hunter, F. J., "The Value of Time in Modern Drama", *Journal of Aesthetics and Art Criticism*, 16:194-201, 1957

Illustrated London News, 226:982, May 28, 1955

Jamois, Marguerite, "Images de l'Alouette", *Cahiers de la Compagnie Madeleine Reynaud-Jean Louis Barrault*, #26:29-30, 1959

Langemann, Ingeborg, "Die Darstellung der Jeanne d'Arc in Anouilh's 'L'Alouette'", *Die Neueren Sprachen* (1969), 18:157-65

Lenski, B. A., *Jean Anouilh; Stages in Rebellion*. 1975. Pp. 35-46

Linke, Hansjurgen, "Dramaturgie des Wunders in Jean Anouilhs Schauspiel 'L'Alouette'", *Zeitschrift für Französische Sprache und Literatur*, Pp. 46-80, 129-49, 1959

Lumley, Frederick, *New Trends in Twentieth Century Drama; A Survey Since Ibsen and Shaw*. 1967. Pp. 170-81

Moore, Harry T., *Twentieth Century French Literature to World War II*. 1966. Vol. 2, Pp. 17-22

Pronko, Leonard Cabell, *The World of Jean Anouilh*. 1961. Pp. 37-40

Rattunde, E., "Die Bedeutung des Titelsymbols in Jean Anouilhs Drama 'L'Alouette'", *Zeitschrift für Französische Sprache und Literatur* (1971), 81:243-66

Legend of Lovers   *SEE*   Eurydice

Leocadia   *SEE*   Time Remembered

Medee, 1946
Hamburger, Käte, *From Sophocles to Sartre; Figures from Greek Tragedy, Classical and Modern.* 1969. Pp. 123-34
Heiney, Donald, "Jean Anouilh: The Revival of Tragedy", *College English,* 16:331-35, 1955
Lapp, J. C., "Anouilh's 'Medee': A Debt to Seneca", *Modern Language Notes,* 69:183-87, March, 1954
Lyons, Charles R., "The Ambiguity of the Anouilh 'Medea' ", *French Review,* 37:312-19, 1964
Pronko, Leonard Cabell, *The World of Jean Anouilh.* 1961. Pp. 30-33 and 207-210
Scott-James, Paule, "The Theatre of Jean Anouilh", *Contemporary Review,* 179:302-08, 1951

Ne Réveillez pas Madame   *SEE*   Don't Awaken Madam

Ornifle, ou le Courant d'Air   *SEE*   Ornifle, or The Draft

Ornifle, or The Draft, 1955
Abirached, Robert, "Chronique du Théâtre: 'Ornifle' de Jean Anouilh", *Etudes,* 288:434-38, 1956
_____ ," 'Ornifle' de Jean Anouilh", *Etudes,* 291:114-6, 1956
Pronko, Leonard Cabell, *The World of Jean Anouilh.* 1961. Pp. 52-53

Pauvre Bitos, ou Le Diner des Têtes   *SEE*   Poor Bitos

Poor Bitos, or The Masked Dinner, 1956
Brustein, Robert, *The Third Theatre.* 1969. Pp. 91-95
Clurman, Harold, *The Naked Image; Observations on the Modern Theatre.* 1966. Pp. 33-36
Lenski, B. A., *Jean Anouilh; Stages in Rebellion.* 1975. Pp. 47-57
Lumley, Frederick, *New Trends in Twentieth Century Drama; A Survey Since Ibsen and Shaw.* 1967. Pp. 170-81
Novick, Julius, *Beyond Broadway; The Quest for Permanent Theatres.* 1968. Pp. 59-61
Pronko, Leonard Cabell, *The World of Jean Anouilh.* 1961. Pp. 52-53
Randot, Pierre, "Anouilh et les règlements de comptes", *Etudes,* 292:29-53, 1957
Rischbieter, H., "Anouilhs 'Der Arme Bitos' in Wien und Berlin", *Theater Heute* (1962), 3:5-11
Saturday Review, 47:43, Dec. 5, 1964, and 49:55, March 5, 1966
Time, 84:104, Nov. 27, 1964
Tynan, Kenneth, *Curtains; Selections from the Drama Criticism and Related Writings.* 1961. Pp. 395-96

The Rehearsal, 1950
Bentley, Eric Russell, *Dramatic Event; An American Chronicle,* Horizon, 1954, p. 66-69
Commonweal, 79-194, Nov. 8, 1963
Hudson Review, 16:583, Winter, 1963-64
Nation, 197:245, Oct. 19, 1963

National Review, 15:406-07, Nov. 5, 1963
New Republic, 127:23, Dec. 22, 1952
New Statesman, 61:599, April 14, 1961
New Yorker, 39:133-34, Oct. 5, 1963
Newsweek, 62:96, Oct. 7, 1963
Pronko, Leonard Cabell, *The World of Jean Anouilh*. 1961. Pp. 45-47
Saturday Review, 35:26, Dec. 13, 1952, 46:30, Oct. 12, 1963
Seilacher, H., "Bühnenwirklichkeit und Lebensauffassung bei Jean Anouilh",
    Die Neueren Sprachen, #12:572-9, 1960
Steinberg, R. and H. H. Mowshowitz, "'La Répétition' par Jean Anouilh:
    Une Nouvelle Lecture", *Etudes Francaises* (1973), 9:115-28
Theatre Arts, 47:10-11, Dec., 1963
Time, 82:63, Oct. 4, 1963

Le Rendezvous de Senlis   *SEE*   Dinner with the Family

The Restless Heart, 1934
    Les Annales Politiques et Littéraires, 111:71-72, Jan. 25, 1938
    Glénisson, E., "Vision du Monde du Héros d'Anouilh dan 'Eurydice', 'An-
        tigone', et 'La Sauvage'", *Culture*, 12:263-75, 1961
    L'Illustration, 199:94, Jan. 22, 1938
    Lumley, Frederick, *New Trends in Twentieth Century Drama; A Survey Since
        Ibsen and Shaw*. 1967. Pp. 170-81
    Pronko, Leonard Cabell, *The World of Jean Anouilh*. 1961. Pp. 9-11
    Revue Politique et Littéraire, 76:73-4, Feb., 1938
    Reynaud, Jean-Pierre, "Jean Anouilh: 'La Sauvage'", *Le Francais dans le
        Monde* (1968), 56:36-40
    Scott-James, Paule, "The Theatre of Jean Anouilh", *Contemporary Review*,
        179:302-08, 1951
    Spectator, 198:652, May 17, 1957
    Stevens, L. C., "Hybris in Anouilh's 'L'Hermine and La Sauvage'", *French
        Review*, 37:658-63, 1964

Ring Round the Moon, 1947

    Catholic World, 172:307, Jan., 1951
    Christian Science Monitor Magazine, Pp. 13, Dec. 2, 1950
    Commonweal, 53:253, Dec. 5, 1950
    Moore, Harry T., *Twentieth Century French Literature to World War II*.
        1966. Vol. 2, Pp. 17-22
    Nathan, George Jean, *Theatre Book of the Year, 1950-51*. Pp. 126-29
    Nation, 171:514, Dec. 2, 1950
    New Republic, 122:21, June 5, 1950 and 123:22, Dec. 25, 1950
    New Yorker, 26:78-79, Dec. 2, 1950
    Newsweek, 36:74, Dec. 4, 1950
    Pronko, Leonard Cabell, *The World of Jean Anouilh*. 1961. Pp. 41-44
    Saturday Review of Literature, 33:25-26, Dec. 16, 1950
    Theatre Arts, 32:30, Feb., 1948 and 34:29, Dec., 1950 and 35:12, Feb., 1951
    Time, 56:64, Dec. 4, 1950
    Valency, Maurice, "The World of Jean Anouilh", *Theatre Arts*, 41:31-32,
        92-93, 1957

Romeo et Jeanette, 1947
    New Statesman and Nation, 38:271, Sept. 10, 1949

Pronko, Leonard Cabell, *The World of Jean Anouilh*. 1961. Pp. 28-30
Theatre Arts, 31:44, May, 1947 and 34:40-41, Nov., 1950

La Sauvage   *SEE*   Restless Heart

Thieves' Carnival, 1932
  Catholic World, 181:148-49, May, 1955
  Commonweal, 62:183, May 20, 1955
  New Republic, 132:28-29, Feb. 21, 1955
  New Yorker, 31:77-78, Feb. 19, 1955
  Pronko, Leonard Cabell, *The World of Jean Anouilh*. 1961. Pp. 14-15
  Saturday Review, 38:38, Dec. 3, 1955
  Theatre Arts, 40:18-19, Jan., 1956
  Valency, Maurice, "The World of Jean Anouilh", *Theatre Arts*, 41:31-32,
    92-93, 1957

Time Remembered, 1939
  America, 98:355, Dec. 14, 1957
  Catholic World, 186:304, Jan., 1958
  Christian Century, 74:1448, Dec. 4, 1957
  Dance Magazine, 32:9, Feb., 1958
  English, 10:185, Summer, 1955
  L'Illustration, 207:401, Dec. 14, 1940
  Life, 43:73-74, Dec. 9, 1957
  Nation, 185:415-16, Nov. 30, 1957
  New York Times Magazine, Pp. 71, Oct. 27, 1957
  New Yorker, 32:77, Nov. 23, 1957
  Newsweek, 50:84, Nov. 25, 1957
  Pronko, Leonard Cabell, *The World of Jean Anouilh*. 1961. Pp. 16
  Reporter, 17:35, Dec. 12, 1957
  Saturday Review, 40:23, Nov. 30, 1957
  Spectator, 193:754, Dec. 10, 1954
  Theatre Arts, 41:71-72, Oct., 1957 and 42:19, Jan., 1958
  Time, 70:91, Nov. 25, 1957

Traveller Without Luggage, 1936
  Clurman, Harold, *The Naked Image; Observations on the Modern Theatre*.
    1966. Pp. 31-33
  Commonweal, 81:73, Oct. 9, 1964
  Illustrated London News, 234:274, Feb. 14, 1959
  Nation, 199:202, Oct. 5, 1964
  Newsweek, 64:90-91, Sept. 28, 1964
  Pronko, Leonard Cabell, *The World of Jean Anouilh*. 1961. Pp. 12-14
  Saturday Review, 47:28, Oct. 3, 1964
  Spectator, 202:224, Feb. 13, 1959
  Time, 84:96, Sept. 25, 1964
  Vogue, 144:66, Nov. 1, 1964
  Valency, Maurice, "The World of Jean Anouilh", *Theatre Arts*, 41:31-32,
    92-93, 1957

La Valse des Toreadors   *SEE*   The Waltz of the Toreadors

Le Voyageur Sans Bagage   *SEE*   The Traveller Without Luggage

Waltz of the Toreadors, 1951
  America, 96:656, March 9, 1957
  Catholic World, 184:469, March, 1957 and 187:146, May, 1958
  Christian Century, 74:201, Feb. 13, 1957
  English, 11:57, Summer, 1956
  Gassner, John, *Dramatic Soundings; Evaluations and Retractions Culled from Thirty Years of Dramatic Criticism*. 1968. Pp. 294-96
  Gassner, John, *Theatre at the Crossroads; Plays and Playwrights of the Mid-century American Stage*. 1960. Pp. 249-52
  Lambert, J. W., "Waltz of the Toreadors", *Plays and Players* (1974) 21:43-44
  Lumley, Frederick, *New Trends in Twentieth Century Drama; A Survey Since Ibsen and Shaw*. 1967. Pp. 170-81
  Mannes, Marya, "Three London Plays: Satire, Sex, and a Song", *Reporter*, 15:38, Nov. 1, 1956
  Nation, 186:261, March 22, 1958, (10-8-73), 217:349
  New Republic, 136:21, Feb. 11, 1957
  New Statesman and Nation, 47:128, Jan. 30, 1954
  New York Times Magazine, p. 58, Jan. 6, 1957
  New Yorker, 32:68, Jan. 26, 1957, (10-1-73), 49:59
  Newsweek, 49:84, Jan. 28, 1957, (9-24-73), 82:127
  Pronko, Leonard Cabell, *The World of Jean Anouilh*. 1961. Pp. 49-52
  Reporter, 15:38, Nov. 1, 1956
  Saturday Review, 39:30, Oct. 13, 1956 and 40:24, Feb. 2, 1957
  Spectator, 196:314, March 9, 1956
  Theatre Arts, 41:21, 79-80, March, 1957
  Time, 69:50, Jan. 28, 1957, (9-24-73), 102:91
  Valency, Maurice, "The World of Jean Anouilh", *Theatre Arts*, 41:31-32, 92-93, 1957

SOLOMON ANSKY (pseud.)

SEE

SOLOMON RAPPOPORT

ALEKSEL NIKOLAEVICH ARBUSOV

The Irkutsk Story, 1963
  Clurman, Harold, *The Naked Image; Observations on the Modern Theater*. 1966. Pp. 215-19

Irkutskaya Istodiya   *SEE*   The Irkutsk Story

Moi Bednyi Narat   *SEE*   The Promise

Promise, 1967
  Commonweal, 87:358-59, Dec. 15, 1967
  Nation, 205:605-06, Dec. 4, 1967
  New Yorker, 43:149, Nov. 25, 1967
  Newsweek, 70:105, Nov. 27, 1967
  Saturday Review, 50:24, Dec. 2, 1967
  Vogue, 151:62, Jan. 1, 1968

WILLIAM ARCHER

Green Goddess, 1921
  Armstrong, M., "Green Goddess", *Spectator*, 131:354, Sept. 15, 1923
  Arns, K., "Green Goddess: Kritik", *English Studies*, 59:63-65, 1925
  Broun, H., "Green Goddess", *Collier's*, 67:14, Feb. 19, 1921
  Firkins, O. W., "Green Goddess", *Review*, 4:112, Feb. 2, 1921
  Lewisohn, Ludwig, "Green Goddess", *Nation*, 112: 250, Feb. 9, 1921
  _____ , *Drama and the Stage*, Harcourt, 1922, Pp. 179-83
  New Statesman, 21:644-46, Sept. 15, 1923
  Outlook, 127:330-31, March 2, 1921
  Shipp, H., "Green Goddess", *English Review*, 37:528-31, Oct., 1923

JOHN ARDEN

Armstrong's Last Goodnight, 1964
  Bonfond, François, "Falstaffian Characters in Two Plays by John Arden", *Revue des Langues Vivantes* (1972), 38:164-74
  Gilman, Richard, *Common and Uncommon Masks; Writings on the Theatre, 1961-70.* 1971. Pp. 173-76
  Kennedy, Andrew K., *Six Dramatists in Search of a Language.* 1975. Pp. 220-28
  Mack, Karin E., "Freedom and Order: A Stylistic and Thematic Study of the Drama of John Arden", *Dissertation Abstracts International* (1973), 34: 2638A
  New Statesman, 67:782-83, May 15, 1964
  New Yorker, 41:102-03, Aug. 14, 1965

The Happy Haven, 1960
  Epstein, Arthur D., "John Arden's Fun House", *University Review* (1970), 36:243-51
  Mack, Karin E., "Freedom and Order; A Stylistic and Thematic Study of the Drama of John Arden", *Dissertation Abstracts International* (1973), 34: 2638A
  Novick, Julius, *Beyond Broadway; the Quest for Permanent Theatres.* 1968. Pp. 172-74
  New Statesman, 59:554, Apr. 16, 1960
  New Statesman, 60:430, Sept. 24, 1960

Harold Muggins Is a Martyr, 1968
  Trussler, Simon, "Political Progress of a Paralyzed Liberal; The Community Dramas of John Arden", *TDR: The Drama Review* (Summer 1969), 13: 181-91

The Hero Rises Up, 1969
  Brown, John Russell, *Theatre Language; A Study of Arden, Osborne, Pinter and Wesker.* 1972. Pp. 190-234
  Trussler, Simon, "Political Progress of a Paralyzed Liberal; The Community Dramas of John Arden", *TDR: The Drama Review* (Summer 1969), 13: 181-91

Island of the Mighty, 1973
  New Republic (Jan. 6, 1973), 168:25

Left-Handed Liberty, 1965
  Mack, Karin E., "Freedom and Order; A Stylistic and Thematic Study of the
    Drama of John Arden", *Dissertation Abstracts International* (1973), 34:
    2638A
  Saturday Review, 51:45, Feb. 3, 1968

Live Like Pigs, 1958
  Mack, Karin E., "Freedom and Order; A Stylistic and Thematic Study of the
    Drama of John Arden", *Dissertation Abstracts International* (1973), 34:
    2638A

Serjeant Musgrave's Dance, 1959
  Adler, Thomas P., "Religious Ritual in John Arden's 'Sergeant Musgrave's
    Dance' ", *Modern Drama* (1973), 16:163-66
  Brown, John Russell, ed., *Modern British Dramatists; A Collection of Critical
    Essays.* 1968. Pp. 38-46
  Brown, John Russell, *Theatre Language; A Study of Arden, Osborne, Pinter
    and Wesker.* 1972. Pp. 190-234
  Clayton, Philip T., "The Drama of John Arden as Communal Ritual", *Dis-
    sertation Abstracts International* (1974), 34:5162A
  Clinton, Craig D., "John Arden: A Playwright's Evolution", *Dissertation
    Abstracts International* (1973), 34:2065A
  Dort, Bernard, *Théâtre Réel, 1967-1970.* 1971. Pp. 207-11
  Gassner, John, *Dramatic Soundings; Evaluations and Retractions Culled
    from Thirty Years of Dramatic Criticism.* 1968. Pp. 617-19
  Gilman, Richard, *Common and Uncommon Masks; Writings on the Theatre,
    1961-70.* 1971. Pp. 124-26 and 130-32
  Hoke, M. A., "John Arden's 'Serjeant Musgrave's Dance': A Highly Relevant
    Play for Young People", *English Journal* (May 1970), 59:633-37
  Jordan, R. J., "Serjeant Musgrave's Problem", *Modern Drama* (May 1970),
    13:54-62
  Kennedy, Andrew K., *Six Dramatists in Search of a Language.* 1975. Pp.
    220-28
  McMillan, Grant E., "The Bargee in 'Sergeant Musgrave's Dance' ", *Educa-
    tional Theatre Journal* (1973), 25:500-03
  Mack, Karin E., "Freedom and Order; A Stylistic and Thematic Study of the
    Drama of John Arden", *Dissertation Abstracts International* (1973),
    34:2638A
  Matthews, Honor, *The Primal Curse; The Myth of Cain and Abel in the
    Theatre.* 1967. Pp. 190-93
  Messenger, Ann P., "John Arden's Essential Vision; Tragical-Historical-
    Political", *Quarterly Journal of Speech* (1972), 58:307-12
  Mills, John, "Love and Anarchy in 'Serjeant's Musgrave's Dance' ", *Drama
    Survey* (Winter 1968-69), 7:45-51
  O'Connell, M. B., "Ritual Elements in John Arden's 'Serjeant Musgrave's
    Dance' ", *Modern Drama* (Feb. 1971), 13:356-59
  Page, Malcolm, "The Motives of Pacifists: John Arden's 'Sergeant Musgrave's
    Dance' ", *Drama Survey* (1967), 6:66-73
  Page, Malcolm, "Some Sources of Arden's 'Sergeant Musgrave's Dance' ",
    Melanges de Science Religieuse (1973), 67:332-41
  Roy, Emil, *British Drama Since Shaw.* 1972. Pp. 109-10
  Williams, Raymond, *Drama from Ibsen to Brecht.* 1968. Pp. 325-28

Squire Jonathan, 1968
  Page, Malcolm and Virginia Evans, "Approaches to John Arden's 'Squire
  Johnathan'", *Modern Drama* (Feb. 1971), 13:360-65

The Waters of Babylon, 1957
  Brown, John Russell, Ed., *Modern British Dramatists; A Collection of Critical
  Essays*. 1968. Pp. 83-97
  Mack, Karin E., "Freedom and Order; A Stylistic and Thematic Study of the
  Drama Of John Arden", *Dissertation Abstracts International* (1973), 34:
  2638A

The Workhouse Donkey, 1963
  Bonfond, François, "Falstaffian Characters in Two Plays by John Arden",
  Revue des Langues Vivantes (1972), 38:164-74
  Brown, John Russell, *Theatre Language; A Study of Arden, Osborne, Pinter
  and Wesker*. 1972. Pp. 190-234
  Clayton, Philip T., "The Drama of John Arden as Communal Ritual", *Dis-
  sertation Abstracts International* (1974), 34:5162A
  Mack, Karin E., "Freedom and Order; A Stylistic and Thematic Study of the
  Drama of John Arden", *Dissertation Abstracts International* (1973), 34:
  2638A

JOHN ARDEN AND MARGARETTA D'ARCY

The Ballygombeen Bequest, 1972
  Brustein, Robert Sanford, *The Culture Watch; Essays on Theatre and Society,
  1969-1974*. 1975. Pp. 53-56

The Island of the Mighty, 1973
  Brustein, Robert Sanford, *The Culture Watch; Essays on Theatre and Society,
  1969-1974*. 1975. Pp. 74-79
  Clayton, Philip T., "The Drama of John Arden as Communal Ritual", *Dissertation Abstracts International* (1974), 34:5162A

ARISTOPHANES

Acharnians, 426 B. C.
  Harsh, Philip Whaley, *A Handbook of Classical Drama*. 1944. Pp. 270-73
  Miller, Harold W., "Comic Iteration in Aristophanes", *American Journal of
  Philology*, 66:398-408, 1945
  Sifakis, G. M. *Parabasis and Animal Choruses*. 1971. Pp. 26-29

Batrachoi   *SEE*   The Frogs

The Birds, 414 B. C.
  Allen, H. W., "The Real Cyrano, Chantecler, and 'The Birds'", *Cornhill
  Magazine*, 101:832-45, June, 1910
  Arrowsmith, W., "Aristophanes's 'Birds'; The Fantasy Politics of Eros",
  Arion (1973), n. s. 1:119-67
  Blake, W. E., "The Aristophanic Bird Chorus—a Riddle", *American Journal
  of Philology*, 64:87-91, 1943
  Bonner, Campbell, "Ornithiaka", *Classical Philology*, 20:210-15, 1925
  Borthwick, E. K., "Two Notes on the 'Birds' of Aristophanes", *Classical Re-
  view* (1967), 17:248-50

Downs, Herbert Bingham, *Famous Books, Ancient and Medieval*. 1964. Pp. 76-81

Harsh, Philip Whaley, *A Handbook of Classical Drama*. 1944. Pp. 288-91

Higham, T. F., "Two Notes on Aristophanes' 'Birds' ", *Classical Quarterly*, 26:103-15, 1932

Jackson, C. N., "Decree-seller in the 'Birds' and the Professional Politicians at Athens", *Harvard Studies in Classical Philology*, 30:89-102, 1919

McCollom, William G., *The Diving Average; A View of Comedy*. 1971. Pp. 125-38

Miller, Harold W., "Comic Iteration in Aristophanes", *American Journal of Philology*, 66:398-408, 1945

Pollard, J. R. T., " 'Birds' of Aristophanes—A Source Book for Old Beliefs", *American Journal of Philology*, 69:353-76, 1948

Quiggin, E. C., ed., *Essays and Studies Presented to William Ridgeway on His Sixtieth Birthday, August 6, 1913*. 1913. Pp. 213-21

Robertson, D. S., "Three Passages of 'The Birds' ", *Classical Review*, 55:67-69, 1941

Rose, H. J., "Aristophanes' 'Birds' ", *Classical Review*, 54:79, 1940

Rosenmeyer, T. G., "Notes on Aristophanes' 'Birds' ", *American Journal of Philology* (Jan. 1972), 93:169-89

Schlesinger, Alfred C., "Identification of Parodies in Aristophanes", *American Journal of Philology*, 58:294-305, 1937

Schreiber, F., "Double-Barreled Joke: Aristophanes' 'Birds' ", *American Journal of Philology* (1974), 95:95-99

Thompson, D. W., "Aristophanes' 'Birds' ", *Classical Review*, 54:188, 1940

VanHook, LaRue, "Crime and Criminals in the Plays of Aristophanes", *Classical Journal*, 23:275-85, 1927-28

Wycherley, R. E., "Birds", *Classical Quarterly*, 31:22-31, 1937

The Clouds, 423 B. C.

Bolling, G. M., "Two Recensions of 'The Clouds' ", *Classical Philology*, 15: 83-85, 1920

Borthwick, E. K., "Aristophanes' 'Clouds' ", *Classical Review* (Dec. 1971), n. s. 21:318-20

" 'Clouds' of Aristophanes", *Living Age*, 244:752-54, March 25, 1905

Downs, Robert Bingham, *Famous Books, Ancient and Medieval*. 1964. Pp. 76-81

Dracoulides, N. N., "Aristophanes' 'The Clouds' and 'The Wasps' ", *American Imago* (Spr. 1966), 23:48-62

Dracoulides, N. N., "Origine de la Psychoanalyse et du Psychodrame dans les 'Nuées' et les Guêpes d'Aristophanes", *Histoire des Sciences Médicales* (1967), 2-3:101-12

Harsh, Philip Whaley, *A Handbook of Classical Drama*. 1944, Pp. 278-81

Havelock, E. A., "The Socratic Self as It Is Parodied in Aristophanes' 'Clouds' ", *Yale Classical Studies* (1972), 22:1-18

Lewis, D. M., "Aristophanes' Clouds' ", *Classical Review* (Dec. 1970), n. s. 20:288-89

Méautis, G., "La Scène de l'Initiation Dans les 'Nuées' d'Aristophane", *Revue de l'Histoire des Religions*, 118:92-97, 1938

Sifakis, G. M., *Parabasis and Animal Choruses*. 1971. Pp. 100-02

VanHook, LaRue, "Crime and Criminals in the Plays of Aristophanes", *Classical Journal*, 23:275-85, 1927-28

Ecclesiazusae; or, The Women in Council, 392 B. C.
   Greek Poetry and Life; Essays Presented to Gilbert Murray on His 70th Birthday, January 2, 1936. 1936. Pp. 257-76
   Harsh, Philip Whaley, *A Handbook of Classical Drama.* 1944. Pp. 307-08
   Miller, Harold W., "Comic Iteration in Aristophanes", *American Journal of Philology*, 66:398-408, 1945
   Pecirka, J., "Aristophanes 'Ekklesiazusen und die Utopien in der Krise der Polis", *Zeitschrift, Wissenschaftliche, der Humboldt-Universitat, Berlin* (1963), 12:215-20
   VanHook, LaRue, "Crime and Criminals in the Plays of Aristophanes", *Classical Journal*, 23:275-85, 1927-28

The Frogs, 405 B. C.
   Beerbohm, Max, *Around Theatres.* 1953. Pp. 538-40
   Campbell, A. Y., "Aristophanes' 'Frogs'", *Classical Review*, n. s. 3:137-38, 1953
   Dearden, C. W., "What Happened to the Donkey? Aristophanes' 'Frogs'", *Mnemosyne. Bibliotheca Classica Batava* (1970), 23:17-22
   Demand, Nancy, "The Identity of the 'Frogs'", *Classical Philology* (1970), 65:83-88
   Denniston, J. D., "Technical Terms in 'The Frogs' of Aristophanes", *Classical Quarterly*, 21:113-21, 1927
   Downs, Robert Bingham, *Famous Books, Ancient and Medieval.* 1964. Pp. 76-81
   Harsh, Philip Whaley, *A Handbook of Classical Drama.* 1944. Pp. 299-306
   MacDowell, Douglas M., "The Frog's Chorus", *Classical Review* (1972), n. s. 22:3-5
   Redfield, James, "Die 'Frosche' des Aristophanes. Komodie und Tragodie als Spiegel der Politik", *Antaios* (1963), 4:422-39
   Sifakis, G. M., *Parabasis and Animal Choruses.* 1971. Pp. 94-96
   Sommerstein, A. H., "Aristophanes's 'Frogs'", *Classical Quarterly* (1974), 24:24-27
   VanHook, LaRue, "Crime and Criminals in the Plays of Aristophanes", *Classical Journal*, 23:275-85, 1927-28
   Wycherley, R. E., "Aristophanes' 'Frogs'", *Classical Review*, 59:34-38, 1945

Hippes   *SEE*   The Knights

The Knights, 424 B. C.
   Harsh, Philip Whaley, *A Handbook of Classical Drama.* 1944. Pp. 274-77
   Littlefield, D. J., "Metaphor and Myth; the Unity of Aristophanes's 'Knights'", *Studies in Philology* (1968), 65:1-22
   Sifakis, G. M., *Parabasis and Animal Choruses.* 1971. Pp. 56-58

Lysistrata, 411 B. C.
   Bookman, 72:298, Nov., 1930
   Commonweal, 12:225-26, June 25, 1930
   Downs, Robert Bingham, *Famous Books, Ancient and Medieval.* 1964. Pp. 76-81
   Elderkin, G. W., "Aphrodite and Athena in the 'Lysistrata' of Aristophanes", *Classical Philology*, 35:387-96, 1940
   Harsh, Philip Whaley, *A Handbook of Classical Drama.* 1944. Pp. 292-94

Miller, Harold W., "Comic Iteration in Aristophanes", *American Journal of Philology*, 66:398-408, 1945
Nathan, George Jean, *Theatre Book of the Year, 1946-47.* Pp. 125-28
Radt, S. L., "Zu Aristophanes 'Lysistrate'", *Mnemosyne* (1974), 27, fasc. 1:7-16
Schlesinger, Alfred C., "Identification of Parodies in Aristophanes", *American Journal of Philology*, 58:294-305, 1937
Theatre Arts, 14:891-92, Oct., 1930 and 30:697, Dec., 1946
Vaio, John, "The Manipulation of Theme and Action in Aristophanes' 'Lysistrata'", *Greek, Roman and Byzantine Studies* (1973), 14:369-80
VanHook, LaRue, "Crime and Criminals in the Plays of Aristophanes", *Classical Journal*, 23:275-85, 1927-28
Wilson, Edmund, *American Earthquake: A Documentary of the Twenties and Thirties*, 1958, Pp. 116-20
Young, Stark, *Immortal Shadows: A Book of Dramatic Criticism.* 1948. Pp. 123-26

Nephelai   *SEE*   The Clouds

Ornithes   *SEE*   The Birds

Peace, 421 B. C.
Borthwick, E. K., "Beetle, Bell, Goldfinch and Weasel in Aristophanes's 'Peace'", *Classical Review* (1968), 18:134-39
Harsh, Philip Whaley, *A Handbook of Classical Drama.* 1944. Pp. 286-87

Pluto, 388 B. C.
Albihi, U., "La Struttura del 'Pluto' di Aristofane", *La Parola del Passato. Rivista di Studi Antichi* (1965), #105:427-42
Harsh, Philip Whaley, *A Handbook of Classical Drama.* 1944. Pp. 309-12

Spekes   *SEE*   The Wasps

Thesmophoriazusae, 412 B. C.
Harsh, Philip Whaley, *A Handbook of Classical Drama.* 1944. Pg. 295-98
Miller, H. W. "On the Parabasis of the 'Thesmophoriazusae'", *Classical Philology*, 42:180-81, 1947
Schlesinger, Alfred C., "Identification of Parodies in Aristophanes", *American Journal of Philology*, 58:294-305, 1937
VanHook, LaRue, "Crime and Criminals in the Plays of Aristophanes", *Classical Journal*, 23:275-85, 1927-28

The Wasps, 424 B. C.
Crosby, H. L., "Unappreciated Joke in Aristophanes", *Classical Philology*, 10:326 30, 1915
Dracoulides, N. N., "Aristophanes' 'The Clouds' and 'Wasps'", *American Imago* (Spr. 1966), 23:48-62
Harsh, Philip Whaley, *A Handbook of Classical Drama.* 1944. Pp. 282-85
Long, T. "Two Questions of Attribution in Aristophanes's 'Vespae'", *American Journal of Philology* (1972), 93:462-67
Post, L. A., "Catana the Cheese-Grater in Aristophanes' 'Wasps'", *American Journal of Philology*, 53:265, 1932
Sifakis, G. M., *Parabasis and Animal Choruses.* 1971. Pp. 97-99

VanHook, LaRue, "Crime and Criminals in the Plays of Aristophanes", *Classical Journal*, 23:275-85, 1927-28

Wilson, N. G., "Aristophanes's 'Wasps' ", *Classical Review* (1972), n. s. 22:313

WYSTAN HUGH AUDEN

For the Time Being, 1944

Driver, Tom F., "Auden's View of History in 'For the Time Being' ", *Journal of Bible and Religion* (Jan. 1963), 31:3-8

Morse, Donald E., "Meaning of Time in Auden's 'For the Time Being' ", *Renascence* (1970), 22:162-68

Morse, Donald E., "Two Major Revisions in W. H. Auden's 'For the Time Being' ", *English Language Notes* (1970), 7:294-97

WYSTEN HUGH AUDEN AND CHRISTOPHER ISHERWOOD

Ascent of F6, 1937

Bruehl, William J., " 'Polus Naufrangia': A Key Symbol in 'The Ascent of F6' ", *Modern Drama* (Sept. 1967), 10:161-64

Donoghue, Denis, *Third Voice; Modern British and American Verse Drama.* 1959. Pp. 62-75

Forster, Edward Morgan, *Two Cheers for Democracy.* 1951. Pp. 263-65

Forum, 97:355, June, 1937

Hazard, Forrest E., " 'The Ascent of F6': A New Interpretation", *Tennessee Studies in Liberature* (1970), 15:165-75

London Mercury, 35:619, April, 1937

New Republic, 141:16-17, Nov. 23, 1959

New Statesman and Nation, 13:368, March 6, 1937 and 18:13, July 1, 1939

Oppel, Horst, *Das Moderne Englische Drama: Interpretationen.* 1963. Pp. 203-219

Saturday Review of Literature, 16:20, May 8, 1937

Scholastic (High School Teacher's Edition), 31:23E, Jan. 15, 1938

Scribner's Magazine, 102:66, Sept. 1937

Spectator, 158:403, March 5, 1937

Stebner, Gerhard, "W. H. Auden: The Ascent of F6, Interpretation eines Drames", *Die Neueren Sprachen*, Pp. 397-413, 1961

Theatre Arts, 21:355-56, May, 1937

Wilde, Alan, *Christopher Isherwood.* 1971. Pp. 78-83

Williams, Raymond, *Drama from Ibsen to Brecht.* 1968. Pp. 199-205

Wilson, Edmund, *Shares of Light; A Literary Chronicle of the Twenties and Thirties.* 1952. Pp. 669-73

Cabaret, 1966

Blades, Joe, "The Evolution of 'Cabaret' ", *Literature/Film Quarterly* (1973), 1:226-38

Dog Beneath the Skin; or, Where is Francis?, 1935

London Mercury, 33:529, March, 1936

New Republic, 141:16-17, Nov. 23, 1959

Saturday Review of Literature, 13:16, Nov. 30, 1935

Spectator, 156:211, Feb. 7, 1936

Wilde, Alan, *Christopher Isherwood.* 1971. Pp. 78-83

Williams, Raymond, *Drama from Ibsen to Brecht.* 1968. Pp. 199-206

On the Frontier, 1938
  New Statesman and Nation, 16:826-27, Nov. 19, 1938
  Spectator, 161:858, Nov. 18, 1938
  Theatre Arts, 23:20, Jan., 1939
  Wilde, Alan, *Christopher Isherwood*. 1971. Pp. 78-83
  Williams, Raymond, *Drama from Ibsen to Brecht*. 1968. Pp. 199-206

ENID BAGNOLD

The Chalk Garden, 1955
  America, 94:195, Nov. 12, 1955
  Catholic World, 182:227, Dec., 1955
  Clay, James H. and Daniel Krempel, *The Theatrical Image*. 1967. Pp. 56-57
  Collier's, 137:6, March 2, 1956
  Commonweal, 63:616, March 16, 1956
  Holiday, 19:85, May, 1956
  Illustrated London News, 228:420, April 28, 1956
  Life, 39:164-66, Dec. 5, 1955
  Nation, 181:426-27, Nov. 12, 1955 and 182:477-78, June 2, 1956
  New Republic, 134:21, March 26, 1956
  New Statesman, 51:414, April 21, 1956
  New Yorker, 31:77, Nov. 5, 1955
  Saturday Review, 38:24, Nov. 12, 1955
  Spectator, 196:547, April 20, 1956
  Theatre Arts, 40:16, Jan., 1956 and 40:66-67, Feb., 1956, and 41:25, May, 1957
  Time, 66:96, Nov. 7, 1955
  Tynan, Kenneth, *Curtains; Selections from the Drama Criticism and Related Writings*. 1961. Pp. 127-28
  Weales, Gerald, "The Madrigal in the Garden", *Tulane Drama Review* (1958), 3:43-50

The Chinese Prime Minister, 1964
  America, 110:148, Jan. 25, 1964
  Hudson Review, 17:86-87, 1964
  Nation, 198:80, Jan. 20, 1964
  New Republic, 150:28, Feb. 1, 1964
  New Yorker, 39:69, Jan. 11, 1964
  Newsweek, 63:70, Jan. 13, 1964
  Saturday Review, 47:22, Jan. 18, 1964
  Time, 83:52, Jan. 10, 1964

Gertie, 1952
  Commonweal, 55:470, Feb. 15, 1952
  Nathan, George Jean, *Theatre in the Fifties*. 1953. Pp. 148-50
  New Yorker, 27:56, Feb. 9, 1952
  Newsweek, 39:82, Feb. 11, 1952
  Theatre Arts, 36:71, April, 1952
  Time, 59:79, Feb. 11, 1952

Last Joke, 1960
  Illustrated London News, 237:666, Oct. 15, 1960
  New Statesman, 60:520, Oct. 8, 1960
  Spectator, 205:521, Oct. 7, 1960

Lottie Dundass, 1943
   New Statesman and Nation, 26:71, July 31, 1943
   Spectator, 171:106, July 30, 1943

A Matter of Gravity, 1976
   Newsweek, (2-16-76), 87:77
   New Yorker (2-16-76), 51:52
   Time (2-16-76), 107:65

Poor Judas, 1951
   New Statesman and Nation, 42:96, July 28, 1951

JAMES M. BARRIE

Admirable Crichton, 1902
   Beaty, John Owen, and others, eds., *Facts and Ideas for Students of English
      Composition*. 1930. Pp. 200-205
   Beerbohm, Max, *Around Theatres*. 1953. Pp. 231-34
   Catholic World, 133:210, May, 1931
   Commonweal, 13:581, March 25, 1931
   Drama, 21:10, April, 1931
   Lamacchia, Grace A., "Textual Variations for Act IV of 'The Admirable
      Crichton' ", *Modern Drama* (1970), 12:408-18
   Literary Digest, 108:17, March 28, 1931
   Nation, 132:336, March 25, 1931
   Theatre Arts, 15:373-74, May, 1931
   Walkley, Arthur Bingham, *Drama and Life*. 1908. Pp. 198-208

Alice Sit by the Fire, 1905
   Bookman, 33:135-37, April, 1911
   Catholic World, 135:77, April, 1932
   Commonweal, 15:579, March 23, 1932
   New Republic, 70:153-54, March 23, 1932
   New Statesman, 22:480, Feb. 2, 1924
   Outlook (London), 53:76, Feb. 2, 1924
   Saturday Review, 137:103, Feb. 2, 1924
   Theatre Arts, 16:353-54, May, 1932

Barbara's Wedding, 1931
   New Republic, 68:300, Oct. 28, 1931

Boy David, 1937
   London Mercury, 35:315-16, Jan., 1937
   New Statesman and Nation, 12:1028, Dec. 19, 1936
   Spectator, 157:1081, Dec. 18, 1936
   Theatre Arts, 21:4, Jan., 1937 and 21:193, March, 1937

Dear Brutus, 1917
   Bellman, 26:12-15, Jan. 4, 1919
   Current Opinion, 66:91-94, Feb., 1919
   Fortnightly, 118:342-45, Aug., 1922
   Forum, 61:243-44, Feb., 1919
   Mais, Stuart Petre Brodie, *Some Modern Aurhors*, 1923. Pp. 252-63
   Nation, 108:30, Jan. 4, 1919

New Republic, 17:285-86, Jan. 4, 1919
New Statesman, 10:86-87, Oct. 27, 1917
New Statesman and Nation, 21:109, Feb. 1, 1941
Spectator, 166:87, Jan. 24, 1941

Kiss for Cinderella, 1916
Bellman, 22:44-46, Jan. 13, 1917
Catholic World, 155:216, May, 1942
Commonweal, 35:561, March 27, 1942
Hackett, Francis, *Horizons; A Book of Cricicism*. 1918. Pp. 208-12
Nation, 102:523-24, May 11, 1916 and 154:348-49, March 21, 1942
New Republic, 9:269, Jan. 6, 1917 and 106:398, March 23, 1942
New Yorker, 18:29, March 21, 1942
Newsweek, 19:59, March 23, 1942
North American Review, 205:296-99, Feb., 1917
Theatre Arts, 26:289-90, May, 1942
Time, 39:46, March 23, 1942
Young, Stark, *Immortal Shadows; A Book of Criticism*. 1948. Pp. 227-29

Mary Rose, 1920
Baring, Maurice, *Punch and Judy and Other Essays*. 1924. Pp. 349-54
Catholic World, 173:148-49, May, 1951
Commonweal, 53:589, March 23, 1951
Current Opinion, 69:63-65, July, 1920
Fortnightly, 113:955-59, June, 1920
Lewisohn, Ludwig, *Drama and the Stage*. 1922. Pp. 174-78
Living Age, 305:492-94, May 22, 1920
Nathan, George Jean, *Theatre Book of the Year, 1950-51*. Pp. 237-40
Nation, 112:48, Jan. 12, 1921
New Statesman, 15:104-05, May 1, 1920 and 33:212, May 25, 1929
New Yorker, 27:54, March 17, 1951
Outlook, 127:11-12, Jan. 5, 1921
Review, 4:18-19, Jan. 5, 1921
School and Society, 73:185, March 24, 1951
Spectator, 124:759-60, June 5, 1920
Theatre Arts, 35:17, May, 1951
Touchstone, 8:335, Feb., 1921

Peter Pan, 1904
Beerbohm, Max, *Around Theatres*. 1953. Pp. 357-61
Catholic World, 171:226-27, June, 1950
Christian Science Monitor Magazine, Pp. 4, April 29, 1950
Commonweal, 52:127-28, May 12, 1950
Illustrated London News, 225:1173, Dec. 25, 1954
Life, 28:89-90, May 22, 1950
Literary Digest, 84:26-27, Jan. 17, 1925
Musical America, 70:4, May, 1950
Nathan, George Jean, *Theatre Book of the Year, 1949-50*. Pp. 270-73
New Republic, 122:20, May 8, 1950
New Yorker, 26:50, May 6, 1950
Newsweek, 35:80, May 8, 1950
Outlook, 139:51-52, Jan. 14, 1925

Saturday Review of Literature, 33:24-26, May 13, 1950
Stevenson, Lionel, "A Source for Barrie's 'Peter Pan'", *Philological Quarterly*, 8:210-14, 1929
Theatre Arts, 34:14, July, 1950
Time, 55:49, May 8, 1950
Walkley, Arthur Bingham, *Drama and Life*. 1908. Pp. 209-13

Quality Street, 1902
Beerbohn, Max, *Around Theatres*. 1953. Pp. 220-23
Nathan, George Jean, *Theatre Book of the Year, 1950-51*. Pp. 84-86
Nation (London), 29:775-76, Aug. 27, 1921
Spectator, 127:269, Aug. 27, 1921
Walkley, Arthur Bingham, *Drama and Life*. 1908. Pp. 194-97

Rosalind, 1915
Harper's Weekly, 61:302, Sept. 23, 1915
New Republic, 4:185, Sept. 18, 1915

Rosy Rapture, 1915
Nation, 100:423, April 15, 1915

Shall We Join The Ladies, 1922
Ward, Alfred Charles, ed., *Specimens of English Dramatic Criticism, 17th - 20th Centuries*. 1945. Pp. 290-93

What Every Woman Knows, 1908
America, 92:406, Jan. 15, 1955
Catholic World, 164:260, Dec., 1946 and 180:389, Feb., 1955
Commonweal, 45:144, Nov. 22, 1946
Nathan, George Jean, *Theatre Book of the Year, 1946-47*. Pp. 290-93
Nation, 163:593, Nov. 23, 1946 and 180:37, Jan. 8, 1955
New Republic, 115:723, Dec. 2, 1946
New Statesman, 21:268-69, June 9, 1923
New Yorker, 22:59, Nov. 16, 1946 and 30:44, Jan. 1, 1955, (6-16-75), 51:50
Newsweek, 28:97, Nov. 18, 1946 and 45:43, Jan. 3, 1955
O'Connor, G., "What Every Woman Knows", *Plays and Players* (Feb. 1975), 22:24-25
Saturday Review, 38:25, Jan. 8, 1955
Spectator, 101:444-45, Sept. 26, 1908
Theatre Arts, 30:692, Dec., 1946 and 31:23, Jan., 1947 and 39:91, March, 1955
Time, 65:35, Jan. 3, 1955

VICKI BAUM

Grand Hotel, 1930
Bookman, 72:515-16, Jan., 1931
Catholic World, 132:460-61, Jan., 1931
Commonweal, 13:497, March 4, 1931
Drama, 21:12, Jan., 1931
L'Europe Nouvelle, 15:13, Jan. 2, 1932
Journal des Débats, 39 pt. 1:84-85, Jan. 15, 1932
Literary Digest, 107:19, Dec. 13, 1930
Mercure de France, 234:130-34, Feb. 15, 1932
New Republic, 65:72, Dec. 3, 1930

New Statesman and Nation, 2:308-09, Sept. 12, 1931
Saturday Review, 152:325, Sept. 12, 1931
Spectator, 147:320, Sept. 12, 1931
Theatre Magazine, 53:24, 28-29, Jan., 1931
Theatre Arts, 15:896-98, Nov., 1931

VICKI BAUM AND BENJAMIN F. GLAZER

Summer Night, 1939
Commonweal, 31:96, Nov. 17, 1939
Newsweek, 14:32, Nov. 13, 1939

PIERRE AUGUSTIN CARON BEAUMARCHAIS

Barber Of Seville, 1775
Arnold, E. J., " 'Le Barbier de Seville', et la critique", *French Studies*, 16:334-347, 1962
Besterman, Theodore, ed., *Studies on Voltaire and the 18th Century. Transactions of the 2nd International Congress on the Enlightment.* 1967. Pp. 1081-91
Canadian Forum, 12:238-39, March, 1932
Cox, Cynthia, *The Real Figaro; The Extraordinary Career of Caron de Beaumarchais.* 1962. Pp. 42-43, 62-63, 84-88
Pomeau, René, " 'Le Barbier de Seville': De l'Intermède à la comédie", *Revue d'Histoire Littéraire de la France* (1974), #6:963-76
Pugh, Anthony R., "Beaumarchais, the Drame Bourgeois and the Piece Bien Faite", *Modern Language Review* (1966), 61:416-21

Le Barbier de Seville *SEE* "The Barber of Seville"

Eugenie, 1767
Morton, B. N., "Beaumarchais's First Play, 'Eugenie' ", *Romanic Review* (1966), 57:81-87

The Guilty Mother, 1791
Cox, Cynthia, *The Real Figaro; The Extraordinary Career of Caron de Beaumarchais.* 1962. Pp. 173-77

Le Mariage de Figaro *SEE* "Marriage Of Figaro"

Marriage of Figaro, 1784
Les Annales Politiques et Littéraires, 113:242-43, March 10, 1939
Cox, Cynthia, *The Real Figaro; The Extraordinary Career of Caron de Beaumarchais.* 1962. Pp. 135-46, 196
Department de Francis Recherches et Travaux. Supp. au Bull. D'Information du Service de Documentation. (Oct.-Dec. 1968), 19-20:36-38
Hampton, John, "Research on 'Le Mariage de Figaro' ", *French Studies*, 16:24-32, 1962
Howarth, W. D., "The Recognition Scene in 'Le Mariage de Figaro' ", *Modern Language Review* (1969), 64:301-11
Landry, Rémy, "Le 'Mariage' et les 'Noces': Notes Pour Figaro", *L'Information Littéraire* (1974), 26:76-79
MacCary, W. T., "The Significance of a Comic Pattern in Plautus and Beaumarchais", *Modern Language Notes* (1973), 88:1262-87

Missions et Démarches de la Critique: Mélanges Offerts au Professeur J. A. Vier. 1973. Pp. 529-35

Musso, Noël, "Le Vocabulaire de Figaro dans 'Le Mariage' ", *Etudes de Linguistique Appliquée* (1972), n. s. 6:89-98

Nurse, Peter H., ed., *The Art of Criticism; Essays in French Literary Analysis.* 1969. Pp. 155-67

Pugh, Anthony R., "Beaumarchais, the Drame Bourgeois and the Piece Bien Faite", *Modern Language Review* (1966), 61:416-21

Ubersfeld, Annie, "Un Balcon Sur la Terreur: 'Le Mariage de Figaro' ", *Europe* (1973), 528:105-15

Rex, Walter E., "Figaro's Games", *Modern Language Association. Publication* (1974), 89:524-29

La Mère Coupable *SEE* The Guilty Mother

FRANCIS BEAUMONT AND JOHN FLETCHER

Barnavelt, 1620
Schelling, Felix E., *Elizabethan Drama: 1558-1642.* 1959. vol. l, Pp. 440-41

The Beggar's Bush, 1640
Briggs, W. D., "First Song in 'The Beggar's Bush' ", *Modern Language Notes*, 39:379-80, 1924

Bonduca, 1647
Maxwell, Baldwin, "The Hungry Knave in the Beaumont and Fletcher Plays", *Philological Quarterly*, 5:299-305, 1926
Waith, Eugene M., *Ideas of Greatness; Heroic Drama in England.* 1971. Pp. 153-55

The Chances, 1620
MacCarthy, D., "Chances", *New Statesman*, 18:502, Feb. 4, 1922

Coxcomb, 1647
Gossett, Suzanne, "Term 'Masque' in Shakespeare and Fletcher and 'The Coxcomb' ", *Studies in English Literature, 1500-1900* (1974), 14:285-95
Shaw, George Bernard, *Plays and Players; Essays on the Theatre.* 1952. Pp. 307-12
Ward, C. E., "Note on Beaumont and Fletcher's 'Coxcomb' ", *Philological Quarterly*, 9:73-76, 1930

Cupid's Revenge, 1615
Savage, J. E., "Beaumont and Fletcher's 'Philaster' and Sidney's 'Arcadia'; Also the Use They Made of the Material in 'Cupid's Revenge' ", *Journal of English Literary History* (ELH), 14:194-206, 1947
Wells, W., "Birth of Merlin", *Modern Language Review*, 16:129-37, 1921

The Custom of the Country, 1619
Schraibman, José, ed., *Homenaje a Sherman H. Eoff.* 1970. Pp. 203-20

The Faithful Shepherdess. 1608
Beerbohm, Max, *Around Theatres.* 1953. Pp. 264-67
Birrell, F., "Faithful Shepherdess", *Nation* (London), 33:434-36, 1923
Podewils, Robert A., "A Critical Study of the Tragicomedies of Beaumont and Fletcher", *Dissertation Abstracts International* (1973), 34:1866A
Schelling, Felix E., *Elizabethan Drama, 1558-1642.* 1959. vol. 2, Pp. 158-61

Strachey, J. St. L., 'Faithful Shepherdess", *Spectator*, 130:1042, June 23, 1923

Turner, W. J., "Faithful Shepherdess", *New Statesman*, 21:363-64, June 30, 1923

Waith, Eugene M., "Characterization in John Fletcher's Tragicomedies", *Review of English Studies*, 19:141-64, 1943

Wallis, Lawrence Bergmann, *Fletcher, Beaumont and Company; Entertainers to the Jacobean Gentry*. 1947. Pp. 177-99

The Humorous Lieutenant, 1625
Waith, Eugene M., "Characterization in John Fletcher's Tragicomedies". *Review of English Studies*, 19:141-64, 1943

The Island Princess, 1621
Waith, Eugene M., "Characterization in John Fletcher's Tragicomedies", *Review of English Studies*, 19:141-64, 1943

King and No King, 1647
Bluestone, Max and Norman Rabkin, eds., *Shakespeare's Contemporaries; Modern Studies in English Renaissance Drama*. 2nd ed. 1970. Pp. 342-62

Griffiths, L. M., "Shakespearian Qualities of 'A King and No King", *Poet-Lore*, 3:169-77, 1891

Mizener, A., "High Design for 'A King and No King'", *Modern Philology*, 38:133-54, 1940

Podewils, Robert A., "A Critical Study of the Tragicomedies of Beaumont and Fletcher", *Dissertation Abstracts International* (1973), 34:1866A

Turner, Robert K., Jr., "The Morality of 'A King and No King'", *Renaissance Papers*, Pp. 93-103, 1958-60

Waith, Eugene M., *Ideas of Greatness; Heroic Drama in England*. 1971. Pp. 151-53

Knight of Malta, 1647
Sherbo, Arthur, "'The Knight of Malta' and Bocaccio's 'Filocolo'", *English Studies*, 33:254-57, 1952

Waith, Eugene M., *Ideas of Greatness; Heroic Drama in England*. 1971. Pp. 149-51

Knight of the Burning Pestle, 1613
Cunningham, John E., *Elizabethan and Early Stuart Drama*. 1965. Pp. 86-88

Doebler, John, "Beaumont's 'The Knight of the Burning Pestle' and the Prodigal Son", *Studies in English Literature, 1500-1900* (1965), 1:333-44

_____ , "Francis Beaumont's 'The Knight of the Burning Pestle'", *Dissertation Abstracts*, 21:3096-97, 1961

Fleming, P., "The Knight of the Burning Pestle", *Spectator*, 148:46, Jan. 9, 1932

Gale, Steven H., "The Relationship Between Beaumont's 'The Knight of the Burning Pestle' and 'Don Quixote'", *Anales Cervantinos* (1972), 11:87-96

Leimberg, Inge, "Das Spiel Mit Der Dramatischen Illusion in Beaumonts 'The Knight of the Burning Pestle'", *Anglia*, 81:142-74, 1963

Maxwell, Baldwin, *Studies in Beaumont, Fletcher and Massinger*. 1939. Pp. 14-16

_____ , "'Twenty Good-Nights'—'The Knight of the Burning Pestle' and Middleton's 'Family of Love'", *Modern Language Notes*, 63:233-37, 1948

Taylor, Marion A., "Lady Arabella Stuart and Beaumont and Fletcher", *Papers on Language and Literature* (1972), 8:252-60

Wallis, Lawrence Bergmann, *Fletcher, Beaumont and Company; Entertainers to the Jacobean Gentry.* 1947. Pp. 177-99

Withington, R., " 'F. S., Which is to Say . . . ' The First Act of 'The Knight of the Burning Pestle' ", *Studies in Philology*, 22:226-33, 1925

Lover's Progress, 1647

Maxwell, Baldwin, *Studies in Beaumont, Fletcher and Massinger.* 1939. Pp. 14-16

—————————— , "The Hungry Knave in the Beaumont and Fletcher Play's", *Philological Quarterly*, 5:299-305, 1926

Love's Cure; or, The Martial Maid, 1647

Maxwell, Baldwin, "The Hungry Knave in the Beaumont and Fletcher Plays", *Philological Quarterly,* 5:299-305, 1926

Mad Lover, 1616

Gossett, Suzanne, "Masque Influence on the Dramaturgy of Beaumont and Fletcher", *Modern Philology* (1971/72), 69:199-208

The Maid in the Mill, 1623

English Association, *Essays and Studies, 1967; Being Volume 20 of the New Series of Essays and Studies Collected for the English Association by Martin Holmes.* 1967. Pp. 47-63

The Maid's Tragedy, 1619

Cunningham, John E., *Elizabethan and Early Stuart Drama.* 1965. Pp. 77-82

Gossett, Suzanne, "Masque Influence on the Dramaturgy of Beaumont and Fletcher", *Modern Philology* (1972), 69:199-208

Herndl, George C., *The High Design; English Renaissance Tragedy and the Natural Law.* 1970. Pp. 244-47

McCarthy, D., "Maid's Tragedy", *New Statesman*, 18:196-98, Nov. 19, 1921

"Maid's Tragedy", *Spectator*, 127:456-57, Oct. 8, 1921, and 127:667, Nov. 19, 1921

Praz, M., "John Webster and 'The Maid's Tragedy' ", *English Studies*, 37:252-28, 1956

Ribner, Irving, *Jacobean Tragedy; The Quest for Moral Order* 1962. Pp. 15-17

Stillman, Donald G., "A Critical Textual Study of Beaumont and Fletcher's 'The Maid's Tragedy' ", *Microfilm Abstracts*, 5 #1:22-23, 1944

Tomlinson, Thomas Brian, *A Study of Elizabethan and Jacobean Tragedy.* 1964. Pp. 253-50

Turner, Robert Kean, "A Textual Study of Beaumond and Fletcher's 'The Maid's Tragedy' ", *Dissertation Abstracts*, 19:1369-70, 1958

Wallis, Lawrence Bergmann, *Fletcher, Beaumont and Company; Entertainers to the Jacobean Gentry.* 1947. Pp. 200-40

Noble Gentleman, 1647

Maxwell, Baldwin, *Studies in Beaumont, Fletcher, and Massinger.* 1939. Pp. 147-65

Philaster, 1620

Adkins, M. G. M., "Citizens in 'Philaster'; Their Function and Significance", *Studies in Philology*, 43:203-12, 1946

Bluestone, Max and Norman Rabkin, eds., *Shakespeare's Contemporaries; Modern Studies in English Renaissance Drama.* 2nd ed. 1970. Pp. 330-42

Cunningham, John E., *Elizabethan and Early Stuart Drama.* 1965. Pp. 82-86

Davison, P., "Serious Concerns of 'Philaster'", *Journal of English Literary History* (ELH), 30:1-15, 1963

English Institute Essays, 1951. 1951. Pp. 146-67

Gossett, Suzanne, "Masque Influence on the Dramaturgy of Beaumont and Fletcher", *Modern Philology* (1971/72), 69:199-208

Morgan, Shirley V., "The Regal Figures in Two Jacobean Dramas", *Dissertation Abstracts International* (1972), 32:5799A

Podewils, Robert A., "A Critical Study of the Tragicomedies of Beaumont and Fletcher", *Dissertation Abstracts International* (1973), 34:1866A

Savage, J. E., "Beaumont and Fletcher's 'Philaster' and Sidney's 'Arcadia'; Also the Use They Made of the Material in 'Cupid's Revenge'", *Journal of English Literary History* (ELH), 14:194-206, 1947

————————— , "The 'Gaping Wounds' in the Text of 'Philaster'", *Philological Quarterly*, 28:443-57, 1949

Schutt, J. H., "'Philaster' Considered as a Work of Literary Art", *English Studies* (1924), 6:81-87

The Prophetess, 1647

Maxwell, Baldwin, "The Hungry Knave in the Beaumont and Fletcher Plays", *Philological Quarterly*, 5:299-305, 1926

The Queen of Corinth, 1647

Maxwell, Baldwin, "The Hungry Knave in the Beaumont and Fletcher Plays", *Philological Quarterly*, 5:299-305, 1926

Rule a Wife and Have a Wife, 1624

Grand, R. P., "Cervantes' 'El Casamiento Engañoso' and Fletcher's 'Rule a Wife and have a Wife'", *Hispanic Review*, 12:330-38, 1944

Levin, Richard, *The Multiple Plot in English Renaissance Drama.* 1971. Pp. 51-54

Scornful Lady, 1647

Maxwell, Baldwin, *Studies in Beaumont, Fletcher and Massinger.* 1939. Pp. 17-28

Thierry and Theodoret, 1621

Turner, Robert K., Jr., "Notes on the Text of 'Thierry and Theodoret'", *Studies in Bibliography: Papers of the Bibliographical Society of the University of Virginia*, 14:218-31, 1961

Two Noble Kinsmen, 1612

Brown, I., "Two Noble Kinsmen", *Saturday Review*, 145:348-49, March 24, 1928

Edwards, Philip, "On the Design of 'The Two Noble Kinsmen'", *Review of English Literature* (1964), 5:89-105

Freehafer, John, "A Textual Crux in 'The Two Noble Kinsmen'", *English Language Notes* (1970), 7:254-57

Horsnell, H., "Two Noble Kinsmen", *Outlook* (London), 61:382, March 24, 1928

Spencer, Theodore, *Theodore Spencer: Selected Essays.* 1966. Pp. 220-41

Valentinian, 1614
  Wallis, Lawrence Bergmann, *Fletcher, Beaumont and Company; Entertainers to the Jacobean Gentry.* 1947. Pp. 200-40

Wild Goose Chase, 1621
  Lister, Rotraud, "A Critical Edition of John Fletcher's Comedy 'The Wild Goose Chase'", *Dissertation Abstracts International* (1972), 33:727A

A Wife for a Month, 1624
  Waith, Eugene M., "Characterization in John Fletcher's Tragicomedies", *Review of English Studies*, 19:141-64, 1943

Wit at Several Weapons, n.d.
  Savage, James E., "The effect of Revision in the Beaumont and Fletcher Play 'Wit at Several Weapons'", *University of Mississippi Studies in English* (1960), 1:32-50

Wit Without Money, 1614
  Forker, Charles R., "'Wit Without Money';; A Fletcherian Antecedent to 'Keep the Widow Waking'", *Comparative Drama* (1974), 8:172-83
  James, Katherine H., "The Widow in Jacobean Drama", *Dissertation Abstracts International* (1973), 34:1246A

The Woman Hater; or, The Hungry Courtier, 1606
  Commonweal (Aug. 7, 1970), 92:390
  Levin, Richard, *The Multiple Plot in English Renaissance Drama.* 1971. Pp. 151-54
  Maxwell, Baldwin, "The Hungry Knave in the Beaumont and Fletcher Plays", *Philological Quarterly*, 5:299-305, 1926
  Podewils, Robert A., "A Critical Study of the Tragicomedies of Beaumont and Fletcher", *Dissertation Abstracts International* (1973), 34:1866A
  Upton, A. W., "Allusions to James I and His Court in Marston's 'Fawn' and Beaumont's 'Woman Hater'", *Modern Language Association. Publications* (PMLA), 44:1048-65, 1929

SAMUEL BECKETT

Act Without Words, 1957
  Habicht, Werner, "Becketts Baum und Shakespeares Walder", *Deutsche Shakespeare-Gesellschaft West. Jahrbuch* (1970), Pp. 77-98
  New Yorker (Dec. 2, 1972), 48:123
  Newsweek (Dec. 4, 1972), 80:70
  Spectator, 209:115, July 27, 1962
  Time (Dec. 11, 1972), 100:122
  Tynan, Kenneth, *Curtains; Selections from the Drama Criticism and Related Writings.* 1961. Pp. 401-03

Acte Sans Paroles   *SEE*   Act Without Words

All That Fall, 1957
  Alpaugh, David J., "The Symbolic Structure of Samuel Beckett's 'All That Fall'", *Modern Drama* (1966), 9:324-32
  Alvarez, A., *Samuel Beckett.* 1973. Pp. 112-15
  Barnard, G. C., *Samuel Beckett; A New Approach.* 1970. Pp. 110-13

Doherty, Francis, "Samuel Beckett's 'All That Fall'; or, All the Oppressions",
Recherches Anglaises et Americaines (1972), 5:80-84
Fletcher, John and John Spurling, *Beckett; A Study of His Plays.* 1972.
Pp. 82-87
Grossvogel, David I., *Four Playwrights and a Postcript: Brecht, Ionesco,
Beckett, and Genet.* 1962. Pp. 120-22
Kennedy, Andrew K., *Six Dramatists in Search of a Language.* 1975. Pp. 154-
59
Kenner, Hugh, *A Reader's Guide to Samuel Beckett.* 1973. Pp. 159-73
Kenner, Hugh, *Samuel Beckett; A Critical Study.* 1968. Pp. 167-76
O'Brien, Justin, *Contemporary French Literature.* 1971. Pp. 5-6
Roitman, Betty, "Mahaze-Kipolin: (Be-Shulei 'Kol ha-Noflim Shel Beckett)",
Bama (1974), 61-62:71-75
Serreau, Geneviève, *Histoire du Nouveau Théâtre.* 1966. Pp. 106-07
Webb, Eugene, *The Plays of Samuel Beckett.* 1972. Pp. 42-53

Cascando, 1964
Alvarez, A., *Samuel Beckett.* 1973. Pp. 119-22
Fletcher, John and John Spurling, *Beckett; A Study of His Plays.* 1972.
Pp. 95-100
Kenner, Hugh, *A Reader's Guide to Samuel Beckett.* 1973. Pp. 159-73
Webb, Eugene, *The Plays of Samuel Beckett.* 1972. Pp. 109-12

Cendres *SEE* Embers

Come and Go, 1966
Fletcher, John and John Spurling, *Beckett; A Study of His Plays.* 1972.
Pp. 114-19
Kenner, Hugh, *A Reader's Guide to Samuel Beckett.* 1973. Pp. 174-75
McAuley, Gay, "Samuel Beckett's 'Come and Go'", *Educational Theatre
Journal* (1966), 18:438-42
Melese, Pierre, *Samuel Beckett.* 1972. Pp. 88-89
Webb, Eugene, *The Plays of Samuel Beckett.* 1972. Pp. 113-19

Comédie *SEE* Play

La Dernière Bande *SEE* Krapp's Last Tape

Eh Joe, 1966
Alvarez, A., *Samuel Beckett.* 1973. Pp. 99-102
Fletcher, John and John Spurling, *Beckett: A Study of His Plays.* 1972.
Pp. 95-100
Kenner, Hugh, *A Reader's Guide to Samuel Beckett.* 1973. Pp. 159-73
Webb, Eugene, *The Plays of Samuel Beckett.* 1972. Pp. 127-30

Embers, 1959
Alpaugh, David, "'Embers' and the sea; Beckettian Intimations of Mortality",
Modern Drama (1973), 16:317-28
Alvarez, A., *Samuel Beckett.* 1973. Pp. 116-18
Barnard, G. C., *Samuel Beckett; A New Approach.* 1970. Pp. 116-18
Fletcher, John and John Spurling, *Beckett; A Study of His Plays.* 1972.
Pp. 95-100
Grossvogel, David I., *Four Playwrights and a Postscript: Brecht, Ionesco,
Beckett, and Genet.* 1962. Pp. 120-24

Kenner, Hugh, *A Reader's Guide to Samuel Beckett.* 1973. Pp. 159-73
Kenner, Hugh, *Samuel Beckett; A Critical Study.* 1968. Pp. 167-76
Reid, Alec, "Becket and the Drama of Unknowing", *Drama Survey,* 2:130-38, 1962
Webb, Eugene, *The Plays of Samuel Beckett.* 1972. Pp. 77-85
Zilliacus, Clas, "Samuel Beckett's 'Embers': A Matter of Fundamental Sounds", *Modern Drama* (Sept. 1970), 13:216-25

En Attendant Godot   *SEE*   Waiting For Godot

End of the Party, 1957
Mayoux, Jean-Jacques, "Le Théâtre de Samuel Beckett", *Etudes Anglaises* (1957), 10:350-66

Endgame, 1957
Abel, Lionel, "Joyce the Father, Beckett the Son", *New Leader,* Dec. 14, 1959, Pp. 26-27
Abel, Lionel, *Metatheatre; A New View of Dramatic Form.* 1963. Pp. 134-40
Ahrens, R., "Kompositionsprinzpien in Samuel Becketts 'Waiting for Godot' and 'Endgame'", *Archiv für das Studium der Neueren Sprachen und Literaturen* (1972), 209:363-68
Anderson, Irmgard Z., "Beckett's 'Tabernacle' in 'Fin de Partie'", *Romance Notes* (1973), 14:417-20
Alvarez, A., *Samuel Beckett.* 1973. Pp. 87-94
Barbour, Thomas, "Beckett and Ionesco", *Hudson Review,* 11:271-77, 1958
Barnard, G. C., *Samuel Beckett; A New Approach.* 1970. Pp. 101-09
Baxter, K. M., *Speak What We Feel; A Christian Looks at the Contemporary Theatre.* 1964. Pp. 80-83
Brick, Allan, "A Note on Perception and Communication in Beckett's 'Endgame'", *Modern Drama,* 4:20-22, 1961
Brook, Peter, "'Endgame' as King Lear; or, How to Stop Worrying and Love Beckett", *Encore* (Jan.-Feb. 1965), 12:8-12
Chambers, Ross, "Vers une Interpretation de 'Fin de Partie'", *Studi Francesi* (1967), #31:90-96
Cohn, Ruby, "The Beginning of 'Endgame'", *Modern Drama* (1966), 9:319-23
_____ , "Beckett and Shakespeare", *Modern Drama* (1972), 15:223-30
_____ , *Currents in Contemporary Drama.* 1969. Pp. 33-36 and 226-29
_____ , "'Endgame'; The Gospel According to Sam Beckett", *Accent,* 20:223-34, 1960
_____ , "Play and Player in the Plays of Samuel Beckett", *Yale French Studies,* 29:43-48, 1962
_____ , "Tempest in an Endgame", *Symposium,* 19:328-34, 1965
Corvin, Michael, *Le Theatre Nouveau en France.* 1963. Pp. 67-72
Deming, Barbara, "John Osborne's War Against the Philistines", *Hudson Review* (1958), 11:411-19
Easthope, Anthony, "Hamm, Llov, and Dramatic Method in 'Endgame'", *Modern Drama* (1968), 10:424-33
Eastman, Richard M., "The Strategy of Samuel Beckett's 'Endgame'", *Modern Drama,* 2:36-44, 1959
Ehevigny, Bell J., *Twentieth Century Interpretations of "Endgame".* 1969

Esslin, Martin, *The Theatre of the Absurd.* 1961. Pp. 10-11 and 27-39

Evans, Ilfor, *A Short History of English Drama.* 1965. Pp. 201-02

Fletcher, John and John Spurling, *Beckett; A Study of His Plays.* 1972. Pp. 69-81

Fowlie, Wallace, "The New French Theatre: Artaud, Beckett, Genet, Ionesco", *Sewanee Review*, 67:648-51, 1959

Frisch, Jack E., " 'Endgame': A Play as a Poem", *Drama Survey*, 3:257-263, 1963

Gaskell, Ronald, *Drama and Reality; The European Theatre Since Ibsen.* 1972. Pp. 147-54

Gassner, John, *Theatre at the Crossroads; Plays and Playwrights of the Mid-century American Stage.* 1960. Pp. 256-61

Gilliam, Nina, "Endgame", *Icarus* (May 1964), 43:58-59

Gilman, Richard, "Beckett", *Partisan Review* (1974), 41:56-76

Gilman, Richard, *Common and Uncommon Masks; Writings on the Theatre, 1961-1970.* 1971. Pp. 23-25

Grossvogel, David I., *Four Playwrights and a Postscript: Brecht, Ionesco, Beckett, and Genêt.* 1962. Pp. 109-20

Heitmann, Klaus, "Die Welt als Wüste; Becketts 'Endspiel' ", *Neueren Sprachen* (Jan. 1970), 19:14-41

Hubert, Renée R., "The Paradox of Silence; Samuel Beckett's Plays", *Mundus Artium* (1969), 2:82-90

Kennedy, Andrew K., *Six Dramatists in Search of a Language.* 1975. Pp. 144-47

Kenner, Hugh, *A Reader's Guide to Samuel Beckett.* 1973. Pp. 120-28

Kenner, Hugh, *Samuel Beckett; A Critical Study.* 1968. Pp. 155-65

Kott, J., " 'King Lear' or 'Endgame' ", *Evergreen Review*, 33:53-65, 1965

Lamont, Rosette C., "The Metaphysical Farce: Beckett and Ionesco", *French Review*, 32:319-28, 1958-1959

Leventhal, A. J., "Reflections on Samuel Beckett's New Work for the French Theatre", *Dublin Magazine*, 32:18, 1957

Life, 42:143, April 22, 1957

Lumley, Frederick, *New Trends in Twentieth Century Drama; A Survey Since Ibsen and Shaw.* 1967. Pp. 202-08

Lyons, Charles R., "Beckett's 'Endgame': An Anti-Myth of Creation", *Modern Drama*, 7:204-09, 1964

Lyons, Charles R., "Beckett's Major Plays and the Trilogy", *Comparative Drama* (1971-72), 5:254-68

Mayoux, Jean-Jacques, "The Theatre of Samuel Beckett", *Perspective*, 11:142-55, 1959

Melese, Pierre, *Samuel Beckett.* 1972. Pp. 49-64

Mercier, Vivian, "How to read 'Endgame' ", *Griffin*, Pp. 10-14, June, 1959

Moore, J. R., "Some Night Thoughts on Beckett", *Massachusettes Review* (1967), 8:529-39

Moore, Harry T., *Twentieth Century French Literature to World War II.* 1966. Vol. 2. Pp. 170-76

Porter, Thomas F., "Samuel Beckett; Dramatic Tradition and the Auslander", *(Eire) Ireland* (Spr. 1969), 4:62-75

Schneider, Alan, "Reality is Not Enough", *Tulane Drama Review*, 9:118-52, 1964-65

Schneider, Ruth M., "The Interpolated Narrative in Modern Drama", *Dissertation Abstracts International* (1974), 34:6605A

Schoell, Konrad, "The Chain and the Circle: A Structural Comparison of 'Waiting for Godot' and 'Endgame'", *Modern Drama* (1968), 11:48-53

Schram, Ulf, "Kritik der Theorie vom Kunstwerk als Negation: Beobachtungen an Becketts 'Endspiel' und an Bildern von Vasarely und Fontana", *Philosophisches Jahrbuch im Auftrag der Görres-Gesellschaft Herausgegeben* (1968/69), 76:349-75

Serreau, Genevieve, *Histoire du Nouveau Théâtre*. 1966. Pp. 97-104

Sheedy, John J., "The Comic Apocalypse of King Hamm", *Modern Drama* (1966), 9:310-18

Tynan, Kenneth, *Curtains; Selections from the Drama Criticism and Related Writings*, Atheneum, 1961, Pp. 225-28

Wagner, Marlene S., "The Game-Play in Twentieth Century Absurdist Drama; Studies in Dramatic Technique", *Dissertation Abstracts International* (1972), 32:4637A

Walker, Roy, "Love, Chess and Death", *Twentieth Century*, 164:533-44, 1958

Weales, Gerald, "The Language of 'Endgame'", *Tulane Drama Review* (1962), 6:107-17

Webb, Eugene, *The Plays of Samuel Beckett*. 1972. Pp. 54-65

West, Alick, "How Shall We Judge?", *Zeitschrift für Anglistik und Amerikanistik*, 15 (1967): 341-42

Wolber, Maria Josefinia, "Becketts 'Endspiel': Ein Versuch einer Gesellschaftlichen Deutung", *Der Deutschunterricht* (1973), 25:83-91

Worth, Katharine, *Beckett the Shape Changer*. 1975. Pp. 188-93

Film, 1964

Fletcher, John and John Spurling, *Beckett; A Study of His Plays*. 1972. Pp. 114-19

Kenner, Hugh, *A Reader's Guide to Samuel Beckett*. 1973. Pp. 159-73

Webb, Eugene, *The Plays of Samuel Beckett*. 1972. Pp. 120-26

Worth, Katharine, *Beckett the Shape Changer*. 1975. Pp. 161-82

Fin de Partie   *SEE*   Endgame

Happy Days, 1961

Abirached, R., "La Voix Tragique de Samuel Beckett", *Les Etudes* (Paris), 320:85-88, 1964

Alpaugh, D. J., "Negative Definition in Samuel Beckett's 'Happy Days'", *Twentieth Century Literature*, 11:202-10, Jan., 1966

Alvarez, A., *Samuel Beckett*. 1973. Pp. 106-10

Barnard, G. C., *Samuel Beckett; A New Approach*. 1970. Pp. 120-24

Brustein, Robert Sanford, *Seasons of Discontent; Dramatic Opinions, 1959-1965*. 1965. Pp. 53-56

Brustein, Robert Sanford, *The Theatre of Revolt; An Approach to the Modern Drama*. 1964. Pp. 29

Clurman, Harold, *The Divine Pastime; Theatre Essays*. 1974. Pp. 119-24

Clurman, Harold, *The Naked Image; Observations on the Modern Theatre*. 1966. Pp. 40-42

Cohn, Ruby, "Beckett and Shakespeare", *Modern Drama* (1972), 15:223-30

_____ , *Currents in Contemporary Drama*. 1969. Pp. 33-36, 194-96 and 229-31

_____ , "Play and Player in the Plays of Samuel Beckett", *Yale French Studies*, 29:43-48, 1962

Collins, P. H., "Proust, Time and Beckett's 'Happy Days'", *French Review* (1974) Special Issue 6:105-19

Eastman, Richard M., "Samuel Beckett and 'Happy Days'", *Modern Drama*, 6:417-24, 1964

Educational Theatre Journal, 13:293-94, Dec. 1961

Fletcher, John and John Spurling, *Beckett; A Study of His Plays*. 1972. Pp. 101-05

Gascoigne, Bomber, "Dying of the Light: 'Happy Days'", *Spectator* (Nov. 9, 1962), Pp. 715-17

Gassner, John, *Dramatic Soundings; Evaluations and Retractions Culled from Thirty Years of Dramatic Criticism*. 1968. Pp. 503-07

Gilman, Richard, "Beckett", *Partisan Review* (1974), 41:56-76

Gilman, Richard, *Common and Uncommon Masks; Writings on the Theatre, 1961-70*. 1971. Pp. 90-92

Grossvogel, David I., *Four Playwrights and a Postscript: Brecht, Ionesco, Beckett and Genet*. 1962. Pp. 128-31

Hubert, Renée R., "The Paradox of Silence; Samuel Beckett's Plays", *Mundus Artium* (1969), 2:82-90

Hudson Review, 14:589, Winter, 1961-62

Hughes, Catherine, "Beckett and the Game of Life", *Catholic World*, 195:163-68, 1962

Hughes, Catherine, "Beckett's World; Wherein God is Continually Silent", *Critic* (1962), 20:40-42

Kennedy, Andrew K., *Six Dramatists in Search of a Language*. 1975. Pp. 148-51

Kenner, Hugh, *A Reader's Guide to Samuel Beckett*. 1973. Pp. 147-52

Kern, Edith, "Beckett's Knight of Infinite Resignation", *Yale French Studies*, 29:49-56, 1962

Kott, Jan, *Theatre Notebook: 1947-1967*. 1968. Pp. 241-45

Lamont, Rosette, "Death and Tragi-Comedy: Three Plays of the New Theatre", *Massachusettes Review* (1965), 6:381-402

Lumley, Frederick, *New Trends in Twentieth Century Drama; A Survey Since Ibsen and Shaw*. 1967. Pp. 202-08

Lyons, Charles R., "Some Analogies Between the Epic Brecht and the Absurdist Beckett", *Comparative Drama* (1967-68), 1:297-304

Marowitz, Charles, "A View from the Gods", *Encore* (1963), 10:6-7

Melese, Pierre, *Samuel Beckett*. 1972. Pp. 71-88

Moore, Harry T., *Twentieth Century French Literature to World War II*. 1966. Vol. 2. Pp. 170-76

Moore, J. R., "Some Night Thoughts on Beckett", *Massachusettes* Review (1967), 8:529-39

Nation, 193:234-35, Oct. 7, 1961 and 201:258-89, Oct. 18, 1965, (Dec. 11, 1972), 215:597

New Republic, 145:45-46, Oct. 2, 1961

New Statesman, 64:679, Nov. 9, 1962

New Yorker, 37:119, Sept. 30, 1961 and 40:102, Feb. 22, 1964, (Dec. 2, 1972), 48:123

Reid, Alec, "Beckett and the Drama of Unknowing", *Drama Survey*, 2:130-38, 1962

Saturday Review, 44:38, Oct. 7, 1961

Serreau, Genevieve, *Histoire du Nouveau Théâtre*. 1966. Pp. 108-16

Spectator, 209:715, Nov. 9, 1962

Theatre Arts, 45:57-58, Nov. 1961
Time, 78:74, Sept. 29, 1961, (Dec. 11, 1972), 100:122
Webb, Eugene, *The Plays of Samuel Beckett*. 1972. Pp. 91-101
Weiss, Jonathan M., "The Dialectic of Movement in Beckett's 'Happy Days'",
    Adam; International Review (1970), 337-339:67-69
Worth, Katharine, *Beckett the Shape Changer*. 1975. Pp. 196-200

Krapp's Last Tape, 1960
    Alvarez, A., *Samuel Beckett*. 1973. Pp. 95-98
    Barnard, G. C., *Samuel Beckett; A New Approach*. 1970. Pp. 113-16
    Baxter, K. M., *Speak What We Feel; A Christian Looks at the Contemporary
        Theatre*. 1964. Pp. 83-84
    Christian Century, 77:256, March 2, 1960
    Clurman, Harold, *The Naked Image; Observations on the Modern Theatre*.
        1966. Pp. 13-15
    Corvin, Michel, *Le Théâtre Nouveau en France*. 1963. Pp. 67-72
    Downer, Alan S., ed., *The American Theater Today*. 1967. Pp. 104-05
    Dukore, Bernard F., "'Krapp's Last Tape' as Tragicomedy" *Modern Drama*
        (1972) 15:351-54
    Esslin, Martin, *The Theatre of the Absurd*. 1961. Pp. 42-46
    Fletcher, John and John Spurling, *Beckett; A Study of His Plays*. 1972.
        Pp. 88-94
    Gilbert, Sandra M., "'All the Dead Voices': A Study of 'Krapp's Last Tape'",
        Drama Survey (1968), 6:244-57
    Grossvogel, David I., *Four Playwrights and a Postscript: Brecht, Ionesco,
        Beckett, and Genêt*. 1962. Pp. 124-31
    Harward, Timothy Blake, ed., *European Patterns; Contemporary Patterns
        in European Writing*. 1967. Pp. 38-43
    Hubert, Renée R., "The Paradox of Silence; Samuel Beckett's Plays", *Mundus
        Artium* (1969), 2:82-90
    Kenner, Hugh. *A Reader's Guide to Samuel Beckett*. 1973. Pp. 129-35
    Lumley, Frederick, *New Trends in Twentieth Century Drama; A Survey
        Since Ibsen and Shaw*. 1967. Pp. 202-08
    Lyons, Charles R., "Beckett's Major Plays and Trilogy", *Comparative Drama*
        (1971-72), 5:254-68
    Melese, Pierre, *Samuel Beckett*. 1972. Pp. 65-71
    Moore, Harry T., *Twentieth Century French Literature to World War II*.
        1966. Vol. 2. Pp. 170-76
    Moore, J. R., "Some Night Thoughts on Beckett", *Massachusettes* Review
        (1967), 8:529-39
    Nation, 190:153, Feb. 13, 1960
    New Republic, 142:21, Feb. 22, 1960
    New Yorker, 35:75, Jan. 23, 1960, (Dec. 2, 1972), 48:123
    Newsweek (Dec. 4, 1972), 80:70
    Oberg, Arthur K., "'Krapp's Last Tape' and the Proustian Vision", *Modern
        Drama* (1966), 9:333-38
    Reid, Alec, *All I Can Manage, More Than I Could; An Approach to the
        Plays of Samuel Beckett*. 1972. Pp. 21-34
    Reid, Alec, "Beckett and the Drama of Unknowing", *Drama Survey*, 2:130-
        38, 1962
    Saturday Review, 43:28, Jan. 30, 1960
    Serreau, Geneviève, *Histoire du Nouveau Théâtre*. 1966. Pp. 104-06

Spectator, 201:609, Nov. 7, 1958

Time (Dec. 11, 1972), 100-122

Tynan, Kenneth, *Curtains; Selections from the Drama Criticism and Related Writings*. 1961. Pp. 225-28

Walker, Roy, "Love, Chess and Death", *Twentieth Century*, 164:533-44, 1958

Webb, Eugene, *The Plays of Samuel Beckett*. 1972. Pp. 66-76

Weightman, John, "Spool, Stool, Drool", *Encounter* (Apr. 1973), 40:37-38

Worth, Katharine, *Beckett the Shape Changer*. 1975. Pp. 192-96

Lost Ones, 1975

Newsweek, (4-7-75), 85:80

Mots et Musique *SEE* Words and Music

Not I, 1972

America (Dec. 16, 1972), 127:525-26

Brater, Enoch, "The 'I' in Beckett's 'Not I'", *Twentieth Century Literature* (1974), 20:189-200

Brater, Enoch, "Noah, 'Not I', and Beckett's 'Incomprehensibly Sublime'", *Comparative Drama* (1974), 8:254-63

Nation (Dec. 11, 1972), 215:597

New Republic (Dec. 16, 1972), 167:24

New Yorker (Dec. 2, 1972), 48:124

Newsweek (Dec. 4, 1972), 80:70

Perez Navarro, Francisco, "'Yo No'; Un Nuevo Drama de Samuel Beckett", *Indice* (1973), 324:36-38

Time (Dec. 11, 1972), 100:122

Weightman, John, "Spool, Stool, Drool", *Encounter* (April 1973), 40:37-38

Oh les Beaux Jours *SEE* Happy Days

Play, 1963

Admussen, Richard L., "The Manuscripts of Beckett's 'Play'", *Modern Drama* (1973), 16:23-27

Alvarez, A., *Samuel Beckett*. 1973. Pp. 103-05

Barnard, G. C., *Samuel Beckett; A New Approach*. 1970. Pp. 125-28

Clurman, Harold, *The Naked Image; Observations on the Modern Theatre*. 1966. Pp. 112-14

Cohn, Ruby, *Currents in Contemporary Drama*. 1969. Pp. 74-77

Commonweal, 79:484-85, Jan. 24, 1964

Dukore, Bernard F., "Beckett's Play 'Play'", *Educational Theater Journal* (1965), 17:19-23

Fischer, Ernst, "Samuel Beckett: 'Play' and 'Film', *Mosaic* (1969), 2:96-116

Fletcher, John and John Spurling, *Beckett; A Study of His Plays*. 1972. Pp. 106-13

Gilman, Richard, *Common and Uncommon Masks; Writings on the Theatre, 1961-70*. 1971. Pp. 111-13

Hubert, Renée Riese, "Beckett's 'Play' Between Poetry and Performance", *Modern Drama* (1966), 9:339-46

Kenner, Hugh, *A Reader's Guide to Samuel Beckett*. 1973. Pp. 153-58

Moore, J. R., "Some Night Thoughts on Beckett" *Massachusettes* Review (1967), 8:529-39

Nation, 198:106, Jan. 27, 1964

New Republic, 150:30, Feb. 1, 1964
Newsweek (4-7-75), 85:80
Reid, Alec, *All I Can Manage, More Than I Could; An Approach to the Plays of Samuel Beckett.* 1972. Pp. 35-48
Saturday Review, 47:25, Jan. 25, 1964
Time, 81:48-50, June 28, 1963 and 83:64, Jan. 17, 1964
Vogue, 143:22, Feb. 15, 1964
Webb, Eugene, *The Plays of Samuel Beckett.* 1972. Pp. 113-19
Worth, Katharine, *Beckett the Shape Changer.* 1975. Pp. 200-05

Tous Ceux qui Tombent *SEE* All That Fall

Va-et-Vient *SEE* Come and Go

Waiting for Godot, 1953
Abel, Lionel, "Joyce the Father, Beckett the Son", *New Leader*, Dec. 14, 1959. Pp. 26-27
Ahrens, R., "Kompositionsprinzpien in Samuel Becketts 'Waiting for Godot' and 'Endgame'", *Archiv für das Studium der Neueren Sprachen und Literaturen* (1972), 209:363-68
Alvarez, A., *Samuel Beckett.* 1973. Pp. 76-86
America, 95:182, May 12, 1956 and 95:265, June 9, 1956
Armstrong, William A., ed., *Experimental Drama*, London, G. Bell, 1963, Pp. 128-46
Ashmore, J., "Philosophical Aspects of Godot", *Symposium*, 16:296-304, 1962
Atkins, Anselm, "Lucky's Speech in Beckett's 'Waiting for Godot'; A Punctuated Sense-Line Arrangement", *Educational Theatre Journal* (1967), 19:426-32
_____ , "A Note on the Structure of Lucky's Speech", *Modern Drama* (1966), 9:309
Bajomee, Danielle, "Beckett Devant Dieu", *Les Lettres Romanes* (1971), 25:350-57
Barnard, G. C., *Samuel Beckett; A New Approach.* 1970. Pp. 89-100
Baxter, K. M., *Speak What We Feel; A Christian Looks at the Contemporary Theatre.* 1964. Pp. 9-19
Beckett at 60; A Festschrift. 1967. Pp. 25-28
Bergonzi, Bernard, ed., *The Twentieth Century.* (History of Literature in the English Language). vol. 7. 1970. Pp. 325-27
Bigsby, C. W. E., *Confrontation and Commitment; A Study of Contemporary American Drama, 1959-66.* 1968. Pp. 51-53
Blau, Herbert, "Politics and the Theatre", *Wascana Review* (1967), 2:5-23
Bleck, Manfred, "Warten auf Godot. Eine Psychologisch-kunstlerische Studie zu dem Buhnenstuck von Samuel Beckett", *Die Therapie des Monats* (1962), 12:306-19
Bodart, Roger, "En Attendant Godot", *Bulletin de l'Academie Royale de Langue et de Litterature Francaises* (1969), 47:209-27
Bonczek, Jane C., "Being and Waiting; A Sign of Our Times", *Lit* (1964), #5:6-10
Bradbrook, Muriel Clara, *Literature in Action; Studies in Continental and Commonwealth Society.* 1972. Pp. 13-33
Brater, Enoch, "'Waiting for Godot': A Modern 'Don Quixote'", *Hispania* (1974) 57:876-85

Brereton, Geoffrey, *Principles of Tragedy; A Rational Examination of the Tragic Concept in Life and Literature.* 1968. Pp. 244-65

Breuer, Horst, "Ordnung und Chaos in Luckys 'Think'" (Zu Samuel Becketts 'Warten auf Godot'), *Germanish-Romanische Monatsschrift* (1971), 21: 344-49

Brooke, Curtis M., "The Mythic Pattern in 'Waiting for Godot'", *Modern Drama* (1966), 9:292-99

Brooks, Mary E., "The British Theatre of Metaphysical Despair", *Literature and Ideology* (1972), 12:49-58

Brown, John Russell, "Mr. Beckett's Shakespeare", *Critical Quarterly* (1963), 5:310-26

Brown, John Russell, ed., *Modern British Dramatists; A Collection of Critical Essays.* 1968. Pp. 58-70

Brustein, Robert Sanford, *The Theatre of Revolt; An Approach to the Modern Drama.* 1964. Pp. 28-30

Busi, F., "Advents of Godot", *Religion in Life* (1973), 42:168-78

Busi, Frederick, "The Transfigurations of Godot", *Research Studies* (1972), 40:290-96

Butler, Harry L., "Balzac and Godeau, Beckett and Godot: A Curious Parallel", *Romance Notes.* 3:13-20, 1962

Catholic World, 183-227-28, June, 1956

Chadwick, C., "'Waiting for Godot'; A Logical Approach", *Symposium*, 14:252-57, 1960

Champigny, R., "Interpretation de 'En Attendant Godot'", *Modern Language Assocation. Publications* (PMLA), 75:329-31, June, 1960

Chase, N. C., "Images of Man; 'Le Malentendu' and 'En Attendant Godot'", *Wisconsin Studies in Contemporary Literature* (1966), 7:295-302

Chiari, J., *Landmarks of Contemporary Drama.* 1965. Pp. 68-78

Christian Century (May 12, 1971), 88:603-04

Clurman, Harold, *The Divine Pastime; Theatre Essays.* 1974. Pp. 63-65

Cohen, Robert S., "Parallels and the Possibility of Influence Between Simone Weil's 'Waiting for God' and Samuel Beckett's 'Waiting for Godot'", *Modern Drama*, 6:425-36, 1964

Cohn, Ruby, "The Absurdly Absurd; Avatars of Godot", *Comparative Literature Studies* (1965), 2:233-40

————— , *Currents in Contemporary Drama.* 1969. Pp. 186-95

————— , "Waiting is All", *Modern Drama*, 3:162-67, 1960-61

Commentary (April 1971), 51:78

Commonweal, 61:365-66, Dec. 31, 1954 and 64:203, May 25, 1956

Corvin, Michel, *Le Theatre Nouveau en France.* 1963. Pp. 67-72

Cowell, Raymond, *Twelve Modern Dramatists.* 1967. Pp. 113-15

Darmstadt, K. S., "Die Zeitproblematik in Samuel Becketts 'En Attendant Godot'", *Die Neueren Sprachen* (1967), 13:201-08

Dimic, Moma, "Godou", *Delo* (1968), 14:543-48

Dort, Bernard, "En Attendant Godot", *Les Temps Modernes*, Pp. 1842-45, May, 1953

Douglas, Dennis, "The Drama of Evasion in 'Waiting for Godot'", *Komos: A Quarterly of Drama and Arts of the Theatre* (1968), 1:140-46

Dubois, Jacques, "Beckett and Ionesco; The Tragic Awareness of Pascal and the Ironic Awareness of Flaubert", *Modern Drama* (1966), 9:283-91

Dukore, Bernard F., "Controversy: A Non-interpretation of 'Godot'", *Drama Survey* (Minneapolis), 3:117-19, 1963

_____ , "Gogo, Didi, and the Absent Godot", *Drama Survey* (Minneapolis), 1:301-07, 1962

_____ , "The Other Pair in 'Waiting for Godot' ", *Drama Survey* (1969), 7:133-37

English, 11:18, Spring, 1956

Esslin, Martin, *The Theatre of the Absurd*. 1961. Pp. 9-10, 13-27, 39-42

Evans, Ifor, *A Short History of English Drama*. 1965. Pp. 200-01

Federman, Raymond, *Journey to Chaos; Samuel Beckett's Early Fiction*. 1965. Pp. 168-70

Findlay, Robert R., "Confrontation in Waiting: 'Godot' and the Wakefield Play", *Renascence* (1969), 21:195-202

Fletcher, John and John Spurling, *Beckett; A Study of His Plays*. 1972. Pp. 55-68

Flood, Ethelbert, "A Reading of Beckett's 'Godot' ", *Culture* (1961), 22:257-62

Fowlie, Wallace, "The New French Theatre: Artaud, Beckett, Genet, and Ionesco", *Sewanee Review*, 67:648-51, 1959

Francis, Richard Lee, "Beckett's Metaphysical Tragi-comedy", *Modern Drama*, 8:259-67, 1965

French, Judith Ann., "The Destruction of Action", *Kerygma* (1963), 3:9-12

"French Theatre; 'Waiting for Godot' and the Conventions of the Drama", *Prompt* (1964), 4:19-23

French, Warren, ed., *The Thirties; Fiction, Poetry, Drama*. 1967. Pp. 193-94

Friedman, Melvin J., "Critic!", *Modern Drama* (1966), 9:300-08

Frye, Northrup, "The Nightmare Life in Death", *Hudson Review* (1960), 13:442-49

Gassner, John, *Directions in Modern Theatre and Drama*. 1965. Pp. 318-25

_____ , *Theatre at the Crossroads; Plays and Playwrights of the Midcentury American Stage*. 1960. Pp. 252-56

Geiser, Judith K., "The Quest for Personal Identity; A Study of Themes in the Theatre of Samuel Beckett", *Dissertation Abstracts International* (1974), 34:6639A

Gilliatt, Penelope, *Unholy Fools; Wits, Comics, Disturbers of the Peace*. 1973. Pp. 20-23

Gilman, Richard, "Beckett", *Partisan Review* (1974), 41:56-76

Gold, Herbert, "Beckett; Style and Desire", *Nation*, 183:397-99, 1956

Gold, Margaret C., "Upon 'Waiting for Godot' A Study in Dramatic Form", *Dissertation Abstracts International* (1972), 33:1167A

Goldsmith, Helen H., "Waiting for Godeau", *Forum* (Houston), (Wint.-Spr. 1970), 8:15-18

Gray, Ronald, " 'Waiting for Godot': A Christian Interpretation", *Listener*, 57:160-61, 1957

Grossvogel, David I., *Four Playwrights and a Postscript: Brecht, Ionesco, Beckett and Genet*. 1962. Pp. 88-110

Habicht, Werner, "Becketts Baum und Shakespeares Walder", *Deutsche Shakespeare-Gesellschaft West. Jahrbuch* (1970), Pp. 77-98

Halloran, Stephen M., "The Anti-Aesthetics of 'Waiting for Godot' ", *Centennial Review* (1972), 16-69-81

Harvey, Lawrence E., "Art and the Existential in 'En Attendant Godot' ", *Modern Language Association. Publications* (PMLA), 75:137-46, 1960

Hecht, W., "Brecht und Beckett. Ein Absurder Vergleich", *Theatre Zeit* (1966), 21:28-30

Higgins, David M., "Existential Valuation in Five Contemporary Plays", *Dissertation Abstracts International* (1972), 32:4612A

Hooker, Ward, "Irony and Absurdity in the Avant-Garde Theatre", *Kenyon Review*, 22:43-54, 1960

Hubert, Renee R., "The Paradox of Silence; Samuel Beckett's Plays", *Mundus Artium* (1969), 2:82-90

Hughes, Catharine, "Beckett and the Game of Life", *Catholic World*, 195:163-68, 1962

Jessup, Bertrand, "About Beckett, Godot, and Others", *Northwest Review*, 1:25-30, 1957

Jones, Louisa, "Narrative Salvation in 'Waiting for Godot'", *Modern Drama* (1974), 17:179-88

Josbin, Raoul, " 'Waiting for Godot' ", *Cross Currents*, 6:204-07, 1956

Kennedy, Andrew K., *Six Dramatists in Search of a Language*. 1975. Pp. 139-44

Kenner, Hugh, *A Reader's Guide to Samuel Beckett*. 1973. Pp. 23-38

————————— , *Samuel Beckett, A Critical Study*. 1968 Pp. 133-55

Kern, E. "Drama Stripped for Inaction: Beckett's 'Waiting for Godot' ", *Yale French Studies*, #14:41-47, 1954-55

Kernodle, George R., *Invitation to the Theatre*. 1967. Pp. 315-17, 328-30

Kolve, V. A., "Religious Language in 'Waiting for Godot' ", *The Centennial Review* (1967), 11:102-27

Kostelanetz, Richard, *On Contemporary Literature; An Anthology of Critical Essays on the Major Movements of Contemporary Literature*. 1964. Pp. 262-85

Lenson, David R., "Examples of Modern Tragedy", *Dissertation Abstracts International* (1972), 32:6433A

Lewis, Allan, *The Contemporary Theatre; The Significant Playwrights of Our Time*. 1962. Pp. 259-81

Life, 40:155-56, May 7, 1956

Lumley, Frederick, *New Trends in Twentieth Century Drama; A Survey Since Ibsen and Shaw*. 1967. Pp. 202-08

Lyons, Charles R., "Beckett's Major Plays and the Trilogy", *Comparative Drama* (1971-72), 5:254-68

Mabley, Edward, *Dramatic Construction; An Outline of Basic Principles*. 1972. Pp. 314-32

McCoy, C. S., " 'Waiting for Godot'; A Biblical Appraisal", *Religion in Life*, 28:595-603, Fall, 1959

Marinello, Leone J., "Samuel Beckett's 'Waiting for Godot' ", *Drama Critique* (1963), 6:75-81

Markus, Thomas B., "Bernard Dukore and 'Waiting for Godot' ", *Drama Survey*, 2.360-63, 1963

Matthews, Honor, *The Primal Curse; The Myth of Cain and Abel in the Theatre*. 1967. Pp. 154-60

Mayoux, Jean-Jacques, "Le Théâtre de Samuel Beckett", *Etudes Anglaises* (1957), 10:350-66

————————— , "The Theatre of Samuel Beckett", *Perspective*, 11:142-55, 1959

Melese, Pierre, *Samuel Beckett*. 1972. Pp. 21-48

Mews, Siegfried and Herbert Knust, eds., *Essays on Brecht; Theater and Politics*. 1974. Pp. 71-78

Michaelis, Rolf, "Godot-Artistisch Oder Realistisch?", *Theater Heute* (1965), 6:43-45

Mihalyi, Gabor, "Beckett's 'Godot' and the Myth of Alienation", *Modern Drama* (1966), 9:277-82

Moore, J. R., "Some Night Thoughts on Beckett", *Massachusetts Review* (1967), 8:529-39

Moore, Harry T., *Twentieth Century French Literature to World War II.* Vol. II. 1966. Pp. 170-76

Moore, John, "A Farewell to Something", *Tulane Drama Review* (1960), 5:49-60

Nation, 182:387, May 5, 1956, (Feb. 22, 1971), 212:253-54

New Republic, 134:20-21, May 14, 1956

New Statesman, 50:184, Aug. 13, 1955

New York Times Magazine, p. 36, Sept. 21, 1958

New Yorker, 32:25-26, May 18, 1956 and 32:89, May 5, 1956, (Feb. 13, 1971), 46:78

Newsweek, 47:76, April 30, 1956 and 48:102, Sept. 24, 1956

Nicol, Bernard de Bear, ed., *Varieties of Dramatic Experience.* 1969. Pp. 249-62

Olson, Elder, *The Theory of Comedy.* 1968. Pp. 125-35

O'Nan, Martha, *The Role of Mind in Hugo, Faulkner, Beckett and Grass.* 1969. Pp. 23-25

Ormerod, Beverly, "Beckett's 'Waiting for Godot'", *Explicator* (May 1974), 32:70

Paris, Jean, "The Clock Struck 29", *Reporter*, 15:39-40, Oct. 4, 1956

Pearce, Richard, "The Limits of Realism", *College English* (Jan. 1970), 31:335-43

Politzer, Heinsz, "The Egghead Waits for Godot", *Christian Scholar*, 42:46-50, 1959

Porter, Thomas E., "Samuel Beckett; Dramatic Tradition and the Auslander", *(Erie) Ireland* (Spr. 1969), 4:62-75

"Puzzling About Godot", *Times Literary Supplement*, 221:2824, April 13, 1956

Radke, Judith J., "The Theatre of Samuel Beckett: 'Une Duree a Animer'", *Yale French Studies*, 29:57-64, 1962

Rechtien, Brother John, "Time and Eternity Meet in the Present", *Texas Studies in Literature and Language*, 6:5-21, 1964

Reid, Alec, *All I Can Manage, More Than I Could; An Approach to the Plays of Samuel Beckett.* 1972. Pp. 21-34 and 50-58

_____ , "Beckett and the Drama of Unknowing", *Drama Survey*, 2:130-38, 1962

_____ , "Samuel Beckett and the Failed Form—An Introduction to 'Waiting for Godot'", *Forum* (Houston) (1973), 11, iii:54-58

Reiter, Seymour, "The Structure of 'Waiting for Godot'", *Costerus; Essays in English and American Language and Literature* (1972), 3:181-95

_____ , *World Theater; The Structure of Drama.* 1973. Pp. 214-28

Reporter, 13:43, Oct. 20, 1955

Rhodes, S. A., "From Godeau to Godot", *French Review*, 36:260-65, 1963

Rosenberg, Marvin, "A Metaphor for Dramatic Form", *Journal of Aesthetics and Art Criticism* (1958), 17:174-80

Rutherford, Malcolm, "Camp Tramps: 'Waiting for Godot'", *Spectator*, Jan. 8, 1965, Pp. 42

Saturday Review, 39:32, May 5, 1956 and 39:46, May 19, 1956 and 40:25, Feb. 9, 1957

Schechner, Richard, "There's Lots of Time in 'Godot'", *Modern Drama* (1966), 9:268-76

Schneider, Alan, "Reality Is Not Enough", *Tulane Drama Review*, 9:118-52, 1964-65

Schoell, Konrad, "The Chain and the Circle: A Structural Comparison of 'Waiting for Godot' and 'Endgame'", *Modern Drama* (1968), 11:48-53

Schwarz, Karl, "Das Theater Samuel Becketts", *Deutschunterricht* (1971), 23, H.5:24-32

─────────── , "Zeitproblematik in Samuel Becketts 'En Attendant Godot'", *Die Neueren Sprachen* (1967), 16:201-08

Serreau, Genevieve, *Histoire du Nouveau Théâtre*. 1966. Pp. 85-97

Sherrell, Richard, *The Human Image; Avant-Garde and Christian*. 1969. Pp. 45-64

Spectator, 195:222, Aug. 12, 1955

Stein, Karen F., "Metaphysical Silence in Absurd Drama", *Modern Drama* (Feb. 1971), 13:423-31

Strauss, Walter A., "Dante's Belacqua and Beckett's Tramps", *Comparative Literature*, 11:250-61, 1959

Taylor, Andrew, "The Minimal Affirmation of 'Godot'", *The Critical Review* (1969), 12:3-14

Theatre Arts, 40:18, June, 1956 and 40:33-35, Aug. 1956 and 41:16, April, 1957

Theology Today, 13:521-26, Jan. 1957

"They Also Serve", *Times Literary Supplement*, Pp. 84, Feb. 10, 1956

Time, 67:55, April 30, 1956, (Feb. 15, 1971), 97:61

Todd, Robert E., "Proust and Redemption in 'Waiting for Godot'", *Modern Drama* (1967), 10:175-81

Toor, David, "Beckett's 'Waiting for Godot'", *Explicator* (1970), 29: Item 1

Torrance, R. M., "Modes of Being and Time in the World of Godot", *Modern Language Quarterly* (1967), 28:77-95

Trousdale, M., "Dramatic Form: The Example of Godot", *Modern Drama* (1968), 11:1-9

Tynan, Kenneth, *Curtains; Selections from the Drama Criticism and Related Writings*. 1961. Pp. 101-03 and 272

Verkein, Lea, "Wachten met Beckett", *De Vlaamse Gids* (1959), 43:842-45

Wagner, Marlene S., "The Game-Play in Twentieth Century Absurdist Drama; Studies in Dramatic Technique", *Dissertation Abstracts International* (1972), 32:4637A

Webb, Eugene, *The Plays of Samuel Beckett*. 1972. Pp. 26-41

Webner, Helene L., "'Waiting for Godot' and the New Theology", *Renascence* (1968), 2:3-9

Williams, Raymond, *Drama from Ibsen to Brecht*. 1968. Pp. 299-305

─────────── , *Modern Tragedy*. 1966. Pp. 153-55

Zilliacus, Clas, "Three Times 'Godot': Beckett, Brecht, Bulatovic", *Comparative Drama* (1970), 4:3-17

Words and Music, 1962

Alvarez, A., *Samuel Beckett*. 1973. Pp. 119-22

Fletcher, John and John Spurling, *Beckett; A Study of His Plays*. 1972. Pp. 95-100

Kenner, Hugh, *A Reader's Guide to Samuel Beckett.* 1973. Pp. 159-73
Webb, Eugene, *The Plays of Samuel Beckett.* 1972. Pp. 102-08

HENRI FRANCOIS BECQUE

The Buffoons, (Unfinished)
Hyslop, Lois Boe, *Henry Becque.* 1972. Pp. 69-76

Les Corbeaux   *SEE*   The Vultures

Les Honnêtes Femmes   *SEE*   Virtuous Women

L'Enfant Prodigue   *SEE*   The Prodigal Son

The Merry-go-round, 1878
Hyslop, Lois Boe, *Henry Becque.* 1972. Pp. 31-34
Journal des Débats, 39 pt. 1:973-74, June 17, 1932
L'Europe Nouvelle, 15:766, June 18, 1932
Revue Politique et Littéraire, 70:375, June 18, 1932

Michel Pauper, 1870
Hyslop, Lois Boe, *Henry Becque.* 1972. Pp. 23-27

La Navette   *SEE*   The Merry-go-round

La Parisienne   *SEE*   The Woman of Paris

Les Polichinelles   *SEE*   The Buffoons

The Prodigal Son, 1868
Hyslop, Lois Boe, *Henry Becque.* 1972. Pp. 19-23

Virtuous Women, 1880
Hyslop, Lois Boe, *Henry Becque.* 1972. Pp. 34-36

The Vultures, 1882
Hyslop, Lois Boe, *Henry Becque.* 1972. Pp. 36-53
Journal des Débats, 32 pt. 1:408-09, March 6, 1925
Theatre Arts, 21:737, Sept. 1937

The Woman of Paris, 1885
L'Europe Nouvelle, 18:129, Feb. 9, 1935
Hyslop, Lois Boe, *Henry Becque.* 1972. Pp. 54-68
Journal des Débats, 39 pt. 1:442-45, March 18, 1932

BRENDAN BEHAN

Hostage, 1958
America, 104:130, Oct. 22, 1960
Aragnio, Riccardo, "Do-it-yourself Drama", *Gemini/Dialogue* (1960), 3:31-34
Brustein, Robert Sanford, *Seasons of Discontent; Dramatic Opinions* 1959-1965. 1965. Pp. 177-80
Catholic World, 192:126-27, Nov., 1960
Clurman, Harold, *The Naked Image; Observations on the Modern Theatre.* Pp. 43-44
Commonweal, 75:389, Jan. 5, 1962

Essays and Studies, 1971; Being Volume 24 of the New Series of Essays and Studies Collected for the English Association by Bernard Harris. 1971. Pp. 69-82

Hogan, Robert, *After the Irish Renaissance; A Critical History of the Irish Drama Since 'The Plough and the Stars'*. 1967. Pp. 203-05

Horizon, 3:113-14, Jan., 1961

Hudson Review, 13:587-88, Winter, 1960-61

Illustrated London News, 233:764, Nov. 1, 1958

Kerr, Walter, *The Theatre in Spite of Itself*. 1963. Pp. 108-12

Lumley, Frederick, *New Trends in Twentieth Century Drama; A Survey Since Ibsen and Shaw*. 1967. Pp. 303-04

Maulnier, Thierry, "Un Otage", *Revue de Paris*, Pp. 152-55, 1962

Nation, 191:236, Oct. 8, 1960

New Republic, 143:20-21, Oct. 3, 1960

New Statesman, 56:560, Oct. 25, 1958

New Yorker, 35:156, April 18, 1959 and 36:128, Oct. 1, 1960 and 37:57-58, Dec. 23, 1961

Newsweek, 56:57, Oct. 3, 1960

Porter, Raymond J., *Brendan Behan*. 1973. Pp. 3-47

Reporter, 23:45, Nov. 24, 1960

Saturday Review, 43:32, Oct. 8, 1960 and 45:30, May 19, 1962

Sewanee Review, 69:335-37, Spring, 1961

Spectator, 201:513, Oct. 17, 1958

Sullivan, Kevin, "Last Playboy of the Western World", *Nation* (1965), 200: 283-87

Theatre Arts, 44:8-9, Nov., 1960

Time, 76:59, Oct. 3, 1960

Twentieth Century, 166:174-75, Sept., 1959

Tynan, Kenneth, *Curtains; Selections from the Drama Criticism and Related Writings*. 1961. Pp. 218-20

The Quare Fellow, 1954

Catholic World, 188:420, Feb., 1959

Commonweal, 69:438-39, Jan. 23, 1959

Evans, Ifor, *A Short History of English Drama*. 1965. Pp. 205-06

Hynes, Sam, "An Irish Success", *Commonweal*, 71:627-29, March 4, 1960

Illustrated London News, 229:238, Aug. 11, 1956

Lumley, Frederick, *New Trends in Twentieth Century Drama; A Survey Since Ibsen and Shaw*. 1967. Pp. 303-04

McMahon, Sean, "The Quare Fellow", *(Eire) Ireland: A Journal of Irish Studies* (1969), 4:143-57

New Statesman, 51:624, June 2, 1956

New Yorker, 34:119-20, Dec. 6, 1958

Newsweek, 52:66-67, Dec. 8, 1958

Porter, Raymond J., *Brendan Behan*. 1973. Pp. 3-47

Saturday Review, 41:27-28, Dec. 13, 1958

Spectator, 196:761, June 1, 1956

Sullivan, Kevin, "Last Playboy of the Western World", *Nation* (1965), 200: 283-87

Theatre Arts, 43:66, Feb., 1959

Time, 70:82, July 29, 1957 and 72:78, Dec. 8, 1959

Tynan, Kenneth, *Curtains; Selections from the Drama Criticism and Related Writings.* 1961. Pp. 136-38
Vogue, 133:95, Jan. 1, 1959

BRENDAN BEHAN AND ALAN SIMPSON

Richard's Cork Leg, 1972 (Begun by Brendan Behan in 1961—completed by Alan Simpson)
Brustein, Robert, *The Culture Watch; Essays on Theatre and Society, 1969-1974.* 1975. Pp. 53-56

JACINTO BENAVENTE Y MARTINEZ

The Alien Nest, 1893
Starkie, Walter, "Benavente, the Winner of the Nobel Prize", *Contemporary Review*, 123:93-100, 1923

Alma Triunfante *SEE* The Soul Triumphant

The Angora Cat, 1900
Starkie, Walter, "Benavente, the Winner of the Nobel Prize", *Contemporary Review*, 123:93-100, 1923

Bonds of Interest, 1909
Alonso, Dámaso, "De 'El Caballero de Ellescas' a 'Los Intereses Creados'", *Revista de Filología Española* (1970), 50:1-24
Chandler, Frank W., *Modern Continental Playwrights.* 1931. Pp. 503-28
Glass, E., "Bonds of Interest", *Poet Lore*, 32:244-50, June, 1921
Hamilton, Clayton Meeker, *Seen on the Stage.* 1920. Pp. 132-37
Lumley, Frederick, *New Trends in Twentieth Century Drama; A Survey Since Ibsen and Shaw.* 1967. Pp. 366-67
New Republic, 19:25, May 3, 1919
Porterfield, Allen W., "Three Spaniards", *Bookman*, 57:576-79, 1923
Starkie, Walter, "Benavente, the Winner of the Nobel Prize", *Contemporary Review*, 123:93-100, 1923
Vila Selma, José, "Notas en Torno a 'Los Intereses Creados' y Sus Posibles Fuentes", *Cuadernos Hispanoamericanos* (1970), 243:588-611

Lo Cursi *SEE* Vulgarity

The Evil Done to Us, 1917
Spaulding, R. K., "Benavente and Campoamor: Is 'El Mal Que Nos Hacen' a Literary Reminiscence?", *Hispanic Review*, 6:258-60, 1938

La Gata de Angora *SEE* The Angora Cat

Gente Conocido *SEE* People of Our Acquaintance

Los Intereses Creados *SEE* Bonds of Interest

The Magic of an Hour, n. d.
Chandler, Frank W., *Modern Continental Playwrights.* 1931. Pp. 503-28

El Mal Que Nos Hacen   *SEE*   The Evil Done To Us

La Malquerido   *SEE*   Passion Flower

El Nido Ajeno   *SEE*   The Alien Nest

La Noche del Sabado   *SEE*   Saturday Night

Passion Flower, 1913
  Field, H. E., " 'Passion Flower' ", *Arts and Decoration*, 12:344, March, 1920
  Hamilton, Clayton Meeker, *Seen on the Stage*. 1920. Pp. 132-37
  Lewisohn, Ludwig, "Passion Flower", *Nation*, 110:152-53, Jan. 31, 1920
  Starkie, Walter, "Benavente, the Winner of the Nobel Prize", *Contemporary Review*, 123:93-100, 1923
  Villegas, Juan, "La Originalidad Tecnica de 'La Malquerida' ", *Hispania* (1967), 50:54-62

People of Our Acquaintance, 1895
  Starkie, Walter, "Benavente, the Winner of the Nobel Prize", *Contemporary Review*, 123:93-100, 1923

La Princesa Bebe   *SEE*   Princess Bebe

Princess Bebe, 1904
  Saturday Review, 143:244-45, Feb. 23, 1929

Rosas de Otoño, 1905
  Young, Raymond A., "A Comparison of Benavente's 'Rosas de Otono' and Martinez Sierra's 'Primavera en Otono' ", *College Language Association Journal* (1968), 11:206-20

Saturday Night, 1903
  Young, Stark, "Saturday Night", *New Republic*, 48:323, Nov. 10, 1926

The Soul Triumphant, 1902
  Starkie, Walter, "Benavente, the Winner of the Nobel Prize", *Contemporary Review*, 123:93-100, 1923

Vulgarity, 1901
  Starkie, Walter, "Benavente, the Winner of the Nobel Prize", *Contemporary Review*, 123:93-100, 1923

ARNOLD BENNETT

Body and Soul, 1922
  Nation (London), 31:803-04, Sept. 16, 1922
  New Statesman, 19:634-35, Sept. 16, 1922
  Spectator, 129:368, Sept. 16, 1922

Bright Island, 1925
  Outlook (London), 55:125, Feb. 21, 1925
  Saturday Review, 139:185, Feb. 21, 1925

Don Juan, 1923
  New Statesman, 27:47-48, Oct. 20, 1923

Great Adventure, 1911
  New Statesman, 23:38, July 5, 1924

Roby, Kinley, *A Writer at War: Arnold Bennett, 1914-1918.* 1972. Pp. 162-66

Honeymoon, 1911
English Review, 9:706-07, Nov., 1911

Judith, 1919
New Statesman, 13:167, May 17, 1919

Love Match, 1922
Nation (London), 31:32-34, April 1, 1922
New Statesman, 18:702, March 25, 1922
Spectator, 128:465, April 15, 1922

Return Journey, 1928
English Review, 47:485-86, Oct., 1928
Nation (London), 43:731-32, Sept. 8, 1928
New Statesman, 31:728-29, Sept. 22, 1928
Saturday Review, 146:295, Sept. 8, 1928

Sacred and Profane Love, 1919
New Statesman, 14:247-48, Nov. 29, 1919
Review, 2:312-14, March 27, 1920

The Title, 1918
Living Age, 298:688-89, Sept. 14, 1918

ARNOLD BENNETT AND EDWARD KNOBLOCK

London Life, 1924
Nation (London), 35:352-53, June 14, 1924
Outlook (London), 53:411, June 14, 1924

Milestones, 1912
Commonweal, 12:192, June 18, 1930

Mister Prohack, 1927
English Review, 46:113-14, Jan., 1928
Nation (London), 42:317-18, Nov. 26, 1927
New Statesman, 30:284-85, Dec. 10, 1927
Outlook (London), 60:702, Nov. 26, 1927
Saturday Review, 144:733-34, Nov. 26, 1927
Spectator, 139:918-19, Nov. 26, 1927

RUDOLF BESIER

Barretts of Wimpole Street, 1930
Arts and Decoration, 34:46, April, 1931
Bookman, 73:182-3, April, 1931
Brown, John Mason, *Seeing Things.* 1946. Pp. 153-59
Canadian Forum, 12:316, May, 1932
Catholic World, 133:79-80, April, 1931 and 161:169, May, 1945
Commonweal, 13:469, Feb. 25, 1931 and 41:648, April 13, 1945
Cornhill, 70:87-93, Jan., 1931
English Review, 51:520-21, Oct., 1930
Golden Book, 13:64-66, May, 1931
Isaacs, E. J. R., "Barretts of Wimpole Street", *Theatre Arts*, 19:258, 1935

Life, 18:105-08, April 16, 1945
Literary Digest, 108:18-19, Feb. 7, 1931
Mercure de France, 255:582, Nov. 1, 1934
Nathan, George Jean, *Theatre Book of the Year, 1944-45*. Pp. 318-19
Nation, 132:224-5, Feb. 25, 1931
New Republic, 112:477, April 9, 1945
New Statesman, 35:643-44, Aug. 30, 1930 and 35:676, Sept. 6, 1930
Outlook, 157:311, Feb. 25, 1931
Revue des Deux Mondes, 24:200-04, Nov. 1, 1934
Revue Politique et Litteraire, 72:832-33, Nov. 3, 1934
Saturday Review, 150:521, Oct. 25, 1930
Saturday Review of Literature, 7:726, April 11, 1931 and 28:20-22, April 7, 1945
Theatre Arts, 15:273-77, April, 1931
Theatre Magazine, 53:24, April, 1931
Time, 45:88, April 9, 1945
Woman's Journal, n. s. 16:12-13, March, 1931

UGO BETTI

Acque Turbate   *SEE*   Troubled Waters

L'Aiuola Bruciata   *SEE*   The Burnt Flower-Bed

The Burnt Flower-Bed, 1953
Illustrated London News, 227:538, Sept. 24, 1955
New Statesman, 50:360, Sept. 24, 1955
Spectator, 195:361, Sept. 16, 1955

La Casa Sull' Acqua   *SEE*   The House on the Water

Corruption in the Palace of Justice, 1949
Catholic World, 198:199-200, Dec., 1963
Nation, 197:306, Nov. 9, 1963
New Republic, 149:26, Dec. 21, 1963
New Yorker, 39:100, Dec. 19, 1963
Newsweek, 62:72, Nov. 18, 1963
Theatre Arts, 48:68, Jan., 1964
Time, 82:75, Oct. 25, 1963

Corruzione al Palazzo di Giustizia   *SEE*   Corruption in the Palace of Justice

Crime on Goat Island, 1950
Lumley, Frederick, *New Trends in Twentieth Century Drama; A Survey Since Ibsen and Shaw*. 1967. Pp. 363-65
New Statesman, 54:814, Dec. 14, 1957 and 61:228, Feb. 10, 1961
New Yorker, 31:81, Oct. 15, 1955
Strem, George G., "Death and the Will to Redeem; The Theatre of Ugo Betti", *Texas Quarterly* (1966), 9:112-21
Theatre Arts, 39:23, Dec., 1955

Delitto all Isola delle Capre   *SEE*   Crime on Goat Island

Frana Allo Scalo Nord   *SEE*   Landslide at North Station

The Gambler, 1951
  Nathan, George Jean, *Theatre in the Fifties*. 1953. Pp. 173-74

Il Giocatore   *SEE*   The Gambler

The House on the Water, 1928
  Stream, George G., "Death and the Will to Redeem; The Theatre of Ugo
  Betti", *Texas Quarterly* (1966), 9:112-21

L'Isola Meravigliosa, 1930
  Nuova Antologia, 388:351-53, Dec. 1, 1936

Landslide at North Station
  Strem, George G., "Death and the Will to Redeem; The Theatre of Ugo Betti",
  Texas Quarterly (1966), 9:112-21

A Night in the Rich Man's House, 1942
  Strem, George G., "Death and the Will to Redeem; The Theatre of Ugo Betti"
  Texas Quarterly (1966), 9:112-21

Notte in Casa del Ricco   *SEE*   A Night in the Rich Man's House

The Queen and the Rebels, 1951
  Lumley, Frederick, *New Trends in Twentieth Century Drama: A Survey Since
  Ibsen and Shaw*. 1967. Pp. 363-65
  New Yorker, 41:80, March 6, 1965
  Spectator, 195:590, Nov. 4, 1955
  Twentieth Century, 159:72-75, Jan., 1956
  Tynan, Kenneth, *Curtains, Selections from the Drama Criticism and Related
  Writings*. 1961. Pp. 108-19
  Wadsworth, Frank W., "Magnanimous Despair: Ugo Betti and 'The Queen
  and the Rebels'", *Drama Survey*, 1:165-77, 1961

La Regina e Gli Insorti   *SEE*   The Queen and the Rebels

Summertime, 1955
  New Statesman, 50:658, Nov. 19, 1955
  Spectator, 195:651, Nov. 18, 1955

Time of Vengeance, 1950
  Gassner, John, *Dramatic Soundings; Evaluations and Retractions Culled
  from Thirty Years of Dramatic Criticism*. 1968. Pp. 485-86

Troubled Waters, 1965
  Nation, 200:681, June 21, 1965
  Salmon, Eric, "Ugo Betti's 'Troubled Waters'", *Modern Drama* (1968),
  11:97-108
  Strem, George G., "Death and the Will to Redeem; The Theatre of Ugo Betti",
  Texas Quarterly (1966), 9:112-21

Wonderful Island *SEE* L'Isola Meravigliosa

ROBERT BOLT

Flowering Cherry, 1957
  Barnett, Gene A., "The Theatre of Robert Bolt", *Dalhousie Review* (Spring
  1968), 48:13-23

Illustrated London News, 231:998, Dec. 7, 1957
New Statesman, 54:725, Nov. 30, 1957
New Yorker, 35:136, Oct. 31, 1959
Spectator, 199:747, Nov. 29, 1957
Theatre Arts, 43:88, Dec., 1959
Time, 74:30, Nov. 2, 1959
Tynan, Kenneth, *Curtains; Selections from the Drama Criticism and Related Writings*. 1961. Pp. 189-90

Gentle Jack, 1963
Barnett, Gene A., "The Theatre of Robert Bolt", *Dalhousie Review* (Spring 1968), 48:13-23
Illustrated London News, 243:1004, Dec. 14, 1963
Spectator, 211:754, Dec. 6, 1963

Man For All Seasons, 1960
America, 106:452, Jan. 6, 1962 and 107:184-87, April 28, 1962
Atkins, Anselm, "Robert Bolt: Self, Shadow and the Theater of Recognition", *Modern Drama* (1967), 10:182-88
Barnett, Gene A., "The Theatre of Robert Bolt", *Dalhousie Review* (Spring 1968), 48:13-23
Brustein, Robert Sanford, *Seasons of Discontent; Dramatic Opinions 1959-1965*. 1965. Pp. 184-86
Catholic World, 194:255-56, Jan., 1962
Christian Century, 79:87-89, Jan. 17, 1962
Clurman, Harold, *The Naked Image; Observations on the Modern Theatre*. 1966. Pp. 48-50
Cohn, Ruby, *Currents in Contemporary Drama*. 1969. Pp. 121-23
Commonweal, 75:317-18, Dec. 15, 1961
Contemporary Review, 198:568-70, Oct., 1960
Driver, Tom F., "A Play of Conscience", *Christian Century* (1962), 79:87-89
Driver, Tom F., "Seeing Man as Man", *Christian Century* (1962), 79:576-77
Duprey, Richard A., *Just Off the Aisle; The Ramblings of a Catholic Critic*. 1962. Pp. 96-101
Educational Theatre Journal, 14:64-66, March, 1962
English, 13:148, Spring, 1961
Fehse, Klaus-Dieter, "Robert Bolts 'A Man for All Seasons': Eine Interpretation", *Neusprachliche Mitteilungen aus Wissenschaft und Praxis* (1973), 26:131-40
Fosbery, M. W., "A Man for All Seasons", *English Studies in Africa* (1963), 6:164-72
French, Judith Ann, "The Destruction of Action", *Kerygma* (1963), 3:9-12
Gassner, John, *Dramatic Soundings; Evaluations and Retractions Culled from Thirty Years of Dramatic Criticism*. 1968. Pp. 508-10
Hudson Review, 14:100-02, Spring, 1961 and 15:117-19, Spring, 1962
Illustrated London News, 237:124, July 16, 1960
Kerr, Walter, *The Theater in Spite of Itself*. 1963. Pp. 161-65
Laufe, Abe, *Anatomy of a Hit; Long-run Plays on Broadway from 1900 to the Present Day*. 1966. Pp. 282-87
Life, 52:55-57, Jan. 12, 1962
Lumley, Frederick, *New Trends in Twentieth Century Drama; A Survey Since Ibsen and Shaw*. 1967. Pp. 299-300

Mabley, Edward, *Dramatic Construction; An Outline of Basic Principles*. 1972. Pp. 379-91
McElrath, Joseph R. J., "Bolt's 'A Man For All Seasons'", *Explicator* (1969), 28:Item 10
—————————, "Metaphoric Structure of 'A Man For All Seasons' ", *Modern Drama* (May 1971), 14:84-92
Nation, 193:480, Dec. 9, 1961
New Republic, 145:28-30, Dec. 11, 1961
New Statesman, 60:46, July 9, 1960
New Yorker, 37:117, Dec. 2, 1961
Newsweek, 58:78, Dec. 4, 1961
Reporter, 26:38, Jan. 4, 1962
Reynolds, E. E., "The Significance of 'A Man For All Seasons' ", *Moreana* (1969), 23:34-39
Saturday Review, 44:27, Dec. 16, 1961 and 45:27, Sept. 15, 1962
Spectator, 205:64, July 8, 1960
Tees, Arthur Thomas, "The Place of the Common Man: Robert Bolt's 'A Man For All Seasons' ", *University Review* (Oct. 1969), 36:67-71
Theatre Arts, 46:10-11, Feb., 1962
Time, 78:64, Dec. 1, 1961

The Tiger and the Horse, 1960
New Statesman, 60:304, Sept. 3, 1960
Spectator, 205:403, Sept. 16, 1960

Vivat! Vivat Regina!, 1970
America (Feb. 19, 1972), 126:181-82
Catholic World (March 1971), 212:313-14
Nation (Feb. 7, 1972), 214:189
New Yorker (Nov. 14, 1970), 46:160-61 and (Jan. 29, 1972), 47:72
Newsweek (Jan. 31, 1972), 79:83
Saturday Review (Feb. 12, 1972), 55:62
Time (Jan. 31, 1972), 99:71

JOHN GRIFFITH BOWEN

After the Rain, 1967
America, 117:723-24, Dec. 9, 1967
Christian Century, 84:1527-28, Nov. 29, 1967
New Statesman, 73:312, Mar. 8, 1968
New Yorker, 43:81, Oct. 21, 1967
Newsweek, 70:113, Oct. 23, 1967
Saturday Review, 50:46, Oct. 28, 1967

BERTOLT BRECHT

Antigone of Sophocles, 1948
Cohn, Ruby, *Currents of Contemporary Drama*. 1969. Pp. 98-100
Elwood, William R., "Hasenclever and Brecht: A Critical Comparison of Two 'Antigones' ", *Educational Theatre Journal* (1972), 24:48-68
Weisstein, Ulrich, "Imitation, Stylization, and Adaptation; The Language of Brecht's 'Antigone' and Its Relation to Hölderlin's Version of Sophocles", *German Quarterly* (1973), 46:581-604

Der Aufhaltsame Aufstieg des Arturo Ui *SEE* The Resistible Rise of Arturo Ui

Aufstieg und Fall der Stadt Mahagonny *SEE* Rise and Fall of the City of Mahagonny

Baal, 1923
Anders, W., "Notes sur 'Baal', première pièce de Brecht", *Revue d' Histoire du Theatre* (Paris), 11:213-21, 1959
Bentley, Eric Russell, *Theatre of War; Comments on Thirty-two Occasions.* 1972. Pp. 123-30
Clurman, Harold, *The Naked Image; Observations on the Modern Theatre.* 1966. Pp. 181-84
Epstein, Leslie, "Beyond the Baroque; The Role of the Audience in the Modern Theater", *Tri-Quarterly* (Spr. 1968), 12:213-24
Hill, Claude, *Bertolt Brecht.* 1975. Pp. 42-45
Hermann, Hans P., "Von "Baal' Zur 'Heiligen Johanna de Schachthöfe': Die Dramatische Produktion des Jungen Brecht als Ort Gesellschaftlicher Erfahrung", *Poetica* (1972), 5:191-211
Jens, W., "Protokoll über Brecht", *Merkur*, 104:943-65, 1956
Krispyn, Egbert, "Brecht and Expressionism. Notes on a Scene from 'Baal' ", *Revue des Langues Vivantes* (1965), 31:211-17
Lyons, Charles R., *Bertolt Brecht; The Despair and the Polemic.* 1968. Pp. 3-24
Lyons, C. R., "Bertolt Brecht's 'Baal'; The Structure of Images", *Modern Drama*, 8:311-23, Dec., 1965
Matthews, Honor, *The Primal Curse; The Myth of Cain and Abel in the Theatre.* 1967. Pp. 184-86
Nation, 196:381, May 4, 1963
Nelson, Gordon, " 'Baal', The Foundation of Brecht's Style", *Dissertation Abstracts International* (1970), 30:3471A
New Yorker, 41:158, May 15, 1965
Time, 85:64, May 14, 1965
Weisstein, Ulrich, "Lonely Baal: Brecht's First Play as a Parody of Hanns Johst's 'Der Einsame' ", *Modern Drama* (Dec. 1970), 13:284-303

Das Badener Lehrstueck vom Einverständnis *SEE* The Didactic Play of Baden: On Consent

The Caucasian Chalk Circle, 1948
America, 114:603-04, April 23, 1966
Bentley, E., "Un-American Chalk Circle?", *Tulane Drama Review* (1966), 10:64-77
Bentley, Eric Russell, *Theatre of War: Comments on Thirty-two Occasions.* 1972. Pp. 172-82
Bosc, R., "Le Théâtre Epique de Bertolt Brecht", *Les Etudes* (Paris), 288:79-93, 1956
Brustein, Robert Sanford, *The Theatre of Revolt; An Approach to the Modern Drama.* 1964. Pp. 255-76
Brustein, Robert, *The Third Theatre.* 1969. Pp. 169-73
Bunge, Hans Joachim, "Brecht Probiert: Notizen and Gedanken zu Proben in Bertolt Brechts Stück 'Der Kaukasische Kreidekreis' ", *Sinn und Form*, 9:322-36, 1957
Cohn, Ruby, *Currents of Contemporary Drama.* 1969. Pp. 204-07
Commonweal, 84:177, April 29, 1966

Daste, Jean, "De Copeau au 'Cercle de Craie'", *Théâtre Populaire*, #29:1-6, 1958

_____ , "Uber die Inszenierunge des 'Kaukasischen Kreidekreises'", *Geist und Zeit*, 4:31-36, 1957

Demetz, Peter, ed., *Brecht; A Collection of Critical Essays*. 1962. Pp. 151-56

Fuegi, John, "Toward a Theory of Dramatic Literature for a Technological Age", *Educational Theatre Journal* (1974), 26:433-40

Gaskell, Ronald, *Drama and Reality; The European Theatre since Ibsen*. 1972. Pp. 139-46

Gaskell, R., "Form of 'The Caucasian Chalk Circle'", *Modern Drama* (1967), 10:195-201

Gassner, John, *Dramatic Soundings; Evaluations and Retractions Culled from Thirty Years of Dramatic Criticism*. 1968. Pp. 512-13

Grossvogel, David I., *Four Playwrights and a Postscript; Brecht, Ionesco, Beckett and Genet*. 1962. Pp. 22-44

Hill, Claude, *Bertolt Brecht*. 1975. Pp. 132-39

Hunnigher, B., "Shaw en Brecht", *Forum der Letteren* (1971), 12:173-90

Illustrated London News. 229:436, Sept. 15, 1956

Jacobs, Jürgen, "Die Rechtspflege des Azdak; Zu Brechts 'Kaukasischen Kreidekreis'", *Euphorion* (1968), 62:421-24

Keeley, Edmund and Peter Adolph Bien, eds., *Modern Greek Writers; Solomos, Calvos, Matesis, Paferis, Cavafy, Kazantzakis, Seferis, Elytis*. 1972. Pp. 191-215

Kerr, Walter, *Thirty Plays Hath November; Pain and Pleasure in the Contemporary Theater*. 1969. Pp. 277-83

Kernodle, George R., *Invitation to the Theatre*. 1967. Pp. 48-53

Life, 60:15, April 22, 1966

Lumley, Frederick, *New Trends in Twentieth Century Drama; A Survey Since Ibsen and Shaw*. 1967. Pp. 80-90

Lupi, S., "L'Antiestetica di Brecht", *Rivista di Estetica*, 8:321-417, 1963

Lyons, Charles R., *Bertolt Brecht; The Despair and the Polemic*. 1968. Pp. 132-54

Mabley, Edward, *Dramatic Construction; An Outline of Basic Principles*. 1972. Pp. 254-69

Mueller, G. H. S., "The Narrator in Brecht's 'Der Kaukasische Kreiderkreis'", *Furman Studies* (1974), 21, iv:41-46

Nation, 183:202, Sept. 8, 1956 and 202:436-37, April 11, 1966

New Republic, 119:27-28, Sept. 6, 1948 and 154:30, April 16, 1966

New Statesman, 52:40, July 14, 1956 and 63:502, April 6, 1962

New Yorker, 31:62-64, July 16, 1955 and 38:159-60, May 12, 1962 and 42:122, April 2, 1966

Newsweek, 67:90-91, April 4, 1966

Read, Malcolm, "Brecht, Klabund and the 'Chalk Circle'", *Modern Languages* (1972), 53:28-32

Reiter, Seymour, *World Theater; The Structure and Meaning of Drama*. 1973. Pp. 50-56

Sagar, K. M., "Brecht in Neverneverland: 'The Caucasian Chalk Circle'", *Modern Drama* (1966), 9:11-17

Saturday Review, 44:39, Nov. 18, 1961 and 49:53, April 9, 1966

Spectator, 197:322, Sept. 7, 1956

Steer, W. A. J., "Brecht's Epic Theater", *Modern Language Review* (1968), 63:636-49

——————— , "The Thematic Unity of Brecht's 'Der Kaukasische Kreidekreis' ", *German Life and Letters* (1967), 21:1-10

Suvin, Darko, "Brecht's 'Caucasian Chalk Circle' and Marxist Figuralism; Open Dramaturgy as Open History", *Clio; An Interdisciplinary Journal of Literature, History and the Philosophy of History* (1974), 3:257-76

Suvin, Darko, "Brechtov 'Kavkaski Krug Kredom' Kao Marksisticki Figuralizam", *Praxis* (1971), 8:733-43

Theatre at Work; Playwrights and Productions in Modern British Theatre, ed. by Charles Marowitz and Simon Trussler. 1968. Pp. 123-32

Time, 87:63, April 1, 1966

Tscharchalaschili, Surab, " 'Der Kaukasische Kreidekreis': Seine Geschichte und die Verfremdungstheorie von Bertolt Brecht", *Weimarer Beitrage* (1968), Heft S:171-84

Tynan, Kenneth, *Curtains; Selections from the Drama Criticism and Related Writings*. 1961. Pp. 452-54

Coriolan, 1957

Gebhardt, Peter, "Brechts 'Coriolan'—Bearbeitung", *Shakespeare Jahrbuch* (1972), Pp. 113-35

Willson, A. Leslie, ed., *A Gunter Gross Symposium*. 1972. Pp. 18-31

Dreigroschenoper *SEE* Threepenny Opera

The Days of the Commune, 1956

Reitz, Leonard, "The Historical Dramas of Brecht", *Dissertation Abstracts International* (1972), 32:4019A

The Didactic Play of Baden: On Consent, 1929

Baxandall, Lee, "Bertolt Brecht's J. B.", *Tulane Drama Review*, 4:113-17, 1960

Drums in the Night, 1919

Bathrick, David, " 'Anschauungsmaterial' for Marx; Brecht Returns to 'Trommeln in der Nacht' ", *Brecht Heute—Brecht Today; Jahrbuch de Internationalen Brecht Gesellschaft* (1972), 2:136-48

Hill, Claude, *Bertolt Brecht*. 1975. Pp. 45-47

Hunnigher, B., "Shaw en Brecht", *Forum der Letteren* (1971), 12:173-90

Lumley, Frederick, *New Trends in Twentieth Century Drama; A Survey Since Ibsen and Shaw*. 1967. Pp. 80-90

Mews, Siegfried and Herbert Knust, eds., *Essays on Brecht; Theater and Politics*. 1974. Pp. 71-78

Reimer, Robert C., "The Tragedy of the Revolutionary; A Study of the Drama of Revolution of Ernst Toller, Friedrich Wolf and Bertolt Brecht, 1918-1933", *Dissertation Abstracts International* (1972), 32:5802A

Stern, Guy, "Brechts 'Trommeln in der Nacht' als Literarische Satire", *Monatshefte für Deutschen Unterricht* (1969), 61:241-59

Edward II, 1924

Bentley, Eric Russell, *Theatre of War; Comments on Thirty-two Occasions*. 1972. Pp. 131-45

Grunninger, Hans Werner, "Brecht und Marlowe", *Comparative Literature* (Summer 1969), 21:232-44

Laboulle, Louise J., "A Note on Bertolt Brecht's Adaptation of Marlowe's 'Edward II' ", *Modern Language Review* (1959), 54:214-20

Svendsen, J., "Queen is Dead: Brecht's Edward II' ", *T. D. R. Drama Review* (1966), 10:160-76

Weisstein, Ulrich, "The First Version of Brecht/Feuchtwanger's 'Leben Eduards des Zweiten von England' and Its Relation to the Standard Text", *Journal of English and Germanic Philology* (1970), 69:193-210

Frau Carrars Gewehre *SEE* Senora Carrar's Rifles

Furcht und Elend des Dritten Reiches *SEE* Private Life of the Master Race

Galileo, 1943

Bauland, Peter, *The Hooded Eagle; Modern German Drama on the New York Stage*. 1968. Pp. 164-67

Baxter, K. M., *Speak What We Feel; A Christian Looks at the Contemporary Theatre*. 1964. Pp. 27-29

Bentley, Eric Russell, *Theatre of War; Comments on Thirty-two Occasions*. 1972. Pp. 146-64

Bezerchen, Alan D., "The Basis for Political Dictatorship as Revealed in Three Works of Bertolt Brecht", *German Life and Letters* (1971/72), n. s. 25:354-59

Catholic World, 166:74, Oct., 1947

Chiari, J., *Landmarks of Contemporary Drama*. 1965. Pp. 161-83

Cohen, M. A., "History and Moral in Brecht's 'The Life of Galileo' ", *Contemporary Literature* (Wint. 1970), 11:80-97

Cohn, Ruby, *Currents in Contemporary Drama*. 1969. Pp. 117-20

Commonweal, 47:255-56, Dec. 19, 1940

Dahl, Helmer, "Brechts 'Galilei' og den Virkelige", *Samtiden* (1967), 76:539-56

Demetz, Peter, ed., *Brecht; A Collection of Critical Essays*. 1962. Pp. 117-26

Dort, Bernard, "'La Vie de Galilee', Parabole et Drame Historique", *Marche Romane* (1971), 20, iii:7-20

Fuegi, John, "Toward a Theory of Dramatic Literature for a Technological Age", *Educational Theatre Journal* (1974), 26:433-40

Groseclose, John Sidney, "Scene Twelve of Bertolt Brecht's 'Galilei': A Structural Study", *Monatshefte fur Deutschen Unterricht* (1970), 62:367-82

Grossvogel, David I., *Four Playwrights and a Postscript: Brecht, Ionesco, Beckett, and Genet*. 1962. Pp. 39-42

Hill, Claude, *Bertolt Brecht*. 1975. Pp. 112-21

Holloway, R., "Galileo", *Plays and Players* (1974), 21:58-59

Hunnigher, B, "Shaw en Brecht", *Forum der Letteren* (1971), 12:173-90

Kelsch, Wolfgang, "Bert Brecht: Leben des Galilei", *Provinz* (1963), 17:274-85

Lucke, Hans, "Schulpraktischer Kommentar zu Brechts 'Leben des Galilei' ", *Der Deutschunterricht* (1968), 20:67-84

Lumley, Frederick, *New Trends in Twentieth Century Drama; A Survey Since Ibsen and Shaw*. 1967. Pp. 80-90

Lupi, S., "L'Antiestetica di Brecht", *Rivista di Estetica*, 8:321-417, 1963

Lyons, Charles R., *Bertolt Brecht; The Despair and the Polemic*. 1968. Pp. 110-31

_____ , " 'Life of Galileo': The Focus of Ambiguity in the Villain Hero", *Germanic Review* (1966), 41:57-71

Mews, Siegfried and Herbert Knust, eds., *Essays on Brecht; Theater and Politics*. 1974. Pp. 174-89

Nagele, Rainer, "Zur Struktur von Brechts 'Leben des Galilei' ", *Der Deutschunterrichter. Beitrage zu Seiner Praxis und Wissenschaftlichen Grundlegung* (1971), 23:86-99

Nathan, George Jean, *Theatre Book of the Year, 1947-48*. Pp. 177-80

New Republic, 117:36, Dec. 29, 1947

Newsweek, 30:60, Dec. 29, 1947

Regnaut, M., and Dort, B., " 'La Vie de Galilee' de Bertolt Brecht", *Théâtre Populaire*, #24:62-74, 1957

Reitz, Leonard, "The Historical Dramas of Brecht", *Dissertation Abstracts International* (1972), 32:4019A

Schumacher, Ernst, "Brechts 'Galilei'; Form and · Einfuhlung", *Sinn und Form*, 12:510-30, 1960

_____ , "Brecht's 'Lebendes Galilei' as a Literary Product of the Age of Science", *Neue Deutsche Literatur*, 8:115-29, 1960

_____ , "The Dialectics of 'Galileo' ", *T. D. R., Drama Review (1968), 12:124-33*

_____ , "Schöne Literatur im Zeitalter der Wissenschaft", *Geist und Zeit*, 2:16-30, 1960

_____ , "Verfremdung Durch Historisierung. Bertolt Brechts 'Leben des Galilei' ", *Kommunitat* (1961), 5:67-74

Sorensen, Otto M., "Brecht's 'Galileo': Its Development from Ideational into Ideological Theater", *Modern Drama* (1969), 11:410-22

Stern, Guy, "The Plight of the Exile; A Hidden Theme in Brecht's 'Galileo Galilei' ", *Brecht Heute—Brecht Today* (1971), 1:110-16

Theatre Arts, 32:12-13, Feb., 1948

Valazzi, Ivy, "Relaciones entre la Teoria Dramatica de Brecht y su Obra, 'Galileo Galilei' ", *Revista de Pacifico* (1967), 4:90-105

Veca, S., "Brecht e la Contraddizione di 'Galileo' ", *Aut Aut. Rivista di Filosofia e di Cultura* (Milano), #81:89-101, 1964

Weimar, K. S., "The Scientist and Society. A Study of Three Modern Plays", *Modern Language Quarterly* (1966), 27:431-48

White, Alfred D., "Brecht's 'Leben des Galilei': Armchair Theatre?", *German Life and Letters* (1974), 27:124-32

Williams, Raymond, *Modern Tragedy*. 1966. Pp. 199-202

Good Woman of Setzuan, 1943

Alter, Maria P., "Bertolt Brecht und die Rassischen Minderheiten", *German Quarterly* (1967), 40:58-67

Bosc, R., "Le Théâtre Epique de Bertolt Brecht", *Les Etudes* (Paris), 288:79-93, 1956

Catholic World, 184:385-86, Feb., 1957

Christian Century, 74:138, Jan. 30, 1957

Cowell, Raymond, *Twelve Modern Dramatists*. 1967. Pp. 79-81

Freedman, Morris, *The Moral Impulse; Modern Drama from Ibsen to the Present*. 1967. Pp. 99-114

Gassner, John, *Dramatic Soundings; Evaluations and Retractions Culled from Thirty Years of Dramatic Criticism*. 1968. Pp. 217-18

_____ , *Theatre at the Crossroads; Plays and Playwrights of the Midcentury American Stage.* 1960. Pp. 264-70

Grossvogel, David I., *Four Playwrights and a Postscript: Brecht, Ionesco, Beckett and Genet.* 1962. Pp. 22-25

Harvey, Franke O., "Ein Vergleich; Brechts 'Der Gute Mensch von Sezuan' und Dostojewskis 'Der Grosinquisitor' ", *Dissertation Abstracts International* (1972), 32:4001A

Henss, Rudolf and Hugo Moser, eds., *Germanistik in Forschung und Lehre.* Vortrage und Diskussionen des Germanistentages in Essen, 21-25. Oktober, 1964. 1965. Pp. 184-91

Hill, Claude, *Bertolt Brecht.* 1975. Pp. 121-26

Hunnigher, B., 'Shaw en Brecht", *Forum der Letteren* (1971), 12:173-90

Illustrated London News, 229:854, Nov. 17, 1956

Ivernel, P., "Deux Pieces de Brecht", *Lettres Nouvelles* (Paris), 9:148-51, 1961

Lau, Franz, "Bert Brecht und Luther. Ein Versuch der Interpretation des 'Guten Menschen von Sezuan' ", *Luther-Jahrbuch* (1962), 29:92-110

Lewis, Allan, *The Contemporary Theatre; The Significant Playwrights of Our Time.* 1962. Pp. 218-42

_____ , "El Teatro Epico—Bertolt Brecht, 'La Buena Mujer de Setzuan' ", *Cuadernos Americanos*, 16:208-31, 1957

Loeb, E., "Sartre's 'No Exit' and Brecht's 'The Good Woman of Setzuan': A Comparison", *Modern Language Quarterly*, 22:283-91, Sept. 1961

Loomis, E. R., "A re-interpretation of Bertolt Brecht", *Univ. of Kansas City Review*, 27:51-56, 1960

Lumley, Frederick, *New Trends in Twentieth Century Drama; A Survey Since' Ibsen and Shaw.* 1967. Pp. 80-90

Mews, Siegfried and Herbert Knust, eds., *Essays on Brecht; Theater and Politics.* 1974. Pp. 190-96

Nation, 184:27, Jan. 5, 1957, (Nov. 23, 1970), 211:524

New Republic (3-13-76), 174:28

New Yorker (2-24-75), 51:96-97

Nicol, Bernard de Bear, ed., *Varieties of Dramatic Experience.* 1969. Pp. 210-14

Saturday Review, 40:24, Jan. 5, 1957 and 49:55, June 4, 1966

Smiley, Sam, *Playwriting; The Structure of Action.* 1971. Pp. 88-103

Spectator, 197:648, Nov. 9, 1956

Tynan, Kenneth, *Curtains; Selections from the Drama Criticism and Related Writings*, 1961. Pp. 146-48

Williams, Raymond, *Modern Tragedy.* 1966. Pp. 196-98

Der Gute Mensch von Sezuan   *SEE*   The Good Woman of Setzuan

Die Heilige Johanna der Schlachthöfe   *SEE*   Saint Joan of the Stockyards

Herr Puntila und Sein Knecht Matti   *SEE*   Mr. Puntila and His Hired Man, Matti

Der Hofmeister   *SEE*   The Tutor

Im Dickicht der Städte   *SEE*   In the Jungle of the Cities

In the Jungle of the Cities, 1923

Alter, Maria P., "Bertolt Brecht und die Rassischen Minderheiten", *German Quarterly* (1967), 40:58-67

Brustein, Robert Sanford, *Seasons of Discontent; Dramatic Opinions 1959-1965.* 1965. Pp. 39-42

_____ , *The Theatre of Revolt; An Approach to the Modern Drama.* 1964. Pp. 241-49

Clurman, Harold, *The Naked Image; Observations on the Modern Theatre.* 1966. Pp. 56-58

Demetz, Peter, ed., *Brecht; A Collection of Critical Essays.* 1962. Pp. 51-58

Hill, Claude, *Bertolt Brecht.* 1975. Pp. 47-53

Lyons, Charles R., *Bertolt Brecht; The Despair and the Polemic.* 1968. Pp. 25-44

Lyons, C. R., "Two Projections of the Isolation of the Human Soul: Brecht and Albee", *Drama Survey* (1965), 4:121-38

Mews, Siegfried and Herbert Knust, eds., *Essays on Brecht; Theater and Politics.* 1974. Pp. 79-98

Nation, 192:18-19, Jan. 7, 1961

New Republic, 14:30-31, Jan. 9, 1961

New Yorker, 36:42-43, Dec. 31, 1960

Theatre Arts, 45:10-11, March, 1961

Der Kaukasische Kreidekreis *SEE* The Caucasian Chalk Circle

Leben des Galilei   *SEE*   Galileo

Mann ist Mann   *SEE*   Man's a Man

Man's a Man, 1926
Brustein, Robert Sanford, *Seasons of Discontent; Dramatic Opinions 1959-1965.* 1965. Pp. 71-74

Buskens, Herman, "Man is Man", *Valodas un Literaturas Instituta Raksti* (1968), 52:17-18

Clurman, Harold, *The Naked Image; Observations on the Modern Theatre.* 1966. Pp. 58-61

Commonweal, 77:72, Oct. 12, 1962

Demetz, Peter, ed., *Brecht; A Collection of Critical Essays.* 1961. Pp. 51-58

Douglas, Mary, ed., *Witchcraft, Confessions and Accusations.* (A. S. A. Monographe 9), 1970. Pp. 180-99

Gilman, Richard *Common and Uncommon Masks; Writings on the Theatre, 1961-70.* 1971. Pp. 49-53

Grossvogel, David I., *Four Playwrights and a Postscript: Brecht, Ionesco, Beckett and Genet.* 1962. Pp. 21-38

Hill, Claude, *Bertolt Brecht.* 1975. Pp. 53-55

Lyons, Charles R., *Bertolt Brecht; The Despair and the Polemic.* 1968. Pp. 45-67

Mews, Siegfried and Herbert Knust, eds., *Essays on Brecht; Theater and Politics.* 1974. Pp. 99-113

Nation, 195:207-08, Oct. 6, 1962

New Republic, 147:26, Oct. 1, 1962

New Yorker, 39:98, Sept. 29, 1962

Onderdelinden, J. W., "Brechts 'Mann Ist Mann': Lustspiel oder Lehrstuck?", *Neophilologus* (1970), 54:149-66

Shaw, L. R., *The Playwright and Historical Change; Dramatic Strategies in Brecht, Hauptmann, Kaiser, and Wedekind.* 1970. Pp. 117-68

Theatre Arts, 47:67, Feb., 1963

Time, 80:91, Sept., 28, 1962

Mann Ist Mann   *SEE*   Man's a Man

Die Massnahme   *SEE*   The Measures Taken

Measures Taken, 1930
Angermeyer, Hans Christoph, *Zuschauer Im Drama*. 1971. Pp. 55-58
Chiari, J., *Landmarks of Contemporary Drama*. 1965. Pp. 161-83
Grossvogel, David I., *Four Playwrights and a Postscript: Brecht, Ionesco, Beckett and Genêt*. 1962. Pp. 16-21
Hill, Claude, *Bertolt Brecht*. 1975. Pp. 76-79
Kaiser, Joachim, "Brechts 'Massnahme' und die Linke Angst; Warum ein 'Lehrstuck' so Viel Verlegenheit und Verlogenheit Provozierte", *Neue Rundschau* (1973), 84:96-125
Lyons, Charles R., *Bertolt Brecht; The Despair and the Polemic*. 1968. Pp. 68-88
Nation (6-7-75), 220:698-700, and (11-2-74), 219:445
New Yorker (10-28-74), 50:66
Nelson, Gordon E., "The Birth of Tragedy Out of Pedagogy; Brecht's 'Learning Play' 'Die Massnahme' ", *German Quarterly* (1973), 46:566-80

Mr. Puntila and His Hired Man, Matti, 1948
Berckman, Edward M., "Comedy and Parody of Comedy in Brecht's 'Puntila' ". *Essays in Literature* (1974), 1:248-60
Bosc, R., "Le Théâtre Epique de Bertolt Brecht", *Les Etudes* (Paris), 288:79-93, 1956
Gilliatt, Penelope, *Unholy Fools; Wits, Comics, Disturbers of the Peace*. 1973. Pp. 234-35
Hein, Jürgen, ed., *Theater und Gesellschaft; Das Volksstück im 19. und 20. Jahrhundert*. 1973. Pp. 187-200
Hermand, Jose, "Herr Puntila und sein Knecht Matti", *Brecht Heute—Brecht Today* (1971), 1:117-36
Hill, Claude, *Bertolt Brecht*. 1975. Pp. 126-32
Lumley, Frederick, *New Trends in Twentieth Century Drama; A Survey Since Ibsen and Shaw*. 1967. Pp. 80-90
Saturday Review, 45:22, June 9, 1962
Speidel, E., "Brecht's 'Puntila': A Marxist Comedy", *Modern Language Review* (April 1970), 65:319-32

The Mother; Life of the Revolutionary Pelagea Vlassova from Tver, 1932
Barthes, Roland, *Critical Essays*. 1972. Pp. 139-42
Thomas, Emma L., "Bertolt Brecht's Drama 'Die Mutter'; A Case of Double Adaptation", *Dissertation Abstracts International* (1972), 33:2955A

Mother Courage and Her Children, 1941
Barthes, Roland, *Critical Essays*. 1972. Pp. 33-36
Bauland, Peter, *The Hooded Eagle; Modern German Drama on the New York Stage*. 1968. Pp. 190-93
Bentley, Eric Russell, *Theatre of War; Comments on Thirty-two Occasions*. 1972. Pp. 165-71
Blau, Herbert, "Brecht's 'Mother Courage'; The Rite of War and the Rhythm of Epic", *Educational Theatre Journal*, 9:1-10, 1957

Block, Haskell M. and Salinger, Herman, eds., *Creative Vision; Modern European Writers on Their Art.* 1960. Pp. 158-61

Boeddinghaus, Walter, "Bestie Mensch in Brechts 'Mutter Courage'", *Acta Germanica* (1968), 2:81-88

Bosc, R., "Le Théâtre Epique de Bertolt Brecht", *Les Etudes* (Paris), 288:79-93, 1956

Bremer, J. M., "Euripides' 'Hecuba' en Brechts 'Mutter Courage'", *Filosofs'ka Dumka* (1970), 11:50-65

Brustein, Robert Sanford, *The Theatre of Revolt; An Approach to the Modern Drama.* 1964. Pp. 267-76

───────────── , *Seasons of Discontent; Dramatic Opinions 1959-1965.* Pp. 152-55

Brustein, Robert, *The Third Theatre.* 1969. Pp. 117-22

Burnshaw, Stanley, ed., *Varieties of Literary Experience; Eighteen Essays in World Literature.* 1962. Pp. 45-62

Catholic World, 142:469, Jan., 1936 and 197:143-44, May, 1963

Chiari, J., *Landmarks of Contemporary Drama.* London. 1965. Pp. 161-83

Clurman, Harold, *The Divine Pastime; Theatre Essays.* 1974. Pp. 125-33

───────────── , *The Naked Image; Observations on the Modern Theatre.* 1966. Pp. 61-64

Cole, Toby and Chinoy, Helen Krich, eds., *Directors on Directing; A Source Book of the Modern Theatre*, Rev. ed., 1963. Pp. 333-50

Commonweal, 23:162, Dec. 6, 1935 and 78:141-42, April 26, 1963

Dehem, Paul, "'Mère Courage' et l'Efficacité du Théâtre de Brecht", *Langues Modernes.* (1970), 64:75-82

Demetz, Peter, ed., *Brecht; A Collection of Critical Essays.* 1962. Pp. 138-50

Dickson, Keith, "Brecht: An Aristotelian 'Malgre Lui'", *Modern Drama* (1968), 11:111-21

Dumur, G., "Autour de 'Mère Courage'", *La Table Ronde*, #80:166-69, 1956

Fergusson, Francis, "Three Allegorists: Brecht, Wilder and Eliot", *Sewanee Review*, 65:544-73, 1956

Fuegi, John, "Toward a Theory of Dramatic Literature for a Technological Age", *Educational Theatre Journal* (1974), 26:433-40

Gilman, Richard, *Common and Uncommon Masks; Writings on the Theatre, 1961-70.* 1971. Pp. 41-45

Gray, Ronald, "'Mother Courage'", *Cambridge Review*, 78:43-45, 1956

Grossvogel, David I., *Four Playwrights and a Postscript: Brecht, Ionesco, Beckett and Genêt.* 1962. Pp. 41-42

Hill, Claude, *Bertolt Brecht.* 1975. Pp. 105-12

Illustrated London News, 229:400, Sept. 8, 1956

Lumley, Frederick, *New Trends in Twentieth Century Drama; A Survey Since Ibsen and Shaw.* 1967. Pp. 80-90

Lupi, S., "L'Antiestetica di Brecht", *Rivista di Estetica*, 8:321-417, 1963

Lyons, Charles R., *Bertolt Brecht; The Despair and the Polemic.* 1968. Pp. 89-109

───────────── , "Some Analogies Between the Epic Brecht and the Absurdist Beckett", *Comparative Drama* (1967-68), 1:297-304

Matthews, Honor, *The Primal Curse; The Myth of Cain and Abel in the Theatre.* 1967. Pp. 24-26

Nation, 141:659-60, Dec. 4, 1935 and 182:557-58, June 30, 1956 and 196:314-15, April 13, 1963

New Republic, 35:175, Dec. 18, 1935 and 148:35-36, April 13, 1963

New Statesman, 50:66-68, July 16, 1955 and 52:274, Sept. 8, 1956

New Yorker, 39:71, April 6, 1963

Newsweek, 61:85, April 8, 1963, (4-7-75), 85:80

Reporter, 28:39-40, May 9, 1963

Saturday Review, 46:20, April 13, 1963

Schäfer, Walter, "War der Weg uber die Lieder ein Umweg? Bert Brecht: 'Mutter Courage und ihre Kinder' ", *Wirkendes Wort* (1964), 14:407-13

Shunami, Gideon, "Mahaze ha-Kronika ba-Sherut ha-Teatron ha-Epic", *Bama* (1974), 60:68-75

Spectator, 196:579, April 27, 1956 and 197:322, Sept. 7, 1956

Speidel, E., "The Mute Person's Voice: 'Mutter Courage and Her Daughter' ", *German Life and Letters* (1970), 23:332-39

Steer, W. A. J., "Brecht's Epic Theater", *Modern Language Review* (1968), 63:636-49

Theatre Arts, 20:13-15, Jan., 1936 and 26:251-52, April, 1942 and 33:26-27, June, 1949 and 46:19-22, June, 1962 and 47:14-15, May, 1963

Time, 26:68, Dec. 2, 1935 and 81:56, April 5, 1963

Tynan, Kenneth, *Curtains; Selections from the Drama Criticism and Related Writings*. 1961. Pp. 99-101, 452-54

Williams, Raymond, *Drama from Ibsen to Brecht*. 1968. Pp. 285-87

——————————— , *Modern Tragedy*. 1966. Pp. 198-99

Woodland, Ronald S., "The Danger of Empathy in 'Mother Courage' ", *Modern Drama* (1972), 15:125-29

Die Mutter: Leben der Revolutionafen Pelegea Wlassowa aus Twer   *SEE*   The Mother: Life of the Revolutionary Pelagea Vlassova from Tver

Mutter Courage und Ihre Kinder   *SEE*   Mother Courage and Her Children

Pauken und Trompeten   *SEE*   Trumpets and Drums

The Private Life of the Master Race; Fear and Misery in the 3rd Reich, 1938
Beyerchen, Alan D., "The Basis for Political Dictatorship as Revealed in Three Works of Bertolt Brecht", *German Life and Letters* (1971/72), n. s. 25:354-59

Hill, Claude, *Bertolt Brecht*. 1975. Pp. 87-89

Nathan, George Jean, *Theatre Book of the Year*, 1945-46. Pp. 27-29

The Private Tutor, 1950
Angermeyer, Hans Christoph, *Zuschauer Im Drama*. 1971. Pp. 94-98

Kitching, Laurence P., " 'Der Hofmeister': A Critical Analysis of Bertolt Brecht's Adaptation of Lenz's Drama", *Dissertation Abstracts International* (1973), 34:1918A

Theatre Arts, 47:58-59, Oct. 1963

Der Prozess der Jeanne d'Arc zu Rouen 1431   *SEE*   The Trial of Joan of Arc at Rouen, 1431

The Resistible Rise of Arturo Ui, 1958
Beyerchen, Alan D., "The Basis for Political Dictatorship as Revealed in Three Works of Bertolt Brecht", *German Life and Letters* (1971/72), n. s. 25:354-59

Brustein, Robert, *The Third Theatre*. 1969. Pp. 131-40
Catholic World, 198:263-64, Jan., 1964
Clurman, Harold, *The Naked Image; Observations on the Modern Theatre*. 1966. Pp. 64-66
Commonweal, 79:314, Dec. 6, 1963, (Jan. 24, 1969), 89:528
Florenne, V., "Brecht au T. N. P.", *La Revue Française* (Paris), #128:33-34, 1961
Gilman, Richard, *Common and Uncommon Masks; Writings on the Theatre, 1961-70*. 1971. Pp. 46-48
Ivernel, P., "Deux Pièces de Brecht", *Lettres Nouvelles* (Paris), 9:148-51, 1961
Kott, Jan, *Theatre Notebook; 1947-1967*. 1968. Pp. 108-10
Nation, 197:403-04, Dec. 7, 1963
New Republic, 149:26, Dec. 21, 1963
Newsweek, 62:71, Nov. 25, 1963
Roy, C., "Les Grandes Distances", *Nouvelle Revue Francaise*, 9:110-18, 1961
Saturday Review, 46:24, Nov. 30, 1963
Time (5-26-75), 105-59

Rise and Fall of the City of Mahagonny, 1929
Nation (3-16-74), 218:349
Newsweek (3-11-74), 83:91

The Roundheads and the Peakheads, 1936
Alter, Marie P., "Bertolt Brecht und die Rassischen Minderheiten", *German Quarterly* (1967), 40:58-67
Hill, Claude, *Bertolt Brecht*. 1975. Pp. 84-87

Die Rundköpfe und die Spitzköpfe   *SEE*   The Roundheads and the Peakheads

St. Joan of the Stockyards, 1932
Ansorge, P., "St. Joan of the Stockyards", *Plays and Players* (1974), 21:45
Berendsohn, Walter A., "Bertolt Brecht, 'Die Heilige Johanna der Schlacht-hofe'", *Colloquia Germanica. Internationale Zeitschrift für Germanische Sprache-und Literaturwissenschaft* (1970), Pp. 46-61
Demetz, Peter, ed., *Brecht; A Collection of Critical Essays*. 1962. Pp. 51-58
Dukore, Bernard F. and Daniel C. Gerould, "Explosions and Implosions; Avant-Garde Drama Between World Wars", *Educational Theatre Journal* (Mar. 1969), 21:1-16
Hermann, Hans P., "Von 'Baal' Zur 'Heiligen Johanna der Schlachthofe': Die Dramatische Produktion des Jungen Brecht als Ort Gesellschaftlicher Erfahrung", *Poetica* (1972), 5:191-211
Hill, Claude, *Bertolt Brecht*. 1975. Pp. 70-76
Mews, Siegfried and Herbert Knust, eds., *Essays on Brecht; Theater and Politics*. 1974. Pp. 114-40
Muller, Gerd, "Brechts 'Heilige Johanna der Schlachthöfe' und Schillers 'Jungfrau von Orleans': Zur Auseinandersetzung des Modernen Theaters mit der Klassischen Tradition", *Orbis Litterarum* (1969), 24:182-200
Neuland, Brunhild, "Bemerkungen Zur Funktion der Parodie in Bertolt Brechts Stück 'Die Heilige Johanna der Schlachthöfe'", *Wissenschaftliche Zeitschrift der Friedrich Schiller* (1974), 23, i:119-24

Newsweek (May 10, 1971), 77:123
Wagner, Peter, "Bertolt Brechts 'Die Heilige Johanna der Schlachthöfe'",
Jahrbuch der Deutschen Schiller-Gesellschaft (1968), 12:493-519

Schweyk in the Second World War, 1957
Knust, Herbert, "Brechts Braver Schweyk", *Modern Language Association,
Publications* (1973), 88:219-29

Schweyk im Zweiten Weltkrieg   *SEE*   Schweyk in the Second World War

Señora Carrar's Rifles, 1937
Hill, Claude, *Bertolt Brecht*. 1975. Pp. 89-91
Mews, Siegfried and Herbert Knust, eds., *Essays on Brecht; Theater and
Politics*. 1974. Pp. 156-73

Seven Deadly Sins, 1933
Loomis, Emerson Robert, "A Re-Interpretation of Bertolt Brecht: The moral Choice in 'Die Sieben Todsunden'", *Univ. of Kansas City Review*,
27:51-56, 1960
Studies in the German Drama; A Festschrift in Honor of Walter Silz. Ed.
by Donald H. Crosby and George C. Schoolfield. 1974. Pp. 235-52

Die Sieben Todsünden der Kleinbürger   *SEE*   The Seven Deadly Sins

Der Tage de Commune   *SEE*   The Days of the Commune

Three Penny Opera, 1928
Bauland, Peter, *The Hooded Eagle; Modern German Drama on the New
York Stage*. 1968. Pp. 180-83
Brustein, Robert Sanford, *The Theatre of Revolt; An Approach to the Modern
Drama*. 1964. Pp. 259-67
Brustein, Robert, *The Third Theatre*. 1969. Pp. 131-40
Dukore, Bernard F., "The Averted Crucifixion of Macheath", *Drama Survey*
4:51-56, 1965
Grossvogel, David I., *Four Playwrights and a Postscript: Brecht, Ionesco,
Beckett and Génêt*. 1962. Pp. 25-44
Hill, Claude, *Bertolt Brecht*. 1975. Pp. 55-59
Lumley, Frederick, *New Trends in Twentieth Century Drama; A Survey
Since Ibsen and Shaw*. 1967. Pp. 80-90
Marx, Robert, "The Operatic Brecht", *American Scholar* (1974/75), 44:
283-90
Sherwin, Judith Johnson, "'The World is Mean and Man Uncouth'",
Virginia Quarterly Review, 35:258-70, 1959
Swados, Harvey, *A Radical's America*. 1962. Pp. 184-90
Weisstein, Ulrich, "Brecht's Victorian Version of Gay: Imitation and Orig-
inality in the 'Dreigroschenoper'", *Comparative Literature Studies* (1970),
7:314-35
Williams, Raymond, *Modern Tragedy*. 1966. Pp. 191-95

The Trial of Joan of Arc at Rouen, 1431, 1952
Reitz, Leonard, "The Historical Plays of Brecht", *Dissertation Abstracts
International* (1972), 32:4019A

The Trial of Lucullus, 1940
Hill, Claude, *Bertolt Brecht*. 1975. Pp. 91-93

Trommeln in der Nacht   *SEE*   Drums in the Night

Trumpets and Drums, 1956
  Ferran, Peter W., "Brecht and Farquhar; The Critical Art of Dramatic Adaptation", *Dissertation Abstracts International* (1973), 33:6353A
  Tynan, Kenneth, *Curtains; Selections from the Drama Criticism and Related Writings.* 1961. Pp. 452-54

Turandot oder der Kongress der Weisswascher   *SEE*   Turandot, or the Congress of The Whitewashers

Turandot, or The Congress of the Whitewashers, 1953
  Kostic, Predrag, " 'Turandot': Das Letzte Dramatische Werk Bertolt Brechs", *Weimarer Beitrage* (1968), Heft S:185-94

Das Verhör des Lukullus   *SEE*   Trial of Lucullus

GEORG BÜCHNER

Danton's Death, 1902
  America, 113:647-48, Nov. 20, 1965
  Bach, Anneliese, "Verantwortlichkeit und Fatalismus in Georg Büchners Drama 'Dantons Tod' ", *Wirkendes Wort*, 6:217-29, 1956
  Baxandall, Lee, "George Büchner's 'Danton's Death' ", *Tulane Drama Review*, 6:136-49, 1962
  Beacham, Richard, "Büchner's Use of Sources in Danton's Death' ", *Yale/Theatre* (1972), 3, iii:45-55
  Bell, Gerda E., "Windows: A Study of a Symbol in Georg Büchner's Work", *Germanic Review* (1972), 47:95-108
  Bodi, Leslie, " 'Sensualism' and 'Spiritualism' in Büchner's 'Danton's Death' ", *Komos: A Quarterly of Drama and Arts of the Theatre* (1973), 3:17-19
  Brustein, Robert. *The Third Theatre.* 1969. Pp. 160-64
  Catholic World, 148:345, Dec., 1938
  Christian Century, 82:1578, Dec. 22, 1965
  Commentary, 41:55-56, Jan., 1966
  Commonweal, 29:104, Nov. 18, 1938, and 83:191-92, Nov. 12, 1965
  Cowen, R. C., "Grabbe's 'Don Juan und Faust' and Büchner's 'Dantons Tod': Epicureanism and Weltschmerz", *Modern Language Association. Publications* (1967), 82:342-51
  _____ , "Grabbe's Napoleon, Büchner's Danton and the Masses", *Symposium* (1967), 21:316-23
  Donoghue, Denis, *The Ordinary Universe; Soundings in Modern Literature.* 1968. Pp. 146-68
  Fleissner, E. M., "Revolution as Theatre; 'Danton's Death' and 'Marat/Sade' ", *Massachusetts Review* (1966), 7:543-56
  Gassner, John, *Dramatic Soundings; Evaluations and Retractions Culled from Thirty Years of Dramatic Criticism.* 1968. Pp. 552-53
  Goldstein, Melvin, ed., *Metapsychological Literary Criticism; Theory and Practice; Essays in Honor of Leonard Falk Manheim.* 1973. Pp. 46-48
  Hamburger, Michael, *Art as Second Nature; Occasional Pieces, 1950-1974.* 1975. Pp. 64-67
  Helbig, Louis F., "Zitatprobleme und Historische Wahrheit in Georg Büchners 'Dantons Tod' ", *Dissertation Abstracts International* (1970), 31:1758A

Holmes, T. M., "The Ideology of the Moderates in Büchner's 'Danton's Death'", *German Life and Letters* (1974), 27:93-100

Hörnigk, Frank, "Über den Umgang Mit dem Erbe", *Weimarer Beiträge* (1974), 20, vii:161-70

Illustrated London News, 234:224, Feb. 7, 1959

Kerr, Walter, *Thirty Plays Hath November; Pain and Pleasure in the Contemporary Theater*. 1969. Pp. 273-77

Lazarowicz, Klaus and Kron, Wolfgang, eds., *Unterscheidung und Bewahrung; Festschrfit für Hermann Kunisch zum 60 Geburtstag*, Berlin, deGruyter, 1961, Pp. 1-11

Mayer, Thomas, "Zur Revision der Quellen für 'Dantons Tod' von Georg Büchner", *Studi Germanici* (1971), 9:223-33

Milburn, Douglas, Jr., "Social Conscience and Social Reform; The Political Paradox of 'Danton's Death'", *Rice University Studies* (Fall 1967), 53:23-31

Nation, 182:538, June 23, 1956, and 201:370-71, Nov. 15, 1965

New Republic 53:194-95, Jan. 4, 1928 and 97:100, Nov. 30, 1938 and 153:37-38, Nov. 6, 1965

New Statesman, 57:186, Feb. 7, 1959

New Yorker, 41:108, Oct. 30, 1965

Newsweek, 12:28, Nov. 14, 1938

Novick, Julius, *Beyond Broadway; The Quest for Permanent Theatres*. 1968. Pp. 198-201

Roche, Reinhard, "Stilus Demagogicus. Beobachtungen an Robespierres Rede im Jakobinerklub", *Wirkendes Wort* (1964), 14:244-54

Saturday Review, 48:41, Nov. 6, 1965

Schonauer, Franz, "Das Drama und die Geschichte. Versuch über Georg Büchners 'Danton'", *Du. Kulturelle Monatsschrift* (1965), 25:790-93

Simon, John, "On 'Danton's Death'", *Yale/Theatre* (1972), 3,iii:35-44

Spectator, 202:183-84, Feb. 6, 1959

Studies in the German Drama; A Festschrift in Honor of Walter Silz. 1974. Pp. 169-78

Szondi, Peter, "Dantons Tod", *Neue Rundschau*, 71:652-57, 1960

Teichmann, Max, "'Danton's Death': An Early Psychodrama", *Komos: A Quarterly of Drama and Arts of the Theatre* (1973), 3:21-23

Theatre Arts, 23:13-14, Jan., 1939

Theatre Arts Anthology; A Record and A Prophecy, ed. by Rosamond Gilder. 1950. Pp. 609-13

Time, 32:61, Nov. 14, 1938 and 86:84, Oct. 29, 1965

Vogue, 146:146, Dec., 1965

Waldeck, Peter B., "Georg Büchner's 'Dantons Tod': Dramatic Structure and Individual Necissity", *Susquehanna University Studies* (1974), 9, iv:211-25

Wessel, Leonard P., "Eighteenth Century Theodicy and the Death of God in Büchner's 'Dantons Tod'", *Seminar, A Journal of Germanic Studies* (1972), 8:198-218

Williams, Raymond, *Drama from Ibsen to Brecht*. 1968. Pp. 236-39

Worrall, G. S., 'The Historical Background to 'Danton's Death'", *Komos: A Quarterly of Drama and Arts of the Theatre* (1973), 3:19-21

Dantons Tod *SEE* Danton's Death

Leonce and Lena, 1885
Bell, Gerda E., "Windows: A Study of a Symbol in Georg Büchner's Work", *Germanic Review* (1972), 47:95-108
Fink, Gauthier-Louis, "Léonce et Lena: Comédie et Réalisme Chez Büchner", *Etudes Germaniques*, 16:223-34, 1961
Hauser, Ronald, "Georg Büchners 'Leonce und Lena'", *Monatshefte*, 53: 338-46, 1961
Hinze, Klaus-Peter, "Zusammenhange Zwischen Diskrepanter Information und Dramatischen Effekt. Theoretische Grundlegung des Problems und Nachweis in George Buchners 'Leonce und Lena'", *Germanisch-Romanische Monatsschrift* (1970), 20:205-13
Kayser, Wolfgang Johannes, *The Grotesque in Art and Literature*. 1963. Pp. 48-99
Mattenklott, Gert and Klaus R. Scherpe, eds., *Demokratisch-Revolutionàre Literatur in Deutschland: Vormarz*. 1974. Pp. 85-115
Maveety, Beth E., "Three Phases of Comedy; A Study of the Archetypal Patterns in 'Leonce und Lena', 'Der Zerbrochene Krug' and 'Die Physiker'", *Dissertation Abstracts International* (1970), 30:3469A
Nation, 202:26-27, Jan. 3, 1966
Newsweek (4-22-74), 83:117
Pfafferdot, Hans G. and Sloane Bosniak, "Büchner's 'Leonce and Lena' at the Arena Stage, Washington", *Theatre Quarterly* (1974), 4:70-84
Shaw, Leroy R., "Symbolism of Time in Büchner's 'Leonce und Lena'", *Monatshefte für Deutsche Unterricht, Deutsche Sprache und Literatur* (Wisconsin), 48:221-30, 1956
Steffen, Hans, ed., *Das Deutsche Lustspiel*. 1968. Pp. 225-42
Studies in the German Drama; A festschrift in Honor of Walter Silz. 1974. Pp. 169-78

Pietro Aretino, n. d.
Schechter, Joel, "'Pietro Aretino': Georg Büchner's Lost Play", *Yale/ Theatre* (1972), 3,iii:94-98

Woyzeck, 1913
Bell, Gerda E., "Windows; A Study of a Symbol in Georg Büchner's Work", *Germanic Review* (1972), 47:95-108
Bornscheuer, Lothar, "Neue Beurteilung der "Wozzeck' Handschriften", *Germanisch-Romanische Monatsschrift* (1972), 22:113-23
Cox, C. B. and A. E. Dyson, eds., *The Twentieth Century Mind: History, Ideas, and Literature in Britain*. 1972. Pp. 309-26
Hamann, Holger, "Zum Namen der Weiblichen Hauptperson in Büchners 'Woyzeck'", *Orbis Litterarum* (1970), 25:259-60
Kanzog, Klaus, "Wozzeck, Woyzeck und Kein Ende: Zur Standortbestimmung de Editionsphilologie", *Deutsche Vierteljahrsschrift für Literaturwissenschaft und Geistesgeschichte* (1973), 47:420-42
Kayser, Wolfgang Johannes, *The Grotesque in Art and Literature*. 1963. Pp. 48-99
Lambrechts, Luc, "Zur Struktur von Büchners 'Woyzeck': Mit Einer Darstellung des Dramaturgischen Verhaltnisscs Büchner-Brecht", *Amsterdamer Beiträge zur Neueren Germanistik* (1972), 1:119-28
Lehmann, Werner I., "Beiträge zu Einem Steitgespräch über den Woyzeck'", *Euphorion. Zeitschrift für Literaturgeschichte* (1971), 65:58-83

Messenger, A. P., "Barefoot into Hell; Clothing Imagery in 'Woyzeck'",
     Modern Drama (Feb. 1971), 13:393-97
Nation (4-10-76), 222:446
New Yorker (4-5-76), 52:96
Newsweek, 67:96, April 18, 1966
Paulus, U., "Georg Büchners 'Wozzeck'", *Jahrbuch der Deutschen Schiller-
     gesellschaft* (1964), 8:226-46
Stein, Jack M., "From Woyzeck to Woyzeck; Alban Berg's Adaptation to
     Buchner", *Germanic Review* (May 1972), 47:168-80
Stodder, J. H., "Influences of 'Othello' on Büchner's 'Woyzeck'", *Modern
     Language Review* (1974), 69:115-20
Studies in the German Drama; A Festschrift in Honor of Walter Silz. 1974.
     Pp. 169-78
Wiles, Timothy, "'Wozzeck', Immer Zu", *Yale/Theatre* (1972), 3,iii:83-89
Williams, Raymond, *Drama from Ibsen to Brecht.* 1968. Pp. 233-36
Zetler, Greta L, "Büchners Weg zu 'Wozzeck'", *Language Quarterly* (1974),
     12,iii-iv:29-32

PEDRO CALDERÓN DE LA BARCA

Absalom's Hair, 1628
     Edwards, Gwynne, "Calderón's 'Los Cabellos de Absalón': A Reappraisal",
          Bulletin of Hispanic Studies (1971), 48:218-38
     Edwards, Gwynne, "Sobre la Transmission del Texto de 'Los Cabellos de
          Absalon'", *Revista de Archivos, Bibliotecas y Museos* (1973), 76:109-20
     Gates, Eunice Joiner, "Proverbs in the Plays of Calderon", *Romanic Re-
          view*, 38:204-05, 1947
     Hesse, Everett W., *Calderon de la Barca.* 1967. Pp. 64-70

El Alcalde de su Mismo   *SEE*   His Own Judge

El Alcalde de Zalamea   *SEE*   The Mayor of Zalamea

El Alcalde de Zalamea   *SEE*   The Mayor of Zalamea

El Astrologo Fingido   *SEE*   The False Astrologer

Basta Callar   *SEE*   It is Enough to Keep Silent

Beware of Smooth Water, 1649
     Hayes, F. C., "The Use of Proverbs as Titles and Motives in the Siglo de
          Oro Drama; Calderon", *Hispanic Review*, 15:453-63, 1947

Bien Vengas, Mal, Si Vienes Solo   *SEE*   Welcome, Trouble, If You Come Alone

The Blush of the Rose, 1660
     Hesse, Everett W., "Court References in Calderon's Zarzuelas", *Hispanic
          Review*, 15:365-77, 1947
     Stevenson, Robert, "The First New World Opera", *Américas*, 16:33-35, 1964

Los Cabellos de Absalón   *SEE*   Absalom's Hair

Casa con Dos Puertas, Mala Es de Guardar   *SEE*   A House with Two Doors
     is Difficult to Guard

La Cisma de Inglaterra *SEE* The Schism of England
El Conde Lucanor *SEE* Count Lucanor

The Constant Prince, 1629
Gilman, Richard, *Common and Uncommon Masks; Writings on the Theatre, 1961-70*. 1971. Pp. 308-10
Hesse, Everett W., *Calderón de la Barca*. 1967. Pp. 70-82
Loftis, John, " 'El Principe Constante' and 'The Indian Emperour': A Reconsideration", *Modern Language Review* (Oct. 1970), 65:761-67
Loftis, John, *The Spanish Plays of Neo-Classical England*. 1973. Pp. 178-208
Norval, Maria, "Another Look at Calderón's 'El Principe Constante' ", *Bulletin of the Comediantes* (1973), 25:18-28
Reichenberger, A. G., "Calderón's 'El Principe Constante'; A Tragedy?", *Modern Language Notes*, 75:668-70, 1960
Rivers, Elias L., "Fenix's Sonnet in Calderón's 'Principe Constante' ", *Hispanic Review* (1969), 37:452-58
Salley, W. C., "A Possible Influence of the 'Abencerraje' Story on Calderón's 'El Principe Constante' ", *Romanic Review*, 23:331-33, 1932
Shergold, N. D. and Peter Ure, "Dryden and Calderón: A New Spanish Source for "The Indian Emperor' ", *Modern Language Review* (1966), 61:369-83
Sloane, Robert, "Action and Role in 'El Principe Constante' ", *Modern Language Notes* (1970), 85:167-83
Sloane, Robert A., "Character and Role: The Problem of Identity in Four Plays of Pedro Calderón de la Barca", *Dissertation Abstracts International* (1973), 33:6376A
Truman, R. W., "Theme of Justice in 'El Principe Constante' ", *Modern Language Review*, 59:43-52, 1964
Wardropper, Bruce W., "Christian and Moor in Calderón's 'El Principe Constante' ", *Modern Language Review*, 53:512-20, 1958
——————————— , *Critical Essays on the Theatre of Calderón*. 1964. Pp. 137-66
Whitby, William M., "Calderón; 'El Principe Constante': Fenix's Role in the Ransom of Fernando's Body", *Bulletin of the Comediantes*, 8:1-4, 1956
Whitby, William M., "Structural Symbolism in Two Plays of Pedro Calderón de la Barca", *Dissertation Abstracts International* (1972), 32:989A
Wilson, E. M. and Entwistle, W. J., "Calderón's 'Principe Constante'; Two Appreciations", *Modern Language Review*, 34:207-22, 1939
——————————— , "Early Rehash of Calderón's 'El Principe Constante' ", *Modern Language Notes*, 76:785-94, 1961

Count Lucanor, 1661
Ashcom, B. B., "The Two Versions of Calderón's 'El Conde Lucanor' ", *Hispanic Review* (1973), Special Issue 41:151-60

La Dama Duende *SEE* The Fairy Lady

Darlo Todo y No Dar Nada *SEE* Give Everything or Nothing

The Daughter of the Air, 1653
Brancaforte, Benito, "Croce on Lope and Calderón; The Application of an Aesthetic Theory", *Symposium* (Sum. 1969), 23:101-15

Edwards, G., "Calderón's 'La Hija del Aire' in the light of his sources", *Bulletin of Hispanic Studies* (1966), 43:177-96

_____ , "Calderón's 'La Hija del Aire' and the Classical Type of Tragedy", *Bulletin of Hispanic Studies* (1967), 44:161-94

Hesse, Everett W., *Calderón de la Barca*. 1967. Pp. 94-103

Rogers, Daniel, "Cielos! Quien en Ninias Habla?': The Mother-Son Impersonation in 'La Hija del Aire' ", *Bulletin of the Comediantes* (1968), 20:1-4

La Devoción de la Cruz, 1633

Hesse, Everett W., "The Alienation Problem in Calderón's 'La Devoción de la Cruz' ", *Revista de Estudios Hispanicos* (1973), 7:361-81

Honig, Edwin, *Calderón and the Seizures of Honor*. 1972. Pp. 53-80

Honig, Edwin, "Calderón's Strange Mercy Play", *Massachusetts Review* (Univ. Mass.), 3:80-107, 1961

Sloane, Robert A., "Character and Role; The Problem of Identy in Four Plays of Pedro Calderón de la Barca", *Dissertation Abstracts International* (1973), 33:6376A

Smieja, Florián, "Julia's Reasoning in Calderón's 'La Devoción de la Cruz' ", *Bulletin of the Comediantes* (1973), 25:37-39

Wardropper, Bruce W., ed., *Critical Essays on the Theatre of Calderón*. 1964. Pp. 169-92

Echo and Narcissus, 1661

Cros, Edmond, "Paganisme et Christianisme dans 'Eco y Narciso' de Calderón", *Revue des Langues Romanes* (Montpellier), 75:39-74, 1962

Groult, P., "Sur 'Eco y Narciso' de Calderón", *Les Lettres Romanes*, 16: 103-13, 1962

Hesse, Everett W., *Calderón de la Barca*, 1967. Pp. 129-36

_____ , "Estructura e Interpretación d una Comedia de Calderón: 'Eco y Narciso' ", *Filologia* (Buenos Aires), 7:61-76, 1963

_____ , "The 'Terrible Mother' Image in Calderón's 'Eco y Narciso' ", *Romance Notes*, 1:133-36, 1960

Kossoff, A. David and Jose Amor y Vásquez, eds., *Homenaje a William L. Fichter: Estudios Sobre el Teatro Antigua Hispanico y Otros Ensayos*. 1971. Pp. 47-58

Eco y Narciso *SEE* Echo and Narcissus

En Esta Vida Todo Es Verdad y Todo Mentira *SEE* In This Life, Everything is Both True and False

La Estatua de Prometeo *SEE* Prometheus' Statue

The Fairy Lady, 1629

Dalbor, John B., " 'La Dama Duende' de Calderón y 'The Parson's Wedding' de Killigrew", *Hispanofila* (Madrid), 2:41-50, 1958

Fucilla, Joseph G., " 'La Dama Duende' and 'La Vinda Valenciana' ", *Bulletin of the Comediantes* (1970), 22:29-32

Honig, Edwin, *Calderón and the Seizures of Honor*. 1972. Pp. 110-57

_____ , "Flickers of Incest on the Face of Honor; Calderón's 'Phantom Lady' ", *Tulane Drama Review*, 6:69-105, 1962

Kuehne, Alyce de, "Los Planos de la Realidad Aparente y la Realidad Auténtica en 'La Dama Duende' de Calderón", *Pacific Coast Philology* (1967), 2:40-46

Sloane, Robert A., "Character and Role; The Problem of Identity in Four Plays of Pedro Calderón de la Barca", *Dissertation Abstracts International* (1973), 33:6376A

The False Astrologer, 1624
Oppenheimer, Max, Jr., "The Burla in Calderón's 'El Astrologo Fingido'", *Philological Quarterly*, 27:241-63, 1948
Lorenz, Erika, "Calderón und die Astrologie", *Romanistisches Jahrbuch*, 12:265-77, 1961

Las Fortunas de Andromeda y Perseo *SEE* The Fortunes of Andromeda and Perseus

The Fortunes of Andromeda and Perseus, 1653
Flasche, Hans, "Antiker Mythos in Christlichen Umprägung: 'Andromeda und Perseus' bei Calderón", *Romanistisches Jahrbuch* (1965), 16:290-317
Martin, H. M., "Corneille's 'Andromede' and Calderón's 'Las Fortunas'", *Modern Philology* (1926), 23:407-15
─────── , "The Perseus Myth in Lope de Vega and Calderón with Some Reference to Their Sources", *Modern Language Association. Publications* (PMLA), 46:450-60, 1931
Merrick, C. A., "Education and Art: Calderón's 'La Vida es Sueño' and 'Las Fortunas de Andromeda y Perseo'", *Dissertation Abstracts International* (1973) 33:3658A
─────── , "Neoplatonic Allegory in Calderón's 'Las Fortunas de Andromeda y Perseo'", *Modern Language Review* (1972), 67:319-27

From Bad to Worse, 1630
Hogan, Floriana T., "Notes on Savage's 'Love in a Veil' and Calderón's 'Peor Está que Estaba'", *Restoration and 18th Century Theatre Research* (1969), 8:23-29

Give Everything or Nothing, 1651
Portera, John J., "Estudio y Edicion Critica de la Comedia 'Darlo Todo y No Dar Nada' de Pedro Calderón de la Barca", *Dissertation Abstracts International* (1971), 32:929A

El Golfo de las Sirenas *SEE* The Gulf of the Sirens

El Gran Duque de Gandia *SEE* The Grand Duke of Gandia

The Grand Duke of Gandia, 1639?
Calvo, Juan A., "Aportación al Estudio de la Métrica de 'El Gran Duque de Gandía'", *Bulletin of the Comediantes* (1969), 21:12-15
Hornedo, Rafael M. de., "La Comedia 'El Gran Duque de Gandía'", *Razón y Fe* (Madrid), 169:131-44, 1964
Liebenmann, Gustav, "El Gran Duque de Gandia. Ein Nenentdecktes Drama von Calderón", *Germanisch-Romanisch Monatsschrift* (1965), 15:262-75
Novak, O., "Une Pièce de Pedro Calderón de la Barca Retrouvée en Tchecoslovaquie", *Sbornik Prac; Filosoficke Fakulty Brnĕnske University. Rady Literarnevĕdne*, 13:165-77, 1964
Whitaker, Shirley B., "Schoolboy Actors in 'El Gran Duque de Gandia'", *Bulletin of the Comediantes* (1970), 22:3-5

El Gran Teatro del Mundo *SEE* The Great Theatre of the World

Great Theatre of the World, 1633
  Fiore, Robert L., "Calderón's 'El Gran Teatro del Mundo': An Ethical In-
  terpretation", *Hispanic Review* (1972), 40:40-52
  Hesse, Everett W., *Calderón de la Barca*. 1967. Pp. 152-55
  Perez, Louis C., "Perspectiva Dramatica en 'El Gran Teatro del Mundo'",
  Hispanofila (1967), 10:30:1-6

Guardate del Agua Mansa *SEE* Beware of Smooth Water

The Gulf of the Sirens, 1657
  Hesse, Everett W., "Court References in Calderón's Zarzuelas", *Hispanic
  Review*, 15:365-77, 1947

La Hija del Aire *SEE* The Daughter of the Air

His Own Judge, 1636
  Nagy, Edward, "La Parodia y la Sátira en el 'Alcaide de si Mismo' de Pedro
  Calderón de la Barca", *Romanische Forschungen* (1971), 83:201-19

El Hombre Pobre Todo Es Trazas *SEE* Poverty Sharpens the Wits

A House with Two Doors Is Difficult to Guard, 1636
  Hayes, F. C., "The Use of Proverbs as Titles and Motives in the Siglo de Oro
  Drama: Calderón", *Hispanic Review*, 15:453-63, 1947
  Hesse, Everett W., *Calderon de la Barca*. 1967. Pp. 47-56
  Varez, J. E., "'Casa Con Dos Puertas': Towards a Definition of Calderón's
  View of Comedy", *Modern Language Review* (1972), 67:83-94

In This Life Everything is Both True and False, 1659
  Boivin, Carmelito, "Voltaire's Criticism of Calderón's 'Todo Es Verdad y
  Todo Mentira'", *Romanische Forschungen* (1973), 85:348-55
  Schramm, E., "Corneilles 'Heraclius' und Calderóns 'En Esta Vida Todo Es
  Verdad y Todo Mentira'; Ein Beitrage zur Geschichte der Literarischen
  Beziehungen Zwischen Frankreich und Spanien in 17. Jahrhundert",
  Revue Hispanique (1927), 71:225-308

It Is Enough to Keep Silent, 1682
  Trevino, S. N., "Versos Desconocidos de Una Comedia de Calderón",
  Modern Language Association. Publications (PMLA), 52:682-704, 1937

El Laurel de Apolo, 1658
  Hesse, Everett W., "Court References in Calderón's Zarzuelas", *Hispanic
  Review*, 15:365-77, 1947

La Lepra de Constantino *SEE* Constantine's Leprosy

Life is a Dream, 1634
  Bandera, Cesáreo, "El 'Confuso Abismo' de 'La Vida es Sueño'", *Modern
  Language Notes* (1972), 87:214-31
  Bandera, C., "El Itinerio de Segismundo en 'La Vida es Sueño'", *Hispanic
  Review* (1967), 35:69-84
  Bandera, Cesareo, "Significacion de Clarin en 'La Vida es Sueño'", *Atlantida*
  (1971), 9:638-46
  Brody, Ervin C., "Poland in Calderón's 'Life Is a Dream': Poetic Illusion
  or Historical Reality", *Polish Review* (1969), 14:21-62

Buchanan, M. A., "Calderón's 'Life is a Dream'.", *Modern Language Association. Publications* (PMLA), 47:1303-21, 1933
————— , "'Culteranismo' in Calderón's 'La Vida es Sueño'", *Homenaje a Menendez Pidal*, 1:545-55, 1926
————— , "Segismundo's Soliloquy on Liberty in Calderón's 'La Vida es Sueño'", *Modern Language Association. Publications* (PMLA), 23: 240-53, 1908
Cape, J. I., "Platonic Metamorphoses of Calderón's 'La Vida Es Sueño'", *Modern Language Notes* (Mar. 1971), 86:225-41
Cargo, Robert T. and Emanuel J. Mickel, Jr., eds., *Studies in Honor of Alfred G. Engstrom*. 1972. Pp. 81-86
Casalduero, Joaquin, "Sentido y Forma de 'La Vida es Sueño'", *Cuadernos del Congreso por la Libertad de la Cultura*, #51:3-13, 1961
Cilveta, Angel L., "La Function de la Metáfora en 'La Vida es Sueño'", *Nueva Revista de Filologia Hispanica* (1973), 22:17-38
Cope, Jackson I., *The Theater and the Dream; From Metaphor to Form in Renaissance Drama*. 1973. Pp. 245-60
Crocker, L. G., "'Hamlet', 'Don Quijote', and 'La Vida es Sueño'; The Quest for Values", *Modern Language Association. Publications* (PMLA), 69: 278-313, 1954
Dale, George I., "Augustin de Rojas and 'La Vida es Sueño'", *Hispanic Review*, 2:319-26, 1934
Feal, Gisèle and Carlos Feal-Deibe, "'La Vida es Sueño': De la Psicologiá al mito", *Reflexion II* (1972), 1, i:35-55
Halkhorce, Premraj, "A Note on the Ending of 'La Vida es Sueño'", *Bulletin of the Comediantes* (1972), 24:8-11
Hall, H. B., "Poetic Justice in 'La Vida Es Sueño'", *Bulletin of Hispanic Studies* (1969), 46:128-31
Heiple, Daniel L., "The Tradition Behind the Punishment of the Rebel Soldier in 'La Vida es Sueño'", *Bulletin of Hispanic Studies* (1973), 50:1-17
Hesse, Everett W., *Calderón de la Barca*. 1967. Pp. 38-40, 137-48, and 178-81
————— , "La Conception Calderoniana del Príncipe Perfecto en 'La Vida es Sueño'", *Clavileño*, 4:204-12, 1953
————— , "'La Vida es Sueño' and the Paradox of Violence", *Revista de Estudios Hispanicos* (1971), 5:3-17
Honig, Edwin, *Calderón and the Seizures of Honor*. 1972. Pp. 158-77
Honig, Edwin, "Reading What's in 'La Vida es Sueño'", *Théâtre Annual*, 20:63-71, 1963
Jacquot, Jean, ed., *Dramaturgie et Société; Rapports entre l'Oeuvre Théâtrale, Son Interpretation et Son Public aux XVI et XVII Siecles*. 1968. Pp. 93-109
Johnson, Carroll B., "Segismundo en Palacio; Nota Sobre 'La Vida Es Sueño, Jornada II", *Duquesne Hispanic Review* (1969), 8:7-17
Knoke, Ulrich, "Calderóns Drama 'La Vida Es Sueño' und Seine Kritiker", *Romanistischen Jahrbuch* (1969), 20:239-89
Kossoff, A. David and José Amor y Vasquez, eds., *Homenaje a William L. Fichter: Estudios Sobre el Teatro Antigua Hispanico y Otros Ensayos*. 1971. Pp. 307-17
Maurin, N. S., "Monster, The Sepulchre and the Dark; Related Patterns of Imagery in 'La Vida es Sueño'", *Hispanic Review* (1967), 35:161-78

Merrick, C. A., "Clotaldo's Role in 'La Vida es Sueño'", *Bulletin of Hispanic Studies* (1973), 50:256-69

————————, "Education and Art; Calderón's 'La Vida es Sueño' and 'Las Fortunas de Andromeda y Perseo'". *Dissertation Abstracts International* (1973), 33:3658A

Papini, Giovanni, *Four and Twenty Minds*. 1922. Pp. 296-307

Paterson, Alan K. G., "The Traffic of the Stage in Calderón's 'La Vida es Sueño'", *Renaissance Drama* (1971), 4:155-83

Porrata, Francisco E., "El Sueño in 'La Vida es Sueño'", *Abside* (1972), 36:305-19

Renaissance Drama, 1971: Essays Principally on the Playhouse and Staging; ed. S. Schoenbaum. 1971. Pp. 155-83

Risco, A. L., "El Sigismundo Historico de 'La Vida es Sueño'", *University of Buenos Aires*, 2:379-464, 1949

Rubio, David, "La Fuente de 'La Vida es Sueño' de Calderón", *Bol. del Inst. Caro y Cuervo*, 5:301-07, 1951

Salvador, A., "Concepción de la Vida Como Sueño" *Cuadernos Hispanoamericanos* (Madrid), 42:370-76, 1961

Suárez-Galbán, Eugenio, "Astolfo: La Moral y su Illustración Dramática en 'La Vida Es Sueño'", Hispanófila (1970), 38:1-12

Sauvage, M., "Le Symbole dans la Dramaturgie de Calderón", *Recherches et Débats du Centre, Catholique des Intellectuals Français*, #29:104-11, 1959

Schevill, R., "'Virtudes Vencen Senales' and 'La Vida es Sueño'", *Hispanic Review*, 1:181-95, 1933

Seward, Patricia M., "Calderón and Aphra Behn: Spanish Borrowings in '.The Young King'", *Bulletin of Hispanic Studies* (1972), 49:149-64

Sloman, A. E., "Structure of Calderón's 'La Vida es Sueño'", *Modern Language Review*, 48:293-300, 1953

Sturm, Harlan G., "From Plato's Cave to Segismundo's Prison; The Four Levels of Reality and Experience", *Modern Language Notes* (1974), 89:280-89

Urrutia, Jorge, "Una Escena de 'La Vida Es Sueño: Su Organización Dramática", *Cuadernos Hispanoamericanos* (1970), 247:173-91

Wardropper, Bruce W., ed., *Critical Essays on the Theatre of Calderon*. 1964. Pp. 63-136

Weiger, John G., "Rebirth in 'La Vida Es Sueño'", *Romance Notes* (1968), 10:119-21

Whitby, William M., "Rosaura's Role in the Structure of 'La Vida es Sueño'", *Hispanic Review*, 28:16-27, 1960

————————, "Structural Symbolism in Two Plays of Pedro Calderón de la Barca", *Dissertation Abstracts International* (1972), 32:989A

El Magico Prodigioso   SEE   The Wonder-Working Magician

Mañanas de Abril y Mayo   SEE   Mornings in April and May

El Mayor Monstruo los Celos   SEE   No Monster Like Jealousy

Mayor of Zalamea, 1640

Aguirre, José M., "'El Alcalde de Zalamea': Venganza or Justicia?", *Estudios Filologicos* (1971), 7:119-32

Beardsley, Theodore S., Jr., "Socrates, Shakespeare, and Calderón: Advice to a Young Man", *Hispanic Review* (1974), 42:185-98

Casanova, Wilfredo O., "Honor, Patrimonio del Alma y Opinión Social, Patrimonio de Casta en 'El Alcalde de Zalamea'", *Hispanófila* (1968), 33:17-33

Catholic World, 162:554, March 1946

Cornejo, S., "Observaciones a la Critica de un Libro: Calderón's 'El Alcalde de Zalamea'", *Revue Hispanique*, 60:532-45, 1924

Halkhoree, Premraj, "The Four Days of 'El Alcalde de Zalamea'", *Romanistisches Jahrbuch* (1971), 22:284-96

Hayes, F. C., "The Use of Proverbs as Titles and Motives in the Siglo de Oro Drama: Calderón", *Hispanic Review*, 15:453-63, 1947

Hesse, Everett W., *Calderón de la Barca*. 1967. Pp. 57-63

Honig, Edwin, *Calderón and the Seizures of Honor*. 1972. Pp. 81-109

Honig, E., "Calderón's 'Mayor': Honor Humanized", *Tulane Drama Review* (1966), 10:134-55

Leavitt, Sturgis, E., "Pedro Crespo and the Captain in Calderón's 'Alcalde de Zalamea'", *Hispania*, 38:430-31, 1955

Jones, C. A., "Honor in 'El Alcalde de Zalamea'", *Modern Language Review*, 50:444-49, Oct. 1955

"Scene Division in Calderón's 'El Alcalde de Zalamea'", *Hispanic Review*, 19:66-71, 1951

Pincus Sigele, Rizel and Gonzalo Sobejano, eds., *Homenaje a Casalduero: Critica y Poesia. Ofrecido por Sus Amigos y Discipulos*. 1972. Pp. 263-73, and 411-18

Soons, C. A., "Caracteres e Imagenes en 'El Alcalde de Zalamea'", *Romanische Forschungen*, 72:104-07, 1960

Thompson, Francis, *Literary Criticisms; Newly Discovered and Collected by Terence L. Connally*. 1948. Pp. 530-33

Wardropper, Bruce W., ed., *Critical Essays on the Theatre of Calderón*. 1964. Pp. 193-223

El Médico de su Honra   SEE   The Surgeon of His Honor

Mornings in April and May, 1637

Hayes, F. C., "The Use of Proberbs as Titles and Motives in the Siglo de Oro Drama: Calderón", *Hispanic Review*, 15:453-63, 1947

No Hay Más Fortuna Que Dios, 1653

Danker, Frederick E., "Emblematic Technique in the 'Auto Sacramenta': Calderón's 'No Hay Más Fortuna Que Dios'", *Comparative Drama* (1972), 6:40-50

No Monster Like Jealousy, 1634

Chang-Rodriguez, R. and E. J. Martin, "Tema e Imágenes en 'El Mayor Monstruo del Mundo'", *Modern Language Notes* (1975), 90:278-82

Friedman, Edward H., "Dramatic Perspective in Calderón's 'El Mayor Monstruo de los Celos'", *Bulletin of the Comediantes* (1974), 26:43-49

Hesse, Everett W., *Calderón de la Barca*. 1967. Pp. 104-10

Sabin, Elenora R., "The Identities of the Monster in Calderón's 'El Mayor Monstruo del Mundo'", *Hispania* (1973), 56:269-75

Smith, Carolyn F., "Imagination and Ritual in the Honor Tragedies of Calderón", *Dissertation Abstracts Internatonal* (1973), 34:1295A

Pcor Está Que Estaba   SEE   From Bad to Worse

The Painter of His Own Dishonor, 1650
   Fisher, Susan L., "The Function and Significance of the 'Gracioso' in Cal-
      derón's 'El Pinto de su Deshonra' ", *Romance Notes* (1972),   14:334-40
   Patterson, Alan K. G., "The Comic and Tragic Melancholy of Juan Roca:
      A Study of Calderón's 'El Pintor de su Deshonra' ", *Forum for Modern
      Language Studies* (1969), 5:244-61
   Sloane, Robert A., "Character and Role; The Problem of Identity in Four
      Plays of Pedro Calderón de la Barca", *Dissertation Abstracts Inter-
      national* (1973), 33:6376A
   Thompson, Francis, *Literary Criticisms; Newly Discovered and Collected by
      Terence L. Connolly.* 1948. Pp. 530-33
   Wardropper, B. W., "Unconscious Mind in Calderón's 'El Pintor de su
      Deshonra' ", *Hispanic Review*, 18:285-301, 1950
   Watson, A. Irvine, " 'El Pintor de su Deshonra' and the Neo-Aristotelian
      Theory of Tragedy", *Bulletin of Hispanic Studies*, 40:17-34, 1963

El Pintor de Su Deshonra   *SEE*   The Painter of His Own Dishonor

Poverty Sharpens the Wits, 1628
   Nagy, Edward, "El Aspecto Picaresco-Cortesano en 'El Hombre Pobre Todo
      Es Trazas' de Pedro Calderón de la Barca", *Ibero-Romania* (1971), 3:
      44-59

El Principe Constante   *SEE*   The Constant Prince

Prometheus' Statue, 1669
   Hesse, Everett W., *Calderón de la Barca.* 1967. Pp. 123-29

La Purpura de la Rosa   *SEE*   The Blush of the Rose

The Schism of England, 1634
   Bacigalupo, Mario Ford, "Calderón's 'La Cisma de Inglaterra' and Spanish
      Seventeenth Century Political Thought", *Symposium* (1974), 28:212-27

Secret Vengeance for a Secret Insult, 1635
   Honig, Edwin, *Calderon and the Seizures of Honor.* 1972. Pp. 37-52
   Kossoff, A. David and José Amor y Vásquez, eds., *Homenaje a William
      L. Fichter; Estudios Sobre el Teatro Antigua Hispanico y Otros Ensayos.*
      1971. Pp. 295-306
   Smith, Carolyn F., "Imagination and Ritual in the Honor Tragedies of
      Calderon", *Dissertation Abstracts International* (1973), 34:1295A
   Wardropper, Bruce W., *Critical Essays on the Theatre of Calderón.* 1964.
      Pp. 169

A Secreto Agravio, Secreta Venganza *SEE* Secret Vengeance for a Secret Insult

La Sibila de Oriente   *SEE*   The Sibyl of the Orient

The Sibyl of the Orient, 1634
   Glaser, Edward, "Calderón de la Barca's 'La Sibila del Oriente' y 'Gran Reina
      de Saba' ", *Romanische Forschungen*, 72:381-403, 1960

Sueños Hay Que Verdad Son   *SEE*   There Are Dreams That Are True

Surgeon of his Honor, 1635
   Les Annales Politiques et Littéraires, 105:185-88, Feb. 25, 1935
   L'Europe Nouvelle, 18:286, March 23, 1935

Hesse, Everett W., *Calderón de la Barca.* 1967. Pp. 110-22

Kossoff, A. D., "El Medico de su Honra' and 'La Amiga del Bernal Frances' ", *Hispanic Review*, 24:66-70, 1956

Kossoff, A. David and José Amor y Vasquez, eds., *Homenaje a William L. Fichter; Estudios Sobre el Teatro Antigua Hispanico y Otros Ensayos.* 1971. Pp. 127-37

Reiter, Seymour, *World Theater; The Structure and Meaning of Drama.* 1973. Pp. 170-94

Rogers, D., "Tienen los Celos Pasos de Ladrones; Silence in Calderón's 'El Medico de su Honra' ", *Hispanic Review*, 33:273-89, 1965

Sloman, Albert E., "Calderón's 'El Medico' and 'La Amiga de Bernal Francis' ", *Bulletin of Hispanic Studies*, 34:168-69, 1957

Smith, Carolyn F., "Imagination and Ritual in the Honor Tragedies of Calderón", *Dissertation Abstracts International* (1973), 34:1295A

Soons, A., "The Convergence of Doctrine and Symbol in 'El Medico de su Honra' ", *Romanische Forschungen*, 72:370-80, 1960

Thiher, Roberta J., "The Final Ambiguity of 'El Medico de su Honra' ", *Studies in Philology* (1970), 67:237-44

Todd Memorial Volumes; Philological Studies, ed. by J. D. Fitzgerald and P. Taylor, vol. 1. 1930. Pp. 201-09

Wardropper, Bruce W., "Poetry and Drama in Calderón's 'El Medico de su Honra' ", *Romanic Review*, 49:3-11, 1958

There Are Dreams That Are True, 1670
Glaser, Edward, "Calderón de la Barca's 'Suenos Hay Que Verdad Son' ", *Zeitschrift fur Romanische Philologie* (1966) 82:41-77

The Three Greatest Marvels, 1636
Kossoff, A. David and José Amor y Vásquez, eds., *Homenaje a William L. Fichter; Estudios Sobre el Teatro Antigua Hispanico y Otros Ensayos.* 1971. Pp. 773-83

La Torre de Babilonia   *SEE*   The Tower of Babylon

The Tower of Babylon, 1650
Foster, David W., "Calderón's 'La Torre de Babilonia' and Christian Allegory", *Criticism* (1967), 9:142-54

Los Tres Mayores Prodigios   *SEE*   The Three Greatest Marvels

La Vida es Sueño   *SEE*   Life Is a Dream

Welcome, Trouble, If You Come Alone, 1635
Hayes, F. C., "The Use of Proverbs as Titles and Motives in the Siglo de Oro Drama: Calderón", *Hispanic Review*, 15:453-63, 1947

The Wonder-Working Magician, 1637
Entwistle, William J., "Justina's Temptation: An Approach to the Under-standing of Calderón", *Modern Language Review*, 40:180-91, 1945

Fucilla, Joseph G., "Una Imitazione dell 'Aminta' nel 'Magico Prodigioso' di Calderón", *Studi Tassiani*, 6:29-33, 1956

Heaton, Harry C., "Calderón and 'El Mágico Prodigioso' " *Hispanic Review*, 19:11-36, 93-103, 1951

——————————— , "Passage in Calderón's 'Mágico Prodigioso' ", *Modern Language Notes*, 46.31-33, 1931

Hesse, Everett W., *Calderón de la Barca*. 1967. Pp. 82-93

Julien, L., "Calderón de la Barca, Ecrivain Manichéen", *Cahiers d'Etudes Cathares*, 6:138-44, 1955

May, T. E., "Symbolism of 'El Mágico Prodigioso' ", *Romanic Review*, 54:95-112, 1963

Moczkowska, Katarzyna, "l'Analyze Comparée de l'Emploi de la Parodie et du mélange du Tragique et du Comique dans 'El Magico Prodigioso' de Calderon et 'The Tragical History of Dr. Faustus' de Marlowe", *Kwartalnik Neofilologiczny* (1974), 21:499-505

Moulton, Richard G., *World Literature and Its Place in General Culture*. 1911. Pp. 231-37

Oppenheimer, Max, Jr., "The Baroque Impasse in Calderonian Drama", *Modern Language Association, Publications* (PMLA), 65:1146-65, 1950

Studia Iberica, Festschrift für Hans Flasche. Hrsg. v. Karl-Herman Körner und Klaus Rühl. 1973. Pp. 35-46

Wardropper, B. W., "Interplay of Wisdom and Saintliness in 'El Mágico Prodigioso' ", *Hispanic Review*, 11:116-24, 1943

ALBERT CAMUS

Caligula, 1944

Alter, André, "De 'Caligula' aux 'Justes': De l'Absurde a la Justice", *Revue d'Histoire du Théâtre*, 12:321-36, 1960

America, 102:775, March 26, 1960

Arnold, A. James, "Camus' Dionysian Hero: 'Caligula' in 1938", *South Atlantic Bulletin* (1973), 38:45-53

Brustein, Robert Sanford, *Seasons of Discontent; Dramatic Opinions 1959-1965*. 1965. Pp. 104-07

Christian Century, 77:352-54, March 23, 1960

Clancy, James H., "Beyond Despair: A New Drama of Ideas", *Educational Theatre Journal*, 13:157-66, 1961

Clurman, Harold, *The Naked Image; Observations on the Modern Theatre*. 1966. Pp. 67-69

Cohn, Ruby, *Currents in Contemporary Drama*. 1969. Pp. 126-30

——————, "Four Stages of the Absurdist Hero", *Drama Survey*, 4:195-208, 1965

Freedman, Morris, *The Moral Impulse; Modern Drama from Ibsen to the Present*. 1967. Pp. 117

Freeman, E., *The Theatre of Albert Camus; A Critical Study*. 1971. Pp. 34-55

Gassner, John, *Dramatic Soundings; Evaluations and Retractions Culled from Thirty Years of Dramatic Criticism*. 1968. Pp. 485-86

Gay-Crosier, Raymond, *Le Théâtre d'Albert Camus*. 1967. Pp. 55-75

Gilles, Janine, " 'Caligula': De Suétone à Camus", *Etudes Classiques* (1974), 42:393-403

Gouhier, H., "Albert Camus et le Théâtre", *La Table Ronde*, #146:61-66, 1960

Grossvogel, David I., *Four Playwrights and a Postscript: Brecht, Ionesco, Beckett and Genêt*. 1962. Pp. 59-66

Hammer, L. Z., "Impossible Freedom in Camus's 'Caligula' ", *Personalist*, 44:322-36, 1963

Harrow, Kenneth, " 'Caligula': A Study in Aesthetic Despair", *Contemporary Literature* (1973), 14:31-48

Illustrated London News, 214:420, March 26, 1949

Jones, Robert Emmet, "Caligula, the Absurd, and Tragedy", *Kentucky Foreign Language Quarterly*, 5:123-27, 1958

Kermauner, Taras, "Človek-Bog-Clovek-Zločinec (Ob Camusovi Drami 'Kaligula')", *Dialogi; Mesečnik za Vprašanja Kulturnega in Javnega Zivljenja* (1974), 10:257-65

Lewis, Allan, *The Contemporary Theatre; The Significant Playwrights of Our Time.* 1962. Pp. 191-217

Lewis, R. W. B., "'Caligula': Or The Realm of the Impossible", *Yale French Studies*, 25:52-58, 1960

Life, 48:85-88, March 7, 1960

Minou, J. M., "Sources et Remaniements du 'Caligula' d'Albert Camus", *Revue de L'Université de Bruxelles*, 12:145-49, 1958-60

Nation, 190:213-14, March 5, 1960

New Republic, 142:21-22, Feb. 29, 1960

New Yorker, 36:100, Feb. 27, 1960

Newsweek, 55:90, Feb. 29, 1960

Onimus, T., "D'Ubu à Caligula ou la Tragédie de l'Intelligence", *Les Etudes* (Paris), 297:328-38, 1958

Rattared, Janine, "Points de Vue sur 'Caligula'", *Praxis* (1968), 15:243-55

Reck, Rima Drell, "The Theatre of Albert Camus", *Modern Drama*, 4:42-53, 1961

Rosenfeld, L. B., "The Absurd in Camus' 'Caligula'", *New Theatre Magazine* (1968), 8:10-16

Ross, Aden, "Tragedy of the Absurd: Marlowe's 'Tamburlaine' and Camus's 'Caligula'", *Thoth* (1973), 13:3-9

Saturday Review, 43:36, March 5, 1960

Simpson, Lurline V., "Tensions in the Works of Albert Camus", *Modern Language Journal*, 38:186-90, 1954

Spectator, 182:358, March 18, 1949

Theatre Arts, 44:59, April, 1960

Time, 75:51, Feb. 29, 1960

Tynan, Kenneth, *Curtains; Selections from the Drama Criticism and Related Writings.* 1961. Pp. 340-43

University of North Carolina Studies in Romance Languages and Literatures (1972), #119:105-36

Walker, I. H., "Composition of 'Caligula'", *Symposium* (1966), 20:263-77

Williams, Raymond, *Modern Tragedy.* 1966. Pp. 177-78

La Devotion à la Croix   *SEE*   Devotion to the Cross

Devotion to the Cross, 1953
Freeman, E., *The Theatre of Albert Camus; A Critical Study.* 1971. Pp. 127-30

L'Etat de Siège   *SEE*   State of Siege

The Just Assassins, 1949
Alter, André, "De 'Caligula' aux 'Justes': De l'Absurde à la Justice", *Revue d'Histoire du Théâtre*, 12:321-36, 1960

Baxter, K. M., *Speak What We Feel; A Christian Looks at the Contemporary Theatre.* 1964, Pp. 43-44

Freeman, F., "Camus' 'Les Justes': Modern Tragedy or Old-Fashioned Melodrama", *Modern Language Quarterly* (Mar. 1970), 31:78-91

Freeman, E., *The Theatre of Albert Camus; A Critical Study.* 1971. Pp. 99-118
Gay-Crosier, Raymond, *Le Théâtre d'Albert Camus.* 1967. Pp. 185-220
Mercure de France, 308:319-21, Feb., 1950
Merton, Thomas, "Three Saviors in Camus", *Thought* (1968), 43:5-23
Moore, Harry T., *Twentieth Century French Literature to World War II.* 1966. Vol. 2, Pp. 58-73
Pollmann, Leo, *Sartre and Camus; Literature and Existence.* 1970. Pp. 148-54
Reck, Rima Drell, "The Theatre of Albert Camus", *Modern Drama*, 4:42-53, 1961
Simpson, Lurline V., "Tensions in the Works of Albert Camus", *Modern Language Journal*, 38:186-90, 1954

Les Justes *SEE* The Just Assassins

Le Malentendu *SEE* The Misunderstanding

The Misunderstanding, 1944
Amer, Henry, "Une Source du 'Malentendu'?", *Revue d'Histoire Litteraire de la France* (1970), 70:98-102
Behrens, Ralph, "Existential 'Character-Ideas' in Camus' 'The Misunderstanding' ", *Modern Drama*, 7:210-12, 1964
Cancel, Rafael A., "Two Studies on Theatre", *Revista de Letras* (1972), 4:257-79
Chase, N. C., "Images of Man: 'Le Malentundu' and 'En Attendant Godot' ", *Wisconsin Studies in Contemporary Literature* (1966), 7:294-302
Church, D. M., " 'Le Malentendu': Search for Modern Tragedy", *French Studies* (1966), 20:33-46
Freeman, Edward, *The Theatre of Albert Camus*; A Critical Study. 1971. Pp. 56-75
Gay-Crosier, Raymond, *Le Théâtre d'Albert Camus.* 1967. Pp. 95-132
Lumley, Frederick, *New Trends in Twentieth Century Drama; A Survey Since Ibsen and Shaw.* 1967. Pp. 347-49
Merton, Thomas, "Three Saviors in Camus", *Thought* (1968), 43:5-23
Moenkemeyer, Heinz, "The Son's Fatal Homecoming in Werner and Camus", *Modern Language Quarterly* (1966), 27:51-67
Mordaunt, Jerrold L., ed., *Proceedings; Pacific Northwest Conference on Foreign Languages, 20th Annual Meeting, April 11-12*, Vol. 20. 1969. Pp. 27-33
Reck, Rima Drell, "The Theatre of Albert Camus", *Modern Drama*, 4:42-53, 1961
Simpson, Lurline V., "Tensions in the Works of Albert Camus", *Modern Language Journal*, 38:186-90, 1954
Verdier, Paul, "Pour une Autre 'Lecture' du 'Malentendu' d'Albert Camus", *Presence Francophone* (1972), 4:139-46
Virtanen, Reino, "Camus' 'Le Malentendu' and Some Analogues", *Comparative Literature*, 10:232-40, 1958
Whittington, Curtis, Jr., "The Earned Vision: Robert Penn Warren's 'The Ballad of Billie Potts' and Albert Camus' 'Le Malentendu' ", *Four Quarters* (1972), 21, iv:79-90
Williams, Raymond, *Modern Tragedy.* 1966. Pp. 178-82

Possessed, 1944 (dramatization of novel by Dostoevsky)
New Yorker, 35:106-07, March 7, 1959

Time, 73:61, Feb. 9, 1959
Yale Review, 48:634-40, June, 1959

Requiem for a Nun, 1956
Blair, John G., "Camus' Faulkner; 'Requiem for a Nun'", *Bulletin de la Faculte des Lettres de Strasbourg* (1969), 47:249-57

State of Siege, 1948
Freeman, Edward, *The Theatre of Albert Camus; A Critical Study*. 1971. Pp. 76-98
Gay-Crosier, Raymond, *Le Théâtre d'Albert Camus*. 1967. Pp. 133-64

JOSEF CAPEK

SEE

KAREL CAPEK AND JOSEF CAPEK

KAREL CAPEK

Makropoulos Secret, 1922
America, 98:484, Jan. 4, 1958
Catholic World, 186:386, Feb. 1958
Christian Century, 75:17, Jan. 1, 1958
Commonweal, 67:336-37, Dec. 27, 1957
Nation, 185:483, Dec. 21, 1957
New Yorker, 33:84-85, Dec. 14, 1957
Saturday Review, 152:356, Sept. 19, 1931
Saturday Review, 40:22, Dec. 28, 1957
Theatre Arts, 42:26, Feb. 1958
Time, 70:45, Dec. 16, 1957

Matka *SEE* The Mother

Mother, 1938
Commonweal, 30:76, May 12, 1939
London Mercury, 39:629, April 1939
New Statesman and Nation, 17:357-58, March 11, 1939
Theatre Arts, 23:402-03, June, 1939

RUR: Rossum's Universal Robots, 1921
Bookman, 56:478-80, Dec., 1922
Catholic World, 116:504-05, Jan., 1923
Christian Century, 40:845-47, July 5, 1923
Collier's, 70:23, Dec. 9, 1922
Darlington, William Aubrey, *Literature in the Theatre, and Other Essays*. 1925. Pp. 137-44
Drama, 13:90-91, Dec., 1922
English Review, 36:588-92, June, 1923
Independent, 109:321-22, Nov. 25, 1922
Literary Digest, 73:30-31, Nov. 4, 1922
Nathan, George Jean, *Theatre Book of the Year, 1942-43*. Pp. 161 62
Nation, 115:478, Nov. 1, 1922
New Republic, 32:251-52, Nov. 1, 1922
New Statesman, 21:110-11, May 5, 1923

Outlook (London), 51:370, May 5, 1923
Pletnev, R., "The Concept of Time and Space in 'R. U. R.' by Karel Capek",
    Etudes Slaves et Est-Européenes (1967), 12:17-24
Spectator, 130:755-56, May 5, 1923

KAREL CAPEK AND JOSEF CAPEK

Insect Play, 1921
    Commonweal, 48:235, June 18, 1948
    Forum, 110:20-22, July, 1948
    Nathan, George Jean, *Theatre Book of the Year, 1948-49*. Pp. 47-50
    New Republic, 118:28-29, June 21, 1948
    New Statesman and Nation, 12:466, Oct. 3, 1936 and 15:766-68, May 7, 1938
    School and Society, 67:478, June 26, 1948
    Spectator, 136:579, March 27, 1926

Več Makropulos *SEE* The Makropoulous Secret

World We Live In, 1921
    Catholic World, 116:501-03, Jan. 1923
    English Review (London), 36:588-92, June, 1923
    Drama, 13:130-31, Jan., 1923
    Independent, 109:320-21, Nov. 25, 1922
    Living Age, 313:619-20, June 3, 1922
    Nation (London), 33:248, May 19, 1923
    New Statesman, 21:198-99, May 26, 1923
    Outlook (London), 51:408, May 19, 1923
    Spectator, 130:800-01, May 12, 1923

PAUL VINCENT CARROL

The Devil Came From Dublin, 1951
    Theatre Arts, 35:66-67, Nov., 1951

Kindred, 1940
    Commonweal, 31:266, Jan. 12, 1940
    Newsweek, 13:34, June 19, 1939 and 15:38, Jan. 8, 1940
    Theatre Arts, 24:165-66, March, 1940

Old Foolishness, 1940
    Commonweal, 33:282-83, Jan., 1934
    New Statesman and Nation, 25:336, May 22, 1943
    New Yorker, 16:30, Dec. 28, 1940
    Spectator, 170:451, May 14, 1943
    Theatre Arts, 25:97, Feb., 1941

Shadow and Substance, 1938
    America, 102:254-55, Nov. 21, 1959
    Brown, John Mason, *Two on the Aisle; Ten Years of the American Theatre
        in Performance*. 1938. Pp. 130-32
    Catholic World, 146:724-25, March, 1938
    Commonweal, 27:440, Feb. 11, 1938 and 27:525, March 4, 1938
    Conway, John D., "The Plays of John Vincent Carroll", *Dissertation Ab-
        stracts International* (1972), 32:6419A
    Independent Woman, 17:147, May, 1938

Literary Digest, 125:22, Feb. 19, 1938
Nation, 146:162, Feb. 5, 1938
New Republic, 94:45, Feb. 16, 1938
New Statesman and Nation, 25:368, June 5, 1943
Newsweek, 11:24, Jan. 31, 1938
Robinson, Lennox, ed., *Irish Theatre*. 1939. Pp. 199-227
Scribner's Magazine, 102:66, Sept., 1937
Spectator, 170:523, June 4, 1943
Theatre Arts, 22:171-72, March, 1938
Time, 31:38, Feb. 7, 1938

Strings, My Lord, Are False, 1942
Commonweal, 36:159, June 5, 1942
Nation, 154:637, May 30, 1942
New Yorker, 18:32, May 30, 1942
Newsweek, 19:67, June 1, 1942
Theatre Arts, 26:659, Oct., 1942

Things That Are Caesar's, 1932
Conway, John Dennis, "The Plays of John Vincent Carroll", *Dissertation Abstracts International* (1972), 32:6419A
Spectator, 149:339, Sept. 17, 1932

Wayward Saint, 1955
America, 92:629-30, March 12, 1955
Catholic World, 181:68, April, 1955
Commonweal, 61:655, March 25, 1955
Nation, 180:226, March 12, 1955
New Yorker, 31:69-70, March 5, 1955
Newsweek, 45:58-59, Feb. 28, 1955
Saturday Review, 38:26, March 5, 1955
Theatre Arts, 39:20, 87, May, 1955
Time, 65:60, Feb. 28, 1955

White Steed, 1939
Brown, John Mason, *Broadway in Review*. 1940. Pp. 205-08
Catholic World, 148:727-28, March, 1939
Commonweal, 29:386, Jan. 27, 1939
Conway, John Dennis, "The Plays of John Vincent Carroll", *Dissertation Abstracts International* (1972), 32:6419A
Nation, 148:100-02, Jan. 21, 1939
New Republic, 98:17, Feb. 8, 1939
Newsweek, 13:24-25, Jan. 23, 1939 and 12:20, Aug. 29, 1938
North American Review, 247: #2:371, June, 1939
Theatre Arts, 23:172-73, March, 1939
Time, 33:20, Jan. 23, 1939

Wise Have Not Spoken, 1946
New Yorker, 30:66, Feb. 20, 1954
Theatre Arts, 30:356, June, 1946

CASTLE OF PERSEVERANCE

SEE

MIRACLE, MORALITY AND MYSTERY PLAYS

GEORGE CHAPMAN

The Blind Beggar of Alexandria, 1596

Reese, J. E., " 'Potiphar's Wife' and Other Folk Tales in Chapman's 'Blind Beggar of Alexandria' ", *Tennessee Studies in Literature* (1973), 18:33-48

Waith, Eugene M., *Ideas of Greatness; Heroic Drama in England.* 1971. Pp. 124-25

Yamada, Akihero, "Bibliographical Studies of George Chapman's 'The Blind Beggar of Alexandria' ", *Shakespeare Studies* (1967-68), 6:147-65

Bussy d'Ambois, 1610

Adams, Robert P., "Critical Myths and Chapman's Original 'Bussy d'Ambois' ", *Renaissance Drama* (1966), 9:141-61

Barber, C. L., "The Ambivalence of 'Bussy d'Ambois' ", *Review of English Literature* (1961), 2:38-44

Bement, P., "The Imagery of Darkness and of Light in Chapman's 'Bussy d'Ambois' ", *Studies in Philology* (1967), 64:187-98

Bergson, Allen, "The Ironic Tragedies of Marston and Chapman; Notes on Jacobean Tragic Form", *Journal of English and Germanic Philology* (Oct. 1970), 69:613-30

Bluestone, Max and Norman Rabkin, eds., *Shakespeare's Contemporaries; Modern Studies in English Renaissance Drama.* 1970. 2nd ed. Pp. 292-306

Braunmuller, Albert R., "The Natural Course of Light Inverted; An 'Impresa' in Chapman's 'Bussy d'Ambois' ", *Journal of the Warburg and Courtald Institute* (1971), 34:356-60

Burbridge, Roger T., "Speech and Action in Chapman's 'Bussy d'Ambois' ", *Tennessee Studies in Literature* (1972), 17:59-65

Craig, Hardin, ed., *Essays in Dramatic Literature; The Parrott Presentation Volume.* 1935. Pp. 25-46

Craig, Jane K., "The Self in Four Plays by George Chapman", *Dissertation Abstracts International* (1974), 35:2934A

Dean, William, "Chapman's 'Bussy d'Ambois': A Case for the Aesthetic and Moral Priority of the 1607 Version", *Journal of the Australasian Universities Language and Literature Association* (1972), 38:159-76

Decap, Roger, "Bussy d'Amboise Héros Tragique; Sur le 'Bussy d'Ambois' de George Chapman", *Caliban, Sp. Issue: Homage à Paul Dottin; Annales Publiées Trimestriellement par la Faculte des Lettres et Sciences Humaines de Toulouse* (1966), n. s. 2:97-114

Ferguson, A. S., "The Plays of George Chapman", *Modern Language Review* (1918), 13:1-24

Freehafer, John, "The Contention for 'Bussy d'Ambois', 1622-41", *Theatre Notebook* (1968), 23:61-69

Goldstein, Leonard, "George Chapman and the Decadence in Early 17th Century Drama", *Science and Society* (Wint. 1962), 26:23-48

Higgins, Michael H., "The Development of the 'Senecal Man': Chapman's 'Bussy d'Ambois' and Some Precursors", *Review of English Studies* (1947), 23:24-42

Ide, Richard S., "The Soldier Theme in Chapman and Shakespeare, 1604-09", *Dissertation Abstracts International* (1973), 34:3345A

Lever, J. W., *The Tragedy of State.* 1971. Pp. 37-58

McCollom, William G., "The Tragic Hero and Chapman's 'Bussy d'Ambois' ", *University of Toronto Quarterly* (1949), 18:227-33

McDonald, Charles Osborne, *The Rhetoric of Tragedy; Form in Stuart Drama.* 1966. Pp. 179-224

Orange, Linwood E., "Bussy d'Ambois: The Web of Pretense", *The Southern Quarterly* (1969), 8:37-56

Perkinson, Richard H., "Nature and the Tragic Hero in Chapman's Bussy Plays", *Modern Language Quarterly* (1942), 3:263-85

Rees, Ennis, *The Tragedies of George Chapman; Renaissance Ethics in Action.* 1954. Pp. 29-50

Ribner, Irving, "Character and Theme in Chapman's 'Bussy d'Ambois'", *ELH* (1959), 26:482-96

Ribner, Irving, *Jacobean Tragedy; The Quest for Moral Order.* 1962. Pp. 23-35

Schwartz, Elias, "Seneca, Homer and Chapman's 'Bussy d'Ambois'", *Journal of English and Germanic Philology* (1957), 56:163-76

Tomlinson, Thomas Brian, *A Study of Elizabethan and Jacobean Tragedy.* 1964. Pp. 257-61

Tricomi, Albert H., "The Hero and the Upstart in Chapman's Comedies and 'Bussy d'Ambois'", *Dissertation Abstracts International* (1970), 30:2981A-82A

Tricomi, Albert H., "The Revised 'Bussy d'Ambois' and 'The Revenge of Bussy d'Ambois': Joint Performance in Thematic Counterpoint", *English Language Notes* (1972), 9:253-62

Tricomi, Albert H., "The Revised Version of Chapman's 'Bussy d'Ambois': A Shift in Point of View", *Studies in Philology* (1973), 70:288-305

Waddington, Raymond B., "Prometheus and Hercules; The Dialectic of 'Bussy d'Ambois", *ELH* (1967), 34:21-48

Waith, Eugene M., *Ideas of Greatness; Heroic Drama in England.* 1971. Pp. 125-31

Chabot, Admiral of France, 1635

Braunmuller, A. R., "Greater Wound: Corruption and Human Frailty in Chapman's 'Chabot, Admiral of France'", *Modern Language Review* (1975), 70:241-59

Rees, Ennis, *The Tragedies of George Chapman; Renaissance Ethics in Action.* 1954. Pp. 156-78

Ribner, Irving, *Jacobean Tragedy; The Quest for Moral Order.* 1962. Pp. 35-49

The Conspiracy and the Tragedy of Charles, Duke of Byron, 1608

Braunmuller, A. R., "Chapman's Use of Plutarck's 'De Fortuna Romanorum' in 'The Tragedy of Charles, Duke of Byron'", *Review of English Studies* (May, 1972), n. s. 23:173-79

Craig, Jane K., "The Self in Four Plays by George Chapman", *Dissertation Abstracts International* (1974), 35:2934A

Freije, George F., "Chapman's 'Byron' and Bartholomaeus Anglicus", *English Language Notes* (1975), 12:168-171

Gabel, John B., "The Date of Chapman's 'Conspiracy and Tragedy of Byron'", *Modern Philology* (1969), 6:330-32

Ide, Richard S., "The Soldier Theme in Chapman and Shakespeare, 1604-09", *Dissertation Abstracts International* (1973), 34:3345A

Rees, Ennis, *The Tragedies of George Chapman; Renaissance Ethics in Action.* 1954. Pp. 51-92

Ure, Peter, *Elizabethan and Jacobean Drama; Critical Essays.* 1974. Pp. 123-44.

Waith, Eugene M., *Ideas of Greatness; Heroic Drama in England*, 1971. Pp. 133-38

The Gentleman Usher, 1602?
Smith, John Hazel, "The Genesis of the Strozza Subplot in George Chapman's 'The Gentleman Usher'", *Modern Language Association. Publications* (Oct. 1968), 83:1448-53

Monsieur D'Olive, 1604
Craig, Jane K., "The Self in Four Plays by George Chapman", *Dissertation Abstracts International* (1974), 35:2934A
Hogan, A. P., "Thematic Unity in Chapman's 'Monsieur D'Olive'", *Studies in English Literature, 1500-1900* (Spr. 1971), 11:295-306

The Revenge of Bussy d'Ambois, 1613
Aggeler, Geoffrey, "The Unity of Chapman's 'The Revenge of Bussy d'Ambois'", *Pacific Coast Philology* (1969), 4:5-18
Bement, Peter, "Stoicism of Chapman's Clermont d'Ambois'", *Studies in English Literature, 1500-1900* (Spr. 1972), 12:345-57
Bergson, Allen, "The Ironic Tragedies of Marston and Chapman; Notes on Jacobean Tragic Form", *Journal of English and Germanic Philology* (Oct. 1970), 69:613-30
Broude, Ronald, "George Chapman's Stoic-Christian Revenger", *Studies in Philology* (1973), 70:51-61
Craig, Hardin, ed., *Essays in Dramatic Literature; The Parrott Presentation Volume*. 1935. Pp. 25-46
Goldstein, Leonard, "George Chapman and the Decadence in Early 17th Century Drama", *Science and Society* (Wint. 1962), 26:23-48
Lever, J. W., *The Tragedy of State*. 1971. Pp. 37-58
O'Callaghan, James F., "The Judging Mind of George Chapman; One Aspect of the Jacobean Temper", *Dissertation Abstracts International* (1973), 33:6879A
Perkinson, Richard H., "Nature and the Tragic Hero in Chapman's Bussy Plays", *Modern Language Quarterly* (1942), 3:263-85
Rees, Ennis, *The Tragedies of George Chapman; Renaissance Ethics in Action*. 1954. Pp. 93-125
Tomlinson, Thomas Brian, *A Study of Elizabethan and Jacobean Tragedy*. 1964. Pp. 261-63
Tricomi, Albert H., "The Revised 'Bussy d'Ambos' and 'The Revenge of Bussy d'Ambois': Joint Performance in Thematic Counterpoint", *English Language Notes* (1972), 9:253-62

The Tragedy of Caesar and Pompey, 1631
Crawley, D., "Decision and Character in Chapman's 'The Tragedy of Caesar and Pompey'", *Studies in English Literature, 1500-1900* (1967), 7:277-97

The Wars of Pompey and Caesar, 1631
Lever, Julius Walter, *The Tragedy of State*. 1971. Pp. 59-77
O'Callaghan, James F., "The Judging Mind of George Chapman; One Aspect of the Jacobean Temper", *Dissertation Abstracts International* (1973), 33: 6879A
Rees, Ennis, *The Tragedies of George Chapman; Renaissance Ethics in Action*. 1954. Pp. 126-55

The Widow's Tears, 1603
  Craig, Jane K., "The Self in Four Plays by George Chapman", *Dissertation Abstracts International* (1974), 35:2934A
  James, Katherine H., "The Widow in Jacobean Drama", *Dissertation Abstracts International* (1973), 34:1246A
  Tricomi, Albert H., "The Social Disorder of Chapman's 'The Widow's Tears'", *Journal of English and Germanic Philology* (1973), 72:350-59

ANTON PAVLOVICH CHEKHOV

The Bear, 1888
  Royde-Smith, N. G., "Bear", *Outlook* (London), 57:393, June 5, 1926

Chayka *SEE* The Sea Gull

The Cherry Orchard, 1904
  America, 94:167, Nov. 5, 1955 and 108:121-22, Jan. 19, 1963, (2-3-73) 128:103
  Beckerman, Bernard, *Dynamics of Drama; Theory and Method of Analysis*. 1970. Pp. 101-12
  Bennett, Arnold, *Books and Persons; Being Comments on a Past Epoch*. 1917. Pp. 321-24
  Brown, John Mason, *Two on the Aisle; Ten Years of the American Theatre in Performance*. 1938. Pp. 84-88
  Brustein, Robert Sanford, *The Theatre of Revolt; An Approach to the Modern Drama*. 1964. Pp. 167-78
  Catholic World, 129:79-80, April, 1929 and 158:584-85, March, 1944
  Clay, James J. and Daniel Krempel, *The Theatrical Image*. 1967. Pp. 114-18
  Commonweal, 39:420, Feb. 11, 1944 and 63:223-25, Dec. 2, 1955
  D'Amico, S., "Cherry Orchard", *Nuova Antologia*, 366:474-75, April 1, 1933
  Deer, Irving, "Speech as Action in Chekhov's 'The Cherry Orchard'", *Educational Theatre Journal*, 10:30-34, 1958
  Fergusson, F., *Idea of a Theatre; A Study of Ten Plays; The Art of Drama in Changing Perspective*. 1949. Pp. 146-77
  Freedman, Morris, *The Moral Impulse; Modern Drama from Ibsen to the Present*. 1967. Pp. 31-44
  Gaskell, Ronald, *Drama and Reality; The European Theatre Since Ibsen*. 1972. Pp. 94-98
  Gerould, Daniel Charles, "'The Cherry Orchard' as a Comedy", *Journal of General Education*, 11:109-22, 1958
  Gilman, Richard, *Common and Uncommon Masks; Writings on the Theatre, 1961-70*. 1971. Pp. 284-87
  Hahn, Beverly, "Chekhov's 'The Cherry Orchard'", *Critical Review* (1973), 16:56-72
  Jackson, Robert Louis, *Chekhov; A Collection of Critical Essays*. 1967. Pp. 136-60
  Kerr, Walter, *Thirty Plays Hath November; Pain and Pleasure in the Contemporary Theater*. 1969. Pp. 151-58
  King, G. B., "Tchekhov's 'Cherry Orchard'", *New Republic*, 3:207, June 26, 1915
  Kronenberger, L., *Republic of Letters; Essays on Various Writers*. 1955. Pp. 178-204

Lahr, John, "Pinter and Chekhov; The Bond of Naturalism", *TDR; The Drama Review* (Wint. 1968), 13:137-45

Latham, Jacqueline E. M., " 'The Cherry Orchard' as Comedy", *Educational Theatre Journal*, 10:21-29, March 1958

Lau, J. S. M., "Ts'ao Yu, the Reluctant Disciple of Chekhov; A Comparative Study of 'Sunrise' and 'The Cherry Orchard' ", *Modern Drama* (1967), 9:358-72

Lewis, A., *The Contemporary Theatre; The Significant Playwrights of Our Time.* 1962. Pp. 59-80

Life, 16:101-02, Feb. 28, 1944

Lindstrom, Thais S., *A Concise History of Russian Literature.* 1966. Pp. 213-15

Literary Digest, 99:27, Dec. 8, 1928

Mabley, Edward, *Dramatic Construction; An Outline of Basic Principles.* 1972. Pp. 139-52

Magarshack, David, *The Real Chekhov; An Introduction to His Last Plays.* 1972. Pp. 187-244

Melnick, Burton, "Theatre and Performance; 'The Cherry Orchard' and 'Henry V' ", *Tulane Drama Review* (Sum. 1967), 11:92-98

Mendelsohn, Michael J., "The Heartbreak Houses of Shaw and Chekhov", *Shaw Review* (1963), 6:89-95

Moses, Montrose Jonas and Brown, John Mason, eds., *American Theatre as Seen by its Critics*, 1752-1934. 1934. Pp. 178-84

Nathan, George Jean, *Theatre Book of the Year, 1943-44.* Pp. 221-25

Nation, 158:167, Feb. 5, 1944 and 181:406, Nov. 5, 1955 and 201:87-88, Aug. 16, 1965, (1-29-73), 216:157-58

New Republic, 110:180-81, Feb. 7, 1944 and 110:211, Feb. 14, 1944 and 133:30, Nov. 21, 1955 and 152:26-28, Feb. 27, 1965

New Statesman, 15:446-47, July 24, 1920 and 27:706, Oct. 2, 1926

New Yorker, 38:118, Nov. 24, 1962 and 41:544, Feb. 20, 1965, (1-20-73), 48:59

Newsweek, 65:93-94, Feb. 22, 1965, (1-22-73), 81:65

Nicol, Bernard de Bear, ed., *Varieties of Dramatic Experience.* 1969. Pp. 178-91

Oates, Joyce Carol, *The Edge of Impossibility; Tragic Forms in Literature.* 1972. Pp. 117-37

Rayfield, Donald, *Chekhov; The Evolution of His Art.* 1975. Pp. 211-28

Remaly, Peter B., "Chekhov's 'The Cherry Orchard' ", *South Atlantic Bulletin (1973), 38:16-20*

Saturday Review, 139:582-83, May 30, 1925

Saturday Review, 38:37, Nov. 19, 1955

Scholastic, 44:20, April 10, 1944

Shimomura, Masao, "Kigeki: 'Sakura no Sono Oboegaki' ", *Bungaku* (1972), 40:141-60

Silverstein, Norman, "Chekhov's Comic Spirit and 'The Cherry Orchard' ", *Modern Drama*, 1:91-100, 1958

Spectator, 134:924-25, June 6, 1925 and 181:729, Dec. 3, 1948

States, Bert O., "Chekhov's Dramatic Strategy", *Yale Review* (1966-67), 56:212-24

Styan, J. L., *The Elements of Drama.* 1960. Pp. 64-85

Swinnerton, F., "Cherry Orchard", *Nation* (London), 27:498-99, July 17, 1920

Theatre Arts, 28:199-202, April, 1944

Time, 43:94, Feb. 7, 1944, (1-29-73), 101:56

Tynan, Kenneth, *Curtains: Selections from the Drama Criticism and Related Writings*. 1961. Pp. 433-37

Valency, Maurice, *The Breaking String; The Plays of Anton Chekhov*. 1966. Pp. 251-88

Valency, Maurice, *The Flower and the Castle; Introduction to Modern Drama*. 1963. Pp. 384-85

Weightman, John, "Chekhov and Chekhovian", *Encounter* (Aug. 1973), 41:51-53

Williams, Raymond, *Drama from Ibsen to Brecht*. 1968. Pp. 107-09

Williams, Raymond, *Modern Tragedy*. 1966. Pp. 143-45

Wright, Edward A. and Lenthiel H. Downs, *A Primer for Playgoers*. 1969. 2nd ed. Pp. 92-96

Young, Stark, *Immortal Shadows; A Book of Dramatic Criticism*. 1948. Pp. 206-10

Dyadya Vanya   *SEE*   Uncle Vanya

Ivanov, 1887
Brown, J., "Ivanoff", *Saturday Review*, 140:698-99, Dec. 12, 1925

Commonweal, 69:496-97, Feb. 6, 1959

Gilliatt, Penelope, *Unholy Fools; Wits, Comics, Disturbers of the Peace; Film and Theater*. 1973. Pp. 336-38

Jackson, Robert Louis, *Chekhov; A Collection of Critical Essays*. 1967. Pp. 88-98

MacCarthy, Desmond, "Ivanoff", *New Statesman*, 26:301, Dec. 19, 1925
————————— , *Theatre*. 1955. Pp. 102-04

New Republic, 123:21, July 3, 1950

New Yorker, 34:58, Oct. 18, 1958

Royde-Smith, N. G., "Ivanoff", *Outlook* (London), 56:405, Dec. 12, 1925

Saturday Review, 41:26, Dec. 25, 1958

Valency, Maurice, *The Breaking String; The Plays of Anton Chekhov*. 1966. Pp. 82-100

Leshy   *SEE*   The Wood Demon

Medved   *SEE*   The Bear

Na Bolshoy Doroge   *SEE*   On the Highroad

On The High Road, 1885
Journal des Debats, 41 pt. 1:885, June 1, 1934

Nation, 192:419, May 13, 1961

Roche, D., "On the High Road", *L'Europe Nouvelle*, 17:588, June 9, 1934

Platonov, or A Country Scandal, 1881
America, 103:362, June 11, 1960

Pyesa Bez Nazvaniya   *SEE*   Platonov, or A Country Scandal

The Sea Gull, 1896
America, 91:257, May 29, 1954 and 96:310, Dec. 8, 1956

Arts and Decoration, 32:67, Nov. 1929

Brown, John Mason, *Two on the Aisle; Ten Years of the American Theatre in Performance*. 1938. Pp. 88-91

Brustein, Robert Sanford, *The Theatre of Revolt; An Approach to the Modern Drama*. 1964. Pp. 140-41

Catholic World, 130:330-31, Dec. 1929 and 147:214-15, May 1938 and 179:307, July 1954 and 184:227, Dec., 1956

Commonweal, 10:21, May 8, 1929 and 10:564, Oct. 2, 1929 and 27:692, April 15, 1938, and 60:269, June 18, 1954 and 76:87, April 20, 1962

Curtis, James M., "Spatial Form in Drama: 'The Sea Gull'", *Canadian-American Slavic Studies* (1972), 6:13-37

English Review, 41:879-80, Dec., 1925

Freedman, Morris, *The Moral Impulse; Modern Drama from Ibsen to the Present*. 1967. Pp. 31-44

Ganz, Arthur, "Arrivals and Departures; The Meaning of the Journey in the Major Plays of Chekhov", *Drama Survey* (1966), 5:5-23

Jackson, Robert Louis, *Chekhov; A Collection of Critical Essays*. 1967. Pp. 99-111

Jones, W. G., "'Sea Gull'—Second Symbolist Play-Within-The-Play", *Slavonic and East European Review* (1975), 53:17-26

Kendle, B., "Elusive Horses in 'The Sea Gull'", *Modern Drama* (May 1970), 13:63-66

Kernan, Alvin B., "Truth and Dramatic Mode in the Modern Theater: Chekhov, Pirandello and Williams", *Modern Drama* (1958), 1:101-14

Kronenberger, Louis, *Republic of Letters; Essays on Various Writers*. 1955. Pp. 178-204

Lahr, John, "Pinter and Chekhov: The Bond of Naturalism", *TDR; The Drama Review* (Wint. 1968), 13:137-45

Lykiardopoulos, M., "Chekhov's 'Seagull' in London", *New Statesman*, 13:238-39, June 7, 1919

MacCarthy, Desmond, "Seagull", *New Statesman*, 26:143, Nov. 14, 1925

McCarthy, M. T., *Sights and Spectacles, 1937-1956*. 1956. Pp. 39-45

Magarshack, David, *The Real Chekhov; An Introduction to Chekhov's Last Plays*. 1972. Pp. 21-78

Moravcevich, Nicholas, "The Dark Side of the Chekhovian Smile", *Drama Survey* (1966), 5:237-51

Nation, 129:366-67, Oct. 2, 1929 and 146:422-23, April 9, 1938, and 178:469-70, May 29, 1954 and 183:415, Nov. 10, 1956

Nation (London), 38:180, Oct. 31, 1925

New Republic, 7:175, June 17, 1916 and 60:205, Oct. 9, 1929 and 94:305, April 13, 1938 and 146:37, May 14, 1962

New Statesman, 32:497, Jan. 26, 1929

New Statesman and Nation, 11:858-60, May 30, 1936

New Yorker, 30:70, May 22, 1954 and 38:115-16, April 7, 1962, (1-20-75), 50:62

Newsweek, 11:22, April 11, 1938

Rayfield, Donald, *Chekhov; The Evolution of His Art*. 1975. Pp. 202-12

Sagar, Keith, "Chekhov's Magic Lake: A Reading of 'The Seagull'", *Modern Drama* (1973), 15:441-47

Saturday Review, 140:472-73, Oct. 24, 1925 and 146:378-79, Oct. 5, 1929

Saturday Review, 37:22-23, May 29, 1954

Seyler, Dorothy U., "'The Sea Gull' and 'The Wild Duck': Birds of a Feather?", *Modern Drama*, 8:167-73, 1965

Spectator, 135:753-54, Oct. 31, 1925

Squire, J. C., "Sea Gull", *London Mercury*, 13:200-01, Dec., 1925

States, Bert O., "Chekhov's Dramatic Strategy", *Yale Review* (1966-67), 56:212-24

Stroud, T. A., "Hamlet and 'The Seagull' ", *Shakespeare Quarterly*, 9:367-72, Summer, 1958

Theatre Arts, 13:401-02, June, 1929 and 22:327-28, May, 1938 and 38:33, Aug., 1954 and 41:26, May, 1957

Time, 31:36, April 11, 1938 and 63:71, May 24, 1954

Valency, Maurice, *The Breaking String; The Plays of Anton Chekhov*. 1966. Pp. 119-78

Williams, Raymond, *Drama from Ibsen to Brecht*. 1968. Pp. 101-04

Winner, T. G., "Chekhov's 'Seagull' and Shakespeare's 'Hamlet'; A Study of Dramatic Device", *American Slavic Review*, 15:103-11, Feb., 1956

Young, Stark, *Immortal Shadows; A Book of Dramatic Criticism*.   1948. Pp. 200-205

Svadba *SEE* The Wedding

Three Sisters, 1901

America, 102:55, Oct. 10, 1959 and 111:54, July 11, 1964, (Sept. 6, 1969), 121:145-46

Bauer, G., "Les Trois Soeurs; Critique", *Annales Politiques et Litteraires*, 92:239, March 1, 1929

Brown, I., "Three Sisters", *Saturday Review*, 141:257-58, Feb. 27, 1926

_____ , "Three Sisters", *Saturday Review*, 148:508, Nov. 2, 1929

Brown, John Mason, *Broadway in Review*. 1940. Pp. 230-33

Brustein, Robert Sanford, *Seasons of Discontent; Dramatic Opinions 1959-1965*. 1965. Pp. 165-68

Catholic World, 156:597-98, Feb., 1943

Commonweal, 31:14, Oct. 27, 1939 and 37:326, Jan. 15, 1943 and 62:127, May 6, 1955

Current History, n.s. 3:548, Feb. 1943

Fraenkl, Pavel, "Cechovs Sceniske Billed-Fantase i 'Tre Søstre' ", *Edda* (1974), 74:235-55

Freedman, Morris, *The Moral Impulse; Modern Drama from Ibsen to the Present*. 1967. Pp. 31-44

Ganz, Arthur, "Arrivals and Departures; The Meaning of the Journey in the Major Plays of Chekhov", *Drama Survey* (1966), 5:5-23

Gilman, Richard, *Common and Uncommon Masks; Writings on the Theatre*, 1961-70. 1971. Pp. 284-87

Hahn, Beverly, "Chekhov: 'The Three Sisters' ", *Critical Review* (1972), 15:3-22

Harper, 231:32, Sept., 1965

Hubbs, Clayton A., "Chekhovian Ritual in the Avant-'Garde Theatre", *Dissertation Abstracts International* (1972), 32:2692A

Jackson, Robert Louis, *Chekhov; A Collection of Critical Essays*.   1967. Pp. 121-35

Kosny, Witold, "Bedeutung und Funktion der Literarischen Zitate in A. P. Cechovs 'Tri Sestry' ", *Die Welt der Slaven* (1971), 16:126-50

Kronenberger, Louis, *Republic of Letters; Essays on Various Writers*.   1955. Pp. 178-204

Life, 14:33-35, Jan. 4, 1943

MacCarthy, Desmond, *Theatre*. 1955. Pp. 98-101

McCarthy, M. T., *Sights and Spectacles, 1937-1956*. 1956. Pp. 57-62.

Magarshack, David, *The Real Chekhov; An Introduction to Chekhov's Last Plays*. 1972. Pp. 125-86

Moravcevich, Nicholas, "The Dark Side of the Chekhovian Smile", *Drama Survey* (1966), 5:237-51

Mordaunt, Jerrold L., ed., *Proceedings; Pacific Northwest Conference on Foreign Languages, 20th Annual Meeting, April 11-12*. 1969. vol. 20. Pp. 94-102.

Nathan, George Jean, *Theatre Book of the Year, 1942-43*. 1943. Pp. 174-84

Nation, 156:31, Jan. 2, 1943 and 180:293-94, April 2, 1955 and 189:218-19, Oct. 10, 1959 and 199:37-39, July 27, 1964, (Nov. 3, 1969), 209:486

New Republic, 100:369, Nov. 1, 1939 and 107:857, Dec. 28, 1942 and 132:22, March 21, 1955 and 133:30, Nov. 21, 1955 and 152:26-28, Feb. 27, 1965, (Nov. 1, 1969), 161:33 and (Mar. 21, 1970), 162:31

New Statesman, 14:676-77, March 13, 1920 and 34:263-64, Nov. 30, 1929

New Statesman and Nation, 15:205-07, Feb. 5, 1938

New Yorker, 18:32, Jan. 2, 1943 and 35:96-98, Oct. 3, 1959 and 40:56, July 4, 1964 and 41:96, Feb. 27, 1965, (Oct. 18, 1969), 45:149, (12-31-73), 49:42

Newsweek, 21:64, Jan. 4, 1943 and 64:45, July 6, 1964 and 65:94, Feb. 22, 1965

Nicol, Bernard de Bear, ed., *Varieties of Dramatic Experience*. 1969. Pp. 175-78

Oates, Joyce Carol, *The Edge of Impossibility: Tragic Forms in Literature*, 1972. Pp. 117-37

Paul, Barbara, "Chekhov's Five Sisters", *Modern Drama* (Feb. 1972), 14:436-40

Rayfield, Donald, *Chekhov: The Evolution of His Art*. 1975. Pp. 211-20

Saturday Review, 46:34, Aug. 24, 1963 and 47:25, July 18, 1964. (July 5, 1969), 52:20

Spectator, 136:363-64, Feb. 27, 1926 and 160:179, Feb. 4, 1938

Swinnerton, F., "Three Sisters", *Nation* (London), 26:806, March 13, 1920

Theatre Arts, 22:407-10, June, 1938 and 23:862-63, Dec., 1939 and 27:73-76, Feb., 1943 and 39:87, May, 1955 and 47:13, Aug. 1963

Time, 40:45-46, Dec. 21, 1942 and 84:72, July 3, 1964, (Feb. 23, 1970), 95:68

Tovstonogev, Georgii, "Chekhov's 'Three Sisters' at the Gorky Theatre", *TDR: The Drama Review* (1968), 13:146-55

Tynan, Kenneth, *Curtains; Selections from the Drama Criticism and Related Writings*. 1961. Pp. 433-37

Valency, Maurice, *The Breaking String: The Plays of Anton Chekhov*. 1966. Pp. 206-50

Williams, Raymond, *Drama from Ibsen to Brecht*. 1968. Pp. 105-07

Tri Sestry   *SEE*   The Three Sisters

Uncle Vanya, 1899

Agate, J. E., *English Dramatic Critics; An Anthology, 1660-1932*. 1958. Pp. 300-06

America, 94:646, March 10, 1956

Bardinat, Philip, "Dramatic Structure in Cexov's 'Uncle Vanya'", *Slavic and East European Journal*, 16:195-210, 1958

Bentley, E. R., *In Search of Theater*. 1953. Pp. 342-64

Bookman (London), 61:167-70, Dec., 1921

Catholic World, 163:357, July, 1946 and 183:65, April, 1956

Commonweal, 11:742-43, April 30, 1930 and 44:166, May 31, 1946 and 64:75-76, April 20, 1956

Cowell, Raymond, *Twelve Modern Dramatists*. 1967. Pp. 36-38
Freedman, Morris, *The Moral Impulse; Modern Drama from Ibsen to to the Present*. 1967. Pp. 31-44
Ganz, Arthur, "Arrivals and Departures; The Meaning of the Journey in the Major Plays of Chekhov", *Drama Survey* (1966), 5:5-23
Gassner, John, *Dramatic Soundings; Evaluations and Retractions Culled from Thirty Years of Dramatic Criticism*. 1968. Pp. 537-38
─────────────── , *Theatre at the Crossroads; Plays and Playwrights of the Midcentury American Stage*. 1960. Pp. 188-93
Hubbs, Clayton A., "Chekhovian Ritual in the Avant-Garde Theatre", *Dissertation Abstracts International* (1972), 32:2692A
Jackson, Robert Louis, *Chekhov; A Collection of Critical Essays*. 1967. Pp. 112-20
Kronenberger, Louis, *Republic of Letters; Essays on Various Writers*. 1955. Pp. 178-204
Magarshack, David, *The Real Chekhov; An Introduction to Chekhov's Last Plays*. 1972. Pp. 79-124
Nation, 130:554, May 7, 1930 and 162:671, June 1, 1946 and 182:147, Feb. 18, 1956, (Sept. 22, 1969), 209-293, (6-25-73), 216:827-28
Nation (London), 38:583-84, Jan. 23, 1926
New Republic, 62:299-300, April 30, 1930 and 114:805, June 3, 1946, (6-30-73), 168:24
New Statesman, 18:254-55, Dec. 3, 1921
New Statesman and Nation, 13:241-42, Feb. 13, 1937
New Yorker, 22:44-46, May 25, 1946, (6-9-73), 49:88
Newsweek, 27:84, May 27, 1946 and 62:45, Aug. 5, 1963 (6-18-73), 81:112
Oates, Joyce Carol, *The Edge of Impossibility; Tragic Forms in Literature*. 1972. Pp. 117-37
O'Connor, G., "Uncle Vanya", *Plays and Players* (Mar. 1975), 22:34
Rayfield, Donald, *Chekhov; The Evolution of His Art*. 1975. Pp. 211-15
Royde-Smith, N. G., "Uncle Vanya", *Outlook* (London), 57:150, Feb. 27, 1926
Saturday Review, 39:24, Feb. 18, 1956, (Nov. 15, 1969), 52:20
Saturday Review of Literature, 29:32-34, June 1, 1946
Spectator, 136:124-25, Jan. 23, 1926
Theatre Arts, 27:721-22, Dec., 1943
Time, 47:66, May 27, 1946 and 67:48, Feb. 13, 1956, (Feb. 22, 1971), 97:52, (6-18-73), 101:70
Tynan, Kenneth, *Curtains; Selections from the Drama Criticism and Related Writings*. 1961. Pp. 437-39
Valency, Maurice, *The Breaking String; The Plays of Anton Chekhov*. 1966. Pp. 179-205
World, 131:338-39, June, 1930

Vishnyovy Sad   *SEE*   The Cherry Orchard

Wedding, 1889
New Yorker, 37:123, May 6, 1961
Tynan, Kenneth, *Curtains; Selections from the Drama Criticism and Related Writings*. 1961. Pp. 6-8

The Wood Demon, 1889
Lambert, J. W., "Wood Demon", *Drama* (1974), #113.53-54

Valency, Maurice, *The Breaking String; The Plays of Anton Chekhov*. 1966.
   Pp. 101-18
America (2-23-74), 130:133
Nation (2-16-74), 218:222
New Yorker (2-11-74), 49:71
Time (2-18-74), 103:95

CHESTER PLAYS

SEE

MIRACLE, MORALITY, AND MYSTERY PLAYS

HENRY CHETTLE

SEE

THOMAS DEKKER, HENRY CHETTLE
AND WILLIAM HAUGHTON

AGATHA MILLER CHRISTIE

Hidden Horizons, 1947
   Nathan, George Jean, *Theatre Book of the Year, 1946-47.* Pp. 67-69

The Hollow (1951)
   Illustrated London News, 218:1036, June 23, 1951

Mousetrap, 1952
   Shorter E., "Quite a Nice Run", *Drama* (1974), No. 112:51-53

Ten Little Indians, 1944
   Nathan, George Jean, *Theatre Book of the Year, 1944-45.* Pp. 31-34

Unexpected Guest, 1958
   Illustrated London News, 233:358, Aug. 30, 1958
   Spectator, 201:249, Aug. 22, 1958

Witness for the Prosecution, 1953
   America, 92:366, Jan. 1, 1955
   Commonweal, 61:406, Jan. 14, 1955
   Illustrated London News, 223:786, Nov. 14, 1953
   Life, 38:95-96, Jan. 24, 1955
   Nation, 180:18, Jan. 1, 1955
   New Yorker, 30:42, Dec. 25, 1954
   Newsweek, 45:43, Jan. 3, 1955
   Saturday Review, 38:24, Jan. 8, 1955
   Time, 64:32, Dec. 27, 1954

AGATHA MILLER CHRISTIE AND GERALD VERNER

Towards Zero, 1956
   Illustrated London News, 229:482, Sept. 22, 1956

COLLEY CIBBER

The Careless Husband, 1704
Ashley, Leonard R. N., *Colley Cibber*. 1965. Pp. 55-59
Bisanz, Adam J., "Stoff als Motiv in Colley Cibbers 'The Careless Husband'",
Fabula. Zeitschrift für Erzähl Forschung (1972), 13:122-34
Glicksman, H., "Stage History of Colley Cibber's 'The Careless Husband'",
Modern Language Association. Publications (PMLA), 36:245-50, 1921
Griffith, R. H., "A 'Wildfrau' Story in a Cibber Play, 'The Careless Husband'",
Philological Quarterly, 12:298-302, July, 1933
Sullivan, Maurine, ed., *Colley Cibber; Three Sentimental Comedies*. 1973.
Pp. 85-174
Tierney, James E., "Cibber's 'The Careless Husband'", *Explicator* (1973), 32:
Item 17

Damon and Phillida, 1729
Ashley, Leonard R. N., *Colley Cibber*. 1965. Pp. 77-78

The Double Gallant; or, The Sick Lady's Cure, 1707
Ashley, Leonard R. N., *Colley Cibber*. 1965. Pp. 60-61

The Lady's Last Stake; or, The Wife's Resentment, 1707
Ashley, Leonard R. N., *Colley Cibber*. 1965. Pp. 62-63
Sullivan, Maurine, ed., *Colley Cibber; Three Sentimental Comedies*. 1973.
Pp. 175-276
_____ , "Two Early Comedies of Colley Siber, A Critical Edition,"
Dissertation Abstracts (1968), 29:880A-81A

Love Makes a Man; or, The Fop's Fortune, 1700
Ashley, Leonard R. N., *Colley Cibber*. 1965. Pp. 52-53

Love's Last Shift; or, The Fool in Fashion, 1696
Ashley, Leonard R. N., *Colley Cibber*. 1965. Pp. 39-44
Fone, B. R., "Colley Cibber's 'Love's Last Shift' and Sentimental Comedy",
Restoration and Eighteenth Century Theatre Research (1968), 7:33-43
Fone, B. R. S., "'Love's Last Shift' and Sentimental Comedy", *Restoration
and 18th Century Theatre Research* (1970), 9:11-23
Parnell, P. E., "Equivocation in Cibber's 'Love's Last Shift'", *Studies in Philol-
ogy*, 57:519-34, July, 1960
Roper, Alan, "Language and Action in 'The Way of the World', 'Love's Last
Shift', and 'The Relapse'", *Journal of English Literary History* (1973), 40:
44-69
Sullivan, Maurine, ed., *Colley Cibber; Three Sentimental Comedies*. 1973.
Pp. 1-84
_____ , "Two Early Comedies of Colley Siber, a Critical Edition",
Dissertation Abstracts (1968), 29:880A-81A

The Non-Juror, 1717
Ashley, Leonard R. N., *Colley Cibber*. 1965. Pp. 65-69
Miles, D. H., "Original of 'The Non-Juror': Moliere's 'Tartuffe'" *Modern Lan-
guage Association Publications* (PMLA), 30:195-214, 1915
_____ , "Political Satire of 'The Non-Juror'", *Modern Philology*,
13:281-304, 1915
Peterson, W. M., "Pope and Cibber's 'The Non-Juror'", *Modern Language
Notes*, 70:332-35, 1955

Perolla and Izadora, 1705
Ashley, Leonard R. N. *Colley Cibber*. 1965. Pp. 59-60

The Provok'd Husband; or, A Journey to London, 1728
Ashley, Leonard R. N., *Colley Cibber*. 1965. Pp. 72-75

The Refusal; or, The Ladies Philosophy, 1721
Ashley, Leonard R. N., *Colley Cibber*. 1965. Pp. 70-71
Hainsworth, J. D., "The Scriblerians and the South Sea Bubble; A Hit by Cibber", *Review of English Studies* (1973), 24:452-60
Hunt, Leigh, *Leigh Hunt's Dramatic Criticism, 1808-1831*, ed. by Lawrence Huston Houtchens and Carolyn Washburn Houtchens. 1949. Pp. 157-62

The Rival Fools, 1709
Ashley, Leonard R. N., *Colley Cibber*. 1965. Pp. 64-65

The Rival Queens, With the Humours of Alexander the Great, 1703
Ashley, Leonard R. N., *Colley Cibber*. 1965. Pp. 75-76

The School Boy; or, The Comical Rivals, 1707
Ashley, Leonard R. N., *Colley Cibber*. 1965. Pp. 45-46

She Wou'd and She Wou'd Not; or, the Kind Imposter, 1702
Ashley, Leonard R. N., *Colley Cibber*. 1965. Pp. 53-55.
Loftis, John, "Spanish Drama in Neo-Classical England", *Comparative Literature* (1959), 11:29-34
Peterson, W. M., "Cibber's 'She Wou'd and She Wou'd Not' and Vanbrugh's 'Aesop' ", *Philological Quarterly*, 35:429-35, Oct., 1956

The Tragical History of King Richard III, 1700
Ashley, Leonard R. N., *Colley Cibber*. 1965. Pp. 47-52
Donohue, Joseph Walter, *Dramatic Character in the English Romantic Age*. 1970. Pp. 126-42

Woman's Wit; or, The Lady in Fashion, 1697
Ashley, Leonard R. N., *Colley Cibber*. 1965. Pp. 45-56

Xerxes, 1699
Ashley, Leonard R. N., *Colley Cibber*. 1965. Pp. 46-47

Ximena; or, The Heroick Daughter, 1719
Ashley, Leonard R. N., *Colley Cibber*. 1965. Pp. 60-70

PAUL LOUIS CHARLES CLAUDEL

And on the Seventh Day God Rested, 1895
Bateman, M., "Claudel's Great Mystic Drama, 'Le Repos du Septième Jour' ", *Catholic World* (June 1917), 105:361-75
Bateman, May, "Paul Claudel, Mystic", *Catholic World* (1916-17), 104:484-95
Brunel, Pierre, "Un Drame 'Chinois' de Paul Claudel: 'Le Repos du Septième Jour' ", *L'Information Littéraire* (1974), 26:17-23
_____ , Jacques Houriez, et als, "Sur Quelques Difficultes", *Revue des Lettres Modernes* (1973), 366-69:131-66
Houriez, Jacques, "Etudes Sur la Genèse", *Revue des Lettres Modernes* (1973), 366-69:9-44
Malicet, Michel, " 'Le Repos du Septième Jour' ou 'La Sublimation d'un Rêve de Désir' ", *Revue des Lettres Modernes* (1973), 366-69: 89-129

Olivero, Federico, "Paul Claudel", *Poet Lore* (1918), 29:110-20

Petit, Jacques, "Structure du Drame", *Revue des Lettres Modernes* (1973), 366-69:65-87

Ross, D. J. A., "A Study of Fire Imagery in Some Plays of Paul Claudel", *French Studies* (1965), 19:144-63

Waters, Harold A., *Paul Claudel.* 1970. Pp. 70-71

L'Annonce Faite à Marie   SEE   The Tidings Brought to Mary

The Book of Christopher Columbus, 1927

Bidou, H., " 'Christophe Colomb': Criticism", *Journal des Debats* (May 2, 1930), 37 Pt. 1:724-25

"Claudel Turns Opera: 'Christoph Colomb' ", *Living Age* (June 1, 1930), 338: 408-09

Longree, Georges H., "Epic Theater: A Marxist and a Catholic Interpretation", *South Central Bulletin* (1966), 26:51-57

Lumley, Frederick, *New Trends in Twentieth Century Drama; A Survey Since Ibsen and Shaw.* 1967. Pp. 61-77

Tynan, Kenneth, *Curtains; Selections from the Drama Criticism and Related Writings.* 1961. Pp. 392-94

America, 90:420-21, Jan. 23, 1954

Catholic World, 185:67, April 1957

France Illustration, #404:100, Nov. 1953

Mercure de France, 319:691, 698-701, Dec. 1953

Nation, 184:147, Feb. 16, 1957

New Republic, 136:20, March 18, 1957

New Yorker, 29:74, Oct. 24, 1953

Newsweek, 49:67, Feb. 11, 1957

Saturday Review, 40:22, Jan 26, 1957

Theatre Arts, 41:21, April 1957

Time, 69:70, Feb. 11, 1957

Break of Noon, 1948

Brereton, Geoffrey, *Principles of Tragedy; A Rational Examination of the Tragic Concept in Life and Literature.* 1968. Pp. 226-43

Deguy, Michel, "Reprise du 'Partage de Midi' ", *Nouvelle Revue Francaise* (1962), 10:174-76

Devel, Mildred, "A Study of the Dramatic Structure of 'Partage de Midi' from 1905-1949", *French Review* (1972), 45:964-70

Fowlie, Wallace, "Claudel as Dramatist", *Sewanee Review* (1956), 64:218-37

Griffiths, Richard, ed., *Claudel; A Reappraisal.* 1968. Pp. 19-33

LeHardouin, Maria, " 'Partage de Midi', ou la Vocation de l'Impossible", *La Table Ronde* (1956), #97:96-101

Lumley, Frederick, *New Trends in Twentieth Century Drama; A Survey Since Ibsen and Shaw.* 1967. Pp. 61-77

Tynan, Kenneth, *Curtains; Selections from the Drama Criticism and Related Writings.* 1961. Pp. 383-84

Waters, Harold A., *Paul Claudel.* 1970. Pp. 77-80

The City, 1890

Emmanuel, Pierre, "Au Coeur de 'La Ville' ", *Esprit* (Jan. 1956), Pp. 77-83

Fowlie, Wallace, "Claudel as Dramatist", *Sewanee Review* (1956), 64:218-37

Gruenberg, Peter, " 'La Ville': Une Représentation à Bruxelles", *Claudel Studies* (1974), 1,v:60-64

Lumley, Frederick, *New Trends in Twentieth Century Drama; A Survey Since Ibsen and Shaw*. 1967. Pp. 61-77

Malicet, Michael and Jacques Petit, "Quelques Obscurities de 'La Ville' ", *La Revue Des Lettres Modernes* (1969), 209-11:79-98

Petit, J., "A Propos de 'La Ville' ", *La Revue des Lettres Modernes* (1967), 4:105-06, 150-52

Ross, D. J. A., "A Study of Fire Imagery in some Plays of Paul Claudel", *French Studies* (1965), 19:144-63

Waters, Harold A., *Paul Claudel*. 1970. Pp. 63-64, and 71-73

Crusts, 1949

France Illustration, 5:305-06, March 26, 1949

" 'Le Pain Dur': Criticism", *Living Age*, 300:361-63, Feb. 8, 1919

Lumley, Frederic, *New Trends in Twentieth Century Drama; A Survey Since Ibsen and Shaw*. 1967. Pp. 61-77

"Sur 'Le Pain Dur' de Paul Claudel", *Mercure de France* (May 1949), 306:11-13

Waters, Harold A., *Paul Claudel*. 1970. Pp. 86-88

L'Échange   SEE   The Exchange

The Exchange, 1894

Lumley, Frederic, *New Trends in Twentieth Century Drama; A Survey Since Ibsen and Shaw*. 1967. Pp. 61-77

Ly-Thei-Nhi, Madeleine, " 'L'Échange' et le Mobile de l'Echange", *Claudel Studies* (1973), 1,iii:63-72

Mercure de France, 280:567-69, Dec. 15, 1937

Mercure de France, 314:326-27, Feb-1952

Waters, Harold A., *Paul Claudel*. 1970. Pp. 67-69

L'Histoire de Tobie et Sara   SEE   Tobias and Sara

The Hostage, 1908-08

Angst, Bertrand, " 'L'Otage' de Paul Claudel", *Romanic Review* (1962), 53: 32-51

Bateman, May, "The Catholic Note in Modern Drama", *Catholic World* (1916-17), 104:164-76

Bauer, G., " 'L'Otage': Critique", *Les Annales Politiques et Littéraires* (Nov. 25, 1934) 104:190-92

Boatto, Alberto, "Attorno all 'Ostaggio' di Claudel", *Ultima* (1968), 10:373-78

Bregy, K., "Claudel's Play of Paradox: 'L'Hotage' ", *Commonweal* (Oct. 9, 1929), 10:581-82

"French Drama Extraordinary: L'Otage' of Paul Claudel and 'Brebis Egarée' F. Jammes", *Nation* (July 2, 1914), 99:25-26

Lievre, P., " 'L'Otage' Vient d'Entrer a la Comédie-Francaise", *Mercure de France* (Dec. 1, 1934), 256:364-68

Lumley, Frederick, *New Trends in Twentieth Century Drama; A Survey Since Ibsen and Shaw*. 1967. Pp. 61-77

MacCarthy, D., " 'Hostage': Criticism", *New Statesman* (April 5, 1919), 13: 16-17

Rouveyre, A., "A Propos d'Une Reprise de 'L'Otage' ", *Mercure de France* (July 1-15, 1930), 221:169-74 and 429-35

Rageot, G., "L'Otage': Critique", *Revue Politique et Littéraire* (Nov. 17, 1934), 72:872-73

Revue Politique et Littéraire, 61:389-90, June 2, 1923
Waters, Harold A., *Paul Claudel*. 1970. Pp. 80-83

The Humiliation of the Father, 1916
Lumley, Frederick, *New Trends in Twentieth Century Drama; A Survey Since Ibsen and Shaw*. 1967. Pp. 61-77
Waters, Harold A., *Paul Claudel*. 1970. Pp. 88-91

Jeanne d'Arc au Bûcher   *SEE*   Joan of Arc at the Stake

La Jeune Fille Violaine   *SEE*   The Maid Violaine

Joan of Arc at the Stake, 1939
Brunel, P., "Trois Anachronismes de Claudel à Propos de la Guerre de Cent Ans", *Revue des Lettres Modernes* (1967), 4:150-52, 107-10
Griffiths, Richard M., ed., *Claudel; A Reappraisal*. 1970. Pp. 63-78
Waters, Harold A., *Paul Claudel*. 1970. Pp. 97

Le Livre de Christophe Colomb   *SEE*   The Book of Christopher Columbus

The Maid Violaine, 1893
Waters, Harold A., *Paul Claudel*. 1970. Pp. 64-67 and 73-75

L'Otage   *SEE*   The Hostage

L'Ours et la Lune, 1917
Lumley, Frederick, *New Trends in Twentieth Century Drama; A Survey Since Ibsen and Shaw*. 1967. Pp. 61-77

Le Pain Dur   *SEE*   Crusts

Partage de Midi   *SEE*   Break of Noon

Le Père Humilie   *SEE*   The Humiliation of the Father

Protee   *SEE*   Proteus

Proteus, 1926
Jost, Francois, ed., *Proceedings of the 4th Congress of the International Comparative Literature Association*. Fribourg, 1964. V.2. 1966. Pp. 1084-96
Lumley, Frederick, *New Trends in Twentieth Century Drama; A Survey Since Ibsen and Shaw*. 1967. Pp. 61-77

Le Repos du Septième Jour   *SEE*   And on the Seventh Day God Rested

The Satin Slipper; or, The Worst is Not Sure, 1943
Barko, Ivan, " 'Le Soulier de Satin': Ouverture et Référent", *Degrés: Revue de Synthèse à Orientation Semiologique* (1973), 4:i-i-15
Baudot, Alain, " 'Le Soulier de Satain' Est il une Antitragédie", *Etudes Françaises* (1969), 5:115-37
Brethenoux, Michel, "L'Espace dans 'Le Soulier de Satin' ", *Revue des Lettres Modernes* (1972), 310-14:33-66
Buovolo, Huguette, "A Propos d'une Analyse Structurale de la Quatrième Journée", *Revue des Lettres Modernes* (1972), 310-14:67-87
Burghardt, L. S., "Paul Claudel's 'Le Soulier de Satin' as a Baroque Drama", *Modern Drama* (May 1971), 14:63-71
Cellier, Leon, "Notes Pour 'Le Soulier de Satin' ", *Revue des Sciences Humaines* (1965), #118:285-88

Cernij, Václao, "La 'Baroquisme' du 'Soulier de Satin' ", *Revue de Littérature Comparée* (1970), 44:472-98

Chambers, Ross, "La Quatrième Journée du 'Soulier de Satin' ", *Cahiers de la Compagnie Madeleine Renaud-Jean-Louis Barrault* (1972), 80:11-37

Clerc, Jean-Marie, "A Propos du 'Soulier de Satin': Dialogue et Lyrisme dans le Théâtre de Claudel", *L'Information Littéraire* (1972), 24:12-17

Cohn, Ruby, *Currents in Contemporary Drama.* 1969. Pp. 113-16

Cox, Sister Fidelia Maria, "Prayer and Sacrifice: Claudel's 'Satin Slipper' ", *Renascence* (1961), 13:78-83

D'Estournelles, Paul, "Paul Claudel; The Poet as Playwright", *Theatre Arts* (1946), 30:301-04

Erwin, John W., "Hero as Audience: 'Antony and Cleopatra' and 'Le Soulier de Satin' ", *Modern Language Studies* (1974), 4,ii:65-77

Fowlie, Wallace, "Claudel as Dramatist", *Sewanee Review* (1956), 64:218-37

——————————— , *Climate of Violence; The French Literary Tradition from Baudelaire to the Present.* 1967. Pp. 138-53

The France of Claudel, ed. Henri Peyre. 1973. Pp. 73-82

Freilich, Joan S., "Paul Claudel's 'Le Soulier de Satin': A Stylistic Study of the Imagery and a Structuralist Interpretation", *Dissertation Abstracts International* (1973), 34:2662A

Freilich, Joan S., " 'Le Soulier de Satin': Four Levels Through Imagery", *Claudel Studies* (1972), 1,i:44-55

Griffiths, Richard, ed., *Claudel; A Reappraisal.* 1968. Pp. 48-62

Henriot, Jacques, "Le Thème de la Quête dans 'Le Soulier de Satin' ", *Revue des Lettres Modernes* (1972), 310-14:89-116

Ince, W. N., "The Unity of Claudel's 'Le Soulier de Satin' ", *Symposium* (1968), 22:35-53

Landry, Jean Noel, "Chronologie et Temps dans 'Le Soulier de Satin' ", *Revue des Lettres Modernes* (1972), 310-14:7-31

Lumley, Frederick, *New Trends in Twentieth Century Drama; A Survey Since Ibsen and Shaw.* 1967. Pp. 61-77

Malicet, Michel, "La Peur de la Femme 'Le Soulier de Satin' ", *Revue des Lettres Modernes* (1974), 391-97:119-87

Mazzega, A. M., "Une Parabole Historique: 'Le Soulier de Satin' ", *Revue des Lettres Modernes* (1967), 4:150-52 and 43-60

Missions et Démarches de la Critique: Mélanges Offerts au Professeur J. A. Vier. 1973. Pp. 411-21

Moscovici, Jacques, "Paul Claudel et Richard Wagner", *Nouvelle Revue Francaise* (1964), 12:323-34

Petit, Jacques, et al, "Etude des Images", *Revue des Lettres Modernes* (1974), 391-97:7-53

Petit, Jacques, "Les Jeux du Double dans 'Le Soulier de .Satin' ", *Revue des Lettres Modernes* (1972), 310-14:117-38

Selna, Barbara, "Paul Claudel: Prison and the Satin Slipper", *Renascence* (1955), 7:171-80

Smith, Winifred, "Mystics in Modern Theatre", *Sewanee Review* (1942), 50:46-48

Vanderploeg, Barbara A., "The Function and Evolution of the Comic in Claudel's Theatre", *Dissertation Abstracts International* (1972), 33:2398A

Waters, Harold A., *Paul Claudel.* 1970. Pp. 91-94

Watson, Harold, "Fire and Water, Love and Death in 'Le Soulier de Satin'", *French Review* (1972), 45:971-79

Wood, Michael, "The Theme of the Prison in 'Le Soulier de Satin'", *French Studies* (1968), 22:225-38

France Illustration 5:454, May 7, 1949

Saturday Review of Literature 28:13, June 30, 1945

Le Soulier de Satin; ou, La Pire N'est Pas Toujours Sur   *SEE*   The Satin Slipper; or, The Worst Is Not Sure

Tête d'Or, 1919

Approaches: Essais sur la Poésie Moderne de Langue Française, (Annales de la Faculte des Lettres et Sciences Humaines de Nice 15). 1971. Pp. 25-40

Barrault, Jean-Louis, "Le Lecon de 'Tête d'Or'", *Cahiers de la Compagnie Madeleine Renaud-Jean Louis Barrault* (1959), #27:41-48

Becker, Aime, "'Tete d'Or' et 'Cebes' ou Le Drame de l'Adolescence", *Revue des Lettres Modernes* (1971), 271-75·53-67

Blanchet, Andre, "'Tete d'Or' est-il Paien?", *Études* (1959), 303:289-305

Fowlie, Wallace "Claudel as Dramatist", *Sewanee Review* (1956), 64:218-37

Harry, Ruth N., "Claudel's 'Tête d'Or'", *French Review* (1962), 35:279-86

Lumley, Frederick, *New Trends in Twentieth Century Drama; A Survey Since Ibsen and Shaw.* 1967. Pp. 61-77

Morisot, Jean-Claude, "L'Histoire et le Mythe dan 'Tête d'Or'", *La Revue des Lettres Modernes* (1967), 4:7-29 and 150-52

——————— , "'Tête d'Or' ou les Adventures ele la Volonte", *La Revue des Lettres Modernes* (1960), 6:117-96

Olivero, Federico, "Paul Claudel", *Poet Lore* (1918), 29:110-20

Østerud, Svein, "Paul Claudel og 'Tête d'Or'", *Vinduet* (1960), 14:223-26

Oswald, Werner, "Die Symbolischen Bezüge in Paul Claudels 'Tête d'Or': Versuch einer Deutung", *Die Neueren Sprachen* (1963), 12:61-72

Waters, Harold A., *Paul Claudel.* 1970. Pp. 58-62

The Tidings Brought to Mary, 1912

"'L'Annonce Faite à Marie': Criticism", *New Statesman* (March 30, 1929), 32:792

Bateman, Mary, "Paul Claudel, Mystic", *Catholic World* (1916-17), 104:484-95

Bidou, J., "'L'Annonce Faite à Marie': Critique", *Journal des Débats* (Oct. 28, 1927), 34 Pt. 2:733-34

Brunel, P., "Trois Anachronismes de Claudel à Propos de la Guerre de Cent Ans", *Revue des Lettres Modernes* (1967), 4:150-52 and 107-10

d'Amico, S., "'Annonce a Marie': Critica", *Nouva Antologia* (May 16, 1933), 367:308-09

Devel, Mildred, "The Structure of the Different Versions of 'L'Annonce Faite à Marie'", *Modern Language Review* (1972), 67:543-49

Espiau de la Maëstre, A., "Paul Claudel, 'L'Annonce Faite à Marie'", *Les Lettres Romanes* (1962), 16:3-26, 149-71 and 241-65

D'Estournelles, Paul, "Paul Claudel; The Poet as Playwright", *Theatre Arts* (1946), 30:301-04

Fowlie, Wallace, "Claudel as Dramatist", *Sewanee Review* (1956), 64: 218-37

The France of Claudel, ed. Henri Peyre. 1973. Pp. 73-82

Gerrard, Thomas J., "The Art of Paul Claudel", *Catholic World* (1916-17), 104: 471-83

Griffiths, Richard M., ed., *Claudel; A Reappraisal.* 1970. Pp. 34-47

Jennings, R., " 'L'Annonce Faite à Marie' ", *Spectator* (March 30,1929), 142:503
Jones, Tobin H., "The Alchemical Language of Paul Claudel's 'L'Annonce Faite à Marie' ", *Symposium* (1973), 27:35-45
Lowe, R. W., "La Doctrine du Corps Mystique dans 'L'Annonce Faite à Marie' ", *Georgetown University French Review* (1938), 6:14-22
Lewisohn, Ludwig, " 'Tidings Brought to Mary': Criticism", *Nation* (Jan. 24, 1923), 116-102
Lumley, Frederick, *New Trends in Twentieth Century Drama; A Survey Since Ibsen and Shaw*. 1967. Pp. 61-77
MacCarthy, D., " 'L'Annonce Faite à Marie': Criticism", *New Statesman* (June 6, 1917), 9:254-56
Melcher, Edith, "A Study of 'L'Annonce Faite à Marie' ", *French Review* (1949), 23:1-9
Olivero, Federico, "Paul Claudel", *Poet Lore* (1918), 29:110-20
Pallister, Janis L., "Presentation Motifs in the Prologue of Claudel's 'La Annonce Faite à Marie' ", *Romance Notes* (1972), 13:409-13
Ross, D. J. A., "A Study of Fire Imagery in some Plays of Paul Claudel", *French Studies* (1965), 19:144-63
Theisen, Josef, "Paul Claudels 'Annonce Faite à Marie': Opfer-Oder Sühne-drama?", *Die Neueren Sprachen* (1962), 11:509-20
" 'Tidings Brought to Mary': Criticism", *Outlook* (Jan. 17, 1923), 133:119-20
Waters, Harold A., *Paul Claudel*. 1970. Pp. 69-70 and 83-86
_____ , "Paul Claudel and the Sensory Paradox", *Modern Language Quarterly* (1959), 20:267-72
Wright, C., " 'Tidings Brought to Mary': Criticism", *Freeman* (Jan. 24, 1923), 6:472-73

Tobias and Sara, 1938
Waters, Harold A., *Paul Claudel*. 1970. Pp. 97-98

La Ville *SEE* The City

JEAN COCTEAU

L'Aigle a Deux Tetes *SEE* The Eagle Has Two Heads

Antigone, 1922
Knapp, Bettina L., *Jean Cocteau*. 1970. Pp. 70-72
Steegmuller, Francis, "A Propos de 'l'Antigone' de Cocteau", *Revue des Lettres Modernes* (1972), 298-303:167-22

Bacchus, 1951
France Illustration, 325:23, Jan. 5, 1952
Knapp, Bettina L., *Jean Cocteau*. 1970. Pp. 144-50
Lumley, Frederick, *New Trends in Twentieth Century Drama; A Survey Since Ibsen and Shaw*. 1967. Pp. 105-14
Mauriac, Francois, *Letters on Art and Literature*. 1953. Pp. 109-20
Mercure de France, 314:327-28, Feb., 1952

Le Boeuf sur le Toit *SEE* The Ox on the Roof

Les Chevaliers de la Table Ronde *SEE* Knights of the Round Table

The Eagle Has Two Heads, 1946
Commonweal, 45:613-14, April 4, 1947

Knapp, Bettina L., *Jean Cocteau*. 1970. Pp. 130-37
Lumley, Frederick, *New Trends in Twentieth Century Drama; A Survey Since Ibsen and Shaw*. 1967. Pp. 105-14
Nathan, George Jean, *Theatre Book of the Year, 1946-47*. Pp. 345-48
Nation, 164:403, April 5, 1947
New Republic, 116:38, March 31, 1947
New Statesman and Nation, 32:187, Sept. 14, 1946
New Yorker, 23:52, March 29, 1947
Newsweek, 29:84, March 31, 1947
Saturday Review of Literature, 30:40-44, April 12, 1947
Theatre Arts, 30:705-06, Dec., 1946, and 31:16, May, 1947
Time, 49:78, March 31, 1947

The Holy Terrors, 1940
Knapp, Bettina L., *Jean Cocteau*. 1970. Pp. 119-24

The Human Voice, 1930
Knapp, Bettina L., *Jean Cocteau*. 1970. Pp. 87-88
Mercure de France, 218:645-47, March 15, 1930
Revue Politique et Littéraire, 68:251, April 19, 1930

Infernal Machine, 1934
America, 98:614, Feb. 22, 1958
Les Annales Politiques et Littéraires, 102:432-33, April 20, 1934
Belli, Angela, *Ancient Greek Myths and Modern Drama; A Study in Continuity*. 1971. Pp. 3-19
Catholic World, 187:69, April, 1958
Christian Century, 75:283, March 5, 1958
Dickinson, Hugh, *Myth on the Modern Stage*. 1969. Pp. 96-112
English Institute Essays, 1946-1952. Pp. 55-72
L'Europe Nouvelle, 17:490-91, May 12, 1934
Fergusson, Francis; *Idea of a Theater, A Study of Ten Plays; The Art of Drama in Changing Perspective*. 1949. Pp. 194-228
Feynman, Alberta E., " 'The Infernal Machine', 'Hamlet', and 'Ernest Jones' ", *Modern Drama* (1963), 6:72-83
From the N. R. F. An Image of the Twentieth Century from the Pages of the 'Nouvelle Revue Francaise', ed. Justin O'Brien. 1958. Pp. 199-201
Gassner, John, *Theatre in Our Times; A Survey of the Men, Materials and Movements in the Modern Theatre*. 1954. Pp. 182-206
Journal des Débats, 41:pt. 1:643-44, April 20, 1934
Kallich, Martin, "Oedipus: From Man to Archetype", *Comparative Literature Studies* (1966), 3:33-46
Knapp, Bettina L., *Jean Cocteau*. 1970. Pp. 138-40
Locke, Louis Glenn; Gibson, William Merriam; and Arms, George Warren eds., *Readings for Liberal Education*. 1952. vol. 2, Pp. 710-19
Lumley, Frederick, *New Trends in Twentieth Century Drama; A Survey Since Ibsen and Shaw*. 1967. Pp. 105-14
Mercure de France, 252:354-57, June 1, 1934
Moore, M., *Predilections*, 1955, Pp. 126-29
New Republic, 119:27, July 5, 1948
Nation, 164:403, April 5, 1947
New Republic, 116:38, March 31, 1947

New Statesman and Nation, 32:187, Sept. 14, 1946
New Yorker, 23:52, March 29, 1947
Newsweek, 29:84, March 31, 1947
Saturday Review of Literature, 30:40-44, April 12, 1947
Theatre Arts, 30:705-06, Dec., 1946 and 31:16
Wimsatt, William Kurtz, ed., *Literary Criticism; Idea and Act*. 1974. Pp. 590-601

Intimate Relations, 1938
Knapp, Bettina L., *Jean Cocteau*. 1970. Pp. 113-17
Lumley, Frederick, *New Trends in Twentieth Century Drama; A Survey Since Ibsen and Shaw*. 1967. Pp. 105-14
New Statesman and Nation, 19:667-68, May 25, 1940

Knights of the Round Table, 1937
L'Illustration, 198:240, Oct. 23, 1937
Knapp, Bettina L., *Jean Cocteau*. 1970. Pp. 106-112
Muir, Lynette, "Cocteau's 'Les Chevaliers de la Table Ronde': A Baroque Play", *Modern Languages*, 40:115-20, 1959
Revue Politique et Littéraire, 75:692-93, Nov. 6, 1937

La Machine à Ecrire   *SEE*   The Typewriter

La Machine Infernale   *SEE*   The Infernal Machine

Les Mariés de la Tour Eiffel   *SEE*   The Wedding on the Eiffel Tower

Les Monstres Sacrés   *SEE*   The Holy Terrors

Oedipus Rex, 1927
Knapp, Bettina L., *Jean Cocteau*. 1970. Pp. 84-85

Orphée   *SEE*   Orpheus

Orpheus, 1926
Les Annales Politiques et Littéraires, 86:690, June 27, 1926
Dickinson, Hugh, *Myth on the Modern Stage*. 1969. Pp. 85-91
L'Illustration, 84 pt. 1:667, June 26, 1926
Journal des Debats, 33 pt. 2:45-47, July 2, 1926
Knapp, Bettina L., *Jean Cocteau*. 1970. Pp. 78-84
Long, Chester Clayton, "Cocteau's 'Orphée': From Myth to Drama and Film", *Quarterly Journal of Speech* (1965), 51:311-25
Lumley, Frederick, *New Trends in Twentieth Century Drama: A Survey Since Ibsen and Shaw*. 1967. Pp. 105-14
MacCarthy, Desmond, *Humanities*. 1954. Pp. 105-09
Moore, Harry T., *Twentieth Century French Literature to World War II*. 1966. Vol. I. Pp. 120-25
Nathan, George Jean, *Theatre Book of the Year, 1946-47*. Pp. 41-42
New Statesman, 31:45-46, April 21, 1928
New Yorker, 38:77, Jan. 12, 1963
Porter, David H., "Ancient Myth and Modern Play; A Significant Counterpoint", *Classical Bulletin* (Nov. 1971), 48:1-9
Spectator, 140:594, April 21, 1928

The Ox on the Roof, 1920
"Le Boeuf sur le Toit", *The Drama Review* (Sept. 1972), 16:27-45

Les Parents Terribles *SEE* Intimate Relations

The Typewriter, 1941
  Commonweal, 62:613, Sept. 23, 1955
  Knapp, Bettina L., *Jean Cocteau*. 1970. Pp. 124-26

La Voix Humaine *SEE* The Human Voice

The Wedding on the Eiffel Tower, 1921
  Cole, Toby, ed., *Playwrights on Playwriting; The Meaning and Making of Modern Drama from Ibsen to Ionesco*. 1960. Pp. 240-46

WILLIAM CONGREVE

Double Dealer, 1693
  Corman, Brian, "The Mixed Way of Comedy: Congreve's 'The Double Dealer' ", *Modern Philology* (1974), 71:356-65
  Cunningham, John E., *Restoration Drama*. 1966. Pp. 116-21
  Edgar, Irving I., *Essays in English Literature and History*. 1972. Pp. 52-70
  Evans, Ifor, *A Short History of English Drama*. 1965. Pp. 116-17
  Holland, Norman N., *The First Modern Comedies*. 1959. Pp. 149-160
  Nickles, Mary A., "The Women in Congreve's Comedies: Characters and Caricatures", *Dissertation Abstracts International* (1973), 33:6321A
  Palmer, John Leslie, *The Comedy of Manners*. 1962. Pp. 141-200
  Sharma, Ram Chandra, *Themes and Conventions in the Comedy of Manners*. 1965. Pp. 52-53, 295-96
  Ward, Adolphus William, *A History of English Dramatic Literature*, v. 3. 1966. Pp. 472-473

Love for Love, 1695
  Agate, James E., *English Dramatic Critics; An Anthology 1660-1932*. 1958. Pp. 3-4 and 28-29
  Brown, John Mason, *Broadway in Review*. 1940. Pp. 79-83
  _____ , *Seeing More Things*. 1948. Pp. 221-27
  Commonweal, 32:170, June 14, 1940 and 46:216, June 13, 1947
  Edgar, Irving I., *Essays in English Literature and History*. 1972. Pp. 52-70
  Forum, 108:123-27, Aug., 1947
  Gilliatt, Penelope, *Unholy Fools; Wits, Comics, Disturbers of the Peace; Film and Theater*. 1973. Pp. 65-66
  Gosse, Anthony, "The Omitted Scene in Congreve's 'Love for Love' ", *Modern Philology* (1963), 61:40-42
  Hawkins, Harriett, *Likeness of Truth in Elizabethan and Restoration Drama*. 1972. Pp. 98-114
  Holland, Norman N., *The First Modern Comedies*. 1959. Pp. 161-74
  Jarvis, F. P. The Philosophical Assumptions of Congreve's 'Love for Love' ", *Texas Studies in Literature and Language* (1972), 14:423-34
  Life, 22:59, June 23, 1947
  McCarthy, M. T., *Sights and Spectacles, 1937-1956*. 1956. Pp. 116-20
  Miner, Earl, ed., *Restoration Dramatists; A Collection of Critical Essays*. 1966. Pp. 151-64
  Nathan, George Jean, *Theater Book of the Year, 1947-48*. Pp. 13-17

Nation, 120:444, April 15, 1925 and 150:739, June 15, 1940 and 164:691-92, June 7, 1947, (11-30-74), 219:572

New Republic, 42:237-38, April 23, 1925 and 116:31-32, June 16, 1947

New Statesman, 16:756, April 2, 1921

New Statesman and Nation, 7:409-10, March 17, 1934

New Yorker, 23:55, June 7, 1947, (11-18-74), 50:113

Newsweek, 29:87, June 9, 1947

Nickles, Mary A., "The Women in Congreve's Comedies: Characters and Caricatures", *Dissertation Abstracts International* (1973), 33:6321A

Palmer, John Leslie, *The Comedy of Manners*. 1962. Pp. 141-200

Saturday Review of Literature, 30:20-22, June 14, 1947

School and Society, 66:65, July 26, 1947

Sharma, Ram Chandra, *Themes and Conventions in the Comedy of Manners*. 1965. Pp. 53-54, 59-60, and 335-36

Spectator, 152:407, March 16, 1934

Theatre Arts, 27:632, 662-68, Nov. 1943

Theatre Arts Anthology, A Record and a Prophecy, ed. by Rosamond Gilder. 1950. Pp. 665-68

Time, 35:52, June 17, 1940 and 49:54, June 9, 1947, (11-25-74), 104:108

Turner, Darwin T., "The Servant in the Comedies of William Congreve", *CLA Journal* (1958), 1:68-74

Ward, Alfred Charles, ed., *Specimens of English Dramatic Criticism, 17th-20th Centuries*. 1945. Pp. 473-74

Williams, Aubrey L., "The 'Utmost Tryal' of Virtue and Congreve's 'Love for Love' ", *Tennessee Studies in Literature* (1972), 17:1-18

Mourning Bride, 1697

Carrigan, Beatrice, "Congreve's 'Mourning Bride' and Caltellini's 'Almerica' ", *Annali Instituto Universitario Orientale*, Napoli, Sezione Romanza, 4:145-66, 1962

Evans, Ifor, *A Short History of English Drama*. 1965. Pp. 118-19

Palmer, John Leslie, *The Comedy of Manners*. 1962. Pp. 141-200

Rothstein, Eric, *Restoration Tragedy; Form and the Process of Change*. 1967. Pp. 173-80

Spectator, 135:967, Nov. 28, 1925

Ward, Adolphus William, *A History of English Dramatic Literature*, v. 3. 1966. Pp. 476-77

The Old Bachelor, 1693

Edgar, Irving I., *Essays in English Literature and History*. 1972. Pp. 52-70

Holland, Norman N., *The First Modern Comedies*. 1959. Pp. 132-48

Nickles, Mary A., "The Women in Congreve's Comedies: Characters and Caricatures", *Dissertation Abstracts International* (1973), 33:6321A

Novak, Maxmillan E., "Congreve's 'The Old Bachelor': From Formula to Art", *Essays in Criticism* (Apr. 1970), 20:182-99

Palmer, John Leslie, *The Comedy of Manners*. Pp. 141-200, 1962

Saturday Review, 152:428, Oct. 3, 1931

Sharma, Ram Chandra, *Themes and Conventions in the Comedy of Manners*. 1965. Pp. 257-58, 281-82, and 307-08

Spectator, 132:914-15, June 7, 1924

Turner, Darwin T., "The Servant in the Comedies of William Congreve", *CLA Journal* (1958), 1:68-74

Ward, Adolphus William, *A History of English Dramatic Literature*, v. 3. 1966. Pp. 471-72

Weales, Gerald, "The Shadow on Congreve's Surface", *Educational Theatre Journal* (1966), 18:33-40

Way of the World, 1700

Agate, James Evershed, comp., *English Dramatic Critics; An Anthology, 1660-1932*. 1958. Pp. 32-34

Bookman, 73:523, July, 1931

Catholic World, 133:464-65, July, 1931

Commonweal, 61:167, Nov. 12, 1954

Cunningham, John E., *Restoration Drama*. 1966. Pp. 126-31

Donaldson, Ian, *The World Upside-Down: Comedy from Jonson to Fielding*. 1970. Pp. 119-58

Edgar, Irving I., *Essays in English Literature and History*. 1972. Pp. 52-70.

Evans, Ifor, *A Short History of English Drama*. 1965. Pp. 117-18

Fox, James H., "The Actor-Audience Relationship in Restoration Comedy, with Particular Reference to the Aside", *Dissertation Abstracts International* (1973), 33:6308A

Hawkins, Harriett, *Likenesses of Truth in Elizabethan and Restoration Drama*. 1972. Pp. 115-38

Holland, Norman N., *The First Modern Comedies*. 1959. Pp. 175-98

Hurley, P. J., "Law and the Dramatic Rhetoric of 'The Way of the World' ", *South Atlantic Quarterly* (Spr. 1971), 70:191-202

Kaufman, Anthony, "Language and Character in Congreve's 'The Way of the World' ", *Texas Studies in Literature and Language* (1973), 15:411-27

Kaul, A. N., *The Action of English Comedy; Studies in the Encounter of Abstraction and Experience from Shakespeare to Shaw*. 1970. Pp. 98-103

Kronenberger, Louis, *The Polished Surface*. 1969. Pp. 55-72

Lambert, J. W., "The Way of the World", *Drama* (1974), No. 113:53-54

Leech, C. "Congreve and the Century's End", *Philological Quarterly*, 41:275-93, 1962

Life, 58:8, June 4, 1965

Miner, Earl, ed., *Restoration Dramatists; A Collection of Critical Essays*. 1966. Pp. 165-74

Nation, 119:606-07, Dec. 3, 1924 and 179:349, Oct. 16, 1954

Nation (London), 34:700, Feb. 16, 1924

New Statesman, 22:543-44, Feb. 16, 1924

New Yorker, 29:87, May 2, 1953, (2-25-74), 50:85

Nickles, Mary A., "The Women in Congreve's Comedies; Characters and Caricatures", *Dissertation Abstracts International* (1973), 33:6321A

Nolan, Paul T., " 'The Way of the World': Congreve's Moment of Truth", *Southern Speech Journal* (1959), 25:75-95

Palmer, John Leslie, *The Comedy of Manners*. 1962. Pp. 141-200

Ricks, Christopher, ed., *English Drama to 1710*. (History of Literature in the English Language) vol. 3. 1971. Pp. 399-401

Roper, Alan, "Language and Action in 'The Way of the World', 'Love's Last Shift', and 'The Relapse' ", *Journal of English Literary History* (1973), 40:44-69

Sharma, Ram Chandra, *Themes and Conventions in the Comedy of Manners*. 1965. Pp. 54-56

Spectator, 132:242, Feb. 16, 1924 and 139:919, Nov. 26, 1927

Tennessee Studies in Literature, 13:75-80, 1968

Teyssandier, H., "Congreve's 'Way of the World': Decorum and Morality", *English Studies* (Apr. 1971), 52:124-31

Theatre Arts, 39:12, Oct., 1955

Turner, Darwin T., "The Servant in the Comedies of William Congreve", *CLA Journal* (1958), 1:68-74

Tynan, Kenneth, *Curtains: Selections from the Drama Criticism and Related Writings*, 1961, Pp. 38-39

Van Voris, William, "Congreve's Gilded Carousel", *Educational Theatre Journal* (1958), 10:211-17

Walkley, Arthur Bingham, *Drama and Life*. 1908. Pp. 304-08

———————————— , *Still More Prejudice*. 1925. Pp. 39-43

Ward, Adolphus William, *A History of English Dramatic Literature*, v. 3. 1966. Pp. 475-76

Ward, Alfred Charles, ed., *Specimens of English Dramatic Criticism. 17th-20th Centuries*. 1945. Pp. 302-06

JOSEPH CONRAD

Secret Agent, 1929

Hartsell, Robert L., "Conrad's Left Symbolism in 'The Secret Agent' ", *Conradiana* (1972), 4,i:57-59

Ryf, R. S., " 'Scret Agent' on Stage", *Modern Drama* (May 1972), 15:54-67

Sullivan, Walter, "Irony and Discorder; 'The Secret Agent' ", *Sewanee Review* (1973), 81:124-31

Thornton, Weldon, "An Episode from Anglo-Irish History in Conrad's 'The Secret Agent' ", *English Language Notes* (1973), 10:286-89

Zyle, Wolodymr T. and Wendell M. Aycock, eds., *Joseph Conrad; Theory and World Fiction*, 1974. Pp. 151-66

Victory, 1919

Ryf, Robert S., "Conrad's Stage 'Victory' ", *Modern Drama* (1964), 7:148-60

PIERRE CORNEILLE

Agésilas, 1666

Abraham, Claude, *Pierre Corneille*. 1972. Pp. 129-31

Gérard, Albert, " 'Agésilas': Tragédie Optimiste", *Revue d'Histoire du Théâtre* (1967), 19:360-70

Andromeda, 1650

Abraham, Claude, *Pierre Corneille*. 1972. Pp. 98-99

Lapp, John C. "Metamorphosis in Corneille's 'Andromeda' ", *University of Toronto Quarterly* (1970), 39:164-81

Martin, H. M., "Corneille's 'Andromède' and Calderon's 'Las Fortunas' ", *Modern Philology*, 23:407-15, 1926

Attila, 1667

Abraham, Claude, *Pierre Corneille*. 1972. Pp. 131-35

Demorest, Jean-Jacques, ed., *Studies in 17th Century French Literature Presented to Morris Bishop*. 1962. Pp. 98-131

Hughes, Kaye V., "The Influence of Prediction in Corneille's 'Attila' and 'Surena' ", *Romance Notes* (1969), 11:350-54

Le Cid, 1636
Abraham, Claude, *Pierre Corneille*. 1972. Pp. 54-60

Ault, Harold C., "The Tragic Genius of Corneille", *Modern Langauge Review*, 45:164-76, 1950

Emigh, John S., "Love and Honor: A Comparative Study of Corneille's 'Le Cid' and Calderon's Honor Plays", *Dissertation Abstracts International* (1972), 32:3949A

Fowlie, Wallace, *Love in Literature; Studies in Symbolic Expression*. 1965. Pp. 37-57

Gerard, Albert S., "Baroque and the Order of Love: Structural Parallels in Corneille's 'Le Cid' and Vondel's 'Jephtha' ", *Neophilologus*, 49:118-31, 210-20, 1965

Haas, Gerhard, ed., *Kinder-und Jugendliteratur: Zur Typologie und Funktion einer Literarischen Gattung*. 1974. Pp. 159-72

Jones, L. E., "The Position of the King in 'Le Cid' ", *French Review* (1967), 40: 643-46

Kirsch, Arthur C., "Dryden, Corneille and the Heroic Play", *Modern Philology*, 59:248-64, 1961-62

Knudsen, Nils L., et als, eds., *Subjekt og Tekst: Bidrag til Semiotikkens Teori*. (Nordisk Sommeruniversitets Skriftserie, 5) 1974. Pp. 455-66

Knutson, Harold C., " 'Le Cid' de Corneille: Un Heros se Fait", *Studi Francesi* (1972), 16:26-33

Koenig, Waldemar, "Un Type Universal de la Littérature Française: 'Le Cid' ", *Die Neueren Sprachen*, 14:369-76, 1965

Krause, Gerd, "Der Heroische Idealismus in Corneilles 'Cid' ", *Die Neueren Sprachen* (1967), 16:362-75

Lancaster, Henry Carrington, *Adventures of a Literary Historian; A Collection of His Writings Presented to H. C. Lancaster by His Former Students and Other Friends in Anticipation of His Sixtieth Birthday, Nov. 10, 1942*. 1942. Pp. 267-71

——————— , " 'The Cid' - 1637", *French Review*, 23:450-51, 1950

Margritic, Milorad, "Ambiguités Cornéliennes: Etude de la Mythologie du 'Cid' ", *Dissertation Abstracts International* (1972), 32:6436A

Matthews, B., " 'Cid' and 'Horace' ", *International Quarterly*, 7:20-25, 1903

Mony, G., ed., *Corneille: Le Cid, La Chanson de Rodrigue: Explication and Commentaire*, Paris, Gabriel Mony, 1964

Nelson, Robert J., "The Denouement of 'Le Cid' ", *French Studies*, 14:141-47, 1960

Richards, K. R., "The First English Performance of Corneille's 'Le Cid' ", *Etudes Anglaises*. (1971), 24:77-78

Sainte-Beuve, Charles Augustin, *Selected Essays;* Trans. and ed. by Francis Steigmuller and Norbert Guterman. 1963. Pp. 29-61

Sedgwick, M., "Richelieu and the 'Querelle du Cid' ", *Modern Language Review*, 48:143-50, 1953

Sellestrom, A. D., "The Structure of Corneille's Masterpieces:, *Romanic Review*, 49:269-77, 1958

Studies in Honor of Alfred G. Engstrom, ed. Robert T. Cargo and Emanuel J. Mickel, Jr. 1972. Pp. 45-51

Valency, Maurice, *The Flower and the Castle; Introduction to Modern Drama*. 1963. Pp. 31-40

Wang, Leonard, "The 'Tragic' Theatre of Corneille", *French Review*, 25:182-91, 1951-52

Yarrow, P. J., "Denouement of 'Le Cid'", *Modern Language Review*, 50:270-73, 1955

Yost, C. A., "Historical Truth in the Dramas of Corneille", *South Atlantic Quarterly*, 16:56-59, 1917

Cinna, or, the Clemency of Augustus, 1640

Abraham, Claude, *Pierre Corneille*. 1972. Pp. 67-73

Ault, Harold C., "The Tragic Genius of Corneille", *Modern Language Review*, 45:164-76, 1950

Bartkus, Gvidonas, "Politiceskiu Smysl Tragedü Kornelja 'Cinna", *Literature: Lietuvos T. S. R. Aukštuju Mokyklu Mokslo Darbai* (1967), 10:127-48

Clarke, D. R., "Heroic Prudence and Reason in the 17th Century—Auguste's Pardon of Cinna", *Forum for Modern Language Studies* (Univ. of St. Andrews, Scotland), 1:328-38, 1965

Doubrovsky, Serge, " 'Cinna' et la Dialectique du Monarque", *La Table Ronde*. #164:29-63, 1961

Ehrmann, Jacques, "Les Structures de l'Echange dans 'Cinna'", *Temps Modernes* (1966), 22:929-60

Garrity, Henry A., "Le Commun Bonheur; Limits of Personal Freedom in Corneille's Later Plays", *French Review* (1974), 48:65-73

Herland, Louis, "Le Pardon d'Auguste dans Cinna", *La Table Ronde*,#158:113-26, 1961

Huther, J., "Rouen und Ludwig XIII; Ein Beitrag zur Genese des 'Cinna' ", *Zeitschrift für Franzosische Sprache und Literatur* (1970), 80:107-30

Jasinski, Rene, "Sur 'Cinna'", *Europe* (1974), 540-41:114-30

Kirsch, Arthur C., "Dryden, Corneille, and the Heroic Play", *Modern Philology*. 59:248-64, 1961-62

Nelson, Robert J., "Kinship and Kingship in 'Cinna'", *Forum for Modern Language Studies* (Univ. of St. Andrews, Scotland), 1:311-27, 1965

Stephan, R., "Cinna, ou, Une Conspiration Sous Richelieu", *Revue Politique et Littéraire*, 67:137-40, March 2, 1929

Van Roosbroeck, G. L., "Corneille's 'Cinna' and the 'Conspiration des Dames' ", *Modern Philology*, 20:1-17, 1922

Yost, C. A., "Historical Truth in the Dramas of Corneille", *South Atlantic Quarterly*, 16:56-59, 1917

Cinna, ou La Clémence d'Auguste   *SEE*   Cinna, or, The Clemency of Augustus

Clitandre, 1630

Koch, Philip, "The Hero in Corneille's Early Comedies", *Modern Language Association. Publications* (PMLA), 78:196-200, 1963

The Comic Illusion, 1635/36

Les Annales Politiques et Littéraires, 109:173-74, Feb. 25, 1937

Cherpack, C., "Captive Audience in 'L'Illusion Comique' ", *Modern Language Notes* (1966), 81:342-44

Cosnier, Colette, "Un Etrange Monstre: 'L'Illusion Comique' ", *Europe* (1974), 540-41:103-13

L'Illustration, 196:240, Feb. 27, 1937

Koch, Philip, "Cornelian Illusion", *Symposium*, 14:85-99, 1960

Lancaster, Henry Carrington, *Adventures of a Literary Historian; A Collection of His Writings Presented to H. C. Lancaster by His Former Students and Other Friends in Anticipation of His Sixtieth Birthday, Nov. 10, 1942*. 1942. Pp. 259-63

_____ , "Corneille's 'L'Illusion Comique': Mahelot's 'Mémoire' and Rampalle's 'Belinde' ", *Studies in Philology*, 18:10-14, 1921

Meier, Harri and Hans Sckommoday, eds., *Wort und Text. Festschrift für Fritz Schalk* (1963), Pp. 281-93

Nelson, Robert J., "Pierre Corneille's 'L'Illusion Comique'; The Play as Magic", *Modern Language Association. Publications* (PMLA), 71:1127-40, 1956

Revue des Deux Mondes, s8, 38:226-28, March 1, 1937

Sellestrom, A. D., " 'L'Illusion Comique' of Corneille: The Tragic Scenes of Act V", *Modern Language Notes*, 73:421-27, 1958

Simon, Alfred, "La Puissance de 'L'Illusion Comique' ", *Cahiers de la Companie Madeleine Renaud—Jean Louis Barrault* (1959), #26:8-12

Walters, Gordon, Jr., "Society and the Theatre in Corneille's 'L'Illusion Comique' ", *Romance Notes* (1969), 10:325-31

Wang, Leonard, "The 'Tragic' Theatre of Corneille", *French Review*, 25:182-91, 1951-52

Death of Pompey, 1642

Brown, Elynor P., "Shakespeare and Corneille: The Roman Patriot as Hero", *Dissertation Abstracts International* (1972), 33:2910A

Gerrard, Albert, " 'Vice ou Vertu': Modes of Self-Assertion in Corneille's 'La Mort de Pompée' ", *Revue des Langues Vivantes* (1965), 31:323-52

Revue de l'Université Laval (Quebec), 15:348-57, 1960

Don Sanche d'Aragon, 1649

Marek, Joseph C., "La Grandeur d'Ame Dans 'Rodogune', 'Don Sanche d'Aragon', et 'Surena' ", *Revue de l'Université Laval*, 15:348-57, 1960

La Galerie du Palais; ou, L'Amie Rivale *SEE* The Palace Corridor; or The Rival Friend

Heraclius, 1646

Schramm, E., "Corneilles 'Heraclius' und Calderons 'En Esta Video Todo Es Verdad y Todo Mentira'; Ein Beitrag zur Geschichte der Literarischen Beziehungen Zwischen Frankreich und Spanien im 17. Jahrhundert", *Revue Hispanique*, 17:225-308, 1927

Horace *SEE* Horatius

Horatius, 1640

Abraham, Claude, *Pierre Corneille*. 1972. Pp. 60-66

Ault, Harold C., "The Tragic Genius of Corneille", *Modern Language Review*, 45:164-76, 1950

Barber, W. H., "Patriotism and Gloire in Corneille's 'Horace' ", *Modern Language Review*, 46:368-78, 1951

Bouvet, Ph., "La Tendresse dans 'Horace' ", *L'Information Littéraire*, 17:139-44, 1965

Brown, Elynor P., "Shakespeare and Corneille: The Roman Patriot as Hero", *Dissertation Abstracts International* (1972), 33:2910A

Charlton, D. G., "Corneille's Dramatic Theories and the Didactism of 'Horace' ", *French Studies*, 15:1-11, 1961

Demorest, Jean-Jacques, ed., *Studies in 17th Century French Literature Presented to Morris Bishop*. 1962. Pp. 65-97

Forsyth, E., "The Tragic Dilemma in 'Horace' ", *Australian Journal of French Studies* (1967), 4:162-76

François, Carlo R., "En Relisant 'Horace' ou les Objections de la Conscience", *French Review*, 28:471-76, 1955

Goodman, Paul, *The Structure of Literature*. 1954. Pp. 257-66

Grant, Elliott M., "Reflections on Corneille's 'Horace' ", *French Review*, 37: 537-41, 1964

Matthews, B., " 'Cid' and 'Horace' ", *International Quarterly*, 7:20-25, 1903

Mazzara, Richard A., "More on Unity of Character of Action in 'Horace' ", *French Review*, 36:588-94, 1963

Mélanges d'Histoire Littéraire (XVI-XVII Siecle); Offerts à Raymond Lebèque par ses Collegues, Ses Elèves et Ses Amis. 1969. Pp. 195-200

Moore, W., "Corneille's 'Horace' and the Interpretation of French Classical Drama", *Modern Language Review*, 34:382-95, 1939   ^

Moore, W. G., ' "Horace' et 'Wilhelm Tell' ", *Revue de Littérature Comparée*, 19:444-51, 1939

Morel, J., "A Propos du Plaidoyer d'Horace: Reflexions sur le Sens de la Vocation Historique Dans le Théâtre de Corneille", *Romanic Review*, 51:27-32, 1960

Newmark, Peter, "A New View of 'Horace' ", *French Studies*, 10:1-10, 1956

Nitze, W. A., "Vertu as Patriotism in Corneille's 'Horace' ", *Modern Language Association. Publications* (PMLA), 67:1167-72, 1952

Scott, J. W., "The 'Irony' of 'Horace' ", *French Studies*, 12:11-17, 1959

Sellestrom, A. D., "The Structure of Corneille's Masterpieces", *Romanic Review*, 49:269-77, 1958

Trafton, Dain A., "On Corneille's 'Horace,' ", *Interpretation; A Journal of Political Philosophy* (1972), 2:183-93

Whiting, Charles G., "The Ambiguity of the Hero in Corneille's 'Horace' ", *Symposium* (1969), 23:163-70

Yost, C. A., "Historical Truth in the Dramas of Corneille", *South Atlantic Quarterly*, 16:56-59, 1917

L'Illusion Comique   SEE   The Comic Illusion

The Liar, 1642

Abraham, Claude, *Pierre Corneille*. 1972. Pp. 81-85

Reiss, I. J., " 'Le Menteur' de Corneille: Langage, Volanté, Societé", *Romance Notes* (1973), 15:284-96

The Maidservant, 1634

Abraham, Claude, *Pierre Corneille*. 1972. Pp. 40-42

Choiński, Krzystof, " 'La Suivante'—Niedoceniona Sztuka Corneille 'a", *Acta Philologica* (1974), 6:5-24

Harvey, L. E., "Intellectualism in Corneille; The Symbolism of Proper Names in 'La Suivante' ", *Symposium*, 13:290-93, 1959

Koch, Philip, "The Hero in Corneille's Early Comedies' ", *Modern Language Association. Publications* (PMLA), 78:196-200, 1963

Médée, 1634

Abraham, Claude K., "Corneille's 'Médée': A Tragedy?", *South Atlantic Bulletin* (1967), 32:7-9

Abraham, Claude, *Pierre Corneille*. 1972. Pp. 50-54

Birnbaum, Neil, "The Place of 'Médée' in the Cornelian Canon", *Dissertation Abstracts International* (1969), 30:2475A

Molk, Ulrich, "Corneilles 'Médée' und die Tragikomödie des Französischen Barock", *Romanistisches Jahrbuch* (1966), 17:82-97

Tobin, Ronald W., " 'Médée' and the Hercules Tradition of the Early Seventeenth Century", *Romance Notes* (1966), 8:65-69

Willez, W. L., "Corneille's First Tragedy: 'Médée' and the Baroque", *L'Esprit Createur* (Minneapolis), 4:135-48, 1964

Melite, or the False Letters, 1629

Abraham, Claude, *Pierre Corneille*. 1972. Pp. 32-38

Harvey, L. E., "Denouement of 'Melite' and the Role of the Nourrice", *Modern Language Notes*, 71:200-03, 1956

Koch, Philip, "The Hero in Corneille's Early Comedies", *Modern Language Association. Publications* (PMLA), 78:196-200, 1963

Van Roosbroeck, G. L., "Commonplace in Corneille's 'Melite': The Madness of Eraste", *Modern Philology*, 17:141-49, 1919

Mélite, ou Les Fausses Lettres   *SEE*   Mélite, or the False Letters

Le Menteur   *SEE*   The Liar

La Mort de Pompee   *SEE*   The Death of Pompey

Nicomède, 1650

Abraham, Claude, *Pierre Corneille*. 1972. Pp. 102-110

Griffiths, Bruce, " 'La Fourbe' and 'La Générosité': Fair and Foul Play in 'Nicomède' ", *Forum for Modern Language Studies* (Univ. of St. Andrews, Scotland), 1:339-51, 1965

Oedipe, 1659

Abraham, Claude, *Pierre Corneille*. 1972. Pp. 114-17

Dauphine, James, " 'Oedipe' de Corneille; Une Experience de la Liberté", *Europe* (1974), 540-41:151-61

Garrity, Henry A., "Le Commun Bonheur; Limits of Personal Freedom in Corneille's Later Plays", *French Review* (1974), 48:65-73

Othon, 1664

Abraham, Claude, *Pierre Corneille*. 1972. Pp. 126-29

Kellenberger, Hunter, " 'Tallemant' des Reaur and Corneille's 'Othon' ", *Modern Language Notes*, 76:130-32, 1961

The Palace Corridor, or, The Rival Friend, 1633

Abraham, Claude, *Pierre Corneille*. 1972. Pp. 38-41

Koch, Philip, "The Hero in Corneille's Early Comedies", *Modern Language Association. Publications* (PMLA), 78:196-200, 1963

Petharite, Roi des Lombards   *SEE*   Petharites, King of the Lombards

Petharites, King of the Lombards, 1652

Abraham, Claude, *Pierre Corneille*. 1972. Pp. 109-13

Hubert, J. D. "Pertharite et la Nouvelle Critique", *Kentucky Romance Quarterly* (1967), 14:17-23

Scott, J. W., " 'Pertharite': A Re-Examination", *Forum for Modern Language Studies* (Univ. of St. Andrew, Scotland), 1:352-57, 1965

Place Royale; or, The Extravagant Lover, 1634

Abraham, Claude, *Pierre Corneille*. 1972. Pp. 42-47

Koch, Philip, "The Hero in Corneille's Early Comedies", *Modern Language Association. Publications* (PMLA), 78:196-200, 1963 .

Larroutis, M., "Corneille et Montaigne: L'Egotisme dans 'La Place Royale' ", *Revue d'Histoire Littéraire de la France*, 62:321-28, 1962

Moisan-Morteyrol, Christine, "Les Premieres Comédies de Corneille: Prelude a 'La Place Royale' ", *Europe* (1974), 540-41:91-99

La Place Royale; ou, l'Amoureux Extravagant *SEE* Place Royale; or The Extravagant Lover

Polyeucte, 1641

Abraham, Claude, *Pierre Corneille*. 1972. Pp. 71-76

Angers, J. E. d', " 'Polyeucte', Tragédie Chrétienne", *Dix-Septieme Siècle* (1967), #75:49-69

Ault, Harold C., "The Tragic Genius of Corneille", *Modern Language Review*, 45:164-76, 1950

Beaujour, Michel, " 'Polyeucte' et la Monarchie du Droit Divin", *French Review*, 36:443-49, 1963

Blechmann, Wilhelm, "Göttliche und Menschliche Motivierung in Corneilles 'Polyeucte' ", *Zeitschrift für Französische Sprache und Literatur*, 75:109-34, 1965

Bouffard, Odoric, "Polyeucte Est-Il Encore Chrétien?", *Culture*, 20:296-306, 1959

Daniel, George B., ed., *Renaissance and other studies in Honor of William Leon Wyley*. 1968. Pp. 115-21

Doubrovsky, Serge, " 'Polyeucte' ou la Conquête de Dieu", *Nouvelle Revue Francaise*, 12:443-58, Sept., 1964, and 12:621-41, Oct., 1964

Falk, Eugene H., *Renunciation as a Tragic Focus; A Study of Five Plays*. 1954. Pp. 34-72

Ginestier, Paul, " 'Polyeucte', Essai de Critique Esthétique", *Revue d'Esthetiqye* (Paris), 13:128-39, 1960

Haley, M. P., " 'Polyeucte' and the 'De Imitatione Christi' ", *Modern Language Association. Publications* (PMLA), 75:174-83, 1960

Harvey, L. E., "Role of Emulation in Corneille's 'Polyeucte' ", *Modern Langauge Association. Publications*. (1967), 82:314-24

Hepp, Noemi, "Sur une Scène Négligee de Polyeucte", *Bulletin des Jeunes Romanistes* (1965), 11-12:1-6

Melanges d'Histoire Littéraire (XVI-XVII Siècle): Offerts a Raymond Lebeque par Ses Collègues, Ses Élèves et Ses Amis. 1969. Pp. 201-10

Moore, W. G., "Note on Corneille's 'Polyeucte' " *Modern Language Review*, 36:508-10, 1941

Picard, M., "Le Personnage de Félix dans 'Polyeucte' de Corneille", *L'Information Littéraire*, 11:223-25, 1959

Prevot, Jacques, "Une Problématique de 'Polyeucte' ", *Europe* (1974), 540-41: 131-39

Spiers, A. G. H., "Corneille's 'Polyeucte' Technically Considered", *Modern Language Review*, 14:44-56, 1919

Thomas, J. H., "Note on Corneille's 'Polyeucte' ", *Modern Language Review*, 35:216-20, 1940

Valentin, J. M., "Une Répresentation Inconnue de 'Polyeucte': Corneille, le Theatre des Jesuites e la Théâtre Allemand au Milieu du XVIII Siècle", *Revue de Litterature Comparee* (1968), 42:562:70

Woodbridge, B. M., "A New Interpretation of Corneille's 'Polyeucte' ", *Romanic Review*, 26:57-59, 1935

Yost, C. A., "Historical Truth in the Dramas of Corneille", *South Atlantic Quarterly*, 16:56-59, 1917

Pulcherie, 1672
Abraham, Claude, *Pierre Corneille*. 1972. Pp. 139-43

Rodogune, Princess of Parthia, 1645
Abraham, Claude, *Pierre Corneille*. 1972. Pp. 85-91

Goldmann, Lucien, "Das Problem des Bösen. Gedanken zu Corneilles 'Rodogune'·und Claudels 'Maria Verkundingunz' ", *Theater und Zeit* (1962-63), 10: 149-56

Hubert, Judd D., "The Conflict Between Chance and Morality in 'Rodogune' ", *Modern Language Notes*, 74:234-39, 1959

Marek, Joseph C., "La Grandeur d'Ame dans 'Rodogune', 'Don Sanche d'Aragon', et 'Surena' ", *Revue de l'Universite Laval* (Quebec), 15: 348-57, 1960

Valency, Maurice, *The Flower and the Castle; Introduction to Modern Drama*. 1963. Pp. 40-41

Sequel to the Liar, 1644
Abraham, Claude, *Pierre Corneille*. 1972. Pp. 83-85

Sertorius, 1662
Abraham, Claude, *Pierre Corneille*. 1972. Pp. 119-23

Garrity, Henry A., "Le Commun Bonheur; Limits of Personal Freedom in Corneille's Later Plays", *French Review* (1974), 48:65-73

Sophonisbe, 1663
Abraham, Claude, *Pierre Corneille*. 1972. Pp. 123-25

La Suite de Menteur   *SEE*   Sequel to the Liar

La Suivante   *SEE*   The Maidservant

Surena, 1674
Abraham, Claude, *Pierre Corneille*. 1972. Pp. 144-49

Hughes, Kaye V., "The Influence of Prediction in Corneille's 'Attila' and 'Surena' ", *Romance Notes* (1969), 11:350-54

La Charite, Raymond C. and Virginia A., "Corneille's 'Surena': An Option to a New Dramaturgy", *Romance Notes* (1968), 10:103-05

Marek, Joseph C., "La Grandeur d'Ame dans 'Rodogune', 'Don Sanche d'Aragon', et 'Surena' ", *Revue de L'Universite Laval* (Quebec), 15:348-57, 1960

Theodora, Virgin and Martyr, 1645
Abraham, Claude, *Pierre Corneille*. 1972. Pp. 92-94

Tite et Berenice, 1670
Abraham, Claude, *Pierre Corneille*. 1972. Pp. 135-40

Garrity, Henry A., "Le Commun Bonheur: Limits of Personal Freedom in Corneille's Later Plays", *French Review* (1974), 48:65-73

Gerard, S. A., "Self-love in Lope de Vega's 'Fuente Ovejuna' and Corncille's 'Tite et Berenice' ", *Australian Journal of French Studies* (1967), 4:177-97

La Veuve; ou, La Traître Trahi   SEE   The Widow; or, The Betrayer Betrayed

The Widow; or, The Betrayer Betrayed, 1631
  Abraham, Claude, *Pierre Corneille*. 1972. Pp. 36-39
  Harvey, Lawrence E., "The Noble and the Comic in Corneille's 'La Veuve'",
    Symposium, 10:291-95, 1956
  Koch, Philip, "The Hero in Corneille's Early Comedies", *Modern Language
    Association. Publications* (PMLA) 78:196-200, 1963

PIERRE CORNEILLE, MOLIERE, AND PHILIPPE QUINAULT

Psyche, 1671
  Abraham, Claude, *Pierre Corneille*. 1972. Pp. 160-61
  Lapp, John, "Corneille's 'Psyche' and the Metamorphosis of Love", *French
    Studies* (1972), 26:395-404

PHILIPPE QUINAULT

SEE

PIERRE CORNEILLE, MOLIERE, AND PHILIPPE QUINAULT

COVENTRY PLAYS

SEE

MIRACLE, MORALITY, AND MYSTERY PLAYS

NOEL COWARD

Ace of Clubs, 1950
  Spectator, 185:46, July 14, 1950

Bittersweet, 1929
  Bellamy, F. R., "Bittersweet", *Outlook*, 154:32, Jan. 1, 1930
  Brown, I., "Bittersweet", *Saturday Review*, 148:155-56, Aug. 10, 1929
  Morse, Clarence R., "Mad Dogs and Englishmen; A Study of Noel Coward",
    Emporia State Research Studies (1973), 31,iv:15-44
  Nation (London), 45:564, July 27, 1929
  New Statesman, 33:497-98, July 27, 1929
  Shipp, H., "Bittersweet", *English Review*, 49:377-79, Sept., 1929

Blithe Spirit, 1941
  Catholic World, 154:335-36, Dec., 1941
  Commonweal, 35:123-24, Nov. 21, 1941
  Kernodle, George R., *Invitation to the Theatre*. 1967. Pp. 251-52
  Laufe, Abe, *Anatomy of a Hit; Long Run Plays on Broadway from 1900 to the
    Present Day*. 1966. Pp. 95-97
  Life, 11:69-71, Sept. 29, 1941
  Morse, Clarence R., "Mad Dogs and Englishmen: A Study of Noel Coward",
    Emporia State Research Studies (1973), 31,iv:15-44
  Nation, 153:491, Nov. 15, 1941
  New Republic, 105:701, Nov. 24, 1941
  New Statesman and Nation, 22:35, July 12, 1941
  New Yorker, 17:37, Nov. 15, 1941
  Newsweek, 18:57, Nov. 17, 1941

Spectator, 167:34, July 11, 1941
Theatre Arts, 26:8-9, Jan., 1942
Time, 38:67, Nov. 17, 1941

Cavalcade, 1931
Dukes, A., "Cavalcade", *Theatre Arts*, 16:26-29, Jan., 1932
Jennings, R., "Cavalcade", *Spectator*, 147:525, Oct. 24, 1931
MacCarthy, Desmond, "Cavalcade", *New Statesman and Nation*, 2:576, Nov. 7, 1931
Wakefield, G., "Cavalcade", *Saturday Review*, 152:526-27, Oct. 24, 1931

Conversation Piece, 1934
Catholic World, 140:340-41, Dec., 1934
Fleming, R., "Conversation Piece", *Spectator*, 152:270, Feb. 23, 1934
Literary Digest, 118:20, Nov. 3, 1934
MacCarthy, Desmond, "Conversation Piece" *New Statesman and Nation 7:301,
March 3, 1934
_____ , *Theatre*. 1955. Pp. 140-43
Theatre Arts, 18:899-90, Dec., 1934

Design for Living, 1932
Arts and Decoration, 38:41, March, 1933
Brown, John Mason, *Two on the Aisle; Ten Years of the American Theatre in
Performance*. 1938. Pp. 114-16
Catholic World, 136:715-16, March 1933
Commonweal, 17:441, Feb. 15, 1933
deCoquet, J., "Design for Living", *Les Annales Politiques et Littéraires*, 105:
294-95, March 25, 1935
Gordon, Max, *Max Gordon Presents*. 1963. Pp. 154-56 and 165-71
Literary Digest, 115:162, Feb. 11, 1933
London Mercury, 39:530, March, 1939
Morse, Clarence R., "Mad Dogs and Englishmen; a study of Noel Coward",
Emporia State Research Studies (1973), 31, iv:15-44
Nathan, George Jean, *Passing Judgments*. 1935. Pp. 140-76
Nation, 136:187-88, Feb. 15, 1933
New Republic, 73:350-52, Feb. 8, 1933
New Statesman and Nation, 17:169, Feb. 4, 1939
Spectator, 162:128, Jan. 27, 1939
Theatre Arts, 17:257-58, April, 1933
Wilson, S., "Design for Living", *Plays and Players* (1974), 21:45-47

Easy Virtue, 1925
Brown, I., "Easy Virtue", *Saturday Review*, 141:744, June 19, 1926
Macdonell, A. G., "The Plays of Noel Coward", *Living Age*, 341:439-46, 1932
Nation, 121:739-40, Dec. 23, 1925
New Republic, 45:133-34, Dec. 23, 1935
Royde-Smith, N. G., "Easy Virtue", *Outlook* (London), 58:10, July 3, 1926
Shipp, H., "Easy Virtue", *English Review*, 43:127-28, July, 1926
Spectator, 136:1038, June 19, 1926
Taylor, John Russell, *The Rise and Fall of the Well-made Play*. 1967. Pp. 137-40
Waldman, M., "Easy Virtue", *London Mercury*, 14:420-21, Aug., 1926

Fallen Angels, 1925
   Brown, I., "Fallen Angels", *Saturday Review*, 139:486-87, May 9, 1925
   Commonweal, 63:542, Feb. 24, 1956
   Holms, J. F., "Fallen Angels", *New Statesman*, 25:74, May 2, 1925
   Illustrated London News, 215:959, Dec. 17, 1949
   Macdonell, A. G., "The Plays of Noel Coward", *Living Age*, 341:439-46, 1932
   Nation, 182:125, Feb. 11, 1956
   New Yorker, 31:58-60, Jan. 28, 1956
   Newsweek, 47:43-44, Feb. 6, 1956
   Royde-Smith, N. G., "Fallen Angels", *Outlook* (London), 55:297, May 2, 1925
   Sayler, O. M., "Fallen Angels", *Saturday Review of Literature*, 4:452, Dec. 17,
      1927
   Spectator, 134:718-19, May 2, 1925
   Theatre Arts, 40:17, March, 1956
   Time, 67:34, Jan. 30, 1956

Hay Fever, 1925
   Gilliatt, Penelope, *Unholy Fools; Wits, Comics, Disturbers of the Peace; Film
      and Theater.* 1973. Pp. 242-43
   McCarthy, Desmond, "Hay Fever", *New Statesman*, 25:449, Aug. 1, 1925
   Morse, Clarence R., "Mad Dogs and Englishmen; A Study of Noel Coward",
      Emporia State Research Studies (1973), 31,iv:15-44
   Nation (Nov. 30, 1970), 211:572
   New Yorker, 40:200-01, Nov. 21, 1964, (Nov. 21, 1970), 46:103
   Newsweek (Nov. 23, 1970), 76:137
   Royde-Smith, N. G. "Hay Fever", *Outlook* (London), 55:413, June 20, 1925
   Wyatt, E. V., "Hay Fever", *Catholic World*, 134:590-91, Feb., 1932

Home Chat, 1927
   Birrell F., "Home Chat", *Nation* (London), 42:184, Nov. 5, 1927
   Horsnell, H., "Home Chat", *Outlook* (London), 60:649, Nov. 12, 1927
   Jennings, R., "Home Chat", *Spectator*, 139:763, Nov. 5, 1927
   Saturday Review, 144:582-83, Oct. 29, 1927
   Shipp, H., "Home Chat", *English Review*, 45:728-30, Dec., 1927

I'll Leave It to You, 1920
   Morse, Clarence R., "Mad Dogs and Englishmen: A Study of Noel Coward",
      Emporia State Research Studies (1973), 31,iv:15-44

Island Fling, 1951
   Theatre Arts, 35:24-25, Sept., 1951

Look After Lulu, 1959 (adaptation of 'Occupe Toi d'Amélie' by G. L. Feydeau)
   America, 100:726, March, 21, 1959
   Catholic World, 189:157, May, 1959
   Commonweal, 70:24-25, April 3, 1959
   Nation, 188:262, March 21, 1959
   New Yorker, 35:80, March 14, 1959
   Newsweek, 53:90, March 16, 1959
   Theatre Arts, 43:24, May, 1959
   Time, 73:59, March 16, 1959
   Tynan, Kenneth, *Curtains; Selections from the Drama Criticism and Related
      Writings.* 1961. Pp. 303-05

Marquise, 1927
  Brown, I., "Marquise", *Saturday Review*, 143:305-06, Feb. 26, 1927
  Horsnell, H., "Marquise", *Outlook* (London), 59:211, Feb. 26, 1927
  Jennings, R., "Marquise", *Spectator*, 138:323, Feb. 26, 1927
  MacCarthy, Desmond, "Marquise", *New Statesman*, 28:602, Feb. 26, 1927
  Sayler, O. M., "Marquise", *Saturday Review of Literature*, 4:452, Dec. 17, 1927

Nude With A Violin, 1956
  America, 98:355, Dec. 14, 1957
  Catholic World, 186:308, Jan., 1958
  Christian Century, 74:1449, Dec. 4, 1957
  Commonweal, 67:489, Feb. 7, 1958
  Dance Magazine, 32:9, Feb., 1958
  Illustrated London News, 229:908, Nov. 24, 1956
  Nation, 185:416, Nov. 30, 1957
  New Statesman, 52:621, Nov. 17, 1956
  New Yorker, 33:78-80, Nov. 23, 1957
  Newsweek, 50:84, Nov. 25, 1957
  Reporter, 17:35-36, Dec. 12, 1957
  Saturday Review, 40:23, Nov. 30, 1957
  Spectator, 197:684, Nov. 16, 1956
  Theatre Arts, 41:30-31, May, 1957 and 42:20, January, 1958
  Time, 70:91, Nov. 25, 1957
  Tynan, Kenneth, *Curtains; Selections from the Drama Criticism and Related Writings*. 1961. Pp. 148-49

On With the Dance, 1925
  Brown, I., "On With the Dance", *Saturday Review*, 139:487, May 9, 1925
  Royde-Smith, N. G., "On With the Dance", *Outlook* (London), 55:313, May 9, 1925

Operette, 1938
  New Statesman and Nation, 15:528, May 26, 1938

Peace In Our Time, 1947
  New Statesman and Nation, 34:90, Aug. 2, 1947
  New York Times Magazine, Pp. 48-49, Sept. 4, 1947
  Spectator, 179:140, Aug. 1, 1947
  Theatre Arts, 31:45, Nov., 1947

Point Valaine, 1935
  New Republic, 81:363, Feb. 6, 1935 and 82:49, Feb. 20, 1935
  New Statesman and Nation, 34:208, Sept. 13, 1947
  Newsweek, 5:26, Jan. 26, 1935
  Spectator, 179:332, Sept. 12, 1947
  Theatre Arts, 19:170, March, 1935

Post Mortem, 1931
  Literary Digest, 109:19, June 6, 1931
  Macdonell, A. G., "The Plays of Noel Coward", *Living Age*, 341:439-46, 1932

Present Laughter, 1942
  Brown, John Mason. *Dramatis Personae; A Retrospective Show*. 1963. Pp. 183-90

_____ , "English Laughter, Past and Present", *Saturday Review of Literature*, 29:24-26, Nov. 23, 1946
_____ , *Seeing More Things*. 1948. Pp. 200-08
Catholic World, 164:261, Dec., 1946
Commonweal, 45:116, Nov. 15, 1946
Morse, Clarence R., "Mad Dogs and Englishmen; A Study of Noel Coward", *Emporia State Research Studies* (1973), 31,iv:15-44
Nathan, George Jean, *Theatre Book of the Year, 1946-47*. Pp. 142-45
Nation, 163:565, Nov. 16, 1946
New Republic, 115:628, Nov. 11, 1946
New Statesman and Nation, 25:335-36, March 22, 1943 and 33:292, April 26, 1947
New Yorker, 22:56, Nov. 9, 1946
Spectator, 170:427, May 7, 1943 and 176:461, April 25, 1947
Theatre Arts, 31:18, Jan., 1947
Time, 41:65, May 10, 1943 and 48:55, Nov. 11, 1946, (6-9-75), 105:68

Private Lives, 1930
America (Jan. 17, 1970), 122:54 and (Dec. 2, 1972), 127:470
Arts and Decoration, 35:83, July, 1931
Bookman, 73:523, July, 1931
Bourget-Pailleron, R., "Private Lives", *Revue des Deux Mondes*, s.8, 27:706-07, June 1, 1935
Catholic World, 132:719-20, March, 1931 and 168:160, Nov., 1948
Commonweal (Jan. 7, 1970), 91:409
Jennings, R., "Private Lives", *Spectator*, 145:488-89, Oct. 11, 1930
MacCarthy, Desmond, "Private Lives", *New Statesman*, 36:14-15, Oct. 11, 1930
Macdonell, A. G., "The Plays of Noel Coward", *Living Age*, 341:439-46, 1932
Morse, Clarence R., "Mad Dogs and Englishmen: A Study of Noel Coward", *Emporia State Research Studies* (1973), 31,iv:15-44
Mortimer, R., "Private Lives", *Nation* (London), 48:15, Oct. 4, 1930
Nathan, George Jean, *Theatre Book of the Year, 1948-49*. Pp. 110-13
Nation, 167:444, Oct. 16, 1948, (Dec. 22, 1969), 209:704
New Republic, 119:27, Nov. 1, 1948
New Yorker, 24:53, Oct. 16, 1948, (Dec. 13, 1969), 45:115, (2-17-75), 50:84
Newsweek, 32:88, Oct. 18, 1948, (Dec. 15, 1969), 94:117, (2-17-75), 85:66
Outlook, 157:234, Feb. 11, 1931
Saturday Review of Literature, 31:30-32, Oct. 23, 1948, (Dec. 20, 1969), 52:36
Theatre Magazine, 58:25, April, 1931
Time, 52:82, Oct. 18, 1948, (Dec. 12, 1969), 94:84
Wakefield, G. "Private Lives", *Saturday Review*, 150:370, Sept. 27, 1930

Quadrille, 1952
America, 92:283, Dec. 4, 1954
Catholic World, 180:307, Jan., 1955
Commonweal, 61:288, Dec. 10, 1954
Illustrated London News, 221:421, Sept. 13, 1952
Life, 33:166, Oct. 13, 1952
Morse, Clarence R., "Mad Dogs and Englishmen: A Study of Noel Coward", *Emporia State Research Studies* (1973), 31,iv:15-44
Nation, 79:450, Nov. 20, 1954

New Statesman and Nation, 44:316, Sept. 20, 1952
New Yorker, 30:103, Nov. 13, 1954
Newsweek, 44:98, Nov. 15, 1954
Saturday Review, 37:27, Nov. 27, 1954
Spectator, 189:359, Sept. 19, 1952
Theatre Arts, 38:20-25, Nov., 1954 and 39:16, 90, Jan., 1955
Time, 64:62, Nov. 15, 1954
Tynan, Kenneth, *Curtains; Selections from the Drama Criticism and Related Writings.* 1961. Pp. 30-32
Vogue, 124:125, Dec., 1954

Queen Was in the Parlor, 1926
Brown, I., "Queen Was in the Parlor", *Saturday Review*, 142:225-26, Aug. 28, 1926
MacCarthy, Desmond, "Queen Was in the Parlor", *New Statesman*, 27:581-82, Sept. 4, 1926
Royde-Smith, N. G., "Queen Was in the Parlor", *Outlook* (London), 58:211, Sept. 4, 1926
Spectator, 137:377, Sept. 11, 1926

Rat Trap, 1926
Brown I., "Rat Trap", *Saturday Review*, 142:467, Oct. 23, 1926
Nation (London), 40:146, Oct. 30, 1926
Spectator, 137:735, Oct. 30, 1926

Relative Values, 1951
Morse, Clarence R., "Mad Dogs and Englishmen: A Study of Noel Coward", *Emporia State Research Studies* (1973), 31,iv:15-44
New Statesman and Nation, 42:664, Dec. 8, 1951
New Yorker, 27:78, Jan. 19, 1952
Spectator, 187:770, Dec. 7, 1951

Sigh No More, 1945
New Statesman and Nation, 30:160, Sept. 8, 1945

Sirocco, 1927
Brown, I., "Sirocco", *Saturday Review*, 144:771-72, Dec. 3, 1927
Jennings, R., "Sirocco", *Spectator*, 139:972, Dec. 3, 1927

A Song at Twilight, 1966
Taylor, John Russell, *The Rise and Fall of the Well-made Play.* 1967. Pp. 124-26
New Yorker, 42:70, July 23, 1966
Vogue, 148:50, Aug. 15, 1966

This Happy Breed, 1942
New Statesman and Nation, 25:335, May 22, 1943
Time, 41:65, May 10, 1943

This Year of Grace, 1928
Bennett, A., "This Year of Grace", *New Statesman*, 30:792-93, March 31, 1928
Brown, I., "This Year of Grace", *Saturday Review*, 145:389-90, March 31, 1928
Horsnell, H., "This Year of Grace", *Outlook* (London), 61:438, April 7, 1928
Jennings, R. "This Year of Grace", *Spectator*, 140:528, April 7, 1928

Macdonell, A. G., "This Year of Grace", *London Mercury*, 18:88, May, 1928
Nathan, George Jean, "This Year of Grace", *American Mercury*, 16:120-21, Jan., 1929
Shipp, H., "This Year of Grace", *English Review*, 46:604, May, 1928
Young, Stark, "This Year of Grace", *New Republic*, 57:15-16, Nov. 21, 1928

Tonight At 8:30, 1935
  Catholic World, 144:471-72, Jan., 1937 and 167:72-73, April, 1948
  Commonweal, 25:193, Dec. 11, 1936 and 47:521, March 5, 1948 and 47:546, March 12, 1948
  Fleming, P., "Tonight at 8:30", *Spectator*, 156:91, Jan. 17, 1936
  Nathan, George Jean, *Theatre Book of the Year, 1947-48.* Pp. 287-94
  Nation, 166:285, March, 6, 1948
  New Republic, 89:217, Dec. 16, 1936
  New Yorker, 24:50, March 6, 1948
  Newsweek, 8:20-22, Dec. 5, 1936
  Saturday Review of Literature, 15:5, Dec. 19, 1936
  Theatre Arts, 21:18, Jan., 1937
  Time, 28:39, Dec. 7, 1936

Vortex, 1924
  Canfield, Mary Cass, *Grotesques and Other Reflections.* 1927. Pp. 223-29
  Macdonell, A. G., "The Plays of Noel Coward", *Living Age*, 341:439-46, 1932
  Shipp, H., "Vortex", *English Review*, 40:261, Feb., 1925
  Spectator, 188:326, March 14, 1952
  Taylor, John Russell, *The Rise and Fall of the Well-made Play.* 1967. Pp. 134-37
  Wright, R., "Vortex", *New Statesman*, 24:234, Nov. 29, 1924

Waiting In the Wings, 1960
  Illustrated London News, 237:534, Sept. 24, 1960

Words and Music, 1932
  Living Age, 343:272-73, Nov., 1932
  Theatre Arts, 16:878-80, Nov., 1932

Young Idea, 1923
  Agate, J., "Young Idea", *Saturday Review*, 135:216-17, Feb. 17, 1923
  Spectator, 130:366, March 3, 1923

ANTHONY CREIGHTON

SEE

JOHN OSBORNE

MARGARETTA D'ARCY

SEE

JOHN ARDEN AND MARGARETTA D'ARCY

WILLIAM DAVENANT

Rivals, 1664
  Spencer, Christopher, "Macbeth and Davenant's 'The Rivals'", *Shakespeare Quarterly* (Spr. 1969), 20:225-29

The Siege of Rhodes, 1656
   Waith, Eugene M., *Ideas of Greatness; Heroic Drama in England.* 1971. Pp. 194-
   98

The Wits, 1634
   Blattes, Robert, "Elements Parodiques Dans 'The Wits' de Sir William Davenant", *Caliban* (1974), 10:127-40

LAWRENCE H. DAVISON (pseud.)

SEE

DAVID HERBERT LAWRENCE

JEANNE DECASALIS

SEE

ROBERT CEDRIC SHERRIFF AND JEANNE DECASALIS

THOMAS DEKKER

The Honest Whore, 1604
   Berlin, Normand, "Thomas Dekker: A Partial Reappraisal", *Studies in English
   Literature*, 1500-1900 (1966), 6:263-77
   Champion, L. S., "From Melodrama to Comedy; A Study of the Dramatic
   Perspective in Dekker's 'The Honest Whore'", *Studies in Philology* (Apr.
   1972), 69:192-209
   English Association. *Essays and Studies*, 1966. 1966. Pp. 18-40
   Keyishian, Harry, "Dekker's 'Whore' and Marston's 'Courtesan'", *English
   Language Notes* (1967), 4:261-66
   Kistner, A. L. and M. K., "'Honest Whore': A Comedy of Blood", *Humanities
   Association Bulletin* (1972), 23,iv:23-27
   Raspa, Richard, "Christian-Humanism and Naturalism in the Plays of Thomas
   Dekker", *Dissertation Abstracts International* (1972), 32:4631A
   Schwartz, Sanford M., "The Comedies of Thomas Dekker", *Dissertation Ab-
   stracts* (1968), 29:1879A-80A
   Spivack, Charlotte, "Bedlam and Bridewell: Ironic Design in 'The Honest
   Whore'", *Komos; A Quarterly of Drama and Arts of the Theater* (1973),
   3:10-16
   Ure, Peter, *Elizabethan and Jacobean Drama; Critical Essays.* 1974. Pp. 187-
   208

Keep the Widow Waking, 1624
   Forker, C. R., "Wit Without Money; A Fletcherian Antecedent to 'Keep the
   Widow Waking'", *Comparative Drama* (1974), 8:172-83

Old Fortunatus, 1600
   Adams, Henry Hatch, *English Domestic or Homiletic Tragedy, 1575 to 1642*
   (Studies in English and Comparative Literature, No. 159). 1943. Pp. 75-99
   Bose, Tirthanker, "Dekker's Response to Tradition in 'Old Fortunatus'", *Pan-
   jab University Research Bulletin* (1972), 3:19-33
   Homan, S. R., "'Dr. Faustus', Dekker's 'Old Fortunatus' and the Morality
   Plays", *Modern Language Quarterly* (1965), 26:497-505
   Raspa, Richard, "Christian-Humanism and Naturalism in the Plays of Thomas
   Dekker", *Dissertation Abstracts International* (1972), 32:4631A

Schwartz, Sanford M., "The Comedies of Thomas Dekker", *Dissertation Abstracts* (1968), 29:1879A-80A

The Shoemaker's Holiday; or, The Gentle Craft, 1600

Berlin, Normand, "Thomas Dekker; A Partial Reapparaisal", *Studies in English Literature, 1500-1900* (1966), 6:263-77

Bluestone, Max and Norman Rabkin, eds., *Shakespeare's Contemporaries; Modern Studies in English Renaissance Drama.* 2nd ed. 1970. Pp. 184-93

Boas, Frederick S., *An Introduction to Stuart Drama.* 1946. Pp. 147-65

Bradbrook, Muriel C., *The Growth and Structure of Elizabethan Comedy.* 1955. Pp. 119-32

Brown, John Mason, *Two on the Aisle; Ten Years of the American Theatre in Performance.* 1938. Pp. 201-04

Burelbach, Frederick M., Jr., "War and Peace in 'The Shoemaker's Holiday'", *Tennessee Studies in Literature* (1968), 13:99-107

Camille, Georgette, et al, *Le Théâtre Elizabethain.* 1940. Pp. 248-54

Catholic World, 146:595-96, Feb., 1938

Commonweal, 27:327, Jan. 14, 1938

Evans, Ifor, *A Short History of English Drama.* 1965. Pp. 75-76

Gayley, Charles Mills, *Representative English Comedies.* vol. 3, 1912-1914. Pp. 3-17

Grayburn, William F., ed., *Studies in the Humanities.* 1969. Pp. 50-54

Hunt, Mary Leland, *Thomas Dekker; A Study.* 1911. Pp. 56-59

Jones-Davies, Marie Therese, *Un Peintre de la Vie Londonienne: Thomas Dekker (circa 1572-1632).* 1958. vol. 1. Pp. 126-29

Kaplan, Joel H., "Virtue's Holiday; Thomas Dekker and Simon Eyre", *Renaissance Drama* (1969), 2:103-22

Knights, Lionel Charles, *Drama and Society in the Age of Jonson.* 1937. Pp. 236-40

Nation, 146:80-81, Jan. 15, 1938

New Republic, 93:310, Jan. 19, 1938

Newsweek, 11:24, Jan. 17, 1938

Novarr, David, "Dekker's Gentle Craft and the Lord Mayor of London", *Modern Philology* (1960), 57:233-39

Pocock, Guy Noel, *Little Room,* 1926, Pp. 218-29

Raspa, Richard, "Christian-Humanism and Naturalism in the Plays of Thomas Dekker", *Dissertation Abstracts International* (1972), 32:4631A

Schwartz, Sanford M., "The Comedies of Thomas Dekker", *Dissertation Abstracts* (1968), 29:1879A-80A

Spender, Constance, "The Plays of Thomas Dekker", *Contemporary Review* (1926), 130:332-39

Steane, J. B., ed., *The Shoemaker's Holiday.* 1965. Pp. 1-23

Theatre Arts, 22:94-96, Feb., 1938

Thomson, Patricia, "The Old Way and the New Way in Dekker and Massinger", *Modern Language Review* (1956), 51:168-78

Time, 31:30, Jan. 10, 1938

The Whore of Babylon, 1606

Pineas, Rainer, "Biblical Allusion in 'The Whore of Babylon'", *American Notes and Queries* (1972), 11:22-24

THOMAS DEKKER AND JOHN FORD

The Witch of Edmonton, 1621
  Brodwin, L. L., "The Domestic Tragedy of Frank Thorney in 'The Witch of
    Edmonton' ", *Studies in English Literature* (1967), 7:311-28
  MacCarthy, D., " 'Witch of Edmonton' at the Old Vic", *New Statesman and
    Nation* (Dec. 19, 1936), 12:1026-28
  Sackville-West, Edward, *Inclinations*. 1967. Pp. 117-25

THOMAS DEKKER, HENRY CHETTLE
AND WILLIAM HAUGHTON

Patient Grissil, 1600
  Levin, Richard, *The Multiple Plot in English Renaissance Drama*. 1971. Pp. 49-
    54

SHELAGH DELANEY

The Lion in Love, 1960
  America, 109:63-64, July 13, 1963
  "Dishing the Dirt at Twenty-one", *Newsweek*, 56:109-10, Sept. 26, 1960
  Illustrated London News, 238:76, Jan. 14, 1961
  New Statesman, 60:377, Sept. 17, 1960 and 61:28, Jan. 6, 1961
  New Yorker, 39:90, May 4, 1963
  Newsweek, 61:83, May 6, 1963
  Spectator, 206:13, Jan. 6, 1961
  Theatre Arts, 47:64-65, June, 1963
  Time, 81:76, May 3, 1963

A Taste of Honey, 1959
  Aragno, Riccardo, "Do-it-yourself Drama", *Gemini/Dialogue* (1960), 3:31-34
  Catholic World, 193:127-28, May, 1961
  Clurman, Harold, *The Naked Image; Observations on the Modern Theatre*.
    1966. Pp. 70-71
  Commonweal, 74:496, Sept. 8, 1961
  Ebony, 16:71-74, Feb., 1961
  English, 12:185, 1959
  Gassner, John, *Dramatic Soundings; Evaluations and Retractions Culled from
    Thirty Years of Dramatic Criticism*. 1968. Pp. 499-500
  Hays, H. R., "Transcending Naturalism", *Modern Drama* (1962), 5:27-36
  Horizon, 3:102-03, March, 1961
  Ippolito, G. J., "Shelagh Delaney", *Drama Survey* (1961), 1:86-91
  Kerr, Walter, *The Theater in Spite of Itself*. 1963. Pp. 126-29
  Lumley, Frederick, *New Trends in Twentieth Century Drama; A Survey Since
    Ibsen and Shaw*. 1967. Pp. 310
  Nation, 188:461-62, May 16, 1959 and 191:334, Oct. 29, 1960
  "Never Underestimate Eighteen Year Old Girls", *New York Times Magazine*,
    Pp. 30, May 28, 1961
  New Republic, 143:22, Oct. 17, 1960
  New Statesman, 57:252, Feb. 21, 1959
  New Yorker, 34:97-98, Feb. 7, 1959 and 36:73, Oct. 15, 1960
  Newsweek, 56:102, Oct. 17, 1960

Noel, J., "Some Aspects of Shelagh Delaney's Use of Language in 'A Taste of Honey' ", *Revue des Langues Vivantes* (1960), 26:284-90

Oberg, A. K., " 'Taste of Honey' and the Popular Play", *Wisconsin Studies in Contemporary Literature* (1966), 7:160-67

"People on the Way Up", *Saturday Evening Post*, 234:30, Oct. 21, 1961

Popkin, Henry, "Theatre Chronicle", *Sewanee Review*, 69:337-38, 1961

Reporter, 23:46, Nov. 24, 1960

Saturday Review, 43:22, Oct. 22, 1960

Simon, John, "Theatre Chronicle", *Hudson Review*, 14:88-89, 1961

Spectator, 200:729, June 6, 1958

Theatre Arts, 43:16-17, May, 1959, and 44:10-11, Dec., 1960

"Three Woman Triumph", *Life*, 50:52, March 10, 1961

Time, 76:54, Oct. 17, 1960

Tynan, Kenneth, *Curtains; Selections from the Drama Criticism and Related Writings*. 1961. Pp. 212-14

JACQUES DEVAL

L'Age de Juliette, 1934
Bourget-Pailleron, R., "L'Age de Juliette", *Revue des Deux Mondes*, s.8 25:212-13, Jan. 1, 1935

deCoquet, J., "L'Age de Juliette", *Les Annales Politiques et Littéraires*, 104:303-04, Dec. 25, 1934

Barricou, 1930
Vidou, H., *Journal des Débats*, 37 Pt. 1:565-66, April 4, 1930

Doumic, R., "Barricou", *Revue des Deux Mondes*, s. 7 57:225-26, May 1, 1930

Rouveyre, A., "Barricou", *Mercure de France*, 219:660, May 1, 1930

Bathsheba, 1947
Catholic World, 165:168, May, 1947

Commonweal, 45:647, April 11, 1947

Nathan, George Jean, *Theatre Book of the Year, 1946-47*. Pp. 349-51

New Republic, 116:42, April 7, 1947

New Yorker, 23:50, April 5, 1947

Newsweek, 29:80, April 7, 1947

Time, 49:77, April 7, 1947

La Beauté du Diable, 1924
Bidou, H., "La Beauté du Diable", *Journal des Débats*, 32 Pt. 1:160-62, Jan. 22, 1925

Brisson, P., "La Beauté du Diable", *Les Annales Politiques et Littéraires*, 84:88, Jan. 25, 1925

Ce Soir à Samarcande   *SEE*   Tonight at Samarkand

Dans sa Candeur Nâive   *SEE*   Her Cardboard Lover

Errand For Bernice, 1945
Theatre Arts, 29:14, Jan., 1945

Etienne, 1930
Bidou, H., "Etienne", *Journal des Débats*, 37 Pt. 1:605-06, April 11, 1930

Doumic, R., "Etienne", *Revue des Deux Mondes*, s. 7 57:226-27, May 1, 1930

Her Cardboard Lover, 1926
  Bellessort, A., "Dans sa Candeur Nâive", *Journal des Débats*, 40 Pt. 1:125-26, Jan. 20, 1933
  L'Illustration, 84 Pt. 1:87, Jan. 23, 1926
  Rageot, G., "Dans sa Candeur Nâive", *Revue Politique et Littéraire*, 64:118, Feb. 20, 1926
  Rouveyre, A., "Dans sa Candeur Nâive", *Mercure de France*, 186:181, Feb. 15, 1926
  Young, Stark, "Her Cardboard Lover", *New Republic*, 50:194-95, April 6, 1927

Il Etait Une Gare, 1953
  France Illustration, No. 388:414, March 21, 1953

Lorelei, 1938
  Catholic World, 184:472, Jan., 1939
  Nation, 147:637, Dec. 10, 1938
  Theatre Arts, 23:95-96, Feb., 1939

Mademoiselle, 1932
  Les Annales Politiques et Littéraires, 98:106-07, Feb. 1, 1932
  Arts and Decoration, 38:57, Dec., 1932
  Catholic World, 136:336-37, Dec., 1932
  Commonweal, 17:49, Nov. 9, 1932
  L'Europe Nouvelle, 15:112-13, Jan. 23, 1932
  New Republic, 73:128-29, Dec. 14, 1932
  Nuova Antologia, 360:134-36, March 1, 1932
  Revue des Duex Mondes, s. 8 7:702-05, Feb. 1, 1932
  Revue Politique et Littéraire, 70:60, Jan. 16, 1932
  Sharp, Mary E., "Le Théâtre de Jacques Deval", *French Review*, 12:469-75, 1938-39
  Theatre Arts, 17:17-18, Jan., 1933

Marriage Story, 1949
  Illustrated London News, 214:704, May 21, 1949

Oh, Brother!, 1945
  Nathan, George Jean, *Theatre Book of the Year, 1945-46*. Pp. 30-35
  New Yorker, 21:32, June 30, 1945

Ombre Chère, 1952
  France Illustration, no. 325:23, Jan. 5, 1952

Le Onzième Commandement, 1932
  Bellessort, A., "Le Onzième Commandement", *Journal des Débats*, 39 pt. 1:684-86, April 29, 1932

Prayer for the Living, 1933
  Bellessort, A., "Prière Pour les Vivants", *Journal des Débats*, 40 pt. 2:556-58, Oct. 6, 1933
  Lievre, P., "Prière Pour les Vivants", *Mercure de France*, 247:672-74, Nov. 1, 1933
  Marcel, G., "Prière Pour les Vivants", *L'Europe Nouvelle*, 16:960, Oct. 7, 1933

Prière Pour les Vivantes *SEE* Prayer for the Living

La Rose de Septembre, 1926
  L'Illustration, 84 pt. 1:253, March 13, 1926

Tovaritch, 1933
  Les Annales Politiques et Litteraires, 101:478-79, Oct. 27, 1933
  Catholic World, 144:335-36, Dec., 1936
  Commonweal, 25:20, Oct. 30, 1936
  Journal des Débats, 40 pt. 2:678-80, Oct. 27, 1933
  Literary Digest, 122:22, Oct. 31, 1936
  Mercure de France, 248:412-14, Dec. 1, 1933
  New Republic, 89:21, Nov. 4, 1936
  Newsweek, 8:40, Oct. 24, 1936
  Revue des Deux Mondes, s.8 18:228-29, Nov. 1, 1933
  Revue Politique et Littéraire, 71:666-67, Nov. 4, 1933
  Theatre Arts, 19:481, July, 1935 and 20:919-23, Dec., 1936
  Time, 28:47, Oct. 26, 1936
  Verschoyle, D., "Tovaritch", *Spectator*, 154:731, May 3, 1935

Ventôse, 1927
  Bidou, H., "Ventôse", *Journal des Débats*, 34 pt. 2:950, Dec. 2, 1927

JACQUES DEVAL AND LORENZO SEMPLE, JR.

Tonight in Samarkand, 1955
  America, 92:657, March 19, 1955
  Catholic World, 181:66-67, April, 1955
  France Illustration, 6:449, Oct. 21, 1950
  Nation, 180:226, March 12, 1955
  New Yorker, 31:50, Feb. 26, 1955
  Newsweek, 45:58, Feb. 28, 1955
  Saturday Review, 38:26, March 5, 1955
  Theatre Arts, 39:15, 22, May, 1955
  Time, 65:60, Feb. 28, 1955

JOHN DRYDEN

All for Love; or, The World Well Lost, 1678
  Agate, James Evershed, *English Dramatic Critics; An Anthology, 1660-1932*.
    1958. Pp. 310-14
  Boase, T. S. R., "All for Love", *New Statesman*, 18:531, Feb. 11, 1922
  Catholic World, 174:393, Feb., 1952
  Creed, Howard, ed., *Essays in Honor of Richebourg Gaillard McWilliams*.
    1970. Pp. 21-28
  Cunningham, John E. *Restoration Drama*. 1966. Pp. 71-74
  Davies, H. Neville, "Dryden's 'All for Love' and Thomas May's 'The Tragedie
    of Cleopatra, Queen of Egypt' ", *Notes and Queries*, 12:139-44, 1965
  Davies, H. Neville, "Dryden's 'All for Love' and Sedley's 'Antony and Cleopa-
    tra' ", *Notes and Queries* (1967), 14:221-27
  Elwin, Malcolm, *Handbook of Restoration Drama*. 1966. Pp. 92-94
  Everett, W., " 'All for Love; or, The World Well Lost' and Shakespeare's 'Cleo-
    patra' ", *Atlantic Monthy*, 95:258-60, Feb., 1905
  Faas, K. E., "Some Notes on Dryden's 'All for Love' ", *Anglia; Zeitschrift für
    Englische Philologie* (1970), 88:341-46

Forker, Charles R., " 'Romeo and Juliet' and the 'Cydnus' Speech in Dryden's 'All for Love' ", *Notes and Queries*, 9:382-83, 1962

Freedman, Morris, " 'All for Love' and 'Samson Agonistes' ", *Notes and Queries*, ns3:514-17, 1956

Hughes, R. E., "Dryden's 'All for Love': The Sensual Dilemma", *Drama Critique* (1960), 3:68-74

Huntley, Frank L., "Dryden, Rochester, and the Eighth Satire of Juvenal", *Philological Quarterly*, 18:269-84, 1939

Hyman, Stanley Edgar, *Poetry and Criticism; Four Revolutions in Literary Taste*. 1961. Pp. 39-84

Jackson, Wallace, "Dryden's Emperor and Lillo's Merchant: The Relevant Bases of Action", *Modern Language Quarterly* (1965), 26:536-44

Jaquith, William G., "Dryden's 'Tyrannick Love' and 'All for Love': A Study of Comic and Tragic Dialects", *Dissertation Abstracts International* (1973), 34:3345A

Kearful, Frank J., " 'Tis Past Recovery: Tragic Consciousness in 'All for Love' ", *Modern Language Quarterly* (1973), 34:227-46

King, Bruce, *Dryden's Major Plays*. 1966. Pp. 133-47

Klima, S., "Some Unrecorded Borrowings from Shakespeare in Dryden's 'All for Love' ", *Notes and Queries* (1963), 10:415-18

Miner, Earl Roy, ed., *Restoration Dramatists; A Collection of Critical Essays*. 1966. Pp. 51-62

Nation (London), 30:952, March 25, 1922

Nazareth, Peter, " 'All for Love': Dryden's Hybrid Play", *English Studies in Africa* (1963), 6:154-63

Nicol, Bernard de Bear, ed., *Varieties of Dramatic Experience*. 1969. Pp. 113-41

Petit, Herbert H., ed., *Essays and Studies in Language and Literature*. 1964. Pp. 49-86

Rostvig, Maren-Sofie, et. al., *The Hidden Sense and Other Essays*. 1963. Pp.159-95

Spectator, 128:368, March 25, 1922

Starnes, D. T., "Imitation of Shakespeare in Dryden's 'All for Love' ", *Texas Studies in Language and Literature*, 6:39-46, 1964

Tritt, Carleton S., "Wit and Paradox in Dryden's Serious Plays", *Dissertation Abstracts* (1968), 29:882A-83A

Visser, Colin Wills, "Dryden's Plays; A Critical Assessment", *Dissertation Abstracts* (1968), 29:1520A-21A

Waith, Eugene M., *The Herculean Hero in Marlowe, Chapman, Shakespeare, and Dryden*. 1962. Pp. 152-201

——————————— , *Ideas of Greatness; Heroic Drama in England*. 1971. Pp. 231-35

Wallerstein, Ruth, "Dryden and the Analysis of Shakespeare's Techniques", *Review of English Studies*, 19:165-85, 1943

Weinbrot, J. D., "Alexas in 'All for Love': His Genealogy and Function", *Studies in Philology* (1967), 64:625-39

Worsley, T. C., "Heroic Tragedy", *New Statesman*, 56:14-15, July 5, 1958

Amboyna; or, The Cruelties of the Dutch to the English Merchants, 1673

Bredvold, Louis I., et. al., *Essays and Studies in English Comparative Literature by Members of the English Department of the University of Michigan*. 1932. Pp. 119-32

Amphytryon, or, The Two Socias, 1690
  Barden, Thomas E., "Dryden's Aim in 'Amphytryon' ", *Costerus; Essays in English and American Language and Literature* (1973), 9:1-8
  Bondurant, A. L., " 'Amphitruo' of Plautus, Moliere's 'Amphitryon' and 'Amphitryon' of Dryden", *Sewanee Review*, 33:455-68, 1925
  Davis, Floyd H., Jr., "The Dramaturgical Functions of Song, Dance and Music in the Comedies of John Dryden", *Dissertation Abstracts International* (1972), 33:2888A
  Spectator, 128:686, June 3, 1922

An Evening's Love, 1668
  O'Regan, M. J., "Two Notes on French Reminiscences in Restoration Comedy", *Hermathena*, 93:63-70, 1959

Assignation; or, Love in a Nunnery, 1672
  Birrell, F., "Assignation", *Nation* (London), 36:611, Jan. 31, 1925
  Brown, I., "Assignation", *Saturday Review*, 139:100, Jan. 31, 1925
  Davis, Floyd H., Jr., "The Dramaturgical Functions of Song, Dance, and Music in the Comedies of John Dryden", *Dissertation Abstracts International* (1972), 33:2888A
  Loftis, John, *The Spanish Plays of Neo-Classical England.* 1973. Pp. 97-130
  Moore, Frank H., "Heroic Comedy; A New Interpretation of Dryden's 'Assignation' ", *Studies in Philology*, 51:585-98, 1954
  Zamonski, John A., "The Spiritual Nature of Carnal Love in Dryden's 'Assignation' ", *Educational Theatre Journal* (1973), 25:189-92

Aureng-Zebe, 1675
  Alssid, M. W., "Design of Dryden's 'Aureng-Zebe' ", *Journal of English and Germanic Philology*, 64:452-69, 1962
  Brooks, Harold F., "Dryden's 'Aureng-Zebe': Debts to Corneille and Racine", *Revue de Littérature Comparée* (1972), 46:5-34
  Fujimura, Thomas H., "The Appeal of Dryden's Heroic Plays", *Modern Language Association. Publications* (PMLA), 75:37-45, 1960
  King, Bruce, *Dryden's Major Plays.* 1966. Pp. 116-32
  Kirsch, A. C., "Significance of Dryden's 'Aureng-Zebe' ", *Journal of English Literary History* (ELH), 29:160-74, 1962
  Law, Richard A., "Admiration and Concernment in the Heroic Plays of John Dryden", *Dissertation Abstracts International* (1974), 35:3688A
  Loftis, John Clyde, ed., *Restoration Drama; Modern Essays in Criticism.* 1966. Pp. 180-94
  Lynch, Kathleen M., "Conventions of Platonic Drama in the Heroic Plays of Orrery and Dryden", *Modern Language Association. Publications* (PMLA), 44:456-71, 1929
  Martin, L. H., " 'Aureng-Zebe' and the Ritual of the Persian King", *Modern Philology* (1973), 71:169-71
  Martin, Leslie H., "The Consistency of Dryden's 'Aureng-Zebe' ", *Studies in Philology* (1973), 70:306-28
  Miner, Earl Roy, ed., *Restoration Dramatists; A Collection of Critical Essays*, 1966. Pp. 37-49
  Newman, Robert S., "Irony and the Problem of Tone in Dryden's 'Aureng-Zebe' ", *Studies in English Literature, 1500-1900* (Sum. 1970), 10:439-58
  Osborn, Scott C., "Heroical Love in Dryden's Heroic Drama", *Modern Language Association. Publications* (PMLA), 73:480-90, 1958

Tritt, Carleton S., "Wit and Paradox in Dryden's Serious Plays", *Dissertation Abstracts* (1968), 29:882A-83A

Waith, Eugene M., *The Herculean Hero in Marlowe, Chapman, Shakespeare, and Dryden.* 1962. Pp. 152-201

_____ , *Ideas of Greatness; Heroic Drama in England.* 1971. Pp. 223-31

Wallerstein, Ruth, "Dryden and the Analysis of Shakespeare's Techniques", *Review of English Studies*, 19:165-85, 1943

Winterbottom, John, "The Development of the Hero in Dryden's Tragedies", *Journal of English and Germanic Philology*, 51:161-73, 1953

_____ , "The Place of Hobbesian Ideas in Dryden's Tragedies", *Journal of English and Germanic Philology*, 57:665-83, 1958

_____ , "Stoicism in Dryden's Tragedies", *Journal of English and Germanic Philology*, 61:868-83, 1962

Cleomenes, The Spartan Hero, 1692

Archer, Stanley, "Performance of Dryden's 'Cleomenes'", *Notes and Queries* (Dec. 1971), 18:460-61

Visser, Colin Wills, "Dryden's Plays; A Critical Assessment", *Dissertation Abstracts* (1968), 29:1520A-21A

Conquest of Granada by the Spaniards, 1672

Ball, Alice D., "An Emendation of Dryden's 'Conquest of Granada'", *Journal of English Literary History* (ELH), 6:217-18, 1939

Campbell, Dowling G., "Background and Application of the Honor Code in Dryden's Four Spanish-Oriented Heroic Plays", *Dissertation Abstracts International* (1974), 35:1041A

Elwin, Malcolm, *Handbook of Restoration Drama.* 1966. Pp. 89-90

Gagen, Jean, "Love and Honor in Dryden's Heroic Plays", *Modern Language Association. Publications* (PMLA), 77:208-20, 1962

King, Bruce, *Dryden's Major Plays.* 1966. Pp. 59-81

Kirsch, Arthur C., "Dryden, Corneille and the Heroic Play", *Modern Philology*, 59:248-64, 1961-62

Law, Richard A., "Admiration and Concernment in the Heroic Plays of John Dryden", *Dissertation Abstracts International* (1974), 35:3688A

Lynch, Kathleen M., "Conventions of Platonic Drama in the Heroic Plays of Orrery and Dryden", *Modern Language Association. Publications* (PMLA), 44:456-71, 1929

Miner, Earl, ed., *Restoration Dramatists; A Collection of Critical Essays.* 1966. Pp. 19-35

Osborn, Scott C., "Heroical Love in Dryden's Heroic Drama", *Modern Language Association. Publications* (PMLA), 73:480-90, 1958

Price, Martin, *To the Palace of Wisdom; Studies in Order and Energy from Dryden to Blake.* 1964. Pp. 28-78

Tritt, Carleton S., "Wit and Paradox in Dryden's Serious Plays", *Dissertation Abstracts* (1968), 29:882A-83A

Waith, Eugene M., *The Herculean Hero in Marlowe, Chapman, Shakespeare, and Dryden.* 1962. Pp. 152-201

_____ , *Ideas of Greatness; Heroic Drama in England.* 1971. Pp. 216-23

Winterbottom, John A., "The Place of Hobbesian Ideas in Dryden's Tragedies", *Journal of English and Germanic Philology*, 57:665-83, 1958

_____ , "Stoicism in Dryden's Tragedies", *Journal of English and Germanic Philology*, 61:868-83, 1962

Don Sebastian, 1689

King, Bruce, " 'Don Sebastian': Dryden's Moral Fable", *Sewanee Review*, 70: 651-70, 1962

Moore, John Robert, "Political Allusions in Dryden's Later Plays", *Modern Language Association. Publications* (PMLA), 73:36-42, 1958

Price, Martin, *To the Palace of Wisdom; Studies in Order and Energy from Dryden to Blake.* 1964. Pp. 28-78

Rothstein, Eric, *Restoration Tragedy; Form and the Process of Change.* 1967. Pp. 147-52

Tritt, Carleton S., "Wit and Paradox in Dryden's Serious Plays", *Dissertation Abstracts* (1968), 29:882A-83A

Visser, Colin Wills, "Dryden's Plays; A Critical Assessment", *Dissertation Abstracts* (1968), 29:1520A-21A

Waith, Eugene M., *Ideas of Greatness; Heroic Drama in England.* 1971. Pp. 258-63

Winterbottom, John A., "The Place of Hobbesian Ideas in Dryden's Tragedies", *Journal of English and Germanic Philology*, 57:665-83, 1958

An Evening's Love; or, The Mock Astrologer, 1668

Davis, Floyd H., Jr., "The Dramaturgical Functions of Song, Dance and Music in the Comedies of John Dryden", *Dissertation Abstracts International* (1972), 33:2888A

Loftis, John, *The Spanish Plays of Neo-Classical England.* 1973. Pp. 97-130

Indian Emperor; or, The Conquest of Mexico by the Spaniards, 1665

Alssid, Michael W., "The Perfect Conquest: A Study of Theme, Structure and Characters in Dryden's 'The Indian Emperor' ", *Studies in Philology*, 59:539-59, 1962

Campbell, Dowling G., "Background and Application of the Honor Code in Dryden's Four Spanish-Oriented Heroic Plays", *Dissertation Abstracts International* (1974), 35:1041A

Freehafer, John, "Dryden's 'Indian Emperor' ". *Explicator* (1968), 27:Item 24

Fujimura, Thomas H., "The Appeal of Dryden's Heroic Plays", *Modern Language Association. Publications* (PMLA), 75:37-45, 1960

Gagen, Jean, "Love and Honor in Dryden's Heroic Plays", *Modern Language Association. Publications* (PMLA), 77:208-20, 1962

Loftis, John, " 'El Principe Constante' and 'The Indian Emperour': A Reconsideration", *Modern Language Review* (1970), 65:761-67

_____ , "Exploration and Enlightenment: Dryden's 'Indian Emperpr' and Its Background", *Philological Quarterly* (1966), 45:71-84

_____ , *The Spanish Plays of Neo-Classical England.* 1973. Pp. 178-208

Lynch, Kathleen M., "Conventions of Platonic Drama in the Heroic Plays of Orrery and Dryden", *Modern Language Association. Publications* (PMLA), 44:456-71, 1929

Osborn, Scott C., "Heroical Love in Dryden's Heroic Drama", *Modern Language Association. Publications* (PMLA), 73:480-90, 1958

Shergold, N. D. and Peter Ure, "Dryden and Calderon: A New Spanish Source for 'The Indian Emperor' ", *Modern Language Review* (1966), 61:369-83

Tritt, Carleton S., "Wit and Paradox in Dryden's Serious Plays", *Dissertation Abstracts* (1968), 29:882A-83A

Waith, Eugene M., *Ideas of Greatness; Heroic Drama in England.* 1971. Pp. 209-11

Winterbottom, John, "The Development of the Hero in Dryden's Tragedies", *Journal of English and Germanic Philology*, 52:161-73, 1953

────────── , "The Place of Hobbesian Ideas in Dryden's Tragedies", *Journal of English and Germanic Philology*, 57:665-83, 1958

────────── , "Stoicism in Dryden's Tragedies", *Journal of English and Germanic Philology*, 61:868-83, 1962

The Kind Keeper; or, Mr. Limberham, 1678

Baker, Van R., "Heroic Posturing Satirized; Dryden's 'Mr. Limberham' ", *Papers on Language and Literature* (1972), 8:370-79

Davis, Floyd H., Jr., "The Dramaturgical Functions of Song, Dance, and Music in the Comedies of John Dryden", *Dissertation Abstracts International* (1972), 33:2888A

King Arthur; or, The British Worthy, 1691

Gottesman, Lillian, "The Arthurian Romance in English Opera and Pantomime, 1660-1800", *Restoration and 18th Century Theatre Research* (Nov. 1969), 8: 47-53

Moore, John Robert, "Political Allusions in Dryden's Later Plays", *Modern Language Association. Publications* (PMLA), 73:36-42, 1958

Love Triumphant; or, Nature Will Prevail, 1694

King, Bruce, *Dryden's Major Plays.* 1966. Pp. 190-208

Rodney, Caroline C., "Dryden's Tragicomedy", *Dissertation Abstracts International* (1973), 34:1253A

Marriage à-la-Mode, 1672

Davis, Floyd H., Jr., "The Dramaturgical Functions of Song, Dance and Music in the Comedies of John Dryden", *Dissertation Abstracts International* (1972), 33:2888A

Gore-Browne, R., "Marriage à la Mode", *Saturday Review*, 150:485, Oct. 18, 1930

King, Bruce, *Dryden's Major Plays.* 1966. Pp. 82-94

────────── , "Dryden's 'Marriage à la Mode' ", *Drama Survey*, 4:28-37, 1965

Rodney, Caroline C., "Dryden's Tragicomedy", *Dissertation Abstracts International* (1973), 34:1253A

Spectator, 177:115, Aug. 2, 1946

The Mistaken Husband, 1675

Davis, Floyd H., Jr., "The Dramaturgical Functions of Song, Dance and Music in the Comedies of John Dryden", *Dissertation Abstracts International* (1972), 33:2888A

The Rival Ladies, 1664

Loftis, John, *The Spanish Plays of Neo-Classical England.* 1973. Pp. 97-130

Scott, F. R., "Lady Honoria Howard and the Name of the Chief Female Character in 'The Rival Ladies' ", *Review of English Studies*, 20:158-59, 1944

Secret Love; or, The Maiden Queen, 1667

Lynch, Kathleen M., "Conventions of Platonic Drama in the Heroic Plays of

Orrery and Dryden", *Modern Language Association. Publications* (PMLA), 44:456-71, 1929

Martin, Leslie H., "Dryden and the Art of Transversion", *Comparative Drama* (1972), 6:3-13

Rodney, Caroline C., "Dryden's Tragicomedy", *Dissertation Abstracts International* (1973), 34:1253A

Sir Martin Mar-All; or, The Feign'd Innocence, 1667
Davis, Floyd H., Jr., "The Dramaturgical Functions of Song, Dance and Music in the Comedies of John Dryden", *Dissertation Abstracts International* (1972), 33:2888A

The Spanish Friar; or, The Double Discovery, 1680
Bredvold, Louis I., et. al., *Essays and Studies in English and Comparative Literature by Members of the English Department of the University of Michigan.* 1932. Pp. 119-32

King, Bruce, *Dryden's Major Plays.* 1966. Pp. 148-64

Osborn, Scott C., "Heroical Love in Dryden's Heroic Drama", *Modern Language Association. Publications* (PMLA), 73:480-90, 1958

Rodney, Caroline C., "Dryden's Tragicomedy", *Dissertation Abstracts International* (1973), 34:1253A

Ward, Charles E., "Dryden's 'Spanish Friar' and a Provincial Touring Company", *Notes and Queries*, 178:96-97, 1939

Winterbottom, John A., "The Place of Hobbesian Ideas in Dryden's Tragedies", *Journal of English and Germanic Philology*, 57:665-83, 1958

The State of Innocence and Fall of Man, 1674
King, Bruce, *Dryden's Major Plays.* 1966. Pp. 95-115

Troilus and Cressida; or, Truth Found Too Late, 1679
Bernhardt, W. W., "Shakespeare's 'Troilus and Cressida' and Dryden's 'Truth Found Too Late' ", *Shakespeare Quarterly* (Spr. 1969), 20:129-41

Tyrannick Love; or, The Royal Martyr, 1669
Gagen, Jean, "Love and Honor in Dryden's Heroic Plays", *Modern Language Association. Publications* (PMLA), 77:208-20, 1962

Jaquith, William G., "Dryden's 'Tyrannick Love' and 'All for Love': A Study of Comic and Tragic Dialects", *Dissertation Abstracts International* (1973), 34:3345A

King, Bruce, "Dryden, Tillotson and 'Tyrannic Love' ", *Drama Survey*, 4:28-37, 1965

King, Bruce, *Dryden's Major Plays.* 1966. Pp. 37-58

Novack, Maximillian E., "The Demonology of Dryden's 'Tyrannick Love' and 'Anti-Scott' ", *English Language Notes* (1966), 4:95-98

Osborn, Scott C., "Heroical Love in Dryden's Heroic Drama", *Modern Language Association. Publications* (PMLA), 73:480-90, 1958

Tritt, Carleton S., "Wit and Paradox in Dryden's Serious Plays", *Dissertation Abstracts* (1968), 29:882A-83A

Waith, Eugene M., *Ideas of Greatness; Heroic Drama in England.* 1971. Pp. 212-16

Winterbottom, John, "The Development of the Hero in Dryden's Tragedies", *Journal of English and Germanic Philology*, 52:161-73, 1953

――――――――― , "The Place of Hobbesian Ideas in Dryden's Tragedies", *Journal of English and Germanic Philology*, 57:665-83, 1958

———————————— ,"Stoicism in Dryden's Tragedies", *Journal of English and Germanic Philology*, 61:868-83, 1962

The Wild Gallant, 1663

Davis, Floyd H., Jr., "The Dramaturgical Functions of Song, Dance and Music in the Comedies of John Dryden", *Dissertation Abstracts International* (1972), 33:2888A

Lynch, Kathleen M., "D'Urfe's 'L'Astree' and the 'Proviso' Scences in Dryden's Comedy", *Philological Quarterly*, 4:302-08, 1925

Osenburg, F. C., "The Prologue to Dryden's 'The Wild Gallant' Re-Examined", *English Language Notes* (Sept. 1969), 7:35-39

JOHN DRYDEN AND WILLIAM DAVENANT

The Tempest; or, The Enchanted Island, 1667

Davis, Floyd H., Jr., "The Dramaturgical Functions of Song, Dance and Music in the Comedies of John Dryden", *Dissertation Abstracts International* (1972), 33:2888A

JOHN DRYDEN AND ROBERT HOWARD

Indian Queen, 1664

Campbell, Dowling G., "Background and Application of the Honor Code in Dryden's Spanish-Oriented Heroic Plays", *Dissertation Abstracts International* (1974), 35:1041A

Fujimura, Thomas H., "The Appeal of Dryden's Heroic Plays", *Modern Language Association. Publications* (PMLA), 75:37-45, 1960

Gagen, Jean, "Love and Honor in Dryden's Heroic Plays", *Modern Language Association. Publications* (PMLA), 77:208-20, 1962

Osborn, Scott C., "Heroical Love in Dryden's Heroic Drama", *Modern Language Association. Publications* (PMLA), 73:480-90, 1958

Stroup, T. B., "Scenery for 'The Indian Queen' ", *Modern Language Notes*, 52:408-09, 1937

Waith, Eugene M., *Ideas of Greatness; Heroic Drama in England.* 1971. Pp. 203-06

JOHN DRYDEN AND NATHANIAL LEE

Duke of Guise, 1682

Bachorik, Lawrence L., " 'Duke of Guise' and Dryden's 'Vindicator': A New Consideration", *English Language Notes* (1973), 10:208-12

Hinnant, Charles H., "The Background of the Early Version of Dryden's 'The Duke of Guise' ", *English Language Notes* (Dec. 1968), 6:102-06

King, Bruce, "Anti-Whig Satire in 'The Duke of Guise' ", *English Language Notes* (Univ. of Colorado), 2:190-93, 1965

ALEXANDRE DUMAS, FILS

Camille, 1852

Catholic World, 133:83-84, April, 1931 and 184:147-48, Nov., 1956

Commonweal, 13:637-38, April 8, 1931

Marek, George Richard, *Front Seat at the Opera.* 1948. Pp. 80-86

Nation, 135:512-13, Nov. 23, 1932

New Republic, 49:190, Jan. 5, 1927 and 73:214-16, Jan. 4, 1933

New Statesman, 35:13, April 12, 1930
Revue des Deux Mondes, s. 8 52:451-52, July 15, 1939
Saturday Review, 149:290-91, March 8, 1930
Theatre Arts, 17:15-16, Jan., 1933
Theatre Magazine, 53:26, April, 1931
Tynan, Kenneth, *Curtains; Selections from the Drama Criticism and Related Writings*. 1961. Pp. 132-33
Young, Stark, *Immortal Shadows; A Book of Dramatic Criticism*. 1948. Pp. 67-71

La Dame Aux Camelias   *SEE*   Camille

The Lady with the Camelias   *SEE*   Camille

ALEXANDRE DUMAS, PÈRE

Angèle, 1833
    Bassan, Fernande and Sylvie Chevalley, *Alexandre Dumas, Père, et la Comèdia Francaise*. 1972. Pp. 82-86

Antony, 1831
    Bassan, Fernande and Sylvie Chevalley, *Alexandre Dumas, Père, et la Comèdia Francaise*. 1972. Pp. 46-66
Behind a Conspiracy; or, The Son of Black Donald, 1860
    Bassan, Fernande and Sylvie Chevalley, *Alexandre Dumas, Père, et la Comèdia Francaise*. 1972. Pp. 207-08

Caligula, 1837
    Bassan, Fernande and Sylvie Chevalley, *Alexandre Dumas, Père, et la Comèdia Francaise*. 1972. Pp. 87-99

Le Bourgeois de Gand; ou, Le Secrétaire du Duc d'Albe *SEE* The Man from Ghent; or, The Duke of Alba's Secretary

Charles VII and His Chief Vassals, 1837
    Bassan, Fernande and Sylvie Chevalley, *Alexandre Dumas, Père, et la Comèdia Francaise*. 1972. Pp. 67-75

Charles VII Chez Ses Grands Vassaux   *SEE*   Charles VII and His Chief Vassals

Christine à Fontainebleau, 1830
    Bassan, Fernande and Sylvie Chevalley, *Alexandre Dumas, Père, et la Comèdia Francaise*. 1972. Pp. 11-22

La Dame de Monsoreau   *SEE*   The Lady from Monsoreau

Les Demoiselles de Saint-Cyr   *SEE*   The Ladies of Saint-Cyr

L'Envers d'Une Conspiration; ou, Le Fils de Donald le Noir *SEE* Behind a Conspiracy, or The Son of Black Donald

Une Fille du Régent   *SEE*   The Regent's Daughter

Hamlet, Prince of Denmark, 1847
    Bassan, Fernande and Sylvie Chevalley, *Alexandre Dumas, Père, et la Comèdia Francaise*, 1972. Pp. 161-77

Henry III and His Court, 1829
Bassan, Fernande and Sylvie Chevalley, *Alexandre Dumas, Père, et la Comèdia Francaise.* 1972. Pp. 23-45
Bassan, Fernande, "Alexandre Dumas, Père, et le Théâtre Romantique", *French Review* (1974), 47:767-72

L'Invitation à la Valse, 1857
Bassan, Fernande and Sylvie Chevalley, *Alexandre Dumas, Père, et la Comèdia Francaise.* 1972. Pp. 204-06

La Jeunesse de Louis XIV *SEE* The Youth of Louis XIV

The Ladies of Saint-Cyr, 1843
Bassan, Fernande and Sylvie Chevalley, *Alexandre Dumas, Père, et la Comèdia Francaise.* 1972. Pp. 139-49

The Lady from Belle-Isle, 1839
Bassan, Fernande and Sylvie Chevalley, *Alexandre Dumas, Père, et la Comèdia Francaise*, 1972. Pp. 105-22

The Lady from Monsoreau, 1860
Bassan, Fernande and Sylvie Chevalley, *Alexandre Dumas, Père, et la Comèdia Francaise.* 1972. Pp. 209-15

Lorenzino, 1842
Bassan, Fernande and Sylvie Chevalley, *Alexandre Dumas, Père, et la Comèdia Francaise.* 1972. Pp. 135-38

Mademoiselle de Belle-Isle *SEE* The Lady from Belle-Isle

The Man from Ghent; or, The Duke of Alba's Secretary, 1838
Bassan, Fernande and Sylvie Chevalley, *Alexandre Dumas, Père, et la Comèdia Francaise.* 1972. Pp. 100-04

Le Mari de la Veuve *SEE* The Widow's Husband

Un Mariage Sous Louis XV *SEE* A Marriage of Convenience: Period Louis XV

A Marriage of Convenience: Period Louis XV, 1841
Bassan, Fernande and Sylvie Chevalley, *Alexandre Dumas, Père, et la Comèdia Francaise.* 1972. Pp. 123-34

The Regent's Daughter, 1845
Bassan, Fernande and Sylvie Chevalley, *Alexandre Dumas, Père, et la Comèdia Francaise.* 1972. Pp. 152-60

Romulus, 1854
Bassan, Fernande and Sylvic Chevalley, *Alexandre Dumas, Père, et la Comèdia Francaise.* 1972. Pp. 192-96

La Testament de Cesar, 1849
Bassan, Fernande and Sylvic Chevalley, *Alexandre Dumas, Père, et la Comèdia Francaise*, 1972. Pp. 178-85

Le Vampire, 1851
Aldridge, A. Owen, "The Vampire Theme: Dumas, Père, and the English Stage", *Revue des Langues Vivantes* (1973), 39:312-324

The Widow's Husband, 1832
   Bassan, Fernande and Sylvie Chevalley, *Alexandre Dumas, Père, et la Comèdia Francaise.* 1972. Pp. 76-81

The Youth of Louis XIV, 1854
   Bassan, Fernande and Sylvie Chevalley, *Alexandre Dumas, Père, et la Comèdia Francaise.* 1972. Pp. 197-200

LAWRENCE DURRELL

Acte, 1961
   Fraser, G. S., *Lawrence Durrell; A Critical Study.* 1968. Pp. 101-02 and 107-09

An Irish Faustus, 1963
   Cole, Douglas, "Faust and Anti-Faust in Modern Drama", *Drama Survey* (1966), 5:39-52
   Fraser, G. S., *Lawrence Durrell; A Critical Study.* 1968. Pp. 109-17

Sappho, 1961
   Fraser, G. S., *Lawrence Durrell; A Critical Study.* 1968. Pp. 101-07

FRIEDRICH DÜRRENMATT

The Anabaptists, 1967
   Durzak, Manfred, *Dürrenmatt, Frisch, Weiss: Deutsches Drama der Gegenwart Zwischen Kritik und Utopie.* 1972. Pp. 55-57
   Hammer, John C. "Friedrich Dürrenmatt and the Tragedy of Bertolt Brecht: An Interpretation of 'Die Wiedertaufer' ", *Modern Drama* (1969), 12:204-09

An Angel Comes to Babylon, 1953
   Daviau, Donald G., "The Role of 'Zufall' in the Writings of Friedrich Dürrenmatt", *Germanic Review* (1972), 47:281-93
   Durzak, Manfred, *Dürrenmatt, Frisch, Weiss: Deutsches Drama der Gegenwart Zwischen Kritik und Utopie.* 1972. Pp. 80-90
   Fickert, Kurt J., *To Heaven and Back; The New Morality in the Plays of Friedrich Dürrenmatt.* 1972. Pp. 33-37
   Holzapfel, Robert, "The Divine Plan Behind the Plays of Friedrich Dürrenmatt", *Modern Drama* (1965-66), 8:237-46
   Lumley, Frederick, *New Trends in Twentieth Century Drama; A Survey Since Ibsen and Shaw.* 1967. Pp. 239-46

Der Besuch der Alten Dame   *SEE*   The Visit

The Blind One, 1948
   Fickert, Kurt J., *To Heaven and Back; The New Morality in the Plays of Friedrich Dürrenmatt.* 1972. Pp. 20-25
   Grosclose, Sidney, "The Murder of Gnadenbrot Suppe: Language and Levels of Reality in Friedrich Dürrenmatt's 'Der Blinde' ", *German Life and Letters* (1974), 28:64-72
   Holzapfel, Robert, "The Divine Plan Behind the Plays of Friedrich Dürrenmatt", *Modern Drama* (1965-66), 8:237-46

Lumley, Frederick, *New Trends in Twentieth Century Drama; A Survey Since Ibsen and Shaw.* 1967. Pp. 239-46

Madler, Herbert P., "Dürrenmatts Konzeption des Mutigen Menschen; Eine Untersuchung der Buchnenwerke Friedrich Dürrenmatts unter Besonderer Berücksichtigung des 'Blinden' ", *Schweizer Rundschau* (1970), 69:314-25

Der Blinde   *SEE*   The Blind One

Die Ehe des Herrn Mississippi   *SEE*   The Marriage of Mr. Mississippi

Ein Engel Kommt nach Babylon   *SEE*   An Angel Comes to Babylon

Es Steht Gescrieben   *SEE*   It is Written

Frank der Fünfte   *SEE*   Frank the Fifth

Frank the 5th, Opera of a Private Bank, 1959
    Daviau, Donald G., "The Role of 'Zufall' in the Writings of Friedrich Dürrenmatt", *Germanic Review* (1972), 47:281-93
    Diller, Edward, "Human Dignity in a Materialistic Society; Friedrich Dürrenmatt and Bertolt Brecht", *Modern Language Quarterly* (1964), 25:451-60
    Durzak, Manfred, *Dürrenmatt, Frisch, Weiss: Deutsches Drama der Gegenwart Zwischen Kritik und Utopie.* 1972. Pp. 102-14
    Fickert, Kurt J., *To Heaven and Back; The New Morality in the Plays of Friedrich Dürrenmatt.* 1972. Pp. 44-49
    Holzapfel, Robert, "The Divine Plan Behind the Plays of Friedrich Dürrenmatt", *Modern Drama* (1965-66), 8:237-46
    Lumley, Frederick, *New Trends in Twentieth Century Drama, A Survey Since Ibsen and Shaw.* 1967. Pp. 239-46

Greek Man Seeks Greek Maiden, 1955
    Diller, Edward, "Despair and the Paradox: Friedrich Dürrenmatt", *Drama Survey* (1966), 5:131-36

Grieche Sucht Griechin   *SEE*   Greek Man Seeks Greek Maiden

Hercules and the Augean Stables, 1963
    Fickert, Kurt J., *To Heaven and Back; The New Morality in the Plays of Friedrich Dürrenmatt.* 1972. Pp. 58-61

It is Written, 1947
    Diller, Edward, "Despair and the Paradox: Friedrich Dürrenmatt", *Drama Survey* (1966), 5:131-36
    _____ , "Dürrenmatt's Use of the Stage as a Dramatic Element", *Symposium* (1966), 20:197-206
    Fickert, Kurt J., *To Heaven and Back; The New Morality in the Plays of Friedrich Dürrenmatt.* 1972. Pp. 15-19
    Holzapfel, Robert, "The Divine Plan Behind the Plays of Friedrich Dürrenmatt", *Modern Drama* (1965-66), 8:237-46
    Lumley, Frederick, *New Trends in Twentieth Century Drama: A Survey Since Ibsen and Shaw.* 1967. Pp. 239-46

The Marriage of Mr. Mississippi, 1952
    Daviau, Donald G., "The Role of 'Zufall' in the Writings of Friedrich Dürrenmatt", *Germanic Review* (1972), 47:281-93
    Diller, Edward, "Aesthetics and the Grotesque: Friedrich Dürrenmatt", *Wisconsin Studies in Contemporary Literature* (1966), 7:328-35

_____ , "Despair and the Paradox: Friedrich Dürrenmatt" *Drama Survey* (1966), 5:131-36

_____ ,"Dürrenmatt's Use of the Stage as a Dramatic Element", *Symposium* (1966), 20:197-206

Durzak, Manfred, *Dürrenmatt, Frisch, Weiss; Deutsches Drama der Gegenwart Zwischen Kritik und Utopie.* 1972. Pp. 69-79

Fickert, Kurt J., *To Heaven and Back; The New Morality in the Plays of Friedrich Dürrenmatt.* 1972. Pp. 26-32

Grimm, Reinhold, "Nach Zwanzig Jahren: Friedrich Dürrenmatt und Seine 'Ehe des herrn Mississippi' ", *Basis: Jahrbuch für Deutsche Gegenwartsliteratur* (1972), 3:214-37

Holzapfel, Robert, "The Divine Plan Behind the Plays of Friedrich Dürrenmatt", *Modern Drama* (1965-66), 8:237-46

Illustrated London News, 235:456, Oct. 17, 1959

Johnson, Peter, "Grostequeness and Injustice in Dürrenmatt", *German Life and Letters* n. s. (1961-62), 15:264-73

Lumley, Frederick, *New Trends in Twentieth Century Drama; A Survey Since Ibsen and Shaw.* 1967. Pp. 239-46

New Statesman, 58:469, Oct. 10, 1959

Phelps, Leland R., "Dürrenmatt's 'Die Ehe des Herrn Mississippi': The Revision of a Play", *Modern Drama* (1965), 8:156-60

Spectator, 203:473, Oct. 9, 1959

The Meteor, 1966

Durzak, Manfred, *Dürrenmatt, Frisch, Weiss: Deutsches Drama der Gegenwart Zwischen Kritik und Utopie.* 1972. Pp. 126-34

Fickert, Kurt J., "Morality in Dürrenmatt's 'Der Meteor' ", *University of Dayton Review* (1969), 6:29-33

_____ , *T o Heaven and Back; The New Morality in the Plays of Friedrich Dürrenmatt.* 1972. Pp. 62-66

Freund, Winfried, "Modernes Welttheater: Eine Studie zu Friedrich Dürrenmatts Komodie 'Der Meteor' ", *Dissertation Abstracts International* (1972), 33:2932A

Usmiani, Renate, "Friedrich Dürrenmatt as Wolfgang Schwitten; An Autobiographical Interpretation of the 'Meteor' ", *Modern Drama* (1968), 11:143-50

The Physicists, 1962

Baxter, Kay, "Dürrenmatt as Prophet", *Religion in Life* (1968), 37:292-99

Christian Century, 80:301-02, March 6, 1963

Clurman, Harold, *The Naked Image; Observations on the Modern Theatre.* 1966. Pp. 181-84

Commonweal, 81:237-38, Nov. 13, 1964

Corrigan, Robert W., *The Theatre in Search of a Fix.* 1973. Pp. 247-52

Daviau, Donald G., "The Role of 'Zufall' in the Writings of Friedrich Dürrenmatt", *Germanic Review* (1972), 47:281-93

Diller, Edward, "Aesthetics and the Grotesque: Friedrich Dürrenmatt", *Wisconsin Studies in Contemporary Literature* (1966), 7:328-35

_____ ,"Dürrenmatt's Use of the Stage as a Dramatic Element", *Symposium* (1966), 20:197-206

Drama, #68:20, Spring, 1963

Durzak, Manfred, *Dürrenmatt, Frisch, Weiss: Deutsches Drama Gegenwart Zwischen Kritik und Utopie.* 1972. Pp. 115-25

Esslin, Martin, *Reflections; Essays on Modern Theatre*. 1969. Pp. 110-12

Fickert, Kurt J., "The Curtain Speech in Dürrenmatt's 'The Physicists'", *Modern Drama* (1970), 13:40-46

———————, *To Heaven and Back; The New Morality in the Plays of Friedrich Dürrenmatt*. 1972. Pp. 50-57

Forest, George C., "The 'Cosmonauts' Song in Dürrenmatt's 'Physicists'", *Hartford Studies in Literature* (1970), 2:229-37

Holzapfel, Robert, "The Divine Plan Behind the Plays of Friedrich Dürrenmatt", *Modern Drama* (1965-66), 8:237-46

Illustrated London News, 242:134, Jan. 26, 1963

Kahn, Robert L., ed., *Studies in German; In Memory of Andrew Louis*. (Rice University Studies, 55). 1969. Pp. 115-30

Kaiser, J., " 'Die Physiker' in Zurich", *Theater Heute* (1962), 3:5-7

Life, 57:89-90, Nov. 20, 1964

Morley, M., "Dürrenmatt's Dialogue with Brecht; A Thematic Analysis of 'Die Physiker'", *Modern Drama* (Sept. 1971), 14:232-42

Muschg, Walter, "Dürrenmatt und die Physiker", *Moderna Sprak* (1962), 56:280-83

Nation, 196:380, May 4, 1963 and 199:340, Nov. 9, 1964

New Statesman, 65:88, Jan. 18, 1963

Newsweek, 64:102, Oct. 26, 1964

Saturday Review, 47:31, Oct. 31, 1964

Saurel, Renée, "Le Public, Cet Inconnu. II: 'Les Physiciens' de Friedrich Dürrenmatt, a la Comédie de l'Est", *Temps Modernes* (1964), 20:943-54

Spectator, 210:69, Jan. 18, 1963

Time, 84:67, Oct. 23, 1964

Vogue, 144:152, Dec., 1964

Weimar, K. S., "The Scientist and Society. A Study of Three Modern Plays", *Modern Language Quarterly* (1966), 27:431-48

Williams, Raymond, *Drama From Ibsen to Brecht*. 1968. Pp. 312-15

Die Physiker *SEE* The Physicists

Play Strindberg, 1969

Boyd, Ursel D., "Friedrich Dürrenmatt und Sein Drama 'Play Strindberg'", *Germanic Notes* (1972), 3, iii:18-21

Nation (Oct. 18, 1971), 213:380

New Yorker (June 12, 1971), 47:84

Rubinstein, Hilde, "Der Schaukampf des Friedrich Dürrenmatt", *Frankfurter Hefte. Zeitschrift für Kultur und Politik* (1970), 25:202-06

Portrait of a Planet, 1970

Durzak, Manfred, *Dürrenmatt, Frisch, Weiss: Deutsches Drama Gegenwart Zwischen Kritik und Utopie*. 1972. Pp. 135-44

New Republic (3-17-73), 168:23

Romulus der Grosse *SEE* Romulus the Great

Romulus the Great, 1949

Daviau, Donald G., "The Role of 'Zufall' in the Writings of Friedrich Dürrenmatt", *Germanic Review* (1972), 47:281-93

Durzak, Manfred, *Dürrenmatt, Frisch, Weiss: Deutsches Drama der Gegenwart Zwischen Kritik und Utopie*. 1972. Pp. 58-69

Fickert, Kurt J., *To Heaven and Back; The New Morality in the Plays of Friedrich Dürrenmatt.* 1972. Pp. 20-25

Holzapfel, Robert, "The Divine Plan Behind the Plays of Friedrich Dürrenmatt", *Modern Drama* (1965-66), 8:237-46

Kott, Jan, *Theatre Notebook*: 1947-1967. 1968. Pp. 94-99

Lumley, Frederick, *New Trends in Twentieth Century Drama; A Survey Since Ibsen and Shaw.* 1967. Pp. 239-46

Educational Theatre Journal, 14:68, March 1962

Hudson Review, 15:264-65, 1962

The Visit, 1956

America, 99:299, May 31, 1958

Askew, Melvin W., "Dürrenmatt's 'The Visit' of the Old Lady", *Tulane Drama Review*, Vol. 5 #4:89-105, 1961

Catholic World, 187:312, July, 1958

Christian Century, 75:668-69, June 4, 1958

Commonweal, 68:377-79, July 11, 1958

Cohn, Ruby, *Currents in Contemporary Drama.* 1969. Pp. 170-73

Daviau, Donald G. and Harvey I. Dunkle, "Friedrich Dürrenmatt's 'Der Besuch der Alten Dame': A Parable of Western Society in Transition", *Modern Language Quarterly* (1974), 35:302-16

Dick, E. S., "Durrenmatts 'Der Besuch der Alten Dame': Welttheater und Ritualspiel", *Zeitschrift für Deutsche Philologie* (1968), 87:498-509

Durzak, Manfred, *Dürrenmatt, Frisch, Weiss; Deutsches Drama der Gegenwart Zwischen Kritik und Utopie.* 1972. Pp. 91-98

Fickert, Kurt J., "Dürrenmatt's 'The Visit' and Job", *Books Abroad* (1967), 41:389-92

_____ , *To Heaven and Back; The New Morality in the Plays of Friedrich Dürrenmatt.* 1972. Pp. 38-43

Gassner, John, *Theatre at the Crossroads; Plays and Playwrights of the Mid-century American Stage.* 1960. Pp. 271-73

Goodman, Randolph, *Drama on Stage.* 1961. Pp. 378-89

Guth, Hans P., "Dürrenmatt's 'Visit': The Play Behind the Play", *Symposium* (1962), 16:94-102

Holzapfel, Robert, "The Divine Plan Behind the Plays of Friedrich Dürrenmatt", *Modern Drama* (1965-66), 8:237-46

Hortenbach, Jenny C., "Biblical Echoes in Dürrenmatt's 'Der Besuch der Alten Dame' ", *Monatshefte* (1965), 57:145-51

Kott, Jan, *Theatre Notebook: 1947-1967.* 1968. Pp. 87-93

Kraft, Walter C., ed., *Proceedings: Pacific Northwest Conference on Foreign Languages.* 1974. Pp. 114-17

Lefcourt, Charles R., "Dürrenmatt's 'Gullen' and Twain's 'Hadleyburg': The Corruption of Two Towns", *Revue des Langues Vivantes* (1967), 33:303-08

Life, 44:91-94, June 2, 1958

Loram, Ian C., " 'Der Besuch der Alten Dame': On 'The Visit' ", *Monatshefte* (1961), 53:15-21

Lumley, Frederick, *New Trends in Twentieth Century Drama; A Survey Since Ibsen and Shaw.* 1967. Pp. 239-46

Nation, 186:455-56, May 17, 1958, (12-17-73), 217:668

New Statesman, 60:14, July 2, 1960

New Yorker, 34:87, May 17, 1958 and 36:118, March 19, 1960, (12-10-73), 49:111

Pfefferkorn, Eli, "Dürrenmatt's Mass Play", *Modern Drama* (1969), 12:30-37
Punte, Maria Luisa, "La Justicia en 'La Visita de la Anciana Dama' de Friedrich Dürrenmatt", *Boletín de Estudios Germánicos* (1972), 9:95-112
Reporter, 18:27, June 12, 1958
Spectator, 205:20, July 1, 1960
Saturday Review, 41:30-31, May 24, 1958
Speidel, E., "'Aristotelian' and 'Non 'Aristotelian' Elements in Dürrenmatt's 'Der Besuch der Alten Dame'", *German Life and Letters* (1974), 28:14-24
Theatre Arts, 42:17, May, 1958
Time, 71:83, May 19, 1958, (12-10-73), 102:86
Tynan, Kenneth, *Curtains; Selections from the Drama Criticism and Related Writings.* 1961. Pp. 344-46
Weimar, Karl S., ed., *Views and Reviews of Modern German Literature; Festschrift für Adolf D. Klarmann.* 1974. Pp. 251-56

Die Wiedertäufer   *SEE*   The Anabaptists

CHARLES DYER

Staircase, 1966
Commonweal, 87:592, Feb. 16, 1968
Nation, 206:156, Jan. 29, 1968
New Statesman, 72:715-16, Nov. 11, 1966
New Yorker, 43:82, Jan. 20, 1968
Newsweek, 71:96, Jan. 22, 1968
Saturday Review, 51:41, Jan. 27, 1968
Time, 91:66, Jan. 19, 1968
Vogue, 151:104, March 1, 1968

THOMAS STEARNS ELIOT

The Cocktail Party, 1949
American Mercury, 70:557-58, March, 1950
Arrowsmith, William, "Eliot and Euripides" *Arion* (1965), 4:21-35
Arrowsmith, W., "Transfigurations in Eliot and Euripides", *Sewanee Review*, 63:421-42, 1955
Bergonzi, Bernard, *Thomas Stearns Eliot.* 1972. Pp. 146-49
Browne, E. Martin, *The Making of a Play; T. S. Eliot's "The Cocktail Party"* (Wilson Lecture). 1966. Pp. 1-48
Browne, E. Martin, *The Making of T. S. Eliot's Plays.* 1969. Pp. 172-248
_____ , "T. S. Eliot in the Theatre; The Director's Memories", *Sewanee Review*, 74:136-52, 1966
Catholic World, 170:466, March, 1950 and 171:469-70, Sept., 1950
Chiari, J., *Landmarks of Contemporary Drama.* 1965. Pp. 96-98
Chiari, Joseph, *Thomas Stearns Eliot; Poet and Dramatist.* 1972. Pp. 133-39
Christian Science Monitor Magazine, Pp. 6, May 27, 1950
Colby, R. A., "The Three Worlds of 'The Cocktail Party'; The Wit of T. S. Eliot", *Univ. of Toronto Quarterly*, 24:56-64, 1954
Commonweal, 51:463, Feb. 3, 1950 and 51:507-08, Feb. 17, 1950
Davenport, Gary, "Eliot's 'The Cocktail Party'; Comic Perspective as Salvation", *Modern Drama* (1974), 17:301-06
Dierickx, J., "T. S. Eliot, Dramaturge", *Revue des Langues Vivantes* (1960), 26:96-123

Eliot in Perspective; A Symposium; ed. by Graham Martin. 1970. Pp. 148-65

Fortnightly, 174 (n. s. 168):391-98, Dec., 1950

France Illustration, 5:263, Sept. 10, 1949

Gardner, Helen, "The Comedies of T. S. Eliot", *Sewanee Review*, 74:153-75, 1966

——————, "The Comedies of T. S. Eliot", *Essays by Divers Hands, Being the Transactions of the Royal Society of Literature* (1966), 34:55-73

Hanzo, Thomas, "Eliot and Kierkegaard: 'The Meaning of Happening' in 'The Cocktail Party'", *Modern Drama*, 3:52-59, 1960-61

Harding, D. W., "Progression of Theme in Eliot's Plays", *Kenyon Review*, 18:345-52, 1956

Hardy, John Edward, "An Antic Disposition", *Sewanee Review*, 65:50-60, 1957

Heilman, Robert B., "'Alcestis' and 'The Cocktail Party'", *Comparative Literature*, 5:105-116, 1953

Heywood, Robert, "Everybody's Cocktail Party", *Renascence*, 3:28-30, 1950

Holland, Joyce M., "Human Relations in Eliot's Drama", *Renascence* (1970), 22:151-61

Hovey, Richard B., "Psychiatrist and Saint in 'The Cocktail Party'", *Literature and Psychology* (1959), 9:51-55

Illustrated London News, 215:388, Sept. 10, 1949 and 216:792, May 20, 1950

Kennedy, Andrew K., *Six Dramatists in Search of a Language*. 1975. Pp. 111-13 and 130-32

Kintanar, Thelma B., "T. S. Eliot's 'The Cocktail Party'", *Diliman Review* (1959), 7:440-47

Kirk, Russell, *Eliot and His Age; T. S. Eliot's Moral Imagination in the 20th Century*. 1971. Pp. 337-53

Levine, George, "'The Cocktail Party' and 'Clara Hopgood'", *Graduate Student of English*, 1:4-11, 1958

Life, 27:16, Sept. 26, 1949

Lightfoot, M. J., "Uncommon Cocktail Party", *Modern Drama* (Feb. 1969), 11:382-95

Lumley, Frederick, *New Trends in Twentieth Century Drama; A Survey Since Ibsen and Shaw*. 1967. Pp. 126-36

Manheim, Leonard Falk and Eleanor B. Manheim, eds., *Hidden Patterns; Studies in Psychoanalytic Literary Criticism*. 1966. Pp. 230-42

Munz, P., "Devil's Dialectic or 'The Cocktail Party'", *Hibbert Journal*, 49:256-63, April, 1951

Nathan, George Jean, *Theatre Book of the Year, 1949-50*. Pp. 197-203

Nation, 170:94-95, Jan. 28, 1950

New Republic, 122:30, Feb. 13, 1950

New Statesman and Nation, 38:243, Sept. 3, 1949 and 39:543, May 13, 1950

New Yorker, 25:47, Jan. 28, 1950 and 26:26-29, April 1, 1950

Newsweek, 35:66, Jan. 30, 1950

Oberg, Arthur K., "'The Cocktail Party' and the Illusion of Autonomy", *Modern Drama* (1968), 11:187-94

Partisan Review, 17:354-59, April, 1950

Porter, Thomas E., *Myth and Modern American Drama*. 1969. Pp. 53-76

Reckford, Kenneth J., "Heracles and Mr. Eliot", *Comparative Literature* (1964), 16:1-18

Rexine, J. E., "Classical and Christian Foundation of T. S. Eliot's 'The Cocktail Party' ", *Books Abroad*, 39:21-26, Winter, 1965

Robbins, Rossell Hope, "A Possible Analogue for 'The Cocktail Party' ", *English Studies*, 34:165-67, 1953

Rottiers, A. K., "Bij de Dood van een Dichter: T. S. Eliot", *De Vlaamse Gids* (1965), 49:200-03

Roy, Emil, *British Drama Since Shaw*. 1972. Pp. 91-93

Sarkar, Subhas, *Thomas Stearns Eliot the Dramatist*. 1972. Pp. 157-88

Saturday Review, 33:28-30, Feb. 4, 1950 and 33:48, Feb. 11, 1950 and 33:23, Feb. 25, 1950

Schmidt, Gerd, "Die Asketische Regel: Zum Verhältnis von Poesie und Drama bei T. S. Eliot", *Die Neueren Sprachen* (1965), 14:153-59

School and Society, 72:180-82, Sept. 16, 1950

Schwartz, E., "Eliot's 'Cocktail Party' and the New Humanism", *Philological Quarterly*, 32:58-68, Jan., 1953

Scott, N. A., "T. S. Eliot's 'The Cocktail Party'; Of Redemption and Vocation", *Religion in Life*, 20 no. 2:274-85, 1951

Scruggs, Charles E., "T. S. Eliot and J. P. Sartre: Toward the Definition of the Human Condition," *Appalachian State Teachers College Faculty Publications* (1965), Pp. 24-29

Sena, Vinod, "Ambivalence of 'The Cocktail Party' ", *Modern Drama* (Feb. 1972), 14:392-404

Shuman, R. Baird, "Buddhist overtones in Eliot's 'The Cocktail Party' ", *Modern Language Notes*, 72:426-27, 1957

————————— , "Eliot's 'The Cocktail Party' ", *Explicator*, 16:#46, 1959

Spectator, 183:294, Sept. 2, 1949 and 184:541, April 21, 1950 and 184:569, April 28, 1950 and 184:645, May 12, 1950

Stelzman, Rarnulf, "The Theology of T. S. Eliot's Dramas", *Xavier University Studies* (1963), 1:7-18

Theatre Arts, 34:8, May, 1950

Thrash, Lois G., "A Source for the Redemption Theme in 'The Cocktail Party' ", *Texas Studies in Literature and Language* (1968), 9:547-53

Time, 54:58, Sept. 5, 1949

Toms, Newby, "Eliot's 'The Cocktail Party': Salvation and the Common Routine", *Christian Scholar*, 47:125-38, 1964

Virginia Quarterly Review, 30 no. 3:431-51, 1954

Ward, David, *Thomas Stearns Eliot: Between Two Worlds*. 1973. Pp. 205-13

Wasson, Richard, "The Rhetoric of Theatre: The Contemporaneity of T. S. Eliot", *Drama Survey* (1968), 6:231-43

Weisstein, Ulrich, " 'The Cocktail Party'; An Attempt at Interpretation on Mythological Grounds", *Western Review*, 16:232-41, 1952

Williams, Raymond, *Drama from Ibsen to Brecht*. 1968. Pp. 188-94

————————— , *Modern Tragedy*. 1966. Pp. 156-73

————————— , "Tragic Resignation and Sacrifice", *Critical Quarterly* (1963), 5:5-19

Wimsatt, W. K., Jr., "Eliot's Comedy", *Sewanee Review*, 58:666-78, Oct. 1950

Wimsatt, William Kurtz, *Hateful Contraries; Studies in Literature and Criticism*. 1965. Pp. 184-200

Winter, Jack, " 'Prufrockism' in 'The Cocktail Party' ", *Modern Language Quarterly*, 22:135-48, 1961

Wren-Lewis, John, "The Passing of Puritanism", *Critical Quarterly* (1963), 5:295-305

The Confidential Clerk, 1953
America, 90:608, March 6, 1954
Arrowsmith, William, "Eliot and Euripides", *Arion* (1965), 4:21-35
Browne, E. Martin, *The Making of T. S. Eliot's Plays*. 1969. Pp. 249-94
_____ , "T. S. Eliot in the Theatre; The Director's Memories",
Sewanee Review, 74:136-52, 1966
Catholic World, 179:68-69, April, 1954
Commentary, 17:367-72, April, 1954
Commonweal, 59:475-76, Feb. 12, 1954 and 59:599, March 19, 1954
Fergusson, Francis, "Three Allegorists: Brecht, Wilder and Eliot", *Sewanee Review*, 64:544-73, 1956
Gardner, Helen, "The Comedies of T. S. Eliot", *Sewanee Review*, 74:153-75, 1966
_____ , "The Comedies of T. S. Eliot", *Essays by Divers Hands, Being the Transactions of the Royal Society of Literature* (1966), 34:55-73
Harding, D. W., "Progression of Theme in Eliot's Plays", *Kenyon Review*, 18:352-360, 1956
Holland, Joyce M., "Human Relations in Eliot's Drama", *Renascence* (1970), 22:151-61
Illustrated London News, 223:353, Sept. 5, 1953
Kenyon Review, 16:463-67, 1954
Kirk, Russell, *Eliot and His Age; T. S. Eliot's Moral Imagination in the 20th Century*. 1971. Pp. 369-73
Life, 36:56-58, Feb. 1, 1954
Lumley, Frederick, *New Trends in Twentieth Century Drama; A Survey Since Ibsen and Shaw*. 1967. Pp. 126-36
Nation, 178:184, Feb. 27, 1954
New Republic, 129:17-18, Sept. 21, 1953 and 130:22, Feb. 22, 1954 and 131:124-25, Nov. 22, 1954
New Statesman and Nation, 46:256, Sept. 5, 1953 and 47:373, March 20, 1954
New York Times Mag., Pp. 36-37, Sept, 6, 1953 and Pp. 16, Feb. 21, 1954
New Yorker, 29:110-11, Oct. 10, 1953 and 30:62, Feb. 20, 1954
Newsweek, 43:94, Feb. 22, 1954
Partisan Review, 21:313-15, May, 1954
Sarkar, Subhas, *Thomas Stearns Eliot the Dramatist*. 1972. Pp. 189-224
Saturday Review, 36:26-28, Aug. 29, 1953 and 36:44-46, Sept. 12, 1953 and 37:26-28, Feb. 27, 1954
Sewanee Review, 62:117-31, Jan., 1954
Spectator, 191:238, Sept. 4, 1953 and 192:364-65, March 26, 1954
Theatre Arts, 37:81-82, Nov., 1953 and 38:22-23, April, 1954 and 38:22-25, May, 1954
Time, 63:80, Feb. 22, 1954
Twentieth Century, 154:302-10, Oct., 1953 and 154:311-16, Oct., 1953
Vogue, 123:30, March 1, 1954
Ward, David, *Thomas Stearns Eliot: Between Two Worlds*. 1973. Pp. 213-17
Williams, Raymond, *Drama from Ibsen to Brecht*. 1968. Pp. 194-97

Elder Statesman, 1958
Balakanian, Nona, "Affirmation and Love in Eliot", *New Leader* (1959), 42:20-21

Boardman, Gwenn R., "Restoring the Hollow Men", *Review* (1962), #4:35-45
Browne, E. Martin, *The Making of T. S. Eliot's Plays*. 1969. Pp. 307-44
────────── , "T. S. Eliot in the Theatre: The Director's Memories", *Sewanee Review*, 74:136-52, 1966
Chiari, J., *Landmarks of Contemporary Drama*. 1965. Pp. 100-01
Chiari, Joseph, *Thomas Stearns Eliot: Poet and Dramatist*. 1972. Pp. 141-43
Contemporary Review, 194:199-201, Oct., 1958
Dobrée, Bonamy, "The London Stage", *Sewanee Review* (Jan.-Mar. 1959), 67:109-17
Eliot in Perspective; A Symposium; ed. Graham Martin. 1970. Pp. 148-65
English (Oxford), 12:139, Spring, 1959
Fleming, Rudd, " 'The Elder Statesman' and Eliot's 'Programme for the Métier of Poetry' ", *Wisconsin Studies in Contemporary Literature* (1960), 1:54-64
Gardner, Helen, "The Comedies of T. S. Eliot", *Sewanee Review*, 74:153-75, 1966
Holland, Joyce M., "Human Relations in Eliot's Drama", *Renascence* (1970), 22:151-61
Illustrated London News, 233:398, Sept. 6, 1958
Kennedy, Andrew K., *Six Dramatists in Search of a Language*. 1975. Pp. 111-20
Kenner, Hugh, "For Other Voices", *Poetry* (1959), 95:36-40
Kirk, Russell, *Eliot and His Age; T. S. Eliot's Moral Imagination in the 20th Century*. 1971. Pp. 403-10
Life, 45:108, Nov. 24, 1958
Lumley, Frederick, *New Trends in Twentieth Century Drama; A Survey Since Ibsen and Shaw*. 1967. Pp. 126-36
Menon, K. P. K., *Literary Studies: Homage to Dr. A. Sivaramasubramionia Aiyer*. 1973. Pp. 70-77
Moffa, Marisa, "Ibsen e 'The Elder Statesman' ", *Studi Americani* (Roma), 8:201-11, 1962
New Statesman, 56:245-46, Aug. 30, 1958
New Yorker, 34:168, Nov. 1, 1958
Oppel, Horst, ed., *Das Moderne Englische Drama: Interpretationen*. 1963. Pp. 332-44
Sampley, Arthur M., "The Woman Who Wasn't There; Lacuna in T. S. Eliot," *South Atlantic Quarterly* (Aut. 1968), 62-603-10
Sarkar, Subhas, *Thomas Stearns Eliot the Dramatist*. 1972. Pp. 225-58
Saturday Review, 41:130-31, Sept. 13, 1958
Smith, Grover, Jr., "The Ghosts in T. S. Eliot's 'The Elder Statesman' ", *Notes and Queries*, 7:233-35, 1960
Spectator, 201:305, Sept. 5, 1958
Stanford, Derek, "T. S. Eliot's New Play", *Queen's Quarterly*, 65:682-89, 1959
Time, 72:43, Sept. 8, 1958
Twentieth Century, 164:342-44, 1958
Unger, Leonard, "Deceptively Simple—and Too Simple", *Virginia Quarterly Review* (1959), 35:501-04
Ward, David, *Thomas Stearns Eliot: Between Two Worlds*. 1973. Pp. 217-22
Wasson, Richard, "The Rhetoric of the Theatre: The Contemporancity of T. S. Eliot", *Drama Survey* (1968), 6:231-43

Family Reunion, 1938
America, 100:174, Nov. 8, 1958

Avery, Helen P., " 'The Family Reunion' Reconsidered", *Educational Theatre Journal* (1965), 17:10-18

Baeroe, Per Richard "T. S. Eliots Eksistensielle Holdning", *Kirke og Kultur* (1959), 64:409-19

Barber, C. L., "T. S. Eliot After Strange Gods; 'Family Reunion' ", *Southern Review* (L. S. U.), 6 no. 2:387-416, 1940

Battenhouse, R. W., "Eliot's 'The Family Reunion' as Christian Prophecy", *Christendom*, 10 no. 3:307-21, 1945

Belli, Angela, *Ancient Greek Myths and Modern Drama; A Study in Continuity*, 1971. Pp. 51-70

Bergonzi, Bernard, *Thomas Stearns Eliot*. 1972. Pp. 146-49

Browne, E. Martin, *The Making of T. S. Eliot's Plays*. 1969. Pp. 90-151

——————— , "T. S. Eliot as Dramatist", *Drama* (1965), #72:41-43

——————— , "T. S. Eliot in the Theatre; The Director's Memories", *Sewanee Review*, 74:136-52, 1966

Catholic World, 188:331, Jan., 1959

Chiari, J., *Landmarks of Contemporary Drama*. 1965. Pp. 95-96

Chiari, Joseph, *Thomas Stearns Eliot: Poet and Dramatist*. 1972. Pp. 123-33

Christian Century, 75:1380-82, Nov. 26, 1958

Cohn, Ruby, *Currents in Contemporary Drama*. 1969. Pp. 87-88 and 180-82

Commonweal, 69:232-34, Sept. 28, 1958

Eliot in Perspective; A Symposium; ed. Graham Martin. 1970. Pp. 148-65

Evans, Ifor, *A Short History of English Drama*. 1965. Pp. 189-90

Gardner, Helen, "The Comedies of T. S. Eliot", *Sewanee Review*, 74:153-75, 1966

Gaskell, Ronald, *Drama and Reality; The European Theatre since Ibsen*. 1972. Pp. 128-38

——————— , " 'The Family Reunion' ", *Essays in Criticism* (Oxford), 12:292-301, 1962

Hamalian, Leo, "Wishwood Revisited", *Renascence* (1960), 12:167-73

Harding, D. W., "Progression of Theme in Eliot's Plays", *Kenyon Review*, 18:337-345, 1956

Hausermann, H. W., " 'East Coker' and 'The Family Reunion' ", *Life and Letters Today*, 47:32-38, Oct., 1945

Isaacs, J. I., "Eliot the Poet-Playwright. As See in 'The Family Reunion' ", *English* (1966), 16:100-05

Jamil, Maya, " 'Hamlet' and 'The Family Reunion' ", *Venture* (June 1968), 5:21-29

Kennedy, Andrew K., *Six Dramatists in Search of a Language*. 1975. Pp. 116-19

Kirk, Russell, *Eliot and His Age; T. S. Eliot's Moral Imagination in the 20th Century*. 1971. Pp. 261-70

Lightfoot, Marjorie J., " 'Purgatory' and 'The Family Reunion': In Pursuit of Prosodic Description", *Modern Drama*, 7:256-66, 1964

Lumley, Frederick, *New Trends in Twentieth Century Drama; A Survey Since Ibsen and Shaw*. 1967. Pp. 126-36

Maccoby, H. Z., "Difficulties in the Plot of 'The Family Reunion' ", *Notes and Queries* (Aug. 1968), 15:296-302

Margolis, John D., *T. S. Eliot's Intellectual Development, 1922-1939*. 1972. Pp. 215-18

Menon, K. P. K., *Literary Studies: Homage to Dr. A. Sivaramasubramonia Aiyer*. 1973. Pp. 229-55

Nation, 187:347, Nov. 8, 1958

New Statesman and Nation, 17:455-56, March 25, 1939 and 25:124, Feb. 20, 1943 and 32:337, Nov. 9, 1946

New Yorker, 34:99-101, Nov. 1, 1958

Oppel, Horst, ed., *Das Moderne Englische Drama; Interpretationen*, 1963, Pp. 220-41

Palmer, Richard E., "Existentialism in T. S. Eliot's 'The Family Reunion'", *Modern Drama*, 5:174-86, 1962

Plewka, K., "'The Family Reunion'; A Play by T. S. Eliot", *Die Neueren Sprachen*, #6:264-76, 1955

Porter, David H., "Ancient Myth and Modern Play; A Significant Counterpoint", *Classical Bulletin* (Nov. 1971), 48:1-9

Reporter, 19:35, Nov. 27, 1958

Rillie, John A. M., "Melodramatic Device in T. S. Eliot", *Renaissance and Modern Studies* (1962), 6:267-81

Roy, Emil, *British Drama since Shaw*. 1972. Pp. 89-92

Sarkar, Subhas, *Thomas Stearns Eliot the Dramatist*. 1972. Pp. 113-56

Saturday Review, 41:25, Nov. 8, 1958

Saturday Review of Literature, 19:12, April 1, 1939

Schmidt, Gerd, "Die Asketische Regel: Zum Verhältnis von Poesie und Drama bei T. S. Eliot", *Die Neueren Sprachen* (1965), 14:153-59

Scrimgeour, C. A., "'The Family Reunion'", *Essays in Criticism* (Oxford), 13:104-06, 1963

Sena, Vinod, "Eliot's 'The Family Reunion': A Study in Disintegration", *Southern Review* (LSU) (1967), 3:895-921

Southern Review, (L. S. U.), 5 no. 3:562-64, 1940

Spanos, William V., *The Christian Tradition in Modern British Verse Drama; The Poetics of Sacramental Time*. 1967. Pp. 184-218

Spanos, W. V., "T. S. Eliot's 'The Family Reunion': The Strategy of Sacramental Transfiguration", *Drama Survey*, 4:3-27, Spring, 1965

Spectator, 162:484, March 24, 1939

Stelzman, Rarnulf, "The Theology of T. S. Eliot's Dramas", *Xavier University Studies* (1963), 1:7-18

Theatre Arts, 41:23-24, May, 1957, and 42:64, Dec., 1958

Time, 72:48, Nov. 3, 1958

Ward, A., "Speculations on Eliot's Time-World: An Analysis of 'The Family Reunion' in Relation to Hulme and Bergson", *American Literature*, 21:18-34, March, 1949

Ward, David, *Thomas Stearns Eliot: Between Two Worlds*. 1973. Pp. 197-205

Wasson, Richard, "The Rhetoric of Theatre; The Contemporaneity of T. S. Eliot", *Drama Survey* (Spr. 1968), 6:231-43

Williams, Raymond, *Drama from Ibsen to Brecht*. 1968. Pp. 183-88

Murder in the Cathedral, 1935

Adams, John F. "The Fourth Temptation in 'Murder in the Cathedral'", *Modern Drama*, 5:381-88, 1963

Bergonzi, Bernard, *Thomas Stearns Eliot*. 1972. Pp. 133-35 and 143-46

Boulton, J. T., "Use of Original Sources for the Development of a Theme: Eliot in 'Murder in the Cathedral'", *English* (Oxford), 11:2-8, 1956

Brooks, Cleanth, ed., *Tragic Themes in Western Literature*. 1955. Pp. 150-78

Browne, E. Martin, *The Making of T. S. Eliot's Plays*. 1969. Pp 34-79

_____ , "The Permanent Contribution of T. S. Eliot to the Drama",
Gordon Review (1958), 4:150-66
_____ , "T. S. Eliot as Dramatist", *Drama* (1965), #72:41-43
_____ , "T. S. Eliot in the Theatre; The Director's Memories",
Sewanee Review, 74:136-52, 1966
Burton, Thomas G., ed., *Essays in Memory of Christine Burleson in Language
and Literature by Former Colleagues and Students*. 1969. Pp. 59-70
Callahan, Elizabeth Amidon, "The Tragic Hero in Contemporary Secular and
Religious Drama", *Literary Half-Yearly* (Jan.-July 1967), 8:42-49
Catholic World, 143:209-11, May, 1936
Chang, Wang-Rok, "An Analysis of 'Murder in the Cathedral' ", *English Lan-
guage and Literature* (1961), 10:280-91
Chiari, J., *Landmarks of Contemporary Drama*. 1965. Pp. 91-94
Chiari, Joseph, *Thomas Stearns Eliot: Poet and Dramatist*. 1972. Pp. 199-23
Christian Century, 52:1636, Dec. 18, 1935
Cohn, Ruby, *Currents in Contemporary Drama*. 1969. Pp. 103-05
Commonweal, 23:636, April 3, 1936 and 27:524, March 4, 1938
Cutts, John P., "Evidence for Ambivalence of Motives in 'Murder in the Cathe-
dral' ", *Comparative Drama* (1974), 8:199-210
Dierickx, J., "King and Archbishop: Henry II and Becket from Tennyson to
Fry", *Revue des Langues Vivantes* (1962), 28:424-35
Eliot in Perspective; A Symposium; ed. Graham Martin. 1970. Pp. 148-65
Evans, R. Wallis, "Cymdeithaseg y Ddrama", *Y Genhinen* (Wint. 1967-68), 18:42-
46
Fergusson, Francis, "Action as Passion: 'Tristan' and 'Murder in the Cathedral' ",
Kenyon Review, 4:201-221, 1947
Forum, 95:346-47, June, 1936
Friedman, Melvin J. and John B. Vickery, eds., *The Shaken Realist; Essays in
Modern Literature in Honor of Friedrick J. Hoffman*. 1970. Pp. 72-99
Galinsky, Hans, "T. S. Eliots 'Murder in the Cathedral'; Versuch Einer Inter-
pretation", *Die Neueren Sprachen*, 7:305-23, 1958
Geraldine, Sister M., "The Rhetoric of Repetition in 'Murder in the Cathedral' ",
Renascence (1967), 19:132-41
Gerstenberger, Donna, "The Saint and the Circle: The Dramatic Potential of an
Image", *Criticism* (1949), 1:336-41
Gross, John, "Eliot: From Ritual to Realism", *Encounter* (1965), 24:48-50
Guidubalbi, E., "T. S. Eliot Vicino Alla 'Meta' Teatrale", *Civiltà Cattolica*,
110:379-91, 1959
Honninghausen, L., "Die Verwendung der Dies-Irae-Sequenz in Eliots 'Murder
in the Cathedral' ", *Die Neueren Sprachen* n. f. (1965), 11:497-508
Kantra, Robert A., "Satiric Theme and Structure in 'Murder in the Cathedral' ",
Modern Drama (1968), 10:387-93
Kennedy, Andrew K., *Six Dramatists in Search of a Language*. 1975. Pp. 104-08
Kernodle, George R., *Invitation to the Theatre*. 1967. Pp. 234-36
Kirk, Russell, *Eliot and His Age; T. S. Eliot's Moral Imagination in the 20th
Century*. 1971. Pp. 239-48
Kivimaa, Kirsti, "Aspects of Style in T. S. Eliot's 'Murder in the Cathedral' ",
Annales Universitatis Turkuensis (1969), Bull. 111:1-96
Kliewer, Warren, "An Alternative to Realistic Forms", *Response* (1966), 7:163-
70
Kornbluth, Martin L., "A Twentieth Century 'Everyman' ", *College English*
(1959), 21:26-29

Kosok, Heinz, "Gestaltung und Funktion der 'Rechtfertigungsszene' in T. S. Eliots 'Murder in the Cathedral' ", *Die Neueren Sprachen*, 12:49-61, 1963

Kreiger, Murray, *The Classic Vision; The Retreat from Extremity in Modern Literature*. 1971. Pp. 337-62

Langslet, Lars Rvar, "Tre Dikteres Møte med Helgenen", *Kirke og Kultur* (1958), 63:406-15

Life, 123:7, Oct. 1, 1945

Lumley, Frederick, *New Trends in Twentieth Century Drama; A Survey Since Ibsen and Shaw*. 1967. Pp. 126-36

McCarthy, Patrick A., "Eliot's 'Murder in the Cathedral' ", *Explicator* (1974), 33:Item 7

Maccoby, J. Z., "Two Notes on 'Murder in the Cathedral' ", *Notes and Queries* (1967), 14:253-56

Margolis, John D., *T. S. Eliot's Intellectual Development, 1922-1939*. 1972. Pp. 187-89

Maxfield, Malinda R., "A Comparative Analysis of T. S. Eliot's 'Murder in the Cathedral' and Jean Anouilh's 'Becket' in the Light of Medieval and Contemporary Religious Drama in England and France", *Dissertation Abstracts International* (1970), 30:4458A

Mueller, W. R., " 'Murder in the Cathedral': An Imitation of Christ", *Religion in Life*, 27:414-26, 1958

Nation, 142:459-60, April 8, 1936

New Republic, 85:290, Jan. 15, 1936 and 86:253, April 8, 1936 and 94:101, March 2, 1938

New Yorker, 29:87, May 2, 1953

Newsweek, 7:26, March 28, 1936

Nicholas, C., "Murders of Doyle and Eliot", *Modern Language Notes*, 70:269-71, April, 1955

Nicholson, Norman, "Modern Verse-Drama and the Fold Tradition", *Critical Quarterly* (1960), 2:166-70

Novick, Julius, *Beyond Broadway; The Quest for Permanent Theatres*. 1968. Pp. 312-13

Pankow, Edith, "The 'Eternal Design' of 'Murder in the Cathedral' ", *Papers on Language and Literature* (1973), 9:35-47

Peter, J., " 'Murder in the Cathedral' ", *Sewanee Review*, 61:362-83, 1953

Pickering, Jerry V., "Form as Agent: Eliot's 'Murder in the Cathedral' ", *Educational Theatre Journal* (1968), 20:198-207

Rahv, Philip, *Literature and the Sixth Sense*. 1969. Pp. 309-15

Rehak, L. R., "On the Use of Martyrs: Tennyson, Eliot on Thomas Becket", *Univ. of Toronto Quarterly*, 33:43-60, 1963

Roy, Emil, "The Becket Plays: Eliot, Fry and Anouilh", *Modern Drama*, 8:268-76, 1965

———————— , *British Drama since Shaw*. 1972. Pp. 87-90

Sarkar, Subhas, *Thomas Stearns Eliot the Dramatist*. 1972. Pp. 83-112

Sharoni, Edna G., " 'Peace' and 'Unbar the Door': T. S. Eliot's 'Murder in the Cathedral' and Some Stoic Forbears", *Comparative Drama* (1972), 6:135-53

Shorter, Robert N., "Becket as Job: T. S. Eliot's 'Murder in the Cathedral' ", *South Atlantic Quarterly* (1968), 67:627-35

Spanos, William V., *The Christian Tradition in Modern British Verse Drama; The Poetics of Sacramental Time*. 1967. Pp. 81-134

———————— , " 'Murder in the Cathedral': The Figura as Mimetic Principle", *Drama Survey* (Minneapolis), 3:206-23, 1963

Speaight, Robert, "With Becket in 'Murder in the Cathedral' ", *Sewanee Review*, 74:176-87, 1966
Stelzman, Rarnulf, "The Theology of T. S. Eliot's Dramas", *Xavier University Studies* (1963), 1:7-18
Tate, Allen, ed., *T. S. Eliot; The Man and His Work; A Critical Evaluation.* 1966. Pp. 182-93
Theatre Arts, 20:25-26, Jan., 1936 and 20:341-43, May, 1936 and 22:254-55, April, 1938
Time, 31:34, Feb. 28, 1938
Turner, A. J., "Note on 'Murder in the Cathedral' ", *Notes and Queries* (Feb. 1970), 17:51-53
Virsis, Rasma, "Christian Concept in 'Murder in the Cathedral' ", *Modern Drama* (Feb. 1972), 14:405-07
Ward, David, *Thomas Stearns Eliot Between Two Worlds.* 1973. Pp. 180-97
Wasson, Richard, "The Rhetoric of the Theatre: The Contemporaneity of T. S. Eliot", *Drama Survey* (1968), 6:231-43
Williams, Pieter D., "The Function of the Chorus in T. S. Eliot's 'Murder in the Cathedral' ", *American Benedictine Review* (1972), 23:499-511
Williams, Raymond, *Drama from Ibsen to Brecht.* 1968. Pp. 179-83
_____ , *Modern Tragedy.* 1966. Pp. 156-63
_____ , "Tragic Resignation and Sacrifice", *Critical Quarterly* (1963), 5:5-19
Wills, Garry, "No Habitation, No Name", *Modern Age* (1963-64), 8:89-92
Wingate, Gifford W., " 'Murder in the Cathedral': A Step Toward Articulate Theatre", *Greyfriar* (1960), Pp. 22-35
Zizola, G., "Orgoglio e Sàntità nel Tomaso Becket di Eliot", *Studium*, 55:649-58, 1959

The Rock, 1934
Browne, E. Martin, *The Making of T. S. Eliot's Plays.* 1969. Pp. 1-33
Olshin, Toby A., "A Consideration of the 'Rock' ", *University of Toronto Quarterly* (1979), 39:310-23
Spanos, William V., *The Christian Tradition in Modern British Verse Drama; The Poetics of Sacramental Time.* 1967. Pp. 52-80

Sweeney Agonistes, 1933
Bergonzi, Bernard, *Thomas Stearns Eliot.* 1972. Pp. 105-09
Browne, E. Martin, "T. S. Eliot in the Theatre; The Director's Memories", *Sewanee Review*, 74:136-52, Winter, 1966
Chiari, Joseph, *Thomas Stearns Eliot: Poet and Dramatist.* 1972. Pp. 110-14
Eliot in Perspective; A Symposium; ed. Graham Martin. 1970. Pp. 148-65
Gwynn, F. L., "Sweeney Among the Epigraphs", *Modern Language Notes*, 69:572-74, 1954
Jayne, S., "Mr. Eliot's 'Agonistes' ", *Philological Quarterly*, 34:395-414, 1955
Kermode, Frank, "What Became of Sweeney?", *Spectator*, 202:513, April 10, 1959
Smith, Carol Hertzig, "From Sweeney 'Agonistes' to 'The Elder Statesman': A Study of the Dramatic Theory and Practice of T. S. Eliot", *Dissertation Abstracts*, 23:635-36, 1962
Spanos, W. V., " 'Wanna Go Home, Baby?'; 'Sweeney Agonistes' as Drama the Absurd", *Modern Language Association. Publications* (Jan. 1970), 85:8-20

Ward, David, *Thomas Stearns Eliot: Between Two Worlds.* 1973. Pp. 173-80
Williams, Raymond, *Drama from Ibsen to Brecht.* 1968. Pp. 176-78

GEORGE ETHEREGE

The Comical Revenge; or, Love in a Tub, 1664
  Holland, Norman N., *The First Modern Comedies.* 1959. Pp. 20-27
  Miner, Earl Roy, ed., *English Criticism in Japan; Essays by Younger Japanese Scholars on English and American Literature.* 1972. Pp. 156-69
  Miner, Earl, ed., *Restoration Dramatists; A Collection of Critical Essays.* 1966 Pp. 63-70
  Palmer, John Leslie, *The Comedy of Manners.* 1962. Pp. 64-91
  Ricks, Christopher, ed., *English Drama to 1710.* (History of Literature in the English Language), vol. 3. 1971. Pp. 381-85

The Man of Mode; or, Sir Fopling Flutter, 1676
  Auffret, J. M., " 'The Man of Mode' and 'The Plain Dealer': Common Origins and Parallels", *Etudes Anglaises* (Jan.-Mar. 1966), 19:209-22
  Berman, R. "The Comic Passions of 'The Man of Mode' ", *Studies in English Literature, 1500-1900* (Sum. 1970), 10:459-68
  Cox, R. S., Jr., "Richard Flecknoe and 'The Man of Mode' ", *Modern Language Quarterly* (June 1968), 29:183-89
  Cunningham, John E., *Restoration Drama.* 1966. Pp. 53-58
  Davies, Paul C., "The State of Nature and the State of War; A Reconstruction of 'The Man of Mode' ", *University of Toronto Quarterly* (1969), 39:53-62
  Elwin, Malcolm, *Handbook of Restoration Drama.* 1966. Pp. 62-68
  Hawkins, Harriett, *Likenesses of Truth in Elizabethan and Restoration Drama.* 1972. Pp. 79-97
  Hayman, John G., "Dorimant and the Comedy of 'A Man of Mode' ", *Modern Language Quarterly* (June 1969), 30:183-97
  Holland, Norman N., *The First Modern Comedies.* 1959. Pp. 86-95
  Hume, R. D., "Reading and Misreading 'The Man of Mode' ", *Criticism* (Wint. 1972), 14:1-11
  Kaul, A. N., *The Action of English Comedy; Studies in the Encounter of Abstraction and Experience from Shakespeare to Shaw.* 1970. Pp. 119-22
  Krause, David, "The Defaced Angel; A Concept of Satanic Grace in Etherege's 'The Man of Mode' ", *Drama Survey* (1969), 7:87-103
  Loftis, John Clyde, ed., *Restoration Drama; Modern Essays in Criticism.* 1966. Pp. 57-81
  Miner, Earl, ed., *Restoration Dramatists; A Collection of Critical Essays.* 1966. Pp. 76-103
  Palmer, John Leslie, *The Comedy of Manners.* 1962. Pp. 64-91
  Ricks, Christopher, ed., *English Drama to 1710.* (History of Literature in the English Language), vol. 3. 1971. Pp. 385-87
  Sherbo, A., "A Note on 'The Man of Mode' ", *Modern Language Notes* (1949), 64:343-44
  Vieth, David M., "Etherege's 'Man of Mode' and Rochester's 'Artemisa to Cloe' ", *Notes and Queries* (1958), 5:473-74

She Would If She Could, 1668
  Cunningham, John E., *Restoration Drama.* 1966. Pp. 49-53
  Elwin, Malcolm, *Handbook of Restoration Drama.* 1966. Pp. 64-68

Holland, Norman N., *The First Modern Comedies*. 1959. Pp. 28-37
Miner, Earl, ed., *Restoration Dramatists; A Collection of Essays*. 1966. Pp. 70-76 and 94-103
Palmer, John Leslie, *The Comedy of Manners*. 1962. Pp. 64-91
Sir Fopling Flutter   *SEE*   The Man of Mode; or, Sir Fopling Flutter

EURIPIDES

Alcestis, 438 B.C.
Anderson, Quentin and Mazzeo, Joseph Anthony, eds., *The Proper Study, Essays on Western Classics*. 1962. Pp. 102-20
Betts, G. G., "The Silence of 'Alcestis' ", *Mnemosyne* (1965), 18:181-82
Beye, G. R., "Alecstis and His Critics", *Greek, Roman and Byzantine Studies* (1959), 2:109-27
Burnett, Anne Pippin, *Catastrophe Survived; Euripides' Plays of Mixed Reversals*. 1971. Pp. 22-46
——————————— , "The Virtue of Admetus", *Classical Philology* (1965), 60: 240-55
Classical Review, 62:50-55, Sept., 1948
Croiset, M., "Observations sur le Rôle d'Admète", *Revue des Études Grecques* 25:1-11
Drew, D. L., "Euripides' 'Alcestis' ", *American Journal of Philology* (1931). 52:295-319
Driver, Tom Faw, *Sense of History in Greek and Shakespearean Drama*. 1960. Pp. 168-98
Ebeling, H. L., "The Admetus of Euripides Viewed in Relation to Admetus of the Tradition", *Transactions and Proceedings of the American Philological Association* (1898), 29:65-85
Goodell, Thomas Dwight, *Athenian Tragedy; A Study in Popular Art*. 1969. Pp. 280-83
Hamburger, Käte, *From Sophocles to Sartre; Figure from Greek Tragedy, Classical and Modern*. 1969. Pp. 103-05
Harsh, Philip Whaley, *A Handbook of Classical Drama*. 1944. Pp. 163-70
Heilman, Robert B., " 'Alcestis' and 'The Cocktail Party' ", *Comparative Literature*, 5:105-16, 1953
Jones, I. D. M.,"Euripides' 'Alcestis' ", *Classical Review* (1948), 62:50-55
Kott, Jan, *The Eating of the Gods; An Interpretation of Greek Tragedy*. 1973. Pp. 78-108
Kullmann, W., "Zum Sinngehalt der Euripideischen Alkestis' ", *Antike und Abenbland* (1967), 13:127-49
Myers, J. L., "The Plot of the 'Alcestis' ", *Journal of the Hellenic Society* (1917), 37:195-218
Nevinson, Henry Woodd, *Books and Personalities*. 1905. Pp. 136-41
Paton, J. A., "The Story of Alcestis in Ancient Literature and Art", *American Journal of Archeology* (1900), 4:150-51
Rivier, André, "En Marge d'Alceste' et de Quelques Interpretations récentes", *Museum Helveticum* (1973), 30:130-43
Rosenmeyer, Thomas Gustav, *The Masks of Tragedy, Essays on Six Greek Dramas*. 1963. Pp. 199-248
Schwinge, E. R., "Zwei Sprachliche Bemerkungen Zu Euripides 'Alkestis' ", *Glotta. Zeitschrift für Griechische und Lateinische Sprach* (1970), 48:36-39
Smith, W. D., "The Ironic Structure in 'Alcestis' ", *Phoenix* (1960), 14:127-45

Alkestis *SEE* Alcestis

Andromache, 426 BC?
Burnett, Anne Pippen, *Catastrophe Survived; Euripides' Plays of Mixed Reversals.* 1971. Pp. 130-56
Ferrari, Franco, "Stuttura e Personaggi Nella 'Andromaca' di Euripide", *Maia* (1971), n. s. 23:209-29
Garzya, A., "Interpretazione dell 'Andromaca' di Euripide", *Dioniso* (1951), 14:109-38
_____ , "Quelques Notes sur l'Andromaque' d'Euripide", *Revue Belge de Philologie et d'Histoire* (1951), 29:1142-50
Greek Poetry and Life; Essays Presented to G. Murray on His 70th Birthday. 1936. Pp. 206-30
Harsh, Philip Whaley, *A Handbook of Classical Drama.* 1944. Pp. 190-92
Johnson, V., "Euripides' 'Andromache' ", *Classical Weekly*, 48:9-13, 1955
Robertson, D. S., "Euripides and Tharyps", *Classical Review* (1923) 37:58-60
Verrall, A. W., *Essays on Four Plays of Euripides*, 1905. Pp. 1-42

Bacchae, 405 B.C.
Adams, Robert Martin, *Strains of Discord; Studies in Literary Openness.* 1958. Pp. 19-33
America (12-13-75), 133:419-22
Arthur M., "The Choral Odes of the 'Bacchae' of Euripides, *Yale Classical Studies* (1972), 22:63-82 and 145-79
Bather, A. G., "The Problem of Euripides' 'Bacchae' ", *Journal of the Hellenic Society* (1894), 14:244-63
Bellinger, A. R., " 'The Bacchae' and 'Hippolytus' ", *Yale Classical Studies*, 6:15-27, 1928-52
Birrell, F., " 'Bacchae' ", *Nation* (London), 46:800-01, March 15, 1930
Borthwick, E. K., "Three Notes on Euripides' 'Bacchae' ", *Classical Review* n. s. (1966), 16:136-38
Classical Review 44:6-8, Feb., 1930, and 44:56, May, 1930 and 57:69, Sept. 1943 and n. s. 8:204-06, Dec., 1958
Deichgraber, K., "Die Kadmos-Teiresiasszene in Euripides' 'Bakchen' ", *Hermes* (1935), 70:322-49
Dracoulides, N. N., "Interpretation Psychoanalytique des 'Bacchantes' d'Euripide", *Acta Psychotherapeutica, Psychosomatica et Orthopaedagogica* (1963), 11:14-27
Fleming, W., *Arts and Ideas.* 1955. Pp. 35-45
Florenne, Z., "L'Aurore du Soir", *Mercure de France*, 344:421-38, 1962
Grube, G. M. A., "Dionysus in the 'Bacchae' ", *Transactions and Proceedings of the American Philological Association* (1935), 66:37-54
Hagopian, J. V., "Literary Aesthetics and Euripides' 'The Bacchae' ", *Classical Journal*, 50:67-71, 1954
Harsh, Philip Whaley, *A Handbook of Classical Drama.* 1944. Pp. 236-45
Hathorn, Richmond Y., *Tragedy, Myth and Mystery.* 1962. Pp. 113-42
Jepsen, L., *Ethical Aspects of Tragedy; A Comparison of Certain Tragedies by Aeschylus, Sophocles, Euripides, Seneca and Shakespeare.* 1953. Pp. 89-95
Kott, Jan, *The Eating of the Gods; An Interpretation of Greek Tragedy.* 1973. Pp. 186-230
Lejnieks, V., "Interpolations in the 'Bacchae' ", *American Journal of Philology* (1967), 88:332-39

Murray, Gilbert, *Tradition and Progress.* 1922. Pp. 56-87
Nation (London), 30:109-10, Oct. 15, 1921
Nicol, Bernard de Bear, ed., *Varieties of Dramatic Experience.* 1969. Pp. 28-32
Nihard, R., "Le Problème des 'Bacchantes' d'Euripides", *Musées Royaux des Beaux-Arts de Belgique* (1912), 16:91-120 and 297-375
Norwood, Gilbert, *Essays on Euripidean Drama.* 1954. Pp. 52-73
Rohde, E., *Psyche.* Tr. W. B. Hillis. 1925. Pp. 253-334
Romilly, Mme J. de, "Le thème du Bonheur dans les 'Bacchantes' ", *Revue des Etudes Greques* (Paris), 70:361-80, 1963
Rosenmeyer, Thomas Gustav, *The Masks of Tragedy. Essays on Greek Dramas.* 1963. Pp. 103-52
Savage, E. B., " 'The Bacchae' as Theatre of Spectacle", *Drama Survey,* 3: 477-89, 1964
Spectator, 144:421-22, March 15, 1930
Stanford, W. B., *Ambiguity in Greek Literature.* 1939. Pp. 174-79
Stewart, Z., "The 'Amphitruo' of Plautus and Euripides' 'Bacchae' ", *Transactions and Proceedings of the American Philological Association,* 89:348-73, 1958
Willink, C. W., "On the Transmission of the 'Bacchae' ", *Classical Quarterly* (1966), 16:347

Cyclops, 423 BC
Arnott, P. D., "The Overworked Playwright", *Greece and Rome* (1961), 8:164-69
Grene, D. and R. Lattimore, eds., *The Complete Greek Tragedies.* vol. 3, 1959. Pp. 224-30
Harsh, Philip Whaley, *A Handbook of Classical Drama.* 1944. Pp. 196-98
Kassel, R., "Bemerkungen zum 'Kyklops' des Euripides", *Rheinisches Museum für Philologie* (1955), 98:279-86
Masqueray, P., " 'Le Cyclope' d'Euripide et Celui d'Homère", *Revue des Études Anciennes* (1902), 4:164-90
Pathmanathan, R. S., "A Playwright Relaxed or Overworked?", *Greece and Rome* (1963), 10:123-30
Rossi, Luigi Enrico, "Il 'Ciclope' di Euripide come Comos 'Mancato' ", *Maia* (1971), n. s. 23:10-38
Ussher, R. G., "The 'Cyclops' of Euripides", *Greece and Rome* (1971), 18:166-79

Electra, 413 BC
Adams, S. M., "Two Plays of Euripides", *Classical Review* (1935), 49:118-22
Baldry, H. C., *The Greek Tragic Theatre.* 1971. Pp. 117-22
Burnshaw, S., ed., *Varieties of Literary Experience; Eighteen Essays in World Literature.* 1962. Pp. 259-82
England, T., "The 'Electra' of Euripides", *Classical Review* (1926), 40:97-104
Hamburger, Käte, *From Sophocles to Sartre; Figures from Greek Tragedy, Classical and Modern.* 1969. Pp. 22-44
Harsh, Philip Whaley, *A Handbook of Classical Drama.* 1944. Pp. 212-18
Jones, Henry John Franklin, *On Aristotle and Greek Tragedy.* 1962. Pp. 239-45
Kott, Jan, *The Eating of the Gods; An Interpretation of Greek Tragedy.* 1973. Pp. 240-67

Kubo, M., "The Norm of Myth; Euripides' 'Electra'", *Harvard Studies in Classical Philology* (1966), 71:15-39

Lesky, Albin, *Greek Tragedy*. 1967. Pp. 169-72

O'Brien, M. J., "Orestes and the Gorgon; Euripides 'Electra'", *American Journal of Philology* (1964), 85:13-39

Sedgewick, G. G., *Of Irony, Especially in Drama*. 1967. Pp. 76-79

Sheppard, J. T., "The 'Electra' of Euripides", *Classical Review* (1918), 32:137-41

Solmsen, F., "Electra and Orestes. Three Recognitions in Greek Tragedy", *Medelingen de Koninklijke Nederlanse Akademie van Wetenschappen afd. Letterkunde* (1967), 30:3-34

Steiger, H., "Warum Schrieb Euripides Seine 'Elektra'?", *Philologus* (1897), 56:561-600

Stevens, P. T., "Euripides' 'Electra' and 'Alcestis'", *Classical Review*, 60:101-02, Dec., 1946

Stoessel, F., "Die 'Elektra' des Euripides", *Rheinisches Museum für Philologie* (1956), 99:47-92

Walkley, Arthur Bingham, *Drama and Life*. 1908. Pp. 127-31

Wilamowitz-Moellendorff, V. Von, "Die Beiden 'Elektren'", *Hermes* (1883), 18:214-63

Hecuba, 417 BC

Abrahamson, E. L., "Euripides' Tragedy of 'Hecuba'", *Transactions and Proceedings of the American Philological Association* (1952), 83:120-29

Adkins, A. W. H., "Basic Greek Values in Euripides' 'Hecuba' and 'Hercules Furens'", *Classical Quarterly* (1966), 16:193-219

Conacher, D. J., "Euripides' 'Hecuba'", *American Journal of Philology*, 82:1-26, Jan. 1961

Grene D. and R. Lattimore, eds., *The Complete Greek Tragedies*. vol. 3, 1959. Pp. 488-93

Harsh, Philip Whaley, *A Handbook of Classical Drama*. 1944. Pp. 193-95

Lesky, Albin, *Greek Tragedy*. 1967. Pp. 155-59

Pearson, L., *Popular Ethics in Ancient Greece*. 1962. Pp. 144-48

Spranger, J. A., "The Problem of 'Hecuba'", *Classical Quarterly* (1927), 21:155-58

Vandaele, H., "L'Unité d'Hēcuba'", *Xenia* (1912), Pp. 10-24

Hekabē *SEE* Hecuba

Helen, 412 BC

Alt, K., "Zur Anagnorisis in der 'Helena'", *Hermes* (1962), 90:6-24

Burnett, Anne Pippen, *Catastrophe Survived; Euripides' Plays of Mixed Reversals*. 1971. Pp. 77-100

Drew, D. L., "The Political Purpose in Euripides' 'Helena'", *Classical Philology* (1930), 25:187-89

Golann, C. P., "The Third Stasimon of Euripides' 'Helen'", *Transactions and Proceedings of the American Philological Association* (1945), 76:31-46

Griffiths, J., "Some Thoughts on the 'Helena'", *Journal of the Hellenic Society* (1953), 73:36-41

Hamburger, Käte, *From Sophocles to Sartre; Figures from Greek Tragedy, Classical and Modern*. 1969. Pp. 94-96

Harsh, Philip Whaley, *A Handbook of Classical Drama*. 1944. Pp. 225-28

Jesi, F., "L'Egitto Infero nell' 'Elena' de Euripide", *Aegyptus* (1965), 45:56-69

Kessels, A. H. M., "Euripides' 'Helen'", *Mnemosyne* (1975), 28:63-65

Pippin, A. N., "Euripides' 'Helen': A Comedy of Ideas", *Classical Philology*, 55:151-63, July, 1960

Segal, Charles P., "Les Deux Mondes de 'l'Helene' d'Euripide", *Revue des Etudes Greques* (1972), 85:293-311

Solmsen, F., "'Onoma' and 'Pragma' in Euripides' 'Helen'", *Classical Review* (1934), 48:119-21

Verrall, A. W., *Essays on Four Plays of Euripides.* 1905. Pp. 43-133

Young, Douglas C. C., "The Text of the Recognition Duet in Euripides' 'Helen'", *Greek, Roman and Byzantine Studies* (1974), 15:39-56

Heraclaidae *SEE* Heracles

Heracles, 421 BC

Adkins, A. W. H., "Basic Greek Values in Euripides' 'Hecuba' and 'Hercules Furens'", *Classical Quarterly* (1966), 16:193-219

Classical Studies in Honor of Charles Forster Smith. 1919. Pp. 11-29

Conacher, D. J., "Theme, Plot and Technique in the 'Heracles' of Euripides", *Phoenix* (1955), 9:139-52

Fitton, J. W., "The 'Suppliant Women' and the 'Heraclaidai' of Euripides", *American Journal of Philology* (1934), 55:197-224

Greenwood, L. H. G., *Aspects of Euripidean Drama.* 1953. Pp. 59-91

Grene, D. and R. Lattimore, eds., *The Complete Greek Tragedies.* 1959. vol. 3. Pp. 266-81

Kamerbeek, J. C., "The Unity and Meaning of Euripides' 'Heracles'", *Mnemosyne* (1966), 19:1-16

Kott, Jan, *The Eating of the Gods; An Interpretation of Greek Tragedy.* 1973. Pp. 147-62

Sheppard, J. T., "The Formal Beauty of the 'Hercules Furens'", *Classical Quarterly* (1916), 10:72-79

Spranger, J. A., "The Political Element in the 'Heracleidae' of Euripides", *Classical Quarterly* (1925), 19:117-64

Verrall, A. W., *Essays on Four Plays of Euripides.* 1905. Pp. 134-98

West, Martin L., "Critical Notes on Euripides' 'Heracles'", *Philologus. Zeitschrift für das Klassische Altertum* (1973), 117:145-51

Wilamowitz, Moellendorff, V. Von, "Excurse zu Euripides 'Heraklidai'", *Hermes* (1882), 17:337-64

Zuntz, G., "Is the 'Heraclidae' Mutilated?", *Classical Quarterly* (1947), 41:46-52

Hēraklēs *SEE* Heracles

Hiketides *SEE* The Suppliants

Hippolytus, 428 BC

Adams, S. M., "Two Plays of Euripides", *Classical Review* (1935), 49:118-22

Bellinger, A. R. "'The Bacchae' and 'Hippolytus'", *Yale Classical Studies*, 6:15-27, 1928-52

Berns, Gisela, "Nomos and Physis. An Interpretation of Euripides' 'Hippolytos'", *Hermes. Zeitschrift für Klassische Philologie* (1973), 101:165-86

Conacher, D. J., "A Problem in Euripides' 'Hippolytus'", *Transactions and Proceedings of the American Philological Association* (1961), 92:37-44

Crocker, L. G., "On Interpreting 'Hipplytus'", *Philologus* (1961), 101:238-46

Edwards, D., "'Tess of the d'Urbervilles' and 'Hippolytus'", *Midwest Quarterly* (1974), 15:392-405

Frischer, Bernard D., "Concordia Discors and Characterization in Euripides' 'Hippolytus'", *Greek, Roman, and Byzantine Studies* (1970), 11:85-100

Graham, H. F., "The 'Escape-Ode' in 'Hippolytus'", *Classical Journal* (1947), 42:275-76

Grene, D., "The Interpretation of 'Hippolytus' of Euripides", *Classical Philology* (1939), 34:45-58

Grube, G. M. A., *The Drama of Euripides.* 1941. Pp. 177-97

Hamburger, Käte, *From Sophocles to Sartre; Figures from Greek Tragedy. Classical and Modern.* 1969. Pp. 117-22

Harsh, Philip Whaley, *A Handbook of Classical Drama.* 1944. Pp. 180-87

Hathorn, Richmond Yancey, "Rationalism and Irrationalism in Euripides' 'Hippolytus'", *Classical Journal*, 52:211-18, 1957

Herter, H., "Theseus and Hippolytus", *Rheinisches Museum für Philologie* (1940), 89:273-92

Jepsen, L., *Ethical Aspects of Tragedy; A Comparison of Certain Tragedies by Aeschylus, Sophocles, Euripides, Seneca and Shakespeare.* 1953. Pp. 76-84

Knox, B. M. W., "The 'Hippolytus' of Euripides", *Yale Classical Studies* (1952), 13:3-31

Lattimore, R., "Phaedra and Hippolytus", *Arion* (1962), 13:5-18

Linforth, I. M., "Hippolytus and Humanism", *Transactions and Proceedings of the American Philological Association* (1914), 45:5-11

Lucas, D. W., "'Hippolytus'", *Classical Quarterly*, 40:65-69, July, 1946

McCollom, William G., "The Downfall of the Tragic Hero", *College English* (1957), 19:51-56

Meron, Evelyne, "D'l'Hippolyte' d'Euripide a la 'Phèdre' de Racine: Deux Conceptions du Tragique", *XVIIe Siecle* (1973), 100:34-54

Norwood, C., *Essays on Euripidean Drama.* 1954. Pp. 74-112

Parry, Hugh, "The Second Stasimon of Euripides' 'Hippolytus'", *Transactions and Proceedings of the American Philological Association* (1966), 97:317-26

Rexroth, Kenneth, *The Elastic Retort; Essays in Literature and Ideas.* 1973. Pp. 12-15

Rudd, Niall, ed., *Essays on Classical Literature.* 1972. Pp. 19-32

Sechan, L., "La Légende d'Hippolyte' dans l'Antiquité", *Revue des Etudes Grecques* (1911), 24:105-51

Segal, Charles, "Shame and Purity in Euripides' 'Hippolytus'", *Hermes* (1970), 98:278-99

Segal, Charles P., "The Tragedy of the 'Hippolytus': The Waters of the Ocean and the Untouched Meadow", *Harvard Studies in Classical Philology* (1965), 70:117-69

Snell, Bruno, *Scenes from Greek Drama.* 1964. Pp. 23-46

Soury, G., "Euripide; Rationaliste et Mystique d'Après 'Hippolyte'", *Revue des Etudes Grecques* (1943), 56:29-52

Spranger, J. A., "The Art of Euripides in 'Hippolytus'", *Classical Review* (1919), 33:9-15

——————— , "The Meaning of the 'Hippolytus' of Euripides", *Classical Quarterly* (1927), 21:18-19

Stallknecht, N. R. and H. Frenz, eds., *Comparative Literature; Method and Perspective.* 1971. Pp. 218-47

Stanford, W. B., "The 'Hippolytus' of Euripides", *Hermathena* (1944), 63: 11-17

Valgiglio, E., " 'L'Ippolito' di Euripide", *Humanitas* (Port.), 5:37-39, 1957

Walkley, Arthur Bingham, *Drama and Life.* 1908, Pp. 120-26

Whitaker, J., "Hypothesis of Euripides' 'Hippolytus'", *Classical Review* (Mar. 1971), n. s. 21:9

Willink, C. W., "Some Problems in 'Hippolytus' ", *Classical Quarterly* (1968), 18:11-43

Ion, 411 BC

Burnett, Anne Pippen, *Catastrophe Survived; Euripides' Plays of Mixed Reversals.* (1971), Pp. 101-29

Colardeau, T., "Ion a Delphes", *Revue des Etudes Grecques* (1916), 29:430-34

Conacher, D. J., "The Paradox of Euripides' 'Ion' ", *Transactions and Proceedings of the American Philological Association*, 90:20-39, 1959

Grube, G. M. A., *The Drama of Euripides.* 1941. Pp. 261-79

Harry, J. E., " 'Ion' of Euripides", *American Journal of Philology*, 44:56-61, 1923

Harsh, Philip Whaley, *A Handbook of Classical Drama.* 1944. Pp. 202-04

Imhof, Max, "Euripides' 'Ion' und Sophokles 'Oedipus auf Kolonis' ", *Museum Helveticum* (1970), 27:65-89

Nicol, Bernard de Bear, ed., *Varieties of Dramatic Experience.* 1969. Pp. 24-28

Rosenmeyer, Thomas Gustav, *The Masks of Tragedy; Essays on Six Greek Dramas.* 1963. Pp. 103-52

Solmsen, F., "Euripides' 'Ion' im Vergleich mit Anderen Tragodian", *Hermes* (1934), 69:390-419

Wassermann, F. M., "Divine Violence and Providence in Euripides' 'Ion' ", *Transactions and Proceedings of the American Philological Association* (1940), 71:587-604

Wolff, Christian, "The Design and Myth in Euripides' 'Ion' ", *Harvard Studies in Classical Philology* (1965), 69:169-94

Iphigenèia è en Taurois   *SEE*   Iphigenia Taurica

Iphigenèia è en Aulidi   *SEE*   Iphigenia in Aulis

Iphigenia in Aulis, 405 BC

Bellinger, A. R., "Achilles' Son and Achilles", *Yale Classical Studies*, 6:1-13, 1928-52

Bonnard, A., *Greek Civilization: From Euripides to Alexandria.* 1961. Pp. 27-38

——————— , " 'Iphigenia in Aulis': Tragique et Poésie", *Museum Helvetium* (1945), 2:87-107

Ferguson, J., "Iphigenia at Aulis", *Transactions and Proceedings of the American Philological Association* (1968), 99:157-64

Hamburger, Käte, *From Sophocles to Sartre; Figures from Greek Tragedy, Classical and Modern.* 1969. Pp. 69-90

Harsh, Philip Whaley, *A Handbook of Classical Drama.* 1944. Pp. 246-49

Jones, Henry John Franklin, *Aristotle and Greek Tragedy.* 1962. Pp. 245-70

Knox, B. M. W., "Euripides' 'Iphigenia in Aulis' ", *Yale Classical Studies* (1972), 22:239-61

Lesky, Albin, *Greek Tragedy.* 1967. Pp. 193-96

Meunier, J., "Pour une Lecture Candide d'Iphigénie à Aulis' ", *Musées Royaux des Beaux Arts de Belgique* (1927), 31:21-35

Parmentier, L., "L'Iphigénia à Aulis' d'Euripide", *Academie Royale de Belgique, Bulletin de la Classe des Lettres* (1926), 5th ser., 12:266-73

Roussel, P., "Le Role d'Achille dans l'Iphigénie à Aulis' ", *Revue des Etudes Grecques* (1915), 28:234-50

Vretska, Helmuth, "Agamemnon in Euripides' 'Iphigenie in Aulis' ", *Studien, Wiener. Zeitschrift fur Klassische Philologie* (1961), 74:18-39

Wassermann, F. M., "Agamemnon in the 'Iphigeneia at Aulis' ", *Transactions and Proceedings of the American Philological Association* (1949), 80:174-86

Will, F., "Remarks on Counterpoint Characterization in Euripides", *Classical Journal*, 55:328-44, 1960

Willink, C. W., "The Prologue of 'Iphigenia at Aulis' ", *Classical Quarterly* (1972), 21:343-64

Iphigenia in Tauris, 412 BC

Burnett, Anne Pippen, *Catastrophe Survived; Euripides' Plays of Mixed Reversals.* 1971. Pp. 47-72

Goodell, Thomas Dwight, *Athenian Tragedy; A Study in Popular Art.* 1969. Pp. 145-49

Hamburger, Käte, *From Sophocles to Sartre; Figures from Greek Tragedy, Classical and Modern.* 1969. Pp. 69-90

Harsh, Philip Whaley, *A Handbook of Classical Drama.* 1944. Pp. 219-24

Verrall, A. W., *Euripides the Rationalist.* 1895. Pp. 166-230

Kyklóps *SEE* Cyclops

Medea, 431 BC

Birrell, F., "Medea", *New Statesman*, 20:74-75, Oct. 21, 1922

Blaiklock, E. M., "The Nautical Imagery of Euripides' 'Medea' ", *Classical Philology* (1955), 50:233-37

Bonnard, A., *Greek Civilization: From Euripides to Alexandria.* 1961. Pp. 15-26

Burnett, A., " 'Medea' and the Tragedy of Revenge", *Classical Philology* (1973), 68:124

Buttrey, T. V., "Accident and Design in Euripides' 'Medea' ", *American Journal of Philology*, 79:1-17, Jan., 1958

Classical Review, 58:11-13, May, 1944 and n. s. 14:1-2, March, 1964

Colby, R. A., "The Sorcery of 'Medea' ", *Univ. of Kansas City Review*, 25:249-55, 1959

Commonweal, 20:183, June 15, 1934

Davison, J. A., "Medea", *Classical Review*, n. s. 14:240-41, Dec., 1964

Goodman, Randolph, *Drama on Stage.* 1961. Pp. 3-5

Hamburger, Käte, *From Sophocles to Sartre; Figures from Greek Tragedy, Classical and Modern.* 1969. Pp. 124-26

Hamilton, Clayton Meeker, *Seen on the Stage.* 1920. Pp. 204-14

Harsh, Philip Whaley, *A Handbook of Classical Drama.* 1944. Pp. 171-79

Hyman, Stanley Edgar, *Poetry and Criticism; Four Revolutions in Literary Taste.* 1961. Pp. 5-37

Kott, Jan, *The Eating of the Gods; An Interpretation of Greek Tragedy.* 1973. Pp. 233-39

Lesky, Albin, *Greek Tragedy.* 1967. Pp. 142-48

Lewisohn, Ludwig, *Drama and the Stage*. 1922. Pp. 121-44

Maddalena, A., "La 'Medea' di Euripide", *Revista di Filologia e di Instruzione Classica*, 91:129-52, 1963

Mead, L. M., "A Study in the 'Medea' ", *Greece and Rome* (1943), 12:15-20

Masurillo, H., "Euripides' 'Medea': A Reconsideration", *American Journal of Philology* (1966), 87:52-74

Nation, 110:525-26, April 17, 1920 (2-5-73), 216:186-87

New Statesman and Nation, 36:303, Oct. 9, 1948

New Yorker (1-27-73), 48:50

Palmer, R. B., "An Apology for Jason: A Study of Euripides' 'Medea' ", *Classical Journal*, 53:49-55, 1957

Reckford, K. J., "Medea's First Exit", *Transactions and Proceedings of the American Philological Association* (1968), 99:329-59

Schlesinger, E., "Zu Euripides' 'Medea' ", *Hermes* (1966), 94:26-53

Sheppard, J. T., "The Garden of the Muses; A Chorus from the 'Medea' ", *Essays by Divers Hands* (1973), 26:43-58

Snell, Bruno, *Scenes from Greek Drama*. 1964. Pp. 47-69

Tarditi, G., "Euripide e il Dramma di 'Medea' ", *Revista di Filologia die Instruzione Classica* (1957), 25-354-71

Thompson, E. A., "Neophron and Euripides' 'Medea' ", *Classical Quarterly* (1944), 38:10-14

Turner, W. J., "Medea", *Spectator*, 129:555-6, Oct. 21, 1922

Usscher, R. G., "Notes on Euripides' 'Medea' ", *Eranos* (1961), 59:1-7

Walton, F. R., "Euripides' 'Medea'; A New Interpretation", *American Journal of Philology*, 70:411-13, Oct., 1949

Orestes, 408 BC

Biehl, Werner, "Zur Darstellung des Menschen in Euripides 'Orestes' ", *Helikon. Rivista di Tradizione e Cultura Classica dell Università di Messina* (1968), 8: 197-221

Burnett, Anne Pippen, *Catastrophe Survived; Euripides' Plays of Mixed Reversals*. 1971. Pp. 183-222

Feaver, D. D., "The Musical Setting of Euripides' 'Orestes' ", *American Journal of Philology* (1960), 81:1-15

Greenberg, N. A., "Euripides' 'Orestes'; An Interpretation", *Harvard Studies in Classical Philology*, 66:157-92, 1962

Grene, D. and R. Lattimore, eds., *The Complete Greek Tragedies*. v. 4, 1959. Pp. 186-91

Hamburger, Käte, *From Sophocles to Sartre; Figures from Greek Tragedy, Classical and Modern*. 1969. Pp. 22-44

Harsh, Philip Whaley, *A Handbook of Classical Drama*. 1944. Pp. 232-35

Lesky, Albin, *Greek Tragedy*. 1967. Pp. 189-93

Lesky, A., "Zum 'Orestes' des Euripides", *Wiener Studien* (1935), 53:37-47

Mullens, H. G., "The Meaning of Euripides' 'Orestes' ", *Classical Quarterly* (1940), 34:153-58

Verrall, A. W. *Essays on Four Plays of Euripides*. 1905. Pp. 199-264

Phoenician Women, 411 BC

Conacher, D. J., "Themes in the 'Exodus' of Euripides' 'Phoenissae' ", *Phoenix* (1967), 21:92-101

Ebener, D., "Die 'Phönizierinnen' des Euripides als Spiegelbild Geschichtlicher Wirklichkeit", *Ceskoslovenski Akademie Vêd, Sekce Jazyka a Literatury. Eirene. Studia Graeca et Latina* (Prague), 2:71-79, 1964

Harsh, Philip Whaley, *A Handbook of Classical Drama*. 1944. Pp. 229-31
Lesky, Albin, *Greek Tragedy*. 1967. Pp. 178-81
Meredith, H. W., "The End of the Phoenissae'", *Classical Review* (1937), 51:97-103
Podlecki, A. J., "Some Themes in Euripides' 'Phoenissae'", *Transactions and Proceedings of the American Philological Association* (1967), 93:355-73
Rebuffat, René, "Le Sacrifice de Créon dans les 'Phéniciennes' d'Euripide", *Annales de la Faculté des Lettres de Bordeaux. Revue des Études Anciennes* (1972), 74:14-31
Romilly, I, de, "Les 'Phéniciennes' d'Euripides ou l'Actualité dans la Tragédie Grecque", *Revue de Philologie, de Litterature et d'Histoire Anciennes* (1965), 39:28-47
Treves, P., "'Le Fenicia' di Euripide", *Atene e Roma* (1930), Pp. 171-95
Verrall, A. W., *Euripides the Rationalist*. 1895. Pp. 231-61
Wallach, L., *Three Plays by Euripides*. 1966. Pp. 83-97

Phoinissai *SEE* The Phoenician Woman

Rhesus, n.d.
Barlow, C. W., "Rhetorical Elements in the 'Rhesus'", *Transactions and Proceedings of the American Philological Associations* (1941), 72:XXVII
Bates, W. N., "Notes on the 'Rhesus'", *Transactions and Proceedings of the American Philological Association* (1916), 47:5-11
Bjork, G., "The Authenticity of 'Rhesus'", *Eranos* (1957), 55:7-17
Elderkin, G. W., "Dolon's Disguise in the 'Rhesus'", *Classical Philology* (1935), 30:349-50
Goossens, R., "La Date du 'Rhesos'", *Archaeologia Classica* (1932), 1:93-134
Gregoire, H., "L'Authenticité du 'Rhesos' d'Euripide", *Archaeologia Classica* (1933), 2:91-133
Gregoire, H. and R. Goossens, "Sitalkes et Athènes dans le 'Rhesos' d'Euripide", *Archaeologia Classica* (1934), 3:431-46
Macurdy, G., "The Dawn Songs in 'Rhesus' and in the Parodos of 'Phaeton'", *American Journal of Philology* (1943), 64:408-16
Mierow, H. E., "The Sophoclean Character of the 'Rhesus'", *American Journal of Philology* (1928), 49:375-78
Nock, A. D., "The End of the 'Rhesus'", *Classical Review* (1926), 40:184-86
——————— , "The 'Rhesus'", *Classical Review* (1930), 44:173-74
Parry, H., "The Approach of Dawn in the 'Rhesus'", *Phoenix* (1964), 18:283-93
Pearson, A. C., "The Rhesus", *Classical Quarterly* (1926), 20:80-81
Porter, W. H., "The Euripidean 'Rhesus' in the Light of Recent Criticism", *Hermathena* (1913), 17:348-80
Richards, G. C., "The Problems of the 'Rhesus'", *Classical Quarterly* (1916), 10:192-97
Ridgeway, W., "Euripides in Macedon", *Classical Quarterly* (1926), 20:1-19
Rolfe, J. C., "The Tragedy of 'Rhesus'", *Harvard Studies in Classical Philology* (1893), 4:61-97
Steadman, S. H., "A Note on the 'Rhesus'", *Classical Review* (1945), 59:6-8
Strohm, H., "Beobachtungen zum 'Rhesos'", *Hermes* (1959), 87:257-74

The Suppliants, 420-418 BC
Collard, C., "The Funeral Oration in Euripides' 'Supplices'", *Bulletin of the Institute of Classical Studies of the University of London* (1972), 19:39-53
——————— , "Notes on Euripides' 'Supplices'", *Classical Quarterly* (1963), 13:178-87

Conacher, D. J., "Religious and Ethical Attitudes in Euripides' 'Suppliants' ", *Transactions and Proceedings of the American Philological Association* (1956), 87:8-26

Fitton, J. W., "The 'Suppliant Women' and the 'Heracleidai' of Euripides", *Hermes* (1961), 89:430-61

Gamble, R. B., "Euripides 'Suppliant Women': Decision and Ambivalence", *Hermes* (1970), 98:385-405

Giles, P., "Political Allusions in the 'Suppliants' of Euripides", *Classical Review* (1890), 4:95-98

Goossens, R., "Périclès et Thésée; À Propos des 'Suppliantes' d'Euripide", *Bulletin de l'Association Guillaume Budé* (1932), 35:9-40

Greenwood, L. H. G., *Aspects of Euripidean Tragedy.* 1953. Pp. 92-120

Harsh, Philip Whaley, *A Handbook of Classical Drama.* 1944. Pp. 202-04

Koster, W. J. W., "De Euripides' 'Supplicibus' ", *Mnemosyne* (1942), 3rd ser. 10:161-203

Kuiper, G., "De Euripidis 'Supplicibus' ", *Mnemosyne* (1923), n. s. 51:102-28

Lesky, Albin, *Greek Tragedy.* 1967. Pp. 159-61

Longman, G. A., "Professor Norwood and the 'Supplices' of Euripides", *Durham University Journal* (1959-60), 21:29-32

Norwood, G., *Essays in Euripidean Tragedy.* 1954. Pp. 112-81

Paduano, G., "Interpretazione delle 'Supplici' di Euripide", *Annali della Scuola Normale Superiore di Pisa. Lettere, Storia e Filosofia* (1966), 35:193-249

Smith, W. D., "Dramatic Structure and Technique in Euripides' 'Suppliants' ", *Harvard Studies in Classical Philology*, 62:152-54, 1957

———————————, "Expressive Form in Euripides 'Suppliants' ", *Harvard Studies in Classical Philology* (1966), 71:151-70

Zunts, G., "Ueber Euripides 'Hiketiden' ", *Museum Helveticum* (1955), 12:20-34

Tròiades   *SEE*   The Trojan Women

The Trojan Women, 415 BC

Clay, James H., and Daniel Krempel, *The Theatrical Image.* 1967. Pp. 39-40

Gilmartin, Kristine, "Talthybius in the 'Trojan Women' ", *American Journal of Philology* (1970), 91:213-22

Hamburger, Käte, *From Sophocles to Sartre; Figures from Greek Tragedy, Classical and Modern.* 1969. Pp. 9-23

Hanson, J. O. deG., "Reconstruction of Euripides' Alexandros", *Hermes* (1964), 92:171-81

Harsh, Philip Whaley, *A Handbook of Classical Drama.* 1944. Pp. 208-11

Nation, 198:58-59, Jan. 13, 1964

New Republic, 150:30, Feb. 1, 1964

New Yorker, 39:70, Jan. 11, 1964 and 41:183-84, April 17, 1965

Newsweek, 63:61, Jan. 6, 1964

Reiter, Seymour, *World Theater; The Structure and Meaning of Drama.* 1973. Pp. 120-37

Segal, E., *Euripides.* 1968. Pp. 115-27

Steiger, H., "Warum Schrieb Euripides Seine 'Troerinnen' ", *Philologus* (1900), n.f. 13:363-66

EVERYMAN

Everyman

Adolf, Helen, "From 'Everyman' and 'Elckerlijc' to Hofmansthal and Kafka", *Comparative Literature*, 9:204-214, 1957

Cary, Elizabeth Luther, " 'Everyman', a Morality Play", *Critic*, 42:42-45, Jan., 1903

——————— , "Summoning of 'Everyman' ", *Independent*, 55:906-11, April 16, 1903

Conley, J., "Phrase 'The Oyle of Forgyenes' in 'Everyman': A Reference to Extreme Unction?", *Notes and Queries* (March 1975), 22:105-06

The Darker Vision of the Renaissance; Beyond the Fields of Reason. 1974. Pp. 147-96

Goldhamer, Allen D., " 'Everyman': A Dramatization of Death", *Quarterly Journal of Speech* (1973), 59:87-98

Kuala, David, "Time and the Timeless in 'Everyman' and 'Dr. Faustus' ", *College English*, 22:9-14, 1960

Mayer, Hans, *Steppenwolf and Everyman*. 1971. Pp. 300-25

Moran, Dennis V., "The Life of 'Everyman' ", *Neophilologus* (1972), 56:324-30

Ryan, Lawrence V., "Doctrine and Dramatic Structure in 'Everyman' ", *Speculum*, 32:722-35, 1957

Sticca, Sandro, ed., *The Medieval Drama; Papers of the 3rd Annual Conference of the Center for Medieval and Early Renaissance Studies*. 1972. Pp. 69-88

Takaku, Shinichi, "Disappearance of Death in 'Everyman' ", *Studies in English Literature* (Japan) (1974), Pp. 232-34

Thomas, Helen S., "The Meaning of the Character Knowledge in 'Everyman' ", *Mississippi Quarterly*, 14:3-13, 1961

Velz, John W., "Episodic Structure in Four Tudor Plays: A Virtue of Necessity", *Comparative Drama* (1972), 6:87-102

Warren, Michael J., "Everyman: Knowledge Once More", *Dalhousie Review* (1974), 54:136-46

Wasson, John M., "Interpolation in the Text of 'Everyman' ", *Theatre Notebook* (1973), 27:14-20

GEORGE FARQUHAR

Beaux Strategem, 1707

America, 100:725, March 21, 1959

Commonweal, 70:25-26, April 3, 1959

Cunningham, John E., *Restoration Drama*. 1966. Pp. 144-47

Elwin, Malcolm, *Handbook of Restoration Drama*. 1966. Pp. 192-95

Evans, Ifor, *A Short History of English Drama*. 1965. Pp. 120-21

Fox, James H., "The Actor-Audience Relationship in Restoration Comedy, with Particular Reference to the Aside", *Dissertation Abstracts International* (1973), 33:6308A

Gravitt, Garland J., "A Primer of Pleasure: Neo-Epicureanism in Farquhar's 'The Beaux' Strategem' ", *Thoth* (1972), 12:38-49

Miner, Earl, ed., *Seventeenth Century Imagery; Essays on Uses of Figurative Language from Donne to Farquhar*. 1971. Pp. 169-86

Nation, 188:234, March 14, 1959

New Republic, 122:20, June 19, 1950

New Statesman, 35:363-64, June 28, 1930

New Yorker, 35:82, March 7, 1959

Olshen, Barry N., " 'Beaux's Strategen' on the 19th Century London Stage", *Theatre Notebook* (1974), 28,ii:70-80

Palmer, John Leslie, *The Comedy of Manners*. 1962. Pp. 242-74

Sharma, Ram Chandra, *Themes and Conventions in the Comedy of Manners*. 1965. Pp. 329-30

Theatre Arts, 43:63, April, 1959

Ward, Adolphus William, *A History of English Dramatic Literature*, v. 3. 1966.
Pp. 484-85

Young, Stark, "Beaux Strategem", *New Republic*, 55:122-23, June 20, 1928

The Constant Couple; or, A Trip to the Jubilee, 1699

Cope, J. I., "'Constant Couple': Farquhar's Four Plays in One", *ELH* (1974),
41:477-93

Elwin, Malcolm, *Handbook of Restoration Drama*. 1966. Pp. 187-89

Sharma, Ram Chandra, *Themes and Conventions in the Comedy of Manners*.
1965. Pp. 184-85

Ward, Adolphus William, *A History of English Dramatic Literature*, v. 3. 1966.
Pp. 482

The Inconstant; or, The Way to Win Him, 1703

Elwin, Malcolm, *Handbook of Restoration Drama*. 1966. Pp. 189-91

Ward, Adolphus William, *A History of English Dramatic Literature*, v. 3. 1966.
Pp. 483-84

Love and a Bottle, 1698

James, Eugene Nelson, "The Burlesque of Restoration Comedy in 'Love and a
Bottle' ", *Studies in English Literature, 1500-1900* (1965), 5:469-90

Ward, Adolphus William, *A History of English Dramatic Literature*, v. 3. 1966,
Pp. 482

The Recruiting Officer, 1706

Ferran, Peter W., "Brecht and Farquhar; The Critical Art of Dramatic Adaptation", *Dissertation Abstracts International* (1973), 33:6353A

Hunt, Leigh, *Leigh Hunt's Dramatic Criticism, 1808-1831*, ed. by Lawrence
Huston Houtchens and Carolyn Washburn Houtchens. 1949. Pp. 206-08

Nation (Feb. 23, 1870), 210:220

New Yorker, 39:117-18, Feb. 15, 1964

Ward, Adolphus William, *A History of English Dramatic Literature*, v. 3. 1966.
Pp. 484

Wertheim, Albert, "Bertolt Brecht and George Farquhar's 'The Recruiting
Officer' ", *Comparative Drama* (1973), 7:179-90

Sir Harry Wildair, Being the Sequel of a Trip to the Jubilee, 1701

Ward, Adolphus William, *A History of English Dramatic Literature*, v. 3. 1966.
Pp. 482-83

The Twin Rivals, 1705

Elwin, Malcolm, *Handbook of Restoration Drama*. 1966. Pp. 191-92

Rothstein, Eric, "Farquhar's 'Twin Rivals' and the Reform of Comedy", *Modern Language Association. Publications* (PMLA), 79:33-41, 1964

Ward, Adolphus William, *A History of English Dramatic Literature*, v. 3. 1966.
Pp. 484

NATHAN FIELD

SEE

PHILIP MASSINGER AND NATHAN FIELD

JOHN FLETCHER

SEE

FRANCIS BEAUMONT AND JOHN FLETCHER

JOHN FORD

The Broken Heart, 1627/31

Anderson, Donald K., Jr., "The Heart and the Banquet: Imagery in Ford's 'Tis Pity' and 'The Broken Heart' ", *Studies in English Literature, 1500-1900* (1962), 2:209-17

Blayney, G. H., "Convention, Plot, and Structure in 'The Broken Heart' ", *Modern Philology* (1958), 56:1-9

Bluestone, Max and Norman Rabkin, eds., *Shakespeare's Contemporaries; Modern Studies in English Renaissance Drama.* 1970. Pp. 399-404

Boas, Frederick S. *An Introduction to Stuart Drama.* 1946. Pp. 342-47

Burbridge, R. T., "Moral Vision of Ford's 'The Broken Heart' ", *Studies in English Literature, 1500-1900* (Spr. 1970), 10:315-23 and 397-407

Burelbach, Frederick M., Jr., " 'The Truth' in John Ford's 'The Broken Heart' Revisited", *Notes and Queries* (1967), 14:211-12

Carsaniga, M., "Truth in John Ford's 'The Broken Heart' ", *Comparative Literature* (1958), 10:344-48

Ewing, S. Blaine, *Burtonian Melancholy in the Plays of John Ford.* 1940. Pp. 55-64

Greenfield, T. N., "Languages of Process in Ford's 'The Broken Heart' ", *Modern Language Association. Publications* (May 1972), 87:397-405

Herndl, George C., *The High Design; English Renaissance Tragedy and the Natural Law.* 1970. Pp. 272-77

Jordan, R., "Calantha's Dance in 'The Broken Heart' ", *Notes and Queries* (Aug. 1969), 16:294-95

Kistner, Arthur L. and M. K., "The Dramatic Functions of Love in the Tragedies of John Ford", *Studies in Philology* (1973), 70:62-76

McDonald, Charles O., "The Design of John Ford's 'The Broken Heart' ", *Studies in Philology* (1962), 59:141-61

McDonald, Charles Osborne, *The Rhetoric of Tragedy; Form in Stuart Drama.* 1966. Pp. 314-33

Malouf, David, "The Dramatist as Critic: John Ford and 'The Broken Heart' ", *Southern Review; An Australian Journal of Literary Studies* (1972), 5:197-206

Pellizzi, Giovanna, "The Speech of Ithocles on Ambition in Ford's 'Broken Heart' ", *English Miscellany* (1969), 20:93-99

Ribner, Irving, *Jacobean Tragedy; The Quest for Moral Order.* 1962. Pp. 156-63

Roberts, Jeanne Addison, "John Ford's Passionate Abstractions", *Southern Humanities Revue* (1973), 7:322-32

Schneider, Steven A., "The Dissonant Design: John Ford and the Art of Tragedy", *Dissertation Abstracts International* (1974), 35:1060A

Sensabaugh, G. F., "John Ford and Elizabethan Tragedy", *Philological Quarterly* (1941), 20:442-53

———————— ,"John Ford and Platonic Love in the Court", *Studies in Philology* (1939), 36:206-26

———————— , "John Ford Revisited", *Studies in English Literature, 1500-1900* (1964), 4:195-216

Sherman, S. P., "Stella and 'The Broken Heart' ", *Modern Language Association. Publications* (1909), 24 No. 17:274-85

Stavig, Mark, *John Ford and the Traditional Moral Order*. 1968. Pp. 144-67

Tomlinson, Thomas Brian, *A Study of Elizabethan and Jacobean Tragedy*. 1964. Pp. 270-72

Ure, Peter, *Elizabethan and Jacobean Drama; Critical Essays*. 1974. Pp. 146-65

The Chronicle Historie of Perkin Warbeck   *SEE*   Perkin Warbeck

The Fancies, Chaste and Noble, 1631

Hart, Dominick J., "A Critical Edition of John Ford's 'The Fancies, Chaste and Noble' ", *Dissertation Abstracts International* (1972), 32:5739A

Noletti, Arthur E., "The Form and Dramaturgy of John Ford's Tragi-Comedy", *Dissertation Abstracts International* (1974), 34:6600A

Sensabaugh, G. F., "John Ford and Platonic Love in the Court", *Studies in Philology* (1939), 36:206-26

Sutton, Juliet, "Platonic Love in Ford's 'The Fancies, Chaste and Noble' ", *Studies in English Literature, 1500-1900* (1967), 7:299-309

An Ill Beginning Has a Good End, 1613

Parrott, T. N., "Note on John Ford: Discussion of the Lost Comedy 'An Ill Beginning Has a Good End' ", *Modern Language Notes* (1943), 58:247-53

The Lady's Trial, 1638

Noletti, Arthur E., "The Form and Dramaturgy of John Ford's Tragi-Comedy", *Dissertation Abstracts International* (1974), 34:6600A

Sensabaugh, G. F., "John Ford and Platonic Love in the Court", *Studies in Philology* (1939), 36:206-26

Love's Sacrifice, 1632

Kistner, Arthur L. and M. K., "The Dramatic Functions of Love in the Tragedies of John Ford", *Studies in Philology* (1973), 70:62-76

Roberts, Jeanne Addison, "John Ford's Passionate Abstractions", *Southern Humanities Review* (1973), 7:322-32

Schneider, Steven A., "The Dissonant Design: John Ford and the Art of Tragedy", *Dissertation Abstracts International* (1974), 35:1060A

Sensabaugh, G. F., "John Ford and Elizabethan Tragedy", *Philological Quarterly* (1941), 20:442-53

_____ , "John Ford and Platonic Love in the Court", *Studies in Philology* (1939), 36:206-26

_____ , "John Ford Revisited", *Studies in English Literature, 1500-1900* (1964), 4:195-216

Stavig, Mark, *John Ford and the Traditional Moral Order*. 1968. Pp. 122-43

Lover's Melancholy, 1628

Noletti, Arthur E., "The Form and Dramaturgy of John Ford's Tragi-Comedy", *Dissertation Abstracts International* (1974), 34:6600A

Perkin Warbeck, 1622

Anderson, Donald K., Jr., "Kingship in Ford's 'Perkin Warbeck' ", *ELH* (1960), 28:177-93

_____ , " 'Richard II' and 'Perkin Warbeck' ", *Shakespeare Quarterly* (1962), 13:260-63

Babb, L., "Abnormal Psychology in John Ford's 'Perkin Warbeck'", *Modern Language Notes* (1936), 51:234-37

Barish, Jonas A., "'Perkin Warbeck' as Anti-History", *Essays in Criticism* (Apr. 1970), 20:151-71

Bennett, Josephine Waters, Oscar Cargill and Vernon Hall, ed., *Studies in the English Renaissance Drama in Memory of Karl Julius Holzknecht.* 1959. Pp. 125-41

Kistner, A. L., "The Fine Balance of Imposture in John Ford's 'Perkin Warbeck'", *English Studies. A Journal of English Letters and Philology* (1971), 52:419-23

Sanna, Vittoria, "Problemi e Aspetti del 'Perkin Warbeck'", *Annali Instituto Universitario Orientale, Napoli, Sezione Germanica* (1965), 8:117-73

Schneider, Steven A., "The Dissonant Design: John Ford and the Art of Tragedy", *Dissertation Abstracts International* (1974), 35:1060A

Stavig, Mark, *John Ford and the Traditional Moral Order.* 1968. Pp. 168-84

Struble, M. D., "Indebtedness of Ford's 'Perkin Warbeck'", *Anglia* (Jan. 1925), 49:80-91

Ure, Peter, "A Pointer to the Date of Ford's 'Perkin Warbeck'", *Notes and Queries* (1970), 17:215-17

Weathers, Winston, "'Perkin Warbeck': A Seventeenth Century Psychological Play", *Studies in English Literature, 1500-1900* (1964), 4:217-26

The Queen; or, The Excellency of Her Sex, 1632

Noletti, Arthur E., "The Form and Dramaturgy of John Ford's Tragi-Comedy", *Dissertation Abstracts International* (1974), 34:6600A

'Tis Pity She's a Whore, 1629/33?

Adams, Henry Hitch, "English Domestic or, Homiletic Tragedy, 1575-1642" *Studies in English and Comparative Literature. Columbia* (1943), 159:160-83

Anderson, Donald K., Jr., "The Heart and the Banquet: Imagery in Ford's 'Tis Pity' and 'The Broken Heart'", *Studies in English Literature, 1500-1900* (1962), 2:209-17

Andriev, Lucette, "'Dommage qu'Elle Soit Une P. . . . ' de John Ford: Vitalité et Devenir Scemique de la Tragédie", *Cahiers, Elisabéthans: Etudes sur la Pre-Renaissance et la Renaissance Anglaises* (1973), 3:16-40

Bauer, G., "'Dommage qu'Elle Soit Une Prostituée: Critique", *Les Annales Politiques et Littéraires* (April 13, 1934), 102-414

Bawcutt, N. W., "Seneca and Ford's 'Tis Pity She's a Whore'", *Notes and Queries* (1967), 14:215

Bellessort, A., "'Dommage qu 'Elle Soit une Prostituée': Critique", *Journal des Debats* (April 13, 1934), 41 pt. 1:601-03

Bluestone, Max and Norman Rabkin, eds., *Shakespeare's Contemporaries; Modern Studies in English Renaissance Drama.* 2nd ed. 1970. Pp. 387-405

Boas, Frederick S., *An Introduction to Stuart Drama.* 1946. Pp. 342-47

Champion, L. S., "Ford's 'Tis Pity She's a Whore' and the Jacobean Tragic Perspective", *Modern Language Association. Publications.* (1975), 90:78-87

Ewing, S. Blaine, *Burtonian Melancholy in the Plays of John Ford.* 1940. Pp. 70-76

Hastings, William Thomson, ed., *Contemporary Essays.* 1928. Pp. 385-95

Herndl, George C., *The High Design; English Renaissance Tragedy and the Natural Law.* 1970. Pp. 259-67

Homan, Sidney R., Jr., "Shakespeare and Dekker as Keys to Ford's 'Tis Pity She's a Whore'", *Studies in English Literature, 1500-1900* (1967), 7:269-76

Hoy, Cyrus, "'Ignorance in Knowledge: Marlowe's Faustus and Ford's Giovanni", *Modern Philology* (Feb. 1960), 57:145-54

Kaufmann, R. J., "Ford's Tragic Perspective", *Texas Studies in Literature and Language* (Wint. 1960), 1:522-37

Kistner, Arthur L. and M. K., "The Dramatic Functions of Love in the Tragedies of John Ford", *Studies in Philology* (1973), 70:62-76

Levin, Richard, *The Multiple Plot in English Renaissance Drama*. 1971. Pp. 85-87

Lièvre, P., "'Dommage qu 'Elle Soit une Prostituée': Critique", *Mercure de France* (May 15, 1934), 252:137-39

MacCarthy, D., "'Tis Pity She's a Whore': Criticism", *New Statesman* (Feb. 3, 1923) 20:514-15

Matthews, Honor, *The Primal Curse; The Myth of Cain and Abel in the Theatre*. 1967. Pp. 74-81

Ornstein, Robert, *The Moral Vision of Jacobean Tragedy*. 1960. Pp. 203-13

Putt, S. Gorley, "The Modernity of John Ford", *English* (Sum. 1969), 18:47-52

Requa, Kenneth A., "Music in the Ear; Giovanni as Tragic Hero in Ford's 'Tis Pity She's a Whore'", *Papers on Language and Literature* (Wint. 1971), 7:13-25

Ribner, Irving, "By Nature's Light: The Morality of 'Tis Pity She's a Whore'", *Tulane Studies in English* (1960), 10:39-50

_____ , *Jacobean Tragedy; The Quest for Moral Order*. 1962. Pp. 163-74

Roberts, Jeanne Addison, "John Ford's Passionate Abstractions", *Southern Humanities Review* (1973), 7:322-32

Rosen, Carol C., "Language of Cruelty in Ford's 'Tis Pity She's a Whore'", *Comparative Drama* (1974-75), 8:356-68

Schneider, Steven A., "The Dissonant Design: John Ford and the Art of Tragedy", *Dissertation Abstracts International* (1974), 35:1060A

Sensabaugh, G. F., "John Ford and Elizabethan Tragedy", *Philological Quarterly* (1941), 20:442-53

_____ , "John Ford and Platonic Love in the Court", *Studies in Philology* (1939), 36:206-26

_____ , "John Ford Revisited", *Studies in English Literature, 1500-1900* (1964), 4:195-216

Shanks, E., "'Tis Pity She's a Whore': Criticism", *Outlook* (Feb. 3, 1923), 51:97

"'Tis Pitty Shees a Whore': Criticism", *Spectator* (Feb. 3, 1923), 130:184-85

Stavig, Mark, *John Ford and the Traditional Moral Order*. 1968. Pp. 95-121

Tomlinson, Thomas Brian, *A Study of Elizabethan and Jacobean Tragedy*. 1964. Pp. 272-76

Turner, W. J., "'Tis Pity She's a Whore': Criticism", *London Mercury* (March 1923), 7:534-36

Woolf, Virginia Stephen, *Collected Essays*. 1967. Pp. 54-61

JOHN FORD, WILLIAM ROWLEY AND THOMAS DEKKER

The Witch of Edmonton, 1621

Noletti, Arthur E., "The Form and Dramaturgy of John Ford's Tragi-Comedy", *Dissertation Abstracts International* (1974), 34:6600A

MAX FRISCH

Als der Krieg zu Ende War   *SEE*   When the War Came to an End

Andorra, 1961
Beckermann, Thomas, *Über Max Frisch*. 1971. Pp. 147-91
Christian Century, 79:1098, Sept. 12, 1962
deGroot, Hans, "Andorra", *Prompt* (1964), 4:37-38
Durzak, Manfred, *Dürrenmatt, Frisch, Weiss: Deutsches Drama Gegenwart Zwischen Kritik und Utopie*. 1972. Pp. 219-30
Esslin, Martin, *Reflections; Essays on Modern Theatre*. 1969. Pp. 90-104
Hammer, J. C., "The Humanism of Max Frisch; An Examination of Three of the Plays", *German Quarterly* (1969), 42:718-26
Hegele, Wolfgang "Max Frisch: 'Andorra' ", *Der Deutschunterricht* (1968), 20: 35-50
Hilty, Hans Rudolf, "Tabu 'Andorra'?", *Die Kulturelle Monatsschrift* (1962), 22 #5:52-54
Horst, Karl August "Andorra Mit Anderen Augen", *Merkur* (1962), 16:396-99
Jōsai Kinbun Kenkyu, *Studies in the Humanities*. 1973. Pp. 159-64
Kustow, Michael, "Andorra", *Encore* (Mar.-Apr. 1964), 11:49-50
Lumley, Frederick, *New Trends in Twentieth Century Drama; A Survey Since Ibsen and Shaw*. 1967. Pp. 233-39
Meinert, Dietrich, "Objektivität und Subjectivität des Existenzbewussteins in Max Frischs 'Andorra' ", *Acta Germanica* (1968), 2:117-24
New Republic, 148:28-29, March 9, 1963
New Yorker, 38:114, Feb. 16, 1963
Newsweek, 61:60, Feb. 25, 1963
Novick, Julius, *Beyond Broadway; The Quest for Permanent Theatres*. 1968. Pp. 130
"A Primer on Max Frisch", *Esquire*, 58:108, Oct., 1962
Rischbieter, H., " 'Andorra' in München, Frankfurt, und Düsseldorf", *Theatre Heute* (1962), 3:5-13
Saturday Review, 46:29, March 2, 1963
Schau, Albrecht, *Max Frisch; Beiträge zur Wirkungsgeschichte*. 1971. Pp. 248-99
Seiser, Robert, "Noch Einmal: Andorra. Ein Lehrstück Ohne Lehre", *Christengemeinschaft* (1962), 34:348-49
Time, 81:75, Feb. 22, 1963
Ziolkowski, Theodore, "Max Frisch; Moralist Without a Moral", *Yale French Studies*, #29:132-41, 1962

Biedermann and the Firebugs, 1958
Bauland, Peter, *The Hooded Eagle; Modern German Drama on the New York Stage*. 1968. Pp. 208-09
Beckermann, Thomas, *Über Max Frisch*. 1971. Pp. 137-46
Brewer, J. T., "Max Frisch's 'Biedermann und die Brandstifter' as the Documentation of an Author's Frustration", *Germanic Review* (Mar. 1971), 46:119-28
Cohn, Ruby, *Currents in Contemporary Drama*. 1969. Pp. 173-77
─────────── , "Hell on the 20th Century Stage", *Wisconsin Studies in Contemporary Literature* (Wint.-Spr. 1964), 5:48-53
Denk, Rudolf, "Vom Regiebuch zum Inzenierungsversuch mit dem Videorecorder. 'Biedermann und die Brandstifter' von Max Frisch als Einführung in das Verständnis des Theatralischen im Deutschunterricht", *Das Deutschunterricht* (1973), 25,H.5:129-42

Dàvišon, Dennis, "Max Frisch's 'The Fire Raisers' ", *Komos: A Quarterly of Drama and Arts of the Theatre* (1968), 1:147-51

Durzak, Manfred, *Dürrenmatt, Frisch, Weiss: Deutsches Drama Gegenwart Zwischen Kritik und Utopie.* 1972. Pp. 207-18

Esslin, Martin, *Brief Chronicles; Essays on Modern Theatre.* 1970. Pp. 101-03
————————, *Reflections; Essays on Modern Theatre.* 1969. Pp. 91-93

Harward, Timothy Blake, ed., *European Patterns; Contemporary Patterns in European Writing.* 1967. Pp. 54-59

Hill, Philip G., "A Reading of 'The Firebugs' ", *Modern Drama* (Sept. 1970), 13:184-90

Illustrated London News, 240:72, Jan. 13, 1962

Lumley, Frederick, *New Trends in Twentieth Century Drama; A Survey Since Ibsen and Shaw.* 1967. Pp. 233-39

McCormick, Dennis R., "Max Frisch's Dramaturgical Development", *Dissertation Abstracts International* (1973), 33:5186A

Neinert, Dietrich, "Das Absurde als Mittel der Verfremdung in Frischs 'Biedermann und die Brandstifter' ", *Acta Germanica* (1970), 5:227-35

New Republic, 148:29, March 9, 1963

New Statesman, 62:997, Dec. 29, 1961

New Yorker, 39:114, Feb. 23, 1963

Newsweek, 61:60, Feb. 25, 1963

Pickar, Gertrud B., "Biedermann und die Brandstifter: The Dilemma of Language," *Modern Languages* (1969), 50:99-105

Saturday Review, 46:29, March 2, 1963

Schau, Albrecht, *Max Frisch: Beiträge zur Wirkungsgeschichte.* 1971. Pp. 240-47

Spectator, 207:951, Dec. 29, 1961

Time, 81:75, Feb. 22, 1963

Weber, Brom, ed., *Sense and Sensibility in 20th Century Writing.* 1970. Pp. 57-74

Williams, Raymond, *Drama from Ibsen to Brecht.* 1968. Pp. 308-12

Bidermann und die Brandstifter   *SEE*   Biedermann and the Firebugs

Biografie   *SEE*   Biography

Biography, 1968
Cohn, Ruby, *Currents in Contemporary Drama.* 1969. Pp. 213-16

Durzak, Manfred, *Dürrenmatt, Frisch, Weiss; Deutsches Drama Gegenwart Zwischen Kritik und Utopie.* 1972. Pp. 231-42

McCormick, Dennis R., "Max Frisch's Dramaturgical Development", *Dissertation Abstracts International* (1973), 33:5186A

Musgrave, M. E., "Kurmann, His Wives and Helen, the Mulatta in Max Frisch's 'Biografie; Ein Spiel' ", *CLA Journal* (1975), 18:341-47

Pickar, Gertrud B., "From Place to Stage—An Evolution in the Dramatic Works of Max Frisch", *Seminar* (1973). 9:134-47
————————, "Max Frisch's 'Biografie': Image as 'Life-Script' ", *Symposium* (1974), 28:166-74

Schau, Albrecht, *Max Frisch: Beiträge zur Wirkungsgeschichte.* 1971. Pp. 300-20

The Chinese Wall, 1955
Beckermann, Thomas, *Über Max Frisch.* 1971. Pp. 116-36

Cohn, Ruby, *Currents in Contemporary Drama.* 1969. Pp. 210-12

Contrum, Peter, "Max Frisch's 'Die Chinesische Mauer': A New Approach to World Literature", *Revue des Langes Vivantes* (1970), 36:35-44

Durzak, Manfred, *Dürrenmatt, Frisch, Weiss: Deutsches Drama Gegenwart Zwischen Kritik und Utopie.* 1972. Pp. 174-84

Glaettli, Walter, "Max Frisch: A New German Playwright", *German Quarterly*, 25:248-54, 1952

Lumley, Frederick, *New Trends in Twentieth Century Drama; A Survey Since Ibsen and Shaw.* 1967. Pp. 233-39

Mordaunt, Jerrold L., ed., *Proceedings: Pacific Northwest Conference on Foreign Languages. 19th Annual Meeting, April 19-20, 1968.* 1968. Pp. 30-36

Novick, Julius, *Beyond Broadway; The Quest for Permanent Theatres.* 1968. Pp. 55-56

Schau, Albrecht, *Max Frisch: Beiträge zur Wirkungsgeschichte.* 1971. Pp. 211-33

Wagner, Marie, "Timeless Relevance; Max Frisch's 'The Chinese Wall' ", *Modern Drama* (1973), 16:149-56

Waldmann, G., "Das Verhängnis der Geschichtlichkeit, Max Frischs 'Die Chinesische Mauer' ", *Wirkend. Wort* (1967), 17:264-71

Ziolkowski, Theodore, "Max Frisch: Moralist Without a Moral", *Yale French Studies*, #29:132-41, 1962

Die Chinesische Mauer   SEE   The Chinese Wall

Count Öderland, 1951

Beckermann, Thomas, *Über Max Frisch.* 1971. Pp. 113-15

Durzak, Manfred. *Dürrenmatt, Frisch, Weiss: Deutsches Drama Gegenwart Zwischen Kritik und Utopie.* 1972. Pp. 185-95

Glaettli, Walter, "Max Frisch: A New German Playwright", *German Quarterly*, 25:248-54, 1952

Lumley, Frederick, *New Trends in Twentieth Century Drama; A Survey Since Ibsen and Shaw.* 1967. Pp. 233-39

Pickar, Gertrud B., "From Place to Stage—An Evolution in the Dramatic Works of Max Frisch", *Seminar* (1973), 9:134-47

Don Juan; oder, Die Liebe zur Geometrie   SEE   Don Juan; or The Love of Geometry

Don Juan; or, The Love of Geometry, 1953

Durzak, Manfred, *Dürrenmatt, Frisch, Weiss; Deutsches Drama Gegenwart Zwischen Kritik und Utopie.* 1972. Pp. 196-206

Elizalde, Ignacio, "El Teatro de Max Frisch", *Arbor* (1972), 81, #316:51-58

Franz, Hertha, "Der Intellektuelle in Max Frischs 'Don Juan' und 'Homo Faber' ", *Zeitschrift für Deutsche Philologie* (1971), 90:555-63

Gontrum, Peter, "Max Frisch's 'Don Juan'; A New Look at a Traditional Hero", *Comparative Literature Studies* (Univ. of Maryland), 2:117-23, 1965

Lumley, Frederick, *New Trends in Twentieth Century Drama; A Survey Since Ibsen and Shaw.* 1967. Pp. 233-39

Matthews, Robert J., "Theatricality and Deconstruction in Max Frisch's 'Don Juan' ", *Modern Language Notes* (1972), 87:742-52

Schau, Albrecht, *Max Frisch: Beiträge zur Wirkungsgeschichte.* 1971. Pp. 234-39

Graf Öderland   SEE   Count Öderland

Now They Sing Again, 1945
  Durzak, Manfred, *Dürrenmatt, Frisch, Weiss: Deutsches Drama Gegenwart Zwischen Kritik und Utopie*. 1972. Pp. 165-73
  Lumley, Frederick, *New Trends in Twentieth Century Drama; A Survey Since Ibsen and Shaw*. 1967. Pp. 233-39
  Hammer, J. C., "The Humanism of Max Frisch; An Examination of Three of the Plays", *German Quarterly* (1969), 42:718-26
  Pickar, Gertrud B., "From Place to Stage—An Evolution in the Dramatic Works of Max Frisch", *Seminar* (1973), 9:134-47
  Schau, Albrecht, *Max Frisch: Beiträge zur Wirkungsgeschichte*. 1971. Pp. 198-210
  Ziolkowski, Theodore, "Max Frisch; Moralist Without a Moral", *Yale French Studies*, #29:132-41, 1962

Nun Singen Sie Wieder   *SEE*   Now They Sing Again

Santa Cruz, 1946
  Durzak, Manfred, *Dürrenmatt, Frisch, Weiss; Deutsches Drama Gegenwart Zwischen Kritik und Utopie*. 1972. Pp. 156-64
  Lumley, Frederick, *New Trends in Twentieth Century Drama; A Survey Since Ibsen and Shaw*. 1967. Pp. 233-39
  Pickar, Gertrud B., "From Place to Stage—An Evolution in the Dramatic Works of Max Frisch", *Seminar* (1973), 9:134-47

When the War Came to an End, 1948
  Glaettli, Walter, "Max Frisch: A New German Playwright", *German Quarterly*, 25:248-54, 1952
  Hammer, J. C., "The Humanism of Max Frisch; An Examination of Three of the Plays", *German Quarterly* (1969), 42:718-26
  Lumley, Frederick, *New Trends in Twentieth Century Drama; A Survey Since Ibsen and Shaw*. 1967. Pp. 233-39
  Pickar, Gertrud B., "From Place to Stage—An Evolution in the Dramatic Works of Max Frisch", *Seminar* (1973), 9:134-47

CHRISTOPHER FRY

Boy With a Cart, 1950
  Ferguson, John, " 'The Boy with a Cart' ", *Modern Drama*, 8:284-92, 1965
  Lecky, Eleazer, "Mystery in the Plays of Christopher Fry", *Tulane Drama Review*, 4:80-87, 1960
  Redman, Ben Ray, "Christopher Fry: Poet-Dramatist", *College English*, 14:191-97, 1953
  Roy, Emil, *Christopher Fry*. 1968. Pp. 31-36
  Saturday Review, 37:32, May 1, 1954
  Spears, M. K., "Christopher Fry and the Redemption of Joy", *Poetry*, 78:28-43, April 1951

Curtmantle, 1961
  Becker, Siegfried, "Christopher Fry: 'Curtmantle' ", *Die Neueren Sprachen* (1967), 16:545-51
  Browne, E. Martin, "Henry II as Hero: Christopher Fry's New Play: 'Curtmantle' ", *Drama Survey* (1962), 2:63-71
  Cohn, Ruby, *Currents in Contemporary Drama*. 1969. Pp. 104-06
  Dierickx, J., "King and Archbishop: Henry II and Becket from Tennyson to Fry", *Revue des Langues Vivantes* (1962), 28:424-35

English (Oxford), 14:150-51, Spring, 1963
Illustrated London News, 241:622, Oct. 20, 1962
"Kritische Ruckschau", *Forum* (1961), 8:379
Lumley, Frederick, *New Trends in Twentieth Century Drama; A Survey Since Ibsen and Shaw*. 1967. Pp. 283-89
New Statesman, 64:333, Sept. 14, 1962
Parker, Gerald, "A Study of Christopher Fry's 'Curtmantle'", *Dalhousie Review* (1963), 43:200-11
Roy, Emil, *Christopher Fry*. 1968. Pp. 122-39
_____ , "Christopher Fry as Tragicomedian", *Modern Drama* (1968), 11:40-47
_____ , "The Beckett Plays: Eliot, Fry and Anouilh", *Modern Drama*, 8:268-76, 1965
Spectator, 209:596, Oct. 19, 1962
Time, 77:84, March 10, 1961
Woodfield, J., "Christopher Fry's 'Curtmantle': The Form of Unity", *Modern Drama* (1974), 17:307-18

The Dark Is Light Enough, 1954
America, 92:657, March 19, 1955
Baxter, K. M., *Speak What We Feel: A Christian Looks at the Contemporary Theatre*, London, 1964. Pp. 72-74, 76-80
Catholic World, 181:65, April, 1955
Chiari, J., *Landmarks of Contemporary Drama*, London, 1965, Pp. 103-04
Commonweal, 62:78, April 22, 1955
Donoghue, Denis, "Christopher Fry's Theatre of Words", *Essays in Criticism* (1959), 9:37-49
Hudson Review, 8:258-63, Summer, 1955
Illustrated London News, 224:806, May, 15, 1954
Lecky, Eleazer, "Mystery in the Plays of Christopher Fry", *Tulane Drama Review*, 4:80-87, 1960
Life, 38:105-06, April 11, 1955
Lumley, Frederick, *New Trends in Twentieth Century Drama; A Survey Since Ibsen and Shaw*. 1967. Pp. 283-89
Nation, 180:226, March 12, 1955
New Statesman, 47:596, May 8, 1954 and 48:262-63, Sept. 4, 1954
New Yorker, 30:58, May 29, 1954 and 31:67, March 5, 1955
Newsweek, 45:85, March 7, 1955
Oppel, Horst, *Das Moderne Englische Drama; Interpretationen*, 1963, Pp. 303-16
Roy, Emil, *Christopher Fry*. 1968. Pp. 110-21
Saturday Review, 37:39, April 3, 1954 and 38:26, March 12, 1955
Sewanee Review, 63:270-80, Spring, 1955
Spectator, 192:541, May 7, 1954
Theatre Arts, 39:72-75, Feb., 1955 and 39:26, March, 1955 and 39:17, 22 May, 1955
Time, 65:92, March 7, 1955
Twentieth Century, 156:179-83, Aug., 1954

Firstborn, 1948
Alexander, John, "Christopher Fry and Religious Comedy", *Meanjin*, 15:77-81, 1956
America, 99:243-44, May 17, 1958

Catholic World, 187:310, July, 1958

Christian Century, 74:201, Feb. 13, 1957 and 75:646, May 28, 1958

Clurman, Harold, *The Divine Pastime; Theatre Essays*. 1974. Pp. 45-49

Commonweal, 68:205-06, May 23, 1958

Lecky, Eleazer, "Mystery in the Plays of Christopher Fry", *Tulane Drama Review*, 4:80-87, 1960

Mandel, O., "Theme in the Drama of Christopher Fry", *Etudes Anglaises* (1957), 10:335-49

Nation, 186:456, May 17, 1958

New Statesman, 43:152, Feb. 9, 1952

New Yorker, 34:83-84, May 10, 1958

Redman, Ben Ray, "Christopher Fry: Poet-Dramatist", *College English*, 14:191-97, 1953

Roy, Emil, *Christopher Fry*. 1968. Pp. 37-48

_____ , "Christopher Fry as Tragicomedian", *Modern Drama* (1968), 11:40-47

Saturday Review, 41:29, May 17, 1958

Spears, M. K., "Christopher Fry and the Redemption of Joy", *Poetry*, 78:28-43, April, 1951

Spectator, 188:173, Feb. 8, 1952

Stanford, Derek, "Comedy and Tragedy in Christopher Fry", *Modern Drama* (1959), 2:3-7

_____ , "Comedy and Tragedy in Christopher Fry", *Month* (1959), 207:307-12

Time, 71:66, May 12, 1958

Lady's Not for Burning, 1948

Adler, Jacob H., "Shakespeare and Christopher Fry", *Educational Theatre Journal* (1959), 11:85-98

America, 96:656, March 9, 1957

Astre, Georges-Albert, "Christopher Fry et la Résurrection du Poème Dramatique", *Critique*, 7:16-25, 1951

Barnes, Lewis W., "Christopher Fry; The Chestertonian Concept of Comedy", *Xavier University Studies* (Mar. 1963), 2:30-47

Catholic World, 172:306, Jan., 1951

Christian Science Monitor Magazine, Pp. 4, Nov. 18, 1950

Commonweal, 53:196, Dec. 1, 1950

Kernodle, George R., *Invitation to the Theatre*. 1967. Pp. 232-33

Life, 29:141-42, Nov. 27, 1950

Life and Letters, 62:220-24, Sept., 1949

Lumley, Frederick, *New Trends in Twentieth Century Drama; A Survey Since Ibsen and Shaw*. 1967. Pp. 283-89

Morgenstern, Charles, "Fantastical Banquet," *Theatre Arts*, 35:26-30, 1951

Nation, 171:466, Nov. 18, 1950

New Republic, 123:22, Nov. 27, 1950

New Statesman and Nation, 35:233, March 20, 1948

New Yorker, 26:77, Nov. 18, 1950

Newsweek, 36:90, Nov. 20, 1950

Redman, Ben Ray, "Christopher Fry: Poet-Dramatist", *College English*, 14:191-97, 1953

Roy, Emil, *British Drama Since Shaw*. 1972. Pp. 95-97

_____ , *Christopher Fry*. 1968. Pp. 59-75

_____ , "Christopher Fry as Tragicomedian", *Modern Drama* (1968), 11:40-47

Saturday Review of Literature, 33:46, Dec. 2, 1950

School and Society, 73:180-81, March 24, 1951

Scott-James, R. A., "Christopher Fry's Poetic Drama", *Nation*, 171:315-16, 1950

Selz, J., "Christopher Fry et le Théâtre Confidentiel", *Lettres Nouvelles* (Paris), 9:152-55, 1961

Spears, M. K., "Christopher Fry and the Redemption of Joy", *Poetry*, 78:28-43, April, 1951

Spectator, 182:678, May 20, 1949

Stanford, Derek, "Comedy and Tragedy in Christopher Fry", *Modern Drama* (1959), 2:3-7

Stemmler, Theo, "Zur Deutung der Eigennamen in der Komödien Christopher Frys", *Archiv für das Studium der Neueren Sprachen und Literaturen* (1963), 200:198-201

Theatre Arts, 35:13, Jan., 1951

Time, 56:58-64, Nov. 20, 1950

Urang, Gunnar, "The Climate is the Comedy; A Study of Christopher Fry's 'The Lady's Not for Burning' ", *Christian Scholar*, 46:61-86, 1963

Vox, Nelvin, "The Comedy of Faith: The Drama of Christopher Fry", *Gordon Review* (1964-65), 8:139-50

Wiersma, S. M., "Spring and Apocalypse, Law and Prophets; A Reading of Christopher Fry's 'The Lady's Not for Burning' ", *Modern Drama* (Feb. 1971), 13:432-47

Woodbury, John, "The Witch and the Nun: A Study of 'The Lady's Not for Burning' ", *Manitoba Arts Review*, 10:41-54, 1956

A Phoenix Too Frequent, 1946

Cabaniss, Allen, "The Matron of Ephesus Again", *University of Mississippi Studies in English* (1961), 2:41-53

Catholic World, 171:227, June, 1950

Christian Science Monitor Magazine, Pp. 9, May 6, 1950

Commonweal, 52:152, May 19, 9150

Koziol, H., "Les Drames de Christopher Fry", *Die Neueren Sprachen*, #1:1-14, 1955

Lecky, Eleazer, "Mystery in the Plays of Christopher Fry", *Tulane Drama Review*, 4:80-87, 1960

Morgenstern, Charles, "Fantastical Banquet", *Theatre Arts*, 35:26-30, 1951

Nation, 170:457, May 13, 1950

New Republic, 122:21, May 15, 1950

New Yorker, 26:52, May 6, 1950

Newsweek, 35:80, May 8, 1950

Redman, Ben Ray, "Christopher Fry: Poet-Dramatist", *English Journal*, 42:1-7, 1953

Roy, Emil, *Christopher Fry*. 1968. Pp. 49-58

_____ , "Christopher Fry as Tragicomedian", *Modern Drama* (1968), 11:40-47

Stemmler, Theo, "Bukolische Elemente in Christopher Frys 'A Phoenix Too Frequent' ", *Monatsschrift* (1963), 13:209-13

_____ , "Zur Deutung der Eigennamen in den Komödien Christopher Frys", *Archiv für das Studium der Neueren Sprachen und Literaturen* (1963), 200:198-201

Theatre Arts, 34:15, July, 1950
Wiersma, Stanley M., "'A Phoenix Too Frequent': A Study in Source and Symbol", *Modern Drama*, 8:293-302, 1965

A Sleep of Prisoners, 1951
Catholic World, 174:226, Dec., 1951
Commonweal, 55:92, Nov. 2, 1951
Kernodle, George R., *Invitation to the Theatre*. 1967. Pp. 233-34
Kleiwar, Warren, "An Alternative to Realistic Form", *Response* (1966), 7:163-70
Koziol, H., "Les Drames de Christopher Fry", *Die Neueren Sprachen*, #1:1-14; 1955
Lecky, Eleazer, "Mystery in the Plays of Christopher Fry", *Tulane Drama Review*, 4:80-87, 1960
Life, 31:73-75, Nov. 12, 1951
Lumley, Frederick, *New Trends in Twentieth Century Drama; A Survey Since Ibsen and Shaw*. 1967. Pp. 283-89
Matthews, Honor, *The Primal Curse; The Myth of Cain and Abel in the Theatre.* 1967. Pp. 187-89
Nation, 173:381, Nov. 3, 1951
New Republic, 124:23, June 11, 1951 and 125:22, Nov. 12, 1951
New Statesman and Nation, 41:591, May 26, 1951
New York Times Magazine, Pp. 58-59, May 20, 1951
New Yorker, 27:66, Oct. 27, 1951
Newsweek, 38:84, Oct. 29, 1951
Oppel, Horst, *Das Moderne Englische Drama; Interpretationen*, 1963, Pp. 267-88
Redman, Ben Ray, "Christopher Fry: Poet-Dramatist", *English Journal*, 42:1-7, 1953
Roy, Emil, *Christopher Fry*. 1968. Pp. 98-109
_____ , "Christopher Fry as Tragicomedian", *Modern Drama* (1968), 11:40-47
Saturday Review, 35:22, March 1, 1952
Saturday Review of Literature, 34:60, Nov. 17, 1951
School and Society, 74:406-07, Dec. 22, 1951
Spanos, William V., *The Christian Tradition in Modern British Verse Drama; The Poetics of Sacramental Time*. 1967. Pp. 294-324
Spanos, W. V., "Christopher Fry's 'A Sleep of Prisoners': The Choreography of Comedy", *Modern Drama*, 8:58-72, May, 1965
Survey, 87:526, Dec., 1951
Theatre Arts, 35:3, Dec., 1951 and 36:20, Jan., 1952
Time, 57:70-71, May 28, 1951 and 58:38, Oct. 29, 1951

Thor, With Angels, 1948
Christian Century, 73:1453, Dec. 12, 1956
Commonweal, 65:175, Nov. 16, 1956
Roy, Emil, *Christopher Fry*. 1968. Pp. 76-82
_____ , "Christopher Fry as Tragicomedian", *Modern Drama* (1968), 11:40-47
Spears, M. K., "Christopher Fry and the Redemption of Joy", *Poetry*, 78:28-43, 1951

Venus Observed, 1950
Adler, Jacob H., "Shakespeare and Christopher Fry", *Educational Theatre Journal* (1959), 11:85-98
Astre, Georges-Albert, "Christopher Fry et la Résurrection du Poème Dramatique", *Critique*, 7:16-25, 1951
Barnes, Lewis W., "Christopher Fry: The Chestertonian Concept of Comedy", *Xavier University Studies* (Mar. 1963), 2:30-47
Catholic World, 175:69, April, 1952
Clurman, Harold, *The Divine Pastime; Theatre Essays*. 1974. Pp. 45-49
Commonweal, 55:543, March 7, 1952
Erzgräber, Willi, "Zur Liebesthematik in Christopher Frys Komödie 'Venus Observed' ", *Die Neueren Sprachen*, 1961, Pp. 57-74
Illustrated London News, 216:228, Feb. 11, 1950
Life and Letters, 65:54-59, April, 1950
Nation, 17:237, March 8, 1952
New Republic, 122:21-22, June 5, 1950 and 126:23, March 3, 1952
New Statesman and Nation, 39:96-97, Jan. 28, 1950
New Yorker, 25:85, Feb. 11, 1950 and 28:58, Feb. 23, 1952
Newsweek, 39:95, Feb. 25, 1952
Oppel, Horst, *Das Moderne Englische Drama: Interpretationen*. 1963, Pp. 242-66
Roy, Emil, *Christopher Fry*. 1968. Pp. 83-97
_____ , "Christopher Fry as Tragicomedian", *Modern Drama* (1968), 11:40-47
Saturday Review, 35:20-22, March 1, 1952 and 35:26, May 10, 1952
School and Society, 75:183-84, March 22, 1952
Scott-James, R. A., "Christopher Fry's Poetic Drama", *Nation*, 171:315-16, 1950
Selz, J., "Christopher Fry et le Théâtre Confidentiel", *Lettres Nouvelles* (Paris), 9:152-55, 1961
Spears, M. K., "Christopher Fry and the Redemption of Joy", *Poetry*, 78:28-43, 1951
Stemmler, Theo, "Zur Deutung der Eigennamen in der Komödie Christopher Frys", *Archiv für das Studium der Neueren Sprachen und Literaturen* (1963), 200:198-201
Theatre Arts, 34:29, Dec., 1950 and 36:18-19, April, 1952
Time, 59:80, Feb. 25, 1952

JOHN GALSWORTHY

Bit of Love, 1915
Nation, 120:635-36, June 3, 1925

Escape, 1926
American Mercury, 13:118-20, Jan., 1928
Catholic World, 126:379-80, Dec., 1927
English Review, 43:471, Oct., 1926
Living Age, 330:673-76, Sept. 25, 1926 and 331:340-45, Nov. 15, 1926
Nation, 125:553-54, Nov. 16, 1927
Nation (London), 39:584-85, Aug. 21, 1926
New Republic, 52:311-12, Nov. 9, 1927
New Statesman, 27:642, Sept. 18, 1926

Outlook, 147:308-09, Nov. 9, 1927
Outlook (London), 58:177, Aug. 21, 1926
Saturday Review, 142:200-01, Aug. 21, 1926
Saturday Review of Literature, 4:299-300, Nov. 12, 1927
Spectator, 137:275, Aug. 21, 1926
Theatre Arts Anthology; A Record and a Prophecy, Theatre Arts Books, 1950,
   Pp. 606-09

Exiled, 1929
   English Review, 243:4, Aug., 1929
   Nation (London), 45:432, June 29, 1929
   New Statesman, 33:402-03, July 6, 1929
   Saturday Review, 147:860-61, June 29, 1929
   Spectator, 142:1005-06, June 29, 1929

Family Man, 1922
   New Statesman, 29:711, Sept. 17, 1927

Forest, 1924
   English Review, 38:599-602, April, 1924
   New Statesman, 22:667, March 15, 1924
   Outlook (London), 53:176, March 15, 1924
   Saturday Review, 137:258-59, March 15, 1924

Fugitive, 1913
   English Review, 15:625-27, Nov., 1913
   Yale Review, n. s. 11:298-303, 1922

Justice, 1910
   Bache, William B., " 'Justice': Galsworthy's Dramatic Tragedy", *Modern Drama*,
      3:138-42, 1960
   Beerbohm, Max, *Around Theatres*, 1953, Pp. 563-68
   Bookman, 43:340-42, May, 1916
   Current Opinion, 60:324-28, May, 1916
   Harper's Weekly, 62:440, April 22, 1916
   Literary Digest, 52:1220-21, April 29, 1916
   Nation, 102:419-20, April 13, 1916
   New Republic, 6:294, April 15, 1916
   Oppel, Horst, *Das Moderne Englische Drama; Interpretationen*. 1963. Pp. 109-
      25
   Outlook, 113:246-48, May 31, 1916
   Spectator, 104:339, Feb. 26, 1910 and 128:207, Feb. 18, 1922 and 154:654,
      April 19, 1935

Loyalties, 1922
   Bookman, 56:476-78, Dec., 1922 and 63:161-65, April, 1926
   Catholic World, 116:507-09, Jan., 1923
   English Review, 47:485, Oct., 1928
   Fortnightly, 118:349-52, Aug., 1922
   Independent, 110:32-34, Jan. 6, 1923
   Nation, 115:420, Oct. 18, 1922
   New Republic, 32:277-78, Nov. 8, 1922
   New Statesman, 31:588-89, Aug. 18, 1928
   Spectator, 128:398, April 1, 1922

The Mob, 1914
  MacCarthy, Sir Desmond, *Theatre.*   1955. Pp. 107-12
  New Republic, 1:27-28, Nov. 7, 1914

Old English, 1924
  English Review, 39:861-63, Dec., 1924
  Nation, 120:49-50, Jan. 14, 1925
  Outlook (London), 54:313, Nov. 1, 1924
  Saturday Review, 138:444-46, Nov. 1, 1924
  Spectator, 133:734, Nov. 15, 1924

Roof, 1929
  Catholic World, 134:333, Dec., 1931
  English Review, 49:764-66, Dec., 1929
  Saturday Review, 148:508, Nov. 2, 1929
  Spectator, 143:711-12, Nov. 16, 1929
  Theatre Arts, 16:19, Jan., 1932

Show, 1925
  English Review, 41:288-90, Aug., 1925
  Living Age, 326:337, Aug. 8, 1925
  Outlook (London), 56:25, July 11, 1925
  Saturday Review, 140:38-39, July 11, 1925
  Spectator, 135:100, July 18, 1925

Silver Box, 1906
  Saturday Review, 146:604-05, Nov. 10, 1928
  Spectator, 128:398, April 1, 1922

Skin Game, 1920
  Drama, 12:122, Jan., 1922
  Fortnightly, 113:961-65, June, 1920
  Literary Digest, 67:30, Nov. 6, 1920
  Nation (London), 27:137-38, May 1, 1920
  New Statesman, 15:134-35, May 8, 1920
  Review, 3:454-55, Nov. 10, 1920

Windows, 1922
  Freeman, 8:186, Oct. 31, 1923
  Nation (London), 31:202-04, May 6, 1922
  New Statesman, 19:94-95, April 29, 1922
  New Statesman and Nation, 3:93-94, Jan. 23, 1932
  Spectator, 128:559, May 6, 1922

FEDERICO GARCÍA LORCA

El Amor de Don Perlimplin con Belisa en su Jardin   *SEE*   The Love of Don Perlimplin for Belisa in His Garden

Así Que Pasen Cinco Años   *SEE*   When Five Years Passes

The Audience, 1934
  Higginbotham, Virginia, *The Comic Spirit of Federico Garcia Lorca.*   1976.
    Pp. 64-68.

Lumley, Frederick, *New Trends in Twentieth Century Drama; A Survey Since Ibsen and Shaw*. 1967. Pp. 92-104

Newberry, Wilma, "Aesthetic Distance in García Lorca's 'El Público' and Pirandello and Ortega", *Hispanic Review* (1969), 37:276-96

Blood Wedding, 1933

Allen, Rupert C., *Psyche and Symbol in the Theater of Federico Garcia Lorca*. 1974. Pp. 161-212

Barnes, Robert, "The Fusion of Poetry and Drama in 'Blood Wedding' ", *Modern Drama*, 2:395-402, 1960

Burton, Julianne, "Society and the Tragic Vision in Federico Garcia Lorca", *Dissertation Abstracts International* (1972), 33:2362A

Catholic World, 169:65, April, 1949

Cobb, Carl W., *Federico Garcia Lorca*. 1967. Pp. 130-35

Commonweal, 49:542-43, March 11, 1949 and 62:473, Aug. 12, 1955

Cuadra Pinto, Fernando, "Para un Analisis de 'Bodas de Sangre' ", *Revista Signos de Valparaiso* (1969), 3:97-116

Dickson, Ronald J., "Archetypal Symbolism in Lorca's 'Bodas de Sangre,' ", *Literature and Psychology* (New York), 10:76-79, 1960

Durzak, Manfred, et als, *Texte und Kontexte: Studien zur Deutschen und Vergleichenden Literaturwissenschaft. Festschrift für Norbert Fuerst zum 65. Geburtstag*. 1973. Pp. 43-79

Forum, 3:164, March, 1949

Freedman, Morris, *The Moral Impulse; Modern Drama from Ibsen to the Present*. 1967. Pp. 89-98

Gaskell, Ronald, *Drama and Reality; The European Theatre since Ibsen*. 1972. Pp. 106-16

Goldfaden, Bruce M., " 'Bodas de Sangre' and 'La Dama del Alba' ", *Hispania*, 54:234-36, 1961

Gonzalez-del-Valle, Luis, " 'Bodas de Sangre' y Sus Elementos Tragicos", *Archivum* (1971), 21:95-120

_____ , "Justicia Poetica en 'Bodas de Sangre' ll, *Romance Notes* (1972), 14:236-41

Halliburton, Charles L., "Garcia Lorca, the Tragedian; An Aristotelian Analysis of 'Bodas de Sangre' ", *Revista de Estudios Hispánicos* (1968), 2:35-40

Higginbotham, Virginia, *The Comic Spirit of Federico Garcia Lorca*. 1976. Pp. 90-97

Hutman, Norma L., "Inside the Circle; On Rereading 'Blood Wedding' ", *Modern Drama* (1973), 16:329-36

Kernodle, George R., *Invitation to the Theatre*. 1967. Pp. 231-32

Lewis, Allan, *The Contemporary Theatre; The Significant Playwrights of Our Time*. 1962. Pp. 242-58

Lumley, Frederick, *New Trends in Twentieth Century Drama; A Survey Since Ibsen and Shaw*. 1967. Pp. 92-104

Nathan, George Jean, *Theatre Book of the Year, 1948-49*. Pp. 266-69

Nonoyama, Minako, "Vida y Muerte en 'Bodas de Sangre' ", *Arbor: Revista General de Investigacion y Cultura* (1972), 324:5-13

Palley, Julian, "Archetypal Symbols in 'Bodas de Sangre' ", *Hispania* (1967), 50:74-79

Platt, Joseph, "The Maternal Theme in Garcia Lorca's Folk Tragedies", *Dissertation Abstracts International* (1973), 34:787A

School and Society, 69:155, Feb. 26, 1949

Theatre Arts, 33:24, 26, May, 1949

Timm, John T. H., "Some Critical Observations on Garcia Lorca's 'Bodas de Sangre'", Revista de Estudios Hispanicos (1973), 7:255-88

Villegas, Juan, "El Leitmotiv del Caballo en 'Bodas de Sangre'", Hispanófila (1967), 29:21-36

Williams, Raymond, Drama from Ibsen to Brecht. 1968. Pp. 167-70

Zimbardo, R. A., "The Mythic Pattern in Lorca's 'Blood Wedding'", Modern Drama (1968), 10:364-71

Bodas de Sangre SEE Blood Wedding

La Casa de Bernarda Alba SEE The House of Bernarda Alba

Doña Rosita the Spinster; or, The Language of the Flowers, 1935

Cobb, Carl W., Federico Garcia Lorca, 1967. Pp. 127-30

Devoto, D., "'Doña Rosita la Soltera': Estructura y Fuentes", Bulletin Hispanique (1967), 69:407-35

Higginbotham, Virginia, The Comic Spirit of Federico Garcia Lorca. 1976. Pp. 102-11

Higginbotham, Virginia, "Lorca and Twentieth Century Spanish Theater: Three Precursors", Modern Drama (1972), 15:164-74

Lumley, Frederick, New Trends in Twentieth Century Drama; A Survey Since Ibsen and Shaw. 1967. Pp. 92-104

Wells, C. Michael, "The Natural Norm in the Plays of Federico Garcia Lorca", Hispanic Review (1970), 38:299-313

The House of Bernarda Alba, 1936

Alvarez-Altman, Grace, "Charactonyms in Garcia Lorca's 'House of Bernarda Alba'", Onomastica Canadiana (1973), 46:3-11

Arce de Vázquez, Margot, "La Casa de Bernarda Alba", Sin Nombre (1970), 1,ii:5-14

Bahner, Werner, ed., Beiträge zur Französischen Aufklärung und zur Spanischen Literatur: Festgabe für Werner Kraus zum 70. Geburtstag. 1971. Pp. 555-84

Bentley, Eric Russell, In Search of Theatre. 1953. Pp. 215-32

Bluefarb, S., "Life and Death in Garcia Lorca's 'House of Bernarda Alba'", Drama Survey, 4:109-20 Summer, 1965

Bull, Judith M., "'Saneta Barbara' and 'La Casa de Bernarda Alba'", Bulletin of Hispanic Studies (1970), 47:117-23

Burton, Juliane, "Society and the Tragic Vision in Federico Garcia Lorca", Dissertation Abstracts International (1972), 33:2362A

Christian Science Monitor Magazine, Pp. 8, May 20, 1950

Cobb, Carl W., Federico Garcia Lorca. 1967. Pp. 138-41

Commonweal, 53:398, Jan. 26, 1951 and 62:475, Aug. 1955

Freedman, Morris, The Moral Impulse; Modern Drama from Ibsen to the Present. 1967. Pp. 89-98

Goldfaden, Bruce M., "'Bodas de Sangre' and 'La Dama del Alba'", Hispania, 44:234-36, 1961

Greenfield, Sumner M., "Poetry and Stagecraft in 'La Casa de Bernarda Alba'", Hispania, 38:456-61, 1955

Higginbotham, Virginia, "Bernarda Alba: A Comic Character", Drama Survey (1968), 6:258-65

——————————— , *The Comic Spirit of Frederico Garcia Lorca*. 1976. Pp. 111-19

——————————— , "Lorca and Twentieth Century Spanish Theater: Three Precursors", *Modern Drama* (1972), 15:164-74

Jimenez Vera, Arturo, "Violence in 'La Casa de Bernarda Alba' ", *Rivista di Letterature Moderne e Comparate* (1974), 27:45-49

Lumley, Frederick, *New Trends in Twentieth Century Drama; A Survey Since Ibsen and Shaw*. 1967. Pp. 92-104

"La Maison de Bernarda Alba", *New Statesman and Nation*, 31:469, June 29, 1946

Nathan, George Jean, *Theatre Book of the Year, 1950-51*, Pp. 175-80

Nation, 172:66, Jan. 20, 1951

New Republic, 124:22, Feb. 5, 1951

New Yorker, 26:54, Jan. 20, 1951

Platt, Joseph, "The Maternal Theme in Garcia Lorca's Folk Tragedies", *Dissertation Abstracts International* (1973), 34:787A

Samatan, M. E., "El Tema de la Mujer en Garcia Lorca", *Universidad* (Argent.), #60:55-69, 1964

School and Society, 73:100, Feb. 17, 1951

Sharp, Thomas F., "The Mechanics of Lorca's Drama in 'La Casa de Bernarda Alba' ", *Hispania*, 44:230-33, 1961

Theatre Arts, 35:17, March, 1951

Young, R. A., "Garcia Lorca's 'La Casa de Bernarda Alba': A Microcosm of Spanish Culture", *Modern Languages* (1969), 50:66-72

The Love of Don Perlimplin for Belisa in His Garden, 1933

Allen, Rupert C., *Psyche and Symbol in the Theater of Federico Garcia Lorca*. 1974. Pp. 3-112

Bogard, Travis and Oliver, William Irvin, eds., *Modern Drama; Essays in Criticism*. 1965. Pp. 209-18

Feal-Deibe, Carlos, "Lorca's Two Farces: 'Don Perlimplin' and 'Don Cristobal' ", *American Imago* (Wint. 1970), 27:358-78

Fergusson, F., " 'Don Perlimplin': Lorca's Theatre Poetry", *Kenyon Review*, 17:337-48, 1955

Higginbotham, Virginia, *The Comic Spirit of Federico Garcia Lorca*. 1976. Pp. 32-39

Josephs, Frederick A., "An Analysis of Dramatic Technique in Garcia Lorca's Early Theater", *Dissertation Abstracts International* (1973), 34:320A

Lumley, Frederick, *New Trends in Twentieth Century Drama; A Survey Since Ibsen and Shaw*. 1967. Pp. 92-104

El Maleficio de la Mariposa SEE The Witchery of the Butterfly

Mariana Pineda, 1927

Cobb, Carl W., *Federico Garcia Lorca*. 1967. Pp. 119-21

Cole, Toby, ed., *Playwrights on Playwriting; The Meaning and Making of Modern Drama from Ibsen to Ionesco*. 1960. Pp. 228-31

Doménech, Ricardo, "A Propósito de 'Mariana Pineda' ", *Cuadernos Hispano-americanos* (1967), 70:608-13

Josephs, Frederick A., "An Analysis of Dramatic Technique in Garcia Lorca's Early Theater", *Dissertation Abstracts International* (1973), 34:320A

Lumley, Frederick, *New Trends in Twentieth Century Drama; A Survey Since Ibsen and Shaw.* 1967. Pp. 92-104
Nation, 184:508, June 8, 1957

El Publico *SEE* The Audience

The Puppet Play of Don Cristóbal, 1933
Higginbotham, Virginia, *The Comic Spirit of Federico García Lorca.* 1976. Pp. 74-79
Josephs, Frederick A., "An Analysis of Dramatic Technique in Garcia Lorca's Early Theater", *Dissertation Abstracts International* (1973), 34:320A
Lumley, Frederick, *New Trends in Twentieth Century Drama; A Survey Since Ibsen and Shaw.* 1967. Pp. 92-104

El Retabillo de Don Cristóbal *SEE* The Puppet Play of Don Cristobal

The Shoemaker's Prodigious Wife, 1931
Cobb, Carl W., *Federico Garcia Lorca.* 1967. Pp. 124-27
Cole, Toby, ed., *Playwrights on Playwriting; The Meaning and Making of Modern Drama from Ibsen to Ionesco.* 1960. Pp. 231-32
Higginbotham, Virginia, *The Comic Spirit of Federico Garcia Lorca.* 1976. Pp. 30-32
Josephs, Frederick A., "An Analysis of Dramatic Technique in Garcia Lorca's Early Theater", *Dissertation Abstracts International* (1973), 34:320A
Lumley, Frederick, *New Trends in Twentieth Century Drama; A Survey Since Ibsen and Shaw.* 1967. Pp. 92-104
Muller, Gerd, "Lorcas 'La Zapatera Prodigiosa' als Manifest Dichterischer Verfemdung", *Die Neueren Sprachen* (1973), 22:439-47
Rincón, Carlos, " 'La Zapatera Prodigioso' de Federico Garcia Lorca—Ensayo de Interpretación", *Ibero-Romania* (1970), 2:290-313

When Five Years Passes, 1936
Higginbotham, Virginia, *The Comic Spirit of Federico Garcia Lorca.* 1976. Pp. 54-64
Knight, R. G., "Federico Garcia Lorca's 'Asi Que Pasen Cinco Años' ", *Bulletin of Hispanic Studies* (1966), 43:32-46
Lumley, Frederick, *New Trends in Twentieth Century Drama; A Survey Since Ibsen and Shaw.* 1967. Pp. 92-104
New Yorker, 38:103-04, May 19, 1962
Theatre Arts, 46:57, Aug. 1962

The Witchery of the Butterfly, 1920
Josephs, Frederick A., "An Analysis of Dramatic Technique in Garcia Lorca's Early Theater", *Dissertation Abstracts International* (1973), 34:320A
Klein, Dennis A., " 'El Maleficio de la Mariposa': The Cornerstone of Garcia Lorca's Theatre", *Garcia Lorca Review* (1974), 2
Lumley, Frederick, *New Trends in Twentieth Century Drama; A Survey Since Ibsen and Shaw.* 1967. Pp. 92-104
Wells, C. Michael, "The Natural Norm in the Plays of Federico Garcia Lorca", *Hispanic Review* (1970), 38:299-313

Yerma, 1934
Allen, Rupert C., *Psyche and Symbol in the Theater of Federico Garcia Lorca.* 1974. Pp. 113-60

Baumgarten, Murray, "Body's Image: 'Yerma', 'The Player Queen', and the Upright Posture", *Comparative Drama* (1974), 8:290-99

Burton, Julianne, "Society and the Tragic Vision in Federico Garcia Lorca", *Dissertation Abstracts International* (1972), 33:2362A

Cannon, C., "Imagery of Lorca's 'Yerma'", *Modern Language Quarterly*, 21:122-30, 1960

Cobb, Carl W., *Federico Garcia Lorca*. 1967. Pp. 135-38

Commonweal, 62:474, Aug. 12, 1955

Correa, Gustavo, "Honor, Blood and Poetry in 'Yerma'", *Tulane Drama Review*, 7:96-110, 1962-63

Falconieri, John V., "Tragic Hero in Search of a Role: Yerma's Juan", *Revista de Estudios Hispánicos* (1967), 1:17-33

Freedman, Moris, *The Moral Impulse; Modern Drama from Ibsen to the Present*. 1967. Pp. 89-98

Gassner, John, *Dramatic Soundings; Evaluations and Retractions Culled from Thirty Years of Dramatic Criticism*. 1968. Pp. 557-58

Higginbotham, Virginia, *The Comic Spirit of Federico Garcia Lorca*. 1976. Pp. 97-102

Lott, Robert E., "'Yerma': The Tragedy of Unjust Barrenness", *Modern Drama*, 8:20-27, 1965

Lumley, Frederick, *New Trends in Twentieth Century Drama; A Survey Since Ibsen and Shaw*. 1967. Pp. 92-104

Morris, C. B., "Lorca's 'Yerma': Wife Without an Anchor", *Neophilologus* (1972), 56:285-97

Nation (Nov. 6, 1972), 215: 144-45

New Statesman, 54:171, Aug. 10, 1957

New Yorker (Oct. 28, 1972), 48:119

Parr, James A., "La Escena Final de 'Yerma'", *Duquesne Hispanic Review* (1971), 10:23-29

Pinto V., Patricia, "El Simbolo del Agua y el Motivo de la Sed en 'Yerma'", *Boletín del Instituto de Filología de la Universidad de Chile* (1972-73), 23-24:283-304

Platt, Joseph, "The Maternal Theme in Garcia Lorca's Folk Tragedies", *Dissertation Abstracts International* (1973), 34:787A

Samatan, M. E., "El Tema de la Mujer en Garcia Lorca", *Universidad* (Argent.), #60:55-69, 1964

Saturday Review (Nov. 11, 1972), 55:80

Skloot, R., "Theme and Image in Lorca's 'Yerma'", *Drama Survey* (1966), 5:151-61

Spectator, 199:192, Aug. 9, 1957

Sullivan, Patricia L., "The Mythic Tragedy of 'Yerma'", *Bulletin of Hispanic Studies* (1972), 265-78

Vázquez Zamora, Rafael, "Garcia Lorca en el Eslava: 'Yerma'", *Insula* (Madrid), 15:19, 1962

Williams, Raymond, *Drama from Ibsen to Brecht*. 1968. Pp. 170-72

La Zapatera Prodigiosa   SEE   The Shoemaker's Prodigious Wife

JOHN GAY

The Beggar's Opera, 1728

Agate, James Evershed, *Alarums and Excursions*. 1922. Pp. 139-52

Aldrich, Richard, *Musical Discourse from The New York Times*, 1928. Pp. 103-25

Baring, Maurice, *Punch and Judy and Other Essays*. 1924. Pp. 343-48

Benerjee, Santi Ranjan, "'The Beggar's Opera' and the Comic Tradition", *Bulletin of the Department of English* (1968-69), 4:51-54

Bentley, Eric Russell, *Dramatic Event; An American Chronicle*. 1954. Pp. 140-43

Brockway, Wallace and Weinstock, Herbert, *Opera; A History of Its Creation and Performance*. 1941. Pp. 27-47

Bronson, B. H., and Others, *Studies in the Comic*. 1941. Pp. 197-231

Burdett, Osbert, *Critical Essays*. 1925. Pp. 66-77

Burgess, C. F., "The Genesis of 'The Beggar's Opera'", *Cithara*, 2:1:6-12, 1962

_____ , "Political Satire: John Gay's 'The Beggar's Opera'", *Midwest Quarterly*, 6:265-76, Spring, 1965

Carr, Mrs. C., "'Beggar's Opera' in the Eighteenth Century", *Blackwood's Magazine*, 211:790-97, June, 1922

Catholic World, 171:390, Aug., 1950 and 185:148-49, May, 1957

Christian Science Monitor Magazine, Pp. 9, June 17, 1950

Colles, Henry Cope, *Essays and Lectures; With a Memoir of the Author by H. J. C.* 1945. Pp. 52-54

Donaldson, Ian, *The World Upside-Down; Comedy from Jonson to Fielding*. 1970. Pp. 159-82

Drama, 11:227-31, April, 1921

Empson, William, *English Pastoral Poetry*. 1938. Pp. 195-205

Firkins, O. W., "The Beggar's Opera", *Review*, 4: 161-63, Feb. 16, 1921

Goberman, M., "Mr. John Gay's 'The Beggar's Opera'", *Music Review*, 24:3-12, Feb., 1963

Goulding, S., "Eighteenth Century French Taste and 'The Beggar's Opera'", *Modern Language Review*, 24:276-93, July, 1929

Herbert, A. P., "London of the 'Beggar's Opera'; Court Reports of 1733", *London Mercury*, 5:156-71, Dec., 1921

Hewlett, Maurice Henry, *Extemporary Essays*. 1922. Pp. 47-51

Hunt, Leigh, *Leigh Hunt's Dramatic Criticism, 1808-1831*, ed. by Lawrence Huston Houchens and Carolyn Washburn Houchens. 1949. Pp. 75-77

Kern, J. B., "Note on 'The Beggar's Opera'", *Philological Quarterly*, 17: 411-13, Oct., 1938

Lewisohn, Ludwig, "The Beggar's Opera", *Nation*, 112:91, Jan. 19, 1921

_____ , *Drama and the Stage*. 1922. Pp. 121-44

Literary Digest, 115:18, Feb. 4, 1933

Loftis, John C., *Comedy and Society from Congreve to Fielding*. 1959. Pp. 101-32

Loftis, John Clyde, ed., *Restoration Drama; Modern Essays in Criticism*. 1966. Pp. 298-327

McIntosh, William A., "Handel, Walpole and Gay; The Aims of 'The Beggar's Opera'", *Eighteenth Century Studies* (1974), 7:415-33

Mais, Stuart Petre Brodie, *Why We Should Read*. 1921. Pp. 58-62

Mark, J., "Ballad Opera and Its Significance in the History of English Stage-Music", *London Mercury*, 8:265-78, July, 1923

Meltzer, C. H., "Beggar's Opera", *Review*, 3:660, Dec. 29, 1920

Moriarity, John J., "Subversive John Gay: Satiric Intention and Technique in His Major Works", *Dissertation Abstracts International* (1973), 33: 6878A

Moss, Harold G., "Imitation and Allusion in John Gay's 'The Beggar's Opera' ", *Notes and Queries* (1974), 21:48-49

Musical America, 70:10, April, 1950 and 74:16, May, 1954

Nation, 171:45, July 8, 1950

Nation (London), 27:340-41, June 12, 1920

National Review, 114:414-15, April, 1940

New Statesman, 15:279-80, June 12, 1920

New Yorker, 30:116, April 17, 1954

Newsweek, 32:75, July 19, 1948 and 36:80, July 10, 1950

Ould, H., "Old Wine in New Bottles", *English Review*, 36:142-43, Feb., 1923

Preston, J., "Ironic Mode; A Comparison of 'Jonathan Wild' and 'The Beggar's Opera' ", *Essays in Criticism* (1966), 16:268-80

Rafroidi, Patrick, "Les Fortunes d'Un Queux", *Bulletin de la Faculté des Lettres de Strasbourg* (1967), 46:355-62

Rees, Christine, "Gay, Swift and the Nymphs of Drury Lane", *Essays in Criticism* (1973), 23:1-21

Rutter, F., "Charles Dickens and 'The Beggar's Opera' ", *Bookman* (London), 61:286-87, March, 1922

Saturday Review, 36:28-29, Aug. 15, 1953

Seldes, G., "The Beggar's Opera", *Dial*, 70:303-06, March, 1921

Sherwin, Judith Johnson, " 'The World is Mean and Man Uncouth' ", *Virginia Quarterly Review*, 35:258-70, 1959

Siegmund-Schultze, Dorothea, "Betrachtungen zur Satirisch-Polemischen Tendenz in John Gays 'Beggar's Opera' ", *Wissenschaftliche Zeitschrift der Martin Luther Universitat Halle-Wittenberg Gesellschafts-und Sprachwissenschafliche Reihe*, 12:1001-14, 1963

Smith, Robert A., "The 'Great Man' Motif in 'Jonathan Wild' and 'The Beggar's Opera' ", *CLA Journal* (1959), 2:183-84

Spectator, 125:304-05, Sept. 4, 1920 and 164:361, March 15, 1940

Stevens, D. H., *Manly Anniversary Studies in Language and Literature*. 1923. Pp. 180-89

Theatre Arts, 41:21, May, 1957

Time, 52:70, Sept. 27, 1948

Walkley, Arthur Bingham, *Pastiche and Prejudice*. 1921. Pp. 127-32

Ward, Alfred Charles, ed., *Specimens of English Dramatic Criticism, XVII-XX Centuries*. 1945. Pp. 69-83, 93-95, 273-75

Wardler, R. M., "Hazlitt on 'The Beggar's Opera' ", *South Atlantic Quarterly* (Spr. 1971), 70:256-64

Wood, R. K., "Play That Has Run for Two Centuries", *Mentor*, 15:48-51, Jan., 1928

The Mohocks, 1712

Lewis, Peter E., "Another Look at John Gay's 'The Mohocks' ", *Modern Language Review* (1968), 63:790-93

Stroup, Thomas B., "Gay's 'Mohocks' and Milton", *Journal of English and Germanic Philology*, 46:164-67, 1947

Polly, 1729

Aitken, G. A., "Gay's 'Polly' ", *Atheneum*, 102:202-03, Aug. 5, 1893

Burgess, C. F., "John Gay and 'Polly' and a Letter to the King", *Philology Quarterly* (1968), 47:596-98

Conolly, L. W., "Anna Margaretta Larpent, the Duchess of Queensberry and Gay's 'Polly' in 1777", *Philological Quarterly* (1972), 51:955-57

Owen, Joan H., "'Polly' and the Choice of Virtue", *Bulletin of the New York Public Library* (1974), 77:393-406

"Polly Goes to Court", *Literary Digest*, 78:35-36, Aug. 4, 1923

Straus, H., "'Polly' and The British National Opera", *Nation*, 116:372, March 28, 1923

Sutherland, J. R., "Polly Among the Pirates", *Modern Language Review*, 37:291-303, July, 1942

The What D'Ye Call It, 1715

Lewis, Peter E., "Gay's Burlesque Method in 'The What D'Ye Call It'", *Durham University Journal* (1967), 29:13-25

JEAN GENÊT

Le Balcon *SEE* The Balcony

The Balcony, 1956

Abel, Lionel, "Metatheater", *Partisan Review* (1960), 27:324-30

Blau, Herbert, "Politics and the Theatre", *Wascana Review* (1967), 2:5-23

Brustein, Robert Sanford, *Seasons of Discontent; Dramatic Opinions, 1959-1965.* 1965. Pp. 33-36

——————————— , *The Theatre of Revolt; An Approach to the Modern Drama.* 1964. Pp. 394-402

Chesneau, Albert C., "Idée de Révolution et Principe de Réversibilité dans 'Le Balcon' et 'Les Nègres' de Jean Genêt", *Modern Language Association. Publications* (1973), 88:1137-45

Christian Century, 77:546-48, May 4, 1960

Cismaru, Alfred, "The Antitheism of Jean Genêt", *Antioch Review*, 24:387-401, 1964-65

Clurman, Harold, *The Naked Image; Observations on the Modern Theatre.* 1966. Pp. 72-73

Coe, Richard N., *The Vision of Jean Genêt.* 1968. Pp. 251-81

Cohn, Ruby, *Currents in Contemporary Drama.* 1969. Pp. 233-39

Corvin, Michel, *Le Théâtre Nouveau en France.* 1963. Pp. 72-76

Cruickshank, John, "Jean Genêt; The Aesthetics of Crime", *Critical Quarterly*, 6:202-10, 1964

Curtis, Jerry L., "The World Is a Stage; Sartre Versus Genêt", *Modern Drama* (1974), 17:33-41

Dort, B., "Le Jeu de Genêt", *Les Temps Modernes* (Paris), 15:1875-84, 1960

Ehrmann, Jacques, "Genêt's Dramatic Metamorphosis From Appearance to Freedom", *Yale French Studies*, 29:33-42, 1962

Eskin, Stanley, G., "Theatricality in the Avant-Garde Drama; A Reconsideration of a Theme in the Light of 'The Balcony' and 'The Connection'", *Modern Drama*, 7:213-22, 1964

Esslin, Martin, *The Theatre of the Absurd.* 1961. Pp. 152-60

Goldmann, Lucien, "The Theatre of Genêt: A Sociological Study", *T. D. R., Drama Review* (1967-68), 12:51-61

Goldmann, L., "Une Pièce Réaliste: 'Le Balcon' de Genêt", *Les Temps Modernes* (Paris), 15:1884-96, 1960

Grossvogel, David, I., *Four Playwrights and a Postscript; Brecht, Ionesco, Beckett and Genêt.* 1962. Pp. 157-66

Higgins, David M., "Existential Valuation in Five Contemporary Plays", *Dissertation Abstracts International* (1972), 32:4612A

Hillard, G., "Das Drama von Jean Genêt", *Merkur*, 16:172, 596-600, 1962

Jeffrey, David K., Genêt and Gelber; Studies in Addiction", *Modern Drama* (Sept. 1968), 11:151-56

Lewis, Allan, *The Contemporary Theatre; The Significant Playwrights of Our Time*. 1962. Pp. 259-81

Luccioni, G., "De Somptueuses Funérailles", *Méditations* (Paris), #4:149-53, 1962

Lumley, Frederick, *New Trends in Twentieth Century Drama; A Survey Since Ibsen and Shaw*. 1967. Pp. 214-16

Markus, Thomas B., "Jean Genêt: The Theatre of the Perverse", *Educational Theatre Journal*, 14:209-14, Oct., 1962

McMahon, Joseph H., "Keeping Faith. and Holding Firm", *Yale French Studies*, 29:26-32, 1962

Melcher, Edith, "The Pirandellism of Jean Genêt", *French Review*, 36:32-36, 1962

Moore, Margaret A., "The Theatre of Jean Genêt; A Study in the Neo-Baroque", *Dissertation Abstracts International* (1973), 33:4426A

Nation, 185:18, July 6, 1957 and 190:282-83, March 26, 1960

Nelson, Benjamin, "'The Balcony' and Parisian Existentialism", *Tulane Drama Review*, 7:60-79, 1963

New Republic, 36:116, March 12, 1960 and 142:21-22, March 28, 1960

New Statesman, 53:542, 568, 1957

New Yorker, 36:116, March 12, 1960

Novick, Julius, *Beyond Broadway; The Quest for Permanent Theatres*. 1968. Pp. 56-57

Popa, Dan, "Modalităţii de Structurare in Teatrue lui Jean Genêt 'Le Balcon'", *Analele Universităţiik Bucuresti, Limbi Romanice* (1973), 22:103-12

Reck, Rima Drell, "Appearance and Reality in Genêt's 'Le Balcon'", *Yale French Studies*, #29:20-25, 1962

Saturday Review, 43:34, March 26, 1960

Serreau, Geneviève, *Histoire du Nouveau Théâtre*. 1966. Pp. 124-25

Sherzer, Dina, "Les Appelatifs dans 'Le Balcon' de Genêt", *French Review* (1974), 48:95-107

Sohlich, W. F., "Genêt's Drama; Rites of Passage of the Anti-Hero: From Alienated Existence to Artistic Alienation", *Modern Language Notes* (1974), 89:641-53

Spectator, 198:587, May 3, 1957

Stewart, H. E., "Jean Genêt's Mirror Images in 'Le Balcon'", *Modern Drama* (Sept. 1969), 12:197-203

Stewart, H. E., "Jean Genêt's Saintly Preoccupation in 'Le Balcon'", *Drama Survey* (1967), 6:24-30

Stewart, H. E., "A Note on Verbal Play in Genêt's 'Le Balcon'", *Contemporary Literature* (1969), 10:389-95

Strem, George S., "The Theatre of Jean Genêt: Facets of Illusion—The Anti-Christ and the Underdog", *Minnesota Review*, 4:226-36, 1963-64

Time, 75:54, April 18, 1962

Tynan, Kenneth, *Curtains; Selections from the Drama Criticism and Related Works*. 1961. Pp. 170-72

Vernois, Paul, ed., *L'Onirisme et l'Insolite dans le Théâtre Francaise Contemporain*. (Actes et Colloques 14), 1974. Pp. 231-51

Williams, Raymond, *Drama from Ibsen to Brecht*. 1968. Pp. 305-08

Zanotto, I. M., "Audience-Structure for 'The Balcony'", *Drama Review* (1973), 17:58-65

The Blacks, 1959

America, 105:671, Aug. 26, 1961

Bogard, Travis and Oliver, William Irvin, eds., *Modern Drama; Essays in Criticism*. 1965. Pp. 152-67.

Brustein, Robert Sanford, *Seasons of Discontent; Dramatic Opinions, 1959-1965*. 1965. Pp. 49-52

———————— , *The Theatre of Revolt; An Approach to the Modern Drama*. 1964. Pp. 391-394 and 402-10

Catholic World, 194:62-64, Oct., 1961

Cetta, Lewis T., "Myth, Magic and Play in Genêt's 'The Blacks'", *Contemporary Literature* (1970), 11:511-25

Chesneau, Albert C., "Idée de Révolution et Principe de Réversibilité dans 'Le Balcon' et 'Les Negres' de Jean Genêt", *Modern Language Association. Publications* (1973), 88:1137-45

Christian Century, 78:744-45, June 14, 1961

Cismaru, Alfred, "The Antitheism of Jean Genêt", *Antioch Review*, 24:387-401, 1964-65

Clurman, Harold, *The Naked Image; Observations on the Modern Theatre*. 1966. Pp. 74-76

Coe, Richard N., *The Vision of Jean Genêt*. 1968. Pp. 282-96

Corvin, Michel, *Le Théâtre Nouveau en France*. 1963. Pp. 72-76

Dort, B., "Le Jeu de Genêt", *Les Temps Modernes* (Paris), 15:1875-84, 1960

Drama, #62:21, Fall, 1961

Ebony, 17:47-48, Sept., 1962

Educational Theatre Journal, 13:217-20, Oct., 1961

Esslin, Martin, *The Theatre of the Absurd*. 1961. Pp. 160-67

Florence, Jean, "Les Espaces Scéniques et Dramaturgiques dan 'Les Negres' de Jean Genet", *Marche Romane* (1970), 20,iii:39-58

Goldman, Lucien, "Micro-Structures dans les 25 Premières Répliques des 'Negres' de Jean Genêt", *Revue de l'Institut de Sociologie* (1969), 3:363-80

———————— , "The Theatre of Genet: A Sociological Study", T. D. R., *Drama Review* (1967-68), 12:51-61

Grossvogel, David I., *Four Playwrights and a Postscript: Brecht, Ionesco, Beckett and Genêt*. 1962. Pp. 166-72

Kerr, Walter, *The Theatre in Spite of Itself*. 1963. Pp. 119-22

Luccioni, G., "De Somptueuses Funérailles", *Méditations* (Paris), #4:149-53, 1962

Lumley, Frederick, *New Trends in Twentieth Century Drama; A Survey Since Ibsen and Shaw*. 1967. Pp. 214-16

McMahon, Joseph H., "Keeping Faith and Holding Firm", *Yale French Studies*, #29:26-32, 1962

Mailer, Norman, *The Presidential Papers*. 1963. Pp. 200-12

Markus, Thomas B., "Jean Genêt; The Theatre of the Perverse", *Educational Theatre Journal*, 14:209-14, Oct., 1962

Matthews, Honor, *The Primal Curse; The Myth of Cain and Abel in the Theatre.* 1967. Pp. 179-83

Melcher, Edith, "The Pirandellism of Jean Genêt", *French Review*, 36:32-36, 1962

Moore, Margaret A., "The Theatre of Jean Genêt: A Study in the New Baroque", *Dissertation Abstracts International* (1973), 33:4426A

Murch, Anne C., "Je Mime Donc Je Suis: 'Les Negres' de Jean Genêt", *Revue des Sciences Humaines* (1973), 150:249-59

Nation, 192:447-48, May 20, 1961

New Republic, 144:21-22, May 29, 1961

New Statesman, 58:706, Nov. 21, 1959

New Yorker, 37:93-94, May 13, 1961

Newsweek, 57:68, May 15, 1961

Partisan Review, 28:662-68, 1961

Piemme, Michel, "Les Espaces Scéniques et Dramaturgiques dans 'Les Nègres' de Genêt", *Marche Romane* (1971), 20,iii:39-52

Pritchett, V. S., "Black and White Murder Show", *New Statesman*, 61:928, June 9, 1961

Regnaut, M., " 'Les Nègres' de Jean Genêt", *Theatre Populaire* (Paris), #36:50-53, 1959

Saturday Review, 44:29, June 3, 1961

Selz, J., " 'Les Nègres': Tragédie ou Exorcisme?", *Lettres Nouvelles* (Paris), 7:37-38, 1959

Serreau, Geneviève, *Histoire du Nouveau Théâtre.* 1966. Pp. 125-30

Sherrell, Richard, *The Human Image; Avant-Garde and Christian.* 1969. Pp. 99-109

Simon, A., "Genêt, le Négre et la Réprobation", *Esprit* (Paris), 28:170-72, 1960

Spectator, 206:835, June 9, 1961

Stremm, George S., "The Theatre of Jean Genêt: Facets of Illusion—The Anti-Christ and the Underdog", *Minnesota Review*, 4:226-36, 1963-64

Swander, Honor D., "Illusion and Comic Form in Genêt's 'The Blacks' ", *Yale Review* (1966), 55:209-26

Taubes, Susan, "The White Mask Falls", *Tulane Drama Review*, 7:85-92, Spring, 1963

Theatre Arts, 45:8-9, July, 1961

Time, 77:64, May 12, 1961

Vernois, Paul, ed., *L'Onirisme et l'Insolite dans le Théâtre Francaise Contemporain.* 1974. Pp. 231-51

Yale Review, 55:209-26, Dec., 1965

Zimbardo, R. A. "Genêt's Black Mass", *Modern Drama*, 8:247-258, 1965

Les Bonnes   *SEE*   The Maids

Deathwatch, 1949

Brustein, Robert Sanford, *The Theatre of Revolt; An Approach to the Modern Drama.* 1964. Pp. 391-92

Cismaru, Alfred, "The Antitheism of Jean Genêt", *Antioch Review*, 24: 387-401, 1964-65

Coe, Richard N., *The Vision of Jean Genêt.* 1968. Pp. 225-36

Cohn, Ruby, *Currents in Contemporary Drama.* 1969. Pp. 37-40 and 63-69

Corvin, Michel, *Le Théâtre Nouveau en France*.   1963. Pp. 72-76
Ehrmann, Jacques, "Genêt's Dramatic Metamorphosis; From Appearance
  to Freedom", *Yale French Studies*, #29:33-42, 1962
Esslin, Martin, *The Theatre of the Absurd*. 1961. Pp. 144-46
Fowlie, Wallace, "The New French Theatre: Artaud, Beckett, Genêt and
  Ionesco", *Sewanee Review*, 67:651-54, 1959
Goldmann, Lucien, "The Theatre of Genêt; A Sociological Study", *T. D. R.,*
  Drama Review (1967-68),^12:51-61
Grossvogel, David I., *Four Playwrights and a Postscript: Brecht, Ionesco,*
  Beckett and Genêt. 1962. Pp. 151-57
Lumley, Frederick, *New Trends in Twentieth Century Drama; A Survey*
  Since Ibsen and Shaw. 1967. Pp. 214-16
Moore, Margaret A., "The Theatre of Jean Genêt: A Study in the New-Ba-
  roque", *Dissertation Abstracts International* (1973), 33:4426A
Partisan Review, 26:100-06, Winter, 1959
Saturday Review, 41:28, Nov. 1, 1958
Serreau, Geneviève, *Histoire du Nouveau Théâtre*. 1966. Pp. 119-20
Sohlich, W. F., "Genêt's Drama; Rites of Passage of the Anti-Hero: From
  Alienated Existence to Artistic Alienation", *Modern Language Notes*
  (1974), 89:641-53
Stewart, Harry E., "The Case of the Lilac Murders: Jean Genêt's 'Haute
  Surveillance' ", *French Review* (1974), 48:87-94
Stewart, Harry E., "In Defense of LeFranc as a 'Hero' of 'Haute Surveillance' ",
  French Review (1972), 45:365-72

Haute Surveillance   *SEE*   The Deathwatch

The Maids, 1947
Brustein, Robert Sanford, *The Theatre of Revolt; An Approach to the*
  Modern Drama. 1964. Pp. 378-82 and 391-92
Cismaru, Alfred, "The Antitheism of Jean Genêt", *Antioch Review*, 24:387-
  401, 1964-65
Coe, Richard N., *The Vision of Jean Genêt*. 1968. Pp. 236-50
Cohn, Ruby, *Currents in Contemporary Drama*. 1969. Pp. 63-69
Commonweal, 62:398-99, July 22, 1955
Dort, B., "Le Jeu de Genêt", *Les Temps Modernes* (Paris), 15:1875-84, 1960
Ehrmann, Jacques, "Genêt's Dramatic Metamorphosis; From Appearance
  to Freedom", *Yale French Studies*, 29:33-42, 1962
Esslin, Martin, *The Theatre of the Absurd*. 1961. Pp. 146-52
Fowlie, Wallace, "The New French Theatre; Artaud, Beckett, Genêt, Ionesco",
  Sewanee Review, 67:651-54, 1959
Goldman, Lucien, "The Theatre of Genêt; A Sociological Study", *T. D. R.,*
  Drama Review (1967-68), 12:51-61
Grossvogel, David I., *Four Playwrights and a Postscript: Brecht, Ionesco,*
  Beckett and Genêt. 1962. Pp. 140-51
Hillard, G., "Das Drama von Jean Genêt", *Merkur*, 16:172, 596-600, 1962
Hubert, Renée, "The Maids as Children; A Commentary on Genêt's "Les
  Bonnes' ", *Romance Notes* (1969), 10:204-09
Leighton, L., "Ecstasy Through Compulsion", *Kenyon Review*, 17:639-42,
  1955
Lumley, Frederick, *New Trends in Twentieth Century Drama; A Survey*
  Since Ibsen and Shaw. 1967. Pp. 214-16

Markus, Thomas B., "Jean Genêt: The Theatre of the Perverse", *Educational Theatre Journal*, 14:209-14, Oct., 1962

Marowitz, C., "Maids", *Plays and Players* (Ap. 1974), 21:45-46

Matthews, Honor, *The Primal Curse; The Myth of Cain and Abel in the Theatre*. 1967. Pp. 172-79

Murch, Anne C., "Genêt-Triana-Kopit: Ritual as 'Danse Macabre'", *Modern Drama* (1972), 15:369-81

Nation, 180:469-70, May 28, 1955

New Yorker, 39:143-44, Nov. 23, 1963

Pucciani, Oreste F., "Tragedy, Genêt, and 'The Maids'", *Tulane Drama Review*, 7:42-59, 1963

Serreau, Geneviève, *Histoire du Nouveau Théâtre*. 1966. Pp. 120-24

Sherrell, Richard, *The Human Image; Avant-Garde and Christian*. 1969. Pp. 89-99

Sohlich, W. F., "Genêt's Drama: Rites of Passage of the Anti-Hero: From Alienated Existence to Artistic Alienation", *Modern Language Notes* (1974), 89:641-53

Strem, George S., "The Theatre of Jean Genêt: Facets of Illusion—The Anti-Christ and the Underdog", *Minnesota Review*, 4:226-36, 1963-64

Zimbardo, R. A., "Genêt's Black Mass", *Modern Drama*, 8:247-58, 1965

Les Nègres   *SEE*   The Blacks

Les Paravents   *SEE*   The Screens

The Screens, 1961
Brustein, Robert Sanford, *The Theatre of Revolt; An Approach to the Modern Drama*. 1964. Pp. 380-82 and 390-94

Calarco, N. Joseph, "Vision Without Compromise: Genêt's 'The Screens'", *Drama Survey*, 4:44-50, 1965

Cismaru, Alfred, "The Antitheism of Jean Genêt", *Antioch Review*, 24:387-401 1964-65

Clurman, Harold, *The Divine Pastime; Theatre Essays*. 1974. Pp. 305-08

Coe, Richard N., *The Vision of Jean Genêt*. 1968. Pp. 296-315

Cohn, Ruby, *Currents in Contemporary Drama*. 1969. Pp. 138-40

Cruickshank, John, "Jean Genêt; the Aesthetics of Crime", *Critical Quarterly*, 6:202-10, 1964

Goldmann, Lucien, "The Theatre of Genêt; A Sociological Study", *T. D. R., Drama Review* (1967-68), 12:51-61

Grossvogel, David I., *Four Playwrights and a Postscript: Brecht, Ionesco, Beckett and Genêt*. 1962. Pp. 171-74

Luccioni, G., "De Somptueuses Funérailles", *Méditations* (Paris), #4:149-53, 1962

Lumley, Frederick, *New Trends in Twentieth Century Drama; A Survey Since Ibsen and Shaw*. 1967. Pp. 214-16

McMahon, Joseph H., "Keeping Faith and Holding Firm", *Yale French Studies*, #29:26-32, 1962

Milne, Tom, "Reflections on 'The Screens'", *Encore* (July-Aug. 1964), 11:21-25

Moore, Margaret A., "The Theatre of Jean Genêt; A Study in the Neo-Baroque", *Dissertation Abstracts International* (1973), 33:4426A

Nation (Dec. 27, 1971), 213:701-02

Newsweek (Dec. 20, 1971), 78:58

Pierret, Marc, "Genêt's New Play: 'The Screens'", *Tulane Drama Review*, 7:93-97, 1963

Pronko, Leonard C., "Jean Genet's 'Les Paravents'", *L'Esprit Créateur* (Minneapolis), 2:181-88, 1962

Scarborough, Margaret, "The Radical Idealism of 'The Screens'", *Modern Drama* (1973), 15:355-68

Serreau, Geneviève, *Histoire du Nouveau Théâtre.* 1966. Pp. 130-37

Strem, George S., "The Theatre of Jean Genêt: Facets of Illusion—The Anti-Christ and the Underdog", *Minnesota Review*, 4:226-36, 1963-64

Time (Dec. 27, 1971), 98:55

MICHEL DE GHELDERODE

Barabbas, 1928

Kliewer, Warren, "An Alternative to Realistic Forms", *Response* (1966), 7:163-70

Mercure de France, 309:317-19, June, 1950

Moore, Harry T., *Twentieth Century French Literature to World War II.* 1966. Vol. II. Pp. 31-33

The Death of Dr. Faust, 1925

Cole, Douglas, "Faust and Anti-Faust in Modern Drama", *Drama Survey* (1966), 5:39-52

Escurial, 1929

Debedt-Malaquais, Elisabeth, "Le Roi et le Bouffon dans l'Escurial' de Michel de Ghelderode", *Australian Journal of French Studies* (1966), 3:196-204

Novick, Julius, *Beyond Broadway; The Quest for Permanent Theatres.* 1968. Pp. 142

Skolnikov, Channa, " 'Escurial'—Mahaze-Avant-Garde al ha-Meah ha-16", *Bama* (1974), 60:39-42

Vandegans, André, " 'Escurial' et 'Hop-Frog' ", *Revue des Langues Vivantes* (1968), 34:616-19

Hop, Signor!, 1962

Commonweal, 76:259-60, June 1, 1962

New Yorker, 38:104, May 19, 1962

Theatre Arts, 46:58, Aug. 1962

Vandegans, André, " 'Escurial' et 'Hop-Frog' ", *Revue des Langues Vivantes* (1968), 34:616-19

Mademoiselle Jaire, 1957

New Statesman, 54:648, Nov. 16, 1957

Magie Rouge *SEE* Red Magic

Pantagleizc, 1930

Gilman, Richard, *Common and Uncommon Masks; Writings on the Theatre, 1961-70.* 1971. Pp. 295-98

Novick, Julius, *Beyond Broadway; The Quest for Permanent Theatres.* 1968. Pp. 221-22

Theatre Arts, 46:26-27, Aug., 1962

Red Magic, 1934
Fraidstern, Iska, "Ghelderode's 'Red Magic': Gold and the use of the Christian Myth", *Modern Drama* (Feb. 1969), 11:376-81

Splendors of Hell, 1949
Hellman, Helen, "'Splendors of Hell'; A Tragic Farce", *Renascence* (1967), 20:30-38

ANDRÉ GIDE

Bethsabé, 1912
Johns Hopkins Studies in Romance Literatures and Languages. 1953 (Extra Vol. #28), Pp. 3-115
Les Caves du Vatican   *SEE*   The Vatican Swindle

King Candaules, 1901
Church, D. M., "Structure and Dramatic Technique in 'Saul' and 'Le Roi Candaule'", *Modern Language Association.* *Publications* (1969), 84: 1639-43
Cordle, Thomas, *Andre Gide.* 1969. Pp. 78-81
Dickinson, Hugh, *Myth on the Modern Stage.* 1969. Pp. 46-57
McLaren, James C., "The Theatre of André Gide", *Johns Hopkins Studies in Romance Literatures and Languages* (1953), Extra 28:1-94
San Juan, E. J., "Pattern and Significance in Two Plays of André Gide", *Discourse* (1965), 8:350-61

Oedipus, 1931
Balmas, Enea, "A Propos d'Oedipe': Notes Sur le Théâtre de Gide", *Revue d'Histoire Littéraire de la France* (1970), 70:244-54
Conacher, D. J., "Theme and Technique in the 'Philoctètes' and 'Oedipus' of André Gide", *University of Toronto Quarterly* (1955), 24:121-35
Cordle, Thomas, *Andre Gide.* 1969. Pp. 150-56
Dickinson, Hugh, *Myth on the Modern Stage.* 1969. Pp. 57-66 and 69-71
Johns Hopkins Studies in Romance Literatures and Languages. 1953 (Extra Vol. #28), Pp. 3-115
The Persistent Voice; Essays on Hellenism in French Literature Since the Eighteenth Century in Honor of Professor Henri M. Peyre, ed. Walter G. Langlois. 1971. Pp. 117-21
Tynan, Kenneth, *Curtains; Selections from the Drama Criticism and Related Writings.* 1961. Pp. 383-84

Perséphone, 1934
McLaren, James C., "The Theatre of André Gide", *Johns Hopkins Studies in Romance Literatures and Languages* (1953), Extra 28:1-94

Philoctètes, 1919
Conacher, D. J., "Theme and Technique in the 'Philoctètes' and 'Oedipus' of André Gide", *University of Toronto Quarterly* (1955), 24:121-35
Cordle, Thomas, *Andre Gide.* 1969. Pp. 59-62
McLaren, James C., "The Theatre of André Gide", *Johns Hopkins Studies in Romance Literatures and Languages* (1953), Extra 28:1-94

Robert, ou l'Intérêt Général, 1946
McLaren, James C., "The Theatre of André Gide", *Johns Hopkins Studies in Romance Literatures and Languages* (1953), Extra 28:1-94

La Roi Candaule *SEE* King Candaules

Säul, 1922

Church, D. M., "Structure and Dramatic Technique in 'Saul' and 'Le Roi Candaule' ", *Modern Language Association. Publications* (1969), 84: 1639-43

Cordle, Thomas, *Andre Gide*. 1969. Pp. 74-78

McLaren, James C., "The Theatre of André Gide", *Johns Hopkins Studies in Romance Literatures and Languages* (1953), Extra 28:1-94

San Juan, E. J., "Pattern and Significance in Two Plays of André Gide", *Discourse* (1965), 8:350-61

Vidal, Georges G., "Pour une Etude des Masques de Gide: 'Saul' ", *La Revue des Lettres Modernes* (1973), 374-79:85-97

Le Treizième Arbre, 1935

McLaren, James C., "The Theatre of André Gide", *Johns Hopkins Studies in Romance Literatures and Languages* (1953), Extra 28:1-94

The Vatican Swindle, 1933

Cancalon, Elaine D., "La Creation des Fantoches dans 'Les Caves du Vatican' ", *Rivista di Letterature Moderne e Comparate* (1972), 25:137-39

Christensen, M. T., "L'Humour Gidien dans 'Les Caves du Vatican' ", *Theoria* (1970), 34:57-76

Cordle, Thomas, *Andre Gide*. 1969. Pp. 108-15

Johns Hopkins Studies in Romance Literatures and Languages. 1953. (Extra Vol. #28), Pp. 3-115

McClelland, John, "The Lexicon of 'Les Caves du Vatican' ", *Modern Language Association. Publications*. (1974), 89:256-67

JEAN GIRAUDOUX

Amphytryon 38, 1929

Amon, Renée Z., "Le Traitement des Mythes dans le Théâtre de Jean Giraudoux", *Dissertation Abstracts International* (1972), 32:3288A

Bauer, G., "Amphitryon 38", *Annales Politiques et Littéraires*, 93:530, Dec. 1, 1929

Behrman, S., "Amphitryon 38", *New Statesman and Nation*, 15:950-52, June 4, 1938

Bidou, H., "Amphitryon 38", *Journal des Débats*, 36:pt. 2:812-13, Nov. 15, 1929

Cohen, Robert, *Giraudoux; Three Faces of Destiny*. 1968. Pp. 45-50

Dickinson, Hugh, *Myth on the Modern Stage*. 1969. Pp. 184-88

Ellis, J. R., ed., *Australasian Universities Language and Literature Association: Proceedings and Papers of the 13th Congress held at Monash University 12-18 August, 1970*. 1971. Pp. 201-02

Gassner, John, *Dramatic Soundings; Evaluations and Retractions Culled from Thirty Years of Dramatic Criticism*. 1968. Pp. 288-90

Knudsen, H., "Amphitryon 28", *Preussische Jahrbücher*, 223:222-23, Feb., 1931

Lemaitre, George, *Jean Giraudoux; The Writer and His Work*. 1971. Pp. 101-05

Lumley, Frederick, *New Trends in Twentieth Century Drama; A Survey Since Ibsen and Shaw*. 1967. Pp. 35-58

Mankin, Paul A., *Precious Irony; The Theatre of Jean Giraudoux.* 1971. Pp. 60-83

Marcel, Gabriel, "Amphitryon 38", *Nouvelles Littéraires*, 14:8, 1957

Morel, Jacques, "Amphitryon 38 a Là Comédie des Champs-Elysées", *Etudes*, 293:109-16, 1957

Rageot, G., "Amphitryon 38", *Revue Politique et Littéraire*, 68:123-24, Feb. 15, 1930

Rouveyre, A., "Amphitryon 38", *Mercure de France*, 216:657-61, Dec. 15, 1929

Spectator, 160:911, May 20, 1938

Szarmach, Marian, "'Amfitrion 38' Jean Giraudoux w Teatrze Polskim w Bydgoszczy", *Meander* (1972), 27:293-95

Szondi, Peter, "Zu Jean Giradoux' 'Amphitryon 38'", *Neophilologus*, 41: 180-84, 1957

The Apollo of Bellac, 1942
Cohen, Robert, *Giraudoux; Three Faces of Destiny.* 1968. Pp. 76-82
Lemaitre, George, *Jean Giraudoux; The Writer and His Work.* 1971. Pp. 135-37

L'Apollon de Bellac   *SEE*   The Apollo of Bellac

L'Apollon de Marsac, 1940
Theatre Arts, 31:25, Nov., 1947
Tynan, Kenneth, *Curtains; Selections from the Drama Criticism and Related Writings.* 1961. Pp. 177-78

Cantique de Cantiques   *SEE*   Song of Songs

Duel of Angels, 1953
America, 103:266, May 14, 1960
Christian Century, 77:672-73, June 1, 1960
Clurman, Harold, *The Naked Image; Observations on the Modern Theatre.* 1966. Pp. 77-79
Cohen, Robert, *Giraudoux; Three Faces of Destiny.* 1968. Pp. 30-42
Lemaitre, George, *Jean Giraudoux; The Writer and His Work.* 1971. Pp. 142-45
Life, 48:95, May 16, 1960
Lumley, Frederick, *New Trends in Twentieth Century Drama; A Survey Since Ibsen and Shaw.* 1967. Pp. 35-58
Mankin, Paul A., *Precious Irony: The Theatre of Jean Giraudoux.* 1971. Pp. 164-80
Nation, 190:411-12, May 7, 1960
New Yorker, 29:85, Dec. 19, 1953 and 36:83, April 30, 1960
Newsweek, 55:54, May 2, 1960
Saturday Review, 43:26, May 7, 1960
Time, 75:78, March 2, 1960

Electra, 1937
Albert, Walter, "Structures of Revolt in Giraudoux's 'Electre' and Anouilh's 'Antigone'", *Texas Studies in Literature and Language* (1970), 12:137-50
Amon, Renée Z., "Le Traitement des Mythes dans le Théâtre de Jean Giraudoux", *Dissertation Abstracts International* (1972), 32:3288A

Les Annales Politiques et Littéraires, 109:517-18, May 25, 1937

Auber, M., "A Propos d' Electre'", *Nouvelle Revue Française*, #88:754-59, 1960

Beli, Angela, *Ancient Greek Myths and Modern Drama; A Study in Continuity.* 1971. Pp. 111-25

Burdick, D. M., "Concept of Character in Giraudoux's 'Electre' and Sartre's 'Les Mouches'", *French Review* 33:31-36, 1960

Cohen, Robert, *Giraudoux; Three Faces of Destiny.* 1968. Pp. 104-15

Cohn, Ruby, *Currents in Contemporary Drama.* 1969. Pp. 88-91

Dickinson, Hugh, *Myth on the Modern Stage.* 1969. Pp. 196-205

Dobbs, Bryan Griffith, "'Electra': Significant Structures", *L'Esprit Créatur* (1969), 9:93-103

Dumur, G. "'Electre' de Jean Giraudoux", *Théâtre Populaire* (Paris), #36: 56-58, 1959

Ganz, Arthur, "Human and Superhuman; Ambiguity in the Tragic World of Jean Giraudoux", *Modern Language Association. Publications* (1972), 87:284-93

Hamburger, Käte, *From Sophocles to Sartre; Figures in Greek Tragedy, Classical and Modern.* 1969. Pp. 50-55

Herrmann, Michael, "'se declarer'—Zur Bedeutung eines Schlüsselwortes in Giraudoux 'Electre' and Racines 'Bajazet'", *Die Neueren Sprachen* (1969), 18:277-82

L'Illustration, 197:224, June 5, 1937

Lemaitre, George, *Jean Giraudoux; The Writer and His Work.* 1971. Pp. 123-28

Lenson, David R., "Examples of Modern Tragedy", *Dissertation Abstracts International* (1972), 32:6433A

Lumley, Frederick, *New Trends in Twentieth Century Drama; A Survey Since Ibsen and Shaw.* 1967. Pp. 35-58

Mankin, Paul A., *Precious Irony; The Theatre of Jean Giraudoux.* 1971. Pp. 134-52

Martin, F., "'Electre' de Jean Giraudoux", *Conjonction* (Port au Prince), #79-80:70-9, 1960

Mercure de France, 277:150-52, July 1, 1937

Nueva Antologia, 393:347-49, Oct. 1, 1937

Revue Politique et Littéraire, 75:393-94, June 5, 1937

The Enchanted, 1933

Les Annales Politiques et Littéraires, 100:255, March 3, 1933

Blinoff, M., "Remarques sur le Comique de Giraudoux", *French Revue*, 32:337-40, 1959

Catholic World, 185:68, April, 1957

Cohen, Robert, *Giraudoux; Three Faces of Destiny.* 1968. Pp. 51-63

L'Europe Nouvelle, 16:229-30, March 11, 1933

Journal des Débats, 40 pt. 1:420-22, March 10, 1933

Lemaitre, George, *Jean Giraudoux; The Writer and His Work.* 1971. Pp. 112-15

Lumley, Frederick, *New Trends in Twentieth Century Drama; A Survey Since Ibsen and Shaw.* 1967. Pp. 35-58

Mankin, Paul A., *Precious Irony; The Theatre of Jean Giraudoux.* 1971. Pp. 84-95

Mercure de France, 243:159-62, April 1, 1933
New Republic, 136:21, March 18, 1957
Revue des Deux Mondes, s8 14:463-66, March 15, 1933
Rychner, M., "Eine Dramatische Legende vom Humanen Staat. Giraudoux: 'Intermezzo' ", *Schweizer Monatshefte*, 43:92-94, 1963
Schweig, Gunter, "Jean Giraudoux: 'Intermezzo' in Fach-Wissenschaftlicher und Erziehungswissenschaftlicher Sicht", *Die Neueren Sprachen* n. s. (1968), Pp. 109-21
Theatre Arts, 41:82, April, 1957
Tynan, Kenneth, *Curtains; Selections from the Drama Criticism and Related Writings*. 1961. Pp. 392-94

La Folle de Chaillot   *SEE*   The Madwoman of Chaillot

For Lucretia, 1954
Nation, 178:489-90, June 5, 1954

La Guerre de Troie n'Aura pas Lieu   *SEE*   Tiger at the Gates

l'Impromptu de Paris   *SEE*   Paris Impromptu

Intermezzo   *SEE*   The Enchanted

Judith, 1931
Abirached, Robert, "La 'Judith' de Giraudoux au Théâtre de France", *Etudes*, 312:248-52, 1962
Les Annales Politiques et Litteraires, 97:532-33, Dec. 15, 1931
Brustein, Robert, *The Third Theatre*. 1969. Pp. 157-59
Cohen, Robert, *Giraudoux; Three Faces of Destiny*. 1968. Pp. 6-15
L'Europe Nouvelle. 14:1562-63, Nov. 21, 1931
Ganz, Arthur, "Human and Superhuman; Ambiguity in the Tragic World of Jean Giraudoux", *Modern Language Association., Publications* (1972), 87:284-93
Journal des Débats, 38 pt. 2:804-06, Nov. 13, 1931
Leefmans, B. M. P., "Giraudoux's Other Muse", *Kenyon Review*, 16:611-27, 1954
Lemaitre, George, *Jean Giraudoux; The Writer and His Work*. 1971. Pp. 105-12
Lumley, Frederick, *New Trends in Twentieth Century Drama; A Survey Since Ibsen and Shaw*. 1967. Pp. 35-58
Mankin, Paul A., *Precious Irony; The Theatre of Jean Giraudoux*. 1971. Pp. 134-52
Mercure de France, 232:620-24, Dec. 15, 1931
Nation, 200:403-04, April 12, 1965
New Republic, 152:23-24, April 10, 1965
New Yorker, 41:86, April 3, 1965
Reporter, 32:38-40, May 6, 1965
Revue des Deux Mondes, s8 6:939-42, Dec. 15, 1931
Revue Politique et Littéraire, 69:705-07, Nov. 21, 1931
Saturday Review, 48:58, April 10, 1965
Time, 85:79, April 9, 1965
Vogue, 145:68, June, 1965

The Madwoman of Chaillot, 1945
Brée, Germaine, "The Madwoman of Chaillot: A Modern Masque", *Tulane Drama Review*, 3, #4:51-56, 1959

Clurman, Harold, *The Divine Pastime; Theatre Essays.* 1974. Pp. 58-62
Cohen, Robert, *Giraudoux; Three Faces of Destiny.* 1968. Pp. 116-29
Cohen, Robert, "Some Political Implications of 'The Mad Woman of Chaillot'", *Wisconsin Studies in Contemporary Literature* (1968), 9:210-22
Illustrated London News, 218:346, March 3, 1951
Kernodle, George R., *Invitation to the Theatre.* 1967. Pp. 317-19
Lemaitre, George, *Jean Giraudoux; The Writer and His Work.* 1971. Pp. 140-42
LeSage, L., "Giraudoux and Big Business: An Element of Reminiscence in 'La Folle de Chaillot'", *French Review*, 31:278-82, 1958
Lewis, Allan, *The Contemporary Theatre; The Significant Playwrights of Our Time.* 1962. Pp. 191-217
Lumley, Frederick, *New Trends in Twentieth Century Drama; A Survey Since Ibsen and Shaw.* 1967. Pp. 35-58
Mabley, Edward, *Dramatic Construction; An Outline of Basic Principles.* 1972
Mankin, Paul A., *Precious Irony; The Theatre of Jean Giraudoux.* 1971. Pp. 153-63
New Statesman and Nation, 41:214, Feb. 24, 1951
New Yorker, 21:46-48, Feb. 9, 1946, (Apr. 4, 1970), 46:64
Reboussin, M., "Giraudoux and the 'Madwoman of Chaillot'", *Educational Theatre Journal*, 13:11-17, March, 1961
Theatre Arts, 41:67-68, March, 1957
Wagenknecht, Edward Charles, *Preface to Literature.* 1954. Pp. 360-62

Ondine, 1939
Les Annales Politiques et Littéraires, 113:521-22, May 25, 1939
Bentley, E. R., *Dramatic Event; An American Chronicle.* 1954. Pp. 200-204
Brosse, Monique, "Personnages et Situation Mythique dans L'Ondine' de Giraudoux", *Rivista di Litterature Moderne e Comparate* (1969), 22: 181-203
Clurman, Harold, *The Divine Pastime; Theatre Essays.* 1974. Pp. 24-26
Cohen, Robert, *Giraudoux; Three Faces of Destiny.* 1968. Pp. 64-75
L'Europe Nouvelle, 22:633, June 10, 1939
Ganz, Arthur, "Human and Superhuman; Ambiguity in the Tragic World of Jean Giraudoux", *Modern Language Association. Publications* (1972), 87:284-93
Harvey, Lawrence E., "Art and Nothingness in 'Antigone' and 'Ondine'", *l'Esprit Créateur* (1969), 9:118-27
L'Illustration, 203:64, May 13, 1939
Lemaitre, George, *Jean Giraudoux; The Writer and His Work.* 1971. Pp. 129-34
Lumley, Frederick, *New Trends in Twentieth Century Drama; A Survey Since Ibsen and Shaw.* 1967. Pp. 35-58
Mankin, Paul A., *Precious Irony; The Theatre of Jean Giraudoux.* 1971. Pp. 96-113
Mercure de France, 292:634-39, June 15, 1939
Revue des Deux Mondes, s8 51:687-91, June 1, 1939
Revue Politique et Litteraire, 77:237, June, 1939
Tynan, Kenneth, *Curtains; Selections from the Drama Criticism and Related Writings.* 1961. Pp. 106-08

Paris Impromptu, 1938
  Annales Politiques et Littéraires, 110:652-53, Dec. 25, 1937
  Revue Politique et Littéraire, 75:797, Dec. 18, 1937
  Theatre Arts, 22:88, Feb., 1938

Pour Lucrèce   *SEE*   Duel of Angels

Siegfried, 1928
  Albères, R. M., "Siegfried et le Limousin et Siegfried" *La Revue des Lettres Modernes*, #63:264-78, 1961
  Batôt, Raymond, "Comparaison Stylistique entre 'Siegfried et le Limousin' et 'Siegfried' de Jean Giraudoux", *Bulletin des Jeunes Romanistes* (1964), 10:43-48
  Bauer, G., "Siegfried", *Les Annales Politiques et Littéraires*, 90:460, May 15, 1928
  Bidou, H., "Siegfried", *Journal des Débats*, 35 pt. 1:916-17, June 1, 1928
  Bookman, 72:513-14, Jan., 1931
  Catholic World, 132:337, Dec., 1930
  Cohen, Robert, *Giraudoux; Three Faces of Destiny*. 1968. Pp. 85-93
  Commonweal, 13:49, Nov. 12, 1930
  Doumic, R., "Siegfried", *Revue des Deux Mondes*, s7 45:705-08, June 1, 1928
  Inskip, Donald, "Some Notes on the First Production of Jean Giraudoux' 'Siegfried' ", *French Studies*, 12:143-46, 1958
  Lemaitre, George, *Jean Giraudoux; The Writer and His Work*. 1971. Pp. 93-100
  Lumley, Frederick, *New Trends in Twentieth Century Drama; A Survey Since Ibsen and Shaw*. 1967. Pp. 35-58
  Macdonell, A. G., "Siegfried", *London Mercury*, 19:196, Dec., 1928
  Mankin, Paul A., *Precious Irony; The Theatre of Jean Giraudoux*. 1971. Pp. 41-59
  Nation, 131:506, Nov. 5, 1930
  Palmer, J., "Siegfried", *Saturday Review*, 146:77, July 21, 1928
  Richard, Lionel, "Giraudoux Entre Deux Nationalismes; Quelques Aspects de la Réception Critique de 'Siegfried' ", *Mosiac* (1972), 5,iv:103-08
  Rouveyre, A., "Siegfried", *Mercure de France*, 205:163-68, July 1, 1928

Sodom and Gomorrah, 1943
  Cohen, Robert, *Giraudoux; Three Faces of Destiny*. 1968. Pp. 21-29
  Lemaitre, George, *Jean Giraudoux; The Writer and His Work*. 1971. Pp. 137-40
  Lumley, Frederick, *New Trends in Twentieth Century Drama; A Survey Since Ibsen and Shaw*. 1967. Pp. 35-58

Song of Songs, 1938
  Cohen, Robert, *Giraudoux; Three Faces of Destiny*. 1968. Pp. 16-20
  Mercure de France, 288:172-74, Nov. 15, 1938
  Revue des Deux Mondes, s8 48:217-19, Nov. 1, 1938
  Revue Politique et Littéraire, 76:435, Nov., 1938

Supplemént au Voyage de Cook   *SEE*   Virtuous Island

Tiger at the Gates, 1935
  America, 94:258, Nov. 26, 1955

Amon, Renée Z., "Le Traitement des Mythes dans le Théâtre de Jean Gir-
audoux", *Dissertation Abstracts International* (1972), 32:3288A
Les Annales Politiques et Littéraires, 106:578-79, Dec. 10, 1935
Belli, Angela, *Ancient Greek Myths and Modern Drama; A Study in Con-
tinuity*. 1971. Pp. 139-45
Catholic World, 182:223-24, Dec., 1955
Cohen, Robert, *Giraudoux; Three Faces of Destiny*. 1968. Pp. 94-103
Commonweal, 63:200-01, Nov. 25, 1955
Desroches, R. H., "Reality Behind the Myth in Giraudoux's 'La Guerre de
Troie N'Aura pas Lieu' ", *Revue des Langues Vivantes* (1968), 34:239-44
Dickinson, Hugh, *Myth on the Modern Stage*. 1969. Pp. 185-96
Eerde, John Van, "Giraudoux' 'Tiger at the Gates' ", *Explicator*, 15:item
25, 1957
English, 10:225, Fall, 1955
L'Europe Nouvelle, 18:1195, Dec. 7, 1935
Ganz, Arthur "Human and Superhuman; Ambiguity in the Tragic World
of Jean Giraudoux", *Modern Language Association. Publications* (1972),
87:284-93
Hamburger, Käte, *From Sophocles to Sartre; Figures in Greek Tragedy,
Classical and Modern*. 1969. Pp. 91-101
Illustrated London News, 226:1112, June 18, 1955
Kenyon Review, 18:128-30, Winter, 1956
Lemaitre, George, *Jean Giraudoux; The Writer and His Work*. 1971. Pp.
116-20
Lewis, Roy, "Giraudoux; 'La Guerre de Troie n'Aura pas Lieu' ", *Studies
in French Literature* (1971), 19:6-63
Life, 39:164-65, Oct. 17, 1955
Living Age, 349:457-58, Jan., 1936
Lumley, Frederick, *New Trends in Twentieth Century Drama; A Survey
Since Ibsen and Shaw*. 1967. Pp. 35-58
Mankin, Paul A., *Precious Irony; The Theatre of Jean Giraudoux*. 1971.
Pp. 114-33
Mercure de France, 264:572-77, Dec. 15, 1935
Moore, Harry T., *Twentieth Century French Literature to World War II*.
1966. vol. I. Pp. 144-49
Nation, 181:348, Oct. 22, 1955
New Republic, 133:22, Oct. 24, 1955
New Statesman, 49:811, June 11, 1955
New York Times Magazine, Pp. 20, Sept. 11, 1955
New Yorker, 31:61, July 30, 1955 and 31:76, Oct. 15, 1955
Newsweek, 46:103, Oct. 17, 1955
Oxenhandler, Neal, "Dialectic and Rhetoric in 'La Guerre de Troie n'Aura
pas Lieu' ", *L'Esprit Créateur* (1969), 9:93-103
Reporter, 13:42, Oct. 20, 1955
Revue des Deux Mondes, s8 31:460-62, Jan. 15, 1936
Revue Politique et Littéraire, 74:34, Jan. 4, 1936
Saturday Review, 38:27, Oct. 22, 1955
Schweig, Gunter, "Jean Giraudoux, 'La Guerre de Troie n'Aura pas Lieu' ",
Die Neueren Sprachen n. s. (1966), Pp. 332-41
Spectator, 194:742, June 10, 1955

Theatre Arts, 20:361-63, May, 1936 and 39:22, Dec., 1955
Time, 66:51-52, Oct. 17, 1955
Tynan, Kenneth, *Curtains; Selections from the Drama Criticism and Related Writings*. 1961. Pp. 96-98

The Trojan War Will Not Take Place   *SEE*   The Tiger at the Gates

Virtuous Island, 1935
Life, 37:117-18, Dec. 13, 1954

BENJAMIN F. GLAZER

SEE

VICKI BAUM and BENJAMIN F. GLAZER

JOHANN WOLFGANG VON GOETHE

Egmont, 1789
Barnasch, H., "Goethes 'Egmont'. Zu Einigen Problemen der Unterrichtlichen Erschliessung", *Deutschunterricht* (1962), 15:273-87
Burckhardt, Sigurd, " 'Egmont' and 'Prinz Friedrich von Homburg': Expostulation and Reply", *German Quarterly*, 36:113-19, 1963
Glaesener, H., "Goethe et la Belgique", *Revue de Littérature Comparée*, 12:217-37, Jan., 1932
Halle, H. G., "Goethe's Political Thinking and 'Egmont' ", *Germanic Review* (1967), 42:96-107
Hartmann, Horst, "Goethes 'Egmont': Eine Analyse", *Weimarer Beitrage* (1967), Pp. 48-75
Ittner, Robert T., "Klarchen in Goethes 'Egmont' ", *Journal of English and Germanic Philology*, 62:252-61, 1963
Nicholls, Roger A., " 'Egmont' and the Vision of Freedom", *German Quarterly* (1970), 43:188-98
Rehder, Helmut, " 'Egmont' and 'Faust' ", *Monatshefte*, 55:203-15, 1963
Sammons, J. L., "On the Structure of Goethe's 'Egmont' ", *Journal of English and Germanic Philology*, 62:241-51, April, 1963
Schaum, Konrad, "Dämonie und Schicksal in Goethes 'Egmont' ", *Germanische-Romanische Monatschrift*, Neue Folge 10:139-57, 1960
Schwartländer, Johannes, Michael Landmann and Werner Loch, eds., *Verstehen und Vertrauen: Otto Friedrich Bollnow zum 65. Geburtstag*. 1968. Pp. 272-92
Swales, M. W., "Questionable Politician; A Discussion of the Ending to Goethe's 'Egmont' ", *Modern Language Review* (Oct. 1971), 66:832-40
Van Abbé, Derek, *Goethe; New Perspectives on a Writer and His Time*. 1972. Pp. 67-69
Waldeck, Marie-Luise, "Klärchen; An Examination of her role in Goethe's 'Egmont' ", *Publications of the English Goethe Society* (1964), 35:68-91

Faust, 1808
Allen, Gay W., "Jurgen and Faust", *Sewanee Review*, 39:485-492, 1931
Andrews, W. P., "Goethe's Key to 'Faust' ", *Atlantic Monthly*, 67:538-46, 676-87, 820-38, April-June, 1891
Arndt, Karl J. R., "Zu den 'Lücken' in der Gretchen-Tragödie", *Monatshefte*, 56:174-76, 1964
Atkins, Stuart P., "The Evaluation of Romanticism in Goethe's 'Faust' ", *Journal of English and Germanic Philology*, 54:9-38, 1955

———————— , "A 'Faust' Miscellany", *Modern Language Notes*, 72:286-87, 1957

———————— , "Goethe, Calderon and 'Faust: Der Tragödie Zweiten Teil' ", *Germanic Review*, 28: 83-98, 1953

Atkins, Stuart, "The Interpretation of Goethe's 'Faust' ", *Orbis Litterarum* (1965), 20:239-67

———————— , "The Mothers, the Phorcides, and the Cabiri in Goethe's 'Faust' ", *Monatshefte*, 45:289-96. 1953

———————— , "Reconsideration of Some Misunderstood Passages in the Gretchen Tragedy of Goethe's 'Faust' ", *Modern Language Review*, 48: 421-34, 1953

———————— , "Studies of Goethe's 'Faust' ", *German Quarterly* (1966), 31:303-10

———————— , "Visions of Leda and the Swan in Goethe's 'Faust' ", *Modern Language Notes*, 68:340-44, 1953

Baldensperger, F., "Pour une Interpretation Correcte de L'Episode D'Euphorion", *Revue de Littérature Comparée*, 12:142-58, Jan., 1932

Barrack, Charles M., "Mephistopheles; 'Ein Teil Jener Kraft, die Stets das Böse Will und Stets das Gute Schafft' ", *Seminar. A Journal of Germanic Studies* (1971), 7,iii:163-74

Barzun, J., *Energies of Art; Studies of Authors, Classic and Modern*. 1956. Pp. 23-48

Bémol, M., "Goethe, Rousseau et 'Faust' ", *Etudes Germaniques*, 13:1-17, 1958

Bencze, E., "La Tragédie de L'Homme Est-Elle le Faust Hongrois?", *Revue de Littérature Comparée*, 14:142-52, Jan., 1934

Bennett, James O'Donnell, *Much Loved Books; Best Sellers of the Ages*. 1924. Pp. 141-47

Benson, A. B., "English Criticism of the Prologue in Heaven in Goethe's 'Faust' ", *Modern Philology*, 19:225-43, Feb., 1922

Bergstraesser, A., *Goethe and the Modern Age; the International Convocation at Aspen, Colorado, 1949*. 1950. Pp. 38-49

Berman, Marshall, "Sympathy for the Devil: Faust, the '60s, and the Tragedy of Development", *American Review* (1974), 19:23-75

Bianquis, G., "Le Second Faust; Note Fragmentaire", *Revue Philosophique*, 118:295-321, Nov., 1934

Binder, Wolfgang, "Goethes Klassische Faust-Konzeption", *Deutsche Vierteljahrsschrift für Literaturwissenschaft und Geistesgeschichte* (1968), 42:55-88

Birchler, Linus, "Uber die Form von Goethes 'Faust' ", *Schweizer Rundschau*, 58:259-62, 1958

Bluhm, H. S., "Reception of Goethe's 'Faust' in England after the Middle of the Nineteenth Century", *Journal of English and Germanic Philology*, 34:201-12, April, 1935

Boudout, J., "Faust et Ahasuerus", *Revue de Littérature Comparée*, 16:691-709, 1936

Browning, R. M., "On the Structure of the 'Urfaust' ", *Modern Language Association. Publications* (PMLA), 68:458-95, 1953

Bruns, Friedrich, "Der Prolog im Himmel in Goethes 'Faust' ", *Monatshefte*, 45:171-80, 1953

———————— , "Die Hexenküche", *Monatshefte*, 46:260-66, 1954

———————— , "Die Mutter in Goethes 'Faust': Versuch Einer Deutung", *Monatshefte*, 43:365-89, 1951

Bub, Douglas F., "The Crown Incident in the 'Hexenküche': A Reinterpretation", *Modern Language Notes*, 73:200-06, 1958

_____ , "Denial, Affirmation and Escape in the Wager and Hexenkueche Scenes of Goethe's 'Faust'", *Modern Language Notes*, 76:39-43, 1961

_____ , "The 'Hexenküche' and the 'Mothers' in Goethe's 'Faust'", *Modern Language Notes* (1968), 83:775-79

_____ , "Intermediate Spirits in Goethe's 'Faust'", *Modern Language Notes*, 78:413-18, Oct., 1963 and 79:428-31, Oct. 1964

_____ , "New Solution to the Nacht Offen Feld Scene of Goethe's 'Faust'", *Modern Language Notes*, 74:440-44, May, 1959

_____ , "Vision and Revelation in Goethe's 'Faust'", *Modern Language Notes* (1973), 88:598-602

Burke, Kenneth, *Language as Symbolic Action; Essays on Life, Literature and Method.* 1966. Pp. 139-85

Cardinal, Clive K., "Polarity in Goethe's 'Faust'", *Modern Language Association. Publications* (PMLA), 54:445-61, 1949

Carriere, Ludwig, "Satan, Mephisto und die 'Wetten' bei Hiob und im 'Faust'", *Goethe*, 20:285-87, 1958

Carus, P., "Significance of Goethe's 'Faust'", *Open Court*, 22:147-72, March, 1908

Catholy, Eckeh and Winifred Hellmann, eds., *Festschrift für Klaus Ziegler.* 1968. Pp. 133-58

Contemporary Review 178:364-68, Dec., 1950

Cottrell, Alan P., "Zoilo-Thersites: Another 'Sehr Ernster Scherz' in Goethe's 'Faust II'", *Modern Language Quarterly* (1968), 29:29-41

Courthion, Pierre, *Romanticism*, tr. by Stuart Gilbert. 1961. Pp. 57-72

Crosby, Donald H. and George C. Schoolfield, eds., *Studies in German Drama; A Festschrift in Honor of Walter Silz.* 1974. Pp. 89-101

d'Amico, S., "Il 'Faust' di Goethe Inscenato da Max Reinhardt ai Festspiel de Salisburgo", *Nuovo Antologia*, 369:309-12, Sept. 16, 1933

Deering, R. W., "'Faust': Critical Study", *Chautauguan*, 35:66-75, 170-77, April-May, 1902

Della Volpe, Galvano, "Saggio di Una Lettura Sociologica del 'Faust'", *Società*, 15:207-15, 1959

Delp, W. E., "Earth Spirit in 'Faust'", *Modern Language Review*, 37:193-97, April, 1942

Dietze, Walter, "Der Walpurgisnachstraum in Goethes 'Faust': Entwurf, Gestallung, Funktion", *Modern Language Association. Publications* (1969), 84:476-91

Druian, Michael G., "Visual Imagination in Blake's 'Jerusalem' and Goethe's 'Faust'", *Dissertation Abstracts International* (1973), 34:1238A

Dshinoria, Otar, "Die Beschwörung der Helena in Goethes 'Faust'", *Goethe* (1970), 32:91-114

_____ , "Das Ende von Goethes 'Faust'", *Goethe Jahrbuch* (1973) 90:57-106

Dunn, Hough-Lewis, "The Language of the Magician as Limitation and Transcendence in The Wolfenbuttel 'Faustbuch', Greene's 'Friar Bacon', Marlowe's 'Dr. Faustus', Shakespeare's 'Tempest', and Goethe's 'Faust'", *Dissertation Abstracts International* (1974), 35:444A

Earll, M., "Faust Problem; What Was the Homunculus?", *Poet-Lore*, 13: #2:269-75, April, 1901

Ehrlich, G., "Ubersetzungen von Faust-Stellen Als Offenbarungen des Französischen Geistes", *Journal of English and Germanic Philology*, 35: 112-26, Jan., 1936

Eiserhardt, Ewald, "Zur Funktion und Psychologie der Valentinszene", *Germanic Review*, 12:223-29, 1937

Elston, Fred G., "Das Hexen-Einmaleins in Goethes 'Faust'", *Germanic Review*, 22:230-32, 1949

Emrich, Wilhelm, *The Literary Revolution and Modern Society and Other Essays*. 1971. Pp. 97-138

Engelberg, Edward, *The Unknown Distance, from Consciousness to Conscience; Goethe to Camus*. 1972. Pp. 47-57

Engelsing, Rolf, "Die Enstehung von Goethes 'Faust' im Sozialgeschichtlichen Zusammenhang", *Colloquia Germanica. International Zeitschrift für Germanische Sprach- und Literaturwissenschaft* (1972), 6: 126-64

The Era of Goethe; Essays Presented to James Boyd, Dufour, 1959. Pp. 81-105

Erbes, P. H., "Essence of Goethe's 'Faust'", *Poet-Lore*, 4:#10:504-10, Oct., 1892

Fairley, Barker, "On Translating 'Faust'", *German Life and Letters* (1969), 23:54-62

Faust, A. B., "Concerning the Changes in the Completed Part I (1808) as Compared with the Earlier Versions of Goethe's 'Faust'", *Journal of English and Germanic Philology*, 38:247-57, April, 1939

———————— , "On the Origin of the Gretchen-Theme in 'Faust'", *Modern Philology*, 20:181-88, Nov., 1922

Feise, Ernst, "Goethes 'Faust' als Hörspiel", *German Quarterly*, 32:211-16, 1959

———————— , "Intermediate Spirits in Goethe's 'Faust'", *Modern Language Notes*, 78:413-18 Oct., 1963

———————— , "Once Again: The Spirit Choruses in Goethe's 'Faust'", *Modern Language Notes*, 79:428-31, 1964

Fiedler, H. G., "Why Goethe Altered Faust's Christian Name", *Modern Language Review*, 38: 347-48, Oct., 1943

Fischer-Lamberg, Hanna, "Mephistopheles und die Handlungsfreiheit", *Chronik Wiener Goetheverein*, 60:37-40, 1956

Flatter, Richard, "The Veil of Beauty; Some Aspects of Verse and Prose in Shakespeare and Goethe", *Journal of English and Germanic Philology*, 50:437-50, 1951

Forster, Leonard "Lynkeus' Masque in 'Faust II'", *German Life and Letters* (1969), 23:62-71

Fuchs, Albert, "La Personnalité de Faust: Essai d'Analyse Psychologique", *Bulletin de la Faculté des Lettres de Strasbourg*, 40:499-506, 1963

Fuerst, Norbert, "Zur Gestaltenfülle des Faust", *Monatshefte*, 39:296-303, 1947

Fuller, Edmund, *A Pageant of the Theatre*. 1965. Pp. 177-201

Funke, Erich, "Goethes 'Faust' als Kunstpädogogische Aufgabe", *Monatshefte für Deutschen Unterricht*, 32:289-95, 1940

Ganz, Peter F., ed., *The Discontinuous Tradition; Studies in German Literature in Honour of Ernest Ludwig Stahl*. 1971. Pp. 54-66

Gausewitz, Walter, "A Re-View of Faust's Last Hours", *Monatshefte*, 41: 405-14, 1949

Gejman, B. Ja., "O 'Fausti' Gёte", *Filologiceskie Nauki* (1969), 12:42-55

German Studies Presented to Walter H. Bruford on His Retirement by His Pupils, Colleagues and Friends. 1962. Pp. 81-101

Gilbert, Mary E., "Ein Bisher Unbekanntes Paralipomenon zu Faust II'", *Jahrbuch des Freien Deutschen Hochstifts* 1971: 22-31

Gillies, A., "Macrocosmos-Sign in Goethe's 'Faust' and Herder's Mystic Hexagon", *Modern Language Review*, 36:397-99, July, 1941

Görne, Dieter, "'Faust' Auf der Bühne Unserer Zeit", *Goethe* (1970), 32: 151-76

Göetze, Alfred, "Gothes Begegnung mit den 'Faust Illustrationen' von Delacroix", *Philobiblon. Eine Vierteljahrsschrift für Buchund Graphik Sammler* (1970), 14:43-56

Götze, Alfred, "Goethes 'Faust' und Madame de Staël", *Archiv für das Studium der Neueren Sprachen und Literaturen* (1967), 204:184-91

Goldsmith, V. K., "Ambiguities in Goethe's 'Faust': A Lecture for the General Reader", *German Quarterly* (1966), 39:311-28

Goodrum, William D., "Ecclesiastes in Goethe's 'Faust'", *McNeese Review* (McNeese State College, Lake Charles, Louisiana), 14:74-79, 1963

Grafe, L. F., "On the Date and Idea of Faust's First Monologue in Faust II", *Modern Language Review*, 40:115-19, April, 1945

Gudde, E. G. "Goethe and His 'Faust'", *South Atlantic Quarterly*, 49:219-25, April, 1950

Hagen, F., and Mahlendorf, U., "Commitment, Concern and Memory in Goethe's 'Faust'", *Journal of Aesthetics and Art Criticism*, 21:473-84, 1963

Hamilton, Edith, *The Ever-Present Past*, 1964. Pp. 89-106

_____ , "Goethe and 'Faust'", *Theatre Arts*, 25: 451-61, June, 1941

Hamm, Heinz, "Zum Symbolbegriff im Zweiten Teil des 'Faust'", *Goethe* (1970), 32:142-50

Hammer, Carl, Jr., "Faust's Taciturnity in Dialogue", *The South Central Bulletin* (Tulsa, Okla., Studies by Members of the South Central MLA), 22:4, 42-46, 1962

Hankamer, E. T., "Faust's Redemption in the Light of Goethe's Own Myth of the Creation", *German Quarterly*, 26:143-49, 1953

Hannedouche, S., "Le Faust de Goethe au Goetheanum", *Cahiers d'Etudes Cathares*, 4:171-78, 1953

Hartwig, Hellmut A., ed., *The Southern Illinois Celebration; A Collection of Nine Papers*. 1950. Pp. 37-48

Haslinger, Adolf, ed., *Sprachkunst als Weltgestaltung: Festschrift für Herbert Seidler*. 1966. Pp. 172-90

Hatfield, J. T., "Note on the Prison-Scene in Goethe's 'Faust'", *Modern Language Association, Publications* (PMLA), 16:117-22, 1901

Heller, Erich, *Disinherited Mind; Essays in Modern German Literature and Thought*. 1952. Pp. 29-49

_____ , "Faust's Damnation; The Morality of Knowledge", *Listener*, 67:59-61, 121-23, 168-70, 1962

_____ , "Faust's Uerdamnis", *Merkur*, 17:32-56, 1963

Heller, Otto, *'Faust' and 'Faustus'; A Study of Goethe's Relationship to*

Marlow, Washington University Studies in Language and Literature, n. s. #2, 1931

Hendel, Charles W., "Goethe's 'Faust' and Philosophy", *Philosophy and Phenomenological Research*, 10:157-71, 1949

Henning, Hans, "Goethes 'Faust' in Japonischen Ubersetzung", *Marginalien: Blätter der Pirckheimer-Gesellschaft* (1968), 31:43-44

Hess, Mrs. John A., "A Leibnizian Philosophy in the Poetic Drama 'Faust' ", *Monatshefte für Deutschen Unterricht*, 24:247-52, 1932

Highet, Gilbert, *Powers of Poetry*. 1960. Pp. 315-22

Hippe, Robert, "Der 'Walpurgisnachstraum' in Goethes 'Faust': Versuch Einer Deutung", *Goethe: Neue Folge des Jahrbuchs der Goethe-Gesellschaft* (1966), 28:67-75

Höhle, Thomas, " 'Faust': Der Tragödie Zweiter Teil", *Weimarer Beiträge. Zeitschrift für Literaturwissenschaft* (1974), 20,H.6:49-89

Hohlfeld, A. R., "Pact and Wager in Goethe's 'Faust' ", *Modern Philology*, 18:513-36, Feb., 1921

Holtzhauer, Helmut, "Aufklärung, Kunst und 'Faust': Der "Übergang vom Ersten zum Zweiten Teil der Tragödie", *Weimarer Beiträge*. Pp. 275-97, 1963

Holtzhauer, Helmut, Bernard Zeller and Hans Henning, eds., *Studien zur Goethezeit; Festschrift für Lieselotte Blumenthal*. 1968. Pp. 165-77

Homan, S. R., " 'Dr. Faustus', Dekker's 'Old Fortunatus' and the Morality Plays", *Modern Language Quarterly* (1965), 26:497-505

Horn, Francis H., ed. *Literary Masterpieces of the Western World*. 1953. Pp. 185-207

Horvoy, Frank D., "Attempt of Relevance in Discussing Goethe's 'Faust' ", *Die Unterrichtspraxis* (1970), 3:79-87

Hoslett, Schuyler D., "The Superman in Nietzsche's Philosophy and in Goethe's 'Faust' ", *Monatshefte für Deutschen Unterricht*, 31:294-300, 1939

Humphrey, George, "Mephisto's Riddle", *Queen's Quarterly*, 40:99-106, Feb., 1933

Huneker, James Gibbons, *Variations*. 1921. Pp. 189-94

Hungerford, Edward Buell, *Shores of Darkness*. 1941. Pp. 240-91

Ide, Heinz, "Faust und Mephistopheles. Faust Program", *Jahrbuch der Wittheit zu Bremen* (1968), 12:59-77

Jacob, C. F., "The 'Faust' Attitude Toward Women", *Sewanee Review*, 26: 417-33, Oct., 1918

Jaeger, Hans, "Faust und Die Natur", *Modern Language Association. Publications* (PMLA), 62:436-71, 707-34, 1947

————— , "Die Szene 'Nacht Offen Feld' in Goethes 'Faust' ", *Monatshefte für Deutschen Unterricht*, 24:99-102, 1932

————— , "The 'Wald und Höhle' Monologue in 'Faust' ", *Monatshefte*, 41:395-404, 1949

James, Henry, *Literary Reviews and Essays; On American, English and French Literature*, ed. by Albert Mordell. 1957. Pp. 110-18

Jantz, Harold, "Faust's Vision of the Macrocosm", *Modern Language Notes*, 68:348-51, May, 1953

————— , "The Function of the 'Walpurgis Night's Dream' in the Faust Drama", *Monatshefte*, 44:397-408, 1952

————— , "Goethe, Faust, Alchemy and Jung", *German Quarterly*, 35.129-41, 1962

_____ , "Goethe's 'Faust' as a Renaissance Man; Sources and Prototypes", *Comparative Literature*, 1:337-48, 1949

Jantz, Harold, "Patterns and Structures in 'Faust': A Preliminary Inquiry", *Modern Language Notes* (1968), 83:359-89

_____ , "Place of the 'Eternal Womanly' in Goethe's 'Faust' Drama", *Modern Language Association. Publications* (PMLA), 68:791-805, 1953

Jockers, Ernst, "Faust und Meister, Zwei Polare Gestalten", *Germanic Review*, 21:118-31, 1946

Jonas, Klaus W., ed., *Deutsche Weltliteratur; Von Goethe bis Ingeborg Bachmann: Festgabe für J. Alan Pfeffer*. 1972. Pp. 28-44

Kahn, Ludwig W., "Voltaire's 'Candide' and the Problem of Secularization", *Modern Language Association. Publications* (PMLA), 67:886-88, 1952

Kaiser, K., "Goethe's 'Faust' in Its Entirety", *World Theatre* (1966), 15:#1:58-59

Kaufmann, M., "Job and the 'Faust' ", *Living Age*, 214:691-707, Sept. 11, 1897

Kaufmann, Walter A., "Faust and Jacob", *Germanic Review*, 26:124, 1951

_____ , *From Shakespeare to Existentialism; Studies in Poetry, Religion and Philosophy*. 1959. Pp. 56-70

_____ , "Goethe's Faith and Faust's Redemption", *Monatshefte*, 41:365-75, 1949

Keller, W. J., "Goethe's 'Faust', Part I as a Source of Part II", *Modern Language Notes*, 33:342-52, July, 1918

Kelman, John, *Among Famous Books*. 1912. Pp. 63-88

Kleinschmit von Lengefeld, Wilhelm, "Goethes 'Faust', Tragödie oder Fabeldichtung?", *Jahrbuch des Freien Deutschen Hochstifts* (1970), Pp. 98-126

Knight, A. H. J., "Some Points Concerning Goethe's 'Faust' ", *Publications of the English Goethe Society*, 31:24-37, 1961

Knoche, Grace, "Goethe, Weimar, and Faust", *Theosophical Forum*, 27:451-75, 1949

Koch, Freidrich, "Christliches und Scheinchristliches in Goethes 'Faust' ", *Germanisch-Romanische Monatsschrift* n. s. (1966), 16:244-63

Koller, Werner, "Goethes 'Faust' im Schwedischer Übersetzung", *Moderna Språk* (1972), 66:258-66

Kruger, Manfred, "Zur Geschichte der 'Faust'-Auffuhrungen", *Die Drei* (1963), 33:263-69

Krumpelman, J. T., "Goethe's 'Faust' ", *Modern Language Notes*, 41:107-14, Feb., 1926

Lange, Victor, ed., *Goethe: A Collection of Critical Essays*. 1968. Pp. 99-109 and 132-44

Laine, B., "By Water and By Fire: The Thales-Anaxagoras Debate in Goethe's 'Faust' ", *Germanic Review* (1975), 50:99-110

Latimer, Dan, "Homunculus as Symbol: Semantic and Dramatic Functions of the Figure in Goethe's 'Faust' ", *Modern Language Notes* (1974), 89:812-21

Lehner, Frederick, "Goethes 'Faust' auf der Bühne", *Germanic Review*, 25:95-102, 1952

Lopéz-Martín, Alfonso, "Concepción del Lenguaje en el 'Fausto' de Goethe", *Revista de la Universidad de Costa Rica* (1973), 35:67-71

Ludwig, Robert, "Der 'Lubecker Faust' von Goethe. Ein Verfremdetes Mysterium in Jahre 1937", *Lübeckische Blätter. Zeitschrift der Gesellschaft zu Förderung Gemeinnütziger Tätigkeit* (1970), 130:230-34

Maché, Ulrich, "Zu Goethes 'Faust': Studierzimmer I und Geisterchor", *Euphorion. Zeitschrift für Literaturgeschichte* (1971), 65:200-05

McClain, W. H., "Goethe's Chorus Mysticus as Significant Form", *Modern Language Notes*, 74:43-49, Jan., 1959

McEachran, F., "Goethe's 'Faust' and Dante's 'Divine Comedy'", *Hibbert Journal*, 30:638-44, July, 1932

——————, "Idea of Progress and Goethe's 'Faust'", *Nineteenth Century*, 101:862-70, 1927

McNeir, Waldo F., *Studies in Comparative Literature*. 1962. Pp. 199-218

Mahal, Günther, ed., *Ansichten zu Faust; Karl Theens zum 70. Geburtstag*. 1973. Pp. 35-48, 69-98 and 169-94

Maier, Hans Albert, "Goethes Gretchen-Mythos", *Monatshefte*, 45:401-18, 1953

——————, "Goethes Phantasiearbeit am Faustoff im Jahre 1771", *Modern Language Association. Publications* (PMLA), 67:125-47, 1952

Manacorda, G., "Problemi Eterni del Faust", *Nuova Antologia*, 356:196-207, 359:487-504, 363:161-71, 1931-32

Mann, Thomas, *Essays of Three Decades*, tr. by H. T. Lowe-Porter. 1947. Pp. 3-42

Marek, George Richard, ed., *World Treasury of Grand Opera; Its Triumphs, Trials, and Great Personalities*. 1957. Pp. 203-20

Masclaux, P., "L'Idée de Faust", *Mercure de France*, 182:94-105, Aug. 15, 1925

Mason, E. C., "Erdgeist Controversy Reconsidered", *Modern Language Review*, 55:66-78, Jan., 1960

Merezkovskiu, D., "L'Avvenire del Christianesimo", *Nuova Antologia*, 393:423-30, Oct. 16, 1937

Merkel, Gottfried F., ed., *On Romanticism and the Art of Translation: Studies in Honor of Edwin Hermann Zeydel*. 1956. Pp. 7-27

Metzger, Lore, "A Note on the Meaning of Activity in Goethe's 'Faust'", *History of Ideas Newsletter*, 1:#2:13, 1955

Meyer, H., "A New Interpretation of 'Faust'", *Univ. of Toronto Quarterly*, 23:425-26, 1954

Michelsen, Peter, "Fausts Erblindung", *Deutsche Vierteljahrsschrift für Literaturwissenschaft und Geistesgeschichte*, 36:26-35, 1962

Morgan, Bayard Q., "Goethe on Goethe's 'Faust'", *Symposium*, 8:102-12, 1954

Moulton, Richard G., *World Literature and Its Place in General Literature*. 1911. Pp. 237-88

Mueller, Gustav Emil, *Philosophy of Literature*. 1948. Pp. 125-63

Müller, Joachim, "Die Figur des Homunculus in Goethes 'Faust'", *Berichte uber die Verhandlungen des Sachsischen Akademie der Wissenschaften zur Leipzig*, 108:#4, 1963

——————, "Goethe's 'Faust' und Holderlins 'Empedokles': Vision und Utopie in der Dichtung", *Goethe*, 20:118-39, 1958

Nabholz, Johannes, "A Note on the Mothers in Goethe's 'Faust'", *Symposium*, 15:198-203, 1961

——————, "Who Was Gretchen?", *German Quarterly*, 27:239-40, 1954

Nedden, Otto C. A., *Europäische Akzente; Ansprachen und Essays*. 1968. Pp. 57-66

Neilson, Francis, *Cultural Tradition and Other Essays*. 1957. Pp. 65-77

Nollendorfs, Valters, "Die 'Lücken' in der Gretchentragödie", *Monatshefte*, 55:254-64, 1963

Osherson, S., "An Adlerian Approach to Goethe's 'Faust'", *Journal of Individual Psychology* (1965), 21:194-98

Paul, Fritz, "Gebirge und Meer in der Szenerie des Vierten Aktes von Faust II' ", *Orbis Litterarum* (1970), 25:230-43

Pfeiler, Wilhelm K., "Faust als Reprasentativer Mensch", *Germanic Review*, 6:8-26, 1931

Politzer, Heinz, "Of Time and Doctor Faustus", *Monatshefte*, 51:145-55, 1959

Porterfield, A. W., "Faust: Echoes of Part I in Part II", *Philological Quarterly*, 15:53-69, 1936

Puknat, Siegfried B., "Literature and Theology: A Comment on Goethe's 'Faust' ", *Research Studies* (1968), 36:1-14

Rather, L. J., "Some Reflections on the Philemon and Baucis Episode in Goethe's 'Faust' ", *Diogenes*, #25:60-73, 1959

Rehder, Helmut, "Classical Walpurgis Night in Goethe's 'Faust' ", *Journal of English and Germanic Philology*, 54:591-611, Oct., 1955

——————— , " 'Egmont' and 'Faust' ", *Monatshefte*, 55:203-15, 1963

Reinhard, J., "Goethe's Mephistopheles", *Sewanee Review*, 5:80-94, Jan. 1897

Reps, A., "Les Deux Expressions du Mal dans le 'Faust' de Goethe", *Triades*, 11:39-53, 1963

Reps, Albert, "Die Gestalt des Bösen Goethes 'Faust' ", *Die Drei* (1965), 35:366-85

Rihouët-Coroze, S., "Actualité de 'Faust' ", *Triades*, 11:1-3, 1963

Riola, Dionisia A., ed., "World Literature", *General Education Journal* (1968), 13:108-17

Rossi, Dominick, "Parallels in Wilde's 'The Picture of Dorian Gray' and Goethe's 'Faust' ", *College Language Association Journal* (1969), 13:188-91

Rüdiger, Ulrich, "Zu Einigen Beinamen des Mephistopheles in Goethes 'Faust' ", *Arcadia. Zeitschrift für Vergleichen de Literaturwissenschaft* (1970), 5:195-96

Ryder, F. G., "George Ticknor and Goethe—Boston and Gottingen", *Modern Language Association. Publications* (PMLA), 67:960-72, 1952

Salm, P., "Faust and Irony", *Germanic Review*, 40:192-204, May, 1965

——————— , "Faust, Eros, and Knowledge", *German Quarterly* (1966), 39:329-39

Santayana, George, *Little Essays Drawn from the Writings of George Santayana* by L. P. Smith. 1920. Pp. 196-99

——————— , *Three Philosophical Poets*, (Harvard Studies in Comparative Literature). 1910. Pp. 139-99

Sargeaunt, G. M., "Faust and Helen of Troy", *Nineteenth Century*, 100:908-17, 1926

Saunders, G., "Faust and the German Character", *Nineteenth Century*, 80:718-39, Oct., 1916

Saupe, Paul, "Konzeption zur Behandlung von Goethes 'Faust' im Unterricht eines Ifl,", *Deutschunterricht* (1970), 23:638-40

Schadewaldt, Wolfgang, "Faust und Helena: Zu Goethes Auffassung vom Schönen und der Realität des Realen im Zweiten Teil des 'Faust' ", *Deutsche Vierteljahrsschrift für Literaturwissenschaft und Geistesgeschichte*, 30:1-40, 1956

Scheibe, Siegfried, "Zur Enstehungsgeschichte der Walpurgisnacht in 'Faust I' ", *Forschungen u. Fortschritte* (1963), 37:245-49

Scheu, W., "Wer ist der tragische Held in Goethes 'Faust'? Eine Untersuchung", *Preussische Jahrbucher*, 220:157-82, May, 1930

Schiller, Ferdinand Canning Scott, *Our Human Truths*. 1935. Pp. 124-39

Schmitt, Albert R., ed., *Festschrift für Detlev W. Schumann zum 70. Geburtstag.* 1970. Pp. 145-72

Scholz, Albert, "Goethe's Homonculus", *German Quarterly*, 17:23-27, 1944

School and Society, 69:336-37, May 7, 1949

Schreiber, William I., "'Faust' in Germany in 1951", *German Quarterly*, 26:123-26, 1953

Schuchard, G. C. L., "Fausts Vorschau im Lichte von Schillers Aesthetischen Briefen", *Journal of English and Germanic Philology*, 48:533-42, Oct., 1949

——————————— , "The Last Scene in Goethe's 'Faust'", *Modern Language Association. Publications* (PMLA), 64:417-44, 1949

Sehrt, E. H., "Goethe's 'Faust'", *Modern Language Notes*, 42:323-24, May, 1927

Seibert, Philipp, "Das Element des Romantischen in Goethe", *Journal of English and Germanic Philology*, 26:33-41, 1928

Seidlin, Oskar, *Essays in German and Comparative Literature.* 1961. Pp. 60-69

——————————— , "Helena; Vom Mythos zur Person; Versuch Einer Neu Interpretation des Helena-Aktes, Faust II", *Modern Language Association. Publications* (PMLA), 62:183-212, 1947

Selinger, M., "Homunculus Motif and the End of the Classical Walpurgis Night", *Modern Language Review*, 41:177-85, 1946

Speck, W. A., "George Borrow and Goethe's 'Faust'", *Modern Language Association. Publications* (PMLA), 41:167-78, 1926

Stahl, E. L., "Schiller and the Composition of Goethe's 'Faust'", *Germanic Review*, 34:185-99, Oct., 1959

Stebbins, Sara A., "The Poodle in Goethe's 'Faust'", *Language Quarterly* (1969), 81:15-16 and 42

Steffen, Hans, ed., *Das Deutsche Lustspiel.* 1968. Pp. 94-119

Steinhauer, H., "Faust's Pact with the Devil", *Modern Language Association. Publications* (PMLA), 71:180-200, 1956

Stemfer, René, "'Wer Immer Strebend Sich Bemuht': Essai d'Interpretation de Faust", *Les Langues Modernes* (1969), 63:633-36

Stock, Frithjof, "Vom Ariel in Shakespeares 'The Tempest' zum Ariel in Goethes 'Faust II'", *Arcadia* (1972), 7:274-80

Stocklein, Paul, "Wie Beginnt und Wie Endet Goethes 'Faust'?", *Jahrbuch. Literaturwissenschaftliches* n. s. (1962), 3:29-51

Strelka, Joseph, ed., *Perspectives in Literary Symbolism.* 1968. Pp. 181-98

Strindberg, August, *Open Letters to the Intimate Theater.* 1966. Pp. 279-89

Sveino, Per, "Er 'Faust' et Kristent Frelsesdrama?", *Kirke og Kultur* (1972) 77:358-61

Theatre Arts, 45:21-23, Feb., 1961 and 45:11, April, 1961

Thieme, K., "Faust im Zweilicht", *Schweizer Ründschau*, 51:438-40, 1951

Thomas, Calvin, *Scholarship and Other Essays.* 1924. Pp. 135-58

Thurnan, H. C., "Faust and the Good Life", *Philological Quarterly*, 12:269-79, July, 1933

Time, 77:81-2, Feb. 17, 1961

Time was Away; The World of Louis MacNeice, ed. Terence Brown and Alec Reid. 1974. Pp. 67-71

Traditions and Transitions; Studies in Honor of Harold Jantz, ed. Lieselotte E. Kurth, et als. 1972. Pp. 132-41

Tuschel, Karl-Heinz, "Der Knittelvers in Goethes 'Faust'", *Neue Deutsche Literatur*, 9:9:86-109, 1961

Van Abbe, Derek, *Goethe; New Perspectives on a Writer and His Time*. 1972. Pp. 114-28

Van Doren, Mark, ed., *New Invitation to Learning*. 1942. Pp. 59-73

VonTaube, O., "Gedanken zu Goethes 'Faust'", *Preussische Jahrbucher*, 240:65-9, April, 1935

Walheim, Alfred, "Noten und Abhandlungen zu Goethes 'Faust'. Zweiten Teil", *Chronik Wiener Goetheverein*, 57:17-52, 1958

Walz, J. A., "Faust I: 'Nacht, Offen Feld'", *Modern Language Notes*, 34: 285-91, May, 1919

——————————, "Hexenfexen, Faust II", *Modern Language Notes*, 55:117-23, Feb., 1940

Warde, Anton R., "A Consideration of the Views of Nature Held by Goethe and His Faust", *Dissertation Abstracts International* (1970), 31:407A

——————————, "The Identity of Real and Ideal in Goeth's 'Faust': A Unifying Irony", *German Quarterly* (1974), 47:544-55

Wasserman, Earl Reeves, ed., *Aspects of the Eighteenth Century*. 1965. Pp. 281-304

Watson, F., "Goethe and Faust; with Some Illustrations for Faust by N. Leeder", *Bookman* (London), 82:22-24, April, 1932

Weigand, Hermann John, *Surveys and Soundings in European Literature*. 1966. Pp. 175-200

Weigand, Hermann, "Wetten und Pakt in Goethes 'Faust'", *Monatshefte*, 53:325-37, 1961

Wells, B. W., "Goethe's 'Faust'", *Sewanee Review*, 2:385-412, Aug., 1894

Wicksteed, P. H., "Magic in Faust", *Hibbert Journal*, 9:754-64, July, 1911

Wilkinson, Elizabeth M., "Goethe's 'Faust': Tragedy in the Diachronic Mode", *Publications of the English Goethe Society* (1972), 42:116-74

Wittkowski, Wolfgang, "Faust und der Kaiser: Goethes Letztes Wort zum 'Faust'", *Deutsche Vierteljahrsschrift für Literaturwissenschaft und Geistesgeschichte* (1969), 43:631-51

——————————, "'Gedenke zu Leben!' Schuld und Sorge in Goethes 'Faust'", *Publications of the English Goethe Society* (1968), 38:114-45

Workman, M. T., "Was Goethe a Christian?", *Religion in Life*, 19 No. 2: 224-36, 1950

Yearbook of Comparative and General Literature, 1961. 1962. Pp. 33-38

Ziegischmid, A. J. F., "Zur Quelle von Goethes Faust II, Akt 5: Bergschlichten", *Journal of English and Germanic Philology*, 40:229-56, April, 1941

Zorn, Otto Manthey, "Goethe's 'Faust' in Rickert's Interpretation", *Germanic Review*, 8:10-16, 1933

Gotz Von Berlichingen Mit der Eisernen Hand *SEE* Götz von Berlichingen with the Iron Hand

Goetz von Berlichingen with the Iron Hand, 1774

Applebaum Graham, Ilse, "Götz von Berlichingen's Right Hand", *German Life and Letters*, 16:212-28, 1963

Haile, H. G., "Herr, Er Will Uns Fressen: The Spirit of Götz", *Journal of English and Germanic Philology*, 64:610-34, Oct., 1965

Ryder, Frank G., "Toward a Revaluation of Goethe's 'Goetz': Features of Recurrence", *Modern Language Association. Publications* (PMLA), 79:58-66, March, 1964

————————— , "Toward a Revaluation of Goethe's 'Goetz': the Protagonist", *Modern Language Association. Publications* (PMLA), 77:58-70, 1962

Schumann, Detlev W., "Goethe and Friedrich Carl von Moser: A Contribution to the Study of 'Götz von Berlichingen'", *Journal of English and Germanic Philology*, 53:1-22, 1954

Iphigenie auf Taurus, 1779

Adorno, Theodor W., "Zum Klassizismus von Goethes 'Iphigenie'", *Neue Rundschau* (1967), 78:586-99

Allison, D. E., "The Spiritual Element in Schiller's 'Jungfrau' and Goethe's 'Iphigenie'", *German Quarterly*, 32:316-29, 1959

Atkins, Stuart P., "On the Opening Lines of Goethe's 'Iphigenie'", *Germanic Review*, 24:116-23, 1949

Baker, G. M., "Healing of Orestes in Goethe's 'Iphigenie auf Taurus'", *Modern Philology*, 15:349-54, Oct., 1917

Browning, R. M., "The Humanity of Goethe's 'Iphigenie'", *German Quarterly*, 30:98-113, 1957

Burckhart, Sigurd, *The Drama of Language; Essays on Goethe and Kleist.* 1970. Pp. 33-56 and 66-93

Burckhardt, Sigurd, "Die Stimme der Wahrheit und der Menschlichkeit': Goethes 'Iphigenie'", *Monatshefte*, 48:49-71, 1956

Burger, Heinz-Otto, "Zur Interpretation von Goethes 'Iphigenie'", *Germanisch-Romanische Monatsschrift*, Neue Folge 9:266-77, 1959

Colby, Ursula J., "The Sorrows of Iphigenie", *Publications of the English Goethe Society* (1964-65), 35:38-67

Dencker, Klaus, "Zur Entstehunggeschichte von Goethes 'Iphigenie auf Taurus'", *Jahrbuch des Wiener Goethe-Vereins* (1967), 71:69-82

The Era of Goethe; Essays Presented to James Boyd. 1959. Pp. 106-17

Fowler, Frank M., "Storm and Thunder in Gluck's and Goethe's 'Iphigenia auf Taurus' and in Schillers's 'Die Jungfrau von Orleans'", *Publications of the English Goethe Society* (1973), 43:1-27

Goessler, Lisette, "Zu Goethes 'Iphigenie'", *Antike und Abendland. Beitrage zum Verstandnis der Griechen und Romer und Ihres Nachlebens* (1973), 18:161-72

Goldsmith, Ulrich K., "The Healing of Orestes in Goethe's 'Iphigenie auf Taurus'", *Far Western Forum; A Review of Ancient and Modern Letters* (1974), 1:209-20

Grimm, Reinhold and Conrad Wildemann, eds., *Literatur und Geistesgeschichte: Festgabe für Heinz Otto Burger.* 1968. Pp. 140-57

Gundolf, Friedrich, *Dem Lebendigen Geist. Aus Reden, Aufsatzen und Buchern Ausgewahlt von D. Berger u. M. Frank.* 1962. Pp. 221-38

Hall, F. A., "Comparison of the Iphigenias of Euripides, Goethe and Racine", *Classical Journal*, 9:371-84, June, 1914

Henckel, Arthur, "iphigenie Auf Taurus", *Das Deutsche Drama*, 1:169-92, 1958

Henkel, A., "Die 'Verteufelt Humane' Iphigenie", *Euphorion. Zeitschrift für Literatur Geschichte* (1965), 59:1-17

Herenger, A., "La Religion de la Vérité Dans Iphigenie", *Revue de Littérature Comparée*, 12:43-48, Jan., 1932

Hritzu, J. N., "Dramatic Irony in Goethe's 'Iphigenie auf Taurus' ", *Monatshefte für Deutsche Unterricht*, 36:217-23, 1944

Lange, Victor, ed., *Goethe: A Collection of Critical Essays*. 1968. Pp. 50-64

Lindenau, Herbert, "Die Geistesgeschichtlichen Voraussetzungen von Goethes 'Iphigenie' ", *Zeitschrift für Deutsche Philologie*, 75:113-53, 1956

Ludwig, W., "Goethes 'Iphigenie', Kleists 'Amphitryon' und Kierkegaard", *Monatshefte* (1947), 39:234-36

Manasse, Ernst M., "Iphigenie und die Götter", *Modern Language Quarterly*, 13:377-91, 1952

May, Kurt, "Goethe's 'Iphigenie' ", *Form und Bedeutung*, Pp. 73-88, 1957

Melchinger, Siegfried, "Das Theater Goethes; Am Beispiel der 'Iphigenie' ", *Jahrbuch der Deutschen Schillergesellschaft* (1967), 11:297-319

Morford, Mark, ed., *The Endless Fountain; Essays on Classical Humanism; Symposium in Honor of Clarence Allen Forbes*. 1972. Pp. 127-35

Müller, J., "Goethes 'Iphigenie' ", *Wissenschaftliche Zeitschrift der Friedrich Schiller Universität Jena, Gessellschäfts- und Sprachwissenschaftliche Reihe*, 9:309-20, 1959-60

Mueller, Martin, "Time and Redemption in 'Samson Agonistes' and 'Iphigenie auf Taurus' ", *University of Toronto Quarterly* (1972), 41:227-45

New Yorker, 35:136-8, Oct. 17, 1959

Politzer, Heinz, "No Man is an Island; A Note on Image and Thought in Goethe's 'Iphigenie' ", *Germanic Review*, 37:42-54, 1962

Pollak, Hans, "Der Schluss von Goethes 'Iphigenie auf Taurus' ", *Germanisch-Romanische Monatsschrift*, Neue Folge 9:427-30, 1959

Scarborough, W. S., "One Heroine—Three Poets", *Education*, 19:285-93, Jan., 1899

Seidlin, Oskar, "Goethe's 'Iphigenie' and the Humane Ideal", *Modern Language Quarterly*, 10:307-20, 1949

_____ , "Goethes 'Iphigenie'—Verteufelt Human?' ", *Wirkendes Wort*, 5:272-80, 1955

Stahl, Ernest L., "Fluch und Entsühnung in Goethes 'Iphigenie auf Taurus' ", *Germanisch-Romanische Monatsschrift*, Neue Folge 11:179-84, 1961

Sternberg, T. T., "Ibsen's 'Catilina' and Goethe's 'Iphigenie auf Taurus' ", *Modern Language Notes*, 39:329-36, June, 1924

Studies in German Drama; A Festschrift in Honor of Walter Silz. 1974. Pp. 71-87. Crosby, Donald H., and George C. Schoolfield, eds.

Van Abbe, Derek, *Goethe; New Perspectives on a Writer and His Time*. 1972. Pp. 100-02

Wagner, H., "Goethes 'Iphigenie', 'Helena', 'Pandora' ", *Glaube und Gewissen. Eine Protestantische Monatsschrift* (1963), 9:55-56

Waldmann, Walter, "Zur Gestaltung des Klassisch-Humanistischen Menschenbildes am Beispiel von Goethes Schauspiel 'Iphigenie auf Taurus' ", *Wissenschaftliche Zeitschrift der U. Rostock* (1973), 22:405-13

Weiss, H. F., "Image Structures in Goethe's 'Iphigenie auf Tauris' ", *Modern Language Notes* (Apr. 1972), 87:433-49

Werner, Hans-Georg, "Antinomien der Humanitá Tskonzeption in Goethes 'Iphigenie' ", *Weimarer Beiträge* (1968), Pp. 361-84

The Natural Daughter, 1803
  Crosby, Donald H. and George C. Schoolfield, eds., *Studies in German Drama;
  A Festschrift in Honor of Walter Silz*. 1974. Pp. 71-87

Die Natürliche Tochter   *SEE*   The Natural Daughter

Stella, 1806
  Bidou, H., "Stella", *Journal des Débats*, 38 pt. 2:515-17, Sept. 25, 1931
  Castle, Edward, " 'Stella': Ein Schauspiel für Liebende", *Jahrbuch des Wiener
  Goethe-Vereins* (1969), 73:125-46
  Hess, Günter H., " 'Stella' und 'Die Wahlverwandtschaften' ", *Seminar; A Jour-
  nal of Germanic Studies* (1970), 6:216-24

Torquato Tasso, 1807
  Bevilacqua, Giuseppe, " 'Tasso' Eroe Positivo?", *Studi Germanici* (1971), 9:71-
  82
  Blumenthal, Liselotte, "Arkadien in Goethe's 'Tasso' ", *Goethe*, 21:1-24, 1959
  Boulby, Mark, " Judgment, by Epithet, in Goethe's 'Torquato Tasso' ", *Modern
  Language Association. Publications* (Mar. 1972), 87:167-81
  Burckhardt, Sigurd, "The Consistency of Goethe's 'Tasso' ", *Journal of English
  and Germanic Philology*, 57:394-402, 1958
  _____ , *The Drama of Language; Essays on Goethe and Kleist.*
  1970. Pp. 57-65
  Cooper, W. A., "Goethe's Revision and Completion of his 'Tasso' ", *Modern
  Language Association. Publications* (PMLA), 34:14-29, March, 1919
  Cotet, Pierre, "Goethe et la Tragédie Racinienne: 'Torquato Tasso' ", *Cahiers
  Raciniens*, #14:56-82, 1963
  DeLaura, David J., ed., *Victorian Prose; A Guide to Research*. 1973. Pp. 5-23
  Hodeige, Fritz and Rothe, Carl, eds., *Atlantische Begegnungen: Eine Freundes-
  gabe für Arnold Bergstraesser*. 1964. Pp. 173-81
  Holmes, T. M., "Homage and Revolt in Goethe's 'Torquato Tasso' ", *Modern
  Language Review* (1970), 65:813-19
  Holtzhauer, Helmut, Bernhard Zeller and Hans Henning, eds., *Studien zur
  Goethezeit: Festschrift für Lieselotte Blumenthal*. 1968. Pp. 285-301
  Magill, C. P., " 'Torquato Tasso' oder die Feindlichen Brüder", *German Life
  and Letters* (1969), 23:39-47
  Ossar, Michael, "Die Kunstlergestalt in Goethes 'Tasso' und Grillparzars
  'Sapho' ", *German Quarterly* (1972), 45:645-61
  Poggioli, Renato, *The Oaten Flute; Essays on Pastoral Poetry and the Pastoral
  Ideal*. 1975. Pp. 220-40
  Rasch, W., "Goethes 'Torquato Tasso': Die Tragödie des Dichters", *Germanic
  Review*, 32:155-57, April, 1957
  Redslob, Edwin, "Torquato Tasso", *Neue Deutsche Hefte* (1974), 143:521-31
  Sammons, Jeffrey L. and Ernst Schürer, eds., *Lebendige form; Interpretationen
  zur Deutschen Literatur. Festschrift für Heinrich E. K. Henel*. 1970. Pp. 89-
  99
  Scholl, Margaret A., "German 'Bildungsroman': Schiller's 'Don Carlos',
  Goethe's 'Torquato Tasso' and Kleist's 'Prinz Friedrich von Homburg' ",
  Dissertation Abstracts International (1973), 34:1934A
  Schultz, H. Stefan, "Hofmannsthal's 'Die Schwierige' and Goethe's 'Torquato
  Tasso' ", *Publications of the English Goethe Society* (1963), 33:130-49
  Silz, Walter, "Ambivalences in Goethe's 'Tasso' ", *Germanic Review* 31:243-68,
  1956

Van Abbe, Derek, *Goethe; New Perspectives on a Writer and His Time.* 1972. Pp. 97-100

White, Alfred D., "The Elysian Vision in Goethe's 'Tasso' and Its Implications", *Trivium* (1972), 7:129-34

Wilkinson, Elizabeth M., "Tasso—ein Gesteigerter Werther in the Light of Goethe's Principle of Steigerung", *Modern Language Review*, 44:305-28, 1949

——————————, "Torquato Tasso", *Das Deutsche Drama*, 1:193-214, 1958

NIKOLAI VASILYEVICH GOGOL

The Gamblers, 1843
Rowe, William Woodin, *Through Gogol's Looking Glass.* 1976. Pp. 150-54

Igroki   *SEE*   The Gamblers

Inspector General, 1836
Bookman, 73:71, March, 1931

Börtnes, Jostein, "Gogol's 'Revizor': A Study in the Grotesque", *Social Science Information* (1969), 15:47-63

Catholic World, 141:89, April, 1935

Cole, Toby and Chinoy, Helen Krich, eds., *Directing the Play; A Source Book of Stagecraft.* 1953. Pp. 259-72

——————————, *Directors on Directing; A Source Book of the Modern Theater*, Rev. ed. 1963. Pp. 311-25

Gassner, John and Allen, Ralph G., eds., *Theatre and Drama in the Making.* 1964. Pp. 743-50

Karlinsky, Simon, "The Alogical and Absurdist Aspects of Russian Realist Drama", *Comparative Drama* (Fall 1969), 3:147-55

Kott, J., "Eating of 'The Inspector General' ", *Theatre Quarterly* (1975), 5:21-29

London Mercury, 14:196-97, June, 1926

Maguire, Robert A., ed., *Gogol from the 20th Century; Eleven Essays.* 1975. Pp. 200-65

Nation (London), 27:107-08, April 24, 1920

New Statesman, 27:107-08. May 8, 1926

Nordby, Edward L., "Gogol's Comic Theory and Practice in 'The Inspector General' ", *Dissertation Abstracts International* (1972), 32:4627

Novick, Julius, *Beyond Broadway; The Quest for Permanent Theatres.* 1968. Pp. 295-296

Ostrander, Sheila and Lynn Schroeder, "Off Stage with 'The Inspector General' in the USSR", *Texas Quarterly* (1968), 11:209-16

Outlook, 157:31, Jan. 7, 1931

Rowe, William Woodin, *Through Gogol's Looking Glass.* 1976. Pp. 135-43

Spectator, 124:551-52, April 24, 1920, and 136:846, May 15, 1926

Symons, James M., *Meyerhold's Theatre of the Grotesque; The Post-Revolutionary Productions, 1920-1932.* 1971. Pp. 145-68

Theatre Arts, 15:95-96, Feb., 1931, and 19:256, April, 1935

Theatre Magazine, 53:26, Feb., 1931

Zelinsky, Bodo, "Gogols 'Revizor': Eine Tragödie?" *Zeitschrift für Slavische Philologie* (1971), 36:1-40

The Marriage, An Utterly Incredible Occurrence, 1842
Karlinsky, Simon, "The Alogical and Absurdist Aspects of Russian Realist Drama", *Comparative Drama* (Fall 1969), 3:147-55

London Mercury, 38:253, July, 1938
New Statesman and Nation, 15:1027, June 18, 1938
Rowe, William Woodin, *Through Gogol's Looking Glass*. 1976. Pp. 144-49

Revizor *SEE* Inspector General

Zhenitba; Sovershenno Neveroyatnoye Sobytiye *SEE* The Marriage, An Utterly
Incredible Occurrence

CARLO GOLDONI

Baruffe Chiozzotte *SEE* The Chioggian Brawls

The Boars, 1760
DeMonticelli, Roberto, "Squarzina Ripropone i 'Rusteghi' di Goldoni", *Epoca*
(1969), 994-1000
Nuova Antologia, 388:349-51, Dec. 1, 1936

La Bottega del Caffe *SEE* The Coffee House

Il Bugiardo *SEE* The Liar

La Cameriera Brillante *SEE* The Clever Lady's Maid

Il Campiello *SEE* The Public Square

La Casa Nova *SEE* The New House

The Chioggian Brawls, 1762
Bosisio, Achille, "Carlo Goldoni a 'Chioggia' ", *Ateneo Veneto*, 141:13-18, 1957
Dazzi, Manlio, "Goldoni e 'Le Baruffe Chiozzotte' ", *Nuova Antologia*, 493:78-
97, 1965
Dort, Bernard, *Théâtre Reel, 1967-1970*. 1971. Pp. 78-91
Nuova Antologia, 386:352-54, Aug. 1, 1936
Ortolani, Giuseppe, "Appunti sulle 'Baruffe Chiozotte' ", *Ateneo Veneto*, 141:
1-36, 1957
"Playwright of the Heart", *Times Literary Supplement*, July 26, 1957, Pp. 456
Scarpa, Attilia, "Il 'Chiozzotto' del Goldoni fra Realtã e Convenzione", *Atti
del R. Istituto Veneto di Scienze, Lettere ed Arti. Venezia. Classe di Scienze
Morali e Lettere*, 117:325-71, 1958-59
Studi in Memoria di Luigi Russo. 1974. Pp. 100-28

The Clever Lady's Maid, 1757
Dazzi, Manlio, "La Cameriera Brilliante", *Studi Goldoniani* (1968), 1:127-32

The Coffee House, 1750
Marletta, Paola, "Introduzione alla 'Bottega del Caffe' ", *Iniziative*, 7:30-33,
1958
Nuova Antologia, 374:473-75, Aug. 1, 1934

The Fan, n.d.
Fido, Franco, "Carlo Goldoni; From 'La Locandiera' to 'Il Ventaglio' ", *Italian
Quarterly*, 8:21-32, 1964
Nuova Antalogia 386:350-52, Aug. 1, 1936 and 404:459-60, Aug. 16, 1939

The Father of a Family, 1750
Reizov, Boris, " 'Il Padre di Famiglia' e la 'Commedia d'Educazione' Europea",
Studi Goldoniani (1968), 1:117-26

La Guerra *SEE* The War

The Liar, 1750
Nuova Antologia, 392:350-53, Aug. 1, 1937

La Locandiera *SEE* The Mistress of the Inn

Mine Hostess *SEE* The Mistress of the Inn

The Mistress of the Inn, 1753
Caccia, Ettore, "Le Varianti de 'La Locandiera' ", *Annali di Ca'Foscari* (Venezia), 3:21-22, 1965
Dort, Bernard, *Théâtre Reel, 1967-1970*. 1971. Pp. 78-91
Fido, Franco, "Carlo Goldoni: From 'La Locandiera' to 'Il Ventaglio' ", *Italian Quarterly*, 8:21-32, 1964
Journal des Débats, 38 pt. 2:676-77, Oct. 23, 1931
Leo, Ulrich, "Goldonis 'Locandiera' und Molieres 'Misanthrope': Zwei Motiv-Entwicklungen", *Romanische Forschungen*, 70:323-65, 1958
Mercure de France, 168:711-12, Dec. 15, 1923 and 232:154-56, Nov. 15, 1931
New Republic, 49:75, Dec. 8, 1926
Rossi, Patrizio, "Considerazioni Sulla 'Locandiera' di Carlo Goldoni", *Studi Goldoniani* (1971), 2:158-67
Young, Stark, *Immortal Shadows; A Book of Dramatic Criticism*. 1948. Pp. 37-40

The New House, 1761
Klefisch, Walter, " 'La Casa Nova' di Goldoni", *Studi Goldoniani* (1968), 1: 33-34
Ringger, Kurt, "Riflessi Della Drammaturgia Goldoniana nella 'La Casa Nova' ", *Studi Goldoniani* (1971), 2:168-78

Il Padre di Famiglia *SEE* The Father of a Family

The Public Square, 1756
Nuova Antologia, 404:457-59, Aug. 16, 1939

Rusteghi *SEE* The Boars

Servant of Two Masters, 1743
Dazzi, Manlio, "Il Servo di Due Padroni", *Studi Goldoniani* (1968), 1:105-09
Harper, 220:24-25, May, 1960
Nation (London), 43:359-60, June 16, 1928
New Yorker, 36:122, March 5, 1960
Novick, Julius, *Beyond Broadway; The Quest for Permanent Theatres*. 1968. Pp. 164-66

Il Servitore de Due Padroni *SEE* The Servant of Two Masters

The True Friend, 1753
Batusic, Slavko, "La Prima Opera di Goldoni Tradotta in Croato: 'Il Vero Amico' ", *Studi Goldoniani* (1968), 1:143-52

Il Ventaglio *SEE* The Fan

Il Vero Amico *SEE* The True Friend

War, 1761
Momo, Arnaldo, " 'La Guerra' di Carlo Goldoni", *Studi Goldoniani* (1968), 1:67-104

OLIVER GOLDSMITH

Good Natur'd Man, 1768
Hassert, Margaret, "Appraisals; The Plays of Oliver Goldsmith", *Journal of Irish Literature* (1974), 3,iii:39-48
New Statesman and Nation, 18:519, Oct. 14, 1939
Schang, William J., "Goldsmith's Development as Comic Dramatist", *Dissertation Abstracts International* (1972), 32:6942A
Sells, A. Lytton, *Oliver Goldsmith; His Life and Works.* 1974. Pp. 329-46
Studies for William A. Read; A Miscellany Presented by Some of His Colleagues and Friends, ed. by N. M. Caffee and T. A. Kirby. 1940. Pp. 237-53
Yearling, Elizabeth M., "The Good-Natured Heroes of Cumberland, Goldsmith, and Sheridan", *Modern Language Review* (1972), 67:490-500

She Stoops to Conquer; or, The Mistakes of a Night, 1773
America, 104:328, Nov. 26, 1960
Catholic World, 170:385, Feb., 1950
Commonweal, 51:414-15, Jan. 20, 1950
English Review, 47:484-85, Oct., 1928
Hassert, Margaret, "Appraisals; The Plays of Oliver Goldsmith", *Journal of Irish Literature* (1974), 3,iii:39-48
Itkowitz, Martin E., "A Fielding Echo in 'She Stoops to Conquer'", *Notes and Queries* (1973), 20:22
Nathan, George Jean, *Theatre Book of the Year, 1949-50.* Pp. 158-63
Nation, 170:18, Jan. 7, 1950
New Statesman, 18:394-95, Jan. 7, 1922
New Yorker, 25:45-46, Jan. 7, 1950 and 36:105-07, Nov. 12, 1960
Newsweek, 35:62, Jan. 9, 1950
Saturday Review, 146:240, Aug. 25, 1928
Saturday Review, 43:38, Nov. 19, 1960
Schang, William J., "Goldsmith's Development as Comic Dramatist", *Dissertation Abstracts International* (1972), 32:6942A
Sells, A. Lytton, *Oliver Goldsmith: His Life and Works.* 1974. Pp. 157-69
Spectator, 127:859-60, Dec. 24, 1921 and 141:238, Aug. 25, 1928
Theatre Arts, 34:12, March, 1950
Time, 55:55, Jan. 9, 1950

PETER GOLDSMITH (PSEUD)

SEE

JOHN BOYNTON PRIESTLEY

MAXIM GORKI

Children of the Sun, 1905
Levin, Dan, *Stormy Petrel; The Life and Work of Maxim Gorky.* 1965. Pp. 117-119

Country People, 1910
Nation (Feb. 9, 1970), 210:157
Newsweek (Jan. 26, 1970), 75:74
Saturday Review (Feb. 7, 1970), 53:24

Dachniki *SEE* Summerfolk

Deti Solntsa *SEE* The Children of the Sun

Dostigaeff and the Others, 1933
  Spectator, 166:630, June 13, 1941

Egor Bulychev and Others *SEE* Yegor Bulichev and Others

The Lower Depths, 1902
  Arts and Decoration, 32:75, March, 1930
  Beerbohm, Max, *Around Theatres*. 1953. Pp. 302-05
  Bhatti, Anil ed., *Language and Literature in Society*. *Journal of the School
    of Languages*. 1973-74. Pp. 28-54
  Cargill, Oscar; Fagin, Nathan Bryllion and Fisher, William, eds., *O'Neill
    and His Plays; Four Decades of Criticism*. 1961. Pp. 431-42
  Cole, Toby and Chinoy, Helen Kritch, *Directors on Directing; A Source
    Book on the Modern Theatre*. 1963. Pp. 281-95
  Commonweal, 11:342, Jan. 22, 1930
  Gassner, John, ed., *O'Neill; A Collection of Critical Essays*. 1964. Pp. 99-
    109
  Levin, Dan, *Stormy Petrel; The Life and Work of Maxim Gorky*. 1965. Pp.
    86-95
  Muchnic, Helen, *Russian Writers; Notes and Essays*. 1971. Pp. 233-48
  Nathan, George Jean, *Theatre Book of the Year, 1947-48*. Pp. 255-57
  Nation, 198:404, April 20, 1964
  New Yorker, 40:95-97, April 11, 1964
  Outlook, 154:229, Feb. 5, 1930

Na Dne *SEE* The Lower Depths

Nachtasyl *SEE* Night Lodging

Night Lodging, 1920
  Current Opinion, 68:195-97, Feb., 1920
  Hackett, Francis, *Invisible Censor*. 1921. Pp. 101-05
  Hamilton, Clayton Meeker, *Seen on the Stage*. 1920. Pp. 138-43
  Jacobsohn, Siegfried, "Zu Maxim Gorkis 'Nachtasyl'", *Die Volksbühne*
    (1965-66), 16:13
  Lewisohn, Ludwig, *Drama on the Stage*. 1922. Pp. 72-77
  Nation, 110:49-50, Jan. 10, 1920
  New Republic, 21:173, Jan. 7, 1920
  Stanislawski, K. S., "Unsere Uraffuhrung von Gorkis 'Nachtasyl'", *Die
    Volksbühne* (1965-66), 16:6-8

Somov and Others, 1930-31
  Levin, Dan, *Stormy Petrel; The Life and Work of Maxim Gorky*. 1965. Pp.
    278-90
  Stauche, Ilse, "Gor'kijs Drama 'Somov i Drugie' und Seine Aüffuhrung in
    Deutschen Theater Berlin 1954", *Wissenschaftliche Zeitschrift der Hum-
    boldt-Universitat zu Berlin. Gesselschafts-u. Sprachwissenschaftliche
    Reihe* (1965), 14:263-68

Somov i Drugie *SEE* Somov and Others

Summerfolk, 1914
  America (3-22-75), 132:219
  Nation (3-29-75), 220:380-81
  New Yorker (2-24-75), 51:95-96
  Newsweek (2-17-75), 85:66
  Esslin, M., "Summerfolk", *Plays and Players* (Oct. 1974), 22:28-29
  Lambert, J. W., "Summerfolk", *Drama* (1974), 115:53-55

The Survivors, n.d.
  Levin, Dan, *Stormy Petrel; The Life and Work of Maxim Gorky*. 1965. Pp. 307-
  10

Yegor Bulichev and Others, 1932
  Block, Anita Cahn, *Changing World in Plays and Theatre*. 1939. Pp. 352-411
  Levin, Dan, *Stormy Petrel; The Life and Work of Maxim Gorky*. 1965. Pp. 280-
  87
  Lewis, Allan, *The Contemporary Theatre; The Significant Playwrights of Our
  Time*. 1962. Pp. 111-27
  Living Age, 343:367, Dec., 1932

Zykovy, 1913
  New Yorker (4-21-75), 51:103

HARLEY GRANVILLE GRANVILLE-BARKER

SEE

LAURENCE HOUSMAN

GUNTER GRASS

Die Bösen Köche   *SEE*   The Wicked Cooks

The Flood, 1957
  Yowell, Robert L., "Pre-Production Analyses of Selected Non-Realistic Plays
  of Gunter Grass in Their English Translation", *Dissertation Abstracts International* (1972), 33:2547A

Hochwasser   *SEE*   The Flood

Mister, Mister, 1958
  Yowell, Robert L., "Pre-Production Analyses of Selected Non-Realistic Plays
  of Gunter Grass in Their English Translation", *Dissertation Abstracts International* (1972), 33:2547A

Onkel, Onkel   *SEE*   Uncle, Uncle, 1958

Die Plebejer Proben den Aufstand   *SEE*   The Plebians Rehearse for the Uprising

The Plebians Rehearse for the Uprising, 1966
  A Gunter Grass Symposium, ed. A. Leslie Willson. 1972. Pp. 18-31
  Hughes, Catharine, *Plays, Politics, and Polemics*. 1973. Pp. 175-81
  Metzger, Lore, "Gunter Grass's Rehearsal Play", *Contemporary Literature*
  (1973), 14:197-212
  New Statesman, 75:215, Feb. 16, 1968

Yowell, Robert L., "Pre-Production Analyses of Selected Non-Realistic Plays of Gunter Grass in Their English Translation", *Dissertation Abstracts International* (1972), 33:2547A

Thirty-Two Teeth, n.d.
Esslin, Martin, *The Theatre of the Absurd*. 1961. Pp. 195

Uncle, Uncle, 1958
Esslin, Martin, *The Theatre of the Absurd*. 1961. Pp. 195-96

The Wicked Cooks, 1962
Esslin, Martin, *The Theatre of the Absurd*. 1961. Pp. 196
Spycher, P., " 'Die Bösen Köche' von Gunter Grass—Ein Absurdes Drama?", *Germanisch-Romanische Monatsschrift* (1966), 16:161-90
Yowell, Robert L., "Pre-Production Analyses of Selected Non-Realistic Plays of Gunter Grass in Their English Translation", *Dissertation Abstracts International* (1972), 33:2547A

Zweiunddreissig Zähne   *SEE*   Thirty-two Teeth

GRAHAM GREENE

Carving a Statue, 1964
Kunkel, Francis L., *The Labyrinthine Way of Graham Greene*. 1973. Pp. 176-82
Lumley, Frederick, *New Trends in Twentieth Century Drama; A Survey Since Ibsen and Shaw*. 1967. Pp. 289-92
New Statesman, 68:462, Sept. 25, 1964
Spectator, 213:402, Sept. 25, 1964
Turnell, Martin, *Graham Greene; A Critical Essay*. 1976. Pp. 38-42

Complaisant Lover, 1959
Christian Century, 78:1532, Dec. 20, 1961
Commonweal, 75:233-34, Nov. 24, 1961
Educational Theatre Journal, 14:67, March, 1962
Kunkel, Francis L., *The Labyrinthine Way of Graham Greene*. 1973. Pp. 172-76
Lumley, Frederick, *New Trends in Twentieth Century Drama; A Survey Since Ibsen and Shaw*. 1967. Pp. 289-92
Nation, 193:437, Nov. 25, 1961
New Yorker, 35:80, Aug. 29, 1959 and 37:117-18, Nov. 11, 1961
Newsweek, 58:95, Nov. 13, 1961
Novick, Julius, *Beyond Broadway; The Quest for Permanent Theatres*. 1968. Pp. 30
Pujals, Esteban, "The Globe Theatre, Londres", *Filologia Moderne* (Univ. do Madrid), 1:59-63, 1960
Reporter, 25:62, Dec. 7, 1961
Saturday Review, 42:25, July 4, 1959 and 44:36, Dec. 2, 1961
Schoonderwoerd, N., "Heeft Graham Greene Ons Weer Teleurgested?", *Kultuurleven* (1959), 26:703-04
Spectator, 203:7, July 3, 1959 and 203:907, Dec. 18, 1959
Spinucci, Pietro, "L'Ultimo Dramma di Graham Greene", *Humanitas* (Brescia), 15:820-25, 1960
Theatre Arts, 43:22, Dec., 1959 and 46:15, Jan., 1962

Time, 73:53-54, June 29, 1959 and 78:66, Nov. 10, 1961

Turnell, Martin, *Graham Greene; A Critical Essay.* 1976. Pp. 38-42

The Living Room, 1953

America, 90:600-02, March 6, 1954 and 92:386-87, Jan. 8, 1955 and 93:433-35, July 30, 1955

Baxter, K. M., *Speak What We Feel: A Christian Looks at the Contemporary Theatre.* 1964. Pp. 19-25

Catholic World, 177:406-10, Sept., 1953

Commonweal, 59:477-78, Feb. 12, 1954 and 61:278, Dec. 10, 1954 and 61:333, Dec. 24, 1954, and 61:354-55, Dec. 31, 1954, and 71:123-24, Oct. 30, 1959 and 77:316-17, Dec. 14, 1962

Cottrell, Beekman W., "Second Time Charm: The Theatre of Graham Greene", *Modern Fiction Studies* (1957), 3:249-55

Davies, Horton, "Catching the Conscience; Graham Greene's Plays", *Religion in Life* (1967), 36:605-14

Illustrated London News, 222:704, May 2, 1953

Kunkel, Francis L., *The Labyrinthine Way of Graham Greene.* 1973. Pp. 164-68

Lumley, Frederick, *New Trends in Twentieth Century Drama; A Survey Since Ibsen and Shaw.* 1967. Pp. 289-92

Nation, 177:138, Aug. 15, 1953 and 179:496-97, Dec. 4, 1954

New Republic, 131:22, Dec. 13, 1954

New Yorker, 29:69, July 18, 1953 and 30:156, Oct. 23, 1954 and 30:86, Nov. 27, 1954

Newsweek, 44:92, Nov. 29, 1954

Robertson, Roderick, "Toward a Definition of Religious Drama", *Educational Theatre Journal*, 9:99-105, 1957

Saturday Review, 36:24, Aug. 1, 1953 and 37:24-25, Dec. 18, 1954

Theatre Arts, 39:12, 90, Feb., 1955

Time, 64:50 Nov. 29, 1954 and 64:55, Dec. 20, 1954

Turnell, Martin, *Graham Greene; A Critical Essay.* 1976. Pp. 38-42

The Potting Shed, 1957

America, 96:594-95, Feb. 23, 1957 and 97:168-70, May 4, 1957 and 97:293, June 8, 1957

Boyd, John D., "Earth Imagery in Graham Greene's 'The Potting Shed' ", *Modern Drama* (1973), 16:69-80

Kunkel, Francis L., *The Labyrinthine Way of Graham Greene.* 1973. Pp. 164-71

Catholic World, 185:66, April, 1957

Christian Century, 74:262, Feb. 27, 1957

Commonweal, 65:613-14, March 15, 1957

Cottrell, Beekman W., "Second Time Charm; The Theatre of Graham Greene", *Modern Fiction Studies* (1957), 3:249-55

Davies, Horton, "Catching the Conscience; Graham Greene's Plays", *Religion in Life* (1967), 36:605-14

Engelborghs, Maurits, "Engelse Letteren, Graham Greene: 'The Potting Shed' ", *Dietsche Warande en Belfort* (1958), 58:306-10

English, 12:58, Summer, 1958

H., T., " 'The Potting Shed'. Figmentum Fidei" *Dublin Review*, 232:71-73, 1958

Illustrated London News, 232:314, Feb. 22, 1958

Life, 42:65-66, April 1, 1957
Lumley, Frederick, *New Trends in Twentieth Century Drama; A Survey Since Ibsen and Shaw*. 1967. Pp. 289-92
Meshet, M. B., "Le Potting Shed de Graham Greene", *Les Etudes* (Paris), 298: 238-47, 1958
Murphy, John P., " 'The Potting Shed' ", *Renascence*, 12:43-49, 1959
Nation, 184:146, Feb. 16, 1958
New Statesman, 55:196, Feb. 15, 1958
New Yorker, 32:70, Feb. 9, 1957
Newsweek, 49:67, Feb. 11, 1957
Partisan Review, 24:270-74, Spring, 1957
Rewak, W. J., " 'The Potting Shed', Maturation of Graham Greene's Vision", *Catholic World*, 186:210-13, Dec., 1957
Reporter, 16:41, March 7, 1957
Saturday Review, 40:26-27, Feb. 16, 1957
Spectator, 200:203, Feb. 14, 1958
Stanford, Derek, "The Potting Shed", *Contemporary Review*, 193:#1110:301-03, June 1958
Stratford, Philip, "Unlocking the Potting Shed", *Kenyon Review*, 24:129-43, 1962
Theatre Arts, 41:15, April, 1957
Time, 69:70, Feb. 11, 1957
Turnell, Martin, *Graham Greene; A Critical Essay*. 1976. Pp. 38-42

The Return of A. J. Raffles, 1976
New Yorker (1-26-76), 51:100-01

ROBERT GREENE

Alphonsus, King of Arragon, 1587
Sulzman, Sister Mary J., "A Critical Edition of Robert Greene's 'The Commicall Historie of Alphonsus, King of Aragon' ", *Dissertation Abstracts* (1969), 29:2687A

Friar Bacon and Friar Bungay, 1589
Allen, Don Cameron, ed., *Studies in Honor of T. W. Baldwin*. 1958. Pp. 136-49
Assarsson-Rizzi, Kerstin, " 'Friar Bacon and Friar Bungay': A Structural Analysis of Robert Greene's Play", *Lund Studies in English* (1972), Vol. 44
Bluestone, Max and Norman Rabkin, eds., *Shakespeare's Contemporaries; Modern Studies in English Renaissance Drama*. 2nd ed., 1970. Pp. 42-46
Dunn, Hough-Lewis, "The Language of the Magician as Limitation and Transcendence in The Wolfenbuttel 'Faustbuch', Greene's 'Friar Bacon', Marlowe's 'Faustus', Shakespeare's 'Tempest' and Goethe's 'Faust' ", *Dissertation Abstracts International* (1974), 35:444A
Hosley, Richard, ed., *Essays on Shakespeare and Elizabethan Drama in Honor of Hardin Craig*. 1962. Pp. 45-54
McCallum, J. D., "Greene's 'Friar Bacon and Friar Bungay' ", *Modern Language Notes* (1920), 35:212-17
McNeir, Waldo F., "Traditional Elements in the Character of Greene's Friar Bacon", *Studies in Philology* (1948), 45:172-79
Mehl, Dieter, *The Elizabethan Dumb Show*. 1966. Pp. 85-87

Mortenson, Peter, "'Friar Bacon and Friar Bungay': Festive Comedy and 'Three-Form'd Luna'", *English Literary Renaissance* (1972), 2:194-207

Round, P. Z., "Greene's Materials for 'Friar Bacon and Friar Bungay'", *Modern Language Review* (1926), 21:19-23

Schelling, F. E., "'Dr. Faustus' and 'Friar Bacon'", *Nation* (July 1, 1915), 101:12-13

Senn, W., "Robert Greene's Handling of Source Material in 'Friar Bacon and Friar Bungay'", *English Studies* (1973), 54:544-53

Towne, F., "White Magic in 'Friar Bacon and Friar Bungay'?", *Modern Language Notes* (1952), 67:9-13

Wertheim, Albert, "The Presentation of Sin in 'Friar Bacon and Friar Bungay'", *Criticism* (1974), 16:273-86

West, Robert H., "White Magic in 'Friar Bacon'", *Modern Language Notes* (1952), 67:499-500

Historie of Orlando Furioso, One of the Twelve Peeres of France   *SEE*   Orlando Furioso

Honorable Historie of Friar Bacon and Friar Bungay   *SEE*   Friar Bacon and Friar Bungay

James IV, 1591

Braunmuller, A. R., "The Serious Comedy of Greene's 'James IV'", *English Literary Renaissance* (1973), 3:335-50

Hudson, R., "Greene's 'James IV' and Contemporary Allusions to Scotland", *Modern Language Association Publications* (1932), 47:652-67

Mehl, Dieter, *The Elizabethan Dumb Show*. 1966. Pp. 83-85

Stein, Charles H., "Robert Greene's 'James IV': A Critical Edition", *Dissertation Abstracts* (1968), 29:1215A

Orlando Furioso, 1591

Babula, William, "Fortune or Fate; Ambiguity in Robert Greene's 'Orlando Furioso'", *Modern Language Review* (1972), 67:481-85

Chakrabarti, Dipendu, ed., "Essays Presented to Professor Amalendu Bose", *Bulletin of the Department of English, Calcutta University* (1972-73), 8:22-26

Gelber, Norman, "Robert Greene's 'Orlando Furioso': A Study of Thematic Ambiguity", *Modern Language Review* (1969), 64:264-66

Houk, R. A., "Shakespeare's Shrew and Greene's Orlando", *Modern Language Association. Publications* (1947), 62:657-71

Morrison, M. R., "Greene's Use of Ariosto in 'Orlando Furioso'", *Modern Language Notes* (1934), 49:449-51

Waith, Eugene M., *Ideas of Greatness; Heroic Drama in England*. 1971. Pp. 68-70

Scottish Historie of James IV   *SEE*   James IV

WALTER GREENWOOD

SEE

DAVID HERBERT LAWRENCE

and

WALTER GREENWOOD

FRANZ SERAFIN GRILLPARZER

Die Ahnfrau   *SEE*   The Ancestress

The Ancestress, 1817
  Angress, Ruth K., "Das Gespenst in Grillparzers 'Ahnfrau' ", *German Quarterly*
  (1972), 45:606-19
  Bauer, Roger, " 'Die Ahnfrau' et la Querelle de la Tragedie Fataliste", *Etudes
  Germaniques* (1972), 27:165-92
  _____ , "Grillparzers 'Ahnfrau': Ihre Kritiker und Ihr Publikum",
  Grillparzer Forum Forchtenstein (1973), Pp. 141-63
  Fielder, H. G., "Notes by George Meredith on Grillparzer's 'Ahnfrau' ", *Modern
  Language Review* (1931), 26:450-53
  Haeussermann, Ernst, "Zur Forchtensteiner Inszenierung der 'Ahnfrau' ", *Grill-
  parzer Forum Forchtenstein* (1973), Pp. 182-85
  Krispyn, E., "Grillparzer and his 'Ahnfrau' ", *Germanic Review* (1963), 38:209-
  25
  Lorenz, Frieder, "Franz Grillparzers 'Ahnfrau': Eine Schicksalstragödie", *Grill-
  parzer Forum Forchtenstein* 1968, Pp. 79-99
  McDonald, Edward R., " 'Die Ahnfrau': Franz Grillparzers Metaphor des
  Schicksalhaften Lebens", *Maske und Kothern* (1972), 18:3-22
  Michailow, Alexander V., "Vorläufiges zur 'Ahnfrau', Zum Lebensbegriff",
  Grillparzer Forum Forchtenstein (1973), Pp. 103-32
  Morris, I. V., "Ahnfrau Controversy", *Modern Language Review* (1967), 62:
  284-91
  _____ , "Grillparzer's Individuality as a Dramatist", *Modern Lan-
  guage Quarterly* (June 1957), 18:83-99
  Rismondo, Piero, "Die Politische Vision in Grillparzer's 'Ahnfrau' ", *Grillparzer
  Forum Forchtenstein* (1973), Pp. 164-81
  Seeba, Heinrich C., "Das Schicksal der Grillen und Parzen. Zu Grillparzers
  'Ahnfrau' ", *Euphorion. Zeitschrift für Literaturgeschichte* (1971), 65:132-61
  Thompson, Regina B., " 'Die Ahnfrau' by Franz Grillparzer and 'Paramater'
  by Aleksandr Blok", *Germano-Slavica* (1973), 1:45-63
  Wolff, Hans M., "Zum Problem der Ahnfrau", *Zeitschrift für Deutsche Philol-
  . ogy* (1937), 62:303-17
  Yates, W. E., *Grillparzer; A Critical Introduction*. 1972. Pp. 47-58
  _____ , "Die Jugendeindrücke Wird Man Nicht los . . . : Grill-
  parzer's Relation to the Viennese Popular Theatre", *Germanic Review* (1973),
  48:132-49

Blanca from Castile, 1809
  Bandet, J. L., " 'Blanka von Kastilien' ou les Ambiguités de la Vertu", *Etudes
  Germaniques* (1972), 27:193-206
  Schmitt, Albert R., ed., *Festschrift für Detlev W. Schumann zum 70. Geburts-
  tag*. 1970. Pp. 281-93
  Tönz, Leo, "Grillparzers 'Blanka von Kastilien' und Schillers 'Don Carlos' ",
  Grillparzer Forum Forchtenstein 1970 Pp. 65-84

Blanka von Kastilien   *SEE*   Blanca from Castile

Ein Bruderzwist in Habsburg   *SEE*   Family Strife in Hapsburg

A Dream Is Life, 1834
  Haider-Pregler, Hilde, "Zur Bühnengeschichte von Grillparzers 'Traum ein
  Leben' ", *Grillparzers Forum Forchtenstein* (1973), Pp. 125-44

Lindtberg, Leopold, "Notizen Zu Einer Inszenierung von Grillparzers 'Traum ein Leben' für die Burgspiele auf Forchtenstein", *Grillparzer Forum Forchtenstein* (1973), Pp. 156-61

Mühler, Robert, "Lebenstraum und Geist der Musik in Grillparzers Dramatischen Märchen 'Der Traum ein Leben' ", *Osterreich in Geschichte und Literatur* (1963), 7:320-32

O'Connell, Richard B., "'Rivers' 'El Desengaño en un Sueño' and Grillparzer's 'Der Traum ein Leben': A Problem in Assessment of Influence", *Philological Quarterly* (1961), 40:569-76

Robertson, J. G., "Rustan and Mirza in Grillparzer's 'Der Traum ein Leben' ", *Modern Langauge Review* (1925), 20:80-82

Yates, W. E., *Grillparzer; A Critical Introduction*. 1972. Pp. 114-31

Esther, 1848

Yates, W. E., *Grillparzer; A Critical Introduction*. 1972. Pp. 189-93

A Faithful Servant of His Master, 1828

Baumann, Gerhart, "Ein Treuer Diener Seines Herrn", *Grillparzer Forum Forchtenstein* 1966, Pp. 26-36

Himmel, Hellmuth, "Tragoedia Christianissima. Zu Grillparzers Trauerspiel 'Ein Treur Diener Seines Herrn' ", *Österreich in Geschichte und Literatur* (1972), 16:36-48

Kautek, Rudolf, " 'Ein Treuer Diener Seines Herrn': Eine Aufführung des Grazer Schauspiels", *Grillparzer Forum Forchtenstein* 1967, Pp. 61-73

Reichert, H. W., "Characterization of Bancbanus in Grillparzer's 'Ein Treuer Diener Seines Herrn' ", *Studies in Philology* (1949), 46:70-78

Schaum, Konrad, "Grillparzer's Drama 'Ein Treuer Seines Herrn' ", *Jahrbuch der Grillparzer-Gesellschaft* (1960), 3:72-94

——————— , "Zum Probleme des Tragischen in Grillparzers 'Treuem Diner' ", *German Quarterly* (1958), 31:6-15

Yates, W. E., *Grillparzer; A Critical Introduction*. 1972. Pp. 132-45

Family Strife in Hapsburg, 1872

Crosby, Donald H. and George C. Schoolfield, eds., *Studies in German Drama; A Festschrift in Honor of Walter Silz*. 1974. Pp. 149-61

David, Claude, "Grillparzers 'Bruderzwist in Habsburg' ", *Literatur und Kritik* (1972), 61:17-34

Hering, Gerhard F., "Zum Thema 'Bruderzwist' ", *Grillparzer Forum Forchtenstein* (1966), Pp. 37-42

Johannessen, K. Langvik, " 'Ein Bruderzwist in Habsburg': Versuch einer Offenlegung der Inneren Handlung", *Grillparzer Forum Forchtenstein* (1967), Pp. 34-42

Langvik-Johannessen, Kare, " 'Ein Bruderzwist in Habsburg': Versuch einer Offenlegung der Inneren Handlung", *Grillparzer Forum Forchtenstein* (1968), Pp. 43-57

Mason, Eve, "A New Look at Grillparzer's 'Bruderzwist' ", *German Life and Letters* (1972), 25:102-15

Naumann, Walter, "Grillparzer's Drama 'Ein Bruderzwist in Habsburg' ", *Euphorion. Zeitschrift für Literaturgeschichte* (1954), 48:412-34

Øhrgaard, Per, " 'Aus Eignem Schoss Ringt los Sich der Barbar': Der Zusammenbruch des Herrschaftsanspruchs in Grillparzers 'Ein Bruderzwist in Habsburg' ", *Text und Kontext* (1974), 2,i:64-76

Sanders, Erwin P., "Franz Grillparzer's 'Ein Bruderzwist in Habsburg' ", *Dissertation Abstracts* (1967), 28:1827A

Schwarz, Egon, Hunter G. Hannum, and Edgar Lohner, eds., *Festschrift für Bernhard Blume: Aufsätze zur Deutschen und Europäischen Literatur*. 1967. Pp. 173-94

Traditions and Transitions; Studies in Honor of Harold Jantz, ed. Lieselotte E. Kurth, et als. 1972. Pp. 210-27

Wassermann, Felix M., "Kaiser Rudolf und Seine Umwelt in Grillparzers 'Bruderzwist: Die Tragödie des Herrschers Zwischen Weisheit und Tat", *Monatschefte für Deutschen Unterricht* (1951), 43:271-78

Wells, G. A., "The Problem of Right Conduct in Grillparzer's 'Ein Bruderzwist in Habsburg' ", *German Life and Letters* (1958), 11:161-72

Wiese, Benno von, *Das Deutsche Drama; Vom Barock bis Zur Gegenwart*. Vol. 1. 1958. Pp. 422-50

Yates, W. E. *Grillparzer; A Critical Introduction*. 1972. Pp. 237-51

The Golden Fleece, 1821

Baker, Christa S., "Unifying Imagery Patterns in Grillparzer's 'Das Goldene Vlies'", *Modern Language Notes* (1974), 89:392-403

Dunham, T. C., "The Monologue as Monodrama in Grillparzer's Hellenic Dramas", *Journal of English and Germanic Philology* (1938), 37:513-23

—————— , "Symbolism in Grillparzer's 'Das Goldene Vliess' ", *Modern Language Association. Publications* (1960), 75:75-82

Morris, I. V., "Grillparzer's Individuality as a Dramatist", *Modern Language Quarterly* (June 1957), 18:83-99

Myth and Reason; A Symposium, ed. Walter D. Wetzels. 1973. Pp. 71-100

Rismondo, Piero, "Das 'Zweite Gesicht' in Grillparzers 'Das Goldene Vliess' ", *Jahrbuch der Grillparzer-Gesellschaft* (1966), 5:129-41

Seidler, Herbert, " 'Das Goldene Vliess': Forschungslage und Interpretationsaufgaben", *Grillparzer Forum Forchtenstein* 1967, Pp. 64-77

Stevens, Henry H., "Description in the Dramas of Grillparzer", *Modern Language Association. Publications* (1918), 30:30-72

Stiefel, Rudolph, "Grillparzers 'Goldene Vlies': Ein Dichterisches Bekenntnis", *Basler Studien zur Deutschen Sprache und Literatur* 1958, #21

Traditions and Transitions; Studies in Honor of Harold Jantz, ed. Lieselotte E. Kurth, et als. 1972. Pp. 210-27

Yates, W. E., *Grillparzer; A Critical Introduction*. 1972. Pp. 84-96

Das Goldene Vliess *SEE* The Golden Fleece

Hero and Leander, 1828-29

Binger, Norman H. and A. Wayne Wonderley, eds., *Studies in 19th Century and Early 20th Century German Literature; Essays in Honor of Paul K. Whitaker*. 1974. Pp. 22-28

Dunham, T. C., "The Monologue as Monodrama in Grillparzer's Hellenic Dramas", *Journal of English and Germanic Philology* (1938), 37:513-23

Morris, I. V., "Grillparzer's Individuality as a Dramatist", *Modern Language Quarterly* (June 1957), 18:83-99

Murdoch, Brian, "Das Tragische Netz in Grillparzers 'Des Meeres und der Liebe Wellen' ", *Etudes Germaniques* (1972), 27:232-42

Stevens, Henry H., "Description in the Dramas of Grillparzer", *Modern Language Association. Publications* (1918), 30:30-72

Straubinger, O. Paul, " 'Des Meeres und der Liebe Wellen' Im Urteil der Zeit", *Grillparzer Forum Forchtenstein* 1968, Pp. 12-23

Traditions and Transitions; Studies in Honor of Harold Jantz, ed. Lieselotte E. Kurth, et als. 1972. Pp. 210-27

Yates, D., "Grillparzer's Hero and Shakespeare's Juliet", *Modern Language Review* (1926), 21:419-25

Yates, W. E., *Grillparzer; A Critical Introduction.* 1972. Pp. 165-77

The Jewess of Toledo, 1872

Baumann, Gerhart, " 'Die Jüdin von Toledo': Zum Spätwerk Franz Grillparzers", *Grillparzer Forum Forchtenstein* 1967, Pp. 7-23

Beinke, Lothar, "Unterschiede in den Auffassungen von Grillparzer und Hebbel: Untersuchungen an 'Die Jüdin von Toledo' und 'Agnes Bernauer' ", *Jahrbuch der Grillparzer-Gesellschaft* (1972), 9:171-86

Cowen, Roy C., "The Tragedy of 'Die Jüdin von Toledo' ", *German Quarterly* (1964), 37:39-53

German Studies Presented to Walter H. Bruford on His Retirement by His Pupils, Colleagues, and Friends. 1961. Pp. 193-206

Kenter, Heinz Dietrich, "Über Meine Inszenierung von Grillparzers 'Die Jüdin von Toledo' ", *Grillparzer Forum Forchtenstein* 1967, Pp. 24-33

Krispyn, E., "Grillparzer's Tragedy 'Die Jüdin von Toledo' ", *Modern Language Review* (1965), 60:405-15

Lippuner, Heinz, "Grillparzers 'Jüdin von Toledo': Untersuchung Eines Paradigmas", *Orbis Litterarum* (1972), 27:202-23

Politzer, Heinz, "Franz Grillparzers Spiel vom Fall: 'Die Jüdin von Toledo' ", *Zeitschrift für Deutsche Philologie* (1967), 86:509-33

Thompson, B. "An Ironic Tragedy; An Examination of Grillparzer's 'Die Jüdin von Toledo' ", *German Life and Letters* (1972), 25:210-18

Thurnber, Eugen, "Staat und Liebe: Racines 'Berenice' und Grillparzers 'Jüdin von Toledo' ", *Lituraturwissenschaftliches Jahrbuch der Gorres-Gesellschaft* (1961), 2:117-23

Yates, W. E., *Grillparzer; A Critical Introduction.* 1972. Pp. 178-88

Die Jüdin von Toledo *SEE* The Jewess of Toledo

King Ottakar, His Rise and Fall, 1825

Dornberg, Otto, "Grillparzer's Use of Historical Sources in 'König Ottakars Glück und Ende' ", *Colloquia Germanica. International Zeitschrift für Germanische Sprach- und Literaturwissenschaft* (1972), 6:165-78

Geitz, Henry, "Grillparzer's Turn to the Historical Drama; 'König Ottakars Glück und Ende' ", *Dissertation Abstracts* (1961), 22:868-69

Morris, I. V., "Grillparzer's Individuality as a Dramatist", *Modern Language Quarterly* (June 1957), 18:83-99

Partl, Kurt, "Friedrich Schillers 'Wallenstein' und Franz Grillparzers 'König Ottakars Glück und Ende': Eine Vergleichenede Interpretation Auf Geschichtlicher Grundlage", *Abhandlungen Zur Kunst, Musik- und Literaturwissenschaft* (1960), Vol. 8

Silz, Walter, "Grillparzer's 'Ottakar' ", *German Review* (Nov. 1964), 39:243-61

Wiese, Benno von, *Das Deutsche Drama; Vom Barock bis Zur Gegenwart.* Vol. 1. 1958. Pp. 405-21

Yates, W. E. *Grillparzer; A Critical Introduction.* 1972. Pp. 97-113

König Ottakars Glück und Ende *SEE* King Ottakar, His Rise and Fall

Libussa, 1874

Barlow, John D., "The Dramatic Structure of Grillparzer's 'Libussa' ", *Dissertation Abstracts* (1968), 29:252A-53A

Dunham, T. C., "Circle Image in Grillparzer's 'Libussa' ", *Germanic Review* (1961), 36:125-46

" 'Libussa': Versuch Einer Deutung", *Jahrbuch der Grillparzer Gesellschaft* (1967), 6:75-93

Wassermann, Felix M., "Grillparzers 'Libussa': Selbstekenntnis und Kultur-kritik", *Monatshefte für Deutschen Unterricht* (1953), 45:90-98

Wiese, Benno von, *Das Deutsche Drama; Vom Barock bis Zur Gegenwart.* Vol. 1. 1958. Pp. 451-74

Yates, W. E. *Grillparzer: A Critical Introduction.* 1972. Pp. 252-64

Des Meeres und der Liebe Wellen   *SEE*   Hero and Leander

Sappho, 1818

Baker, Christa S., "Structure and Imagery in Grillparzer's 'Sappho' ", *Germanic Review* (1973), 48:44-55

Brundrett, Ralph B., Jr., "The Role of the Ego in Grillparzer's 'Sappho' and Schiller's 'Jungfrau' ", *German Quarterly* (1958), 31:16-23

Cowen, Roy C., "Zur Struktur von Grillparzers 'Sappho' ", *Grillparzer Forum Forchtenstein* 1968, Pp. 58-71

Crosby, Donald H. and George C. Schoolfield, eds., *Studies in German Drama; A Festschrift in Honor of Walter Silz.* 1974. Pp. 125-47

Dunham, T. C., "The Monologue as Monodrama in Grillparzer's Hellenic Dramas", *Journal of English and Germanic Philology* (1938), 37:513-23

Dyck, J. W., "Goethes Humanitätsidee und Grillparzers 'Sappho' ", *Jahrbuch der Grillparzer Gesellschaft* (1966), 4:65-79

German Studies; Presented to Professor H. G. Fiedler by Pupils, Colleagues, and Friends on His 75th Birthday, 28 April, 1937. 1938. Pp. 459-92

Harris, S. C., "Figure of Melitta in Grillparzer's 'Sappho' ", *Journal of English and German Philology* (1961), 60:102-10

Kenter, Heinz D., "Überlegungen zu Einer Freilicht-Inszenierung des Trauer-spiels 'Sappho' ", *Grillparzer Forum Forchtenstein* 1968, Pp. 72-78

Klarmann, Adolf D., "Psychological Motivation in Grillparzer's 'Sappho' ", *Monatsheft für Deutschen Unterricht* (1948), 40:271-78

Krispyn, Egbert, "Grillparzer and the Chorus", *Modern Language Quarterly* (March 1964), 25:46-56

Morikawa, Kokyo, "Grillparzers 'Sappho': Entstehung und Erlauterung", *Jahr-buch der Grillparzer-Gesellschaft* (1967), 6:101-19

Morris, I. V., "Grillparzer's Individuality as a Dramatist", *Modern Language Quarterly* (June 1957), 18:83-99

Ossar, Michael, "Die Kunstlergestalt in Goethes 'Tasso' und Grillparzers 'Sap-pho' ", *German Quarterly* (1972), 45:645-61

Root, Winthrop H., "Grillparzer's 'Sappho' and Thomas Mann's 'Tonio Krö-ger' ", *Monatshefte für Deutschen Unterricht* (1937), 29:59-64

Stevens, Henry H., "Description in the Dramas of Grillparzer", *Modern Lan-guage Association. Publications* (1918), 30:30-72

Wurm, Ernst, "Grillparzer's 'Sappho' und Ihre Berühmten Darstellerinnen", *Jahrbuch der Grillparzer-Gesellschaft* (1970), 8:117-29

Yates, W. E., *Grillparzer: A Critical Introduction.* 1972. Pp. 59-73

Thou Shalt Not Lie, 1838

Angress, R. K., " 'Weh Dem, Der Lügt': Grillparzer and the Avoidance of Trag-edy", *Modern Language Review* (April 1971), 66:355-64

Birbaumer, Ulf, " 'Weh dem, der Lügt': Von Hanzwurzst zu Leon", *Grill-parzer Forum Forchtenstein* (1971), Pp. 45-63

Gladt, Karl, " 'Weh Dem, Der Lugt': Gedanken zu Einem Bricfkonzept", *Jahrbuch der Grillparzer-Gesellschaft* (1960), 3:31-38

Haeusserman, Ernst, "Ist 'Weh dem, der Lügt' ein Lustspiel? Überlegungen des Regisseurs", *Grillparzer Forum Forchtenstein* (1971), Pp. 125-31

Jones, Sheila, " 'Weh dem, der Lügt': Reconsidered in the Light of Some Basic Character Types in Grillparzer's Work:, *New German Quarterly* (1974), 2:171-91

Krispyn, Egbert, "The Fiasco of 'Weh dem, der Lügt' ", *German Life and Letters* (1972), 25:201-09

Schimmerl, Erich, "Die Spanischen Einflüsse in Grillparzers Lustspiel "Weh Dem, Der Lügt' ", *Modern Language Quarterly* (1951), 12:67-71

Seidler, Herbert, "Grillparzers Lustspiel 'Weh Dem, Der Lugt' ", *Jahrbuch der Grillparzer-Gesellschaft* (1965), 4:7-29

Steffen, Hans, ed., *Das Deutsche Lustspiel.* 1968. Pp. 143-65

Traditions and Transítions; Studies in Honor of Harold Jantz, ed. Lieselotte E. Kurth, et als. 1972. Pp. 210-27

Die Wissenschaft von Deutsches Sprache und Dichtung: Methoden, Probleme, Aufgaben. Festschrift für Friedrich Maurer zum 65. Geburtstag am 5. January, 1963. 1963. Pp. 438-57

Yates, W. E., *Grillparzer: A Critical Introduction.* 1972. Pp. 201-15

——————— , "Die Jugendeindrucke Wird Man Nicht los . . . : Grillparzer's Relation to the Viennese Popular Theatre", *Germanic Review* (1973), 48:132-49

Der Traum ein Leben   *SEE*   A Dream Is Life

Ein Treuer Diener Seines Herrn   *SEE*   A Faithful Servant of His Master

Weh Dem, Der Lugt!   *SEE*   Thou Shalt Not Lie

PATRICK HAMILTON

Angel Street, 1941
  Clay, James H. and Daniel Krempel, *The Theatrical Image.* 1967. Pp. 157-65
  Laufe, Abe, *Anatomy of a Hit; Long Run Plays on Broadway from 1900 to the Present Day.* 1966. Pp. 131-34
  Catholic World, 154:600, Feb. 1942
  Colliers, 109:14, Apr. 11, 1942
  Commonweal, 35:221, Dec. 19, 1941
  Commonweal, 47:424, Feb. 6, 1948
  Nation, 153:649, Dec. 20, 1941
  New Yorker, 23:40, Jan. 31, 1948
  Theatre Arts, 26:87, Feb. 1942
  Time, 38:73, Dec. 15, 1941

Duke in Darkness, 1944
  Nathan, George Jean, *Theatre Book of the Year, 1943-1944.* Pp. 218-20
  Commonweal, 39:420, Feb. 11, 1944
  Spectator, 169:359, Oct. 16, 1942
  Theatre Arts, 28:208, Apr. 1944

Rope's End, 1930
  Catholic World, 130:467-68, Jan., 1930
  Review of Reviews, 80:158, Dec. 1929

WILLIAM HAUGHTON

SEE

THOMAS DEKKER, HENRY CHETTLE
AND WILLIAM HAUGHTON

GERHART HAUPTMANN

The Beaver Coat, 1893
  Beerbohm, Max, *Around Theatres*. 1953. Pp. 365-69
  Harris, Frank, *Contemporary Portraits*, 4th Series. 1923. Pp. 252-61
  Heydebrand, Renate von and G. Just Klaus, eds., *Wissenschaft als Dialog; Studien zur Literatur und Kunst seit der Jahrhundertwende*. 1969. Pp. 83-111
  Koester, Rudolf, "The Ascent of the Criminal in German Comedy", *German Quarterly* (May 1970), 43:376-93
  Osborne, John, *The Naturalist Drama in Germany*. 1971. Pp. 136-40
  Steffen, Hans, ed., *Das Deutsche Lustspiel*. II. 1969. Pp. 25-60

Before Sunrise, 1889
  Osborne, John, *The Naturalist Drama in Germany*. 1971. Pp. 76-87

Before Sunset, 1932
  McInnes, Edward, "The Domestic Dramas of Gerhart Hauptmann: Tragedy or Sentimental Pathos?", *German Life and Letters* n. s. (1966-67), 20:53-59
  New Statesman and Nation, 6:413-14, Oct. 7, 1933
  Preussische Jahrbucher, 227:277-79, March, 1932
  Saturday Review, 156:371, Oct. 7, 1933
  Spectator, 151:441, Oct. 6, 1933
  Westermanns Monatshefte, 152:183-85, April, 1932

Biberpelz   *SEE*   The Beaver Coat

Conflagration, 1901
  Osborne, John, *The Naturalist Drama in Germany*. 1971. Pp. 136-39
  Steffen, Hans, ed., *Das Deutsche Lustspiel*. II. 1969. Pp. 25-60

Darkness, 1947
  Stirk, S. D., "Gerhart Hauptmann's Play 'Die Finsternisse'", *Modern Language Quarterly*, 9:146-51, 1948

The Daughter of the Cathedral, 1940
  Heuser, Frederick W. J., "Gerhart Hauptmanns 'Die Tochter der Kathedrale'", *Germanic Review*, 15:137-45, 1940
  Westermanns Monatshefte, 167:303, Jan., 1940

Dorothea Angermann, 1926
  McInnes, Edward, "The Domestic Dramas of Gerhart Hauptmann: Tragedy or Sentimental pathos?', *German Life and Letters* n. s. (1966-67), 20:53-59
Drayman Henschel, 1898
  Osborne, John, *The Naturalist Drama in Germany*. 1971. Pp. 146-52

Einsame Menschen   *SEE*   Lonely Lives

Elektra, 1947
  Cohn, Ruby, *Currents in Contemporary Drama*. 1969. Pp. 92-93

Untersuchungen zur Literatur al Geschichte. Festschrift für Benno von Wiese, Hrsg. v. Vincent J. Gunther. 1973. Pp. 418-30

Die Finsternisse *SEE* Darkness

Florian Geyer, 1896
McInnes, Edward, "The Domestic Dramas of Gerhart Hauptmann: Tragedy or Sentimental Pathos?", *German Life and Letters* n. s. (1966-67), 20:53-59
——————— , "The Image of the Hunt in Hauptmann's Dramas", *German Life and Letters* (1965-66), n. s. 19:190-96
Osborne, John, *The Naturalist Drama in Germany.* 1971. Pp. 121-23
Rippley, LaVern J., "Dramatic Structure in Gerhart Hauptmann's 'Florian Geyer' ", *University of Dayton Review* (1973), 10:39-47
Scholz, Albert "Gerhart Hauptmanns 'Florian Geyer' in der Literaturgeschichte", *German Quarterly,* 20:49-56, 1947
——————— , "Zur Quellenforschung von Gerhart Hauptmanns 'Florian Geyer' ", *Modern Langauage Notes,* 58:292-93, 1943
Weigand, Hermann J., "Auf den Spuren von Hauptmanns 'Florian Geyer' ", *Modern Language Association. Publications* (PMLA), 58:797-848, 1948

Das Friedensfest *SEE* The Reconciliation

Fuhrmann Henschel *SEE* Drayman Henschel

Germanen und Römer, 1880-1881
Heuser, F. W. J., "Hauptmann's 'Germanen und Römer' ", *Germanic Review,* 17:174-96, 1942
Reichart, Walter A., "Gerhart Hauptmann's 'Germanen und Römer' ", *Modern Language Association. Publications* (PMLA), 44:901-10, 1929

The Golden Harp, 1933
Westermanns Monatshefte, 155:493-94, Jan., 1934

Die Goldene Harfe *SEE* The Golden Harp

Hamlet, 1927
Busse, A., "The Case of Hauptmann's 'Hamlet' ", *Monatshefte für Deutsche Unterricht,* 30:163-170, 1938
Heuser, F. W. J., "A Modern German Hamlet", *Journal of English and Germanic Philology,* 31:27-50, 1932
Philological Quarterly, 16:124-38, 1937

Hamlet in Wittenberg, 1935
Theatre Arts, 20:90, Feb., 1936
Westermanns Monatshefte, 159:587-88, Feb., 1936

Iphigenia in Delphi, 1941
Hamburger, Kate, *From Sophocles to Sartre; Figures in Greek Tragedy, Classical and Modern.* 1969. Pp. 80-85
Reichart, W. C., "Iphigenie in Delphi", *Germanic Review,* 17:221-37, 1942
Ziolkowsky, T., "Hauptmann's 'Iphigenie in Delphi': A Travesty?", *Germanic Review,* 34:105-23, 1959

Lonely Lives, 1891
Batley, E. N. "Functional Idealism in Gerhart Hauptmann's 'Einsame Menschen'; An Interpretation", *German Life and Letters* (1969), 23:243-54

De Jenkinson, "Satirical Elements in Hauptmann's 'Einsame Menschen' ", *New German Studies* (1974), 2:145-56

Lea, Henry A., "The Specter of Romanticism; Hauptmann's Use of Quotations", *Germanic Review* (1974), 49:267-83

McInnes, Edward, "The Domestic Dramas of Gerhard Hauptmann: Tragedy or Sentimental Pathos?", *German Life and Letters* n. s. (1966-67), 20:53-59

Osborne, John, *The Naturalist Drama in Germany*. 1971. Pp. 104-18

Shaw, LeRoy Robert, *The Playwright and Historical Change*. 1970. Pp. 20-48

Michael Kramer, 1900

Bachman, Charles R., "Life Into Art: Gerhart Hauptmann and 'Michael Kramer' ", *German Quarterly* (1969), 42:381-92

Osborne, John, *The Naturalist Drama in Germany*. 1971. Pp. 143-46

Schmidt, Hugo, "Hauptmann's 'Michael Kramer' and Joyce's 'The Dead' ", *Modern Language Association. Publications* (1965), 80:141-42

The Rats, 1911

McInnes, Edward, "The Domestic Dramas of Gerhart Hauptmann: Tragedy or Sentimental Pathos?", *German Life and Letters* n. s. (1966-67), 20:53-59

Osborne, John, *The Naturalist Drama in Germany*. 1971. Pp. 147-50

Wiese, Benno von, "Wirklichkeit und Drama in Gerhart Hauptmanns Tragikomödie, 'Die Ratten' ", *Jahrbuch der Deutschen Schiller-Gesellschaft*, 6:311-25, 1962

Die Ratten *SEE* The Rats

The Reconciliation, 1890

Osborne, John, "Hauptmann's Family Tragedy: Das Friedensfest", *Forum for Modern Language Studies* (1968), 4:223-33

Osborne, John, *The Naturalist Drama in Germany*. 1971. Pp. 88-103

Rose Bernd, 1903

Drama, 13:59-60, No. 1922

Osborne, John, *The Naturalist Drama in Germany*. 1971. Pp. 147-56

Nation, 155:392-4, Oct. 11, 1922

New Republic, 32:251-52, Nov. 1, 1922

Theatre Arts, 17:27-28, Jan., 1933

Der Rote Hahn *SEE* The Conflagration

Vor Sonnenaufgang *SEE* Before Sunrise

The Sunken Bell, 1896

Allen, Genieve, M., "The Problem of Individualism in Relation to Society in Ibsen, Maeterlinck, and Hauptmann", *Poet-Lore*, 32:262-66, 1921

Huneker, James Gibbons, *Ivory Apes and Peacocks*. 1915. Pp. 203-21

Weisert, John J., "Critical Reception of Gerhart Hauptmann's 'The Sunken Bell' on the American Stage", *Monatshefte*, 43:221-34, 1951

Die Tochter der Kathedrale *SEE* The Daughter of the Cathedral

Veland, 1925

Crosby, Donald H. and George C. Schoolfield, eds., *Studies in German Drama; A Festschrift in Honor of Walter Silz*. 1974. Pp. 199-211

Die Versunkene Glocke *SEE* The Sunken Bell

The Weavers, 1893
  Bauland, Peter, *The Hooded Eagle; Modern German Drama on the New York Stage*. 1968. Pp. 19-22
  Blankenagel, John C., "Early Reception of Hauptmann's 'Die Weber' in the United States", *Modern Language Notes*, 69:334-40, 1953
  Cole, Toby and Chinoy, Helen Krich, *Directing the Play; A Source Book of Stagecraft*. 1953. Pp. 273-78
  _____ , *Directors on Directing; A Source Book of the Modern Theatre*. 1963. Pp. 326-32
  Dobie, Ann B., "Riot, Revolution and 'The Weavers' ", *Modern Drama* (1969), 12:165-72
  Harper's Weekly, 62:16, Jan. 1, 1916
  Mandel E., "Gerhart Hauptmanns 'Weber' in Russland", *Zeitschrift für Slawistik* (1967), 12:5-19
  McInnes, Edward, "The Image of the Hunt in Hauptmann's Dramas", *German Life and Letters* n. s. (1965-66), 19:190-96
  Nation 101:786, Dec. 30, 1915
  New Republic, 5:200, Dec. 25, 1915
  Osborne, John, *The Naturalist Drama in Germany*. 1971. Pp. 119-31
  Survey, 35:372, Jan. 1, 1916
  Urner, H., "Neuer Blick auf 'Die Weber' ", *Zeichender Zeit* (1963), 17:234-35
  Williams, Raymond, *Drama from Ibsen to Brecht*. 1968. Pp. 240-43

Die Weber   *SEE*   The Weavers

J. H. HAWKES

SEE

JOHN BOYNTON PRIESTLEY AND J. H. HAWKES

THOMAS HEYWOOD

The Captives, or The Lost Recovered, 1624
  Townsend, Freda L., "The Artistry of Thomas Heywood's Double Plots", *Philological Quarterly* (1946), 25:97-119

A Challenge for Beauty, 1634-35
  Levin, Richard, *The Multiple Plot in English Renaissance Drama*. 1971. Pp. 158-60
  Townsend, Freda L., "The Artistry of Thomas Heywood's Double Plots", *Philological Quarterly* (1946), 25:97-119

The English Traveller, 1627?
  Bluestone, Max and Norman Rabkin, eds., *Shakespeare's Contemporaries: Modern Studies in English Renaissance Drama*. 2nd ed. 1970. Pp. 203-18
  Townsend, Freda L., The Artistry of Thomas Heywood's Double Plots", *Philological Quarterly* (1946), 25:97-119

King Edward the Fourth, 1599
  Adams, Henry Hitch, *English Domestic or Homiletic Tragedy, 1575 to 1642*. 1943. Pp. 75-99

A Maidenhead Well Lost, 1625
   Townsend, Freda L., "The Artistry of Thomas Heywood's Double Plots,"
   Philological Quarterly (1946), 25:97-119

The Rape of Lucrece, 1611
   Ribner, Irving, *Jacobean Tragedy; The Quest for Moral Order.* 1962. Pp.
   59-71

The Royal King and the Loyal Subject, 1602?
   Townsend, Freda L., "The Artistry of Thomas Heywood's Double Plots",
   Philological Quarterly (1946), 25:97-119

A Woman Killed with Kindness, 1603
   Adams, Henry Hitch, *English Domestic or Homiletic Tragedy, 1575 to 1642.*
   1943. Pp. 144-59
   Bennett, Josephine Waters; Cargill, Oscar; and Hall, Vernon, eds., *Studies
   in the English Renaissance Drama; In Memory of Karl Julius Holzknecht.*
   1959. Pp. 189-211
   Berry, Lloyd E., "A Note on Heywood's 'A Woman Killed with Kindness'",
   Modern Language Review, 58:64-65, 1963
   Bluestone, Max and Norman Rabkin, eds., *Shakespeare's Contemporaries;
   Modern Studies in English Renaissance Drama.* 2nd ed. 1970. Pp. 194-
   203
   Bryan, Margaret B., "Food Symbolism in 'A Woman Killed with Kindness'",
   Renaissance Papers (1974), Pp. 9-17
   Canuteson, John, "A Woman Killed with Kindness", *Renaissance Drama*
   (1969), 2:123-41
   Cary, Cecile W., "'Go Break this Lute': Music in Heywood's 'A Woman
   Killed with Kindness'", *Huntington Library Quarterly* (1974), 37:111-22
   Cook, D. J., "A Woman Killed with Kindness': An Unshakespearian Trag-
   edy", *English Studies* (Amsterdam), 45:353-72, 1964
   Coursen, Herbert R., Jr., "The Subplot of 'A Woman Killed with Kindness'",
   English Language Notes (1965), 2:180-85
   Herndl, George C., *The High Design; English Renaissance Tragedy and
   the Natural Law*. 1970. Pp. 169-74
   Hooper, A. G., "Heywood's 'A Woman Killed with Kindness'", *English
   Studies in Africa* (1961), 4:54-57
   Johnston, George Burke, "The Lute Speech in 'A Woman Killed with Kind-
   ness'", *Notes and Queries*, 5:525-26, 1958
   Levin, Richard, *The Multiple Plot in English Renaissance Drama.* 1971.
   Pp. 93-97
   McDermott, John J., "Henryson's 'Testament of Cresseid' and Heywood's
   'A Woman Killed with Kindness'", *Renaissance Quarterly* (1967), 20:
   16-21
   Ribner, Irving, *Jacobean Tragedy; The Quest for Moral Order.* 1962. Pp.
   51-58
   Smith, Hallett D., "A Woman Killed with Kindness", *Modern Language
   Association. Publications* (1939), 53:138-47
   Spacks, Patricia Meyer, "Honor and Perception in 'A Woman Killed with
   Kindness'", *Modern Language Quarterly*, 20:321-32, 1959
   Sturgess, K. M., "The Early Quartos of Heywood's 'A Woman Killed with
   Kindness'", *Library* (June 1970), 25:93-104

Townsend, Freda L., "The Artistry of Thomas Heywood's Double Plots",
Philological Quarterly (1946), 25:97-119

Ure, Peter, *Elizabethan and Jacobean Drama; Critical Essays.* 1974. Pp.
145-65

THOMAS HEYWOOD AND WILLIAM ROWLEY

Fortune By Land and Sea, 1607

Adams, Henry Hitch, *English Domestic or Homiletic Tragedy, 1575 to 1642.*
1943. Pp. 160-83

Townsend, Freda L., "The Artistry of Thomas Heywood's Double Plots",
Philological Quarterly (1946), 25:97-119

ROLF HOCHHUTH

The Deputy, 1963

Alexander, E., "Rolf Hochhuth· Equivocal Deputy", *America*, 109:416-18,
Oct. 12, 1963

America, 108:730-31, May 25, 1963, and 109:70, July 20, 1963, and 109:187,
Aug. 24, 1963, and 109:570-3, Nov. 9, 1963 and 110:139-40, Jan. 25, 1964,
and 110:304-05, March 7, 1964 and 110:341-42, March 14, 1964 and 110:
400, March 28, 1964 and 110:495-96, April 4, 1964

Beckman, Heinz, "Rolf Hochhuth: 'Der Stellvertreter'", *Zeitwende. Die
Neue Furche* (1963), 34:280-82

Bentley, Eric Russell, *The Theatre of Commitment and Other Essays on
Drama in Our Society.* 1967. Pp. 190-231

Brustein, Robert Sanford, *Seasons of Discontent; Dramatic Opinions 1959-
1965.* 1965. Pp. 204-07

Buchheim, Hans, "Hochhuths 'Stellvertreter' in der Sicht of Historikers",
Zeitwende. Die Neue Furche (1964), 35:253-58

Carew, Rivers, "The Representative", *The Dubliner* (1964), 3:73-75

Catholic World, 197:380-85, Sept., 1963 and 199:135-6, May 1964

Christian Century, 80:980-81, Aug. 7, 1963 and 80:1269-70, Oct. 16, 1963
and 81:349, March 11, 1964

Clurman, Harold, *The Naked Image; Observations on the Modern Theatre.*
1966. Pp. 80-82

Commonweal, 79:647-62, Feb. 28, 1964, and 79:749-51, March 20, 1964
and 80:174-76, May 1, 1964

"Danish Rabbi Speaks Concerning Hochhuth's Play 'The Deputy'", *America*,
110:30, Jan. 11, 1964

"Deputy Controversy", *Christian Century*, 81:507-08, April 22, 1964

Drama, #71:20-2, 1963

Educational Theatre Journal, 16:180, May, 1964

Flynn, Edward and Patricia Flynn, "The Representative", *Aylesford Review*
(1964), 6:160-65

Gilman, Richard, *Common and Uncommon Masks; Writings on the Theatre,
1961-70.* 1971. Pp. 163-66

Grenzmann, Wilhelm, "Der Umstrittene Papst. Zu Rolf Hochhuths Drama
'Der Stellvertreter'", *Orientierung* (1963), 27:106-10

Hansen, Christian, "War der Papst Mitschuldiz? Lefhafte Diskussion um
das Zeitdrama 'Der Stellvertreter'", *Die Kommenden* (1963), 17:21-24

Hildebrandt, Dieter, "Musste der Papst Reden? Zur Diskussion um den 'Stellvertreter'", *Kirche* (1963), 24:230-32

Hill, Leonidas E., "History and Rolf Hochhuth's 'The Deputy'", *Mosaic* (1967), 1:118-31

Hudson Review, 17:237-38, Summer, 1964

Hughes, Catharine, *Plays, Politics and Polemics.* 1973. Pp. 127-38

Illustrated London News, 243:652, Oct. 19, 1963

Kerr, Walter, *Thirty Plays Hath November; Pain and Pleasure in the Contemporary Theater.* 1969. Pp. 88-92

Kleinschmidt, K., "Prüfing und Bewährung 'Auschwitz und die Frage nach Gott'", *Glaube und Gewissen. Eine Protestantische Monatschrift* (1963), 9:162-66

Lefevre, H., "'Stedfortroederen's historieforfalskning", *Catholica* (Denmark), 21:67-73, 1963

Life, 56:28, March 13, 1964

Lumley, Frederick, *New Trends in Twentieth Century Drama; A Survey Since Ibsen and Shaw.* 1967. Pp. 361-62

Martin, Bernhard, "Papst Pius XII vor Gericht. Zu Hochhuths Schauspiel 'Der Stellvertreter'", *Die Neue Schau* (1963), 24:133-34

Mydans, C., "Footnote to 'The Deputy' Dispute: Jews of Rome, the Nazis, and the Vatican", *Life*, 56:21, May 1, 1964

Nation, 197:287-88, Nov. 2, 1963 and 198:270-72, and 198:277-78, March 16, 1964

New Republic, 150:23-25, March 14, 1964

New Statesman, 66:460-61, Oct. 4, 1963

New Yorker, 39:54, Dec. 28, 1963 and 40:118, March 7, 1964

Newsweek 61:65, March 11, 1963 and 63:78-79, March 2, 1964 and 63:78-79, March 9, 1964

"Nothing More Unjust: Pope Paul's Allusion to the Attack Upon Pope Pius XII in 'The Deputy'", *America*, 110:68-69, Jan. 18, 1964

Novick, Julius, *Beyond Broadway; The Quest for Permanent Theatres.* 1968. Pp. 98-99

"Als die Offiziellen Kirchen Schwiegen. Hochhuths Bühnenstuck 'Der Stellvertreter' und Bischof Dibelius", *Glaube und Gewissen. Eine Protestantische Monatschrift* (1963), 9:166-67

Otto, H., "Gedanken zu Rolf Hochhuths 'Stellvertreter'", *Quäker, Der Monatshefte der Deutschen Freunde* (1963), 37:215-22

Partisan Review, 31:288-89, Spring, 1964

Perry, R. C., "Historical Authenticity and Dramatic Form: Hochhuth's 'Der Stellvertreter' and Weiss's 'Die Ermittlung'", *Modern Language Review* (Oct. 1969), 64:828-39

"Pius Defended: English Version of 'Der Stellvertreter'" *Newsweek*, 62:97, Oct. 7, 1963

"P. O. A. U. on Trial: Tempest over 'Der Stellvertreter'", *Christian Century*, 80:1124, Sept. 18, 1963

Randall, A., "Tragic Dilemma of Pope Pius XII", *Wiseman Review*, 277:101-13, 1963

Reporter, 30:46, Jan. 30, 1964 and 30:40, April 9, 1964

Riquet, M., "Du Vicaire au Bouc Émissaire," *La Table Ronde*, #193:7-18, 1964

"Rolf Hochhuth's 'The Deputy': Symposium", *Commonweal*, 79:647-62, Feb. 28, 1964

Saturday Evening Post, 237:36, 39, Feb. 29, 1964

Saturday Review, 47:16, March 14, 1964 and 47:41-42, March 21, 1964

Scharz, E., "Rolf Hochhuth's 'The Representative'", *Germanic Review*, 39:211-30, 1964

Schroers, Rolf and Wolfgang Hildesheimer, "Unbewältigtes Schweigen. Zu Rolf Hochhuths 'Stellvertreter'", *Merkur. Deutsche Zeitschrift für Europaisches Denken* (1963), 17:807-11

"See or Read It First!", *Christian Century*, 81:294, March 4, 1964

Simmel, Oskar, 'Der Stellvertreter", *Stimmen der Zeit* (1963), 172:66-69

Sontag, Susan, *Against Interpretation and Other Essays*. 1966. Pp. 124-31

Spectator, 211:417, Oct. 4, 1963

T. L. S. Essays and Reviews from The Times Literary Supplement, 1963. 1964. Pp. 90-95

Taeni, R., "'Der Stellvertreter': Episches Theatre oder Christliche Tragödie?", *Seminar: A Journal of Germanic Studies* (1966), 2:15-35

Time, 82:85-86, Nov. 1, 1963 and 83:50, March 6, 1964

United States News, 56:60, March 16, 1964

Vogue, 143:54, April 15, 1964

Werner, H., "Hochhuts 'Stellvertreter' und Kein Ende", *Kirche in der Zeit* (1963), 18:485-87

Wieser, Gottlob, "Die Katholiken und der 'Stellvertreter'", *Kirchenblatt für die Reformierte* (1963), 119:392

"Zur Diskussion um Hochhuths 'Stellvertreter'", *Herder-Korrespondenz. Orbis Catholicus* (1963), 17:373-81

Guerillas, 1970

Eckstein, Georg Gunther, "Zu Hochhuth's 'Guerillas': Eine Amerikanische Stimme", *Merkur* (1970), 24:993-96

Karasek, Hellmuth, "Zur Uraufführung von Rolf Hochhuths Neuem Stück, 'Guerillas'", *Die Zeit. Wochenzeiting für Politik, Wirtschaft, Handel und Kultur* (Jan. 25, 1970), #21:13-14

Taeni, Rainer, "Revolution by Inflation", *Meanjin* (March 1971), 30:114-17

Die Soldaten   *SEE*   The Soldiers

The Soldiers, 1967

America, 118:752-54, June 8, 1968

America, 119:140, Aug. 31, 1968

Commonweal, 88:182-84, April 26, 1968

Commonweal, 88:335, May 31, 1968

Esslin, Martin, *Brief Chronicles; Essays on Modern Theatre.* 1970. Pp. 139-49

Hughes, Catharine, *Plays, Politics and Polemics.* 1973. Pp. 117-24

Life, 64:12, June 7, 1968

Mering, Otto von and Leonard Kasdan, eds., *Anthropology and the Behavioral and Health Sciences.* 1970. Pp. 242-61

Nation, 205:700-01, Dec. 25, 1967

Nation, 206:678, May 20, 1968

New Yorker, 44:83-84, May 11, 1968

New Statesman, 74:479, Oct. 13, 1967

New York Times Magazine, Pp. 48-49, Nov. 19, 1967

Newsweek, 71:105, Mar. 11, 1968

Newsweek, 71:109, May 13, 1968

Reporter, 38:38-39, May 30, 1968
Saturday Review, 50:27, Dec. 2, 1967
Saturday Review, 51:32, May 18, 1968
Stumm, Reinhardt, "Modell einen Revolution. Ein Gesprach mit Rolf
  Hochhuth über Sein Neues Stuck 'Guerillas'", *Weltwoche* (1970), 38:
  31-33
Time, 90:82, Oct. 20, 1967
Time, 91:72, May 10, 1968
Vogue, 151:158, May 1968
Weightman, John, "Dirty Hands or the Higher Cleanliness", *Encounter*
  (Feb. 1969), 32:55-56
Zipes, J. D., "Guilt-Ridden Hochhuth: 'The Soldiers'", *New Theatre Mag-*
  azine (1968), 9:17-20

Die Stellvertreter *SEE* The Deputy

HUGO VON HOFMANNSTHAL

Der Abenteurer und die Sängerin *SEE* The Adventurer and the Singer

The Adventurer and the Singer, 1899
  Rey, W. H., "Eros und Ethos in Hofmannsthals Lustspielen; Eine Studie
    zur Kunst der Konfiguration in 'Der Abenteur', 'Cristinas Heimreise', und
    'Der Rosenkavalier'", *Deutsche Vierteljahrsschrift für Literaturwissenschaft*
    und Geistesgeschichte (1956), 30:449-73

Die Aegyptische Helen *SEE* The Egyptian Helen

Alcestis, 1916
  Hamburger, Kate, *From Sophocles to Sartre; Figures from Greek Tragedy,*
    Classical and Modern. 1969. Pp. 105-07
  Nuchtern, Eva-Maria, "Hofmannsthal's 'Alcestis'", *Frankfurter Beitrage*
    zur Germanistik (1968), Special Issue Vol. 6
  Wellesz, Egon, *Essays on Opera.* 1950. Pp. 145-52

Alkestis *SEE* Alcestis

Arabella, 1933
  Bie, O., "Der Weg der 'Arabella'", *Neue Rundschau* (Dec. 1933), 44 pt.2:
    820-23
  Dieckmann, Friedrich, "Zweimal 'Arabella'", *Die Neue Rundschau* (1974),
    85:96-112
  Koch, Hans-Albrecht, "Die Schluss-Szene der 'Arabella'. Textkritische
    Bemerkungen", *Hofmannsthal Blatter* (1972), 8/9:173-77
  Masur, Gerhard, "Hugh von Hofmannsthal's 'Arabella'", *American-Ger-*
    man (1956), 22:24-26
  Tumler, Franz, "Rosenkavalier und Arabella", *Neue Deutsche Hefte* (1956),
    29:359-78

Ariadne auf Naxos *SEE* Ariadne in Naxos

Ariadne in Naxos, 1912
  Colleville, Maurice, et als, *Un Dialogue des Nations: Albert Fuchs zum 70.*
    Geburtstag. 1967. Pp. 159-74

Daviau, Donald G., "Hugo von Hofmannsthal's 'Ariadne in Naxos': An Analysis and Interpretation of the 'Vorspiel'", *Modern Austrian Literature; Journal of the International Arthur Schnitzler Research Association* (1973), 6:41-71

Dumesmil, R., "Ariadne auf Naxos", *Mercure de France* (Oct. 15, 1937), 279:409-11

Interpretationen zur Österreichischen Literatur. 1971. Pp. 63-79

Konneker, Barbara, "Die Funktion des Vorspiels in Hofmannsthals 'Ariadne auf Naxos'", *Germanische-Romanische Monatschrift* (1972), n. f. 22:124-41

Lewis, Hanna B., "Hofmannsthal and Milton", *Modern Language Notes* (1972), 87:732-41

Winder, Marianne, "The Psychological Significance of Hosmannsthal's 'Ariadne auf Naxos'", *German Life and Letters* (1961), 15:100-09

Wittmann, Horst, "Hofmannsthals Lustspielsprache; Die Sprachkrise und Ihre Überwindung in den Komödien 'Der Schwierige', 'Der Rosenkavalier' und 'Ariadne auf Naxos'", *Dissertation Abstracts* (1969), 30:741A-42A

Die Beiden Götter, 1917-18

Misty, Frenz, "Toward Buddhahood; Some Remarks on the Sigismund Figure in the Hofmannsthall 'Turm' Plays", *Modern Language Review* (1974), 69:337-47

Cavalier of the Rose, 1911

Gilbert, M. E., "Painter and Poet: Hogarth's 'Marriage à la Mode' and Hofmannsthal's 'Der Rosenkavalier'", *Modern Language Review* (Oct. 1969), 64:818-27

Giordano, Charles B., "On the Significance of Names in Hofmannsthal's 'Rosenkavalier'", *German Quarterly* (1963), 36:258-68

Herz, Joachim and Rudolf, "Entwurf einer 'Rosenkavalier' Inszenierung", *Hofmannsthal Blatter* (1971), 7:76-88

Kleine-Kreutzmann, Alfred, "Time and Change in 'Die Rosenkavalier'", *University of Dayton Review* (1972), 9,i:25-33

Rey, W. H., "Eros und Ethos in Hofmannsthals Lustspielen: Eine Studie Zur Kunst der Konfiguration in 'Der Abenteurer', 'Cristinas Heimreise', und 'Der Rosenkavalier'", *Deutsche Vierteljahrsschrift für Literaturwissenschaft und Geistesgeschichte* (1956), 30:449-73

Schwarz, Egon, "Hofmannsthal and the Problem of Reality", *Wisconsin Studies in Contemporary Literature* (1967), 8:484-504

Stenberg, P. A., "'Die Rosenkavalier': Hofmannsthal's 'Märchen' of Time", *German Life and Letters* (1973), 26:24-32

Tumler, Franz, "Rosenkavalier und Arabella", *Neue Deutsche Hefte* (1956), 29:359-78

Wandruszka, Adam, "Das Zeit-und Sprachkostum von Hofmannsthals 'Rosenkavalier'", *Zeitschrift für Deutsche Philologie* (1967), 86:561-70

Wittmann, Horst, "Hofmannsthals Lustspielsprache; Die Sprachkrise und Ihre Überwindung in den Komödien 'Der Schwierige', 'Der Rosenkavalier' und 'Ariadne auf Naxos'", *Dissertation Abstracts* (1969), 30:741A-42A

Christinas Heimreise *SEE* Cristina's Journey Home

Cristina's Journey Home, 1910

Naumann, Walter, "'Cristinas Heimreise' und ihr Vorbild", *Modern Language Notes* (1944), 59:104-06

Rey, W. H., "Eros und Ethos in Hofmannsthals Lustspielen: Eine Studie zur Kunst der Konfiguration in 'Der Abenteuer', 'Cristinas Heimreise', und 'Der Rosenkavalier'", *Deutsche Vierteljahrsschrift für Literaturwissenschaft und Geistesgeschichte* (1956), 30:449-73

Death and the Fool, 1898
Alewyn, Richard, "Hofmannsthals 'Tor und Tod'", *Monatshefte für Deutsche Unterricht* (1944), 36:409-24
Porter, Michael, "Hugo von Hofmannsthal's 'Death and the Fool': The Poet as Fool", *Modern Austrian Literature; Journal of the International Arthur Schnitzler Research Association* (1972), 5,i-ii:14-29
Siefken, Hinrich, "Hugo von Hofmannsthal's 'Der Tor und der Tod': The Paradox of the 'Nahe Ferne'", *German Life and Letters* (1970), 24:78-88

The Death of Titian, 1901
Fuchs, Albert, "Hugo von Hofmannsthal: 'Der Tod des Tizian'; Interpretation, Problemes de la Forme", *Recherches Germaniques* (1973), 3:135-52
White, J. J., "A Reappraisal of the Treatment of Aestheticism in Hugo von Hofmannsthal's 'Der Tod des Tizian'", *New German Studies* (1974), 2:30-47

The Difficult Man, 1921
Bauer, Sibylle, ed., *Hugo von Hofmannsthal*. 1968. Pp. 402-47
Bilou, H., "'Der Schwierige': Critique", *Journal des Debats* (Oct. 2, 1931), 38 pt. 2:555-58
Burckhardt, Carl J., "Zu Hugo von Hofmannsthals Lustspiel 'Der Schwierige'", *Neue Rundschau* (1960), 71:133-37
Carter, T. E., "Structure in Hofmannsthal's 'Der Schwierige'", *German Life and Letters* (1964), 18:15-24
Cohn, Hilde D., "Die Beiden Schwierigen in Deutschen Lustspiel: Lessing, 'Minna von Barnhelm'—Hofmannsthal, 'Der Schwierige'", *Monatshefte* (1952), 44:257-69
Gray, Ronald D., *The German Tradition in Literature, 1871-1945.* 1965. Pp. 301-26
Hirsch, Rudolf, "Zwei Briefe Uber den 'Schwierige'", *Hofmannsthal Blätter* (1971), 7:70-75
Joyce, Douglas A., "Some Uses of Irony in Hofmannsthal's 'Der Schwierige'", *Modern Language Quarterly* (1969), 30:402-16
Kleen, Tebbe, "Zur Arbeit am 'Schwierigen'", *Hofmannsthal Blatter* (1969), 2:152-56
Manger, Philip, "One More 'Praeexistenz-Tyche-Existenz' in Hofmannsthal's 'Der Schwierige'", *Seminar; A Journal of Germanic Studies* (1970), 6:48-62
Norton, R. C., "Hugo von Hofmannsthal's 'Der Schwierige' and Granville-Barker's 'Waste'", *Comparative Literature* (1962), 14:272-79
——————, "Inception of Hofmannsthal's 'Der Schwierige': Early Plans and Their Significance", *Modern Language Association. Publications* (1964), 79:97-103
Schultz, H. Stefan, "Hofmannsthal's 'Der Schwierige' and Goethe's 'Torquato Tasso'", *Publications of the English Goethe Society* (1963), 33:130-49
Steffen, Hans, ed., *Das Deutsche Lustspiel.* 1968. Pp. 125-58
Stern, Martin, "In Illo Tempore: Uber Notizen und Varianten zu Hofmannsthalls Lustspiel 'Der Schwierige'", *Wirkendes Wort* (1957-58), 8:115-19

Weigel, Hans, "Triumph der Wortlosigkeit: Ein Versuch uber Hugo von Hofmannsthals Lustspiel 'Der Schwierige'", *Neue Deutsche Hefte* (1963), 95:30-44

Wittmann, Horst, "Hofmansthals 'Der Schwierige': Die Potentialitat des Leichten", *Seminar. A Journal of Germanic Studies* (1974), 10:274-97

———————— , "Hofmannsthals Lustspielsprache; Die Sprachkrise und Ihre Überwindung in den Komodien 'Der Schwierige', 'Der Rosenkavalier' und 'Ariadne auf Naxos'". *Dissertation Abstracts* (1969), 30:741A-42A

Wucherpfenning, Wolf, " 'Der Schwierige' und 'Der Manschenfeind': Zur Auffassung des Individuums bei Molière und Hofmannsthal", *Colloquia Germanica; Internationale Zeitschrift für Germanische Sprach- und Literaturwissenschaft* (1969), 3:269-301

The Egyptian Helen, 1928

Glenn, Jerry, "Hofmannsthal, Hacks and Hildesheimer; Helen in the Twentieth Century", *Seminar; A Journal of Germanic Studies* (Spring 1969), 5:1-20

Hamburger, Käte, *From Sophocles to Sartre; `Figures from Greek Tragedy, Classical and Modern.* 1969. Pp. 96-100

Hodeige, Fritz and Carl Rothe, eds., *Atlantische Begegnungen: Eine Freundesgabe für Arnold Bergstraesser.* 1964. Pp. 103-33

Electra, 1903

Bauer, Sibylle, ed., *Hugo von Hofmannsthal.* 1968. Pp. 274-310

Baumann, Gerhart, "Hugo von Hofmannsthals 'Elektra'", *Germanisch-Romanische Monatshefte* n. s. (1959), 9:157-81

Breuer, R., "Strauss's 'Elektra' as seen by Hugo von Hofmannsthal", *Musical America* (Jan. 15, 1952), 72:8

Corrigan, Robert W., "Character as Destiny in Hofmannsthal's 'Elektra'", *Modern Drama* (1959), 2:17-28

———————— , *The Theatre in Search of a Fix.* 1973. Pp. 147-60

Doswald, H. K., "Nonverbal Expression in Hofmannsthal's 'Elektra'", *Germanic Review* (May 1969), 44:199-210

Hamburger, Käte, *From Sophocles to Sartre; Figures from Greek Tragedy, Classical and Modern.* 1969. Pp. 45-68

Newiger, Hans-Joachim, "Hofmannsthals 'Elektra' und Griechische Tragödie", *Arcadia* (1969), 4:138-63

Politzer, Heinz, "Hugo von Hofmannsthals 'Elektra': Geburt der Tragödie aus dem Geiste der Psychopathologie", *Deutsche Vierteljahrsschrift für Literaturwissenschaft Geistesgeschichte* (1973), 47:95-119

Untersuchungen zur Literatur also Geschichte. Festschrift für Benno von Wiese, Hrsg. v. Vincent j. Gunther. 1973. Pp. 418-30

The Emperor and the Witch, 1897

Michelsen, Peter, "Zu Hugo von Hofmannsthal: 'Der Kaiser und die Hexe'", *Zeitschrift für Deutsche Philologie* (1964), 83:113-41

Everyman, 1911

d'Amico, S., " 'Jedermann': Critica", *Nuova Antologia* (Aug. 1, 1933), 368:468-70

Bidou, H., "Jedermann': Critique", *Journal des Debats* (Sept 5, 1930), 37 pt. 2:404-06

Hirsch, Rudolf, "Zum Verständnis des 'Jedermann'", *Hofmannsthal Blatter* (1970), 4:289-93

Koester, Rudolf, "Everyman and Mammon—The Persistence of a Theme in Modern German Drama", *Revue des Langues Vivantes* (1969), 35:368-80

Schwarz, Alfred, "The Allegorical Theatre of Hugo von Hofmannsthal", *Tulane Drama Review* (1959-60), 4:65-76

Young, S., "'Jedermann': Criticism", *New Republic* (Dec. 28, 1927), 53:164-65

Die Frau Ohne Schatten *SEE* The Woman Without a Shadow

Das Gerettete Venedig *SEE* Venice Preserv'd

Gestern, 1891

Alewyn, Richard, "Hofmannsthals Aufang: 'Gestern'", *Trivium* (1948), 6:241-62

The Great World Theatre of Salzburg, 1922

Bergstraesser, Arnold, "The Holy Beggar: Religion and Society in Hugo von Hofmannsthal's 'Great World Theatre of Salzburg'", *Germanic Review* (1946), 20:261-86

Best, A. J., "'Great Theatre of the World': Criticism", *Spectator* (Jan. 19, 1924), 132:80

Düsel, F., "'Grosses Welttheatre': Kritik", *Westermanns Monatshefte* (1933), 154-281-83

Misty, Frenz, "Toward Buddhahood; Some Remarks on the Sigismund Figure in the Hofmannsthal 'Turm' Plays", *Modern Language Review* (1974), 69:337-47

Schwarz, Alfred, "The Allegorical Theatre of Hugo von Hofmannsthal", *Tulane Drama Review* (1959-60), 4:65-76

Schwarz, Egon, "Hofmannsthal and the Problem of Reality", *Wisconsin Studies in Contemporary Literature* (1967), 8:484-504

Sterne, M., "'Great World Theatre': Criticism", *Theatre Arts* (Jan. 1923), 7:15-20

Annales Politiques et Litteraires, 110:77-78, July 25, 1937

The Incorruptible Man, 1923

Düsel, F., "'Der Unbestechliche': Kritik", *Westermanns Monatshefte* (1923), 135:307

Erken, Gunther, Max Fritzsche and Leonardi Fiedler, "'Der Unbestechliche' in Bochum und Wien" *Hofmannsthal Blatter* (1970), 4:296-304

Jedermann *SEE* Everyman

Der Kaiser und die Hexe *SEE* The Emperor and the Witch

Das Kleine Welttheatre *SEE* The Little Theatre of the World

Das Leben ein Traum, 1902-10

Misty, Frenz, "Toward Buddhahood; Some Remarks on the Sigismund Figure in the Hofmannsthal 'Turm' Plays", *Modern Language Review* (1974), 69:337-47

The Little Theatre of the World, 1897

Baumann, Gerhart, "Hugo von Hofmannsthal: 'Das Kleine Welttheatre'", *Germanisch-Romanische Monatschrift* n. s. (1957), 7:106-30

Ost, Hans, "Ein Motif Michelangelos bei Hofmannsthal: 'Die Schlacht von

Cascina' und 'Das Kleine Welttheatre'", *Euphorion. Zeitschrift für Literatur Geschichte* (1965), 59:173-77

Steiner, Herbert, "Zu Hofmannsthals 'Kleinem Weltheatre'", *Monatshefte für Deutsche Unterricht* (1943), 35:224-25

Wiese, Bruno von, *Das Deutsche Drama; Vom Barock bis zur Gegenwart.* 1958. Vol. II. Pp. 229-43

Oedipus and the Sphinx, 1906

Hamburger, Käte, *From Sophocles to Sartre; Figures from Greek Tragedy. Classical and Modern.* 1969. Pp. 135-46

Rey, W. H., "Geist und Blut in Hofmannsthals 'Opedipus und die Sphinx'", *German Quarterly* (1958), 31:84-93

Steffen, Hans, "Die Paradoxie von Selbstbehauptung und Selbsthingabe in 'Oedipus und die Sphinx' von Hofmannsthal", *Etudes Germaniques* (1974), 29:206-23

Der Rosenkavalier *SEE* The Cavalier of the Rose

Das Salzburger Grosse Welttheatre *SEE* The Great World Theatre of Salzburg

Der Schwierige *SEE* The Difficult Man

Der Tod des Tizian *SEE* The Death of Titian

Der Tor und der Tod *SEE* Death and the Fool

The Tower, 1928

Bauer, Sibylle, ed., *Hugo von Hofmannsthal.* 1968. Pp. 448-64

Düsel, F., "'Der Turm': Kritik", *Westermanns Monatshefte* (May 1928), 144:313-15

Llewellyn, R. T., "Hofmannsthal's Nihilism", *Modern Language Review* (1966), 61:250-59

Misty, Frenz, "Towards Buddhahood; Some Remarks on the Sigismund Figure in the Hofmannsthal 'Turm' Plays", *Modern Language Review* (1974), 69:337-47

Peschken, Bernd, "Zur Entwicklungsgeschichte von Hofmannsthal's 'Turm', mit Ideologiekritische Absicht", *Germanisch-Romanishe Monatsschrift* (1969), 19:152-78

Rey, W. H., "Der Turm", *Das Deutsche Drama* (1958), 2:265-83

Schwarz, Alfred, "The Allegorical Theatre of Hugo von Hofmannsthal", *Tulane Drama Review* (1959-60), 4:65-76

Schwarz, Egon, "Hofmannsthal and the Problem of Reality", *Wisconsin Studies in Contemporary Literature* (1967), 8:484-504

Der Turm *SEE* The Tower

Der Unbestechliche *SEE* The Incorruptible Man

Venice Preserv'd, 1905

Crowhurst, Griseldis, "Der Dramatische Schluss in Hugh von Hofmannsthals 'Das Gerettete Venedig'", *Acta Germanica* (1970), 5:153-59

Hietsch, Otto, ed., *Osterreich und die Angelsächsische Welt: Kulturbegegnungen und Vergleiche.* 1961. Pp. 418-31

Klieneberger, H. R., "Otway's 'Venice Preserv'd' and Hofmannsthal's 'Das Gerettete Venedig'", *Modern Language Review* (1967), 62:292-97

Lewis, Hanna B., "Hofmannsthal and Milton", *Modern Language Notes* (1972), 87:732-41

Der Weisse Fächer   *SEE*   The White Fan

The White Fan, 1897
   Ritter, Ellen, "Die Chinesische Quelle von Hofmannsthal's Dramolette 'Der Weisse Fächer' ", *Arcadia* (1968), 3:299-305
   Szondi, Peter, "Hofmannsthals 'Weisser Fächer' ", *Neue Rundschau* (1964), 75:81-87

Woman Without a Shadow, 1919
   Colleville, Maurice, et als, *Un Dialogue des Nations: Albert Fuchs zum 70. Geburtsag.* 1967. Pp. 175-87
   Koch, Hans-Albrecht, " 'Fast Kontrapunktlich Streng': Beobachtungen zur Form von Hugh von Hofmannsthal Operndichtung 'Die Frau Ohne Schatten' ", *Jahrbuch des Freien Deutschen Hochstifts* (1971), 456-78
   Naumann, Walter, "Die Quelle Hofmannsthals 'Frau Ohne Schatten' ", *Modern Language Notes* (1944), 59:386-87

LUDVIG HOLBERG

Jeppe of the Hill, 1722
   Anker, Oyvind, "Holbergs 'Jeppe' und Wiers-Jenssens 'Anne Pederstochter' ", *Maske und Kothurn* (1965), 11:20-29
   Myhrman, Gustaf, "Alkoholisten Jeppe", *Bonniers Litterara Magasin* (1961), 30:622-24
   Sprinchorn, Evert, ed., *The Genius of the Scandinavian Theater.* 1964. Pp. 537-47

Jeppe paa Bjerget   *SEE*   Jeppe of the Hill

ARNO HOLZ AND JOHANNES SCHLAF

Die Familie Selicke, 1890
   Osborne, John, *The Naturalistic Drama in Germany.* 1971. Pp. 51-54
   Ritchie, James MacPherson, ed., *Periods in German Literature.* 1970. Pp. 193-219

WILLIAM DOUGLAS HOME

Aunt Edwina, 1959
   Illustrated London News, 235:714, Nov. 21, 1959
   Spectator, 203:667, Nov. 13, 1959
   Twentieth Century, 167:254-58, March, 1960

Bad Soldier Smith, 1961
   Illustrated London News, 239:30, July 1, 1961
   New Statesman, 61:1020, June 23, 1961
   Spectator, 206:917, June 23, 1961

Iron Duchess, 1957
   Illustrated London News, 230:518, March 30, 1957
   New Statesman, 53:375, March 23, 1957
   Spectator, 198:378, March 22, 1957

Reluctant Debutant, 1955
 America, 96:111, Oct. 27, 1956
 Catholic World, 184:226-27, Dec. 1956
 Commonweal, 65:151, Nov. 9, 1956
 Illustrated London News, 226:1072, June 11, 1955
 Nation, 183:354, Oct. 27, 1956
 New Yorker, 31:61, July 30, 1955 and 32:109, Oct. 20, 1956
 Newsweek, 48:75, Oct. 29, 1956
 Reporter, 13:43, Oct. 20, 1955
 Saturday Review, 38:33, Sept. 17, 1955 and 39:30, Nov. 3, 1956
 Spectator, 194:706, June 3, 1955
 Theatre Arts, 40:19, Dec. 1956
 Time, 68:60, Oct. 22, 1956

Yes, M'Lord, 1949
 Catholic World, 170:147, Nov., 1949
 New Republic, 121:20, Oct. 24, 1949
 New Yorker, 25:54, Oct. 15, 1949
 Newsweek, 34:81, Oct. 17, 1949
 School and Society, 70:361, Dec. 3, 1949
 Theatre Arts, 33:11, Dec. 1949
 Time, 54:89, Oct. 17, 1949

LAURENCE HOUSMAN

Victoria Regina, 1935
 Laufe, Abe, *Anatomy of a Hit; Long Run Plays on Broadway from 1900 to the Present*. 1966. Pp. 155-57
 Catholic World, 142:589-99, Feb. 1936
 Commonweal, 23:301, Jan. 10, 1936
 Literary Digest, 121:19, Jan. 11, 1936
 Nation, 142:83-84, Jan. 15, 1936
 New Republic, 85:286, Jan. 15, 1936
 Newsweek, 6:25, Dec. 28, 1935
 Pictorial Review, 37:50, April 1936
 Theatre Arts, 20:98, Feb. 1936 and 467, June 1936
 Theatre Arts, 21:769-70, Oct. 1937
 Time, 26:22, Dec. 20, 1935

LAURENCE HOUSMAN AND
HARLEY GRANVILLE GRANVILLE-BARKER

Prunella, or Love in a Garden, 1906
 Beerbohm, Max, *Around Theatres*. 1953. Pp. 466-69
 Boyce, N., "Love in a Dutch Garden", *Harper's Weekly* (Jan. 10, 1914), 58:27
 "Play Without a 'Punch'", *Literary Digest* (Nov. 15, 1913), 47:944-45

ROBERT HOWARD

SEE

JOHN DRYDEN AND ROBERT HOWARD

VICTOR MARIE HUGO

Les Burgraves, 1843

Houston, John Porter, *Victor Hugo*. 1975. Pp. 64-66

Smith, Hugh Allison, *Main Currents of Modern French Drama*. 1925. Pp. 15-35

Cromwell, 1827

Houston, John Porter, *Victor Hugo*. 1975. Pp. 44-50

See, H., "Le Cromwell de Victor Hugo et le Cromwell de l'Histoire", *Mercure de France*, 200:5-17, Nov. 15, 1927

Simon, G., "Va-t-on Jouer Cromwell au Théâtre-Francais?" *Les Annales Politiques et Littéraires*, 85:353, Oct. 4, 1925

Smith, Hugh Allison, *Main Currents of Modern French Drama*. 1925. Pp. 15-35

Studies in Speech and Drama in Honor of Alexander M. Drummond. 1944. Pp. 152-66

Tournier, C., "Les Pointes de Départ du Cromwell de Victor Hugo", *Revue de Littérature Comparée*, 7:87-110, Jan., 1927

Hernani, 1830

Baguley, David, "Drama and Myth in Hugo's 'Hernani'", *Modern Languages* (1971), 52:16-22

Bruner, J. D., "Character of Victor Hugo's 'Hernani'", *Sewanee Review*, 13:209-15, 444-53, 1905

Carlson, Marvin, "'Hernani's' Revolt from the Tradition of French Stage Composition", *Theatre Survey* (1972), 13:1-27

Charlier, G., "'Hernani' et le Figaro", *Mercure de France*, 305:459-65, March, 1949

Clark, R. J. B., "'Hernani' Reconsidered or Don Carlos Vindicatus", *Modern Languages* (1972), 53:168-74

Essays Contributed in Honor of President William Alan Neilson (Smith College Studies in Modern Languages, vol. 21, #1-4), 1939. Smith College, Northampton, Mass., Pp. 103-09

Evans, D. O. "Hegelian Idea in 'Hernani'", *Modern Language Notes*, 63:171-73, 1948

——————— , "Hernani", *Modern Language Notes*, 47:21-4, Jan., 1932

——————— , "Source of 'Hernani'; Le Paria, by Casimir Delavigne", *Modern Language Notes*, 47:514-19, Dec., 1932

Grant, Elliott M., "'Car le Géant est Pris . . . '", *Modern Language Notes*, 44:458-59, 1929

Hess, J. A., "Goethe's 'Egmont' as a Possible Source of Hugo's 'Hernani'", *Modern Philology*, 27:193-99, Nov., 1929

Houston, John Porter. *Victor Hugo*. 1975. Pp. 53-55

Kemp, R. and Gandon, Y., "La Bataille d'Hernani", *France Illustration*, #334:235-37, March 8, 1952

Lancaster, Henry Carrington, *Adventures of a Literary Historian; A Collection of His Writings Presented to H. C. Lancaster by His Former Students and Other Friends in Anticipation of His 60th Birthday, Nov. 10, 1942*. 1942. Pp. 353

McLean, Malcolm D., "The Historical Accuracy of Hugo's 'Hernani'", *The South Central Bulletin* (Tulsa, Okla. Studies by Members of the South Central MLA), 22:4:26-30, 1962

Morand, H., "Les Suspiciens dans la Maison d'Hernani", *Journal des Debats*, 37 pt. 1:436-37, March 14, 1930

Smith, Hugh Allison, *Main Currents of Modern French Drama*. 1925. Pp. 15-35

Stocker, Leonard, "Hugo's 'Hernani' and Verdi's 'Ernani'", *Southern Quarterly* (1970), 8:357-81

Warren, F. M., "Some Notes on 'Hernani'", *Modern Language Notes*. 42:523-25, Dec., 1927

Williams, M. A., "A Precursor of Hernani", *French Studies*, 13:18-27, 1959

Marion de Lorme, 1831

Houston, John Porter, *Victor Hugo*. 1975. Pp. 50-53

Smith, Hugh Allison, *Main Currents of Modern French Drama*. 1925. Pp. 15-35

Mary Tudor, 1833

Fitch, G. B., "Favras and Hugo's 'Marie Tudor'", *Modern Language Notes*, 55:24-30, Jan. 1940

Mercure de France, 286:169-70, Aug. 15, 1938

Ruy Blas, 1838

Les Annales Politiques et Littéraires, 111:591-92, June 10, 1938

Beerbohm, Max, *Around Theatres*. 1953. Pp. 308-10

Bruner, J. D., "Character of Victor Hugo's 'Ruy Blas'", *Sewanee Review*, 14:306-23, 1906

Florenne, Yves, "'Ruy Blas': La Vision et le Songe", *Medicine de France* (1969), Pp. 43-48

Houston, John Porter, *Victor Hugo*. 1975. Pp. 55-64

La Force, "A Propos de Ruy Blas", *Revue des Deux Mondes*, 45:937-40, June 15, 1938

Lancaster, Henry Carrington, *Adventures of a Literary Historian; A Collection of His Writings Presented to H. C. Lancaster by His Former Students and Other Friends in Anticipation of His 60th Birthday, Nov. 10, 1942*. 1942. Pp. 354-60

Lyons, Constance L., "Tragedy and the Grotesque: Act IV of 'Ruy Blas'", *French Review* (1972), 45 (Special Issue):75-84

Mercure de France, 285:428-31, July 15, 1938

Moore, O. H. "How Victor Hugo Altered the Characters of Don Cesar and Ruy Blas", *Modern Language Association. Publications* (PMLA), 47:827-33, 1932

Revue des Deux Mondes, 45:911-14, June 15, 1938

Showalter, E., "De 'Madame de la Pommeraye' a 'Ruy Blas'", *Revue d'Histoire Litteraire de la France* (1966), 66:238-53

Smith, Hugh Allison, *Main Currents of Modern French Drama*. 1925. Pp. 15-35

DOUGLAS HYDE

SEE

WILLIAM BUTLER YEATS, LADY GREGORY AND
DOUGLAS HYDE

HENRIK IBSEN

Brand, 1885

Anderson, Marilyn A., "Norse Trolls and Ghosts in Ibsen", *Journal of Popular Culture* (1971), 5:349-67

Auden, Wystan Hugh, *The Dyer's Hand and Other Essays.* 1962. Pp. 433-55

Baxter, K. M., *Speak What We Feel; A Christian Looks at the Contemporary Theatre.* 1964. Pp. 30-31

Bollerup, Erik, "Om Ibsens 'Brand' och Rydbergs 'Prometeus och Ahasverus'", *Nordisk Tidskrift* (1967), 63:269-90

Brustein, Robert Sanford, *The Theatre of Revolt; An Approach to the Modern Drama.* 1964. Pp. 46-59

Cross, W. L., "Ibsen's 'Brand'", *Arena*, 3:81-90, Dec., 1890

Dahlstrom, Carl E. W. L., "Brand—Ibsen's Bigot?", *Scandinavian Studies* (1956), 22:1-13

de Selincourt, Aubrey, *Six Great Playwrights.* 1960. Pp. 143

Egan, Michael, ed., *Ibsen; The Critical Heritage.* 1972. Pp. 255-58

Fjelde, Rolf, ed., *Ibsen; A Collection of Critical Essays.* 1965. Pp. 52-62

Hurt, James, *Catiline's Dream; An Essay on Ibsen's Plays.* 1972. Pp. 12-20, 24-31, and 37-58

Kjøller-Ritzu, Mette, "Sull' Unita Strutturale del 'Brand' di Ibsen", *Studi Germanici* (1972), 10:121-56

La Chesnais, P. G., "A Propos du Centenaire d'Ibsen; La Genèse de 'Brand'", *Revue des Deux Mondes*, s. 7 44:199-225, March 1, 1928

Lorch-Falch, Even, "Menneskets Forhold Til Gud i 'Brand'", *Samtiden* (1972), 81:31-38

Lyons, Charles R., *Henrik Ibsen; The Divided Consciousness.* 1972. Pp. 1-24

Matthews, Honor, *The Primal Curse; The Myth of Cain and Abel in the Theatre.* 1967. Pp. 89-95

Meyer, Hans Georg, *Henrik Ibsen.* 1972. Pp. 19-32

New Yorker, 35:79, May 30, 1959

Nicol, Bernard de Bear, ed., *Varieties of Dramatic Experience.* 1969. Pp. 169-71

Northam, John, *Ibsen; A Critical Study.* 1973. Pp. 32-75

Palmer, A. H., "Henrik Ibsen's 'Brand'", *New Englander*, 53 (ns 17): 340-73, Oct., 1890

Skard, Eiliv, "Sluttreplikkene in Ibsens 'Brand'", *Edda* (1964), 51: 154-56

Stobart, M. A., "New Lights on Ibsen's 'Brand'", *Fortnightly Review*, 72 (ns. 66):227-39, Aug., 1899

Stone, J. D., "Ibsen's 'Brand'", *Poet-Lore*, 17 #3:60-68, Sept., 1906

Svennson, Sven, "Idéproblematik och Tegner' Inflytande i Ibsens 'Brand'", *Edda* (1972), 72:1-26

Valency, Maurice, *The Flower and the Castle; Introduction to Modern Drama.* 1963. Pp. 124-36

Williams, Raymond, *Drama from Ibsen to Brecht.* 1968. Pp. 34-39

Wood, Forrest, Jr., "Kierkegaardian Light on Ibsen's 'Brand' ", *Personalist* (1970), 51:393-400

Zucker, A. E., "Ibsen-Hettner-Coriolanus-Brand", *Modern Language Notes*, 51:99-106, Feb., 1936

Bygmester Solness   *SEE*   The Master Builder

Catiline, 1881

deSelincourt, Aubrey, *Six Great Playwrights.* 1960. Pp. 136-37

Haakonsen, Daniel, et als, eds., *Ibsenforbundet: Arbok 1967.* 1968. Pp. 61-71

Hurt, James, *Catiline's Dream; An Essay on Ibsen's Plays.* 1972. Pp. 9-19 and 25-33

Joyce, James, *Critical Writings of James Joyce*, ed. by Ellsworth Mason and Richard Ellmann. 1959. Pp. 98-101

Larson, Philip E., "Vision and Structure in Ibsen's Early Plays", *Dissertation Abstracts International* (1974), 34:7762A

Lervik, Ase Hiorth, "Ibsens Verkunst: 'Catalina' ", *Edda* (1963), 50: 269-86

Stenberg, T. T., "Ibsen's 'Catilina' and Goethe's 'Iphigenie auf Taurus' ", *Modern Language Notes*, 39:329-36, June, 1924

Theatre Arts, 20:170, March, 1936

The Doll's House, 1879

Adams, Robert Martin, *Strains of Discord; Studies in Literary Openness.* 1958. Pp. 34-51

Allen, Genieve M., "The Problem of Individualism in Relation to Society in Ibsen, Maeterlinck and Hauptmann", *Poet-Lore*, 32:262-66, 1921

Brockett, Oscar G., *Perspectives on Contemporary Theatre.* 1971. Pp. 62-64

Brown, John Mason, *Two on the Aisle; Ten Years of the American Theatre in Performance.* 1938. Pp. 76-79

Brustein, Robert Sanford, *The Culture Watch; Essays on Theater and Society, 1969-1974.* 1975. Pp. 79-81

——————— , *The Theatre of Revolt; An Approach to the Modern Drama.* 1964. Pp. 67-68 and 105-06

Catholic World, 146:596-97, Feb., 1938

Cole, Toby, ed., *Playwrights on Playwriting; The Meaning and Making of Modern Drama from Ibsen to Ionesco.* 1960. Pp. 151-54

deSelincourt, Aubrey, *Six Great Playwrights.* 1960. Pp. 145-46

Downs, Robert Bingham, *Molders of the Modern Mind; One Hundred and Eleven Books that Shaped Western Civilization.* 1961. Pp. 311-14

Egan, Michael, ed., *Ibsen; The Critical Heritage.* 1972. Pp. 101-25

Freedman, Morris, *The Moral Impulse; Modern Drama from Ibsen to the Present.* 1967. Pp. 3-18

Gassner, John, *Dramatic Soundings; Evaluations and Retractions Culled from Thirty Years of Dramatic Criticism.* 1968. Pp. 24-27

Gilman, Richard, *Common and Uncommon Masks; Writings on the Theatre, 1961-1970.* 1971. Pp. 61-63

Hardwick, Elizabeth, *Seduction and Betrayal; Women and Literature.* 1974. Pp. 33-48

Hurt, James, *Catiline's Dream; An Essay on Ibsen's Plays.* 1972. Pp. 10-19 and 102-09

Jennings, Ann S., "The Reaction of London's Drama Critics to Certain Plays by Henrik Ibsen, Harold Pinter and Edward Bond", *Dissertation Abstracts International* (1973), 34:2067A

Kaasa, Harris, "Ibsen and the Theologians", *Scandinavian Studies* (1971), 43:356-84

Literary Digest, 125:22-23, Jan. 15, 1938

Meyer, Hans Georg, *Henrik Ibsen.* 1972. Pp. 48-55

Nation, 146:53-54, Jan. 8, 1938

New Republic, 93:338, Jan. 26, 1938

New Yorker, 38:68, Feb. 9, 1963

Newsweek, 11:28, Jan. 10, 1938 and 61:56, Feb. 18, 1963

Olivarius, Peder, "Kvindesag og Kvindelyst; Om Henrik Ibsens 'Et Dukkehjem' og 'Hedda Gabler'", *Kritik* (1972), 22:27-42

Pearce, Richard, "The Limits of Realism", *College English* (Jan. 1970), 31:335-43

Rosenberg, M., "Ibsen vs. Ibsen: Or, Two Versions of 'A Doll's House'", *Modern Drama* (Spring 1969), 12:187-96

Scribner's Magazine, 103:71, March, 1938

Spacks, Patricia Meyer, "Confrontation and Escape in Two Social Dramas", *Modern Drama* (May 1968), 11:61-72

Theatre Arts, 22:92, Feb., 1938 and 22:384, May, 1938 and 47:12-13, April, 1963

Theatre Arts Anthology; A Record and a Prophecy, ed. by Rosamond Gilder and others. 1950. Pp. 265-77

Time, 31:32, Jan. 10, 1938

Valency, Maurice, *The Flower and the Castle; Introduction to Modern Drama.* 1963: Pp. 149-59

Warnken, William P., "Kate Chopin and Henrik Ibsen: A Study of 'The Awakening' and 'A Doll's House'", *Massachusetts Studies in English* (1974), 4,iv-5, i:43-49

Weigand, Hermann, *The Modern Ibsen; A Reconsideration.* 1960. Pp. 26-75

Weintraub, Stanley, "Ibsen's 'Doll House'; Metaphor Foreshadowed in Victorian Fiction", *Nineteenth Century Fiction,* 13:67-69, 1958

Williams, Raymond, *Drama from Ibsen to Brecht.* 1968. Pp. 47-50

——————— , *Modern Tragedy.* 1966. Pp. 97-101

Zucker, A. E., "The Forgery in Ibsen's 'Doll House'", *Scandinavian Studies,* 17:309-12, 1943

Et Dukkehjem   *SEE*   The Doll's House

The Emperor and the Galilean, 1896

Fjelde, Rolf, ed., *Ibsen; A Collection of Critical Essays.* 1965. Pp. 80-90

Hurt, James, *Catiline's Dream; An Essay on Ibsen's Plays.* 1972. Pp. 77-99

Johnston, Brian, "The Mythic Foundation of Ibsen's Realism", *Comparative Drama* (Spring 1969), 3:27-41

Lyons, Charles R., *Henrik Ibsen; The Divided Consciousness.* 1972. Pp. 51-74

Valency, Maurice, *The Flower and the Castle; Introduction to Modern Drama*. 1963. Pp. 141-44
Williams, Raymond, *Drama from Ibsen to Brecht*. 1968. Pp. 44-47

An Enemy of the People, 1883
Allen, Genieve M., "The Problem of Individualism in Relation to Society in Ibsen, Maeterlinck and Hauptmann", *Poet-Lore*, 32:262-66, 1921
Bronson, David, "'An Enemy of the People': A Key to Arthur Miller's Art and Ethics", *Comparative Drama* (1968-69), 2:229-47
Brustein, Robert Sanford, *The Theatre of Revolt; An Approach to the Modern Drama*. 1964. Pp. 71-74
Catholic World, 172:387, Feb., 1951
Christian Science Monitor Magazine, Pp. 6, Jan. 6, 1951
Commonweal, 53:374, Jan. 19, 1951
deSelincourt, Aubrey. *Six Great Playwrights*. 1960. Pp. 151
Egan, Michael, ed., *Ibsen; The Critical Heritage*. 1972. Pp. 298-311
Esslin, Martin, *Brief Chronicles; Essays on Modern Theatre*. 1970. Pp. 39-44
_____ , *Reflections; Essays on Modern Theatre*. 1969. Pp. 29-48
Freedman, Morris, *The Moral Impulse; Modern Drama from Ibsen to the Present*. 1967. Pp. 3-18
Halsey, Martha I., "The Rebel Protagonist: Ibsen's 'An Enemy of the People' and Buero's 'Un Soñador para un Pueblo'", *Comparative Literature Studies* (1969), 6:462-71
Hurt, James, *Catiline's Dream; An Essay on Ibsen's Plays*. 1972. Pp. 115-20
Kaasa, Harris, "Ibsen and the Theologians", *Scandinavian Studies* (1971), 43:356-84
Lambert, Robert G., "'An Enemy of the People': A Friend of the Teacher", *English Journal* (1965), 54:626-28
Meyer, Hans Georg, *Henrik Ibsen*. 1972. Pp. 78-92
Nation, 172:18, Jan. 6, 1951
New Republic, 90:139, March 10, 1937 and 124:22, Jan. 22, 1951
New Yorker, 26:44, Jan. 13, 1951
Newsweek, 37:67, Jan. 8, 1951
School and Society, 73:105, Feb. 17, 1951
Theatre Arts 35:15, March, 1951
Time, 57:31, Jan. 8, 1951
Weigand, Hermann, *The Modern Ibsen; A Reconsideration*. 1960. Pp. 101-33
Williams, Raymond, *Modern Tragedy*. 1966. Pp. 97-101

En Folkenfiend   SEE   An Enemy of the People

The Feast at Solhaug, 1856
Larson, Philip E., "Vision and Structure in Ibsen's Early Plays", *Dissertation Abstracts International* (1974), 34:7762A

Fru Inger til Ostraat   SEE   Lady Inger of Ostraat

Fruen fra Havet   SEE   The Lady from the Sea

Gengangere   SEE   Ghosts

Ghosts, 1882

Adams, Robert Martin, *Strains of Discord; Studies in Literary Openness.* 1958. Pp. 34-51

America, 106:29, Oct. 7, 1961

Anderson, Marilyn A., "Norse Trolls and Ghosts in Ibsen", *Journal of Popular Culture* (1971), 5:349-67

Arestad, Sverre, "Ibsen, Strindberg and Naturalistic Tragedy", *Theatre Annual* (1968), 24:6-13

Bermel, Albert, *Contradictory Characters; An Interpretation of Modern Theatre.* 1973. Pp. 15-36

Brustein, Robert Sanford, *The Theatre of Revolt; An Approach to the Modern Drama.* 1964. Pp. 67-71, 74-75, and 349-50

——————— , *Seasons of Discontent; Dramatic Opinions 1959-1965.* 1965. Pp. 57-60

Catholic World, 142:601, Feb., 1936

Cole, Toby, ed., *Playwrights on Playwriting; the Meaning and Making of Modern Drama from Ibsen to Ionesco.* 1960. Pp. 154-55

Commonweal, 23:244, Dec. 27, 1935 and 75:94, Oct. 20, 1961

Corrigan, Robert W., "The Sun Always Rises; Ibsen's 'Ghosts' as Tragedy?", *Educational Theatre Journal*, 11:172-80, 1959

Corrigan, Eric Russell, *The Theatre in Search of a Fix.* 1973. Pp. 98-110

Cowell, Raymond, *Twelve Modern Dramatists.* 1967. Pp. 15-17

Deer, Irving, "Ibsen's Aim and Achievement in 'Ghosts'", *Speech Monographs* (1957), 24:264-74

deSelincourt, Aubrey, *Six Great Playwrights.* 1960. Pp. 150

Egan, Michael, ed., *Ibsen; The Critical Heritage.* 1972. Pp. 182-208

Field, B. S., Jr., "Ibsen's 'Ghosts': Repetitions and Repetitions", *Papers on Language and Literature* (1972), 8 (Supplement):26-38

Fjelde, Rolf, ed., *Ibsen; A Collection of Critical Essays.* 1965. Pp. 109-19

Freedman, Morris, *The Moral Impulse; Modern Drama from Ibsen to the Present.* 1967. Pp. 3-18

Gassner, John and Allen, Ralph G., eds., *Theatre and Drama in the Making.* 1964. Pp. 963-67

Gilbert, W. S., "Ghosts", *Plays and Players* (March 1974), 21:36-39

Gilman, Richard, *Common and Uncommon Masks; Writings on the Theatre, 1961-1970.* 1971. Pp. 59-63

Grove, Robin, "Ibsen's Ghosts", *Critical Review* (1968), 11:8-14

Howells, William Dean, *Criticism and Fiction, and Other Essays.* 1959. Pp. 139-47

Hurt, James, *Catiline's Dream; An Essay on Ibsen's Plays.* 1972. Pp. 6-19 and 109-15

Jennings, Ann S., "The Reaction of London's Drama Critics to Certain Plays by Henrik Ibsen, Harold Pinter and Edward Bond", *Dissertation Abstracts International* (1973), 34:2067A

Johnston, Brian, "Archetypal Repetition in 'Ghosts'", *Scandinavian Studies* (1969), 41:93-125

Kaasa, Harris, "Ibsen and the Theologians", *Scandinavian Studies* (1971), 43:356-84

Lecky, Eleazer, "'Ghosts' and 'Mourning Becomes Electra': Two Versions of Fate", *Arizona Quarterly*, 13:320-38, 1957

Lewis, Allan, *The Contemporary Theatre; The Significant Playwrights of Our Time.* 1962. Pp. 8-41

Mabley, Edward, *Dramatic Construction; An Outline of Basic Principles.* 1972. Pp. 98-109

Mayer, Hans Georg, *Henrik Ibsen.* 1972. Pp. 56-77

Nathan, George Jean, *Theatre Book of the Year, 1947-48.* Pp. 275-78

Nation, 166:256, Feb. 28, 1948 and 193:459, Dec. 2, 1961

New Republic, 85:230, Jan. 1, 1936 and 145:30-31, Oct. 9, 1961

New Yorker, 37:120, Sept. 30, 1961

Newsweek, 6:39, Dec. 21, 1935

Northam, John, *Ibsen; A Critical Study.* 1973. Pp. 76-112

——————— , "Some Uses of Rhetoric in 'Ghosts' ", *Ibsenforbundet; Årbok.* 1972. Pp. 7-31

O Hehir, Diana F., "Ibsen and Joyce; A Study of Three Themes", *Dissertation Abstracts International* (1971), 31:3515A·

Osborne, John, *The Naturalistic Drama in Germany.* 1971. Pp. 28-33

Sedgewick, G. G., *Of Irony, Especially in Drama.* 1967. Pp. 44-48

Shaw, George Bernard, *Plays and Players; Essays on the Theatre.* 1952. Pp. 257-65

Stern, Walter, "No Need of this Hypothesis: 'Ghosts' and the Death of God", *Critical Quarterly* (1967), 9:109-19

Theatre Arts, 20:97-98, Feb., 1936 and 45:59-60, Nov., 1961

Time, 26:32, Dec. 23, 1935 and 78:88, Oct. 6, 1961

Valency, Maurice, *The Flower and the Castle; Introduction to Modern Drama.* 1963. Pp. 159-65

Ward, Alfred Charles, ed., *Specimens of English Dramatic Criticism, 17th-20th Centuries* (World Classics). 1945. Pp. 182-89

Weigand, Hermann, *The Modern Ibsen; A Reconsideration.* 1960. Pp. 76-100

West, Ray Benedict, ed., *Essays in Modern Literary Criticism.* 1952. Pp. 548-59

Williams, Raymond, *Drama from Ibsen to Brecht.* 1968. Pp. 50-53

Wright, Edward A. and Lenthiel H. Downs, *A Primer for Playgoers.* 1969. 2nd ed. Pp. 289-93

Young, Stark, *Immortal Shadows; A Book of Dramatic Criticism.* 1948. Pp. 29-32

Zucker, A. E., "Southern Critics of 1903 on Ibsen's 'Ghosts' ", *Philological Quarterly*, 19:392-99, Oct., 1940

Gildet Paa Solhaug   *SEE*   The Feast at Solhaug

Gjengangere   *SEE*   Ghosts

Haermaendene Paa Helgeland   *SEE*   The Vikings of Helgeland

Hedda Gabler, 1891

Allen, Genieve M., "The Problem of Individualism in Relation to Society in Ibsen, Maeterlinck and Hauptmann", *Poet-Lore*, 32:262-66, 1921

Beckerman, Bernard, *Dynamics of Drama; Theory and Method of Analysis.* 1970. Pp. 87-97, 189-96 and 198-205

Beerbohm, Max, *Around Theatres.* 1953. Pp. 277-81

Blau, Herbert, " 'Hedda Gabler': The Irony of Decadence", *Educational Theatre Journal*, 1953, Pp. 112-16

Bonnevie, Margarete, "'Hedda Gabler': Et Kvinnesynspunkt", *Samtiden*, 68:330-36, 1959

Brereton, Geoffrey, *Principles of Tragedy; A Rational Examination of the Tragic Concept in Life and Literature.* 1968. Pp. 198-200

Brockett, Oscar G., ed., *Studies in Theatre and Drama; Essays in Honor of Hubert C. Heffner.* 1973. Pp. 64-72

Catholic World, 144:469, Jan., 1937

Clurman, Harold, *The Divine Pastime; Theatre Essays.* 1974. Pp. 265-66

Colby, Frank Moore, "Analogies of a Disagreeable Heroine", *Bookman*, 25:467-71, July, 1907

_____ , *Constrained Attitudes.* 1910. Pp. 57-86

Cole, Toby, ed., *Playwrights on Playwriting; The Meaning and Making of Modern Drama from Ibsen to Ionesco.* 1960. Pp. 156-70

Commonweal, 9:460, Feb. 20, 1929 and 21:207, Dec. 14, 1934 and 25:134, Nov. 27, 1936 and 35:417, Feb. 13, 1942 and 74:304-05, June 16, 1961

Cross, W. L., "Ibsen's Latest Work 'Hedda Gabler'", *New Englander*, 55 (ns. 19):14-18, July, 1891

Dorcy, Michael M., "Ibsen's 'Hedda Gabler': Tragedy as Denouement", *College English* (1967), 29:223-27

Durbach, E., "Apotheosis of 'Hedda Gabler'", *Scandinavian Studies* (Spring 1971), 43:143-59

Egan, Michael, ed., *Ibsen; The Critical Heritage.* 1972. Pp. 218-44

Esslin, Martin, *Brief Chronicles; Essays on Modern Theatre.* 1970. Pp. 44-51

_____ , *Reflections; Essays on Modern Theatre.* 1969. Pp. 29-48

Faguet, Emile, "The Symbolical Drama", *International Quarterly*, 8:329-41, 1904

Fjelde, Rolf, ed., *Ibsen; A Collection of Critical Essays.* 1965. Pp. 131-38

Fleischmann, Wolfgang B., "Hedda Gabler: A Cascade of Triangles", *Scandinavica* (1969), 8:49-53

Frederickson, G. M., "Ibsen's Anti-Christ: A Study of 'Hedda Gabler'", *Symposium*, 12:1-2, 117-32, 1958

Goodman, Randolph, "Playwatching with a Third Eye; Fun and Games with Albee, Ibsen and Strindberg", *Columbia University Forum* (1967), 10:18-22

Gosse, E. W., "Ibsen's New Drama: With Excerpts", *Fortnightly Review*, 55 (ns. 49):4-13, Jan., 1891

Haakonsen, Daniel, et als, ed., *Ibsenforbundet: Arbok 1968-69.* 1970. Pp. 60-81

Haaland, Arild, "Ibsen og 'Hedda Gabler'", *Samtiden*, 67:566-77, 1958

Hallman, A., "Greater Courage in Ibsen's 'Hedda'", *Poet-Lore*, 22:134-36, 1911

Hardwick, Elizabeth, *Seduction and Betrayal; Women and Literature.* 1974. Pp. 49-68

Henry, Stuart, *French Essays and Profiles.* 1921. Pp. 173-86

Holtan, Orley I., *Mythic Patterns in Ibsen's Last Plays.* 1970. Pp. 64-96

Houm, Philip, "Nytt Eys Over en Hundjevel: Artikell om 'Hedda Gabler'", *Bonniers Litterara Magasin*, 27:571-74, 1958

Huneker, James Gibbon, "Hedda", *Forum*, 52:765-69, Nov., 1914

_____ , *Ivory Apes and Peacocks.* 1915. Pp. 311-328

Hurt, James, *Catiline's Dream; An Essay on Ibsen's Plays.* 1972. Pp. 14-19 and 146-53

Jacobs, Elizabeth, "Henrik Ibsen and the Doctrine of Self-Realization", *Journal of English and Germanic Philology*, 38:416-30, 1939

Jennings, Ann S., "The Reaction of London's Drama Critics to Certain Plays by Henrik Ibsen, Harold Pinter, and Edward Bond", *Dissertation Abstracts International* (1973), 34:2067A

Jessen, Heinrich, "'Ja um Gottes Willen—So Etwas Tut Man Doch Nicht?' Anmerkumgen zur einer Norwegischen Aufführung von Ibsens 'Hedda Gabler'", *Ausblick; Mitteilungsblatt der Deutschen Auslandgesellschaft* (1971), 22:30-32

Johnston, Brian, "The Mythic Foundation of Ibsen's Realism", *Comparative Drama* (Spring 1969), 3:27-41

Kildahl, Erling E., "The Social Conditions and Principles of 'Hedda Gabler'", *Educational Theatre Journal*, 13:207-13, 1961

Koht, Halvdan, "'Hedda Gabler': Forhistorie og Symbol", *Nordisk Tidskrift*, 34:353-61, 1958

Magnus, Gunnar, "Hedda Gabler: Almenmenneskelig Skikkelse Eller Historisk Bundet Person?", *Minerva* (1969), 13:366-78

Mayer, Hans Georg, *Henrik Ibsen.* 1972. Pp. 123-41

Mayerson, Caroline W., "Thematic Symbols in 'Hedda Gabler'", *Scandinavian Studies*, 22:151-60, 1950

Moe, Ola, "'Hedda Gabler' og den Moderne Tragedies Dilemma", *Edda* (1972), 72:41-50

Monleón, José, "Ibsen Ahora: El Testimonio de 'Hedda Gabler'", *Primer Acto* (1972), 141:35-38

Nathan, George Jean, *Theatre Book of the Year, 1947-48.* Pp. 300-05

Nation, 139:720, Dec. 19, 1934 and 143:641-42, Nov. 28, 1936 and 191:462-63, Dec. 10, 1960

New Republic, 106:204, Feb. 9, 1942 and 143:39, Nov. 28, 1960

New Yorker, 36:94, Nov. 19, 1960 and 38:175-76, Dec. 15, 1962

Newsweek, 8:19, Nov. 28, 1936

Northam, John, *Ibsen; A Critical Study.* 1973. Pp. 147-85

Novick, Julius, *Beyond Broadway; The Quest for Permanent Theatres.* 1968. Pp. 135-36

O Hehir, Diana F., "Ibsen and Joyce; A Study of Three Themes", *Dissertation Abstracts International* (1971), 31:3515A

Olivarius, Peder, "Kvindesag og Kvindelyst; Om Henrik Ibsens 'Et Dukkehjem' og 'Hedda Gabler'", *Kritik* (1972), 22:27-42

Outlook, 151:299, Feb. 20, 1929

Raphael, Robert, "From 'Hedda Gabler' to 'When We Dead Awaken': The Quest for Self-Realization", *Scandinavian Studies* (1964), 36:34-47

Ryvold, Arnt, "'Hedda Gabler' Som Sosialt Drama", *Samtiden* (1972), 81:39-51

Rønning, Helge, "Könets Fånge och Klassens: Om Ibsens 'Hedda Gabler'", *Ord och Bild* (1973), 82:491-99

Saturday Review, 44:27, Jan. 28, 1961

Simonsen, Peter, "Om 'Hedda Gabler', 'Lille Eyolf' og Lord Byron", *Edda* (1962), 62:176-84

Smedley, C., "'Hedda Gabler' of Today", *Fortnightly Review*, 88:77-90, July, 1907

————————, "In Defense of 'Hedda Gabler'", *Fortnightly Review*, 89:565-67, March, 1908

Solensten, John M., "Time and Tragic Rhythm in Ibsen's 'Hedda Gabler'",
Scandinavian Studies (Nov. 1969), 41:315-19
Spacks, Patricia Meyer, "The World of Hedda Gabler", *Tulane Drama Review* (1962), 7:155-64
Swanson, Carl A., "Ibsen and the Comédie Francaise", *Scandinavian Studies*, 19:70-78, 1946
Theatre Arts, 21:11, Jan., 1937 and 26:226, April, 1942 and 27:50-51, January, 1943 and 45:72, Jan., 1961
Tucker, Edward L., "Faulkner's Drusilla and Ibsen's Hedda", *Modern Drama* (1973), 16:157-61
Tynan, Kenneth, *Curtains; Selections from the Drama Criticism and Related Writings*. 1961. Pp. 77-78
Valency, Maurice, *The Flower and the Castle; Introduction to Modern Drama*. 1963. Pp. 192-201
Webb, Eugene, *The Dark Dove; The Sacred and Secular in Modern Literature*. 1975. Pp. 34-87
—————————— , "The Radical Irony of 'Hedda Gabler'", *Modern Language Quarterly* (1970), 31:53-63
Weigand, Hermann, *The Modern Ibsen; A Reconsideration*. 1960. Pp. 242-73
Williams, Raymond, *Drama from Ibsen to Brecht*. 1968. Pp. 62-64
Wilson, E., "Hedda Gabler", *New Republic*, 45:356-57, Feb. 17, 1926
Xrapovickaja, G. N., "Henrik Ibsen's Drama 'Hedda Gabler'", *Moskovsky Gosudarstvennyi Pedagogiceskij Institut Ucenye Zapiski* (1964), 218:251-68
Zucker, A. E., "Ibsen's Bardach Episode and 'Hedda Gabler'", *Philological Quarterly*, 8:288-95, July, 1929

John Gabriel Borkman, 1897
Dawson, H., "John Gabriel Borkman", *Plays and Players* (March 1975), 22:22-23
deSelincourt, Aubrey, *Six Great Playwrights*. 1960. Pp. 155
Egan, Michael, ed., *Ibsen; The Critical Heritage*. 1972. Pp. 359-74
Grene, David, *Reality and the Heroic Pattern; Last Plays of Ibsen, Shakespeare, and Sophocles*. 1967. Pp. 24-27
Haslund, Fredrik J., "Ibsens Diktning Avgir Stadig Nye Signaler: Ein Strukturanalyse av 'John Gabriel Borkman'", *Forskningsnytt* (1972), 5:39-46
Holtan, Orley I., *Mythic Patterns in Ibsen's Last Plays*. 1970. Pp. 134-76
Hurt, James, *Catiline's Dream; An Essay on Ibsen's Plays*. 1972. Pp. 183-92
James, Henry, *Scenic Art; Notes on Acting and the Drama; 1872-1901*. 1948. Pp. 291-94
Kjellen, A., "'John Gabriel Borkman': Ensamhetens Tragedi", *Ord Och Bild* (Stockholm), 68:27-38, 1959
Lyons, Charles R., "The Function of Dream and Reality in 'John Gabriel Borkman'", *Scandinavian Studies* (1973), 45:293-309
MacCarthy, Desmond, *Theatre*. 1955. Pp. 77-80
Meyer, Hans Georg, *Henrik Ibsen*. 1972. Pp. 152-70
Shaw, George Bernard, *Plays and Players; Essay on the Theatre*. 1952. Pp. 170-78 and 221-30
Weigand, Hermann, *The Modern Ibsen; A Reconsideration*. 1960. Pp. 356-77

Katilina *SEE* Catiline

Kejser og Galilaeer *SEE* The Emperor and the Galilean

Kjaemphøien *SEE* The Warrior's Barrow

Kjaerlighedens Komodie *SEE* Love's Comedy

Kongs-Emnerne *SEE* The Pretenders

Lady From The Sea, 1889
  Beerbohm, Max, *Around Theatres*. 1953. Pp. 205-08
  Catholic World, 139:344-45, June, 1934 and 172:69-70, Oct., 1950
  deSelincourt, Aubrey, *Six Great Playwrights*. 1960. Pp. 156
  Egan, Michael, ed., *Ibsen; The Critical Heritage*. 1972. Pp. 245-50
  Faguet, Emile, "The Symbolical Drama", *International Quarterly*, 8:329-41, 1904
  Fjelde, Rolf, ed., *Ibsen; A Collection of Critical Essays*. 1965. Pp. 120-30
  Holtan, Orley I., *Mythic Patterns in Ibsen's Last Plays*. 1970. Pp. 64-96
  Hurt, James, *Catiline's Dream; An Essay on Ibsen's Plays*. 1972. Pp. 15-19 and 139-46
  Nation, 171:174, Aug. 19, 1950
  New Republic, 79:22, May 16, 1934 and 123:23, Aug. 28, 1950
  O Hehir, Diana F., "Ibsen and Joyce; A Study of Three Themes", *Dissertation Abstracts International* (1971), 31:3515A
  Raphale, Robert, "Illusion and the Self in 'The Wild Duck' and 'Rosmersholm' and 'Lady from the Sea' ", *Scandinavian Studies* (1963), 35:37-50
  Skinner, R. D., "Lady from the Sea", *Commonweal*, 9:626-27, April 3, 1929
  Weigand, Hermann, *The Modern Ibsen; A Reconsideration*. 1960. Pp. 209-41
  Young, Stark, *Immortal Shadows; A Book of Dramatic Criticism*. 1948. Pp. 29-32

Lady Inger of Østeraad, 1855
  Egan, Michael, ed. *Ibsen; The Critical Hertiage*. 1972. Pp. 439-41
  Larson, Philip E., "Vision and Structure in Ibsen's Early Plays", *Dissertation Abstracts International* (1974), 34:7762A

The League of Youth, 1869
  Valency, Maurice, *The Flower and the Castle; Introduction to Modern Drama*. 1963. Pp. 146-47

Lille Eyolf *SEE* Little Eyolf

Little Eyolf, 1895
  Arestad, Sverre, " 'Little Eyolf' and Human Responsibility", *Scandinavian Studies*, 32:140-52, 1960
  Bogard, Travis and Oliver, William Irvin, eds., *Modern Drama; Essays in Criticism*. 1965. Pp. 192-208
  deSelincourt, Aubrey, *Six Great Playwrights*. 1960. Pp. 155
  Egan, Michael, ed., *Ibsen; The Critical Heritage*. 1972. Pp. 334-58
  Ericsson, Kjersti, "Lille Eyolf og Familie Myten", *Samtiden* (1972), 81:8-19
  Grene, David, *Reality and the Heroic Pattern; Last Plays of Ibsen, Shakespeare, and Sophocles*. 1967. Pp. 20-24
  Holtan, Orley I., *Mythic Patterns in Ibsen's Last Plays*. 1970. Pp. 115-33
  Hurt, James, *Catiline's Dream; An Essay on Ibsen's Plays*. 1972. Pp. 14-18 and 169-83

Matthews, Honor, *The Primal Curse; The Myth of Cain and Abel in the Theatre*. 1967. Pp. 110-13

Nation, 198:355-56, April 6, 1964

New Yorker, 40:138, March 28, 1964

Northam, John, *Ibsen; A Critical Study*. 1973. Pp. 186-220

Shaw, George Bernard, *Plays and Players; Essays on the Theatre*. 1952. Pp. 124-33

_____ , *Selected Prose*, selected by Diarmuid Russell. 1952. Pp. 463-78

Simonsen, Peter, "Om 'Hedda Gabler', 'Lille Eyolf' og Lord Byron", *Edda* (1962), 62:176-84

Valency, Maurice, *The Flower and the Castle; Introduction to Modern Drama*. 1963. Pp. 213-17

Weigand, Hermann, *The Modern Ibsen; A Reconsideration*. 1960. Pp. 310-55

Williams, Raymond, *Drama from Ibsen to Brecht*. 1968. Pp. 67-70

Wilson, E., "Little Eyolf", *New Republic*, 45:356-57, Feb. 17, 1926

Love's Comedy, 1873

deSelincourt, Aubrey, *Six Great Playwrights*. 1960. Pp. 139-40

Northam, John, *Ibsen; A Critical Study*. 1973. Pp. 10-31

The Master Builder, 1893

Agate, James Evershed, comp., *English Dramatic Critics; An Anthology, 1660-1932*. 1958. Pp. 283-87

Allen, Genieve M., "The Problem of Individualism in Relation to Society in Ibsen, Maeterlinck and Hauptmann", *Poet-Lore*, 32:262-66, 1921

America, 93:25-26, April 2, 1955

Anderson, Marilyn A., "Norse Trolls and Ghosts in Ibsen", *Journal of Popular Culture* (1971), 5:349-67

Bager, Poul, "Uendelighedens Tilbageslag", *Kritik* (1969), 11:46-68

Barranger, M. S., "Ibsen's 'Strange Story' in 'The Master Builder': A Variation in Technique", *Modern Drama* (1972), 15:175-84

Berulfsen, Bjarne, "Spraklig Differensiering i 'Bygmester Solness'", *Maal og Minne* (1968), Pp. 74-95

Brereton, Geoffrey, *Principles of Tragedy; A Rational Examination of the Tragic Concept in Life and Literature*. 1968. Pp. 204-09

Brustein, Robert Sanford, *The Theatre of Revolt; An Approach to the Modern Drama*. 1964. Pp. 75-83

Catholic World, 181:68, April 1955

Commonweal, 62:127, May 6, 1955

Egan, Michael, ed., *Ibsen; The Critical Heritage*. 1972. Pp. 266-92

Esslin, Martin, *Brief Chronicles; Essays on Modern Theatre*. 1970. Pp. 52-58

_____ , *Reflections; Essays on Modern Theatre*. 1969. Pp. 29-48

Grene, David, *Reality and the Heroic Pattern; Last Plays of Ibsen, Shakespeare, and Sophocles*. 1967. Pp. 10-19

Haakonsen, Daniel, et als, eds., *Ibsenforbrundet: Arbok, 1967*. 1968. Pp. 72-102

Hinden, M., "Ibsen and Nietzsche; A Reading of 'The Master Builder'", *Modern Drama* (1973), 15:403-10

Holtan, Orley I., *Mythic Patterns in Ibsen's Last Plays*. 1970. Pp. 97-114

Hurst, J. S., "Interpreting 'The Master Builder'", *Forum for Modern Language Studies* (1968), 4:207-16

Hurt, James, *Catiline's Dream; An Essay on Ibsen's Plays.* 1972. Pp. 156-69

Jennings, Ann S., "The Reaction of London's Drama Critics to Certain Plays by Henrik Ibsen, Harold Pinter and Edward Bond", *Dissertation Abstracts International* (1973), 34:2067A

Kaasa, Harris, "Ibsen and the Theologians", *Scandinavian Studies* (1971), 43:356-84

Kaufman, Michael W., "Nietzsche, Georg Brandes and Ibsen's 'The Master Builder'", *Comparative Drama* (1972), 6:169-86

LaVictoire, A. L., "Message of the 'Master Builder'", *North American Review*, 196:254-63, Aug., 1912

Lyons, Charles R., *Henrik Ibsen; The Divided Consciousness.* 1972. Pp. 119-35

——————————— , " 'The Master Builder' as Drama of the Self", *Scandinavian Studies* (1967), 39:329-39

Mailly, W., "Ibsen's 'Master Builder' ", *Arena*, 39:160-65, Feb., 1908

Matthews, Honor, *The Primal Curse; The Myth of Cain and Abel in the Theatre.* 1967. Pp. 106-10

Meyer, Hans Georg, *Henrik Ibsen.* 1972. Pp. 142-51

Nation, 180:246, March 19, 1955

New Republic, 132:27-28, March 14, 1955

New Yorker, 31:64, March 12, 1955

Price, T. R., "Solness; A Study of Ibsen's Dramatic Method", *Sewanee Review*, 2:257-81, 1894

Quirino, Leonard, "Ibsen's Daedalus: 'The Master Builder' ", *Modern Drama* (1970), 12:238-41

Saturday Review, 38:30, April 2, 1956

Sechmsdorf, Henning K., "Two Legends about St. Olaf, 'The Master Builder': A Clue to the Dramatic Structure of Henrik Ibsen's 'Bygmester Solness' ", *Edda* (1967), 54:263-71

Sprinchorn, Evert, ed., *The Genius of the Scandinavian Theater.* 1964. Pp. 555-82

Theatre Arts, 39:87, May, 1955

Tornqvist, Egil, "The Illness Pattern in 'The Master Builder' ", *Scandinavica* (1972), 11:1-12

Valency, Maurice, *The Flower and the Castle; Introduction to Modern Drama.* 1963. Pp. 202-12 and 383-85

Walkley, A. B. "Some Plays of the Day", *Fortnightly Review*, 59 (ns. 53): 468-73, April, 1893

Weigand, Hermann, *The Modern Ibsen; A Reconsideration.* 1960. Pp. 274-309

Wyatt, E. V., "The Master Builder", *Catholic World*, 122:663-64, Feb., 1926

Nar Vi Döde Vagner   SEE   When We Dead Awaken

Olaf Liljekrans, 1857
Larson, Philip E., "Vision and Structure in Ibsen's Early Plays", *Dissertation Abstracts International* (1974), 34:7762A

Peer Gynt, 1876
America, 102:539, Jan. 30, 1960

Anderson, Marilyn A., "Norse Trolls and Ghosts in Ibsen", *Journal of Popular Culture* (1971), 5:349-61

Anstensen A., "Notes on the Text of Ibsen's 'Peer Gynt'", *Journal of English and Germanic Philology*, 29:53-73, Jan., 1930

Arestad, Sverre, "'Peer Gynt' and the Idea of Self", *Modern Drama*, 3:103-22, 1960

Auden, Wystan Hugh, *The Dyer's Hand and Other Essays*. 1962. Pp. 433-55

Bergholz, Harry, "Peer Gynt's Redemption, *Edda* (1969), 56:10-20

Bishop, W. S., "Ibsen's Peer Gynt'; A Philosophy of Life", *Sewanee Review*, 17:475-87, Oct., 1909

Brereton, Geoffrey, *Principles of Tragedy; A Rational Examination of the Tragic Concept in Life and Literature*. 1968. Pp. 192-97

Brustein, Robert Sanford, *Seasons of Discontent; Dramatic Opinions 1959-1965*. 1965. Pp. 218-21

Catholic World, 172:464, March, 1951

Commonweal, 53:468-69, Feb. 16, 1951

deSelincourt, Aubrey, *Six Great Playwrights*. 1960. Pp. 144

Dilla, G. P., "Different Hallowe'en Play: 'Peer Gynt'", *English Journal*, 11: 108-10, Feb., 1922

Eaton, W. P., "Peer Gynt", *The Freeman*, 7:16-17, March 14, 1923

Edwards, Mrs. L. R., "Structural Analysis of 'Peer Gynt'", *Modern Drama*, 8:28-38, May, 1965

Egan, Michael, ed., *Ibsen; The Critical Heritage*. 1972. Pp. 45-49

Engberg, Harald, "'Peer Gynt' Udsat for Gruppeteatret", *Ibsenforbundet: Årbok* (1972), Pp. 130-32

Engelberg, Edward, *The Unknown Distance; From Consciousness to Conscience, Goethe to Camus*. 1972. Pp. 111-16

Faguet, Emile, "The Symbolical Drama", *International Quarterly*, 8:329-41, 1904

Fjelde, Rolk, "Peer Gynt, Naturalism and the Dissolving Self", *The Drama Review* (1968), 13:28-43

Fjelde, Rolf and Sverre Arestad, "Translating 'Peer Gynt'", *Modern Drama* (1967), 10:104-10

Gaskell, Ronald, *Drama and Reality; The European Theatre since Ibsen*. 1972. Pp. 75-82

_____ , "Symbol and Reality in 'Peer Gynt'", *Drama Survey*, 4:57-64, 1965

"Gleanings from 'Peer Gynt'", *Scandinavian Studies and Notes*, 9:224-30, 1928

Green, Paul, *Plough and Furrow; Some Essays and Papers on Life and the Theatre*. 1963. Pp. 133-41

Haakonsen, D., "Genre-problemet i 'Peer Gynt'", *Vinduet*, 8:199-210, 1954

Haakonsen, Daniel, et als, eds., *Ibsenforbundet: Arbok, 1967*. 1968. Pp. 32-47 and 109-18

Heinrichs, Ann, "Henrik Ibsen, 'Peer Gynt': Ein Schauspiel Aus dem Neunzehnten Jahrhundert", *Skandinavistik* (1971), 1:100-04

Highet, Gilbert, *Explorations*. 1971. Pp. 36-42

Hurt, James R., *Catiline's Dream; An Essay on Ibsen's Plays*. 1972. Pp. 9-17 and 59-76

_____ , "Fantastic Scenes in 'Peer Gynt'", *Modern Drama* (1962), 5:37-42

Konner, L., "Psychiatric Study of Ibsen's 'Peer Gynt'", *Journal of Abnormal Psychology*, 19:373-82, Jan., 1925

Larsen, Svend E., "Symbol og Fiktion i Ibsens 'Peer Gynt'", *Exil: Tidsskrift für Literatur og Semiologi* (1972), 6:15-50

Lewisohn, Ludwig, "Peer Gynt", *Nation*, 116:250, Feb. 28, 1923

Literary Digest, 76:30-31, March 3, 1923

Lyons, Charles R., *Henrik Ibsen; The Divided Consciousness*. 1972. Pp. 25-50

Meyer, Hans Georg, *Henrik Ibsen*. 1972. Pp. 33-47

Michl, Josef B., "Ibsenuv 'Peer Gynt': Problém Literarní a Divadelní", *Crosscurrents/Modern Fiction* (1969), 51:1-12

Moen, Einar Gabriel, "Et Mischandlet Kunstverk", *Samtiden* (March 1968), 73:190-98

Nation, 30:952-54, March, 1922 and 172:139-40, Feb. 10, 1951 and 190:106, Jan. 30, 1960

New Republic, 124:22-23, March 5, 1951 and 142:21, Feb. 1, 1960

New Yorker, 26:61, Feb. 10, 1951 and 35:72, Jan. 23, 1960

Parker, R. A., "Peer Gynt", *The Independent*, 110:141-42, Feb. 17, 1923

Pitman, R., "William Archer and 'Peer Gynt'", *Notes and Queries* (1973), 20:255-57

Roellenbleck, Ewald, "'Peer Gynt' als Erotischer Typus Sui Generis" *Psyche. Zeitschrift fur Psychoanalyse und Ihre Anwendungen* (1969), 23:929-46

School and Society, 73:184, March 24, 1951

Simon, J., "On Producing 'Peer Gynt'", *Hudson Review* (Winter 1969-70), 22:675-86

Smith, Denzell, "The Relationship of Setting and Idea in 'Peer Gynt'", *Modern Drama* (1970), 13:169-73

Stone, J. D., "'Peer Gynt': An Interpretation", *Poet-Lore*, 18:383-92, 1907

Theatre Arts, 19:908-09, Dec., 1935 and 29:147, March, 1945 and 35:14, April, 1951

Tveteras, Harald, "Botten—Hansens 'Huldrebrylluppet' og Ibsens 'Peer Gynt'", *Edda* (1967), 54:247-62

Tysdahl, Bjørn, "Ener Eller Medmenneske? En Nløst Konflict i 'Peer Gynt'", *Edda* (1973), 73:61-72

Valency, Maurice, *The Flower and the Castle; Introduction to the Modern Drama*. 1963. Pp. 136-41

Ward, Alfred Charles, ed., *Specimens of English Dramatic Criticism, 17th-20 Centuries* (World Classics). 1945. Pp. 294-96

Williams, Raymond, *Drama from Ibsen to Brecht*. 1968. Pp. 39-43

Young, Stark, "Peer Gynt", *New Republic*, 34:46-47, March 7, 1923

Zentner, Jules, "Figures and Estrangement—Peer Gynt's Other Selves", *Edda* (1973), 73:73-78

——————— , "Peer Gynt: The Quest for Shine and the Giving Way of a Loop", *Scandinavica* (1970), 9:116-26

The Pillars of Society, 1878

Commonweal, 14:639-40, Oct. 28, 1931

Egan, Michael, ed., *Ibsen; The Critical Heritage*. 1972. Pp. 126-32

Johnston, Brian, "The Mythic Foundation of Ibsen's Realism", *Comparative Drama* (Spring 1969), 3:27-41

Theatre Arts, 15:989-90, Dec., 1931

Valency, Maurice, *The Flower and the Castle; Introduction to the Modern Drama*. 1963. Pp. 147-49

Weigand, Hermann, *The Modern Ibsen; A Reconsideration.*   1960.
Pp. 3-25

Williams, Raymond, *Modern Tragedy.* 1966. Pp. 97-101

The Pretenders, 1863
Ward, Alfred Charles, eds., *Specimens of English Dramatic Criticism,
17th -20th Centuries* (World Classics).   1945. Pp. 264-72

Rosmersholm, 1887
Anderson, Marilyn A., "Norse Trolls and Ghosts in Ibsen", *Journal of
Popular Culture* (1971), 5:349-67

Arestad, Sverre, "Ibsen, Strindberg and Naturalistic Tragedy", *Theatre
Annual* (1968), 24:6-13

Beerbohm, Max, *Around Theatres.* 1953. Pp. 497-501

Brereton, Geoffrey, *Principles of Tragedy; A Rational Examination of
the Tragic Concept in Life and Literature.*   1968. Pp. 202-04

Brustein, Robert Sanford, *Seasons of Discontent; Dramatic Opinions
1959-1965.* 1965. Pp. 64-67

Carlson, Marvin, "Patterns of Structure and Character in Ibsen's 'Rosmersholm'", *Modern Drama* (1974), 17:267-75

Chamberlain, John S., "Tragic Heroism in 'Rosmersholm'", *Modern
Drama* (1974), 17:277-88

Commonweal, 23:218, Dec. 20, 1935 and 76:175, May 11, 1962

deSelincourt, Aubrey, *Six Great Playwrights.* 1960. Pp. 154

Downs, Brian Westerdale, *Modern Norwegian Literature, 1860-1918.*
1966. Pp. 116-32

Egán, Michael, ed., *Ibsen; The Critical Heritage.* 1972. Pp. 158-80

Faguet, Emile, "The Symbolical Drama," *International Quarterly,* 8:
329-41, 1904

Farris, Jon R., "The Evolution of the Dramatic Functions of the Sec-
ondary Characteristics in 'Rosemersholm'", *Educational Theatre
Journal* (1969), 21:439-48

Fjelde, Rold, ed., *Ibsen: A Collection of Critical Essays.* 1965. Pp. 120-30

Frenz, Horst, "Eugene O'Neill's 'Desire Under the Elms' and Henrik
Ibsen's 'Rosmersholm'", *Jahrbuch fur Amerikastudien* (1964), 9:160-
65

Gaskell, Ronald, *Drama and Reality; The European Theatre since Ibsen.*
1972. Pp. 83-93

Gilman, Richard, *Common and Uncommon Masks; Writings on the
Theatre, 1961-1970.* 1971. Pp. 53-56

Haakonsen, Daniel, et als, eds., *Ibsenforbundet; Arbok 1968-69.*   1970.
Pp. 82-112

Hardwick, Elizabeth, *Seduction and Betrayal; Women and Literature.*
1974. Pp. 69-83

The Idiom of Drama. 1970. Pp. 44-61

Holtan, Orley I., *Mythic Patterns in Ibsen's Last Plays.* 1970. Pp. 35-63

Hurrell, John D., "'Rosmersholm', the Existential Drama, and the
Dilemma of Modern Tragedy", *Educational Theatre Journal* (1963),
15:118-24

Hurt, James, *Catiline's Dream; An Essay on Ibsen's Plays.* 1972. Pp.
130-39

Johnston, Brian, "The Dialectic of 'Rosmersholm'", *Drama Survey* (1967), 6:181-220

Kaasa, Harris, "Ibsen and the Theologians", *Scandinavian Studies* (1971), 43:356-84

Krutch, J. W., "Rosmersholm", *Nation*, 120:578-79, May 20, 1925

Lyons, Charles R., *Henrik Ibsen; The Divided Consciousness.* 1972. Pp. 100-18

MacCarthy, Desmond, *Humanities.* 1954. Pp. 65-70

Matthews, Honor, *The Primal Curse; The Myth of Cain and Abel in the Theatre.* 1967. Pp. 100-06

Meyer, Hans Georg, *Henrik Ibsen.* 1972. Pp. 111-22

Nation, 194:407-08, May 5, 1962

New Republic, 146:20-22, April 30, 1962

New Yorker, 38:85-87, April 21, 1962

Raphael, Robert, "Illusion and the Self in 'The Wild Duck', 'Rosmersholm', and 'Lady from the Sea'", *Scandinavian Studies* (1963), 35:37-50

Skipenes, D., "Fra Drøm til Død og Fra Kall til Plikt", *Vinduet*, 12: 235-40, 1958

Theatre Arts, 20:98, Feb., 1936 and 46:59, June, 1962

Van Laan, Thomas F., "Art and Structure in 'Rosmersholm'", *Modern Drama* (1963), 6:150-63

Weigand, Hermann, *The Modern Ibsen; A Reconsideration.* 1960. Pp. 167-208

Williams, Raymond, *Drama from Ibsen to Brecht.* 1968. Pp. 58-62

St. John's Eve, 1853
Larson, Philip E., "Vision and Structure in Ibsen's Early Plays", *Dissertation Abstracts International* (1974), 34:7762A

Samfundets Støtter   SEE   The Pillars of Society

Sancthansnatten   SEE   St. John's Eve

De Unges Forbund   SEE   The League of Youth

Vikings at Helgeland, 1858
Commonweal, 12:109, May 28, 1930

Egan, Michael, ed., *Ibsen; The Critical Heritage.* 1972. Pp. 405-18

Larson, Philip E., "Vision and Structure in Ibsen's Early Plays", *Dissertation Abstracts International* (1974), 34:7662A

Nation, 130:633, May 28, 1930

Young, Stark, "Vikings at Helgeland", *New Republic*, 63:42-43, May 28, 1930

Vildanden   SEE   The Wild Duck

Warrior's Barrow, 1850
Larson, Philip E., "Vision and Structure in Ibsen's Early Plays", *Dissertation Abstracts International* (1974), 34:7762A

When We Dead Awaken, 1900
Arestad, Sverre, "'When We Dead Awaken' Reconsidered", *Scandinavian Studies* (1958), 30:117-30

Barranger, M. S., "Ibsen's 'Endgame': A Reconsideration of 'When We Dead Awaken'", *Modern Drama* (1974), 17:289-99

_____ , "Ibsen's 'When We Dead Awaken' ", *Explicator* (1975), 33: 61

Bermel, Albert, *Contradictory Characters; An Interpretation of Modern Theatre.* 1973. Pp. 269-86

Brooks, Harold F., " 'Pygmalion' and 'When We Dead Awaken' ", *Notes and Queries* (1960), 7:469-71

Brustein, Robert Sanford, *The Theatre of Revolt; An Approach to the Modern Drama.* 1964. Pp. 75-83

deSelincourt, Aubrey, *Six Great Playwrights.* 1960. Pp. 156-57

Egan, Michael, ed., *Ibsen; The Critical Heritage.* 1972. Pp. 385-404

Fraenkl, Pavel, "Tabu og Drama i 'Nar vi Döde Vagner' ", *Nordisk Tidskrift* (1967), 43:340-63

Grabowski, Simon, "Livets Kunstverk", *Samtiden* (1972), 81:20-30

Grene, David, *Reality and the Heroic Pattern; Last Plays of Ibsen, Shakespeare, and Sophocles.* 1967. Pp. 27-36

Haakonsen, Daniel, et als, eds., *Ibsenforbundet: Arbok 1968-69.* 1969. Pp. 22-37

Holtan, Orley I., *Mythic Patterns in Ibsen's Last Plays.* 1970. Pp. 134-76

Hurt, James, *Catiline's Dream; An Essay on Ibsen's Plays.* 1972. Pp. 15-20, 30-33 and 193-303

Johnston, Brian, "The Mythic Foundations of Ibsen's Realism", *Comparative Drama* (Spring 1969), 3:27-41

Joyce, James, *Critical Writings of James Joyce,* ed. by Ellsworth Mason and Richard Ellmann. 1959. Pp. 47-67

Kaasa, Harris, "Ibsen and the Theologians", *Scandinavian Studies* (1971), 43:356-84

Lyons, Charles R., *Henrik Ibsen; The Divided Consciousness.* 1972. Pp. 136-54

Mayer, Hans Georg, *Henrik Ibsen.* 1972. Pp. 171-84

Raphael, Robert, "From 'Hedda Gabler' to 'When We Dead Awaken': The Quest for Self-Realization", *Scandinavian Studies* (1964), 36:34-47

Valency, Maurice, *The Flower and the Castle; Introduction to Modern Drama.* 1963. Pp. 223-35

Weigand, Hermann, *The Modern Ibsen; A Reconsideration.* 1960. Pp. 378-412

Williams, Raymond, *Drama from Ibsen to Brecht.* 1968. Pp. 70-74

The Wild Duck, 1885

Abirached, R., "La Comedie de l'Est et 'Le Canard Sauvage' d'Ibsen", *Les Etudes* (Paris), 306:100-03, 1960

Adler, Jacob H., "Ibsen, Shaw and 'Candida' ", *Journal of English and Germanic Philology* (1960), 59:50-58

_____ , "Two Hamlet Plays: 'The Wild Duck' and 'The Sea Gull' ", *Journal of Modern Literature* (1970), 1:226-48

Arestad, Sverre, " 'The Iceman Cometh' and 'The Wild Duck' ", *Scandinavian Studies,* 20:1-11, 1948

Berulfsen, Bjarne, " 'Vildanden': 'Hun' eller 'Den'?", *Maal og Minne* (1963), Pp. 47-59

Bookman, 62:678-81, Feb., 1926

Brustein, Robert Sanford, *The Theatre of Revolt; An Approach to the Modern Drama.* 1964. Pp. 72-74

Catholic World, 174:464, March, 1952

Commonweal, 55:349, Jan. 11, 1952

Crompton, Louis, "The 'Demonic' in Ibsen's 'The Wild Duck'", *Tulane Drama Review*, 4:96-103, 1959

deSelincourt, Aubrey, *Six Great Playwrights*. 1960. Pp. 151-53

Dial, 78:430-33, May, 1925

Downs, B. W., *Modern Norwegian Literature*, 1860-1918. 1966. Pp. 116-32

Dukes, A., "The Wild Duck", *Theatre Arts*, 15:634-37, Aug., 1937

Durbach, Erroll, "Sacrifice and Absurdity in 'The Wild Duck'", *Mosaic* (1974), 7, iv:99-107

Egan, Michael, ed., *Ibsen: The Critical Heritage*. 1972. Pp. 317-22

Faguet, Emile, "The Symbolical Drama", *International Quarterly*, 8:329-41, 1904

Fjelda, Rolf, ed., *Ibsen: A Collection of Critical Essays*. 1965. Pp. 120-30

Freedman, Morris, *The Moral Impulse; Modern Drama from Ibsen to the Present*. 1967. Pp. 3-10

Hallett, C. A., "'Wild Duck' and Critical Cliché", *Papers on Language and Literature* (1975), 11:54-70

Halsey, Martha T., "Reality vs. Illusion: Ibsen's 'The Wild Duck' and Buero Vallejo's 'En La Ardiente Oscuridad'", *Contemporary Literature* (1970), 11:48-57

Harmer, R., "Character Conflict and Meaning in 'The Wild Duck'", *Modern Drama* (Feb. 1970), 12:419-27

Holtan, Orley I., *Mythic Patterns in Ibsen's Last Plays*. 1970. Pp. 35-63

Hurt, James, *Catiline's Dream; An Essay on Ibsen's Plays*. 1972. Pp. 12-14, 25-31 and 121-29

Institute for Religious and Social Studies, *Great Moral Dilemmas in Literature, Past and Present*, ed. by R. M. MacIver. 1956. Pp. 47-60

Johnston, Brian, "The Mythic Foundation of Ibsen's Realism", *Comparative Drama* (Spring 1969), 3:27-41

Lyons, Charles R., *Henrik Ibsen; The Divided Consciousness*. 1972. Pp. 75-99

McCarthy, Mary Therese, *Sights and Spectacles, 1937-1956*. Pp. 168-78

Matthews, Honor, *The Primal Curse; The Myth of Cain and Abel in the Theatre*. 1967. Pp. 117-18

Mendel, S., "The Revolt Against the Father: 'Hamlet' and 'The Wild Duck'", *Essays in Criticism* (G.B.), 14:171-78, 1964

Meyer, Hans Georg, *Henrik Ibsen*. 1972. Pp. 93-110

Mueller, Janel M., "Ibsen's 'Wild Duck'", *Modern Drama* (1969), 11:347-55

Nation, 120:299, March 18, 1925, 204:156-57, Jan. 30, 1967

New Republic, 42:70-71, March 11, 1925 and 126:23, Jan. 21, 1952

Northam, John, *Ibsen; A Critical Study*. 1973. Pp. 113-46

Novick, Julius, *Beyond Broadway; The Quest for Permanent Theatres*. 1968. Pp. 219-30

Raphael, Robert, "Illusion and the Self in 'The Wild Duck', 'Rosmersholm' and 'Lady From the Sea'", *Scandinavian Studies* (1963), 35:37-50

Reinert, O., "Sight Imagery in 'The Wild Duck'", *Journal of English and Germanic Philology*, 55:457-62, July, 1956

Seeger, Lothar G., "Ibsen's 'Wildente' und Mussils 'Kafanien'", *German Quarterly* (1970), 43:47-54

Seyler, Dorothy U., "'Sea Gull' and 'The Wild Duck': Birds of a Feather?", *Modern Drama*, 8:167-73, Sept., 1965

Syre, Sivert, "'Den Trettende Mann Til Bords'", *Samtiden* (1972), 81:52-62

Theatre Arts, 36:70, March, 1952

Time, 59:44, Jan. 7, 1952, 89:70-71, Jan. 20, 1967

Tynan, Kenneth, *Curtains; Selections from the Drama Criticism and Related Writings*. 1961. Pp. 112-13

Urdal, Bjorn, "'Vildanden'", *Edda* (1958), 58:155-60

Valency, Maurice, *The Flower and the Castle; Introduction to Modern Drama*. 1963. Pp. 168-77 and 380-83

Van Doren, Mark, ed., *New Invitation to Learning*. 1942. Pp. 74-88

Ward, Alfred Charles, ed., *Specimens of English Dramatic Criticism, 17th-20th Centuries* (World Classics). 1945. Pp. 237-41

Watts, C. T., "The Unseen Catastrophe in Ibsen's 'Vildanden'", *Scandinavica* (1973), 12:137-41

Weigand, Hermann, *The Modern Ibsen; A Reconsideration*. 1960. Pp. 134-66

Williams, Raymond, *Drama from Ibsen to Brecht*. 1968. Pp. 56-58

Zucker, A. E., "Courtiers in 'Hamlet' and 'The Wild Duck'", *Modern Language Notes*, 54:196-98, March, 1939

EUGENE IONESCO

Amédée, ou Comment s'en Débarrasser   *SEE*   Amedee, or How to Get Rid of It

Amédée, or How To Get Rid of It, 1954

Abastado, Claude, "'Amédée, ou Comment s'en Débarasser' de Eugene Ionesco", *Le Francaise dans le Monde* (1974), 99, Sept.:6-13

Abastado, Claude, "Pages Commentees de 'Amédée' d'Eugene Ionesco", *La Francaise dans la Monde* (1973), 99, Sept.:28-31

Coe, Richard N., *Ionesco; A Study of His Plays*. 1971. Pp. 96-99

Corvin, Michel, *Le Théâtre Nouveau en France*. 1963. Pp. 59-67

Esslin, Martin, *The Theatre of the Absurd*. 1961. Pp. 109-10

Hayman, Ronald, *Eugene Ionesco*. 1972. Pp. 50-55

Jacobs, Willis D., "Ionesco's 'Amédée'", *Explicator* (1972), 31:14

Kister, Daniel, "Some Imaginative Motifs from Primitive Sacred Myths in the Theatre of Eugene Ionesco", *Dissertation Abstracts International* (1974), 34:4267A

Lamont, Rosette C., ed., *Ionesco; A Collection of Critical Essays*. 1973. Pp. 38-54

Lewis, Allan, *Ionesco*. 1972. Pp. 55-66

Serreau, Geneviève, *Histoire du Nouveau Théâtre*. 1966. Pp. 50-51

Tynan, Kenneth, *Curtains; Selections from the Drama Criticism and Related Writings*. 1961. Pp. 167-79

Vos, Nelvin, *Eugene Ionesco and Edward Albee; A Critical Essay*. 1968. Pp. 14-29

L'Avenir est dans les Oeufs, ou Il Faut de Tout pour Faire un Monde   *SEE*   The Future is in Eggs, or It Takes all Sorts to Make a World

The Bald Soprano, 1950

Catholic World, 187:387, Aug. 1958

Clurman, Harold, *The Naked Image; Observations on the Modern Theatre*. 1966. Pp. 83-85

Coe, Richard N., *Ionesco; A Study of His Plays*. 1971. Pp. 22-24 and 152-54

Cole, Toby, ed., *Playwrights on Playwriting; The Meaning and Making of Modern Drama from Ibsen to Ionesco*. 1960. Pp. 282-84

Demaitre, Ann, "The Idea of Commitment in Brecht's and Ionesco's Theories of the Theater", *Symposium* (1968), 22:215-23

Dukore, Bernard F., "The Theatre of Ionesco: A Union of Form and Substance", *Educational Theatre Journal*, 13:174-81, 1961

Esslin, Martin, *The Theatre of the Absurd*. 1961. Pp. 90-94 and 128-39

Fowlie, Wallace, "The New French Theatre: Artaud, Beckett, Genet, Ionesco", *Sewanee Review*, 67:654-57, 1959

Freedman, Morris, *The Moral Impulse; Modern Drama from Ibsen to the Present*. 1967. Pp. 119-22

Gilman, Richard, *Common and Uncommon Masks; Writings on the Theatre, 1961-1970*. 1971. Pp. 87-89

Grossvogel, David I., *Four Playwrights and a Postscript; Brecht, Ionesco, Beckett and Genet*. 1962. Pp. 52-56

Hayman, Ronald, *Eugene Ionesco*. 1972. Pp. 9-15

Hooker, Ward, "Irony and Absurdity in the Avant-Garde Theatre", *Kenyon Review*, 22:436-54, 1960

Illustrated London News, 229:854, Nov. 17, 1956

Lamont, Rosette C., ed., *Ionesco; A Collection of Critical Essays*. 1973. Pp. 21-37

Lewis, Allan, *Ionesco*. 1972. Pp. 33-42

Lumley, Frederick, *New Trends in Twentieth Century Drama; A Survey Since Ibsen and Shaw*. 1967. Pp. 209-14

Moore, Harry T., *Twentieth Century French Literature to World War II*. 1966. Vol. II. Pp. 154-61

Murray, Jack, "Ionesco and the Mechanics of Memory", *Yale French Studies*, 29:82-90, 1962

Nation, 187:50, Aug. 2, 1958

New Yorker, 39:94, Sept. 28, 1963

Newsweek, 62:60, Sept. 30, 1963

Oates, Joyce Carol, *The Edge of Impossibility; Tragic Forms in Literature*. 1972. Pp. 225-49

Serreau, Genevieve, *Histoire du Nouveau Théâtre*. 1966. Pp. 37-41

Sherrell, Richard, *The Human Image; Avant-Garde and Christian*. 1969. Pp. 65-73

Tarrab, Gilbert, "Essai de Sociologie du Théâtre: 'La Cantatrice Chauve' et 'Les Chaises' de Ionesco", *L'Homme et la Société. Revue Internationale de Recherche et de Synthese Sociologique* (1967), #6:161-70

Tynan, Kenneth, *Curtains; Selections from the Drama Criticism and Related Writings*. 1961. Pp. 149-50

Vos, Nelvin, *Eugene Ionesco and Edward Albee; A Critical Essay*. Pp. 8-14

Vuletic, B., "Le Langage Universal d'Eugene Ionesco", *Studia Romanica et Anglica Zagrebiensa*, #12:97-104, 1961

La Cantatrice Chauve   *SEE*   The Bald Soprano

The Chairs, 1952

Abirached, R., "Ionesco et 'Les Chaises'", *Les Etudes* (Paris), 290:116-20, 1956

Catholic World, 186:469, March, 1958

Checroun, Sylvia L., "Philémon, Baucis et Sémiramis dans 'Les Chaises' de Ionesco", *French Review* (1972), 45 (Special Issue 4):116-22

Christian Century, 75:137, Jan. 29, 1958

Coe, Richard, *Ionesco; A Study of His Plays*. 1971. Pp. 152-56

Cohn, Ruby, *Currents in Contemporary Drama*. 1969. Pp. 164-66

Corvin, Michel, *Le Théâtre Nouveau en France*. 1963. Pp. 59-67

DeFuria, Richard, "At the Intersection of Freud and Ionesco", *Modern Language Notes* (1972), 87:971-76

Dubois, Jacques, "Beckett and Ionesco: The Tragic Awareness of Pascal and the Ironic Awareness of Flaubert", *Modern Drama* (1966), 9:283-91

Esslin, Martin, *The Theatre of the Absurd*. 1961. Pp. 99-103

Gassner, John, *Theatre at the Crossroads; Plays and Playwrights of the Mid-century American Stage*. 1960. Pp. 261-64

Hayman, Ronald, *Eugene Ionesco*. 1972. Pp. 29-36

Illustrated London News, 230:868, May 25, 1957

Jacobs, Willis D., "Ionesco's 'The Chairs'", *Explicator*, 22: Item 42, 1964

Kister, Daniel, "Some Imaginative Motifs from Primitive Sacred Myths in the Theater of Eugene Ionesco", *Dissertation Abstracts International* (1974), 34:4267A

Lamont, Rosette C., ed., *Ionesco: A Collection of Critical Essays*. 1973. Pp. 64-98

_____ , "The Metaphysical Farce: Beckett and Ionesco", *French Review*, 32:319-28, 1958-59

Lewis, Allan, *The Contemporary Theatre; The Significant Playwrights of Our Time*. 1962. Pp. 259-81

_____ , *Ionesco*. 1972. Pp. 33-42

Lumley, Frederick, *New Trends in Twentieth Century Drama; A Survey Since Ibsen and Shaw*. 1967. Pp. 209-14

Moore, Harry T., *Twentieth Century French Literature to World War II*. 1966. Vol. II. Pp. 154-61

Nation, 185:17, July 6, 1957

New Statesman, 53:669, May 25, 1957

New Yorker, 33:68, Jan. 18, 1958

Newsweek, 51:84, Jan. 20, 1958

Oates, Joyce Carol, *The Edge of Impossibility; Tragic Forms in Literature*. 1972. Pp. 225-49

Saturday Review, 41:26, Jan. 25, 1958

Schechner, Richard, "The Enactment of the 'Not' in Ionesco's 'Les Chaises'", *Yale French Studies*, 29:65-72, 1962

Schneider, Ruth M., "The Interpolated Narrative in Modern Drama", *Dissertation Abstracts International* (1974), 34:6605A

Seresia, C., "Les Chances d'Ionesco", *Revue Nouvelle*, 23:89-92, 1956

Serreau, Genevieve, *Histoire du Nouveau Théâtre*. 1966. Pp. 44-48

Tarrab, Gilbert, "Essai de Sociologie du Theatre: 'La Cantatrice Chauve' et 'Les Chaises' de Ionesco", *L'Homme et la Société. Revue Internationale de Recherche et de Synthese Sociologique* (1967), #6:161-70

Theatre Arts, 42:14, March, 1958

Time, 71:42, Jan. 20, 1958

Tolpin, Marian, "Eugene Ionesco's 'The Chairs' and the Theater of the Absurd", *American Imago* (1968), 25:119-39

Tynan, Kenneth, *Curtains; Selections from the Drama Criticism and Related Writings*. 1961. Pp. 177-78, 407-09

Vox, Nelvin, *Eugene Ionesco and Edward Albee; A Critical Essay*. 1968. Pp. 8-14

Williams, E. W., "God's Share; A Mythic Interpretation of 'The Chairs'", *Modern Drama* (Dec. 1969), 12:298-307

Les Chaises *SEE* The Chairs

Exit the King, 1962
Abirached, R., "Ionesco et l'Obsession de la Mort", *Les Etudes* (Paris), 317: 88-91, 1963
America, 109:512-14, Nov. 2, 1963
Cohn, Ruby, *Currents in Contemporary Drama*. 1969. Pp. 142-45 and 166-68
Gilliatt, Penelope, *Unholy Fools; Wits, Comics, Disturbers of the Peace; Film and Theater*. 1973. Pp. 23-25
Hayman, Ronald, *Eugene Ionesco*. 1972. Pp. 90-96
Illustrated London News, 243:484, Sept. 28, 1963
Kerr, Walter, *Thirty Plays Hath November; Pain and Pleasure in the Contemporary Theater*. 1969. Pp. 83-87
Kister, Daniel A., "Some Imaginative Motifs from Primitive Sacred Myths in the Theater of Eugene Ionesco", *Dissertation Abstracts International* (1974), 34:4267A
Lamont, Rosette, "Death and Tragi-Comedy; Three Plays of the New Theatre", *Massachusettes Review* (1965), 6:381-402
Lewis, Allan, *Ionesco*. 1972. Pp. 75-77
Nation, 196:57-58, Jan. 19, 1963
New Statesman, 66:330, Sept. 13, 1963, 206:155-56, Jan. 29, 1968
New Yorker, 38:102, Jan. 12, 1963, 43:82, Jan. 20, 1968
Newsweek, 71:96, Jan. 22, 1968
Reporter, 38:46, Feb. 22, 1968
Roy, Claude, "Le Roi se Meurt", *Nouvelle Revue Francaise*, 11:348-350, 1963
Saturday Review, 51:41, Jan. 27, 1968
Senat, Philippe, "Ionesco: 'Le Roi se Meurt'", *Revue des Deux Mondes*, Jan. 15, 1967. Pp. 283-87
Serreau, Genevieve, *Histoire du Nouveau Théâtre*. 1966. Pp. 59-61
Spectator, 211:292, Sept. 6, 1963
Theatre Arts, 48:31-32, Jan., 1964
"Theatre-Ionesco: Ab mit Thron", *Der Spiegel* (1963), 17:106-07
Time, 91:67, Jan. 19, 1968

The Future is in Eggs, or It Takes all Sorts to Make a World, 1953
Esslin, Martin, *The Theatre of the Absurd*. 1961. Pp. 98-99
Hayman, Ronald, *Eugene Ionesco*. 1972. Pp. 21-28
Vos, Nelvin, *Eugene Ionesco and Edward Albee; A Critical Essay*. 1968. Pp. 8-14

Hunger and Thirst, 1964
Atlas, 11:311-13, May, 1966
Cismaru, Alfred, "Ionesco's Latest: 'Hunger and Thirst'", *Laurel Review* (1967), 7, pt.2:63-70
Hayman, Ronald, *Eugene Ionesco*. 1972. Pp. 97-105
Kister, Daniel A., "Some Imaginative Motifs from Primitive Sacred Myths in the Theater of Eugene Ionesco", *Dissertation Abstracts International* (1974), 34:4267A
Lewis, Allan, *Ionesco*. 1972. Pp. 79-88
New Yorker, 42:101-02, July 16, 1966

Serreau, Genevieve, *Histoire du Nouveau Theatre*. 1966. Pp. 61-65
Vernois, Paul, ed., *l'Onirisme et l'Insolite dans le Théâtre Francais Contemporain*. 1974. Pp. 159-70

L'Impromptu de L'Alma, ou Le Caméléon du Berger   *SEE*   Improvisation, or The Shepherd's Chameleon

Improvisation, or The Shepherd's Chameleon, 1956
Esslin, Martin, *The Theatre of the Absurd*. 1961. Pp. 114-18
Grossvogel, David I., *Four Playwrights and a Postscript: Brecht, Ionesco, Beckett and Genet*. 1962. Pp. 68-81
Hayman, Ronald, *Eugene Ionesco*. 1972. Pp. 58-60
Lamont, Rosette C., ed., *Ionesco; A Collection of Critical Essays*. 1973. Pp. 120-34
Serreau, Genevieve, *Histoire du Nouveau Theatre*. 1966. Pp. 50-52

Jack, or The Submission, 1955
Clurman, Harold, *The Naked Image; Observations on the Modern Theatre*. 1966. Pp. 83-85
Hayman, Ronald, *Eugene Ionesco*. 1972. Pp. 21-28
Illustrated London News, 237:162, July 23, 1960 and 238:600, April 8, 1961
Issacharoff, Michael, "Métaphore et Metamorphose dans 'Jacques ou La Soumission'", *French Review* (1974), 48:108-18
Lewis, Allan, *Ionesco*. 1972. Pp. 43-45
Nation, 187:59, Aug. 2, 1958
Oates, Joyce Carol, *The Edge of Impossibility; Tragic Forms in Literature*. 1972. Pp. 225-49
Vos, Nelvin, *Eugene Ionesco and Edward Albee; A Critical Essay*. 1968. Pp. 8-14

Jacques, ou La Soumission   *SEE*   Jack, or the Submission

Jeux de Massacre   *SEE*   Wipe Out Games

The Killer, 1959
Corvin, Michel, *Le Théâtre Nouveau en France*. 1963. Pp. 59-67
Czarnecki, J., "Au Théâtre: Temoignage Pour l'Homme", *Christianisme Social*, 68:5-6, 410-17, 1960
Doubrovsky, J. S., "Ionesco and the Comic of Absurdity", *Yale French Studies*. #23, 3-10, 1959
Engellhardt, Klaus, "Une Source Roumaine du 'Tueur Sans Gages' d'Eugene Ionesco", *Die Neueren Sprachen* (1972), 21:9-14
Esslin, Martin, *The Theatre of the Absurd*. 1961. Pp. 119-24
Fernandez, A., "Une Longue Piece de Ionesco", *Revue Nouvelle*, 23:89-92, 1956
Gassner, John, *Dramatic Soundings; Evaluations and Retractions Culled from Thirty Years of Dramatic Criticism*. 1968. Pp. 490-91
Grossvogel, David I., *Four Playwrights and a Postscript: Brecht, Ionesco, Beckett and Genet*. 1962. Pp. 72-83
Hayman, Ronald, *Eugene Ionesco*. 1972. Pp. 61-68
Kister, Daniel A., "Some Imaginative Motifs from Primitive Sacred Myths in the Theater of Eugene Ionesco", *Dissertation Abstracts International* (1974), 34:4267A

Lamont, Rosette C., "The Hero in Spite of Himself", *Yale French Studies*, 29:73-80, 1962

Lewis, Allan, *Ionesco*. 1972. Pp. 55-66

Martin, George, "Bérenger and His Counterpart in 'La Photo du Colonel' ", *Modern Drama* (1974), 17:189-97

Moore, Harry T., *Twentieth Century French Literature to World War II.* 1966. Vol. II. Pp. 154-61

New Yorker, 36:82, April 2, 1960

Oates, Joyce Carol, *The Edge of Impossibility; Tragic Forms in Literature.* 1972. Pp. 225-49

Purdy, Strother B., "A Reading of Ionesco's 'The Killer' ", *Modern Drama* (1968), 10:416-23

Saturday Review, 43:37, April 9, 1960

Schwartz, Barry N., "Golgotha Again?", *Modern Drama* (Sept. 1971), 14: 224-26

Vos, Nelvin, *Eugene Ionesco and Edward Albee; A Critical Essay.* 1968. Pp. 14-29

La Lecon *SEE* The Lesson

The Lesson, 1951

Barbour, Thomas, "Beckett and Ionesco", *Hudson Review*, 11:271-77, 1958

Catholic World, 186:468-69, March 1958

Christian Century, 75:137, Jan. 29, 1958

Corvin, Michel, *Le Theatre Nouveau en France*. 1963. Pp. 59-67

DeFuria, Richard, "At the Intersection of Freud and Ionesco", *Modern Language Notes* (1972), 87:971-76

Dukore, Bernard F., "The Theatre of Ionesco: A Union of Form and Substance", *Educational Theatre Journal*, 13:174-81, 1961

Esslin, Martin, *The Theatre of the Absurd.* 1961. Pp. 94-98

Fowlie, Wallace, "The New French Theatre: Artaud, Beckett, Genet, Ionesco", *Sewanee Review*, 67:654-57, 1959

Fricke, Dietmar, " 'La Lecon. Les Messes Noires de la Bonne Auberge': Neue Lehrstücke für Eugene Ionescos Publikum?", *Neusprachliche Mitteilungen aus Wissenschaft und Praxis* (1973), 26:140-48

Gassner, John, *Theatre at the Crossroads; Plays and Playwrights of the Midcentury American Stage.* 1960. Pp. 261-64

Gilman, Richard, *Common and Uncommon Masks; Writings on the Theatre, 1961-1970.* 1971. Pp. 87-89

Grossvogel, David I., *Four Playwrights and a Postscript: Brecht, Ionesco, Beckett and Genet.* 1962. Pp. 69-82

Hayman, Ronald, *Eugene Ionesco.* 1972. Pp. 16-20

Illustrated London News, 226:566, March 26, 1955

Lamont, Rosette C., ed., *Ionesco; A Collection of Critical Essays.* 1973. Pp. 21-37

Lewis, Allan, *Ionesco*. 1972. Pp. 24-26 and 33-42

Murray, Jack, "Ionesco and the Mechanics of Memory", *Yale French Studies*, 29:82-90, 1962

Nation, 186:87, Jan. 25, 1958

New Yorker, 33:68, Jan. 18, 1958 and 39:96, Sept. 28, 1963

Newsweek, 51:84, Jan. 20, 1958

Novick, Julius, *Beyond Broadway; The Quest for Permanent Theatres.* 1968. Pp. 142-45

Oates, Joyce Carol, *The Edge of Impossibility; Tragic Forms in Literature.* 1972. Pp. 225-49

Saturday Review, 41:26, Jan. 25, 1958

Seresia, C., "Les Chances d'Ionesco", *Revue Nouvelle*, 23:89-92, 1956

Serreau, Geneviève, *Histoire du Nouveau Théâtre.* 1966. Pp. 41-44

Sherrell, Richard, *The Human Image; Avant-Garde and Christian.* 1969. Pp. 73-75 and 84-88

Smith, J. Oates, "Ionesco's Dances of Death", *Thought* (1965), 40:415-31

Theatre Arts, 42:14, March, 1958

Time, 71:42, Jan. 20, 1958

Vos, Nelvin, *Eugene Ionesco and Edward Albee; A Critical Essay.* 1968. Pp. 8-14

Williams, Raymond, *Drama from Ibsen to Brecht.* 1968. Pp. 296-99

The New Tenant, 1955
Corrigan, Robert W. and James L. Rosenberg, eds., *The Art of the Theatre; A Critical Anthology of Drama.* 1964. Pp. 596-609

Esslin, Martin, *The Théâtre of the Absurd.* 1961. Pp. 94-98

Hayman, Ronald, *Eugene Ionesco.* 1972. Pp. 48-49

Illustrated London News, 229:854, Nov. 17, 1956

Kister, Daniel A., "Some Imaginative Motifs from Primitive Sacred Myths in the Theater of Eugene Ionesco", *Dissertation Abstracts International* (1974), 34:4267A

Lewis, Allan, *Ionesco.* 1972. Pp. 47-48

Tynan, Kenneth, *Curtains; Selections from the Drama Criticism and Related Writings.* 1961. Pp. 149-50

Le Nouveau Locataire   *SEE*   The New Tenant

The Picture, 1955
Esslin, Martin, *The Theatre of the Absurd.* 1961. Pp. 112-14

Hayman, Ronald, *Eugene Ionesco.* 1972. Pp. 56-57

Le Piéton de l'Air   *SEE*   The Stroller in the Air

The Rhinoceros, 1959
Abirached, R., " 'Rhinoceros' d'Eugène Ionesco", *Les Etudes* (Paris), 304: 341-94, 1960

America, 104:576-77, Jan. 28, 1961 and 104:593-95, Feb. 4, 1961

Americas, 17:6-10, Feb. 1965

Brustein, Robert Sanford, *Seasons of Discontent; Dramatic Opinions 1959-1965.* 1965. Pp. 119-22

Catholic World, 192:380-81, March, 1961

Christian Century, 78:274, March 1, 1961

Clurman, Harold, *The Divine Pastime; Theatre Essays.* 1974. Pp. 134-37
——————— , *The Naked Image; Observations on the Modern Theatre.* 1966. Pp. 85-87

Cohn, Ruby, *Currents in Contemporary Drama.* 1969. Pp. 142-45

Corvin, Michel, *Le Théâtre Nouveau en France.* 1963. Pp. 59-67

Cowell, Raymond, *Twelve Modern Dramatists.* 1967. Pp. 124-26

Czarnecki, J., "Au Théâtre: Témoignage Pour L'Homme, *Christianisme Social*, 68:5-6, 410-17, 1960

Dusane, A., "'Rhinoceros' d'Eugene Ionesco", *Mercure de France*, #1159: 499, 1960

Esslin, Martin, *The Theatre of the Absurd.* 1961. Pp. 124-28

French, Judith Ann, "The Destruction of Action", *Kerygma* (1963), 3:9-12

Gassner, John, *Dramatic Soundings; Evaluations and Retractions Culled from Thirty Years of Dramatic Criticism.* 1968. Pp. 501-02

Hayman, Ronald, *Eugene Ionesco.* 1972. Pp. 69-77

Hudson Review, 14:260, Summer, 1961

Illustrated London News, 236:850, May 14, 1960

Kerr, Walter, *The Theatre in Spite of Itself.* 1963. Pp. 112-16

Knowles, Dorothy, "Eugene Ionesco's Rhinoceroses: Their Romanian Origin and Their Western Fortunes", *French Studies* (1974), 28:294-307

Lamont, Rosette C., "The Hero in Spite of Himself", *Yale French Studies*, 29:73-80, 1962

Lewis, Allan, *Ionesco.* 1972. Pp. 67-73

Lumley, Frederick, *New Trends in Twentietch Century Drama; A Survey Since Ibsen and Shaw.* 1967. Pp. 209-14

Mabley, Edward, *Dramatic Construction; An Outline of Basic Principles.* 1972. Pp. 365-78

Martin, George, "Bérenger and His Counterpart in 'La Photo du Colonel'", *Modern Drama* (1974), 17:189-97

Moore, Harry T., *Twentieth Century French Literature to World War II.* 1966. Vol. II. Pp. 154-61

Nation, 192:85-86, Jan. 28, 1961

National Review, 10:157-58, March 11, 1961

New Republic, 144:22-23, Jan. 30, 1961

New Statesman, 59:666, May 7, 1960

New Yorker, 36:103, May 28, 1960 and 36:66, Jan. 21, 1961

Newsweek, 57:57, Jan. 23, 1961

Oates, Joyce, *The Edge of Impossibility; Tragic Forms in Literature.* 1972. Pp. 225-49

Parsell, David B., "A Reading of Ionesco's 'Rhinoceros'", *Furman Studies* (1974), 21,iv:13-15

Saturday Review, 44:51, Jan. 21, 1961

Serreau, Genevieve, *Histoire du Nouveau Théâtre.* 1966. Pp. 55-59

Sewanee Review, 69:341, Spring, 1961

Smith, J. Oates, "Ionesco's Dances of Death", *Thought* (1965), 40:415-31

Spectator, 204:661, May 6, 1960

Theatre Arts, 45:9-10, March, 1961

Time, 75:56, May 23, 1960 and 77:77, Jan. 20, 1961

Vos, Nelvin, *Eugene Ionesco and Edward Albee; A Critical Essay.* 1968. Pp. 14-29

Le Roi Se Meurt *SEE* Exit the King

Le Soif et la Faim *SEE* Hunger and Thirst

The Stroller in the Air, 1962

Gerrard, Charlotte F., "Bergsonian Elements in Ionesco's 'Le Piéton de l'Air'", *Papers on Language and Literature* (1973), 9:297-310

Hayman, Ronald, *Eugene Ionesco.* 1972. Pp. 80-89

Kaiser, J., "'Fussgänger der Luft': Ionescos Neues Stuck", *Theater Heute* (1963), 4.8-10

Kister, Daniel A., "Some Imaginative Motifs from Primitive Sacred Myths in the Theater of Eugene Ionesco", *Dissertation Abstracts International* (1974), 34:4267A

Martin, George, "Berenger and His Counterpart in 'La Photo du Colonel'", *Modern Drama* (1974), 17:189-97

Newsweek, 63:96-97, March 16, 1964

Saturday Review, 49:53, Feb. 5, 1966

Time, 81:34, Jan. 4, 1963

Le Tableau   *SEE*   The Picture

Tueur sans Gages   *SEE*   The Killer

Victimes du Devoir   *SEE*   Victims of Duty

Victims of Duty, 1953

Chambers, Ross, "Detached Committal: Eugene Ionesco's 'Victims of Duty'", *Meanjin*, 22:23-33, 1963

Cohn, *Ruby, Currents in Contemporary Drama*. 1969. Pp. 162-64

Corvin, Michel, *Le Théâtre Nouveau en France*. 1963. Pp. 59-67

Esslin, Martin, *The Theatre of the Absurd*. 1961. Pp. 103-09

Hayman, Ronald, *Eugene Ionesco*. 1972. Pp. 37-44

Kister, Daniel A., "Some Imaginative Motifs from Primitive Sacred Myths in the Theater of Eugene Ionesco", *Dissertation Abstracts International* (1974), 34:4267A

Lewis, Allan, *Ionesco*. 1972. Pp. 29-30 and 48-52

Mast, G., "Logic of Illogic; Ionesco's 'Victims of Duty'", *Modern Drama* (1970, 13:133-38

Murray, Jack, "Ionesco and Mechanics of Memory", *Yale French Studies*, #29:82-90, 1962

New Yorker, 40:88-89, June 6, 1964

Sherrell, Richard, *The Human Image; Avant-Garde and Christian*. 1969. Pp. 75-88

Wipe Out Games, 1970

Hayman, Ronald, *Eugene Ionesco*. 1972. Pp. 106-14

Lewis, Allan, *Ionesco*. 1972. Pp. 79-88

CHRISTOPHER ISHERWOOD

SEE

WYSTAN HUGH AUDEN AND CHRISTOPHER ISHERWOOD

ANN JELLICOE

The Knack, 1961

Clurman, Harold, *The Naked Image; Observations on the Modern Theatre*. 1966. Pp. 88-89

Hudson Review, 17:428-29, 1964

Illustrated London News, 240:554, April 7, 1962

Lumley, Frederick, *New Trends in Twentieth Century Drama; A Survey Since Ibsen and Shaw*. 1967. Pp. 311-12

Nation, 198:612, June 15, 1964

New Statesman, 63:537, April 13, 1962

New Yorker, 40:86, June 6, 1964
Newsweek, 63:90, June 15, 1964
Prickett, Stephen, "Three Modern English Plays", *Philologica Pragensia.
Academia Scientiarum Bohemo-Slovenico* (1967), 10:12-21
Saturday Review, 47:28, June 20, 1964
Spectator, 208:445, April 6, 1962
Vogue, 144:30, Aug. 1, 1964

The Sport of My Mad Mother, 1958
Lumley, Frederick, *New Trends in Twentieth Century Drama; A Survey
Since Ibsen and Shaw*. 1967. Pp. 311-12
New Statesman, 55:301, March 8, 1958
Spectator, 200:296, March 7, 1958

JEROME KLAPKA JEROME

The Passing of the Third Floor Back, 1908
Beerbohm, Max, *Around Theatres*. 1953. Pp. 516-19
Chesterton, Gilbert K., *Miscellany of Men*. 1912. Pp. 277-83
Fortnightly, 90:679-80, 1908
Forum, 42:440-41, Nov., 1909
Living Age. 259:332-33, Nov. 7, 1908

BENJAMIN JONSON

The Alchemist, 1610
America, 115:668, Nov. 19, 1966
Arnold, Judd, "Lovewit's Trimph and Jonsonian Morality; A Reading of 'The
Alchemist'", *Criticism* (Spring 1969), 11:151-66
Barish, Jonas A., "Feasting and Judging in Jonsonian Comedy", *Renaissance
Drama* (1972), 5:3-36
Blissett, William, "Venter Tripartite in 'The Alchemist'", *Studies in English
Literature, 1500-1900* (1968), 8:323-34
Bluestone, Max and Norman Rabkin, eds., *Shakespeare's Contemporaries;
Modern Studies in English Renaissance Drama*. 2nd ed. 1970. Pp. 240-52
Bookman, 73:632, Aug., 1931
Brustein, Robert Sanford, *The Third Theatre*. 1969. Pp. 173-77
Bryant, J. A., Jr., *The Compassionate Satirist; Ben Jonson and His Imperfect
World*. 1973. Pp. 92-133
Catholic World, 133:463, July, 1931 and 167:267, July, 1948
Child, C. C., "Source of Ben Jonson's 'Alchemist'", *Nation*, 79:74-75, July
29, 1904
Clurman, Harold, *The Naked Image; Observations on the Modern Theatre*.
1966. Pp. 178-81
Commonweal, 48:139, May 21, 1948 and 81:73, Oct. 9, 1964
Dessen, Alan C., "'The Alchemist': Jonson's 'Estates' Play", *Renaissance
Drama* (1964), 7:35-54
Duncan, E. H., "Jonson's 'Alchemist' and the Literature of Alchemy", *Modern
Language Association. Publications* (PMLA), 61:699-710, 1946
Dutton, A. Richard, "'Volpone' and 'The Alchemist': A Comparison in
Satiric Techniques", *Renaissance and Modern Studies* (1974), 18:36-62

Empson, William, "The Alchemist", *Hudson Review* (Winter 1969-1970), 22:595-608

Fredeman, Patsy D., "Ben Jonson: Principles of Criticism and Creation", *Dissertation Abstracts International* (1972), 33:1140A

Goodman, Paul, *Structure of Literature*. 1954. Pp. 82-103

Halleran, James V., "Character Transmutation in 'The Alchemist'", *College Language Association Journal* (1968), 11:221-27

Helton, Tinsley, "Theme as a Shaping Factor in 'Volpone' and 'The Alchemist'", *English Record* (1963), 13:38-46

Hibbard, George R., ed., *The Elizabethan Theatre IV*. 1974. Pp. 1-21

Hill, Edgar Duncan, "Jonson's 'Alchemist' and the Literature of Alchemy", *Modern Language Association. Publications* (1945), 61:699-710

Hoy, Cyrus, "The Pretended Piety of Jonson's Alchemist", *Renaissance Papers* (1955), Pp. 15-19

Jacobs, Henry E., "Theaters Within Theaters; Levels of Dramatic Illusion in Ben Jonson's Comedies", *Dissertation Abstracts International* (1974), 34:7707A

James, Katherine H., "The Widow in Jacobean Drama", *Dissertation Abstracts International* (1973), 34:1246A

Jones, Myrddin, "Sir Epicure Mammon: A Study in 'Spiritual Fornication'", *Renaissance Quarterly* (Autumn 1969), 22:233-42

Kennedy, Dennis E., "Character and Disguise in Ben Jonson's Major Plays", *Dissertation Abstracts International* (1972), 33:2381A

Knights, L. C., *Drama and Society in the Age of Jonson*. 1962. Pp. 206-10

Knoll, Robert E., "How to Read 'The Alchemist'", *College English*, 21:456-60, 1960

Knowlton, Edgar C., "The Plots of Ben Jonson", *Modern Language Notes*, 44:77-86, 1929

Levin, Harry, "Two Magian Comedies: 'The Tempest' and 'The Alchemist'", *Shakespeare Survey* (1969), 22:47-58

Macdonald, Andrew F., "Rhetorical Strategy in Ben Jonson's Comedy", *Dissertation Abstracts International* (1973), 34:731A

Miner, Earl, ed., *Seventeenth Century Imagery; Essays of Figurative Language from Donne to Farquhar*. 1971. Pp. 69-82

Nathan, George Jean, *Theatre Book of the Year, 1948-49*. Pp. 12-14.

Nation, 203:460, Oct. 21, 1966

New Republic, 155:32-33, Oct. 29, 1966

New Yorker, 24:50, May 15, 1948 and 40:160, Sept. 26, 1964, 42:83, Oct. 22, 1966

Newsweek, 64:91, Sept. 28, 1964, 68:108, Oct. 24, 1966

Papenhausen, Richard W., "Identity and Sexuality in Ben Jonson; A Psychoanalytic Reading of Three Comedies and a Masque", *Dissertation Abstracts International* (1974), 35:1631A

Parr, J., "Non-Alchemical Pseudo-Sciences in 'The Alchemist'", *Philological Quarterly*, 24:85-89, Jan., 1945

Parr, Johnstone, *Tamburlaine's Malady and Other Essays on Astrology in Elizabethan Drama*. 1953. Pp. 107-11

Petronella, Vincent, "Teaching Ben Jonson's 'The Alchemist': Alchemy and Analysis", *Humanities Association Bulletin* (Spring 1970), 21:19-23

Rankin, Dave, "Ben Jonson: Semanticist", *Etc* (1962), 19:289-97

Ricks, Christopher, ed., *English Drama to 1710*. (History of Literature in the English Language, vol. 3). 1971. Pp. 293-302

Saturday Review, 49:49, Oct. 29, 1966

Savage, James E., *Ben Jonson's Basic Comic Characters and Other Essays*. 1973. Pp. 36-39, and 74-76

Schelling, Felix E., *Elizabethan Drama, 1558-1642*. 1959. Pp. 539-42

Shaaber, M. A., "Unclean Birds in 'The Alchemist'", *Modern Language Notes*, 65:106-09, Feb., 1950

Slocum, Keith D., "The Problem of Judgment in Ben Jonson's Plays, 1598-1614", *Dissertation Abstracts International* (1973), 34:1868A

South, Malcolm H., "The 'Uncleane Birds, in Seventy-Seven': 'The Alchemist'", *Studies in English Literature*, 1500-1900 (1973), 13:331-43

Targan, Barry, "The Dramatic Structure of 'The Alchemist'", *Discourse* (1963), 6:315-24

Thayer, C. G., "Theme and Structure in 'The Alchemist'", *English Literary History* (ELH), 26:23-35, March, 1959

Tillotson, Geoffrey, *Essays in Criticism and Research*. 1942. Pp. 41-48

Time, 51:88, May 17, 1948, 85:85, Oct. 21, 1966

Vogue, 148:161, Dec. 1966

Bartholomew Fair, 1614
Barish, J. A., "'Bartholomew Fair' and Its Puppets", *Modern Language Quarterly*, 20:3-17, March, 1959

Beaurline, L. A., "Ben Jonson and the Illusion of Completeness", *Modern Language Association. Publications* (Jan. 1969), 84:51-59

Bryant, J. A., Jr., *The Compassionate Satirist; Ben Jonson and His Imperfect World*. 1973. Pp. 134-59

Donaldson, Jan, *The World Upside-Down; Comedy from Jonson to Fielding*. 1970. Pp. 46-77

Fredeman, Patsy D., "Ben Jonson; Principles of Criticism and Creation", *Dissertation Abstracts International* (1972), 33:1140A

Gardiner, J. K., "Infantile Sexuality, Adult Critics, and 'Bartholomew Fair'", *Literature and Psychology* (1974), 24,iii:124-31

Hamel, Guy, "Order and Judgment in 'Bartholomew Fair'", *University of Toronto Quarterly* (1973), 43:48-67

Hibbard, George R., ed., *The Elizabethan Theatre IV*. 1974. Pp. 80-105

Jacobs, Henry E., "Theaters Within Theaters; Levels of Dramatic Illusion in Ben Jonson's Comedies", *Dissertation Abstracts International* (1974), 34:7707A

James, Katherine H., "The Widow in Jacobean Drama", *Dissertation Abstracts International* (1973), 34:1246A

Kennedy, Dennis E., "Character and Disguise in Ben Jonson's Major Plays", *Dissertation Abstracts International* (1972), 33:2381A

Latham, Jacqueline E. M., "Form in 'Bartholomew Fair'", *English* (1972), 21:8-11

Levin, Lawrence L., "Replication as Dramatic Strategy in the Comedies of Ben Jonson", *Renaissance Drama* (1972), 5:37-74

Levin, Richard, *The Multiple Plot in English Renaissance Drama*. 1971. Pp. 191-93 and 202-14

Levin, R., "Structure of 'Bartholomew Fair'", *Modern Language Association. Publications* (PMLA), 80:172-79, 1965

McCollom, William G., *The Divine Average; A View of Comedy*. 1971. Pp. 153-64

Macdonald, Andrew F., "Rhetorical Strategy in Ben Jonson's Comedy", *Dissertation Abstracts International* (1973), 34:731A

Mager, Don, "The Paradox of Tone in 'Bartholomew Fayre'", *Thoth* (1968), 9:39-47

Papenhausen, Richard W., "Identity and Sexuality in Ben Jonson: A Psychoanalytic Reading of Three Comedies and a Masque", *Dissertation Abstracts International* (1974), 35:1631A

Parker, R. B., "The Themes and Staging of 'Bartholomew Fair'", *University of Toronto Quarterly* (1970), 39:293-309

Paster, Gail Kern, "Ben Jonson's Comedy of Limitations", *Studies in Philology* (1973), 72:51-71

Petronella, Vincent F., "Jonson's 'Bartholomew Fair': A Study in Baroque Style", *Discourse* (1970), 13:325-37

Ricks, Christopher, ed., *English Drama to 1710.* (History of Literature in the English Language, vol. 3). 1971. Pp. 280-302

Robinson, James E., "'Bartholomew Fair': Comedy of Vapors", *Studies in English Literature, 1500-1900* (Rice Univ.), 1:65-80, 1961

Smith, Calvin C., "Bartholomew Fair: Cold Decorum", *South Atlantic Quarterly* (1972), 71:548-56

Theatre Arts, 43:79, Dec., 1959

Tynan, Kenneth, *Curtains; Selections from the Drama Criticism and Related Writings.* 1961. Pp. 3-6

Umphrey, Lee, "Jonson's 'Bartholomew Fair' and the Popular Dramatic Tradition", *Louisburg College Journal of Arts and Sciences* (June 1967), 1:6-16

Wimsatt, William Kurtz, ed., *English Stage Comedy.* 1955. Pp. 74-97

———————— , ed., *Literary Criticism; Idea and Act.* 1974. Pp. 346-61

The Case Is Altered, 1609

Fredeman, Patsy D., "Ben Jonson; Principles of Criticism and Creation", *Dissertation Abstracts International* (1972), 33:1140A

Catiline, His Conspiracy, 1611

Brandes, George, *William Shakespeare; A Critical Study*, Vol. I. 1963. Pp. 398-99

Brown, John Russell and Harris, Bernard, eds., *Jacobean Theatre* (Stratford on Avon Studies, 1). 1960. Pp. 113-31

Bryant, Joseph A., Jr., "'Catiline' and the Nature of Jonson's Tragic Fable", *Modern Language Association. Publications* (PMLA), 69:265-77, 1954

DeLuna, Barbara N., *Jonson's Romish Plot: A Study of 'Catiline' and Its Historical Context.* 1967. 415 pages

deVilliers, Jacot I., "Ben Jonson's Tragedies", *English Studies* (1964), 45:432-42

Dorenkamp, Angela G., "Jonson's 'Catiline': History as the Trying Faculty", *Studies in Philology* (1970), 67:210-20

Echeruo, Michael J. C., "The Conscience of Politics and Jonson's 'Catiline'", *Studies in English Literature, 1500-1900* (1966), 6:263-77

Harris, L. H., "Local Color in Ben Jonson's 'Catiline' and Historical Accuracy of the Play", *Classical Philology*, 14:273-83, 1919

———————— , "Lucan's 'Pharsalia' and Jonson's 'Catiline'", *Modern Language Notes*, 34:397-402, 1919

Mustard, W. P., "Notes on Ben Jonson's 'Catiline'", *Modern Language Notes*, 36:154-57, 1921

Santa Lucia, Gaetano F., "Irony in 'Sejanus' and 'Catiline'", *Dissertation Abstracts International* (1974), 35:416A

Williams, W. M., "Influence of Ben Jonson's 'Catiline' Upon John Oldham's 'Satyrs Upon the Jesuits'", *Journal of English Literary History* (ELH), 11:38-62, March, 1944

Cynthia's Revels, or The Fountain of Self-Love, 1600-01

Bryant, J. A., Jr., "Jonson's Satirist Out of His Humor", *Ball State Teachers College Forum* (1962), 3:31-36

Carr, Joan C., "Poetry and the Nature of Satire in Jonsonian Comedy; A Study of Comicall Satyre", *Dissertation Abstracts International* (1973), 34:1851A

Kallich, M., "Unity of Time in 'Every Man in His Humor' and 'Cynthia's Revels'", *Modern Language Notes*, 57:445-49, June, 1942

Knowlton, Edgar C., "The Plots of Ben Jonson", *Modern Language Notes*, 44:77-86, 1929

Levin, Lawrence L., "Replication as Dramatic Strategy in the Comedies of Ben Jonson", *Renaissance Drama* (1972), 5:37-74

Savage, James E., "Ben Jonson in Ben Jonson's Plays", *University of Mississippi Studies in English* (1962), 3:1-17

——————————— , *Ben Jonson's Basic Comic Characters and Other Essays.* 1973. Pp. 134-37

Shibata, Toshihiko, "On the Palinodial Ending of 'Cynthia's Revels'", *Shakespeare Studies* (Japan) (1971-72), 10:1-15

Thron, E. M., "Jonson's 'Cynthia's Revels': Multiplicity and Unity", *Studies in English Literature, 1500-1900* (Spring 1971), 11:235-47

The Devis Is An Ass, 1616

Knights, L. C., *Drama and Society in the Age of Jonson.* 1962. Pp. 210-18

Ledford, Ted R., "A Critical Study of Ben Jonson's Last Plays", *Dissertation Abstracts International* (1974), 35:2945A

Levin, Lawrence L., "Replication as Dramatic Strategy in the Comedies of Ben Jonson", *Renaissance Drama* (1972), 5:37-74

Potta, R., "Three Jacobean Devil Plays", *Studies in Philology*, 28:730-36, Oct., 1931

Savage, James E., *Ben Jonson's Basic Comic Characters and Other Essays.* 1973. Pp. 24-27 and 38-48

Epicoene; or, The Silent Woman, 1609

Anderson, Mark A., "The Successful Unity of 'Epicoene'; A Defense of Ben Jonson", *Studies in English Literature, 1500-1900* (1970), 10:349-66

Beaurline, L. A., "Ben Jonson and the Illusion of Completeness", *Modern Language Association. Publications* (Jan. 1969), 84:51-59

Bryant, J. A., Jr., *The Compassionate Satirist; Ben Jonson and His Imperfect World.* 1973. Pp. 92-133

Campbell, Oscar J. "The Relation of 'Epicoene' to Aretino's 'Il Marescalco'", *Modern Language Association. Publications* (PMLA), 46:752-62, 1931

Donaldson, Ian, "A Martyr's Resolution: Jonson's 'Epicoene'", *Review of English Studies* (1967), 18:1-15

——————————, *The World Upside-Down; Comedy from Jonson to Field-ing*. 1970. Pp. 24-45

Ferns, John, "Ovid, Juvenal, and 'The Silent Woman': A Reconsideration", *Modern Language Review* (1970), 65:248-53

Graves, T. S., "Jonson's 'Epicoene' and Lady Arabella Stuart", *Modern Philology*, 14:525-30, Jan., 1917

Kennedy, Dennis E., "Character and Disguise in Ben Jonson's Major Plays", *Dissertation Abstracts International* (1972), 33:2381A

Levin, Lawrence L., "Replication as Dramatic Strategy in the Comedies of Ben Jonson", *Renaissance Drama* (1972), 5:37-74

Macdonald, Andrew F., "Rhetorical Strategy in Ben Jonson's Comedy", *Dissertation Abstracts International* (1973), 34:731A

Partridge, Edward B., "The Allusiveness of 'Epicoene'", *Journal of English Literary History* (ELH), 22:93-107, 1955

Paster, Gail Kern, "Ben Jonson's Comedy of Limitations", *Studies in Philology* (1973), 72:51-71

Ricks, Christopher, ed., *English Drama to 1710*. (History of Literature in the English Language, vol. 3). 1971. Pp. 284-301

Salinger, L. G., "Farce and Fashion in 'The Silent Woman'", *Essays and Studies* (1967), 20:29-46

Shapiro, Michael, "Audience vs. Dramatist in Jonson's 'Epicoene' and Other Plays of the Children's Troupes", *English Literary Renaissance* (1973), 3:400-17

Slights, William W. E., "'Epicoene' and the Prose Paradox", *Philological Quarterly* (1970), 49:178-87

Slocum, Keith D., "The Problem of Judgment in Ben Jonson's Plays, 1598-1614", *Dissertation Abstracts International* (1973), 34:1868A

Wimsatt, William Kurtz, ed., *English Stage Comedy*. 1955. Pp. 74-97

——————————, ed., *Literary Criticism; Idea and Act*. 1974. Pp. 346-61

Every Man in His Humor, 1598

Barish, Jonas A., "Feasting and Judging in Jonsonian Comedy", *Renaissance Drama* (1972), 5:3-36

Bluestone, Max and Norman Rabkin, eds., *Shakespeare's Contemporaries: Modern Studies in English Renaissance Drama*. 2nd ed. 1970. Pp. 219-27

Bryant, J. S., Jr., "Jonson's Revision of 'Every Man in His Humor'", *Studies in Philology* (1962), 59:641-50

Colley, John S., "Opinion, Poetry and Folly in 'Every Man In His Humor'", *South Atlantic Bulletin* (1974), 39,iv:3-9

Cunningham, John E., *Elizabethan and Early Stuart Drama*. 1965. Pp. 61-65

Dutton, A. Richard, "The Significance of Jonson's Revision of 'Every Man In His Humor'", *Modern Language Review* (1974), 69:241-49

Foltinek, Herbert, "Uber die Methode des Motivvergleichs: Dargestellt an Englischen Literaturwerken", *English Miscellany* (1964), 15:103-33

Fredeman, Patsy D., "Ben Jonson: Principles of Criticism and Creation", *Dissertation Abstracts International* (1972), 33:1140A

Hardison, O. B., "Three Types of Renaissance Catharsis", *Renaissance Drama* (1969), 2:3-22

Kallich, M., "Unity of Time in 'Every Man In His Humor' and 'Cynthia's Revels'", *Modern Language Notes*, 57:445-49, June, 1942

Knowlton, Edgar C., "The Plots of Ben Jonson", *Modern Language Notes*, 44:77-86, 1929

Levin, Lawrence L., "Clement Justice in 'Every Man In His Humor'", *Studies in English Literature, 1500-1900* (1972), 12:291-307

——————, "Replication as Dramatic Strategy in the Comedies of Ben Jonson", *Renaissance Drama* (1972), 5:37-74

Rankin, Dave, "Ben Jonson: Semanticist", *Etc* (1962), 19:289-97

Ricks, Christopher, ed., *English Drama to 1710*. (History of Literature in the English Language, vol. 3). 1971. Pp. 282-302

Rollin, Roger B., "Images of Libertinism in 'Every Man In His Humour' and 'To His Coy Mistress'", *Papers on Language and Literature* (1970), 6: 188-91

Savage, James E., *Ben Jonson's Basic Comic Characters and Other Essays*. 1973. Pp. 129-31

Slocum, Keith D., "The Problem of Judgment in Ben Jonson's Plays, 1598-1614", *Dissertation Abstracts International* (1973), 34:1868A

Every Man Out of His Humor, 1599

Barish, Jonas A., "Feasting and Judging in Jonsonian Comedy", *Renaissance Drama* (1972), 5:3-36

Beaurline, L. A., "Ben Jonson and the Illusion of Completeness", *Modern Language Association. Publications* (Jan. 1969), 84:51-59

Bryant, J. A., Jr., "Jonson's Satirist Out of His Humor", *Ball State Teachers College Forum* (1962), 3:31-36

Carr, Joan C., "Poetry and the Nature of Satire in Jonsonian Comedy; A Study of Comicall Satyres", *Dissertation Abstracts International* (1973), 34:1851A

Clubb, Roger L., "The Relationship of Language to Character in Ben Jonson's 'Every Man Out of His Humour'", *Dissertation Abstracts International* (1969), 30:274A

Enck, J. J., "The Peace of the Poet Omachia", *Modern Language Association. Publications* (PMLA), 77:386-96, 1962

Essays Contributed in Honor of President William Allan Neilson, ed. by C. B. Bourland and others (Smith College Studies in Modern Languages, v. 21, #1-4), 1939. Pp. 64-80

Fredeman, Patsy D., "Ben Jonson; Principles of Criticism and Creation", *Dissertation Abstracts International* (1972), 33:1140A

Gilbert, A. H., "Italian Names in 'Every Man Out of His Humor'", *Studies in Philology*, 44:195-208, April, 1947

Jacobs, Henry E., "Theaters Within Theaters; Levels of Dramatic Illusion in Ben Jonson's Comedies", *Dissertation Abstracts International* (1974), 34:7707A

Kernan, Alvin, *The Cankered Muse: Satire of the English Renaissance*. 1959. Pp. 158-62

Knowlton, Edgar C., "The Plots of Ben Jonson", *Modern Language Notes*, 44:77-86, 1929

Savage, James E., "Ben Jonson in Ben Jonson's Plays", *University of Mississippi Studies in English* (1962), 3:1-17

——————, *Ben Jonson's Basic Characters and Other Essays*. 1973. Pp. 15-21, 105-07 and 131-34

Slocum, Keith D., "The Problem of Judgment in Ben Jonson's Plays, 1598-1614", *Dissertation Abstracts International* (1973), 34:1868A

For the Honour of Wales, 1618
Cutts, John P., "Seventeenth Century Illustrations of Three Masques by Jonson", *Comparative Drama* (1972), 6:125-34

Gypsies Metamorphosed, 1621
Cutts, John P., "Seventeenth Century Illustrations of Three Masques by Jonson", *Comparative Drama* (1972), 6:125-34

The Magnetic Lady; or, Humours Reconciled, 1629
Champion, Larry S., " 'The Magnetic Lady': The Close of Ben Jonson's Circle", *Southern Humanities Review* (Winter 1968), 2:104-21
Knights, L. C., *Drama and Society in the Age of Jonson*. 1962. Pp. 223-27
Ledford, Ted R., "A Critical Study of Ben Jonson's Last Plays", *Dissertation Abstracts International* (1974), 35:2945A
McFarland, Ronald E., "Jonson's 'Magnetic Lady' and the Reception of Gilbert's 'De Magnete'", *Studies in English Literature, 1500-1900* (1971), 11:283-93
Savage, James E., *Ben Jonson's Basic Comic Characters and Other Essays*. 1973. Pp. 76-86

The Masque of Augurs, 1622
Cutts, John P., "Seventeenth Century Illustrations of Three Masques by Jonson", *Comparative Drama* (1972), 6:125-34

Mortimer, His Fall, 1640
Studies in Honor of John Wilcox, by Members of the English Department, ed. by A. Doyle Wallace and Woodburn O. Ross. 1958. Pp. 9-22

The New Inn; or, The Light Heart, 1629
Duncan, Douglas, "A Guide to 'The New Inn'", *Essays in Criticism* (July 1970), 20:311-26
Essays in Honor of Walter Clyde Curry. (Vanderbilt Studies in the Humanities, 2). 1954. Pp. 133-42
Hawkins, Harriett, "The Idea of a Theatre in Jonson's 'The New Inn'", *Renaissance Drama* (1966), 9:205-26
Jacobs, Henry E., "Theaters Within Theaters; Levels of Dramatic Illusion in Ben Jonson's Comedies", *Dissertation Abstracts International* (1974), 34:7707A
Ledford, Ted R., "A Critical Study of Ben Jonson's Last Plays", *Dissertation Abstracts International* (1974), 35:2945A
Levin, Richard, "The New 'New Inne' and the Proliferation of Good Bad Drama", *Essays in Criticism* (1972), 22:41-47 and 327-29 and (1974), 24:312-16
Maxwell, Baldwin, *Studies in Beaumont, Fletcher and Massinger*. 1939. Pp. 107-15

Pleasure Reconciled to Virtue, 1618
Papanhausen, Richard W., "Identity and Sexuality in Ben Jonson; A Psychoanalytic Reading of Three Comedies and a Masque", *Dissertation Abstracts International* (1974), 35:1631A

Poetaster; or, The Arraignment, 1601

Barish, Jonas A., "Feasting and Judging in Jonsonian Comedy", *Renaissance Drama* (1972), 5:3-36

Brandes, George, *William Shakespeare; A Critical Study*, Vol. I. 1963. Pp. 392-93

Bryant, J. A., Jr., "Jonson's Satirist Out of His Humor", *Ball State Teachers College Forum* (1962), 3:31-36

Carr, Joan C., "Poetry and the Nature of Satire in Jonsonian Comedy; A Study of Comicall Satyre", *Dissertation Abstracts International* (1973), 34:1851A

Levin, Lawrence L., "Replication as Dramatic Strategy in the Comedies of Ben Jonson", *Renaissance Drama* (1972), 5:37-74

Mardswardt, Albert H., "A Fashionable Expression: Its Status in 'Poetaster' and 'Satiromastix'", *Modern Language Notes*, 44:93-96, 1929

Platz, Norbert H., "Jonson's 'Ars Poetica': An Interpretation of 'Poetaster' in Its Historical Context" *Elizabethan Studies* (1973), 12:1-42

Ricks, Christopher, *English Drama to 1710*. (History of Literature in the English Language, vol. 3). 1971. Pp. 289-96

Savage, James E., "Ben Jonson in Ben Jonson's Plays", *University of Mississippi Studies in English* (1962), 3:1-17

——————————— , *Ben Jonson's Basic Comic Characters and Other Essays*. 1973. Pp. 59-62, 108-10, and 137-44

Sejanus, His Fall, 1603

Barish, Jonas A., "Feasting and Judging in Jonsonian Comedy" *Renaissance Drama* (1972), 5:3-36

Boughner, Daniel C., "Jonson's Use of Lipsius in 'Sejanus'", *Modern Language Notes*, 73:247-55, April, 1958

——————————— , "'Sejanus' and Machiavelli", *Studies in English Literature, 1500-1900* (Rice Univ.), 1:81-100, 1961

Brandes, George, *William Shakespeare; A Critical Study*, Vol. I. 1963. Pp. 395-98

Brown, I., "Sejanus", *Saturday Review*, 145:190-91, Feb. 18, 1928

Brown, John Russell and Harris, Bernard, ed., *Jacobean Theatre* (Stratford Upon Avon Studies, 1). 1960. Pp. 113-31

deVilliers, Jacob I., "Ben Jonson's Tragedies", *English Studies* (1964), 45: 432-42

Evans, K. W., "'Sejanus' and the Ideal Prince Tradition", Studies in English Literature, 1500-1900 (Spring 1971), 11:249-64

Gilbert, A., "The Eavesdroppers in Jonson's 'Sejanus'", *Modern Language Notes*, 69:164-66, 1954

Hamilton, Gary D., "Irony and Fortune in 'Sejanus'", *Studies in English Literature, 1500-1900* (Spring 1971), 11:265-81

Knights, L. C., *Drama and Society in the Age of Jonson*. 1962. Pp. 180-85

Knowlton, Edgar C., "The Plots of Ben Jonson", *Modern Language Notes*, 44:77-86, 1929

Lever, J. W., *The Tragedy of State*. 1971. Pp. 59-77

Levin, Lawrence L., "Justice and Society in 'Sejanus' and 'Volpone'", *Discourse* (1970, 13:19-24

Lindsay, Barbara N., "The Structure of Tragedy in 'Sejanus'", *English Studies* (Anglo-American Supp.) (1969), xliv-1

Marotti, Arthur F., "The Self-Reflexive Art of Ben Jonson's 'Sejanus'", *Texas Studies in Literature and Language* (1970), 12:197-220

Ricks, Christopher, ed., *English Drama to 1710*. (History of Literature in the English Language, vol. 3). 1971. Pp. 284-302

————————, "'Sejanus' and Dismemberment", *Modern Language Notes*, 76:301-08, 1961

Santa Lucia, Gaetano F., "Irony in 'Sejanus' and 'Catiline'", *Dissertation Abstracts International* (1974), 35:416A

Slocum, Keith D., "The Problem of Judgment in Ben Jonson's Plays, 1598-1614", *Dissertation Abstracts International* (1973), 34:1868A

Staple of News, 1626

Barish, Jonas A., "Feasting and Judging in Jonsonian Comedy", *Renaissance Drama* (1972), 5:3-36

A Celebration of Ben Jonson; Papers Presented at the University of Toronto in October 1972. 1973. Pp. 83-128

Janicka, Irena, "Jonson's 'Staple of News': Sources and Traditional Devices", *Kwartalnik Neofilologiczny* (1968), 15:301-07

Kifer, Devra R., "'The Staple of News': Jonson's Festive Comedy", *Studies in English Literature, 1500-1900* (1972), 12:329-44

————————, "Too Many Cookes: An Addition to the Printed Text of Jonson's 'Staple of Newes'", *English Language Notes* (1974), 11:264-71

Knights, L. C., *Drama and Society in the Age of Jonson*. 1962. Pp. 218-23

Ledford, Ted R., "A Critical Study of Ben Jonson's Last Plays", *Dissertation Abstracts International* (1974), 35:2945A

Levin, Richard, *The Multiple Plot in English Renaissance Drama*. 1971. Pp. 184-91

Mills, Lloyd L., "A Clarification of Broker's Use of 'A Perfect Sanguine' in 'The Staple of Neues'", *Notes and Queries* (1967), 14:208-09

The Vision of Delight, 1617

Hawkins, Harriett, "Jonson's Use of Traditional Dream Theory in 'The Vision of Delight'", *Modern Philology.* (1967), 64:285-92

Volpone, or the Fox, 1606

America, 96:566, Feb. 16, 1957

Arnold, Judd, "The Double Plot in 'Volpone': A Note on Jonsonian Dramatic Structure", *Seventeenth Century News* (1965), 23:47-52

Barish, J. A., "Double Plot in Volpone", *Modern Philology*, 51:83-92, 1953

Bennett, Josephine Waters; Cargill, Oscar; and Hall, Vernon, eds., *Studies in English Renaissance Drama; In Memory of Karl Julius Holzknecht.* 1959. Pp. 310-21

Bluestone, Max and Norman Rabkin, eds., *Shakespeare's Contemporaries; Modern Studies in English Renaissance Drama.* 2nd ed. 1970. Pp. 227-40

Boughner, Daniel C., "Lewkenor and 'Volpone'", *Notes and Queries*, 9:124-30, 1962

Bryant, J. A., Jr., *The Compassionate Satirist; Ben Jonson and His Imperfect World.* 1973. Pp. 56-91

Catholic World, 166:457-58, Feb., 1948

Clary, Frank N., Jr., "The Volpone and the Pone; A Reconsideration of Jonson's 'Volpone'", *English Language Notes* (1972), 10:102-09

Clurman, Harold, *The Naked Image; Observations on the Modern Theatre.* 1966. Pp. 178-81

Cox, Gerard H., III, "Celia, Bonario, and Jonson's Indebtedness to the Medieval Cycles", *Etudes Anglaises* (1972), 25:506-11

Craik, T. W., "Volpone's Young Antinous", *Notes and Queries* (June 1970), 17:213-14

Cunningham, John E., *Elizabethan and Early Stuart Drama.* 1965. Pp. 65-67

Davison, P. H., "Volpone and the Old Comedy", *Modern Language Quarterly*, 24:151-57, June, 1963

Deniz, Jose A. G., "Aspectos del Humor en 'Volpone' de Ben Jonson," *Filología Moderna* (1972), 12:281-97

Dessen, A. C., "Volpone and the Late Morality Tradition", *Modern Language Quarterly*, 25:383-99, Dec., 1964

Donaldson, Ian, "Jonson's Tortoise", *Review of English Studies* (1968), 19: 162-66

Donaldson, I., "'Volpone': Quick and Dead", *Essays in Criticism* (April 1971), 21:121-34 and 411-12

Duncan, Douglas, "Audience Manipulation in 'Volpone'", *Wascana Review* (1970), 5:23-37

——————— , "Ben Jonson's Lucianic Irony", *Ariel: A Review of International English Literature* (April 1970), 1:42-53

Dutton, A. Richard, "'Volpone' and 'The Alchemist': A Comparison in Satiric Techniques", *Renaissance and Modern Studies* (1974), 18:36-62

Empson, William, "Volpone", *Hudson Review* (Winter 1968-1969), 21:651-66

Freeman, Arthur, "The Earliest Allusion to Volpone", *Notes and Queries* (1967), 14:207-08

Gianakaris, C. J., "Identifying Ethical Values in 'Volpone'", *Huntington Library Quarterly* (1968), 32:45-57

——————— , "Jonson's Use of 'Avocatori' in 'Volpone'", *English Language Notes* (1974), 12:8-14

Goldberg, S. L., "Folly Into Crime: The Catastrophe of 'Volpone'", *Modern Language Quarterly*, 20:233-42, 1959

Hallett, Charles A., "Jonson's Celia: A Reinterpretation of 'Volpone'", *Studies in Philology* (Jan. 1971), 68:50-69

——————— , "The Satanic Nature of Volpone", *Philological Quarterly* (Jan. 1970), 49:41-55

Hammond, Emily E., "A Directorial Analysis of Ben Jonson's 'Volpone'", *Dissertation Abstracts International* (1972), 33:1878A

Hans, Pierre, "'Tabarine' in Ben Jonson's 'Volpone'", *Seventeenth Century News* (1970), 28:4-5

Hawkins, Harriett, "Folly, Disease, and Volpone", *Studies in English Literature, 1500-1900* (1968), 8.335-38

Helton, Tinsley, "Theme as a Shaping Factor in 'Volpone' and 'The Alchemist'", *English Record* (1963), 13:38-46

Hibbard, George R., ed., *The Elizabethan Theatre IV.* 1974. Pp. 1-21

Hill, W. Speed, "Biography, Autobiography and 'Volpone'", *Studies in English Literature, 1500-1900* (1972), 12:309-28

Hoffmann, Gerhard, "Zur Form der Satirischen Kömodie; Ben Jonson's 'Volpone'", *Deutsche Vierteljahrsschrift für Literaturwissenschaft und Geistesgeschichte* (1972), 46:1-27

Jacobs, Henry E., "Theaters Within Theaters: Levels of Dramatic Illusion in Ben Jonson's Comedies", *Dissertation Abstracts International* (1974), 34: 7707A

Kennedy, Dennis E., "Character and Disguise in Ben Jonson's Major Plays", *Dissertation Abstracts International* (1972), 33:2381A

Kernan, Alvin B., ed., *Ben Jonson: Volpone.* 1962. Pp. 1-26

––––––––––––, *The Cankered Muse; Satire of the English Renaissance.* 1959. Pp. 164-68

Knights, L. C., *Drama and Society in the Age of Jonson.* 1962. Pp. 200-06

Knowlton, Edgar C., "The Plots of Ben Jonson", *Modern Language Notes*, 44:77-86, 1929

Leggatt, Alexander, "The Suicide of Volpone", *University of Toronto Quarterly* (1969), 39:19-32

Levin, Harry, "Jonson's Metempsychosis", *Philological Quarterly* (1943), 22:231-39

Levin, Lawrence L., "Justice and Society in 'Sejanus' and 'Volpone'", *Discourse* (1970), 13:19-24

––––––––––––, "Replication as Dramatic Strategy in the Comedies of Ben Jonson", *Renaissance Drama* (1972), 5:37-74

Litt, Dorothy E., "Unity of Theme in 'Volpone'", *Bulletin of the New York Public Library* (1969), 73:218-26

Lyle, Alexander W., "Volpone's Two Worlds", *Yearbook of English Studies* (1974), 4:70-76

MacCarthy, Desmond, *Humanities.* 1954. Pp. 54-59

Macdonald, Andrew, "Rhetorical Strategy in Ben Jonson's Comedy", *Dissertation Abstracts International* (1973), 34:731A

Miller, Joyce, "'Volpone': A Study of Dramatic Ambiguity", *Scripta Hierosolymitana* (1966), 17:35-95

Mills, Lloyd L., "Barish's 'The Double Plot' Supplemented: The Tortoise Symbolism", *Serif* (1967), 4:25-28

Nash, R., "Comic Intent of 'Volpone'", *Studies in Philology*, 44:26-40, 1947

Nathan, George Jean, *Theatre Book of the Year, 1947-48.* Pp. 217-19

Nation, 166:108-09, Jan. 24, 1948 and 184:174, Feb. 23, 1957 and 199:59, Aug. 10, 1964

New Republic, 136:20, March 18, 1957

New Yorker, 23:42, Jan. 17, 1948

Papanhausen, Richard W., "Identity and Sexuality in Ben Jonson: A Psychoanalytic Reading of Three Comedies and a Masque", *Dissertation Abstracts International* (1974), 35:1631A

Parfitt, George A. E., "Some Notes on the Classical Borrowings in 'Volpone'", *English Studies* (1974), 55:127-32

Paster, Gail Kern, "Ben Jonson's Comedy of Limitations", *Studies in Philology* (1973), 72:51-71

Perkinson, R. H., "'Volpone' and the Reputation of Venetian Justice", *Modern Language Review*, 35:11-18, Jan., 1940

Pineas, Rainer, "The Morality Vice in 'Volpone'", *Discourse* (1962), 5:451-59

Rankin, Dave, "Ben Jonson: Semanticist", *Etc* (1962), 19:289-97

Ricks, Christopher, ed., *English Drama to 1710.* (History of Literature in the English Language, vol. 3). 1971. Pp. 287-302

Saturday Review, 40:26, March 2, 1957

Savage, James E., *Ben Jonson's Basic Comic Characters and Other Essays.* 1973. Pp. 31-48, 87-90 and 114-16

Schene, D. A., "Jonson's 'Volpone' and Traditional Fox Lore", *Review of English Studies*, n. s. 1:242-44, July, 1950

School and Society, 67:87, Jan. 31, 1948

Shalvi, Alice and A. A. Mendilov, ed., *Studies in English Language and Literature*. 1966. Pp. 35-95

Slocum, Keith D., "The Problem of Judgment in Ben Jonson's Plays, 1598-1614", *Dissertation Abstracts International* (1973), 34:1868A

South, Malcolm H., "Animal Imagery in 'Volpone'", *Tennessee Studies in Literature* (1965), 10:141-50

Theatre Arts, 41:21, April, 1957

Tulip, James, "Comedy as Equivocation; An Approach to the Reference of 'Volpone'", *Southern Review; An Australian Journal of Literary Studies* (1972), 5:91-101

Tynan, Kenneth, *Curtains; Selections from the Drama Criticism and Related Writings*. 1961. Pp. 34-35

Weld, John S., "Christian Comedy: 'Volpone'", *Studies in Philology*, 51: 172-93, 1954

Westcott, Robert, "Volpone? Or the Fox?", *The Critical Review* (1974), 17:82-96

Woodard, Lawrence E., "A Study of the Argumentation Used in Four Selected Elizabethan Plays: 'Julius Caesar', 'Volpone', 'Dr. Faustus', and 'The Spanish Tragedy'", *Dissertation Abstracts International* (1974), 35:3935A

JAMES JOYCE

Exiles, 1919

Adams, Robert M., "Light on Joyce's 'Exiles'? A New MS, a Curious Analogue and some Speculations", *Studies in Bibliography* (1964), 17: 83-105

Aitken, D. J. F., "Dramatic Archetypes in Joyce's 'Exiles'", *Modern Fiction Studies* (Spring 1958), 4:42-52

Bandler, Bernard, "Joyce's 'Exiles'", *Hound and Horn* (Jan.-Mar. 1933), 6:266-85

Beebe, Maurice, *Ivory Towers and Sacred Founts: The Artist as Hero in Fiction from Goethe to Joyce*. 1964. Pp. 290-93

Benstock, Bernard, "'Exiles', Ibsen and the Play's Function in the Joyce Canon", *Ball State University Forum* (1970), 11:26-37

——————, "'Exiles': 'Paradox Lust' and 'Lost Paladays'", *ELH* (1969), 36:739-56

Brivic, Sheldon R., "Structure and Meaning in Joyce's 'Exiles'", *James Joyce Quarterly* (Fall 1968), 6:29-52

Clark, Earl John, "James Joyce's 'Exiles'", *James Joyce Quarterly* (Fall 1968), 6:69-78

Cohn, Ruby, "Absurdity in English: Joyce and O'Neill", *Comparative Drama* (Fall 1969), 3:156-61

Cunningham, Frank R., "Joyce's 'Exiles': A Problem of Dramatic Stasis", *Modern Drama* (Feb. 1970), 12:399-407

Douglass, James W., "James Joyce's 'Exiles': A Portrait of the Artist", *Renascence* (Winter 1963), 15:82-87

Ellmann, Richard, "James Joyce, Irish European", *Tri-Quarterly* (Winter 1967), #8:199-204

_____ , "A Portrait of the Artist as Friend", *Kenyon Review* (Winter 1956), 18:53-67

Fergusson, Francis, "'Exiles' and Ibsen's Work", *Hound and Horn* (April-June 1932), 5:345-53

Ferris, William R., Jr., "Rebellion Matured: Joyce's 'Exiles'", (Eire) *Ireland; A Journal of Irish Studies* (Winter 1969), 4:73-83

Givens, Sean, ed., *James Joyce; Two Decades of Criticism.* 1948. Pp. 95-131

Goldberg, S. L., *The Classical Temper; A Study of James Joyce's "Ulysses".* 1961. Pp. 111-13

_____ , *James Joyce.* 1962. Pp. 63-67

Golding, Louis, *James Joyce.* 1933. Pp. 69-82

Gordman, Herbert, *James Joyce; His First Forty Years.* 1924. Pp. 101-15

Harmon, Maurice, "Richard Rowan, His Own Scapegoat", *James Joyce Quarterly* (Fall 1965), 3:34-40

Jacquot, J., "Réflexions sur 'Les Exiles' de Joyce", *Etudes Anglaises,* 9:338-43, 1956

Jolas, Maria, ed., *A James Joyce Yearbook.* 1949. Pp. 47-67

Kenner, Hugh, *Dublin's Joyce.* 1956. Pp. 69-94

_____ , "Joyce and Ibsen's Naturalism", *Sewanee Review* (Jan. 1951), 59:75-96

_____ , "Joyce's 'Exiles'", *Hudson Review,* 5:389-403, 1952

Levin, Harry, *James Joyce; A Critical Introduction.* 1941. Pp. 37-40

Little Review Anthology, ed. by Margaret Anderson. 1953. Pp. 215-21

Litz, Walton, *James Joyce.* 1966. Pp. 73-76

MacCarthy, Desmond, *Humanities.* 1954. Pp. 88-93

Mac Nicholas, John, "Joyce's 'Exiles': The Argument for Doubt", *James Joyce Quarterly* (1973), 11:33-40

Magalaner, Marvin and Richard M. Kain, *Joyce: The Man, the Work, and the Reputation.* 1956. Pp. 130-45

Maher, R. A., "James Joyce's 'Exiles': The Comedy of Discontinuity", *James Joyce Quarterly* (1972), 9:461-74

Majault, Joseph, *James Joyce.* 1963. Pp. 61

Metzger, Deena P., "Variations on a Theme: A Study of 'Exiles' by James Joyce and 'The Great God Brown' by Eugene O'Neill", *Modern Drama,* 8;174-84, 1965

Moseley, Virginia, *Joyce and the Bible.* 1967. Pp. 45-56

Moseley, Virginia Douglas, "Joyce's 'Exile' and the Prodigal Son", *Modern Drama* (1959), 1:218-27

Nation, 120:272, March 11, 1925

New Statesman, 11:492-93, Sept. 21, 1918 and 26:581-82, Feb. 20, 1926

New Statesman and Nation, 36:602-03, May 27, 1950

O'Brien, Darcy, *The Conscience of James Joyce.* 1967. Pp. 60-64

O Hehir, Diana F., "Ibsen and Joyce; A Study of Three Themes", *Dissertation Abstracts International* (1971), 31:3515A

Outlook (London), 57:170, March 6, 1926

Pound, Ezra, *Pound/Joyce; The Letters of Ezra Pound to James Joyce with Pound's Essays on Joyce,* ed. Forrest Read. 1967. Pp. 49-56

Studies in Bibliography; Papers of the Bibliographical Society of the Univ. of Virginia, ed. by Fredson Bowers, v. 14-17, The Society, 1961-64 , v. 17:83-105

Tindall, William York, *A Reader's Guide to James Joyce.* 1959. Pp. 104-32

Tysdahl, Bjorn, *James Joyce and Ibsen; A Study in Literary Influence.* 1968.
Pp. 87-102

———————— , "Joyce's 'Exiles' and Ibsen", *Orbis Litterarum* (1964), 19:
176-86

Williams, Raymond, "The 'Exiles' of James Joyce", *Politics and Letters*
(Summer 1948), 1:13-21

———————— , *Drama from Ibsen to Brecht.* 1968. Pp. 141-46

Finnegan's Wake, 1952
Theatre Arts, 36:88-89, Sept., 1952

HEINRICH VON KLEIST

Amphitryon, 1899

Crosby, Donad H. and George C. Schoolfield, eds., *Studies in German Drama;
A Festschrift in Honor of Walter Silz.* 1974. Pp. 103-14

Gadamer, Hans-Georg, "Der Gott des Innersten Gefühls", *Neue Rundschau*
(1961), 72:340-49

Henkel, Arthur, "Die Zentrale Szene in Kleists 'Amphitryon'", *Sitzungberichte der Heidelberger Akademie der Wissenschaften. Mathematisch-
Naturwissenschaftliche Klasse* (1968). Pp. 76-77

Hogg, James, ed., *Romantic Reassessment XI.* 1973. Pp. 151-70

Jancke, Gerhard, "Zum Problem des Identischen Selbst in Kleists Lustspiel
'Amphitryon'", *Colloquia Germanica; Internationale Zeitschrift für
Germanische Sprache- und Literaturwissenschaft* (1969), 3:87-110

Jetter, Marianne R., "Some Thoughts on Kleist's 'Amphitryon' and Kaiser's
'Zweimal Amphitryon'", *German Life and Letters* (1960), 13:178-89

Lindsay, J. M., "Figures of Authority in the Works of Heinrich von Kleist",
Forum for Modern Language Studies (1972), 8:107-19

Ludwig, W., "Goethes 'Iphigenie', Kleists 'Amphitryon' und Kierkegaard",
Monatshefte (1947), 39:234-36

Mann, Thomas, *Essays of Three Decades.* 1947. Pp. 202-40

Muller-Seidel, Walter, ed., *Kleist und Frankreich.* 1968. Pp. 27-121

———————— , "Die Vermischung des Komischen mit dem Tragischen
in Kleists Lustspiel 'Amphitryon'", *Jahrbuch der Schiller-Gesellschaft*
(1961), 5:118-35

Nordmeyer, Henry W., "Kleists 'Amphitryon': *Zur Deutung der Komedie*",
(1941), 39:89-125

Plard, Henri, " 'Gottes Ehebruch'? Sur L'Arrière-plan Rélieieux de
'L'Amphitryon' de Kleist", *Etudes Germaniques* (1961), 16:335-74

Sembdner, Helmut, "Kleist und Falk; Zur Entstehungsgeschichte von Kleists
'Amphitryon'", *Jahrbuch der Deutschen Schiller-Gesellschaft* (1969),
13:361-96

Silz, Walter, *Heinrich von Kleist; Studies in His Works and Literary Characters.* 1961. Pp. 45-68

Szarota, E. M., "Antike und Modernes in Kleists 'Amphitryon'", *Kwartalnik
Neofilologiczny* (1961), 8:389-410

Szondi, Peter, "L'Amphitryon' de Kleist, une Comedie d'Apres Moliere",
Revue des Sciences Humaines (1964), #113:37-49

———————— , " 'Amphitryon': Kleists 'Lustspiel nach Moliere'", *Euphorion. Zeitschrift für Literatur Geschichte* (1961), 55:249-59

Thalmann, Marianne, "Das Jupiterspiel in Kleists 'Amphitryon'", *Maske und Kothern* (1963), 9:56-67

Van Stockum, T. C., "Kleists 'Amphitryon' und Rotrous 'Les Sosies'", *Neophilologus* (1950), 34:157-62

The Battle of Arminius, 1839

Burckhart, Sigurd, *The Drama of Language; Essays on Goethe and Kleist.* 1970. Pp. 116-62

Graebel, Frederick, "A Note on the Character of Ventidius in Kleist's Hermannsschlacht'", *Modern Language Forum* (1941), 24:190-91

Mathieu, Gustave, "Kleist's 'Hermannsschlacht': The Portrait of the Artist in Propaganda", *German Life and Letters* n. s. (1953), 7:1-10

Samuel, Richard, "Kleists 'Hermannsschlacht' und der Freiherr vom Stein", *Jahrbuch der Schiller-Gesellschaft* (1961), 5:64-101

Schlosser, Horst D., "Zur Entstehungsgeschichte von Kleists 'Hermannsschlacht'", *Euphorion. Zeitschrift für Literatur Geschichte* (1967), 61:170-74

Sinn, Rolf, "Comical and Humorous Elements in Kleist's 'Die Hermannschlacht'", *Germanic Review* (1972), 47:159-67

The Broken Jug, 1808

Atkins, Stuart, "Some Notes to Kleist's 'Der Zerbrochene Krug'", *Philological Quarterly* (1943), 22:278-83

Delbrück, Hansgerd, "Zur Dramentypologischen Funktion von Sündenfall und Recht-Fertigung in Kleists 'Zerbrochene Krug'", *Deutsche Vierteljahrsschrift für Literaturwissenschaft und Geistesgeschichte* (1971), 45:706-56

Flygt, Sten, "Kleist's Struggle with the Problem of Feeling", *Modern Language Association. Publications* (1943), 58:514-36

Goldammer, Peter, "Variante oder Urfassung? Ein Patriotisches Motiv in Kleists 'Zerbrochene Krug'", *Neue Deutsche Literatur* (1956), 4:115-24

Graham, Ilse A., "'The Broken Pitcher': Hero of Kleist's Comedy", *Modern Language Quarterly* (1955), 16:99-113

Guthke, Karl, "Kleists 'Zerbrochene Krug' und Sartres 'La Putain Respectueuse'", *Die Neueren Sprachen* n. s. (1959), 10:466-70

Koester, Rudolf, "The Ascent of the Criminal in German Comedy", *German Quarterly* (May 1970), 43:376-93

Krumpelmann, John T., "Kleist's 'Krug' and Shakespeare's 'Measure for Measure'", *Germanic Review* (1951), 26:13-21

——————————, "Shakespeare's Falstaff Dramas and Kleist's 'Zerbrochener Krug'", *Modern Language Quarterly* (1951), 12:462-72

Lindsay, J. M., "Figures of Authority in the Works of Heinrich von Kleist", *Forum for Modern Language Studies* (1972), 8:107-19

Martini, Fritz, "Kleists 'Der Zerbrochene Krug': Bauformen des Lustspiels", *Jahrbuch der Deutschen Schiller-Gesellschaft* (1965), 9:373-419

Maveetz, Beth E., "Three Phases of Comedy; A Study of the Archetypal Patterns in 'Leonce und Lena', 'Der Zerbrochene Krug' and 'Die Physiker'", *Dissertation Abstracts International* (1970), 30:3469A

Milfull, John, "Oedipus and Adam: Greek Tragedy and Christian Comedy in Kleist's 'Der Zerbrochene Krug'", *German Life and Letters* (1974), 27:7-17

Nicholls, Roger A., "Kleist's 'Der Zerbrochene Krug', Oedipus and the Comic Tradition", *Theater Annual* (1964), 21:23-28

Russ, Colin, "Human Error in 'Der Zerbrochene Krug': A Typological Approach", *Publications of the English Goethe Society* (1971), 41:65-90

Schmidt, Ernst-Joachim, ed., *Kritische Bewahrung. Beiträge zur Deutschen Philologie. Festschrift für Werner Schröder zum 60. Geburtstag.* 1974. Pp. 434-75

Scholz, A., "Zur Textkritik von Kleists 'Der Zerbrochene Krug'", *Modern Language Notes* (1957), 72:200-02

Schunicht, Manfred, "Heinrich von Kleist: 'Der Zerbrochene Krug'", *Zeitschrift für Deutsche Philologie* (1965), 84:550-62

Steffen, Hans, ed., *Das Deutsche Lustspiel.* 1968. Pp. 166-80

Ulvestad, Bjarne, "A Fairy Tale Motive in Kleist's 'Der Zerbrochene Krug'", *Journal of American Folklore* (1965), 68:290 and 312

Wolff, Hans M., "'Der Zerbrochene Krug' und 'Konig Oidipus'", *Modern Language Notes* (1939), 54:267-72

Zimmerman, H. J., "Noch Einmal: Kleists 'Zerbrochener Krug' und Sartres 'La Putain Respectueuse'", *Die Neueren Sprachen* n. s. (1960), 10:485-88

Cathy from Heilbronn; or, The Trial by Fire, 1810

Crosby, Donald H. and George C. Schoolfield, eds., *Studies in German Drama; A Festschrift in Honor of Walter Silz.* 1974. Pp. 115-23

Hubbs, V. C., "The Plus and Minus of 'Penthesilea' and 'Katchen'", *Seminar. A Journal of Germanic Studies* (1970), 6:187-94

Schwerte, Hans, "Das Katchen von Heilbronn", *Der Deutschunterricht* (1961), 8:5-26

Tymms, Ralph, "Alternation of Personality in the Dramas of Heinrich von Kleist and Zacharias Werner", *Modern Language Review* (1942), 37:64-73

Die Familie Schroffenstein   SEE   The Feud of the Schroffensteins

The Feud of the Schroffensteins, 1804

Flygt, Sten, "Kleist's Struggle with the Problem of Feeling", *Modern Language Association. Publications* (1943), 58:514-36

Hubbs, V. C., "The Concept of Fate in Kleist's 'Schroffenstein'", *Monatshefte* (1964), 56:339-45

Scholl, J. W., "Cave Scenes in 'Die Familie Schroffenstein'", *Modern Philology* (1921), 18:537-43

Seeba, Hinrich, "Des Sündenfall des Verdachts; Identitätskrise und Sprachskepsis in Kleists 'Familie Schroffenstein'", *Deutsche Viertel-Jahrsschrift für Literaturwissenschaft und Geistesgeschichte* (1970), 44:64-100

Die Hermannschlacht   SEE   The Battle of Arminius

Das Kätchen von Heilbronn; oder, Die Feuerprobe   SEE   Cathy from Heilbronn, or, The Trial by Fire

Penthesilea, 1876

Adel, Kurt, "Grillparzer's Hero-Drama and Kleist's 'Penthesilea'", *Jahrbuch der Grillparzer-Gesellschaft* (1967), 7:143-201

Binger, Norman H. and A. Wayne Wonderley, eds., *Studies in 19th Century and Early 20th Century German Literature; Essays in Honor of Paul K. Whitaker.* 1974. Pp. 50-51

Brown, Hilda, "'Penthesilea': Nightingale and Amazon", *Oxford German Studies* (1972/73), 7:24-33

Crosby, Donald H., "Psychological Realism in the Works of Kleist: 'Penthesilea' and 'Die Marquise von O. . . .'", *Literature and Psychology* (1969), 19:3-16

Durzak, Manfred, "Das Gesetz der Athene und das Gesetz der Tanais. Zur Funktion des Mythischen in Kleists 'Penthesilea'", *Jahrbuch des Freien Deutschen Hochstifts* (1973), Pp. 354-70

Dyer, Denys, "The Imagery in Kleist's 'Penthesilea'", *Publications of the English Goethe Society* (1961). 31:1-23

Flygt, Sten, "Kleist's Struggle with the Problem of Feeling", *Modern Language Association. Publications* (1943), 58:514-36

Fricke, Gerhard, "Penthesilea", *Das Deutsche Drama* (1958), 1:363-84

Gray, Ronald, "'Jenseits von Sinn und Unsinn': Kleist's 'Penthesilea' and Its Critics", *Publications of the English Goethe Society* (1967), 37:57-82

Hubbs, V. C., "The Plus and Minus of 'Penthesilea' and 'Katchen'", *Seminar. A Journal of Germanic Studies* (1970), 6:187-94

Kraft, Walter C., ed., *Proceedings; Pacific Northwest Conference on Foreign Languages.* 1974. Pp. 236-41

May, Kurt, *Form und Bedeutung; Interpretationen Deutscher Dichtung des 18. und 19. Jahrhunderts.* 1957. Pp. 243-51

Mersand, Joseph, "Kleist's 'Penthesilea': A Modern Tragic Heroine", *Germanic Review* (1937), 12:233-41

Papu, Edgar, "Heinrich von Kleist: 'Penthesilea'", *Luceäfarul* (March 22, 1969), Pp. 8

St. Leon R., "The Question of Guilt in Kleist's 'Penthesilea'", *Seminar. A Journal of Germanic Studies* (1974), 10:19-37

Salmon, P. B., "'Hellenistic' Diction in Kleist's 'Penthesilea'", *German Life and Letters* (1961), 15:89-99

Streller, Siegfried, "Zur Problematik von Kleists 'Penthesilea'", *Weimarer Beitrage* (1959), Pp. 496-512

Tymms, Ralph, "Alternating Personality in the Dramas of Heinrich von Kleist and Zacharias Werner", *Modern Language Review* (1942), 37:64-73

Whitaker, Paul, "Penthesilea and the Problem of Bad Faith", *Colloquia Germanica; Internationale Zeitschrift für Germanische Sprach- und Literaturwissenschaft* (1972), 6:59-77

Wolff, Hans M., "Der Bruch in Kleists 'Penthesilea'", *Modern Language Notes* (1937), 52:330-38

——————— , "Kleists Amazonenstat im Lichte Rousseaus", *Modern Language Association. Publications* (1938), 53:189-206

Prinz Friedrich von Homburg, 1810

Baumgartel, G., "Zur Frage der Wandlung in Kleists 'Prinz Friedrich von Homburg'", *Germanisch-Romanische Monatsschrift* (1966), 16:264-76

Benson, J. M., "Kleist's 'Prinz Friedrich von Homburg'", *Modern Languages* (1965), 46:98-103

Blankenagel, J. C., "'Prinz Friedrich von Homburg' and Freedom of Initiative", *Modern Language Notes* (1937), 52:339-41

Bruns, F., "Kleists 'Prinz von Homburg': Eine Duplik", *Monatshefte für Deutsche Unterricht* (1941), 33:33-36

Burkholz, Gerhard, "Uber Kleists Stück 'Der Prinz von Homburg'; Eine Interpretation", *Der Deutschunterricht* (1973), 25:31-33

Burckhart, Sigurd, *The Drama of Language; Essays on Goethe and Kleist.* 1970. Pp. 94-100

Chiarini, Paolo, et al, eds., *Miscellanea di Studi in Onore di Bonaventura Tecchi.* 1969. 2 vols. Pp. 349-66

Crosby, Donald H., "Kleist's 'Prince von Homburg': An Intensified Egmont?", *German Life and Letters* (1969), 23:315-22

Flygt, Sten, "Kleist's Struggle with the Problem of Feeling", *Modern Language Association. Publications* (1943), 58:514-36

Frey-Staiger, Eleonore, "Das Problem des Todes bei Kleist"; *Modern Language Notes* (1968), 83:821-47

Garland, Mary, *Kleist's "Prinz Friedrich von Homburg"; An Interpretation Through Word Patterns.* 1968

Gearey, John, "Character and Idea in 'Prinz Friedrich von Homburg'", *Germanic Review* (1967), 42:276-92

Hackert, Fritz, "Kleists 'Prinz Friedrich von Homburg' in der Nachkriegs-Interpretation 1947-1972; Ein Literaturbericht", *LiLi; Zeitschrift für Literaturwissenschaft und Linguistik* (1973), 12:53-80

Henkel, Arthur, "Traum und Gesetz in Kleists 'Prinz von Homburg'", *Neue Rundschau* (1962), 73:438-64

Herd, E. W., "Form and Intention in Kleist's 'Prinz Friedrich von Homburg'", *Seminar. A Journal of Germanic Studies* (1967), 2:1-13

Hohendahl, Peter U., "Der Pass des Grafen Horn: Ein Aspekt des Politischen in 'Prinz Friedrich von Homburg'", *German Quarterly* (1968), 41:167-76

Hubbs, V. C., "Heinrich von Kleist and the Symbol of the Wise Man", *Symposium* (1962), 16:165-79

Kaufmann, F. W., "Kleist und Fichte", *Germanic Review* (1934), 9:1-8

Lindsay, J. M., "Figures of Authority in the Works of Heinrich von Kleist", *Forum for Modern Language Studies* (1972), 8:107-19

Mathieu, G., "The Struggle for a Man's Mind: A Modern View of Kleist's 'Prinz von Homburg'", *German Life and Letters* (1960), 13:169-77

Müller-Seidel, Walter and Wolfgang Preisendanz, ed., *Formenwandel: Festschrift zum 65. Geburtstag von Paul Bockmann.* 1964. Pp. 351-62

———————— , "Prinz Friedrich von Homburg", *Das Deutsche Drama* (1958), 1:385-404

Parker, John J., "A Motif and Certain Peculiarities of Style in Heinrich von Kleist's 'Prinz Friedrich von Homburg'", *Journal of the Australasian Universities Language and Literature Association* (1965), #23:103-110

———————— , "Kleists Schauspiel 'Prinz Friedrich von Homburg': Ein in Jeder Hinsicht Politisches Werk?", *Germanisch-Romanische Monatschrift* (1966), 16:43-52

Politizer, Heinz, "Kleists Trauerspeil von Traum; 'Prinz Friedrich von Homburg'", *Euphorion* (1970), 64:200-20

Salm, Peter, "'Confidence' and the 'Miraculous' in Kleist's 'Prinz Friedrich von Homburg'", *German Quarterly* (1961), 34:238-47

Scholl, Margaret A., "German 'Bildungsroman': Schiller's 'Don Carlos', Goethe's 'Torquato Tasso' and Kleist's 'Prinz Friedrich von Homburg'", *Dissertation Abstracts International* (1973), 34:1934A

Sembdner, Helmut, "Noch Einmal zur Manuskript-Lage Des 'Prinz von Homburg'", *Euphorion. Zeitschrift für Literatur Geschichte* (1967), 61:163-69

Silz, Walter, *Heinrich von Kleist, Studies in His Works and Literary Characters.* 1961. Pp. 199-246

——————————— , "On the Interpretation of Kleist's 'Prinz Friedrich von Homburg'", *Journal of English and Germanic Philology* (1936), 35:500-16

——————————— , "Zur Bühnenkunst in Kleists 'Prinz Friedrich von Homburg'", *Der Deutschunterricht* (1961), 8:72-91

Sinn, R. N., "Die Prästabilierte Harmonie in Heinrich von Kleists 'Prinz von Homburg'", *Modern Language Notes* (1973), 88:1029-34

Studies in German Literature of the 19th and 20th Centuries; Festschrift for Frederic E. Coenen. 1971. Pp. 24-34

Tatar, Marie M., "Psychology and Poetics: J. C. Reil and Kleist's 'Prinz Friedrich von Homburg'", *Germanic Review* (1973), 48:21-34

Thalheim, Hans-Günther, "Kleists 'Prinz Friedrich von Homburg'", *Weimarer Beiträge* (1965), Pp. 483-550

Tymms, Ralph, "Alternation of Personality in the Dramas of Heinrich von Kleist and Zacharias Werner", *Modern Language Review* (1942), 37:64-73

Wiegenstein, Roland H., "Der Widerspruch des 'Prinzen von Homburg'; Zu Zwei Berliner Inszenzierungen", *Merkur. Deutsche Zeitschrift für Europaisches Denken* (1973), 27:63-72

Wittkowski, Wolfgang, "Absolutes Gefuhl und Absolute Kunst in Kleists 'Prinz Friedrich von Homburg'", *Der Deutschunterricht* (1961), 8:72-91

Wolff, Hans M., "Rotrous 'Venceslas' und Kleists 'Prinz Friedrich von Homburg'", *Modern Philology* (1939), 37:201-12

Zucker, A. E., "Biographical Elements in Homburg's Todesfurchtsszene", *Studies in Philology* (1937), 34:564-75

Der Zerbrochene Krug   *SEE*   The Broken Jug

Robert Guiskard, 1808

Kreuzer, Helmut and Käte Hamburger, eds., *Gestaltungsgeschichte und Gesellschaftsgeschichte. Literatur-Kunst-und Musikwissenschaftliche Studien. Fritz Martini zum 60. Geburtstag.* 1969. Pp. 242-64

FREDERICK KNOTT

Dial "M" for Murder, 1952

Catholic World, 176:229, Dec. 1952

Commonweal, 57:164, Nov. 21, 1952

Hobson, L. E., "Harrowing History of 'Dial 'M' for Murder'", *Saturday Review* (Aug. 1, 1953), 36:5

Life, 33:73-76, Nov. 10, 1952

Nathan, George Jean, *Theatre in the Fifties.* 1953. Pp. 136-40

Nation, 175:454, Nov. 15, 1952

New Yorker, 28:86, Nov. 8, 1952

Newsweek, 40:94, Nov. 10, 1952

Saturday Review, 35:30, Nov. 15, 1952

Theatre Arts, 37:22-3, Jan. 1953 and 66:67, June 1953

Time, 60:71, Nov. 10, 1952

Mr. Fox of Venice, 1959

Illustrated London News, 234:720, Apr. 25, 1959

Wait Until Dark, 1961

Kerr, Walter, *Thirty Days Hath November; Pain and Pleasure in the Contemporary Theater.* 1969. Pp. 15-20

Look, 30:112-13, May 17, 1966
Newsweek, 67:88, Feb. 14, 1966
Saturday Review, 49:52-53, Feb. 19, 1966
Time, 87:66, Feb. 11, 1966

Write Me a Murder, 1961
America, 106-375, Dec. 9, 1961
New Yorker, 37:126, Nov. 4, 1961
Newsweek, 58:69, Nov. 6, 1961
Saturday Review, 44:39, Nov. 18, 1961
Theatre Arts, 46:12-13, Jan. 1962
Time, 78:44, Nov. 3, 1961

THOMAS KYD

Cornelia, 1595
Maguin, Jean-Marie, "Of Ghosts and Spirits Walking by Night; A Joint Examination of the Ghost Scenes in Robert Garnier's 'Cornelia', Thomas Kyd's 'Cornelia', and Shakespeare's 'Hamlet' in the Light of Reformation Thinking as Presented in Lavater's Book", *Cahiers Elisabéthans: Etudes sur la Pré-Renaissance et la Renaissance Anglaises* (1972), 1:25-46

The Spanish Tragedy, 1589
Adams, Barry B., "Audiences of 'The Spanish Tragedy' ", *Journal of English and Germanic Philology* (April 1969), 68:221-36
Anderson, M. J., ed., *Classical Drama and Its Influence; Essays Presented to H. D. F. Kitto, B.A., D.-es-L., F.B.A., F.R.S.L., Pro. Emeritus of Greek at the University of Bristol.* 1965. Pp. 121-34
Baker, Howard, "Ghosts and Guides; Kyd's 'Spanish Tragedy' and the Medieval Tragedy", *Modern Philology*, 33:27-35, 1935
―――――――――― , "*Induction to Tragedy; A Study in a Development of Form in 'Gorboduc', 'The Spanish Tragedy', and 'Titus Andronicus'* ". 1965. Pp. 106-53
Bennett, Gilbert, "Conventions of the Stage Villain", *Anglo-Welsh Review* (1963), 13:92-102
Bluestone, Max and Norman Rabkin, eds., *Shakespeare's Contemporaries: Modern Studies in English Renaissance Drama.* 1970. P. 47-73
Bowers, Fredson T., *Elizabethan Revenge Tragedy, 1587-1642.* 1959. Pp. 65-73
Broude, R., "Time, Truth and Right in 'The Spanish Tragedy' ", *Studies in Philology* (April 1971), 68:130-45
Brown, John Russell and Bernard Harris, ed., *Elizabethan Theatre.* (Stratford Upon Avon Studies, #9), 1966. Pp. 59-85
Burrows, Ken C., "The Dramatic and Structural Significance of the Portuguese Sub-Plot in 'The Spanish Tragedy' ", *Renaissance Papers* (1966), Pp. 25-35
Cannon, Charles K., "The Relations of the Additions of 'The Spanish Tragedy' to the Original Play", *Studies in English Literature*, 1500-1900 (1962), 2: 229-39
Carrère, Felix, *Le Théâtre de Thomas Kyd; Contribution à l'Etude du Drame Elizabéthain.* 1951. Pp. 67-80

Chickera, Ernst de, "Divine Justice and Private Revenge in 'The Spanish Tragedy'", *Modern Language Review*, 57:228-32, 1962

Cole, Douglas, *Suffering and Evil in the Plays of Christopher Marlowe*. 1962. Pp. 62-70

Colley, John S., "'The Spanish Tragedy' and the Theatre of God's Judgment", *Papers on Language and Literature* (1974), 10:241-53

Coursen, Herbert R., Jr., "The Unity of 'The Spanish Tragedy'", *Studies in Philology* (1968), 65:768-82

Cunningham, John E., *Elizabethan and Early Stuart Drama*. 1965. Pp. 51-54

The Elizabethan Theatre, V; Papers Given at the 5th International Conference on Elizabethan Theatre Held at the University of Waterloo, Ontario, in July, 1973. 1974. Pp. 112-23

Faber, M. D., and C. Skinner, "Spanish Tragedy", *Philological Quarterly* (Oct. 1970), 49:444-59

Farnham, Willard, *The Medieval Heritage of Elizabethan Tragedy*. 1936. Pp. 391-95

Freeman, Arthur, *Thomas Kyd; Facts and Problems*. 1967. Pp. 80-115

Fuzier, Jean, "Thomas Kyd et l'Ethique du Spectacle Populaire", *Langues Modernes* (1965), 59:43-50

Hamilton, Donna B., "'The Spanish Tragedy': A Speaking Picture", *English Literary Renaissance* (1974), 4:203-17

Hapgood, R., "The Judge in the Firie Tower: Another Virgilian Passage in 'The Spanish Tragedy'", *Notes and Queries* (1966), 13:287-88

Hawkins, Harriett, "Fabulous Counterfeits; Dramatic Construction and Dramatic Perspectives in 'The Spanish Tragedy', 'A Midsummer Night's Dream' and 'The Tempest'", *Shakespeare Studies* (1970), 6:51-65

——————— , *Likenesses of Truth in Elizabethan and Restoration Drama*. 1972. Pp. 27-50

Homan, Sidney R., "The Uses of Silence; The Elizabethan Dumb Show and the Silent Cinema", *Comparative Drama* (Winter 1968-69), 2:213-28

Hosley, Richard, ed., *Essays on Shakespeare and Elizabethan Drama in Honor of Hardin Craig*. 1962. Pp. 23-36

Jacquot, Jean, et als., eds., *Dramaturgie et Société; Rapports entre L'Oeuvre Théâtrale, son Interprétation et son Public aux XVI et XVII Siecles*. 1968. Pp. 589-606, 607-31, and 633-53

Jensen, Ejner J., "Kyd's 'Spanish Tragedy': The Play Explains Itself", *Journal of English and Germanic Philology* (1965), 64:7-16

Kaufmann, Ralph James, *Elizabethan Drama; Modern Essays in Criticism*. 1961. Pp. 60-80

Kistner, A. L. and M. K., "The Senecan Background of Despair in 'The Spanish Tragedy' and 'Titus Andronicus'", *Shakespeare Studies* (Univ. of Cincinnati) (1974), 7:1-10

Kohler, Richard C., "The Dramatic Artistry of Thomas Kyd's 'The Spanish Tragedy': A Study in Context, Meaning and Effect", *Dissertation Abstracts International* (1969), 30:4950A

Kolb, Edward and Jörg Hasler, eds., *Festschrift Rudof Stamm zu Seinem Sechzigsten Geburtstag*. 196. Pp. 163-87

Leggatt, Alexander, "The Three Worlds of 'The Spanish Tragedy'", *Southern Review; An Australian Journal of Literary Studies* (1973), 6:35-47

Levin, H., "Echo from 'The Spanish Tragedy'", *Modern Language Notes*, 64:297-302, 1949

Levin, Michael Henry, " 'Vindicta Mihi!': Meaning, Morality and Motivation in 'The Spanish Tragedy' ", *Studies in English Literature, 1500-1900* (Rice Univ.), 4:307-24, 1964

McMillin, Scott, "Book of Seneca in 'The Spanish Tragedy' ", *Studies in English Literature, 1500-1900* (1974), 14:201-08

────────────── , "The Figure of Silence in 'The Spanish Tragedy' ", *Journal of English Literary History* (1972), 39:27-48

Mehl, Dieter, *The Elizabethan Dumb Show*. 1966. Pp. 63-71

Price, Hereward T., " 'Titus Andronicus' and the Additions to 'The Spanish Tragedy' ", *Notes and Queries*, 9:331, 1962

Prior, Moody Erasmus, *The Language of Tragedy*. 1947. Pp. 46-59

Ratliff, John D., "Hieronimo Explains Himself", *Studies in Philology* (1957), 54:112-18

Renaissance Drama; Essays Principally on Comedy, ed. by S. Schoenbaum and Alan C. Dessen. 1972. Pp. 89-121

Ricks, Christopher, ed., *English Drama to 1710*. (History of Literature in the English Language, vol. 3). 1971. Pp. 217-26

Ross, Thomas W., "Kyd's 'The Spanish Tragedy': A Bibliographical Hypothesis", *Bulletin of the Rocky Mountain Modern Language Association* (1968), 22 pt. 2:13-21

Talbert, Ernest William, *English Drama and Shakespeare's Early Plays; An Essay in Historical Criticism*. 1963. Pp. 62-64, 72-79 and 133-40

Tomlinson, Thomas Brian, *A Study of Elizabethan and Jacobean Tragedy*. 1964. Pp. 73-85

Willbern, David P., "The Elizabethan Revenge Play; A Psychoanalytic Inquiry", *Dissertation Abstracts International* (1973), 34:1261A

────────────── , "Thomas Kyd's 'The Spanish Tragedy': Inverted Vengeance", *American Imago* (Fall 1971), 28:247-67

Wittig, Kurt, *Strena Anglica; Otto Ritter zum 80. Geburtstag*. 1956. Pp. 133-77

Woodard, Lawrence E., "A Study of the Argumentation Used in Four Selected Elizabethan Plays: 'Julius Caesar', 'Volpone', 'Dr. Faustus', and 'The Spanish Tragedy' ", *Dissertation Abstracts International* (1974), 35: 3935A

LADY GREGORY

SEE

WILLIAM BUTLER YEATS

PÄR FABIAN LAGERKVIST

Barrabas, 1953
  Beijer, Agne, "Two Swedish Dramatists", *World Theatre* (Spring 1955), 4:14-24

Bödeln *SEE* The Hangman

L'Etre Invisible *SEE* The Invisible One

Han Som Fick Leva Oun Sitt Liv *SEE* The Man Who Was Given Life to Live Over Again

The Hangman, 1933
  Benson, Adolph B., "Pär Lagerkvist: Nobel Laureate", *English Journal* (1952), 41:231-38
  Hannevik, Arne, "Pär Lagerkvists Drama 'Bödeln' ", *Edda* (1964), 51:1-17
  Johannesson, Eric O., "Pär Lagerkvist and the Art of Rebellion", *Scandinavian Studies* (1958), 30:19-29
  Paulson, A., " 'The Hangman': Criticism", *Theatre Arts* (March 1935), 19:191-95
  Weathers, Winston, *Pär Lagerkvist: A Critical Essay*. 1968. Pp. 10-18
  Spectator, 155:718, Nov. 1, 1935

Himlens Hemlighet *SEE* The Secret of Heaven

The Invisible One, 1923
  Beijer, Agne, "Two Swedish Dramatists", *World Theatre* (Spring 1955), 4:14-24
  Mjöberg, Joran, "Pär Lagerkvist and the Ancient Greek Drama", *Scandinavian Studies* (1953), 25:46-51

The King, 1932
  Ahlenius, Holger, "The Dramatic Works of Pär Lagerkvist", *American-Scandinavian Review* (1940), 28:301-08
  Mjöberg, Joran, "Pär Lagerkvist and the Ancient Greek Drama", *Scandinavian Studies* (1953), 25:46-51
  Weathers, Winston, *Pär Lagerkvist; A Critical Essay*. 1968. Pp. 10-18

The Last Man, 1917
  Ahlenius, Holger, "The Dramatic Works of Pär Lagerkvist", *American-Scandinavian Review* (1940), 28:301-08
  Björklof, Eva. "Lagerkvists 'Sista Mänskan' och Verkligheten", *Nordisk Tidskrift* (1968), 44:475-76
  Mjöberg, Joran, "Pär Lagerkvist and the Ancient Greek Drama", *Scandinavian Studies* (1953), 25:46-51
  Rovinsky, Robert T., "Pär Lagerkvist's Development as a Dramatist; A Study in Theory and Practice", *Dissertation Abstracts International* (1972), 33:2342A

Låt Manniskan Leva *SEE* Let Man Live

Let Man Live, 1949
  Spector, Robert Donald, "The Limbo World of Pär Lagerkvist", *American-Scandinavian Review* (1955), 43:271-74

Livet, 1911
  Rovinsky, Robert T., "Pär Lagerkvist's Development as a Dramatist; A Study in Theory and Practice", *Dissertation Abstracts International* (1972), 33:2342A
  _____ , "The Path to Self-Realization; An Analysis of Lagerkvist's 'Livet' ", *Scandinavian Studies* (1973), 45:107-27

The Man Who Was Given His Life to Live Again, 1928
  Beijer, Agne, "Two Swedish Dramatists", *World Theatre* (Spring 1955), 4:14-24
  Mjöberg, Joran, "Pär Lagerkvist and the Ancient Greek Drama", *Scandinavian Studies* (1953), 25:46-51

The Man Without a Soul, 1936
  Beijer, Agne, "Two Swedish Dramatists", *World Theatre* (Spring 1955), 4:14-24
  Spector, Robert Donald, "The Limbo World of Pär Lagerkvist", *American-Scandinavian Review* (1955), 43:271-74

Mannen Utan Själ   *SEE*   The Man Without a Soul

Midsommardröm i Fattighuset   *SEE*   Midsummer Night's Dream in the Workhouse

Midsummer Night's Dream in the Workhouse, 1941
  Beijer, Agne, "Two Swedish Dramatists", *World Theatre* (Spring 1955), 4:14-24

Den Osynlige   *SEE*   The Invisible One

The Philosopher's Stone, 1947
  Beijer, Agne, "Two Swedish Dramatists", *World Theatre* (Spring 1955), 4:14-24

The Secret of Heaven, 1919
  Benson, Adolph B., "Pär Lagerkvist: Nobel Laureate", *English Journal* (1952), 41:231-38
  Weathers, Winston, *Pär Lagerkvist; A Critical Essay.* 1968. Pp. 10-18
  Sprinchorn, Evert, ed., *The Genius of the Scandinavian Theater.* 1964. Pp. 428-35

Sista Mänskan   *SEE*   The Last Man

Den Svåra Stunden   *SEE*   The Trying Hour

The Trying Hour, 1918
  Benson, Adolph B., "Pär Lagerkvist: Nobel Laureate", *English Journal* (1952), 41:231-38

Den Vises Sten   *SEE*   The Philosopher's Stone

DAVID HERBERT LAWRENCE

A Collier's Friday Night, 1906
  Sagar, Keith, "D. H. Lawrence: Dramatist", *D. H. Lawrence Review* (Summer 1971), 4:154-82
  Williams, Raymond, *Drama from Ibsen to Brecht.* 1958. Pp. 257-59

The Daughter-in-Law, 1912
  Sagar, Keith, "D. H. Lawrence: Dramatist", *D. H. Lawrence Review* (Summer 1971), 4:154-82

David, 1927
  Christian Century, 75:511, April 23, 1958
  Jennings, R., "David", *Spectator*, 138:939-40, Mary 28, 1927
  Nation (London), 41:261, Mary 28, 1927
  Panichas, George A., "D. H. Lawrence's Biblical Play 'David'", *Modern Drama*, 6:164-76, 1963

Merry-Go-Round, 1912
  Davies R., "Merry-Go-Round", *Plays and Players* (1974), 21:50-52
  Lambert, J. W., "Merry-Go-Round", *Drama* (1973), 111:26-28

Touch and Go, 1920
  Lowell, Amy, *Poetry and Poets; Essays.* 1930. Pp. 175-86

The Widowing of Mrs. Holroyd, 1920
  Brown, I., "The Widowing of Mrs. Holroyd", *Saturday Review*, 142:767,
    Dec. 18, 1926
  Delavenay, Emile, *D. H. Lawrence; The Man and His Work; The Formative
    Years, 1885-1919.* 1972. Pp. 107-09
  MacCarthy, Desmond, "The Widowing of Mrs. Holroyd", *New Statesman*,
    28:310, Dec. 18, 1926
  Outlook (London), 28:629, Dec. 24, 1926
  Sagar, Keith, "D. H. Lawrence: Dramatist", *D. H. Lawrence Review* (Sum-
    mer 1971), 4:154-82
  Shipp, H., "The Widowing of Mrs. Holroyd", *English Review*, 44:120-21,
    Jan., 1927
  Williams, Raymond, *Drama from Ibsen to Brecht.* Pp. 258-60

D. H. LAWRENCE AND WALTER GREENWOOD

My Son's My Son, 1936
  London Mercury, 34:249-50, July, 1936

NATHANIEL LEE

Lucius Junius Brutus, 1680
  Skrine, Peter N., "Blood, Bombast and Deaf Gods; The Tragedies of Lee
    and Lohenstein", *German Life and Letters* (Oct. 1970), 24:14-30

The Rival Queens; or, The Death of Alexander the Great, 1677
  Waith, Eugene M. *Ideas of Greatness; Heroic Drama in England.* 1971.
    Pp. 239-41

Sophonisba; or, Hannibal's Overthrow, 1675
  Skrine, Peter N., "Blood, Bombast and Deaf Gods; The Tragedies of Lee and
    Lohenstein", *German Life and Letters* (Oct. 1970), 24:14-30
  Waith, Eugene, *Ideas of Greatness; Heroic Drama in England.* 1971. Pp.
    236-39

Tragedy of Nero, Emperior of Rome, 1674
  Skrine, Peter N., "Blood, Bombast and Deaf Gods; The Tragedies of Lee
    and Lohenstein", *German Life and Letters* (Oct. 1970), 24:14-30

ERNEST LEGOUVE

SEE

AUGUSTIN EUGENE SCRIBE AND ERNEST LEGOUVE

GOTTHOLD EPHRAIM LESSING

Emilia Galotti, 1772
  Angress, R. K., "The Generations in 'Emilia Galotti'", *Germanic Review*
    (1968), 43:15-23

Bauer, Gerhard and Sibylle, eds., *Gotthold Ephraim Lessing.* 1968. Pp. 214-44 and 362-75

Bostock, J. K., "Death of Emilia Galotti", *Modern Language Review*, 46:69-71, 1951

Brown, F. Andrew, *Gotthold Ephraim Lessing.* 1971. Pp. 114-30

Cowen, Roy C., "On the Dictates of Logic in Lessing's 'Emilia Galotti' ", *German Quarterly* (1969), 42:11-20

DeLaura, David, ed., *Victorian Prose; A Guide to Research.* 1973. Pp. 279-94

Desch, Joachim, "Emilia Galotti—A Victim of Misconceived Morality", *Trivium* (1974), 9:88-99

Diamond, W., "Does Emilia Love the Prince?", *Modern Philology*, 19:199-209, 1921

Durzak, Manfred, "Das Gesellschaftsbild in Lessing's 'Emilia Galotti' ", *Lessing Yearbook* (1969), 1:60-87

Dvoretzky, Edward, *The Engima of 'Emilia Galotti'.* 1963.

——————, "Modern German Writers; View of Lessing's 'Emilia Galotti' ", *The South Central Bulletin* (Tulsa, Okla., Studies by Members of the South Central MLA), 23:51-59, 1963

Feise, E., "Lessings 'Emilia Galotti' und Goethes 'Werther' ", *Modern Philology*, 15:321-38, 1917

Gerber, Richard, "Von Geheimnis der Namen; Eine Onomastische Studie uber Lessings Dramatische Werke", *Die Neue Rundschau* (1965), 76:573-86

Graham, Illse Appelbaum, "Minds Without Medium; Reflections on 'Emilia Galotti' and 'Werthers Leiden' ", *Euphorion* (Heidelberg), 56:3-24, 1962

Hatfield, M., "Emilia's Guilt Once More", *Modern Language Notes*, 71:287-96, 1956

Heitner, R. R., " 'Emilia Galotti': An Indictment of Bourgeois Passivity", *Journal of English and Germanic Philology*, 52:480-90, 1953

——————, "Lessing's Manipulation of a Single Comic Theme", *Modern Language Quarterly*, 18:183-98, 1957

Ittner, R. T., " 'Werther' and 'Emilia Galotti' ", *Journal of English and Germanic Philology*, 41:418-26, 1942

Kahn, Robert L., ed., *Studies in German; In Memory of Andrew Lewis.* 1969. Pp. 9-32

Kaufmann, F. W., "Zu Lessings 'Emilia Galotti' ", *Monatshefte für Deutsche Unterricht*, 27:50-53, 1935

Kraft, Werner, "Emilia Galotti", *Neue Rundschau*, 72:198-232, 1961

Labroisse, Gerd, "Emilia Galottis Wollen und Sollen", *Neophilologus* (1972), 56:311-23

Muller, Klaus-Detlef, "Das Erbe der Komödie im Burgerlichen Trauerspiel— Lessings 'Emilia Galotti' und die Comedia dell'arte", *Deutsche Viertel-jahrsschrift für Literaturwissenschaft und Geistesgeschichte* (1972), 46:28-60

Muller-Seidel, Walter; Hans Fromm; and Karl Richter, eds., *Historizität in Sprach und Literaturwissenschaft; Vorträge und Berichte der Stuttgarter Germanistentagung 1972.* 1974. Pp. 259-75

Nolte, Fred O., "Lessing and the Bourgeois Drama", *Journal of English and Germanic Philology*, 31:66-83, 1932

——————, "Lessing's 'Emilia Galotti' in the Light of his Hamburgische Dramaturgie", *Harvard Studies and Notes in Philology and Literature*, 19:175-97, 1937

Rieck, Werner, "Lessings 'Emilia Galotti': Versuch einer Analyse", *Wissenschaftliche Zeitschrift der Padagogischen Hochschule Potsdam. Gesellschafts-u. Sprachwissenschaftliche Reihe* (1967), 11:121-28
Ryder, Frank G., "Emilia Galotti", *German Quarterly* (1972), 45:329-47
Schneider, H., "Emilia Galotti's Tragic Guilt", *Modern Language Notes*, 71:353-55, 1956
Schröder, Jürgen, *Gotthold Ephraim Lessing; Sprache und Drama.* 1972. Pp. 189-221
Stahl, Ernest L., "Emilia Galotti", *Das Deutsche Drama*, 1:101-12, 1958
Steinhauer, H., "The Guilt of Emilia Galotti", *Journal of English and Germanic Philology*, 48:173-85, 1949
Stockert, Franz von, "'Emilia Galotti': Ein Beitrage zu Lessings Theorie und Praxis der Tragodie", *Meddelelser fra Gymnasieskolernes Tyskloererforening* (May 1972), 47:57-71
Weigand, H. J., "Warum Stirbt Emilia Galotti?", *Journal of English and Germanic Philology*, 28:467-81, 1929
Wessell, Leonard P., Jr., "The Function of Odoardo in Lessing's 'Emilia Galotti'", *Germanic Review* (1972), 47:243-58
Wierlacher, Alois, "Das Haus der Frende oder Warum Stirbt Emilia Galotti?", *Lessing Yearbook* (1973), 5:147-62
_____ , "Zum Gebrauch der Begriffe 'Burger' et 'Bürgerlich' bei Lessing", *Neophilologus* (1967), 51:147-56

The Freethinker, 1767
Benseler, Frank, ed., *Festschrift zum Achtzigsten Geburtstag von Geary Lukacs.* 1965. Pp. 374-91
Brown, F. A., "Conversion of Lessing's 'Freigeist'", *Journal of English and Germanic Philology*, 56:186-202, 1957
Heitner, R. R., "Lessing's Manipulation of a Single Comic Theme", *Modern Language Quarterly*, 18:183-98, 1957
Kies, Paul P., "Lessing's Relation to Early English Sentimental Comedy", *Modern Language Association. Publications* (PMLA), 47:807-26, 1932
Moser, Hugh; Rudolf Schützeichel and Karl Stackmann, eds., *Festschrift Josef Quint Anlässlich Seines 65. Geburtstages Überreicht.* 1964. Pp. 83-120

Der Freigeist *SEE* The Freethinker

The Jews, 1775
Dunkle, Harvey, J., "Lessing's 'Die Juden'; An Original Experiment", *Monatshefte*, 49:323-29, 1957
Heitner, Robert R., "Lessing's Manipulation of a Single Comic Theme", *Modern Language Quarterly*, 18:183-98, 1957
Kies, Paul P., "Lessing's Relation to Early English Sentimental Comedy", *Modern Language Association. Publications* (PMLA), 47:807-26, 1932
_____ , "The Sources of Lessing's 'Die Juden'", *Philological Quarterly*, 6:406-10, 1927

Die Juden *SEE* The Jews

Der Junge Gelehrte *SEE* The Young Scholar

Die Matrone von Ephesus, n. d.
Stockum, Th. C. van, "Lessings Dramenentwurf 'Die Matrone von Ephesus'", *Neophilologus*, 46:125-34, 1962

Minna von Barnhelm; or, Das Soldatenglück *SEE* Minna von Barnhelm; or, The Soldier's Fortune

Minna von Barnhelm; or, The Soldier's Fortune, 1767
Bauer, Gerhard and Sibylle, eds., *Gotthold Ephraim Lessing*. 1968. Pp. 376-447
Brewer, Edward V., "Lessing and 'The Corrective Virtue in Comedy' ", *Journal of English and Germanic Philology*, 26:1-23, 1927
Brown, F. Andrew, *Gotthold Ephraim Lessing*. 1971. Pp. 92-102
Cohn, Hilde D., "Die Beiden Schwierigen im Deutschen Lustspiel: Lessing, 'Minna von Barnhelm'—Hofmannsthal, 'Der Swierige' ", *Monatshefte*, 44:257-69, 1952
Colleville, Maurice, ed., *Un Dialogue des Nations: Albert Fuchs zum 70. Geburtstag*. 1967. Pp. 21-31
Duncan, Bruce, "Hand, Heart, and Language in 'Minna von Barnhelm' ", *Seminar. A Journal of Germanic Studies* (1972), 8:15-30
Fricke, Gerhard, *Studien und Interpretationen: Ausgewählte Schriften zur Deutschen Dichtung*. 1956. Pp. 25-46
Gerber, Richard, "Von Geheimnis der Namen; Eine Onomastische Studie über Lessings Dramatische Werke", *Die Neue Rundschau* (1965), 76:573-86
Graham, Ilse Appelbaum, "The Currency of Love; A Reading of Lessing's 'Minna von Barnhelm' ", *German Life and Letters*, 18:270-78, 1965
Kaufman, F. W., "Lessings 'Minna von Barnhelm' ", *Monatshefte für Deutsche Unterricht*, 24:136-40, 1932
Lukács, George, "Lessing's 'Minna von Barnhelm' ", *International Social Science Journal* (1967), 19:570-80
_____ , "Minna von Barnhelm", *Belfagor*, 19:501-16, 1964
Mann, Otto, "Minna von Barnhelm", *Das Deutsche Drama*, 1:79-100, 1958
Michelsen, Peter, "Die Verbergung der Kunst; Über die Exposition in Lessings 'Minna von Barnhelm' ", *Jahrbuch der Deutschen Schiller-Gesellschaft* (1973), 17:192-252
Möckel, Manfred, "Über Theaterarbeit an Klassikern; Was Interessiert Junge Zuschauer an 'Minna von Barnhelm' ", *Weimarer Beiträge* (1972), 18:121-41
Müller-Seidel, Walter and Preisendanz, Wolfgang, eds., *Formenwandel: Festschrift zum 65. Geburtstag von Paul Böckmann*. 1964. Pp. 193-235
Nagel, Bert, " 'Ein Unerreichbares Muster'; Lessings 'Minna von Barnhelm' ", *Heidelberger Jahrbucher* (1973), 17:47-85
Schröeder, Jürgan, "Das Parabolische Geschehen der 'Minna von Barnhelm' ", *Deutsche Vierteljahrsschrift für Literaturwissenschaft und Geistesgeschichte* (1969), 43:222-59 ·
_____ , *Gotthold Ephraim Lessing; Sprach und Drama*. 1972. Pp. 222-46
_____ , " 'Minna von Barnhelm': Asthetische Struktur und 'Sprache des Herzens' ", *Lessing Yearbook* (1971), 3:84-107
Schwann, Werner, "Justs Streit mit dem Wirt; Zur Frage des Lustspielbeginns und der Exposition in Lessings 'Minna von Barnhelm' ", *Jahrbuch der Deutschen Schiller-Gesellschaft* (1968), 12:170-93
Steffen, Hars, ed., *Das Deutsche Lustspiel*. I. 1968. Pp. 27-47
Thalheim, Hans-Gunther and Ursula Werthem, eds., *Studien zur Literaturgeschichte und Literaturtheorie. Gerhard Scholz Anlässlich Seines 65. Geburtstages Gewidmet von Seinen Schülern und Freunded*. 1970. Pp. 10-57

Ulmer, Bernhard, "The Leitmotiv and Musical Structure in Lessing's Dramas", *Germanic Review*, 22:13-31, 1947

Waldeck, Peter B., "Lessing's 'Minna von Barnhelm' and Plautus' 'Amphitruo'", *Orbis Litterarum* (1969), 24:16-34

Wessell, Leonhard P., Jr., and Charles M. Barrack, "The Tragic Background to Lessing's Comedy 'Minna von Barnhelm'", *Lessing Yearbook* (1970), 2:149-61

Zinnecker, W. D., "Lessing the Dramatist", *German Quarterly*, 2:48-53, 1929

Miss Sara Sampson, 1755

Bornkamm, Heinrich, "Die Innere Handlung in Lessings 'Miss Sara Sampson'", *Euphorion* (Heidelberg), 41:385-96, 1958

Brown, F. Andrew, "Sara Sampson; The Dilemma of Love", *Lessing Yearbook* (1970), 2:135-48

Durzak, Manfred, "Äussere und Innere Handlung in 'Miss Sara Sampson': Zur Ästhetischen Geschlossenheit von Lessings Trauerspiel", *Deutsche Vierteljahrsschrift für Literaturwissenschaft und Geistesgeschichte* (1970), 44:47-63

Gerger, Richard, "Von Geheimnis der Namen; Eine Onomastische Studie uber Lessings Dramatische Werke", *Die Neue Rundschau* (1965), 76:573-86

Heitner, Robert R., "Lessing's Manipulation of a Single Comic Theme", *Modern Language Quarterly*, 18:183-98, 1957

Ingen, Ferdinand van, "Tugend bei Lessing; Bemerkungen zu 'Miss Sara Sampson'", *Amsterdamer Beitrage zur Neueren Germanistik* (1972), 1:43-73

Kahn, Robert L., ed., *Studies in German; In Memory of Andrew Lewis.* 1969. Pp. 9-32

Kies, Paul P., "Lessing and English Domestic Tragedy", *Research Studies of the State College of Washington*, 2:130-47, 1931

Labroisse, Gerd, "Zum Gestaltungsprinzip von Lessings 'Miss Sara Sampson'", *Amsterdamer Beitrage zur Neueren Germanistik* (1972), 1:75-102

Moser, Hugo; Schützeichel, Rudolf and Stackmann, Karl, eds., *Festschrift Josef Quint Anlässlich Seines 65. Geburtstages Überreicht.* 1964. Pp. 83-120

Nolte, Fred O., "Lessing and the Bourgeois Drama", *Journal of English and Germanic Philology*, 31:66-83, 1932

Schröder, Jürgen, *Gotthold Ephraim Lessing; Sprache und Drama.* 1972. Pp. 162-88

Scott, Alison, "The Rôle of Mellefont in Lessing's 'Miss Sara Sampson'", *German Quarterly* (1974), 47:394-408

Sommer, D., "Die Gesellschaftliche Problematik in Lessings Burgerlichen Trauerspiel 'Miss Sara Sampson'", *Zeitschrift Wissenschaftliche der Martin Luther Universität* (1961), 10:959-64

Ziolkowski, T., "Language and Mimetic Action in Lessing's 'Miss Sara Sampson'", *Germanic Review*, 40:261-76, 1965

Nathan der Weise   *SEE*   Nathan the Wise

Nathan the Wise, 1783

Adolf, Helen, "Wesen und Art des Rings: Lessings Parabel, Nach Mittelalterlichen Quellen Gedeutet", *German Quarterly*, 34:228-34, 1961

Angress, R. K., "'Dreams That Were More Than Dreams' in Lessing's 'Nathan'", *Lessing Yearbook* (1971), 3:108-27

Atkins, Stuart, "The Parable of the Pimp in Lessing's 'Nathan der Weise'", *Germanic Review* (1951), 26:259-67

Batley, E. M., "Lessing's 'Nathan der Weise': Transcending Reason in Dramatic Motivation", *Publications of the English Goethe Society* (1972), 42:1-36

Bauer, Gerhard and Sibylle, eds., *Gotthold Ephraim Lessing*. 1968. Pp. 74-82 and 302-11

Bohler, Michael J., "Lessings 'Nathan der Weise' als Spiel vom Grunde", *Lessing Yearbook* (1971), 3:128-50

Bradfield, T., "Lessing's Story of the Three Rings", *Westminster Review*, 144:666-69, Dec., 1895

Brown, F. Andrew, *Gotthold Ephraim Lessing*. 1971. Pp. 151-61

Buehne, Sheema Z., James L. Hodge, and Lucille B. Pinto, eds., *Helen Adolf Festschrift*. 1968. Pp. 166-86

Buschmann, Wolfgang, "Betrachtungen zur Struckturproblematik von Lessings Dramatischen Gedicht 'Nathan der Weise'", *Wissenschaftliche Zeitschrift der Padogogischen Hochschule Potsdam. Gesellschats-u. Sprachwissenschaftliche Reihe.* (1968). 12:723-38

Carruth, W. H., "Lessing's Treatment of the Story of the Ring and its Teaching", *Modern Language Association. Publications* (PMLA), 16:107-16, 1901

Catholic World, 155:214-15, May, 1942

Commonweal, 35:647-48, April 17, 1942

Daemmrich, Horst S., "The Incest Motif in Lessing's 'Nathan der Weise' and Schiller's 'Braut von Messina'", *Germanic Review* (1967), 42:184-96

Deering, R. W., "Nathan the Wise: A Critical Study", *Chautauguan*, 34:519-28, Feb., 1902

Diekhoff, T., "Lessing's Boastfulness of 'Good Works'", *Monatshefte für Deutsche Unterricht*, 23:65-71, 1931

Fischer, Uve, "La Storia Dei Tre Anelli: Dal Mito all'Utopia", *Annali della Scuola Normale Superiore di Pisa* (1973), n. s. 3:955-98

Flajole, Edward S., "Lessing's Retrieval of Lost Truths", *Modern Language Association. Publications* (PMLA), 74:52-66, 1959

Friedrich, Wolf-Hartmut, "Menander Redivivus; Zur Wiedererkennung im 'Nathan'", *Euphorion* (1970), 64:167-80

Fuller, Edmund, *A Pageant of the Theatre*. 1965. Pp. 177-201

Fuchs, Heinz Ph., "Eine Klasse der Berufsaufbauschule Erarbertet und Erlebt Lessings 'Nathan'", *Die Berufsbildende Schule* (1963), 15:299-302

Gruener, G., "Genesis of the Characters in Lessing's 'Nathan der Weise'", *Modern Language Association. Publications* (PMLA), 7:75-88, 1892

Heitner, Robert R., "Lessing's Manipulation of a Single Comic Theme", *Modern Language Quarterly*, 18:183-98, 1957

Kaufmann, F. W., "Nathan's Crisis", *Monatshefte*, 48:277-80, 1956

Lenz, Harold, "Der Deutschlehrer und Lessings 'Nathan'", *German Quarterly*, 14:121-27 and 170-75, 1941

Ley-Piscator, Maria, *The Piscator Experiment: The Political Theatre*. 1967. Pp. 169-71

Martin, Bernhard, "Lessings Parabel von den Drei Ringen", *Schau* (1963), 24:243-47

Maurer, Warren R., "The Integration of the Ring Parable in Lessing's 'Nathan der Weise' ", *Monatshefte*, 54:49-57, 1962

Mordaunt, Jerreol L., ed., *Proceedings. Pacific Northwest Conference on Foreign Languages. Nineteenth Annual Meeting, April 19 and 20, 1968.* 1968. Pp. 81-85

Müller, Joachim, "Zur Dialogstruktur und Sprachfiguration in Lessings 'Nathan'-Drama", *Sprachkunst. Beitrage zur Literaturwissenschaft* (1970), 1:42-69

Nathan, George Jean, *Theatre Book of the Year, 1943-44*, Pp. 248

New Yorker, 13:31, April 11, 1942

Newsweek, 19:68, April 13, 1942

Politzer, Heinsz, "Das Paradoxe in der Parabel: Untersucht am Beispiel von Lessings Ringerzählung," *Forum*, 5:453-55, 1958

Primer, S., "Lessing's Religious Development with Special Reference to his 'Nathan the Wise' ", *Modern Language Association. Publications (PMLA)*, 8:335-79, 1893

Roedder, Edwin, "Lessings 'Nathan der Weise' auf der Englischen Bühne", *Monatshefte für Deutsche Unterricht*, 34:235-40, 1942

Rohrmoser, Günter, "Nathan der Weise", *Das Deutsche Drama*, 1:113-26, 1958

Schimpfke, Gerhard, " 'Nathan der Weise': Ein Parabelstück. Gedanken zum Strukturprinzip des Werkes", *Deutschunterricht* (1970), 23:695-706

Schmitt, Albert R., ed., *Festschrift für Detlev W. Schumann zum 70. Geburtstag.* 1970. Pp. 89-96

Schröder, Jürgen, *Gotthold Ephraim Lessing; Sprache und Drama.* 1972. Pp. 247-67

Schweitzer, Christoph E., "Die Erziehung Nathans", *Monatshefte*, 53:277-84, 1961

Spann, Meno, "Wie? Auf Nathan Argwohn?" *German Quarterly*, 14:211-16, 1941

Theatre Arts, 26:290-91, May, 1942

Thomas, Werner, "Opus Supererogatum: Didaktische Skizze zur Interpretation von Lessings 'Nathan der Weise' ", *Der Deutschunterricht*, 11:41-70, 1959

Time, 39:57, April 13, 1942

Ulmer, Bernhard, "The Leitmotiv and Musical Structure in Lessing's Dramas", *Germanic Review*, 22:13-31, 1947

Wernsing, Armin V., "Nathan der Spieler; Über den Sinn vom Spiel in Lessings 'Nathan der Weise' ", *Wirkendes Work* (1970), 20:52-59

Wirtz, Erika A., "Lessing's Religion and 'Nathan der Weise' ", *Modern Languages* (1968), 49:62-67

Zinnecker, W. D., "Lessing the Dramatist", *German Quarterly*, 2:48-53, 1929

Zitzmann, Rudolf, "Zur Interpretation von Lessings Dramatischem Gedicht 'Nathan der Weise' im Unterricht der Höheren Schule", *Wort, Wirkendes. Deutsches Sprachschaften in Lehre und Leben* (1963), 13:229-39

Philotas, 1780

Bauer, Gerhard and Sibylle, eds., *Gotthold Ephraim Lessing.* 196. Pp. 196-213

Hofacker, Erich and Dieckmann, Liselotte, eds., *Studies in Germanic Languages and Literatures; In Memory of Fred O. Nolte*. 1963. Pp. 35-42

Kahn, Robert L., ed., *Studies in German; In Memory of Andrew Lewis*. 1969. Pp. 9-32

Wiedamann, Conrad, "Ein Schones Ungeheuer; Zur Deutung von Lessings Einakter 'Philotas'", *Germanisch-Romanische Monatsschrift* (1967), 17:381-97

Der Schatz   *SEE*   The Treasure

The Treasure, 1749

Heitner, Robert R., "Lessing's Manipulation of a Single Comic Theme", *Modern Language Quarterly*, 18:183-98, 1957

The Young Scholar, 1748

Borden, Charles E., *The Original Model for Lessing's 'Der Junge Gelehrte'*. 36:#3. Pp. 113-27, 1952

Ulmer, Bernhard, "The Leitmotiv and Musical Structure in Lessing's Dramas", *Germanic Review*, 22:13-31, 1947

JOHN LYLY

Alexander, Campaspe, and Diogenes, 1584

Bevington, David M., "John Lyly and Queen Elizabeth; Royal Flattery in 'Campaspe' and 'Sapho and Phao'", *Renaissance Papers* (1966), Pp. 37-67

Bluestone, Max and Norman Rabkin, eds., *Shakespeare's Contemporaries; Modern Studies in English Renaissance Drama*. 2nd ed. 1970. Pp. 12-22

Mustard, W. P., "Agrippa's Shadows in Lyly's 'Campaspe'", *Modern Language Notes*, 43:325, 1928

Saccio, Peter, *The Court Comedies of John Lyly; A Study in Allegorical Dramaturgy*. 1969. Pp. 26-94

Turner, Robert Y., "Some Dialogues of Love in Lyly's Comedies", *Journal of English Literary History* (ELH), 29:276-88, 1962

Whiting, G. W., "Canary Wine and 'Campaspe'", *Modern Language Notes*, 45:148-51, 1930

Endimion, the Man in the Moon, 1586

Bennett, Josephine W., "Oxford and 'Endimion'", *Modern Language Association. Publications* (PMLA), 57:354-69, 1942

Bluestone, Max and Norman Rabkin, eds., *Shakespeare's Contemporaries; Modern Studies in English Renaissance Drama*. 2nd ed. 1970. Pp. 12-22

Bond, S., "John Lyly's 'Endimion'", *Studies in English Literature, 1500-1900* (1974), 14:189-99

Boughner, Daniel C., "The Background of Lyly's Tophas", *Modern Language Association. Publications* (PMLA), 54:967-73, 1939

Braendel, Doris B., "The Limits of Clarity: Lyly's 'Endimion', Bronzino's 'Allegory of Venus and Cupid', Webster's 'White Devil', and Botticelli's 'Primavera'", *Hartford Studies in Literature* (1972), 4:197-215

Bryant, J. A., Jr., "The Nature of the Allegory in Lyly's 'Endimion'", *Renaissance Papers* (1956), Pp. 4-11

The Elizabethan Theatre, V; Papers Given at the 5th International Conference on Elizabethan Theatre held at the University of Waterloo, Ontario, in July, 1973. 1974. Pp. 92-111

Huppe, Bernard F., "Allegory of Love in Lyly's Court Comedies", *Journal of English Literary History* (ELH), 14:93-113, 1947

Long, P. W., "Lyly's 'Endimion'", *Modern Philology*, 8:509-605, 1911
_____ , "Purport of Lyly's 'Endimion'", *Modern Language Association. Publications* (PMLA), 24:164-84, 1909

Mehl, Dieter, *The Elizabethan Dumb Show.* 1966. Pp. 86-87

Saccio, Peter, *The Court Comedies of John Lyly; A Study in Allegorical Dramaturgy.* 1969. Pp. 175-86

Weltner, Peter, "The Antinomic Vision of Lyly's 'Endimion'", *English Literary Renaissance* (1973), 3:5-29

Galathea, 1585

Saccio, Peter, *The Court Comedies of John Lyly; A Study in Allegorical Dramaturgy.* 1969. Pp. 95-160

Turner, Robert Y., "Some Dialogues of Love in Lyly's Comedies", *Journal of English Literary History* (ELH), 29:276-88, 1962

Love's Metamorphosis, 1589/90?

Edge, D., "Salamints in John Lyly's 'Love's Metamorphoses'", *Notes and Queries* (August 1974), 21:286

Huppe, Bernard F., "Allegory of Love in Lyly's Court Comedies", *Journal of English Literary History* (ELH), 14:93-113, 1947

Parnell, P. E., "Moral Allegory in Lyly's 'Love's Metamorphosis'", *Studies in Philology*, 52:1-16, 1955

Saccio, Peter, *The Court Comedies of John Lyly; A Study in Allegorical Dramaturgy.* 1969. Pp. 161-64

Tilley, N. P., "'Maid's Metamorphosis' and Ovid's 'Metamorphosis'", *Modern Language Notes*, 46:139-43, 1931

Midas, 1589

Allen, D. C., "Note on Lyly's 'Midas'", *Modern Language Notes*, 60:326-27, 1945

Best, Michael R., "A Theory of the Literary Genesis of Lyly's 'Midas'", *Review of English Studies* (1966), 17:133-40

Hilliard, Stephen S., "Lyly's 'Midas' as an Allegory of Tyranny", *Studies in English Literature, 1500-1900* (1972), 12:243-58

Lancashire, Anne C., "Lyly and Shakespear on the Ropes", *Journal of English and Germanic Philology* (April 1969), 68:237-44

Mustard, W. P., "Note on John Lyly's 'Midas'", *Modern Language Notes*, 41:193, 1926

Saccio, Peter, *The Court Comedies of John Lyly; A Study in Allegorical Dramaturgy.* 1969. Pp. 192-201

Mother Bombie, 1594

Turner, Robert Y., "Some Dialogues of Love in Lyly's Comedies", *Journal of English Literary History* (ELH), 29:276-88, 1962

Sapho and Phao, 1582-84

Bevington, David M., "John Lyly and Queen Elizabeth; Royal Flattery in 'Campaspe' and 'Sapho and Phao'", *Renaissance Papers* (1966), Pp. 37-67

Huppe, Bernard F., "Allegory of Love in Lyly's Court Comedies", *Journal of English Literary History* (ELH), 14:93-113, 1947

Saccio, Peter, *The Court Comedies of John Lyly; A Study in Allegorical Dramaturgy.* 1969. Pp. 165-68

Teggert, F. J., "Plot of Lyly's 'Sapho and Phao'", *Poet-Lore*, 8:29-33, 1896
Turner, Robert Y., "Some Dialogues of Love in Lyly's Comedies", *Journal of English Literary History* (ELH), 29:276-88, 1962

Woman in the Moon, 1590-95?
Huppe, Bernard F., "Allegory of Love in Lyly's Court Comedies", *Journal of English Literary History* (ELH), 14:93-113, 1947
Saccio, Peter, *The Court Comedies of John Lyly; A Study in Allegorical Dramaturgy*. 1969. Pp. 200-06

MICHEAL MACLIAMMOIR

Ill Met by Moonlight, 1946
Hogan, Robert, *After the Irish Renaissance; A Critical History of the Irish Drama Since "The Plough and the Stars"*. 1967. Pp. 116-19

Where Stars Walk, 1940
Hogan, Robert, *After the Irish Renaissance; A Critical History of the Irish Drama Since "The Plough and the Stars"*. 1967. Pp. 116-17
Nathan, George Jean, *Theatre Book of the Year. 1947-48*. 1948. Pp. 295-99

MAURICE MAETERLINCK

l'Abbe-Setubal   *SEE*   Father Setubal

Aglavaine et Selysette, 1896
Falk, Eugene H., *Renunciation as a Tragic Focus; A Study of Five Plays*. 1954. Pp. 73-81
Jervey, Huger, "Maeterlinck Versus Conventional Drama", *Sewanee Review*, 11:187-204, 1903
Knapp, Bettina, *Maurice Maeterlinck*. 1975. Pp. 88-92
Rouveyre, A., "Aglavaine et Selysette", *Mercure de France*, 228:400-02, June 1, 1931
Smith, Hugh Allison, *Main Currents of Modern French Drama*. Pp. 283-307

Alladine and Palomides, 1894
Knapp, Bettina, *Maurice Maeterlinck*. 1975. Pp. 78-82

Ariadne and Bluebeard; or, The Useless Deliverance, 1901
Knapp, Bettina, *Maurice Maeterlinck*. 1975. Pp. 98-101
Smith, Hugh Allison, *Main Currents of Modern French Drama*. Pp. 283-307

Ariane et Barbe-Bleue; ou, La Délivrance Inutile   *SEE*   Ariadne and Bluebeard; or, The Useless Deliverance

Les Aveugles   *SEE*   The Blind

The Betrothal, 1922
Hamilton, Clayton Meeker, *Seen on the Stage*. Pp. 114-21
Knapp, Bettina, *Maurice Maeterlinck*. 1975. Pp. 151-52
Literary Digest, 59:28-29, Dec. 7, 1918
New Republic, 17:313, Jan. 11, 1919
North American Review, 209:117-23, Jan., 1919
Smith, Hugh Allison, *Main Currents of Modern French Drama*. Pp. 283-307

The Blind, 1891

Hadar, Tayitta, "L'Angoisse Métaphysique dans 'Les Aveugles' de Maeterlinck", *Nineteenth Century French Studies* (1974), 2:68-74

Knapp, Bettina, "Maeterlinck's 'The Blind'; Or, The Dying Complex", *Yale Theatre* (1974), 5,iii:79-86

————————— , *Maurice Maeterlinck*. 1975. Pp. 49-59

Smith, Hugh Allison, *Main Currents of Modern French Drama*. Pp. 283-307

The Blue Bird, 1908

" 'Blue Bird': A Lovely Fairy Tale", *Delineator*, 77:256, March, 1911

" 'Blue Bird' as a Féerie", *Scribner's Magazine*, 48:765, Dec., 1910

"Blue Bird's Song Flight", *Literary Digest*, 64:32-34, Jan. 17, 1920

Brisson, P., " 'L'Oiseau Bleu': Critique", *Les Annales Politiques et Littéraires*, 81:690-91, Dec. 9, 1923

Firkins, O. W., "The Drama of Maeterlinck", *Nation*, 93:246-49, 1911

Hamblen, E. S., "Significance of Maeterlinck's 'Blue Bird' ", *Poet-Lore*, 22:460-68, Nov., 1911

Knapp, Bettina, *Maurice Maeterlinck*. 1975. Pp. 119-27

"Maeterlinck's Fairy Tale: 'The Blue Bird' ", *Independent*, 69:1023-25, Oct. 10, 1910

Outlook, 96:339-40, Oct. 15, 1910

Phelps, William Lyon, "An Estimate of Maeterlinck", *North American Review*, 213:98-108, 1921

Ruhl, A., "The Blue Bird", *Collier's*, 46:24, Oct. 22, 1910

Smith, Hugh Allison, *Main Currents of Modern French Drama*. Pp. 283-307

Southerland, L., "Blue Bird for Happiness", *St. Nicholas*, 38:335-40, Feb., 1911

Spectator, 104:18-19, Jan. 1, 1910

Stanislavsky, C., "The Blue Bird", *Theatre Arts*, 7:29-40, Jan., 1923

Syford, E., "Maeterlinck's 'Blue Bird' ", *New England Magazine*, n. s. 43:36-42, Sept., 1910

Tassin, A., "Blue Bird of Maeterlinck", *Good Housekeeping*, 51:708-09, Dec., 1910

Winter, W., "The Blue Bird", *Harper's Weekly*, 54:20, Oct. 29, 1910

Le Bourgmestre de Stilemonde   *SEE*   The Burgomaster of Stilemonde

Burgomaster of Stilemonde, 1918

Literary Digest, 60:31-32, Feb. 22, 1919

Moses, Montrose Jonas, "Burgomaster", *Bellman*, 26:436-39, April 19, 1919

Nation, 108:511, April 5, 1919

Phelps, William Lyon, "An Estimate of Maeterlinck", *North American Review*, 213:98-108, 1921

"War Play by Maeterlinck: 'The Burgomaster of Stilemonde' ", *Living Age*, 299:440-42, Nov. 16, 1918

The Death of Tintagiles, 1905

Knapp, Bettina, *Maurice Maeterlinck*. 1975. Pp. 84-86

Father Setubal, 1941

Knapp, Bettina, *Maurice Maeterlinck*. 1975. Pp. 169-70

Les Fiançailles   *SEE*   The Betrothal

Interior, 1894

Knapp, Bettina, *Maurice Maeterlinck*. 1975. Pp. 83-85

The Intruder, 1891
  Henderson, Archibald, "Maurice Maeterlinck as a Dramatic Artist", *Sewanee Review*, 12:207-16, 1904
  Jervey, Huger, "Maeterlinck Versus Conventional Drama", *Sewanee Review*, 11:187-204, 1903
  Knapp, Bettina, *Maurice Maeterlinck*. 1975. Pp. 40-49

l'Intruse *SEE* The Intruder

Joyzelle, 1903
  Knapp, Bettina, *Maurice Maeterlinck*. 1975. Pp. 111-17

Le Jugement Dernier *SEE* The Last Judgment

The Last Judgment, 1944
  Knapp, Bettina, *Maurice Maeterlinck*. 1975. Pp. 171-72

Mary Magdalene, 1909
  Knapp, Bettina, *Maurice Maeterlinck*. 1975. Pp. 129-33

Monna Vanna, 1902
  Archer, William, "Monna Vanna", *Nation*, 99:171, 1914
  Bellesort, A., "Monna Vanna", *Journal des Débats*, 41 pt. 1:363-65, March 2, 1934
  Cooper, Frederic Taber, "Maeterlinck and the Forbidden Play", *Bookman*, 16:46-49, 1902
  Firkins, O. W., "The Dramas of Maeterlinck", *Nation*, 93:246-49, 1911
  Hale, E. E., Jr., "Monna Vanna", *Dial*, 35:257-58, Oct. 16, 1902
  Henderson, Archibald, "Maurice Maeterlinck as a Dramatic Artist", *Sewanee Review*, 12:207-16, 1904
  Knapp, Bettina, *Maurice Maeterlinck*. 1975. Pp. 107-11
  Lord, W. F., "Monna Vanna", *Nineteenth Century*, 52:72-75, July, 1902
  Phelps, William Lyon, "An Estimate of Maeterlinck", *North American Review*, 213:98-108, 1921
  Rageot, G., "Monna Vanna—Critique", *Revue Politique et Littéraire*, 62:25-26, Jan. 5, 1924
  Scott, Evelyn, "A Critic of the Threshold", *Dial*, 68:311-25, 1920
  Smith, Hugh Allison, *Main Currents of Modern French Drama*. 1925. Pp. 283-307
  Tadema, L. A., "Monna Vanna", *Living Age*, 234:378-80, Aug. 9, 1902

La Mort de Tintagiles *SEE* *The Death of Tintagiles*

L'Oiseau Bleu *SEE* The Blue Bird

Pelléas and Mélisande, 1893
  Baring, Maurice, *Punch and Judy and Other Essays*. 1924. Pp. 325-26
  Beerbohm, Max, *Around Theatres*. 1953. Pp. 91-94
  Dubois, Jacques, "La Répetition dans 'Pelléas et Mélisande' ", *Revue des Langues Vivantes* (Bruxelles), 28:483-89, 1962
  Evans, Calvin, "Maeterlinck and the Quest for a Mystic Tragedy of the 20th Century", *Modern Drama*, 4:54-59, 1961
  Jervey, Huger, "Maeterlinck Versus Conventional Drama", *Sewanee Review*, 11:187-204, 1903
  Kellock, H., "Pelléas et Mélisande", *Freeman*, 8:353-54, Dec. 9, 1923
  Kerchove, Arnold de, "Méditation", *Revue Générale Belge*, Pp. 21-34; 1962

Knapp, Bettina, "Pélleas and Mélisande; The Spirit of Eros and Anteros", *Language Quarterly* (1974), 13, i-iii:15-18
————————— , *Maurice Maeterlinck*. 1975. Pp. 67-76
Lewisohn, Ludwig, "Pelléas et Mélisande", *Nation*, 117:46-47, Dec. 26, 1923
Lievre, P., "Pelleas et Melisande de Maurice Maeterlinck", *Mercure de France*, 291:383-86, April 15, 1939
Smith, Hugh Allison, *Main Currents of Modern French Drama*. 1925. Pp. 283-307
Spectator, 102:936-37, June 12, 1909
Woollcott, Alexander, *Enchanted Isles*. 1924. Pp. 224-26
Young, Stark, "Pélleas et Mélisande", *New Republic*, 37:123, Dec. 26, 1923

The Power of the Dead, 1926
Knapp, Bettina, *Maurice Maeterlinck*. 1975. Pp. 158-60

Princess Maleine, 1889
Henderson, Archibald, "Maurice Maeterlinck as a Dramatic Artist", *Sewanee Review*, 12:207-16, 1904
Jervey, Huger, "Maeterlinck Versus Conventional Drama", *Sewanee Review*, 11:187-204, 1903
Knapp, Bettina, *Maurice Maeterlinck*. 1975. Pp. 28-39

La Puissance des Morts   *SEE*   The Power of the Dead

Les Sept Princesses   *SEE*   The Seven Princesses

The Seven Princesses, 1891
Jervey, Huger, "Maeterlinck Versus Conventional Drama", *Sewanee Review*, 11:187-204, 1903
Knapp, Bettina, *Maurice Maeterlinck*. 1975. Pp. 60-67
Smith, Hugh Allison, *Main Currents of Modern French Drama*. 1925. Pp. 283-307

Sister Beatrice, 1901
Allen, Genieve M., "The Problem of Individualism in Relation to Society in Ibsen, Maeterlinck and Hauptmann", *Poet-Lore*, 32:262-66, 1921
Knapp, Bettina, *Maurice Maeterlinck*. 1975. Pp. 103-06

Soeur Beatrice   *SEE*   Sister Beatrice

VLADIMIR VLADIMIROVICH MAIAKOVSKII

Banya   *SEE*   The Bathhouse

The Bathhouse, 1930
Symons, James M., *Meyerhold's Theatre of the Grotesque; The Post-Revolutionary Productions, 1920-1932*. 1971. Pp. 184-89

The Bedbug, 1929
Symons, James M., *Meyerhold's Theatre of the Grotesque; The Post-Revolutionary Productions, 1920-1932*. 1971. Pp. 175-85

Klop   *SEE*   The Bedbug

Misteriya-Buff   *SEE*   Mystery-Bouffe

Mystery-Bouffe, 1918
Symons, James M., *Meyerhold's Theatre of the Grotesque; The Post-Revolutionary Productions, 1920-1932.* 1971. Pp. 49-56

HEINRICH MANN

Madame Legros, 1917
Weisstein, U., "Heinrich Mann's 'Madame Legros': Not a Revolutionary Drama", *Germanic Review* (1960), 35:39-49

FRANK MARCUS

Green Room, n. d.
"Green Room: Enter the Dramaturg", *Plays and Players* (Sept. 1974), 21:12-13

The Killing of Sister George, 1965
Christian Century, 84:16-17, Jan. 4, 1967
Commonweal, 85:106, Oct. 28, 1966
Downer, Alan S., "The Doctor's Dilemma: Notes on the New York Theatre, 1966-1967", *Quarterly Journal of Speech* (1967), 53:219-20
Encounter, 25:42-43, Oct. 1965
Esquire, 66:8, Nov. 1966
Kerr, Walter, *Thirty Plays Hath November; Pain and Pleasure in the Contemporary Theatre.* 1969. Pp. 301-04
Nation, 203:459-60, Oct. 31, 1966
National Review, 19:100, Jan. 24, 1967
Newsweek, 68:98, Oct. 17, 1966
Reporter, 35:62-63, Nov. 17, 1966
Saturday Review, 49:72-73, Oct. 22, 1966
Simon, Neil, "Theatre Chronicle", *Hudson Review* (1966-67), 19:633-34
Time, 88:93, Oct. 14, 1966
Vogue, 149:99, Nov. 15, 1966

Mrs. Mouse Are You Within?, 1968
New Statesman, 75:492, April 12, 1968

PIERRE CARLET DE CHAMBLAIN DE MARIVAUX

Les Acteurs de Bone Foi   *SEE*   Actors in Good Faith

Actors in Good Faith, 1757
Spinelli, Donald Carmen, "The Dramaturgy of Marivaux; Three Elements of Technique", *Dissertation Abstracts International* (1972), 32:4025A

L'Amour et la Vérité   *SEE*   Love and Truth

Annibal   *SEE*   Hannibal

The Argument, 1744
Burgess, J., "La Dispute", *Plays and Players* (Apr. 1974), 21:54-55
Haac, Oscar A., *Marivaux*. 1973. Pp. 110-11
Nelson, Robert J., "The Trials of Love in Marivaux's Theatre", *University of Toronto Quarterly* (1966-67), 36:237-48
Revue des Deux Mondes s. 8, 45:455-56, May 15, 1938

Arlequin Poli par l'Amour   *SEE*   Harlequin Polished by Love

A Case of Mistaken Identity, 1734
   Haac, Oscar A., *Marivaux*, 1973. Pp. 91

A Case of Sincerity, 1739
   Haac, Oscar A., *Marivaux*. 1973. Pp. 102-03

La Colonie   *SEE*   The Colony

The Colony, 1750
   Gilot, Michel, "Marivaux dans la Société de son Temps", *Revue des Sciences Humaines* (1974), 153:79-101
   Haac, Oscar A., *Marivaux*. 1973. Pp. 113-15
   Kraft, Walter C., ed., *Proceedings; Pacific Northwest Conference on Foreign Languages*. 1974. Pp. 208-11

La Commère   *SEE*   The Gossip

La Dénouement Imprévu   *SEE*   The Unforeseen Solution

La Dispute   *SEE*   The Argument

Double Inconstancy, 1723
   Bauer, G., " 'La Double Inconstance': Critique", *Les Annales Politiques et Litteraires* (March 16, 1934), 102:304
   Gilot, Michel, "Marivaux dans la Société de Son Temps", *Revue des Sciences Humaines* (1974), 153:79-101
   Haac, Oscar S., *Marivaux*. 1973. Pp. 49-50
   Lievre, P., " 'La Double Inconstance': Critique", *Mercure de France* (April 1, 1934), 251:144-47
   McCollom, William G., *The Divine Average; A View of Comedy*. 1971. Pp. 180-97
   Mason, Hayden, T., "Cruelty in Marivaux's Theatre", *Modern Language Review* (1967), 62:238-47
   Tchalekian, Chavarche, "Social Criticism in Marivaux' Plays", *Humanities Association Bulletin* (Winter 1969), 20:20-26

l'Ecole des Meres   *SEE*   A School for Mothers

l'Épreuve   *SEE*   The Test

The Faithful Wife, 1755
   Haac, Oscar A., *Marivaux*. 1973. Pp. 118-19
   Mason, Hayden, T., "Cruelty in Marivaux's Theatre", *Modern Language Review* (1967), 62:238-47

False Confessions, 1737
   Bentley, Eric Russell, *Dramatic Event; An American Chronicle*. 1954. Pp. 58-61
   Catholic World, 176:389, Feb. 1953
   Cismaru, Alfred, "The 'Molieresque' Origins of 'Les Fausses Confidences' " *Kentucky Romance Quarterly* (1968), 15:223-29
   Commonweal, 57:223, Dec. 5, 1952
   Gilot, Michel, "Marivaux dans la Société de Son Temps", *Revue des Sciences Humaines* (1974), 153:79-101

Haac, Oscar A., *Marivaux*. 1973. Pp. 98-101
Mason, Hayden T., "Cruelty in Marivaux's Theatre", *Modern Language Review* (1967), 62:238-47
Mercure de France, 275:588-91, May 1, 1937
Nelson, Robert J., "The Trials of Love in Marivaux's Theatre", *University of Toronto Quarterly* (1966-67), 36:237-48
New Republic, 127:22, Dec. 1, 1952
New Yorker, 28:95, Nov. 22, 1952
Newsweek, 40:88, Nov. 24, 1952
Saturday Review, 35:27, Nov. 29, 1952
Scherer, Jacques, "Analyse et Mecanisme des 'Fausses Confidences'" *Cahiers de la Compagnie Madeleine Renaud—Jean Louis Barrault* (1960), #28:11-19
School and Society, 76:402, Dec. 20, 1952
Time, 60:68, Nov. 24, 1952

The False Servant, 1724
Haac, Oscar A., *Marivaux*. 1973. Pp. 53-55

A Father, Prudent and Just; or, Crispin the Jolly Rogue, 1712
Haac, Oscar A., *Marivaux*. 1973. Pp. 21-22

Les Fausses Confidences   SEE   False Confessions

La Fausse Suivante   SEE   The False Servant

Félicie, 1757
Haac, Oscar A., *Marivaux*. 1973. Pp. 119-20

La Femme Fidèle   SEE   The Faithful Wife

The Fop Reformed, 1734
Haac, Oscar A., *Marivaux*. 1973. Pp. 91-93

The Game of Love and Chance, 1730
Barrera-Vidal, Albert, "Les Differents Niveaux de Langue dans les 'Jeux de l'Amour et du Hasard'", *Die Neueren Sprachen* (1966), 15:378-84
Haac, Oscar A., *Marivaux*. 1973. Pp. 67-69
McCollom, William G., *The Divine Average; A View of Comedy*. 1971. Pp. 180-97
Theatre Arts, 21:730, 1937
Wernsing, Von Armin Volkmar, "Die Verkleidete Wahrheit: Das Speil im Theater Marivaux", *Die Neueren Sprachen* (1972), N. F. 21:716-26

The Gossip, 1741
Haac, Oscar A., *Marivaux*. 1973. Pp. 106-07

Hannibal, 1720
Haac, Oscar A., *Marivaux*. 1973. Pp. 41-42

Harlequin Polished by Love, 1720
Haac, Oscar A., *Marivaux*. 1973. Pp. 40-41

l'Héritier du Village   SEE   The Village Heir

l'Heureux Stratagème   SEE   The Lucky Strategem

l'Ile de la Raison   SEE   The Island of Reason

L'Ile des Esclaves *SEE* The Island of Slaves

The Inheritance, 1736
  Haac, Oscar A., *Marivaux*. 1973. Pp. 95-98

The Island of Reason, 1727
  Haac, Oscar A., *Marivaux*. 1973. Pp. 61-63

The Island of Slaves, 1725
  Haac, Oscar A., *Marivaux*. 1973. Pp. 56-57
  Mercure de France, 294:115-17, Aug. 15, 1939
  Revue des Deux Mondes, s. 8, 52:938-39, Aug. 15, 1939

Le Jeu de L'Amour et du Hasard *SEE* The Game of Love and Chance

La Joie Imprévue *SEE* Joy Unforeseen

Joy Unforeseen, 1738
  Haac, Oscar A., *Marivaux*. 1973. Pp. 101-02

Le Legs *SEE* The Inheritance

Love and Truth, 1720
  Haac, Oscar A., *Marivaux*. 1973. Pp. 38-39
  Tchalekian, Chavarche, "Social Criticism in Marivaux' Plays", *Humanities
    Association Bulletin* (Winter 1969), 20:20-26

The Lucky Strategem, 1733
  Haac, Oscar A., *Marivaux*. 1973. Pp. 81-83
  Mason, Hauden T., "Cruelty in Marivaux's Theatre", *Modern Language Review* (1967), 62:238-47

La Méprise *SEE* A Case of Mistaken Identity

La Mere Confidente *SEE* The Mother as a Confidante

The Mother as a Confidante, 1735
  Haac, Oscar A., *Marivaux*. 1973. Pp. 93-95

Oaths All Too Rashly Taken, 1732
  Frederick, E. C., "Marivaux and Musset: 'Les Serments Indiscrets' and 'On
    ne Badine Pas Avec L'Amour'", *Romanic Review* (1940), 31:259-64
  Haac, Oscar A., *Marivaux*. 1973. Pp. 77-79

Le Pere Prudent et Equitable *SEE* A Father, Prúdent and Just

Le Petit-Maître Corrige *SEE* The Fop Reformed

Plutus Triumphant, 1728
  Haac, Oscar A., *Marivaux*. 1973. Pp. 65-66

Le Préjugé Vaincu *SEE* Victory Over Prejudice

The Prince in Disguise; or, The Illustrious Imposter, 1724
  Bellessort, J., "'Le Prince Travesti': Critique", *Journal des Debats* (Dec. 16,
    1932), 39 pt. 2:1035-37
  Haac, Oscar A., *Marivaux*. 1973. Pp. 50-53
  LeVerrier, C., "'Le Prince Travesti': Critique", *L'Europe Nouvelle* (Jan. 14,
    1933), 16:36

Missions et Demarches de la Critique; Melanges Offerts au Professeur J. A. Vier. 1973. Pp. 367-70

Le Prince Travesti, ou l'Illustre Aventurier *SEE* The Prince in Disguise; or, The Illustrious Imposter

The Provincial Lady, 1761
Haac, Oscar A., *Marivaux*. 1973. Pp. 122-23

La Provinciale *SEE* The Provincial Lady

La Réunion des Amours *SEE* Two Kinds of Love Reconciled

A School for Mothers, 1732
Haac, Oscar A., *Marivaux*. 1973. Pp. 79-80

The (Second) Surprise of Love, 1727
Haac, Oscar A., *Marivaux*. 1973. Pp. 63-65
McCollom, William G., *The Divine Average; A View of Comedy.* 1971. Pp. 180-97

La Seconde Surprise de L'Amour *SEE* The Second Surprise of Love

Les Serments Indiscrets *SEE* Oaths All Too Rashly Taken

The Sincere Ones, 1739
Cismaru, Alfred, " 'Les Sinceres' and 'Le Misanthrope': An Attempt to Settle The Relationship", *French Review* (May 1969), 42:865-70

Les Sinceres *SEE* The Sincere Ones

La Surprise de l'Amour *SEE* The Surprise of Love

The Surprise of Love, 1722
Haac, Oscar A., *Marivaux*. 1973. Pp. 46-49

The Test, 1740
Haac, Oscar A., *Marivaux*. 1973. Pp. 103-06
Mason, Hayden T., "Cruelty in Marivaux's Theatre", *Modern Language Review* (1967), 62:238-47

Le Triomphe de l'Amour *SEE* The Triumph of Love

Le Triomphe de Plutus *SEE* The Triumph of Plutus

The Triumph of Love, 1732
Haac, Oscar A., *Marivaux*. 1973. Pp. 76-77

The Triumph of Plutus, 1728
Desvignes, Lucette, "Genèse du 'Triomphe de Plutus' ", *Studi Francesi* (1970), 14:90-96

Two Kinds of Love Reconciled, 1731
Haac, Oscar A., *Marivaux*. 1973. Pp. 75-76

The Unforeseen Solution, 1724
Haac, Oscar A., *Marivaux*. 1973. Pp. 55-56

Victory Over Prejudice, 1746
Haac, Oscar A., *Marivaux*. 1973. Pp. 111-13

The Village Heir, 1725
  Haac, Oscar A., *Marivaux*. 1973. Pp. 57-58

CHRISTOPHER MARLOWE

Dr. Faustus *SEE* The Tragical History of Dr. Faustus

Edward II, 1592
  Ahrends, Gunter, "Die Bildersprache in Marlowes 'Edward II' ", *Germanisch-Romanische Monatsschrift* (Oct. 1969), 19:353-79
  Bentley, Eric Russell, *Theatre of War; Comments on Thirty-two Occasions*. 1972. Pp. 131-45
  Berdan, John M., "Marlowe's 'Edward II", *Philological Quarterly* (1924), 3:197-207
  Bevington, David M., *From Mankind to Marlowe; Growth of Structure in the Popular Drama of Tudor England*. 1962. Pp. 234-44
  Bluestone, Max and Norman Rabkin, eds., *Shakespeare's Contemporaries; Modern Studies in English Renaissance Drama*. 2nd ed. 1970. Pp. 74-172
  Bobin, Donna, "Marlowe's Humor", *Massachusetts Studies in English* (Fall 1969), 2:29-40
  Box, Terry J., "Irony and Objectivity in the Plays of Christopher Marlowe", *Dissertation Abstracts International* (1973), 33:4333A
  Brodwin, Leonora Leet, " 'Edward II': Marlowe's Culminating Treatment of Love", *Journal of English Literary History* (ELH), 31:139-55, 1964
  Bynum, James J., "Isolation, Metamorphosis and Self-Destruction in the Plays of Christopher Marlowe", *Dissertation Abstracts International* (1973), 34:719A
  Craig, Hardin, "The Origin of the History Play", *Arlington Quarterly* (Spring 1968), 1:5-11
  Fraser, Russell, "On Christopher Marlowe", *Michigan Quarterly Review* (1973), 12:136-59
  Fricker, Robert, "The Dramatic Structure of 'Edward II' ", *English Studies* (1953), 34:204-17
  Grüninger, Hans Werner, "Brecht und Marlowe", *Comparative Literature* (Summer 1969), 21:232-44
  Johnson, S. F., "Marlowe's 'Edward II' ", *Explicator*, 10:item 53, 1952
  Kuriyama, Constance B., "Hammer or Anvil; A Psychoanalytic Study of the Plays of Christopher Marlowe", *Dissertation Abstracts International* (1974), 34:7710A
  Kurokawa, Takashi, " 'De Casibus' Theme and Machiavellism—In Connection with the Theme of 'Edward II' ", *Shakespeare Studies* (Japan) (1968-69), 7:61-80
  Leech, Clifford, ed., *Marlowe; A Collection of Critical Essays*. 1964. Pp. 120-43
  _____ , "Marlowe's 'Edward II': Power and Suffering", *Critical Quarterly* (1959), 1:181-96
  Manheim, Michael, "The Weak King History Play of the Early 1590's' ", *Renaissance Drama* (1969), 2:71-80
  Masinton, Charles G., *Christopher Marlowe's Tragic Vision; A Study in Damnation*. 1972. Pp. 86-112
  _____ , "Marlowe's Artists; The Failure of Imagination", *Ohio University Review* (1969), 11:22-35

Mills, L. J., "The Meaning of 'Edward II' ", *Modern Philology*, 32:11-31, 1934
Perret, M., " 'Edward II': Marlowe's Dramatic Technique", *Review of English Literature* (1966), 7:87-91
Ribner, Irving, *The English History Play in the Age of Shakespeare*. 1957. Pp. 127-36
——————— , "Marlowe's 'Edward II' and the Tudor Historical Plays", *Journal of English Literary History (ELH)*, 22:243-53, 1955
Ricks, Christopher, ed., *English Drama to 1710*. (History of Literature in the English Language) Vol. 3, 1971. Pp. 143-45
Sampley, A. M., "Peele's 'Discensus Astraeae' and Marlowe's 'Edward II' ", *Modern Language Notes*, 50:506, Dec., 1935
Schelling, Felix Emmanuel, *The English Chronicle Play; A Study in the Popular Historical Literature Environing Shakespeare*. 1902. Pp. 64-74
Shanks, E., "Edward II", *Outlook* (London), 52:394, Nov. 24, 1923
Studies in Bibliography. Papers of the Bibliographical Society of the Univ. of Virginia, ed. by Fredson Bowers, v. 16-17, 1963-64, Pp. 197-98
Summers, Claud J., "Isabella's Plea for Gaveston in Marlowe's 'Edward II' ", *Philological Quarterly* (1973), 52:308-10
Waith, Eugene M., " 'Edward II': The Shadow of Action", *Tulane Drama Review*, 8:59-76, 1964
Ward, Adolphus William, *A History of English Dramatic Literature*, vol. l. 1966. Pp. 347-54
World Shakespeare Congress, 1st, Vancouver, B. C., *Shakespeare, 1971; Proceedings*. 1972. Pp. 123-32
Wright, R., "Edward II", *New Statesman*, 22:210-11, Nov. 24, 1923

The Jew of Malta, 1589
Babb, Howard, "Policy in Marlowe's 'The Jew of Malta' ", *Journal of English Literary History* (ELH), 24:85-94, 1957
Bawcult, N. W., "Marlowe's 'Jew of Malta' and Foxe's 'Acts and Monuments' ", *Notes and Queries* (1968), 15:250
Bennett, Gilbert, "Conventions of a Stage Villain", *Anglo-Welsh Review* (1963), 13:92-102
Bevington, David, M., *From Mankind to Marlowe; Growth of Structure in the Popular Drama of Tudor England*. 1962. Pp. 218-33
Blackwood's Magazine, 212:833-34, Dec., 1922
Bluestone, Max and Norman Rabkin, eds., *Shakespeare's Contemporaries; Modern Studies in English Renaissance Drama*. 2nd ed. 1970. Pp. 74-172
Bobin, Donna, "Marlowe's Humor", *Massachusetts Studies in English* (Fall 1969), 2:29-40
Box, Terry J., "Irony and Objectivity in the Plays of Christopher Marlowe", *Dissertation Abstracts International* (1973), 33:4333A
Bynum, James J., "Isolation, Metamorphosis and Self-Destruction in the Plays of Christopher Marlowe", *Dissertation Abstracts International* (1973), 34: 719A
Clarke, Peter P., II, "The Pastoral/Anti-Pastoral Dialectic in the Plays of Christopher Marlowe", *Dissertation Abstracts International* (1972), 32:5176A
Cunningham, John E., *Elizabethan and Early Stuart Drama*. 1965. Pp. 40-43
D'Andrea, Antonio, "Studies in Machiavelli and His Reputation in the 16th Century, I: Marlowe's Prologue to 'The Jew of Malta' ", *Medieval and Renaissance Studies* (1961), 5:214-48

Davidson, I., "Shylock and Barabas; A Study in Character", *Sewanee Review*, 9:337-48, 1901

Flosdorf, J. W., "The 'O di et Amo' Theme in 'The Jew of Malta' ", *Notes and Queries* (1960), 8:10-14

Fraser, Russell, "On Christopher Marlowe", *Michigan Quarterly Review* (1973), 12:136-59

Friedman, Alan Warren, "The Shackling of Accidents in Marlowe's 'The Jew of Malta' ", *Texas Studies in Literature and Language* (1966), 8:155-67

Harbage, A., "Innocent Barabas", *Tulane Drama Review*, 8:47-58, 1964

Hunt, Leigh, *Leigh Hunt's Dramatic Criticism, 1808-1831*, ed. by Lawrence Huston Houtchens and Carolyn Washburn Houtchens. 1949. Pp. 190-98

Hunter, G. K., "The Theology of Marlowe's 'The Jew of Malta' ", *Journal of the Warburg and Courtauld Institute* (1964), 27:211-40

Illíc, Aleksa Č., "Slike i Problem Jedinstva u Marloovom 'Jevrejinu sa Malte' " (Imagery and the Problem of Unity in 'The Jew of Malta'. Summary in English) *Godisnjak Filozofskog Fakulteta u Novom Sadu* (1968), ll:423-43

Jensen, Ejner J., "Marlowe Our Contemporary", *College English* (May 1969), 30:627-32

Kay, Donald, "The Appearance-Reality Theme in 'The Jew of Malta' ", *Studies in English Literature* (Japan) (1972), English No.:200-01

Kocher, Paul H., "English Legal History in Marlowe's 'Jew of Malta' ", *Huntington Library Quarterly*, 26:155-63, 1963

————————— , "Marlowe's Art of War", *Studies in Philology*, 39:207-25, 1942

Leech, Clifford, ed., *Marlowe; A Collection of Critical Essays*. 1964. Pp. 120-27 and 144-58

Levin, Harry, ed., *Veins of Humor*. 1972. Pp. 69-91

London Mercury, 20:175, Nov. 11, 1922

Masinton, Charles G., *Christopher Marlowe's Tragic Vision; A Study in Damnation*. 1972. Pp. 56-86

————————— , "Marlowe's Artists; The Failure of Imagination", *Ohio University Review* (1969), 11:22-35

Maxwell, J. C., "How Bad is the Text of 'The Jew of Malta'?", *Modern Language Review*, 48:435-38, 1953

New Statesman, 20:175, Nov. 11, 1922

Peavy, Charles E., " 'The Jew of Malta'—Anti-Semitic or Anti-Catholic?", *McNeese Review* (1959-60), 11:57-60

Purcell, H. D., "Whetstone's 'English Myrror' and Marlowe's 'The Jew of Malta' ", *Notes and Queries* (1966), 13:288-90

Renaissance Drama: Essays Principally on Comedy, ed. by S. Schoenbaum and Alan C. Dessen. 1972. Pp. 93-104

Ricks, Christopher, ed., *English Drama to 1710*. (History of Literature in the English Language) Vol. 3. 1971. Pp. 141-45

Rothstein, Eric, "Structure as Meaning in 'The Jew of Malta' ", *Journal of English and Germanic Philology* (1966), 65:260-73

Schuman, Samuel, "Occasion's Bald Behind; A Note on the Sources of an Emblematic Image in 'The Jew of Malta' ", *Modern Philology* (1973), 70:234-35

Simmons, J. L., "Elizabethan Stage Practice and Marlowe's 'Jew of Malta' ", *Renaissance Drama* (1971), 4:93-104

Speaight, Robert, "Marlowe: The Forerunner", *Review of English Literature* (1966), 7:25-41

Spectator, 129:695-96, Nov. 11, 1922

Stephens, Rosemary, "In Another Country: Three as Symbol", *University of Mississippi Studies in English* (1966), 7:77-83

Swan, A., "Jew That Marlowe Drew", *Sewanee Review*, 19:483-97, 1911

Tomlinson, Thomas Brian, *A Study of Elizabethan and Jacobean Tragedy.* 1964. Pp. 87-93

Ward, Adolphus William, *A History of English Dramatic Literature*, vol. 1. 1966. Pp. 337-47

Willberg, David P., "The Elizabethan Revenge Play; A Psychoanalytic Inquiry", *Dissertation Abstracts International* (1973), 34:1261A

The Massacre at Paris, 1593
Bobin, Donna, "Marlowe's Humor", *Massachusetts Studies in English* (Fall 1969), 2:29-40

Bynum, James J., "Isolation, Metamorphosis and Self-Destruction in the Plays of Christopher Marlowe", *Dissertation Abstracts International* (1973), 34:719A

Galloway, David, "The Ramus Scene in Marlowe's 'The Massacre at Paris'", *Notes and Queries*, 198:146-47, 1953

Glenn, John R., "The Martyrdom of Ramus in Marlowe's 'Massacre at Paris'", *Papers on Language and Literature* (1973), 9:365-79

Kocher, Paul H., "Contemporary Pamphlet Backgrounds for Marlowe's 'The Massacre at Paris'", *Modern Language Quarterly*, 8:151-73, 309-18, 1947

Leech, Clifford, ed., *Marlowe; A Collection of Critical Essays.* 1964. Pp. 128-37

Ward, Adolphus William, *A History of English Dramatic Literature*, vol. 1, 1966. Pp. 354-56

Tamburlaine the Great, 1587
Allen, Don C., "Marlowe's 'Tamburlaine'", *Times Literary Supplement*, Pp. 730, Sept. 24, 1931

"Renaissance Remedies for Fortune: Marlowe and the 'Fortunati'", *Studies in Philology*, 38:188-97, 1941

America, 94:541, Feb. 11, 1956

Barber, C. L., "The Death of Zenocrate 'Conceiving and Subduing Both' in Marlowe's 'Tamburlaine'", *Literature and Psychology* (1966), 16:2-14

Battenhouse, Roy W., "Protestant Apologetics and the Subplot of the Second Tamburlaine", *English Literary Renaissance* (1973), 3:30-43

——————— , "The Relation of Henry V to Tamburlaine", *Shakespeare Survey* (1974), 27:71-79

——————— , "Tamburlaine, the Scourge of God", *Modern Language Association. Publications* (1941), 56:337-48

Beckett, R. D., "Themes in 'Tamburlaine II'", *Univ. of Colorado Studies, Language and Literature,* #9:19-31, 1963

Benaquist, Lawrence M., "The Ethical Structure of 'Tamburlane'", *Thoth* (1969], 10:3-19

Bevington, David, *From Mankind to Marlowe: Growth of Structure in the Popular Drama of Tudor England.* 1962. Pp. 198-217

Bluestone, Max and Norman Rabkin, eds., *Shakespeare's Contemporaries; Modern Studies in English Renaissance Drama,* 2nd ed. 1970. Pp. 74-172

Bobin, Donna, "Marlowe's Humor", *Massachusetts Studies in English* (Fall 1969), 2:29-40

Boas, Frederick S., *University Drama in the Tudor Age*. 1966. Pp. 270-71

Box, Terry J., "Irony and Objectivity in the Plays of Christopher Marlowe", *Dissertation Abstracts International* (1973), 33:4333A

Brooks, Charles, "'Tamburlaine' and Attitudes Toward Women", *Journal of English Literary History* (ELH), 24:1-11, 1957

Bynum, James J., "Isolation, Metamorphosis and Self-Destruction in the Plays of Christopher Marlowe", *Dissertation Abstracts International* (1973), 34:719A

Camden, Carroll, Jr., "Tamburlaine: The Choleric Man", *Modern Language Notes*, 44:430-35, 1929

Catholic World, 182:467, March, 1956

Clarke, Peter P., II, "The Pastoral/Anti-Pastoral Dialectic in the Plays of Christopher Marlowe", *Dissertation Abstracts International* (1972), 32:5176A

Commonweal, 63:593, March 9, 1956

Cunningham, John E., *Elizabethan and Early Stuart Drama*. 1965. Pp. 35-40

Daiches, David, *More Literary Essays*. 1968. Pp. 42-69

Egan, Robert, "The Muse of Fire; 'Henry V' in the Light of 'Tamburlaine'", *Modern Language Quarterly* (March 1968), 29:15-28

Elizabethan Studies and Other Essays in Honor of George F. Reynolds (Univ. of Colorado Studies in the Humanities, Ser. 3, v. 2, #4). 1945. Pp. 126-31

English Association, London, *Essays and Studies by Members of the Association*. 1924. v. 10, Pp. 13-35

―――――――― , *Essays and Studies by Members of the Association*. 1948. 1:101-26

Friedenreich, Kenneth, "'Hugh Greatnesse' Overthrown: The Fall of the Empire in Marlowe's Tamburlaine Plays", *Clio; An Interdisciplinary Journal of Literature, History and Philosophy of History* (1972), 1:37-48

Gardner, H. L., "Second Part of Tamburlaine the Great", *Modern Language Review*, 37:18-24, 1942

Gilbert, Allan, "Tamburlaine's 'Pampered Jades'", *Rivista di Letterature Moderne y Comparate*, 4:208-10, 1953

Jacquot, Jean, "La Pensée de Marlowe dans 'Tamburlaine the Great'", *Études Anglaises* (1953), 6:322-45

Kaufmann, Ralph James, *Elizabethan Drama; Modern Essays in Criticism*. 1961. Pp. 81-94

Kimbrough, Robert, "'Tamburlaine': A Speaking Picture in a Tragic Glass", *Renaissance Drama* (Northwestern), 7:20-34, 1964

Kocher, Paul H., "Marlowe's Art of War", *Studies in Philology*, 39:207-25, 1942

Korninger, Siegfried, ed., "Studies in English Language and Literature Presented to Prof. Dr. Karl Brunner", *Wiener Beiträge zur Englischen Philologie* (1957), Pp. 232-51

Kuriyama, Constance B., "Hammer or Anvil; A Psychoanalytic Study of the Plays of Christopher Marlowe", *Dissertation Abstracts International* (1974), 34:7710A

Leech, Clifford, ed., *Marlowe; A Collection of Critical Essays*. 1964. Pp. 57-91

―――――――― , "The Structure of 'Tamburlaine'", *Tulane Drama Review*, 8:32-46, 1964

LePage, Peter V., "The Search for Godhead in Marlowe's 'Tamburlaine'", *College English* (1965), 26:604-09

Lever, K., "Image of Man in 'Tamburlaine', Part I", *Philological Quarterly*, 35:421-27, Oct., 1965

Masinton, Charles G., *Christopher Marlowe's Tragic Vision; A Study in Damnation*. 1972. Pp. 14-55

——————— , "Marlowe's Artists; The Failure of Imagination", *Ohio University Review* (1969), 11:22-35

Mezzadri, Piero, "Nota su 'Tamburlaine'", *Rivista di Letterature Moderne y Comparate*, 6:611-21, 1956

Mills, L. J., "Note on 'Tamburlaine'", *Modern Language Notes*, 52:101-03, Feb., 1937

Nation, 182:99-100, Feb. 4, 1956

Nelson, Timothy G. A., "Marlowe and His Audience; A Study of 'Tamburlaine'", *Southern Review* (Adelaide) (1969), 3:249-63

New Yorker, 31:58, Jan. 28, 1956

Newsweek, 47.91, Jan. 30, 1956

Nicol, Bernard DeBear, ed., *Varieties of Dramatic Experience*. 1969. Pp. 60-66

Parr, Johnstone, "The Horoscope of Mycetes in Marlowe's 'Tamburlaine I'" *Philological Quarterly*, 25:371-77, 1946

——————— , "Tamburlaine's Malady", *Modern Language Association, Publications* (PMLA), 59:696-714, 1944

Pearce, T. M., "Marlowe and Castiglione", *Modern Language Quarterly*, 12:3-12, 1951

——————— , "Tamburlaine's 'Discipline to His Three Sonnes': An Interpretation of 'Tamburlaine, Part II'", *Modern Language Quarterly* (1954), 15:18-27

Peet, C. Donald, "Rhetoric of 'Tamburlaine'", *Journal of English Literary History* (ELH), 26:137-55, June, 1959

Prior, Moody Erasmus, *The Language of Tragedy*. 1947. Pp. 33-46

Quinn, Michael, "The Freedom of Tamburlaine", *Modern Language Quarterly*, 21:315-20, 1960

Rattenhouse, R. W., "Tamburlaine, the 'Scourge of God'", *Modern Language Association. Publications* (PMLA), 56:337-48, 1941

Renaissance Drama; Essays Principally on Comedy, Ed. by S. Schoenbaum and Alan C. Dessen. 1972. Pp. 105-20

Ribner, Irving, "Idea in Marlowe's 'Tamburlaine'", *Journal of English Literary History* (ELH), 20:251-66, 1953

——————— , "'Tamburlaine' and 'The Wars of Cyrus'", *Journal of English and Germanic Philology*, 53:569-73, 1954

Richards, Susan, "Marlowe's 'Tamburlaine II'; A Drama of Death", *Modern Language Quarterly*, 26:375-87, 1965

Rickey, Mary E., "Astronomical Imagery in 'Tamburlaine'", *Renaissance Papers*, Pp. 63-70, 1954

Ricks, Christopher, ed., *English Drama to 1710*. (History of Literature in the English Language) Vol. 3. 1971. Pp. 134-45

Ross, Adan, "Tragedy of the Absurd; Marlowe's 'Tamburlaine' and Camus's 'Caligula'", *Thoth* (1973), 13:3-9

Saturday Review, 39:20, Feb. 4, 1956

Schuster, Erika and Horst Oppel, "Die Bankett-Szene in Marlowes "Tamburlaine'", *Anglia* (1959), 77:310-45

Scudder, Harold H., "An Allusion in 'Tamburlaine'", *Times Literary Supplement*, March 2, 1933, Pp. 147

Simpson, Percy, *Studies in Elizabethan Drama*. 1955. Pp. 95-111

Smith, Warren D., "The Substance of Meaning in 'Tamburlaine Part I'", *Studies in Philology* (1970), 67:156-66

Spence, Leslie, "Influence of Marlowe's Sources on Tamburlaine", *Modern Philology*, 24:181-99, 1926

_____ , "'Tamburlaine' and Marlowe", *Modern Language Association. Publications* (PMLA), 42:604-22, 1927

Sternlicht, Sanford, "'Tamburlaine' and Iterative Sun-Image", *English Record* (1966), 16:23-29

Summers, C. J., "Tamburlaine's Opponents and Machiavelli's Prince", *English Language Notes* (1974), 11:256-58

Taylor, Robert T., "Maximinus and 'Tamburlaine'", *Notes and Queries*, 4:417-18, 1957

Theatre Arts, 40:21-23, Feb., 1956 and 40:18-19, March, 1956

Thorp, Willard, "The Ethical Problem in Marlowe's 'Tamburlaine'", *Journal of English and Germanic Philology*, 29:385-89, 1930

Time, 67:34, Jan. 30, 1956

Tomlinson, Thomas Brian, *A Study of Elizabethan and Jacobean Tragedy*. 1964. Pp. 48-72

Velz, John W., "Episodic Structure in Four Tudor Plays; A Virtue of Necessity", *Comparative Drama* (1972), 6:87-102

Waith, Eugene M., *The Herculean Hero in Marlowe, Chapman, Shakespeare, and Dryden*. 1962. Pp. 60-87

_____ , *Ideas of Greatness; Heroic Drama in England*. 1971. Pp. 48-64

Ward, Adolphus William, *A History of English Dramatic Literature*, Vol. 1. 1966. Pp. 321-29

Watson-Williams, Helen, "The Power of Words: A Reading of 'Tamburlaine the Great'", *English* (1973), 22:13-18.

Wehling, Mary Meller, "Marlowe's Mnemonic Nominology, with Especial Reference to 'Tamburlaine'", *Modern Language Notes*, 73:243-47, 1958

Wild, Friedrich, "Studien zu Marlowes 'Tamburlaine'", *Wiener Beiträge zur Englischen Philologie Weltstimmen*, 65:232-51, 1958

Wyler, Siegfried, "Marlowe's Technique of Communicating with His Audience as Seen in His 'Tamburlaine'", *English Studies* (1967), 48:306-16

The Tragical History of Dr. Faustus, 1594

Alexander, Nigel, "The Performance of Christopher Marlowe's 'Dr. Faustus'", *Proceedings of the British Academy* (1971), 57:331-49

America, 96:655, March 9, 1957

Baker, Donald C., "Ovid and Faustus"; The 'Noctus Equi'", *Classical Journal*, 55:126-28, 1959

Banarjee, Chinmoy, "'Dr. Faustus': A Christian Re-Interpretation", *Quest* (July-Sept. 1966), #50:60-67

Barber, C. L., "'The Form of Faustus; Fortunes Good or Bad'", *Tulane Drama Review*, 8:92-119, 1964

Beall, Charles N., "Definition of Theme by Unconsecutive Event: Structure as Induction in Marlowe's 'Dr. Faustus'", *Renaissance Papers* (1962), Pp. 53-61

Bluestone, Max and Norman Rabkin, eds., *Shakespeare's Contemporaries; Modern Studies in English Renaissance Drama.* 2nd ed. 1970. Pp. 74-172

Bowe, Elaine C., "Doctrines and Images of Despair in Christopher Marlowe's 'Dr. Faustus' and Edmund Spencer's 'The Faerie Queene' ", *Dissertation Abstracts* (1969), Pp. 2206A

Bowers, R. H., "Marlowe's 'Dr. Faustus', Tirso's 'El Condenado por Desconfiado' and the Secret Cause", *Costerus* (1972), 4:9-27

Box, Terry J., "Irony and Objectivity in the Plays of Christopher Marlowe", *Dissertation Abstracts International* (1973), 33:4333A

Brahmer, Mieczyslav, Stanislaw Helsztynski and Julian Krzyzanowski, *Studies in Language in Honour of Margaret Schlauch.* 1966. Pp. 293-305

Briggs, W. D., "Marlowe's 'Faustus' ", *Modern Language Notes*, 38:385-93, 1923

Brooke, C. F. Tucker, "Notes on Marlowe's 'Dr. Faustus' ", *Philological Quarterly*, 12:17-23, 1933

Brooke, Nicholas, "The Moral Tragedy of Dr. Faustus", *Cambridge Journal* (1952), 5:662-87

Brooks, Cleanth, *A Shaping Joy; Studies in the Writer's Craft.* 1972. Pp. 367-80

Brown, Beatrice D., "Marlowe, Faustus and Simon Magus", *Modern Language Association. Publications* (PMLA), 54:82-121, 1939

Burwick, Frederick, "Marlowe's 'Dr. Faustus'; Two Manners, the Argumentative and the Passionate", *Neuphilologische Mitteilungen* (1969), 70:121-45

Bynum, James J., "Isolation, Metamorphosis and Self-Destruction in the Plays of Christopher Marlowe", *Dissertation Abstracts International* (1973), 34:719A

Campbell, Lily B., " 'Dr. Faustus': A Case of Conscience", *Modern Language Association. Publications*, (PMLA) 67:219-39, 1952

Carpenter, Nan C., " 'Miles' Versus 'Clericus' in Marlowe's 'Faustus' ", *Notes and Queries*, 197:91-93, 1952

Carreres, F. deA., "El Movimento Pendular en la 'Faustus' de Marlowe", *Filología Moderna* (1973), 13:29-64

Catholic World, 144:602, Feb., 1937 and 185:149, May, 1957

Clarke, Peter P., II, "The Pastoral/Anti-Pastoral Dialectic in the Plays of Christopher Marlowe", *Dissertation Abstracts International* (1972), 32:5176A

Commonweal, 25:360, Jan. 22, 1937 and 81:167, Oct. 30, 1964

Cox, Gerald H., III, "Marlowe's 'Dr. Faustus' and 'Sin Against the Holy Ghost' ", *Huntington Library Quarterly* (1973), 36:119-37

Crabtree, John H., Jr., "The Comedy in Marlowe's 'Dr. Faustus' ", *Furman Studies*, 9:#1:1-9, 1961

Craik, T. W., "Faustus' Damnation Reconsidered", *Renaissance Drama* (1969), n. s. 2:189-96

Cunningham, John E., *Elizabethan and Early Stuart Drama.* 1965. Pp. 45-50

Davidson, Clifford, "Dr. Faustus at Rome", *Studies in English Literature, 1500-1900* (Spring 1969), 9:232-39

Davidson, C., "Dr. Faustus of Wittenberg", *Studies in Philology*, 59:514-23, July, 1962

Dent, R. W., "Ramist Faustus or Ramist Marlowe?", *Neuphilologische Mitteilungen* (1972), 73:63-74

Dunn, Hough-Lewis, "The Language of the Magician as Limitation and Transcendence in the Wolfenbuttel 'Faustbuch', Greene's 'Friar Bacon', Marlowe's

'Dr. Faustus', Shakespeare's 'Tempest', and Goethe's 'Faust' ", *Dissertation Abstracts International* (1974), 35:444A

Duthie, G. I., "Some Observations on Marlowe's 'Dr. Faustus' ", *Archiv für das Studium der Neueren Sprachen und Literaturen* (1966), 118:81-96

Fabian, Bernhard, "A Note on Marlowe's 'Faustus' ", *English Studies*, 41: 365-68, 1960

Flasdieck, H. M., "Zur Datierung von Marlowes 'Faust' ", *English Studies*, 64 #2-3:320-51, 1929 and 65 #1:1-25, 1930

Forum, 97:355, June, 1937

Fraser, Russell, "On Christopher Marlowe", *Michigan Quarterly Review* (1973), 12:136-59

French, A. L., "Philosophy of 'Dr. Faustus' ", *Essays in Criticism* (April 1970), 20:123-42 and 21 (Jan. 1971): 101-06

French, William W., "Double View in 'Dr. Faustus' ", *West Virginia University Philological Papers* (1970), 17:3-15

Frey, Leonard H., "Antithetical Balance in the Opening and Close of 'Dr. Faustus' ", *Modern Language Quarterly* (1963), 24:350-53

Frye, R. M., "Marlowe's 'Dr. Faustus': The Repudiation of Humanity", *South Atlantic Quarterly*, 55:322-28, July, 1956

———— , "Theological and Non-Theological Structures in Tragedy", *Shakespeare Studies* (1968), 4:132-48

Gardner, Helen, "Milton's Satan and the Theme of Damnation in Elizabethan Tragedy", *Essays and Studies by Members of the English Association* (1948), n. s. 1:48-53

Gemzøe, Anker, "Faustus og Historien; En Sammenlignende Analyse af 'Historia von D. Johann Fausten' of Marlowe's 'Dr. Faustus' ", *Poetik* (1974), 22:5-44

Giamatti, Bartlett, "Marlowe: The Arts of Illusion", *Yale Review* (1972), 61: 530-43

Goldfarb, Russell and Clare, "The Seven Deadly Sins of 'Dr. Faustus' ", *College Language Association Journal* (1970), 13:350-63

Gonzalez, LaVerne D. K., "The Faustian Motif in Genêt: A Comparison of Marlowe's 'Dr. Faustus' and Genêt's 'Notre Dame des Fleurs' ", *Dissertation Abstracts International* (1972), 33:723A

Green, Clarence, " 'Dr. Faustus': Tragedy of Individualism", *Science and Society*, 10 #3:275-85, 1946

Greg, W. W., "Damnation of Faustus", *Modern Language Review*, 41:97-107, 1946

Hawkins, Sherman, "The Education of Faustus", *Studies in English Literature, 1500-1900* (1966), 6:193-209

Heilman, Robert B., "The Tragedy of Knowledge; Marlowe's Treatment of Faustus", *Quarterly Review of Literature*, 2:316-32, 1946

Heller, Otto, *"Faust" and "Faustus": A Study of Goethe's Relationship to Marlowe*, Washington Univ. Studies, n. s., Language and Literature, #2, 1931

Homan, Sidney R., Jr., " 'Dr. Faustus', Dekker's 'Old Fortunatus' and the Morality Plays", *Modern Language Quarterly* (1965), 26:497-505

Honderich, Pauline, "John Calvin and Dr. Faustus", *Modern Language Review* (1973), 68:1-13

Hosley, Richard, ed., *Essays on Shakespeare and the Elizabethan Drama in Honor of Hardin Craig*. 1962. Pp. 83-90

Houk, R. A., " 'Dr. Faustus' and 'A Shrew' ", *Modern Language Association. Publications* (PMLA), 62:950-57, 1947

Hoy, Cyrus, " 'Ignorance in Knowledge': Marlowe's Faustus and Ford's Giovanni", *Modern Philology* (Feb. 1960), 57:145-54

Hunter, G. K., "Five-Act Structure in 'Dr. Faustus' ", *Tulane Drama Review*, 8:77-91, 1964

Jarrett, Hobart S., "Verbal Ambiguities in Marlowe's 'Dr. Faustus' ", *College English*, 5:339-40, 1944

Kaula, David, "Time and the Timeless in 'Everyman' and 'Dr. Faustus' ", *College English* (1960), 22:9-14

Kawasaki, Junnosuke, "The Tragical Composition of 'Dr. Faustus' ", *Shakespeare Studies* (Japan) (1967-68), 6:103-21

Kiessling, N., "Dr. Faustus and the Sin of Demoniality", *Studies in English Literature* (1975), 15:205-11

Kirschbaum, Leo, "Marlowe's 'Faustus'; A Reconsideration", *Review of English Studies*, 19:225-41, July, 1943

―――――――――― , "Mephistophilis and the Lost Dragon", *Review of English Studies*, 18:312-15, 1942

Kocher, Paul H., "English Faust Book and the Date of Marlowe's 'Faustus' ", *Modern Language Notes*, 55:95-101, Feb., 1940

―――――――――― , "The Witchcraft Basis in Marlowe's 'Faustus' ", *Modern Philology*, 38:9-36, 1940

Lambert, J. W., "Dr. Faustus", *Drama* (1974), 115:56

Leech, Clifford, ed., *Marlowe; A Collection of Critical Essays*. 1964. Pp. 92-107, 112-19

Levin, Richard, *The Multiple Plot in English Renaissance Drama*. 1971. Pp. 119-23

Longo, Joseph A., "Marlowe's 'Dr. Faustus: Allegorical Parody in Act 5", *Greyfriar; Siena Studies in Literature* (1974), 15:38-49

Lynner, Darwin T., II, "The Dramatic Form of Christopher Marlowe's 'Dr. Faustus' ", *Dissertation Abstracts International* (1973), 33:4552A

McAlindon, T., "Classical Mythology and Christian Tradition in Marlow's 'Dr. Faustus' ", *Modern Language Association. Publications* (1966), 81:214-23

McCloskey, John C., "The Theme of Despair in Marlowe's 'Faustus' ", *College English*, 4:110-13, 1942

McCullen, Joseph T., "Dr. Faustus and Renaissance Learning", *Modern Language Review*, 51:6-16, Jan., 1956

Manley, Frank, "The Nature of Faustus", *Modern Philology* (Feb. 1969), 66:218-31

Masinton, Charles G., *Christopher Marlowe's Tragic Vision; A Study in Damnation*. 1972. Pp. 113-42

Matalene, H. W., III, "Marlowe's 'Faustus' and the Comforts of Academicism", *Journal of English Literary History* (1972), 39:495-520

Maxwell, J. C., "The Sin of Faustus", *The Wind and the Rain* (Summer 1947), 4:49-52

Mizener, Arthur, "The Tragedy of Marlowe's 'Dr. Faustus' ", *College English* (1943), 5:70-75

Morgan, Gerald, "Harlequin Faustus: Marlowe's Comedy of Hell", *Humanities Association Bulletin* (Spring 1967), 18:22-34

Moulton, Richard G., *World Literature*. 1911. Pp. 224-31

Mroczkowska, Katarzyna, "l'Analyse Comparée de l'Emploi de la Parodie et due Mélange du Tragique et du comique dans 'El Magico Prodigioso' de Calderon et 'The Tragical History of Dr. Faustus' de Marlowe", *Kwartalnik Neofilologiczny* (1974), 21:499-505

Muir, K., "Marlowe's 'Dr. Faustus'", *Philological Pragensia. Academia Scientiarum Bohemo-Slovenico* (1966), 9:395-468

Nagarajan S., "Philosophy of 'Dr. Faustus'", *Essays in Criticism* (Oct. 1970), 20:485-87

Nation, 199:285-86, Oct. 26, 1964

New Republic, 90:46-47, Feb. 17, 1937

New Yorker, 40:108, Oct. 17, 1964

Newsweek, 9:30-31, Jan. 23, 1937

Nicol, Bernard DeBear, ed., *Varieties of Dramatic Experience*. 1969. Pp. 66-72

O'Brien, Margaret A., "Christian Belief in 'Dr. Faustus'", *ELH* (1970), 37:1-11

O'Connor, G., "Dr. Faustus", *Plays and Players* (Oct. 1974), 22:36-37

Ornstein, Robert, "Comic Synthesis in 'Dr. Faustus'", *Journal of English Literary History* (ELH), 22:165-72, Sept., 1955

Ornstein, Robert, "Marlowe and God: The Tragic Theology of 'Dr. Faustus'", *Modern Language Association. Publications* (Oct. 1968), 83:1378-85

Palmer, D. J., "Magic and Poetry in 'Dr. Faustus'", *Critical Quarterly*, 6:56-67, 1964

Perkinson, Richard H., "A Restoration 'Improvement' of 'Dr. Faustus'", *Journal of English Literary History* (ELH), 1:305-24, 1934

Rabkin, Norman, ed., *Reinterpretations of Elizabethan Drama*. 1969. Pp. 33-88

Ransom, Mariann; Cook, Roderick; and Pearce, T. M., "'German Valdes and Cornelius' in Marlowe's 'Dr. Faustus'", *Notes and Queries*, 9:329-31, 1962

Ricks, Christopher, ed., *English Drama to 1710*. (History of Literature in the English Language), Vol. 3. 1971. Pp. 138-45

Rosador, Kurt Tetzeli von, "Dr. Faustus", *Anglia* (1972), 90:470-93

Sachs, Arich, "The Religious Despair of Dr. Faustus", *Journal of English and Germanic Philology*, 63:625-47, 1964

Sams, Henry W., "Faustus and the Reformation", *Bulletin of the Citadel*, v. 5: #4, Pp. 3-9, 1941

Sanders, Wilbur, "Marlowe's 'Dr. Faustus'", *Melbourne Critical Review* (Univ. of Melbourne), #7:78-91, 1964

Schelling, F. E., "Dr. Faustus and Friar Bacon", *Nation*, 101:12-13, July 1, 1915

Sewall, R., *The Vision of Tragedy*. 1962. Pp. 57-67

Shaw, George Bernard, *Plays and Players; Essays on the Theatre*. 1952. Pp. 105-14

Simpson, Percy, *Studies in Elizabethan Drama*. 1955. Pp. 95-111

Smidt, Kristian, "Two Aspects of Ambition in Elizabethan Tragedy; 'Dr. Faustus' and 'Macbeth'", *English Studies* (1969), 50:235-48

Smith, James, "Marlowe's 'Dr. Faustus'", *Scrutiny* (1939), 8:36-55

Smith, Warren D., "The Nature of Evil in 'Dr. Faustus'", *Modern Language Review*, 60:171-75, 1965

Snyder, Susan, "Marlowe's 'Dr. Faustus' as an Inverted Saint's Life", *Studies in Philology* (1966), 63:565-77

Speaight, Robert, "Marlowe: The Forerunner", *Review of English Literature* (1966), 7:25-41

Stroup, Thomas B., "'Dr. Faustus' and 'Hamlet': Contrasting Kinds of Christian Tragedy", *Comparative Drama* (1971-72), 5:243-53

Studies in English in Honor of Raphael Dorman O'Leary and Selden Lincoln Whitcomb, by Members of the English Department, Univ. of Kansas (Kansas Univ., Humanistic Studies, v. 6, #4), 1940, Pp. 3-7

Summers, Claude J. and Ted-Larry Pebworth, "Marlowe's 'Faustus' and the Earl of Bedford's Motto", *English Language Notes* (1972), 9:165-67

Tapper, Bonno, "Aristotle's 'Sweete Analutikes' in Marlowe's 'Dr. Faustus'", *Studies in Philology*, 27:215-19, 1930

Theatre Arts, 21:184-85, March, 1937

Tibi, Pierre, "'Dr. Faustus' et la Cosmologie de Marlowe", *Revue des Langues Vivantes* (1974), 40:212-27

Time, 84:77, Oct. 16, 1964

Traci, Phillip J., "Marlowe's Faustus as Artist; A Suggestion About a Theme in the Play", *Renaissance Papers* (1966), Pp. 3-9

Versefield, Martin, "Some Remarks of Marlowe's 'Faustus'", *English Studies in Africa* (Johannesburg), 1:134-43, 1958

Walsh, Maureen P., "Demigod, Devil or Man; A Reconsideration of the Character of Faustus", *Nassau Review* (1970), 2:54-65

Ward, Adolphus William, *A History of English Dramatic Literature*, vol. 1. 1966. Pp. 329-37

West, Robert H., "The Impatient Magic of 'Dr. Faustus'", *English Literary Renaissance* (1974), 4:218-40

Westlund, Joseph, "The Orthodox Christian Framework of Marlowe's 'Faustus'", *Studies in English Literature, 1500-1900* (Rice Univ.), 3:191-205, 1963

Woodard, Lawrence E., "A Study of the Argumentation Used in Four Selected Elizabethan Plays: 'Julius Caesar', 'Volpone', 'Dr. Faustus' and 'The Spanish Tragedy'", *Dissertation Abstracts International* (1974), 35:3935A

Wyman, Linda, "How Plot and Sub-Plot Unite in Marlowe's 'Faust'", *CEA Critic* (1974), 37:14-16

Young, Stark, *Immortal Shadows; A Book of Dramatic Criticism.* 1948. Pp. 174-77

Tragedy of Dido, Queen of Carthage, 1594

Bennett, Josephine Waters; Cargill, Oscar; and Hall, Vernon, eds., *Studies in English Renaissance Drama in Memory of Karl Julius Holzknecht.* 1959. Pp. 231-47

Boas, Frederick S., *University Drama in the Tudor Age.* 1965. Pp. 189-91

Bobin, Donna, "Marlowe's Humor", *Massachusetts Studies in English* (Fall 1969), 2:29-40

Brashear, Marion G., Jr., "Marlowe's 'Tragedy of Dido'", *Dissertation Abstracts International* (1973), 33:3574A

Bynum, James J., "Isolation, Metamorphosis, and Self-Destruction in the Plays of Christopher Marlowe", *Dissertation Abstracts International* (1973), 34:719A

Cope, Jackson I., "Marlowe's 'Dido' and the Titillating Children", *English Literary Renaissance* (1974), 4:315-25

Cutts, John P., "'Dido, Queen of Carthage'", *Notes and Queries*, 5:371-74, 1958

Gill, Roma, "Marlowe, Lucan and Sulpitius", *Review of English Studies* (1973), n. s. 14:401-13

Godshalk, W. L., "Marlowe's 'Dido, Queen of Carthage'", *ELH* (March 1971), 38:1-18

Hosley, Richard ed., *Essays on Shakespeare and Elizabethan Drama; In Honor of Hardin Craig.* 1962. Pp. 55-68

Leigh, William, "Marlowe's 'Dido Queen of Carthage'", *Journal of English Literary History* (1971), 38:1-18

Pearce, Thomas, "Marlowe's 'Tragedie of Dido' in Relation to Its Latin Source", *Univ. of Pittsburgh Abstracts of Theses*, 6:141-48, 1930

Rogers, David M., "Love and Honor in Marlowe's 'Dido, Queen of Carthage'", *Greyfriar* (Sierra College, Londonville, N.Y.) 6:3-7, 1963

Rousseau, G. S., "Marlowe's 'Dido' and a Rhetoric of Love", *English Miscellany* (1968), 19:25-49

Ward, Adolphus William, *A History of English Dramatic Literature*, vol. 1. 1966. Pp. 356-58

Xavier, Francis, "Christopher Marlowe's 'Dido Queen of Carthage'", *Dissertation Abstracts International* (1972), 33:1702A

EDUARDO MARQUINO
SEE

GREGORIO MARTINEZ SIERRA AND

EDUARDO MARQUINO

JOHN MARSTON

Antonio and Mellida, 1599

Bergson, Allen, "Dramatic Style as Parody in Marston's 'Antonio and Mellida'", *Studies in English Literature, 1500-1900* (Spring 1971), 11: 307-25

―――――――――, "The Ironic Tragedies of Marston and Chapman: Notes on Jacobean Tragic Form", *Journal of English and Germanic Philology* (Oct. 1970), 69:613-30

Berland, Ellen, "The Function of Irony in Marston's 'Antonio and Mellida'", *Studies in Philology* (Oct. 1969), 66:739-55

Foakes, R. A., "John Marston's Fantastical Plays: 'Antonio and Mellida' and 'Antonio's Revenge'", *Philological Quarterly* (1962), 41:229-39

Kernan, Alvin, *The Cankered Muse; Satire of the English Renaissance.* 1959. Pp. 206-10

Wilson, Alice C., "The Concept of Wealth in the Works of John Marston", *Dissertation Abstracts International* (1972), 33:1701A

Antonio's Revenge, 1599

Ayres, Philip J., "Marston's 'Antonio's Revenge': The Morality of the Revenging Hero", *Studies in English Literature, 1500-1900* (1972), 12:359-74

Bergson, Allen, "The Ironic Tragedies of Marston and Chapman: Notes on Jacobean Tragic Form", *Journal of English and Germanic Philology* (Oct. 1970), 69:613-30

Foakes, R. A., "John Marston's Fantastical Plays: 'Antonio and Mellida' and 'Antonio's Revenge'", *Philological Quarterly* (1962), 41:229-39

Geckle, George L., "'Antonio's Revenge': Never More Woe in Lesser Plot Found", *Comparative Drama* (1972-73), 6:323-35

Lever, J. W., *The Tragedy of State.* 1971. Pp. 18-36

Mehl, Dieter, *The Elizabethan Dumb Show.* 1966. Pp. 125-32

Wilson, Alice C., "The Concept of Wealth in the Works of John Marston", *Dissertation Abstracts International* (1972), 33:1701A

The Dutch Courtesan, 1603/04

Hamilton, Donna B., "Language and Theme in 'The Dutch Courtesan'", *Renaissance Drama* (1972), 5:75-87

Keyishian, Harry, "Dekker's Whore and Marston's Courtesan", *English Language Notes* (1967), 4:261-66

Spencer, Theodore, "Reason and Passion in Marston's 'The Dutch Courtesan'", *Criterion* (1934), 13:586-94

Viebrock, Helmut and Erzgräber, Willie, eds., *Festschrift zum 75. Geburtstag von Theodor Spira.* 1960. Pp. 152-63

Wilson, Alice, "The Concept of Wealth in the Works of John Marston", *Dissertation Abstracts International* (1972), 33:1701A

Yae, Young Soo, "Moral Growth Through Contrived Experience in Selected Plays of John Marston", *Dissertation Abstracts International* (1974), 35: 3779A

Histriomastix; or, The Player Whipt, 1599

Geckle, George L., "John Marston's 'Histriomastix' and the Golden Age", *Comparative Drama* (1972), 6:205-22

Kernan, Alvin, *The Cankered Muse; Satire of the English Renaissance.* 1959. Pp. 143-49

——————————— , "John Marston's Play 'Historiomastix'", *Modern Language Quarterly* (1958), 19:134-40

Jack Drum's Entertainment, 1600

Wilson, Alice C., "The Concept of Wealth in the Works of John Marston", *Dissertation Abstracts International* (1972), 33:1701A

The Malcontent, 1604

Bluestone, Max and Norman Rabkin, eds., *Shakespeare's Contemporaries; Modern Studies in English Renaissance Drama.* 2nd ed. 1970. Pp. 255-69

Geckle, George L., "Fortune in Marston's 'The Malcontent'", *Modern Language Association. Publications* (March 1971), 86:202-09

Houser, D. J., "Purging the Commonwealth: Marston's Disguised Dukes and 'A Knack to Know a Knave'", *Modern Language Association. Publications* (1974), 89:993-1006

Jensen, Ejner J., "Theme and Imagery in 'The Malcontent'", *Studies in English Literature, 1500-1900* (Spring 1970), 10:367-84

Kernan, Alvin, *The Cankered Muse; Satire of the English Renaissance.* 1959. Pp. 211-28

Mehl, Dieter, *The Elizabethan Dumb Show.* 1966. Pp. 135-36

Salomon, Brownell, "The Theological Basis of Imagery and Structure in 'The Malcontent'", *Studies in English Literature, 1500-1900* (1974), 14: 271-84

Slights, W. W. E., "Elder in a Deform'd Church; The Function of Marston's Malcontent'", *Studies in English Literature, 1500-1900* (1973), 13:360-73
——————————, "Political Morality and the Ending of 'The Malcontent'", *Modern Philology* (Nov. 1971), 69:138-39

Stoll, Elmer Edgar, "Shakespeare, Marston and the Malcontent", *Modern Philology* (Jan. 1906), 3:281-303

Tomlinson, Thomas Brian, *A Study of Elizabethan and Jacobean Tragedy*. 1964. Pp. 220-23

Viebrock, Helmut, ed., *Festschrift zum 75. Geburtstag von Theodor Spira*. 1961. Pp. 152-63

West, Herbert F., Jr., "Unifying Devices in Four Globe Plays", *Dissertation Abstracts International* (1970), 30:5424A

Wharton, T. F., "'Malcontent' and Dreams, Visions, Fantasies", *Essays in Criticism* (1974), 24:261-73

Yae, Young Soo, "Moral Growth Through Contrived Experience in Selected Plays of John Marston", *Dissertation Abstracts International* (1974), 35: 3779A

Yagi, Tsuyoshi, "Fushigeki 'The Malcontent'", *Eigo Seinen* (1974), 119: 696-98

The Parasitaster; or, The Fawne, 1604-06

Finkelpearl, Philip J., "The Use of the Middle Temple's Christmas Revels in Marston's 'The Fawne'", *Studies in Philology* (1967), 64:199-209

Houser, D. J., "Purging the Commonwealth; Marston's Disguised Dukes and 'A Knack to Know a Knave'", *Modern Language Association. Publications* (1974), 89:993-1006

Kaplan, Joel, "John Marston's 'Fawn'; A Saturnalian Satire", *Studies in English Literature, 1500-1900* (Spring 1969), 9:335-50

Yae, Young Soo, "Moral Growth Through Contrived Experience in Selected Plays of John Marston", *Dissertation Abstracts International* (1974), 35:3779A

What You Will, 1601

Kernan, Alvin, *The Cankered Muse; Satire of the English Renaissance*. 1959. Pp. 150-54

Rouk, Bruce A., "John Marston; The Growth of a Satirist", *Dissertation Abstracts International* (1972), 32:6390A

The Wonder of Women; or, Sophronisba, 1606

Mehl, Dieter, *The Elizabethan Dumb Show*. 1966. Pp. 133-35

Ure, Peter, *Elizabethan and Jacobean Drama; Critical Essays*. 1974. Pp. 75-92

Wilson, Alice C., "The Concept of Wealth in the Works of John Marston", *Dissertation Abstracts International* (1972), 33:1701A

JOHN MARSTON, GEORGE CHAPMAN AND BEN JONSON

Eastward Ho!, 1605

Adams, J. Q., "'Eastward Hoe' and Its Satire Against the Scots", *Studies in Philology*, 28:689:701, Oct., 1931

Brandes, George, *William Shakespeare; A Critical Study*, Vol. 1. 1963. Pp. 387

Cohen, Ralph A., "The Function of Spelling in 'Eastward Ho'", *Renaissance Papers*, 1973:83-96

GREGORIO MARTINEZ SIERRA

Amanecer *SEE* Dawn

Cada Uno y Su Vida, 1919
O'Connor, Patricia W., "A Spanish Precursor to Women's Lib: The Heroine in Gregorio Martinez-Sierra's Theater", *Hispania* (1972), 55:865-72

El Corazón Ciego, 1919
O'Connor, Patricia W., "A Spanish Precursor to Women's Lib; The Heroine in Gregorio Martinez-Sierra's Theater", *Hispania* (1972), 55:865-72

Dawn, 1915
Starkie, Walter, "Gregorio Martinez Sierra and Modern Spanish Drama", *Contemporary Review*, 125:198-205, 1924

Kingdom of God, 1915
Birrell, F., "Kingdom of God", *Nation* (London), 42:184-85, Nov. 5, 1927
Brown, I., "Kingdom of God", *Saturday Review*, 144:583, Oct. 29, 1927
Catholic World, 128:591-92, Feb., 1929
Commonweal, 9:264-65, Jan. 2, 1929
Horsnell, H., "Kingdom of God", *Outlook* (London), 60:621, Nov. 5, 1927
Jennings, R., "Kingdom of God", 139:763-64, Nov. 5, 1927
Literary Digest, 100:21-22, Jan. 12, 1929
MacCarthy, Desmond, "Kingdom of God", *New Statesman*, 30:110, Nov. 5, 1927
Nation, 128:52, Jan. 9, 1929
New Republic, 57:245-46, Jan. 16, 1929
Outlook, 151:53, Jan. 9, 1929
Shipp, H., "Kingdom of God", *English Review*, 45:728-29, Dec., 1927
Young, Stark, *Immortal Shadows; A Book of Dramatic Criticism*. 1948. Pp. 101-05

Madame Pepita, 1912
Starkie, Walter, "Gregorio Martinez-Sierra and Modern Spanish Drama", *Contemporary Review*, 125:198-205, 1924

Mama, 1912
Starkie, Walter, "Gregorio Martinez-Sierra and Modern Spanish Drama", *Contemporary Review*, 125:198-205, 1924

The Palace of Sadness, 1911
Starkie, Walter, "Gregorio Martinez-Sierra and Modern Spanish Drama", *Contemporary Review*, 125:198-205, 1924

El Palacio Triste *SEE* The Palace of Sadness

Pobrecito Juan *SEE* Poor John

Poor John, 1912
Starkie, Walter, "Gregorio Martinez-Sierra and Modern Spanish Drama", *Contemporary Review*, 125:198-205, 1924

El Reino de Dios   *SEE*   Kingdom of God

The Romantic Young Lady, 1918
  O'Connor, Patricia W., "A Spanish Precursor to Women's Lib; The Heroine in Gregorio Martinez-Sierra's Theater", *Hispania* (1972), 55:865-72
  Swinnerton, Frank, "Romantic Young Lady", *Nation* (London), 28:16, Oct. 2, 1920
  Young, Stark, "Romantic Young Lady", *New Republic*, 47:59-60, June 2, 1926

Sueño de Una Noche de Agosto   *SEE*   Romantic Young Lady

GREGORIO MARTINEZ SIERRA AND EDUARDO MARQUINO

Road to Happiness, 1927
  Young, Stark, "Road to Happiness", *New Republic*, 50:354-55, May 18, 1927

GREGORIO MARTINEZ SIERRA AND MARIA MARTINEZ SIERRA

Cradle Song, 1911
  America, 94:342, Dec. 17, 1955
  Birrell, F., "Cradle Song", *Nation* (London), 40:216-17, Nov. 13, 1926
  Bookman (London), 71:203-06, Dec., 1926
  Catholic World, 124:812-13, March, 1927 and 182:385, Feb., 1956
  Commonweal, 63:457-8, Feb. 3, 1956
  L'Europe Nouvelle, 14:1340, Oct. 3, 1931
  Jennings, R., "Cradle Song", *Spectator*, 137:852-53, Nov. 13, 1926
  MacCarthy, Desmond, "Cradle Song", *New Statesman and Nation*, 2:338, Sept. 19, 1931
  Mercure de France, 268:365-68, June 1, 1936
  Nation, 124:243-44, March 2, 1927
  New Republic, 50:274, April 27, 1927 and 51:18, May 25, 1927 and 134:20, Jan. 2, 1956
  Outlook (London), 58:473, Nov. 13, 1926
  Revue des Deux Mondes, s. 8 33:466-67, May 15, 1936
  Royde-Smith, N. G., "Cradle Song", *Outlook* (London), 59:66, Jan. 15, 1927
  Starkie, Walter, "Gregorio Martinez-Sierra and Modern Spanish Drama", *Contemporary Review*, 125:198-205, 1924
  Theatre Arts, 28:342, June, 1944

MARIA MARTINEZ SIERRA

SEE

GREGORIO MARTINEZ SIERRA AND MARIA MARTINEZ SIERRA

PHILIP MASSINGER

Believe as You List, 1631
  Gill, Roma, "'Necessitie of State': Massinger's 'Believe as You List'", *English Studies* (1965), 46:407-16
  Hogan, Alice P., "Theme and Structure in Massinger's Plays", *Dissertation Abstracts International* (1972), 32:3954A

The Bondman, 1623
  Gross, Allen, "Contemporary Politics in Massinger", *Studies in English Literature* (1966), 6:279-90
  Winston, Florence T., "The Significance of Women in the Plays of Philip Massinger", *Dissertation Abstracts International* (1972), 33:2909A

The City Madam, 1632
  Fothergill, Robert A., "Dramatic Experience of Massinger's 'The City Madam' and 'A New Way to Pay Old Debts' ", *University of Toronto Quarterly* (1973), 43:68-86
  Gibson, C. A., "Massinger's London Merchant and the Date of 'The City Madam' ", *Modern Language Review* (Oct. 1970), 65:737-49
  Gross, Allen, Social Change and Philip Massinger", *Studies in English Literature* (1967), 7:329-42
  Knights, L. C., *Drama and Society in the Age of Jonson*. 1962. Pp. 270-73 and 280-82

The Emperor of the East, 1631
  Winston, Florence T., "The Significance of Women in the Plays of Philip Massinger", *Dissertation Abstracts International* (1972), 33:2909A

The Maid of Honour, 1621
  Gross, Allen, "Contemporary Politics in Massinger", *Studies in English Literature* (1966), 6:279-90
  Mullany, Peter F., "Religion in Massinger's 'The Maid of Honour' ", *Renaissance Drama* (1969), 2:143-56
  Winston, Florence T., "The Significance of Women in the Plays of Philip Massinger", *Dissertation Abstracts International* (1972), 33:2909A

A New Way to Pay Old Debts, 1621/22?
  Birrell, F., " 'A New Way to Pay Old Debts': Criticism", *New Statesman* (Dec. 2, 1922), 20:267-68
  Bluestone, Max and Norman Rabkin, eds., *Shakespeare's Contemporaries; Modern Studies in English Renaissance Drama*. 2nd ed. 1970. Pp. 378-86
  Bowers, R. H., "A Note on Massinger's 'New Way' ", *Modern Language Review* (1958), 53:214-15
  Burelbach, Frederick M., Jr., " 'A New Way to Pay Old Debts': Jacobean Morality", *College Language Association Journal* (1969), 12:205-13
  Craig, Hardin, ed., *Essays in Dramatic Literature; The Parrott Presentation Volume*. 1935. Pp. 277-87
  Cunningham, John E., *Elizabethan and Early Stuart Drama*. 1965. Pp. 103-07
  Essays in Dramatic Literature; The Parrott Presentation Volume by Pupils of Professor T. M. Parrott of Princeton University. Published in His Honor. Ed. by H. Craig. 1935. Pp. 277-87
  Fothergill, R. A., "Dramatic Experience of Massinger's 'The City Madam' and 'New Way to Pay Old Debts' ", *University of Toronto Quarterly* (1973), 43:68-86
  Gross, Alan Gerald, "Social Change and Philip Massinger", *Studies in English Literature* (1967), 7:329-42
  Knights, L. C., *Drama and Society in the Age of Jonson*. 1962. Pp. 273-80
  Levin, Richard, *The Multiple Plot in English Renaissance Drama*. 1971. Pp. 134-36

Thomson, Patricia, "The Old Way and the New Way in Dekker and Massinger", *Modern Language Review* (1956), 51:168-78

Turner, W. J., "'A New Way to Pay Old Debts': Criticism", *Spectator* (Nov. 25, 1922), 129:764

The Picture, 1629

Steiner, A., "Massinger's 'The Picture', Bandello and Hungary", *Modern Language Notes* (1931), 46:401-03

Winston, Florence T., "The Significance of Women in the Plays of Philip Massinger", *Dissertation Abstracts International* (1972), 33:2909A

Renegado; or, The Gentleman of Venice, 1624

Mullany, Peter F. "Massinger's 'The Renegado': Religion in Stuart Tragicomedy", *Genre* (1972), 5:138-52

The Roman Actor, 1626

Crabtree, John Henry, Jr., "Philip Massinger's Use of Rhetoric in 'The Roman Actor'", *Furman Studies* (1960), 7:40-58

Hogan, A. P., "Imagery of Acting in 'The Roman Actor'", *Modern Language Review* (1971), 66:273-81

A Very Woman; or, The Prince of Tarent, 1634

Gill, R., "Collaboration and Revision in Massinger's 'A Very Woman'", *Review of English Studies* (1967), 18:136-48

Maxwell, Baldwin, *Studies in Beaumont, Fletcher and Massinger.* 1939. Pp. 177-93

PHILIP MASSINGER AND NATHAN FIELD

Fatal Dowry, 1619

Bishop, Carol, "A Critical Edition of 'The Fatal Dowry'", *Dissertation Abstracts International* (1972), 33:2885A

Waith, Eugene M., "'Controversia' in the English Drama: Medwall and Massinger", *Modern Language Association. Publications* (1953), 68:286-303

The Virgin Martyr, 1620

Fischer, Uve Christian, "Un Dramma Martirologico Barocco: 'The Virgin Martyr' di Philip Massinger", *Siculorum Gymnasium* (1963), 16:1-19

W. SOMERSET MAUGHAM

Breadwinner, 1930

Arts and Decoration, 36:68, Dec., 1931

Catholic World, 134:209, Nov., 1931

New Republic, 68:209, Oct. 7, 1931

Tate, Michael G., "The Inconsistent Vision; Edwardian Social Theory and the Plays of W. Somerset Maugham", *Dissertation Abstracts International* (1973), 34:342A

Theatre Arts, 15:990, Dec., 1931

Theatre Magazine, 53:30, Feb., 1931

Caesar's Wife, 1919

Review, 1:688, Dec. 20, 1919

Tate, Michael G., "The Inconsistent Vision: Edwardian Social Theory and the Plays of W. Somerset Maugham", *Dissertation Abstracts International* (1973), 34:342A

Camel's Back, 1923
New Statesman, 22:511, Feb., 9, 1924
Spectator, 132:198, Feb. 9, 1924

Caroline, 1916
Nation 103:331, Oct. 5, 1916
Nation (London), 39:352-53, June 26, 1926

Le Cercle   *SEE*   The Circle

The Circle, 1921
Les Annales Politiques et Littéraires, 92:41, Jan. 1, 1929
Bookman (London), 60:45, April, 1921
Catholic World, 147:346-47, June, 1938
Commonweal, 28:48, May 6, 1938
Cordell, Richard A., "The Theatre of Somerset Maugham", *Modern Drama* (1959), 1:211-17
L'Illustration, 86 pt. 2:704, Dec. 8, 1928
Journal des Débats, 35 pt. 2:909-10, Nov. 30, 1928
Lewisohn, Ludwig, *Drama and the Stage*. 1922. Pp. 184-87
MacCarthy, Desmond, *Theatre*. 1955. Pp. 129-31
Mais, Stuart Petre Brodie, *Some Modern Authors*. 1923. Pp. 288-95
Mercure de France, 209:155-58, Jan. 1, 1929
Nation, 113:356, Sept. 28, 1921 and 146:512-13, April 30, 1938
Nation (London), 28:879-80, March 19, 1921
New Republic, 28:161, Oct. 5, 1921
New Statesman, 16:704-05, March 19, 1921
Review, 5:275, Sept. 24, 1921
Rosenblood, Norman, ed., *Shaw; Seven Critical Essays; Seven Papers Presented at the Shaw Seminars, Niagara on the Lake, 1966-68*. 1971. Pp. 36-50
Spectator, 126:396, March 26, 1921 and 146:344, March 7, 1931
Tate, Michael G., "The Inconsistent Vision; Edwardian Social Theory and the Plays of W. Somerset Maugham", *Dissertation Abstracts International* (1973), 34:342A
Theatre Arts, 29:167-69, March, 1945
Time, 31:26, May 2, 1938

The Constant Wife, 1926
Block, Anita Cahn, *Changing World in Plays and Theatre*. 1939. Pp. 76-132
Catholic World, 174:392, Feb., 1952
Commonweal, 55:299, Dec. 28, 1951
Cordell, Richard A., "The Theatre of Somerset Maugham", *Modern Drama* (1959), 1:211-17
London Mercury, 16:85, May, 1927 and 36:278, July, 1937
New Republic, 49:108, Dec. 15, 1926 and 126:22, Jan. 7, 1952
New Statesman and Nation, 13:882, May 29, 1937
New Yorker, 27:72, Dec. 15, 1951
Newsweek, 38:69, Dec. 17, 1951

Saturday Review, 143:598-99, April 16, 1927
Saturday Review of Literature, 34:18-19, Dec. 29, 1951
School and Society, 75:326, May 24, 1952
Spectator, 138:685, April 16, 1927
Taylor, John Russell, *The Rise and Fall of the Well-Made Play*. 1967. Pp. 104-06
Time, 58:76, Dec. 17, 1951
Tynan, Kenneth, *Curtains; Selections from the Drama Criticism and Related Writings*. 1961. Pp. 247-48

East of Suez, 1922
Bookman (London), 63:53-54, Oct., 1922
MacCarthy, Desmond, *Theatre*. 1955. Pp. 131-34
Mais, Stuart Petre Brodie, *Some Modern Authors*. 1923. Pp. 288-95
New Statesman, 20:14, Oct. 7, 1922
Spectator, 129:337, Sept. 9, 1922
Walkley, Arthur Bingham, *More Prejudice*. 1923. Pp. 118-21

The Explorer, 1908
Tate, Michael G., "The Inconsistent Vision; Edwardian Social Theory and the Plays of W. Somerset Maugham", *Dissertation Abstracts International* (1973), 34:342A

For Services Rendered, 1932
Block, Anita Cahn, *Changing World in Plays and Theatre*. 1939. Pp. 302-51
Catholic World, 137:208-10, May, 1933
Commonweal, 17:719, April 26, 1933
English Review, 55:667-69, Dec., 1932
MacCarthy, Desmond, *Theatre*. 1955. Pp. 134-39
Nation, 136:511-12, May 3, 1933
New Statesman and Nation, 4:577-78, Nov. 12, 1932
Newsweek, 1:28, April 22, 1933
Saturday Review, 154:502, Nov. 12, 1932
Spectator, 149:659, Nov. 11, 1932
Tate, Michael G., "The Inconsistent Vision; Edwardian Social Theory and the Plays of W. Somerset Maugham", *Dissertation Abstracts International* (1973), 34:342A
Theatre Arts, 17:416-17, June, 1933

Lady Fredericks, 1907
Taylor, John Russell, *The Rise and Fall of the Well-Made Play*. 1967. Pp. 93-99
Theatre Arts, 31:30, March, 1947

The Land of Promise, 1913
Tate, Michael G., "The Inconsistent Vision; Edwardian Social Theory and the Plays of W. Somerset Maugham", *Dissertation Abstracts International* (1973), 34:342A

Landed Gentry, 1910
Tate, Michael G., "The Inconsistent Vision; Edwardian Social Theory and the Plays of W. Somerset Maugham", *Dissertation Abstracts International* (1973), 34:342A

Letter, 1927
  Nation (London), 40:757, March 5, 1927
  New Republic, 52:207-08, Oct. 12, 1927
  New Statesman, 28:698, March 19, 1927
  Outlook, 147:181-82, Oct. 12, 1927
  Saturday Review, 143:350-51, March 5, 1927
  Saturday Review of Literature, 4:193-94, Oct. 15, 1927
  Spectator, 138:358, March 5, 1927

Man of Honour, 1903
  Atheneum, 1:283, Feb. 28, 1903
  Tate, Michael G., "The Inconsistent Vision; Edwardian Social Theory and
  the Plays of W. Somerset Maugham", *Dissertation Abstracts International*
  (1973), 34:342A

Marriages Are Made in Heaven, 1902
  Tate, Michael G., "The Inconsistent Vision; Edwardian Social Theory and
  the Plays of W. Somerset Maugham", *Dissertation Abstracts International*
  (1973), 34:342A

Our Betters, 1917
  Cordell, Richard A., "The Theatre of Somerset Maugham", *Modern Drama*
  (1959), 1:211-17
  MacCarthy, Desmond, *Theatre*. 1955. Pp. 119-24
  Nation (London), 34:198, Nov. 3, 1923
  New Republic, 10:200, March 17, 1917
  New Statesman, 21:738-39, Oct. 6, 1923
  Outlook, 148:383, March 7, 1928
  Outlook (London), 52:271, Oct. 6, 1923
  Spectator, 131:386-87, Sept. 22, 1923
  Tate, Michael G., "The Inconsistent Vision; Edwardian Social Theory and
  the Plays of W. Somerset Maugham", *Dissertation Abstracts International*
  (1973), 34:342A

Sacred Flame, 1928
  New Statesman and Nation, 30:386, Dec. 8, 1945
  Saturday Review, 147:210-11, Feb. 16, 1929
  Spectator, 142:228-29, Feb. 16, 1929
  Tate, Michael G., "The Inconsistent Vision; Edwardian Social Theory and the
  Plays of W. Somerset Maugham", *Dissertation Abstracts International*
  (1973), 34:342A

Sheppey, 1933
  Commonweal, 40:60-61, May 5, 1944
  MacCarthy, Desmond, *Theatre*. 1955. Pp. 124-28
  Nathan, George Jean, *Theatre Book of the Year, 1943-44*. Pp. 302-04
  New Statesman and Nation, 6:325, Sept. 16, 1933
  New Yorker, 20:44, April 29, 1944
  Saturday Review, 156:327-28, Sept. 23, 1933
  Spectator, 151:369, Sept. 22, 1933
  Theatre Arts, 28:335-36, June, 1944
  Time, 43:58, May 1, 1944

The Tenth Man, 1910
  Tate, Michael G., "The Inconsistent Vision; Edwardian Social Theory and
  the Plays of W. Somerset Maugham", *Dissertation Abstracts International*
  (1973), 34:342A

Unknown, 1920
  Nation (London), 27:637-38, Aug. 21, 1920

ANTHONY MAURICE

SEE

TERRENCE RATTIGAN AND ANTHONY MAURICE

VLADIMIR V. MAYAKOVSKY

SEE

VLADIMIR V. MAIAKOVSKII

SEBASTIAN MELMOTH (pseud.)

SEE

OSCAR WILDE

MENANDER

Arbitration, 4th Cent. B.C.
  Capps, E., "The Plot of 'Epitrepontes'", *American Journal of Philology*,
  29:410-31, 1908 and 30:22-37, 1909
  Harsh, Philip Whaley, *A Handbook of Classical Drama.* 1944. Pp. 322-27
  Verdenius, W. J., "Notes on Menander's 'Epitrepontes'", *Mnemosyne* (1974),
  27,i:17-43
  Weller, Charles, "Menander's 'Arbitrants'", *Classical Journal*, 8:275-78, 1913
  Williams, Thomas, "Menanders 'Epitrepontes' im Spiegel der Griechischen
  Ehevertrage aus Agypten", *Studien, Wiener. Zeitschrift für Klassische
  Philologie* (1961), 74:43-58

Curmudgeon, 316 B.C.
  "Presenting Menander", *Time*, 73:47, June 8, 1959

Dyskolos *SEE* The Grouch

Epitrepontes *SEE* Arbitration

The Girl from Samos, 321/316 B.C.
  Austin, Colin, "Notes on Menander's Aspis and Samia", *Zeitschrift für
  Papyrologie und Epigraphik* (1969), 4:161-70
  Barigazzi, Adelmo, "Sulla Nuova e Vecchia 'Samia' di Menander", *Rivista
  di Filologia e di Istruzione Classica* (1970), Ser. 3, 98:148-71 and 257-73
  Borgogno, Alberto, "Aspis e Epikleros?", *Rivista di Filologia e di Istruzione
  Classica* (1970), Ser. 3, 98:274-77
  Keuls, Eva. "The 'Samos' of Menander; An Interpretation of Its Plot and
  Theme", *Zeitschrift für Papyrologie und Epigraphik* (1973), 10:1-20
  Lloyd-Jones, H., "Menander's 'Samia' in the Light of the New Evidence",
  Yale Classical Studies (1972), 22:119-44

The Grouch, 317 B.C.
Alfonsi, Luigi, "Il 'Querolo' e il 'Dyskolos'", *Aegyptus* (1964), 44:200-05
Blake, W. E., "Menander's 'Dyskolos': Restorations and Emendations", *Classical Philology*, 55:174-76, 1960
Graves, Robert, *Food for Centaurs; Stories, Talks, Critical Studies, Poems.* 1960. Pp. 224-29
Hosek, A., "Tri Poznamky k Menandrovu 'Dyskolu'", *Sbornik Praci Filosofické Fakulty Brnénské Univ. Rady Archeology* (1964), 13:103-06
Kraus, Walther, "Menanders 'Dyskolos': Forschungsbericht", *Anzeiger für die Altertumswissenschaft* (1962), 15:Sp. 1-12
Pack, R. A., "On the Plot of Menander's 'Dyscolus'", *Classical Philology*, 30:151-60, 1935
Post, L. A., "Some Subtleties in Menander's 'Dyscolus'", *American Journal of Philology*, 84:36-51, 1963
Ramage, E. S., "City and Country in Menander's 'Dyskolos'", *Philologus* (1966), 110:194-211
Reckford, K. J., "'Dyskolos' of Menander", *Studies in Philology*, 58:1-24, 1961
Sherk, R. K., "Passage in Menander's 'Dyscolus'", *American Journal of Philology*, 80:400-01, 1959

Perikeiromene *SEE* The Shearing of Glycera

The Sheraring of Glycera, 4th cent. B.C.
Prescott, Henry W., "The Comedy of Errors", *Classical Philology*, 24:32-41, 1929

Samia *SEE* The Girl from Samos

THOMAS MIDDLETON

Blurt, Master Constable; or, The Spaniard's Night Walk, 1601/02
Dodson, Daniel B., "Blurt, Master Constable", *Notes and Queries*, 6:61-65, 1959
Holmes, David M., "Thomas Middleton's 'Blurt, Master Constable; or, The Spaniard's Night Walk'", *Modern Language Review* (1969), 64:1-10
Jenzen, Henry D., "Two Cruxes in Dyce's Edition of Middleton's 'Blurt, Master Constable'", *English Language Notes* (1972), 10:100-01
Kaul, R. K., ed., *Essays Presented to Amy G. Stock, Professor of English, Rajasthan University, 1961-65.* 1965. Pp. 41-57

The Chaste Maid in Cheapside, 1611
Bennett, Josephine W.; Cargill, Oscar; and Hall, Vernon, eds., *Studies in the English Renaissance Drama; in Memory of Karl Julius Holzknecht.* 1959. Pp. 287-309
Brittin, Norman A., *Thomas Middleton.* 1972. Pp. 50-58
Buckingham, E. L., "Campion's 'Art of English Poesie' and Middleton's 'Chaste Maid of Cheapside'", *Modern Language Association. Publications (PMLA)*, 43-784-92, 1928
Covatta, Anthony, *Thomas Middleton's City Comedies.* 1973. Pp. 137-62
Hallett, Charles A., "Middleton's Allwit; The Urban Cynic", *Modern Language Quarterly* (1969), 30:498-507

Holmes, David M., *The Art of Thomas Middleton; A Critical Study*. 1970.
Pp. 90-98

Levin, Richard, "The Four Plots of 'A Chaste Maid in Cheapside'", *Review of English Studies*, 16:14-24, 1965

——————— , "Middleton's Way with Names in 'A Chaste Maid in Cheapside'", *Notes and Queries*, 12:102-03, 1965

——————— , *The Multiple Plot in English Renaissance Drama*. 1971.
Pp. 192-202

Marotti, Arthur F., "Fertility and Comic Form in 'A Chaste Maid in Cheapside'", *Comparative Drama* (Spring 1969), 3:65-74

Mehl, Dieter, *The Elizabethan Dumb Show*. 1966. Pp. 148-49

Tomlinson, Thomas Brian, *A Study of Elizabethan and Jacobean Tragedy*. 1964. Pp. 158-84

Wigler, Martin S., "Thomas Middleton's Drama", *Dissertation Abstracts International* (1973), 33:3681A

Williams, Robert I., "Machiavelli's Mandragola, Touchwood Senior and the Comedy of Middleton's 'A Chaste Maid in Cheapside'", *Studies in English Literature, 1500-1900* (1970), 10:385-96

The Family of Love, 1604/07?

Brittin, Norman A., *Thomas Middleton*. 1972. Pp. 35-37

Covatta, Anthony, *Thomas Middleton's City Comedies*. 1973. Pp. 58-65

Davidson, Clifford, "Middleton and 'The Family of Love'", *English Miscellany* (1969), 20:81-92

Elizabethan Studies and Other Essays in Honor of George F. Reynolds, (Univ. of Colorado Studies in the Humanities, Ser. B, v. 2, #4). 1945. Pp. 195-200

Hengveld, Dennis A., "Thomas Middleton's Early City Comedies", *Dissertation Abstracts International* (1973), 34:1243A

Levin, Richard, "The Elizabethan 'Three Level' Play", *Renaissance Drama* (1969), 2:23-37

——————— , "The Family of Lust and 'The Family of Love'", *Studies in English Literature, 1500-1900* (1966), 6:263-77

——————— , *The Multiple Plot in English Renaissance Drama*. 1971.
Pp. 58-66

——————— , "Name Puns in 'The Family of Love'", *Notes and Queries*, 12:340-42, 1965

Marotti, Arthur F., "The Purgations of Middleton's 'The Family of Love'", *Papers on Language and Literature* (Winter 1971), 7:80-84

Maxwell, Baldwin, "'Twenty Good-Nights'—'The Knight of the Burning Pestle' and Middleton's 'Family of Love'", *Modern Language Notes*, 63:233-37, 1948

Zeidman, Alan E., "The Relationship Between Wit and Justice in Five City Comedies of Thomas Middleton", *Dissertation Abstracts International* (1972), 32:6398A

A Game at Chess, 1624

Brittin, Norman A., *Thomas Middleton*. 1972. Pp. 70-76

Bullough, G., "'Game of Chesse': How it Struck a Contemporary", *Modern Language Review*, 49:156-63, 1954

Moore, J. R., "Contemporary Significance of Middleton's 'Game at Chesse'", *Modern Language Association. Publications* (PMLA), 50:761-68, 1955

Phialas, P. G., "Unpublished Letter About 'A Game at Chesse'", *Modern Language Notes*, 69:398-99, 1954

Price, George R., "The Latin Oration in 'A Game at Chesse'", *Huntington Library Quarterly*, 23:389-93, 1960

Sargent, Roussel, "Theme and Structure in Middleton's 'A Game at Chesse'", *Modern Language Reivew* (Oct. 1971), 66:721-30

Wagner, B. M., "New Allusions to 'A Game at Chesse'", *Modern Language Association. Publications* (PMLA), 44:827-34, 1929

Wilson, E. M., and Turner, O., "Spanish Protest Against 'A Game at Chesse'", *Modern Language Review*, 44:476-82, 1949

Wright, Louis B., "A Game at Chesse", *Times Literary Supplement*, Feb. 16, 1928, Pp. 112

A Mad World, My Masters, 1606?

Brittin, Norman A., *Thomas Middleton*. 1972. Pp. 39-43

Covatta, Anthony, *Thomas Middleton's City Comedies*. 1973. Pp. 120-36

Hallett, Charles A., "Penitent Brothel, the Succubus and Parson's 'Resolution': A Reappraisal of Penitent's Position in Middleton's Canon", *Studies in Philology* (1972), 69:72-86

Hengveld, Dennis A., "Thomas Middleton's Early City Comedies", *Dissertation Abstracts International* (1973), 34:1243A

Levin, Richard, *The Multiple Plot in English Renaissance Drama*. 1971. Pp. 168-73 and 176-78

Marotti, Arthur F., "The Method in the Madness of 'A Mad World, My Masters'", *Tennessee Studies in Literature* (1970), 15:99-108

Miller, David L., "A Study of Ironic Technique in Three of Thomas Middleton's Early Comedies", *Dissertation Abstracts International* (1974), 34:7197A

Rowe, George E., Jr., "'Tis a Plot Shall Vex Him': Middleton's Transformation of New Comedy Conventions", *Dissertation Abstracts International* (1973), 34:3429A

Slights, William W. E., "The Trickster-Hero and Middleton's 'A Mad World, My Masters'", *Comparative Drama* (Summer 1969), 3:89-98

Taylor, Michael, "Realism and Morality in Middleton's 'A Mad World, My Masters'", *Literature and Psychology* (1968), 18:166-78

Wigler, S., "Penitent Brothel Reconsidered: The Place of the Grotesque in Middleton's 'A Mad World, My Masters'", *Literature and Psychology* (1975), 25:17-26

Wigler, Martin S., "Thomas Middleton's Drama", *Dissertation Abstracts International* (1973), 33:3681A

Zeidman, Alan E., "The Relationship Between Wit and Justice in Five City Comedies of Thomas Middleton", *Dissertation Abstracts International* (1972), 32:6398A

The Mayor Quinborough; or, Hengist, King of Kent, 1616/20?

Brittin, Norman A. *Thomas Middleton*. 1972. Pp. 111-18

Schoenbaum, Samuel, "Hengist, King of Kent' and Sexual Preoccupation in Jacobean Drama", *Philological Quarterly*, 29:182-98, 1953

Michaelmas Term, 1606?

Brittin, Norman A., *Thomas Middleton*. 1972. Pp. 43-45

Chatterji, Ruby, "Unity Disparity: 'Michaelmas Term'", *Studies in English Literature, 1500-1900* (1968), 8:349 63

Covatta, Anthony, "Remarriage in 'Michaelmas Term'", *Notes and Queries* (1972), 19:460-61

───────────── , *Thomas Middleton's City Comedies*. 1973. Pp. 79-98

Hengveld, Dennis A., "Thomas Middleton's Early City Comedies", *Dissertation Abstracts International* (1973), 34:1243A

Knights, L. C., *Drama and Society in the Age of Jonson*. 1962. Pp. 263-65

Levin, Richard, *The Multiple Plot in English Renaissance Drama*. 1971. Pp. 168-70 and 173-82

───────────── , "Quomodo's Name in 'Michaelmas Term'", *Notes and Queries* (1973), 20:460-61

Maxwell, Baldwin, "Middleton's 'Michaelmas Term'", *Philological Quarterly*, 22:29-35, 1943

Miller, David L., "A Study of Ironic Technique in Three of Thomas Middleton's Early Comedies", *Dissertation Abstracts International* (1974), 34:7197A

Rowe, George E., Jr., "'Tis a Plot Shall Vex Him': Middleton's Transformation of New Comedy Conventions", *Dissertation Abstracts International* (1973), 34:3429A

Zeidman, Alan E., "The Relationship Between Wit and Justice in Five City Comedies of Thomas Middleton", *Dissertation Abstracts International* (1972), 32:6398A

More Dissemblers Besides Woman, 1615?
Brittin, Norman A., *Thomas Middleton*. 1972. Pp. 64-67

Schoenbaum, Samuel, "Middleton's Tragicomedies", *Modern Philology*, 54:7-19, 1956

No Wit, No Help Like a Woman's, 1613
Brittin, Norman A., *Thomas Middleton*. 1972. Pp. 58-64

The Phoenix, 1604
Bawcutt, N. W., "Middleton's 'The Phoenix' as a Royal Play", *Notes and Queries*, n. s. 3:287-88, 1956

Brittin, Norman A., *Thomas Middleton*. 1972. Pp. 31-35

Brooks, John B., "Middleton's Stepfather and the Captain of 'The Phoenix'", *Notes and Queries*, 8:382-84, 1961

Covatta, Anthony, *Thomas Middleton's City Comedies*. 1973. Pp. 66-72

Davidson, Clifford, "'The Phoenix': Middleton's Didactic Comedy", *Papers on Language and Literature* (1968), 4:121-30

Desser, Alan C., "Middleton's 'The Phoenix' and the Allegorical Tradition", *Studies in English Literature*, 1500-1900 (1966), 6:263-77

Dodson, Daniel B., "King James and 'The Phoenix'—Again", *Notes and Queries*, 5:434-37, 1958

Howell, James F., "The Dramatic Function of the Comic in Thomas Middleton's Tragicomedies and Tragedies", *Dissertation Abstracts International* (1972), 32:5186A

Power, William, "'The Phoenix', Ralegh, and King James", *Notes and Queries*, 5:57-61, 1958

Wigler, Martin S., "Thomas Middleton's Drama", *Dissertation Abstracts International* (1973), 33:3681A

Williamson, Marilyn L., "'The Phoenix': Middleton's Comedy de Regimine Principum", *Renaissance News*, 10:183-87, 1957

Second Maiden's Tragedy, 1611
Levin, Richard, *The Multiple Plot in English Renaissance Drama.* 1971. Pp. 25-38

A Trick to Catch the Old One, 1604/06?
Brittin, Norman A., *Thomas Middleton.* 1972. Pp. 46-49
Bullock, Helene B., "Thomas Middleton and the Fashion in Playmaking", *Modern Language Association. Publications* (PMLA), 42:766-76, 1927
Covatta, Anthony, *Thomas Middleton's City Comedies.* 1973. Pp. 99-119
Falk, S., "Plautus' 'Persa' and Middleton's 'A Trick to Catch the Old One'", *Modern Language Notes*, 66:19-21, 1951
Hengveld, Dennis A., "Thomas Middleton's Early City Comedies", *Dissertation Abstracts International* (1973), 34:1243A
Holmes, David M., *The Art of Thomas Middleton; A Critical Study.* 1970. Pp. 80-84
James, Katherine H., "The Widow in Jacobean Drama", *Dissertation Abstracts International* (1973), 34:1246A
Knights, L. C., *Drama and Society in the Age of Jonson.* 1962. Pp. 262 63
Levin, Richard, "The Dampit Scenes in 'A Trick to Catch the Old One'", *Modern Language Quarterly* (1964), 25:140-52
――――――――, *The Multiple Plot in English Renaissance Drama.* 1971. Pp. 127-37
Miller, David L., "A Study of Ironic Technique in Three of Thomas Middleton's Early Comedies", *Dissertation Abstracts International* (1974), 34:7197A
Wigler, Martin S., "Thomas Middleton's Drama", *Dissertation Abstracts International* (1973), 33:3681A
Zeidman, Alan E., "The Relationship Between Wit and Justice in Five City Comedies of Thomas Middleton", *Dissertation Abstracts International* (1972), 32:6398A

The Viper and Her Brood, 1606
Hillebrand, Harold, "Thomas Middleton's 'The Viper's Brood'", *Modern Language Notes*, 42:35-38, 1927

The Widow, 1616
James, Katherine H., "The Widow in Jacobean Drama", *Dissertation Abstracts International* (1973), 34:1246A
Wigler, Martin S., "Thomas Middleton's Drama", *Dissertation Abstracts International* (1973), 33:3681A

The Witch, 1614
Brittin, Norman A., *Thomas Middleton*, 1972. Pp. 87-90
Holmes, David M., *The Art of Thomas Middleton; A Critical Study.* 1970. Pp. 145-50
Cutts, John P., "The Original Music to Middleton's 'The Witch'", *Shakespeare Quarterly*, 7:203-09, 1956
George, David, "The Problem of Middleton's 'The Witch' and Its Sources", *Notes and Queries* (1967), 14:209-11
Howard-Hill, T. H., "Lizards Braine in Middleton's 'The Witch'", *Notes and Queries* (1973), 20:458-59
Schoenbaum, Samuel, "Middleton's Tragicomedies", *Modern Philology*, 54:7-19, 1956

Women Beware Women, 1625/27?
Batchelor, J. B., "The Pattern of 'Women Beware Women'", *Yearbook of English Studies* (1972), 2:78-82
Binder, Barrett F., "Tragic Satire; Studies in Cyril Tourneur, John Webster, and Thomas Middleton", *Dissertation Abstracts International* (1973), 33:4331A
Bradford, Gamaliel, "The Women of Middleton and Webster", *Sewanee Review*, 29:14-29, 1921
Brittin, Norman A., *Thomas Middleton*. 1972. Pp. 118-32
Core, George, "The Canker and the Muse; Imagery in 'Women Beware Women'", *Renaissance Papers* (1968), Pp. 65-76
Dodson, D., "Middleton's 'Livia'", *Philological Quarterly*, 27:376-81, 1948
Engelberg, E., "Tragic Blindness in 'The Changeling' and 'Women Beware Women'", *Modern Language Quarterly*, 23:20-28, 1962
Ewbank, Inga-Stina, "Realism and Morality in 'Women Beware Women'", *Essays and Studies by Members of the English Assn.* (1969), 22:57-70
Hallett, Charles A., "The Psychological Drama in 'Women Beware Women'", *Studies in English Literature* 1500-1900 (1972), 12:375-89
Hibbard, G. R., "The Tragedies of Thomas Middleton and the Decadence of Drama", *Renaissance and Modern Studies* (1957), 1:35-64
Holmes, David M., *The Art of Thomas Middleton; A Critical Study.* 1970. Pp. 161-71
Howell, James F., "The Dramatic Function of the Comic in Thomas Middleton's Tragicomedies and Tragedies", *Dissertation Abstracts International* (1972), 32:5186A
Krook, Dorothea, "Tragedy and Satire: Middleton's 'Women Beware Women'", *Scripta Hierosolymitana* (1966), 17:96-120
Mehl, Dieter, *The Elizabethan Dumb Show.* 1966. Pp. 149-54
Ribner, Irving, "Middleton's 'Women Beware Women': Poetic Imagery and the Moral Vision", *Tulane Studies in English*, 9:19-33, 1959
Ricks, C., "Word-Play in 'Women Beware Women'", *Review of English Studies*, n. s. 12:238-50, 1961
Simpson, P., "Thomas Middleton's 'Women Beware Women'", *Modern Language Review*, 33:45, 1938
Tomlinson, Thomas Brian, *A Study of Elizabethan and Jacobean Tragedy.* 1964. Pp. 158-84

Your Five Gallants, 1607
Brittin, Norman A., *Thomas Middleton*. 1972. Pp. 37-39
Gross, A. G., "Middleton's 'Your Five Gallants'; The Fifth Act", *Philological Quarterly*, 44:124-29, 1965
Hengveld, Dennis A., "Thomas Middleton's Early City Comedies", *Dissertation Abstracts International* (1973), 34:1243A
Holmes, David M., *The Art of Thomas Middleton; A Critical Study.* 1970. Pp. 27-30 and 54-56
Hoole, W. S., "Thomas Middleton's Use of 'Impresse' in 'Your Five Gallants'", *Studies in Philology*, 31:215-23, 1934
Maxwell, Baldwin, "Thomas Middleton's 'Your Five Gallants'", *Philological Quarterly*, 30:30-39, 1951
Mehl, Dieter, *The Elizabethan Dumb Show.* 1966. Pp. 146-48

Wigler, Martin S., "Thomas Middleton's Drama", *Dissertation Abstracts International* (1973), 33:3681A

Zeidman, Alan E., "The Relationship Between Wit and Justice in Five City Comedies of Thomas Middleton", *Dissertation Abstracts International* (1972), 32:6398A

THOMAS MIDDLETON AND THOMAS DEKKER

The Roaring Girl; or, Moll Cut-Purse, 1610

Brittin, Norman A., *Thomas Middleton*. 1972. Pp. 77-79

Holmes, David M., *The Art of Thomas Middleton; A Critical Study*. 1970. Pp. 100-10

McManaway, James G., "Fortune's Wheel", *Times Literary Supplement*, April 16, 1938, Pp. 264

Power, William, "Double, Double", *Notes and Queries*, 6:4-8, 1959

THOMAS MIDDLETON AND JOHN WEBSTER

Anything for a Quiet Life, 1621

Brittin, Norman A., *Thomas Middleton*. 1972. Pp. 68-70

Holmes, David M., *The Art of Thomas Middleton; A Critical Study*. 1970. Pp. 153-60

Power, William, "Double, Double", *Notes and Queries*, 6:4-8, 1959

Soens, Adolph L., "Lawyers, Collusions and Cudgels; Middleton's 'Anything for a Quiet Life'", *English Language Notes* (1970), 7:248-54

THOMAS MIDDLETON AND WILLIAM ROWLEY

The Changeling, 1622

Arbiteboul, Maurice, "Un Aspect de l'Esthétique dans 'The Changeling': L'Art du Doute et des Ambiguités", *Publications Universitaires. Lettres et Sciences Humaines de l'Université de Provence* (1972), 5:5-22

Barker, Richard Hindry. *Thomas Middleton*. 1958. Pp. 121-31

Berger, Thomas L., "The Petrarchan Fortress of 'The Changeling'", *Renaissance Papers* (1969), Pp. 37-46

Berlin, Normand, "The Finger Image and Relationship of Character in 'The Changeling'", *English Studies in Africa* (Sept. 1969), 12:162-66

Bluestone, Max and Norman Rabkin, eds., *Shakespeare's Contemporaries; Modern Studies in English Renaissance Drama*. 2nd ed. 1970. Pp. 363-76

Boas, Frederick S., *An Introduction to Stuart Drama*. 1946. Pp. 241-45

Bradbrook, Muriel C., *Theme and Conventions of Elizabethan Tragedy*. 1936. Pp. 213-24 and 234-39

Bradford, Gamaliel, "The Women of Middleton and Webster", *Sewanee Review*, 29:14-29, 1921

Brittin, Norman A., *Thomas Middleton*. 1972. Pp. 132-42

Brustein, Robert Sanford, *Seasons of Discontent; Dramatic Opinions 1959-1965*. 1965. Pp. 252-59

Bullock, Helene B., "Thomas Middleton and the Fashion in Playwriting", *Modern Language Association. Publications* (PMLA), 42:766-76, 1927

Burelbach, Frederick M., Jr., "Middleton and Rowley's 'The Changeling'", *Explicator* (March 1968), 26:Item 60

Doob, Penelope B. R., "A Reading of 'The Changeling'", *English Literary Renaissance* (1973), 3:183-206

Duffy, Joseph M., "Madhouse Optics: 'The Changeling'", *Comparative Drama* (1974), 8:184-98

Eliot, Thomas Stearns, *Selected Essays*. 1950. Pp. 140-48

Ellis-Fermor, Una, *Jacobean Drama*. 4th ed. 1958. Pp. 144-49

Empson, William, *Some Versions of Pastoral*. 1935. Pp. 48-52

Engelberg, E., "Tragic Blindness in 'The Changeling' and 'Women Beware Women'", *Modern Language Quarterly*, 23:20-28, 1962

Farr, Dorothy M., "The Changeling", *Modern Language Review* (1967), 62:586-97

Ford, Boris, ed., *A Guide to English Literature*. 1955. Pp. 361-68

Hebert, Catherine A., "A Note on the Significance of the Title of Middleton's 'The Changeling'", *College Language Association Journal* (1968), 12:66-69

Hibbard, G. R., "The Tragedy of Thomas Middleton and the Decadence of Drama", *Renaissance and Modern Studies* (1957), 1:35-64

Holmes, David M., *The Art of Thomas Middleton; A Critical Study*. 1970. Pp. 172-84

Holzknecht, Karl J., "The Dramatic Structure of 'The Changeling'", *Renaissance Papers*, Pp. 77-87, 1954

Jacobs, H. E., "Constancy of Change: Character and Perspective in 'The Changeling'", *Texas Studies in Literature and Language* (1975), 16:651-74

Kehler, Dorothea, "Middleton and Rowley's 'The Changeling'", *Explicator* (Jan. 1968), 26:Item 41

——————— , "Rings and Jewels in 'The Changeling'", *English Language Notes* (1967), 5:15-17

Kerr, Walter, *Thirty Plays Hath November; Pain and Pleasure in the Contemporary Theater*. 1969. Pp. 267-71

Lawrence, Robert G., "A Bibliographical Study of Middleton's and Rowley's 'The Changeling'", *The Library*, 16:37-43, 1961

Levin, Richard, *The Multiple Plot in English Renaissance Drama*. 1971. Pp. 34-48 and 53-55

Matthews, Honor, *The Primal Curse; The Myth of Cain and Abel in the Theatre*. 1967. Pp. 61-65

Novick, Julius, *Beyond Broadway; The Quest for Permanent Theatres*. 1968. Pp. 187-89

Ornstein, Robert, *The Moral Vision of Jacobean Tragedy*. 1960. Pp. 179-90

Pentzell, R. J., "'Changeling': Notes on Mannerism in Dramatic Form", *Comparative Drama* (1975), 9:3-28

Ribner, Irving, *Jacobean Tragedy; The Quest for Moral Order*. 1962. Pp. 126-37

Ricks, Christopher, ed., *English Drama to 1710*. (History of Literature in the English Language) Vol. 3. 1971. Pp. 334-43

——————— , "The Moral and Poetical Structure of 'The Changeling'", *Essays in Criticism* (Oxford), 10:290-306, 1960

Schoenbaum, Samuel, *Middleton's Tragedies; A Critical Study*. 1955. Pp. 132-50

Stafford, T. J., "Middleton's Debt to Chaucer in 'The Changeling'", *Bulletin of the Rocky Mountain Modern Language Association* (1968), 22:4:208-13

Stoll, Elmer E., "Heroes and Villains: Shakespeare, Middleton, Byron, Dickens", *Review of English Studies*, 18:257-69, 1942

Sturm, Dieter, "Hypothesen vor Proben-Beginn zu 'Changeling' von Middleton/Rowley", *Theatre Heute. Zeitschrift für Schauspiel* (1970), 11:33-36

Taylor, J. Chesley, "Metaphors of the Moral World: Structure in 'The Changeling'", *Tulane Studies in English* (1972), 20:41-56

Tomlinson, T. B., "Poetic Naturalism—'The Changeling'", *Journal of English and Germanic Philology*, 63:648-59, 1964

Tomlinson, Thomas Brian, *A Study of Elizabethan and Jacobean Tragedy*. 1964. Pp. 185-212

Wigler, Martin S., "Thomas Middleton's Drama", *Dissertation Abstracts International* (1973), 33:3681A

Fair Quarrel, 1617

Bowers, F. T., "Middleton's 'Fair Quarrel' and the Duelling Code", *Journal of English and Germanic Philology*, 36:40-65, 1937

Brittin, Norman A., *Thomas Middleton*. 1972. Pp. 90-96

Bronstrops, "A Note on 'A Faire Quarrell'", *Modern Language Review*, 35:59-62, 1940

Holdsworth, R. V., "The Medical Jargon in 'A Fair Quarrel'", *Review of English Studies* (1973), 23:448-54

Holmes, David M., *The Art of Thomas Middleton; A Critical Study*. 1970. Pp. 113-21

Levin, Richard, "The Elizabethan 'Three Level' Play", *Renaissance Drama* (1969), 2:23-37

———, *The Multiple Plot in English Renaissance Drama*. 1971. Pp. 7-9, 66-75 and 158-60

Price, George R., "Medical Men in 'A Faire Quarrell'", *Bulletin of the History of Medicine*, 24:38-42, 1956

Schoenbaum, Samuel, "Middleton's Tragicomedies", *Modern Philology*, 54:7-19, 1956

The Spanish Gypsy, 1623

Brittin, Norman A. *Thomas Middleton*. 1972. Pp. 96-102

Burelbach, Frederick M., Jr., "Theme and Structure in 'The Spanish Gipsy'", *Humanities Association Bulletin* (1968), 19 #2:37-41

Kistner, A. L. and M. K., "The Spanish Gypsy", *Humanities Association Bulletin* (1974), 25:211-24

THOMAS MIDDLETON, PHILIP MASSINGER AND WILLIAM ROWLEY

The Old Law; or, A New Way to Please, 1618?

Holmes, David M., *The Art of Thomas Middleton; A Critical Study*. 1970. Pp. 121-29

Howell, James F., "The Dramatic Function of the Comic in Thomas Middleton's Tragicomedies and Tragedies", *Dissertation Abstracts International* (1972), 32:5186A

Rowe, George E., Jr., "'Tis a Plot Shall Vex Him': Middleton's Transformation of New Comedy Conventions", *Dissertation Abstracts International* (1973), 34:3429A

Schoenbaum, Samuel, "Middleton's Tragicomedies", *Modern Philology*, 54:7-19, 1956

ALAN ALEXANDER MILNE

Ariadne, 1925
  Holmes, J.F., "Ariadne", *New Statesman*, 25:74, May, 2, 1925
  Royde-Smith, N. G., "Ariadne", *Outlook* (London), 55:297, May 2, 1925

Dover Road, 1922
  Nation (London), 31:452, June 24, 1922
  Parker, R. A., "Dover Road", *Independent*, 108:41-43, Jan. 14, 1922
  Pollock, J., "Dover Road", *Fortnightly*, 118:339-42, Aug., 1922
  Spectator, 128:782-83, June 24, 1922

The Fourth Wall, 1928
  Brown, I., "The Fourth Wall", *Saturday Review*, 145:285, March 10, 1928
  Horsnell, H., "The Fourth Wall", *Outlook* (London), 61:308, March 10, 1928
  Jennings, R., "The Fourth Wall", *Spectator*, 140:355, March 10, 1928
  New Statesman, 30:694, March 10, 1928

Give Me Yesterday, 1931
  Arts and Decoration, 35:57, May, 1931
  Catholic World, 133:80-81, April, 1931
  Commonweal, 13:694, April 22, 1931
  Nation, 132:306, May 18, 1931
  Outlook, 157:411, March 18, 1931
  Theatre Arts, 15:372-73, May, 1931

The Great Broxopp, 1923
  Nation (London), 32:930-32, March 17, 1923
  Shanks, E., "Great Broxopp", *Outlook* (London), 51:249, March 24, 1923
  Shipp, H., "Great Broxopp", *English Review*, 36:351-54, April, 1923

Ivory Door, 1927
  Jennings, R., "The Ivory Door", *Spectator*, 142:686, May 4, 1929
  New Statesman, 33:148-49, May 11, 1929
  Outlook, 147:465, Dec. 14, 1927
  Saturday Review of Literature, 4:320, Nov. 19, 1927

The Lucky One, 1922
  Darlington, William Aubrey, *Literature in the Theatre and Other Essays*.
    1925. Pp. 197-201

Meet the Prince, 1929
  Arts and Decoration, 31:64, May, 1929
  Catholic World, 129:85, April, 1929
  Commonweal, 9:544-45, March 13, 1929
  Outlook, 151:423, March 13, 1929

Michael and Mary, 1929
  Arts and Decoration, 32:96, Feb., 1930
  Commonweal, 11:257, Jan. 1, 1930
  Drama, 20:138, Feb., 1930
  Jennings, R., "Michael and Mary", *Spectator*, 144:308, March 1, 1930
  Literary Digest, 104:25, Feb. 1, 1930
  Theatre Arts, 14:109-11, Feb., 1930

Mr. Pim Passes By, 1919
Firkins, O. W., *Review*, 4:280, March 23, 1921

Other People's Lives, 1932
Pollock, J., "Other People's Lives", *Saturday Review*, 154:503, Nov. 12, 1932
Verschoyle, D., "Other People's Lives", *Spectator*, 151:80, July 21, 1933

Perfect Alibi, 1928
Commonweal, 10:104, May 29, 1929
Outlook, 150:1355, Dec. 19, 1928

Sarah Simple, 1937
Spectator, 158:903, May 14, 1937

Success, 1923
Armstrong, M., "Success", *Spectator*, 131:51-52, July 14, 1923
Shanks, E., "Success", *Outlook* (London), 52:14, July 7, 1923

They Don't Mean Any Harm, 1932
Hutchens, J., "They Don't Mean Any Harm", *Theatre Arts*, 16:363-64, May, 1932

To Have the Honor, 1924
Spectator, 132:706-07, May 3, 1924

The Truth About Blayds, 1921
Brown, I., "The Truth About Blayds", *New Statesman*, 18:394-95, Jan. 7, 1922
Catholic World, 135:210, May, 1932
Commonweal, 16:49-50, May 11, 1932
Nation (London), 30:538-39, Dec. 31, 1921
Nation, 134:497-98, April 27, 1932
Parker, R. A., "The Truth About Blayds", *Independent*, 108:462-63, May 13, 1922
Spectator, 127:891-92, Dec. 31, 1921
Young, Stark, "The Truth About Blayds", *New Republic*, 30:198-99, April 12, 1922

MIRACLE, MORALITY, AND MYSTERY PLAYS

Abel, J. Gardner, "Theme and Irony in the Wakefield Mactacio", *Modern Language Association. Publications* (PMLA), 80:515-21, 1965
Altieri, J. S., "Ironic Structure of the 'Townley Flagellacio'", *Drama Survey* (Wint. 1968-69), 7:104-12
Baird, Joseph L., "Humility and the Towneley 'Annunciation'", *Philological Quarterly* (1973), 52:301-06
Baugh, Albert Crell, "Recent Theory of the 'Ludus Coventriae'", *Philological Quarterly*, 12:403-06, 1933
Benkovitz, M. J., "Some Notes on the Prologue of 'Ludus Coventriae'", *Modern Language Notes*, 60:78-85, 1945
Bernbrock, J. E., "Notes on the Towneley Cycle 'Slaying of Abel'", *Journal of English and Germanic Philology*, 62:317-22, 1963
Bonnell, J. K., "Serpent With a Human Head in Art and in Mystery Plays", *American Journal of Archeology*, 21:255-91, 1917

Brawer, Robert A., "The Dramatic Function of the Ministry Group in the Townley Cycle", *Comparative Drama* (1970), 4:166-76

Bridges-Adams, William, *Irresistible Theatre.* 1957. Pp. 41-45, and 61-75

Brown, Carleton Fairchild, "Early Mention of a St. Nicholas Play in England", *Studies in Philology,* 28:594-601, 1931

Browne, E. M., "English Mystery Plays", *Drama,* 43:34-36, 1956

Bryant, J. A., Jr., "Chester's Sermon for Catechumens", *Journal of English and Germanic Philology,* 53:399-402, 1954

Burgess, C. F., "Art and Artistry in the 'Brome Miracle Play of Abraham and Isaac'", *Cithara* (1962), 1:37-42

Cady, Frank W., "The Maker of Mak", *Univ. of California Chronicle,* 29: 261-72, 1927

———————— , "Passion Group in Towneley", *Modern Philology,* 10:587-600, 1913

———————— , "Towneley, York, and True-Coventry", *Studies in Philology,* 26:386-400, 1929

Campbell, Josie P., "The Polarization of Authority; A Study of the Towneley Cycle", *Dissertation Abstracts International* (1973), 33:6864A

Carey, Millicent, "'The Wakefield Group in the Towneley Cycle': A Study to Determine the Conventional and Original Elements in Four Plays Commonly Ascribed to the Wakefield Author", *Hesperia,* #11, 1930

Cawley, A. C., "Grotesque Feast in the 'Prima Pastorum'", *Speculum,* 30:213-17, 1955

———————— , "Iak Garcio of the 'Prima Pastorum'", *Modern Language Notes,* 68:169-72, 1953

Chesterton, Gilbert K., *Uses of Diversity; A Book of Essays.* 1921. Pp. 145-51

Chidamian, Claude, "Mak and the Tossing in the Blanket", *Speculum,* 22: 186-90, 1947

Clark, Thomas Blake, "Theory Concerning the Identity and History of the 'Ludus Coventriae' Cycle of Mystery Plays", *Philological Quarterly,* 12: 144-69, 1933

Cohen, G., "Influence of Mysteries on Medieval Art: Abstract", *American Journal of Archeology,* 48:385, 1944

Collins, Fletcher, Jr., "Music in the Craft Cycles", *Modern Language Association. Publications* (PMLA), 47:613-21, 1932

Corder, Jim, "'Everyman': The Way of Life", *Drama Critique* (1963), 6:136-38

Cosby, R. C., "Mak Story and Its Folklore Analogues", *Speculum,* 20:310-17, 1945

Curtiss, Chester G., "York and Towneley Plays on 'The Harrowing of Hell'", *Studies in Philology,* 30:24-33, 1932

Driver, Tom Faw, *Sense of History in Greek and Shakespearean Drama.* 1960. Pp. 404-12

Earl, James W., "The Shape of Old Testament History in the Towneley Plays", *Studies in Philology* (1972), 69:434-52

Eliason, Norman E., "'I Take My Cap in My Lappe' . . . ", *Philological Quarterly,* 14:271-74, 1935

Elliott, J. R., "Sacrifice of Isaac as Comedy and Tragedy in 'Abraham and Isaac'", *Studies in Philology* (Jan. 1969), 66:36-59

Essays and Studies in Honor of Carleton Brown. 1940. Pp. 158-66

Frampton, Mendal Garbutt, "Brewbarret Interpolation in the York Play: 'The Sacrificium Cayme and Abell' ", *Modern Language Association. Publications* (PMLA), 52:895-900, 1937

—————— , "The Towneley 'Harrowing of Hell' ", *Modern Language Association. Publications* (PMLA), 56:105-19, 1941

—————— , "York Play of Christ Led Up to Calvary", *Philological Quarterly*, 20:198-204, 1941

Fry, T., "Unity of the 'Ludus Coventriae' ", *Studies in Philology*, 48:527-70, 1951

Gassner, John and Allen, Ralph G., eds., *Theatre and Drama in the Making.* 1964. Pp. 151-67

Gheon, Henri, "Le Mystère du Roi Saint Louis", *Journal des Débats*, 38 pt. 1:1084-86, June 26, 1931

Gillet, J. E., "Valencian Misterios and Mexican Missionary Plays in the Early Sixteenth Century, *Hispanic Review*, 19:59-61, 1951

Goodman, Randolph, *Drama on Stage.* 1961. Pp. 61-64 and 85-86

Harder, K. B., "Chaucer's Use of the Mystery Plays in the Miller's Tale", *Modern Language Quarterly*, 17:193-98, 1956

Hibbard, L. A., "Guy of Warwick and the Second Mystère of Jean Louvet", *Modern Philology*, 13:181-87, 1915

Hieatt, Constance B., "A Case for 'Duk Moraud' as a Play of the Miracles of the Virgin", *Medieval Studies* (1970), 32:345-51

Holthausen, F., "Das Wakefielder Spiel von Kain und Abel", *English Studies*, 62:132-51, 1927

—————— , "Studien zu den Towneley Plays", *English Studies*, 58:161-78, 1924

Jean Marie, Sister, "The Cross in the Towneley Plays", *Traditio*, 5:331-34, 1947

Jenney, F. G., "Comic in German Folk-Christmas Plays", *Poet-Lore*, 27:680-99, 1916

Kinghorn, A. M., *Medieval Drama.* 1968. Pp. 61-128

Kirk, R., "York and Social Boredom", *Sewanee Review*, 61:664-81, 1953

Kirtlan, E. J. B., "Mystery and Miracle Plays", *London Quarterly Review*, 134:117-19, 1920

Kreutz, I., "Three Collector's Items", *Educational Theatre Journal*, 14:141-47, 1962

Larson, O. K., "Bishop Abraham of Souzdal's Description of 'Sacre Rappresentazioni' ", *Educational Theatre Journal*, 9:208-13, 1957

Lebegue, Raymond, "La Passion d'Arnoul Gréban", *Romania*, 60:218-31, April, 1934

Leeper, J., "York Cycle of Mystery Plays", *Spectator*, 186:748, June 8, 1951

Leigh, D. J., "Doomsday Mystery Play; An Eschatological Morality", *Modern Philology* (Feb. 1970), 67:211-23

Leiter, L. H., "Typology, Paradigm, Metaphor and Image in the York Creation of Adam and Eve", *Drama Survey* (Wint. 1968-69), 7:113-32

Macaulay, P. S., "The Play of the 'Harrowing of Hell' as a Climax in the English Mystery Cycles", *Studia Germanica Gandensia* (1966), 8:115-34

MacDowell, Edward Alexander, *Critical and Historical Essays; Lectures Delivered at Columbia University*, ed. by W. J. Baltzell. 1912. Pp. 205-09

Mackenzie, W. Roy, *The English Moralities from the Point of View of Allegory.* 1966. Pp. 206-10

McNeir, Waldo F., "Corpus Christi Passion Plays as Dramatic Art", *Studies in Philology*, 48:601-28, 1951

Maltman, N., "Pilate—Os Malleatoris", *Speculum*, 36:308-11, 1961

Manly Anniversary Studies in Language and Literature. 1923. Pp. 254-68

Markland, Murray F., "An Observation of Humor and Pathos in the English Mystery Plays", *Theatre Annual* (1968), 24:24-34

Marshall, Linda E., " 'Sacral Parody' in the 'Secunda Pastorum' ", *Speculum*, (1972), 47:720-36

Medievalia et Humanistica; Studies in Medieval and Renaissance Culture, ed. Paul Maurice Clogan. 1974. Pp. 169-82

Mill, Anna Jean, "Hull Noah Play", *Modern Language Review*, 33:489-505, 1938

_____ , "Noah's Wife Again", *Modern Language Association. Publications* (PMLA), 56:613-26, 1941

_____ , "York Baker's Play of the Last Supper", *Modern Language Review*, 30:145-58, 1935

_____ , "York Plays of the Dying Assumption, and Coronation of Our Lady", *Modern Language Association. Publications* (PMLA), 65:866-76, 1950

Miller, F. H., "Metrical Affinities of the Shrewsburg Officium Pastorum and Its York Correspondent", *Modern Language Notes*, 33:91-95, 1918

_____ , "Northern Passion and the Mysteries", *Modern Language Notes*, 34:88-92, 1919

Morgan, M. M., "High Fraud: Paradox and Double-Plot in the English Shepherd Plays", *Speculum*, 39:676-89, 1964

Nelson, A. H., "Principles of Processional Staging; York Cycle", *Modern Philology* (May 1970), 67:303-20

Nelson, Alan H., " 'Sacred' and 'Secular' Currents in 'The Towneley Play of Noah' ", *Drama Survey* (1964), 3:393-401

Nicoll, Allardyce, *World Drama from Aeschelus to Anouilh.* 1949. Pp. 141-73

Oliver, L. M., "John Foxe and 'The Conflict of Conscience' ", *Review of English Studies*, 25:1-9, 1949

Parrott, Thomas Marc, "Mak and Archie Armstrong; What Prof. Kölbing Left Unsolved", *Modern Language Notes*, 59:297-304, 1944

_____ , and Ball, Robert Hamilton, *Short View of Elizabethan Drama, Together With Some Account of Its Principal Playwrights and the Conditions Under Which It Was Produced.* 1943. Pp. 1-26

Paull, Michael, "The Figure of Mahomet in the Towneley Cycle", *Comparative Drama* (1972), 6:187-204

Pennsylvania Univ., *Studies in Medieval Literature; In Honor of Albert Croll Baugh.* 1961. Pp. 229-43

Phillips, R., "Church and Drama", *London Quarterly Review*, 173:213-17, 1948

Read, H., "York Mystery Plays", *New Statesman and Nation*, 41:650, June 9, 1951

Renaissance Studies in Honor of Hardin Craig; ed. by B. Maxwell and Others. 1941. Pp. 13-19

Robinson, J. W., "The Art of the York Realist", *Modern Philology* (1963), 60:241-51

————————— , "Commentary on the York Play of the Birth of Jesus", *Journal of English and Germanic Philology* (April 1971), 70:241-54

Rogers, Genevieve, "Reduction of the Speakers' Parts in the Towneley 'Pharao' ", *Philological Quarterly*, 9:216-18, 1930

Royal Society of Literature of the United Kingdom, London, *Essays by Divers Hands, Being the Transactions of the Society*. 1928. v. 7, Pp. 133-53

Russell, Harry Kitsun, "Tudor and Stuart Dramatization of the Doctrines of Natural and Moral Philosophy", *Studies in Philology*, 31:1-27, 1934

Sanctis, Francesco de, *History of Italian Literature*. v. 1, 1960. Pp. 91-117

Schelling Anniversary Papers by His Former Students. 1923. Pp. 35-63

Severs, J. B., "Relationship Between the Brome and Chester Plays of Abraham and Isaac", *Modern Philology*, 42:137-51, 1945

Simonson, Lee, *The Stage is Set*. 1946. Pp. 172-93

Sisam, C., "Towneley Play of Noah: 'Bere'; 'Lufe' ", *Review of English Studies*, n. s. 13:387-89, 1962

Slote, Bernice, ed., *Literature and Society; by Germaine Brée and Others*. 1964. Pp. 175-86

Smart, W. K., "Mankind and the Mumming Plays", *Modern Language Notes*, 32:21-25, 1917

Smith, John H., "Another Allusion to Costume in the Work of the 'Wakefield Master' ", *Modern Language Association. Publications* (PMLA), 52:901-02, 1937

Smyser, Hamilton Martin, "Analogues to the Mak Story", *Journal of American Folklore*, 47:378-80, 1934

Speaight, R., "York Festival", *New Statesman*, 53:837-38, 1957

Spivack, B., "Falstaff and the Psychomachia", *Shakespeare Quarterly*, 8:449-59, 1957

Stevens, Martin, "Dramatic Setting of the Wakefield Annunciation", *Modern Language Association. Publications* (1966), 81:193-98

Stratman, Carl J., " 'Everyman': The Way to Death", *Drama Critique* (1964), 7:61-64

Strunk, William, Jr., "Two Notes on the Towneley 'Second Shepherds' Play", *Modern Language Notes*, 45:151, 1930

Thomas, C. B. C., "Miracle Play at Dunstable", *Modern Language Notes*, 32:337-44, 1917

Thomas, Helen S., "The Meaning of the Character Knowledge in 'Everyman' ", *Mississippi Quarterly* (1960-61), 14:3-13

————————— , "Some Analogues of 'Everyman' ", *Mississippi Quarterly* (1963), 16:97-103

Trusler, Margaret, "The Language of the Wakefield Playwright", *Studies in Philology*, 33:15-39, 1936

————————— , "York Sacrificium Cayme and Abell", *Modern Language Association. Publications* (PMLA), 49:956-59, 1934

Urwin, Kenneth, "Mystère d'Adam; Two Problems", *Modern Language Review*, 34:70-72, 1939

Van Laan, Thomas F., " 'Everyman': A Structural Analysis", *Modern Language Association. Publications* (1963), 78:465-75

Vane, H., "Old Religion: The York Festival", *Twentieth Century*, 162:174-77, 1957

Villiers, Andre, "Le Vray Mistère dans la Basilique", *Mercure de France*, 294:662-66, Sept. 15, 1939

Wall, C., "York Peasant XLVI and Its Music", *Speculum* (Oct. 1971), 46:687-712

Wann, Louis, "Influence of French Farce on the Towneley Cycle of Mystery Plays", *Wisconsin Academy of Science. Transactions*, 19:356-68, 1918

—————————— , "A New Examination of the Manuscript of the Towneley Plays", *Modern Language Association. Publications (PMLA)*, 43:137-52, 1928

Wells, Henry Willis, "Style in the English Mystery Plays", *Journal of English and Germanic Philology*, 38:360-81, 1939 ·

Wertz, D., "Deadly Sins in a Changing Social Order; An Analysis of the Portrayal of Sin in the Medieval English Theater", *International Journal of Comparative Sociology* (Sept. 1970), 11:240-45

—————————— , "Theology of Nominalism in the English Morality Plays", *Harvard Theological Review* (July 1969), 62:371-74

Wharey, J. B., "Bunyan's Holy War and The Conflict-Type of Morality Play", *Modern Language Notes*, 34:65-73, 1919

Whiting, Bartlett Jere, "Analogue to the Mak Story", *Speculum*, 7:552, 1932

Williamson, C. C. H., "Early Religious Drama", *American Catholic Quarterly*, 46:225-42, 1921

Williamson, Cecile, "The Importance of the Number Three in the Medieval Easter Play", *Universitas* (1966), 4:117-22

Wilson, Robert Henry, "Stanzaic Life of Christ and the Chester Plays", *Studies in Philology*, 28:413-32, 1931

Withington, Robert, "Braggart, Devil and Vice", *Speculum*, 11:124-29, 1936

—————————— , "'Water Fastand'", *Modern Language Notes*, 50:95-96, 1935

Wright, N., "Morality Tradition in the Poetry of Edward Taylor", *American Literature*, 18:1-17, 1946

Wynne, Arnold, *Growth of English Drama*. 1914. Pp. 22-50

Young, Karl, "Interludium for a Gild of Corpus Christi", *Modern Language Notes*, 48:84-86, 1933

Zumwalt, Eugene E., "Irony in the Towneley Shepherds' Plays", *Research Studies of the State College of Washington* (1958), 26:37-53

MOLIÈRE (JEAN BAPTISTE POQUELIN)

Les Amants Magnifiques   SEE   The Magnificent Lovers

The Amorous Quarrel, 1659

Bech, Kirsten, "Le Jeune Molière et la Commedia dell'Arte: Thèmas et Aspects Scéniques dans 'l'Etourdi' et 'Le Dépit Amoureux'", *Revue Romane* (1970), 5:1-16

Hall, H. Gaston, "Comedy and Romance in Molière's 'Depit Amoureux'", *Australian Journal of French Studies* (1971), 8:245-58

Amphytryon, 1668
Bondurant, A. L., "'Amphitruo' of Plautus, Moliere's 'Amphitryon' and the 'Amphitryon' of Dryden", *Sewanee Review*, 33:455-68, 1925
Bugliani, Ivanna, "'Amphitrion' et 'L'Oeuvre' de Molière", *Modern Language Notes* (1969), 84:565-98
Burgess, G. S., "Molière and the Pursuit of Criteria", *Symposium* (Spring 1969), 22:5-15
Cornett, Patricia L., "Doubling in 'Amphytrion'", *Essays in French Literature* (1972), 9:16-29
Forehand, W. E., "Adaptation and Comic Intent: Plautus' 'Amphitruo' and Moliere's 'Amphytrion'", *Comparative Literature Studies* (1974), 11:204-17
Gossman, Lionel, *Men and Masks; A Study of Molière.* 1963. Pp. 1-35
_____ , "Molière's 'Amphitryon'", *Modern Language Association. Publications* (PMLA), 78:201-13, 1963
Hébert, Rodolphe-Louis, "An Episode in Molière's 'Amphitryon' and Cartesian Epistemology", *Modern Language Notes*, 70:416-22, 1955
Howarth, W. D. and Merlin Thomas, ed., *Molière: Stage and Study; Essays in Honor of W. G. Moore.* 1973. Pp. 185-97
Mélanges d'Histoire Littéraire (XVI-XVII Siecle): Offerts à Raymond Lebegues par Ses Collègues, Ses Élèves et Ses Amis. 1969. Pp. 241-48
Nation, 176:18, Jan. 3, 1953
Phelps, Ruth S., "Amphitryon' and Montespan", *Modern Philology*, 24:443-61, 1927
Romer, Paul, *Molières "Amphitrion" und Sein Gesellschaftlicher Hintergrund.* 1967
Shakespeare Survey, ed. Kenneth Muir. 1970. vol. 22. Pp. 15-26
Walker, Hallam. *Molière.* 1971. Pp. 137-42

L'Avare *SEE* The Miser

The Blunderer; or, The Mishaps, 1653
Bech, Kirsten, "Le Jeune Molière et la Commedia dell'Arte: Thèmas et Aspects Scéniques dans 'l'Etourdi' et 'Le Dépit Amoureux'", *Revue Romane* (1970), 5:1-16
Fraser, R. D. and S. F. Rendall, "The Recognition Scene in Molière's Theater", *Romanic Review* (1973), 64:16-31
Potter, Edithe J., "Molière's Comic Artistry in 'l'Etourdi'", *Kentucky Romance Quarterly* (1973), 20:89-97
Sakharoff, Micheline, "'L'Etourdi' de Molière ou l'Écoles des Innocents", *French Review* (1969), 43:240-48
Walker, Hallam, *Molière.* 1971. Pp. 25-27

Le Bourgeoise Gentilhomme *SEE* The Bourgeois Gentleman

The Bourgeois Gentleman, 1670
Barrault, Jean-Louis, "'Le Bourgeois Gentilhomme' ou la Poésie du Rire", *Modern Drama* (1973), 16:113-17
deSelincourt, Aubrey, *Six Great Playwrights.* 1960. Pp. 94-95
Falk, Eugene H., "Molière the Indignant Satirist: 'Le Bourgeois Gentilhomme'", *Tulane Drama Review*, 5:73-88, 1960
Forum, 105:661, March, 1946
Fraser, R. D. and S. F. Rendall, "The Recognition Scene in Molière's Theater", *Romanic Review* (1973), 64:16-31

Ganz, Hans U., "Zur Quellenfrage des 'Bourgeoise Gentilhomme'", *Maske und Kothern* (1968), 14:310-17

Gil, J., "Notes sur un Piège de Moliere", *Revue de Métaphysique et de Morale* (1969), 74:263-67

Girard, René, "Perilous Balance: A Comic Hypothesis", *Modern Language Notes* (1972), 87:811-26

Howarth, W. D. and Merlin Thomas, eds., *Molière: Stage and Study; Essays in Honor of W. G. Moore.* 1973. Pp. 170-84

Life, 39:175-76, Nov. 14, 1955

Maxfield-Miller, Elisabeth, "The Real Monsieur Jourdain of the 'Bourgeois Gentilhomme'", *Studies in Philology*, 56:62-73, 1959

Nation, 162:108, Jan. 26, 1946 and 181:426, Nov. 12, 1955

New Republic, 133:21-22, Nov. 7, 1955

New Yorker, 21:46, Jan. 26, 1946 and 31:81-82, Nov. 5, 1955

Newsweek, 27:87, Jan. 21, 1946

Nicolich, Robert N., "Classicism and Baroque in 'Le Bourgeois Gentilhomme'", *French Review* (1972), 45 (Special Issue):21-30

Oliver, T. E., "Notes on the "Bourgeois Gentilhomme'", *Modern Philology*, 10:407-12, 1913

Rouillard, C. D., "The Background of the Turkish Ceremony in Molière's 'Le Bourgeois Gentilhomme'", *University of Toronto Quarterly* (1969), 39:33-52

Saturday Review, 38:24, Nov. 12, 1955

Saturday Review of Literature, 29:28-30, Feb. 9, 1946

Talamon, R., "La Marquise du 'Bourgeois Gentilhomme'", *Modern Language Notes*, 50:369-75, 1935

Theatre Arts, 30:137, 187, March, 1946 and 39:46-47, Nov., 1955

Time, 66:96, Nov. 7, 1955

Walker, Hallam, "Strength and Style in 'Le Bourgeois Gentilhomme'", *French Review*, 37:282-87, 1964

Le Depit Amoureux *SEE* The Amorous Quarrel

The Doctor in Spite of Himself, 1666
  Scholl, Konrad, "'Le Médecin Malgré Lui' und die Farcenkomik", *Literatur in Wissenschaft und Unterricht* (1972), 5:110-26

Dom Garcie de Navarre ou, Le Prince Jaloux *SEE* Don Garcia of Narvarre; or, The Jealous Prince

Don Garcia of Navarre; or, The Jealous Prince, 1661
  Freudmann, F. R., "Le Comique dan 'Dom Garcie de Navarre'", *Romance Review* (1969), 60:251-64
  Gutwirth, Marcel, "'Dom Garcie de Navarre' et 'Le Misanthrope': De la Comédie Heroique au Comique du Héros", *Modern Language Association. Publications* (1968), 83:118-29
  Hubert, J. D., "Comedy of Incompatibility in Molière's 'Don Garcie de Navarre'", *Modern Language Quarterly*, 21:228-34, Sept., 1960
  Rountree, B., "'Dom Garcie de Navarre': Tentative de Réconciliation Avec Les Precieux", *Romanic Review*, 56:161-70, 1965
  Walker, Hallam, *Molière.* 1971. Pp. 44-47
  Zdanowicz, C. D., "'Don Garcie' and 'Le Misanthrope'", *Modern Philology*, 16:129-42, July, 1918

Don Juan; or, The Feast with the Statue, 1665

Brandt, Per Aage, *Tekstens Teater; Bidrag til en Kritik af den Poetiske Økonomi.* 1972. Pp. 11-56

Brody, Jules, "'Don Juan' and 'Le Misanthrope' or the Esthetics of Individualism in Molière", *Modern Language Association. Publications* (1969), 84:559-76

Buckley, Daniel H., "Metaphor in Four Plays of Molière", *Dissertation Abstracts International* (1974), 35:2981A

Burgess, G. S., "Molière and the Pursuit of Criteria", *Symposium* (Spring 1969), 22:5-15

Cancalon, Elaine D., "l'Inversion de l'Amour Courtois dans Trois Comedies de Molière", *Neophilologus* (1972), 56:134-45

Cole, Toby and Chinoy, Helen Krich, eds., *Directing the Play: A Source Book of Stagecraft.* 1953. Pp. 136-41

——————, *Directors on Directing; A Source Book of the Modern Theatre*, Rev. ed.. 1963. Pp. 179-84

Coquelin, C., "'Don Juan' of Molière", *International Quarterly*, 8:60-92, Sept., 1903

Doolittle, J., "Humanity of Molière's 'Dom Juan'", *Modern Language Association. Publications* (PMLA) 68:509-34, 1953

Dreano, M., "Monsieur de Queriolet et Dom Juan", *Revue d'Histoire Littéraire de la France*, 62:503-13, 1963

Goichot, Emile, "Monsieur de Kériolet, Conti et le 'Dom Juan' de Molière", *Revue de Histoire Littéraire de la France* (1974), 74:29-39

Goode, William O. "Dom Juan and Heaven's Spokesman", *French Review* (1972), 45 (Special Issue):3-12

Gossman, Lionel, *Men and Masks; A Study of Molière.* 1963. Pp. 36-65

Gray, Henry David, "The Treatment of the Villain in Shakespeare and Molière", *Sewanee Review*, 7:68-82, 1889

Gross, Nathan, "The Dialectic of Obligation in Molière's 'Don Juan'", *Romanic Review* (1974), 65:175-200

Guicharnaud, Jacques, ed., *Molière; A Collection of Critical Essays.* 1964. Pp. 79-102

Guitton, Edouard, "Moliere Juriste dans 'Dom Juan'", *Revue d'Histoire Littéraire de la France* (1972), 72:945-53

Hall, H. G., "Comic 'Dom Juan'", *Yale French Studies*, 23:77-84, 1959

Howarth, W. D. and Merlin Thomas, eds., *Molière: Stage and Study; Essays in Honor of W. G. Moore.* 1973. Pp. 61-72

Laufer, R., "Le Comique du Personnage de 'Dom Juan' de Molière", *Modern Language Review*, 58:15-20, 1963

Lawrence, Francis L., "The Ironic Commentator in Molière's 'Don Juan'", *Studi Francesi* (1968), 12:201-07

Leveque, A., "Le Spectre en Femme Voilée dans le 'Dom Juan' de Molière", *Modern Language Notes*, 76:742-48, 1961

Matthews, B., "Molière's 'Don Juan'", *Sewanee Review*, 18:257-67, 1910

Maulnier, Thierry, "'Don Juan' et la Mise en Scene", *Revue de Paris* (1967), 74:140-43

Moore, W. G., "'Don Juan' Reconsidered", *Modern Language Review*, 52:510-17, 1957

Morel, Jacques, "A Propos de la 'Scène du Pauvre' dans 'Dom Juan'", *Revue d'Histoire Littéraire de la France* (1972), 72:938-44

New Yorker, 43:149-51, Mar. 11, 1967

Nelson, Robert J., "The Unreconstructed Heroes of Molière", *Tulane Drama Review*, 4:14-37, 1959-60

Nurse, P. H., "Essai de Definition du Comique Molièresque", *Revue des Sciences Humaines*, 113:9-24, 1964

Nurse, Peter H., ed., *The Art of Criticism; Essays in French Literary Analysis.* 1969. Pp. 69-87

Roussit, Jean, " 'Don Juan' et les Metamorphoses d'Une Structure", *Nouvelle Revue Francaise* (1967), 15:480-90

Schaffer, A., "Thomas Corneille's Reworking of Molière's 'Don Juan' ", *Modern Philology*, 19:163-75, 1921

Singer, I., "Moliere's 'Don Juan' ", *Hudson Review* (Autumn 1971), 24:447-60
_____ , "Shadow of Don Juan in Molière", *Modern Language Notes* (Dec. 1970), 85:838-57
1970), 85:838-57

Stewart, Philip, "An Analysis of the Plot in 'Don Juan' ", *French Review* (1972), 45 (Special Issue): 13-20

Theatre Arts, 33:21, Jan., 1949

Thuel, Francoise, " 'Don Juan' de Molière; Des Mots et Objets 'Mis en Texte' à la Mise en Scène du Sens", *Litterature* (1973), 12:74-85

Truchet, Jacques, "Molière Theologien dans 'Dom Juan' ", *Revue d'Histoire Littéraire de la France* (1972), 72:928-38

Turnell, Martin, *Classical Moment; Studies of Corneille, Molière, and Racine.* 1947. Pp. 78-90

Vier, J., "Oú Va le Théâtre? Le 'Don Juan' de Molière; En Marge d'Une Reprise au Théâtre Français", *Pensée Catholique* (1967), #107:78-83

Walker, Hallam, *Molière.* 1971. Pp. 98-111
_____ , "The Self-Creating Hero in 'Don Juan' ", *French Review*, 36:167-74, 1962

Young, B. E., "Defense and Illustration of the 'Don Juan' of Molière", *South Atlantic Quarterly*, 11:251-58, July, 1912

Don Juan; ou Le Festin de Pierre   SEE   Don Juan; or, The Feast with the Statue

L'École des Femmes   SEE   The School for Wives

l'École des Maris   SEE   The School for Husbands

L'Étourdi; ou, Les Contre-Temps   SEE   The Blunderer; or, The Mishaps

Les Femmes Savantes   SEE   The Learned Ladies

Les Fourberies de Scapin   SEE   The Rogueries of Scapin

George Dandin; or, The Abashed Husband, 1668
Les Annales Politiques et Littéraires, 110:491-92, Nov. 10, 1937

Baader, Renate, " 'George Dandin' Oder die Krise des Komischen", *Archiv für das Studium der Neueren Sprachen und Literaturen* (1973), 210:295-311

Canfield, M. C., "Georges Dandin", *Independent*, 112:259, May 10, 1924

Han, Jean-Pierre, "Notes Pour la Mise en Scène de 'George Dandin' ", *Europe* (1972), 523-24:168-72

Howarth, W. D. and Merlin Thomas, eds., *Molière: Stage and Study: Essays in Honor of W. G. Moore.* 1973. Pp. 3-12

Lewisohn, Ludwig, "Georges Dandin", *Nation*, 118:486, April 23, 1924
New Republic, 38:184, April 9, 1924
Saturday Review, 51:22, July 13, 1968
Walker, Hallam, *Molière*. 1971. Pp. 142-45

Georges Dandin, ou Le Mari Confondu   *SEE*   George Dandin; or, the Abashed Husband

The Imaginary Invalid, 1673
Albert-Fernet, Michel, "La Fiche Médicale d'Argan: 'La Malade Imaginaire'", *Revue des Deux Mondes* (1973), Pp. 320-28
Berk, Philip R., "The Therapy of Art in 'La Malade Imaginaire'", *French Review* (1972), 45 (Special Issue):39-48
Buckley, Daniel H., "Metaphor in Four Plays of Molière", *Dissertation Abstracts International* (1974), 35:2981A
Giula, Dvora, "The Graduation Ceremony of the Medical School in 'The Imaginary Invalid': Moliere's Use of Latin and Its Rendition in the Hebrew Translation by N. Altermann", *Hasifrut; Quarterly for the Study of Literature* (1969), 1:529-37
Guicharnaud, Jacques, ed., *Molière; A Collection of Critical Essays*. 1964. Pp. 160-69
Knowlson, James R., "'Le Malade Imaginaire': The 'Invention Nouvelle' of Cléante", *Modern Language Review*, 58:69-70, 1963
Levrat, E., "La Cas du 'Malade Imaginaire'", *Mercure de France*, 153:387-400, Jan. 15, 1922
Mélanges d'Histoire Littéraire (XVI-XVII Siecle): Offerts à Raymond Lebeque par Ses Collegues, Ses Élèves et Ses Amis. 1969. Pp. 249-58
Stoker, J. T., "Argan's Sickness in Molière's 'La Malade Imaginaire'", *Culture* (1969), 30:122-28
Tynan, Kenneth, *Curtains; Selections from the Drama Criticism and Related Writings*. 1961. Pp. 3-6 and 391-92
Walker, Hallam, *Molière*. 1971. Pp. 167-73
Walkley, Arthur Bingham, *Pastiche and Prejudice*. 1921. Pp. 178-83
Zdanowicz, C. D., "From 'Le Misanthrope' to 'La Malade Imaginaire'", *Modern Philology*, 19:17-32, 1921

The Learned Ladies (1672)
Henning, G. N., "The Dénouement of 'Les Femmes Savantes'", *French Review*, 13:42-45, 1939
Miclău, Paul, et al, "Structura Statistică a Alexandrinului in 'Les Femmes Savantes'", *Analele Universitatii, Bucuresti, Limbi Romanice* (1973), 22:85-92
Nation, 204:285-86, Feb. 27, 1967
Perregaux, Béatrice, "'Les Femmes Savantes' de Molière: Une Mise en Scène d'André Steiger", *Cahiers de l'Association Internationales des Etudes Françaises* (1969), 21:73-85
Suther, Judith D., "The Tricentennial of Molière's 'Femmes Savantes'", *French Review* (1972), 45 (Special Issue):31-38
Walker, Hallam, *Molière*. 1971. Pp. 161-66

The Magnificent Lovers, 1670
Howarth, W. D. and Merlin Thomas, eds., *Moliere; Stage and Study; Essays in Honor of W. G. Moore*. 1973. Pp. 21-42

Walker, Hallam, *Molière*. 1971. Pp. 134-35

La Malade Imaginaire   *SEE*   The Imaginary Invalid

Le Medecin Malgre Lui   *SEE*   The Doctor in Spite of Himself

The Misanthrope, 1666
America, 119:445-47, Nov. 9, 1968
Ampola, Fillippo, "Note sul 'Misantropo' di Molière", *Rivista di Letterature Moderne e Comparate*, 13:89-91, 1960
Les Annales Politiques et Littéraires, 11:528-29, May 25, 1938
Belloc, Hilaire, *On*. 1923. Pp. 66-73
Bookman, 58:416-17, Dec., 1923
Brody, Jules, " 'Don Juan' and 'Le Misanthrope', or the Esthetics of Individualism in Molière", *Modern Language Association. Publications* (May 1969), 84:559-76
Burgess, G. S., "Molière and the Pursuit of Criteria", *Symposium* (Spring 1969), 22:5-15
Cancalon, Elaine D., "l'Inversion de l'Amour Courtois dans Trois Comédies de Molière", *Neophilologus* (1972), 56:134-45
Catholic World, 185:67, April, 1957
Christian Century, 85:1509-10, Nov. 27, 1968
Cismaru, Alfred, " 'Les Sinceres' and 'Le Misanthrope': An Attempt to Settle the Relationship", *French Review* (May 1969), 42:865-70
Demorest, Jean-Jacques, ed., *Studies in 17th Century French Literature Presented to Morris Bishop*. 1962. Pp. 165-84
deSelincourt, Aubrey, *Six Great Playwrights*. 1960. Pp. 101-02
Edmunds, J., "Timon of Athens Blended with 'Le Misanthrope': Shadwell's Recipe for Satirical Tragedy", *Modern Language Review* (July 1969), 64:500-07
Friedson, A. M., "Wycherley and Molière: Satirical Point of View in 'The Plain Dealer' ", *Modern Philology* (1967), 64:189-97
Goethe, Johann W., *Literary Essays; A Selection in English*. 1921. Pp. 212
Goodman, Randolph, *Drama on Stage*. 1961. Pp. 198-207 and 230-32
Gossman, Lionel, *Men and Masks; A Study of Molière*. 1963. Pp. 66-99
Grieve, Artur, "Molière als Versdichter. Zum Alexandriner im 'Misanthrope' ", *Archiv für das Studium der Neueren Sprachen und Literaturen* (1970), 207:81-93
Gutwirth, Marcell, " 'Dom Garcie de Navarre' et 'Le Misanthrope': De la Comédie Heroique au Comique du Héros", *Modern Language Association. Publications* (1968), 83:118-29
Hall, H. Gaston, "The Literary Context of Molière's 'Le Misanthrope' ", *Studi Francesi* (1970), 14:20-38
_____ , "Molière's 'Le Misanthrope' in the Light of d'Aubignac's 'Conseils d'Ariste à Celimène' and Other Contemporary Texts", *Kentucky Romance Quarterly* (1972), 19:347-63
Hope, Q. M., "Society in "Le Misanthrope" ", *French Review*, 32:329-36, 1959
Jasinski R., Molière et 'Le Misanthrope' ", *Romanic Review*, 43:215-22, 1952
Leo, Ulrich, "Goldonis 'Locandiera' and Molières 'Misanthrope': Zwei Motiv-Entwicklungen", *Romanische Forschungen*, 70:323-65, 1958
Lichet, Raymond, " 'Le Misanthrope' et le Language", *Le Francais dans le Monde* (Jan.-Feb. 1967), 46:41-43

Mesnard, Jean, "'Le Misanthrope': Mise en Question de l'Art de Plaire", *Revue d'Histoire Littéraire de la France* (1972), 72:863-89

Michel, Marc, "'Alceste' ou 'Le Misanthrope'", *Nouvelle Revue Francaise*, 11:316-23, 1963

Monod, Richard, "Un 'Misanthrope' Sans Auto-Censure et Sans Héros", *Europe* (1972), 523-24:128-44

Moore, W. G., "Reflections on 'Le Misanthrope'", *Australian Journal of French Studies* (1967), 4:198-203

Nation, 207:510, Nov. 11, 1968

New Yorker, 44:159, Oct. 19, 1968

Nelson, Robert J., "The Unreconstructed Heroes of Molière", *Tulane Drama Review*, 4:14-37, 1959-60

New Statesman and Nation, 13:325-26, Feb. 27, 1937

Nurse, P. H., "Essai de Definition du Comique Molièresque", *Revue des Sciences Humaines*, #113:9-24, 1964

————— ,"La Vie et la Morale dans l'Oeuvre de Molière", *Seventeenth Century* (France), #52:20-35, 1961

Picard, Michel, "Le Personnage d'Alceste dans 'Le Misanthrope' de Molière", *L'Information Littéraire*, 9:134-37, 1957

Regosin, R. L., "Ambiguity and Truth in 'Le Misanthrope'", *Romanic Review* (Dec. 1969), 60:265-72

Rudin, Seymour, "Molière and 'The Misanthrope'", *Educational Theatre Journal*, 17:308-13, 1965

Saturday Review, 49:54, Mar. 5, 1966 and 51:53, Nov. 2, 1968

Scanlan, T., "Molière's 'Le Misanthrope'", *Explicator* (1974), 32:43

Schunk, Peter, "Zur Wirkungsgeschichte des 'Misanthrope'", *Germanisch-Romanische Monatsschrift* (1971), 21:1-15

Seilliere, E., "La Philosophie du 'Misanthrope'; A Propos du Livre 'Le Misanthrope' de Molière", *Journal des Débats*, 36 pt. 1:394-97, March 8, 1929

Shaw, David C., "'Le Misanthrope' and Classicism", *Modern Languages* (1974), 55,i:16-26

Sullivan, E. D., "The Actor's Alceste: Evolution of 'The Misanthrope'", *Modern Language Quarterly*, 9:492-96, 1948

Theatre Arts, 41:82, April, 1957

Time. 92:72, Oct. 18, 1968

Turnell, Martin, *Classical Moment; Studies of Corneille, Molière and Racine.* 1947. Pp. 90-120

Tynan, Kenneth, *Curtains; Selections from the Drama Criticism and Related Writings.* 1961. Pp. 391-92

Vogue, 153:70, Jan. 1, 1969

Wadsworth, P. A., "Recollections of Cicognini's 'Gelosie Fortunate' in 'Le Misanthrope'", *Modern Language Association. Publications* (1974), 89:1099-105

Walker, Hallam, "Action and Illusion in 'Le Misanthrope'", *Kentucky Foreign Language Quarterly*, 9:150-61, 1962

————— , *Molière.* 1971. Pp. 111-25

Wucherpfennig, Wolf, "'Der Schwierige' und 'Der Manschenfeind': Zur Auffassung des Individuums bei Molière und Hofmannsthal", *Colloquia Germanica, Internationale Zeitschrift für Germanische-Sprach-und Literaturwissenschaft* (1969), 3:269-301

Yarrow, P. J., "A Reconsideration of Alceste", *French Studies*, 13:314-31, 1959

Zdanowicz, C. D., " 'Don Garcie' and 'Le Misanthrope' ", *Modern Philology*, 16:129-42, 1918

—————— , "From 'Le Misanthrope' to 'Le Malade Imaginaire' ", *Modern Philology*, 19:17-32, 1921

Zolbrod, Paul G., "Coriolanus and Alceste; A Study in Misanthropy", *Shakespeare Quarterly* (1972), 23:51-62

The Miser, 1668

Buckley, Daniel H., "Metaphor in Four Plays of Molière", *Dissertation Abstracts International* (1974), 35:2981A

Gilman, Richard, *Common and Uncommon Masks; Writings on the Theatre, 1961-70*. 1971. Pp. 274-76

Goode, William O., "The Comic Recognition Scenes in 'l'Avare' ", *Romance Notes* (1972), 14:122-27

Guicharnaud, Jacques, ed., *Molière; A Collection of Critical Essays*. 1964. Pp. 155-59

Gutwirth, M., "Unity of Molière's 'L'Avare' ", *Modern Language Association. Publications* (PMLA), 76:359-66, 1961

Herrick, I. A., "Shylock and Harpagon, Two Specialists in Avarice", *Education*, 14:633-37, 1894

Hubert, Judd D., "Theme and Structure in 'L'Avare' ", *Modern Language Association. Publications* (PMLA), 75:31-36, 1960

Illustrated London News, 216:148, Jan. 28, 1950

Walker, Hallam, "Action and Ending of 'L'Avare' ", *French Review*, 34:531-36, 1961

—————— , *Molière*. 1971. Pp. 146-53

Wells, David J., "The Structure of Laughter in Molière's 'l'Avare' ", *South Central Bulletin* (1972), 32:242-45

Monsieur de Pourceaugnac, 1669

Doumic, R., "Monsieur de Pourceaugnac", *Revue des Deux Mondes*, ser. 8, 13:708-10, Feb. 1, 1933

Garavini, Fausta, "La Fantasi Verbale et le Mimetisme Dialectal dans le Théâtre de Molière: A Propos de 'Monsieur de Pourceaugnac' ", *Revue d'Histoire Littéraire de la France* (1972), 72:806-20

Potter, Edithe J., "Levels of Knowing in 'Monsieur de Pourceaugnac' ", *Orbis Litterarum* (1974), 29:87-92

La Princesse d'Elide, 1664

Walker, Hallam, *Molière*. 1971. Pp. 79-80

Précieuses Ridicules   *SEE*   The Ridiculous Snobs

The Ridiculous Snobs, 1659

Daniel, George B., ed., *Renaissance and Other Studies in Honor of William Leon Wyley*. 1968. Pp. 140-50

deSelincourt, Aubrey, *Six Great Playwrights*. 1960. Pp. 90-94

Pintard, René, "Pour le Tricentenaire des 'Précieuses Ridicules': Préciosité et Classicisme", *Seventeenth Century* (France), #50 and 51, Pp. 8-20, 1961

Walker, Hallam, *Molière*. 1971. Pp. 31-40

Weinrich, Harold, "Zur Szene XI des 'Précieuses Ridicules' ", *Romanische Forschungen* (1967), 79:263-70,

The Rogueries of Scapin, 1672
  Bentley, E. R., *In Search of Theatre*. 1953. Pp. 196-214
  Christian Century, 78:395-96, March 29, 1961
  Garin, Carol, "Contrast in 'Les Fourberies de Scapin'", *Romance Notes* (1968), 9:265-66
  Guicharnaud, Jacques, ed., *Molière; A Collection of Critical Essays*. 1964. Pp. 150-54
  Nation, 176:18, Jan. 3, 1953 and 192:221-22, March 11, 1961
  New Yorker, 37:93, March 4, 1961
  Richardson, J., "Molière and Magic", *Commentary* (Nov. 1974), 58:74-75
  Saturday Review, 44:38, March 11, 1961
  Walker, Hallam, *Molière*. 1971. Pp. 158-61

The School for Husbands, 1661
  Walker, Hallam, *Molière*. 1971. Pp. 47-58

School for Wives, 1662
  Cancalon, Elaine D., "L'Inversion de l'Amour Courtois dans Trois Comedies de Molière", *Neophilologus* (1972), 56:134-45
  Catholic World, 173:148, May, 1951 and 185:388, Aug. 1957
  Commonweal, 53:645, April 6, 1951
  Ehrmann, Jacques, "Notes sur 'L'Ecole des Femmes'", *Revue des Sciences Humaines*, #109:5-10, 1963
  Fraser, R. D. and S. F. Rendall, "The Recognition Scene in Molière's Theater", *Romanic Review* (1973), 64:16-31
  Guitry, L., "L'École des Femmes", *L'Illustration*, 82 pt. 2:341, Oct. 11, 1924
  Hall, G., "Parody in "L'École des Femmes': Agnès's Question", *Modern Language Review*, 57:63-65, 1962
  Howarth, W. D., "Source of 'L'École des Femmes'", *Modern Language Review*, 58:10-14, 1963
  Hubert, Judd D., "'L'Ecole des Femmes', Tragédie Burlesque?', *Revue des Sciences Humaines*, #97:41-52, 1960
  Journal des Débats, 41 pt. 1:1167-69, July 20, 1934
  Kern, Edith, "'l'École des Femmes' and the Spirit of Farce", *l'Esprit Créateur* (1973), 13:220-28
  McBride, Robert, "The Sceptical View of Marriage and the Comic Vision in Molière", *Forum for Modern Language Studies* (1969), 5:26-46
  Magne, Bernard, "'l'École des Femmes' ou la Conquête de la Parole", *Revue des Sciences Humaines* (1972), n. s. 145:125-42
  New Republic, 124:21, April 9, 1951
  New Yorker, 27:53, March 31, 1951
  Nurse, P. H., "Role of Chrysalde in 'L'École des Femmes'", *Modern Language Review*, 56:167-71, 1961
  Porter, Dennis, "Comic Rhythm in 'L'École des Femmes'", *Forum for Modern Language Studies* (1969), 5:205-17
  Revue des Deux Mondes, s. 8, 33:686-89, June 1, 1936.
  Rossat-Mignod, Suzanne, "L'Emancipation des Femmes", *Europe*, May-June, 1961. Pp. 116-22
  Shapherd, James L., III, "Molière and Wycherley's 'Plain Dealer'", *South Central Bulletin* (1963), 23:37-40
  Theatre Arts, 35:23, March, 1951
  Turnell, Martin, *Classical Moment; Studies of Corneille, Molière and Racine*. 1947. Pp. 53-58

Walker, Hallam, *Molière*. 1971. Pp. 62-70

Zwillenberg, Myrna K., "Arnolphe, Fate's Fool", *Modern Language Review* (1973), 68:292-308

Tartuffe; or, The Impostor, 1664

Aastrup, Klaus, " 'Tartuffe' og den Danske Kritik", *Edda* (1970), 70:130-36
America, 112:336, March 6, 1965

Bennett, James O'Donnell, *Much Loved Books; Best Sellers of the Ages*. 1927. Pp. 223-29

Boiadjiev, G. N., " 'Tartuffe' Sur la Scène Sovietique", *Europe* (1972), 523-24:199-218

Bouffard, Odaric, O. F. M., "Tartuffe, Faux Monnayeur en Dévotion", *Culture*, 23:341-58, 1962

Bourdieu, P., "Tartuffe' ou le Drame de la Foi et de la Manuvaise Foi", *Revue de la Méditerranee*, (Alger.), 19:92-93, 453-58, 1959

Brandwajn, R., "Quelques Réflexions sur 'Tartuffe' ", *Europe* (1972), 523-24:109-21

Brisson, P., "Tartuffe", *Les Annales Politiques et Littéraires*, 80:370, April 8, 1923

Brustein, Robert Sanford, *Seasons of Discontent; Dramatic Opinions 1959-, 1965*. 1965. Pp. 263-69

Buckley, Daniel H., "Metaphor in Four Plays of Molière", *Dissertation Abstracts International* (1974), 35:2981A

Burgess, J., "Tartuffe", *Plays and Players* (Jan. 1975), 22:35

Busson, H., "Notes sur 'Tartuffe' ", *Revue de la Méditerranée* (Alger.) 15:136-51, 1955

Cairncross, John, " 'Tartuffe' ou Molière Hypocrite", *Revue d'Histoire Littéraire de la France* (1972), 72:890-901

Chill, Emanuel S., " 'Tartuffe', Religion and Courtly Culture", *French Historical Studies*, 3:151-83, 1963

Commonweal, 81:611-12, Feb. 5, 1965

Couton, Georges, "Réflexions sur 'Tartuffe' et le Peche d'Hypocrisie 'Cas Reserve' ", *Revue d'Histoire Littéraire de la France* (1969), 69:404-13

Defourneaux, M., "Molière et l'Inquisition Espagnole", *Bulletin Hispanique* (Bordeaux), 64:1-2, 30-42, 1962

Deguy, Michel, "Un Vrai Tartuffe", *Critique*, 20:403-10, 1964

Delcourt, Marie, "Tricentenaire de 'Tartuffe, II': Imposteur ou Hypocrite?", *Marche Romane* (1967), 17:205-06

deSelincourt, Aubrey, *Six Great Playwrights*. 1960. Pp. 96-101

Dorenkamp, John H., ed., *Literary Studies: Essays in Memory of Francis A. Drumm*. 1974. Pp. 191-206

Dupriez, Bernard, "Tartuffe et la Sincérité", *Etudes Françaises*, 1:52-67, 1965

Fau, G., "Molière Expurgé", *Le Courrier Rationalists*, 8:96-99, 1961

Fonsny, J., "Du Nouveau sur Molière", *Etudes Classiques*, 22:172-86, 1954

Garboli, Cesare, "Ipotesi sul 'Tartuffe' ", *Paragone* (1973), 282:42-52

Gossman, Lionel, *Men and Masks; A Study of Molière*. 1963. Pp. 100-45
_____ , "Molière and 'Tartuffe': Law and Order in the 17th Century", *French Review* (1970), 43:901-12

Grant, E. M., "Tartuffe Again", *Philological Quarterly* 6:67-74, 1927

Gray, Henry David, "The Treatment of the Villain in Shakespeare and Molière", *Sewanee Review*, 7:68-82, 1889

Harrison, J. A., "'Tartuffe': A Typical Comedy of Molière", *Chautauguan*, 32:297-301, Dec., 1900

Hope, Quentin M., "Place and Setting in 'Tartuffe'", *Modern Language Association. Publications* (1974), 89:42-49

Jubecourt, Gerard S. de, "A Propos du Tricentenaire de 'Tartuffe': Versailles et Son Poete Molière", *Modern and Classical Language Bulletin* (1969), 8:9-13

Laurence, F. L., "The Norm in 'Tartuffe'", *Revue de l'Université d'Ottawa* (1966), 36:698-702

Lawrenson, T. E., and F. E. Sutcliffe and G. F. A. Gadoffe, eds., *Modern Miscellany Presented to Eugene Vinaver by Pupils, Colleagues and Friends*. 1970. Pp. 48-64

Mabley, Edward, *Dramatic Construction; An Outline of Basic Principles*. 1972. Pp. 66-79

MacCarthy, Desmond, "Tartuffe", *New Statesman and Nation*, 30:23, July 14, 1945

McCollom, William G., *The Divine Average; A View of Comedy*. 1971. Pp. 165-79

Mélanges d'Histoire Littéraire (XVI-XVII Siecle): Offerts à Raymond Lebeque par Ses Collegues, Ses Élèves et Ses Amis. 1969. Pp. 227-39

Melese, Pierre, "Un Episode Peu Commun de la Quarelle de Tartuffe", *Seventeenth Century* (France), #53:51-54, 1961

Miles, D. H., "Original of the Non-Juror", *Modern Language Association. Publications* (PMLA), 23:195-214, 1915

Montgomery, Edward D., "'Tartuffe': The History and Sense of a Name", *Modern Language Notes* (1973), 88:838-41

Moore, W. G., "Tartuffe and the Comic Principle in Molière", *Modern Language Review* 43:47-53, 1948

Nation, 200:122, Feb. 1, 1965, 207:61-62, July 22, 1968

Nelson, Robert J., "The Unreconstructed Heroes of Molière", *Tulane Drama Review*, 4:14-37, 1959-60

New Republic, 152:34, Jan. 30, 1965

New Yorker, 37:112, March 11, 1961

Newsweek, 65:86, Jan. 25, 1965

Novick, Julius, *Beyond Broadway; The Quest for Permanent Theatres*. 1968. Pp. 191-93 and 231-33

Orwin, Gifford P., "'Tartuffe' Reconsidered", *French Review* (1968), 41:611-17

Pholien, Georges, "Une Defence du 'Tartuffe'", *Marche Romane* (1967), 17:179-96

Roy, Claude, "Sur Tartuffe", *Nouvelle Revue Francaise*, 12:897-908, 1964

Salomon, H. P., "Tartuffe Devant l'Opinion Francaise", *Romanic Review*, 55:211-13, 1964

Salvan, P., "'Le Tartuffe' de Molière et l'Agitation Anticléricale en 1825", *Revue de'Histoire du Théâtre* (Paris), 12:7-19, 1960

Saturday Review, 48:44, Feb. 6, 1965, 50:28, Oct. 7, 1967 and 51:49, Aug. 24, 1968

Stoll, Elmer Edgar, *Shakespeare, And Other Masters*. 1940. Pp. 334-61

——————— , "'Tartuffe' and the 'Optique du Théâtre'", *Revue Anglo-Americaine*, 13:193-214, 1936

Tiefenbrun, Susan W., "Explication de Texte: Molière's 'Le Tartuffe'; A Play Within a Play", *Newsletter; Teaching Languages Through Literature* (1973), 13:9-22

Time, 85:40, Jan. 22, 1965

Toporkov, V., "Stanislavsky Works with Tartuffe", *Drama Survey* (Spring 1966), 5:73-77

Trollope, H., "What Was Tartuffe?", *Blackwood's Magazine*, 154:641-47, Nov. 18, 1893

Turnell, Martin, *Classical Moment; Studies of Corneille, Molière, and Racine.* 1947. Pp. 58-78

Vogue, 145:95, March 1, 1965

Walker, Hallam, *Molière.* 1971. Pp. 81-98

Wayne, Richard J., "The Relationship of Tartuffe and Orgon in Molière's 'Tartuffe': The Problem Posed by Its Symmetry", *Dissertation Abstracts International* (1972), 32:6946A

Wright, Edward A. and Lenthiel H. Downs, *A Primer for Playgoers.* 1969. Pp. 79-84

Tartuffe; ou, L'Imposteur *SEE* Tartuffe; or, The Impostor

MOLIERE, PIERRE CORNEILLE AND PHILIPPE QUINAULT

Psyché, 1671
Wadsworth, Philip A., "The Composition of 'Psyché'", *Rice University Studies* (1967), 53:69-76

FERENC MOLNAR

Carnival, 1925
Clark, B. H., "Carnival", *Drama*, 15:97, Feb., 1925

Csoda a Hegyek Közt *SEE* Miracle in the Mountains

Delicate Story, 1940
Catholic World, 152:470-71, Jan., 1941
Nation, 151:641, Dec. 21, 1940
Newsweek, 16:66, Dec. 16, 1940
Theatre Arts, 25:97, Feb., 1941

Devil, 1907
Firkins, O. W., "Supernatural in 'The Devil'", *Poet-Lore*, 20:438-48, Nov., 1909
Walker, R., "'Devil': A Powerful Drama of Mental Suggestion", *Arena*, 40:536-46, Dec., 1908

Égi és Földi Szerelem *SEE* Launzi

Egy, Kettö, Három *SEE* One, Two, Three

A Farkas *SEE* The Wolf

Farsang *SEE* Carnival

Good Fairy, 1932
Arts and Decoration, 36:56, Feb., 1932
Bookman, 74:565, Jan., 1932

Catholic World, 134:469, Jan., 1932
Commonweal, 15:187-88, Dec. 16, 1931
London Mercury, 36:181, June, 1937
Nation, 133:678, Dec. 16, 1931
Outlook, 159:470, Dec. 9, 1931
Theatre Arts, 16:97-98, Feb., 1932

The Guardsman, 1910
  Behrman, S. N., "Ferenc Molnar: Playwright", *New Yorker*, 22:32-36, June 1, 1946

A Hattyú   *SEE*   The Swan

Játék a Kastélyban   *SEE*   The Play's the Thing

A Jó Tünder   *SEE*   The Good Fairy

Launzi, 1923
  Young, Stark, "Launzi", *New Republic*, 36:230-31, Oct. 24, 1923

Liliom, 1909
  Behrman, S. N., "Ferenc Molnar: Playwright", *New Yorker*, 22:32-6, June 1, 1946
  Battey, A., "Liliom", *Drama* 12:6-8, Oct., 1921
  ————————— , "Liliom", *Poet-Lore*, 35:43-47, 1924
  Catholic World, 136:463-64, Jan., 1933 and 151:210-11, May, 1940
  Commonweal, 17:75, Nov. 16, 1932 and 31:514, April 5, 1940
  Crawford, J., "Liliom", *Drama*, 11:308-10, June, 1921
  Firkins, O. W. "Liliom", *Review*, 4:444-46, May 7, 1921
  Gassner, John, *Dramatic Soundings; Evaluations and Retractions Culled from Thirty Years of Dramatic Criticism.* 1968. Pp. 218-19
  Literary Digest, 69:24-25, May 21, 1921
  Lewisohn, Ludwig, *Drama and the Stage.* 1922. Pp. 53-71
  ————————— , "Liliom", *Nation*, 112:695, May 11, 1921
  Nation, 150:457, April 6, 1940
  Nation (London), 40:508, Jan. 8, 1927
  New Republic, 102:473, April 8, 1940
  New Yorker, 16:30, April 6, 1940
  Outlook, 128:153-54, May 25, 1921
  Outlook, (London), 59:66, Jan. 15, 1927
  Saturday Review, 143:12, Jan. 1, 1927
  Spectator, 138:38-39, Jan. 8, 1927
  Theatre Arts, 17:14-15, Jan., 1933 and 24:315, May, 1940
  Time, 35:38, April 8, 1940
  Wilson, E., Jr., "Liliom", *New Republic*, 26:299, May 4, 1921

Miracle In the Mountains, 1947
  Nathan, George Jean, *Theatre Book of the Year, 1946-47*, Pp. 373-76
  New Yorker, 23:54, May 3, 1947
  Newsweek, 29:86, May 5, 1957
  Time, 49:76, May 5, 1947

One, Two, Three, 1930
  Catholic World, 132:209, Nov., 1930
  Commonweal, 12:610, Oct. 15, 1930

Az Ördög *SEE* The Devil

The Play's The Thing, 1925
  Catholic World, 167:264-65, June, 1948
  Life, 24:85-86, May 24, 1948
  Nathan, George Jean, *Theatre Book of the Year, 1947-48.* Pp. 358-60
  Nation, 166:577-78, May 15, 1948
  New Republic, 118:34, May 17, 1948
  New Yorker, 24:54, May 8, 1948
  Newsweek, 31:77, May 10, 1948
  Saturday Review of Literature, 31:20-21, May 29, 1948
  Theatre Arts, 32:13, 19, June, 1948
  Time, 51:81, May 10, 1948

The Swan, 1920
  Behrman, S. N., "Ferenc Molnar; Playwright", *New Yorker*, 22:32-6, June
    1, 1946
  Jennings, R., "The Swan", *Spectator*, 145:79-80, July 19, 1930
  Kellock, H., "The Swan", *Freeman*, 8:281-82, Nov. 28, 1923
  Wakefield, G., "The Swan", *Saturday Review*, 150:45, July 12, 1930

A Testör *SEE* The Guardsman

Unknown Girl, 1935
  Wittner, V., "Unknown Girl", *Theatre Arts*, 19:264-67, April, 1935

The Wolf, 1912
  Lambert, J. W., "The Wolf", *Drama* (1973), 111:26

HENRY MILLON DE MONTHERLANT

Brocéliande, 1956
  Haft, Cynthia J., "Montherlant's 'Brocéliande': A Note on a Neglected
    Play", *Language Quarterly* (1974), 12,iii-iv:15-22
  Johnson, Robert B., *Henry de Montherlant.* 1968. Pp. 96-99
  Norrish, P. ,J., "Montherlant's Conception of the Tragic Hero", *French
    Studies*, 14:18-37, 1960
  Von Arx, Paulette, *La Femme dans le Théâtre de Henry de Montherlant.*
    1973. Pp. 117-28

Cardinal d'Espagne *SEE* Cardinal of Spain

Cardinal of Spain, 1960
  Alheinc, Raoul, "La Part de la Simulation Chez la Reine Folle du 'Cardinal
    d'Espagne' ", *L'Âge Nouveau*, #113:135-40, 1962
  Balust, L. S., "Le Moment Espagnol dans l'Oeuvre de Montherlant", *La
    Table Ronde*, #148:34-40, 1960
  Blanchet, André, " 'Le Cardinal d'Espagne' ou le Mystique Manque", *Les
    Etudes* (Paris), 308:328-44, 1961
  Calmel, R. T., "Le Christianisme du 'Cardinal d'Espagne' de Montherlant",
    Itineraires, #59:143-8, 1962
  Cognet, L., "Un Drame de l'Absolu", *La Table Ronde*, #148:33, 1960
  Elizalde, I., "La Tragedia de Cisneros en el Ultimo Drama de Montherlant",
    Razon y Fe, 161:646-49, 1960

Gouhier, H., "Une Tragedie de l'Homme Caché", *La Table Ronde*, #148:20-25, 1960

Johnson, Robert B., *Henry de Montherlant*. 1968. Pp. 120-23

————————— , "Metaphor in Montherlant's 'Le Cardinal d'Espagne' ", *Romance Notes* (1973), 14:425-29

Knutsen, Katharine A., "Symbolism in 'Le Cardinal d'Espagne' ", *French Review* (1974), 48:343-48

Massis, H., "Montherlant, Homme de Théâtre", *La Table Ronde*, #148:45-48, 1960

New Yorker, 36:94, Jan. 21, 1961

Orcibal, J., "De 'Port-Royal' au 'Cardinal d'Espagne' ", *La Table Ronde*, #148:26-32, 1960

Peman, J. N., "Un Tragédie des Conflits", *La Table Ronde*, #148:41-44, 1960

Saint-Robert, P. de, "Une Tragédie de la Grâce", *La Table Ronde*, #148:49-51, 1960

Spiriot, P., " 'Le Cardinal d'Espagne' de Montherlant et les Constantes de l'Oeuvre", *Annales du Centre Universitaire Méditerranéen* (Nice), 14:149-62, 1960-61

Von Arx, Paulette, *La Femme dans le Théâtre de Henry de Montherlant*. 1973. Pp. 153-64

Celles Qu'on Prend dans Ses Bras   *SEE*   Women One Takes in One's Arms

The City Whose Prince Is a Child, 1951
Johnson, Robert, *Henry de Montherlant*. 1968. Pp. 83-86

The Civil War, 1965
Belli, Angela, "The Rugged Individualists of Henry de Montherlant", *Modern Drama* (Sept. 1970), 13:156-68

Johnson, Robert B., *Henry de Montherlant*. 1968. Pp. 123-26

Demain il Fera Jour   *SEE*   Tomorrow the Dawn

Don Juan, 1958
Belli, Angela, "The Rugged Individualists of Henry de Montherlant", *Modern Drama* (Sept. 1970), 13:156-68

Beauchet, André, "Un Don Juan Méconnaissable", *Les Etudes* (Paris), 300:78-82, 1959

Johnson, Robert B., *Henry de Montherlant*. 1968. Pp. 118-20

Von Arx, Paulette, *La Femme dans le Théâtre de Henry de Montherlant*. 1973. Pp. 129-52

l'Exil   *SEE*   The Exile

The Exile, 1929
Johnson, Robert B., *Henry de Montherlant*. 1968. Pp. 86-88

Norrish, P. J., "Montherlant's Conception of the Tragic Hero", *French Studies*, 14:18-37, 1960   ~

Von Arx, Paulette, *La Femme dans le Théâtre de Henry de Montherlant*. 1973. Pp. 13-22

Weiss, Aureliu, "Montherlant et 'L'Exil' ", *Canadian Modern Language Review* (1967), 23:22-25

Fils de Personne   *SEE*   No Man's Son

Un Incompris *SEE* Misunderstood

La Guerre Civile *SEE* The Civil War

Le Maitre de Santiago *SEE* The Master of Santiago

Malatesta, 1950
  Batchelor, John "'Malatesta' ou Imagination et Realité", *Revue de Paris*
    (Feb. 1970), 77:104-11
  Gerrard, Charlotte F., "Montherlant's 'Malatesta': Pagan, Christian, or
    Nietzschean?", *French Review* (1968), 41:831-38
  Illustrated London News, 230:554, April 6, 1957
  Johnson, Robert B., *Henry de Montherlant*. 1968. Pp. 107-10
  Mercure de France, 311:696-97, April, 1951
  Traverso, Leone, "'Malatesta' di Henry de Montherlant", *Studi Urbinati
    di Storia, Filosofia at Literatura* (1971), 45:294-95
  Von Arx, Paulette, *La Femme Dans le Théâtre de Henry de Montherlant*.
    1973. Pp. 51-58

The Master of Santiago, 1948
  Balust, L. S., "Le Moment Espagnol dans l'Ouevre de Montherlant", *La
    Table Ronde*, #148:34-40, 1960
  Belli, Angela, "The Rugged Individualists of Henry de Montherland", *Modern
    Drama* (Sept. 1970), 13:156-68
  English, 11:186, Summer, 1957
  Gobert, David L., "Structural Identity of 'La Reine Morte' and 'Le Maitre de
    Santiago'", *French Review*, 38:30-33, 1964
  Johnson, Robert B., *Henry de Montherlant*. 1968. Pp. 110-14
  Lumley, Frederick, *New Trends in Twentieth Century Drama; A Survey
    Since Ibsen and Shaw*. 1967. Pp. 342-47
  New Statesman, 53:275, March 2, 1957
  Norrish, P. J., "Montherlant's Conception of the Tragic Hero", *French Studies*,
    14:18-37, 1960
  Thiher, Allen, "'Le Maître de Santiago' and Tragic Affirmation", *Romance
    Notes* (1969), 11:238-43
  Von Arx, Paulette, *La Femme dans le Théâtre de Henry de Montherlant*.
    1973. Pp. 59-66

Misunderstood, 1944
  Johnson, Robert B., *Henry de Montherlant*. 1968. Pp. 93-94

No Man's Son, 1949
  Johnson, Robert B., *Henry de Montherlant*. 1968. Pp. 89-93
  Norrish, P. J., "Montherlant's Conception of the Tragic Hero", *French
    Studies* 14:18-37, 1960
  Von Arx, Paulette, *La Femme dans le Théâtre de Henry de Montherlant*.
    1973. Pp. 45-50

Pasiphaë, 1938
  Belli, Angela, *Ancient Greek Myths and Modern Drama; A Study in Con-
    tinuity*. 1971. Pp. 91-97

Port-Royal, 1954
  America, 93:155-56, May 7, 1955
  Belli, Angela, "The Rugged Individualists of Henry de Montherlant", *Modern
    Drama* (Sept. 1970), 13:156-68

Blanc, Andre, "A Propos de 'Port-Royal'", *Revue de Deux Mondes* (1969), 12:612-16

Blanchet, A., "Encore 'Port-Royal'", *Les Etudes*, 284:365-75, 1955

Champomier, Abbe, "Reflexions Auvergnates sur le 'Port-Royal' de Montherlant", *Bulletin Historique et Scientifique d'Auvergne*, 75:89-94, 1955

Frèches, Claude-Henri, "Le 'Port-Royal' de Montherlant", *Annali Instituto Universitario Orientale, Napoli, Sezione Germanica*, 2:1-24, 1960

Johnson, Robert B., *Henry de Montherlant*. 1968. Pp. 114-18

Manduit, J., "Henry de Montherlant: 'Port-Royal'", *Les Etudes* (Paris), 284:232-39, 1955

Moeller, C., "Les Idées: Montherlant et le Drame de 'Port-Royal'" *Revue Nouvelle*, 21:415-21, 1955

Newsweek, 55:84, May 2, 1960

Orcibal, J., "De 'Port-Royal' au 'Cardinal d'Espagne'", *La Table Ronde*, #148:26-32, 1960

Saint-Robert, Phillippe de, "Du Côté de la Souffrance: 'Port-Royal'", *La Table Ronde*, April, 1959, Pp. 155-63

Schweig, G., "Henry de Montherlant und 'Port-Royal'", *Die Neueren Sprachen*, #1:23-31, 1962

Venesoen, Constant, "La Dramaturgie du 'Port-Royal' d'Henry de Montherlant; Une Création par l'Émotion", *Revue de l'Université d'Ottawa* (1970), 40:631-44

Vial, Fernand, "Montherlant's Farewell to the Stage: 'Port-Royal'", *American Society of Legion of Honor Magazine*, 27:33-54, 1958

Von Arx, Paulette, *La Femme dans le Théâtre de Henry de Montherlant*. 1973. Pp. 81-116

Weiss, Auréliu, "Montherlant et Port-Royal; Un Portrait de Soeur Angélique", *Romance Notes* (1968), 10:1-6

Queen After Death; or, How to Kill Women, 1942

Belli, Angela, "The Rugged Individualists of Henry de Montherlant", *Modern Drama* (Sept. 1970), 13:156-68

Cox, Laurence W., "'La Reine Morte' and 'Reinar Despues de Morir'", *Romance Notes* (1972), 13:402-08

Edney, D. B., "Two Stage Versions of Molière's 'La Reine Morte'", *Modern Drama* (1973), 16:13-21

Gobert, David L., "Structural Identity of 'La Reine Morte' and 'Le Maître de Santiago'", *French Review*, 38:30-33, 1964

Johnson, Robert B., "The Ferrante Image in Montherlant's 'La Reine Morte'", *French Review*, 36:255-59, 1963

————, *Henry de Montherlant*. 1968. Pp. 101-07

Moore, Harry T., *Twentieth Century French Literature to World War II*. 1966. Vol. 2, Pp. 198-200

New Republic, 141:31, Aug. 24, 1959

New Statesman, 61:275, Feb. 17, 1961

Von Arx, Paulette, *La Femme dans le Théâtre de Henry de Montherlant*. 1973. Pp. 29-44

La Reine Morte; ou, Comment on tue les Femmes *SEE* Queen After Death; or, How to Kill Women

Tomorrow the Dawn, 1949

Johnson, Robert B., *Henry de Montherlant*. 1968. Pp. 89-93

La Ville Dont le Prince Est un Enfant   *SEE*   The City Whose Prince is a Child

Women One Takes in One's Arms, 1950
  Johnson, Robert B., *Henry de Montherlant*. 1968. Pp. 94-96
  Von Arx, Paulette, *La Femme Dans le Théâtre de Henry de Montherlant*.
    1973. Pp. 67-80

ALBERTO MORAVIA (pseud.)
SEE
ALBERTO PINCHERLE

LOUIS CHARLES ALFRED DE MUSSET

Barberine, 1882
  Hamilton, Clayton, "Alfred de Musset in the Theatre", *Bookman*, 48:668-
    72, 1917-18

Bettine, 1851
  Ganne, Gilbert, *Alfred de Musset; Sa Jeunesse et la Nôtre*. 1970. Pp. 267-96

The Candle-Stick, 1848
  Revue des Deux Mondes, s8, 37:228-29, Jan. 1, 1937
  Sices, David, *Theater of Solitude; The Drama of Alfred de Musset*. 1973.
    Pp. 179-98

A Caprice, 1847
  Ganne, Gilbert, *Alfred de Musset; Sa Jeunesse et la Nôtre*. 1970. Pp. 267-96

Les Caprices de Marianne   *SEE*   The Follies of Marianne

Carmosine, 1865
  Brisson, P., "Carmosine", *Les Annales Politiques et Littéraires*, 80:137-38,
    Feb. 11, 1923
  Revue des Deux Mondes, s8, 48:668-69, Dec. 1, 1938
  Sices, David, *Theater of Solitude; The Drama of Alfred de Musset*. 1973.
    Pp. 220-40

Le Chandelier   *SEE*   The Candle-Stick

La Coupe et les Lèvres   *SEE*   The Cup and the Lip

The Cup and the Lip, 1833
  Revue des Deux Mondes, s8, 25:435-39, Jan. 15, 1935

Fantasio, 1866
  Fiber, L. A., "The Masked Event in Musset's 'Fantasio' and 'Lorenzaccio'",
    French Review (1972), 45(Special Issue):85-94
  King, Russell S., "Linguistic and Stylistic Clues to Characterization in Mus-
    set's 'Fantasio'", *Neophilologus* (1974), 58:187-94
  Ridge, George Ross, "The Anti-Hero in Musset's Drama", *French Review*,
    32:428-34, 1958-59
  Sices, David, "Musset's 'Fantasio': The Paradise of Chance", *Romantic
    Review* (1967), 58:23-37
  —————————— , *Theater of Solitude; The Drama of Alfred de Musset*.
    1973. Pp. 65-89

The Follies of Marianne, 1851

Agudiez, Juan Ventura, "Autour des 'Caprices de Marianne'", *Kentucky Romance Quarterly* (1968), 15:179-94

Amossy, Ruth and Elisheva Rosen, "La Comédie 'Romantique' et la Carnaval: 'La Nuit des Rois' et 'Les Caprices de Marianne'", *Littérature* (1974), 16:37-49

Castex, Pierre-Georges, "Quelques Cadres d'Etude pour 'Les Caprices de Marianne'". *L'Information Littéraire*, 8:76-84, 1956

Ganne, Gilbert, *Alfred de Musset; Sa Jeunesse et la Nôtre.* 1970. Pp. 267-96

Ngoue, Lucienne, "Pour une Etude Dramatique des 'Caprices de Marianne'", *Annales de la Faculté des Lettres et Sciences Humaines* (Univ. of Yaoundé, Cameroun), (1973), 2,v:52-60

Sices, David, *Theater of Solitude; The Drama of Alfred de Musset.* 1973. Pp. 23-64

Il Ne Faut Jurer de Rien *SEE* You Can't Be Sure of Anything

Lorenzaccio, 1896

Callen, A., "Dramatic Construction in Musset's 'Lorenzaccio'", *Forum for Modern Language Studies* (1973), 9:182-91

——————— , "The Place of 'Lorenzaccio' in Musset's Theatre", *Forum for Modern Language Studies* (1969), 5:225-31

Denommé, Robert T., "The Motif of the Poète Maudit in Musset's 'Lorenzaccio'", *L'Esprit Créateur* (Minneapolis), 5:138-46, 1965

d'Houville, G., "Lorenzaccio", *Revue des Deux Mondes*, 7 per .40:209-14, July 1, 1927

Department de Francaise, Recherches et Travaux. Supp. de Bulletin d'Information du Service de Documentation 19-20 (Oct.-Dec. 1968), Pp. 18-21

Dort, Bernard, "Tentative de Description de Lorenzaccio", *Travail Theatral* (Oct.-Dec. 1970), 1:29-37

——————— , *Théâtre Réel, 1967-1970.* 1971. Pp. 92-103

Fiber, L. A., "The Masked Event in Musset's 'Fantasio' and 'Lorenzaccio'", *French Review* (1972), 45(Special Issue):85-94

Frenzel, Elisabeth, "Mussets 'Lorenzaccio'—Ein Mögliches Vorbild für 'Dantons Tod'", *Euphorion. Zeitschrift für Literatur Geschichte* (1964), 58:59-68

Ganne, Gilbert, *Alfred de Musset; Sa Jeunesse et la Nôtre.* 1970. Pp. 267-96

Grimsley, Ronald, "The Character of Lorenzaccio", *French Studies*, 11:16-27, 1957

Hunt, H. J., "Alfred de Musset et la Revolution de Juillet; La Lecon Politique de 'Lorenzaccio'", *Mercure de France*, 251:70-88, April 1, 1934

Jansen, Steen, "L'Unité d'Action dans 'Andromaque' et dans 'Lorenzaccio'", *Revue Romane* (1968), 3:16-29 and 116-35

Lombard, Charles M., "Ducis' 'Hamlet' and Musset's 'Lorenzaccio'", *Notes and Queries*, 5:72-75, 1958

Masson, Bernard, "'Lorenzaccio' Rendu au Théâtre", *l'Information Littéraire* (1974), 26:107-12

Rees, Margaret A., "Imagery in the Plays of Alfred de Musset", *French Review*, 36:245-54, 1962-63

Revue des Deux Mondes, s8, 25:439-40, Jan. 15, 1935

Rutten, Raimund, "Individuum und Gesellschaft in Alfred de Mussets 'Lorenzaccio'", *Germanisch-Romanische Monatsschrift* (1973), nf. 23:67-93

Sices, David, *Theater of Solitude; The Drama of Alfred de Musset.* 1973.
Pp. 109-78
Tarro, Brian J., "An Analytical Study of Structure in 'Lorenzaccio'", *Dissertation Abstracts International* (1972), 32:7009A
Time, 72:84, Oct. 27, 1958
VanTieghem, Phillippe, "L'Evolution de Musset des Débuts à Lorenzaccio", *Revue d'Histoire du Théâtre*, #4:261-75, 1958
Ware, J., "'Lorenzino dei Medici' on the French Stage", *Cornhill Magazine*, 66:680-88, June, 1929

No Trifling With Love, 1861
America, 102:305, Nov. 28, 1959
Frederick, E. C., "Marivaux and Musset: 'Les Serments Indiscrets' and 'On Ne Badine Pas Avec L'Amour'", *Romanic Review*, 31:259-64, 1940
L'Illustration, 205:130, Feb. 10, 1940
Lièvre, P., "On Ne Badine Pas Avec L'Amour", *Mercure de France*, 238:390-93, Sept. 1, 1932
Moreau, Pierre, "A Propos d'On Ne Badine Pas Avec L'Amour'", *L'Information Littéraire*, 8:1-5, 1956
Nation, 189:427, Dec. 5, 1959
New Yorker, 35:117, Nov. 21, 1959
Rees, Margaret A., "Imagery in the Plays of Alfred de Musset", *French Review*, 36:245-54, 1962-63
Sices, David, "Multiplicity and Integrity in 'On ne Badine Pas Avec L'Amour'", *French Review* (1970), 43:443-51
―――――――――― , *Theater of Solitude; The Drama of Alfred de Musset.* 1973. Pp. 91-108
Vial, André, "A Propos d'On Ne Badine Pas Avec L'Amour'", *Revue des Sciences Humaines*, #101:55-67, 1961

La Nuit Vénitienne, ou Les Noces de Laurette   SEE   A Venetian Night; or Laurette's Wedding

On ne Badine Pas Avec L'Amour   SEE   No Trifling with Love

A Venetian Night, or Laurette's Wedding, 1830
Ridge, George Ross, "The Anti-Hero in Musset's Drama", *French Review*, 32:428-34, 1958-59

You Can't Be Sure of Anything, 1848
Sices, David, *Theater of Solitude; The Drama of Alfred de Musset.* 1973. Pp. 199-220

PETER NICHOLS

Chez Nous, 1974
Bryder, R., "Chez Nous", *Plays and Players* (1974), 21:27-29
Lambert, J. W., "Chez Nous", *Drama* (1974), 112:19-20

A Day in the Death of Joe Egg, 1967
America, 118:330-31, Mar. 9, 1968
Commentary, 45:76, Apr. 1968
Commonweal, 87:718-20, Mar. 15, 1968
Life, 63:106, Nov. 24, 1967

Nation, 206:247-49, Feb. 19, 1968
New Statesman, 74:125, July 28, 1967
New Yorker, 43:84, Aug. 19, 1967, and 43:86, Feb. 10, 1968
Newsweek, 71:89, Feb. 12, 1968
Reporter, 38:44, Mar. 7, 1968
Saturday Review, 51:26, Feb. 17, 1968
Taylor, John Russell, *The Second Wave; British Drama for the Seventies.*
   1971. Pp. 16-35
Time, 91:75, Feb. 9, 1968
Vogue. 150:70, Oct. 15, 1967 and 151:44, Mar. 15, 1968

Forget Me Not Lane, 1973
Newsweek (April 30, 1973), 81:87

Freeway, 1974
Lambert, J. W., "Freeway", *Drama* (1974), 115:42-44
Weightman, J., "Freeway", *Encounter* (Dec. 1974), 43:65-66

National Health, 1969
America (Nov. 30, 1974), 131:349
Nation (Nov. 2, 1974), 444:45
New Republic (Nov. 2, 1974), 171:32
New Yorker (Oct. 21, 1974), 50:60
Newsweek (April 22, 1974), 83:117
Time (Oct. 21, 1974), 104:90
Weightman, John, "Life and Death of the Common Man", *Encounter* (Dec.
   1969), 33:51-53

THOMAS NORTON AND
THOMAS SACKVILLE

Gorboduc, or Ferrex and Porrex 1561
Baker, Howard, *Induction to Tragedy; a Study in a Development of Form
   in 'Gorboduc', 'The Spanish Tragedy' and 'Titus Andronicus'*, 1965, Pp.
   9-47
Berlin, Normand, *Thomas Sackville.* 1974. Pp. 33-39, 44-59, and 80-119
Babula W., "Gorboduc as Apology and Critique", *Tennessee Studies in
   Literature* (1972), 17:37-43
Dust, Philip, "The Theme of 'Kinde' in 'Gorboduc'", *Salzburg Studies in
   English Literature: Elizabethan Studies* (1973), Pp. 43-81
Harmen, Stanley A., "An Institutional Drama at Inner Temple; The Concept
   of the Crown and Its Influence on 'Gorboduc'", *Dissertation Abstracts
   International* (1974), 35:1624A
Studies in Speech and Drama in Honor of Alexander M. Drummond. 1944.
   Pp. 78-104

SEAN O'CASEY

Bedtime Story, 1952
Kosok, Heinz, *Sean O'Casey; Das Dramatische Werk.* 1972. Pp. 251-54
Smith, Bobby L., "The Hat, The Whore, and the Hypocrite in O'Casey's
   'Bedtime Story'", *Serif* (1967), 4:2:3-5
Theatre Arts, 43:9, June, 1959

Behind the Green Curtains, 1962
  Snowden, J. A., "Dialect in the Plays of Sean O'Casey", *Modern Drama*
    (1971), 14:387-91

Bishop's Bonfire, 1955
  Atlantic Monthly, 196:96, Oct. 1955
  Cowasjee, Saros, *Sean O'Casey, The Man Behind the Play*. 1963. Pp. 214-31
  Hogan, Robert, *After the Irish Renaissance; A Critical History of the Irish
    Drama Since "The Plough and the Stars"*. 1967. Pp. 244-47
  Kosok, Heinz, *Sean O'Casey; Das Dramatische Werk*. 1972. Pp. 282-95
  Krause, David, *Sean O'Casey; The Man and His Work*. 1975. Pp. 202-12
  Murphy, Robert P., "Stubborn Vison; The Dramaturgy of Sean O'Casey",
    Dissertation Abstracts International (1972), 32:4625A
  New Statesman, 49:320, March 5, 1955 and 62:164, Aug. 4, 1961
  O'Casey, Eileen, *Sean*. 1972. Pp. 236-40
  Spectator, 194:256, March 4, 1955 and 207:204, Aug. 11, 1961
  Time, 65:58, March 14, 1955
  Tynan, Kenneth, *Curtains; Selections from the Drama Criticism and Related
    Writings*. 1960. Pp. 83-85

Cathleen Listens In, 1923
  Cowasjee, Saros, *Sean O'Casey, The Man Behind the Play*. 1963. Pp. 40-42

Cock-a-Doodle-Dandy, 1949
  Cole, Toby, ed., *Playwrights on Playwriting; The Meaning and Making of
    Modern Drama from Ibsen to Ionesco*. 1960. Pp. 247-49
  Cowasjee, Saros, *Sean O'Casey, The Man Behind the Play*. 1963. Pp. 205-14
  Daniel, Walter C., "The False Paradise Pattern in Sean O'Casey's 'Cock-a-
    Doodle Dandy' ", *College Language Association Journal* (1969), 13:137-43
  Kosok, Heinz, *Sean O'Casey; Das Dramatische Werk*. 1972. Pp. 265-76
  Kilroy, Thomas, ed., *Sean O'Casey; A Collection of Critical Essays*. 1975.
    Pp. 35-52
  Krause, David, *Sean O'Casey; The Man and His Work*. 1975. Pp. 187-202
  Murphy, Robert P., "Stubborn Vision; The Dramaturgy of Sean O'Casey",
    Dissertation Abstracts International (1972), 34:4625A
  Nation, 187:416, Nov. 29, 1958
  New Yorker, 34:100-02, Nov. 22, 1958
  Newsweek, 52:78, Nov. 24, 1958
  O'Casey, Eileen, *Sean*. 1972. Pp. 200-02
  Rollins, Ronald G., "Dramatic Symbolism in Sean O'Casey's Dublin Trilogy",
    Philological Papers (1966), 15:49-56
  _____ , "Ritual to Romance in 'Within the Gates' and 'Cock-a-
    Doodle Dandy' ", *Modern Drama* (1974), 17:11-18
  Roy, Emil, *British Drama Since Shaw*. 1972. Pp. 79-81
  Saturday Review, 38:37, Nov. 19, 1955 and 41:37, Dec. 6, 1958
  Smith, Bobby L., "Satire in O'Casey's 'Cock-a-Doodle-Dandy' ", *Renascence*
    (1967), 19:64-73
  Theatre Arts, 42:22-24, Nov. 1958 and 43:64, Jan., 1959
  Time, 72:83, Nov. 24, 1958
  Worth, Katharine J., "O'Casey's Dramatic Symbolism", *Modern Drama*,
    4:260-67, 1961

The Drums of Father Ned, 1962
 Cowasjee, Saros, *Sean O'Casey, The Man Behind the Play*. 1963. Pp. 231-37
 Hogan, Robert, *After the Irish Renaissance; A Critical History of the Irish Drama Since "The Plough and the Stars"*. 1967. Pp. 247-49
 Knight, George Wilson, *The Christian Renaissance; With Interpretations of Dante, Shakespeare and Goethe and New Discussions of Oscar Wilde and the Gospel of Thomas*. 1962. Pp. 341-47
 Kosok, Heinz, *Sean O'Casey; Das Dramatische Werk*. 1972. Pp. 296-309
 Kilroy, Thomas, ed., *Sean O'Casey; A Collection of Critical Essays*. 1975. Pp. 133-38
 Krause, David, *Sean O'Casey; The Man and His Work*. 1975. Pp. 212-24
 Murphy, Robert P., "Stubborn Vision; The Dramaturgy of Sean O'Casey", *Dissertation Abstracts International* (1972), 32:4625A
 New Statesman, 60:782, Nov. 19, 1960
 O'Casey, Eileen, *Sean*. 1972. Pp. 261-63
 Saturday Review, 42:22, May 9, 1959

Drums Under the Window, 1946
 Krause, David, *Sean O'Casey; The Man and His Work*. 1975. Pp. 269-72

The End of the Beginning, 1937
 Murphy, Robert P., "Stubborn Vision; The Dramaturgy of Sean O'Casey", *Dissertation Abstracts International* (1972), 32:4625A

The Hall of Healing, 1952
 Kosok, Heinz, *Sean O'Casey; Das Dramatische Werk*. 1972. Pp. 240-50
 _____ , "Sean O'Casey's 'Hall of Healing'", *Die Neueren Sprachen* (April 1970), 4:168-78

I Knock at the Door, 1939
 Gassner, John, *Theatre at the Crossroads; Plays and Playwrights of the Midcentury American Stage*. 1960. Pp. 286-88
 Krause, David, *Sean O'Casey; The Man and His Work*. 1975. Pp. 260-64

Juno and the Paycock, 1924
 Arts and Decoration, 25:64, May, 1926
 Armstrong, William A., "Integrity of 'Juno and the Paycock'", *Modern Drama* (1974), 17:1-9
 Ayling, Ronald, "Popular Tradition and Individual Talent in Sean O'Casey's Dublin Trilogy", *Journal of Modern Literature* (1972), 2:491-504
 Blitch, Alice F., "O'Casey's Shakespeare", *Modern Drama* (1972), 15:283-89
 Catholic World, 150:730-31, March, 1940
 Cowasjee, Saros, *Sean O'Casey, The Man Behind the Play*. 1963. Pp. 43-60
 Cowell, Raymond, *Twelve Modern Dramatists*. 1967. Pp. 66-67
 Durbach, Errol, "Peacocks and Mothers; Theme and Dramatic Metaphor in O'Casey's 'Juno and the Paycock'", *Modern Drama* (1972), 15:15-25
 Hayes, Una, "An Analogy Between the Painting of the Impressionists and the Dramatic Technique of Sean O'Casey in His Dublin Trilogy", *Dissertation Abstracts International* (1972), 33:1170A
 Kaufman, Michael W., "O'Casey's Structural Design in 'Juno and the Paycock'", *Quarterly Journal of Speech* (1972), 58:191-98
 Kilroy, Thomas ed., *Sean O'Casey; A Collection of Critical Essays*. 1975. Pp. 35-60, 77-89 and 91-112

Kosok, Heinz, *Sean O'Casey; Das Dramatische Werk.* 1972. Pp. 45-66
Krause, David, *Sean O'Casey; The Man and His Work.* 1975. Pp. 68-79
Living Age, 321:869-70, May 3, 1924
Mabley, Edward, *Dramatic Construction; An Outline of Basic Principles.* 1972. Pp. 173-86
MacCarthy, Desmond, "Juno and the Paycock", *New Statesman,* 26:207, Nov. 28, 1925
Malone, Andrew E., *The Irish Drama.* 1965. Pp. 209-19
Murphy, Robert P., "Stubborn Vision; The Dramaturgy of Sean O'Casey", *Dissertation Abstracts International* (1972), 32:4625A
Nation, 122:348, March 31, 1926
O'Casey, Eileen, *Sean.* 1972. Pp. 16-18
Oppel, Horst, *Das Moderne Englische Drama: Interpretationen.* 1963. Pp. 183-202
Rollins, Ronald G., "Dramatic Symbolism in Sean O'Casey's Dublin Trilogy", *Philological Papers* (1966), 15:49-56
───────────── , "Form and Content in Sean O'Casey's Dublin Trilogy", *Modern Drama,* 8:419-25, 1966
Roy, Emil, *British Drama Since Shaw.* 1972. Pp. 72-78
Theatre Arts, 24:162, March, 1940
Time, 35:36, Jan. 29, 1940
Worth, Katharine J., "O'Casey's Dramatic Symbolism", *Modern Drama,* 4:260-67, 1961
Wyatt, Euphemia V. R., "Juno and the Paycock", *Catholic World,* 150: 730-31, 1940

Nannie's Night Out, 1924
Ayling, Ronald, " 'Nannie's Night Out' ", *Modern Drama* (1962), 5:155-63
Kosok, Heinz, *Sean O'Casey; Das Dramatische Werk.* 1972. Pp. 45-66

Oak Leaves and Lavender; or, A World on Wallpaper, 1947
Cowasjee, Saros, *Sean O'Casey, The Man Behind the Play.* 1963. Pp. 195-205
Kosok, Heinz, *Sean O'Casey; Das Dramatische Werk.* 1972. Pp. 221-39

Pictures in the Hallway, 1942
Gassner, John, *Theatre at the Crossroads; Plays and Playwrights of the Midcentury American Stage.* 1960. Pp. 284-86

The Plough and the Stars, 1926
America, 91:488, Aug. 14, 1954
Armstrong, W. A., "The Sources and Themes of 'The Plough and the Stars' ", *Modern Drama,* 4:234-42, 1961
Ayling, Ronald, "Popular Tradition and Individual Talent in Sean O'Casey's Dublin Trilogy", *Journal of Modern Literature* (1972), 2:491-504
Catholic World, 192:320, Feb., 1961
Cowasjee, Saros, Sean O'Casey, *The Man Behind the Play.* 1963. Pp. 61-84
DeBaum, Vincent C., "Sean O'Casey and the Road to Expressionism", *Modern Drama,* 4:254-59, 1961
Freedman, Morris, *The Moral Impulse; Modern Drama from Ibsen to the Present.* 1967. Pp. 67-73
Hayes, Una, "An Analogy Between the Painting of the Impressionists and the Dramatic Technique of Sean O'Casey in His Dublin Trilogy", *Dissertation Abstracts International* (1972), 33:1170A

Kosok, Heinz, *Sean O'Casey; Das Dramatische Werk*. 1972. Pp. 67-75
Kilroy, Thomas ed., *Sean O'Casey; A Collection of Critical Essays*. 1975. Pp. 53-60, 77-89, and 91-112
Krause, David, *Sean O'Casey; The Man and His Work*. 1975. Pp. 69-75
Literary Digest, 95:20-21, Dec. 24, 1927
Living Age, 328:693-94, March 27, 1926
Nation, 176:353, April 25, 1953 and 191:510, Dec. 24, 1960
New Yorker, 36:96-98, Dec. 17, 1960
O'Casey, Eileen, *Sean*. 1972. Pp. 48-51
Outlook, 148:187, Feb. 1, 1928
Reiter, Seymour, *World Theater; Structure and Meaning of Drama*. 1973. Pp. 195-213
Rollins, Ronald G., "Dramatic Symbolism in Sean O'Casey's Dublin Trilogy", *Philological Papers* (1969), 15:49-56
_____, "Form and Content in Sean O'Casey's Dublin Trilogy", *Modern Drama*, 8:419-25, 1966
Roy, Emil, *British Drama Since Shaw*. 1972. Pp. 75-78
Saturday Review, 36:25, June 6, 1953
Saturday Review of Literature, 4:427, Dec. 10, 1927
Smith, Bobby L., "Satire in 'The Plough and the Stars': A Tragedy in Four Acts", *Ball State University Forum* (1969), 10:3-11
Theatre Arts, 45:11, Feb., 1961
Time, 76:63, Dec. 19, 1960
Vernon, G., "The Plough and the Stars", *Commonweal*, 21:122, Nov. 23, 1934

Pound on Demand, 1947
Kosok, Heinz, *Sean O'Casey; Das Dramatische Werk*. 1972. Pp. 131-35
Nathan, George Jean, *Theatre Book of the Year, 1946-47*. Pp. 231-39
Theatre Arts, 43:9, June 1959

Purple Dust, 1944
Catholic World, 184:469-70, March 1957
Cowasjee, Saros, *Sean O'Casey, The Man Behind the Play*. 1963. Pp. 61-84
English (Oxford), 10:139-40, Spring, 1955
Hogan, Robert, *After the Irish Renaissance; A Critical History of the Irish Drama Since "The Plough and the Stars"*. 1967. Pp. 239-43
Kilroy, Thomas, ed., *Sean O'Casey; A Collection of Critical Essays*. 1975. Pp. 61-76
Kosok, Heinz, *Sean O'Casey; Das Dramatische Werk*. 1972. Pp. 174-95
Krause, David, *Sean O'Casey; The Man and His Work*. 1975. Pp. 177-87
McLaughlin, John J., "Political Allegory in O'Casey's 'Purple Dust' ", *Modern Drama* (May 1970), 13:47-53
Murphy, Robert P., "Stubborn Vision; The Dramaturgy of Sean O'Casey", *Dissertation Abstracts International* (1972), 32:4625A
Nation, 184:65, Jan. 19, 1957
Newsweek, 49:67, Jan. 21, 1957
O'Casey, Eileen, *Sean*. 1972. Pp. 213-17
Rollins, Ronald, "O'Casey's 'Purple Dust' ", *Explicator* (Oct. 1967), 26:Item 19
_____, "Shaw and O'Casey: John Bull and His Other Island", *Shaw Review* (1967), 10:60-69
_____, "O'Casey's 'Purple Dust' ", *Explicator* (1967), 26:Item 19
Saturday Review, 40:48, Jan. 19, 1957

Red Roses for Me, 1943
  Beckerman, Bernard, *Dynamics of Drama; Theory and Method of Analysis*.
    1970. Pp. 126-28
  Catholic World, 182:387, Feb., 1956
  Clurman, Harold, *Lies Like Truth; Theatre Reviews and Essays*. 1958. Pp.
    122-24
  Esslinger, Pat M., "Sean O'Casey and the Lockout of 1913: 'Materia Poetica'
    of the Two Red Plays", *Modern Drama* (1963), 6:53-63
  Kilroy, Thomas, ed., *Sean O'Casey; A Collection of Critical Essays*. 1975.
    Pp. 35-52
  Kosok, Heinz, *Sean O'Casey; Das Dramatische Werk*. 1972. Pp. 196-220
  Lewis, Allan, *The Contemporary Theatre; The Significant Playwrights of
    Our Time*. 1962. Pp. 169-91
  ─────────── , "Red Roses for Me", *America*, 94:459-60, Jan. 21, 1956
  Malone, Maureen, " 'Red Roses for Me'; Fact and Symbol", *Modern Drama*
    (1966), 9:147-52
  Murphy, Robert P., "Stubborn Vision; The Dramaturgy of Sean O'Casey",
    Dissertation Abstracts International (1972), 32:4625A
  Nation, 181:555-56, Dec. 24, 1955 and 182:39, Jan. 14, 1956
  New Republic, 134:21, Jan. 30, 1956
  New Statesman and Nation, 31:173, March 9, 1946
  New Yorker, 31:62, Jan. 14, 1956 and 37:162, Dec. 9, 1961
  Newsweek, 47:44-45, Jan. 9, 1956
  Redfern, James, "Red Roses for Me", *Spectator*, 176:244, March 8, 1946
  Saturday Review, 39:20, Jan. 14, 1956
  Theatre Arts, 40:15, March, 1956
  Time, 67:51, Jan. 9, 1956

Shadow of a Gunman, 1923
  America, 100:382, Dec. 20, 1958
  Ayling, Ronald, "Popular Tradition and Individual Talent in Sean O'Casey's
    Dublin Trilogy", *Journal of Modern Literature* (1972), 2:491-504
  Catholic World, 188:417, Feb., 1959
  Christian Century, 75:1463, Dec. 17, 1958
  Cowasjee, Saros, *Sean O'Casey, The Man Behind the Play*. 1963. Pp. 28-39
  Hayes, Una, "An Analogy Between the Painting of the Impressionists and
    the Dramatic Technique of Sean O'Casey in his Dublin Trilogy", *Disser-
    tation Abstracts International* (1972), 33:1170A
  Kilroy, Thomas, ed., *Sean O'Casey; A Collection of Critical Essays*. 1975.
    Pp. 35-60, 77-89, 91-112
  Kosok, Heinz, *Sean O'Casey; Das Dramatische Werk*. 1972. Pp. 14-18
  Krause, David, *Sean O'Casey; The Man and His Work*. 1975. Pp. 66-68, 88-91
  New Yorker, 34:113, Dec. 6, 1958
  Rollins, Ronald G., "Form and Content in Sean O'Casey's Dublin Trilogy",
    Modern Drama, 8:419-25, 1966
  ─────────── , "O'Casey and Synge: The Irish Hero as Playboy and Gunman",
    Arizona Quarterly (1966), 22:217-22
  ─────────── , "Dramatic Symbolism in Sean O'Casey's Dublin Trilogy",
    Philological Papers (1966), 15:49-56
  Saturday Review, 41:37, Dec. 6, 1958
  Snowden, J. A., "Dialect in the Plays of Sean O'Casey", *Modern Drama* (1971),
    14:387-91

Tynan, Kenneth, *Curtains; Selections from the Drama Criticism and Related Writings.* 1960. Pp. 285-88

The Silver Tassie, 1929
Agate, James Evershed, comp., *English Dramatic Critics; An Anthology, 1660-1932.* 1958. Pp. 347-49
Ayling, Ronald, "Feathers Finely Aflutther", *Modern Drama* (1964), 7:135-47
Catholic World, 130:334-35, Dec., 1929
Commonweal, 50:631-32, Oct. 7, 1949
Cowasjee, Saros, *Sean O'Casey, The Man Behind the Play.* 1963. Pp. 102-36
DeBaum, Vincent C., "Sean O'Casey and the Road to Expressionism", *Modern Drama*, 4:254-59, 1961
Fortnightly, 132:851-53, Dec., 1929
Hughes, Catherine, *Plays, Politics and Polemics.* 1973. Pp. 69-76
Jennings, Richard, "The Silver Tassie", *Spectator*, 143:523, 1929
Kilroy, Thomas, ed., *Sean O'Casey; A Collection of Critical Essays.* 1975. Pp. 35-60 and 91-117
Kosok, Heinz, *Sean O'Casey; Das Dramatische Werk.* 1972. Pp. 98-100
Krause, D., "Playwright's Not for Burning", *Virginia Quarterly Review*, 34:60-76, 1958
────────── , *Sean O'Casey; The Man and His Work.* 1975. Pp. 109-22, 128-30, and 354-56
Literary Digest, 98:24-25, Aug. 4, 1928
Murphy, Robert P., "Stubborn Vision; The Dramaturgy of Sean O'Casey", *Dissertation Abstracts International* (1972), 32:4625A
New Republic, 61:17-18, Nov. 27, 1929 and 121:21, Sept. 19, 1949
New Statesman, 34:52-53, Oct. 19, 1929
O'Casey, Eileen, *Sean.* 1972. Pp. 83-103
Rollins, Ronald G., "O'Casey, O'Neill and Expressionism in 'The Silver Tassie'", *Bucknell Review* (1962), 10:364-69
────────── , "O'Casey's 'The Silver Tassie'", *Explicator* (1962), 20:Item 62
Shipp, H., "The Silver Tassie", *English Review*, 49:639, Nov., 1929
Theatre Arts, 14:5, Jan., 1930 and 15:790-92, Oct., 1931
Williams, Raymond, *Drama from Ibsen to Brecht.* 1968. Pp. 151-53

The Star Turns Red, 1940
Cowasjee, Saros, *Sean O'Casey, The Man Behind the Play.* 1963. Pp. 170-80
Esslinger, Pat M., "Sean O'Casey and the Lockout of 1913: 'Materia Poetica' of the Two Red Plays", *Modern Drama* (1963), 6:53-63
Kosok, Heinz, *Sean O'Casey; Das Dramatische Werke.* 1972. Pp. 159-73
Krause, David, *Sean O'Casey; The Man and His Work.* 1975. Pp. 158-61
Newsweek, 13:25, June 26, 1939
O'Casey, Eileen, *Sean.* 1972. Pp. 175-78
Rollins, Ronald G., "Sean O'Casey's 'The Star Turns Red': A Political Prophecy", *Mississippi Quarterly* (1963), 16:67-75
Theatre Arts, 24:410, June, 1940

Time to Go, 1952
Kosok, Heinz, *Sean O'Casey; Das Dramatische Werk.* 1972. Pp. 277-81

Within the Gates, 1934
Ayling, Ronald, "Ritual Patterns in Sean O'Casey's 'Within the Gates'", *Theoria* (1974), 43:19-27

Catholic World, 140:338-40, Dec., 1934

Commonweal, 21:66, Nov. 9, 1934

Goldstone, Herbert, "The Unevenness of O'Casey: A Study of 'Within the Gates' ", *Forum* (Texas) (1965), 4:37-42

Harman, Bill J. and Ronald G. Rollins, "Mythical Dimensions in O'Casey's 'Within the Gates' ", *West Virginia University Philological Papers* (1967), 16:72-78

Kosok, Heinz, *Sean O'Casey; Das Dramatische Werk*. 1972. Pp. 136-54

Krause, David, *Sean O'Casey; The Man and His Work*. 1975. Pp. 138-40

Literary Digest, 118:26, Oct. 27, 1934

Nation, 139:546, Nov. 7, 1934

New Republic, 80:369, Nov. 7, 1934

O'Casey, Eileen, *Sean*. 1972. Pp. 128-44

Rollins, R. G., "O'Casey, O'Neill and the Expressionism in 'Within the Gates' ", *West Virginia Univ. Bulletin, Philological Papers* (Morgantown), 13:76-81, 1961

——————————, "O'Casey's 'Within the Gates' ", *Explicator* (1970), 29:Item 8

——————————, "Ritual to Romance in 'Within the Gates' and 'Cock-a-Doodle Dandy' ", *Modern Drama* (1974), 17:11-18

Saturday Review of Literature, 11:256, Nov. 3, 1934

Snowden, J. A., "Dialect in the Plays of Sean O'Casey", *Modern Drama* (1971), 14:387-91

Theatre Arts, 18:258-59, April, 1934 and 18:894, Dec., 1934

Theatre Arts Anthology; A Record and a Prophecy, ed. by Rosamond Gilder et. al.. 1950. Pp. 630-32

Todd, R. Mary, "The Two Published Versions of Sean O'Casey's 'Within the Gates' ", *Modern Drama* (1968), 10:346-55

Worth, Katharine J., "O'Casey's Dramatic Symbolism", *Modern Drama*, 4:260-67, 1961

JOHN JAMES OSBORNE

The Blood of the Bambergs, 1962

Carter, Alan, *John Osborne*. 1969. Pp. 118-20

Hayman, Ronald, *John Osborne*. 1969. Pp. 53-57

Illustrated London News, 241:190, Aug. 4, 1962

Spectator, 209:115, July 27, 1962

Trussler, Simon, *The Plays of John Osborne; An Assessment*. 1969. Pp. 108-19

A Bond Honoured, 1966

Carter, Alan, *John Osborne*. 1969. Pp. 122-26

Hayman, Ronald, *John Osborne*. 1969. Pp. 73-77

Lumley, Frederick, *New Trends in Twentieth Century Drama; A Survey Since Ibsen and Shaw*. 1967. Pp. 221-32

New Statesman, 71:902, June 17, 1966

Trussler, Simon, *The Plays of John Osborne*. 1969. Pp. 150-58

Vogue, 148:206, Sept. 1, 1966

The Entertainer, 1957

America, 98:736, March 22, 1958 and 114:54, Jan. 8, 1966

Athanason, Arthur N., "John Osborne; From Apprenticeship to Artistic Maturity", *Dissertation Abstracts International* (1973), 33;6898A

Baxter, K. M., *Speak What We Feel; A Christian Looks at the Contemporary Theatre.* 1964. Pp. 62-71

Bonnerot, Louis, "John Osborne", *Etudes Anglaises* (1957), 10:378-91

Brown, John Russell, *Theatre Language; A Study of Arden, Osborne, Pinter, and Wesker.* 1972. Pp. 118-57

Bryden, R., "Entertainer", *Plays and Players* (1975), 22:22-23

Carter, Alan, *John Osborne.* 1969. Pp. 63-71

Catholic World, 187:68, April, 1958

Deming, Barbara, "John Osborne's Man Against the Philistines", *Hudson Review*, 11:411-19, 1959

Gassner, John, *Theatre at the Crossroads; Plays and Playwrights of the Midcentury American Stage.* 1960. Pp. 175-77

Hayman, Ronald, *John Osborne.* 1969. Pp. 23-31

Hollis, Christopher, "Keeping Up with the Rices", *Spectator*, 199:504-05, Oct. 18, 1957

Illustrated London News, 230:702, April 27, 1957 and 231:524, Sept. 28, 1957

Kennedy, Andrew K., *Six Dramatists in Search of a Language.* 1975. Pp. 206-12

Lahr, John, *Up Against the Fourth Wall.* 1970. Pp. 231-45

Life, 44:118, March 10, 1958

Lumley, Frederick, *New Trends in Twentieth Century Drama; A Survey Since Ibsen and Shaw.* 1967. Pp. 221-32

Nation, 186:192-93, March 1, 1958

New Statesman, 53:512, April 20, 1957 and 54:343, Sept. 21, 1957 and 54:464, Oct. 12, 1957

New Yorker, 33:153-54, Sept. 28, 1957 and 34:63, Feb. 22, 1958

Newsweek, 51:62, Feb. 24, 1958

Reporter, 18:39, March 20, 1958

Sahl, Hans, "John Osborne", *Welt and Wort*, 14:36-37, 1959

Saturday Review, 40:26, May 11, 1957 and 41:24, March 1, 1958

Spectator, 198:517, April 19, 1957

Theatre Arts, 42:22-23, April, 1958

Time, 71:52, Feb. 24, 1958

Trussler, Simon, *The Plays of John Osborne.* 1969. Pp. 56-75

Twentieth Century, 161:583-85, June, 1957

Tynan, Kenneth, *Curtains; Selections from the Drama Criticism and Related Writings.* 1961. Pp. 173-76

Verkein, Lea, "'The Entertainer' van John Osborne", *De Vlaamse Gids* (1959), 43:412-14

The Hotel in Amsterdam, 1968

Carter, Alan, *John Osborne.* 1969. Pp. 105-11

Hayman, Ronald, *John Osborne.* 1969. Pp. 78-89

Life, 65:10, Aug. 2, 1968

Trussler, Simon, *The Plays of John Osborne.* 1969. Pp. 180-96

Vogue, 152:268, Sept. 1, 1968

Inadmissible Evidence, 1964

Athanason, Arthur N., "John Osborne; From Apprenticeship to Artistic Maturity", *Dissertation Abstracts International* (1973), 33:6898A

Brown, John Russell, *Theatre Language; A Study of Arden, Osborne, Pinter, and Wesker.* 1972. Pp. 118-57

Brustein, Robert Sanford, *The Third Theatre.* 1969. Pp. 146-48

Carter, Alan, *John Osborne.* 1969. Pp. 87-92

Christian Century, 82:1066, Sept. 1, 1965
Clurman, Harold, *The Divine Pastime; Theatre Essays.* 1974. Pp. 141-44
_____ , *The Naked Image; Observations on the Modern Theatre.*
   1966. Pp. 101-04
Commentary, 41:75, March, 1966
Commonweal, 83:375, Dec. 24, 1965
Gassner, John, *Dramatic Soundings; Evaluations and Retractions Culled from Thirty Years of Dramatic Criticism.* 1968. Pp. 612-14
Harper, 232:125, April, 1966
Hayman, Ronald, *John Osborne.* 1969. Pp. 65-72
Hudson Review, 19:112-13, Spring, 1966
Kaufmann, Stanley, *Figures of Light; Film Criticism and Comment.* 1971. Pp. 91-93
Kerr, Walter, *Thirty Plays Hath November; Pain and Pleasure in the Contemporary Theater.* 1969. Pp. 46-49
Lahr, John, *Up Against the Fourth Wall.* 1970. Pp. 232-45
Life, 60:17, Jan. 14, 1966
Lumley, Frederick, *New Trends in Twentieth Century Drama; A Survey Since Ibsen and Shaw.* 1967. Pp. 221-32
Nation, 201:508-09, Dec. 20, 1965
National Review, 18:325-27, April 5, 1966
New Republic, 154:34-35, Jan. 1, 1966
New Statesman, 68:410, Sept. 18, 1964
New Yorker, 41:176, April 17, 1965 and 41:142, Dec. 11, 1965
Newsweek, 66:90, Dec. 13, 1965
Reporter, 33:38-40, Nov. 4, 1965
Rosselli, John, "England on Trial", *Guardian* (Jan. 7, 1965), Pp. 6
Roy, Emil, *British Drama since Shaw.* 1972. Pp. 104-06
Saturday Review, 48:31, May 29, 1965 and 48:43, Dec. 18, 1965 and 49:96, Jan. 8, 1966
Sheed, Wilfrid, *The Morning After; Selected Essays and Reviews.* 1971. Pp. 154-156
Spectator, 213:369-70, Sept. 18, 1964
Stack, Maureen A., "Inadmissible Evidence", *Aylesford Review* (1965), 7: 193-95
Taylor, John Russell, "Inadmissible Evidence", *Encore* (Nov.-Dec. 1964), 11:43-46
Time, 86:76, Dec. 10, 1965
Trussler, Simon, *The Plays of John Osborne.* 1969. Pp. 120-38
Vogue, 146:51-52, Aug. 15, 1965 and 147:34, Jan. 15, 1966

Look Back in Anger, 1956
   Allsop, Kenneth, *Angry Decade; A Survey of the Cultural Revolt of the Nineteen Fifties.* 1959. Pp. 96-147
   America, 98:146, Nov. 2, 1957
   Aragno, Riccardo, "Do-It-Yourself Drama", *Gemini/Dialogue* (1960), 3:31-34
   Athanason, Arthur N., "John Osborne; From Apprenticeship to Artistic Maturity", *Dissertation Abstracts International* (1973), 33:6898A
   Barker, Clive, " 'Look Back in Anger'—The Turning Point: An Assessment of the Importance of John Osborne's First Play in the Development of the British Theatre", *Zeitschrift für Anglistik und Amerikanistik* (1966), 14: 367-71

Baxter, K. M., *Speak What We Feel; A Christian Looks at the Contemporary Theatre.* 1964. Pp. 62-71

Bonnerot, Louis, "John Osborne", *Etudes Anglaises* (1957), 10:378-91

Brown, John Russell, ed., *Modern British Dramatists; A Collection of Critical Essays.* 1968. Pp. 47-57

Brown, John Russell, *Theatre Language; A Study of Arden, Osborne, Pinter, and Wesker.* 1972. Pp. 118-57

Carter, Alan, *John Osborne.* 1969. Pp. 51-62

Catholic World, 186:226, Dec., 1957, and 188:122-28, Nov., 1958

Christian Century, 74:1262-63, Oct. 23, 1957

Chiari, J., *Landmarks of Contemporary Drama.* 1965. Pp. 109-11

Clurman, Harold, *The Divine Pastime; Theatre Essays.* 1974. Pp. 55-57

Commonweal, 67:232-33, Nov. 29, 1957

Deming, Barbara, "John Osborne's Man Against the Philistines", *Hudson Review*, 11:411-19, 1959

Dyson, A. E., "Look Back in Anger", *Critical Quarterly*, 1:318-26, 1959

Dupee, Frederick Wilcox, *"The King of the Cats" and Other Remarks on Writers and Writing.* 1965. Pp. 196-200

Faber, M. D., "The Character of Jimmy Porter; An Approach to 'Look Back in Anger'", *Modern Drama* (1970), 13:67-77

Freedman, Morris, *The Moral Impulse; Modern Drama from Ibsen to the Present.* 1967. Pp. 115-20

Gassner, John, *Dramatic Soundings; Evaluations and Retractions Culled from Thirty Years of Dramatic Criticism.* 1968. Pp. 212-13

———————— , *Theatre at the Crossroads; Plays and Playwrights of the Mid-century American Stage.* 1960. Pp. 173-77

Hayman, Ronald, *John Osborne.* 1969. Pp. 17-22

Huss, Roy, "John Osborne's Backward Half-Way Look", *Modern Drama*, 6:20-25, 1963

Karrfalt, David H., "The Social Theme in Osborne's Plays", *Modern Drama* (May 1970), 13:78-82

Kerr, Walter, *The Theatre in Spite of Itself.* 1963. Pp. 129-31

Kvam, Ragnar, "Teddy-Boys og Nietzsche-Boys", *Vinduet* (1958), 12:179-87

Lahr, John, *Up Against the Fourth Wall.* 1970. Pp. 231-45

Landstone, Charles, "From John Osborne to Shelagh Delaney", *World Theatre* (1959), 9:203-16

Levidova, I., "A New Hero Appears in the Theatre", *Inostrannaya Literatura* (1962), #1:201-08

Lewis, Allan, *Contemporary Theatre.* 1962. Pp. 77-95

Life, 43:141-42, Oct. 14, 1957

Lumley, Frederick, *New Trends in Twentieth Century Drama; A Survey Since Ibsen and Shaw.* 1967. Pp. 221-32

Mander, John, *The Writer and Commitment.* 1962. Pp. 179-211

Martin, Graham, "A Look Back at Osborne", *Universities and Left Review* (1959), 7:37-40

Nation, 185:272, Oct. 19, 1957

New Republic, 137:16-17, Sept. 9, 1957 and 137:19-21, Dec. 23, 1957 and 138:23-24, Jan. 20, 1958

New Statesman, 51:566, May 19, 1956 and 53:66-67, Jan. 19, 1957

New Yorker, 33:153-54, Sept. 28, 1957 and 33:93, Oct. 12, 1957

Newsweek, 50:114, Oct. 14, 1957

Oppel, Horst, *Das Moderne Englische Drama; Interpretationen.* 1963. Pp. 317-31

Peinert, Dietrich, " 'Bear' and 'Squirrel' in John Osborne's 'Look Back in Anger' ", *Literatur in Wissenschaft und Unterricht* (1968), 1:117-22

Reporter, 15:33-35, Oct. 18, 1956 and 15:7, Nov. 15, 1956 and 17:38, Nov. 14, 1957

Rogers, Daniel, " 'Look Back in Anger'—to George Orwell", *Notes and Queries*, 9:310-11, 1962

Rollins, Ronald F., "Carroll and Osborne; Alice and Alison in Wild Wonderlands", *Forum* (Houston) (Summer 1969), 7:16-20

Roy, Emil, *British Drama Since Shaw.* 1972. Pp. 100-03

Sahl, Hans, "John Osborne", *Welt und Wort*, 14:36-37, 1959

Saturday Review, 39:30, Oct. 13, 1956 and 40:30, Oct. 12, 1957

Schlesinger, Arthur Meier, *The Politics of Hope.* 1963. Pp. 247-53

Selz, Jean, "John Osborne et Jimmy Porter", *Les Lettres Nouvelles* (1958), #61:908-11

Spacks, Patricia Meyer, "Confrontation and Escape in Two Social Dramas", *Modern Drama* (May 1968), 11:61-72

Spectator, 196:688, May 18, 1956

Taylor, John Russell, *Anger and After; A Guide to the New British Drama.* 1962. Pp. 31-45

Theatre Arts, 41:28, May, 1957 and 41:18, Dec., 1957

Time, 69:90, April 22, 1957 and 70:85, Oct. 14, 1957

Trilling, Ossia, "The New English Realism", *Tulane Drama Review* (1962), 7:184-93

Trussler, Simon, *The Plays of John Osborne.* 1969. Pp. 40-55

Twentieth Century, 160:72-74, July, 1956

Tynan, Kenneth, *Curtains; Selections from the Drama Criticism and Related Writings.* 1961. Pp. 130-32

Wardle, Irving, "Looking Back at Osborne's Anger", *New Society* (July 1, 1965), Pp. 22-23

Weiss, Samuel A., "Osborne's Angry Young Play", *Educational Theatre Journal*, 12:285-88, Dec., 1960

Williams, Raymond, *Drama from Ibsen to Brecht.* 1968. Pp. 318-22

Wolfe, Bernard, "Angry at What?", *The Nation* (1958), 187:316-22

Luther, 1961

America, 107:533, July 21, 1962 and 109:496-97, Oct. 26, 1963

Athanason, Arthur N., "John Osborne; From Apprenticeship to Artistic Maturity", *Dissertation Abstracts International* (1973), 33:6898A

Brown, John Russell, ed., *Modern British Dramatists; A Collection of Critical Essays.* 1968. Pp. 117-21

Brown, John Russell, *Theatre Language; A Study of Arden, Osborne, Pinter, and Wesker.* 1972. Pp. 118-57

Brustein, Robert Sanford, *Seasons of Discontent; Dramatic Opinions 1959-1965.* 1965. Pp. 196-200

Carter, Alan, *John Osborne.* 1969. Pp. 76-87

Catholic World, 198:135-36, Nov., 1963

Christian Century, 80:1351, Oct. 20, 1963

Commonweal, 79:103-04, Oct. 18, 1963

Dennis, Nigel, "Out of the Box", *Encounter*, 17:51-53, 1961

Denty, Vera D., "The Psychology of Martin Luther", *Catholic World*, 194: 99-105, Nov., 1961
Drama, #62:18-19, Fall, 1961
Educational Theatre Journal, 15:360-61, Dec., 1963
English, 14:20-21, Spring, 1962
Flint, Martha, "'Le Diable et le Bon Dieu' and an Angry Young Luther", *Journal of European Studies* (1972), 2:247-55
Hausmann, Manfred, "John Osborne und Martin Luther", *Luther. Zeitschrift der Luther Gesellschaft* (1963), 34:91-94
Hayman, Ronald, *John Osborne*. 1969. Pp. 42-52
Hudson Review, 16:584-85, Winter, 1963-64
Ihlenfeld, Kurt, "Osborne's 'Luther'", *Eckart Jahrbuch*, 1961-62, Pp. 312-15
Illustrated London News, 239:266, Aug. 12, 1961
Karrfalb, David H., "The Social Theme in Osborne's Plays", *Modern Drama* (May 1970), 13:78-82
Kennedy, Andrew K., *Six Dramatists in Search of a Language*. 1975. Pp. 202-04
Lumley, Frederick, *New Trends in Twentieth Century Drama; A Survey Since Ibsen and Shaw*. 1967. Pp. 221-32
"Luther", *Tamarack Review* (1962), #25:99-100
Marowitz, Charles, "The Ascension of John Osborne", *Tulane Drama Review*, 7 #2:175-79, 1962
Milne, Tom, "Luther and the Devils", *New Left Review* (1961), #12:55-58
Nation, 193:539-40, Dec. 30, 1961 and 197:245-46, Oct. 19, 1963
National Review, 15:446-48, Nov. 9, 1963
New Republic, 149:28, Oct. 19, 1963
New Statesman, 62:163, Aug. 4, 1961
New Yorker, 37:200-01, Oct. 14, 1961 and 39:133, Oct. 5, 1963
Newsweek, 62:96, Oct. 7, 1963
O'Brien, Charles H., "Osborne's 'Luther' and the Humanistic Tradition", *Renascence* (1969), 21:59-63
Partisan Review, 31:96-97, 1964
Reporter, 25:50, Oct. 12, 1961 and 29:54, Oct. 24, 1963
Rosselli, John, "At Home with Lucifer", *Reporter* (1961), 25:50-53
Rupp, Gordon, "Luther and Mr. Osborne", *Cambridge Quarterly* (Winter 1965/66), 1:28-42
Saturday Review, 46:30, Oct. 12, 1963
Sherman, Franklin, "Angry Young Luther", *Christian Century* (1961), 78: 1561-62
Spectator, 207:171, Aug. 4, 1961
Theatre Arts, 47:12-13, Dec., 1963
Time, 77:58-59, June 30, 1961 and 82:63, Oct. 4, 1963
Trussler, Simon, *The Plays of John Osborne*. 1969. Pp. 95-107
Vogue, 143:20, Jan. 1, 1964
Waugh, Evelyn, "'Luther', John Osborne's New Play", *Critic* (1962), 20: 53-55

A Patriot for Me, 1965
Bryden, Ronald, "Osborne at the Ball", *New Statesman* (July 9, 1965), 69:58
Carter, Alan, *John Osborne*. 1969. Pp. 92-100
Christian Century, (Sept. 1, 1965), 82:1067

Encounter (Oct. 1965), 25:42
Hayman, Ronald, *John Osborne*. 1969. Pp. 58-64
Lahr, John, *Up Against the Fourth Wall*. 1970. Pp. 236-45
Masters, A., "Patriot for Me", *Plays and Players* (1974), 21:54
New Yorker, 41:59-60, July 31, 1965
Reeves, Geoffrey, "A Patriot for Me", *Encore* (Sept.-Oct. 1965), 7:40-44
Reporter, (Nov. 4, 1965), 33:38-40
Trussler, Simon, *The Plays of John Osborne*. 1969. Pp. 139-49
Vogue (Sept. 1, 1965), 146:179

A Subject of Scandal and Concern, 1960
Carter, Alan, *John Osborne*. 1969. Pp. 115-18
Hayman, Ronald, *John Osborne*. 1969. Pp. 37-41
Trussler, Simon, *The Plays of John Osborne*. 1969. Pp. 87-94

Time Present, 1968
Carter, Alan, *John Osborne*. 1969. Pp. 100-05
Hayman, Ronald, *John Osborne*. 1969. Pp. 78-89
Lahr, John, *Up Against the Fourth Wall*. 1970. Pp. 231-45
Life, 65:10, Aug. 2, 1968
Trussler, Simon, *The Plays of John Osborne*. 1969. Pp. 159-79
Vogue, 152:268, Sept. 1, 1968

Under Plain Cover, 1962
Carter, Alan, *John Osborne*. 1969. Pp. 100-05
Hayman, Ronald, *John Osborne*. 1969. Pp. 53-57
Illustrated London News, 241:190, Aug. 4, 1962
Spectator, 209:115, July 27, 1962
Trussler, Simon, *The Plays of John Osborne; An Assessment*. 1969. Pp. 108-19

West of Suez, 1971
Hewes, Henry, "The British Bundle", *Saturday Review* (Sept. 11, 1971), 54:
20 and 54
Weightman, John, "Post-Imperial Blues", *Encounter* (Nov. 1971), 37:56-58

The World of Paul Slickey, 1959
Athanason, Arthur, "John Osborne; From Apprenticeship to Artistic
Maturity", *Dissertation Abstracts International* (1973), 33:6898A
Carter, Alan, *John Osborne*. 1969. Pp. 112-15
Findlater, R., "The Case of Paul Slickey", *Twentieth Century*, 167:29-38, 1960
Marowitz, Charles, "The Ascension of John Osborne", *Tulane Drama Review*
(1962), 7:175-79
Trussler, Simon, *The Plays of John Osborne*. 1969. Pp. 76-86

JOHN OSBORNE AND ANTHONY CREIGHTON

Epitaph for George Dillon, 1958
America, 100:299, Nov. 29, 1958
Carter, Alan, *John Osborne*. 1969. Pp. 71-76
Christian Century, 75:1436, Dec. 10, 1958
English, 12:59, 1958
Gassner, John, *Theatre at the Crossroads; Plays and Playwrights of the
Mid-century American Stage*. 1960. Pp. 175-77
Hayman, Ronald, *John Osborne*. 1969. Pp. 10-16

Hudson Review, 12:98-100, 1959

Marowitz, Charles, "The Ascension of John Osborne", *Tulane Drama Review*, 7 #2:175-79, 1962

Martin, Graham, "A Look Back at Osborne", *Universities and Left Review* (1959), 7:37-40

Nation, 187:394-95, Nov. 22, 1958

New Yorker, 34:101-03, Nov. 15, 1958

Newsweek, 52:75, Nov. 17, 1958

Partisan Review, 26:100-06, 1959

Saturday Review, 41:24-25, Nov. 22, 1958

Spectator, 200:232, Feb. 21, 1958

Theatre Arts, 43:21-23, Jan., 1959 and 45:68, March, 1961

Time, 72:62, Nov. 17, 1958

Trussler, Simon, *The Plays of John Osborne*. 1969. Pp. 21-39

Tynan, Kenneth, *Curtains; Selections from the Drama Criticism and Related Writings*. 1961. Pp. 205-07

ALEXANDER NIKOLAIVICH OSTROVSKY

Bespridannitsa   *SEE*   The Girl with No Dowry

Dokhodnoye Mesto   *SEE*   A Profitable Job

The Forest, 1871
Symons, James M., *Meyerhold's Theatre of the Grotesque; The Post-Revolutionary Productions, 1920-1932*. 1971. Pp. 111-25 and 140-43

The Girl with No Dowry, 1878
Kosteljanec, B., "Razgadyvaja 'Bespridannicu'", *Neva* (1973), 4:185-97

Les Les   *SEE*   The Forest

A Profitable Job, 1863
Symons, James M., *Meyerhold's Theatre of the Grotesque; The Post-Revolutionary Productions, 1920-1932*. 1971. Pp. 110-17 and 131-41

THOMAS OTWAY

The Atheist, 1683
Ross, J. C., "Attack on Thomas Shadwell in Otway's 'The Atheist'", *Philological Quarterly* (1973), 52:753-60
Spurling, Hiliary, "Remember Poor Otway", *Spectator* (Aug. 30, 1968), #7314:293-94

Don Carlos, Prince of Spain, 1676
Waith, Eugene M., *Ideas of Greatness; Heroic Drama in England*. 1971. Pp. 243-45

The Orphan; or, The Unhappy Marriage, 1680
Cunningham, John E., *Restoration Drama*. 1966. Pp. 98-101
London Mercury, 12:200-01, June 1925
MacCarthy, D., "'Orphan': Criticism", *New Statesman* (May 16, 1925), 25: 134-35
Marshall, Georffrey, "The Coherence of Thomas Otway", *Texas Studies in Literature and Language* (1969), 11:931-43

Nabi, Saiyid Ale, "Thomas Otway and the Poetics of Late Seventeenth
Century Tragedy", *Dissertation Abstracts International* (1972), 32:3960A
Royde-Smith, N. G., "'Orphan': Criticism", *Outlook* (London) (May 16,
1925), 55:329
Waith, Eugene M., *Ideas of Greatness; Heroic Drama in England.* 1971.
Pp. 246-50
Warner, Kerestin S., "Thomas Otway's Strumpet Fortune", *Dissertation
Abstracts International* (1973), 34:291A

The Soldier's Fortune, 1680
Cunningham, John E., *Restoration Drama.* 1966. Pp. 101-07
Spurling, Hilary, "Remember Poor Otway", *Spectator* (Aug. 30, 1968), #7314:
293-94
Warner, Kerestin S., "Thomas Otway's Strumpet Fortune", *Dissertation
Abstracts International* (1973), 34:291A

Venice Preserved; or, A Plot Discovered, 1682
Berman, Ronald, "Nature in 'Venice Preserved'", ELH (1969), 36:529-43
Cunningham, John E., *Restoration Drama.* 1966. Pp. 107-10
Durant, Jack D., "'Honour's Toughest Task': Family and State in 'Venice
Preserved'", *Studies in Philology* (1974), 71:484-503
Hansen, D. R., "Otway Preserved: Theme and Form in 'Venice Preserv'd'",
Studies in Philology (1958), 55:481-93
Heitsch, Otto, ed., *Osterreich und die Angelsächsissche Welt: Kulturbegegnun-
gen und Vergleiche.* 1961. Pp. 418-31
Hughes, D. W., "New Look at 'Venice Preserved'", *Studies in English Lit-
erature, 1500-1900* (Summer 1971), 11:437-57
Hughes, R. E., "'Comic Relief' in Otway's 'Venice Preserv'd'", *Notes and
Queries* (1958), 5:65-66
Klieneberger, H. R., "Otway's 'Venice Preserv'd' and Hofmannsthal's 'Das
Gerettete Venedig'", *Modern Language Review* (1967), 62:292-97
Loftis, J. C., ed., *Restoration Drama; Modern Essays in Criticism.* 1966.
Pp. 195-228
McBurney, William H., "Otway's Tragic Muse Debauched: Sensuality in
'Venice Preserved'", *Journal of English and Germanic Philology* (1959),
58:380-99
MacKenzie, Aline, "A Note on Pierre's White Hat", *Notes and Queries* (1947),
192:90-93
_____ , "'Venice Preserv'd' Reconsidered", *Tulane Studies in En-
glish* (1949), 1:81-118
Miner, Earl Roy, ed., *Restoration Dramatists; A Collection of Critical Essays.*
1966. Pp. 139-49
Moore, J. R., "Contemporary Satire in Otway's 'Venice Preserv'd'", *Modern
Language Association. Publications* (1928), 43:166-81
Nabi, Saiyid Ale, "Thomas Otway and the Poetics of Late Seventeenth Cen-
tury Tragedy", *Dissertation Abstracts International* (1972), 32:3960A
Pasquarelli, Robert, "On the Nicky-Nacky Scene of 'Venice Preserved'",
Restoration and 18th Century Theatre Research (Nov. 1969), 8:38-41
Proffitt, Bessie, "Religious Symbolism in Otway's 'Venice   Preserv'd'",
Papers on Language and Literature (Winter 1971), 7:26-37
Saturday Review, 36:24, Aug. 1, 1953

Tynan, Kenneth, *Curtains; Selections from the Drama and Related Writings.* 1961. Pp. 50-51

Van Voris, W., "Tragedy Through Restoration Eyes: 'Venice Preserv'd' in Its Own Theatre", *Hermathena* (1964), 99:55-65

"Venise Sauvée; ou, Les Debiteurs Decouverts", *Mercure de France* (March 1, 1935 and Feb. 1, 1939), 258:297-308 and 289:760-61

Waith, Eugene M., *Ideas of Greatness; Heroic Drama in England.* 1971. Pp. 250-52

Warner, Kerestin S., "Thomas Otway's Strumpet Fortune", *Dissertation Abstracts International* (1973), 34:291A

Williams, Gordon, "The Sex-Death Motive in Otway's 'Venice Preserv'd' ", *Trivium* (1967), 2:59-70

ALBERTO PINCHERLE

Beatrice Cenci, 1957
Boatto, Alberto " 'Beatrice Cenci' di Moravia", *Humanitas* (Brescia), 12: 980-82, 1952

Surchi, Sergio, "La 'Beatrice Cenci' di Moravia e il Dibattito tra Letteratura e Teatro", *Belfagor*, 12:585-87, 1957

ARTHUR WING PINERO

The Amazons, 1893
Lazenby, Walter, *Arthur Wing Pinero.* 1972. Pp. 58-60

The Benefit of the Doubt, 1895
Courtney, W. L., "Realistic Drama", *Living Age*, 278:265-78, 1913
Lazenby, Walter, *Arthur Wing Pinero.* 1972. Pp. 95-97
Miner, Edmund J., "The Theme of Disillusionment in the Drama of Arthur Pinero", *Contemporary Review* (1975), 226:184-90
Rideing, William H., "Some Women of Pinero's", *North American Review*, 188:38-49, 1908 -
Taylor, John Russell, *The Rise and Fall of the Well-Made Play.* 1967. Pp. 73-80

The Big Drum, 1915
Archer, William, "Pinero's New Satire: 'The Big Drum' ", *Nation,* 101:389-91, Sept. 23, 1915
Lazenby, Walter, *Arthur Wing Pinero.* 1972. Pp. 107-09

Child Man, 1930
Lazenby, Walter, *Arthur Wing Pinero.* 1972. Pp. 63-65

A Cold June, 1932
Lazenby, Walter, *Arthur Wing Pinero.* 1972. Pp. 109-11

Dandy Dick, 1887
Lazenby, Walter, *Arthur Wing Pinero.* 1972. Pp. 52-56

Dr. Harmer's Holidays, 1931
Lazenby, Walter, *Arthur Wing Pinero.* 1972. Pp. 144-47

The Enchanted Cottage, 1922
Lazenby, Walter, *Arthur Wing Pinero.* 1972. Pp. 80-82

Littlewood, S. R., "Sir Arthur Pinero—and the Fairies", *Bookman* (London), 62:8-11, April, 1922
Miner, Edmund J., "The Theme of Disillusionment in the Drama of Arthur Pinero", *Contemporary Review* (1975), 226:184-90
Nation (London), 30:868-70, March 11, 1922

The Freaks, 1918
Lazenby, Walter, *Arthur Wing Pinero*. 1972. Pp. 78-80

The Gay Lord Quex, 1899
Hamilton C., "Gay Lord Quex", *Bookman*, 46:475-77, Dec., 1917
Lazenby, Walter, *Arthur Wing Pinero*. 1972. Pp. 101-03
Rideing, William H., "Some Women of Pinero's", *North American Review*, 188:38-49, 1908
Towse, J. R., "Gay Lord Quex", *Critic*, 38:38-42, Jan., 1901

Girls and Boys, 1882
Lazenby, Walter, *Arthur Wing Pinero*. 1972. Pp. 31-33

His House in Order, 1906
Current Literature, 40:403-04, April, 1906
Lazenby, Walter, *Arthur Wing Pinero*. 1972. Pp. 136-39
Miner, Edmund J., "The Theme of Disillusionment in the Drama of Arthur Pinero", *Contemporary Review* (1975), 226:184-90
Rideing, William H., "Some Women of Pinero's", North American Review, 188:38-49, 1908
Tynan, Kenneth, *Curtains; Selections from the Drama Criticism and Related Writings*. 1961. Pp. 12-13
Walkley, Arthur Bingham, *Drama and Life*. 1907. Pp. 185-93

The Hobby Horse, 1886
Lazenby, Walter, *Arthur Wing Pinero*, 1972. Pp. 89-91

Imprudence, 1881
Lazenby, Walter, *Arthur Wing Pinero*. 1972. Pp. 35-37

In Chancery, 1884
Lazenby, Walter, *Arthur Wing Pinero*. 1972. Pp. 45-48

Iris, 1901
Beerbohm, Max, *Around Theatres*. 1953. Pp. 162-67
Colby, F. M., "Iris", *Bookman*, 16:280-82, Nov., 1901
Courtney, W. L., "Iris", *Fortnightly Review*, 76:902-10, Nov., 1901
————— , "Realistic Drama", *Living Age*, 278:265-78, 1913
Lazenby, Walter, *Arthur Wing Pinero*. 1972. Pp. 133-36
Leggatt, Alexander, "Pinero; From Farce to Social Drama", *Modern Drama* (1974), 17:329-44
Living Age, 313:247-48, April 22, 1922
Mais, Stuart Petre Brodie, *Some Modern Authors*. 1923. Pp. 303-10
Sampson, M. W., "Iris", *Dial*, 32:112-14, Feb. 16, 1901
Saturday Review, 139:325-26, March 28, 1925

The Ironmaster, 1884
Lazenby, Walter, *Arthur Wing Pinero*. 1972. Pp. 118-20

Lady Bountiful, 1891
Lazenby, Walter, *Arthur Wing Pinero*. 1972. Pp. 71-73

Letty, 1903
  Beerbohm, Max, *Around Theatres.* 1953. Pp. 281-85
  Walkley, Arthur Bingham, *Drama and Life.* 1907. Pp. 175-84

The Magistrate, 1885
  Lazenby, Walter, *Arthur Wing Pinero.* 1972. Pp. 47-49
  Leggatt, Alexander, "Pinero; From Farce to Social Drama", *Modern Drama* (1974), 17:329-44
  Veszy-Wagner, L., "Pinero's Farce 'The Magistrate' as an Anxiety Dream", *American Imago* (1975), 32:200-15

Mayfair, 1885
  Lazenby, Walter, *Arthur Wing Pinero.* 1972. Pp. 87-89

Mid-Channel, 1909
  Burns, Winifred, "Certain Women Characters of Pinero's Serious Drama", *Poet-Lore*, 54:195-219, 1948
  Lazenby, Walter, *Arthur Wing Pinero.* 1972. Pp. 142-44
  Miner, Edmund J., "The Theme of Disillusionment in the Drama of Arthur Pinero", *Contemporary Review* (1975), 226:184-90
  Nation (London), 32:206-08, Nov. 4, 1922

Notorious Mrs. Ebbsmith, 1895
  Agate, James Evershed, *English Dramatic Critics; An Anthology, 1660-1932.* 1958. Pp. 229-40
  Beerbohm, Max, *Around Theatres.* 1953. Pp. 131-35
  Burns, Winifred, "Certain Women Characters of Pinero's Serious Drama", *Poet-Lore*, 54:195-219, 1948
  Courtney, W. L., "Realistic Drama", *Living Age*, 278:265-78, 1913
  Fromm, Harold, *Bernard Shaw and the Theater in the Nineties; A Study of Shaw's Dramatic Criticism.* 1967. Pp. 82-92
  Lazenby, Walter, *Arthur Wing Pinero.* 1972. Pp. 129-33
  Miner, Edmund J., "The Theme of Disillusionment in the Drama of Arthur Pinero", *Contemporary Review* (1975), 226:184-90
  Shaw, George Bernard, *Plays and Players; Essays on the Theatre.* 1952. Pp. 25-32
  Taylor, John Russell, *The Rise and Fall of the Well-Made Play.* 1967. Pp. 67-69

Preserving Mr. Panmure, 1911
  Lazenby, Walter, *Arthur Wing Pinero.* 1972. Pp. 61-63

The Princess and the Butterfly; or, The Fantastics, 1897
  Courtney, W. L., "Idea of Comedy and Mr. Pinero's New Play", *Fortnightly Review*, 67:746-56, May, 1897
  Lazenby, Walter, *Arthur Wing Pinero.* 1972. Pp. 97-100
  Shaw, George Bernard, *Plays and Players; Essays on the Theatre.* 1952. Pp. 204-14

Playgoers, 1913
  Wearing, J. P., "Two Early Absurd Plays in England", *Modern Drama* (1973), 16:259-64

The Profligate, 1889
  Courtney, W. L., "Realistic Drama", *Living Age*, 278:265-78, 1913
  Lazenby, Walter, *Arthur Wing Pinero.* 1972. Pp. 120-24
  Taylor, John Russell, *The Rise and Fall of the Well-Made Play.* 1967. Pp. 53-66

The Rector; The Story of Four Friends, 1883
  Lazenby, Walter, *Arthur Wing Pinero*. 1972. Pp. 114-16

The School Mistress, 1886
  Beerbohm, Max, *Around Theatres*. 1953. Pp. 15-19
  Lazenby, Walter, *Arthur Wing Pinero*. 1972. Pp. 49-52

A Seat in the Park, 1922
  Wearing, J. P., "Two Early Absurd Plays in England", *Modern Drama* (1973), 16:259-64

The Second Mrs. Tanqueray, 1893
  Archer, W., "Plays and Acting of the Season", *Fortnightly Review*, 60:255-63, 1893
  Burns, Winifred, "Certain Women Characters of Pinero's Serious Drama", *Poet-Lore*, 54:195-219, 1948
  Courtney, W. L., "Realistic Drama", *Living Age*, 278:265-78, 1913
  Krutch, J. W., "The Second Mrs. Tanqueray", *Nation*, 119:551-52, Nov. 19, 1924
  Lazenby, Walter, *Arthur Wing Pinero*. 1972. Pp. 123-29
  Leggatt, Alexander, "Pinero; From Farce to Social Drama", *Modern Drama* (1974), 17:329-44
  Mais, Stuart Petre Brodie, *Some Modern Authors*, 1923. Pp. 303-10
  Miner, Edmund J., "The Theme of Disillusionment in the Drama of Arthur Pinero", *Contemporary Review* (1975), 226:184-90
  Nethercot, Arthur C., " 'Mrs. Warren's Profession' and 'The Second Mrs. Tanqueray' ", *Shaw Review* (1970), 13:26-28
  Pollock, J., "The Second Mrs. Tanqueray", *Fortnightly*, 118:345-48, Aug., 1922
  Rideing, William H., "Some Women of Pinero's", *North American Review*, 188:38-49, 1908
  "Second Mrs. Tanqueray; Lesson of Paula", *English Review*, 14:655-58, 1913
  Shaw, George Bernard, *Plays and Players; Essays on the Theatre*. 1952. Pp. 17-25
  Taylor, John Russell, *The Rise and Fall of the Well-Made Play*. 1967. Pp. 60-88

Sweet Lavender, 1888
  Lazenby, Walter, *Arthur Wing Pinero*. 1972. Pp. 68-71
  MacCarthy, Desmond, "Sweet Lavender", *New Statesman and Nation*, 3:824-25, June 25, 1932
  Nation (London), 32:499, Dec. 23, 1922
  Outlook (London), 51:34, Jan. 13, 1923

The Thunderbolt, 1908
  Hamilton, C., "Pinero's 'Thunderbolt' ", *Bookman*, 32:464-67, Jan., 1911
  Lazenby, Walter, *Arthur Wing Pinero*. 1972. Pp. 139-42
  Winter, W., "Pinero's 'Thunderbolt' ", *Harper's Weekly*, 54:28-29, Dec. 10, 1910

The Times, 1891
  Lazenby, Walter, *Arthur Wing Pinero*. 1972. Pp. 91-94

Trelawney of the "Wells", 1898
  Lazenby, Walter, *Arthur Wing Pinero*. 1972. Pp. 73-76
  London Mercury, 38:553-54, Oct., 1938
  New Republic, 49:357-58, Feb. 16, 1927

Outlook, 145:396-97, March 30, 1927
Saturday Review, 142:645, Nov. 27, 1926
Shaw, George Bernard, *Plays and Players; Essays on the Theatre*. 1952. Pp. 299-307
Taylor, John Russell, *The Rise and Fall of the Well-Made Play*. 1967. Pp. 73-80
Ward, Alfred Charles, ed., *Specimens of English Dramatic Criticism, 17th-20th Centuries*. 1945. Pp. 218-21

The Weaker Sex, 1888
Lazenby, Walter, *Arthur Wing Pinero*. 1972. Pp. 85-87

HAROLD PINTER

The Basement, 1967
Commonweal, 89:350-51, Dec. 6, 1968
Esslin, Martin, *The Peopled Wound; The Work of Harold Pinter*. 1970. Pp. 171-78
Hayman, Ronald, *Harold Pinter*, 1969. Pp. 72-77
Hinschliffe, Arnold P., *Harold Pinter*. 1967. Pp. 135-38
Nation, 207:477, Nov. 4, 1968
New Yorker, 44:140-41, Oct. 26, 1968
Newsweek, 72:135, Oct. 28, 1968
Rosador, Kurt Tetzeli V., "Pinter's Dramatic Method; 'Kullus', 'The Examination', and 'The Basement' ", *Modern Drama* (Sept. 1971), 14:195-204
Time, 92:69, Oct. 25, 1968
Vogue, 152:170, Dec. 1968
Wagner, Marlene S., "The Game-Play in Twentieth Century Absurdist Drama: Studies in Dramatic Technique", *Dissertation Abstracts International* (1972), 32:4637A

The Birthday Party, 1958
Bernhard, F. J., "Beyond Realism; The Plays of Harold Pinter", *Modern Drama* (Sept. 1965), 8:185-91
Brooks, Mary E., "The British Theatre of Metaphysical Despair", *Literature and Ideology* (1972), 12:49-58
Brown, John Russell, ed., *Modern British Dramatists; A Collection of Critical Essays*. 1968. Pp. 38-46
Brown, John Russell, *Theatre Language; A Study of Arden, Osborne, Pinter and Wesker*. 1972. Pp. 15-54
Burghardt, Lorraine H., "Game Playing in Three by Pinter", *Modern Drama* (1974), 17:377-87
Burkman, Katherine H., *The Dramatic World of Harold Pinter; Its Basis in Ritual*. 1971. Pp. 23-39
Carpenter, C. A., What Have I Seen, The Scum or the Essence? Symbolic Fallout in Pinter's 'Birthday Party' ", *Modern Drama* (1974), 17:389-402
Cohn, Ruby, *Currents in Contemporary Drama*. 1969. Pp. 180-82
_____ , "The World of Harold Pinter", *Tulane Drama Review* (March 1962), 6:55-68
Dias, Earl J., "The Enigmatic World of Harold Pinter", *Drama Critique* (Fall 1968), 11:119-24
Dukore, Bernard, "The Theatre of Harold Pinter", *Tulane Drama Review* (March 1962), 6:43-54

Elliott, Susan M., "Fantasy Behind Play: A Study of Emotional Responses to Harold Pinter's 'Birthday Party', 'The Caretaker', and 'The Home-coming'", *Dissertation Abstracts International* (1974), 34:5963A

English, Alan C., "Feeling Pinter's World", *Ball State University Forum* (1973), 14,i:70-75

Esslin, Martin, *Brief Chronicles; Essays on Modern Theatre*. 1970. Pp. 190-92

————————, "Harold Pinter, un Dramaturge Anglais de L'Absurde", *Preuves* (Sept. 1963), #151:45-54

————————, *The Peopled Wound; The Work of Harold Pinter*. 1970. Pp. 74-87

————————, *The Theatre of the Absurd*, 1961. Pp. 204-08

Ganz, Arthur, ed., *Pinter: A Collection of Critical Essays*. 1972. Pp. 78-92, and 123-46

Gilman, Richard, *Common and Uncommon Masks; Writings on the Theatre, 1961-70*. 1971. Pp. 108-10

Hayman, Ronald, *Harold Pinter*. 1969. Pp. 19-27

Herin, Miriam M., "An Analysis of Harold Pinter's Use of Language as Seen in 'The Birthday Party', 'The Caretaker', 'The Homecoming', and 'Old Times'", *Dissertation Abstracts International* (1973), 34:1913A

Hinchliffe, Arnold P., *Harold Pinter*. 1967. Pp. 48-63

Hoefer, Jacqueline, "Pinter and Whiting; Two Attitudes Towards the Alienated Artist", *Modern Drama* (1962), 4:402-08

Hollis, James R., *Harold Pinter; the Poetics of Silence*. 1970. Pp. 31-43

Itzin, C., "Birthday Party", *Plays and Players* (March 1975), 22:26-27

Jennings, Ann S., "The Reaction of London's Drama Critics to Certain Plays by Henrik Ibsen, Harold Pinter and Edward Bond", *Dissertation Abstracts International* (1973), 34:2067A

Jones, Paul D., "The Intruder in the Drama of Harold Pinter: A Functional Analysis", *Dissertation Abstracts International* (1972), 32:4758A

Kaufman, Michael W., "Actions that a Man Might Play: Pinter's 'The Birthday Party'", *Modern Drama* (1973), 16:167-78

Kerr, Walter, *Thirty Plays Hath November; Pain and Pleasure in the Contemporary Theater*. 1969. Pp. 41-45

Kunkel, Francis L., "The Dystopia of Harold Pinter", *Renascence* (Autumn 1968), 21:17-20

Lahr, John, "Pinter and Chekhov; The Bond of Naturalism", *TDR; The Drama Review* (Winter 1968), 13:137-45

Lesser, S. O., "Reflections on Pinter's 'The Birthday Party'", *Contemporary Literature* (Winter 1972), 13:34-43

Lumley, Frederick, *New Trends in Twentieth Century Drama; A Survey Since Ibsen and Shaw*. 1967. Pp. 266-73

Mabley, Edward, *Dramatic Construction; An Outline of Basic Principles*. 1972. Pp. 352-64

Messenger, Ann P., "Blindness and the Problem of Identity in Pinter's Plays", *Die Neueren Sprachen* (1972), n. f. 21:481-90

Morrison, Kristin, "Pinter and the New Irony", *Quarterly Journal of Speech* (Dec. 1969), 55:388-93

New Statesman, 55:692, May 31, 1958 and 58:836, Dec. 12, 1959

O'Casey, Sean, "The Bald Primaqueera", *Atlantic Monthly* (Sept. 1965), 216:69-74

Pesta, John, "Pinter's Usurpers", *Drama Survey* (1967-68), 6:54-65

Roy, Emil, *British Drama Since Shaw*. 1972. Pp. 116-20

Saturday Review, 44:26, Aug. 26, 1961

Schiff, Ellen F., "Pancakes and Soap Suds: A Study of Childishness in Pinter's Plays", *Modern Drama* (1973), 16:91-101

Schwarze, Hans-Wilhelm, "Orientierungslosigkeit und Betroffensein: Spiel-elemente in Harold Pinters 'The Birthday Party' ", *Literatur in Wissenschaft und Unterricht* (1974), 7:98-114

Sheed, Wilfrid, *The Morning After; Selected Essays and Reviews*. 1971. Pp. 227-29

Spectator, 200:687, May 30, 1958

Sprague, Claire, "Possible or Necessary?", *New Theatre Magazine* (1967), 8#1:36-37

Stein, Karen F., "Metaphysical Silence in Absurd Drama", *Modern Drama* (Feb. 1971), 13:423-31

Storch, R. F., "Harold Pinter's Happy Families", *Massachusetts Review* (Aut. 1967), 8:703-12

Talley, Mary Ethel, "The Relationship of Theme and Technique in Plays of Harold Pinter", *Dissertation Abstracts International* (1972), 33:1744A

Weber, Brom, ed., *Sense and Sensibility in 20th Century Writing; A Gathering in Memory of William Van O'Connor*. 1970. Pp. 57-75

Williams, Raymond, *Drama from Ibsen to Brecht*. 1968. Pp. 322-25

Wray, Phoebe, "Pinter's Dialogue; The Play on Words", *Modern Drama* (Feb. 1971), 13:418-22

The Caretaker, 1960

America, 106:376, Dec. 9, 1961

Bernhard, F. J., "Beyond Realism; The Plays of Harold Pinter", *Modern Drama* (Sept. 1965), 8:185-91

Boulton, James T., "Harold Pinter: 'The Caretaker' and Other Plays", *Modern Drama* (1963), 6:131-40

Brown, John Russell, ed., *Modern British Dramatists; A Collection of Critical Essays*. 1968. Pp. 66-70

―――――――――― , *Theatre Language; A Study of Arden, Osborne, Pinter and Wesker*. 1972. Pp. 55-92

Christian Century, 78:1403-06, Nov. 22, 1961

Clurman, Harold, *The Divine Pastime; Theater Essays*. 1974. Pp. 145-57

―――――――――― , *The Naked Image; Observations on the Modern Theatre*. 1966. Pp. 105-07

Cohn, Ruby, "The World of Harold Pinter", *Tulane Drama Review* (March 1962), 6:55-68

Commonweal, 75:122-23, Oct. 27, 1961 and 77:366, Dec. 28, 1962

Cook, David and Harold F. Brooks, "A Room with Three Views: Harold Pinter's 'The Caretaker' ", *Komos* (1967), 1:62-69

Cowell, Raymond, *Twelve Modern Dramatists*. 1967. Pp. 134-35

Deurbergue, Jean, "Sujet, Personnage, Parole dans 'The Caretaker' de Harold Pinter", *Recherches Anglaises et Américaines* (1972), 5:47-62

Dias, Earl J., "The Enigmatic World of Harold Pinter", *Drama Critique* (Fall 1968), 11:119-24

Dick, Kay, "Mr. Pinter and the Fearful Matter", *Texas Quarterly* (1963), 4:257-65

Douglas, Reid, "The Failure of English Realism", *Tulane Drama Review* (1962), 7:180-83

Educational Theatre Journal, 13:294-96, Dec., 1961

Elliott, Susan M., "Fantasy Behind Play; A Study of Emotional Responses to Harold Pinter's 'The Birthday Party', 'The Caretaker', and 'The Homecoming'", *Dissertation Abstracts International* (1974), 34:5963A

Esslin, Martin, *The Peopled Wound; The Work of Harold Pinter*. 1970. Pp. 95-115

—————————— , *The Theatre of the Absurd*. 1961. Pp. 210-14

—————————— , "Harold Pinter, un Dramaturge Anglais de L'Absurde", *Preuves* (Sept. 1963), #151:45-54

Gallagher, K. G., "Harold Pinter's Dramaturgy", *Quarterly Journal of Speech* (1966), 52:242-48

Ganz, Arthur, ed., *Pinter; A Collection of Critical Essays*. 1972. Pp. 72-104 and 123-35

Gassner, John, *Dramatic Soundings; Evaluations and Retractions Culled from Thirty Years of Dramatic Criticism*. 1968. Pp. 503-07

Goodman, Florence Jeanne, "Pinter's 'The Caretaker': 'The Lower Depths' Decended", *Midwest Quarterly* (1964), 5:117-26

Hayman, Ronald, *Harold Pinter*. 1969. Pp. 36-42

Herin, Miriam M., "An Analysis of Harold Pinter's Use of Language as Seen in 'The Birthday Party', The Caretaker', 'The Homecoming', and 'Old Times'", *Dissertation Abstracts International* (1973), 34:1913A

Hinchliffe, Arnold P., *Harold Pinter*. 1967. Pp. 87-107

Hollis, James R., *Harold Pinter; The Poetics of Silence*. 1970. Pp. 77-95

Hudson Review, 14:94-95, Spring, 1961 and 14:590, Winter, 1961-62

Illustrated London News, 236:850, May 14, 1960

Jennings, Ann S., "The Reactions of London's Drama Critics to Certain Plays by Henrik Ibsen, Harold Pinter, and Edward Bond", *Dissertation Abstracts International* (1973), 34:2067A

Jones, Paul D., "The Intruder in the Drama of Harold Pinter; A Functional Analysis", *Dissertation Abstracts International* (1972), 32:4758A

Kennedy, Andrew K., *Six Dramatists in Search of a Language*. 1975. Pp. 169-84

Kerr, Walter, *The Theatre in Spite of Itself*. 1963. Pp. 116-19

Life, 51:195-96, Nov. 17, 1961

Lumley, Frederick, *New Trends in Twentieth Century Drama; A Survey Since Ibsen and Shaw*. 1967. Pp. 266-73

Morrison, Kristin, "Pinter and the New Irony", *Quarterly Journal of Speech* (Dec. 1969), 55:388-93

Murphy, Robert P., "Non-Verbal Communication and the Overlooked Action in Pinter's 'The Caretaker'", *Quarterly Journal of Speech* (1972), 58:41-47

Nation, 193:276, Oct. 21, 1961

National Review, 11:424, Dec. 16, 1961

New Republic, 145:29-30, Oct. 23, 1961

New Statesman, 59:666, May 7, 1960

New Yorker, 36:60, July 9, 1960 and 37:162, Oct. 14, 1961

Newsweek, 58:101, Oct. 16, 1961

Pesta, John, "Pinter's Usurpers", *Drama Survey* (1967-68), 6:54-65

Prickett, Stephen, "Three Modern English Plays", *Philololgica Pragensia* (1967), 10:12-21

Quigley, Austin E., "The Dynamics of Dialogue: The Plays of Harold Pinter", *Dissertation Abstracts International* (1973), 33:6928A

Reporter, 23:48, Oct. 13, 1960

Roy, Emil, *British Drama Since Shaw*. 1972. Pp. 118-20

Salem, Daniel, " 'Le Gardien': Analyse d'un Personnage de Pinter", *Langues Modernes* (1973), 67:67-71

Saturday Review, 44:34, Oct. 21, 1961

Schechner, Richard, "Puzzling Pinter", *Tulane Drama Review* (1966), 11:176-84

Schlegelmilch, Wolfgang, "Der Raum des Humanen; Zu Harold Pinters 'The Caretaker' ", *Die Neueren Sprachen* (1964), 13:328-33

Spectator, 204:661, May 6, 1960 and 204:835, June 10, 1960

Storch, R. F., "Harold Pinter's Happy Families", *Massachusetts Review* (Aut. 1967), 8:703-12

Talley, Mary Ethel, "The Relationship of Theme and Technique in Plays of Harold Pinter", *Dissertation Abstracts International* (1972), 33:1744A

Taylor, John Russell, *Anger and After; A Guide to the New British Drama*. 1962. Pp. 336-40

Theatre Arts, 45:12, Dec., 1961

Time, 78:58, Oct. 13, 1961

Walker, Augusta, "Messages from Pinter", *Modern Drama* (1967), 10:1-10

Wardle, Irving, "There's Music in that Room", *Encore* (1960), 7:32-34

The Collection, 1961

Clurman, Harold, *The Naked Image; Observations on the Modern Theatre*. 1966. Pp. 108-10

Cohn, Ruby, "Latter Day Pinter", *Drama Survey* (1964), 3:367-77

Commonweal, 77:367, Dec. 28, 1962

Dukore, Bernard F., "The Pinter Collection", *Educational Theatre Journal*, (1974), 26:81-85

Esslin, Martin, *The Peopled Wound; The Work of Harold Pinter*. 1970. Pp. 130-37

Gilman, Richard, *Common and Uncommon Masks; Writings on the Theatre, 1961-70*. 1971. Pp. 94-96

Hayman, Ronald, *Harold Pinter*. 1969. Pp. 49-54

Hinchliffe, Arnold P., *Harold Pinter*. 1967. Pp. 114-18

_____ , "Mr. Pinter's Belinda", *Modern Drama* (Sept. 1968), 11:173-79

Hollis, James A., *Harold Pinter; The Poetics of Silence*. 1970. Pp. 70-77

Illustrated London News, 240:1058, June 30, 1962

Lumley, Frederick, *New Trends in Twentieth Century Drama; A Survey Since Ibsen and Shaw*. 1967. Pp. 266-73

Matthews, Honor, *The Primal Curse; The Myth of Cain and Abel in the Theatre*. 1967. Pp. 198-201

Nation, 195:430, Dec. 15, 1962

New Yorker, 38:148-50, Dec. 8, 1962

Saturday Review, 45:30, Dec. 15, 1962

Schechner, Richard, "Puzzling Pinter", *Tulane Drama Review* (1966), 11:176-84

Spectator, 208:857, June 29, 1962

Theatre Arts, 47:10-11, Jan., 1963

Time, 80:73, Dec. 7, 1962

Wagner, Marlene S., "The Game-Play in Twentieth Century Absurdist Drama; Studies in Dramatic Technique", *Dissertation Abstracts International* (1972), 32:4637A

Walker, Augusta, "Messages from Pinter", *Modern Drama* (1967), 10:1-10

The Dumb Waiter, 1959

Burghardt, Lorraine H., "Game Playing in Three by Pinter", *Modern Drama* (1974), 17:377-87

Burkman, Katherine H., *The Dramatic World of Harold Pinter; Its Basis in Ritual.* 1971. Pp. 39-44

Carpenter, Charles A., "The Absurdity of Dread: Pinter's 'The Dumb Waiter' ", *Modern Drama* (1973), 16:279-85

Clurman, Harold, *The Naked Image; Observations on the Modern Theatre.* 1966. Pp. 108-10

Cohn, Ruby, "The Absurdly Absurd; Avators of Godot", *Comparative Literature Studies* (1965), 2:233-40

——————————— , "The World of Harold Pinter", *Tulane Drama Review* (March 1962), 6:55-68

Commonweal, 77:367, Dec. 28, 1962

Dukore, Bernard, "The Theatre of Harold Pinter", *Tulane Drama Review* (March 1962), 6:43-54

English, Alan C., "Feeling Pinter's World", *Ball State University Forum* (1973), 14,i:70-75

Esslin, Martin, *The Peopled Wound; The Work of Harold Pinter.* 1970. Pp. 67-73

——————————— , *The Theatre of the Absurd.* 1961. Pp. 201-04

Ganz, Arthur, ed., *Pinter; A Collection of Critical Essays.* 1972

Gilman, Richard, *Common and Uncommon Masks; Writings on the Theatre, 1961-70.* 1971. Pp. 94-96

Hayman, Ronald, *Harold Pinter*, 1969. Pp. 15-18

Hinchliffe, Arnold P., *Harold Pinter.* 1967. Pp. 63-68

Hollis, James R., *Harold Pinter; The Poetics of Silence.* 1970. Pp. 43-51

Illustrated London News, 236:226, Feb. 6, 1960

Jones, Paul D., "The Intruder in the Drama of Harold Pinter; A Functional Analysis", *Dissertation Abstracts International* (1972), 32:4758A

Matthews, Honor, *The Primal Curse; The Myth of Cain and Abel in the Theatre.* 1967. Pp. 22-23

Morrison, Kristin, "Pinter and the New Irony", *Quarterly Journal of Speech* (Dec. 1969), 55:388-93

Nation, 195:429-30, Dec. 15, 1962

New Statesman, 59:150, Jan. 30, 1960

New Yorker, 38:148-50, Dec. 8, 1962

Pesta, John, "Pinter's Usurpers", *Drama Survey* (Spring-Summer 1967), 6:54-65

Roy, Emil, *British Drama Since Shaw.* 1972. Pp. 116-18

Saturday Review, 45:30, Dec. 15, 1962

Theatre Arts, 47:10-11, Jan., 1963

Time, 80:72-73, Dec. 7, 1962

Towey, Denis J., "Form and Content in Selected Plays of Harold Pinter", *Dissertation Abstracts International* (1973), 34:3609A

Walker, Augusta, "Messages from Pinter", *Modern Drama* (1967), 10:1-10

The Dwarfs, 1960

Brown, John Russell, *Theatre Language; A Study of Arden, Osborne, Pinter and Wesker.* 1972. Pp. 55-92

Burkman, Katherine H., *The Dramatic World of Harold Pinter; Its Basis in Ritual.* 1971. Pp. 68-70

Cohn, Ruby, "Latter Day Pinter", *Drama Survey* (1964), 3:367-77

Esslin, Martin, *The Peopled Wound; The Work of Harold Pinter.* 1970. Pp. 120-30

—————————— , *The Theatre of the Absurd.* 1961. Pp. 214-17

Hayman, Ronald, *Harold Pinter.* 1969. Pp. 46-48

Hinchliffe, Arnold P., *Harold Pinter.* 1967. Pp. 78-86

Jones, Paul D., "The Intruder in the Drama of Harold Pinter; A Functional Analysis", *Dissertation Abstracts International* (1972), 32:4758A

McLaughlin, John, "Harold Pinter and P. B. L.: Analysis of 'The Dwarfs'", *America* (Feb. 10, 1968), 118:193

Quigley, A. E., "'Dwarfs': A Study in Linguistic Dwarfism", *Modern Drama* (1974), 17:413-22

Homecoming, 1965

Blau, Herbert, "Politics and the Theatre", *Wascana Review* (1967), 2:5-23

Brown, John Russell, ed., *Modern British Dramatists; A Collection of Critical Essays.* 1968. Pp. 145-63

Brown, John Russell, *Theatre Language; A Study of Arden, Osborne, Pinter and Wesker.* 1972. Pp. 93-117

Brustein, Robert, *The Third Theatre.* 1969. Pp. 117-22

Burkman, Katherine H., *The Dramatic World of Harold Pinter; Its Basis in Ritual.* 1971. Pp. 108-16

Christian Century, 82:1096-97, Sept. 8, 1965

Clurman, Harold, *The Divine Pastime; Theatre Essays.* 1974. Pp. 210-13

Cohn, Ruby, *Currents in Contemporary Drama.* 1969. Pp. 80-81 and 178-82

Dawick, J., "Punctuation and Patterning in 'The Homecoming'", *Modern Drama* (May 1971), 14:37-46

Dias, Earl J., "The Enigmatic World of Harold Pinter", *Drama Critique* (Fall 1968), 11:119-24

Downer, Alan S., "The Doctor's Dilemma: Notes on the New York Theatre, 1966-1967", *Quarterly Journal of Speech* (1967), 53:215-17

Dukore, Bernard F., "A Woman's Place", *Quarterly Journal of Speech* (1966), 52:237-41

Elliott, Susan M., "Fantasy Behind Play; A Study of Emotional Responses to Harold Pinter's 'The Birthday Party', 'The Caretaker', and 'The Homecoming'", *Dissertation Abstracts International* (1974), 34:5963A

Esslin, Martin, *The Peopled Wound; The Work of Harold Pinter.* 1970. Pp. 143-66

Franzblau, A. N., "A Psychiatrist Looks at 'The Homecoming'", *Saturday Review* (April 8, 1967), 50:58

Free, William J., "Treatment of Character in Harold Pinter's 'The Homecoming'", *South Atlantic Bulletin* (Nov. 1969), 34:1-5

Ganz, Arthur, "A Clue to the Pinter Puzzle; The Triple Self in 'The Homecoming'", *Educational Theatre Journal* (1969), 21:180-87

Ganz, Arthur, ed., *Pinter; A Collection of Critical Essays.* 1972. Pp. 147-60

Gillen, Francis, "'. . . . Apart from the Known and Unknown': The Unreconciled Worlds of Harold Pinter's Characters", *Arizona Quarterly* (1970), 26:17-23

Gilman, Richard, *Common and Uncommon Mask; Writings on the Theatre, 1961-70.* 1971. Pp. 101-07

Goldstone, Herbert, "Not so Puzzling Pinter: 'The Homecoming'", *Theatre Annual* (1969), 25:20-27

Hayman, Ronald, *Harold Pinter*. 1969. Pp. 62-71

Herin, Miriam M., "An Analysis of Harold Pinter's Use of Language as Seen in 'The Birthday Party', 'The Caretaker', 'The Homecoming', and 'Old Times' ", *Dissertation Abstracts International* (1973), 34:1913A

Higgins, David M., "Existential Valuation in Five Contemporary Plays", *Dissertation Abstracts International* (1972), 32:4612A

Hinchliffe, Arnold P., *Harold Pinter*. 1967. Pp. 146-62

————————— , "Mr. Pinter's Belinda", *Modern Drama* (Sept. 1968), 11:173-79

Hirschberg, Stuart, "Pinter's Caricature of 'Howard's End' in 'The Homecoming' ", *Notes on Contemporary Literature* (1974), 4,iv:14-15

Hollis, James R., *Harold Pinter; The Poetics of Silence*. 1970. Pp. 96-111

Hunt, Joseph A., "Interaction Process Analysis of Harold Pinter's 'The Homecoming': Toward a Phenomenological Criticism of Drama", *Dissertation Abstracts International* (1972), 32:4159A

Jiji, V. M., "Pinter's Four Dimensional House; 'The Homecoming' ", *Modern Drama* (1974), 17:433-42

Jennings, Ann S., "The Reactions of London's Drama Critics to Certain Plays of Henrik Ibsen, Harold Pinter, and Edward Bond", *Dissertation Abstracts International* (1973), 34:2067A

Kauffman, S., *Living Images; Film Comment and Criticism*. 1975. Pp. 242-46

Kennedy, Andrew K., *Six Dramatists in Search of a Language*. 1975. Pp. 184-88

Kerr, Walter, "Harold Pinter", *Columbia Essays on Modern Writers* (1967), #27:1-48

Kunkel, Francis L., "The Dystopia of Harold Pinter", *Renascence* (Autumn 1968), 21:17-20

Lahr, John, *Up Against the Fourth Wall*. 1970. Pp. 181-83 and 186-91

Lamont, Rosette C., "Pinter's 'The Homecoming': The Contest of the Gods", *Folktales of the World* (1974), 1:47-73

Lumley, Frederick, *New Trends in Twentieth Century Drama; A Survey Since Ibsen and Shaw*. 1967. Pp. 266-73

Mast, Gerald, "Pinter's 'Homecoming' ", *Drama Survey* (1968), 6:266-77

Morgan, Ricki, "What Max and Teddy Come Home to in 'The Homecoming' ", *Educational Theatre Journal* (1973), 25:490-99

Morris, Kelly, "Homecoming", *Tulane Drama Review* (1966), 11:185-91

New Republic, 152:29-30, June 26, 1965

New Statesman, 69:928, June 11, 1965

New Yorker, 41:59, July 31, 1965

Osherow, A. R., "Mother and Whore; The Role of Woman in 'The Homecoming'.", *Modern Drama* (1974), 17:423-32

Pesta, John, "Pinter's Usurpers", *Drama Survey* (1967-68), 6:54-65

Roland, Alan, "Pinter's 'Homecoming': Imagoes in Dramatic Action", *Psychoanalytic Review* (1974), 61:415-28

Roy, Emil *British Drama Since Shaw*. 1972. Pp. 121-23

Schechner, Richard, "Puzzling Pinter", *Tulane Drama Review* (1966), 11:176-84

Schiff, Ellen F., "Pancakes and Soap Suds; A Study of Childishness in Pinter's Plays", *Modern Drama* (1973), 16:91-101

Schneider, Ruth M., "The Interpolated Narrative in Modern Drama", *Dissertation Abstracts International* (1974), 34:6605A

States, Bert O., "Pinter's 'Homecoming': The Shock of Nonrecognition",
    Hudson Review (Aut. 1968), 21:474-86
Storch, R. F., "Harold Pinter's Happy Families", *Massachusetts Review* (Aut.
    1967), 8:703-12
Talley, May Ethel, "The Relationship of Theme and Technique in Plays
    of Harold Pinter", *Dissertation Abstracts International* (1972), 33:1744A
Towey, Denis J., "Form and Content in Selected Plays of Harold Pinter",
    Dissertation Abstracts International (1973), 34:3609A
Warner, John M., "The Epistemological Quest in Pinter's 'The Homecoming' ",
    Contemporary Literature (1970), 11:340-53
Wray, Phoebe, "Pinter's Dialogue; The Play on Words", *Modern Drama* (Feb.
    1971), 13:418-22
Wright, Edward A. and Lenthiel H. Downs, *A Primer for Playgoers.* 1969.
    Pp. 128-33 and 303-05

Landscape, 1969
Allison, Ralph and Charles Wellborn, "Rhapsody in an Anechoic Chamber:
    Pinter's 'Landscape' ", *Educational Theatre Journal* (1973), 25:215-25
Burkman, Katherine H., *The Dramatic World of Harold Pinter; Its Basis
    in Ritual.* 1971. Pp. 141-45
Eigo, James, "Pinter's 'Landscape' ", *Modern Drama* (1973), 16:179-83
Ganz, Arthur, ed., *Pinter; A Collection of Critical Essays.* 1972. Pp. 161-78
Hayman, Ronald, *Harold Pinter.* 1969. Pp. 78-81
Hollis, James R., *Harold Pinter; The Poetics of Silence.* 1970. Pp. 118-21
Quigley, Austin E., "The Dynamics of Dialogue; The Plays of Harold Pinter",
    Dissertation Abstracts International (1973), 33:6928A
Salmon, Eric, "Harold Pinter's Ear", *Modern Drama* (1974), 17:363-75

The Lover, 1963
Brown, John Russell, *Theatre Language; A Study of Arden, Osborne, Pinter
    and Wesker.* 1972. Pp. 15-54
Burkman, Katherine H., *The Dramatic World of Harold Pinter; Its Basis in
    Ritual.* 1971. Pp. 104-07
Clurman, Harold, *The Naked Image; Observations on the Modern Theatre.*
    1966. Pp. 112-14
Cohn, Ruby, "Latter Day Pinter", *Drama Survey* (1964), 3:367-77
Commonweal, 79:484-85, Jan. 24, 1964
Esslin, Martin, *The Peopled Wound; The Work of Harold Pinter.* 1970. Pp.
    137-43
Gilman, Richard, *Common and Uncommon Masks; Writings on the Theatre,
    1961-70.* 1971. Pp. 111-13
Hayman, Ronald, *Harold Pinter.* 1969. Pp. 55-57
Hinchliffe, Arnold P., *Harold Pinter.* 1967. Pp. 118-24
    _____ , "Mr. Pinter's Belinda", *Modern Drama* (Sept. 1968), 11:173-
79
Hollis, James R., *Harold Pinter; The Poetics of Silence.* 1970. Pp. 62-69
Lumley, Frederick, *New Trends in Twentieth Century Drama; A Survey Since
    Ibsen and Shaw.* 1967. Pp. 266-73
Nation, 198:106, Jan. 27, 1964
New Republic, 150:28, Feb. 1, 1964
New Yorker, 39:69-70, Jan. 11, 1964

Roy, Emil, *British Drama Since Shaw*. 1972. Pp. 117-21
Saturday Review, 47:25, Jan. 25, 1964
Spectator, 211:386, Sept. 27, 1963
Time, 83:64, Jan. 17, 1964
Vogue, 143:22, Feb. 15, 1964
Wagner, Marlene S., "The Game-Play in Twentieth Century Absurdist Drama;
    Studies in Dramatic Technique", *Dissertation Abstracts International* (1972),
    32:4637A

Night, 1969
Hayman, Ronald, *Harold Pinter*. 1969. Pp. 88-90

A Night Out, 1960
Esslin, Martin, *The Peopled Wound; The Work of Harold Pinter*. 1970. Pp.
    91-95
Hayman, Ronald, *Harold Pinter*. 1969. Pp. 32-35
Storch, R. F., "Harold Pinter's Happy Families", *Massachusetts Review* (Aut.
    1967), 8:703-12

Night School, 1961
Esslin, Martin, *The Peopled Wound; The Work of Harold Pinter*. 1970. Pp.
    116-20
Hayman, Ronald, *Harold Pinter*. 1969. Pp. 43-45

No Man's Land, 1975
Atlantic (Feb. 1976), 237:98
Nation (Aug. 16, 1975), 221:124
New Yorker (May 12, 1975), 51:117-18
Time (May 19, 1975), 105:80

Old Times, 1971
Aylwin, Tony, "The Memory of All That; Pinter's 'Old Times'", *English*
    (1973), 22:99-102
Clurman, Harold, *The Divine Pastime; Theatre Essays*. 1974. Pp. 286-88
Ganz, Arthur, ed., *Pinter; A Collection of Critical Essays*. 1972. Pp. 161-78
Herin, Miriam M., "An Analysis of Harold Pinter's Use of Language as Seen
    in 'The Birthday Party', 'The Caretaker', 'The Homecoming', and 'Old
    Times'", *Dissertation Abstracts International* (1973), 34:1913A
Hewes, Henry, "The British Bundle", *Saturday Review* (Sept. 11, 1971), 54:
    20 and 54
——————————— , "Odd Husband Out", *Saturday Review* (Dec. 4, 1971), 54:20-
    22
Hughes, A., "They Can't Take That Away from Me; Myth and Memory in
    Pinter's 'Old Times'", *Modern Drama* (1974), 17:467-76
Martineau, Stephen, "Pinter's 'Old Times': The Memory Game", *Modern Drama*
    (1973), 16:287-97
Towey, Denis J., "Form and Content in Selected Plays of Harold Pinter",
    Dissertation Abstracts International (1973), 34:3609A

The Room, 1957
Burkman, Katherine H., *The Dramatic World of Harold Pinter; Its Basis in
    Ritual*. 1971. Pp. 70-73
Clurman, Harold, *The Naked Image; Observations on the Modern Theatre*.
    1966. Pp. 110-12

Cohn, Ruby, "The World of Harold Pinter", *Tulane Drama Review* (March 1962), 6:55-68

English, Alan C., "Feeling Pinter's World", *Ball State University Forum* (1973), 14,i:70-75

Esslin, Martin, *The Peopled Wound; The Work of Harold Pinter.* 1970. Pp. 57-66

_____ , *The Theatre of the Absurd.* 1961. Pp. 199-201

_____ , "Harold Pinter, un Dramaturge Anglais de L'Absurde", *Preuves* (Sept. 1963), #151:45-54

Ganz, Arthur, ed., *Pinter; A Collection of Critical Essays.* 1972. Pp. 78-92 and 105-35

Hayman, Ronald, *Harold Pinter.* 1969. Pp. 11-14

Hinchliffe, Arnold P., *Harold Pinter.* 1967. Pp. 41-48

Hollis, James R., *Harold Pinter; The Poetics of Silence.* 1970. Pp. 20-31

Illustrated London News, 236:226, Feb. 6, 1960

Jones, Paul D., "The Intruder in the Drama of Harold Pinter: A Functional Analysis", *Dissertation Abstracts International* (1972), 32:4758A

Kerr, Walter, "Harold Pinter", *Columbia Essays on Modern Writers* (1967), #27:1-48

Messenger, Ann P., "Blindness and the Problem of Identity in Pinter's Plays", *Die Neueren Sprachen* (1972), n. f. 21:481-90

Morrison, Kristin, "Pinter and the New Irony", *Quarterly Journal of Speech* (Dec. 1969), 55:388-93

Nation, 199:523, Dec. 28, 1964

New Yorker, 40:68, Dec. 19, 1964

Newsweek, 64:75-76, Dec. 21, 1964

Pesta, John, "Pinter's Usurpers", *Drama Survey* (1967-68), 6:54-65

Quigley, Austin E., "The Dynamics of Dialogue; The Plays of Harold Pinter", *Dissertation Abstracts International* (1973), 33:6928A

Roy, Emil, *British Drama Since Shaw.* 1972. Pp. 116-119

Salmon, Eric, "Harold Pinter's Ear", *Modern Drama* (1974), 17:363-75

Saturday Review, 47:33, Dec. 26, 1964

Spectator, 204:138, Jan. 29, 1960

Talley, Mary Ethel, "The Relationship of Theme and Technique in Plays of Harold Pinter", *Dissertation Abstracts International* (1972), 33:1744A

Time, 84:86, Dec. 18, 1964

Vogue, 145:98, Feb. 1, 1965

Walker, Augusta, "Messages from Pinter", *Modern Drama* (1967), 10:1-10

Silence, 1969

Esslin, Martin, *The Peopled Wound; The Work of Harold Pinter.* 1970. Pp 188-96

Ganz, Arthur, ed., *Pinter; A Collection of Critical Essays.* 1972. Pp. 161-78

Hayman, Ronald, *Harold Pinter.* 1969. Pp. 82-87

Hollis, James R., *Harold Pinter; The Poetics of Silence.* 1970. Pp. 114-18

Imhof, Rüdiger, "Pinter's 'Silence'; The Impossibility of Communication", *Modern Drama* (1974), 17:449-59

New Statesman (July 11, 1969), 78:57

Towey, Denis J., "Form and Content in Selected Plays of Harold Pinter", *Dissertation Abstracts International* (1973), 34:3609A

A Slight Ache, 1959

Burkman, Katherine H., *The Dramatic World of Harold Pinter; Its Basis in Ritual*. 1971. Pp. 47-64

―――――――――― , "Pinter's 'A Slight Ache' ", *Modern Drama* (Dec. 1968), 11:326-35

Clurman, Harold, *The Naked Image; Observations on the Modern Theatre*. 1966. Pp. 110-12

Commonweal, 82:194, April 30, 1965

Esslin, Martin, *The Peopled Wound; The Work of Harold Pinter*. 1970. Pp. 87-91

―――――――――― , *The Theatre of the Absurd*. 1961. Pp. 208

Hayman, Ronald, *Harold Pinter*. 1969. Pp. 28-31

Hinchliffe, Arnold P., *Harold Pinter*. 1967. Pp. 68-71

Hollis, James R., *Harold Pinter; The Poetics of Silence*. 1970. Pp. 52-62

Jones, Paul D., "The Intruder in the Drama of Harold Pinter: A Functional Analysis", *Dissertation Abstracts International* (1972), 32:4758A

Messenger, Ann P., "Blindness and the Problem of Identity in Pinter's Plays", *Die Neueren Sprachen* (1972), n. f. 21:481-90

Midwest Monographs, Series 1:1-8, 1967

Morrison, Kristin, "Pinter and the New Irony", *Quarterly Journal of Speech* (Dec. 1969), 55:388-93

Nation, 199:523, Dec. 28, 1964

New Yorker, 40:68, Dec. 18, 1964

Newsweek, 64:75-76, Dec. 21, 1964

Powlick, Leonard, "A Phenomenological Approach to Harold Pinter's 'A Slight Ache' ", *Quarterly Journal of Speech* (1974), 60:25-32

Salmon, Eric, "Harold Pinter's Ear", *Modern Drama* (1974), 17:363-75

Saturday Review, 47:33, Dec. 26, 1964

Schechner, Richard, "Puzzling Pinter", *Tulane Drama Review* (1966), 11:176-84

Schiff, Ellen F., "Pancakes and Soap Suds; A Study of Childishness in Pinter's Plays", *Modern Drama* (1973), 16:91-101

Spectator, 206:106, Jan. 27, 1961

Stein, Karen F., "Metaphysical Silence in Absurd Drama", *Modern Drama* (Feb. 1971), 13:423-31

Talley, Mary Ethel, "The Relationship of Theme and Technique in Plays of Harold Pinter", *Dissertation Abstracts International* (1972), 33:1744A

Time, 84:86, Dec. 18, 1964

Vogue, 145:98, Feb. 1, 1965

Tea Party, 1965

America, 119:447, Nov. 9, 1968

Burghardt, Lorraine H., "Game Playing in Three by Pinter", *Modern Drama* (1974), 17:377-87

Burkman, Katherine H., *The Dramatic World of Harold Pinter; Its Basis in Ritual*. 1971. Pp. 47-64

Canaday, Nicholas, Jr., "Harold Pinter's 'Tea Party'; Seeing and Not Seeing", *Studies in Short Fiction* (1969), 6:580-85

Commonweal, 89:350-51, Dec. 6, 1968

Esslin, Martin, *The Peopled Wound; The Work of Harold Pinter*. 1970. Pp. 166-71

Gillen, Francis, "'. . . Apart from the Known and Unknown': The Un-
reconciled Worlds of Harold Pinter's Characters", *Arizona Quarterly*
(Spr. 1970), 26:17-24
Hayman, Ronald, *Harold Pinter*. 1969. Pp. 58-61
Hinchliffe, Arnold P., *Harold Pinter*. 1967. Pp. 138-45
Nation, 207:477, Nov. 4, 1968
New Yorker, 44:140-41, Oct. 26, 1968
Newsweek, 72:135, Oct. 28, 1968
Time, 92:69, Oct. 25, 1968
Vogue, 152:170, Dec. 1968

LUIGI PIRANDELLO

All for the Best, 1920
Lumley, Frederick, *New Trends in Twentieth Century Drama; A Survey Since
Ibsen and Shaw*. 1967. Pp. 18-34
Moestrup, Jørn, *The Structural Patterns in Pirandello's Work*. 1972. Pp. 169-
73
Spizzo, Jean, "Répétition e Réformation du Texte Pirandellien 'Tutto per
Benne': De la Forme Narrative à la Forme Dramatique", *Revue des Etudes
Italiennes* (1974), 20:74-104

All'Uscita   *SEE*   At the Gate

l'Altro Figlio   *SEE*   The Other Son

As Before, Better than Before, 1920
Moestrup, Jørn, *The Structural Patterns in Pirandello's Work*. 1972. Pp. 173-
75

As You Desire Me, 1930
Arts and Decoration, 34:84, April, 1931
Bellessort, A., "As You Desire Me", *Journal des Débats*, 39 pt. 2:859-61,
Nov. 18, 1932
Bookman, 73:409-10, June, 1931
Catholic World, 132:721, March, 1931
Commonweal, 13:415, Feb. 11, 1931
Drama, 21:9, April, 1931
Lievre, P., "As You Desire Me", *Mercure de France*, 240:617-18, Dec. 15,
1932
Living Age, 338:290-91, May 1, 1930
Marcel, G., "As You Desire Me", *L'Europe Nouvelle*, 15:1357-58, Nov. 19,
1932
Nation, 132:198, Feb. 18, 1931
New Republic, 66:209, April 8, 1931
Outlook, 158:36, May 13, 1931
Theatre Arts, 15:277, April, 1931
Theatre Magazine, 53:26, April, 1931

At the Gate, 1922
Moestrup, Jørn, *The Structural Patterns in Pirandello's Work*. 1972. Pp.
138-40

Il Berretto a Sonagli   *SEE*   Cap and Bells

But It's Not a Serious Affair, 1918
  Moestrup, Jørn, *The Structural Patterns in Pirandello's Work*. 1972. Pp.
  163-64

Cap and Bells, 1917
  Matthaei, Renate, *Luigi Pirandello*. 1973. Pp. 33-42
  Moestrup, Jørn, *The Structural Patterns in Pirandello's Work*. 1972. Pp. 142-
  45

Ciascuno a Suo Modo   *SEE*   Each in His Own Way

Come Prima, Meglio di Prima   *SEE*   As Before, Better than Before

Come Tu Mi Vuoi   *SEE*   As You Desire Me

Cosi è (Se Vi Pare)   *SEE*   Right You Are If You Think You Are

Diana and Tuda, 1926
  Moestrup, Jørn, *The Structural Patterns in Pirandello's Work*. 1972. Pp.
  218-23

The Doctor's Duty, 1913
  Moestrup, Jørn, *The Structural Patterns in Pirandello's Work*. 1972. Pp.
  136-38

Il Dovere del Medico   *SEE*   The Doctor's Duty

A Dream (But Perhaps It Isn't), 1931
  Moestrup, Jørn, *The Structural Patterns in Pirandello's Work*. 1972.
  Pp. 237-39

Each in His Own Way, 1924
  Dukore, Bernard F. and Daniel C. Gerould, "Explosions and Implosions;
  Avant-Garde Drama Between World Wars", *Educational Theatre Journal*
  (March 1969), 21:1-16
  Freedman, Morris, *The Moral Impulse; Modern Drama From Ibsen to the
  Present*. 1967. Pp. 74-88
  Matthaei, Renate, *Luigi Pirandello*. 1973. Pp. 129-42
  Moestrup, Jørn, *The Structural Patterns in Pirandello's Work*. 1972. Pp.
  208-13

Enrico IV   *SEE*   Henry IV

The Festival of Our Lord of the Ship, 1925
  Moestrup, Jørn, *The Structural Patterns in Pirandello's Work*. 1972. Pp.
  213-14

I Giganti della Montagna   *SEE*   The Mountain Giants

Il Giuoco Delle Parti   *SEE*   The Rules of the Game

Grafting, 1919
  Moestrup, Jørn, *The Structural Patterns in Pirandello's Work*. 1972. Pp. 162-
  63

Henry IV, 1922
  Bentley, Eric Russell, *Theatre of War; Comments on Thirty-Two Occasions*.
  1972. Pp. 32-44

Bidou, H., "Henry IV", *Journal des Débats*, 32 pt. 1:409, March 6, 1925 and 32 pt. 2:73-74, July 10, 1925

Birrell, F., "Henry IV", *Nation* (London), 35:379-80, June 21, 1924 and 35: 407-08, June 28, 1924 and 35:437, July 5, 1924

—————————— , "Henry IV", *Nation* (London), 37:399-400, June 27, 1925

Blasich, Corrado, " 'Enrico IV' di Luigi Pirandello", *Letture* (1972), 27:135-37

Brisson P., "Henry IV", *Les Annales Politiques et Littéraires*, 84:247-48, March 8, 1925

Brustein, Robert Sanford, *The Theatre of Revolt; An Approach to the Modern Drama.* 1964. Pp. 296-301

Cambon, Glauco, ed., *Pirandello; A Collection of Critical Essays.* 1967. Pp. 11-13

Clerici, Roger, "Un Capolavoro Drammatico: 'Enrico IV' ", *Realismo Lirico* (1967-68), 82-88:117-18

deCasseres, B., "Henry IV", *Arts and Decoration*, 20:32, March, 1924

DelMinistro, Manrizio, "Interpretazione di 'Enrico IV' ", *Rassegna della Letteratura Italiana* (1969), 73:16-26

Garzilli, Enrico, *Circle Without Center.* 1972. Pp. 75-88

Kellock, H., "Henry IV", *Freeman*, 8:544-45, Feb. 13, 1924

Kraft, Walter C., ed., *Proceedings: Pacific Northwest Conference on Foreign Languages.* 1974. Pp. 87-92

Lambert, J. W., "Henry IV", *Drama* (1974), 13:47-48

Lewis, Allan, *The Contemporary Theatre; The Significant Playwrights of Our Time.* 1962. Pp. 127-43

Lumley, Frederick, *New Trends in Twentieth Century Drama; A Survey Since Ibsen and Shaw.* 1967. Pp. 18-24

MacCarthy, Desmond, "Henry IV", *New Statesman*, 25:309-10, June 27, 1925

Matthaei, Renate, *Luigi Pirandello.* 1973. Pp. 102-17

Moestrup, Jørn, *The Structural Patterns in Pirandello's Work.* 1972. Pp. 187-95

Palmer, J., "Plays of Luigi Pirandello", *Nineteenth Century*, 97:897-909, June, 1925

Royde-Smith, N. G., "Henry IV", *Outlook* (London), 56:57, July 25, 1925

Seymour, A., "Henry IV", *Plays and Players* (April 1974), 21:36-39

Shipp, H., "Henry IV", *English Review*, 41:437-40, Sept., 1925

Teatro di Pirandello. Convegno di Studi ad Asti il 27 e 28 Maggio, 1967, in Casa d'Alfieri. 1968. Pp. 29-45

Time, 9:77, Feb. 16, 1968

Williams, Raymond, *Drama from Ibsen to Brecht.* 1968. Pp. 164-66

Wolfe, H., "Henry IV", *Spectator*, 132:954-55, June 14, 1924

Young, Stark, *Immortal Shadows; A Book of Dramatic Criticism.* 1948. Pp. 48-51

—————————— , "Henry IV", *New Republic*, 37:287, Feb. 6, 1924

If Not So; or, Other People's Reasons, 1915

Moestrup, Jørn, *The Structural Patterns in Pirandello's Work.* 1972. Pp. 131-34

The Imbecile, 1922

Moestrup, Jørn, *The Structural Patterns in Pirandello's Work.* 1972. Pp. 195-96

L'Imbecille   *SEE*   The Imbecile

l'Innestø   *SEE*   Grafting

Lazarus, 1929
  Moestrup, Jørn, *The Structural Patterns in Pirandello's Work*. 1972. Pp. 223-26

The Life I Gave You, 1923
  Antonucci, Giovanni, "Pirandello Recuperato: 'La Vita che ti Diedi'", *Studium* (1974), 70:127-29
  Lumley, Frederick, *New Trends in Twentieth Century Drama; A Survey Since Ibsen and Shaw*. 1967. Pp. 18-34
  Moestrup, Jørn, *The Structural Patterns in Pirandello's Work*. 1972. Pp. 202-04
  Roberts, R. E., "Life I Gave You", *New Statesman and Nation*, 1:425, May 16, 1931

Liola, 1916
  Bentley, Eric Russell, *In Search of Theatre*. Pp. 296-314
  Freedman, Morris, *The Moral Impulse; Modern Drama From Ibsen to the Present*. 1967. Pp. 74-88
  Moestrup, Jørn, *The Structural Patterns in Pirandello's Work*. 1972. Pp. 145-47 *Nuova Antologia*, 380:304-06, July 16, 1935
  Paolucci, Anne, "Theatre of Illusion; Pirandello's 'Liola' and Machiavelli's 'Mandragola'", *Comparative Literature Studies* (1972), 10:44-58

Lumíe di Sicilia   *SEE*   Sicilian Limes

Ma Non è Una Cosa Seria   *SEE*   But It Is Not a Serious Affair

Man, Beast and Virtue, 1919
  Lumley, Frederick, *New Trends in Twentieth Century Drama; A Survey Since Ibsen and Shaw*. 1967. Pp. 18-34

The Man With the Flower in His Mouth, 1923
  Licastro, Emanuele, "The Anti-Theatre in Pirandello: 'The Man With the Flower in His Mouth'", *Romance Notes* (1974), 15:513-15
  Loriggio, Franco, "Life and Death: Pirandello's 'Man with a Flower in His Mouth'", *Italian Quarterly* (1969), 47-48:151-60
  Moestrup, Jørn, *The Structural Patterns in Piranadello's Work*. 1972. Pp. 204-06
  Royde-Smith, N. G., "The Man with a Flower in His Mouth", *Outlook* (London), 57:393, June 5, 1926

La Morsa   *SEE*   The Vise

Mountain Giants, 1937
  Matthaei, Renate, *Luigi Pirandello*. 1973. Pp. 154-68
  Moestrup, Jørn, *The Structural Patterns in Pirandello's Work*. 1972. Pp. 248-52
  Nuova Antologia, 391:488-91, June 16, 1937
  Theatre Arts, 22:290-3, April, 1938

Mrs. Morli, One and Two, 1920
  Moestrup, Jørn, *The Structural Patterns in Pirandello's Work*. 1972. Pp. 175-77

Naked; To Clothe the Naked, 1922

Naked; To Clothe the Naked, 1922
  Birrell, F., "Naked", *Outlook* (London), 59:330, March 26, 1927
  Krutch, J. W., "Naked", *Nation*, 123:539-40, Nov. 24, 1926
  MacCarthy, Desmond, "Naked", *New Statesman*, 28:732-33, March 26, 1927
  Matthaei, Renate, *Luigi Pirandello*. 1973. Pp. 118-28
  Moestrup, Jørn, *The Structural Patterns in Pirandello's Work*. 1972. Pp. 196-201
  New Yorker, 43:155, May 6, 1967
  Time, 89:58, May 5, 1967

The New Colony, 1928
  Freedman, Morris, *The Moral Impulse; Modern Drama From Ibsen to the Present*. 1967. Pp. 74-88
  Living Age, 334:955-56, June, 1928
  Moestrup, Jørn, *The Structural Patterns in Pirandello's Work*. 1972. Pp. 226-28

No One Knows How, 1934
  Moestrup, Jørn, *The Structural Patterns in Pirandello's Work*. 1972. Pp. 245-48
  Nuova Antologia, 378:307-09, March 16, 1935 and 383:109-12, Jan. 1, 1936

Non Si Sa Come   *SEE*   No One Knows How

La Nuova Colonia   *SEE*   The New Colony

The Other Son, 1923
  Moestrup, Jørn, *The Structural Patterns in Pirandello's Work*. 1972. Pp. 206-08

Pensaci, Giacomino!   *SEE*   Think It Over, Giacomino!

Il Piacere dell 'Onesta   *SEE*   The Pleasure of Honesty

The Pleasure of Honesty, 1917
  Lumley, Frederick, *New Trends in Twentieth Century Drama; A Survey Since Ibsen and Shaw*. 1967. Pp. 18-34
  Matthaei, Renate, *Luigi Pirandello*. 1973. Pp. 68-75
  Moestrup, Jorn, *The Structural Patterns in Pirandello's Work*. 1972. Pp. 154-62

Questa Sera si Recita a Soggetto   *SEE*   Tonight We Improvise

Right You Are, If You Think You Are, 1917
  Bentley, Eric Russell, *In Search of Theatre*. Pp. 296-314
  _____ , *Theatre of War; Comments on Thirty-Two Occasions*. 1972. Pp. 22-31
  Brown, I., "And That's the Truth, If You Think It Is", *Saturday Review*, 140:334-35, Sept. 26, 1925
  Brustein, Robert Sanford, *The Theatre of Revolt; An Approach to the Modern Drama*. 1964. Pp. 293-96
  _____ , *The Third Theatre*. 1969. Pp. 155-57
  Cambon, Glauco, ed., *Pirandello; A Collection of Critical Essays*. 1967. Pp. 15-18
  Dombroski, Robert S., "Laudisi's Laughter and the Social Dimension of 'Right You Are (If You Thank So)", *Modern Drama* (1973), 16:337-46

Freedman, Morris, *The Moral Impulse; Modern Drama from Ibsen to the Present*. 1967. Pp. 74-88

Garzilli, Enrico, *Circles Without Center*. 1972. Pp. 75-88

Lumley, Frederick, *New Trends in Twentieth Century Drama; A Survey Since Ibsen and Shaw*. 1967. Pp. 18-34

Matthaei, Renate, *Luigi Pirandello*. 1973. Pp. 43-67

Moestrup, Jorn, *The Structural Patterns in Pirandello's Work*. 1972. Pp. 148-54

Nation, 203:651, Dec. 12, 1966

New Republic, 156:41-42, Jan. 7, 1967

New Yorker, 40:109, March 14, 1964

Newsweek, 68:96, Dec. 5, 1966

Outlook (London), 56:202, Sept. 26, 1925

Time, 88:84, Dec. 2, 1966

Turner, W. J., "And That's The Truth, If You Think It Is", *New Statesman*, 25:694-95, Oct. 3, 1925

Williams, Raymond, *Drama from Ibsen to Brecht*. 1968. Pp. 162-64

———————————— , *Modern Tragedy*. 1966. Pp. 146-49

Wright, Edward A. and Lenthiel H. Downs, *A Primer for Playgoers*. 1969. Pp. 103-07 and 298-300

Young, Stark, *Immortal Shadows; A Book of Dramatic Criticism*. 1948. Pp. 84-87

———————————— , "Right You Are, If You Think You Are", *New Republic*, 50: 141-42, March 23, 1927

The Rules of the Game, 1918
Moestrup, Jorn, *The Structural Patterns in Pirandello's Work*. 1972. Pp. 164-68

New Yorker, 36:43-44, Dec. 31, 1960

Theatre Arts, 45:68, March, 1961

Sagra del Signore della Nave   SEE   The Festival of Our Lord of the Ship

Se Non Cosi, o La Ragione Degli Altri   SEE   If Not So; or, Other People's Reasons

Sei Personaggi in Cerca d'Autore   SEE   Six Characters in Search of an Author

Sicilian Limes, 1910
Moestrup, Jorn, *The Structural Patterns in Pirandello's Work*. 1972. Pp. 134-36

La Signora Morli, Una e Due   SEE   Mrs. Morli, One and Two

Six Characters in Search of an Author, 1921
America, 94:384, Dec. 31, 1955

Arts and Decoration, 35:46, June, 1931

Bentley, Eric, "Father's Day; In Search of Six Characters in Search of an Author", *TDR* (1968), 13:57-72

———————————— , *Theatre of War; Comments on Thirty-two Occasions*. 1972. Pp. 45-63

Beraud, H., "Six Characters in Search of an Author", *Mercure de France*, 163:754-57, May 1, 1923

Brisson, P., "Six Characters in Search of an Author", *Les Annales Politiques et Littéraires*, 80:459-60, May 6, 1923

Brustein, Robert Sanford, *The Theatre of Revolt; An Approach to the Modern Drama*. 1964. Pp. 309-15

Cambon, Glauco, ed., *Pirandello; A Collection of Critical Essays*. 1967. Pp. 35-42 and Pp. 67-71

Casalbore, Mario, "I 'Sei Personaggi' Sono Stati Traditi da Buazzelli?", *Gazzetta del Mezzogiorno* (March 15, 1972), Pp. 3

Catholic World, 182:385-86, Feb., 1956

Cole, Toby, ed., *Playwrights on Playwriting; The Meaning and Making of Modern Drama from Ibsen to Ionesco*. 1960. Pp. 205-17

Commonweal, 63:483-84, Feb. 10, 1956 and 78:105-6, April 19, 1963

Crawford, J., "Six Characters in Search of an Author", *Drama*, 13:130-1, Jan., 1923

Epstein, Leslie, "Beyond the Baroque; The Role of the Audience in the Modern Theater", *Tri-Quarterly* (Spr. 1968), #12:213-24

Freedman, Morris, *The Moral Impulse; Modern Drama from Ibsen to the Present*. 1967. Pp. 74-88

Garzilli, Enrico, *Circles Without Centers*. 1972. Pp. 75-88

Gaskell, Ronald, *Drama and Reality; The European Theatre since Ibsen*. 1972. Pp. 117-27

Gassner, John, *Theatre at the Crossroads; Plays and Playwrights of the Mid-century American Stage*. 1960. Pp. 242-45

——————————— , *Theatre in Our Time; A Survey of the Men, Materials and Movements in the Modern Theatre*. 1954. Pp. 182-206

Gilliatt, Penelope, *Unholy Fools; Wits, Comics, Disturbers of the Peace*. 1973. Pp. 62-64

Gilman, Richard, *Common and Uncommon Masks; Writings on the Theatre, 1961-70*. 1971. Pp. 81-83

Giudice, G., "L'Ambiguita Nei 'Sei Personaggi in Cerca d'Autori' ", *Paragone* (Firenze), 12:34-35, 1961

Gordon, Jan B., " 'Sei Personaggi in Cerca d'Autore': Myth, Ritual, and Pirandello's Anti-Symbolist Theatre", *Forum Italicum* (1972), 6:333-55

Hudson, L. A., *Life and the Theatre*. 1954. Pp. 34-38

Illiano, Antonio, "Pirandello's 'Six Characters in Search of an Author': A Comedy in the Making", *Italica* (1967), 44:1-12

Kennedy, Andrew K., "Six Characters: Pirandello's Last Tape", *Modern Drama* (1969), 12:1-9

Kernan, Alvin B., "Truth and Dramatic Mode in the Modern Theater: Chekhov, Pirandello and Williams", *Modern Drama* (1958), 1:101-14

Kligerman, C. K., "A Psychoanalytic Study of Pirandello's 'Six Characters in Search of an Author' ", *Journal of American Psychoanalysis Association*, 10:731-44, 1962

Kraft, Walter C., ed., *Proceedings; Pacific Northwest Conference on Foreign Languages*. 1973. Pp. 163-68

Lumley, Frederick, *New Trends in Twentieth Century Drama; A Survey Since Ibsen and Shaw*. 1967. Pp. 18-34

MacCarthy, Desmond, *Theatre*, 1955. Pp. 94-97

——————————— , "Six Characters in Search of an Author", *New Statesman*, 25:282-3, Jan. 20, 1925

Matthaei, Renate, *Luigi Pirandello*. 1973. Pp. 76-101

Meynaud-Jeuland, Maryse, "A Propos des Didiscalies des 'Sei Personaggi in Cerca d'Autore' ", *Revue des Etudes Italiennes* (1968), 14:72-87

Moestrup, Jorn, *The Structural Patterns in Pirandello's Work.* 1972. Pp. 177-87
Montani, F., "La Tragedia dei 'Sei Personaggi'", *Studium*, 55:320-31, 1959
Nation, 181:582, Dec. 31, 1955 and 196:334, April 20, 1963
Needler, Howard I., "On the Art of Pirandello; Theory and Praxis", *Texas Studies in Literature and Language* (1974), 15:735-58
New Republic, 148:30, March 30, 1963
New Yorker, 31:46-47, Dec. 24, 1955 and 39:74-5, March 23, 1963
Newberry, Wilma, *The Pirandellian Mode in Spanish Literature from Cervantes to Sartre.* 1973. Pp. 59-72
Newsweek, 46:53, Dec. 26, 1955
Nicol, Bernard de Bear, ed., *Varieties of Dramatic Experience.* 1969. Pp. 193-203
Ongley, L., "Pirandello Confesses—Why and How He Wrote 'Six Characters in Search of an Author'", *Virginia Quarterly Review*, 1:36-52, April, 1925
Palmer, J., "Plays of Luigi Pirandello", *Nineteenth Century*, 97:897-909, June, 1925
Saturday Review, 38:25, Dec. 31, 1955 and 46:28, March 23, 1963
Shipp, H., "Six Characters in Search of an Author", *English Review*, 47:113-14, July, 1928
Sogliuzzo, A. Richard, "The Uses of the Mask in 'The Great God Brown' and 'Six Characters in Search of an Author'", *Educational Theatre Journal* (1966), 18:224-29
Sypher, W., *Rococo to Cubism in Art and Literature.* 1960. Pp. 289-94
Taylor, William E., ed., *Modern American Drama; Essays in Criticism.* 1968. Pp. 29-37
Theatre Arts, 15:450-51, June, 1931 and 40:75, Feb., 1956 and 47:13-14, March, 1963
Time, 66:30, Dec. 26, 1955
Williams, Raymond, *Drama from Ibsen to Brecht.* 1968. Pp. 157-59
_____ , *Modern Tragedy.* 1966. Pp. 149-52
Wyatt, E., "Six Characters in Search of an Author", *Catholic World*, 116:505-07, Jan., 1923
Young, Stark, "Six Characters in Search of an Author", *New Republic*, 32: 335-36, Nov. 22, 1922 and 33:97, Dec. 20, 1922

Sogno (Ma Forse No)   *SEE*   A Dream (But Perhaps It Isn't)

Stasera Si Recita a Soggetto   *SEE*   Tonight We Improvise

Think It Over, Giacomino!, 1916
Moestrup, Jorn, *The Structural Patterns in Pirandello's Work.* 1972. Pp. 140-42

To Find Oneself, 1932
Horvath, O., "Trovarsi", *Plays and Players* (June 1974), 21:53

Tonight We Improvise, 1930
Les Annales Politiques et Littéraires, 105:135-37, Feb. 10, 1935
Brustein, Robert Sanford, *Seasons of Discontent; Dramatic Opinions 1959-1965.* 1965. Pp. 30-33
Keeley, Edmund and Peter A. Bien, eds., *Modern Greek Writers; Solomos, Calvos, Matesis, Palamas, Cavafy, Kazantzakis, Serferis, Elytis.* 1972. Pp. 191-215

Lumley, Frederick, *New Trends in Twentieth Century Drama; A Survey Since Ibsen and Shaw*. 1967. Pp. 18-34

Matthaei, Renate, *Luigi Pirandello*. 1973. Pp. 143-53

Moestrup, Jorn, *The Structural Patterns in Pirandello's Work*. 1972. Pp. 232-36

New Republic, 71:44-46, May 25, 1932 and 141:22-23, Dec. 7, 1959

New Yorker, 35:122-24, Nov. 14, 1959

Nuova Antologia, 378:305-07, March 16, 1935

Revue des Deux Mondes, s8 25:703-05, Feb. 1, 1935

Seymour, A., "Tonight We Improvise", *Plays and Players* (July 1974), 21:32-33

Trovarsi *SEE* To Find Oneself

Tutto per Bene *SEE* All for the Best

L'Uomo dal Fiore in Bocca *SEE* The Man with the Flower in His Mouth

L'Uomo, La Bestia e La Virtu *SEE* Man, Beast, and Virtue

The Vise, 1910

Moestrup, Jorn, *The Structural Patterns in Pirandello's Work*. 1972. Pp. 130-31

Vestire Gli Egnudi *SEE* Naked, or To Clothe the Naked

La Vita che ti Diedi *SEE* The Life I Gave You

TITUS MACCIUS PLAUTUS

Amphitryon, 186 B.C.

Barnes, H. E., "The Case of Sosia Versus Sosia", *Classical Journal*, 53:19-24, 1957

Bondurant, A. L., "'Amphitruo' of Plautus, Molière's 'Amphitryon' and the 'Amphitryon' of Dryden", *Sewanee Review*, 33:455-68, 1925

Dorey, T. A. and Donald Reynold Dudley, ed., *Roman Drama*. 1965. Pp. 87-122

Fantham, Elaine, "Towards a Dramatic Reconstruction of the Fourth Act of Plautus' 'Amphitryon'", *Philologus. Zeitschrift für das Klassische Altertum* (1973), 117:197-214

Fernandez, R. M. R., "O 'Amphitrio' de Plauto", *Revista da Faculdade de Letras de Lisboa*, 3:146-67, 1959

Galinsky, G. K., "Scipionic Themes in Plautus' 'Amphitruo'", *Transactions and Proceedings of the American Philological Association* (1966), 97:203-35

Hall, F. W., "Repetitions and Obsessions in Plautus", *Classical Quarterly*, 20:20-26, 1926

Harsh, Philip Whaley, *A Handbook of Classical Drama*. 1944. Pp. 338-41

Kent, Roland G., "Variety and Monotony in Plautine Plots", *Philological Quarterly*, 2:164-72, 1923

Levin, Richard, *The Multiple Plot in English Renaissance Drama*. 1971. Pp. 236-39

Little, Alan McN., "Plautus and the Popular Drama", *Harvard Studies in Classical Philology*, 49:205-28, 1938

Prescott, H. W., "'Amphitruo' of Plautus", *Classical Philology*, 8:14-22, 1913

Stewart, Z., "The 'Amphitruo' of Plautus and Euripides' 'Bacchae'", *Transactions and Proceedings of the American Philological Association*, 89:348-73, 1958
——————— , "God Nocturnus in Plautus' 'Amphitruo'", *Journal of Roman Studies*, 50:37-43, 1960

Asinaria, 207 B.C.
Harsh, Philip Whaley, *A Handbook of Classical Drama*. 1944. Pp. 342-44
Hough, J. N., "The Structure of the 'Asinaria'", *American Journal of Philology*, 58:19-37, 1937
Kent, Roland G., "Variety and Monotony in Plautine Plots", *Philological Quarterly*, 2:164-72, 1923

Aulularia, 194 B.C.
Harsh, Philip Whaley, *A Handbook of Classical Drama*. 1944. Pp. 342-44
Kent, Roland G., "Variety and Monotony in Plautine Plots", *Philological Quarterly*, 2:164-72, 1923
Stace, C., "Four Notes on Plautus' 'Aularia'", *Classical Philology* (1975), 70:41-42

Bacchides, 189 B.C.
Bader, Bernd, "Der Verlorene Aufang der Plautinischen 'Bacchides'", *Rheinisches Museum für Philologie* (1970), n. s. 113:304-23
Harsh, Philip Whaley, *A Handbook of Classical Drama*. 1944. Pp. 345-46

Captivi, 188 B.C.
Harsh, Philip Whaley, *A Handbook of Classical Drama*. 1944. Pp. 346-50
Kent, Roland G., "Variety and Monotony in Plautine Plots", *Philological Quarterly*, 2:164-72, 1923

The Carthaginian, 191 B.C.
Harsh, Philip Whaley, *A Handbook of Classical Drama*. 1944. Pp. 364
Yale Classical Studies; ed. for the Dept. of Classics by Christopher M. Dawson and Thomas Cole. Vol. 21. 1969. Pp. 95-123

Casina, 184 B.C.
Levin, Richard, *The Multiple Plot in English Renaissance Drama*. 1971. Pp. 235-38
MacCary, W. T., "Patterns of Myth, Ritual and Comedy in Plautus' 'Casina'", *Texas Studies in Literature and Language* (1974), 15,v:881-89
——————— , "The Significance of a Comic Pattern in Plautus and Beaumarchais", *Modern Language Notes* (1973), 88:1262-87

Curculio, 193 B.C.
Conrad, Clinton C., "The Role of the Cook in Plautus' 'Curculio'", *Classical Philology*, 13:389-400, 1918
Fantham, E., "The 'Curculio' of Plautus: An Illustration of Plautine Methods in Adaptation", *Classical Quarterly* (1965), 15:84-100
Harsh, Philip Whaley, *A Handbook of Classical Drama*. 1944. Pp. 353-54
Kent, Roland G., "Variety and Monotony in Plautine Plots", *Philological Quarterly*, 2:164-72, 1923

Epidicus, 190 B.C.
Duckworth, G. E., "Cretics in the First Scene of Plautus' 'Epidicus'", *Classical Philology*, 34:245-51, 1939

Hall, F. W., "Repetitions and Obsessions in Plautus", 1 *Classical Quarterly*, 20:20-26, 1926

Harsh, Philip Whaley, *A Handbook of Classical Drama*. 1944. Pp. 354-55

Kent, Roland G., "Variety and Monotony in Plautine Plots", *Philological Quarterly*, 2:164-72, 1923

Menaechmi, 186 B. C.

Connely, W., "When Plautus is Greater than Shakespeare; Imprints of 'Menaechmi' on 'Comedy of Errors' ", *Classical Journal*, 19:303-05, 1924, and 20:401-07, 1925

Harsh, Philip Whaley, *A Handbook of Classical Drama*. 1944. Pp. 355-57

Levin, Harry, *Refractions; Essays in Comparative Literature*. 1966. Pp. 128-50

Little, Alan McN., "Plautus and the Popular Drama", *Harvard Studies in Classical Philology*, 49:205-28, 1938

Yale Classical Studies, ed. for the Dept. of Classics by Christopher M. Dawson and Thomas Cole. Vol. 21. 1969. Pp. 75-93

Miles Gloriosus, 205 B.C.

Beare, W., "Plautus' 'Miles Gloriosus' ", *Classical Review*, 41:10-11, 1927

Hall, F. W., "On Plautus, 'Miles Gloriosus' ", *Classical Quarterly*, 17:100-02, 1923

——————— , "Repetitions and Obsessions in Plautus", *Classical Quarterly*, 20:20-26, 1926

Harsh, Philip Whaley, *A Handbook of Classical Drama*. 1944. Pp. 359-60

Haywood, R. M., "On the Unity of the 'Miles Gloriosus' ", *American Journal of Philology*, 65: 382-86, 1944

Kent, Roland G., "Variety and Monotony in Plautine Plots", *Philological Quarterly*, 2:164-72, 1923

Mostellaria, 193 B.C.

Kent, Roland G., "Variety and Monotony in Plautine Plots", *Philological Quarterly*, 2:164-72, 1923

Harsh, Philip Whaley, *A Handbook of Classical Drama*. 1944. Pp. 361-62

Little, Alan McN., "Plautus and the Popular Drama", *Harvard Studies in Classical Philology*, 49:205-28, 1938

Sturtevant, E. H., "Notes on Plautus' 'Mostellaria' ", *American Journal of Philology*, 48:344-49, 1927

Persa, 186 B.C.

Falk, S., "Plautus' 'Persa' and Middleton's "A Trick to Catch the Old One' ", *Modern Language Notes*, 66:19-21, 1951

Harsh, Philip Whaley, *A Handbook of Classical Drama*. 1944. Pp. 363-64

Poenulus SEE The Carthaginian

Pseudolus, 2nd cent. B.C.

DeWitt, N. J., " 'Pseudolus' and Hannibal's Elephant", *Classical Philology*, 36:189-90, 1941

Fuchs, H., "Nachlese im 'Pseudolus' ", *Philologus*, 89:258-60, 1934

Harsh, Philip Whaley, *A Handbook of Classical Drama*. 1944. Pp. 364

Jachmann, G., "Zum 'Pseudolus' des Plautus", *Philologus*, 88:443-56, 1933

Kent, Roland G., "Variety and Monotony in Plautine Plots", *Philological Quarterly*, 2:164-72, 1923

Skutsch, O., "Notes on 'Pseudolus' of Plautus", *Classical Review*, 56:66-68, 1942

Rudens, 189 B.C.
Beare, W., "Plautus and the 'Fabula Atellana'", *Classical Review*, 44:165-68, 1930
Coulter, C. C., "Composition of the 'Rudens' of Plautus", *Classical Philology*, 8:57-64, 1913
Fraenkel, E., "Stars in the Prologue of the 'Rudens'", *Classical Quarterly*, 36:10-14, 1942
Harsh, Philip Whaley, *A Handbook of Classical Drama*. 1944. Pp. 365
Highet, G., "Shipwrecked Slaves in Plautus' 'Rudens'", *American Journal of Philology*, 63:462-66, 1942
Kent, Roland G., "Variety and Monotony in Plautine Plots", *Philological Quarterly*, 2:164-72, 1923
Leach, E. W., "Plautus' 'Rudens': Venus Born from a Shell", *Texas Studies in Literature and Language* (1974), 15,v:915-31
Olson, Elder, *The Theory of Comedy*. 1968. Pp. 77-79
Skutsch, Otto, "Plautus: 'Rudens'", *Classical Review* n. s. (Mar. 1967), 17:11-12

Stichus, 200 B.C.
Levin, Richard, *The Multiple Plot in English Renaissance Drama*. 1971. Pp. 239-45

Trinummus, 187 B.C.
Frank, T., "Some Political Allusions in Plautus' 'Trinummus'", *American Journal of Philology*, 53:152-56, 1932
Green, W. M., "Greek and Roman Law in the 'Trinummus' of Plautus", *Classical Philology*, 24:183-92, 1929
Hall, F. W., "Repetitions and Obsessions in Plautus", *Classical Quarterly*, 20:20-26, 1926
Harsh, Philip Whaley, *A Handbook of Classical Drama*. 1944. Pp. 370-71
Segal, E., "Purpose of the 'Trinummus'", *American Journal of Philology* (1974), 95:252-64

Truculentus, 186 B.C.
Harsh, Philip Whaley, *A Handbook of Classical Drama*. 1944. Pp. 372-74

ALEKSANDAR POPOVIC

Deadly Motorism, 1967
Czerwinski, E. J., "Aleksandar Popovic and Pop-Theater; Beyond the Absurd", *Comparative Drama* (Fall 1969), 3:168-75

Druga Vrata Levo   *SEE*   Second Door Left

The Goldwinged Duck, 1968
Czerwinski, E. J., "Aleksandar Popovic and Pop-Theater; Beyond the Absurd", *Comparative Drama* (Fall 1969), 3:168-75

Hats Off!, 1968
Czerwinski, E. J., "Aleksandar Popovic and Pop-Theater; Beyond the Absurd", *Comparative Drama* (Fall 1969), 3:168-75

Kape Dole *SEE* Hats Off!

Second Door Left, 1969
   Czerwinski, E. J., "Aleksandar Popovic and Pop-Theater; Beyond the
     Absurd", *Comparative Drama* (Fall 1969), 3:168-75
   ——————— , "Alexander Popovic: Sound Images, Metaphor-Scenes, and
   Audience Involvement", *Modern Drama* (1972), 15:449-56

Smrtonosna Motoristika *SEE* Deady Motorism

Utva Ptica Zlatorkrila *SEE* The Goldwinged Duck

JOHN BOYNTON PRIESTLEY

Bees on the Boat Deck, 1936
   Evans, Fareth Lloyd, *J. B. Priestley, the Dramatist.* 1964. Pp. 155-56
   Spectator, 156:879, March 15, 1936

Cornelius, 1935
   Dukes, A., 'Cornelius", *Theatre Arts*, 19:414, June, 1935
   London Mercury, 32:55, May, 1935
   Spectator, 154:529, March 29, 1935

Dangerous Corner, 1932
   Catholic World, 136:334-35, Dec., 1932 and 137:724, Sept., 1933
   Evans, Fareth Lloyd, *J. B. Priestley, the Dramatist.* 1964. Pp. 72-91
   Fleming, P., "Dangerous Corner", *Spectator*, 148:760-61, May 28, 1932
   Nathan, George Jean, *Passing Judgments.* 1935. Pp. 140-76
   New Statesman and Nation, 16:688, Oct. 29, 1938
   Skloot, Robert, "The Time Plays of John Boynton Priestley", *Quarterly
     Journal of Speech* (1970), 56:426-31
   Theatre Arts, 16:712-13, Sept., 1932 and 17:22-23, Jan., 1933
   Wakefield, G., "Dangerous Corner, *Saturday Review*, 153:561, June 4, 1932

Desert Highway, 1943
   New Statesman and Nation, 27:172, March 11, 1944
   Theatre Arts, 28:340, June, 1944

Eden End, 1934
   Commonweal, 23:48, Nov. 8, 1935
   Curtis, A., "Eden End", *Plays and Players* (1974), 21:34-35
   Lambert, J. W., "Eden End", *Drama* (1974), 113:51-52
   London Mercury, 30:576-77, Oct., 1934
   Nation, 141:547-48, Nov. 6, 1935
   Spectator, 153:398, Sept. 21, 1934
   Theatre Arts, 19:894, Dec., 1935

Ever Since Paradise, 1947
   Evans, Fareth Lloyd, *J. B. Priestley, the Dramatist.* 1964. Pp. 153-54
   New Statesman and Nation, 33:432, June 14, 1947
   Spectator, 178:684, June 13, 1947
   Theatre Arts, 31:37, Oct., 1947

The Glass Cage, 1957
   New Statesman, 53:570, May 4, 1957

Spectator, 198:620, May 10, 1957

Goodnight, Children, 1942
New Statesman and Nation, 23:108, Feb. 14, 1942
Spectator, 168:154, Feb. 13, 1942

Home is Tomorrow, 1948
Illustrated London News, 213:588, Nov. 20, 1948
Spectator, 181:629, Nov. 12, 1948

I Have Been Here Before, 1937
Commonweal, 29:21, Oct. 28, 1938
Evans, Fareth Lloyd, *J. B. Priestley, the Dramatist*. 1964. Pp. 103-21
London Mercury, 37:55, Nov., 1937
New Statesman and Nation, 14:486-87, Oct. 2, 1937
Skloot, Robert, "The Time Plays of John Boynton Priestley", *Quarterly Journal of Speech* (1970), 56:426-31
Spectator, 159:547, Oct. 1, 1937
Theatre Arts, 22:858, Dec., 1938
Time, 32:56, Oct. 24, 1938

An Inspector Calls, 1946
Catholic World, 166:265, Dec., 1947
Commonweal, 47:119, Nov. 14, 1947
Forum, 109:25, Jan., 1948
Lumley, Frederick, *New Trends in Twentieth Century Drama; A Survey Since Ibsen and Shaw*. 1967. Pp. 296-98
McCarthy, Mary Therese, *Sights and Spectacles, 1937-1956*. 1956. Pp. 121-30
Nathan, George Jean, *Theatre Book of the Year, 1947-48*. Pp. 113-15
New Republic, 117:35, Nov. 10, 1947
New Yorker, 23:47-48, Nov. 1, 1947
Newsweek, 30:76, Nov. 3, 1947
Oetting, Wilhelm, "J. B. Priestley; 'An Inspector Calls': Eine Erörterung des Schauspielschlusses", *Die Neueren Sprachen* (1966), 15:535-59
School and Society, 66:422-23, Nov. 29, 1947
Spectator, 177:392, Oct. 18, 1946
Theatre Arts, 31:51, Jan., 1947 and 31:61, Dec., 1947 and 32:11, Jan., 1948
Time, 50:71, Nov. 3, 1947

Johnson Over Jordan, 1939
Evans, Fareth Lloyd, *J. B. Priestley, the Dramatist*. 1964. Pp. 35-37 and 122-36
New Statesman and Nation, 17:322, March 4, 1939
Spectator, 162:349, March 3, 1939
Theatre Arts, 23:331-32, May, 1939

Laburnum Grove, 1933
Commonweal, 21:403, Feb. 1, 1935
Galitzine, N., "Laburnum Grove", *Saturday Review*, 156:607, Dec. 9, 1932
MacCarthy, Desmond, "Laburnum Grove", *New Statesman and Nation*, 6:734, Dec. 9, 1933
New Republic, 81:336, June 20, 1935
Verschoyle, D., "Laburnum Grove", *Spectator*, 151:847, Dec. 8, 1933

Linden Tree, 1947
Illustrated London News, 211:306, Sept. 13, 1947

Lumley, Frederick, *New Trends in Twentieth Century Drama; A Survey Since Ibsen and Shaw*. 1967. Pp. 296-98
Nathan, George Jean, *Theatre Book of the Year, 1947-48*. Pp. 311-14
New Republic, 118:28, March 15, 1948
New Statesman and Nation, 34:149, Aug. 23, 1947
New Yorker, 24:48, March 13, 1948
Newsweek, 31:78, March 15, 1948
Spectator, 179:237, Aug. 22, 1947
Theatre Arts, 31:44, 46, Nov., 1947
Time, 51:65, March 15, 1948

The Long Mirror, 1945
Spectator, 164:328, March 8, 1940 and 176:399, April 19, 1946

Music At Night, 1939
Evans, Fareth Lloyd, *J. B. Priestley, the Dramatist*. 1964. Pp. 136-47
London Mercury, 38:455-56, Sept., 1938
New Statesman and Nation, 16:251, Aug. 13, 1938 and 18:519, Oct. 14, 1939
Theatre Arts, 23:866, Dec., 1939

People at Sea, 1937
Spectator, 159:992, Dec. 3, 1937

Roundabout, 1933
Spectator, 154:780, May 10, 1935

The Scandalous Affair of Mr. Kettle and Mrs. Moon, 1955
New Statesman, 50:296, Sept. 10, 1955
Spectator, 195:332, Sept. 9, 1955

Summer Day's Dream, 1949
Illustrated London News, 215:472, Sept. 24, 1949
New Statesman and Nation, 38:299, Sept. 17, 1949
New Yorker, 25:80, Oct. 1, 1949
Spectator, 183:353, Sept. 16, 1949

They Came To a City, 1943
American Mercury, 57:742-45, Dec., 1943
Lumley, Frederick, *New Trends in Twentieth Century Drama; A Survey Since Ibsen and Shaw*. 1967. Pp. 296-98
New Statesman and Nation, 25:287-88, May 1, 1943
Spectator, 170:406, April 30, 1943
Theatre Arts, 27:403-04, July, 1943

Time and the Conways, 1937
Catholic World, 146:598, Feb., 1938
Commonweal, 27:358, Jan. 21, 1938
Evans, Fareth Lloyd, *J. B. Priestley, the Dramatist*. 1964. Pp. 91-103
London Mercury, 36:555, Oct., 1937
New Republic, 93:310, Jan. 19, 1938
New Statesman and Nation, 14:405-07, Sept. 18, 1937
Skloot, Robert, "The Time Plays of John Boynton Priestley", *Quarterly Journal of Speech* (1970), 56:426-31
Spectator, 159:380, Sept. 3, 1937
Theatre Arts, 21:847, Nov., 1937 and 22:97-98, Feb., 1938
Time, 31:61, Jan. 17, 1938

When We Are Married, 1938
  Commonweal, 31:245, Jan. 5, 1940
  Evans, Fareth Lloyd, *J. B. Priestley, the Dramatist*. 1964. Pp. 167-68
  London Mercury, 39:59, Nov., 1938
  New Statesman and Nation, 16:609, Oct. 22, 1938
  Spectator, 161:651, Oct. 21, 1938
  Theatre Arts, 24:168-69, March, 1940

JOHN BOYNTON PRIESTLEY AND J. H. HAWKES

Dragon's Mouth, 1952
  Catholic World, 182:311, Jan., 1956
  New Statesman and Nation, 43:612, May 24, 1952 and 43:647, May 31, 1952

White Countess, 1954
  New Statesman and Nation, 47:434, April 3, 1954
  Twentieth Century, 156:175-79, Aug., 1954

JOHN BOYNTON PRIESTLEY AND EDWARD KNOBLOCK

Good Companions, 1931
  Catholic World, 134:208-09, Nov., 1931
  Jennings, R., "Good Companions", *Spectator*, 146:818-19, May 23, 1931
  Theatre Arts, 15:982-83, Dec., 1931
  Wakefield, G., "Good Companions", *Saturday Review*, 151:794, May 30, 1931

PHILIPPE QUINAULT

SEE

MOLIERE, PIERRE CORNEILLE AND PHILIPPE QUINAULT

JEAN BAPTISTE RACINE

Alexander the Great, 1665
  Adams, Henry Hitch and Hathaway, Baxter, eds., *Dramatic Essays of the Neo-Classic Age*. 1950. Pp. 102-10
  Branan, Alvord G., "The Prince in Racinian Tragedy: Bossuetian and Machiavellian Politics", *Dissertation Abstracts International* (1972), 33:1160A
  Brée, Germaine, "Le Thème de la Violence dans le Monde Tragique Racine", *Romanic Review*, 38:216-25, 1947
  Elledge, Scott and Schier, Ronald Stephen, eds., *The Continental Model; Selected French Critical Essays of the 17th Century in English Translation*. 1960. Pp. 132-39
  Gutwirth, Marcel, "D' 'Alexandré le Grand' à 'Mithradate': Persistance d'une Velleite Racinienne", *Modern Language Notes* (1969), 84:599-604
  Hartle, Robert W., "LeBrun's 'Histoire d'Alexandre' and Racine's 'Alexandre le Grand' ", *Romanic Review*, 48:90-103, 1957
  Knapp, Bettina L., *Jean Racine; Mythos and Renewal in Modern Theater*. 1971. Pp. 46-63
  Mélanges d'Histoire Littéraire (XVI-XVII⁹ Siècle): Offerts à Raymond Lebeque par Ses Collegues, Ses Eleves et Ses Amis. 1969. Pp. 259-68
  Turnell, Martin, *Jean Racine, Dramatist*. 1972. Pp. 41-52

Alexandre la Grand   *SEE*   Alexander the Great

Andromaque, 1667

Branan, Alvord G., "The Prince in Racinian Tragedy; Bossuetian and Machiavellian Politics", *Dissertation Abstracts International* (1972), 33:1160A

Brée, Germaine, "Le Thème de la Violence dans le Monde Tragique Racine", *Romanic Review*, 38:216-25, 1947

"Comparison des Trois Andromaques", *Le Correspondent*, 310:659-81, March 10, 1928

Dagley, Cynthia R., "Racine's 'Andromaque'; A Study of Source", *Modern Language Association. Publications* (PMLA), 52:80-99, 1937

Delacroix, Maurice, "Le Sacré dans les Tragédies Profane de Racine: 'Andromaque'", *Cahiers Raciniens* (1967), 22:13-42

Descotes, Maurice, *Les Grands Rôles du Théâtre de Jean Racine*. 1957. Pp. 1-52

Edwards, Michael, "Racinian Tragedy", *Critical Quarterly* (1971), 13:329-48

France, Peter, "Oreste and Orestes", *French Studies* (April 1969), 23:131-37

Gerard, Albert, "'Andromaque': Une Tragi-Comédie", *Revue Generale Belge* (1968), 103 #1:27-37

Hall, H. Gaston, "Pastoral, Epic and Dynastic Denouement in Racine's 'Andromaque'", *Modern Language Review* (1974), 69:64-78

Han, Pierre, "Racine's Use of the Concept of Myth in 'Andromaque'", *Romance Notes* (1969), 11:339-43

Jacobs, Carolyn L., "Irony in the Tragedies of Racine", *Dissertation Abstracts International* (1974), 35:2271A

Jansen, Steen, "Sur les Rôles des Personnages dans 'Andromaque'", *Orbis Litterarum* (1967), 22:77-87

_____ , "L'Unité d'Action dans 'Andromaquc' et dans 'Lorenzaccio'", *Revue Romane* (1968), 3:16-29 and 116-35

Jausz, H. R., "Racines 'Andromaque' und Anouilhs 'Antigone'", *Die Neueren Sprachen*, #9:428-44, 1960

Knapp, Bettina L., *Jean Racine; Mythos and Renewal in Modern Theater*. 1971. Pp. 64-84

Lockert, Lacy, *Studies in French Classical Tragedy*. 1958. Pp. 295-303

Macchia, Giovanni, "Note su 'Andromaque' e 'Britannicus'", *Galleria*, 13: 65-75, 1963

Monaco, Marion, "Racine and the Problem of Suicide", *Modern Language Association. Publications* (PMLA), 70:441-54, 1955

Patterson, Charles D., "Dramatic Aspects of Versification in Racine", *Dissertation Abstracts International* (1973), 34:1289A

Schweitzer, Jerome W., "Racine's 'Andromaque'; Oreste, Slayer of Pyrrhus?" *Romance Notes* (Univ. of North Carolina), 3:37-39, 1961

Seznec, Alain, "The Uses of 'Enfin' in Racine's 'Andromaque'", *French Review* (1972), 45 (Special Issue):61-64

Studies in French Language, Literature and History Presented to R. L. Graeme Ritchie. 1949. Pp. 107-18

Tobin, Ronald W., "Racine and Seneca", *University of North Carolina Studies in Romance Language and Literature* (1971), 96:91-112

Turnell, Martin, *Classical Moment: Studies of Corneille, Moliere, and Racine*. 1947. Pp. 183-87

_____ , *Jean Racine, Dramatist*. 1972. Pp. 53-90

Vossler, Karl, *Jean Racine.* 1972. Pp. 49-54
Walkley, Arthur Bingham, *Drama and Life.* 1907. Pp. 274-78
Wells, B. W., "Study of Racine's 'Andromaque'", *Sewanee Review*, 6:51-73, Jan., 1898
Wheatley, K. E. "Andromaque as the 'Distrest Mother'", *Romanic Review*, 39:3-21, 1948

Athalie, 1691
Abel, Lionel, *Metatheatre; A New View of Dramatic Form.* 1963. Pp. 11-38
Boerebach, B. M., "Racine en Zéjn Tyd", *Katholiek Cultureel Tydschrift. Streven*, 6:224-31, 1952
Bouffard, Odoric, O. F. M., "'Athalie, Tragédie Biblique", *Culture*, 22:387-91, 1961
Chedozeau, B., "Le Tragique d'Athalie", *Revue d'Histoire Littéraire de la France* (1967), 67:494-501
Chicoteau, Marcel, "'Athalie' ou la Résurrection d'un Enfant", *Bulletin de l'Association Guillaume Budé* (1967), Pp. 307-11
Descotes, Maurice, *Les Grands Rôles du Théâtre de Jean Racine.* 1957. Pp. 173-91
Edwards, Michael, "Racinian Tragedy", *Critical Quarterly* (1971), 13:329-48
Fonsny, Joseph, "'Athalie' et le Dieu des Juifs", *Cahiers Raciniens* (1968), 23:10-30
Geoffroy-Dechaume, R., "Racine et la Musique", *Cahiers Raciniens* (1967), 22:43-50
Harth, Erica, "The Tragic Moment in 'Athalie'", *Modern Language Quarterly* (1972), 33:382-95
Hubert, J. D., "The Timeless Temple in 'Athalie'", *French Studies*, 10:140-53, 1956
Jacobs, Carolyn L., "Irony in the Tragedies of Racine", *Dissertation Abstracts International* (1974), 35:2271A
Knapp, Bettina L., *Jean Racine; Mythos and Renewal in Modern Theater.* 1971. Pp. 218-39
Lapp, J. C., "Athaliah's Dream", *Studies in Philology*, 51:461-69, July, 1954
Lichem, Klaus, "Une Source du Songe d'Athalie; Le Songe d'Armide dans la 'Jerusalem Délivrée'", *Revue d'Histoire Littéraire de la France* (1968), 68:285-90
Lockert, Lacy, *Studies in French Classical Tragedy.* 1958. Pp. 404-14
Missions et Démarches de la Critique; Mélanges Offerts au Professeur J. A. Vier. 1973. Pp. 595-610
Moore, Will Grayburn; Sutherland, Rhoda; and Starkie, Enid, eds., *French Mind; Studies in Honour of Gustave Rudler.* 1952. Pp. 90-108
New Yorker, 31:122, May 21, 1955
Orgel, Vera, "What is Tragic in Racine?", *Modern Language Review*, 45:312-18, 1950
Pavel, T. G., "Parole Sacrée et Action Politique: 'Athalie' de Racine", *Liberté* (1973), 87-88:133-40
Revue des Deux Mondes, 51:932-34, June 15, 1939
Turnell, Martin, *Classical Moment; Studies of Corneille, Moliere and Racine.* 1947. Pp. 215-41
——————————, *Jean Racine, Dramatist.* 1972. Pp. 299-334
Vossler, Karl, *Jean Racine.* 1972. Pp. 92-101

Williams, E. E., "Athalie, the Tragic Cycle and the Tragedy of Joas", *Romanic Review*, 28:36-45, Feb., 1937

Bajazet; or, The Tragedy of Roxane, 1672
Les Annales Politiques et Littéraires, 109:629-30, June 25, 1937
Alzonne, C., "Bajazet, Tragédie de Racine vue d'Istanbul", *Revue Politique et Littéraire*, 75:408-10, June 19, 1937
Branan, Alvord G., "The Prince in Racinian Tragedy; Bossuetian and Machiavellian Politics", *Dissertation Abstracts International* (1972), 33:1160A
Brody, J., "Bajazet; or, The Tragedy of Roxane", *Romanic Review* (Dec. 1969), 60:273-90
Descotes, Maurice, *Les Grands Rôles du Théâtre de Jean Racine.* 1957. Pp. 97-111
France, Peter, *Racine's Rhetoric.* 1965. Pp. 104-09
Hermann, Michal, "'se Declarer'—Zur Bedeutung eines Schlüsselwortes in Giraudoux 'Electre' und Racines 'Bajazet'", *Die Neueren Sprachen* (1969), 18:277-82
Jacobs, Carolyn L., "Irony in the Tragedies of Racine", *Dissertation Abstracts International* (1974), 35:2271A
Josse, R. and R. Haution, "Jean de la Haye et 'Bajazet'", *Cahiers Raciniens* (1967), 21:87-92
Knapp, Bettina L., *Jean Racine; Mythos and Renewal in Modern Theater.* 1971. Pp. 125-36
Kriesel, Rhoda R. S., "Characterization as a Structural Device in the Tragedies of Racine", *Dissertation Abstracts International* (1972), 33:2383A
Lockert, Lacy, *Studies in French Classical Tragedy.* 1958. Pp. 328-47
Mercure de France, 277:360-62, July 15, 1937
Mishriky, Salwa E., "La Trancendance de 'Bajozet'", *Romance Notes* (1973), 15:306-13
Missions et Démarches de la Critique; Mélanges Offerts au Professeur J. A. Vier. 1973. Pp. 595-610
Monaco, Marion, "Racine and the Problem of Suicide", *Modern Language Association. Publications* (PMLA), 70:441-54, 1955
Revue Politique et Litteraire, 75:423-24, June 19, 1937
Saunders, H. R., "Bajazet Speaks", *Modern Languages* (1965), 46:51-54
Tobin, Ronald W., "Racine and Seneca", *University of North Carolina Studies in Romance Language and Literature* (1971), 96-113-29
——————————, "Seneca in 'Bajazet' and 'Mithradate'", *Studi Francesi* (1969), 13:285-90
Turnell, Martin, *Jean Racine, Dramatist.* 1972. Pp. 153-82
Vossler, Karl, *Jean Racine.* 1972. Pp. 57-61

Bérénice, 1670
Branan, Alvord G., "The Prince in Racinian Tragedy; Bossuetian and Machiavellian Politics", *Dissertation Abstracts International* (1972), 33:1160A
Chevalley, Sylvie, "Les Deux 'Bérénice'", *Revue d'Histoire du Théâtre* (1970), 22:91-120
Defrenne, M., "Absence et Présence Chez Racine", *Revue de l'Université de Bruxelles*, 14:2-3, 192-203, 1961-62
Descotes, Maurice, *Les Grands Rôles du Théâtre de Jean Racine.* 1957. Pp. 85-96

Edwards, Michael, "Racinian Tragedy", *Critical Quarterly* (1971), 13:329-48
Evans, William M., "Does Titus Really Love Bérénice?", *Romance Notes* (1974), 15:454-58
Fergusson, Francis, *Idea of a Theatre; A Study of Ten Plays; The Art of Drama in Changing Perspective.* 1949. Pp. 42-67
France, Peter, *Racine's Rhetoric.* 1965. Pp. 185-96
Gossip, C. J., "Le Rôle et les Antécédents de l'Antiochus de Racine", *Cahiers Raciniens* (1967), 21:87-92
Han, Pierre, " 'Vraisement' and 'Decorum': A Note on the Baroque in 'Samson Agonistes' and 'Bérénice' ", *Seventeenth Century News* (1971), Pp. 16-25
Knapp, Bettina L., *Jean Racine; Mythos and Renewal in Modern Theater.* 1971. Pp. 108-24
Kriesel, Rhoda R. S., "Characterization as a Structural Device in the Tragedies of Racine", *Dissertation Abstracts International* (1972), 33:2383A
Lockert, Lacy, "Racine's 'Berenice' ", *Romanic Review*, 30:26-38, Feb. 1939
—————— , *Studies in French Classical Tragedy.* 1958. Pp. 310-27
McBride, Robert, "Le Role de Rome dans Bérénice' ", *Studi Francesi* (1974), 52:86-91
Mélanges d'Histoire Littéraire (XVI-XVIIᵉ Siecle): Offerts à Raymond Lebèque par Ses Collegues, Ses Élèves et Ses Amis. 1969. Pp. 279-91
Mueller, Martin, "The Truest Daughter of Dido: Racine's 'Bérénice' ", *Canadian Review of Comparative Literature* (1974), 1:201-17
Plauchon, Robert, "Bérénice", *La Nouvelle Critique, Revue du Marxisme Militant* (1971), 222:56-59
Razumovskaja, Margarita, "Idejines ir Kompozicines Klasicistiniu Rasino 'Berenikes' bei Kornelio 'Tito ir Berekikes' Pjesiu Ypatybes", *Aukstuju Literatura: Lietuvos T. S. R. Aukstyju Mokyklu Mokslo Darbai* (1972), 14:23-43
Soares, Sandra, "Time in 'Bérénice' ", *Romance Notes* (1973), 15:104-09
Turnell, Martin, *Classical Moment; Studies of Corneille, Moliere and Racine.* 1947. Pp. 188-91
—————— , *Jean Racine, Dramatist.* 1972. Pp. 125-52
Vossler, Karl, *Jean Racine.* 1972. Pp. 61-71
Wagner, N., " 'Bérénice', Tragedie 'Sublime' ", *L'Information Littéraire*, 10:169-78, 1958
Whatley, J., "l'Orient Desert: 'Bérénice' and 'Antony and Cleopatra' ", *University of Toronto Quarterly* (1975), 44:96-114

Britannicus, 1669
    Branan, Alvord G., "The Prince in Racinian Tragedy; Bossuetian and Machiavellian Politics", *Dissertation Abstracts International* (1972), 33:1160A
    Brée, Germaine, "Le Thème de la Violence dans le Monde Tragique Racine", *Romanic Review*, 38:216-25, 1947
    Christian Century, 78:395-96, March 29, 1961
    Defrenne, M., "Absence et Presénce Chez Racine", *Revue de l'Université de Bruxelles*, 14:2-3, 192-203, 1961-62
    Descotes, Maurice, *Les Grands Rôles du Théâtre de Jean Racine.* 1957. Pp. 53-85
    Fortnightly Review, 85:89-91, Jan., 1906
    Gautier, Jean-Jacques, " 'Britannicus' à la Comédie Française", *Cahiers Raciniens*, #9:662-64, 1961

Gilman, Donald, " 'Le Venin Qui Vous Tue': Motif, Metaphor and Mode in Racine's 'Britannicus' ", *Romance Notes* (1973), 15:278-83

Jacobs, Carolyn L., "Irony in the Tragedies of Racine", *Dissertation Abstracts International* (1974), 35:2271A

Kahl, Mary C., "Irony in the Tragedies of Racine", *Harvard Library Bulletin* (1973), 21:144-60

Knapp, Bettina L., *Jean Racine; Mythos and Renewal in Modern Theater.* 1971. Pp. 85-107

Kriesel, Rhoda R. S., "Characterization as a Structural Device in the Tragedies of Racine", *Dissertation Abstracts International* (1972), 33:2383A

Lancaster, Henry Carrington, *Adventures of a Literary Historian; A Collection of His Writings Presented to H. C. Lancaster by His Former Students, and Other Friends in Anticipation of His 60th Birthday, Nov. 10, 1942.* 1942. Pp. 334-38

Lockert, Lacy, *Studies in French Classical Tragedy.* 1958. Pp. 304-09

Macchia, Guovanni, "Note su 'Andromaque' e 'Britannicus' ", *Galleria*, 13: 65-75, 1963

Mélanges d'Histoire Littéraire (XVI-XVIIe Siècle): Offerts à Raymond Lebèque par Ses Collegues, Ses Élèves et Ses Amis. 1969. Pp. 269-77

Nation, 192:242, March 18, 1961

New Yorker, 37:112, March 11, 1961

Pitou, Spire, "The Ghost of Messalina and 'Britannicus' ", *Romance Notes* (1971), 13:296-300

Revue des Deux Mondes, 52:452-55, July 15, 1939

Rombout, A. F., "Le Rôle de la Crainte dans 'Britannicus' ", *Neophilologus* (1968), 52:1-12

Sweetser, M. O., "Racine Rival de Corneille: Innutrition et Innovations dans 'Britannicus' ", *Romanic Review* (1975), 66:13-31

Turnell, Martin, *Jean Racine, Dramatist.* 1972. Pp. 91-124

Vossler, Karl, *Jean Racine.* 1972. Pp. 57-61

Esther, 1689

Descotes, Maurice, *Les Grands Rôles du Théâtre de Jean Racine.* 1957. Pp. 167-72

Geoffroy-Dechaume, R., "Racine et la Musique", *Cahiers Raciniens* (1967), 22:43-50

Knapp, Bettina L., *Jean Racine; Mythos and Renewal in Modern Theater.* 1971. Pp. 193-217

Londré, Felicia H., "The Religious Musicals of Jean Racine", *Thought* (1974), 49:156-86

Turnell, Martin, *Jean Racine, Dramatist.* 1972. Pp. 279-98

Vossler, Karl, *Jean Racine.* 1972. Pp. 85-91

Iphigenie, 1674

Chicoteau, M., "Le Rôle de la Nature dans 'l'Iphigénie' de Racine", *Modern Language Review*, 39:347-56, Oct., 1944

Descotes, Maurice, *Les Grands Rôles du Théâtre de Jean Racine.* 1957. Pp. 129-46

Edwards, Michael, "Racinian Tragedy", *Critical Quarterly* (1971), 13:329-48

France, Peter, *Racine's Rhetoric.* 1965. Pp. 215-18

Hall, F. A., "Comparison of the Iphigenias of Euripides, Goethe and Racine", *Classical Journal*, 9:371-84, June, 1914

Jacobs, Carolyn L., "Irony in the Tragedies of Racine", *Dissertation Abstracts International* (1974), 35:2271A

Kahl, Mary C., "Irony in the Tragedies of Racine", *Harvard Library Bulletin* (1973), 21:144-60

Knapp, Bettina L., *Jean Racine; Mythos and Renewal in Modern Theater.* 1971. Pp. 151-65

Lancaster, H. C., "The 'Denouement en Action' of Racine's 'Iphigenie'", *Modern Language Notes*, 68:356-59, 1953

Lapp, John C., "Time, Space and Symbol in 'Iphigenie'", *Modern Language Association. Publications* (PMLA), 66:1023-32, 1951

Libby, Diane M., "The Double Oracle in Racine's 'Iphigenie'", *Romance Notes* (1973), 15:110-17

Lockert, Lacy, *Studies in French Classical Tragedy.* 1958. Pp. 366-87

Monaco, Marion, "Racine and the Problem of Suicide", *Modern Language Association. Publications* (PMLA), 70:441-54, 1955

Nurse, Peter H., ed., *The Art of Criticism; Essays in French Literary Analysis.* 1969. Pp. 89-99

Plaut, Johanna M., "Characterization Through Style in Racine's 'Iphigenie'", *Dissertation Abstracts International* (1972), 33:2948A

Reiss, T. J., "Classicism, the Individual, and Economic Exchange in Racine's 'Iphigenie'", *l'Esprit Createur* (1973), 13:204-19

Scarborough, W. S., "One Heroine—Three Poets", *Education*, 19:213-21, Dec., 1898

Turnell, Martin, *Jean Racine, Dramatist.* 1972. Pp. 209-38

Vossler, Karl, *Jean Racine.* 1972. Pp. 71-76

The Litigants, 1668

Vossler, Karl, *Jean Racine.* 1972. Pp. 54-57

Mithradate, 1673

Branan, Alvord G., "The Prince in Racinian Tragedy; Bossuetian and Machiavellian Politics", *Dissertation Abstracts International* (1972), 33:1160A

Descotes, Maurice, *Les Grands Rôles du Théâtre de Jean Racine.* 1957

Dickson, Jesse D. J., "Le 'Mithradate' de Racine", *Dissertation Abstracts International* (1973), 34:1901A

Fonsny, Joseph, "Apologie Pour 'Mithradate'", *Etudes Classiques* (1972), 40:191-203

Gutwirth, Marcel, "D'Alexandre le Grande' à 'Mithradate': Persistance d'une Velléite Racienne", *Modern Language Notes* (1969), 84:599-604

Knapp, Bettina L., *Jean Racine; Mythos and Renewal in Modern Theater.* 1971. Pp. 137-50

Kriesel, Rhoda R. S., "Characterization as a Structural Device in the Tragedies of Racine", *Dissertation Abstracts International* (1972), 33:2383A

Lockert, Lacy, *Studies in French Classical Tragedy.* 1958. Pp. 348-65

Monaco, Marion, "Racine and the Problem of Suicide", *Modern Language Association. Publications* (PMLA), 70:441-54, 1955

Revue Politique et Littéraire, 76:35-36, Jan., 1938

Tobin, Ronald W., "Racine and Seneca", *University of North Carolina Studies in Romance Language and Literature* (1971), 96:113-29

——————— , "Seneca in 'Bajazet' and 'Mithradate'", *Studi Francesi* (1969), 13:285-90

Turnell, Martin, *Jean Racine, Dramatist.* 1972. Pp. 183-208

Vossler, Karl, *Jean Racine.* 1972. Pp. 71-76

Phèdre, 1677

Baldensperger, F., "Encore la 'Cabale de Phèdre': Leibniz du Mauvais Cote?" *Modern Language Notes*, 58:523-6, Nov., 1943

Baring, Maurice, *Punch and Judy and Other Essays*. 1924. Pp. 322-24

Barko, J. P., "La Symbolique de Racine: Essai d'Interpretation des Images de Lumière et de Ténèbre dans la Vision Tragique de Racine", *Revue des Sciences Humaines*, #115:353-77, 1964

Bidou, H., "Phèdre et l'Article 64", *Journal des Débats*, 34 pt. 1:969, June 17, 1927

——————— , "Le Procès de Phèdre", *Journal des Débats*, 34 pt. 2:45-47, July 1, 1927

Blanchet, Andre, "Phèdre Entre le Soleil et la Nuit", *Etudes*, 299:55-74, 1958

Brooks, Cleanth, ed., *Tragic Themes in Western Literature*. 1955. Pp. 77-106

Caillois, Roger, " 'Phèdre' et la Mythologie", *Nouvelle Revue Francaise* (1972), 234:7-18

Clary, James H. and Daniel Krempel, *The Theatrical Image*. 1967. Pp. 81-90

Cole, Toby and Chinoy, Helen Krich, eds., *Directing the Play; A Source Book of Stagecraft*. 1953. Pp. 279-90

——————— , *Directors on Directing; A Source Book of the Modern Theatre*. 1963. Pp. 351-63

Commonweal, 83:699, Mar. 18, 1966

Coquillat, Michelle, "Phèdre, ou la Liberté dans l'Acte Héroique", *French Review* (1974), 47:857-64

Crain, William L., "A Problem in Racine's 'Phèdre': Whose Murderous Hand?", *Romance Notes* (1973), 14:528-35

Cruttwell, Patrick, "Six Phaedras in Search of one 'Phèdre' ", *Delos; A Journal On and Of Translation* (1968), 2:198-211

Daniel, George G., ed., *Renaissance and Other Studies in Honor of William Leon Wyley*. 1968. Pp. 107-113

Dedieu, J., "Ambiguité de 'Phèdre' de Racine: Tragédie Antique ou Drame Chrétien?", *Humanitas*, 2:43-49, 1955

Descotes, Maurice, *Les Grands Rôles au Théâtre de Jean Racine*. 1957. Pp. 147-65

Donaldson,-Evans, Lance K., "The 'Récit de Théramène' Reconsidered", *Romance Notes* (1972/73), 14:544-56

Duffy, Joseph M., "Subject and Structure as Cosmology in Racine's 'Phèdre' ", *Mosaic* (1974), 7,iv:155-70

Edwards, Michael, "Racinian Tragedy", *Critical Quarterly* (1971), 13:329-48

Eriksen, Hans Peter Boude, et al, *Trøgedie og Tragik: Til Oparbejdelsen af en Teori om den Borgerlige Bevidsthed*. Pp. 41-53

Eustis, A., "Nineteenth Century Version of the Cabale de 'Phèdre' ", *Modern Language Notes*, 67:446-50, 1952

Fowlie, Wallace, *Love in Literature; Studies in Symbolic Expression*. 1972. Pp. 51-57

France, Peter, *Racine's Rhetoric*. 1965. Pp. 136-40

Francois, Carlo, "Phèdre et les Dieux", *French Review*, 35:269-78, 1962

Gandon, Jean, "Par Vous Aurait Peri les Monstre de la Crète", *Romanic Review* (1972), 63:251-60

Gassner, John, *Dramatic Soundings; Evaluations and Retractions Culled from Thirty Years of Dramatic Criticism*. 1968. Pp. 567-69

Gifford, G. H., "L'Inceste dans 'Phèdre' ", *Revue d'Histoire Littéraire de la France*, 39:560-62, 1933

Gilman, Donald, "The River of Death; Motif and Metaphor in Racine's 'Phèdre' ", *Romance Notes* (1972), 14:326-30

Grossvogel, David I., *Four Playwrights and a Postscript; Brecht, Ionesco, Beckett and Genet.* 1962. Pp. 186-87

Han, Pierre, "A Baroque Marriage; Phèdre's 'Déclaration' and Théraméne's 'Récit' ", *South Atlantic Bulletin* (1974), 39,iv:83-87

————————— , "Innocence and Natural Depravity in 'Paradise Lost', 'Phèdre' and 'Billy Budd' ", *Revue Belge de Philologie et d'Histoire* (1971), 49:856-61

————————— , "The 'Passions' in Descartes and Racine's 'Phèdre' ", *Romance Notes* (1969), 11:107-09

————————— , "The Symbolism of 'Lieu' in Racine's 'Phèdre' ", *South Atlantic Bulletin* (1973), 38,iv:21-25

Handelingen van Het Eenendertigste Nederlands Filologncongres: Gehouden te Groningen op Woensdag 1, Donderdag Two en Vrijdag 3 April 1970. 1971. Pp. 7-23

Hannedouche, S., "Deux Tragédies Manichéennes au XVII Siècle: 'Phèdre' et 'Cinna' ", *Cahiers d'Etudes Cathares*, 7:15-19, 1956

Hartle, Robert W., "Racine's Hidden Metaphors", *Modern Language Notes*, 76:132-39, 1961

Henzey, Jacques, "Le Décor de 'Phèdre' ", *Revue d'Histoire du Theatre*, 14:18-21, 1962

Jacobs, Carolyn L., "Irony in the Tragedies of Racine", *Dissertation Abstracts International* (1974), 35:2271A

Jasenas, Elaine, "Le Thème de la Chasse au Monstre dans la 'Phèdre' de Racine", *Symposium* (1967), 21:118-31

Jouve, Pierre Jean, "La Lecon de 'Phèdre' ", *Mercure de France*, 338:193-98, 754-55, 1960

Kahl, Mary C., "Irony in the Tragedies of Racine", *Harvard Library Bulletin* (1973), 21:144-60

Keller, Abraham C., "Death and Passion in Racine's 'Phèdre' ", *Symposium*, 16:190-92, 1962

Knapp, Bettina L., *Jean Racine; Mythos and Renewal in Modern Theatre.* 1971. Pp. 166-89

Kott, Jan, *Theatre Notebook: 1947-1967.* 1968. Pp. 123-26

Lancaster, Henry Carrington, *Adventures of a Literary Historian; A Collection of His Writings Presented to H. C. Lancaster by His Former Students, and Other Friends in Anticipation of His 60th Birthday, Nov. 10, 1942.* 1942. Pp. 1-13, 339-40

————————— , "Nineteen-Forty", *Modern Language Association. Publications* (PMLA), 54:1314-24, 1940

————————— , "Saint-Réal's 'Don Carlos' and 'Phèdre' ", *Modern Language Notes*, 54:519-20, Nov., 1939

Lapp, John C., "Hippolyte, Phèdre and the 'Récit de Théraméne' ", *Univ. of Toronto Quarterly*, 19:158-64, 1950

Lockert, Lacy, *Studies in French Classical Tragedy.* 1958. Pp. 388-403

Macksey, Richard and Eugenio Donato, eds., *The Languages of Criticism and the Sciences of Man; The Structuralist Controversy.* 1969. Pp. 296-318

Maulnier, Thierry, "Notes Pour Une Mise en Scene; Voici Comment jai vu 'Phèdre' ", *Figaro Littéraire* (1967), 23:16

McCollom, William G., "The Downfall of the Tragic Hero", *College English* (1957), 19:51-56

Mercure de France, 262:579-82, Sept. 15, 1935

Meron, Evelyne, "De 'l'Hippolyte' d'Euripide à la 'Phèdre' de Racine: Deux Conceptions du Tragique", XVII° *Siecle* (1973), 100:34-54

Modern Miscellany Presented to Eugéne Vinaver, by Pupils, Colleagues and Friends; ed. by T. E. Lawrenson, F. E. Sutcliffe and G. F. A. Gadoffre. 1969. Pp. 97-108 and 294-304

Den Moderne Roman og Romanforskning i Norden. Innlegg ved den 8. Studiekonferanse over Skandinavisk Literatur 10-14 August 1970. 1971. Pp. 239-44

Monaco, Marion, "Racine and the Problem of Suicide", *Modern Language Association. Publications* (PMLA), 70:441-54, 1955

Mönch, Walter, "Racines 'Phèdre': Eine Literatur- und Geistesgeschichtliche Betrachtung", *Zeitschrift für Französische Sprache und Literatur*, 66:137-53, 1956

New Yorker, 41.130, Feb. 19, 1966

Nikitine, B., "Phèdre à la Persane", *Revue de Littérature Comparée*, 30:529-31, 1956

Olson, Elder, *Tragedy and the Theory of Drama*. 1966. Pp. 217-36

Orgel, Vera, "What is Tragic in Racine", *Modern Language Review*, 45:312-18, 1950

Partisan Review, *New Partisan Reader, 1945-53*, ed. by William Phillips and Philip Rahv. 1953. Pp. 396-407

Pasternak, Monique, "Racine; Le Probleme de la Responsibilite de 'Phèdre'", *Revue de l'Université d'Ottawa* (1974), 44:58-69

Patterson, Charles D., "Dramatic Aspects of Versification in Racine", *Dissertation Abstracts International* (1973), 34:1289A

Pavel, T. G., "'Phèdre': Outline of a Narrative Grammar", *Language Sciences* (1973), 28:1-6

Pickens, Rupert T., "Hippolyte's Horses; A Study of a Metaphorical Action in Racine's 'Phèdre'", *Romance Notes* (1968), 9:266-77

Pommier, Jean, "A Propos de 'Phèdre'", *Mercure de France*, 336:25-30, 1959

Reiter, Seymour, *World Theater; The Structure and Meaning of Drama.* 1973. Pp. 50-56

Rexroth, Kenneth, *The Elastic Retort; Essays in Literature and Ideas.* 1973. Pp. 51-54

Rogers, J. Hoyt, "The Symmetry of 'Phèdre' and the Role of Aricie", *French Review* (1972), 45 (Special Issue):65-74

Salomon, Herman Prins, "'Phèdre', Pièce Janséniste?", *Cahiers Raciniens*, #15:54-64, 1964

Savin, Maurice, "Psychanalyse de Phèdre (Fantaisie)", *La Table Ronde*, #108:169-77, 1956

Spitzer, Leo, *Linguistics and Literary History; Essays in Stylistics.* 1948. Pp. 87-134

Stoll, Elmer Edgar, *Shakespeare and Other Masters.* 1940. Pp. 317-33

Sutton, Genevieve, "Phedre et Thérése Desqueyroux; Une Communante du Destin", *French Review* (1970), 43:559-70

Tobin, Ronald W., "Racine and Seneca", *University of North Carolina Studies in Romance Language and Literature* (1971), 96:113-29

Turnell, Martin, *Classical Moment; Studies of Corneille, Moliere and Racine.*
1947. Pp. 192-215

—————————— , *Jean Racine, Dramatist.* 1972. Pp. 239-78
Tynan, Kenneth, *Curtains; Selections from the Drama Criticism and Related
Writings.* 1961. Pp. 399-401, and 405-06
Vossler, Karl, *Jean Racine.* 1972. Pp. 76-85
Yarrow, P. J., "Un Temple Sacré: A Note on Racine's 'Phèdre' ", *Modern
Language Notes,* 72:194-99, March, 1957

Les Plaideurs   *SEE*   The Litigants

La Thébaide; ou, Les Freres Ennemis   *SEE*   The Thebans; or, The Enemy
Brothers

The Thebans; or, The Enemy Brothers, 1664
Branan, Alvord G., "The Prince in Racinian Tragedy: Bossuetian and Machi-
avellian Politics", *Dissertation Abstracts International* (1972), 33:1160A
Brody, Jules, "Racine's 'Thébäide'; An Analysis", *French Studies,* 13:199-213,
1959
Delcroix, M., "Le Sacré dans les Tragédies Profanes de Racine: 'Le The-
bäide' ", *Cahiers Raciniens* (1967), 21:9-44
Hartle, Robert W., "Racine's Hidden Metaphors", *Modern Language Notes,*
76:132-39, 1961
Kahl, Mary C., "Irony in the Tragedies of Racine", *Harvard Library Bulletin*
(1973), 21:144-60
Knapp, Bettina L., *Jean Racine; Mythos and Renewal in Modern Theater.*
1971. Pp. 31-45
Lapp, John C., "The Oracle in 'La Thébäide' ", *Modern Language Notes,*
66:462-64, 1951
Merigon, C., "Deux Antigone", *Europe* (1967), 45:130-32
Monaco, Marion, "Racine and the Problem of Suicide", *Modern Language
Association. Publications* (PMLA), 70:441-54, 1955
Orgel, Vera, "What is Tragic in Racine?", *Modern Language Review,* 45:312-
18, 1950
Patterson, Charles D., "Dramatic Aspects of Versification in Racine", *Dis-
sertation Abstracts International* (1973), 34:1289A
Tobin, Ronald W., "Racine and Seneca", *University of North Carolina Studies
in Romance Language and Literature* (1971), 96:79-90
Turnell, Martin, *Jean Racine; Dramatist.* 1972. Pp. 29-40
Vossler, Karl, *Jean Racine.* 1972. Pp. 44-47
Yarrow, P. J., "A Note on Racine's 'Thébäide' ", *French Studies,* 10:20-31,
1956
Zimmerman, Eleonore M., "La Tragédie de Jocaste; Le Problème de Destin
dans 'La Thébäide' de Racine", *French Review* (1972), 45:560-70

SOLOMON RAPPOPORT

The Dybbuk, 1920
Arts and Decoration, 24:66, Feb., 1926
Brown, I., "Dybbuk", *Saturday Review,* 143:559-60, April 9, 1927
Catholic World, 122:665-67, Feb., 1926 and 167:266-67, June, 1948
Dial, 80:255-59, March, 1926
Horsnell, H., "Dybbuk", *Outlook* (London), 54:407, April 16, 1927

Jennings, R., "Dybbuk", *Spectator*, 138:639, April 9, 1927
Literary Digest, 88:29, Jan. 23, 1926
MacCarthy, Desmond, "Dybbuk", *New Statesman*, 28:797-98, April 9, 1927
Nation, 122:16-17, Jan. 6, 1926
New Republic, 45:187-88, Jan. 6, 1926 and 49:190-91, Jan. 5, 1927 and 118: 28-29, May 24, 1948 and 131:21-22, Nov. 15, 1954
New Yorker, 24:55, May 8, 1948
Newsweek, 63:90, Feb. 17, 1964
Outlook (London), 59:407, April 16, 1927
Pichon, J., "Dybbuk", *L'Illustration*, 84 pt. 1:609, June 12, 1926
Powys, J. C., "Dybbuk", *Menorah Journal*, 13:361-65, Aug., 1927
Samuel, M., "Dybbuk", *Menorah Journal*, 13:63-67, Feb., 1927
Saturday Review, 149:559-60, April 9, 1927
Shipp, H., "Dybbuk", *English Review*, 44:632-34, May, 1927
Survey, 55:572, Feb. 1, 1926
Theatre Arts, 32:18, June, 1948
Theatre Arts Anthology; A Record and a Prophecy, ed. by Rosamond Gilder and others. 1950. Pp. 604-06
Waldman, M., "Dybbuk", *London Mercury*, 16:83-84, May, 1927
Woman Citizen, n. s. 10:16, Feb., 1926
Young, Stark, *Immortal Shadows; A Book of Dramatic Criticism.* 1948. Pp. 67-71

TERRENCE RATTIGAN

Adventure Story, 1949
Illustrated London News, 214:488, April 9, 1949
Spectator, 182:394, March 25, 1949
Theatre Arts, 33:4-5, June, 1949

After the Dance, 1939
New Statesman and Nation, 18:13-14, July, 1939

Browning Version, 1948
Catholic World, 170:227, Dec., 1949
Illustrated London News, 213:362, Sept. 25, 1948
Life, 27:93, Oct. 31, 1949
Nathan, George Jean, *Theatre Book of the Year, 1949-1950.* Pp. 50-55
New Republic, 121:21, Nov. 7, 1949
New Yorker, 25:60, Oct. 22, 1949
Newsweek, 34:84, Oct. 24, 1949
Saturday Review of Literature, 32:26-27, Nov. 5, 1949
School and Society, 71:26, Jan. 14, 1950
Spectator, 181:366, Sept. 17, 1948
Theatre Arts, 33:12, Dec., 1949
Time, 54:58, Oct. 24, 1949

Deep Blue Sea, 1952
Catholic World, 176:306-07, Jan., 1953
Commonweal, 57:197-98, Nov. 28, 1952
Lumley, Frederick, *New Trends in Twentieth Century Drama; A Survey Since Ibsen and Shaw.* 1967. Pp. 306-10
Nathan, George Jean, *Theatre in the Fifties.* 1953. Pp. 131-35

Nation, 175:472-3, Nov. 22, 1952
New Statesman, 43:301-02, March 15, 1952
New Yorker, 28:69, Nov. 15, 1952
Newsweek, 40:74, Nov. 17, 1952
Saturday Review, 35:36-37, Nov. 22, 1952
School and Society, 76:402-03, Dec. 20, 1952
Spectator, 188:326, March 14, 1952
Taylor, John Russell, *The Rise and Fall of the Well-Made Play.* 1967.
    Pp. 152-59
Theatre Arts, 37:21-22, Jan., 1953
Time, 60:102, Nov. 17, 1952
Tynan, Kenneth, *Curtains; Selections from the Drama Criticism and Related*
    Writings. 1961. Pp. 18-19

Flare Path, 1942
    Commonweal, 37:326, Jan. 15, 1943
    Current History, n. s. 3:550, Feb., 1943
    Nathan, George Jean, *Theatre Book of the Year, 1942-43.* Pp. 187-89
    New Statesman and Nation, 24:123-24, Aug. 22, 1942
    Spectator, 169:171, Aug. 21, 1942
    Theatre Arts, 24:77-78, Feb., 1943

French Without Tears, 1936
    New Yorker (April 1, 1974), 50:52
    Taylor, John Russell, *The Rise and Fall of the Well-Made Play.* 1967.
        Pp. 148-55

Harlequinade, 1948
    Catholic World, 170:227, Dec., 1949
    Life, 27:94-95, Oct. 31, 1949
    Illustrated London News, 213:362, Sept. 25, 1948
    Nathan, George Jean, *Theatre Book of the Year, 1949-1950.* Pp. 50-55
    School and Society, 71:26, Jan. 14, 1950
    Spectator, 181:366, Sept. 17, 1948
    Theatre Arts, 33:12, Dec., 1949
    Time, 54:58, Oct. 24, 1949

Heart to Heart, 1962
    Lumley, Frederick, *New Trends in Twentieth Century Drama; A Survey*
        Since Ibsen and Shaw. 1967. Pp. 306-10

In Praise of Love, 1973
    Lambert, J. W., "In Praise of Love", *Drama* (1973), 111:23-26
    Nation (Dec. 28, 1974), 219:700
    New Republic (Jan. 4, 1975), 172:33-34
    New Yorker (Dec. 23, 1974), 50:53
    Newsweek (Dec. 23, 1974), 84:56
    Time (Dec. 23, 1974), 104:46-47

Love in Idleness, 1944
    Brown, John Mason, *Dramatis Personae: A Retrospective Show.* 1963. Pp.
        252-56
    Catholic World, 162:551, March, 1946

Forum, 105:659-60, March, 1946
Life, 20:49-50, Feb. 18, 1946
Nathan, George Jean, *Theatre Book of the Year, 1945-1946*. Pp. 290-91
New Republic, 114:158, Feb. 4, 1946
New Statesman and Nation, 28:436, Dec. 30, 1944
New Yorker, 21:34, Feb. 2, 1946
Newsweek, 27:80, Feb. 4, 1946
Spectator, 173:598, Dec. 29, 1944
Theatre Arts, 30:133, March, 1946
Time, 47:61, Feb. 4, 1946

Man and Boy, 1963
New Statesman, 66:368, Sept. 20, 1963
New Yorker, 39:143, Nov. 23, 1963
Newsweek, 62:71, Nov. 25, 1963
Saturday Review, 46:24, Nov. 30, 1963
Spectator, 211:320, Sept. 13, 1963
Time, 82:71, Nov. 22, 1963

Man to Man, 1963
Lumley, Frederick, *New Trends in Twentieth Century Drama; A Survey Since Ibsen and Shaw*. 1967. Pp. 306-10

Ross, 1960
Commonweal, 75:435-36, Jan. 19, 1962
Educational Theatre Journal, 14:66-67, March, 1962
English, 13:148, 1961
Hudson Review, 14:97-99, 1961, and 15:117, 1962
Illustrated London News, 236:944, May 28, 1960
New Republic, 146:20, Jan. 22, 1962
New Statesman, 59:748, May 21, 1960
New Yorker, 36:59-60, July 9, 1960 and 37:55, Jan. 6, 1962
Newsweek, 55:78, May 30, 1960 and 59:44, Jan. 8, 1962
Saturday Review, 45:51, Jan. 13, 1962
Spectator, 204:732, May 20, 1960
Theatre Arts, 45:58-60, Feb., 1961 and 46:57-58, March, 1962
Time, 75:56, May 23, 1960 and 79:52, Jan. 5, 1962
Weintraub, Stanley, "How History Gets Rewritten: Lawrence of Arabia in the Theatre", *Drama Survey* (1963), 2:269-75

Separate Tables, 1956
America, 96:281, Dec. 1, 1956
Catholic World, 184:303, Jan., 1957
Christian Century, 73:1328-29, Nov. 14, 1956
Commonweal, 65:234, Nov. 30, 1956
English, 10:139, 1955
Life, 41:89-90, Dec. 3, 1956
Nation, 183:416, Nov. 10, 1956
New Republic, 135:23, Nov. 12, 1956
New Yorker, 32:68, Nov. 3, 1956
Newsweek, 48:78, Nov. 5, 1956
Reporter, 13:43, Oct. 20, 1955

Saturday Review, 38:33, Sept. 17, 1955 and 39:29, Nov. 3, 1956
Sewanee Review, 63:270-80, 1955
Theatre Arts, 41:19-20, Jan., 1957
Time, 68:75, Nov. 5, 1956
Tynan, Kenneth, *Curtains; Selections from the Drama Criticism and Related Writings.* 1961. Pp. 79-81
Vogue, 128:72, Oct. 15, 1956

Sleeping Prince, 1953
America, 96:359, Dec. 22, 1956
Catholic World, 184:307, Jan., 1957
Commonweal, 65:235, Nov. 30, 1956
Nation, 183:485, Dec. 1, 1956
New Statesman, 46:596-97, Nov. 14, 1953
New Yorker, 29:163, Dec. 12, 1953 and 32:112-14, Nov. 10, 1956
Newsweek, 48:54, Nov. 12, 1956
Saturday Review, 39:28, Nov. 17, 1956
Theatre Arts, 41:24, Jan., 1957
Time, 68:71, Nov. 12, 1956

Variation on a Theme, 1958
New Statesman, 55:633-34, May 17, 1958
Spectator, 200:621, May 16, 1958
Tynan, Kenneth, *Curtains; Selections from the Drama Criticism and Related Writings.* 1961. Pp. 214-16

While the Sun Shines, 1943
Catholic World, 160:169, Nov., 1944
Commonweal, 40:589, Oct. 6, 1944
Nathan, George Jean, *Theatre Book of the Year, 1944-1945.* Pp. 71-75
Nation, 159:389, Sept. 30, 1944
New Statesman and Nation, 27:24, Jan. 8, 1944
New Yorker, 20:38, Sept. 30, 1944
Newsweek, 24:99, Oct. 2, 1944
Spectator, 172:10, Jan. 7, 1944
Theatre Arts, 28:641, Nov., 1944
Time, 44:59, Oct. 2, 1944

Who is Sylvia?, 1950
Illustrated London News, 217:780, Nov. 11, 1950

The Winslow Boy, 1946
Brown, John Mason, *Dramatis Personae; A Retrospective Show.* 1963. Pp. 313-27
Catholic World, 166:264, Dec., 1947
Commonweal, 47:120, Nov. 14, 1947
Forum, 109:25, Jan., 1948
Life, 23:97-98, Nov. 24, 1947
Nathan, George Jean, *Theatre Book of the Year, 1947-1948.* Pp. 121-23
Nation, 165:537-38, Nov. 15, 1947
New Republic, 117:35, Nov. 10, 1947
New Yorker, 23:52, Nov. 8, 1947
Newsweek, 30:74, Nov. 10, 1947

Saturday Review of Literature, 30:24-29, Nov. 29, 1947
School and Society, 67:315-16, April 24, 1948
Spectator, 176:583, June 7, 1946
Theatre Arts, 30:597, Oct., 1946 and 31:43, June, 1947 and 32:12, June, 1948
Time, 50:100, Nov. 10, 1947

TERRENCE RATTIGAN AND ANTHONY MAURICE

Follow My Leader, 1940
New Statesman and Nation, 19:104, Jan. 27, 1940
Spectator, 164:108, Jan. 26, 1940

THOMAS WILLIAM ROBERTSON

Caste, 1867
New Statesman, 25:474, Aug. 8, 1925
Outlook (London), 56:89, Aug. 8, 1925
Saturday Review, 140:157-58, Aug. 8, 1925
Shaw, George Bernard, *Plays and Players; Essays on the Theatre.* 1952. Pp. 250-56
Theatre Arts, 31:28-30, March, 1947
Ward, Alfred Charles, ed., *Specimens of English Dramatic Criticism, 17th-20th Centuries.* 1945. Pp. 132-41

EDMOND ROSTAND

L'Aiglon, 1900
Aldrich, Thomas Bailey, *Ponkapog Papers.* 1907. vol. 7:57-61
Baring, Maurice, *Punch and Judy and Other Essays.* 1924. Pp. 297-301
Beerbohm, Max, *Around Theatres.* 1953. Pp. 151-54
Brown, John Mason, *Two on the Aisle; Ten Years of the American Theater in Performance.* 1938. Pp. 81-84
Catholic World, 72:670-73, Feb., 1901 and 140:337-38, Dec., 1934
Commonweal, 21:96, Nov. 16, 1934
Edmonds, Mary Arms, "A Fisher of the Moon", *Forum*, 51:592-604, 1914
Hale, E. E., Jr., "L'Aiglon", *Dial*, 29:354-55, Nov. 16, 1900
Krutch, J. W., "L'Aiglon", *Nation*, 119:527-28, Nov. 12, 1924
Nation, 139:601, Nov. 21, 1934
New Republic, 81:78, Nov. 28, 1934
Smith, Hugh Allison, *Main Currents of Modern French Drama.* 1925. Pp. 76-107
Theatre Arts, 19:12, Jan., 1935
Van Vorst, B., "Mme Bernhardt in 'L'Aiglon'", *Critic*, 36:429-40, May, 1900

Chantecler, 1910
Allen, H. W., "Real Cyrano, Chantecler, and 'The Birds'", *Cornhill*, 101: 832-45, June, 1910
Ambriere, F., "Une Source Ignorée de Chanticler?", *Mercure de France*, 267:222-23, April 1, 1936 and 267:444-46, April 15, 1936
Anniversary Papers, by Colleagues and Pupils of George Lyman Kittredge Presented in June, 1913. 1913. Pp. 67-72

"'Chantecler' and 'The Birds' of Aristophanes", *Living Age*, 264:696-99, March 12, 1910

deSoissons, S. C., "Chantecler", *Living Age*, 265:37-43, April 2, 1910

Edmonds, Mary Arms, "A Fisher of the Moon", *Forum*, 51:592-604, 1914

English Review, 4:740-47, March, 1910

Frank G., "Politics and the Cock of Dawn", *Century*, 103:637-40, Feb., 1922

Galdemar, A., "Edmond Rostand and 'Chantecler'", *McClure*, 35:523-37, Sept., 1910

Hamilton, C., "Supernatural Plays: 'Chantecler'", *Bookman*, 33:25-27, March, 1911

L'Illustration, 85 pt. 2:444-45, Oct. 22, 1927

Journal des Débats, 34 pt. 2:780-81, Nov. 4, 1927^

MacDonald, J. F., "Paris, Rostand and 'Chantecler'", *Fortnightly*, 93:575-90, March, 1910

Marquand, E., "Rostand's 'Chantecler'", *New England Magazine*, n. s. 42:226-31, April, 1910

Marsh, E. C., "Barnyard Chef-d'Oeuvre", *Bookman*, 32:154-56, Oct., 1910

Nordan, M., "Chantecler", *Bookman*, 31:397-401, June, 1910

Norman, H. D., "Powers of Darkness and the Cock of Dawn", *Poet-Lore*, 34:283-87, 1923

Piggott, F. T., "Season of French Plays; Recollections of 'Chantecler'", *Nineteenth Century*, 88:79-90, July, 1920

Review of Reviews, 41:481-83, April, 1910

Revue des Deux Mondes, s.7 42:223-27, Nov. 1, 1927

Richardot, M., "Chantecler Dans La Viet et Dans L'Oeuvre d'Edmond Rostand", *Revue des Deux Mondes*, s 7 42:624-39, Dec. 1, 1927

Rosenfeld, Paul, "Rostand", *New Republic*, 17:337-39, 1918

Sheldon, C., "Rostand and 'Chantecler'", *Poet-Lore*, 23:74-78, Jan., 1912

Slosson, E. E., "Bird of France", *Independent*, 68:680-85, March 31, 1910

Smith, Hugh Allison, *Main Currents of Modern French Drama*. 1925. Pp. 76-107

Thomas, Eleanor W., "The Romanticism of Rostand", *Poet-Lore*, 32:64-75, 1921

Cyrano de Bergerac, 1897

America, 118:739, June 1, 1968

American Mercury, 64:53-55, Jan., 1947

Les Annales Politiques et Littéraires, 113:20-21, Jan. 10, 1939

Beerbohm, Max, *Around Theatres*. 1953. Pp. 4-7, 73-75

Brenner, C. D., "Rostand's 'Cyrano de Bergerac'; An Interpretation", *Studies in Philology*, 46:603-11, Oct., 1949

Catholic World, 164:168-69, Nov., 1946 and 178:308-09, Jan., 1954

Commonweal, 24:76, May 15, 1936 and 45:70, Nov. 1, 1946, 88:268, May17, 1968

de Beauplan, R., "Cyrano et ses Interprètes", *L'Illustration*, 202:100-07, Jan. 28, 1939

Edmonds, Mary Arms, "A Fisher of the Moon", *Forum*, 51:592-604, 1914

Eliot, Thomas Stearns, *Sacred Wood; Essays on Poetry and Criticism*. 1921. Pp. 71-77

_____ , *Selected Essays, 1917-1932*. 1932. Pp. 25-30

Gerard, R., "Cyrano de Bergerac", *L'Illustration*, 202:97-98, Jan. 28, 1939

L'Illustration, 89 pt. 1:323, March 14, 1931

Journal des Débats, 41 pt. 1:562-63, April 6, 1934

Knight, J. "The Real Cyrano de Bergerac", *Fortnightly Review*, 70 (n. s. 64): 205-15, Aug., 1898

Kobbe, G., "Cyrano de Bergerac", *Forum*, 26:502-12, Dec., 1898

Lievre, P., "Cyrano de Bergerac", *Mercure de France*, 289:648-50, Feb. 1, 1939

Literary Digest, 79:28-29, Nov. 24, 1923 and 109:18, June, 1931

Moskowitz, Samuel, *Explorers of the Infinite; Shapers of Science Fiction.* 1963. Pp. 17-32

Nathan, George Jean, *Theatre Book of the Year, 1946-47.* Pp. 88-92

New Republic, 115:518, Oct. 21, 1946

New Yorker, 22:57-58, Oct. 19, 1946 and 29:88, Nov. 21, 1953, 44:129-30, May 4, 1968

Newsweek, 7:44, May 9, 1936 and 28:93, Oct. 21, 1946 and 42:64, Nov. 23, 1953, 71:94, May 6, 1968

Outlook, 151:299, Feb. 20, 1929

Outlook (London), 60:677, Nov. 19, 1927

Parsons, C. O., "The Nose of Cyrano de Bergerac", *Romanic Review*, 25: 225-35, 1934

Revue des Deux Mondes, 49:445-49, Jan. 15, 1939

Rosenfeld, Paul, "Rostand", *New Republic*, 17:337-39, 1918

Sailens, E., "Une Source de Cyrano: 'L'Orgueil", *Mercure de France*, 282:412-16, March 1, 1938 and 283:243, April 1, 1938

Saturday Review, 45:18, Sept. 1, 1962

Saturday Review of Literature, 29:28-30, Nov. 2, 1946

Saurat, Denis, *Modern French Literature, 1870-1940.* 1946. Pp. 100-06

Smith, Hugh Allison, *Main Currents of Modern French Drama.* 1925. Pp. 76-107

Theatre Arts, 30:690, Dec., 1946 and 31:50, Jan., 1947 and 38:25, Jan., 1954 and 47:69, Aug., 1963

Thomas, Eleanor W., "The Romanticism of Rostand", *Poet-Lore*, 32:64-75, 1921

Time, 48:78, Oct. 21, 1946

Williams, Patricia E., " 'Cyrano de Bergerac' and French Morale in 1897", *South Central Bulletin* (1974), 34:164-65

———————— , "Some Classical Aspects of 'Cyrano de Bergerac' ", *Nineteenth Century Studios* (1973), 1:112-24

Young, Stark, "Cyrano de Bergerac", *New Republic*, 37:18-19, Nov. 28, 1923

———————— , "Cyrano de Bergerac", *Nineteenth Century*, 44:102-15, July, 1898

La Derniere Nuit de Don Juan   *SEE*   The Last Night of Don Juan

The Faraway Princess, 1895

Edmonds, Mary Arms, "A Fisher of the Moon', *Forum*, 51:592-604, 1914

L'Illustration, 87 pt. 2:524-25, Nov. 8, 1929

Smith, Hugh Allison, *Main Currents of Modern French Drama.* 1925. Pp. 76-107

Thomas, Eleanor W., "The Romanticism of Rostand", *Poet-Lore*, 32:64-75, 1921

The Last Night of Don Juan, 1922
  Young, Stark, "The Last Night of Don Juan", *New Republic*, 45:86-87, Dec. 9, 1925

La Princesse Lointaine *SEE* The Faraway Princess

Les Romanesques *SEE* The Romantics

The Romantics, 1894
  Smith, Hugh Allison, *Main Currents of Modern French Drama.* 1925. Pp. 76-107

La Samaritaine *SEE* The Woman of Samaria

The Woman of Samaria, 1897
  Smith, Hugh Allison, *Main Currents of Modern French Drama.* 1925. Pp. 76-107
  Thomas, Eleanor W., "The Romanticism of Rostand", *Poet-Lore*, 32:64-75, 1921

NICHOLAS ROWE

The Ambitious Stepmother, 1700
  Waith, Eugene M., *Ideas of Greatness; Heroic Drama in England.* 1971. Pp. 269-71

The Fair Penitent, 1703
  Waith, Eugene M., *Ideas of Greatness; Heroic Drama in England.* 1971. Pp. 272-74

WILLIAM ROWLEY

SEE

THOMAS HEYWOOD AND WILLIAM ROWLEY

AND

THOMAS MIDDLETON AND WILLIAM ROWLEY

THOMAS SACKVILLE

SEE

THOMAS NORTON AND THOMAS SACKVILLE

ARMAND SALACROU

l'Archipel Lenoir; ou Il ne Faut pas Toucher aux Choses Immobiles *SEE* The Lenoir Archipelago; or, One Must not Touch Immobile Things

Atlas-Hotel, 1931
  Bidou, H., "'Atlas-Hotel': Critique", *Journal des Débats* (May 8, 1931), 38 pt. 1:781-82
  Lumley, Frederick, *New Trends in Twentieth Century Drama; A Survey Since Ibsen and Shaw.* 1967. Pp. 159-70

The Bridge of Europe, 1927
Bidou, H., " 'Le Pont de l'Europe': Critique", *Journal des Débats* (Dec. 9, 1927), 34 pt. 2:988-99

Une Femme Libre   *SEE*   A Free Woman

Les Fiancés du Havre, 1944
Silenieks, Juris, "Circularity of Plot in Salacrou's Plays", *Symposium* (1966), 20:56-62

A Free Woman, 1934
Les Annales Politiques et Littéraires, 104:94, Oct. 25, 1934
Lumley, Frederick, *New Trends in Twentieth Century Drama; A Survey Since Ibsen and Shaw*. 1967. Pp. 159-70
" 'Une Femme Libre': Criticism", *Living Age* (Jan. 1935), 347:458

Les Frenetiques   *SEE*   The Frenzied Ones

The Frenzied Ones, 1934
Les Annales Politiques et Littéraires, 104:302-03, Dec. 25, 1934
Revue des Deux Mondes, s. 8 45:213-15, Jan. 1, 1935

Histoire de Rire   *SEE*   When the Music Stops

Un Homme Comme les Autres   *SEE*   A Man Like the Others

l'Inconnue d'Arras   *SEE*   The Unknown Woman of Arras

The Lenoir Archipelago; or, One Must not Touch Immobile Things, 1947
Silenieks, Juris, "Circularity of Plot in Salacrou's Plays", *Symposium* (1966), 20:56-62
Theatre Arts, (Feb. 1948), 32:29

A Man Like the Others, 1936
Les Annales Politiques et Littéraires, 108:558-60, Dec. 10, 1936
Lumley, Frederick, *New Trends in Twentieth Century Drama; A Survey Since Ibsen and Shaw*. 1967. Pp. 159-70
Revue Politique et Litteraire, Dec. 5, 1936, 74:817-18

Nights of Wrath, 1946
Catholic World, 185:67, April, 1957
Commonweal, 47:4949-95, Feb. 27, 1948
Ley-Piscator, Maria, The *Piscator Experiment; The Political Theatre*. 1967. Pp. 209-11
Lumley, Frederick, *New Trends in Twentieth Century Drama; A Survey Since Ibsen and Shaw*. 1967. Pp. 159-70
Silenieks, Juris, "Circularity of Plot in Salacrou's Plays", *Symposium* (1966), 20:56-62
Theatre Arts, 31:46, May, 1947, and 41:82, Apr. 1957
Tynan, Kenneth, *Curtains; Selections from the Drama Criticism and Related Writings*. 1961. Pp. 383-84

Les Nuits de la Colere   *SEE*   Nights of Wrath

Patchouli, 1934
Bidou, H., " 'Patchouli': Critique", *Journal des Débats* (Jan. 31, 1930), 37 pt. 1:204-05

Le Pont de l'Europe *SEE* The Bridge of Europe

Shore Leave, 1925
Bauer, G., " 'Tour à Terre': Critique", *Les Annales Politiques et Littéraires (Jan. 10, 1926), 86:32*
Bidou, H., " 'Tour à Terre': Critique", *Journal des Débats* (Jan. 1, 1926), 33 pt. 1:1130-31

La Terre Est Ronde *SEE* The World Is Round

Tour à Terre *SEE* Shore Leave

The Unknown Woman of Arras, 1935
Lumley, Frederick, *New Trends in Twentieth Century Drama; A Survey Since Ibsen and Shaw.* 1967. Pp. 159-70
Silenieks, Juris, "Circularity of Plot in Salacrou's Plays", *Symposium* (1966), 20:56-62

When the Music Stops, 1939
L'Europe Nouvelle, Feb. 24, 1940, 23:205

The World Is Round, 1938
Les Annales Politiques et Littéraires, 112:528-29, Nov. 25, 1938
L'Europe Nouvelle, June 10, 1939, 22:633
L'Illustration, 201:427-38, Nov. 26, 1938
Lumley, Frederick, *New Trends in Twentieth Century Drama; A Survey Since Ibsen and Shaw.* 1967. Pp. 159-70
Mercure de France, 288:417-20, Dec. 1, 1938
Revue des Deux Mondes, s. 8 48:662-68, Dec. 1, 1938
Silenieks, Juris, "Circularity of Plot in Salacrou's Plays", *Symposium* (1966), 20:56-62

JEAN PAUL SARTRE

Condemned of Altona, 1959
America, 114:272-73, Feb. 19, 1966
Barnes, Hazel E., *Sartre.* 1974. Pp. 87-97
Brustein, Robert, *The Third Theatre*, 1969. Pp. 165-68
Czarnecki, J., "Au Théâtre: Témoignage pour l'Homme", *Christianisme Social*, 68:5-6, 410-17, 1960
Fields, M., "De la Critique de la Raison Dialectique aux 'Séquestrés d'Altona' ", *Modern Language Association. Publications* (PMLA), 78:622-30, 1963
Galler, Dieter, "The Different Spheres of Sequestration in Jean Paul Sartre's Play 'Les Séquestrés d'Altona' ", *South Central Bulletin* (1971), 31:179-82
_____ , "Jean-Paul Sartre's Drama 'Les Séquéstres d'Altona': Two More Examples of the Schizophrenic Syndrome", *Language Quarterly* (1970), 9:55-60
_____ , "Jean Paul Sartre's 'Les Séquestrés d'Altona': Old Von Gerlach—Portrait of a Schizophrenic", *Language Quarterly* (1969), 8:33-38
_____ , "The Phases of Schizophrenia in Jean Paul Sartre's 'Les Séquestrés d'Altona' ", *Language Quarterly* (1973), 11,iii:5-16
_____ , "Le Portrait d'un Schizophrène dans la Piece de Jean Paul Sartre 'Les Séquéstres d'Altona", *South Central Bulletin* (1969), 29:136-38

———————— , "The Relationship Between Soma and Psyche in Jean-Paul Sartre's Drama 'Les Séquestrés d'Altona' ", *Language Quarterly* (1967), 6:1 pt. 2:35-38

———————— , "Stereotyped Characters in Sartre's Play, 'Les Séquestrés d'Altona' ", *Kentucky Romance Quarterly* (1968), 15:57-68

Gassner, John, *Dramatic Soundings; Evaluations and Retractions Culled from Thirty Years of Dramatic Criticism.* 1968. Pp. 554-57

Gouhier, H., "Le Théâtre. Intrigue et Action; de B. Shaw à J. P. Sartre", *La Table Ronde*, #143:173-78, 1959

Haffter, P., " 'Les Séquestrés d'Altona', Une Oeuvre Engagee?", *French Studies in Southern Africa* (1973), 2:60-67

Kern, Edith, ed., *Sartre, A Collection of Critical Essays.* 1962. Pp. 92-103

Lorris, Robert, " 'Les Séquestrés d'Altona': Terme de la Quête Orestienne", *French Review* (1970), 44:4-14

Lumley, Frederick, *New Trends in Twentieth Century Drama: A Survey Since Ibsen and Shaw.* 1967. Pp. 139-58

McCall, Dorothy, *The Theatre of Jean Paul Sartre.* 1969. Pp. 127-51

Moore, Harry T., *Twentieth Century French Literature to World War II.* 1966. Vol II. Pp. 45-51

Nation, 189:492-93, Dec. 26, 1939 and 202:222-24, Feb. 21, 1966

New Republic, 154:42-43, Feb. 26, 1966

New Statesman, 58:706, Nov. 21, 1959 and 61:680, April 28, 1961

New York Times Magazine, Pp. 84, Nov. 29, 1959.

New Yorker, 41:206, Oct. 2, 1965 and 41:110, Feb. 12, 1966

Newsweek, 67:88, Feb. 14, 1966

O'Brien, Justin, *The French Literary Horizon.* 1967. Pp. 389-92

Palmer, Jeremy N. J., " 'Les Séquestrés d'Altona': Sartre's Black Tragedy", *French Studies* (1970), 24:150-62

Pollmann, Leo, *Sartre and Camus; Literature of Existence.* 1970. Pp. 74-81

Pucciani, Oreste F., " 'Les Séquestrés d'Altona' of Jean Paul Sartre", *Tulane Drama Review,* 5:19-33, 1961

Rose, Marilyn Gaddis, "Sartre and the Ambiguous Thesis Play", *Modern Drama*, 8:12-19, 1965-66

Sartre, J. P., " 'Les Séquestrés d'Altona', Nous Concernent Tous", *Théâtre Populaire*, #36:1-14, 1959

Saturday Review, 49:52, Feb. 19, 1966

"Les Séquestrés d'Altona", *Recherches et Débats du Centre Catholique des Intellectuels Francais*, #32:42-66, 1960

Spectator, 206:608, April 28, 1961

Tembeck, Robert, "Dialectic and Time in 'The Condemned of Altona' ", *Modern Drama* (1969), 12:10-17

Time, 87:67, Feb. 18, 1966

Vogue, 147:58, March 15, 1966

Williams, John S., "Sartre's Dialectic of History; 'Les Séquestrés d'Altona' ", *Renascence* (1970), 22:59-68 and 112

Witt, Mary Ann, "Confinement in 'Die Verwandlung' and 'Les Séquestrés d'Altona' ", *Comparative Literature* (Wint. 1971), 23:32-44

Zivanovic, Judith, "Sartre's Drama; Key to Understanding His Concept of Freedom", *Modern Drama* (Sept. 1971), 14:144-54

Death Without Burial, or Men Without Shadows   *SEE*   The Victors

The Devil and the Good Lord, 1951
Arnold, P., "Jean-Paul Sartre's New Play: 'Le Diable et le Bon Dieu' ", *Theatre Arts*, 35:24-25, Oct., 1951
Cohn, Ruby, *Currents in Contemporary Drama*. 1969. Pp. 134-36
Curtis, Jerry L., "The World is a Stage: Sartre Versus Genêt", *Modern Drama* (1974), 17:33-41
Fagone, V., "Sartre, "Il Diavolo et Il Buon Dio' ", *Civiltà Cattolica*, 114:360-73, 1963
Flint, Martha and Charlotte Genard, " 'Le Diable et le Bon Dieu' and an Angry Young Luther", *Journal of European Studies* (1972), 2:247-55
France Illustration, 7:700, June 30, 1951
Frank, H., "J. P. Sartre: 'Der Teufel und der Liebe Gott' ", *Philosophischer Literatur Anzeiger*, 6:193-95, 1954
"Is God Dead?", *Katholiek Cultureel Tijdschrift. Streven*, 5:97-108, 1951
Lewis, Allan, *Contemporary Theatre; The Significant Playwrights of Our Time*. 1962. Pp. 191-217
Lumley, Frederick, *New Trends in Twentieth Century Drama; A Survey Since Ibsen and Shaw*. 1967. Pp. 139-58
Luthy, Herbert, "Jean Paul Sartre and God", *Twentieth Century*, 150:221-30, Sept., 1951
McCall, Dorothy, *The Theatre of Jean Paul Sartre*. 1969. Pp. 24-42
Marcel, G., "Existentialismus und das Zeitgenössische Theatre", *Wissenschaft und Weltbild*, 9:251-61, 1955
New Republic, 125:22, July 23, 1951 and 125:21-22, Aug. 6, 1951 and 125:9, Sept. 10, 1951
New Yorker, 27:46, June 30, 1951
Partisan Review, 19:202-10, March, 1952
Pollmann, Leo, *Sartre and Camus; Literature of Existence*. 1970. Pp. 89-96
Ricoeur, Paul, "Sartre's 'Lucifer and the Lord' ", *Yale French Studies* (1954-55), #14:85-93
Ridge, George Ross, " 'Le Diable et le Bon Dieu': Sartre's Concept of Freedom", *Shenandoah*, 9:35-38, 1958
Rose, Marilyn Gaddis, "Sartre and the Ambiguous Thesis Play", *Modern Drama*, 8:12-19, 1965-66
Wisser, R., "Jean Paul Sartre und der 'Liebe Gott' ", *Zeitschrift für Religions-und Geistesgeschichte* (1967), 19:235-63
Zivanovic, Judith, "Sartre's Drama; Key to Understanding His Concept of Freedom", *Modern Drama* (Sept. 1971), 14:144-54

Le Diable et le Bon Dieu   SEE   The Devil and the Good Lord

Dirty Hands, 1948
Barnes, Hazel E., *Sartre*. 1974. Pp. 77-96
Bruckner, Rodelinde, "Jean Paul Sartre—'Les Mains Sales': Ihre Verwend-barkeit im Hinblick auf Hernzielouentiertes Testen", *Die Neueren Sprachen* (1973), 22:266-72
Glicksberg, Charles Irving, *The Tragic Vision in Twentieth Century Literature*. 1963. Pp. 126-36
Lumley, Frederick, *New Trends in Twentieth Century Drama; A Survey Since Ibsen and Shaw*. 1967. Pp. 139-58
McCall, Dorothy, *The Theatre of Jean Paul Sartre*. 1969. Pp. 53-78

Moore, Harry T., *Twentieth Century French Literature to World War II.* 1966. Vol. II. Pp. 45-51

Nathan, George Jean, *Theatre Book of the Year, 1948-49,* Pp. 193-96

New Statesman and Nation, 35:520, June 26, 1948

New York Times Magazine, Pp. 20, July 11, 1948

Newsweek, 43:94, May 24, 1954

Pollmann, Leo, *Sartre and Camus; Literature of Existence.* 1970. Pp. 69-74

Ridge, George Ross, "Meaningful Choice in Sartre's Drama", *French Review,* 30:435-41, 1956-57

Rose, Marilyn Gaddis, "Sartre and the Ambiguous Thesis Play", *Modern Drama,* 8:12-19, 1965-66

Scruggs, Charles E., "T. S. Eliot and J. P. Sartre—Toward the Definition of the Human Condition", *Appalachian State Teachers College Faculty Publications* (1965), Pp. 24-29

Smith, Colin, "French Theatre: The Philosophical Drama of Jean Paul Sartre", *Prompt* (1964), 4:25-29

Spectator, 181:205, Aug. 13, 1948

Twentieth Century, 152:362-64, Oct., 1952

The Flies, 1943

Allen, M., "Character Development in the 'Oreste' of Voltaire and 'Les Mouches' of Jean Paul Sartre", *CLA Journal* (1974), 18:1-21

Artinian, Robert W., "Foul Winds in Argos; Sartre's 'Les Mouches' ", *Romance Notes* (1972), 14:7-12

Belli, Angela, *Ancient Greek Myths and Modern Drama; A Study in Continuity.* 1971. Pp. 70-87

Burdick, Dolores Mann, "Concept of Character in Giraudoux's 'Electre' and Sartre's 'Les Mouches' ", *French Review,* 33:131-36, 1960

——————————— , "Imagery of the 'Plight' in Sartre's 'Les Mouches' ", *French Review,* 32:242-46, 1959

Cohn, Ruby, *Currents in Contemporary Drama.* 1969. Pp. 88-91

Commonweal, 46:93-94, May 9, 1947

Curtis, Jerry L., "The World Is a Stage; Sartre Versus Genêt", *Modern Drama* (1974), 17:33-41

Debusscher, Gilbert, "Modern Masks of the Orestes: 'The Flies' and 'The Prodigal' ", *Modern Drama* (1970), 12:308-18

Dickinson, Hugh, *Myth on the Modern Stage.* 1969. Pp. 221-47

Ekman, Hans Goran, "Jean-Paul Sartres 'Les Mouches' ", *Edda* (1968), 55:372-79

Forum, 107:541-45, June, 1947

Gassner, John, *The Theatre in Our Times.* 1954. Pp. 337-41

Hamburger, Käte, *From Sophocles to Sartre; Figures in Greek Tragedy, Classical and Modern.* 1969. Pp. 34-43

Kern, Edith, ed., *Sartre; A Collection of Critical Essays.* 1962. Pp. 54-61

Lerner, Max, *Actions and Passions; Notes on the Multiple Revolution of Our Time.* 1949. Pp. 49-51

Ley-Piscator, Maria, *The Piscator Experiment: The Political Theatre.* 1967. Pp. 204-08

Lumley, Frederick, *New Trends in Twentieth Century Drama; A Survey Since Ibsen and Shaw.* 1967. Pp. 139-58

McCall, Dorothy, *The Theatre of Jean Paul Sartre.* 1969. Pp. 9-24

Marcel, G., "Existentialismus und das Zeitgenössische Theatre", *Wissenschaft und Weltbild*, 9:251-61, 1955

Matthews, Honor, *The Primal Curse; The Myth of Cain and Abel in the Theatre*. 1967. Pp. 137-40

Moore, Harry T., *Twentieth Century French Literature to World War II*. 1966. Pp. 201-05

Mordaunt, Jerrold L., ed. *Proceedings. Pacific Northwest Conference on Foreign Languages. 19th Annual Meeting, April 19-20, 1968*. 1968. Pp. 50-54

New Statesman and Nation, 42:620, Dec. 1, 1951

New Yorker, 23:52, May 24, 1947

Pollmann, Leo, *Sartre and Camus; Literature of Existence*. 1970. Pp. 44-51

Porter, David H., "Ancient Myth and Modern Play: A Significant Counterpoint", *Classical Bulletin* (Nov. 1971), 48:1-9

Rickman, H. P., "Death of God", *Hibbert Journal*, 59:220-26, April, 1961

Ridge, George Ross, "Meaningful Choice in Sartre's Drama", *French Review*, 30:435-41, 1956-57

Rose, Marilyn Gaddis, "Sartre and the Ambiguous Thesis Play", *Modern Drama*, 8:12-19, 1965-66

Royle, Peter, "The Ontological Significance of 'Les Mouches' ", *French Studies* (1972), 26:42-53

Smith, Colin, "French Theatre: The Philosophical Drama of Jean Paul Sartre", *Prompt* (1964), 4:25-29

Williams, Raymond, *Drama from Ibsen to Brecht*. 1968. Pp. 225-27

Williams-Ellis, A., "The Flies", *Spectator*, 175:264, Sept. 21, 1945

Zivanovic, Judith, "Sartre's Drama; Key to Understanding His Concept of Freedom", *Modern Drama* (Sept. 1971), 14:144-54

Hui-Clos   *SEE*   No Exit

Kean, or Disorder and Genius, 1953

Reiss, Timothy J., "Psychical Distance and Theatrical Distancing in Sartre's Drama", *Yale French Studies* (1971), #46:5-16

Kean, ou Désordre et Génie   *SEE*   Kean, or Disorder and Genius

Les Mains Sales   *SEE*   Dirty Hands

Morts Sans Sépulture   *SEE*   The Victors

Les Mouches   *SEE*   The Flies

Nekrassov, 1955

Bensimon, Marc, "Nekrassov ou l'Anti-Théâtre", *French Review*, 31:18-26, 1957

McCall, Dorothy, *The Theatre of Jean Paul Sartre*. 1969. Pp. 87-98

Marcel, G., "Existentialismus und das Zeitgenössische Theatre", *Wissenschaft und Weltbild*, 9:251-61, 1955

Moore, Harry T., *Twentieth Century French Literature to World War II*. 1966. Pp. 45-51

New Statesman, 51:40, Jan. 14, 1956

New Yorker, 31:66, July 2, 1955

Oxenhandler, N., "Nekrassov and the Critics", *Yale French Studies*, #16:8-12, 1955-56

Rose, Marilyn Gaddis, "Sartre and the Ambiguous Thesis Play", *Modern Drama*, 8:12-19, 1965-66

Terrex, J., " 'Nekrassov' ou les Dangers de l'Engagement", *La Table Ronde,* #93:135-37, 1955

No Exit, 1944
Barnes, Hazel E., *Sartre.* 1974. Pp. 73-76
Blitgen, Sister M. J. Carol, B. V. M., " 'No Exit': The Sartrean Idea of Hell", *Renascence* (1967), 19:59-63
Bogard, Travis and Oliver, William Irvin, eds., *Modern Drama; Essays in Criticism.* 1965. Pp. 276-89
Brown, John Mason, *Seeing More Things.* 1948. Pp. 85-91
Cate, Hollis L., "The Final Line in Sartre's 'No Exit' ", *Notes on Contemporary Literature* (1972), 2,v:9-10
Catholic World, 164:358, Jan., 1947
Cohn, Ruby, *Currents in Contemporary Drama.* 1969. Pp. 59-64
——————————— , "Hell on the 20th Century Stage", *Wisconsin Studies in Contemporary Literature* (Wint. Spring 1964), 5:48-53
Commonweal, 45:229, Dec. 13, 1946
Curtis, Jerry L., "The World Is a Stage; Sartre Versus Genêt", *Modern Drama* (1974), 17:33-41
Falk, Eugene H., " 'No Exit' and 'Who's Afraid of Virginia Woolf': A Thematic Comparison", *Studies in Philology* (1970), 67:406-17
Jacquot, Jean, *Le Théâtre Moderne.* 1967. P. 29-36
Kern, E., "Abandon Hope, All Ye . . .", *Yale French Studies,* #30:56-60, 1964
Loeb, E., "Sartre's 'No Exit' and Brecht's 'The Good Woman of Setzuan'; A Comparison", *Modern Language Quarterly,* 22:283-91, Sept., 1961
Lumley, Frederick, *New Trends in Twentieth Century Drama; A Survey Since Ibsen and Shaw.* 1967. Pp. 138-58
Mabley, Edward, *Dramatic Construction; An Outline of Basic Principles.* 1972. Pp. 270-76
McCall, Dorothy, *The Theatre of Jean Paul Sartre.* 1969. Pp. 110-27
Mendel, Sydney, "The Descent into Solitude", *Forum* (Houston) (1961), 3:19-24
Moore, Harry T., *Twentieth Century French Literature to World War II.* 1966. Vol. I. Pp. 201-05
Nathan, George Jean, *Theatre Book of the Year, 1946-47.* Pp. 211-14
——————————— , *Theatre Book of the Year, 1947-48.* Pp. 30-33
Nation, 163:708, Dec. 14, 1946
New Republic, 115:764, Dec. 9, 1946
New Statesman and Nation, 32:63, July 27, 1946
New Yorker, 22:69, Dec. 7, 1946
Newsweek, 28:92, Dec. 9, 1946
Ridge, George Ross, "Meaningful Choice in Sartre's Drama", *French Review,* 30:435-41, 1956-57
Rose, Marilyn Gaddis, "Sartre and the Ambiguous Thesis Play", *Modern Drama,* 8:12-19, 1965-66
Saturday Review of Literature, 29:26-28, Dec. 28, 1946
Sewanee Review, 55:346-47, April, 1947
Sakharoff, Micheline, "The Polyvalence of Theatrical Language in 'No Exit' ", *Modern Drama* (1973), 16:199-205
Smith, Colin, "French Theatre; The Philosophical Drama of Jean Paul Sartre", *Prompt* (1964), 4:25-29

Theatre Arts, 30:641, 674, Nov., 1946 and 31:16, 20, Jan., 1947

Time, 48:83, Dec. 9, 1946

Zanoto, Ilka Marinho, "'Huis Clos': Sartre Trinta Anos Depois", *O Estado de Sao Paula, Suplemento Literario* (1974), June 23:6

Zivanovic, Judith, "Sartre's Drama; Key to Understanding His Concept of Freedom", *Modern Drama* (Sept. 1971), 14:144-54

La Putain Respectueuse *SEE* The Respectful Prostitute

The Respectful Prostitute, 1946

Curtis, Jerry L., "The World Is a Stage; Sartre Versus Genêt", *Modern Drama* (1974), 17:33-41

Ewing, James M., Jr., "Sartre's Existentialism and 'The Respectful Prostitute'", *Southern Quarterly* (1969), 7:167-74

Guthke, K. S., "Kleists 'Zerbrochene Krug' und Sartres 'La Putain Respectueuse'", *Die Neueren Sprachen*, #10:466-70, 1959

Lumley, Frederick, *New Trends in Twentieth Century Drama; A Survey Since Ibsen and Shaw.* 1967. Pp. 139-58

McCall, Dorothy, *The Theatre of Jean Paul Sartre.* 1969. Pp. 79-87

Mendel, Sydney, "The Descent into Solitude", *Forum* (Houston) (1961), 3: 19-24

Moore, Harry T., *Twentieth Century French Literature to World War II.* 1966. Vol. II. Pp. 45-51

Nathan, George Jean, *Theatre Book of the Year, 1947-48.* Pp. 258-61

Pollmann, Leo, *Sartre and Camus; Literature of Existence.* 1970. Pp. 65-69

Ridge, George Ross, "Meaningful Choice in Sartre's Drama", *French Review,* 30:435-41, 1956-57

Rose, Marilyn Gaddis, "Sartre and the Ambiguous Thesis Play", *Modern Drama*, 8:12-19, 1965-66

Theatre Arts, 31:45, Feb., 1947

United Nations World, 1:60, Feb., 1947

Zimmerman, H. J., "Noch Einmal: Kleists 'Zerbrochene Krug' und Sartres 'La Putain Respectueuse'", *Die Neueren Sprachen*, #10:485-88, 1960

Les Séquestrés d'Altona *SEE* The Condemned of Altona

The Victors, 1946

Abraham, Claude K., "A Study in Autohypocrisy: 'Morts Sans Sépulture'", *Modern Drama*, 3:343-47, 1961

Cohn, Ruby, *Currents in Contemporary Drama.* 1969. Pp. 131-33

Curtis, Jerry L., "The World Is a Stage; Sartre Versus Genêt", *Modern Drama* (1974), 17:33-41

Lumley, Frederick, *New Trends in Twentieth Century Drama; A Survey Since Ibsen and Shaw.* 1967. Pp. 139-58

McCall, Dorothy, *The Theatre of Jean Paul Sartre.* 1969. Pp. 43-52

Moore, Harry T., *Twentieth Century French Literature to World War II.* 1966. Vol. II. Pp. 45-51

Nathan, George Jean, *Theatre Book of the Year, 1948-49.* Pp. 221-23

Pollmann, Leo, *Sartre and Camus; Literature of Existence.* 1970. Pp. 56-62

Rose, Marilyn Gaddis, "Sartre and the Ambiguous Thesis Play", *Modern Drama*, 8:12-19, 1965-66

Theatre Arts, 31:44, Feb., 1947

United Nations World, 1:60-61, Feb., 1947

JOHANN CHRISTOPH FRIEDRICH VON SCHILLER

Die Braut von Messina, oder, Die Feinlichen Bruder *SEE* The Bride of Messina

The Bride of Messina, 1803

Atkins, Stuart, "Gestalt als Gehalt in Schillers 'Braut von Messina' ", *Deutsche Vierteljahrsschrift für Literaturwissenschaft und Geistesgeschichte*, 33: 529-64, 1959

Carruth, W. H., "Fate and Guilt in Schiller's 'Die Braut von Messina' ", *Modern Language Association. Publications* (PMLA), 17:105-24, 1902

Cutting, S. W., "Schiller's Treatment of Fate and Dramatic Guilt in His 'Braut von Messina' ", *Modern Philology*, 5:347-60, Jan., 1908

Garland, H. B., *Schiller; the Dramatic Writer*. 1969. Pp. 233-60

Graham, Ilse, *Schiller's Drama; Talent and Integrity*. 1974. Pp. 67-92

Hibberd, J. L., "The Patterns of Imagery in Schiller's Braut von Messina' ", *German Life and Letters* (1967), 20:306-15

Mackay, Alexander T., "Fate and 'Hybris' in 'Die Braut von Messina' ", *Forum For Modern Language Studies* (1970), 6:213-25

Schadewaldt, Wolfgang, "Antikes und Modernes in Schillers 'Braut von Messina' ", *Jahrbuch der Deutschen Schillergesellschaft* (1969), 13:286-307

Sengle, Friedrich, "Die Braut von Messina", *Der Deutschunterricht*, 12:72-89, 1960

Weigand, Hermann John, *Surveys and Soundings in European Literature*. 1966. Pp. 124-63

Weiser, Ernest L., "The Inner Form of Schiller's 'Die Braut von Messina' ", *South Atlantic Bulletin* (1969), 34:10-12

Wells, G. A., "Fate-Tragedy and Schiller's 'Die Braut von Messina' ", *Journal of English and Germanic Philology*, 64:191-212, April, 1965

Demetrius, 1805

Binder, Wolfgang, "Schiller's 'Demetrius' ", *Euphorion* (Heidelberg), 53: 232-80, 1959

Brody, Ervin C., "Schiller's 'Demetrius' and Pushkin's 'Boris Godunov': A Contemporary Interpretation", *Neohelicon; Acta Comparationis Litterarum Universarum* (1973), 1:241-94

——————— , "Schiller's Vision of the Slavic World in His 'Demetrius' Fragment", *Polish Review* (1970), 15:5-45

Fowler, F. M., "The Riddle of Schiller's 'Demetrius' ", *Modern Language Review* (1966), 61:446-54

——————— , "The Significance of Sambor; A Note on Schiller's 'Demetrius' ", *New German Studies* (1973), 1:48-50

Thalheim, Hans Gunter, "Schillers Dramen von 'Maria Stuart' bis 'Demetrius' ", *Weimarer Beiträge. Zeitschrift für Literaturwissenschaft* (1974), 20, H.1:5-33 and 20, H.2:99-130

Witte, William, *Schiller and Burns and Other Essays*. 1959. Pp. 48-56

Don Carlos, Infante of Spain, 1787

Braig, Friedrich, "Schillers 'Philosophische Briefe' und 'Don Carlos' ", *Forschungen und Fortschritte*, 34:106-11, 1960

Brother Gregory, F. S. C., *Catholicism in Schiller's Dramas*. 1949. Pp. 4-6

Chiarini, Paolo, et al, eds., *Miscellanea di Studi in Onore di Bonaventura Tecchi*. 1969. Pp. 324-40

Ebstein, Frances, "In Defense of Marquis Posa", *Germanic Review*, 36:205-20, 1961

Garland, H. B., *Schiller; The Dramatic Writer*. 1969. Pp. 96-137

Graham, Ilse, *Schiller's Drama; Talent and Integrity*. 1974. Pp. 45-66

Gronicka, Andre von, "Friedrich Schiller's Marquis Posa", *Germanic Review*, 26:196-214, 1951

Koch, Herbert, "Zwei Unbekannte Schiller-Rezensionen. Eine 'Don Carlos' Kritik. Eine 'Maria Stuart' Kritik", *Jahrbuch der Deutschen Schiller-Gesellschaft*, 6:178-83, 1962

Maler, A. C., "Zur Methodik der Literargeschichtlichen Forschung", *Germanic Review*, 1:314-35, 1926

Schmitt, Albert R., ed., *Festschrift für Detlev W. Schumann Zum 70. Geburtstag*. 1970. Pp. 281-93

Schwarz, Egon, Hunter G. Hannum, and Edgar Lohner, eds., *Festschrift für Bernhard Blume: Aufsatze zur Deutschen und Europaischen Literatur*. 1967. Pp. 81-89

Seidlin, Oskar, *Essays in German and Comparative Literature*. 1961. Pp. 92-109

Simons, J. D., "Nature of Oppression in 'Don Carlos'", *Modern Language Notes* (April 1969), 84:451-57

————————— , "Schiller's 'Don Carlos'", *Explicator* (1969), 27:Item 22

Storz, Gerhard, "Die Struktur des 'Don Carlos'", *Jahrbuch der Schiller-Gesellschaft*, 4:110-39, 1960

Streurman, G. H., "Schillers 'Don Carlos': Zur Entstehungsgeschichte Eines Freudschaftsdenkmals", *Levende Talen*, 208:77-86 and 209:232-44, 1961

Tönz, Leo, "Grillparzers 'Blanka von Kastilien' und Schillers 'Don Carlos'", *Grillparzer Forum Forchtenstein* (1970), Bd. 1969:65-84

Fiesco; or, The Conspiracy of Genoa, 1784

Graham, Ilse, *Schiller's Drama; Talent and Integrity*. 1974. Pp. 9-44

————————— , *Schiller, Ein Meister der Tragischen Form*. 1974. Pp. 5-69

Phelps, Reginald H., "Schiller's 'Fiesco'; A Republican Tragedy?", *Modern Language Association. Publications* (1974), 89:442-53

Die Jungfrau von Orleans   *SEE*   The Maid of Orleans

Kabale und Liebe   *SEE*   Love and Intrigue

Love and Intrigue, 1784

Abbé, Derek van, " 'Kabale und Liebe' und 'Luisa Millerin'", *Deutschunterricht für Ausländer*, 9:97-100, 1959

Binder, Wolfgang, "Kabale und Liebe", *Das Deutsche Drama*, 1:248-68, 1958

Garland, H. B., *Schiller; The Dramatic Writer*. 1969. Pp. 67-95

Goldhahn, J., "Erfahrungen bei der Unterrichtlichen Arbeit an Schillers Drama 'Kabale und Liebe'", *Deutschunterricht* (1963), 16:379-95

Graham, Ilse Appelbaum, "Passions and Possessions in Schiller's 'Kabale und Liebe'", *German Life and Letters*, n. s. 6:12-20, 1952

————————— , *Schillers's Drama; Talent and Integrity*. 1974. Pp. 110-20

Grenzmann, Wilhelm, "Schillers Fruhe Dramen: 'Die Räuber' und 'Kabale und Liebe': Eine Analyse", *Doitsu Bungaku*, #23:3-34, 1959

Heitner, Robert R., "Luise Millerin and the Shock Motif in Schiller's Early Dramas", *Germanic Review* (1966), 41:27-45

————————— , "Neglected Model for 'Kabale und Liebe'", *Journal of English and Germanic Philology*, 57:72-85, Jan., 1958

McCardle, Arthur W., "Schiller and Swabian Pietism", *Dissertation Abstracts International* (1972), 32:3316A

Schwarz, E., "Manuel Tamayo y Baus and Schiller", *Comparative Literature*, 13:123-37, 1961

Seidlin, Oskar, *Essays in German and Comparative Literature*. 1961. Pp. 131-40

——————— , "Greatness and Decline of the Bourgeois; Dramas by Schiller and Dumas", *Comparative Literature*, 6:123-29, 1954

Wilcke, Gero von, "Genealogische Hintergründe zu Schillers Dramen 'Die Räuber' und 'Kabale und Liebe'", *Genealogie. Deutsche Zeitschrift für Familienkunde* (1970), 10,J.19,H.12:325-36

The Maid of Orleans, 1801

Allison, D. E., "The Spiritual Element in Schiller's 'Jungfrau' and Goethe's 'Iphigenie'", *German Quarterly*, 32:316-29, 1959

Blankenagel, John C., "Shaw's 'Saint Joan' and Schiller's 'Jungfrau von Orleans'", *Journal of English and Germanic Philology*, 25:379-92, 1926

Brother Gregory, F. S. C., *Catholicism in Schiller's Drama*. 1949. Pp. 10-16

Burkart, Carl J., "Der Zauberbaum. Die Mystische Seite der 'Jungfrau von Orleans' von Friedrich v. Schiller", *Natur und Kultur* (1963), 55:147-51

Casselmann, Gerhard Gustav, "Biblical and Catholic Elements in Schiller's 'Jungfrau von Orleans'", *Louisiana State University Thesis*, 1941

Evans, M. Blakemore, "'Die Jungfrau von Orleans'; A Drama of Philosophical Idealism", *Monatshefte für Deutschen Unterricht*, 35:188-94, 1943

Fowler, Frank M., "Sight and Insight in Schiller's 'Die Jungfrau von Orleans'", *Modern Language Review* (1973), 68:367-79

——————— , "Storm and Thunder in Gluck's and Goethe's 'Iphigenie auf Taurus' and Schiller's 'Die Jungfrau von Orleans'", *Publications of the English Goethe Society* (1973), 43:1-27

Garland, H. B., *Schiller; The Dramatic Writer*. 1969. Pp. 210-32

Graham, Ilse, *Schiller's Drama; Talent and Integrity*. 1974. Pp. 171-94

Gutmann, Anna, "Schillers 'Jungfrau von Orleans' und die Schuldfrage", *Zeitschrift für Deutsche Philology* (1969), 88:560-83

Kaiser, Gerhard, "Johannes Sendung; Eine These zu Schillers 'Jungfrau von Orleans'", *Jahrbuch der Deutschen Schiller-Gesellschaft* (1966), 10:205-36

Kaufmann, Friedrich W., "Schillers 'Jungfrau von Orleans': Zur Zeitlichen Struktur des Dramas", *German Quarterly*, 7:1-8, 1934

Krumpelmann, John T., "Schiller's Rehabilitation of Jeanne d'Arc", *American-German Review* (1960), 26:8-9 and 38

Muller, Gerd, "Brechts 'Heilige Johanna der Schlachthöfe' und Schillers 'Jungfrau von Orleans': Zur Auseinandersetzung des Modernen Theaters mit der Klassischen Tradition", *Orbis Litterarum* (1969), 24:182-200

Sammons, Jeffrey L., "Mortimer's Conversion and Schiller's Allegiances", *Journal of English and Germanic Philology* (1973), 72:155-66

Sautermeister, Gert, *Idyllik und Dramatik im Werk Friedrich Schillers*. 1971. Pp. 85-89, 110-16, 139-45, 159-61 and 215-20

Storz, Gerhard, "Die Jungfrau von Orleans", *Das Deutsche Drama*, 1:322-38, 1958

Wagenknecht, Edward Charles, ed., *Joan of Arc; An Anthology of History and Literature*. 1948. Pp. 279-92

Waterman, John T., "'Die Jungfrau von Orleans' in the Light of Schiller's Essays", *Germanic Review*, 25:230-38, 1952

Willan, J. N., "Schiller's 'Jungfrau von Orleans': Its Point of Contact with Shakespeare", *Poet-Lore*, 7:169-83, April, 1895

Maria Stuart, 1800
Abel, Lionel, *Metatheatre; A New View of Dramatic Form*. 1963. Pp. 73-74
Ayrault, Roger, "La Figure de Mortimer dans 'Marie Stuart' et la Conception du Drame Historique chez Schiller", *Etudes Germaniques*, 14:313-24, 1959
Beck, Adolf, "Maria Stuart", *Das Deutsche Drama*, 1:305-21, 1958
Best, Alan, "Schiller's 'Mary Stuart': Masquerade as Tragedy", *Modern Languages* (1972), 53:106-10
Brother Gregory, F. S. C., *Catholicism in Schiller's Dramas*. 1949. Pp. 7-9
Deutung und Bedeutung; Studies in German Comparative Literature Presented to Karl Werner Maurer, ed. by Brigette Scheudermann. 1973. Pp. 100-17
Field, G. S., "Schiller's 'Maria Stuart'", *University of Toronto Quarterly*, 29:326-40, 1960
Fuchs, A. and H. Motekat, *Hans Heinrich Borcherdt zum 75. Geburtstag 14. 8. 1962*. 1962. Pp. 238-50
Garland, H. B., *Schiller; The Dramatic Writer*. 1969. Pp. 190-209
Gassner, John, *Theatre at the Crossroads, Plays and Playwrights of the Mid-century American Stage*. 1960. Pp. 279-82
Graham, Ilse, *Schiller's Drama; Talent and Integrity*. 1974. Pp. 149-70
Koch, Herbert, "Zwei Unbekannte Schiller-Rezensionen. Eine 'Don Carlos' Kritik. Eine 'Maria Stuart' Kritik", *Jahrbuch der Deutschen Schiller-Gesellschaft*, 6:178-83, 1962
Politi, Francesco, "Il Senso Della 'Maria Stuart' di Schiller", *Letterature Moderne*, 10:357-61, 1960
Sammons, Jeffrey L., "Mortimer's Conversion and Schiller's Allegiances", *Journal of English and Germanic Philology* (1973), 72:155-66
Sautermeister, Gert, *Idyllic und Dramatik im Werk Friedrich Schillers*. 1971. Pp. 209-14
Seidlin, Oskar, *Essays in German and Comparative Literature*. 1961. Pp. 92-109
Thalheim, Hans Gunter, "Schillers Dramen von 'Maria Stuart' bis 'Demetrius'", *Weimarer Beiträge. Zeitschrift für Literaturwissenschaft* (1974), 20,H.1:5-33 and 20,H.2:99-130
Witte, William, "Zweimal 'Maria Stuart': Schiller Auf Der Englischen und Schottischen Buhne", *Maske und Kothrun* (Graz-Wien), 5:221-26, 1959

Die Rauber   *SEE*   The Robbers

The Robbers, 1782
Aquila; Chestnut Hill Studies in Modern Languages and Literatures. Vol. 1. 1968. Pp. 110-20
Bohn, William J., "Style and Function of the Monologue in Three Plays by Friedrich Schiller: 'Die Rauber', 'Wallenstein' and 'Wilhelm Tell'", *Dissertation Abstracts International* (1972), 32:6964A
Garland, H. B., *Schiller; The Dramatic Writer*. 1969. Pp. 5-39
Graham, Ilse, *Schiller's Drama; Talent and Integrity*. 1974. Pp. 93-109
Grenzmann, Wilhelm, "Schillers Frühe Dramen: 'Die Räuber' und 'Kabale und Liebe'. Eine Analyse", *Doitsu Bungaku*, #23:3-34, 1959
Heitner, Robert R., "Luise Millerin and the Shock Motif in Schiller's Early Dramas", *Germanic Review* (1966), 41:27-45

Klein, Wolfgang, "Uber die Mathematisch-Linguistische Analyse des Drama: Ein Analyse des Kerne in Schillers 'Räubern'", *Cahiers de Linguistique Théorique et Appliquée* (1973), 10:195-200

Lambert, J. W., "Highwaymen", *Plays and Players* (Jan. 1975), 22:29

McCardle, Arthur W., "Schiller and Swabian Pietism", *Dissertation Abstracts International* (1972), 32:3316A

Oehlmann, Werner, "'Die Räuber' von Giselher Klebe: Opernaüffuhrung in Dusseldorf", *Neue Zeitschrift für Musik*, 118:430-31, 1957

Rieder, Heinz, "Schillers 'Räuber'—Eine Tragodie des Weltgerichts", *Stimmen der Zeit*, 165:94-102, 1959

Rouché, Max, "Nature de la Liberté, Legitimité de l'Insurrection dans 'Les Brigands' et 'Guillaume Tell'", *Etudes Germaniques*, 14:403-10, 1959

Schwerte, Hans, "Schillers 'Räuber'", *Der Deutschunterricht*, 12:18-41, 1960

Stamm, Israel S., "The Religious Aspect of 'Die Räuber'", *Germanic Review*, 27:5-9, 1952

Veit, Philipp F., "Moritz Spiegelberg; Eine Charakterstudie zu Schillers 'Räubern'", *Jahrbuch der Deutschen Schiller-Gesellschaft* (1973), 17:273-90

―――――――― , "The Strange Case of Moritz Spiegelberg", *Germanic Review* (May 1969), 44:171-86

Waltschanow, Alexander, "Schillers 'Räuber' in Bulgarien biz zur Befreiung vom Turkischen Joch", *Goethe-Almanach* (1971), Pp. 264-82

Waterhouse, G., "Schiller's 'Räuber' in England Before 1800", *Modern Language Review*, 30:355-57, July, 1935

Wilcke, Gero von, "Genealogische Hintergründe zu Schillers Dramen 'Die Räubern' und 'Kabale und Liebe'", *Genealogie. Deutsche Zeitschrift für Famielenkund* (1970), 10, J.19, H.12:325-36

Turandot, Princess of China, 1802

Witte, W., "Turandot", *Publications of the English Goethe Society* (1969), 39:123-40

Die Verschworung des Fiesco zu Genua SEE Fiesco; or, The Conspiracy of Genoa

Wallenstein, 1798/99

Barnouw, Jeffrey, "Das 'Problem der Aktion' und 'Wallenstein'", *Jahrbuch der Deutschen Schiller-Gesellschaft* (1972), 16:330-408

Berghahn, Klaus, "'Doch eine Sprache Braucht das Herz'; Beobachtungen zu den Liebesdialogen in Schillers 'Wallenstein'", *Monatshefte für Deutschen Unterricht, Deutsche Sprache und Literatur* (1972), 64:25-32

Blankenagel, J. C., "'Wallenstein' and Prinz Friedrich von Homburg", *Germanic Review*, 2:1-11, 1927

Bohn, William J., "Style and Function of the Monologue in Three Plays by Friedrich Schiller: 'Die Rauber', 'Wallenstein' and 'Wilhelm Tell'", *Dissertation Abstracts International* (1972), 32:6964A

Burkart, Carl J., "Die Mystische Seite des 'Wallenstein' von Friedrich v. Schiller", *Das Edle Leben* (1963), 12:6-13

The Discontinuous Tradition; Studies in German Literature in Honour of Ernest Ludwig Stahl, ed. P. F. Ganz. 1971. Pp. 79-98

Garland, H. B., *Schiller; The Dramatic Writer*. 1969. Pp. 138-89

Gille, Klaus F., "Das Astrologische Motiv in Schillers 'Wallenstein'", *Amsterdamer Beiträge zur Neueren Germanistik* (1972), 1:103-18

Guthke, Karl S., "Die Hamburger Bühnenfassung des 'Wallenstein'", *Jahrbuch der Schiller-Gesellschaft*, 2:68-82, 1958

—————— , "Die Sinnstruktur des 'Wallenstein'", *Neophilologus* (Groninger), 42:109-27, 1958

Hofacker, Erich and Liselotte Dieckmann, eds., *Studies in Germanic Languages and Literature: In Memory of Fred O. Nolte*. 1963. Pp. 77-91

Krausse, Helmut K., "Die Schwägerin Marginalien zu Schillers 'Wallenstein'", *Modern Language Notes* (April 1970), 85:332-44

Lawrenson, T. E., F. E. Sutcliffe, and G. F. A. Gadoffe, eds., *Modern Miscellany Presented to Eugene Vinaver by Pupils, Colleagues and Friends*. 1969. Pp. 65-78

Linn, R. N., "Wallenstein's Innocence", *Germanic Review*, 34:200-08, Oct., 1959

Mann, Michael, "Zur Charackterologie in Schillers "Wallenstein'", *Euphorion* (1969), 63:329-39

Marleyn, R., "'Wallenstein' and the Structure of Schiller's Tragedies", *Germanic Review*, 32:186-99, 1957

Müller, Joachim, "Schillers "Wallenstein' als Beispeil eines Historisch-Literarischen Porträts", *Wissenschaftliche Zeitschrift der Friedrich Schiller-Universitat Leipzig. Gesellschafts-u. Sprachwissenschaftliche Reihe* (1970), 18:165-68

Neubauer, John, "The Idea of History in Schiller's 'Wallenstein'", *Neophilologus* (1972), 56:451-63

Rothman, John, "Octavio and Buttler in Schiller's 'Wallenstein'", *German Quarterly*, 27:110-15, 1954

Sammons, Jeffrey L., "Mortimer's Conversion and Schiller's Allegiances", *Journal of English and Germanic Philology* (1973), 72:155-66

Sautermeister, Gert, *Idyllik und Dramatik im Werk Friedrich Schillers*. 1971. Pp. 67-84, 130-38, 155-58 and 201-08

Seidel, Siegfried, "Neue Positionen in der Theorie Schillers Wahrend der Arbeit am 'Wallenstein'", *Weimarer Beiträge*, Pp. 74-97, 1959

Seidlin, Oskar, *Essays in German and Comparative Literature*. 1961. Pp. 92-109

—————— , "'Wallenstein': Sein und Zeit", *Der Monat*, 15:177:28-36, 1963

Spanner, Werner, "Schillers 'Wallenstein': Ein Beiträge zur Gestalt-Interpretation", *Wirkendes Wort*, 13:87-96, 1963

—————— , "Schillers 'Wallenstein' in Unterprima", *Wirkendes Wort*, (1963), 13:96-105

Vincenti, "Il 'Wallenstein' di F. Schiller", *Atti dell' Academia delle Scienze di Torino*, 95:29-86, 1960

Wells, G. A., "Astrology in Schiller's 'Wallenstein'", *Journal of English and Germanic Philology* (Jan. 1969), 68:100-15

Wiese, Benno von, "Wallenstein", *Das Deutsche Drama*, 1:269-304, 1958

Witte, William, *Schiller and Burns and Other Essays*. 1959. Pp. 38-47

Zucker, A. E., "An 'Ahnfrau' Scene in Schiller's 'Wallenstein'", *Modern Language Notes*, 51:97-98, 1936

William Tell, 1804

Appelbaum, Graham, I., "Schillers Wilhelm Tell: Dankgesang eines Gene-senden", *Neophilologus*, 44: 307-22, 1960

Barnstorff, Hermann, "Individualism and Collectivism in Schiller's 'Wilhelm Tell'; A Classroom Suggestion", *Monatshefte*, 45:166-70, 1953

Berendsohn, Walter A., "Schillers 'Wilhelm Tell' als Kunstwerk; Struktur und Stilstudien", *Studier i Modern Sprakvetenskap*, n. s. 1:5-78, 1960

Bohn, William J., "Style and Function of the Monologue in Three Plays by Friedrich Schiller: 'Die Rauber', 'Wallenstein' and 'Wilhelm Tell'", *Dissertation Abstracts International* (1972), 32:6964A

Brinkmann, Richard, et al, *Deutsche Literatur und Franzosische Revolution; Sieben Studien*. 1974. Pp. 87-128

Busse, A., "Schiller's 'Tell' and the Volksstück", *Modern Language Association. Publications* (PMLA), 32:59-67, 1917

The Discontinuous Tradition; Studies in German Literature in Honour of Ernest Ludwig Stahl, ed. P. F. Ganz. 1971. Pp. 71-112

Field, G. W., "Schiller's Theory of the Idyl and 'Wilhelm Tell'", *Monatshefte*, 42:13-21, 1950

Garland, H. B., *Schiller; The Dramatic Writer*. 1969. Pp. 261-86

German Studies; Presented to Professor H. G. Fiedler by Pupils, Colleagues and Friends on His 75th Birthday, April 28, 1937. 1938. Pp. 278-92

Graham, Ilse, *Schiller Drama; Talent and Integrity*. 1974. Pp. 195-215

Grotegut, E. K., "Schiller's 'Wilhelm Tell': A Dramatic Triangle", *Modern Language Notes* (1965), 80:628-34

Hammer, Carl, Jr., ed., *Studies in German Literature*. 1963. Pp. 72-84

Jetter, Marianne R., "'Wilhelm Tell' and Modern Students", *German Quarterly*, 30:45-48, 1957

Jofen, Jean B., "Elements of Homer and the Bible in Schiller's 'Wilhelm Tell'", *Canadian Modern Language Review*, 16:27-35, 1960

Jordan, Gilbert J., "The Oetigheim 'Wilhelm Tell'", *American-German Review*, 19:28-32, 1952

Kahn, Ludwig W., "Freedom; An Existentialist and Idealist View: Sartre's 'Les Mouches' and Schiller's 'Wilhelm Tell'", *Modern Language Association. Publications* (PMLA), 64:5-14, 1949

Kniffler, Carter, "'Wilhelm Tell'—Heute als Schullektüre?", *Der Deutschunterricht* (1971), 23, H.5:53-65

Martini, Fritz, "'Wilhelm Tell': Der Ästhetische Staat und der "Ästhetische Mensch", *Der Deutschunterricht*, 12:90-118, 1960

Mitchell, Roger E. and Joyce P. Mitchell, "Schiller's 'William Tell': A Folkloristic Perspective", *Journal of American Folklore* (Jan. 1970), 83:44-52

Moore, W. G., "'Horace' et 'Wilhelm Tell'", *Revue de Littérature Comparée*, 19:444-51, July, 1939

Plant, Richard, "Gessler and Tell: Psychological Patterns in Schiller's 'Wilhelm Tell'", *Modern Language Quarterly*, 19:60-70, 1958

Poittner, Barbara, "'Wilhelm Tell': Heute Noch als Lektüre in der 8. Klasse: Eine Möglichkeit der Interpretation", *Der Deutschunterricht* (1973), 25: 92-99

Rischbieter, H. and H. Karasek, "Ein Streit um Tell", *Theatre Heute* (1966), 7:34-37

Rouche, Max, "Nature de la Liberté, Legitimité de l'Insurrection dans 'Les Brigands' et 'Guillaume Tell'", *Etudes Germaniques*, 14:403-10, 1959

Sautermeister, Gert, *Idyllik und Dramatik im Werk Friedrich Schillers*. 1971. Pp. 117-27, 146-52, 162-73, and 221-27

Schnapp, F., "Schiller über Seinen 'Wilhelm Tell'", *Deutsche Rundschau*, 206:101-11, Feb., 1926

Sumberg, S. L., "Continuity of Action in Schiller's 'Wilhelm Tell'", *Germanic Review*, 8:17-29, 1933

Texas University. *A Schiller Symposium; In Observance of the Bicentenary of Schiller's Birth. Essays by Harold Jantz and Others.* 1960. Pp. 65-81

Tisch, J. H., *Proceedings of the Australian Goethe Society, 1963-65.* 1966. Pp. 71-96

Untersuchungen zur Literatur als Geschichte. Festschrift für Benno von Wiese, Hrsg. v. Vincent J. Gunther. 1973. Pp. 112-28

Wiese, Benno von and Rudolf Henes, eds., *Nationalismus in Germanistik und Dichtung; Dokumentation des Germanistentages in München vom 17 bis 22 October, 1966.* 1966. Pp. 285-304

JOHANNES SCHLAF

SEE

ARNO HOLZ AND JOHANNES SCHLAF

ARTHUR SCHNITZLER

Affairs of Anatol, 1892

Bauland, Peter, *The Hooded Eagle; Modern German Drama on the New York Stage.* 1968. Pp. 29-30

Bookman, 73:71, March, 1931

Catholic World, 132:720-21, March, 1931

Commonweal, 13:385, Feb. 4, 1931

Grummann, Paul H., "Arthur Schnitzler", *Poet-Lore*, 23:25-41, 1912

Hill, Claude, "The Stature of Arthur Schnitzler", *Modern Drama*, 4:80-91, 1961

Kilian, Klaus, *Die Komödien Arthur Schnitzler.* 1972. Pp. 53-61

Klarmann, Adolf D., "Die Weise von Anatol", *Forum* (Wien), 9:263-65, 1962

Nation, 132:134-35, Feb. 4, 1931

New Republic, 65:323, Feb. 4, 1931

Outlook, 157:190, Feb. 4, 1931

Theatre Magazine, 53:25, March, 1931

Wilson, Edmund, *Shores of Light; A Literary Chronicle of the Twenties and Thirties.* 1952. Pp. 504-08

Das Bacchusfest *SEE* The Festival of Bacchus

The Call of Life, 1906

Conner, Maurice W., "An Investigation of Three Themes Pertaining to Life and Death in the Works of Arthur Schnitzler, with Particular Emphasis on the Drama 'Der Ruf des Lebens'", *Dissertation Abstracts International* (1974), 34:4250A

Krutch, J. W., "Call of Life", *Nation*, 121:494-95, Oct. 28, 1925

Young, Stark, "Call of Life", *New Republic*, 44:255-56, Oct. 28, 1925

The Comedy of Seduction, 1924

Killian, Klaus, *Die Komödien Arthur Schnitzler.* 1972. Pp. 104-09

Countess Mizzi; or, The Family Reunion, 1909

Kilian, Klaus, *Die Komödien Arthur Schnitzler.* 1972. Pp. 80-83

The Eccentric One, 1932
Swales, Martin, *Arthur Schnitzler; A Critical Study*. 1971. Pp. 155-59

Der Einsame Weg SEE The Lonely Way

Fair Game, 1896
Grummann, Paul H., "Arthur Schnitzler", *Poet-Lore*, 23:25-41, 1912

The Fairy Tale, 1894
Grummann, Paul H., "Arthur Schnitzler", *Poet-Lore*, 23:25-41, 1912

The Festival of Bacchus, 1915
Haynes, William, "The Dramatist of Psychoanalysis", *Dial*, 63:63-64, 1917
Swales, Martin, *Arthur Schnitzler; A Critical Study*. 1971. Pp. 171-77

Fink und Fliederbusch, 1917
Kilian, Klaus, *Die Komödien Arthur Schnitzler*. 1972. Pp. 97-100
Offermanns, Ernst L., "Arthur Schnitzlers Komödie 'Fink und Fliederbusch' ", *Modern Austrian Literature; Journal of the International Arthur Schnitzler Research Assn*. 1970. 3:7-24

Freiwild SEE Fair Game

Der Gang zum Weiher SEE The Walk to the Pond

Die Gefährtin SEE His Helpmate

The Green Cockatoo, 1899
Bauland, Peter, *The Hooded Eagle; Modern German Drama on the New York Stage*. 1968. Pp. 28-29
Friedrichsmeyer, Erhard, "Schnitzlers 'Der Grüne Kakadu' ", *Zeitschrift für Deutsche Philologie* (1969), 88:209-28
Grummann, Paul H., "Arthur Schnitzler", *Poet-Lore*, 23:25-41, 1912
Hill, Claude, "The Stature of Schnitzler", *Modern Drama*, 4:80-91, 1961-62
Kilian, Klaus, *Die Komödien Arthur Schnitzler*. 1972. Pp. 66-72 and 149-51
Schinnerer, Otto P., "The Suppression of Schnitzler's 'Der Grüne Kokadu' by the Burg-Theatre", *Germanic Review*, 6:183-92, 1931
Steffen, Hans, ed., *Das Deutsche Lustspiel*. II. 1969. Pp. 61-78
Stroka, Anna, "Arthur Schnitzler Einakter; 'Paracelsus', 'Die Gefährtin' und 'Der Grüne Kakadu' ", *Germanica Wratislaviensia* (1969), 13:57-66
Swales, Martin, *Arthur Schnitzler; A Critical Study*. 1971. Pp. 273-77

The Great Show, 1906
Swales, Martin, *Arthur Schnitzler; A Critical Study*. 1971. Pp. 266-73

Zum Grossen Wurstel SEE The Great Show

Der Grüne Kakadu SEE The Green Cockatoo

Halbzwei SEE One-Thirty

Hands Around, 1920
Bentley, Eric Russell, *Dramatic Event; An American Chronicle*. 1954. Pp. 209-12
Hannum, Hunter G., " 'Killing Time': Aspects of Schnitzler's 'Reigen' ", *Germanic Review*, 37:190-206, 1962
Hill, Claude, "The Stature of Arthur Schnitzler", *Modern Drama*, 4:80-91, 1961-62

Marcuse, Ludwig, "Der 'Reigen' Prozess; Sex, Politik und Kunst 1920 in Berlin", *Der Monat*, 14:#168:48-55 and #169:34-46, 1962

New Republic, 130:21, April 5, 1954

New Yorker, 36:117, May 21, 1960

Sanders, Jon B., "Arthur Schnitzler's 'Reigen': Lost Romanticism", *Modern Austrian Literature; Journal of the International Arthur Schnitzler Research Assn.* (1968), n. s. 1:56-62

Schinnerer, Otto P., "The History of Schnitzler's 'Reigen' ", *Modern Language Association. Publications* (PMLA), 46:839-59, 1931

Theatre Arts, 39:80, Oct. 1955 and 40:77-78, 1956

His Helpmate, 1898
Grummann, Paul H., "Arthur Schnitzler", *Poet-Lore*, 23:25-41, 1912

Haynes, William, "The Dramatist of Psychoanalysis", *Dial*, 63:63-64, 1917

Stroka, Anna, "Arthur Schnitzler Einakter; 'Paracelsus', 'Die Gefährtin' und 'Der Grüne Kakadu' ", *Germanica Wratislavensia* (1969), 13:57-66

Hour of Recognition, 1915
Swales, Martin, *Arthur Schnitzler; A Critical Study*. 1971. Pp. 167-69

Der Junge Medardus SEE The Young Medardus

Komödie der Verfuhrung SEE The Comedy of Seduction

Komtesse Mizzi; oder, Der Familientag SEE Countess Mizzi; or, The Family Reunion

Last Masks, 1902
Hunningher-Schilling, Erica, ed., *Essays on Drama and Theatre; Liber Amicorum Benjamin Hunningher Presented to Professor Dr. B. Hunningher on the Occasion of His Retirement from the Chair of Drama and Theatre Arts in the University of Amsterdam*. 1973. Pp. 129-39

The Legacy, 1898
Grummann, Paul H., "Arthur Schnitzler", *Poet-Lore*, 23:25-41, 1912

Die Letzten Masken SEE Last Masks

Liebelei SEE Light of Love

Light of Love, 1895
Hill, Claude, "The Stature of Arthur Schnitzler", *Modern Drama*, 4:80-91, 1961-62

Literature, 1901
Haynes, William, "The Dramatist of Psychoanalysis", *Dial*, 63:63-64, 1917

The Lonely Way, 1904
Liptzin, S., "Genesis of Schnitzler's 'Der Einsame Weg' ", *Journal of English and Germanic Philology*, 30:392-404, July, 1931

Sevin, Dieter, "Arthur Schnitzlers Gestalt des Erotischen Abenteurers", *University of Dayton Review* (1973), 10:59-66

Das Märchen SEE The Fairy Tale
New Year's Night, 1926
Swales, Martin, *Arthur Schnitzler; A Critical Study*. 1971. Pp. 164-66

One-Thirty, 1932
Swales, Martin, *Arthur Schnitzler; A Critical Study*. 1971. Pp. 159-63

Paracelsus, 1899 ·
Grummann, Paul H., "Arthur Schnitzler", *Poet-Lore*, 23:25-41, 1912
Stroka, Anna, "Arthur Schnitzler Einakter; 'Paracelsus', 'Die Gefährtin' und 'Der Grüne Kakadu'", *Germanica Wratislaviensia* (1969), 13:57-66

Pierette's Veil, 1910
Swales, Martin, *Arthur Schnitzler; A Critical Study*. 1971. Pp. 264-66

Professor Bernhardi, 1912
Commonweal, 88:144-45, Apr. 19, 1968
English Review, 63:275, Sept. 1936
Huneker, James Gibbons, *Ivory Apes and Peacocks*. 1915, Pp. 203-21
Kilian, Klaus, *Die Komödien Arthur Schnitzler*. 1972. Pp. 88-97 and 102-06
Liptzin, Sol, "The Genesis of Schnitzler's 'Prof. Bernhardi'", *Philological Quarterly*, 10:348-55, 1931
Nation, 206:485, Apr. 8, 1968
New Statesman and Nation, 12:255-56, Aug. 22, 1936
Swales, Martin, *Arthur Schnitzler; A Critical Study*. 1971. Pp. 56-68
Weiss, Robert O., "The 'Hero' in Schnitzler's Comedy 'Professor Bernhardi'", *Modern Austrian Literature; Journal of the International Arthur Schnitzler Research Assn.* (1969), 2:30-34

Reigen *SEE* Hands Around

La Ronde *SEE* Hands Around

Der Ruf des Lebens *SEE* The Call of Life

Der Schleier der Pierrette *SEE* Pierette's Veil

Sie Schwestern; oder, Casanova in Spa *SEE* The Sisters; or, Casanova in Spa

The Sisters; or, Casanova in Spa, 1920
Kilian, Klaus, *Die Komödien Arthur Schnitzler*. 1972. Pp. 110-16

Stunde des Erkennens *SEE* Hour of Recognition

Sylvesternacht *SEE* New Year's Night

The Transformation of Pierrot, 1908
Swales, Martin, *Arthur Schnitzler; A Critical Study*. 1971. Pp. 261-64

Die Überspannte Person *SEE* The Eccentric One

Das Vermachtnis *SEE* The Legacy

Die Verwandlungen des Pierrot *SEE* The Transformation of Pierrot

The Walk to the Pond, 1931
Auernheimer, R., "The Way to the Pond", *Theatre Arts*, 15:406-09, May, 1931
Dickerson, Harold D., Jr., "Water and Vision as Mystical Elements in Schnitzler's 'Der Gang zum Weiher'", *Modern Austrian Literatur; Journal of the International Arthur Schnitzler Research Association* (1971), 4,iii:24-36

Das Weite Land *SEE* The Wide Country

The Wide Country, 1911
Kilian, Klaus, *Die Komödien Arthur Schnitzler*. 1972. Pp. 122-26
Liptzin, Sol, "The Genesis of Schnitzler's 'Das Weite Land'", *Modern Language Association. Publications* (PMLA), 46:860-66, Sept., 1931

The Young Medardus, 1910
Mews, Siegfried, ed., *Studies in German Literature of the 19th and 20th Centuries; Festschrift for Frederic E. Coenen*. 1970. Pp. 149-56

AUGUSTIN EUGENE SCRIBE

La Calomnie   *SEE*   Slander

The Glass of Water; or, Causes and Effects, 1841
Arvin, Neil C., "The Comédie-Vaudeville of Scribe", *Sewanee Review*, 26:474-84, 1918

Le Mariage d'Argent   *SEE*   Marriage for Money

Marriage for Money, 1827
Arvin, Neil C., "The Comédie-Vaudeville of Scribe", *Sewanee Review*, 26:474-84, 1918

Slander, 1840
Gauthier, T., "Scribe's 'Calomnie'", *Theatre Arts*, 21:734, Sept., 1937

Le Verre d'Eau; ou, Les Effets et les Causes   *SEE*   The Glass of Water; or, Causes and Effects

AUGUSTIN EUGENE SCRIBE AND ERNEST LEGOUVE

Adrienne Lecouvreur, 1849
Walkley, Arthur Bingham, *Drama and Life*. 1907. Pp. 279-82

Bataille de Dames; ou, Un Duel en Amour   *SEE*   The Queen's Gambit; or, A Duel of Love

A Queen's Gambit; or, A Duel of Love, 1851
Stanton, Stephen S., "Ibsen, Gilbert and Scribe's 'Bataille de Dames'", *Educational Theatre Journal*, 17:24-30, 1965

LORENZO SEMPLE, JR.

SEE

JACQUES DEVAL AND LORENZO SEMPLE, JR.

LUCIUS ANNAEUS SENECA

Agamemnon, 1st Cent. A.D.
Calder, W. M. III, "Size of the Chorus in Seneca's 'Agamemnon'", *Classical Philology* (1975), 70:32-35

Hercules Furens, 1st cent. A.D.
Henry, D. and Walker, B., "Futility of Action; A Study of Seneca's 'Hercules Furens'", *Classical Philology*, 60:11-22, 1965
Harsh, Philip Whaley, *A Handbook of Classical Drama*. 1944. Pp. 410-12

Tobin, Ronald W., "Racine and Seneca", *University of North Carolina Studies in Romance Language and Literature* (1971), 96:29-43

Traina, A., "Le 'Litanie del Sonno' Nello 'Hercules Furens' di Seneca", *Rivista Filologia e di Istruzione Classica* (1967), 95:169-79

Walker, Henry B., "The Futility of Action: A Study of Seneca's 'Hercules Furens'", *Classical Philology* (1965), 60:11-22

Hercules Oetaeus, 1st Cent. A.D.

Axelson, G., "Korruptelenkult. Studien zur Textkritik der Unechten Seneca-Tragödie 'Hercules Oetaeus'", *Humanistika Vetenskapssamfundet i Lund* (1967), #1:3-121

Harsh, Philip Whaley, *A Handbook of Classical Drama*. 1944. Pp. 432-33

Jepson, Laura, *Ethical Aspects of Tragedy; A Comparison of Certain Tragedies by Aeschylus, Sophocles, Euripides, Seneca, and Shakespeare*. 1953. Pp. 103-11

King, Christine M., "Seneca's 'Hercules Oetaeus'; A Stoic Interpretation of the Greek Myth", *Greece and Rome* (1971), 18:215-22

Médée, 1st cent. A.D.

Bellessort, A., "Médée", *Journal des Débats*, 39 pt. 1:851-53, May 27, 1932

Boyer, Clarence Valentine, *The Villain as Hero in Elizabethan Tragedy*. 1964. Pp. 13-20

Harsh, Philip Whaley, *A Handbook of Classical Drama*. 1944. Pp. 417-19

Shakespeare Survey, (1966), 19:82-94

Tobin, Ronald W., "Racine and Seneca", *University of North Carolina Studies in Romance Language and Literature* (1971), 96:17-28, 33-35

Wimmel, Walter, *Forschungen zur Römischen Literatur. Festschrift zum 60. Geburtstag von Karl Büchner*. 1970. Pp. 158-67

Octavia, 1st Cent. A.D.

Harsh, Philip Whaley, *A Handbook of Classical Drama*. 1944. Pp. 437-39

Marti, B. M., "Seneca's 'Apocolocyntosis' and 'Octavia': A Diptych", *American Journal of Philology*, 73:24-36, 1952

Oedipus, 1st Cent. A.D.

Harsh, Philip Whaley, *A Handbook of Classical Drama*. 1944. Pp. 425-26

Mastronarde, Donald J., "Seneca's 'Oedipus': The Drama in the Word", *Transactions and Proceedings of the American Philological Association* (1970), 101:291-315

Scott-Kilvert, Ian, "Seneca or Scenario?" *Arion* (Aut. 1968), 7:501-11

Phèdre, 1st cent. A.D.

Delcourt, M., "Archaïsmes Religieux dans les Tragédies de Sénèque", *Revue Belge de Philologie et d'Histoire*, 41:74-90, 1964

Ruch, M., "La Langue de la Psychologie Amoureuse dans la 'Phèdre' de Sénèque", *Etudes Classiques* (Belg.), 32:356-63, 1964

————, "Phèdre Romaine et Hippolyte Romain", *L'Information Littéraire*, 16:200-06, 1964

Tobin, Ronald W., "Racine and Seneca", *University of North Carolina Studies in Romance Language and Literature* (1971), 96:17-28

Thyestes, 1st cent. A.D.

Gigon, O., "Bemerkungen zu Senecas 'Tyestes'", *Philologus*, 93#1-2:176-83, 1938

Hadas, Moses, "The Roman Stamp of Seneca's Tragedies", *American Journal of Philology*, 60:220-31, 1939
Harsh, Philip Whaley, *A Handbook of Classical Drama*. 1944. Pp. 427-29

PETER SHAFFER

Black Comedy, 1967
  Commentary, 43:74-75, June 1967
  Gilliatt, Penelope, *Unholy Fools, Wits, Comics, Disturbers of the Peace; Film and Theater*. 1973. Pp. 190-92
  Lawson, Wayne P., "The Dramatic Hunt; A Critical Evaluation of Peter Shaffer's Plays", *Dissertation Abstracts International* (1974), 34:7374A
  Life, 62:70A-70B, Mar. 10, 1967
  Nation, 204:285-86, Feb. 27, 1967
  New Statesman, 75:279, Mar. 1, 1968
  New Yorker, 43:91, Feb. 25, 1967
  Newsweek, 69:102-03, Feb. 20, 1967
  Reporter, 36:50, Mar. 9, 1967
  Saturday Review, 50:59, Feb. 25, 1967
  Time, 89:70, Feb. 25, 1967
  Vogue, 149:54, Mar. 15, 1967

Equus, 1973
  America, Dec. 13, 1975, 133:419-22, and Dec. 8, 1973, 129:443-44
  Christian Century, Dec. 17, 1975, 92:1162
  Commonweal, April 25, 1975, 202:78-79
  Dance Magazine, May, 1975, 49:48-50
  "Equus: Playwright Peter Shaffer Interprets Its Ritual", *Vogue*, (Feb. 1975), 165:136-37
  Glenn, Jules, "Anthony and Peter Shaffer's Plays; The Influence of Twinship on Creativity", *American Imago* (1974), 31:270-91
  Harper's Bazaar, Oct. 1974, 107:133
  Lambert, J. W., "Equus", *Drama* (1973), 111:14-16
  Nation, Nov. 16, 1974, 219:506-07
  National Review, Jan. 31, 1975, 27:114-15
  New Republic, Dec. 7, 1974, 171:18
  New Yorker, Nov. 4, 1974, 50:123, Nov. 12, 1973, 49:184
  New York Times Magazine, April 13, 1975, Pp. 20-21
  Newsweek, Nov. 4, 1974, 84:60 and Nov. 11, 1974, 84:121
  Richardson, J., "Equus", *Commentary* (Feb. 1975), 59:76-78
  Saturday Review, Jan. 25, 1975, 2:54
  Simon, J., "Equus", *Hudson Review* (1975), 28:97-106
  Sports Illustrated, March 3, 1975, 42:9
  Time, Nov. 4, 1974, 104:119
  Weightman, J., "Equus", *Encounter* (March 1975), 44:44-46

Five Finger Exercise, 1958
  America, 102:428, Jan. 9, 1960
  Christian Century, 77:16, Jan. 6, 1960
  Commonweal, 71:395, Jan. 1, 1960
  Lawson, Wayne P., "The Dramatic Hunt: A Critical Evaluation of Peter Shaffer's Plays", *Dissertation Abstracts International* (1974), 34:7374A

Life, 48:93, March 21, 1960
Lumley, Frederick, *New Trends in Twentieth Century Drama; A Survey Since Ibsen and Shaw*. 1967. Pp. 279-83
Nation, 188:462, May 16, 1959 and 189:475-76, Dec. 19, 1959
New Yorker, 34:121, Sept. 6, 1959 and 35:100-02, Dec. 12, 1959
Reporter, 22:36-37, Jan. 7, 1960
Saturday Review, 42:24, Dec. 19, 1959
Taylor, John Russell, *Anger and After; A Guide to the New British Drama*. 1962. Pp. 273-75
Theatre Arts, 44:14, Feb. 1960
Time, 74:77, Dec. 14, 1959
Tynan, Kenneth, *Curtains; Selections from the Drama Criticism and Related Writings*. 1963. Pp. 335-37

The Private Ear and The Public Eye, 1962
America, 109:752, Dec. 7, 1963
Lawson, Wayne P., "The Dramatic Hunt; A Critical Evaluation of Peter Shaffer's Plays", *Dissertation Abstracts International* (1974), 34:7374A
Lumley, Frederick, *New Trends in Twentieth Century Drama; A Survey Since Ibsen and Shaw*. 1967. Pp. 279-83
Nation, 197:306, Nov. 9, 1963
Newsweek, 62:104, Oct. 21, 1963
Theatre Arts, 48:65, Jan. 1964
Time, 82:76, Oct. 18, 1963

The Royal Hunt of the Sun, 1964
America, 113:648, Nov. 20, 1965
Brustein, Robert, *The Third Theatre*. 1969. Pp. 114-16
Commonweal, 83:215, Nov. 19, 1965
Dance Magazine, 39:138-39, Dec. 1965
Gassner, John, *Dramatic Soundings; Evaluations and Retractions Culled from Thirty Years of Dramatic Criticism*. 1968. Pp. 609-12
Glenn, Jules, "Anthony and Peter Shaffer's Plays: The Influence of Twinship on Creativity", *American Imago* (1974), 31:270-91
Illustrated London News, 145:208, Aug. 8, 1964
Lawson, Wayne P., "The Dramatic Hunt; A Critical Evaluation of Peter Shaffer's Plays", *Dissertation Abstracts International* (1974), 34:7374A
Life, 59:134-35, Dec. 10, 1965
Lumley, Frederick, *New Trends in Twentieth Century Drama; A Survey Since Ibsen and Shaw*. 1967. Pp. 279-83
Nation, 201:397, Nov. 22, 1965
National Review, 18:37, Jan. 11, 1966
New Republic, 153:145-46, Nov. 27, 1965
New Statesman, 68:95-96, July 17, 1964
New Yorker, 41:115, Nov. 6, 1965
Novick, Julius, *Beyond Broadway; The Quest for Permanent Theatres*. 1968. Pp. 78-79
Partisan Review, 33:273, Apring 1966
Saturday Review, 48:71, Nov. 13, 1965 and 49:72, Nov. 19, 1966
Simon, John, "Theatre Chronicle", *Hudson Review* (1965-66), 18:573-74
Spectator, 213:82, July 17, 1964
Time, 86:77, Nov. 5, 1965

Vogue, 144:112, Nov. 1, 1961

Winegarten, Renee, "The Anglo-Jewish Dramatist in Search of His Soul", *Mid-stream* (1966), 12:40-52

White Lies/White Liars, 1967

Glenn, Jules, "Anthony and Peter Shaffer's Plays; The Influence of Twinship on Creativity", *American Imago* (1974), 31:270-91

Lawson, Wayne P., "The Dramatic Hunt: A Critical Evaluation of Peter Shaffer's Plays", *Dissertation Abstracts International* (1974), 34:7374A

Nation, 204:286, Feb. 27, 1967

New Yorker, 43:91, Feb. 25, 1967

Reporter, 36:50, Mar. 9, 1967

Saturday Review, 50:59, Feb. 25, 1967

GEORGE BERNARD SHAW

Admiral Bashville, 1901

Catholic World, 183:150, May, 1956

Saturday Review, 39:26, March 17, 1956

Androcles and the Lion, 1913

Agate, James Evershed, comp., *English Dramatic Critics, An Anthology, 1660-1932.* 1958. Pp. 295-99

"Androcles (Oh! I Say!) Potiphar", *English Review*, 15:465-68, Oct., 1913

Berst, Charles A., *Bernard Shaw and the Art of Drama.* 1973. Pp. 175-95

Brown, John Mason, *Seeing More Things.* 1948. Pp. 179-87

Catholic World, 148:601, Feb. 1939

deSelincourt, Aubrey, *Six Great Playwrights.* 1960. Pp. 188

Freedman, Morris, *The Moral Impulse; Modern Drama from Ibsen to the Present.* 1967. Pp. 45-62

Haussler, Franz, "'Androcles'; Shaw's Fable Play", *Shaw Bulletin*, 5:8-9, 1954

Hummert, Paul A., *Bernard Shaw's Marxian Romance.* 1973. Pp. 99-102

MacCarthy, Desmond, "Religious Pantomime: 'Androcles and the Lion'", *New Statesman and Nation*, 25:123, Feb. 20, 1943

——————— , *Shaw's Plays in Review.* 1969. Pp. 102-07

Morgan, Margery M., *The Shavian Playground; An Exploration of the Art of Bernard Shaw.* 1972. Pp. 59-62

Nathan, George Jean, *Theatre Book of the Year, 1946-47.* Pp. 231-39

Nelson, Raymond S., "Wisdom and Power in 'Androcles and the Lion'", *Yearbook of English Studies* (1972), 2:192-204

New Yorker, 37:119, Dec. 2, 1961

School and Society, 65:251, April 5, 1947

Time, 32:25, Dec. 26, 1938

Valency, Maurice, *The Cart and the Trumpet.* 1973. Pp. 304-12

Apple Cart, 1929

America, 96:359, Dec. 22, 1956

Catholic World, 131:78-79, April, 1930 and 184:225, Dec., 1965

Chesterton, Gilbert Keith, *Sidelights on New London and Newer New York and Other Essays.* 1932. Pp. 240-46

Christian Century, 73:1328, Nov. 14, 1956

Commonweal, 10:497-98, Sept. 18, 1929 and 11:535, March 12, 1930 and 65:288, Dec. 14, 1956

Donaghy, Henry J., " 'The Apple Cart': A Chestertonian Play", *Shaw Review* (1968), 11:104-08

Drama, 20:6-8, Oct. 1929

Hummert, Paul A., *Bernard Shaw's Marxian Romance*. 1973. Pp. 153-57

Literary Digest, 102:19-20, July 20, 1929 and 104:23-24, March 15, 1930

MacCarthy, Desmond, *Shaw's Plays in Review*. 1969. Pp. 181-87

McDowell, Frederick P. W., " 'The Eternal Against the Expedient': Structure and Theme in Shaw's 'The Apple Cart' ", *Modern Drama*, 2:99-113, 1959

Morgan, Margery M., *The Shavian Playground; An Exploration of the Art of Bernard Shaw*. 1972. Pp. 303-15

Nation, 130:338, March 19, 1930 and 183:374, Nov. 3, 1956

New Republic, 62:99, March 12, 1930 and 135:21-22, Dec. 3, 1956

New York Times Magazine, Pp. 32, Oct. 7, 1956

New Yorker, 29:66, July 18, 1953 and 32:117-18, Oct. 27, 1956

Newsweek, 48:76, Oct. 29, 1956

Review of Reviews, 81:144-45, April, 1930

Rhondda, Margaret Haig, *Notes on the Way*. 1937. Pp. 186-93

Saturday Review, 6:110, Sept. 7, 1929 and 6:705-06, Feb. 8, 1930 and 36:24, Aug. 1, 1953 and 39:24, Nov. 10, 1956

Silverman, Albert H., "Bernard Shaw's Political Extravaganza", *Drama Survey* (Winter 1966-67), 5:213-22

Theatre Arts, 14:370, May, 1930 and 40:21-22, Dec. 1956

Time, 69:98, Oct. 29, 1956

Arms and the Man, 1894

Agate, James Evershed, comp., *English Dramatic Critics, An Anthology, 1660-1932*. 1958. Pp. 223-28

America, 117:63, July 15, 1967

Beerbohm, Max, *Around Theatres*. 1953. Pp. 491-93

Berst, Charles A., *Bernard Shaw and the Art of Drama*. 1973. Pp. 20-38
_____ , "Romance and Reality in 'Arms and the Man' ", *Modern Language Quarterly* (1966), 27:197-211

Catholic World, 172:227, Dec. 1950

Christian Science Monitor Magazine, Pp. 8, Oct. 28, 1950

Commonweal, 53:121, Nov. 10, 1950

Ganz, Arthur, "The Ascent to Heaven; A Shavian Pattern (Early Plays 1894-1898)", *Modern Drama* (Dec. 1971), 14:253-63

Hummert, Paul A., *Bernard Shaw's Marxian Romance*. 1973. Pp. 70-73

Kaul, A. N., *The Action of English Comedy; Studies in the Encounter of Abstraction and Experience from Shakespeare to Shaw*. 1970. Pp. 286-94

Lockhart, J. H. K., "Shaw, Wilde and the Revival of the Comedy of Manners", *Hermathena; A Dublin University Review* (Spr. 1968), 106:18-22

Morgan, Margery M., *The Shavian Playground; An Exploration of the Art of Bernard Shaw*. 1972. Pp. 47-55

New Republic, 123:20, Nov. 13, 1950

Newsweek, 36:78, Oct. 30, 1950

Novick, Julius, *Beyond Broadway; The Quest for Permanent Theatres*. 1968. Pp. 319-21

Quinn, Michael, "Form and Intention: A Negative View of 'Arms and the Man' ", *Critical Quarterly* (1963), 5:148-54

Shaw, George Bernard, *Selected Non-Dramatic Writings*, ed. by Dan H. Lawrence. 1965. Pp. 323-40

―――――――――― , *Shaw on Theatre*, ed. by E. J. West. 1958. Pp. 212-13

Smiley, Sam, *Playwriting: The Structure of Action*. 1971. Pp. 52-60

Speckhard, Robert R., "Shaw's Therapeutic Satire", *Marab: A Review* (1964), 1:94-99

Valency, Maurice, *The Cart and the Trumpet*. 1973. Pp. 104-09 and 111-17

Ward, Alfred Charles, ed., *Specimens of English Dramatic Criticism 17th—20th Centuries*. 1945. Pp. 190-97

Augustus Does His Bit, 1917

MacCarthy, Desmond, *Shaw's Plays in Review*. 1969. Pp. 124-28

Regan, Arthur E., "The Fantastic Reality of Bernard Shaw: A Look at 'Augustus' and 'Too True' ", *Shaw Review* (1968), 11:2-10

Back to Methuselah, 1922

Baughan, E. A., "Back to Methuselah", *Fortnightly Review*, 120:827-34, Nov. 1923

Brustein, Robert, *The Theatre of Revolt; An Approach to the Modern Drama*. 1964. Pp. 195-204

Catholic World, 187:226-27, June, 1958

Clutton-Brock, Arthur, *Essays on Literature and Life*. 1927. Pp. 182-89

Darlington, William Aubrey, *Literature in the Theatre and Other Essays*. 1925. Pp. 151-56

deSelincourt, Aubrey, *Six Great Playwrights*. 1960. Pp. 177

The Dial, a Dial Miscellany, ed. by William Wasserstrom. 1963. Pp. 47-50

English Association, *Essays and Studies, 1960, being vol. 13 of the new series of Essays and Studies Collected for the English Assn. by M. St. Clare Byrne*. 1960. Pp. 82-98

Ganz, Arthur, "The Ascent to Heaven; A Shavian Pattern (Early Plays 1894-1898)", *Modern Drama* (Dec. 1971), 14:253-63

Geduld, Harry M., "The Lineage of Lility", *Shaw Review* (1964), 7:58-61

Gottesman, Ronald and Scott Boyce, eds., *Art and Error; Modern Textual Editing*. 1970. Pp. 208-18

Hamilton, R., "Philosophy of Bernard Shaw; A Study of 'Back to Methuselah' ", *London Quarterly Review*, 170:333-41, July, 1945

Hummert, Paul A., *Bernard Shaw's Marxian Romance*. 1973. Pp. 135-47

Hunnigher, B., "Shaw en Brecht", *Forum der Letteren* (1971), 12:173-90

Kaufmann, Ralph James, ed., *G. B. Shaw; A Collection of Critical Essays*. 1965. Pp. 130-42

Kaul, A. N., *The Action of English Comedy; Studies in the Encounter of Abstraction and Experience from Shakespeare to Shaw*. 1970. Pp. 286-94

Kennedy, Andrew K., "The Absurd and the Hyperarticulate in Shaw's Dramatic Language", *Modern Drama* (1973), 16:185-92

―――――――――― , *Six Dramatists in Search of a Language*. 1975. Pp. 76-79

Lawrence, Kenneth, "Bernard Shaw; The Career of the Life Forces", *Modern Drama* (1972), 15:130-46

Leary, Daniel and Foster, Richard, "Adam and Eve; Evolving Archetypes in 'Back to Methuselah' ", *Shaw Review*, 4:12-23, 1961

Lewisohn, Ludwig, "Back to Methuselah", *Nation*, 114:323, March 15, 1922

Literary Digest, 73:30-1, April 1, 1922

MacCarthy, Desmond, *Shaw's Plays in Review.* 1969. Pp. 134-42

Morgan, Margery M., "'Back to Methuselah'; The Poet and the City", *Essays and Studies by Members of the English Association*, 13:82-98, 1960

———————, *The Shavian Playground; An Exploration of the Art of Bernard Shaw.* 1972. Pp. 221-38

Nation, 186:349, April 19, 1958

Nelson, Raymond S., "'Back to Methuselah': Shaw's Modern Bible", *Costerus; Essays in English and American Language and Literature* (1972), 5:117-23

———————, "Shaw's Heaven and Hell", *Contemporary Review* (1975), 226:132-36

New Republic, 138:21, April, 1958

New Yorker, 34:62, April 5, 1958

Parker, R. A., "Back to Methuselah", *The Independent*, 108:310, March 25, 1922

Rankin, H. D., "Plato and Bernard Shaw, Their Ideal Communities", *Hermathena* (1959), 93:71-77

Reitemeier, Rüdiger, "Sündenfall und Ubermensch in G. B. Shaws 'Back to Methuselah'", *Germanisch-Romanische Monatschrift* (1966), 16:65-76

Saturday Review, 41:34, April 12, 1958

Squire, John Collings, *Books Reviewed.* 1922. Pp. 122-28

Theatre Arts, 31:35-36, May, 1947 and 38:24-25, June, 1954

Valency, Maurice, *The Cart and the Trumpet.* 1973. Pp. 349-68

Wardle, Irving, "Back to Shaw", *Listener* (1966), 75:56-58

Wisenthal, J. L., *The Marriage of Contraries; Bernard Shaw's Middle Plays.* 1974. Pp. 193-217

Young, Stark, "Back to Methuselah", *New Republic*, 30:80-81, March 15, 1922

Buoyant Billions, 1959

America, 101:438, June 13, 1959

New Yorker, 35:120, June 6, 1959

Caesar and Cleopatra, 1906

Adams, Elsie B., *Bernard Shaw and the Aesthetes.* 1971. Pp. 112-14

Berst, Charles A., "The Anatomy of Greatness in 'Caesar and Cleopatra'", *Journal of English and Germanic Philology* (Jan. 1969), 68:74-91

———————, *Bernard Shaw and the Art of Drama.* 1973. Pp. 75-95

Brown, John Mason, *As They Appear.* 1952. Pp. 89-97

———————, *Dramatis Personae; A Retrospective Show.* 1963. Pp. 136-40

———————, *Still Seeing Things.* 1950. Pp. 160-66

Canfield, May Case, *Grotesques and Other Reflections.* 1927. Pp. 172-81

Catholic World, 170:384, Feb. 1950 and 174:389-90, Feb. 1952

Christian Science Monitor Magazine, Pp. 5, March 4, 1950

Clurman, Harold, *The Divine Pastime; Theatre Essays.* 1974. Pp. 91-93

Colliers, 128:21, Dec. 22, 1951

Commonweal, 51:390, Jan. 13, 1950 and 55:349, Jan. 11, 1952

Conchman, Gordon W., "Comic Catharsis in 'Caesar and Cleopatra'", *Shaw Review*, 3:11-14, 1960

deSelincourt, Aubrey, *Six Great Playwrights*. 1960. Pp. 182-83

Dukore, Bernard F., "'Too Much of a Good Thing?' Structural Features of 'Caesar and Cleopatra'", *Educational Theatre Journal* (1973), 25:193-98

Freedman, Morris, *The Moral Impulse; Modern Drama from Ibsen to the Present*. 1967. Pp. 45-62

Gassner, John, *Dramatic Soundings; Evaluations and Retractions Culled from Thirty Years of Dramatic Criticism*. 1968. Pp. 540-42

Hummert, Paul A., *Bernard Shaw's Marxian Romance*. 1973. Pp. 83-86

Kaul, A. N., *The Action of English Comedy; Studies in the Encounter of Abstraction and Experience from Shakespeare to Shaw*. 1970. Pp. 309-15

Lalou, R., "George Bernard Shaw", *Revue d'Histoire du Théâtre*, 47:49-52, 1951

Larson, Gale K., "Bernard Shaw's 'Caesar and Cleopatra' as History", *Dissertation Abstracts* (1969), 29:4495A

Leary, Daniel J., "The Moral Dialectic in 'Caesar and Cleopatra'", *Shaw Review* (1962), 5:42-53

Life, 28:46-48, Jan. 30, 1950 and 31:82-84, Dec. 17, 1951

MacCarthy, Desmond, *Shaw's Plays in Review*. 1969. Pp. 93-101

Mason, Michael, "'Caesar and Cleopatra': A Shavian Exercise in Both Hero-Worship and Belittlement", *Humanities Association Bulletin* (1974), 25:1-10

Morgan, Margery M., *The Shavian Playground; An Exploration of the Art of Bernard Shaw*. 1972. Pp. 240-44 and 246-48

Nathan, George Jean, *Theatre Book of the Year, 1949-50*. Pp. 130-42

Nation, 120:500, April 29, 1925 and 169:650-51, Dec. 31, 1949 and 174:17-18, Jan. 5, 1952

New Republic, 42:262-63, April 29, 1925 and 122:21, Jan. 2, 1950 and 126:22, Jan. 21, 1952

New York Times Magazine, Pp. 16, Dec. 18, 1949

New Yorker, 25:38, Dec. 31, 1949 and 27:50, Dec. 29, 1951

Newsweek, 35:48, Jan. 2, 1950 and 38:53, Dec. 31, 1951

Reinert, Otto, "Old History and New; Anachronism in 'Caesar and Cleopatra'", *Modern Drama*, 3:37-41, 1960

Saturday Review, 33:26-28, Jan. 14, 1950 and 35:24-27, Jan. 12, 1952

School and Society, 71:215-17, April 8, 1950 and 75:104-06, Feb. 16, 1952

Theatre Arts, 34:8, March, 1950 and 35:10-11, Dec. 1951

Time, 55:52, Jan. 2, 1950 and 58:44-47, Dec. 31, 1951

Tynan, Kenneth, *Curtains; Selections from the Drama Criticism and Related Writings*. 1960. Pp. 8-10

Ure, Peter, "Master and Pupil in Bernard Shaw", *Essays in Criticism* (1969), 19:118-39

Valency, Maurice, *The Cart and the Trumpet*. 1973. Pp. 171-77

Young, Stark, *Immortal Shadows; A Book of Dramatic Criticism*. 1948. Pp. 57-60

Candida, 1897

Adler, Jacob, "Ibsen, Shaw and 'Candida'", *Journal of English and Germanic Philology* (1960), 59:50-58

Bergman, Herbert, "Comedy in 'Candida'", *Shavian* (1972), 4:161-69

Berst, Charles A., *Bernard Shaw and the Art of Drama*. 1973. Pp. 39-74

_____ , "The Craft of 'Candida'", *College Literature* (1974), 1:157-73

Canadian Magazine, 64:74-75, April, 1925
Catholic World, 145:211-13, May, 1937 and 155:338-40, June, 1942
Commonweal, 25:612, March 26, 1937 and 36:135-36, May 29, 1942 and
    56:140, May 16, 1952
Erskine, John, *Delight of Great Books*. 1928. Pp. 277-94
Fortnightly, 177 (ns 171):122-27, Feb. 1952
Freedman, Morris, *The Moral Impulse; Modern Drama from Ibsen to the
    Present*. 1967. Pp. 45-62
Ganz, Arthur, "The Ascent to Heaven; A Shavian Pattern (Early Plays 1894-
    1898)", *Modern Drama* (Dec. 1971), 14:253-63
Hummert, Paul A., *Bernard Shaw's Marxian Romance*. 1973. Pp. 66-70
King, Walter N., "The Rhetoric of 'Candida'", *Modern Drama*, 2:71-83,
    1959
Lalou, R., "George Bernard Shaw", *Revue d'Histoire du Théâtre*, 47:49-52,
    1951
Lauter, Paul, "'Candida' and 'Pygmalion'; Shaw's Subversion of Stereo-
    types", *Shaw Review*, 3:14-19, 1960
Literary Digest, 84:28-29, Feb. 7, 1925 and 123:28, March 20, 1937
McCall's, 90:28, March, 1963
MacCarthy, Desmond, *Shaw's Plays in Review*. 1969. Pp. 19-27
Mais, Stuart Petre Brodie, *Some Modern Authors*. 1923. Pp. 311-17
Mills, John A., "The Comic in Words: Shaw's Cockneys", *Drama Survey*
    (Summer 1966), 5:137-50
Nathan, George Jean, *Theatre Book of the Year, 1945-46*. Pp. 353-57
Nation, 144:361-62, March 27, 1937
Nethercot, Arthur H., "The Truth about Candida", *Modern Language
    Association. Publications* (PMLA), 64:639-47, 1949
New Republic, 90:322, April 21, 1937
New Yorker, 28:68, May 3, 1952
Newsweek, 9:22, March 20, 1937 and 39:94, May 5, 1952
Smith, J. Percy, *The Unrepentant Pilgrim; A Study of the Development
    of Bernard Shaw*. 1965. Pp. 258-60
Speckhard, Robert R., "Shaw's Therapeutic Satire", *Marab: A Review*
    (1964), 1:94-99
Theatre Arts, 21:344, May, 1937 and 26:421-22, July, 1942
Time, 59:54, May 5, 1952
Valency, Maurice, *The Cart and the Trumpet*. 1973. Pp. 18-35
Walkley, Arthur Bingham, *Drama and Life*. 1907. Pp. 214-18
Williams, Raymond, *Drama from Ibsen to Brecht*. 1968. Pp. 249-51
Young, Stark, *Immortal Shadows; A Book of Dramatic Criticism*.   1948.
    Pp. 193-95

Captain Brassbound's Conversion, 1900
    Alexander, D. N., "Captain Brant and Captain Brassbound; The Origin of an
        O'Neill Character", *Modern Language Notes*, 74:306-10, April, 1959
    Catholic World, 172:388, Feb. 1951
    Christian Science Monitor Magazine, Pp. 6, Jan. 6, 1951
    Commonweal, 53:374, Jan. 19, 1951
    Duerksen, Roland A., "Shelleyan Witchcraft; The Unbinding of Brassbound",
        Shaw Review (1972), 15:21-25
    Hummert, Paul A., *Bernard Shaw's Marxian Romance*. 1973. Pp. 105-10
    MacCarthy, Desmond, *Shaw's Plays in Review*. 1969. Pp. 57-65

Mason, Michael, "Captain Brassbound and Governor Eyre", *Shavian* (1963), 2:20-22

Mills, John A., "The Comic in Words: Shaw's Cockneys", *Drama Survey* (Summer 1966), 5:137-50

Morgan, Margery M., *The Shavian Playground: An Exploration of the Art of Bernard Shaw*. 1972. Pp. 55-59

Nathan, George Jean, *Theatre Book of the Year, 1950-51*. Pp. 164-66

Nation, 172:18, Jan. 6, 1951

Nelson, Raymond S., "The Quest for Justice in 'Captain Brassbound's Conversion'", *Iowa English Bulletin Yearbook* (Fall 1971), 21:3-9

Newsweek, 37:67, Jan. 8, 1951

School and Society, 73:101-02, Feb. 17, 1951

Speckhard, Robert R., "Shaw's Therapeutic Satire", *Marab: A Review* (1964), 1:94-99

Theatre Arts, 35:14, March, 1951

Theatre Arts Anthology; A Record and a Prophecy, ed. by Rosamond Gilder, et al. 1950. Pp. 274-77

Time, 57:30, Jan. 8, 1951

Valency, Maurice, *The Cart and the Trumpet*. 1973. Pp. 181-98

The Dark Lady of the Sonnets, 1910
English Review, 7:258-59, Jan. 1911
MacCarthy, Desmond, *Shaw's Plays in Review*. 1969. Pp. 120-23

The Devil's Disciple, 1897
America, 116:880, June 24, 1967
Beerbohm, Max, *Around Theatres*. 1953. Pp. 38-41
Catholic World, 170:468, March, 1950
Christian Science Monitor Magazine, Pp. 5, March 4, 1950
Commonweal, 51:535-36, Feb. 24, 1950
Ganz, Arthur, "The Ascent to Heaven; A Shavian Pattern (Early Plays 1894-1898)", *Modern Drama* (Dec. 1971), 14:253-63
Hummert, Paul A., *Bernard Shaw's Marxian Romance*. 1973. Pp. 92-95
Life, 28:53-54, March 6, 1950
Littell, Robert "The Devil's Disciple", *New Republic*, 34:299-300, May 9, 1923
———————— , *Read America First*. 1933. Pp. 172-82
MacCarthy, Desmond, *Shaw's Plays in Review*. 1969. Pp. 198-202
Nathan, George Jean, *Theatre Book of the Year, 1949-50*. Pp. 210-12
Nation, 170:114, Feb. 4, 1950
New Republic, 122:20, Feb. 27, 1950
New Yorker, 26:58, March 4, 1950
Newsweek, 35:82, March 6, 1950
School and Society, 71:215-17, April 8, 1950
Shaw, George Bernard, *Selected Non-Dramatic Writings*, ed. by Dan H. Lawrence. 1965. Pp. 442-45
Theatre Arts, 34:13, April, 1950
Time, 55:66, Feb. 6, 1950
Valency, Maurice, *The Cart and the Trumpet*. 1973. Pp. 156-68

The Doctor's Dilemma, 1906
Adams, Elsie B., *Bernard Shaw and the Aesthetes*. 1971. Pp. 121-30
Agate, James Evershed, comp., *English Dramatic Critics, An Anthology, 1660-1932*. 1958. Pp. 261-65

America, 92:491, Feb. 5, 1955
Beerbohm, Max, *Around Theatres*. 1953. Pp. 442-46
Catholic World, 153:216, May, 1941 and 180:468-69, March, 1955
Commonweal, 33:574-75, March 28, 1941 and 61:524-25, Feb. 18, 1955
Freedman, Morris, *The Moral Impulse; Modern Drama from Ibsen to the Present*. 1967. Pp. 45-62
Gouhier, H., "Le Théâtre. Intrigue et Action: Bernard Shaw à J. P. Sartre", *La Table Ronde*, #143:173-78, 1959
Hummert, Paul A., *Bernard Shaw's Marxian Romance*. 1973. Pp. 111-15
Lehman, B. H. and Others, "Image of the Work; Essays in Criticism", *Univ. of California Pubs. in English Studies*, 11:189-207, 1955
Life, 10:82-84, May 5, 1941
MacCarthy, Desmond, *Shaw's Plays in Review*. 1969. Pp. 66-76
McCarthy, Mary Therese, *Sights and Spectacles, 1937-1956*. 1956. Pp. 151-62
Morgan, Margery M., *The Shavian Playground; An Exploration of the Art of Bernard Shaw*. 1972. Pp. 158-69
Nation, 152:331, March 22, 1941 and 180:107, Jan. 29, 1955, 203:427-28, Oct. 24, 1966
New Republic, 53:96-97, Dec. 14, 1927 and 104:404, March 24, 1941 and 132:22, Feb. 7, 1955
New Yorker, 17:36, March 22, 1941 and 30:74, Jan. 22, 1955
Newsweek, 17:70, March 24, 1941
Outlook, 147:532, Dec. 28, 1927
Saturday Review, 38:24, Jan. 29, 1955
Saturday Review of Literature, 4:372, Dec. 3, 1927
Smith, J. Percy, "A Shavian Tragedy: 'The Doctor's Dilemma'", *Univ. of Cal. Publications in English Studies*, 11:189-207, 1955
Tedesco, Joseph S., "The Theory and Practice of Tragicomedy in George Bernard Shaw's Dramaturgy", *Dissertation Abstracts International* (1973), 33:4586A
Theatre Arts, 25:327-29, May, 1941 and 39:92, March, 1955
Time, 37:43, March 24, 1941
Turco, Alfred, "Sir Colenso's White Lie", *Shaw Review* (1970), 13:14-25
Valency, Maurice, *The Cart and the Trumpet*. 1973. Pp. 265-79
Walkley, Arthur Bingham, *Drama and Life*. 1907. Pp. 239-44

Fanny's First Play, 1911
Chapman, John Jay, *Memories and Milestones*. 1915. Pp. 31-41
Lorichs, Sonja, *The Unwomanly Woman in Bernard Shaw's Drama and Her Social and Political Background*. 1973. Pp. 113-32
MacCarthy, Desmond, *Shaw's Plays in Review*. 1969. Pp. 203-05

Geneva, 1938
Canadian Forum, 19:288, Dec. 1939
Catholic World, 150:729, March, 1940
Commonweal, 31:367, Feb. 16, 1940
Hummert, Paul A., *Bernard Shaw's Marxian Romance*. 1973. Pp. 189-95
MacCarthy, Desmond, *Shaw's Plays in Review*. 1969. Pp. 193-97
Newsweek, 15:38, Feb. 12, 1940
Nineteenth Century, 125:88-90, Jan. 1939 and 126:449-57, Oct. 1939
Sharp, Sister M. Corona, "The Theme of Masks in 'Geneva'; An Example of Shaw's Later Technique", *Shaw Review*, 5:82-91, 1962

Silverman, Albert H., "Bernard Shaw's Political Extravaganza", *Drama Survey* (Winter 1966-67), 5:213-22

Stone, Susas C., "'Geneva': Paean to the Dictators?", *Shaw Review* (1973), 16:21-40

Theatre Arts, 23:100, Feb. 1939 and 24:238, April, 1940

Time, 34:59-60, Nov. 13, 1939

Getting Married, 1908

Beerbohm, Max, *Around Theatres*. 1953. Pp. 508-12

Catholic World, 133:207, May, 1931

Commonweal, 13:666, April 15, 1931

Dawick, John, "Stagecraft and Structure in Shaw's Disquisitory Drama", *Modern Drama* (1971), 14:276-87

Dervin, Daniel, *Bernard Shaw; A Psychological Study*. 1975. Pp. 268-74

Drama, 21:10, May, 1931

Hackett, Francis, *Horizons; A Book of Criticism*. 1918. Pp. 198-202

Hummert, Paul A., *Bernard Shaw's Marxian Romance*. 1973. Pp. 115-18

MacCarthy, Desmond, *Shaw's Plays in Review*. 1969. Pp. 155-59

Morgan, Margery M., *The Shavian Playground; An Exploration of the Art of Bernard Shaw*. 1972. Pp. 176-86

New Republic, 66:236, April 15, 1931

New Yorker, 35:84, June, 13, 1959

Rosenblood, Norman, ed., *Shaw; Seven Critical Essays*. 1971. Pp. 3-24

Sharp, William, "'Getting Married': New Dramaturgy in Comedy", *Educational Theatre Journal* (1959), 11:103-09

Solomon, Stanley J., "Theme and Structure in 'Getting Married'", *Shaw Review*, 5:92-96, 1962

Valency, Maurice, *The Cart and the Trumpet*. 1973. Pp. 279-86

Heartbreak House, 1920

Agate, James Evershed, *Alarums and Excursions*. 1922. Pp. 187-92

America, 102:218, Nov. 14, 1959

Berst, Charles A., *Bernard Shaw and the Art of Drama*. 1973. Pp. 221-58

Brustein, Robert, *The Theatre of Revolt; An Approach to the Modern Drama*. 1964. Pp. 220-27

Catholic World, 147:344-45, June, 1938 and 171:148, May, 1950

Christian Century, 76:1345, Nov. 18, 1959

Coleman, D. C., "Fun and Games; Two Pictures of 'Heartbreak House'", *Drama Survey* (1966-67), 5:223-36

Commonweal, 28:77, May 13, 1938

Corrigan, Robert W., "'Heartbreak House'; Shaw's Elegy for Europe", *Shaw Review*, 2:2-6, 1959

——————— , *The Theatre in Search of a Fix*. 1973. Pp. 161-74

Crompton, Louis, "Shaw's 'Heartbreak House'", *Prairie Schooner* (1965), 39:17-32

Dawick, John, "Stagecraft and Structure in Shaw's Disquisitory Drama", *Modern Drama* (1971), 14:276-87

Fernald, John, "Vivisection of 'Heartbreak House'", *Shavian* (1961), 2:30-31

Hornby, Richard, "The Symbolic Action of 'Heartbreak House'", *Drama Survey* (Winter 1968-69), 7:5-24

Hoy, Cyrus, "Shaw's Tragicomic Irony; from 'Man and Superman' to 'Heartbreak House'", *Virginia Quarterly Review* (Winter 1971), 47:56-78

Hummert, Paul A., *Bernard Shaw's Marxian Romance*. 1973. Pp. 124-29

Hunnigher, B., "Shaw en Brecht", *Forum der Letteren* (1971), 12:173-90

Jordan, John, "Shaw's 'Heartbreak House'", *Threshold*, 1:50-56, 1957

Kaufman, Michael V., "The Dissonance of Dialectic: Shaw's 'Heartbreak House'", *Shaw Review* (1970), 13:2-9

Kennedy, Andrew K., *Six Dramatists in Search of a Language*. 1975. Pp. 59-61

Kozelka, Paul, "'Heartbreak House' Revived", *Shaw Review*, 3:38-39, 1960

Leary, Daniel J., "Shaw's Blakean Vision: A Dialectic Approach to 'Heartbreak House'", *Modern Drama* (1972), 15:89-103

Lewis, Allan, *The Contemporary Theatre; The Significant Playwrights of Our Time*. 1962. Pp. 80-111

MacCarthy, Desmond, *Shaw's Plays in Review*. 1969. Pp. 143-54

McCarthy, Mary Therese, *Sights and Spectacles, 1937-1956*. 1956. Pp. 39-45

McDowell, Frederick P. W., "Technique, Symbol and Theme in 'Heartbreak House'", *Modern Language Association. Publications* (PMLA), 68:335-56, 1953

Mendelsohn, Michael J., "The Heartbreak Houses of Shaw and Chekhov", *Shaw Review* (1963), 6:89-95

Morgan, Margery M., *The Shavian Playground; An Exploration of the Art of Bernard Shaw*. 1972. Pp. 200-20

Nation, 146:566-67, May 14, 1938 and 177:157, Aug. 22, 1953 and 189:338, Nov. 7, 1959

Nethercot, Arthur H., "Zeppelins Over Heartbreak House", *Shaw Review* (1966), 9:46-51

New Republic, 95:130, June 8, 1938 and 141:20-21, Nov. 2, 1959

New Yorker, 35:131, Oct. 31, 1959

Newsweek, 54:97-98, Nov. 2, 1959

Peters, Sally A., "Shaw: A Formal Analysis of Structural Development Through an Examination of Representative Plays", *Dissertation Abstracts International* (1973), 34:3426A

Reed, Robert R., "Boss Mangan, Peer Gynt and Heartbreak House", *Shaw Review*, 2:6-12, 1959

Reporter, 21:33-35, Nov. 26, 1959

Roy, Emil, *British Drama Since Shaw*. 1972. Pp. 13-18

Saturday Review, 42:26, Oct. 31, 1959

Tedesco, Joseph S., "The Theory and Practice of Tragicomedy in George Bernard Shaw's Dramaturgy", *Dissertation Abstracts International* (1973), 33:4586A

Theatre Arts, 43:85, Dec. 1959

Time, 74:32, Nov. 2, 1959

Tynan, Kenneth, *Curtains; Selections from the Drama Criticism and Related Writings*. 1961. Pp. 327-30

Ure, Peter, "Master and Pupil in Bernard Shaw", *Essays in Criticism* (1969), 19:118-39

Valency, Maurice, *The Cart and the Trumpet*. 1973. Pp. 335-48

Vidal, Gore, "Debate in the Moonlight", *Reporter* (1959), 21:33-35

——————————, *Homage to Daniel Shays; Collected Essays, 1952-1972*. 1972. Pp. 58-66

Weintraub, Stanley, "'Hearbreak House': Shaw's 'Lear'", *Modern Drama* (1972), 15:255-65

Wisenthal, J. L., *The Marriage of Contraries; Bernard Shaw's Middle Plays.*
1974. Pp. 127-29 and 136-71
Young, Stark, *Immortal Shadows; A Book of Dramatic Criticism.* 1948.
Pp. 206-10

In Good King Charles' Golden Days, n. d.
O'Donnell, Norbert F., "Harmony and Discord in 'Good King Charles' ",
Shaw Bulletin, 2:5-8, 1958

John Bull's Other Island, 1904
Beerbohm, Max, *Around Theatres.* 1953. Pp. 353-57
Catholic World, 167:71, April, 1948
Commonweal, 47:494, Feb. 27, 1948
deSelincourt, Aubrey, *Six Great Playwrights.* 1960. Pp. 175-76
Gassner, John, *Dramatic Soundings; Evaluations and Retractions Culled
from Thirty Years of Dramatic Criticism.* 1968. Pp. 641-42
Hummert, Paul A., *Bernard Shaw's Marxian Romance.* 1973. Pp. 86-89
Kaul, A. N., *The Action of English Comedy; Studies in the Encounter of
Abstraction and Experience from Shakespeare to Shaw.* 1970. Pp. 304-09
Leary, Daniel J., "A Deleted Passage from Shaw's 'John Bull's Other Island' ",
Bulletin of the New York Public Library (1970), 74:598-606
MacCarthy, Desmond, *Shaw's Plays in Review.* 1969. Pp. 28-31
McDowell, Frederick P., "Politics, Comedy, Character and Dialectic: The
Shavian World of 'John Bull's Other Island' ", *Modern Language Associa-
tion. Publications* (1967), 82:542-53
Morgan, Margery M., *The Shavian Playground; An Exploration of the Art
of Bernard Shaw.* 1969. Pp. 119-33
Nathan, George Jean, *Theatre Book of the Year, 1947-48.* Pp. 262-66
Nation, 166:219-21, Feb. 21, 1948
New Republic, 118:24, March 1, 1948
New Yorker, 23:53, Feb. 21, 1948
Newsweek, 31:80, Feb. 23, 1948
O'Driscoll, Robert, ed., *Theatre and Nationalism in 20th Century Ireland.*
1971. Pp. 156-78
Robinson, Lennox, ed., *Irish Theatre.* 1939. Pp. 199-227
Rollins, Ronald G., "Shaw and O'Casey: John Bull and His Other Island",
Shaw Review (1967), 10:60-69
Sidnell, M. J., " 'John Bull's Other Island'—Yeats and Shaw", *Modern Drama*
(Dec. 1968), 11:245-51
Time, 51:56, Feb. 23, 1948
Valency, Maurice, *The Cart and the Trumpet.* 1973. Pp. 238-47
Walkley, Arthur Bingham, *Drama and Life.* 1907. Pp. 219-23
Wisenthal, J. L., *The Marriage of Contraries; Bernard Shaw's Middle Plays.*
1974. Pp. 87-108

Major Barbara, 1905
Albert, Sidney P., "In More Ways than One; Major Barbara's Debt to Gilbert
Murray", *Educational Theatre Journal* (1968), 20:123-40
_____ , "The Price of Salvation; Moral Economics in 'Major Bar-
bara' ", *Modern Drama* (Dec. 1971), 14:307-23
America, 96:358, Dec. 22, 1956
Beerbohm, Max, *Around Theatres.* 1953. Pp. 409-14

Bennett, C. A., "Major Barbara", *Bookman*, 63:32-36, March, 1926

Berst, Charles A., "The Devil and Major Barbara", *Modern Language Association. Publications* (1968), 83:71-79

―――――――――― , *Bernard Shaw and the Art of Drama*. 1973. Pp. 154-74

Bree, Germaine, *Literature and Society*. 1964. Pp. 121-41

Catholic World, 184:305, Jan. 1957

Christian Century, 74:658, May 22, 1957

Commonweal, 65:288-89, Dec. 14, 1956 and 60:558, Sept. 10, 1954

Devin, Daniel, *Bernard Shaw; A Psychological Study*. 1975. Pp. 275-78

"The Dramatist's Dilemma; An Interpretation of 'Major Barbara'", *Shaw Bulletin*, 2:18-24, 1958

Dukore, Bernard F., "Revising 'Major Barbara'", *Shaw Review* (1973), 16:2-10

―――――――――― , "Toward an Interpretation of 'Major Barbara'", *Shaw Review* (1963), 6:62-70

Frank, Joseph, "'Major Barbara'; Shaw's 'Divine Comedy'", *Modern Language Association. Publications* (PMLA), 71:61-74, 1956

Freedman, Morris, *The Moral Impulse; Modern Drama from Ibsen to the Present*. 1967. Pp. 45-62

Geduld, J. M., "The Comprehensionist", *Shavian* (1963), 2:22-26

Gelber, Norman, "The 'Misalliance' Theme in 'Major Barbara'", *Shaw Review* (1972), 15:65-70

Hoy, Cyrus, "Shaw's Tragicomic Irony; From 'Man and Superman' to 'Heartbreak House'", *Virginia Quarterly Review* (Wint. 1971), 47:56-78

Hummert, Paul A., *Bernard Shaw's Marxian Romance*. 1973. Pp. 95-99

Institute for Religious and Social Studies, *Great Moral Dilemmas in Literature, Past and Present*, ed. by R. M. MacIver. 1956. Pp. 15-23

Irvine, William, "Major Barbara", *Shavian*, #7, 1956. Pp. 43-47

Jordan, Robert J., "Theme and Character in 'Major Barbara'", *Texas Studies in Literature and Language* (1970), 12:471-80

Ketels, Violet B., "Shaw, Snow and the New Men", *Personalist* (Oct. 1966), 47:520-31

Leary, Daniel J., "Dialectical Action in 'Major Barbara'", *Shaw Review* (1969), 12:46-58

Lefcourt, Charles R., "'Major Barbara'; An Exercise in Shavian Wit and Wisdom", *English Record* (1974), 25,ii:27-29

Life, 41:123-24, Dec. 10, 1956

Lorichs, Sonja, *The Unwomanly Woman in Bernard Shaw's Drama and Her Social and Political Background*. 1973. Pp. 61-88

MacCarthy, Desmond, *Shaw's Plays in Review*. 1969. Pp. 44-56

McCollom, William G., *The Divine Average; A View of Comedy*. 1971. Pp. 198-212

"Major Barbara: Shaw's Apotheosis of Money", *Current Literature*, 43: 193-98, Aug. 1907

Mills, John A., "The Comic in Words; Shaw's Cockneys", *Drama Survey* (Summer 1966), 5:137-50

Morgan, Margery M., *The Shavian Playground; An Exploration of the Art of Bernard Shaw*. 1972. Pp. 134-57

Nation, 127:666-67, Dec. 12, 1928 and 183:439, Nov. 17, 1956

New Republic, 135:22-23, Dec. 3, 1956 and 136:23, May 20, 1957

New Yorker, 32:114, Nov. 10, 1956

Newsweek, 48:54-55, Nov. 12, 1956

Review of Reviews, 79:152-54, Jan. 1929

Rosador, Kurt T. von, "Natural History of 'Major Barbara' ", *Modern Drama* (1974), 17:141-53

Roy, Emil, *British Drama Since Shaw*. 1972. Pp. 6-8

Saturday Review, 39:28, Nov. 17, 1956

Schuchter, J. D., "Shaw's 'Major Barbara' ", *Explicator* (1970), 28:Item 74

Shaw, George Bernard, *Shaw on Theatre*, ed. by E. J. West. 1958. Pp. 118-21

Slote, Bernice, ed., *Literature and Society*. 1964. Pp. 121-41

Tedesco, Joseph S., "The Theory and Practice of Tragicomedy in George Bernard Shaw's Dramaturgy", *Dissertation Abstracts International* (1973), 33:4586A

Theatre Arts, 41:21-22, Jan. 1957

Time, 68:72, Nov. 12, 1956

Ure, Peter, "Master and Pupil in Bernard Shaw", *Essays in Criticism* (1969), 19:118-39

Valency, Maurice, *The Cart and the Trumpet*. 1973. Pp. 247-65

Vogue, 128:118, Sept. 15, 1956

Walkley, Arthur Bingham, *Drama and Life*. 1907. Pp. 233-38

Watson, Barbara Bellow, "Sainthood for Millionaires: 'Major Barbara' ", *Modern Drama* (Dec. 1968), 11:227-44

Wilson, Colin, "Shaw's Existentialism", *Shavian* (1960), 2:4-6

Wisenthal, J. L., *The Marriage of Contraries; Bernard Shaw's Middle Plays*. 1974. Pp. 57-86

——————————, "The Underside of Undershaft; A Wagnerian Motif in 'Major Barbara' ", *Shaw Review* (1972), 15:56-65

Wright, Edward A. and Lenthiel H. Downs, *A Primer for Playgoers*. 1969. Pp. 98-103

Man and Superman, 1905

Adams, Elsie B., *Bernard Shaw and the Aesthetes*. 1971. Pp. 115-19

Barnett, Gene A., "Don Juan's Hell", *Ball State University Forum* (Sept. 1970), 11:47-51

Barr, Alan P., *Victorian Stage Pulpiteer; Bernard Shaw's Crusade*. 1973. Pp. 157-60

Beerbohm, Max, *Around Theatres*. 1953. Pp. 268-72

Bently, Joseph, "Tanner's Decisions to Marry in 'Man and Superman' ", *Shaw Review* (1968), 11:26-28

Berst, Charles A., *Bernard Shaw and the Art of Drama*. 1973. Pp. 96-153

Blanch, Robert L., "The Myth of Don Juan in 'Man and Superman' ", *Revue des Langues Vivantes* (1967), 33:158-63

Boyd, T., "My Favorite Fiction Character: Ann in 'Man and Superman' ", *Bookman*, 63:58-59, March, 1926

Brown, John Mason, *Dramatis Personae; A Retrospective Show*. 1963. Pp. 121-29

Brustein, Robert, *The Theatre of Revolt; An Approach to the Modern Drama*. 1964. Pp. 213-20

Catholic World, 166:169, Nov. 1947

Cohn, Ruby, "Hell on the 20th Century Stage", *Wisconsin Studies in Contemporary Literature* (Wint.-Spring 1964), 5:48-53

Commonweal, 47:41, Oct. 24, 1947

Dervin, Daniel, *Bernard Shaw; A Psychological Study*. 1975. Pp. 237-68

deSelincourt, Aubrey, *Six Great Playwrights*. 1960. Pp. 179-82

Ellis, Havelock, *Views and Reviews; A Selection of Uncollected Articles, 1884-1932*, 1st-2nd ser., 2 vol. in 1, 1932. Pp. 194-203

Freedman, Morris, *The Moral Impulse; Modern Drama from Ibsen to the Present.* 1967. Pp. 45-62

Gassner, John, *Dramatic Soundings; Evaluations and Retractions Culled from Thirty Years of Dramatic Criticism.* 1968. Pp. 564-65

Harrison, George Bagshawe, ed., *Major British Writers.* 1954. vol. 2, Pp. 535-37

Hoy, Cyrus, "Shaw's Tragicomic Irony; from 'Man and Superman' to 'Heartbreak House'", *Virginia Quarterly Review* (Winter 1971), 47:56-78

Hunningher, B., "Shaw en Brecht", *Forum der Letteren* (1971), 12:173-90

Irvine, William "'Man and Superman'; A Step in Shavian Disillusionment", *Huntington Library Quarterly*, 10:209-24, 1947

Kaul, A. N., *The Action of English Comedy; Studies in the Encounter of Abstraction and Experience from Shakespeare to Shaw.* 1970. Pp. 303-14

Kennedy, Andrew K., *Six Dramatists in Search of a Language.* 1975. Pp. 66-70

Lawrence, Kenneth, "Bernard Shaw; The Career of the Life Force", *Modern Drama* (1972), 15:130-46

Leary, Daniel J., "Shaw's Use of Stylized Characters and Speech in 'Man and Superman'", *Modern Drama* (1963), 5:477-90

Life, 23:107-08, Oct. 27, 1947 and 58:10, Jan. 15, 1965

MacCarthy, Desmond, *Shaw's Plays in Review.* 1969. Pp. 32-36

McDowell, F. P. W., "Heaven, Hell and Turn-of-the-Century London: Reflections on Shaw's 'Man and Superman'", *Drama Survey*, 2:245-68, 1963

Miles, Carl H., "'Man and Superman' and the Don Juan Legend", *Comparative Literature* (1967), 19:216-25

Morgan, Margery M., *The Shavian Playground; An Exploration of the Art of Bernard Shaw.* 1972. Pp. 100-18

Nathan, George Jean, *Theatre Book of the Year, 1947-48.* Pp. 84-94

——————— , *World of George Jean Nathan*, ed. by Charles Angoff. 1952. Pp. 417-27

Nation, 165:454, Oct. 25, 1947 and 177:158, Aug. 22, 1953 and 199:522-23, Dec. 28, 1961

Nelson, Raymond S., "Shaw's Heaven and Hell", *Contemporary Review* (1975), 226:132-36

New Republic, 117:38, Oct. 20, 1947 and 152:33, Jan. 30, 1965

New York Times Magazine. Pp. 36-37, Oct. 5, 1947

New Yorker, 23:58-59, Oct. 18, 1947 and 40:66, Dec. 19, 1964

Newsweek, 30:88, Oct. 20, 1947

Peters, Sally A., "Shaw; A Formal Analysis of Structural Development Through an Examination of Representative Plays", *Dissertation Abstracts International* (1973), 34:3426A

Redmond, J., "Misattributed Speech in 'Man and Superman'", *Times Literary Supplement* (Jan. 18, 1974), 73:60

Rosenblood, Norman, ed., *Shaw; Seven Critical Essays.* 1971. Pp. 25-35

Saturday Review, 47:33, Dec. 26, 1964

Saturday Review of Literature, 30:28-32, Nov. 1, 1947

School and Society, 67:314-15, April 24, 1948

Stamm, J. L., "Shaw's 'Man and Superman': His Struggle for Sublimation", *American Imago* (1965), 22:250-54

Stockholder, Fred E., "Shaw's Drawing-Room Hell: A Reading of 'Man and Superman'", *Shaw Review* (1968), 11:42-51
Theatre Arts, 31:18, Nov. 1947 and 31:12, Dec. 1947
Time, 50:73, Oct. 20, 1947
Valency, Maurice, *The Cart and the Trumpet*. 1972. Pp. 200-36
Walkley, Arthur Bingham, *Drama and Life*. 1907. Pp. 224-32
Wisenthal, J. L., "The Cosmology of 'Man and Superman'", *Modern Drama* (1971), 14:298-306
────────── , *The Marriage of Contraries; Bernard Shaw's Middle Plays*. 1974. Pp. 22-56

Man of Destiny, 1897
Hummert, Paul A., *Bernard Shaw's Marxian Romance*. 1973. Pp. 70-73
MacCarthy, Desmond, *Shaw's Plays in Review*. 1969. Pp. 84-85

Millionairess, 1936
Bentley, Eric Russell, *Dramatic Event; An American Chronicle*. 1954. Pp. 50-53
Brown, John Mason, "Katharine Without Petruchio: 'Millionairess'", *Saturday Review*, 35:24-25, Nov. 1, 1952
Catholic World, 176:227, Dec. 1952
Commonweal, 57:198-99, Nov. 28, 1952
Hummert, Paul A., *Bernard Shaw's Marxian Romance*. 1973. Pp. 182-99
Life, 33:163-65, Oct. 13, 1952
Nation, 175:413, Nov. 1, 1952
New Republic, 127:22-23, Nov. 3, 1952
New York Times Magazine, Pp. 17, July 13, 1952
New Yorker, 28:65, July 19, 1952 and 28:74, Oct. 25, 1952
Newsweek, 40:76, Oct. 27, 1952
Saturday Review of Literature, 14:10, June 13, 1936
Theatre Arts, 36:18-20, Nov. 1952
Time, 60:75, Oct. 27, 1952
Tynan, Kenneth, *Curtains; Selections from the Drama Criticism and Related Writings*. 1961. Pp. 26-28

Misalliance, 1910
America, 88:632, March 7, 1953
Beerbohm, Max, *Around Theatres*. 1953. Pp. 561-65
Catholic World, 177:68-69, April, 1953
Commonweal, 57:648-49, April 3, 1953 and 75:389, Jan. 5, 1962
Crane, Gladys M., "Shaw's 'Misalliance': The Comic Journey from Rebellious Daughter to Conventional Womanhood", *Educational Theatre Journal* (1973), 25:480-89
Dawick, John, "Stagecraft and Structure in Shaw's Disquisitory Drama", *Modern Drama* (1971), 14:276-87
Hackett, Francis, *Horizons; A Book of Criticism*. 1918. Pp. 203-07
Life, 34:155-56, April 13, 1953
MacCarthy, Desmond, *Shaw's Plays in Review*. 1969. Pp. 160-61
Morgan, Margery M., "Bernard Shaw on the Tightrope", *Modern Drama* (1962), 4:343-54
────────── , *The Shavian Playground; An Exploration of the Art of Bernard Shaw*. 1972. Pp. 187-99
Nation, 176:212, March 7, 1953

New Yorker, 29:60, March 7, 1953 and 37:132-33, Oct. 21, 1961

Newsweek, 41:84, March 2, 1953

Quinn, Martin, "Dickens and 'Misalliance'", *Shaw Review* (1974), 17:141-43

Saturday Review, 36:34, March 7, 1953

School and Society, 77:186-87, March 21, 1953

Sharp, William L., "'Misalliance'; An Evaluation", *Educational Theatre Journal*, 8:9-16, 1956

Sidnell, Michael J., "'Misalliance': Sex, Socialism and the Collectivist Poet", *Modern Drama* (1974), 17:125-39

Theatre Arts, 37:16, May, 1953 and 45:71, Dec. 1961

Time, 61:74, March 2, 1953 and 78:88, Oct. 6, 1961

Valency, Maurice, *The Cart and the Trumpet*. 1973. Pp. 292-95

Wisenthal, J. L., *The Marriage of Contraries; Bernard Shaw's Middle Plays*. 1974. Pp. 127-35

Mrs. Warren's Profession, 1902

Beerbohm, Max, *Around Theatres*. 1953. Pp. 191-95

———————— , "Mr. Shaw's Profession", *Shaw Review* (1962), 5:5-9

Berst, Charles A., *Bernard Shaw and the Art of Drama*. 1973. Pp. 3-19

———————— , "Propaganda and Art in 'Mrs. Warren's Profession'", *ELH* (1966), 33:390-404

Bullough, Geoffrey, "Literary Relations of Shaw's Mrs. Warren", *Philological Quarterly* (1962), 41:339-58

Catholic World, 172:226-27, Dec. 1950

Christian Science Monitor Magazine, Pp. 6, Nov. 4, 1950

Dukore, Bernard F., "The Fabian and the Freudian", *Shavian*, 2:8-10, 1961

Ganz, Arthur, "The Ascent to Heaven; A Shavian Pattern (Early Plays, 1894-1898)", *Modern Drama* (1971), 14:253-63

Gilliatt, Penelope, *Unholy Fools; Wits, Comics, Disturbers of the Peace; Film and Theater*. 1973. Pp. 58-61

Grecco, Stephen, "Vivie Warren's Profession: A New Look at 'Mrs. Warren's Profession'", *Shaw Review* (1967), 10:93-99

Hummert, Paul A., *Bernard Shaw's Marxian Romance*. 1973. Pp. 62-66

Johnson, Betty F., "Shelley's 'Cenci' and 'Mrs. Warren's Profession'", *Shaw Review* (1972), 15:26-34

Kaul, A. N., *The Action of English Comedy; Studies in the Encounter of Abstraction and Experience from Shakespeare to Shaw*. 1970. Pp. 284-86

LeCorre, P., "Les Cent Ans de George Bernard Shaw", *Pensée Catholique*, #70:32-42, 1956

Morgan, Margery M., *The Shavian Playground; An Exploration of the Art of Bernard Shaw*. 1972. Pp. 36-45

Moses, Montrose Jonas and Brown, John Mason, eds., *American Theatre as Seen by Its Critics, 1752-1934*. 1934. Pp. 163-67

Nathan, George Jean, *Theatre Book of the Year, 1950-51*. Pp. 74-76

Nation, 171:418, Nov. 4, 1950

Nelson, Raymond S., "'Mrs. Warren's Profession' and English Prostitution", *Journal of Modern Literature* (1972), 2:357-66

Nethercot, Arthur C., "'Mrs. Warren's Profession': 'The Second Mrs. Tanqueray'", *Shaw Review* (1970), 13:26-36

Nethercot, Arthur H., "The Vivie-Frank Relationship in 'Mrs. Warren's Profession'", *Shavian*, #15, Pp. 7-9, 1959

New Republic, 123:21, Nov. 13, 1950

New Yorker, 39:93, May 4, 1963

Newsweek, 36:89, Nov. 6, 1950

Oppel, Horst, *Das Moderne Englische Drama; Interpretationen.*   1963. Pp. 11-27

Stozier, Robert, "The Undramatic Dramatist: Mrs. Warren's Shaw", *Shavian* (1965), 3:11-14

Tedesco, Joseph S., "The Theory and Practice of Tragicomedy in George Bernard Shaw's Dramaturgy", *Dissertation Abstracts International* (1973), 33:4586A

Time, 56:58, Nov. 6, 1950

Valency, Maurice, *The Cart and the Trumpet.* 1973. Pp. 92-99

Wasserman, Marlie P., "Vivie Warren; A Psychological Study", *Shaw Review* (1972), 15:71-75

On the Rocks, 1933

   Commonweal, 28:273, July 1, 1938

   Hummert, Paul A., *Bernard Shaw's Marxian Romance.* 1973. Pp. 168-75

   _____ , "Bernard Shaw's 'On the Rocks' ", *Drama Critique* (1959), 2:34-41

   Literary Digest, 118:24, Aug. 18, 1934

   McDowell, F. P. W., "Crisis and Unreason: Shaw's 'On the Rocks' ", *Educational Theatre Journal*, 13:192-200, Oct. 1961

   Morgan, Margery M., *The Shavian Playground; An Exploration of the Art of Bernard Shaw.* 1972. Pp. 272-86

   New Republic, 95:251, July 6, 1938

   Nickson, Richard, "The Art of Shavian Political Drama", *Modern Drama* (1971), 14:324-30

   Silverman, Albert H., "Bernard Shaw's Political Extravaganzas", *Drama Survey* (Wint. 1966-67), 5:213-22

   Theatre Arts, 18:6, Jan. 1934

   Time, 31:33, June 27, 1938

Over-Ruled, 1912

   MacCarthy, Desmond, *Shaw's Plays in Review.* 1969. Pp. 176-80

   Nathan, George Jean, *Theatre Book of the Year, 1945-46.* Pp. 45-51

   " 'Over-Ruled': Dramatic Study", *English Review*, 14:179-97, May, 1913

The Philanderer, 1907

   Beerbohm, Max, *Around Theatres.* 1953. Pp. 449-51

   Drama (1967), 10:69-78

   MacCarthy, Desmond, *Shaw's Plays in Review.* 1969. Pp. 77-83

   Morgan, Margery M., *The Shavian Playground; An Exploration of the Art of Bernard Shaw.* 1972. Pp. 30-35

   Tyson, Brian, "One Man and His Dog; A Study of a Deleted Draft of Bernard Shaw's 'The Philanderer' ", *Modern Drama* (1967) 10:69-78

   Walkley, Arthur Bingham, *Drama and Life.* 1907. Pp. 245-50

Pygmalion, 1913

   Adams, Elsie B., *Bernard Shaw and the Aesthetes.* 1971. Pp. 133-37

   Appia, H., "A Propos de 'Pygmalion', George Bernard Shaw Phonéticien", *Etudes Anglaises* (1974), 27:45-63

   Berst, Charles A., *Bernard Shaw and the Art of Drama.* 1973. Pp. 196-220

Brooks, Harold F., "'Pygmalion' and 'When We Dead Awaken'", *Notes and Queries*, 7:469-71, 1960

Brown, John Mason, *Seeing Things*. 1946. Pp. 160-66

Bryden, R., "Pygmalion", *Plays and Players* (1974), 21:30-31

Commonweal, 27:496, Feb. 25, 1938

Crane, Milton, "'Pygmalion'; Bernard Shaw's Dramatic Theory and Practice", *Modern Language Association. Publications* (PMLA), 66:879-85, 1951

Crompton, Louis, "Improving Pygmalion", *Prairie Schooner* (1967), 41:73-83

Dervin, Daniel, *Bernard Shaw; A Psychological Study*. 1975. Pp. 86-88

Drew, Arnold P., "'Pygmalion' and 'Pickwick'", *Notes and Queries*, n. s. 2:221-22, 1955

Freedman, Morris, *The Moral Impulse; Modern Drama from Ibsen to the Present*. 1967. Pp. 45-62

Hulban, Horia, "Notes on Style and Substance in Shaw's 'Pygmalion'", *Analele Stiintifice ale Universitatii Iasi* (1972), 18:127-35

Hummert, Paul A., *Bernard Shaw's Marxian Romance*. 1973. Pp. 121-23

Kennen, J., "Rond 'Pygmalion' van G. B. Shaw", *Dietsche Warande en Belfort*, 106:392-403, 1961

Lambert, J. W., "Pygmalion", *Drama* (1974), 114:52-54

Lauter, Paul, "'Candida' and 'Pygmalion'; Shaw's Subversion of Stereotypes", *Shaw Review*, 3:14-19, 1960

Lorichs, Sonja, *The Unwomanly Woman in Bernard Shaw's Drama and Her Social and Political Background*. 1973. Pp. 133-54

Mabley, Edward, *Dramatic Construction; An Outline of Basic Principles*. 1972. Pp. 153-72

MacCarthy, Desmond, *Shaw's Plays in Review*. 1969. Pp. 108-13

Mademoiselle, 44:104-06, Dec., 1956

Matlaw, Myron, "The Denouement of 'Pygmalion'", *Modern Drama*, 1: 29-34, 1958

Mills, John A., "The Comic in Words; Shaw's Cockneys", *Drama Survey* (Summer 1966), 5:137-50

Morgan, Margery M., *The Shavian Playground; An Exploration of the Art of Bernard Shaw*. 1972. Pp. 169-75

Nathan, George Jean, *Theatre Book of the Year, 1945-46*. Pp. 242-45

Nation, 123:566-67, Dec. 1, 1926

New Republic, 49:41-42, Dec. 1, 1926

Noyes, E. S., "A Note on 'Peregrine Pickle' and 'Pygmalion'", *Modern Language Notes*, 41:327-30, 1926

O'Donnell, Norbert F., "On the Unpleasantness of 'Pygmalion'", *Shaw Bulletin*, 1:7-10, 1955

Oppel, Horst, *Das Moderne Englische Drama; Interpretationen*. 1963. Pp. 126-48

Pedersen, Lise, "Shakespeare's 'The Taming of the Shrew' vs. Shaw's 'Pygmalion': Male Chauvinism vs. Women's Lib?", *Shaw Review* (1974), 17: 32-39

"'Pygmalion' at Home and Abroad", *English Review*, 17:276-78, May, 1914

Roll-Hansen, Diderik, "Shaw's 'Pygmalion': The Two Versions of 1916 and 1941", *Review of English Literature* (1967), 8 pt. 3:81-90

Roy, Emil, " 'Pygmalion' Revisited", *Ball State University Forum* (1970), 11:38-46

Schotter, Richard D., "Shaw's Stagecraft: A Theatrical Study of 'Pygmalion' ", *Dissertation Abstracts International* (1974), 34:5991A

Solomon, S. J., "Ending of 'Pygmalion'; A Structural View", *Educational Theatre Journal*, 16:59-63, March, 1964

Theatre Arts, 40:29-31, Dec. 1956

Ure, Peter, "Master and Pupil in Bernard Shaw", *Essays in Criticism* (1969), 19:118-39

Valency, Maurice, *The Cart and the Trumpet.* 1973. Pp. 312-28

Vogue, 144:152-55, Nov. 1, 1964

Wainger, Bertrand M., "Henry Sweet—Shaw's 'Pygmalion' ", *Studies in Philology*, 27:558-72, 1930

Weissman, Philip, *Creativity in the Theater; A Psychoanalytic Study.* 1965. Pp. 146-70

Wisenthal, J. L., *The Marriage of Contraries; Bernard Shaw's Middle Plays.* 1974. Pp. 119-31

St. Joan, 1923

America, 6:630-32, Sept. 29, 1956, 118:131, Jan. 27, 1968

Berst, Charles A., *Bernard Shaw and the Art of Drama.* 1973. Pp. 259-92

Bhalla, Alok, "An Obstinate Margin in Tragedy", *Quest* (Summer 1967), #54:45-51

Blankenagel, J. C., "Shaw's 'St. Joan' and Schiller's 'Jungfrau von Orleans' ", *Journal of English and Germanic Philology*, 25:379-92, July, 1926

Brooks, Cleanth, ed., *Tragic Themes in Western Literature; Seven Essays by Bernard Knox and Others.* 1955. Pp. 150-78

Brown, John Mason, *As They Appear.* 1952. Pp. 71-76

_____ , *Dramatis Personae; A Retrospective Show.* 1963. Pp. 141-48

_____ , *Two on the Aisle; Ten Years of The American Theatre in Performance.* 1938. Pp. 102-06

Catholic World, 143:85-86, April, 1936 and 174:147-48, Nov. 1951 and 184:146-47, Nov. 1956

Channing-Pearce, Melville, *Terrible Crystal; Studies in Kierkegaard and Modern Christianity.* 1941. Pp. 194-201

Christian Century, 73:1138, Oct. 3, 1956

Commonweal, 23:609, March 27, 1936 and 55:38, Oct. 19, 1951 and 65:46-47, Oct. 12, 1956 and 75:666-67, March 23, 1962, 87:538-39, Feb. 2, 1968

Connolly, Thomas E., "Shaw's 'St. Joan' ", *Explicator*, 14:Item 19, 1955

Cowell, Raymond, *Twelve Modern Dramatists.* 1967. Pp. 49-50

Crawford, J., "St. Joan", *Drama*, 14:178-79, Feb., 1924

deSelincourt, Aubrey, *Six Great Playwrights.* 1960. Pp. 186-87

Dolis, John J., Jr., "Bernard Shaw's 'St. Joan': Language Is Not Enough," *Massachusettes Studies in English* (1974-75), 4,iv-v:17-25

Fielden, John, "Shaw's 'St. Joan' as Tragedy", *Twentieth Century Literature*, 3:59-67, 1957

Freedman, Morris, *The Moral Impulse; Modern Drama from Ibsen to the Present.* 1967. Pp. 45-62

Gribben, J. L. "Shaw's 'St. Joan': A Tragic Heroine", *Thought* (1965), 40:549-66

Hollis, C., "Some Notes on Mr. Shaw's 'St. Joan'", *Dublin Review*, 182: 177-88, April, 1928

Kaufman, Ralph James, ed., *G. B. Shaw; A Collection of Critical Essays*. 1965. Pp. 143-61

Kaul, A. N., *The Action of English Comedy; Studies in the Encounter of Abstraction and Experience from Shakespeare to Shaw*. 1970. Pp. 321-25

Kellock, H., "St. Joan", *The Freeman*, 8:447-49, Jan. 16, 1924

Lalou, R., "George Bernard Shaw", *Revue d'Histoire du Theatre*, 47:49-52, 1951.

Leary, Daniel J., "The Rest Could Not Be Silence", *Independent Shavian* (1965), 3:40-42

Lewisohn, Ludwig, "St. Joan", *Nation*, 118:96-97, Jan. 23, 1924

Life, 31:141-42, Oct. 22, 1951 and 41:59-60, Sept. 10, 1956 and 41:90-97, Oct. 15, 1956

Literary Digest, 80:26-27, Jan. 19, 1924 and 86:31, July 4, 1925 and 121:19, March 21, 1936

Living Age, 326:73-74, July 4, 1925

Lorichs, Sonja, *The Unwomanly Woman in Bernard Shaw's Drama and Her Social and Political Background*. 1973. Pp. 155-79

MacCarthy, Desmond, "St. Joan", *New Statesman*, 35:332-34, June 21, 1930
——————, *Shaw's Plays in Review*. 1969. Pp. 162-75

McKee, Irving, "Shaw's 'St. Joan' and the American Critics", *Shavian* (1964), 2:13-16

Morgan, Margery M., *The Shavian Playground; An Exploration of the Art of Bernard Shaw*. 1972. Pp. 248-56

Nation, 142:392, March 25, 1936 and 173:360-61, Oct. 27, 1951 and 183:274-75, Sept. 29, 1956 and 194:221, March 10, 1962 and 199:60, Aug. 10, 1964, 206:125-26, Jan. 22, 1968

New Republic, 86:198, March 25, 1936 and 125:29-30, Oct. 29, 1951 and 146: 37-38, March 5, 1962

New Yorker, 27:83, Oct. 13, 1951 and 32:96, Sept. 22, 1956 and 38:93, March 3, 1962, 43:57, Jan. 13, 1968

Newsweek, 7:22, March 21, 1936 and 38:84, Oct. 15, 1951 and 48:102, Sept. 24, 1956, 71:78-79, Jan. 15, 1968

Novick, Julius, *Beyond Broadway; The Quest for Permanent Theatres*. 1968. Pp. 209-11

Oppel, Horst, *Das Moderne Englische Drama; Interpretationen*. 1963. Pp. 166-82

Papajewski, Helmut, "Bernard Shaw's Chronicle Play 'St. Joan'", *Germanisch-Romanische Monatsschrift*, Neue Folge 6:262-77, 1956

Pictorial Review, 37:55, June, 1936

Rascoe, B., "St. Joan", *Arts and Decoration*, 20:17, Feb., 1924

Reade, A. E. E., "St. Joan", *Living Age*, 322:175-78, July 26, 1924

Roy, Emil, *British Drama Since Shaw*. 1972. Pp. 18-20

Saturday Review, 37:32, Oct. 23, 1954 and 39:24-25, Sept. 15, 1956, 51:18, Jan. 20, 1968

Schirmir-Imhoff, Ruth, "'St. Joan'—Die Quelle und Ihre Bearbeitung", *Anglia*. 74:102-32, 1956

School and Society, 74:405-06, Dec. 22, 1951

Searle, William, "Shaw's St. Joan as Protestant", *Shaw Review* (1972), 15: 110-16

Shaw, George Bernard, *Shaw on Theatre*, ed. by E. J. West. 1958. Pp. 243-52
Solomon, Stanley J., "'St. Joan' as Epic Tragedy", *Modern Drama* (1964), 6:437-49
Survey, 87:525-26, Dec., 1951
Tedesco, Joseph S., "The Theory and Practice of Tragicomedy in George Bernard Shaw's Dramaturgy", *Dissertation Abstracts International* (1973), 33:4586A
Tetzeli von Rosador, Kurt, "Shaws St. Joan und die Historiker", *Germanisch-Romanische Monatsschrift* (1973), N. F. 23:342-55
Theatre Arts, 20:333-38, May, 1936 and 20:463-64, June, 1936 and 35:3, 20-21, Dec., 1951 and 36:34-35, Jan., 1952 and 39:70-71, Sept. 1955 and 40:80-81, Nov., 1956 and 41:30, March, 1957
Theatre Arts Anthology: A Record and a Prophecy, ed. by Rosamond Gilder, et al., 1950. Pp. 639-41
Time, 27:55, March 23, 1936 and 58:73, Oct. 15, 1951 and 68:78, Sept. 24, 1956 and 79:64, March 2, 1962 and 83:64, May 22, 1964, 91:40, Jan. 12, 1968
Tynan, Kenneth, *Curtains; Selections from the Drama Criticism and Related Writings*. 1961. Pp. 83
Valency, Maurice, *The Cart and the Trumpt*. 1973. Pp. 368-91
Vogue, 151:42, Feb. 15, 1968
Wagenknecht, Edward Charles, *Joan of Arc; An Anthology of History and Literature*. 1948. Pp. 279-92
Walkley, Arthur Bingham, *Still More Prejudice*. 1925. Pp. 118-22
West, E. J., "'St. Joan'; A Modern Classic Reconsidered", *Quarterly Journal of Speech*, 40:249-59, 1954
Williams, Raymond, *Drama from Ibsen to Brecht*. 1968. Pp. 252-56
Wisenthal, J. L., *The Marriage of Contraries; Bernard Shaw's Middle Plays*. 1974. Pp. 172-92
Wyatt, E. V., "St. Joan", *Catholic World*, 119:196-205, May, 1924
Young, Stark, "St. Joan", *New Republic*, 37:205-06, Jan. 16, 1924

Shewing Up of Blanco Posnet, 1909
MacCarthy, Desmond, *Shaw's Plays in Review*. 1969. Pp. 129-33
Nelson, Raymond S., "Blanco Posnet—Adversary of God", *Modern Drama* (May 1970), 13:1-9
Our Irish Theatre; A Chapter of Autobiography by Lady Gregory. 1972. Pp. 212-21
Valency, Maurice, *The Cart and the Trumpet*. 1973. Pp. 287-91

The Simpleton of the Unexpected Isles, 1935
Catholic World, 141:87-88, April, 1935
Commonweal, 21:542, March 8, 1935
Dukore, Bernard F., "Shaw's Doomsday", *Educational Theatre Journal* (1966), 18:61-71
Hummert, Paul A., *Bernard Shaw's Marxian Romance*. 1973. Pp. 175-81
Lawrence, Kenneth, "Bernard Shaw; The Career of the Life Forces", *Modern Drama* (1972), 15:130-46
Leary, Daniel J., "About Nothing in Shaw's 'Simpleton of the Unexpected Isles'", *Educational Theatre Journal* (1972), 24:139-48
MacCarthy, Desmond, *Shaw's Plays in Review*. 1969. Pp. 206-11
McDowell, Frederick P. W., "Spiritual and Political Reality: 'The Simpleton of the Unexpected Isles", *Modern Drama*, 3:196-210, 1960

Morgan, Margery M., *The Shavian Playground; An Exploration of the Art of Bernard Shaw.* 1972. Pp. 286-302

Nation. 140:287, March 6, 1935

Nelson, Raymond S., " 'The Simpleton of the Unexpected Isles': Shaw's Last Judgment", *Queen's Quarterly* (1969), 76:692-706

New Republic, 82:105, March 6, 1935

Silverman, Albert H., "Bernard Shaw's Political Extravaganzas", *Drama Survey* (Wint. 1966-67), 5:213-22

Theatre Arts, 19:244, April, 1935

Too True to Be Good, 1932

America, 108:591, April 20, 1936

Bookman, 75:75-76, April, 1932

Brustein, Robert, *The Theatre of Revolt; An Approach to the Modern Drama.* 1964. Pp. 204-05

Catholic World, 135:206-07, May, 1932

Commonweal, 15:691, April 20, 1932

Hopwood, Alison L., " 'Too True to be Good': Prologue to Shaw's Later Plays", *Shaw Review* (Sept. 1968), 11:109-18

Hummert, Paul A., *Bernard Shaw's Marxian Romance.* 1973. Pp. 161-66

Literary Digest, 113:14, April 30, 1932 and 114:15, Nov. 12, 1932

MacCarthy, Desmond, *Shaw's Plays in Review.* 1969. Pp. 188-92

Morgan, Margery M., *The Shavian Playground; An Exploration of the Art of Bernard Shaw.* 1972. Pp. 286-302

Nation, 134:447-48, April 20, 1932 and 177:157, Aug. 22, 1953 and 196:275, March 30, 1963

New Republic, 70:271-73, April 20, 1932 and 148:29, March 30, 1963

New Yorker, 39:73, March 23, 1963

Newsweek, 61:97, March 25, 1963

Regan, Arthur E., "The Fantastic Reality of Bernard Shaw: A Look at 'Augustus' and 'Too True' ", *Shaw Review* (1968), 11:2-10

Shaw, George Bernard, *Shaw on Theatre,* ed. by E. J. West. 1958. Pp. 214-17

Silverman, Albert H., "Bernard Shaw's Political Extravaganzas", *Drama Survey* (Wint. 1966-67), 5:213-22

Theatre Arts, 16:437-39, June, 1932 and 16:877-78, Nov., 1932 and 47:69, May, 1963

Time, 81:74, March 22, 1963

Village Wooing, 1933

Newsweek, 3:39, April 28, 1934

Widower's Houses, 1892

Cole, Toby, ed., *Playwrights on Playwriting; The Meaning and Making of Modern Drama from Ibsen to Ionesco.* 1960. Pp. 193-200

Dervin, Daniel, *Bernard Shaw; A Psychological Study.* 1975. Pp. 209-16

deSelincourt, Aubrey, *Six Great Playwrights.* 1960. Pp. 174

Dukore, Bernard F., " 'Widowers Houses': A Question of Genre", *Modern Drama* (1974), 17:27-32

Hummert, Paul A., *Bernard Shaw's Marxian Romance.* 1973. Pp. 54-66

Illinois University English Dept., *Studies by Members of the English Dept., University of Illinois, in Memory of John Jay Parry.* 1955. Pp. 170-82

Morgan, Margery M., *The Shavian Playground; An Exploration of the Art of Bernard Shaw*. 1972. Pp. 23-30 and 36-41

Nelson, Raymond S., "Shaw's 'Widower's Houses' ", *Research Studies* (1969), 37:27-37

Peters, Sally A., "Shaw: A Formal Analysis of Structural Development Through an Examination of Representative Plays", *Dissertation Abstracts International* (1973), 34:3426A

Rosenblood, Norman, ed., *Shaw; Seven Critical Essays*. 1971. Pp. 3-24

Valency, Maurice, *The Cart and the Trumpet*. 1973. Pp. 79-86

You Never Can Tell, 1899
Catholic World, 167:169, May, 1948
Commonweal, 48:635, April 16, 1948
Hummert, Paul A., *Bernard Shaw's Marxian Romance*. 1973. Pp. 73-75
MacCarthy, Desmond, *Shaw's Plays in Review*. 1969. Pp. 37-43
Matlaw, Myron, "'You Never Can Tell' in the Theater", *Regional* (1961), 4:6-7
Morgan, Margery M., *The Shavian Playground; An Exploration of the Art of Bernard Shaw*. 1972. Pp. 83-99
Nation, 166:361, March 27, 1948
New Republic, 118:30, March 29, 1948
New Yorker, 24:49, March 27, 1948
Newsweek, 31:82, March 29, 1948
Saturday Review of Literature, 31:32-34, April 24, 1948
Shaw, George Bernard, *Shaw on Theatre*, ed. by E. J. West. 1958. Pp. 84-89
Speckhard, Robert R., "Shaw's Therapeutic Satire", *Marab: A Review* (1964), 1:94-99
Theatre Arts, 32:47, Jan., 1948
Time, 51:56, March 29, 1948
Valency, Maurice, *The Cart and the Trumpet*. 1973. Pp. 146-54

ROBERT SHAW

The Man in the Glass Booth, 1967
America, 119:336, Oct. 12, 1968
Christian Century, 85:1438, Nov. 13, 1968
Commonweal, 89:253, Nov. 15, 1968
Gilman, Richard, *Common and Uncommon Masks; Writings on the Theatre, 1961-1970*. 1971. Pp. 223-27
Hughes, Catharine, *Plays, Politics, and Polemics*. 1973. Pp. 145-54
Life, 65:20, Oct. 25, 1968
Nation, 207:411-12, Oct. 21, 1968
National Review, 20:1282-83, Dec. 17, 1968
New Republic, 159:37, Oct. 19, 1968
New Yorker, 44:95, Oct. 5, 1968
New Statesman, 74:153-54, Aug. 4, 1967
Newsweek, 72:116, Oct. 7, 1968
Saturday Review, 51:52-53, Oct. 12, 1968
Time, 90:44, Aug. 11, 1967 and 92:65-66, Oct. 4, 1968
Vogue, 150-70, Oct. 15, 1967 and 152:124, Nov. 1, 1968

RICHARD BRINSLEY BUTLER SHERIDAN

The Critic; or, A Tragedy Rehearsed, 1779

Atkins, J. W. H., *English Literary Criticism: 17th and 18th Centuries.* 1951. Pp. 314-55

deSelincourt, Aubrey, *Six Great Playwrights.* 1960. Pp. 125-27

Jason, P. K., "Twentieth Century Response to 'The Critic' ", *Theatre Survey* (1974), 15:51-58

Leff, Leonard J., "Sheridan as Playwright, 1751-1780", *Dissertation Abstracts International* (1972), 32:3955A

Lutard, O., "Des Acharniens d'Aristophae au Critique de Sheridan", *Les Langues Modernes* (July-Aug. 1966), 60:65-70

Duenna, 1775

Armstrong, M., "Duenna", *Spectator*, 133:637-38, Nov. 1, 1924

Birrell, F., "Duenna", *Nation* (London), 36:185, Nov. 1, 1924

Nussbaum, R. D., "Poetry and Music in 'The Duenna' ", *Westerly* (1963), #1:56-63

Shipp, H., "Duenna", *English Review*, 39:861-63, Dec., 1924

Taylor, Garland F., "Richard Brinsley Sheridan's 'The Duenna' ", *Dissertation Abstracts International* (1969), 30:1537A-1538A

Pizarro, 1799

Bahlsen, Leopald, "Kotzebues Peru-Dramen und Sheridans 'Pizarro' ", *Herrigs Archiv*, 81:353-80, 1888

Donohue, Jospeh Walter, *Dramatic Character in the English Romantic Age.* 1970. Pp. 125-56

Kaul, A. N., *The Action of English Comedy; Studies in the Encounter of Abstraction and Experience from Shakespeare to Shaw.* 1970. Pp. 131-43

Matlaw, Myron, " 'This is Tragedy!'; The History of 'Pizarro' ", *Quarterly Journal of Speech*, 43:288-94, 1957

The Rivals, 1775

Auburn, M. S., "Pleasures of Sheridan's 'The Rivals'; A Critical Study in the Light of Stage History", *Modern Philology* (1975), 72:256-71

Beerbohm, Max, *Around Theatres.* 1953. Pp. 72-73

Brown, I., "Rivals", *Saturday Review*, 139:270, March 14, 1925

Catholic World, 131:213, May, 1930

Commonweal, 11:590, March 26, 1930

Daghlian, Philip B., "Sheridan's Minority Waiters", *Modern Language Quarterly*, 6:421-22

deSelincourt, Aubrey, *Six Great Playwrights.* 1960. Pp. 117-21

Gabriel, M. and Mueschke, P., "The Contemporary Sources of Sheridan's 'The Rivals', Garrick's 'Miss in Her Teens' and Coleman's 'Deuce is in Him' ", *Modern Language Association. Publications* (PMLA), 43:237-50, 1928

Hunt, Leigh, *Leigh Hunt's Dramatic Criticism, 1808-1831*, ed. by Laurence Huston Houtchens and Carolyn Washburn Houtchens. 1949. Pp. 248-50

Kaul, A. N., *The Action of English Comedy; Studies in the Encounter of Abstraction and Experience from Shakespeare to Shaw.* 1970. Pp. 140-49

Leff, Leonard J., "Sheridan as Playwright, 1751-1780", *Dissertation Abstracts International* (1972), 32:3955A

Macey, Samuel L., "Sheridan; The Last of the Great Theatrical Satirists", *Restoration and 18th Century Theatre Research* (Nov. 1970), 9:35-45

Sen, Sailendra Kumar, "Sheridan's Literary Debt: 'The Rivals' and 'Humphry Clinker'", *Modern Language Quarterly*, 21:291-300, 1960

Smedley, C., "Undiscovered Heroine: Julia of 'The Rivals'", *Bookman* (London), 72:210-12, July, 1927

Stahlkopf, Carole S., "Rhetoric and Comic Technique in Richard Brinsley Sheridan's 'The Rivals' and 'The School for Scandal'", *Dissertation Abstracts International* (1974), 34:4219A

Theatre Arts, 41:25-26, May, 1957

The School for Scandal, 1777

America, 116:25-26, Jan. 7, 1967

Appleton, 17:556, 1875-76

Beck, Mrs. Lily Moresby Adams, *The Gallants*, 1924. Pp. 247-308

Brustein, Robert Sanford, *The Third Theatre*. 1969. Pp. 155-57

Commonweal, 77:542, Feb. 15, 1963

deSelincourt, Aubrey, *Six Great Playwrights*. 1960. Pp. 121-25

Dolman, John, Jr., "Laugh Analysis of 'The School for Scandal'", *Quarterly Journal of Speech*, 16:432-45, Nov., 1930

Durant, Jack D., "The Moral Focus of 'The School for Scandal'", *South Atlantic Bulletin* (1972), 37:44-53

――――――――――, "Prudence, Providence and the Direct Road of Wrong: 'The School for Scandal' and Sheridan's Westminster Hall Speech", *Studies of Burke and His Time* (1974), 15:241-51

Duthie, G. I., ed., *English Studies Today, Third Series; Lectures and Papers Read at the 5th Conference of the International Association of Professors of English Held at Edinburgh and Glasgow, August 1962*. 1964. Pp. 125-35

Jackson, J. R. deJ., "The Importance of Witty Dialogue in 'The School for Scandal'", *Modern Language Notes*, 76:601-07, 1961

James, Henry, *Scenic Art; Notes on Acting and the Drama, 1872-1901*. ed. by Allan Wade. 1948. Pp. 12-21

Kaul, A. N., *The Action of English Comedy; Studies in the Encounter of Abstraction and Experience from Shakespeare to Shaw*. 1970. Pp. 136-41

Kernodle, George R., *Invitation to the Theatre*. 1967. Pp. 280-81 and 286-88

"Kritische Rückschau", *Forum* (1961), 8:454

Kronenberger, Louis, *The Polished Surface; Essays in the Literature of Worldliness*. 1969. Pp. 73-84

Leff, Leonard J., "The Disguise Motif in 'The School for Scandal'", *Educational Theatre Journal* (1970), 22:350-60

――――――――――, "Sheridan as Playwright, 1751-1780", *Dissertation Abstracts International* (1972), 32:3955A

Life, 29:65-66, Aug. 14, 1950 and 54:47-48, Feb. 22, 1963

London Magazine, 5:481, 1821

Mabley, Edward, *Dramatic Construction; An Outline of Basic Principles*. 1972. Pp. 80-97

MacCarthy, Desmond, "Old Sherry: Revival of 'The School for Scandal'", *New Statesman and Nation*, 14:1100-02, Dec. 25, 1937

――――――――――, "School for Scandal", *New Statesman*, 13:47, April 12, 1919

――――――――――, "School for Scandal", *New Statesman*, 34:329-30, Dec. 14, 1929

Macey, Samuel L., "Sheridan; The Last of the Great Theatrical Satirists", *Restoration and 18th Century Theatre Research* (Nov. 1970), 9:35-45

Malone, K., "Meaningful Fictive Names in English Literature", *Names*, 5: 9-12, March, 1957

Moore, J. R., "Sheridan's Little Bronze Pliny", *Modern Language Notes*, 59:164-65, March, 1944

Nation, 196:126-27, Feb. 9, 1932, 203:651, Dec. 12, 1966

New Republic, 146:38, May 14, 1962 and 148:29, Feb. 23, 1963, 156:41-42, Jan. 7, 1967

New Yorker, 38:122, March 24, 1962 and 38:69, Feb. 2, 1963

Newsweek, 68:96, Dec. 5, 1966

Saturday Review, 45:38, April 28, 1962 and 46:20, Feb. 9, 1963 and 46:52, Feb. 23, 1963

Schiller, A., "'School for Scandal': The Restoration Unrestored", *Modern Language Association. Publications* (PMLA), 71:694-704, 1956

Shaw, George Bernard, *Plays and Players; Essays on the Theatre.* 1952. Pp. 95-104

Stahlkopf, Carole S., "Rhetoric and Comic Technique in Richard Brinsley Sheridan's 'The Rivals' and 'The School for Scandal'", *Dissertation Abstracts International* (1974), 34:4219A

Theatre Arts, 22:185, March, 1938 and 47:57-58, March, 1963

Time, 81:65, Feb. 1, 1963

Yearling, Elizabeth M., "The Good-Natured Heroes of Cumberland, Goldsmith and Sheridan", *Modern Language Review* (1972), 67:490-500

The Stranger, 1798 (adaptation of *Die Spanien in Peur* by August von Kotzebue)
Matlaw, Myron, "Adultery Analyzed; The History of 'The Stranger'", *Quarterly Journal of Speech*, 43:22-28, 1957

ROBERT CEDRIC SHERRIFF

Badger's Green, 1930
Saturday Review, 149:784, June 21, 1930
Spectator, 144:1044, June 28, 1930

Home at Seven, 1950
Christian Science Monitor Magazine, Pp. 4, April 1, 1950

Journey's End, 1928
American Mercury, 17:245-47, 376-77, 1929
Les Annales Politiques et Littéraires, 93:363, Oct. 15, 1929
Block, Anita Cahn, *Changing World in Plays and Theatre.* Pp. 302-51
Bookman, 69:173-96, April, 1929
Catholic World, 129:201-02, May, 1929 and 130:326-27, Dec., 1929 and 150: 214-15, Nov., 1939
Christian Century, 46:1332, Oct. 30, 1929
Commonweal, 9:656-7, April 10, 1929 and 30:519, Scpt. 29, 1939
Colliers, 83:7, June 8, 1929
Cornhill, 67:171-73, Aug., 1929 and 66:740-42, June, 1929
English Review, 49:491-96, Oct., 1929 and 49:620-23, Nov., 1929
Literary Digest, 100:22-23, March 30, 1929
London Mercury, 19:314-15, Jan., 1929
Mercure de France, 216:420-21, Dec. 1, 1929

Nation, 128:434, April 10, 1929 and 149:355-57, Sept. 30, 1939
New Republic, 58:225-26, April 10, 1929
New Statesman, 32:325, Dec. 15, 1928 and 32:531, Feb. 2, 1929
Newsweek, 14:35, Oct. 2, 1939 and 14:44, Oct. 16, 1939
Nineteenth Century, 105:844-48, June, 1929
Nuova Antologia, 274:126-30, Nov. 1, 1930
Saturday Review, 147:106-07, Jan. 26, 1929
Saturday Review of Literature. 5:1021, May 18, 1929
Spectator, 142:154, Feb. 2, 1929
Theatre Arts, 13:325-30, May, 1929 and 23:777-79, Nov., 1939
Time, 34:38, Oct. 2, 1939
West, Rebecca, *Ending in Earnest; A Library Log.* 1931. Pp. 45-51, 75-78
Western Monatshefte, 147:312, Nov. 1929
Woollcott, Alexander, *Portable Woollcott.* 1946. Pp. 318-26
Young, Stark, *Immortal Shadows; A Book of Dramatic Criticism.* 1948. Pp.
   110-13

Long Sunset, 1955
Spectator, 207:765, Nov. 24, 1961

Miss Mabel, 1948
Illustrated London News, 213:712, Dec. 18, 1948
Spectator, 181:694, Nov. 26, 1948

Shred of Evidence, 1960
Illustrated London News, 236:850, May 14, 1960

White Carnation, 1953
Illustrated London News, 222:584, April 11, 1953
Tynan, Kenneth, *Curtains; Selections from the Drama Criticism and Related
   Writings.* 1961. Pp. 48

Windfall, 1933
Spectator, 152:315, March 2, 1934

ROBERT CEDRIC SHERRIFF AND JEANNE DECASALIS

St. Helena, 1935
Catholic World, 144:212-13, Nov. 1936
Commonweal, 24:617, Oct. 23, 1936
London Mercury, 33:528, March, 1936
Nation, 143:457, Oct. 17, 1936
New Republic, 88:314, Oct. 21, 1936
New Statesman and Nation, 11:187, Feb. 8, 1936
Newsweek, 8:28, Oct. 17, 1936
Saturday Review of Literature, 15:17, Oct. 31, 1936
Spectator, 156:575, March 27, 1936
Theatre Arts, 20:843-44, Nov., 1936
Time, 28:44, Oct. 19, 1936

NORMAN FREDERICK SIMPSON

Cresta Run, 1965
New Statesman, 70:708, Nov. 5, 1965

The Hole, 1957
  Esslin, Martin, *The Theatre of the Absurd.* 1961. Pp. 220-21
  New Yorker, 37:76, Apr. 15, 1960
  Twentieth Century, 163:553-54, June 1958
  Tynan, Kenneth, *Curtains; Selections from the Drama Criticism and Related
    Writings.* 1961. Pp. 209-11

One Way Pendulum, 1959
  America, 106:29, Oct. 7, 1961
  Commonweal, 75:94, Oct. 20, 1961
  Educational Theatre Journal, 13:291, Dec. 1961
  Esslin, Martin, *The Theatre of the Absurd.* 1961. Pp. 221-25
  Hudson Review, 14:589-90, 1961-62
  Illustrated London News, 236:110, Jan. 16, 1960
  Lumley, Frederick, *New Trends in Twentieth Century Drama; A Survey Since
    Ibsen and Shaw.* 1972. Pp. 306-08
  New Statesman, 59:12, Jan. 2, 1960
  New Yorker, 36:104, May 28, 1960 and 37:118-20, Sept. 30, 1961
  Saturday Review, 44:38, Oct. 7, 1961
  Spectator, 204:13, Jan. 1, 1960
  Swanson, Michele A., " 'One Way Pendulum': A New Dimension in Farce",
    Drama Survey (1963), 2:322-32
  Theatre Arts, 45:59, Nov. 1961

A Resounding Tinkle, 1957
  Diller, Jans-Jürgen, "N. F. Simpsons 'A Resounding Tinkle' als Philosophische
    Satire", *Die Neueren Sprachen* (1967), 16:357-61
  Esslin, Martin, *The Theatre of the Absurd.* 1961. Pp. 217-20
  Fothergill, C. Z., "Echoes of 'A Resounding Tinkle'; Norman F. Simpson
    Reconsidered", *Modern Drama* (1973), 16:299-306
  Lumley, Frederick, *New Trends in Twentieth Century Drama; A Survey Since
    Ibsen and Shaw.* 1972. Pp. 305-08
  New Yorker, 37:67, Apr. 15, 1961
  Spectator, 200:455, Apr. 11, 1958
  Twentieth Century, 163:551-54, June 1958
  Tynan, Kenneth, *Curtains; Selections from the Drama Criticism and Related
    Writings.* 1961. Pp. 198-200 and 200-11

SOPHOCLES

Ajax, 450/447 B. C.
  Adams, S. M., "The 'Ajax' of Sophocles", *Phoenix* (1955), 9:93-110
  Anderson, Quentin and Mazzeo, Joseph Anthony, eds., *The Proper Study;
    Essays on Western Classics.* 1962. Pp. 78-101
  Biggs, Penelope, "Disease Theme in Sophocles' 'Ajax', 'Philoctetes' and
    'Trachiniae' ", *Classical Philology* (1966), 61:223-35
  Calder, W. M., "The Entrance of Athena in 'Ajax' ", *Classical Philology* (1965),
    60:114-16
  Dalmeyda, G., "Sophocles' 'Ajax' ", *Revue des Etudes Grecques* (1933), 46:
    1-14
  Dalcourt, M., "La Suicide par Vengeance dans la Gréce Ancienne", *Revue de
    l'Histoire des Religions* (1939), 119.154-71

deSelincourt, Aubrey, *Six Great Playwrights*. 1960. Pp. 21-26

Ebeling, R., "Misverstandnisse um den 'Aias' de Sophokles", *Hermes* (1941), 76:283-314

Faber, M. D., "Suicide and the 'Ajax' of Sophocles", *Psychoanalytic Review* (Aut. 1966), 54:49-60

Ferguson, J., "Ambiguity in 'Ajax'", *Dioniso* (1970), 44:12-29

Grene, David, *Reality and the Heroic Pattern; Last Plays of Ibsen, Shakespeare and Sophocles*. 1967. Pp. 118-35

Guthrie, W. K. C., "Odysseus in the 'Ajax'", *Greece and Rome* (1947), 16: 115-19

Harsh, Philip Whaley, *A Handbook of Classical Drama*. 1944. Pp. 95-101

Jones, Henry John Franklin, *On Aristotle and Greek Tragedy*. 1962. Pp. 177-91

Kitto, Humphrey Davy, *Form and Meaning in Drama; A Study of Six Greek Plays and 'Hamlet'*. 1956, Pp. 179-98

Knox, B. M. W., "The 'Ajax' of Sophocles", *Harvard Studies in Classical Philology* (1961), 65:1-37

Kott, Jan, *The Eating of the Gods; An Interpretation of Greek Tragedy*. 1973. Pp. 43-77

Lattimore, Richmond Alexander, *Poetry of Greek Tragedy*. 1958. Pp. 56-80

Lesky, Albin, *Greek Tragedy*. 1967. Pp. 97-103

Lilly, W. S., "Two Plays of Sophocles: 'Ajax' and 'Philoctetes'", *Nineteenth Century and After*, 84:835-58, Nov., 1918

Maddalena, A., "'L'Aiace' di Sofocle", *Filosofia*, 6:3-39, 1955

Nesbit, Lawall S., "Sophocles' 'Ajax': Aristos . . . After Achilles", *Classical Journal*, 54:290-94, 1959

Pearson, A. C. "Ajax", *Classical Quarterly*, 16:124-36, July, 1922

Platt, A., "The Burial of Ajax", *Classical Review* (1912), 25:101-04

Rosenmeyer, Thomas Gustav, *The Masks of Tragedy; Essays on Six Greek Dramas*. 1963. Pp. 153-98

Schlesinger, Eilhard, "Erhaltung im Untergang. Sophokles 'Aias' als 'Pathetische' Tragödie", *Poetica. Zeitschrift für Sprach-und Literaturwissenschaft* (1970), 3:359-87

Seidenberg, R. and Papathomopoulos, E., "Sophocles' 'Ajax': A Morality for Madness", *Psychoanalytic Quarterly*, 30:404-12, 1961

Tyler, J., "Sophocles' 'Ajax' and the Sophoclean Plot Construction", *American Journal of Philology* (1974), 95:24-42

Wigodsky, M. M., "The 'Salvation' of Ajax", *Hermes* (1962), 90:149-58

Woodard, Thomas, ed., *Sophocles; A Collection of Critical Essays*. 1966. Pp. 29-61

Antigone, 442 B.C.

Amacher, Richard E., "'Antigone': The Most Misread of Ancient Plays", *College English* (1959), 20:355-58

Anderson, Quentin and Mazzeo, Jospeh Anthony, eds., *The Proper Study; Essays on Western Classics*. 1962. Pp. 78-101

Arrowsmith, W., "The Criticism of Greek Tragedy", *Tulane Drama Review* (1959), 3:31-56

Brackett, H. D., "Alleged Blemish in the 'Antigone' of Sophocles", *Classical Journal*, 12:522-34, May, 1917

Bradshaw, A. T. von S., "The Watchman Scenes in the 'Antigone'", *Classical Quarterly*, 12:200-11, 1962

Brown, John Mason, *Seeing Things*. 1946. Pp. 167-73

Burton, Richard, *Little Essays in Literature and Life*. 1914. Pp. 209-17

Clay, J. H., "The 'Antigone' of Sophocles: A Production Concept", *Drama Survey*, 3:490-99, 1964

Cole, Toby and Chinoy, Helen Krich, eds., *Directing the Play; A Source Book of Stagecraft*. 1953. Pp. 92-97

———————————— , *Directors on Directing; A Source Book of the Modern Theatre*, Rev. ed. 1963. Pp. 103-08

Corrigan, Robert W. and James L. Rosenberg, eds., *The Art of the Theatre; A Critical Anthology of Drama*. 1966. Pp. 31-57

Coughanawr, E., "Dirke and the Sun's Course in Sophocles' 'Antigone'", *Classical Quarterly* (1973), 23:22-24

Dachmann, A. B., "Zur Composition der Sophokleischer 'Antigone'", *Hermes* (1908), 43:67-76 (Translation by H. A. Siepmann in *Classical Review* (1910), 23:212-16)

deSelincourt, Aubrey, *Six Great Playwrights*. 1960. Pp. 26-31

deWitt, N. W., "Character and Plot in the 'Antigone'", *Classical Journal*, 12:393-96, March, 1917

Di Virgilio, R., "Il 'Ballo' dell' 'Antigone' di Sofocle", *Rivista di Filologia e di Istruzione Classica* (1967), 95:142-56

———————————— , "L'Ironia Tragica nell' 'Antigone' di Sofocle", *Rivista di Filologia e di Istruzione Classica* (1966), 94:26-34

Downs, Robert Bingham, *Famous Books, Ancient and Medieval*. 1964. Pp. 51-56

Eliot, George, *Essays*, ed. by Thomas Pinney. 1963. Pp. 261-65

Falk, Eugene H., *Renunciation as a Tragic Focus; A Study of Five Plays*. 1954. Pp. 25-33

Field, S. B., "Classic Festival at Siracusa: 'Antigone'", *Drama*, 16:47-50, Nov., 1925

Hamburger, Käte, *From Sophocles to Sartre; Figures from Greek Tragedy, Classical and Modern*. 1969. Pp. 147-66

Harsh, Philip Whaley, *A Handbook of Classical Drama*. 1944. Pp. 102-10

Hathorn, Richmond Yancey, "Sophocles' 'Antigone'; Eros in Politics", *Classical Journal*, 54:109-15, 1958

———————————— , *Tragedy, Myth and Mystery*. 1962. Pp. 62-78

Institute for Religious and Social Studies, *Conflict of Loyalties; A Series of Addresses and Discussions*. 1952. Pp. 1-7

———————————— , *Great Moral Dilemmas in Literature, Past and Present*. 1956. Pp. 145-53

Hausman, C. R., "Sophocles and the Metaphysical Question of Tragedy", *Personalist* (1966), 47:509-19

Jepsen, Laura, *Ethical Aspects of Tragedy; A Comparison of Certain Tragedies by Aeschylus, Sophocles, Euripides, Seneca and Shakespeare*. 1953. Pp. 64-68

Johnson, S., "Catastrophe in the 'Antigone' by Sophocles", *Royal Society of Canada. Proc. and Trans.*, s.3 40 Sec. 2:143-59, 1946

Jones, Henry John Franklin, *On Aristotle and Greek Tragedy*. 1962. Pp. 192-214

Joseph, E., "Two Antigones: Sophocles and Anouilh", *Thought*, 38:578-606, 1963

Kitto, Humphrey Davy, *Form and Meaning in Drama, A Study of Six Greek Plays and of 'Hamlet'*. 1956. Pp. 138-78

Knapp, C., "Point in the Interpretation of the 'Antigone' of Sophocles", *American Journal of Philology*, 37:300-16, July, 1916

Lesky, Albin, *Greek Tragedy*. 1967. Pp. 103-08

Levy, Charles S., "Antigone's Motives: A Suggested Interpretation", *Transactions and Proceedings of the American Philological Association* (1963), 94:137-44

Linforth, I. M., "Antigone and Creon", *Univ. of California Publications on Classical Philology* (1961), 15:183-266

McCall, M. H., "Divine and Human Action in Sophocles; The Two Burials of the 'Antigone'", *Yale Classical Studies* (1972), 22:103-17

MacNeice, L., "Antigone of Sophocles", *Spectator*, 162:404, March 10, 1939

Maddalena, A., "'Antigone' di Sofocle", *Filosofia*, 6:309-44, 1955

Manheim, Leonard Falk and Eleanor Manheim, eds., *Hidden Patterns; Studies in Psychoanalytic Literary Criticism*. 1966. Pp. 66-78

Margon, J. S., "Sophocles' 'Antigone'", *Classical Philology* (April 1970), 65:105-07

Molstad, D., "'Mill on the Floss' and 'Antigone'", *Modern Language Association. Publications* (May 1970), 85:527-31

Muller, G., "Uberlegungen zum Chor der 'Antigone'", *Hermes* (1961), 89: 398-422

Nathan, George Jean, *Theatre Book of the Year, 1945-46*. Pp. 313-15

Oxford and Asquith, Herbert Henry Asquith, 1st Earl of, *Studies and Sketches*. 1924. Pp. 155-64

Pastrana, A., "El Primor Estásimo de la 'Antigona' de Sófocles". *Helmántica. Revista de Humanidades Clasicas* (1967), 18:241-72

Pearson, A. C., "Antigone", *Classical Quarterly*, 22:179-90, July, 1928

Robertson, H. G., "Role of the Guard in the 'Antigone'", *Philological Quarterly*, 14:184-87, April, 1935

Rose, H. J., "Antigone and the Bride of Corinth", *Classical Quarterly* (1925), 19:147-51

Rouse, W. H. D., "The Two Burials in 'Antigone'", *Classical Review* (1911), 35:40-42

Roussel, P., "Les Fiancailles d'Haimon et d'Antigone", *Revue des Etudes Grecques* (1922), 85:63-81

Schadewaldt, W., "Aus der Werkstatt Meines Ubersetzens", *Schweizer Monatshefte für Politik, Wortschaft, Kultur* (1966), 46:851-59

Segal, C. P., "Sophocles' Praise of Man and the Conflicts of the 'Antigone'", *Arion* (1964), 3:46-66

Sheldon, W. L., "'Antigone' of Sophocles and Shakespeare's 'Isabel'", *Poet-Lore*, 4:609-12, Dec., 1892

Sturgeon, May C., *Women of the Classics*. 1914. Pp. 185-208

Trousson, R., "La Philosphie du Pouvoir dans 'l'Antigone' de Sophocle", *Revue des Etudes Greques*, 364-5:23-33, 1964

Weissman, Philip, *Creativity in the Theater; A Psychoanalytic Study*. 1965. Pp. 190-203

Woodard, Thomas, ed., *Sophocles; A Collection of Critical Essays*. 1966. Pp. 60-100

Zambrano, M., "La Tumba de Antigona", *Revista de Occidente* (1967), 5:1-13

Ziobro, W. J., "Where Was Antigone?", *American Journal of Philology* (Jan. 1971), 92:81-85

Electra, 409 B.C.

America, 111:266. 12, 1964

Anderson, Quentin and Mazzeo, Jospeh Anthony, eds., *The Proper Study; Essays on Western Classics*. 1962. Pp. 78-101

Baldry, H. C., *The Greek Tragic Theatre*. 1971. Pp. 122-28

Bentley, Eric Russell, *Dramatic Event, An American Chronicle*. 1954. Pp. 62-65

Burnshaw, Stanley, ed., *Varieties of Literary Experience; Eighteen Essays in World Literature*. 1962. Pp. 259-82

Calder, W. M., "The End of Sophocles' 'Electra' ", *Greek, Roman and Byzantine Studies (USA)*, 4:213-16, 1963

Catholic-World, 187:385-86, Aug. 1958

Commonweal, 57:283, Dec. 19, 1952

Corrigan, R. W., "The 'Electra' of Sophocles", *Tulane Drama Review* (1955-57), 1:36-66

Greek Poetry and Life; Essays Presented to Gilbert Murray on his 70th Birthday, Jan. 2, 1936. 1936. Pp. 145-57

Hamilton, Clayton Meeker, *Seen on the Stage*. 1920. Pp. 204-14

Harsh, Philip Whaley, *A Handbook of Classical Drama*. 1944. Pp. 132-41

Heubner, Heinz, "Elektra oder Chrysothemis?", *Rheinisches Museum für Philologie* (1961), 104:152-56

Johansen, H. F., "Die 'Elektra' des Sophokles", *Classica et Mediaevalia* (1964), 25:1-2 and 8-32

Jones, Henry John Franklin, *On Aristotle and Greek Tragedy*. 1962. Pp. 141-59

Kott, Jan, *The Eating of the Gods; An Interpretation of Greek Tragedy*. 1973. Pp. 240-67

Linforth, I. M., "Electra's Day in the Tragedy of Sophocles", *University of California Publications in Classical Philology* (1963), 19:89-126

Maddalena, A., " 'L'Elettra' di Sofocle", *Filosofia*, 7:291-40, 1956

Salmon, A., "L'Ironie Tragique dans l'Exodus de 'l'Electra' de Sophocles", *Etudes Classiques*, 29:241-70, 1961

Saturday Review, 35:42, Dec. 6, 1952 and 35:24-25, Dec. 20, 1952

Schwinge, Ernst-Richard, "Abermals; Die 'Elektren' ", *Rheinisches Museum für Philologie* (1969), NF 112:1-13

Sedgewick, G. G., *Of Irony, Especially in Drama*. 1967. Pp. 34-37 and 79-82

Segal, C. P., "The 'Electra' of Sophocles", *Transactions and Proceedings of the American Philological Association*. (1966), 97:473-545

Sheppard, J. T., "Electra: A Defense of Sophocles", *Classical Review*, 41:2-9, Feb., 1927

———————— , "Electra Again", *Classical Review*, 41:163-65, Nov., 1927

———————— , "The Tragedy of Electra According to Sophocles", *Classical Quarterly* (1918), 12:80-88

Solmsen, F., " 'Electra' and 'Orestes': Three Recognitions in Greek Tragedy", *Mededelingen de Koninklijke Nederlanse Akademie van Wetenschappen afd. Letterkunde* (1967), 30:3-34

Time, 60:78, Dec. 1, 1952 and 78:74, Sept. 29, 1961

Tynan, Kenneth, *Curtains; Selections from the Drama Criticism and Related Writings*. 1961. Pp. 6-8

Wilamowitz-Moellendorff, U. von, "Die Beiden Elektra", *Hermes* (1883), 18:214-63

Winnington, Ingram, R. P., "The 'Electra' of Sophocles; Prolegomena to an Interpretation", *Proceedings of the Cambridge Philological Society*, 1083:20-26, 1954-55

Woodard, T. M., ' "Electra' by Sophocles; The Dialectical Design", *Harvard Studies in Classical Philology*, 68:164-205, 1964

———————————— , *Sophocles; A Collection of Critical Essays*. 1966. Pp. 122-45

Oedipus at Colonus, 404/401 B.C.

Adams, S. M., "Unity of Plot in the 'Oedipus Colonus' ", *Phoenix* (1953), 7:136-47

Currie, R. Hector, "The Energies of Tragedy: Cosmic and Psychic", *Centennial Review* (1967), 11:220-36

Downs, Robert Bingham, *Famous Books, Ancient and Medieval*. 1964. Pp. 51-56

Easterling, P. E., "Oedipus and Polynices", *Proceedings of the Cambridge Philological Society* (1967), #193:1-13

Forrer, R., " 'Oedipus at Colonos': A Crisis in the Greek Notion of Deity", *Comparative Drama* (1974-75), 8:328-46

Grene, David, *Reality and the Heroic Pattern; Last Plays of Ibsen, Shakespeare and Sophocles*. 1967. Pp. 154-69

Harsh, Philip Whaley, *A Handbook of Classical Drama*. 1944. Pp. 152-55

Heiman, N., " 'Oedipus at Colonus'; A Study of Old Age and Death", *American Imago* 19:91-98, 1962

Jepsen, Laura, *Ethical Aspects of Tragedy; A Comparison of Certain Tragedies by Aeschylus, Sophocles, Euripides, Seneca, and Shakespeare*. 1953. Pp. 55-58

Jones, Henry John Franklin, *On Aristotle and Greek Tragedy*. 1962. Pp. 214-35

Lesky, Albin, *Greek Tragedy*. 967. Pp. 126-30

Linforth, I. M., "Religion and Drama in 'Oedipus at Colonus' ", *University of California Publications in Classical Philology* (1951), 14:75-191

Manheim, Leonard Falk and Eleanor Manheim, eds., *Hidden Patterns; Studies in Psychoanalytic Literary Criticism*. 1966. Pp. 66-78

Politzer, Heinz, " 'Oedipus auf Kolonos'; Versuch über eine Gameinsamkeit von Psychoanalyse und Literaturkritik", *Psyche. Zeitschrift für Psychoanalyse und Ihre Anwendungen* (1972), 26:489-519

Rado, C., " 'Oedipus at Colonus'; An Interpretation", *American Imago*, 19:235-42, 1962

Ruitenbeek, Hendrik M., ed., *Psychoanalysis and Literature*. 1964. Pp. 243-50

Shields, H. G., "Sight and Blindness Imagery in 'Oedipus Colonus' ", *Phoenix* (1961), 15:63-73

Wasserstein, A., "Réflexions sur Deux Sophocléenes: 'Oedipe Roi' et 'Oedipe à Colone' ", *Bulletin de l'Association Guillaume Budé* (1969), Ser. 4:189-200

Weissman, Philip, *Creativity in the Theater; A Psychoanalytic Study*. 1965. Pp. 194-203

Woodard, Thomas, ed., *Sophocles; A Collection of Critical Essays*. 1966. Pp. 146-74

Oedipus Rex, 425 B.C.

Adams, Robert Martin, *Strains of Discord; Studies in Literary Openness*. 1958. Pp. 19-33

Agate, James Evershed, comp., *English Dramatic Critics; An Anthology, 1660-1932*. 1958. Pp. 353-56

Alexander, Nigel, "Critical Disagreement about 'Oedipus' and 'Hamlet'",
   Shakespeare Survey (1967), 20:33-40
Ansorge, P., "Oedipus Tyrannus", *Plays and Players* (Aug. 1974), 21:42-43
Atkins, Frances, "The Social Meaning of the Oedipus Myth", *Journal of
   Individual Psychology* (1966), 22:173-84
Ax, W., "Die Parados des 'Oidipus Tyrannos'", *Hermes* (1932), 67:413-37
Boggs, W. Arthur, "'Oedipus' and 'All My Sons'", *Personalist* (1961), 42:
   555-60
Brereton, Geoffrey, *Principles of Tragedy; A Rational Examination of the
   Tragic Concept in Life and Literature.* 1968. Pp. 77-86
Brustein, Robert Sanford, *The Culture Watch; Essays on Theatre and Society,
   1969-1974.* 1975. Pp. 94-96
Calder, W. M., III, "The Blinding, 'Oedipus Tyrannus'", *American Journal
   of Philology*, 80:301-05, July, 1959
_____ , "Oedipus Tyrannus", *Classical Philology*, 57:219-29, Oct.,
   1962
Cameron, A., "The Maker and the Myth", *Antioch Review* (1965), 25:167-
   38
Carroll, J. P., "Some Remarks on the Questions in the 'Oedipus Tyrannus'",
   Classical Journal (1937), 32:406-16
Catholic World, 176:306, Jan., 1953
Chandler, A. R., "Tragic Effect in Sophocles Analyzed According to the Freud-
   ian Method", *Monist*, 23:59-89, Jan., 1913
Clay, James H. and Daniel Krempel, *The Theatrical Image.* 1967. Pp. 103-13
   and 182-91
Commonweal, 57:283, Dec. 19, 1952
Cooper, Lane, ed., *Greek Genius and Its Influences; Select Essays and Extracts.*
   1917. Pp. 156-62
Davydov, I., "Oedipe-Roi: Platon et Aristotle LaTragédie Antique Comme
   Phénomène Esthétique", *Voprosy Literatury*, 8:150-76, 1964
deSelincourt, Aubrey, *Six Great Playwrights.* 1960. Pp. 31-40
Deubner, L., "Oedipusprobleme", *Abhandlung der Preussichen Akademie
   der Wissenschaft.* 1943. Pp. 1-43
Diano, C., "Edipo Figlio Della Tyche", *Dioniso* (1952), 15:56-89
Dodds, E. R., "On Misunderstanding the 'Oedipus Rex'", *Greece and Rome*
   (1906), 13:37-49
Donnelly, Francis Patrick, *Literature the Leading Educator.* 1938. Pp. 14-25
Downs, Robert Bingham, *Famous Books, Ancient and Medieval.* 1964.
   Pp. 51-56
Driver, Thom Faw, *Sense of History in Greek and Shakespearean Drama.*
   1960. Pp. 143-67
Dyson, M., "Oracle, Edict and Curse in 'Oedipus Tyrannus'", *Classical
   Quarterly* (1973), 23:202-13
Faber, Melvyn D., ed., *The Design Within; Psychoanalytic Approaches to
   Shakespeare.* 1970. Pp. 79-86
Faber, Melvin D., "Self-Destruction in 'Oedipus Rex'", *American Imago*
   (1970), 27:41-51
Falk, Eugene H., *Renunciation as a Tragic Focus; A Study of Five Plays.*
   1954. Pp. 7-24
Fergusson, Francis, *Idea of a Theatre; A Study of Ten Plays.* 1949. Pp. 13-41
Festschrift Ernst Kapp, 1958. Pp. 93-108

Frierman, J. and S. Gassel, "The Chorus in Sophocles' 'Oedipus Tyrannus' ", *Psychoanalytic Quarterly* (1950), 19:213-26

Gellie, G. H., "Second Stasimon of the 'Oedipus Tyrannus' ", *American Journal of Philology*, 85:113-23, April, 1964

Gillespie, Patti P., "Plays: Well Constructed and Well Made", *Quarterly Journal of Speech* (1972), 58:313-21

Girard, Rene, "Perilous Balance; A Comic Hypothesis", *Modern Language Notes* (1972), 87:811-26

Goodell, Thomas Dwight, *Athenian Tragedy; A Study in Popular Art.* 1969. Pp. 149-58

Gould, Thomas, "Innocence of Oedipus: The Philosophers on 'Oedipus the King' ", *Arion* (Aut.-Wint. 1965), 4:363-86 and (Wint. 1966), 5:478-525

Greek Poetry and Life; Essays Presented to Gilbert Murray on His 70th Birthday, Jan. 2, 1936. 1936. Pp. 158-63

Hamburger, Käte, *From Sophocles to Sartre; Figures from Greek Tragedy, Classical and Modern.* 1969. Pp. 135-46

Harsh, Philip Whaley, *A Handbook of Classical Drama.* 1944. Pp. 111-28

——————— , "Implicit and Explicit in the 'Oedipus Tyrannus' ", *American Journal of Philology.* 79:243-58, July, 1958

Harshbarger, K., "Who Killed Laius?", *Tulane Drama Review* (1965), 9:120-31

Hathorn, Richmond Yancey, "The Existential Oedipus", *Classical Journal*, 53:223-30, 1958

Hausman, C. R., "Sophocles and the Metaphysical Question of Tragedy", *Personalist* (1966), 47:509-19

Helmbold, W. C., "Paradox of the 'Oedipus' ", *American Journal of Philology*, 72:293-300, July, 1951

Hewitt, W. H., "The 'Oedipus Tyrannus': Sophocles and Mr. Velacott", *Theoria* (Oct. 1964), #23:43-50

Howe, T. P., "Taboo in the Oedipus Theme", *Transactions and Proceedings of the American Philological Association*, 93:124-43, 1962

Hug, A., "Der Doppelsinn in Sophokles 'Oedipus Konig' ", *Philologus* (1871), 31:66-84

Hyman, Stanley Edgar, *Poetry and Criticism; Four Revolutions in Literary Taste.* 1961. Pp. 5-37

The Isenberg Memorial Lecture Series, 1965-1966. 1969. Pp. 193-222

Jepsen, Laura, *Ethical Aspects of Tragedy; A Comparison of Certain Tragedies by Aeschylus, Sophocles, Euripides, Seneca and Shakespeare.* 1953. Pp. 34-46

Jones, Henry John Franklin, *On Aristotle and Greek Tragedy.* 1962. Pp. 192-214

Kernodle, George R., *Invitation to the Theatre.* 1967. Pp. 156-60, 169-71, and 176-78

Kitto, Humphrey Davy Findley, *Poiesis; Structure and Thought.* 1966. Pp. 153-242

Knox, B. M. W., "Why is Oedipus called 'Tyrannus'?", *Classical Journal*, 50:97-102, 1954

La Belle, Maurice M., "Le 'Paradeigma dan 'Oedipe Roi' et 'Roi Lear' ", *Bulletin de l'Association Guillaume Büde* (1969), Ser. 4:343-47

Lattimore, Richmond Alexander, *Poetry of Greek Tragedy.* 1958. Pp. 81-102

Lauter, P., "The Parados of 'Oedipus Tyrannus' ", *Classical Journal*, 57:317, 1962

Lesky, Albin, *Greek Tragedy.* 1967. Pp. 111-17 and 126-28

Lesser, Simon O., "'Oedipus the King': The Two Dramas, the Two Conflicts", *College English* (1967), 29:175-97

Mabley, Edward, *Dramatic Construction; An Outline of Basic Principles.* 1972. Pp. 37-46

McCulloh, W. E., "'Metaphysical Solace' in Greek Tragedy", *Classical Journal*, 59:109-15, 1963

McCollom, William G., "The Downfall of the Tragic Hero", *College English* (1957), 19:51-56

Maddalena, A., "L'Edipo Re", *Filosofia*, 9:369-416, 1958

Manheim, Leonard Falk and Eleanor Manheim, eds., *Hidden Patterns; Studies in Psychoanalytic Literary Criticism.* 1966. Pp. 66-78

Moloney, James Clark, "Oedipus Rex, Cu Chulain, and the Ass", *Psychoanalytic Review* (Summer 1966), 54:5-49

Muller, Herbert Joseph, *In Pursuit of Relevance.* 1971. Pp. 152-64

Nathan, George Jean, *Theatre Book of the Year, 1945-46.* Pp. 234-35

New Yorker, 28:69, Dec. 6, 1952

Owen, E. T., "Drama in Sophocles' 'Oedipus Tyrannus'", *University of Toronto Quarterly* (1940), 10:46-59

Paolucci, A., "The Oracles are Dumb or Cheat. A Study of the Meaning of 'Oedipus Rex'", *Classical Journal*, 58:241-47, 1963

Pfeiffer, Irmgard, "Die Tragödie des Sophokles 'König Oidipus' unter Gruppendynamischen Aspekt", *Gruppenpsychotherapie und Gruppendynamik* (1969), 3:47-62

Pilikian, Hovhanness, "The Swollen-Footed Tyrant", *Drama* (1974), 113:31-36

Powell, J. E., "Notes on the 'Oedipus Tyrannus'", *Classical Philology*, 30:66-72, Jan., 1935

Rosenberg, Harold, *Act and Actor; Making the Self.* 1970. Pp. 58-73

Ruitenbeek, Hendrik M., ed., *Psychoanalysis and Literature.* 1964. Pp. 168-86

Saturday Review, 35:24-25, Dec. 20, 1952

School and Society, 76:401-02, Dec. 20, 1952

Sedgewick, G. G., *Of Irony, Especially in Drama.* 1967. Pp. 39-41

Seidensticker, Bernd, "Beziehungen Zwischen den Beiden Oidipusdramen des Sophokles", *Hermes. Zeitschrift für Klassische Philologie* (1972), 100:255-73

Shakespeare Survey, 20:33-39, 1967

Smiley, Sam, *Playwriting; The Structure of Action.* 1971. Pp. 89-114

Staiger, Emil, "Sophokles: König Odipus", *Scheidewege. Vierteljahrsschrift für Skeptisches Denken* (1973), 3:74-116

Stallknecht, Newton Phelps and Horst Frenz, eds., *Comparative Literature; Method and Perspective.* 1971. Pp. 218-47

Stanford, W. B., *Ambiguity in Greek Literature.* 1939. Pp. 163-73

Stoll, Elmer Edgar, *Shakespeare and Other Masters.* 1940. Pp. 213-29

Thomson, J. A. K., *Irony.* 1926. Pp. 54-69

Tracz, H. L., "Motif in 'Oedipus Rex'", *Queens Quarterly*, 50, #3:269-73, Aug., 1943

Traschen, Isadore, "The Elements of Tragedy", *Centennial Review* (1962), 6:215-29

Vellacott, P. H., "The Chorus in 'Oedipus Tyrannus'", *Greece and Rome* (1967), 14:109-24

—————————— , "The Guilt of Oedipus", *Greece and Rome* (1964), 11:137-48

—————————— , *Sophocles and Oedipus: A Study of "Oedipus Tyrannus".* 1971. Pp. 101-246

Versenzi, Laszlo, *Man's Measure; A Study of the Greek Image of Man from Homer to Sophocles.* 1974. Pp. 208-51

Wachtel, A., "On Analogical Action", *Journal of Aesthetics and Art Criticism,* 22:153-59, 1963

Wasserstein, A., "Réflexions sur Deux Sophocléenes: 'Oedipe Roi' et 'Oedipe à Colone' ", *Bulletin de l'Association Guillaume Budé* (1969), Ser. 4:189-200

Weigand, Hermann John, *Surveys and Soundings in European Literature.* 1966. Pp. 124-63

Weissman, Philip, *Creativity in the Theater; A Psychoanalytic Study.* 1965. Pp. 190-203

Woodard, Thomas, ed., *Sophocles; A Collection of Critical Essays.* 1966. Pp. 101-21

Young, Stark, *Flower in Drama and Glamour; Theatre Essays and Criticisms,* Rev. Ed., 1955. Pp. 208-23

—————————— , *Glamour; Essays on the Art of the Theatre.* 1925. Pp. 183-208

Witlox, A., "De 'Oedipus Rex' ", *Katoliek Cultureel Tijdschrift. Streven,* 11:932-39, 1958

Oedipus the King *SEE* Oedipus Rex

Oedipus Tyrannus *SEE* Oedipus Rex

Philoctetes, 409 B.C.

Bellinger, A. R., "Achilles' Son and Achilles", *Yale Classical Studies,* 6:1-13, 1939

Biggs, Penelope, "Disease Theme in Sophocles' 'Ajax', 'Philoctetes', and 'Trachiniae' ", *Classical Philology* (1966), 61:223-35

Dale, A. M., "Seen and Unseen on the Greek Stage", *Wiener Studien* (1956), 59:96-106

Feder, Lillian, "The Symbol of the Desert Island in Sophocles' 'Philoctetes' ", *Drama Survey,* 3:33-41, 1963

Gelen, S., "Plot Structure in the 'Philoctetes' ", *Educational Theatre Journal,* 11:8-12, March, 1959

Grene, David, *Reality and the Heroic Pattern; Last Plays of Ibsen, Shakespeare and Sophocles.* 1967. Pp. 136-54

Harsh, Philip Whaley, *A Handbook of Classical Drama.* 1944. Pp. 142-51

—————————— , "Role of the Bow in the 'Philoctetes' Of Sophocles", *American Journal of Philology,* 81:408-14, Oct., 1960

Hinds, A. E., "The Prophecy of Helenus in Sophocles' 'Philoctetes' ", *Classical Quarterly* (1967), 17:169-80

Huxley, G., "Thersites in Sophokles 'Philoktetes' ", *Greek, Roman and Byzantine Studies* (1967), 1:33-34

Jameson, M. H., "Politics and the 'Philoctetes' ", *Classical Philology,* 51:217-27, Oct., 1956

Jones, D. M. "Sleep of Philoctetes", *Classical Review,* 63:83-85, Dec., 1949

Kells, J. H., "Philoctetes", *Classical Review,* 13:7-9, March, 1963

Kieffer, J. P., "Philoctetes and Arete", *Classical Philology* (1942), 37:38-50

Kitto, Humphrey Davy, *Form and Meaning in Drama; a Study of Six Greek Plays and of 'Hamlet' ".* 1956. Pp. 87-137

Kott, Jan. *The Eating of the Gods; An Interpretation of Greek Tragedy*. 1973. Pp. 162-85

Lesky, Albin, *Greek Tragedy*. 1967. Pp. 120-26

Lilly, W. S., "Two Plays of Sophocles: 'Ajax' and 'Philoctetes'", *Nineteenth Century and After*, 84:835-58, Nov., 1918

Linforth, I. M., "Philoctetes: The Play and the Man", *University of California Publications in Classical Philology* (1956), 15:95-156

Maddalena, A., "'Filottete' l'Erede di Eracle", *Filosofia*, 8:423-63, 1957

Reiter, Seymour, *World Theater; The Structure and Meaning of Drama*. 1973. Pp. 36-49

Robinson, D. R., "Topics in Sophocles' 'Philoctetes'", *Classical Quarterly* (1969), 19:34-66

Van Nostrand, Albert D., ed., *Literary Criticism in America*. 1957. Pp. 293-310

Vurveris, K., "'Le Philoctète' de Sophocles: Interpretation Humaniste de la Trägedie", *Revista de Filologia di Istruzione Classica* (1965), 93:191-93

Wilson, Edmund, *Wound and the Bow; Seven Studies in Literature*. 1941. Pp. 272-95

Woodhouse, W. J., "The Scenic Arrangements of the 'Philoctetes' of Sophocles", *Journal of the Hellenic Society* (1912), 32:239-49

Trachiniae *SEE* Women of Trachis

Women of Trachis, 440 B.C.
Albini, Umberto, "Dubbi Sulle 'Trachinie'", *La Parola de Passato*. *Rivista di Studi Antichi* (1968), Fasc. 121-262-70

Biggs, Penclope, "Disease Theme in Sophocles' 'Ajax', 'Philoctetes' and 'Trachiniae'", *Classical Philology* (1966), 61:223-35

Greek Poetry and Life; Essays Presented to Gilbert Murray. 1936. Pp. 164-80

Harsh, Philip Whaley, *A Handbook of Classical Drama*. 1944. Pp. 129-31

Hoey, T. F., "The Trachiniae and Unity of Hero", *Arethusa* (1970), 3:1-22

Kirkwood, G. M., "The Dramatic Unit of Sophocles' 'Trachiniae'", *Transactions and Proceedings of the American Philological Association* (1941), 72:203-11

Kitto, Humphrey Davy Findley, *Poieses; Structure and Thought*. 1966. Pp. 153-242

Kott, Jan, *The Eating of the Gods; An Interpretation of Greek Tragedy*. 1973. Pp. 124-47

Lesky, Albin, *Greek Tragedy*. 1967. Pp. 108-11

Lloyd-Jones, Hugh, ed., *The Greeks*. 1962. Pp. 87-108

Lloyd-Jones, H., "Notes on Sophocles' 'Trachiniae'", *Yale Classical Studies* (1972), 22:263-70

Murray, G., *Greek Studies*. 1946. Pp. 106-26

Musurillo, H., "Fortune's Wheel; The Symbolism of Sophocles' 'Women of Trachis'", *Transactions and Proceedings of the American Philological Association*, 92:372-83, 1961

WILLIAM STEVENSON

Gammer Gurton's Needle, 1552-1563?
Bluestone, Max and Norman Rabkin, eds., *Shakespeare's Contemporaries; Modern Studies in English Renaissance Drama*. 2nd ed. 1970. Pp. 1-5

Boas, Frederick S., *University Drama in the Tudor Age*. 1965. Pp. 70-80

Brett-Smith, H. F. B., ed., *Gammer Gurton's Needle*, by Mr. S., Blackwell, 1920 (Pp. v-xv)

Hewlett, Maurice Henry, *Last Essays*. 1924. Pp. 109-14

―――――――― , "Merrie England", *Nation* (London), 29:740-41, Aug. 20, 1921

Humphrey, Grace, "Gammer Gurton's Needle", *English Journal*, 7:24-28, 1918

Ingram, R. W., " 'Gammer Gurton's Needle': Comedy not Quite of the Lowest Order?", *Studies in English Literature* (1967), 7:257-68

Watt, H. A., *Elizabethan Studies and Other Essays in Honor of George F. Reynolds*, (Univ. of Colorado Studies in the Humanities, Ser. B, V. 2, #4). 1945. Pp. 85-92

Whiting, Bartlett Jere, "Diccon's French Cousin", *Studies in Philology*, 42:31-40, Jan., 1945

TOM STOPPARD

Enter a Free Man, 1975
  New Yorker, Jan. 6, 1975, 50:50
  Newsweek, Jan. 6, 1975, 85:64

Jumpers, 1972
  America, May 18, 1974, 130:395
  Hughes, C., "Jumpers", *Plays and Players* (July 1974), 21:50
  National Review, March 29, 1974, 26:377-78
  Nation, Aug. 13, 1973, 217:123-24, May 11, 1974, 218:604, and May 18, 1974, 218:637-38
  New Republic, May 18, 1974, 170:18
  New Yorker, May 6, 1974, 50:75
  Newsweek, March 4, 1974, 83:87
  Richardson, J., "Jumpers", *Commentary* (June 1974), 57:79-80
  Time, March 11, 1974, 103:103
  Weightman, John, "A Metaphysical Comedy", *Encounter* (1972), 38:44-46

The Real Inspector Hound, 1968
  Kennedy, Andrew K., "Old and New in London Now", *Modern Drama* (1969), 11:437-46

Rosencrantz and Guildenstern Are Dead, 1966
  Asmus, Walter D., "Rosencrantz and Guildenstern Are Dead", *Deutsche Shakespeare Gesellschaft West. Jahrbuch*. 1970. Pp. 118-31
  Babula, William, "The Play-Life Metaphor in Shakespeare and Stoppard", *Modern Drama* (1972), 15:279-81
  Berlin, Normand, " 'Rosencrantz and Guildenstern Are Dead': Theater of Criticism", *Modern Drama* (1973), 16:269-77
  Brustein, Robert, *The Third Theatre*. 1969. Pp. 149-53
  Commentary, 44:82-84, Dec. 1967
  Commonweal, 87:171-72, Nov. 10, 1967
  Encounter, 29:38-40, July 1967
  Gianakaris, C. J., "Absurdism Altered: 'Rosencrantz and Guildenstern Are Dead' ", *Drama Survey* (Winter 1968/69), 7:52-58
  Kennedy, Andrew K., "Old and New in London Now", *Modern Drama* (1969), 11:437-46

Lee, R. H., "The Circle and Its Tangent", *Theoria* (1969), 33:37-43
Life, 64:72-73, Feb. 9, 1968
Look, 31:92-96, Dec. 26, 1967
Nation, 205:476, Nov. 6, 1967
National Review, 19:1393-95, Dec. 12, 1967
New Republic, 157:25-26, Nov. 4, 1967
New Yorker, 43:179-80, May 6, 1967 and 105, Oct. 28, 1967 and 43:52, Nov. 4, 1967
Newsweek, 70:90, Oct. 30, 1967
Pasquier, Marie-Claire, "Shakespeare ou le Lieu Commun: A Propos de 'Rosencrantz and Guildenstern Are Dead' de Tom Stoppard", *Recherches Anglaises et Americaines* (1972), 5:110-20
Reporter, 37:39-40, Nov. 16, 1967
Saturday Review, 50:28, Nov. 4, 1967
Taylor, John Russell, *The Second Wave; British Drama for the Seventies.* 1971. Pp. 94-107
Time, 90:84, Oct. 27, 1967
Travel, 128:22, Dec. 1967
Vogue, 150:72, Nov. 15, 1967

Travesties, 1974
America, Dec. 6, 1975, 133:408
Commentary, Jan. 1976, 61:71-74
Commonweal, Feb. 13, 1976, 103:114
Lambert, J. W., "Travesties", *Drama* (1974), 114:38-41
Nation, Nov. 22, 1975, 221:540
New Republic, Nov. 22, 1975, 173:18-19
New Yorker, Nov. 10, 1975, 51:135
Newsweek, June 24, 1974, 83:77 and Nov. 10, 1975, 86:66
O'Connor, G., "Travesties", *Plays and Players* (July 1974), 21:34-35
Saturday Review, Nov. 15, 1975, 3:36-37
Time, Nov. 10, 1975, 106:75

AUGUST STRINDBERG

Advent, 1915
Steene, Birgitta, *The Greatest Fire; A Study of August Strindberg.* 1973. Pp. 88-90

The Bond, 1892
Madsen, Borge Gedso, "Naturalism in Transition; Strindberg's 'Cynical' Tragedy 'The Bond' ", *Modern Drama*, 5:291-98, 1962

Brända Tomten *SEE* The Burned House

The Bridal Crown, 1907
Bentley, Eric Russell, *In Search of Theatre.* 1953. Pp. 134-43
Time, 31:36, Feb. 14, 1938

Brott och Brott *SEE* Crime and Crime

The Burned House, 1907
Valency, Maurice, *The Flower and the Castle; Introduction to Modern Drama.* 1963. Pp. 347-48

Comrades, 1905
  Lambert, J. W., "Comrades", *Drama* (Winter 1974), 115:53
  O'Connor, G., "Comrades", *Plays and Players* (Jan. 1975), 22:30-31

Creditors, 1889
  Beyer, W., "Strindberg Heritage: 'Father' and 'Creditors'", *School and Society*, 71:23-24, Jan. 14, 1950
  Commonweal, 51:267-68, Dec. 1949 and 75:543, Feb. 16, 1962
  Forum, 113:26-27, Jan., 1950
  Gilman, Richard, *Common and Uncommon Masks; Writings on the Theatre, 1961-1970.* 1972. Pp. 78-80
  Nation, 194:126, Feb. 10, 1962
  New Republic, 122:22, Jan. 2, 1950 and 146:20-21, Feb. 19, 1962
  New Yorker, 37:72, Feb. 3, 1962
  Theatre Arts, 46:63, April, 1962
  Valency, Maurice, *The Flower and the Castle; Introduction to Modern Drama.* 1963. Pp. 279-81

Crime and Crime, 1900
  Allen, James L. Jr., "Symbol and Meaning in Strindberg's 'Crime and Crime'", *Modern Drama* (May 1966), 9:62-73
  Benston, Alice N., "From Naturalism to the Dream Play; A Study of the Evolution of Strindberg's Unique Theatrical Form", *Modern Drama*, 7:382-404, 1964-65
  Lamm, Martin, *August Strindberg.* 1971. Pp. 320-23
  Sprinchorn, Evert, ed., *The Genius of the Scandinavian Theater.* 1964. Pp. 599-603
  Sprinchorn, Evert, "'The Zola of the Occult': Strindberg's Experimental Method", *Modern Drama* (1974), 17:251-66
  Valency, Maurice, *The Flower and the Castle; Introduction to Modern Drama.* 1963. Pp. 308-12

Crown Bride, 1906
  Lamm, Martin, *August Strindberg.* 1971. Pp. 376-80
  Syndergaard, Larry E., "The 'Skogsra' of Folklore and Strindberg's 'The Crown Bride'", *Comparative Drama* (1973), 6:310-22

Dance of Death, 1905
  Bronsen, David, "'The Dance of Death' and the Possibilities of Laughter", *Drama Survey* (1967), 6:31-41
  Heltan, Orley I., "The Absurd World of Strindberg's 'The Dance of Death'", *Comparative Drama* (1967), 1:199-206
  Hildeman, Karl-Ivar, "Strindberg, 'The Dance of Death' and Revenge", *Scandinavian Studies* (Nov. 1963), 35:267-94
  Hughes, C., "Dance of Death", *Plays and Players* (June 1974), 21:48-49
  Lamm, Martin, *August Strindberg.* 1971. Pp. 372-76
  Lewisohn, Ludwig, *Drama and the Stage.* 1922. Pp. 53-71
  ———————— , "Dance of Death", *Nation*, 110:774-75, June 5, 1920 and 118:16-17, Jan. 2, 1924
  Nathan, George Jean, *Theatre Book of the Year, 1947-48.* Pp. 241-45
  Reinert, Otto, ed., *Strindberg; A Collection of Critical Essays.* 1971. Pp. 117-24
  Shipp, H., "Dance of Death", *English Review*, 46:355-57, March, 1928

Shunami, Gideon, "Misshak H-Halomot Le-Strindberg; Hazaya o Metsiut", *Bamah; Educational Theatre Review* (1972), 53-54:54-63

Steene, Birgitta, *The Greatest Fire; A Study of August Strindberg.* 1973. Pp. 65-69

Steiner, Donald L., "August Strindberg and Edward Albee: 'The Dance of Death' ", *Dissertation Abstracts International* (1972), 33:766A

Taylor, Marion A., "Edward Albee and August Strindberg; Some Parallels Between 'The Dance of Death' and 'Who's Afraid of Virginia Woolf?' ", *Papers on Language and Literature* (1965), 1:59-71

——————————— , "A Note on Strindberg's 'The Dance of Death' and Edward Albee's 'Who's Afraid of Virginia Woolf?' ", *Papers on Language and Literature* (1966), 2:187-88

Theatre Arts, 44:9, Nov., 1960

Valency, Maurice, *The Flower and the Castle; Introduction to Modern Drama.* 1963. Pp. 315-19

Williams, Raymond, *Modern Tragedy.* 1966. Pp. 108-10

Dödsdansen *SEE* The Dance of Death

A Dream Play, 1907

Adler, Henry, "To Hell with Society", *Tulane Drama Review* (May 1960), 4:53-76

Benston, Alice N., "From Naturalism to the Dream Play; A Study of the Evolution of Strindberg's Unique Theatrical Form", *Modern Drama*, 7:382-404, 1964-65

Brustein, Robert Sanford, *The Theatre of Revolt; An Approach to the Modern Drama.* 1964. Pp. 126-32

Cole, Toby, ed., *Playwrights on Playwriting; the Meaning and Making of Modern Drama from Ibsen to Ionesco.* 1960. Pp. 182-83

Corrigan, Robert W., *The Theatre in Search of a Fix.* 1973. Pp. 111-23

Currie, R. Hector, "The Energies of Tragedy; Cosmis and Psychic", *Centennial Review* (1967), 11:220-36

Even-Zohar, Itamar, "Correlative Position and Correlative Negative Time in Strindberg's 'The Father' and 'A Dream Play' ", *Hasifrut; Quarterly for the Study of Literature* (1969), 1:538-68

Freedman, Morris, *The Moral Impulse; Modern Drama from Ibsen to the Present.* 1967. Pp. 19-30

The Hero in Scandinavian Literature; From Peer Gynt to the Present, ed. by John M. Weinstock and Robert T. Rovinsky. 1975. Pp. 143-55

Jarvi, Raymond, " 'Ett Dromspel'; A Symphony for the Stage", *Scandinavian Studies* (1972), 44:28-42

Johnson, Walter, " 'A Dream Play': Plans and Fulfillment", *Scandinavica* (1971), 10:103-11

Lamm, Martin, *August Strindberg.* 1971. Pp. 387-410

Lawson, Stephen R., "Strindberg's 'Dream Play' and 'Ghost Sonata' ", *Yale Theatre* (1974), 5,iii:95-102

New Yorker, 36:103, Dec. 3, 1960

Passerini, Edward M., "Strindberg's Absurdist Plays—An Examination of the Expressionistic, Surrealistic and Absurd Elements in Strindberg's Drama", *Dissertation Abstracts International* (1972), 32:4628A

Plasberg, Elaine, "Strindberg and the New Poetics", *Modern Drama* (1972), 15:1-14

Reinert, Otto, ed., *Strindberg; A Collection of Critical Essays*. 1971. Pp. 137-51

Reiter, Seymour, *World Theater; The Structure and Meaning of Drama*. Pp. 195-213

Rosenberg, Marvin, "A Metaphor for Dramatic Form", *Journal of Aesthetics and Art Criticism* (1958), 17:174-80

Sprinchorn, Evert, "The Logic of 'A Dream Play' ", *Modern Drama*, 5:352-65, 1962

——————— , "The 'Zola of the Occult'; Strindberg's Experimental Method", *Modern Drama* (1974), 17:251-66

Steene, Birgitta, *The Greatest Fire; A Study of August Strindberg*. 1973. Pp. 97-104

Valency, Maurice, *The Flower and the Castle; Introduction to Modern Drama*. 1963. Pp. 321-42

Ett Drömpsel   *SEE*   A Dream Play

Easter, 1901
America, 96:511, May 2, 1957

Benston, Alice N., "From Naturalism to the Dream Play; A Study of the Evolution of Strindberg's Unique Theatrical Form", *Modern Drama*, 7:382-404, 1964-65

Bergeron, D. M., "Strindberg's 'Easter'; A Musical Play", *Universities Review* (1967), 33:219-32

Hildeman, Karl-Ivar, "Strindberg, the Regenerated", *Journal of English and Germanic Philology* (1930), 29:257-70

Lamm, Martin, *August Strindberg*. 1971. Pp. 367-72

Steene, Birgitta, *The Greatest Fire; A Study of August Strindberg*. 1973. Pp. 92-95

Valency, Maurice, *The Flower and the Castle; Introduction to Modern Drama*. 1963. Pp. 312-15

Fadren   *SEE*   The Father

The Father, 1887
Arts and Decoration, 36:55, Dec., 1931

Bayerschmidt, Carl F. and Erik J. Friis, eds., *Scandinavian Studies; Essays Presented to Dr. Henry Goddard Leach on the Occasion of His 85th Birthday*. 1965. Pp. 247-59

Benston, Alice N., "From Naturalism to the Dream Play; A Study of the Evolution of Strindberg's Unique Theatrical Form", *Modern Drama*, 7:382-404, 1964-65

Beyer, W., "Strindberg Heritage: 'Father' and 'Creditors' ", *School and Society*, 71:23-24, Jan. 14, 1950

Brustein, Robert Sanford, *The Theatre of Revolt; An Approach to the Modern Drama*. 1964. Pp. 103-14

Catholic World, 170:307-08, Jan., 1950

Clarke, Margaret, "Strindberg and Samuel de Constant; The Source of 'The Father' and of Strindbergian Sociology, 1883-1887", *Revue de Littérature Comparée* (1968), 42:583-96

Commonweal, 51:267-68, Dec. 9, 1949

Dahlstrom, Carl E. W. L., "Strindberg's 'Fadren' as an Expressionistic Drama", *Scandinavian Studies and Notes*, 16:83-94, 1940

————————— , "Strindberg's 'The Father' as Tragedy", *Scandinavian Studies*, 27:45-63, 1955

Even-Zohar, Itamar, "Correlative Position and Correlative Negative Time in Strindberg's 'The Father' and 'A Dream Play'", *Hasifrut; Quarterly for the Study of Literature* (1969), 1:538-68

Forum, 113:26, Jan., 1950

Freedman, Morris, *The Moral Impulse; Modern Drama from Ibsen to the Present*. 1967. Pp. 19-30

————————— , "Strindberg's Positive Nihilism", *Drama Survey*, 2:288-96, 1963

Jacobs, Barry, "'Psychic Murder' and Characterization in Strindberg's 'The Father'", *Scandinavica* (1969), 8:19-34

Lyons, Charles L., "The Archetypal Action of Male Submission in Strindberg's 'The Father'", *Scandinavian Studies* (Aug. 1964), 36:218-32

MacCarthy, Desmond, *Humanities*. 1954. Pp. 84-88

————————— , "The Father", *New Statesman*, 33:599-600, Aug. 24, 1929

Nathan, George Jean, *Theatre Book of the Year, 1949-50*. Pp. 95-100

Nation, 169:525, Nov. 26, 1949

New Republic, 68:301, Oct. 28, 1931 and 121:22, Sept. 19, 1949 and 121:21, Dec. 19, 1949

New Yorker, 25:52, Nov. 26, 1949

Newsweek, 34:67, Nov. 28, 1949

Outlook, 159:280, Oct. 28, 1931

Sprinchorn, Evert, "Strindberg and the Greater Naturalism", *TDR: The Drama Review* (Winter 1968), 13:119-29

Steene, Birgitta, *The Greatest Fire; A Study of August Strindberg*. 1973. Pp. 49-51

Styan, J. L., *The Elements of Drama*. 1960. Pp. 158-62

Theatre Arts, 15:981-82, Dec., 1931 and 34:15, Jan., 1950

Time, 54:61, Nov. 28, 1949

Valency, Maurice, *The Flower and the Castle; Introduction to Modern Drama*. 1963. Pp. 260-63

Williams, Raymond, *Drama from Ibsen to Brecht*. 1968. Pp. 78-80

————————— , *Modern Tragedy*. 1966. Pp. 108-10

Fordringsagare *SEE* Creditors

Froken Julie *SEE* Miss Julie

Ghost Sonata, 1908

Benston, Alice N., "From Naturalism to the Dream Play; A Study of the Evolution of Strindberg's Unique Theatrical Form", *Modern Drama*, 7:382-404, 1964-65

Corrigan, Robert W., *The Theatre in Search of a Fix*. 1973. Pp. 111-24

Freedman, Morris, *The Moral Impulse; Modern Drama from Ibsen to the Present*. 1967. Pp. 19-30

Hildeman, Karl Ivar, "Strindberg, the Regenerated", *Journal of English and Germanic Philology* (1930), 29:257-70

Jarvi, Raymond, "Strindberg's 'The Ghost Sonata' and Sonata Form", *Mosaic; A Journal for the Comparative Study of Literature and Ideas* (1972), 5,ii:69-84

Kellock, H., "Ghost Sonata", *The Freeman*, 8:472, Jan. 23, 1924

Knauf, David M., ed., *Papers in Dramatic Theory and Criticism*. 1969. Pp. 54-63

Lawson, Stephen R., "Strindberg's 'Dream Play' and 'Ghost Sonata'", *Yale Theatre* (1974), 5,iii:95-102

Lewis, Allan, *The Contemporary Theatre; The Significant Playwrights of Our Time*. 1962. Pp. 42-59

May, Milton A., "Strindberg's 'Ghost Sonata': Parodied Fairy Tale on Original Sin", *Modern Drama* (Sept. 1967), 10:189-94

Parker, Gerald, "The Spectator Seized by the Theatre: Strindberg's 'The Ghost Sonata'", *Modern Drama* (1971), 14:373-86

Steene, Birgitta, *The Greatest Fire; A Study of August Strindberg*. 1973. Pp. 11-17 and 152-53

Törnquist, Egil, "'Hamlet' and 'The Ghost Sonata'", *Drama Survey* (1969), 7:25-44

Valency, Maurice, *The Flower and the Castle; Introduction to Modern Drama*. 1963. Pp. 348-55

Williams, Raymond, *Drama from Ibsen to Brecht*. 1968. Pp. 96-99
────────────── , *Modern Tragedy*. 1966. Pp. 106-15

Young, Stark, "Ghost Sonata", *New Republic*, 37:231-32, Jan. 23, 1924

The Great Highway, 1910

Myrdahl, Bertil, "'The Highway': Strindberg's Last Drama", *Bulletin of the American Institute of Swedish Arts, Literature and Science*, 4:19-21, 1949

Valency, Maurice, *The Flower and the Castle; Introduction to Modern Drama*. 1963. Pp. 357-60

Gustav III, 1916

Wattman, Ulla, "Strindbergs Drama 'Gustav III'", *Dramaforskning* (1968), 3:330-38

Himmelrikets Nycklar, Eller Sankte Per Vandrar På Jorden   *SEE*   The Keys of Heaven; or St. Peter Wanders on the Earth

Isle of the Dead, 1907

Vowles, Richard B., "Strindberg's 'Isle of the Dead'", *Modern Drama*, 5:366-78, 1962

The Keys of Heaven; or St. Peter Wanders on the Earth, 1892

Passerini, Edward M., "Strindberg's Absurdist Plays—An Examination of the Expressionistic, Surrealistic, and Absurd Elements in Strindberg's Drama", *Dissertation Abstracts International* (1972), 32:4628A

Kamraterna   *SEE*   Comrades

Kronbruden   *SEE*   Crown Bride

Lucky Per's Journey, 1883

Passerini, Edward M., "Strindberg's Absurdist Plays—An Examination of the Expressionistic, Surrealistic, and Absurd Elements in Strindberg's Drama", *Dissertation Abstracts International* (1972), 32:4628A

Valency, Maurice, *The Flower and the Castle; Introduction to Modern Drama*. 1963. Pp. 250-51

Lycko-Pers Resa   *SEE*   Lucky Per's Journey

Marauders, 1910
Valency, Maurice, *The Flower and the Castle; Introduction to Modern Drama.* 1963. Pp. 259-61

Marodörer *SEE* Marauders

Master Olof, 1881
Lamm, Martin, *August Strindberg.* 1971. Pp. 25-40
"Reform och Revolution i 'Master Olof': Ett Grupparbete", *Bonniers Litterära Magasin* (1969), 38:407-22
Stolpe, Jan, "Götebergs 'Master Olof' ", *Bonniers Litterära Magasin* (1969), 38:622-23
Valency, Maurice, *The Flower and the Castle; Introduction to Modern Drama.* 1963. Pp. 245-49

Midsummer, 1901
Lamm, Martin, *August Strindberg.* 1971. Pp. 363-66

Miss Julie, 1889
Arestad, Sverre, "Ibsen, Strindberg and Naturalistic Tragedy", *Theatre Annual* (1968), 24:6-13
Benston, Alice N., "From Naturalism to the Dream Play; A Study of the Evolution of Strindberg's Unique Theatrical Form", *Modern Drama*, 7:382-404, 1964-65
Bergöö, Britta, Marianne Giselsson and Ninne Olsson, "Ett Nytt Slut På 'Froken Julie' ", *Ord och Bild* (1972), 81:196-99
Brustein, Robert Sanford, *The Theatre of Revolt; An Approach to the Modern Drama.* 1964. Pp. 102-04 and 112-19
Catholic World, 183:66, April, 1956
Cole, Toby, ed., *Playwrights on Playwriting; The Meaning and Making of Modern Drama from Ibsen to Ionesco.* 1960. Pp. 171-82
Corrigan, Robert W. and James L. Rosenberg, eds., *The Art of the Theatre; A Critical Anthology of Drama.* 1964. Pp. 321-30
Cowell, Raymond, *Twelve Modern Dramatists.* 1967. Pp. 27-29
Dahlstrom, C. E. W. L., "Strindberg's 'Naturalistiska Sorgespel' and Zola's Naturalism, 'Fröken Julie'", *Scandinavian Studies*, 18:183-94, 1945
Freedman, Morris, *The Moral Impulse; Modern Drama from Ibsen to the Present.* 1967. Pp. 19-30
Gassner, John, *Directions in Modern Theatre and Drama.* 1965. Pp. 259-77
Gassner, John and Allen, Ralph G., eds., *Theatre and Drama in the Making.* 1964. Pp. 558-70
————————— , *Theatre at the Crossroads; Plays and Playwrights of the Mid-Century American Stage.* 1960. Pp. 188-93
Harrison, A. Cleveland, " 'Miss Julie': Essence and Anomaly of Naturalism", *Central States Speech Journal* (1970), 21:87-92
Hayes, Stephen G., "Strindberg's 'Miss Julie'; Lilacs and Beer", *Scandinavian Studies* (1973), 45:59-64
Jaspers, Karl, "Patografia de Strindberg en los Años que Escribió 'La Señorita Julia' ", *Primer Acto* (1973), 154:30-34
MacCarthy, Desmond, *Humanities.* 1954. Pp. 88-93
Nation, 182:205, March 10, 1956
New Yorker, 32:62, March 3, 1956

Offenbacher, Emil, "A Contribution to the Origin of Strindberg's 'Miss Julie' ", *Psychoanalytical Review*, 31:81-87, 1944
Reinert, Otto, ed., *Strindberg; A Collection of Critical Essays*. 1971. Pp. 105-16
Saturday Review, 39:25, March 10, 1956
Sprinchorn, Evert, "Strindberg and the Greater Naturalism", *TDR: The Drama Review* (Wint. 1968), 13:119-29
Steene, Birgitta, *The Greatest Fire; A Study of August Strindberg*. 1973. Pp. 51-58
Time, 67:47, March 5, 1956
Törnqvist, Egil, "Fröken Julie och O'Neill", *Meddelanden fran Strindbergssällskapet* (1969), 42;43:5-16
Valency, Maurice, *The Flower and the Castle; Introduction to Modern Drama*. 1963. Pp. 274-78
Williams, Raymond, *Drama from Ibsen to Brecht*. 1968. Pp. 81-85
_____ , *Modern Tragedy*. 1966. Pp. 110-12
Young, Vernon, "The History of 'Miss Julie' ", *Hudson Review* (Spring 1955), 8:123-30

Pariah, 1889
MacCarthy, Desmond, *Humanities*. 1954. Pp. 88-93

Päsk *SEE* Easter

Den Starkare *SEE* The Stronger

Stora Landsvagen *SEE* The Great Highway

The Stronger, 1889
Saturday Review, 39:25, March 10, 1956
Törnquist, Egil, "Strindberg's 'The Stronger' ", *Scandinavian Studies* (1970), 42:297-308

Svanevit *SEE* Swanwhite

Swanwhite, 1908
Lamm, Martin, *August Strindberg*. 1971. Pp. 380-83

Till Damaskus *SEE* To Damascus

To Damascus, 1916
Brustein, Robert Sanford, *The Theatre of Revolt; An Approach to the Modern Drama*. 1964. Pp. 119-24
Dahlstrom, Carl E. W. L., "Situation and Character in 'Till Damaskus' ", *Modern Language Association. Publications* (PMLA), 53:886-902, 1939
Hildeman, Karl-Ivar, "Strindberg, the Regenerated", *Journal of English and Germanic Philology* (1930), 29:257-70
Lamm, Martin, *August Strindberg*. 1971. Pp. 308-16
Matthews, Honor, *The Primal Curse; The Myth of Cain and Abel in the Theatre*. 1967. Pp. 128-33
Scanlan, David, " 'The Road to Damascus', Part I: A Skeptic's 'Everyman' ", *Modern Drama*, 5:344-51, 1962
Sprinchorn, Evert, ed., *The Genius of the Scandinavian Theater*. 1964. Pp. 583-98
Sprinchorn, Evert, " 'The Zola of the Occult'; Strindberg's Experimental Method", *Modern Drama* (1974), 17:251-66

Steene, Birgitta, *The Greatest Fire; A Study of August Strindberg.* 1973. Pp. 84-88
Valency, Maurice, *The Flower and the Castle; Introduction to Modern Drama.* 1963. Pp. 295-308
Vincentia, Sister M., "Naturalism in 'Road to Damascus' ", *Modern Drama,* 5:335-43, 1962
Williams, Raymond, *Drama from Ibsen to Brecht.* 1968. Pp. 86-93
—————————— , *Modern Tragedy.* 1966. Pp. 112-14

ALEXANDER VASILEALEXANDER VASILEIVICH SUKHOVO-KOBYLIN

The Death of Tarelkin, 1869
Karlinsky, Simon, "The Alogical and Absurdist Aspects of Russian Realist Drama", *Comparative Drama* (Fall 1969), 3:147-55
Symons, James M., *Meyerhold's Theatre of the Grotesque; The Post-Revolutionary Productions, 1920-1932.* 1971. Pp. 88-98 and 104-07

Smert Tarelkin *SEE* The Death of Tarelkin

JOHN MILLINGTON SYNGE

Deirdre of the Sorrows, 1910
America, 102:217, Nov. 14, 1959
Barnett, Pat, "The Nature of Synge's Dialogue", *English Literature in Transition (1880-1920)* (1967), 10:119-29
Bourgeois, Maurice, *John Millington Synge and the Irish Theatre.* 1965. Pp. 212-17
Bushrui, S. B., ed., *A Centenary Tribute to John Millington Synge.* 1972. Pp. 91-106
Fackler, Herbert V., "John Millington Synge's 'Deirdre of the Sorrows': Beauty Only", *Modern Drama* (1969), 11:404-09
Fakacs, Dalma S., "John Millington Synge as Dramatist", *Dissertation Abstracts International* (1972), 32:6457A
Farris, J. R., "Nature of the Tragic Experience in 'Deirdre of the Sorrows' ", *Modern Drama* (Sept. 1971), 14:243-51
Forum, 113:27, Jan., 1950
Greene, David H., "Synge's Unfinished 'Deirdre' ", *Modern Language Association. Publications* (PMLA), 68:1314-21, 1948
Hunter, Jean C., "The Primitive Vision of John Millington Synge", *Dissertation Abstracts International* (1974), 35:1047A
Leech, Clifford, "John Synge and the Drama of His Time", *Modern Drama* (1973), 16:223-37
Murphy, Brenda, "Stoicism, Asceticism, and Ecstasy; Synge's 'Deirdre of the Sorrows' ", *Modern Drama* (1974), 17:155-63
New Yorker, 35:95, Oct. 24, 1959
Orel, Harold D., "Synge's Last Play: And a Story Will be Told Forever", *Modern Drama,* 4:306-13, 1961
Skelton, Robin, *John Millington Synge.* 1972. Pp. 78-85
Stephens, E. M., "Synge's Last Play", *Contemporary Review,* 186:288-93, Nov., 1954
Wickstrom, Gordon M., "The Deirdre Plays of Yeats and Synge: Patterns of Irish Exile", *Dissertation Abstracts* (1969), 29:4027A

Williams, Raymond, *Drama from Ibsen to Brecht*. 1968. Pp. 137-40

In the Shadow of the Glen, 1903
  Barnett, Pat, "The Nature of Synge's Dialogue", *English Literature in Transition (1880-1920)* (1967), 10:119-29
  Beerbohm, Max, *Around Theatres*. 1953. Pp. 314-19
  Bourgeois, Maurice, *John Millington Synge and the Irish Theatre*. 1965. Pp. 145-58
  Bushrui, S. B., ed., *A Centenary Tribute to John Millington Synge*. 1972. Pp. 21-32
  Catholic World, 185:148, May, 1957
  Fakacs, Dalma S., "John Millington Synge as Dramatist", *Dissertation Abstracts International* (1972), 32:6457A
  Ferris, William R., Jr., "Folklore and Folklife in the Works of John Millington Synge", *New York Folklore Quarterly* (1971), 27:339-56
  Fréchet, René, "Le Thème de la Parole dans le Théâtre de John Millington Synge", *Etudes Anglaises* (1968), 21:243-56
  Grene, Nicholas, "Synge's 'The Shadow of the Glen': Repetition and Allusion", *Modern Drama* (1974), 17:19-25
  Hunter, Jean C., "The Primitive Vision of John Millington Synge", *Dissertation Abstracts International* (1974), 35:1047A
  Michie, Donald M., "Synge and His Critics", *Modern Drama* (1972), 15: 427-31
  Orr, Robert H., "The Surprise Ending; One Aspect of John Millington Synge's Dramatic Technique", *English Literature in Transition, 1880-1920* (1972), 15:105-15
  Robinson, Paul N., "The Peasant Play as Allegory; John Millington Synge's 'The Shadow of the Glen'", *CEA Critic* (1974), 36,iv:36-38
  Roy, Emil, *British Drama Since Shaw*. 1972. Pp. 59-62
  Skelton, Robin, *John Millington Synge*. 1972. Pp. 39-44
  _____ , "John Millington Synge and 'In the Shadow of the Glen'", *English* (Aut. 1969), 18:91-97

Playboy of the Western World, 1907
  Bessai, Diane E., "Little Hound in Mayo: Synge's 'Playboy' and the Comic Tradition in Irish Literature", *Drama Review* (1968), 48:372-83
  Bookman (London), 32:181, Aug., 1970
  Bourgeois, Maurice, *John Millington Synge and the Irish Theatre*. 1965. Pp. 193-212 and 311-13
  Bushrui, S. B., ed., *A Centenary Tribute to John Millington Synge*. 1972. Pp. 61-74 and 173-88
  Catholic World, 145:312-13, July, 1938 and 164:263-64, Dec., 1946
  Cole, Toby, ed., *Playwrights on Playwriting; The Meaning and Making of Modern Drama from Ibsen to Ionesco*. 1960. Pp. 201-02
  Commonweal, 45:95, Nov. 8, 1946 and 68:303-04, June 20, 1958
  Cowell, Raymond, *Twelve Modern Dramatists*. 1967. Pp. 57-59
  Current Literature, 50:81-84, Jan., 1911
  Cusack, Cyril, "A Player's Reflections on 'Playboy'", *Modern Drama*, 4:300-05, 1961
  Dalmasso, M., "'The Playboy of the Western World': Langue et Imagination Populaires", *Publications Universitaires. Lettres et Sciences Humaines de l'Université de Provence* (1972), 5:49-68

Day-Lewis, Sean, "Synge's Song", *Drama* (Aut. 1968), #90:35-38

Edwards, Bernard L., "Vision of John Millington Synge; A Study of 'Playboy of the Western World'", *English Literature in Transition, 1880-1920* (1974), 17,i:8-18

Fakacs, Dalma S., "John Millington Synge as Dramatist", *Dissertation Abstracts International* (1972), 32:6457A

Farris, Jon R., "The Hard Birth of 'The Playboy of the Western World'", *Dissertation Abstracts International* (1974), 35:3735A

Ferris, William R., Jr., "Folklore and Folklife in the Works of John Millington Synge", *New York Folklore Quarterly* (1971), 27:339-56

Foster, Leslie D., "Heroic Strivings in 'The Playboy of the Western World'", *Ireland: A Journal of Irish Studies* (1973), 8:85-94

Fréchet, René, "Le Thème de la Parole dans le Théâtre de John Millington Synge", *Etudes Anglaises* (1968), 21:243-56

Gerstenberger, Donna, "Bonnie and Clyde and Christy Malon; Playboys All", *Modern Drama* (Sept. 1971), 14:227-31

Gillie, Christopher, *Movements in English Literature, 1900-1940*. 1975. Pp. 164-82

Gutierrez, Donald, "Coming of Age in Mayo: Synge's 'The Playboy of the Western World' as a Rite of Passage", *Hartford Studies in Literature* (1974), 6:159-66

Harper's Weekly, 51:344, March 9, 1907

Hart, William, "Synge's Ideas on Life and Art; Design and Theory in 'The Playboy of the Western World'", *Yeats Studies* (1972), 2:33-51

Hawkes, Terence, "Playboys of the Western World", *Listener* (1965), 74:991-93

Henry, P. L., "The Playboy of the Western World", *Philologica Pragensia* (1965), 8:189-204

Hunter, Jean C., "The Primitive Vision of John Millington Synge", *Dissertation Abstracts International* (1974), 35:1047A

Johnson, Wallace H., "The Pagan Setting of Synge's 'Playboy'", *Renascence* (1967), 19:119-21 and 150

Kilroy, James F., "The Playboy as Poet", *Modern Language Association. Publications* (1968), 83:439-42

Leech, Clifford, "John Synge and the Drama of His Time", *Modern Drama* (1973), 16:223-37

Lengeler, Rainer, "Phantasie und Komik in Synges 'The Playboy of the Western World'", *Germanisch-Romanische Monatsschrift* (1969), n. s. 19:291-304

Malone, Andrew E., *The Irish Drama*, 1965. Pp. 150-53

Michie, Donald M., "Synge and His Critics", *Modern Drama* (1972), 15:427-31

Nathan, George Jean, *Theatre Book of the Year, 1946-47*. 1947. Pp. 136-39

Nation, 93:376-77, Oct. 19, 1911 and 163:536, Nov. 9, 1946

New Republic, 115:628, Nov. 11, 1946

New Statesman and Nation, 17:169, Feb. 4, 1939

New Yorker, 22:57, Nov. 2, 1946

Newsweek, 28:85, Nov. 4, 1946

Oppel, Horst, *Das Moderne Englische Drama; Interpretationen*. 1963. Pp. 87-108

O'Riordan, John, "Playwright of the Western World", *Library Review* (1971), 23:140-45

Orr, Robert H., "The Surprise Ending; One Aspect of John Millington Synge's Dramatic .Technique", *English Literature in Transition, 1880-1920* (1972), 15:105-15

Our Irish Theatre; A Chapter of Autobiography, by Lady Gregory. 1972. Pp. 97-135

Pearce, Howard D., "Synge's Playboy as Mock-Christ", *Modern Drama*, 8:303-11, 1965

Rollins, Ronald G., "O'Casey and Synge: The Irish Hero as Playboy and Gunman", *Arizona Quarterly* (1966), 22:217-22

Roy, Emil, *British Drama Since Shaw.* 1968. Pp. 61-67

Salmon, Eric, "John Millington Synge's 'Playboy': A Necessary Reassessment", *Modern Drama* (1970), 13:111-28

Sanderlin, R. Reed, "Synge's 'Playboy' and the Ironic Hero", *Southern Quarterly* (April 1968), 6:289-301

Shand, J., "Playboy of the Western World", *New Statesman*, 26:47, Oct. 24, 1925

Sidnell, M. J., "Synge's 'Playboy' and the Champion of Ulster", *Dalhousie Review* (1965), 45:51-59

Skelton, Robin, *John Millington Synge.* 1972. Pp. 57-70

Smith, Harry W., "Synge's 'Playboy' and the Proximity of Violence", *Quarterly Journal of Speech* (Dec. 1969), 55:381-87

Solomont, Susan, *The Comic Effect of "Playboy of the Western World",* 1962

Spacks, Patricia Meyer, "The Making of the Playboy", *Modern Drama*, 4:314-23, 1961

Sullivan, Mary Rose, "Synge, Sophocles and the Un-Making of Myth", *Modern Drama* (Dec. 1969), 12:242-53

Theatre Arts, 31:21-22, Jan., 1947

Time, 48:55, Nov. 4, 1946

Turner, W. J., "Playboy of the Western World", *London Mercury;* 4:537-39, Sept., 1921

Untermeyer, L. J. M., "Synge and 'The Playboy of the Western World'", *Poet-Lore*, 19:364-67, Sept., 1908

Ward, Alfred Charles, ed., *Specimens of English Dramatic Criticism, 17th-20th Centuries.* 1945. Pp. 248-59

Williams, Raymond, *Drama from Ibsen to Brecht.* 1968. Pp. 135-37

Yeats, W. B., *Explorations.* 1962. Pp. 225-30

Riders to the Sea, 1904

Barnett, Pat, "The Nature of Synge's Dialogue", *English Literature in Transition (1880-1920)* (1967), 10:119-29

Beerbohm, Max, *Around Theatres.* 1953. Pp. 314-19

Bourgeois, Maurice, *John Millington Synge and the Irish Theatre.* 1965. Pp. 158-72

Bushrui, S. B., ed., *A Centenary Tribute to John Millington Synge.* 1972. Pp. 32-52

Casey, Daniel J., "An Aran Requiem: Setting in 'Riders to the Sea'", *Antigonish Review* (1972), 9:89-100

Catholic World, 185:148, May, 1957

Collins, R. L., "The Distinction of 'Riders to the Sea'", *University of Kansas City Review*, 13:278-84, 1946-47

Currie, Ryder H., and Martin Bryan, "'Riders to the Sea' Reappraised", *Texas Quarterly* (1968), 11:139-46

Durbach, Errol, "Synge's Tragic Vision of the Old Mother and the Sea", *Modern Drama* (1971), 14:363-72

Fakacs, Dalma S., "John Millington Synge as Dramatist", *Dissertation Abstracts International* (1972), 32:6457A

Ferris, William R., Jr., "Folklore and Folklife in the Works of John Millington Synge", *New York Folklore Quarterly* (1971), 27:339-56

Fréchet, René, "Le Thème de la Parole dans le Théâtre de John Millington Synge", *Etudes Anglaises* (1968), 21:243-56

Gaskell, Ronald, *Drama and Reality; The European Theatre since Ibsen*. 1972. Pp. 99-105

Hunter, Jean C., "The Primitive Vision of John Millington Synge", *Dissertation Abstracts International* (1974), 35:1047A

Leech, Clifford, "John Synge and the Drama of His Time", *Modern Drama* (1973), 16:223-37

Levitt, Paul M., *A Structural Approach to the Analysis of Drama*. 1971. Pp. 84-116

―――――― , "The Structural Craftsmanship of John Millington Synge's 'Riders to the Sea'", *(Eire) Ireland; A Journal of Irish Studies* (1969), 4:53-61

Orr, Robert H., "The Surprise Ending; One Aspect of John Millington Synge's Dramatic Technique", *English Literature in Transition, 1880-1920* (1972), 15:105-15

Pittock, Malcolm, "Riders to the Sea", *English Studies* (Oct. 1968), 49:445-49

Skelton, Robin, *John Millington Synge*. 1972. Pp. 31-38

Van Laan, Thomas F., "Form as Agent in Synge's 'Riders to the Sea'", *Drama Survey*, 3:352-66, 1964

Tinker's Wedding, 1909

Barnett, Pat, "The Nature of Synge's Dialogue", *English Literature in Transition (1880-1920)* (1967), 10:119-29

Bookman (London), 33:260, March, 1908

Bourgeois, Maurice, *John Millington Synge and the Irish Theatre*. 1965. Pp. 176-82

Bushrui, S. B., ed., *A Centenary Tribute to John Millington Synge*. 1972. Pp. 75-90

Catholic World, 184:148, May, 1957

Cole, Toby, ed., *Playwrights on Playwriting; The Meaning and Making of Modern Drama from Ibsen to Ionesco*. 1960. Pp. 202-03

Fréchet, René, "Le Theme de la Parole dans le Théâtre de John Millington Synge", *Etudes Anglaises* (1968), 21:243-56

Greene, D. H., "'Tinker's Wedding': A Revaluation", *Modern Language Association. Publications* (PMLA), 62:824-27, 1947

Hunter, Jean C., "The Primitive Vision of John Millington Synge", *Dissertation Abstracts International* (1974), 35:1047A

Michie, Donald M., "Synge and His Critics", *Modern Drama* (1972), 15:427-31

Orr, Robert H., "The Surprise Ending: One Aspect of John Millington Synge's Dramatic Technique", *English Literature in Transition, 1880-1920* (1972), 15:105-15

Skelton, Robin, *John Millington Synge*. 1972. Pp. 45-50
Williams, Raymond, *Drama from Ibsen to Brecht*. 1968. Pp. 129-33

Well of the Saints, 1905
Alspack, R. K., "Synge's 'Well of the Saints'" *Times Literary Supplement*, Pp. 899, Dec. 28, 1935
Arts and Decoration, 36:42, March, 1932
Barnett, Pat, "The Nature of Synge's Dialogue", *English Literature in Transition (1880-1920)* (1967), 10:119-29
Bourgeois, Maurice, *John Millington Synge and the Irish Theatre*. 1965. 182-93
Bushrui, S. B., ed., *A Centenary Tribute to John Millington Synge*. 1972. Pp. 53-60
Catholic World, 189:243, June, 1959
Eckley, Grace, "Truth at the Bottom of the Well: Synge's 'The Well of the Saints'", *Modern Drama* (1973), 16:193-98
Fakacs, Dalma S., "John Millington Synge as Dramatist", *Dissertation Abstracts International* (1972), 32:6457A
Ferris, William R., Jr., "Folklore and Folklife in the Works of John Millington Synge", *New York Folklore Quarterly* (1971), 27:339-56
Fréchet, René, "Le Thème de la Parole dans le Théâtre de John Millington Synge", *Etudes Anglaises* (1968), 21:243-56
Hunter, Jean C., "The Primitive Vision of John Millington Synge", *Dissertation Abstracts International* (1974), 35:1047A
Nash, Vincent, " 'The Well of the Saints'; Language in a Landscape", *Literatur in Wissenschaft und Unterricht* (1972), 5:267-76
New Yorker, 35:82-83, April 18, 1959
O'Riordan, John, "Playwright of the Western World", *Library Review* (1971), 23:140-45
Orr, Robert H., "The Surprise Ending: One Aspect of John Millington Synge's Dramatic Technique", *English Literature in Transition, 1880-1920* (1972), 15:105-15
Skelton, Robin, *John Millington Synge*. 1972. Pp. 51-56
Williams, Raymond, *Drama from Ibsen to Brecht*. 1968. Pp. 129-35

ANTON TCHEKHOV

SEE

ANTON CHEKHOV

(PUBLIUS TERENTIUS AFTER) TERENCE

Adelphi   *SEE*   Brothers

Andria   *SEE*   Maid of Andros

The Brothers, 160 B.C.
Grant, John N., "The Role of Canthara in Terence's 'Adelphi' ", *Philologus; Zeitschrift für das Klassische Altertum* (1973), 117:70-75
Harsh, Philip Whaley, *A Handbook of Classical Drama*. 1944. Pp. 394-97
Levin, Richard, *The Multiple Plot in English Renaissance Drama*. 1971. Pp. 227-32
Lloyd-Jones, Hugh, "Terentian Technique in the 'Adelphi' and the 'Eunuchus' ", *Classical Quarterly* (1973), 23:279-85

The Eunuch, 161 B.C.
  Harsh, Philip Whaley, *A Handbook of Classical Drama.* 1944. Pp. 386-88
  Kraemer, C. J., Jr., "In Defense of Chaerea in 'The Eunuch' of Terence",
    Classical Journal, 23:662-67, 1928
  Levin, Richard, *The Multiple Plot in English Renaissance Drama.* 1971.
    Pp. 227-32
  Lloyd-Jones, Hugh, "Terentian Technique in the 'Adelphi' and the
    'Eunuchus' ", *Classical Quarterly* (1973), 23:279-85
  Olson, Elder, *The Theory of Comedy.* 1968. Pp. 82-84
  Rouveryre, A., "l'Eunuque", *Mercure de France*, 219:399, April 15, 1930

Heautontimorumenos *SEE* The Self-Tormentor

Hecyra *SEE* Mother-in-Law

Maid of Andros, 166 B.C.
  Harsh, Philip Whaley, *A Handbook of Classical Drama.* 1944. Pp. 381-
    84

Mother-in-Law, 160 B.C.
  Harsh, Philip Whaley, *A Handbook of Classical Drama.* 1944. Pp. 392-93

Phormio, 161 B.C.
  Arnott, W. Geoffrey, " 'Phormio Parasitus': A Study in Dramatic Methods
    of Characterization", *Greece and Rome* (1970), 17:32-57
  Harsh, Philip Whaley, *A Handbook of Classical Drama.* 1944. Pp. 389-91
  Levin, Richard, *The Multiple Plot in English Renaissance Drama.* 1971.
    Pp. 227-32

Self-Tormentor, 163 B.C.
  Harsh, Philip Whaley, *A Handbook of Classical Drama.* 1944. Pp. 385-87
  Levin, Richard, *The Multiple Plot in English Renaissance Drama.* 1971.
    Pp. 227-32

DYLAN MARLAIS THOMAS

Under Milk Wood, 1953
  Brinnin, John Malcolm, ed., *A Casebook on Dylan Thomas.* 1960. Pp. 110-14
  Christian Century, 74:1324, Nov. 6, 1957 and 78:535-37, April 26, 1961
  Cleverdon, Douglas, "Under Milk Wood", *Times Literary Supplement*
    (July 18, 1968). Pp. 761
  Commonweal, 58:297, June 26, 1953 and 67:151, Nov. 8, 1957
  Cox, D. B., ed., *Dylan Thomas; A Collection of Critical Essays.* 1966.
    Pp. 84-116
  Davies, M. Bryn, "Dylan Thomas—An Appraisal", *Literary Half-Yearly*
    (1962), 3:53-56
  ——————— , "A Few Thoughts About 'Milk Wood' ", *Literary Half-
    Yearly* (1963), 4:41-44
  Davies, Walford, ed., *Dylan Thomas; New Critical Essays.* 1972. Pp. 262-82
  Davis, C., "Voices of 'Under Milkwood' ", *Criticism* (1975), 17:74-89
  "Dylan Thomas's Play for Voices", *Critical Quarterly* (1959), 1:18-26
  Hawkes, Terence, "Playboys of the Western World", *Listener* (1965), 74:
    991-93
  Holbrook, David, *Dylan Thomas; The Code of Night.* 1972. Pp. 221-44

Illustrated London News, 226:520, March 19, 1955 and 229:400, Sept. 8, 1956
and 229:566, Oct. 6, 1956

Jenkins, David Clay, "Dylan Thomas's 'Under Milk Wood': The American
Element", *Trace* (1964), 51:325-35

Kerr, Walter, *The Theatre in Spite of Itself*. 1963. Pp. 78-82

Lerner, Laurence, *The Uses of Nostalgia; Studies in Pastoral Poetry*. 1972.
Pp. 81-104

Meller, H., "Zum Literarischen Hintergrund von Dylan Thomas 'Under
Milk Wood'", *Die Neueren Sprachen* (1966), #2:49-58

Morgan, W. J., " 'Under Milk Wood' Under Milk Wood", *Twentieth Century*, 164:275-76, Sept., 1958

Nation, 185:309, Nov. 2, 1957

New Yorker, 33:95, Oct. 26, 1957 and 37:132, April 8, 1961 and 38:132, Dec.
15, 1962

Oppel, Horst, *Das Moderne Englische Drama; Interpretationen*.   1963.
Pp. 289-302

Rea, J., "A Topographical Guide to 'Under Milk Wood' ", *College English*
(1964), 25:535-42

Reporter, 17:39, Nov. 14, 1957

Riesner, Dieter and Helmut Gneuss, *Festschrift für Walter Hubner*.   1964.
Pp. 327-36

Saturday Review, 36:24-25, June 6, 1953 and 39:39, Oct. 6, 1956 and 43:30,
June 4, 1960

Talbot, Norman, "Polly's Milk Wood and Abraham's Bosom", *Southern
Review* (Australia), 1:33-43, 1965

Theatre Arts, 41:92-93, May, 1957 and 41:22-23, Dec., 1957

Time, 70:93, Oct. 28, 1957

Tynan, Kenneth, *Curtains; Selections from the Drama Criticism and Related
Writings*. 1961. Pp. 145-46

Vogue, 130:212-13, Sept. 1, 1957

Williams, Raymond, *Drama·from Ibsen to Brecht*.   1968. Pp. 212-19

ERNST TOLLER

Der Deutsche Hinkemann   *SEE*   Hinkemann

Hinkemann, 1923

Mennemeier, F. N., "Das Idealistische Proletarierdrama", *Deutschunterricht*
(1972), 24,ii:100-16

Ossar, Michael L., "Anarchism in the Dramas of Ernst Toller", *Dissertation Abstracts International* (1974), 34:7773A

Hoppla! Such Is Life!, 1927

Ossar, Michael L., "Anarchism in the Dramas of Ernst Toller", *Dissertation Abstracts International* (1974), 34:7773A

Williams, Raymond, *Drama from Ibsen to Brecht*. 1968. Pp. 261-66

Hoppla! Wir Leben   *SEE*   Hoppla! Such Is Life!

The Machine Wreckers, 1922

Ossar, Michael L., "Anarchism in the Dramas of Ernst Toller", *Dissertation Abstracts International* (1974), 34:7773A

Pittock, Malcolm, "Maschinenstürmer", *Durham University Journal*
(1974), 35:294-305

Maschinenstürmer *SEE* The Machine Wreckers

Masse Mensch *SEE* Masses and Man

Masses and Man, 1920
  Dukore, Bernard F. and Daniel C. Gerould, "Explosions and Implosions; Avant-Garde Drama Betwen World Wars", *Educational Theatre Journal* (March 1969) 21:1-16
  Mennemeier, F. N., "Das Idealistische Proletarierdrama", *Deutschunterricht* (1972), 24,ii:100-16
  Ossar, Michael L., "Anarchism in the Dramas of Ernst Toller", *Dissertation Abstracts International* (1974), 34:7773A
  Pittock, Malcolm, "'Masse Mensch' and the Tragedy of Revolution", *Forum for Modern Language Studies* (1972), 8:162-83

Transfiguration, 1917/18
  Mennemeier, F. N., "Das Idealistische Proletarierdrama", *Deutschunterricht* (1972), 24,ii:100-16
  Ossar, Michael L., "Anarchism in the Dramas of Ernst Toller", *Dissertation Abstracts International* (1974), 34:7773A
  Reimer, Robert C., "The Tragedy of the Revolutionary; A Study of the Drama of Revolution of Ernst Toller, Friedrich Wolf and Bertolt Brecht, 1918-1933", *Dissertation Abstracts International* (1972), 32:5802A

Die Wandlung *SEE* Transfiguration

LEV (LEO) NIKOLAEVICH TOLSTOY

Fruits of Enlightenment, 1890
  Nation (London), 44:208, Nov. 10, 1928
  Spectator, 141:687-88, Nov. 10, 1928

Living Corpse, 1911
  Arts and Decoration, 32:96, Feb., 1930
  Baring, Maurice, *Punch and Judy and Other Essays*. 1924. Pp. 327-32
  Bertensson, S., "History of Tolstoy's Posthumous Play", *American Slavic Review*, 14:265-68, April, 1955
  Commonweal, 11:229, Dec. 25, 1929
  Freling, Roger N., "A Critical Study of Two Tolstoy Plays: 'The Power of Darkness' and 'The Living Corpse'", *Dissertation Abstracts International* (1972), 32:4661A
  Hamilton, Clayton Meeker, *Seen on the Stage*. 1920. Pp. 144-53
  MacGowan, K., "The Living Corpse", *New Republic*, 17:46, Nov. 9, 1918
  Mar'jamov, A., "Ziznennyj Slucaj i Literaturnyj Sjuzet; Zametki o 'Zivom Trupe' L. N. Tolstogo", *Voprosy Literatury* (1970), 14:89-122
  Moses, Montrose J., "Tolstoy Drama in America", *Bellman*, 25:628-31, Dec. 7, 1918
  Nation, 129:785-86, Dec. 25, 1929
  Theatre Arts, 14:107-08, Feb., 1930

Plody Prosveshcheniya *SEE* Fruits of Enlightenment

The Power of Darkness; or, "If a Claw Is Caught, The Bird Is Lost", 1888
  Bailey, L. W., "Tolstoy as Playwright", *Drama* (1973), 110:50-55

Banasevíc, Nikola, ed., *Actes du V Congrès de l'Association Internationale de Litterature Comparée, Belgrade, 1967.* 1969. Pp. 633-39

Bjalyi, G. A., " 'Vlast 't'My' v̌ Tvorčěstve L. N. Tolstogo 80-x Godov", *Russkaja Literatura* (1973), 16:71-92

Firkins, O. W., "Power of Darkness", *Review*, 2:137-38, Feb. 7, 1920

Freling, Roger N., "A Critical Study of Two Tolstoy Plays: 'The Power of Darkness' and 'The Living Corpse' ", *Dissertation Abstracts International* (1972), 32:4661A

Hackett, F., "Power of Darkness", *New Republic*, 21:296, Feb. 4, 1920

Hamilton, Clayton Meeker, *Seen on the Stage.* 1920. Pp. 144-53

Lewisohn, Ludwig, "Power of Darkness", *Nation*, 110:178, Feb. 7, 1920

Matual, David M., "Tolstoy's 'Vlast't'My': History and Analysis", *Dissertation Abstracts International* (1972), 32:3315A

Nabakoff, C., "Tolstoy's 'Power of Darnkess' and 'Alexander III' ", *Spectator*, 138:841-42, May 14, 1927

Nation, 72:47-48, Jan. 17, 1901

Nation (London), 44:208, Nov. 10, 1928

New Yorker, 35:129-30, Oct 10, 1959

Spectator, 141:687-88, Nov. 10, 1928

Vlast Tmy, ili "Kogotok Wyaz, Vsey Pitchke Propast" *SEE* The Power of Darkness; or, "If a Claw Is Caught, The Bird Is Lost"

Zhivoy Trup *SEE* The Living Corpse

CYRIL TOURNEUR

Atheist's Tragedy; or, The Honest Man's Revenge, 1607/11

Ellis-Fermor, Una, "The Imagery of 'The Revenger's Tragodie' and 'The Atheist's Tragodie' ", *Modern Language Review* (1935), 30:289-301

Hérndl, George C., *The High Design; English Renaissance Tragedy and the Natural Law.* 1970. Pp. 223-26

Imai, Sachiko, "The Two Revenge Tragedies: Dramatic Failure in the Revengers", *Ochanomizu University Studies* (1972), 25,ii:49-62

Kaufmann, R. J., "Theodicy, Tragedy and the Psalmist: Tourneur's 'Atheist's Tragedy' ", *Comparative Drama* (Wint. 1969-70), 3:241-62

Levin, Richard, "The Elizabethan 'Three Level' Play", *Renaissance Drama* (1969), 2:23-37

————————, *The Multiple Plot in English Renaissance Drama.* 1971. Pp. 75-85 and 154-58

————————, "The Subplot of 'The Atheist's Tragedy' ", *Huntington Library Quarterly* (1965), 28:17-33

Ribner, Irving, *Jacobean Tragedy; The Quest for Moral Order.* 1962. Pp. 86-96

Ricks, Christopher, ed., *English Drama to 1710.* (History of Literature in the English Language) Vol 3. 1971. Pp. 316-22 and 341-45

Waller, G. F., "Time, Providence and Tragedy in 'The Atheist's Tragedy' and 'King Lear' ", *English Miscellany* (1972), 23:55-74

Revengers Tragedy, 1606/07

Adams, Henry Hitch, "Cyril Tourneur on Revenge", *Journal of English and Germanic Philology* (1949), 48:72-87

Ayres, Philip J., "Parallel Action and Reductive Techniques in 'The Revenger's Tragedy'", *English Language Notes* (1970), 8:103-06

Barker, Richard Hindry, *Thomas Middleton*. 1958. Pp. 64-75

Binder, Barrett F., "Tragic Satire: Studies in Cyril Tourneur, John Webster and Thomas Middleton", *Dissertation Abstracts International* (1973), 33:4331A

Bluestone, Max and Norman Rabkin, eds., *Shakespeare's Contemporaries; Modern Studies in English Renaissance Drama*. 2nd ed. 1970. Pp. 307-27

Boas, Frederick S., *An Introduction to Stuart Drama*. 1946. Pp. 214-18

Bowers, Fredson T., *Elizabethan Revenge Tragedy: 1587-1642*. 1959. Pp. 132-38

Bradbrook, Muriel C., *Themes and Conventions of Elizabetham Tragedy*. 1957. Pp. 165-74

Craig, Hardin, ed., *Essays in Dramatic Literature; The Parrott Presentation Volume*. 1935. Pp. 103-26

Ekeblad, Inga-Stina, "An Approach to Tourneur's Imagery", *Modern Language Review* (1959), 54:489-98

Eliot, Thomas Stearns, *Selected Essays*. 1950. Pp. 159-69

Ellis-Fremor, Una, "The Imagery of 'The Revenger's Tragedy' and 'The Atheist's Tragedy'", *Modern Language Review* (1935), 30:289-301

———————— , *The Jacobean Drama*. 4th rev. ed. 1958. Pp. 153-69

Ford, Boris, ed., *A Guide to English Literature*. vol. 2. 1955. Pp. 334-54

Geckel, George L., "Justice in 'The Revenger's Tragedy'", *Renaissance Papers* (1973), Pp. 75-82

Herndl, George C., *The High Design; English Renaissance Tragedy and the Natural Law*. 1970. Pp. 218-23

Imai, Sachiko, "The Two Revenge Tragedies: Dramatic Failure in the Revengers", *Ochanomizu University Studies* (1972), 25,ii:49-62

Jacobson, Daniel J., "The Language of 'Revenger's Tragedy'", *Dissertation Abstracts International* (1974), 34:5915A

Jenkins, Harold, "Cyril Tourneur", *Review of English Studies* (1941), 17:21-36

Kernan, Alvin, *The Cankered Muse; Satire of the English Renaissance*. 1959. Pp. 221-32

Kistner, Arthur L. and M. K., "Morality and Inevitability in 'The Revenger's Tragedy'", *Journal of English and Germanic Philology* (1972), 71:36-46

Layman, B. J., "Tourneur's Artificial Noon; The Design of 'The Revenger's Tragedy'", *Modern Language Quarterly* (1973), 34:20-35

Legouis, Pierre, "Refléxions sur la Recherche des Sources: A Propos de la 'Tragedie du Vengeur'", *Etudes Anglaises* (1959), 12:47-55

Lever, J. W., *The Tragedy of State*. 1971. Pp. 18-36

McDonald, Charles Osborne, *The Rhetoric of Tragedy; Form in Stuart Drama*. 1966. Pp. 225-66

Mehl, Dieter, *The Elizabethan Dumb Show*. 1966. Pp. 132-33

Murray, Peter B., *A Study of Cyril Tourneur*. 1964. Pp. 173-257

Nicol, Bernard de Bear, ed., *Varieties of Dramatic Experience*. 1969. Pp. 127-32

Oates, J. C., "The Comedy of Metamorphosis in 'The Revenger's Tragedy'", *Bucknell Review* (1962), 10:38-52

Oliphant, E. H. C., "Tourneur and Mr. T. S. Eliot", *Studies in Philology* (1935), 32:546-52

Ornstein, Robert, "The Ethical Design of 'The Revenger's Tragedy'", *ELH* (1954), 21:81-93

——————————— , *The Moral Vision of Jacobean Tragedy.* 1960. Pp. 105-18

Peter, John Desmond, *Complaint and Satire in Early English Literature.* 1956. Pp. 255-73

Prior, Moody Erasmus, *The Language of Tragedy.* 1947. Pp. 135-44

Ribner, Irving, *Jacobean Tragedy; The Quest for Moral Order.* 1962. Pp. 75-86

Ricks, Christopher, ed., *English Drama to 1710.* (History of Literature in the English Language) Vol. 3. 1971. Pp. 101-05 and 314-33

Salingar, L. G., " 'The Revenger's Tragedy' and the Morality Tradition", *Scrutiny* (1938), 6:402-22

Sanders, Leslie, " 'The Revenger's Tragedy': A Play on the Revenge Play", *Renaissance and Reformation* (1974), 10:25-36

Schoenbaum, Samuel, *Middleton's Tragedies: A Critical Study.* 1955. Pp. 3-35

——————————— , " 'The Revenger's Tragedy' and Middleton's Moral Outlook", *Notes and Queries* (1951), 196:8-10

——————————— , " 'The Revenger's Tragedy': Jacobean Dance of Death", *Modern Language Quarterly* (1954), 15:201-07

Sternlicht, Sanford, "Tourneur's Imagery and 'The Revenger's Tragedy' ", *Papers on Language and Literature* (1970), 6:192-97

Tomlinson, Thomas Brian, "The Morality of Revenge; Tourneur's Critics", *Essays in Criticism* (1960), 10:134-47

——————————— , *A Study of Elizabethan and Jacobean Tragedy.* 1964. Pp. 97-131

West, Herbert F., Jr., "Unifying Devices in Four Globe Plays", *Dissertation Abstracts International* (1970), 30:5424A

Wilds, N. G., "Of Rare Fire Compact: Image and Rhetoric in 'The Revenger's Tragedy' ", *Texas Studies in Literature and Language* (1975), 17:61-74

Towneley Plays

SEE

Miracle, Morality and Mystery Plays

IVAN SERGEYVICH TURGENEV

Mesyats v Derevne   *SEE*   A Month in the Country

A Month in the Country, 1897

America, 95:91, April 21, 1956

Arts and Decoration, 33:62, May, 1930

Catholic World, 131:215, May, 1930, and 183:228, June, 1956

Commonweal, 11:622, April 2, 1930 and 64:150, May 11, 1956 and 78:354, June 21, 1963

L'Europe Nouvelle, 15:245, Feb. 20, 1932

Gassner, John, *Theatre at the Crossroads; Plays and Playwrights of the Mid-Century American Stage.* 1960. Pp. 193-94

Illustrated London News, 215:956, Dec. 17, 1949

Journal des Débats, 39 pt. 1:322-24, Feb. 26, 1932

London Mercury, 14:421-22, Aug., 1926

Nation, 130:430, April 9, 1930 and 182:348, April 21, 1956

New Republic, 62:246, April 16, 1930 and 134:21-22, April 23, 1956

New Statesman, 27:358, July 10, 1926
New Yorker, 32:72, April 14, 1956 and 39:126, June 8, 1963
Newsweek, 47:106, April 16, 1956
Outlook, 154:550, April 2, 1930
Outlook (London), 58:389, Oct. 23, 1926
Saturday Review, 142:39-40, July 10, 1936
Saturday Review, 39:24, April 21, 1956
Spectator, 137:46-47, July 10, 1926, and 157:582, Oct. 9, 1936
Theatre Arts, 14:373-74, May, 1930, and 40:82, June, 1956, and 47:10-11, Aug., 1963
Time, 67:63, April 16, 1956

NICHOLAS UDALL

Jacob and Esau, ?
  Thomas, Helen, " 'Jacob and Esau'—'Rigidly Calvinistic?' " *Studies in English Literature, 1500-1900* (Spring 1969), 9:199-213

Ralph Roister Doister, 1552
  Baldwin, T. W. and Linthicum, M. Chenning, "The Date—'Ralph Roister Doister'", *Philological Quarterly*, 6:379-95, 1927
  Plumstead, A. W., "Satirical Parody in 'Roister Doister'", *Studies in Philology* (1963), 60:141-54
  —————— , "Who Pointed Roister's Letter?", *Notes and Queries* (1963), 10:329-31
  Scheurweghs, Gustave, *Nicholas Udall's 'Roister Doister'*, Louvain, Librairie Universitaire, 1939, Pp. vii-lxxxiv
  Stříbrný, Zdenek, "Anglické Školské Drama v Obdobi Humanismu". *Philologica Pragensia* (1963), 6:269-84
  Texas University, Dept. of English, *Studies in English*, 1948. Pp. 222-23

PETER ALEXANDER USTINOV

Banbury Nose, 1943
  New Statesman and Nation, 28:184, Sept. 16, 1944
  Spectator, 173:242, Sept. 15, 1944

Blow Your Own Trumpet, 1941
  Theatre Arts, 27:719-20, Dec., 1943

Halfway Up the Tree, 1967
  America, 117:724, Dec. 9, 1967
  Nation, 205:572-73, Nov. 27, 1967
  New Yorker, 43:131, Nov. 18, 1967
  Saturday Review, 50:70, Nov. 25, 1967
  Time, 90:50, Nov. 17, 1967

High Balcony, 1952
  New Statesman, 44:634, Nov. 29, 1952

House of Regrets, 1940
  Theatre Arts, 27:51-52, Jan., 1943

Life in My Hands, 1963
Spectator, 212:78, Jan. 17, 1964

Love of Four Colonels, 1951
Catholic World, 176:466-67, March, 1953
Commonweal, 57:450, Feb. 6, 1953
Harper, 203:110, Nov., 1951
Illustrated London News, 218:948, June 9, 1951
Life, 34:95-96, Feb. 2, 1953
Look, 17:17, Feb. 24, 1953
Nation, 176:132, Feb. 7, 1953
New Republic, 128:22-23, Feb. 2, 1953
New York Times Magazine, Pp. 38, Jan. 4, 1953
New Yorker, 28:54, Jan. 24, 1953
Newsweek, 41:95, Jan. 26, 1953
Saturday Review, 36:26, Jan. 31, 1953
Spectator, 186:716, June 1, 1951
Theatre Arts, 37:66-68, March, 1953
Time, 61:52, Jan. 26, 1953

Man in the Raincoat, 1949
Illustrated London News, 215:388, Sept. 10, 1949

Moment of Truth, 1951
Illustrated London News, 219:952, Dec. 18, 1951
New Statesman and Nation, 42:620, Dec. 1, 1951

No Sign of the Dove, 1953
New Statesman, 46:758, Dec. 12, 1953

Paris Not So Gay, 1958
Illustrated London News, 232:480, March 22, 1958

Photo Finish, 1962
Drama, #65:20-21, Summer, 1962
English, 14:104, 1962
Hudson Review, 16:269-70, 1963
Illustrated London News, 240:768, May 12, 1962
Lumley, Frederick, *New Trends in Twentieth Century Drama; A Survey Since Ibsen and Shaw*. 1967. Pp. 304-06
Nation, 196:214, March 9, 1963
New Statesman, 63:656, May 4, 1962
New Yorker, 39:112, Feb. 13, 1963
Newsweek, 61:60, Feb. 25, 1963
Saturday Review, 46:30, March 2, 1963
Spectator, 208:585, May 4, 1962
Theatre Arts, 47:10-11, April, 1963
Time, 81:75, Feb. 22, 1963

Romanoff and Juliet, 1956
America, 98:355, Dec. 14, 1957
Catholic World, 186:225, Dec., 1957
Christian Century, 74:1424, Nov. 27, 1957
Commonweal, 67:175, Nov. 15, 1957
Illustrated London News, 228:658, June 2, 1956

Life, 43:111-12, Nov. 25, 1957
Lumley, Frederick, *New Trends in Twentieth Century Drama; A Survey Since Ibsen and Shaw*. 1967. Pp. 304-06
Mannes, Marya, "Three London Plays: Satire, Sex and a Song", *Reporter* 15:38, Nov. 1, 1956
Nation, 185:291, Oct. 26, 1957
New Republic, 137:20, Oct. 28, 1957
New Statesman, 51:596-97, May 26, 1956
New Yorker, 33:81, Oct. 19, 1957
Newsweek, 50:99, Oct. 21, 1957
Reporter, 15:38, Nov. 1, 1956 and 17:39, Nov. 14, 1957
Saturday Review, 39:30, Oct. 13, 1956 and 40:27, Oct. 26, 1957
Spectator, 196:730, May 25, 1956
Theatre Arts, 41:92, May, 1957 and 41:19-20, Dec., 1957
Time, 70:57, Oct. 21, 1957

The Unknown Soldier and His Wife, 1967
America, 117:139, Aug. 5, 1967
Christian Century, 84:1131, Sept. 6, 1967
Commonweal, 86:472-73, July 28, 1967
Life, 63:12, Aug. 25, 1967
New Yorker, 43:94, July 15, 1967
Newsweek, 70:67, July 17, 1967
Saturday Review, 50:48, July 22, 1967
Time, 90:75, July 14, 1967
Vogue, 150:225, Sept. 1, 1967

Who's Who in Hell, 1974
Hughes, C., "Who's Who in Hell", *Plays and Players* (1975), 22:35
New Yorker, 50:53, Dec. 23, 1974
Progressive, 39:39, Apr., 1975

SUTTON VANE

Outward Bound, 1923
Canfield, Mary Cass, *Grotesques and Other Reflections*. 1927. Pp. 204-13
Catholic World, 148:599, Feb., 1939
Commonweal, 29:302, Jan. 6, 1939
Freeman, 8:473, Jan. 23, 1924
Independent, 112:231-32, April 26, 1924
Nation, 148:44, Jan. 7, 1939
New Statesman, 21:739, Oct. 6, 1923
Outlook (London), 52:318, Oct. 27, 1923 and 58:161, Aug. 14, 1926 and 61:178, Feb. 11, 1928
Spectator, 131:592, Oct. 27, 1923
Sutton, Graham, *Some Contemporary Dramatists*. 1925. Pp. 184-208
Theatre Arts, 23:97-98, Feb., 1939
Time, 33:24-25, Jan. 2, 1939
Woman Citizen, n. s. 8:23, March 8, 1924

Overture, 1925
English Review, 40:681-83, May, 1925
Living Age, 325:431, May 23, 1925

Nation (London), 32:104-05, April 25, 1925
New Statesman, 25:42-43, April 25, 1925

LOPE FELIX DE VEGA CARPIO

El Acero de Madrid   *SEE*   The Waters of Madrid

El Arenal de Sevilla, 1603
  Weston, E., "Change and Essence in Lope de Vega's 'El Arenal de Sevilla'",
  Modern Language Notes (March 1971), 86:211-24

The Birth of Urson and Valentin, 1588-95
  Glenn, Richard R., "The Loss of Identity; Towards a Definition of the Dialectic in Lope's Early Drama", *Hispanic Review* (1973), 41:609-26

Las Bizarriás de Belisa   *SEE*   The Gallantries of Belisa

La Buena Guarda   *SEE*   The Good Custodian

El Caballero de Olmedo   *SEE*   The Knight from Olmedo

El Caballero del Milagro   *SEE*   Sir Miracle Comes a Cropper

El Castigo sin Venganza   *SEE*   Justice Without Revenge

Los Cautivos de Argel, 1647
  Kossoff, A. David and José Amor y Vásquez, eds., *Homenaje a William L.
  Fichter: Estudios Sobre el Teatro Antigua Hispanico y Otros Ensayos.*
  1971. Pp. 387-97

El Cerco de Santa Fe   *SEE*   The Siege of Santa Fe

Los Comendadores de Córdoba   *SEE*   The Commanders of Cordoba

The Commanders of Cordoba, 1598
  Kossoff, A. David and José Amor y Vásquez, eds., *Homenaje a William
  L. Fichter: Estudios Sobre el Teatro Antigua Hispanico y Otros Ensayos.*
  1971. Pp. 399-412

La Corona de Hungría   *SEE*   The Hungarian Crown

La Corona Merecida   *SEE*   The Deserved Crown

La Dama Boba   *SEE*   The Idiot Lady

The Deserved Crown, 1620
  Blue, William R., "Sol: Image and Structure in Lope's 'La Corona Mercida'",
  Hispania (1973), 56:1000-06

The Dog in the Manger, 1618
  Tynan, Kenneth, *Curtains; Selections from the Drama Criticism and Related
  Writings.* 1961. Pp. 391-92
  Wilson, Margaret, Lope as Satirist; Two Themes in 'El Perro dell Hortelano'",
  Hispanic Review (1972), 40:371-82

Don Lope de Cardona, 1618
  Bork, A. W., "Lope's 'Don Lope de Cardona', a Defense of the Duke of
  Sessa", *Hispanic Review*, 9:348-58, 1941

Los Donaires de Matico   *SEE*   The Witty Sayings of Matico

The Duke of Viseo, 1608-09
González del Valle, Luis, "Vasallaje Ideal y Justicia poética en 'El Duque de Viseo'", *Hispanófila* (1973), 47:27-37

El Duque de Viseo   *SEE*   The Duke of Viseo

El Ejemplo de Casadas y Prueba de la Paciencia   *SEE*   The Example for Married Women and the Text of Patience

El Esclavo de Roma   *SEE*   The Slave of Rome

The Example for Married Women and the Text of Patience, 1615
Arjona, J. H., "La Fecha de 'Ejemplo de Casadas' y 'Prueba de la Paciencia' de Lope de Vega", *Modern Language Notes*, 52:249-52, 1937

The Fairs of Madrid, 1609
McGrady, Donald, "The Comic Treatment of Conjugal Honor in Lope's 'Las Ferias de Madrid'", *Hispanic Review* (1973), 41:33-42

Las Ferias de Madrid   *SEE*   The Fairs of Madrid

La Fianza Satisfecha   *SEE*   The Outrageous Saint

Lo Fingido Verdadero   *SEE*   Make-Believe Becomes Truth

The Fortunate Son, 1588-95
Glenn, Richard F., "The Loss of Identity; Towards a Definition of the Dialectic in Lope's Early Drama", *Hispanic Review* (1973), 41:609-26

Fuente Ovejuna, 1619
Almasov, Alexey, "'Fuenteovejuna' y el Honor Villanesco en el Teatro de Lope de Vega", *Cuadernos Hispanoamericanos* (Madrid), 54:701-55, 1963
Anibal, C. E., "Historical Elements of Lope de Vega's 'Fuente Ovejuna'", *Modern Language Association. Publications* (PMLA), 49:657-718, 1934
Barbera, Raymond E., "An Instance of Medieval Iconography in 'Fuenteovejuna'", *Romance Notes* (1968), 10:160-62
Behler, Ernst, *Die Europäische Romantik*. 1972. Pp. 338-56
Casalduero, Joaquin, "'Fuenteovejuna': Form and Meaning", *Tulane Drama Review*, 4:83, 1959
Forastieri Braschi, Eduardo, "'Fuenteovejuno' y la Justificación", *Revista de Estudios Hispánicos* (1972), 1-4:89-99
Gerard, Albert S., "Self-Love in Lope de Vega's 'Fuenteovejuna' and Corneille's 'Tete et Bérénice'", *Australian Journal of French Studies* (1967), 4:177-97
Herrero, Javier, "The New Monarchy; A Structural Reinterpretation of 'Fuenteovejuna'", *Revista Hispania Moderna* (1970-71), 36:173-85
Hesse, Everett W., "Los Conceptos del Amor en 'Fuenteovejuna'", *Revista de Archivos, Bibliotecas y Museos* (1968-72), 75:305-23
Kossoff, A. David and José Amor y Vásquez, eds., *Homenaje a William L. Fichter; Estudios Sobre al Teatro Antigua Hispanico y Otros Ensayos*. 1971. Pp. 453-68 and 537-46
McCrary, William C., "'Fuenteovejuna': Its Platonic Vision and Execution", *Studies in Philology*, 58:179-92, 1961
Morley, S. Griswold, "'Fuente Ovejuna' and Its Theme-Parallels", *Hispanic Review*, 4:303-11, 1936

Pazos, J. Robles, "Sobre la Fecha de 'Fuente Ovejuna'", *Modern Language Notes*, 50:179-82, 1935

Pring-Mill, R. D. F., "Sententiousness in 'Fuente Ovejuna'", *Tulane Drama Review*, 7:5-37, 1962

Spitzer, L., "Central Theme and Its Structural Equivalent in Lope's 'Fuente-ovejuna'", *Hispanic Review*, 23:274-92, Oct., 1955

El Galan de La Membrilla   *SEE*   The Gallant of La Membrilla

The Gallant of La Membrilla, 1615
St. John, Bruce, "Possessions and Personality; 'El Galan de la Membrilla' of Lope de Vega", *Bulletin of the Comediantes* (1972), 24:15-21

The Gallantries of Belisa, 1637
Land, Jerry Ann, "The Importance of the Conde Enrique in Lope's 'Las Bizarrias de Belisa'", *Romanic Review* (1974), 65:103-15

The Good Custodian, 1610
Kossoff, A. David and José Amor y Vásquez, eds., *Homenaje a William L. Fichter; Estudios Sobre el Teatro Antigua Hispanico y Otros Ensayos.* 1971. Pp. 413-27

Le Gran Duc de Moscou, 1606
Balachov, H. I., "Lope de Vega et les Problemes du Drame Espagnol du XVII Siecle sur les Themes des Slaves Orientaux", *Izvestija Akademii Nauk. S.S.S.R. Otdel Literatury i Jazyka*, 22:3-18, 1963

The Greatest Virtue of a King, 1625
Silverman, Joseph H., "Lope de Vega's Last Years and His Final Play, 'The Greatest Virtue of a King'", *Texas Quarterly* (Univ. of Texas), 6:174-86, 1963
_____ , and Andres, Alfonso, "La Mayor Virtud de un Rey': Ultima Comedia de Lope de Vega", *Insula* (Madrid), 18:10, 23, 1963

La Hermosa Ester, 1610
Glash, Edward, "Lope de Vega's 'La Hermosa Ester'", *Sefarad* (Madrid; Barcelona), 20:110-35, 1960

El Hijo de Reduán   *SEE*   Reduán's Son

El Hijo Venturoso   *SEE*   The Fortunate Son

La Humildad y La Soberbia   *SEE*   Humility and Pride

Humility and Pride, 1612/14
Jacquot, Jean, et als, ed., *Dramaturgie et Sociéte; Rapports entre l'Oeuvre Théâtrale, son Interprétation et son Public aux XVI et XVII Siècle.* 1968. vol. 1. Pp. 13-30

The Hungarian Crown, 1633
Rennert, H. A. "Lope de Vega's Comedias 'Los Pleitos de Inglaterra' and 'La Corona de Hungria'", *Modern Language Review*, 13:455-64, 1918

The Idiot Lady, 1613
Gerstinger, Heinz, *Lope de Vega and Spanish Drama.* 1974. Pp. 118-22
Holloway, James E., "Lope's Neoplatonism: 'La Dama Boba'", *Bulletin of Hispanic Studies* (1972), 49:236-55
Larson, Donald R., "'La Dama Boba' and the Comic Sense of Life", *Romanische Forschungen* (1973), 85:41-62

The Inn of the Court, 1588-95
  Glenn, Richard R., "The Loss of Identity; Towards a Definition of the Dialectic in Lope's Early Drama", *Hispanic Review* (1973), 41:609-26

Justice Without Revenge, 1632
  May, T. E., "Lope de Vega's 'El Castigo sin Venganza': The Idolatry of the Duque de Ferrara", *Bulletin of Hispanic Studies*, 37:154-82, 1960
  Morris, C. B., "Lope de Vega's 'El Castigo sin Venganza' and Poetic Tradition", *Bulletin of Hispanic Studies*, 40:69-78, 1963

The King and the Farmer, 1617
  Andrews, J. R., S. G. Armistead, and J. H. Silverman, "Two Notes for Lope de Vega's 'El Villano en su Rincón' ", *Bulletin of the Comediantes* (1966), 18:33-35
  Brown, Sandra L., "Goodness and 'El Villano en su Rincón' ", *Romance Notes*, (1973), 14:551-56
  Camp, Jean, "Como Lope de Vega Imaginaba a Francia; Vision de Francia en Lope, y Especialaments en 'El Villano en su Rincón' ", *Cuadernos Hispanoamericanos* (Madrid), 54:421-26, 1963
  Halkhoree, Premraj, "Lope de Vega's 'El Villano en su Rincón'; An Emblematic Play", *Romance Notes* (1972), 14:141-45
  Hesse, Everett W., "The Sense of Lope's 'El Villano en su Rincón' ", *Studies in Philology*, 57:165-77, 1960
  Kossoff, A. David and José Amor y Vásquez, eds., *Homenaje a William L. Fichter; Estudios Sobre el Teatro Antigua Hispanico y Otros Ensayos.* (1971), Pp. 639-45 and 765-72

The King, The Greatest Alcalde, 1620-23
  Diez Borque, José M., "Estructura Social de la Comedia de Lope; A Proposito de 'El Major Alcalde el Rey' ", *Arbor; Revista General de Investigacion y Cultura* (1973), 33-32:121-34

The King Without a Kingdom, 1597-1612
  Perlorson, Jean-Marc, "Lope de Vega et Alonso de Contreras; Une Mise au Foint à Propos de 'El Rey Sin Reino' ", *Annales de la Faculté des Lettres de Bordeaux. Bulletin Hispanique* (1970), 72:253-76

The Knight from Olmedo, 1615-26
  Brancaforte, Benito, "La Tragedia de 'El Caballero de Olmedo' ", *Cuadernos Hispanoamericanos* (1974), 286:93-106
  Gerard, A. S., "Baroque Unity and the Dualities of 'El Caballero de Olmedo' ", *Romanic Review*, 56:92-106, April, 1965
  Giacoman, Helmy F., "Eros y Thanatos: Una Interpretación de 'El Caballero de Olmedo' ", *Hispanofila* (1966), 28:9-16
  Hesse, E. W., "Role of the Mind in Lope's 'El Çaballero de Olmedo' ", *Symposium*, 19:58-66, Spring, 1965
  King, Lloyd, "'The Darkest Justice of Death' in Lope's 'El Caballero de Olmedo' ", *Forum for Modern Language Studies* (1969), 5:388-94
  Kossoff, A. David and José Amor y Vásquez, eds., *Homenaje a William L. Fichter; Estudios Sobre el Teatro Antigua Hispanico y Otros Ensayos.* 1971. Pp. 367-79 and 439-45
  McCrary, William C., "The Goldfinch and the Hawk: A Study of Lope de Vega's 'El Caballero de Olmedo' ", *University of North Carolina Studies in the Romance Languages and Literatures* (1966), #62

Marin, D., "La Ambiguedad Dramatica en 'El Caballero de Olmedo'",
Hispanofilia, 8:1-11, 1965

Mordaunt, Jerrold L., ed., *Proceedings: Pacific Northwest Conference on
Foreign Languages, 20th Annual Meeting, April 11-12, 1969.* vol. 20.
Pp. 121-28

Soons, Alan, "Towards an Interpretation of 'El Caballero de Olmedo'",
Romanische Forschungen, 73:160-68, 1961

Turner, Alison, "Dramatic Function of Imagery and Symbolism in 'Peribañez'
and 'El Caballero de Olmedo'", *Symposium* (1966), 20:174-86

Wardropper, Bruce W., "The Criticism of the Spanish Comedia; 'El Cabellero
de Olmedo' as Object Lesson", *Philological Quarterly* (1972), 51:177-
96

Yates, Donald S., "The Poetry of the Fantastic in 'El Caballero de Olmedo'",
Hispania, (Univ. of Connecticut), 43:503-07, 1960

The Life of St. Peter Nolasco, 1629
*Actes du VI Congrès International de Langue et Littérature d'Oc et d'Etudes
Franco-Provencales.* 1971. Pp. 81-93

Lo Que Ha De Ser   *SEE*   What Must Be, Must Be

Los Locos de Valencia   *SEE*   The Madmen of Valencia

The Madmen of Valencia, 1620
Gerstinger, Heinz, *Lope de Vega and Spanish Drama.* 1974. Pp. 132-39

Make-Believe Becomes Truth, 1608
Trueblood, Alan S., "Role-playing and the Sense of Illusion in Lope de Vega",
Hispanic Review, 32:305-18, 1964

El Mayor Alcalde el Rey   *SEE*   The King, The Greatest Alcalde

El Mayor Imposible, 1614
Bohning, W. H., "Lope's 'El Mayor Imposible' and Boisrobert's 'La Folle
Gagenre'", *Hispanic Review*, 12:248-57, 1944

La Mayor Virtud de un Rey   *SEE*   The Greatest Virtue of a King

El Meson de la Corte   *SEE*   The Inn of the Court

La Moza de Cántaro, 1632
Wilson, William E., "A Note on 'La Moza de Cántaro'", *Hispanic Review*,
10:71-72, 1942

El Nacimiento de Ursón y Valentin   *SEE*   The Birth of Urson and Valentin

The Outrageous Saint, 1616
Barnstone, Willis, "Lope's Leonido: An Existential Hero", *Tulane Drama
Review*, 7:56-57, 1962-63

Pragg-Chantraine, Jacqueline van, "'La Fianza Satisfecha', 'Comedia
Famosa' de Lope de Vega", *Revue Belge de Philologie et d'Histoire*
(1966), 44:945-58

Prat, Angel Valbuena, "A Freudian Character in Lope de Vega", *Tulane
Drama Review*, 7:44-55, 1962-63

Rank, Otto, "The Incest of Amnon and Tamar", *Tulane Drama Review*,
7:38-43, 1962-63

Sanchez Romeralo, Jaime and Norbert Poulussen, eds., *Actas del Segundo Congreso Internacional de Hispanistas. Celebrado en Nywegen del 20 al 25 de Agosto de 1965.* 1967. Pp. 245-52

Las Paces de los Reyes y Judia de Toledo   *SEE*   The Peace of Kings and the Jewess of Toledo

The Peace of Kings and the Jewess of Toledo, 1604/12
  Darst, David H., "The Unity of 'Las Paces de los Reyes y Judiá de Toledo' ", *Symposium* (Fall 1971), 25:225-35
  McCrary, William C., "Plot, Action, and Imitation; The Art of Lope's 'Las Paces de los Reyes' ", *Hispanófila* (1973), 48:1-17
  Soons, C. Alan, "The Emblematic Technique in 'Las Paces de los Reyes' ", *Theatre Annual*, 19:43-45, 1962
  Strout, Lilia D., "Psicomaquia y Hierogamia en 'Las Paces de los Reyes y Judiá de Toledo' de Lope de Vega", *Dissertation Abstracts International* (1974), 34:5205A

Peribañez The Commander of Ocaña, 1609-12
  Araya, Guillermo, "Paralelismo Antitetico en 'Peribañez y el Comendador de Ocaña' ", *Estudios Filologicos* (1969), 5:91-127
  Case, Thomas E., "El Papel de Ines en 'Peribañez' ", *Romanische Forschungen* (1972), 84:546-52
  Correa, Gustavo, "El Doble Aspecto de la Honra en 'Peribañez y el Comendador de Ocaña' ", *Hispanic Review*, 26:188-99, 1958
  Dixon, V., "The Symbolism of 'Peribanez' ", *Bulletin of Hispanic Studies* (1966), 43:11-24
  Guntert, Georges, "Relección del 'Peribañez' ", *Revista de Filologia Española* (1971), 54:37-52
  Randel, Mary G., "The Portrait and the Creation of 'Peribañez' ", *Romanische Forschungen* (1973), 85:145-58
  Turner, Alison, "Dramatic Function of Imagery and Symbolism in 'Peribañez' and 'El Caballero de Olmedo' ", *Symposium* (1966), 20:174-86

El Perro del Hortelano   *SEE*   The Dog in the Manger

El Perseo, 1621
  Martin, Henry M., "The Perseus Myth in Lope de Vega and Calderon with Some Reference to Their Sources", *Modern Language Association. Publications* (PMLA), 46:450-60, 1931

Persistence Until Death, 1636
  Trueblood, Alan S., "Role-playing and the Sense of Illusion in Lope de Vega", *Hispanic Review*, 32:305-18, 1964

Los Pleitos de Ingalaterra, 1638
  Rennert, H. A., "Lope de Vega's Comedias 'Los Pleitos de Ingalaterra' and 'La Corona de Hungria' ", *Modern Language Review*, 13:455-64, Oct., 1918

Porfiar Hasta Morir   *SEE*   Persistence Until Death

Reduán's Son, 1604
  Glenn, Richard, "The Loss of Identity; Towards a Definition of the Dialectic in Lope's Early Drama", *Hispanic Review* (1973), 41:609-26

El Rey Sin Reino *SEE* The King Without a Kingdom

Roma Abrasada *SEE* Rome Burned

Rome Burned, 1625
  Ruser, W., " 'Roma Abrasada'; Ein Echtes Jugendrama; Eine Studie zu Lope de Vega", *Revue Hispanique*, 72:325-411, April, 1928

The Siege of Santa Fe, 1603
  Kossoff, A. David and José Amor y Vásquez, eds., *Homenaje a William L. Fichter; Estudios Sobre el Teatro Antigua Hispanico y Otros Ensayos*. 1971. Pp. 115-25

Sir Miracle Comes a Cropper, 1621
  Fernández-Santos, Angel, " 'Caballero de Milagro' de Lope de Vega", *Indice*, 17: #186:25, 1964

The Slave of Rome, 1617
  Rosado, Gabriel, "Observaciones Sobre las Fuentes de Dos Comedias de Lope de Vega: 'El Esclavo de Roma' y 'Lo Que ha de Ser' ", *Bulletin of the Comediantes* (1972), 24:25-30

The True Lover, 1576
  Morby, Edwin S., "Reflections on 'El Verdadero Amante' ", *Hispanic Review*, 27:317-23, 1959

The Valencian Widow, 1620
  deArmas, Frederick A., "Some Observations on Lope's 'La Viuda Valenciana' ", *Bulletin of the Comediantes* (1973), 25:3-5

El Verdadero Amante *SEE* The True Lover

La Vida de San Pedro Nolasco *SEE* The Life of St. Peter Nolasco

El Villano en su Rincón *SEE* The King and the Farmer

La Viuda Valenciana *SEE* The Valencian Widow

Waters of Madrid, 1608
  Morley, S. Griswold, "El Acero de Madrid", *Hispanic Review*, 13:166-69, 1945

What Must Be, Must Be, 1624
  Rosado, Gabriel, "Observaciones Sobre las Fuentes de Dos Comedias de Lope de Vega: 'El Esclavo de Roma' y 'Lo Que Ha De Ser' ", *Bulletin of the Comediantes* (1972), 24:25-30

The Witty Sayings of Matico, 1604
  Glenn, Richard F., "The Loss of Identity; Towards a Definition of the Dialectic in Lope's Early Drama", *Hispanic Review* (1973), 41:609-26

JOHN WEBSTER

The Devil's Lawcase; or, When Women Go to Law, The Devil is Full of Business, 1610?
  Berry, Ralph, *The Art of John Webster*. 1972. Pp. 151-67

Gunby, D. C., "'The Devil's Lawcase': An Interpretation", *Modern Language Review* (July 1968), 63:545-58

McLeod, Susan M., "Dramatic Imagery in the Plays of John Webster", *Dissertation Abstracts International* (1973), 33:4355A

Tomlinson, Thomas Brian, *A Study of Elizabethan and Jacobean Tragedy.* 1964. Pp. 223-29

The Duchess of Malfi, 1614

Allison, Alexander W., "Ethical Themes in 'Duchess of Malfi' ", *Studies in English Literature. 1500-1900* (1964), 4:263-73

America, 97:55, April 13, 1957

Baldini, Gabriele, *John Webster e il Linguaggio della Tragedia.* 1953. Pp. 151-73

Berry, Ralph, *The Art of John Webster.* 1972. Pp. 107-50

Binder, Barrett F., "Tragic Satire; Studies in Cyril Tourneur, John Webster, and Thomas Middleton", *Dissertation Abstracts International* (1973), 33: 4331A

Bluestone, Max and Norman Rabkin, eds., *Shakespeare's Contemporaries; Modern Studies in English Renaissance Drama.* 1970. Pp. 278-88

Boas, Frederick S., *An Introduction to Stuart Drama.* 1946. Pp. 198-203

Bogard, Travis, *The Tragic Satire of John Webster.* 1955. Pp. 131-41

Boyer, Charence Valentine, *The Villain as Hero in Elizabethan Tragedy.* 1964. Pp. 145-64

Bradbrook, Muriel C., *Themes and Conventions of Elizabethan Tragedy.* 1957. Pp. 195-209

Bradford, Gamaliel, "The Women of Middleton and Webster", *Sewanee Review* (1921), 29:14-29

Brooke, Rupert, *John Webster and the Elizabethan Drama.* 1916. Pp. 123-62

Calderwood, James L., " 'The Duchess of Malfi': Styles of Ceremony", *Essays in Criticism* (1962), 12:133-47

Catholic World, 185:226, June, 1957

Christian Century, 74:456, April 10, 1957

Commonweal, 45:70-71, Nov. 1, 1946

Cunningham, John E., *Elizabethan and Early Stuart Drama.* 1965. Pp. 90-97

Davies, Cecil W., "The Structure of 'The Duchess of Malfi': An Approach", *English* (1958), 12:89-93

Davison, Richard Allan, "John Webster's Moral View Re-Examined", *Moderna Sprak* (1969), 63:213-23

Driscoll, James P., "Integrity of Life in 'The Duchess of Malfi' ", *Drama Survey* (1967), 6:42-53

Ekeblad, Inga-Stena, "The 'Impure Art' of John Webster", *Review of English Studies* (1958), 9:253-67

Fieler, Frank B., "The Eight Madmen in 'The Duchess of Malfi' ", *Studies in English Literature*, 1500-1900 (1967), 7:343-50

Forker, Charles R., "Love, Death and Fame; The Grotesque Tragedy of John Webster", *Anglia; Zeitschrfit für Englische Philologie* (1973), 91: 194-218

_____ , "A Possible Source for the Ceremony of the Cardinal's Arming in 'The Duchess of Malfi' ", *Anglia; Zeitschrift für Englische Philologie* (1969), 87:398-403

Forum, 106:556-60, Dec., 1946

Giannetti, Louis D., "A Contemporary View of 'The Duchess of Malfi' ", *Comparative Drama* (Winter 1969-70), 3:297-307

Grant, George L., "The Imagery of Witchcraft in 'The Duchess of Malfi'", *Dissertation Abstracts International* (1972), 32:5737A

Grusbow, Ira, "Bosola's Dirge in 'The Duchess of Maifi'", *Concerning Poetry* (1973), 6:61-62

Hawkins, Harriett, *Likeness of Truth in Elizabethan and Restoration Drama.* 1972. Pp. 15-17

Herndl, George C., *The High Design; English Renaissance Tragedy and the Natural Law.* 1970. Pp. 194-217

Hunter, G. K. and S. K., eds., *John Webster; A Critical Anthology.* 1969. Pp. 132-56, 266-84 and 295-305

Jacobean Theatre, (Stratford Upon Avon Studies, 1), 1960. Pp. 201-25

Jenkins, Harold, "The Tragedy of Revenge in Shakespeare and Webster", *Shakespeare Survey* (1961), 14:49-53

Kaufman, Ralph James, ed., *Elizabethan Drama; Modern Essays in Criticism.* 1961. Pp. 25-67

Kelleher, Victor M. K., "Notes on 'The Duchess of Malfi'", *Unisa English Studies* (1972), 10,ii:11-15

Kernan, Alvin, *The Cankered Muse; Satire of the English Renaissance.* 1959. Pp. 232-42

Kirsch, Arthur Clifford, *Jacobean Dramatic Perspectives.* 1972. Pp. 97-111

Knight, G. Wilson, "The Duchess of Malfi", *Malahat Review* (1967), 4:88-113

Leech, C., "An Addendum on Webster's 'Duchess'", *Philological Quarterly*, 37:253-56, 1958

Leech, Clifford, *John Webster; A Critical Study.* 1951. Pp. 58-89

Lever, J. W., *The Tragedy of State.* 1971. Pp. 78-97

Luecke, Jane Marie, "'The Duchess of Malfi': Comic and Satiric Confusion in a Tragedy", *Studies in English Literature, 1500-1900* (1964), 4:275-90

Luisi, David, "The Function of Bosola in 'The Duchess of Malfi'", *English Studies; A Journal of English Letters and Philology* (1972), 53:509-13

McLeod, Susan M., "Dramatic Imagery in the Plays of John Webster", *Dissertation Abstracts International* (1973), 33:4355A

Matthews, Honor, *The Primal Curse; The Myth of Cain and Abel in the Theatre.* 1967. Pp. 68-71

Mehl, Dieter, *The Elizabethan Dumb Show.* 1966. Pp. 142-45

Moody, JoAnn, "Britomart, Imogen, Perdita, the Duchess of Malfi; A Study of Women in English Renaissance Literature", *Dissertation Abstracts International* (1972), 33:1146A

Moore, Don D., *John Webster and His Critics, 1617-1964.* 1966. Pp. 15-20, 42-45 and 152-59

Nathan, George Jean, *Theatre Book of the Year, 1946-47.* Pp. 120-22

Nation, 55:348, Nov. 10, 1892 and 163:510, Nov. 2, 1946 and 184:351, April 20, 1957

Nation (London), 34:832-33, March 15, 1924

New Republic, 115:556-57, Oct. 28, 1946

New Statesman, 22:602-03, March 1, 1924

New Yorker, 22:51-53, Oct. 26, 1946

Newsweek, 28:86, Oct. 28, 1946

Nicol, Bernard de Bear, ed., *Varieties of Dramatic Experience.* 1969. Pp. 114-23

Ono, Kyoichi, "Malfi Koshaku Fujin no Higeki", *Eigo Seinen* (1968), 114: 584-85

Ornstein, Robert, *The Moral Vision of Jacobean Tragedy*. 1960. Pp. 129-30 and 140-48

Peterson, Joyce E., "A Counsellor for a King; A Study of the Morality Drama, Commonweal Tragedy and 'The Duchess of Malfi' ", *Dissertation Abstracts International* (1974), 34:7718A

Price, H. T., "The Function of Imagery in Webster", *Modern Language Association. Publications* (PMLA), 70:717-39, 1955

Rabkin, Norman, ed., *Twentieth Century Interpretations of "The Duchess of Malfi": A Collection of Critical Essays*. 1968

Rexroth, Kenneth, "The Duchess of Malfi", *Saturday Review* (1967), 50:21

Ribner, Irving, *Jacobean Tragedy; The Quest for Moral Order*. 1962. Pp. 108-22

Ricks, Christopher, ed., *English Drama to 1710*. (History of Literature in the English Language) vol. 3, 1971. Pp. 320-22 and 341-47

Ridley, Maurice Roy, *Second Thoughts; More Studies in Literature*. 1965. Pp. 90-106, 110-23, and 123-32

Riewald, J. G., "Shakespeare Burlesque in John Webster's 'The Duchess of Malfi' ", *English Studies* (1964), 45:Supp. 177-89

Saturday Review, 40:26, April 6, 1957

Schuman, Samuel, "The Ring and the Jewel in Webster's Tragedies", *Texas Studies in Literature and Language* (1972), 14:253-68

Scott-Kilvert, Ian, *John Webster*. 1964. Pp. 23-29

Sewanee Review, 9:410-34, Oct., 1901

Sullivan, S. W., "The Tendency to Rationalize in 'The White Devil' and 'Duchess of Malfi' ", *Yearbook of English Studies* (1974), 4:77-84

Thayer, C. G., "The Ambiguity of Bosola", *Studies in Philology* (1957), 54:162-71

Theatre Arts, 29:546, 563-70, 1945 and 30:695-96, Dec., 1946 and 41:22, May, 1957

Thornton, R. K. R., "Cardinal's Rake in 'The Duchess of Malfi' ", *Notes and Queries* (Aug. 1969), 16:295-96

Time, 48:63, Oct. 28, 1946 and 69:61, April 1, 1957

Tomlinson, Thomas Brian, *A Study of Elizabethan and Jacobean Tragedy*. 1964. Pp. 132-57

Ure, Peter, " 'Duchess of Malfi': Another Debt to Sir William Alexander", *Notes and Queries* (Aug. 1966), 13:296

Vernon, P. F., "The Duchess of Malfi's Guilt", *Notes and Queries* (1963), 10:335-38

Virginia Univ., Bibliographical Society. *Studies in Bibliography; Papers of the Bibliographical Society of the Univ. of Virginia*, ed. by Fredson Bowers. 1961-64. v. 15, Pp. 57-69

Waddington, R. R. and J. P. Driscoll, "Integrity of Life in 'The Duchess of Malfi' ", *Drama Survey* (1967), 6:42-53

Wadsworth, Frank W., "Some Nineteenth Century Revivals of the 'Duchess of Malfi' ", *Theatre Survey* (1967), 8:67-83

Walkley, Arthur Bingham, *Pastiche and Prejudice*. 1921. Pp. 178-83

Webster, John, *The Duchess of Malfi*, ed. by F. L. Lucas. 1958. Pp. 28-35

The White Devil, 1609/12

Baldini, Gabriele, *John Webster e il Linguaggio della Tragedia*. 1953. Pp. 56-150

Benjamin, Edwin G., "Patterns of Morality in 'The White Devil'", *English Studies* (Amsterdam) (1965), 46:1-15

Berry, Ralph, *The Art of John Webster*. 1972. Pp. 83-105

Bluestone, Max and Norman Rabkin, eds., *Shakespeare's Contemporaries; Modern Studies in English Renaissance Drama*. 2nd ed. 1970. Pp. 271-77

Boas, Frederick S., *An Introduction to Stuart Drama*. 1946. Pp. 194-98

Bowers, Fredson T., *Elizabethan Revenge Tragedy, 1587-1642*. 1959. Pp. 179-83

Bradbrook, Muriel C., *Themes and Conventions of Elizabethan Tragedy*. 1957. Pp. 186-95

Bradford, Gamaliel, "The Women of Middleton and Webster", *Sewanee Review* (1921), 29:14-29

Braendel, Doris B., "The Limits of Clarity; Lyly's 'Endymion', Bronzino's 'Allegory of Venus and Cupid', Webster's 'White Devil', and Botticelli's 'Primavera'", *Hartford Studies in Literature* (1972), 4:197-215

Brooke, Rupert, *John Webster and the Elizabethan Drama*. 1916. Pp. 98-104

Champion, L. S., "Webster's 'The White Devil' and the Jacobean Tragic Perspective", *Texas Studies in Literature and Language* (1974), 16:447-62

Cohen, Hennig, "Melville and Webster's 'The White Devil'", *Emerson Society Quarterly* (1963), #33:33

Cross, Gustav, "A Note on 'The White Devil'", *Notes and Queries*, n. s. 3:99-100, 1956

Dent, R. W., "'The White Devil' or Vittoria Corombona?", *Renaissance Drama* (1966), 9:170-203

Forker, Charles R., "Love, Death and Fame: The Grotesque Tragedy of John Webster", *Anglia; Zeitschrift für Englische Philologie* (1973), 91:194-218

Franklin, H. Bruce, "The Trial Scene of Webster's 'The White Devil' Examined in Terms of Renaissance Rhetoric", *Studies in English Literature, 1500-1900* (1961), 1:35-51

Gill, Roma, "'Quaintly Done': A Reading of 'The White Devil'", *Essays and Studies* (1966), 19:41-59

Hart, Clive, "Wild-Fire, St. Anthony's Fire and 'The White Devil'", *Notes and Queries* (1968), 15:375-76

Herndl, George C., *The High Design; English Renaissance Tragedy and the Natural Law*. 1970. Pp. 187-94

Hogan, Jerome W., "Webster's 'The White Devil'", *Explicator* (1974), 33:25

Holland, George, "The Function of the Minor Characters in 'The White Devil'", *Philological Quarterly* (1973), 52:43-54

Homan, Sidney R., "The Uses of Silence; The Elizabethan Dumb Show and the Silent Cinema", *Comparative Drama* (Wint. 1968-69), 2:213-28

Hunter, G. K. and S. K., eds., *John Webster; A Critical Anthology*. 1969. Pp. 235-55 and 263-65

Hurt, James R., "Inverted Rituals in Webster's 'The White Devil'", *Journal of English and Germanic Philology* (1962), 61:42-47

Jacobean Theatre, St. Martin's Press (Stratford Upon Avon Studies, 1), 1960. Pp. 201-25

Jenkins, Harold, "The Tragedy of Revenge in Shakespeare and Webster", *Shakespeare Survey* (1961), 14:49-53

Kaufmann, Ralph James, *Elizabethan Drama; Modern Essays in Criticism*. 1961. Pp. 225-49

Kirsch, Arthur Clifford, *Jacobean Dramatic Perspectives.* 1972. Pp. 97-111

Kroll, Norma, "The Democritean Universe in Webster's 'The White Devil'", *Comparative Drama* (1973), 7:3-21

Layman, B. D., "The Equilibrium of Opposites in 'The White Devil'", *Modern Language Association. Publications* (PMLA), 74:336-45, 1959

Leech, Clifford, *John Webster; A Critical Study.* 1951. Pp. 29-57

Lever, J. W., *The Tragedy of State.* 1971. Pp. 78-97

Lucas, F. L., ed., *The White Devil.* 1959. Pp. 38-45

McDonald, Charles Osborne, *The Rhetoric of Tragedy; Form in Stuart Drama.* 1966. Pp. 269-313

McLeod, Susan N., "Dramatic Imagery in the Plays of John Webster", *Dissertation Abstracts International* (1973), 33:4355A

Mehl, Dieter, *The Elizabethan Dumb Show.* 1966. Pp. 138-42

Moonschein, Henry, "Note on 'The White Devil'", *Notes and Queries* (1966), 13:296

Moore, Don D., *John Webster and His Critics, 1617-1964.* 1966. Pp. 15-20 and 153-56

Nation, 202:54-55, Jan. 10, 1966

New Republic, 154:35-36, Jan. 1, 1966

New Statesman, 14:708-09, March 20, 1920 and 26:11-13, Oct. 17, 1925

Ornstein, Robert, *The Moral Vision of Jacobean Tragedy.* 1960. Pp. 129-40

Outlook (London, 56:277, Oct. 24, 1925

Pratt, Samuel M., "Webster's 'The White Devil'", *Explicator* (1970), 29:Item 11

Price, H. T., "The Function of Imagery in Webster", *Modern Language Association. Publications* (PMLA), 70:717-39, 1955

Ribner, Irving, *Jacobean Tragedy; The Quest for Moral Order.* 1962. Pp. 100-08

Ricks, Christopher, ed., *English Drama to 1710.* (History of Literature in the English Language) vol. 3. 1971. Pp. 94-97 and 322-26

Ridley, Maurice Roy, *Second Thoughts; More Studies in Literature.* 1965. Pp. 76-90, 108-10 and 123-32

Saturday Review, 38:30, April 2, 1955

Schuman, Samuel, "The Ring and the Jewel in Webster's Tragedies", *Texas Studies in Literature and Language* (1972), 14:253-68

Scott-Kilvert, Ian, *John Webster.* 1964. Pp. 16-23

Sensabaugh, George F., "Tragic Effect in Webster's 'The White Devil'", *Studies in English Literature, 1500-1900* (1965), 1:345-61

Stearns, Stephen J., "A Critical Edition of John Webster's 'The White Devil'", *Dissertation Abstracts International* (1972), 33:441A

Stroup, Thomas B., "Flamineo and the 'Comfortable Words'", *Renaissance Papers* (1964), Pp. 12-16

Sullivan, S. W., "The Tendency to Rationalize in 'The White Devil' and 'The Duchess of Malfi'", *Yearbook of English Studies* (1974), 4:77-84

Theatre Arts, 39:25, Aug., 1955

Time, 86:40, Dec. 17, 1965

Tomlinson, Thomas Brian, *A Study of Elizabethan and Jacobean Tragedy.* 1964. Pp. 229-37

Wadsworth, Frank W., "'The White Devil'; An Historical and Critical Study", *Dissertation Abstracts*, 15:832-33. 1955

Yamamoto, Hiroshi, "'The White Devil' Ni Egakareta Konran no Sekai", *English Literature and Language* (Tokyo) (1972), 9:84-99

PETER WEISS

Die Ermittlung *SEE* The Investigation

Gesang Vom Lusitanischen Papang *SEE* Song of the Lusitanian Bogey

Hölderlin, 1971

Best, Otto F., "O Marx und Business", *Basis; Jahrbuch für Deutsche Gegenwartsliteratur* (1972), 3:238-44

Berghahn, Klaus L., "'Wenn Ich So Singend Fiel. . . .'", *Basis; Jahrbuch für Deutsche Gegenwartsliteratur* (1972), 3:244-56

Brower, Reuben, et al, *I. A. Richards; Essays in His Honor*. 1973. Pp. 218-41

Durzak, Manfred, *Dürrenmatt, Frisch, Weiss; Deutsches Drama Gegenwart Zwischen Kritik und Utopie*. 1972. Pp. 331-44

Håstad, Disa, "'Hölderlin' Börjar med Marats Död; Disa Håstad Samtaler med Peter Weiss", *Ord och Bild* (1972), 81:312-18

Honza, Norbert, "Peter Weiss und das Dokumentarische Theater", *Kwartalnik Neofilologiczny* (1972), 19:389-401

Moreno Castillo, Enrique, "'Hölderlin' de Peter Weiss", *Camp de l'Arpa; Revista de Literatura* (1974), 9:13-16

Raleigh, Peter J., "'Hölderlin': Peter Weiss's Artist in Revolt", *Colloquia Germanica* (1973), 7:193-213

Vennberg, Karl, "Hölderlin i Förvandling; Vid Läsningen av Peter Weiss Drama 'Hölderlin'", *Ord och Bild* (1972), 81:319-20

The Investigation, 1965

America, 115:525, Oct. 29, 1966

"Auschwitz auf der Bühne. 'Die Ermittlung' von Peter Weiss", *Die Zeit. Wochenzeitung für Politik Wirtschaft, Handel und Kultur* (1965), 20:19-22

Best, Otto F., *Peter Weiss; Vom Existentialischen Drama zum Marxistischen Welttheater*. 1971. Pp. 134-47

Carmichael, Joel, "German Reactions to a New Play about Auschwitz", *American-German Review* (1966), 32:30-31

——————— , "Peter Weiss' 'Auschwitz'", *Encounter* (1966), 26 pt. 1:90-93

Castagne, Helmut, "Auschwitz auf der Buhne. Zu dem Oratorium 'Die Ermittlung' von Peter Weiss", *Tribüne. Zeitschrift zum Verständnis des Judentums* (1965), 4:1730

Christian Century, 83:1540-41, Dec. 14, 1966

Commentary, 42:75-76, Dec. 1966

Commonweal, 85:139-41, Nov. 4, 1966

Durzak, Manfred, *Dürrenmatt, Frisch, Weiss: Deutsches Drama Gegenwart Zwischen Kritik und Utopie*. 1972. Pp. 279-93

Esslin, Martin, "'Die Ermittlung' und die Grenzen des Dramas", *Weltwoche* (1965), 33:25

Fiedler, Leslie Aaron, *The Collected Essays of Leslie Fiedler*. vol 2. 1971. Pp. 145-50

Gilman, Richard, *Common and Uncommon Masks; Writings on the Theatre, 1961-70*. 1971. Pp. 170-72

Hädecki, Wolfgang, "Zur 'Ermittlung' von Peter Weiss", *Die Neue Rundschau* (1966), 77:165-69

"Hat 'Die Ermittlung' das Publikum Erreicht? Jeder Regisseur Entdeckte Andere Buhnenmoglichkeiten, das Auschwitz-Drama von Peter Weiss zu Inszenieren", *Christ und Welt* (1965), 18:22

Hoffman, Jens, "Auschwitz in Elf Gesängen. Peter Weiss und ein Oratorium", *Christ und Welt* (1965), 18:23

Honsza, Norbert, "Peter Weiss und das Kokumentarische Theater", *Kwartalnik Neofilologiczny* (1972), 19:389-401

Hudson, Roger, "The Evidence; Reflections on 'The Investigation'", *Jewish Quarterly* (Spring 1966), 14:13-14

Hughes, Catharine, *Plays, Politics and Polemics.* 1973. Pp. 139-44

Ignée, Wolfgang, "Schwierigkeiten, die Wahrheit zu Spielen. Piscator bei den Berliner Proben zum Auschwitz-Drama von Peter Weiss", *Christ und Welt* (1965), 18:27

Karl, Eugen, "Peter Weiss Kontra Gropindustrie. 'Die Ermittlung' Gegen den Kapitalismus", *Der Volkswirt. Wirtschafts-und Finanzzeitung* (1965), 19:2232-33

Life, 61:8, Oct. 28, 1966

Müller, H., "Auschwitz auf dem Theatre", Liberal. *Beiträge zur Entwicklung einer Freiheitlichen Ordnung* (1965), 7:823-29

Nation, 203:395-96, Oct. 17, 1966

New Republic, 155:42-44, Nov. 26, 1966

New Statesman, 70:666, Oct. 29, 1965

New Yorker, 42:118, Oct. 15, 1966

Newsweek, 68:98, Oct. 17, 1966

Nössig, M., "Ermittlung zur 'Ermittlung'", *Theater der Zeit* (1965), 20:4-7

Osses, J. E., "La Conciencia de Peter Weiss Frente a Auschwitz en el Escenario de Francfort", *Mapocho* (1968), 16:37-44

Perry, R. C., "Historical Authenticity and Dramatic Form; Hochhuth's 'Der Stellvertreter' and Weiss's 'Die Ermittlung'", *Modern Language Review* (Oct. 1969), 64:828-39

Salloch, Erika, "Peter Weiss, 'Die Ermittlung': Eine Studie zur Struktur des Dokumentartheaters", *Dissertation Abstracts International* (1970), 31:1291A

Saturday Review, 49:72, Oct. 22, 1966

Schoenberner, Gerhard, "'Die Ermittlung' von Peter Weiss: Requiem oder Lehrstuck?", *Gewerkschaftliche Monatshefte* (1965), 16:738-45

Simon, John, "Theatre Chronicle", *Hudson Review* (1966-67), 19:630-32

Time, 88:93, Oct. 14, 1966

Times Literary Supplement, #3337:103, Feb. 10, 1966

Valentin, Jean M., "d'Une Tour à l'Autre: Evolution et Continuité dans l'Oeuvre Dramatique de Peter Weiss", *Recherches Germaniques* (1972), 2:94-129

Vogue, 148:99, Nov. 11, 1966

Wendt, Ernst, "Was Wird Ermittelt? Peter Weiss 'Ermittlung'", *Theatre Heute Zeitschrift für Schauspiel, Oper, Ballett* (1965), 6:14-18

Weichardt, Jurgen, "Einsicht, Gesinnung, Verwandlung. Zur Berliner Auffuhrung von Peter Weiss: 'Die Ermittlung'", *Europäische* (1965), 5:690

Marat/Sade, 1964

Abel, Lionel, "So Who's not Mad; On Marat/Sade and Nihilism", *Dissent* (1966), 13:166-71 and 425-27

America, 114:181-82, Jan. 29, 1966

Bauland, Peter, *The Hooded Eagle; Modern German Drama on the New York Stage.* 1968. Pp. 220-24

Bayers, Robert, "On the Sanity of Marat/Sade; In Defense of the Young Leftist", *Dissent* (1966), 13:42.'24

Beaujour, Michel, "Peter Weiss and the Futility of Sadism", *Yale French Studies* (1965), #35:114-19

Best, Otto F., *Peter Weiss: Vom Existentialischen Drama zum Marxistischen Welttheater*. 1971. Pp. 79-110

Brook P., L. Fiedler, G. Lust, N. Podhoretz, I. Richardson, and G. Rogoff, "Marat/Sade Forum", *Tulane Drama Review* (1966), 10:214-37

Brustein, Robert Sanford, *The Third Theatre*. 1969. Pp. 140-45

Catholic World, 203:63-64, Apr. 1966

Clurman, Harold, *The Naked Image; Observations on the Modern Theatre*. 1966. Pp. 117-22

Cohn, Ruby, *Currents in Contemporary Drama*. 1969. Pp. 218-23

——————— , "'Marat/Sade': An Education in Theatre", *Educational Theatre Journal* (1967), 19:478-85

Commentary, 41:75-76, Mar. 1966

Commonweal, 83:476-77, Jan. 21, 1966 and 83:636-38, Mar. 4, 1966

Durzak, Manfred, *Dürrenmatt, Frisch, Weiss: Deutsches Drama Gegenwart Zwischen Kritik und Utopie*. 1972. Pp. 266-78

Elliot, George P., "Nihilism in Marat/Sade", *Dissent* (1966), 13:333-35

Enderstein, Carl O., "Gestaltungsformen in Peter Weiss' 'Marat/Sade'", *Modern Language Notes* (1973), 88:582-93

Esslin, Martin, *Brief Chronicles; Essays on Modern Theatre*. 1970. Pp. 184-87

——————— , *Reflections; Essays on Modern Theatre*. 1969. Pp. 154-57

Fleissner, E. M., "Revolution as Theatre; 'Danton's Death' and 'Marat/Sade'", *Massachusettes Review* (1966), 7:543-56

Gassner, John, *Dramatic Soundings; Evaluations and Retractions Culled from Thirty Years of Dramatic Criticism*. 1968. Pp. 614-16

Genno, C. N., "Peter Weiss's 'Marat/Sade'", *Modern Drama* (Dec. 1970), 13:304-15

Gilman, Richard, *Common and Uncommon Masks; Writings on Theatre, 1960-70*. 1971. Pp. 167-70

Grosshans, Henry, ed., *To Find Something New; Studies in Contemporary Literature*. 1969. Pp. 90-101

Habermas, Jürgen, "Ein Verdranungsprozess Wird Enthulet. Noch Einmal: Das 'Marat/Sade'-Drama von Peter Weiss", *Die Zeit. Wochenzeitung für Politik, Wirtschaft, Handel und Kultur* (1964), 19:10

Hampshire, Stuart N., *Modern Writers and Other Essays*. 1970. Pp. 63-70

Harper, 232:124, Apr. 1966

Honsza, Norbert, "Peter Weiss und das Dokumentarische Theater", *Kwartalnik Neofilologiczny* (1972), 19:389-401

Howe, Irving, ed., *The Radical Imagination; An Anthology from "Dissent Magazine"*. 1967. Pp. 150-58

Iriesch, Manfred, "Peter Weiss, Marat and de Sade", *American-German Review* (1964), 30:9-11

——————— , "Peter Weiss: The Murder of Marat", *Books Abroad* (1965), 39:27-29

James, Norman, "The Fusion of Pirandello and Brecht in 'Marat/Sade' and 'The Plebians Rehearse Uprising'", *Educational Theatre Journal* (1969), 21:426-38

Kerr, Walter, *Thirty Plays Hath November; Pain and Pleasure in the Contemporary Theater*. 1969. Pp. 60-63 and 248-49

Life, 60:26B and 27, Mar. 11, 1966

Look, 30:106-10, Feb. 22, 1966

Lumley, Frederick, *New Trends in Twentieth Century Drama; A Survey Since Ibsen and Shaw*. 1967. Pp. 247-53

Mabley, Edward, *Dramatic Construction; An Outline of Basic Principles*. 1972. Pp. 392-402

Mango, Achille, "Peter Weiss, 'Marat/Sade': Storia e Dialettica della Forma", *Il Ponte* (1968), 24:271-83

Milfull, J., "From Kafka to Brecht: Peter Weiss's Development Towards Marxism", *German Life and Letters* (1966), 20:61-71

Miller, L. L., "Peter Weiss, Marat and Sade; Comments on an Author's Commentary", *Symposium* (Spring 1971), 25:39-58

Moeller, Hans-Bernhard, "German Theater 1964; Weiss' Reasoning in the Madhouse", *Symposium* (1966), 20:163-73

Nation, 202:82-84, Jan. 17, 1966

New Republic, 154:23-24, Jan. 22, 1966

New Statesman, 68:332, Sept. 4, 1964

New Yorker, 40.204-06, Sept. 19, 1964 and 41:98, Jan. 8, 1966

Newsweek, 67:63, Jan. 10, 1966 and 69:93, Jan. 16, 1967

Partisan Review, 33:270-71, Spring 1966

Prins, P. de, "En Flamand", *De Vlaamse Gids* (1966), 50:214-25

Reporter, 34:48-49, Jan. 27, 1967

Rischbieter, Henning, "Da Ist Deutsche Drama! Peter Weiss 'Marat' in Schiller-Theater", *Theater Heute. Zeitschrift für Schauspiel, Oper, Ballett* (1964), 5:21-25

Roberts, David, "Peter Weiss, 'Marat/Sade' and the Revolution", *Komos: A Quarterly of Drama and the Arts of the Theatre*. (1969), 2:1-8

Saturday Review, 49:45, Jan. 15, 1966

Schaefer, Hans W., " 'Die Verfolgung und Ermordung Jean Paul Marats' von Peter Weiss: Eine Provokation?'", *Boletin de Estudios Germánicos* (1972), 9:33-45

Schneider, Peter, "Uber das 'Marat'—Stück von Peter Weiss", *Die Neue Rundschau* (1964), 75:666-72

Schumacher, E., "Engagement im Historischen", *Theater der Zeit* (1965), 20:4-7

Sheed, Wilfrid, *The Morning After; Selected Essays and Reviews*. 1971. Pp. 142-46

Simon, John, "Theatre Chronicle", *Hudson Review* (1966), 19:110-12

Simon, K. G., "Marat als Posse", *Theater Heute. Zeitschrift für Schauspiel, Oper, Ballett* (1966), 7:46-47

Sontag, Susan, "Marat/Sade/Artaud", *Partisan Review* (1965), 32:210-19
——————————— , *Against Interpretation and Other Essays*. 1966. Pp. 163-74

Spectator, 213:376, Aug. 28, 1964

Stone, Michal, "Die Verfolgung des Jacques Roux. Premiere in der Zone: 'Marat' von Peter Weiss im Volkstheater Rostock", *Christ und Welt* (1965), 18:18

Taeni, Rainer, "Peter Weiss' 'Marat/Sade' ", *Meanjin Quarterly* (1968), 27: 94-105

Time, 87:51, Jan. 7, 1966

Valentin, Jean M., "d'Une Tour à l'Autre: Evolution et continuité dans l'Oeuvre Dramatique de Peter Weiss", *Recherches Germaniques* (1972), 2:94-129

Vogue, 144:94, Oct. 15, 1964 and 147:102-05, Jan. 1, 1966 and 147:56, Feb. 15, 1966

Waldrop, Rosmarie, "'Marat/Sade': A Ritual of the Intellect", *Bucknell Review* (1970), 18:52-68

Weiss, S. A., "Peter Weiss's 'Marat/Sade'", *Drama Survey* (1966), 5:123-30

White, John J., "History and Cruelty in Peter Weiss's 'Marat/Sade'", *Modern Language Review* (1968), 63:437-48

Wuletich, Sybil, "The Depraved Angel of 'Marat/Sade'", *Wisconsin Studies in Contemporary Literature* (1968), 9:91-99

The Persecution and Assassination of Jean-Paul Marat as Performed by the Inmates of the Asylum at Charenton under the Direction of the Marquis de Sade   *SEE*   Marat/Sade

The Song of the Lusitanian Bogey, 1966
America, 118:132, Jan. 27, 1968

Atlas, 13:54, Apr. 1967

Best, Otto F., *Peter Weiss: Vom Existentialischen Drama zum Marxistischen Welttheater.* 1971. Pp. 148-58

Durzak, Manfred, *Dürrenmatt, Frisch, Weiss: Deutsches Drama Gegenwart Zwischen Kritik und Utopie.* 1972. Pp. 294-305

Honsza, Norbert, "Peter Weiss und das Dokumentarische Theater", *Kwartalnik Neofilologiczny* (1972), 19:389-401

Nation, 206:125, Jan. 22, 1968

New Yorker, 43:57-58, Jan. 13, 1968

Newsweek, 71:79, Jan. 15, 1968

Niemi, Irmeli, "Peter Weiss and Documentary Theatre: 'Song of a Scarecrow'", *Modern Drama* (1973), 16:29-34

Reporter, 38:40, Feb. 8, 1968

Rischbieter, H., "Peter Weiss Dramatisiert Vietnam", *Theater Heute.* (1967), 8:6-7

Saturday Review, 51:18, Jan. 20, 1968

Time, 91:40, Jan. 12, 1968

Valentin, Jean M., "d'Une Tour à l'Autre: Evolution et Continuité dans l'Oeuvre Dramatique de Peter Weiss", *Recherches Germaniques* (1972), 2: 94-129

Trotzky in Exile, 1969
Best, Otto F., *Peter Weiss: Vom Existentialischen Drama zum Marxistischen Welttheater.* 1971. Pp. 172-87

Durzak, Manfred, *Dürrenmatt, Frisch, Weiss: Deutsches Drama Gegenwart Zwischen Kritik und Utopie.* 1972. Pp. 318-30

Honsza, Norbert, "Peter Weiss und das Dokumentarische Theater", *Kwartalnik Neofilologiczny* (1972), 19:389-401

Hughes, Catharine, *Plays, Politics and Polemics.* 1973. Pp. 155-64

Valentin, Jean M., "d'Une Tour à l'Autre: Evolution et Continuité dans l'Oeuvre Dramatique de Peter Weiss", *Recherches Germaniques* (1972), 2:94-129

Der Turm, 1948
Best, Otto F., *Peter Weiss: Vom Existentialischen Drama zum Marxistischen Welttheater.* 1971. Pp. 13-24.

Honsza, Norbert, "Peter Weiss und das Dokomentarische Theater", *Kwartalnik Neofilologiczny* (1972), 19:389-401

Valentin, Jean M., "d'Une Tour à l'Autre: Evolution et Continuité dans l'Oeuvre Dramatique de Peter Weiss", *Recherches Germaniques* (1972), 2:94-129

Die Verfolgung und Ermordung Jean Paul Marats Dargestellt Durch die Schauspielgruppe des Hospizes zu Charenton unter Auleitung des Herrn de Sade *SEE* Marat/Sade

Vietnam Discourse, 1968
Best, Otto F., *Peter Weiss; Vom Existentialischen Drama zum Marxistischen Welttheater.* 1971. Pp. 159-64
Durzak, Manfred, *Dürrenmatt, Frisch, Weiss; Deutsches Drama Gegenwart Zwischen Kritik und Utopie.* 1972. Pp. 306-17

ARNOLD WESKER

Chicken Soup with Barley, 1958
Brown, John Russell, *Modern British Dramatists; A Collection of Critical Essays.* 1968. Pp. 79-81
Goodman, Henry, "Arnold Wesker", *Drama Survey* (1961-62), 1:215-22
Hayman, Ronald, *Arnold Wesker.* 1973. Pp. 18-28
Kleinberg, Robert, "Seriocomedy in 'The Wesker Trilogy'", *Educational Theatre Journal* (March 1969), 21:36-40
Peinert, Dietrich, "'Chicken Soup with Barley': Untersuchungen zur Dramentechnik Arnold Weskers", *Literatur in Wissenchaft und Unterricht* (1970), 3:169-86

Chips with Everything, 1962
Brown, John Russell, *Theatre Language; A Study of Arden, Osborne, Pinter and Wesker.* 1972. Pp. 158-89
Hayman, Ronald, *Arnold Wesker.* 1973. Pp. 68-79
Mathews, Honor, *The Primal Curse; The Myth of Cain and Abel in the Theatre.* 1967. Pp. 193-94
Page, Malcolm, "Whatever Happened to Arnold Wesker? His Recent Plays", *Modern Drama* (Dec. 1968), 11:317-25

The Four Seasons, 1965
Hayman, Ronald, *Arnold Wesker.* 1973. Pp. 93-102
Page, Malcolm, "Whatever Happened to Arnold Wesker? His Recent Plays", *Modern Drama* (Dec. 1968), 11:317-25

The Friends, 1969
Hayman, Ronald, *Arnold Wesker.* 1973. Pp. 103-07
Mannheimer, Monica, "Major Themes in Arnold Wesker's Play, 'The Friends'", *Moderna Språk* (1972), 66:109-16

I'm Talking about Jerusalem, 1959
Goodman, Henry, "Arnold Wesker", *Drama Survey* (1961-62), 1:215-22
Hayman, Ronald, *Arnold Wesker.* 1973. Pp. 57-67
Kleinberg, Robert, "Seriocomedy in 'The Wesker Trilogy'", *Educational Theatre Journal* (March 1969), 21:36-40

The Journalists, 1973
Hayman, Ronald, *Arnold Wesker.* 1973. Pp. 117-23

The Kitchen, 1959
  Brown, John Russell, *Modern British Dramatists; A Collection of Critical Essays.* 1968. Pp. 75-79
  Brown, John Russell, *Theatre Language; A Study of Arden, Osborne, Pinter and Wesker.* 1972. Pp. 158-89
  Goodman, Henry, "Arnold Wesker", *Drama Survey* (1961-62), 1:215-22
  Hayman, Ronald, *Arnold Wesker.* 1973. Pp. 3-17
  Sheed, Wilfrid, *The Morning After; Selected Essays and Reviews.* 1971. Pp. 135-37

The Old Ones, 1972
  Hayman, Ronald, *Arnold Wesker.* 1973. Pp. 108-16

Roots, 1959
  Brown, John Russell, *Modern British Dramatists; A Collection of Critical Essays.* 1968. Pp. 71-75
  _____ , *Theatre Language; A Study of Arden, Osborne, Pinter and Wesker.* 1972. Pp. 158-89
  Cowell, Raymond, *Twelve Modern Dramatists.* 1967. Pp. 103-05
  Goodman, Henry, "Arnold Wesker", *Drama Survey* (1961-62), 1:215-22
  Hayman, Ronald, *Arnold Wesker.* 1973. Pp. 28-37
  Kleinberg, Robert, "Seriocomedy in 'The Wesker Trilogy'", *Educational Theatre Journal* (March 1969), 21:36-40

Their Very Own and Golden City, 1966
  Hayman, Ronald, *Arnold Wesker*, 1973. Pp. 80-92
  Page, Malcolm, "Whatever Happened to Arnold Wesker? His Recent Plays", *Modern Drama* (Dec. 1968), 11:317-25

JOHN WHITING

The Devils, 1963
  Brustein, Robert Sanford, *The Third Theatre.* 1969. Pp. 95-97
  Catholic World, 202:255-56, Jan. 1966
  Commonweal, 79:371, Dec. 20, 1963 and 83:348-49, Dec. 17, 1965
  Gassner, John, *Dramatic Soundings; Evaluations and Retractions Culled from Thirty Years of Dramatic Criticism.* 1968. Pp. 616-17
  Hurrell, John Dennis, "John Whiting and the Theme of Self-Destruction", *Modern Drama* (1965), 8:134-41
  Illustrated London News, 238:362, Mar. 4, 1961
  Lumley, Frederick, *New Trends in Twentieth Century Drama; A Survey Since Ibsen and Shaw.* 1967. Pp. 257-60
  Lyons, Charles R., "The Futile Encounter in the Plays of John Whiting", *Modern Drama* (Dec. 1968), 11:283-98
  Nation, 201:483-84, Dec. 13, 1965
  National Review, 18:38-39, Jan. 11, 1966
  New Republic, 153:28, Dec. 18, 1965
  New Statesman, 61:317-18, Feb. 24, 1961
  New Yorker, 37:168-69, Apr. 22, 1961 and 41:170, Nov. 27, 1965
  Newsweek, 62:77, Nov. 11, 1963 and 66:91, Nov. 29, 1965
  Reporter, 33:46, Dec. 16, 1965
  Roy, Emil, *British Drama since Shaw.* 1972. Pp. 128-31
  Saturday Review, 46:35, Nov. 23, 1963 and 48:76, Dec. 4, 1965 and 50:50, Apr. 15, 1967

Spectator, 206:331-32, Mar. 10, 1961
Time, 86:67, Nov. 26, 1965
Vogue, 147:72, Jan. 1, 1966

Marching Song, 1954
America, 102:483, Jan. 16, 1960
Hurrell, John Dennis, "John Whiting and the Theme of Self-Destruction",
   Modern Drama (1965-66), 8:134-41
Hayman, Ronald, "Tragedy in the Holiday Camp", *London Magazine* (Sept.
   1969), 9:83:92
Lyons, Charles R., "The Futile Encounter in the Plays of John Whiting",
   Modern Drama (Dec. 1968), 11:283-98
New Statesman, 47:500, Apr. 17, 1954
Nightingale, Benedict, "A Private Individual", *New Statesman* (April 3, 1970),
   Pp. 483
Spectator, 192:457, Apr. 16, 1954
Williams, Raymond, *Drama from Ibsen to Brecht*. 1968. Pp. 316-18

A Penny for a Song, 1951
Illustrated London News, 225:1075, Dec. 11, 1954
Spectator, 209:188, Aug. 10, 1962

Saint's Day, 1951
Brown, John Russell, *Modern British Dramatists; A Collection of Critical
   Essays*. 1968. Pp. 38-46
Bryden, Ronald, "Whiting's Way", *New Statesman* (1965), 69:773-74
Hayman, Ronald, "Tragedy in the Holiday Camp", *London Magazine* (Sept.
   1969), 9:83-92
Hoefer, Jacqueline, "Pinter and Whiting: Two Attitudes Towards the Alienated
   Artist", *Modern Drama* (1961-62), 4:402-08
Hurrell, John Dennis, "John Whiting and the Theme of Self-Destruction",
   Modern Drama (1965-66), 8:134-41
Lyons, Charles R., "The Futile Encounter in the Plays of John Whiting",
   Modern Drama (Dec. 1968), 11:283-98
New Statesman and Nation, 42:404, Oct. 13, 1951 and 42:437, Oct. 20, 1951
Nightingale, Benedict, "A Private Individual", *New Statesman* (April 3, 1970),
   Pp. 483
Robinson, Gabriele, "Beyond 'The Waste Land'; An Interpretation of John
   Whiting's 'Saint's Day' ", *Modern Drama* (1971), 14:463-77

OSCAR FINGAL O'FLAHERTIE WILLS WILDE

The Duchess of Padua, 1891
Berland, Ellen, "Form and Content in the Plays of Oscar Wilde", *Dissertation
   Abstracts International* (1973), 33:3631A

An Ideal Husband, 1895
Berland, Ellen, "Form and Content in the Plays of Oscar Wilde", *Dissertation
   Abstracts International* (1973), 33:3631A
Ganz, Arthur, "The Divided Self in the Society Comedies of Oscar Wilde",
   Modern Drama (1960), 3:16-23
Menon, K. P. K., *Literary Studies; Homage to Dr. Sivaramasubramonia Aiyer*.
   1973. Pp. 70-77

Mikhail, E. H., "Self-Revelation in 'An Ideal Husband'", *Modern Drama* (Sept. 1968), 11:180-86

Nassaar, Christopher S., *Into the Demon Universe; A Literary Exploration of Oscar Wilde*. 1974. Pp. 123-29

Shaw, George Bernard, *Plays and Players; Essays on the Theatre*. 1952. Pp. 1-9

The Importance of Being Earnest, 1895

Appleton, W. W., "Making a Masterpiece; 'Importance of Being Earnest'", *Saturday Review*, 39:21, May 12, 1956

Beerbohm, Max, *Around Theatres*. 1953. Pp. 188-91

Berland, Ellen, "Form and Content in the Plays of Oscar Wilde", *Dissertation Abstracts International* (1973), 33:3631A

Brown, John Mason, *Seeing More Things*. 1948. Pp. 209-20

Catholic World, 148:730, March, 1939 and 165:70-71, April, 1947

Commonweal, 29:413, Feb. 3, 1939 and 45:565-66, March 21, 1947

Freedman, Morris, *The Moral Impulse; Modern Drama from Ibsen to the Present*. 1967. Pp. 63-67

Ganz, Arthur, "The Divided Self in the Society Comedies of Oscar Wilde", *Modern Drama* (1960), 3:16-23

_____ , "The Meaning of 'The Importance of Being Earnest'", *Modern Drama* (1963), 6:42-52

Illustrated London News, 237:862, Nov. 12, 1960

Jordan, Robert J., "Satire and Fantasy in Wilde's 'Importance of Being Earnest'", *Ariel; A Review of International English Literature* (1970), 1:101-09

Lambert, J. W., "Importance of Being Earnest", *Drama* (1974), 113:39-51

Life, 22:123-24, March 31, 1947

Mabley, Edward, *Dramatic Construction; An Outline of Basic Principles*. 1972. Pp. 128-38

McCarthy, Mary Therese, *Sights and Spectacles, 1937-1956*. 1956. Pp. 106-10

Mikhail, E. H., "The Four Act Version of 'The Importance of Being Earnest'", *Modern Drama* (1968), 11:263-66

Nassaar, Christopher S., *Into the Demon Universe; A Literary Exploration of Oscar Wilde*. 1974. Pp. 129-45

Nathan, George Jean, *Theatre Book of the Year, 1946-47*. Pp. 328-31

Nation, 148:128, Jan. 28, 1939 and 164:338-39, March 22, 1947

New Republic, 116:41, March 17, 1947

New Statesman, 60:694, Nov. 5, 1960 and 61:190, Feb. 3, 1961

New Statesman and Nation, 17:205, Feb. 11, 1939 and 18:305-07, Aug. 26, 1939

New Yorker, 23:53, March 15, 1947 and 39:132, March 9, 1963

Newsweek, 29:97, March 17, 1947 and 61:86, March 11, 1963

Oppel, Horst, *Das Moderne Englische Drama; Interpretationen*. 1963. Pp. 44-61

Parker, David, "Oscar Wilde's Great Farce; 'Importance of Being Earnest'", *Modern Language Quarterly* (1974), 35:173-86

Partridge, E. B., "The Importance of Not Being Earnest", *Bucknell Review* (1960), 9:143-58

Peinert, Dietrich, "Neuere Aufsätze zu Oscar Wildes Dramen", *Literatur in Wissenschaft und Unterricht* (1968), 1:2-4

Poague, L. A., "'Importance of Being Earnest': The Texture of Wilde's Irony", *Modern Drama* (1973), 16:251-57

Reinert, Otto, "The Courtship Dance in 'The Importance of Being Earnest'", *Modern Drama* (1959), 1:256-57

Richards, Kenneth and Peter Thomson, eds., *Essays on 19th Century British Theatre; The Proceedings of a Symposium Sponsored by the Manchester University Department of Drama.* 1971. Pp. 125-43

Roy, Emil, *British Drama since Shaw.* 1972. Pp. 28-34

Saturday Review of Literature, 30:22-24, March 29, 1947

Shaw, George Bernard, *Plays and Players; Essays on the Theatre.* 1952. Pp. 17-25

Shipp, H., "The Importance of Being Earnest", *English Review,* 51:278-80, Aug. 1930

Spectator, 163:289, Aug. 25, 1939

Sullivan, Kevin, *Oscar Wilde.* 1972. Pp. 23-31

Theatre Arts, 23:174, March, 1939 and 23:253, April, 1939 and 31:16-17, 22, April, 1947 and 47:12-13, April, 1963

Theatre Arts Anthology; A Record and a Prophecy, ed. by Rosamond Gilder et. al., 1950. Pp. 665-68

Time, 33:21, Jan. 23, 1939 and 49:39, March 17, 1947

Toliver, Harold E., "Wilde and the Importance of 'Sincere and Studied Triviality' ", *Modern Drama* (1963), 5:389-99

Vordtriede, W., "Dramatic Devices in 'Faust' and 'The Importance of Being Earnest' ", *Modern Language Notes,* 70:584-85, Dec., 1955

Wakefield, G., "The Importance of Being Earnest", *Saturday Review,* 150:79, July 19, 1930

Lady Windemere's Fan, 1892

Berland, Ellen, "Form and Content in the Plays of Oscar Wilde", *Dissertation Abstracts International* (1973), 33:3631A

Brown, John Mason, "Importance of Not Being Earnest", *Saturday Review of Literature,* 29:34-36, Nov. 9, 1946

——————— , *Seeing More Things.* 1948. Pp. 209-14

Catholic World, 164:262, Dec., 1946

Commonweal, 44:551-52, Sept. 20, 1946

Freedman, Morris, *The Moral Impulse; Modern Drama from Ibsen to the Present.* 1967. Pp. 63-67

Ganz, Arthur, "The Divided Self in the Society Comedies of Oscar Wilde", *Modern Drama* (1960), 3:16-23

Life, 20:119-20, April 15, 1946

Nathan, George Jean, *Theatre Book of the Year, 1946-47.* Pp. 115-19

Nation, 163:510, Nov. 2, 1946

New Republic, 115:556, Oct. 28, 1946

New Yorker, 22:51, Oct. 26, 1946

Newsweek, 28:86, Oct. 28, 1941

Peckham, Morse, *The Triumph of Romanticism; Collected Essays.* 1970. Pp. 226-30

School and Society, 65:182-83, March 8, 1947

Shipp, H., "Lady Windermere's Fan", *English Review,* 51:278-80, Aug., 1930

Theatre Arts, 30:691, 696, Dec., 1946

Time, 48:63, Oct. 28, 1946

Wakefield, G., "Lady Windemere's Fan", *Saturday Review,* 150:79, July 19, 1930

Salome, 1896

Beerbohm, Max, *Around Theatres.* 1953. Pp. 377-80

Bendz, E. P. "A Propos de la 'Salomé' de Oscar Wilde", *English Studies*, 51: 48-70, 1917

Berland, Ellen, "Form and Content in the Plays of Oscar Wilde", *Dissertation Abstracts International* (1973), 33:3631A

Ellman, Richard, "Overtures to Wilde's 'Salome'", *Tri-Quarterly* (1969), 15:45-64

Hamilton, Clayton Meeker, *Seen on the Stage*. 1920. Pp. 122-24

Jennings, P. "Salomé", *Spectator*, 146:894, June 6, 1931

Joost, Nicholas and Franklin E. Court, "'Salomé', the Moon and Oscar Wilde's Aesthetics; A Reading of the Play", *Papers on Language and Literature* (1972), 8 (Supp.):96-111

MacCarthy, Desmond, "Salomé", *New Statesman and Nation*, 1:542, June 6, 1931

Nassaar, Christopher S., *Into the Demon Universe; A Literary Exploration of Oscar Wilde*. 1974. Pp. 80-109

Roof, K. M., "'Salomé'—the Play and the Opera", *Craftsman*, 11:523-38, 1907

Rose, Marilyn Gaddis, "The Daughters of Herodias in 'Herodiade', 'Salomé', and 'A Full Moon in March'", *Comparative Drama* (1967), 1:172-81

Row, A., "Salomé", *Poet-Lore*, 30:433-35, 1919

Saunders, W., "Salomé", *Drama*, 12:335-37, 1922

Snijers, Robert, "Oscar Wildes 'Salomé': Alleen Maar Mooi?", *Kunst en Cultur* (1973), 20:Sept. 18

Vera; or, The Nihilists, 1883
Berland, Ellen, "Form and Content in the Plays of Oscar Wilde", *Dissertation Abstracts International* (1973), 33:3631A

A Woman of No Importance, 1893
Berland, Ellen, "Form and Content in the Plays of Oscar Wilde", *Dissertation Abstracts International* (1973), 33:3631A

Ganz, Arthur, "The Divided Self in the Society Comedies of Oscar Wilde", *Modern Drama* (1960), 3:16-23

Nassaar, Christopher S., *Into the Demon Universe; A Literary Exploration of Oscar Wilde*. 1974. Pp. 109-22

Nation, 102:525, May 11, 1916

Saturday Review, 36:24, Aug. 1, 1953

EMLYN WILLIAMS

Accolade, 1950
Christian Science Monitor Magazine, Pp. 7, Sept. 30, 1950

Spectator, 185:311, Sept. 22, 1950

The Corn is Green, 1938
Arts and Decoration, 53:10, Jan., 1941

Catholic World, 152:469-70, Jan., 1941 and 157:299, June, 1943

Commonweal, 33:209, Dec. 13, 1940

Independent Woman, 20:24, Jan., 1941

Life, 9:25-28, Dec. 23, 1940

Nathan, George Jean, *Theatre Book of the Year, 1942-43*. Pp. 283-84

Nation, 151:585, Dec. 7, 1940

New Republic, 103:789, Dec. 9, 1940

New Statesman and Nation, 16:457, Sept. 24, 1938

New Yorker, 16:49, Dec. 7, 1940
Theatre Arts, 25:91-93, Feb., 1941 and 34:15, March, 1950
Time, 36:69, Dec. 9, 1940

Druid's Rest, 1944
New Statesman and Nation, 27:92, Feb. 5, 1944
Spectator, 172:102, Feb. 4, 1944
Theatre Arts, 28:342, June, 1944

He Was Born Gay, 1937
Spectator, 158:1051, June 4, 1937

Light of Heart, 1940
New Statesman and Nation, 19:273, March 2, 1940
Spectator, 164:284, March 1, 1940

Morning Star, 1941
Commonweal, 36:565, Oct. 2, 1942
Nathan, George Jean, *Theatre Book of the Year, 1942-43*. Pp. 53-61
Nation, 155:278, Sept. 26, 1942
New Republic, 107:381-82, Sept. 28, 1942
New Yorker, 18:34, Sept. 26, 1942
Spectator, 167:578, Dec. 19, 1941
Theatre Arts, 26:677-79, Nov., 1942
Time, 40:47, Sept. 28, 1942

A Murder Has Been Arranged, 1930
Jennings, R., "A Murder Has Been Arranged", *Spectator*, 145:879, Dec. 6, 1930

Night Must Fall, 1935
Catholic World, 144:213, Nov., 1936
Commonweal, 24:560, Oct. 9, 1936
Literary Digest, 122:28, Oct. 10, 1936
Nation, 143:426-27, Oct., 10, 1936
New Republic, 88:284, Oct. 14, 1936
Newsweek, 8:29, Oct. 10, 1936
Theatre Arts, 20:847-48, Nov., 1936
Time, 28:52, Oct. 12, 1936
Verschoyle, D., "Night Must Fall", *Spectator*, 154:974, June 7, 1935

Someone Waiting, 1953
America, 94:646, March 10, 1956
Illustrated London News, 223:982, Dec. 12, 1953
New Yorker, 32:93-94, Feb. 25, 1956
Spectator, 191:658, Dec. 4, 1953
Theatre Arts, 40:21, April, 1956
Time, 67:61, Feb. 27, 1956

Spring 1600, 1934
Brown, I., "Spring, 1600", *New Statesman and Nation*, 7:189-90, Feb. 10, 1934
Fleming, P., "Spring, 1600, *Spectator*, 152:195, Feb. 9, 1934

Trespass, 1946
Theatre Arts, 31:36, Oct., 1947

Vessels Departing, 1933
  Saturday Review, 156:53, July 8, 1933
  Verschoyle, D., "Vessels Departing", 151:12, Spectator, July 7, 1933

Wind of Heaven, 1945
  New Statesman and Nation, 29:256, April 21, 1945
  Spectator, 174:359, April 20, 1945

Yesterday's Magic, 1942
  Catholic World, 155:340, June, 1942
  Commonweal, 36:38, May 1, 1942
  New Yorker, 18:30, April 25, 1942
  Time, 39:61, April 27, 1942

STANISLAW IGNACY WITKIEWICZ

Anonymous Work, 1967
  Gerould, E., " 'Anonymous Work': Four Acts of a Rather Nasty Nightmare",
    Drama and Theatre (1974), 12:23-48
  Wirth, Andrzej, "Brecht and Witkiewicz: Two Concepts of Revolution in the
    Drama of the Twenties", *Comparative Drama* (Fall 1969), 3:198-209

Beelzebub Sonata; or, What Really Happened at Mordowar, 1966
  Pomian, Krzystof, "Konfrontacje: Witkiewicz Zredukowany do Absurdu",
    Dialog (1970), 15:106-15

Bezimienne Dzieto   *SEE*   The Anonymous Work

Kurka Wodna   *SEE*   The Water Hen

The Madman and the Nun; or, There Is Nothing Bad Which Could Not Turn
  Into Something Worse, 1926
  Tarn, Adam, "Witkiewicz, Artaud and the Theatre of Cruelty", *Comparative
    Drama* (Fall 1969), 3:162-67
  Wirth, Andrzej, "Brecht and Witkiewicz: Two Concepts of Revolution in the
    Drama of the Twenties", *Comparative Drama* (Fall 1969), 3:198-209

Oni   *SEE*   They

The Shoemakers, 1957
  Szwecow, Maria, "Elementy Zwarowe w Dramacie 'Szewcy' St. I. Wit-
    kiewicza", *Poradnik Jezykowy* (1969), Pp. 49-69
  Wirth, Andrzej, "Brecht and Witkiewicz: Two Concepts of Revolution in the
    Drama of the Twenties", *Comparative Drama* (Fall 1969), 3:198-209

Sonata Belzebuba, Czyli Prawdziwe Zdarzenie w Mordowarze   *SEE*   The
  Beelzebub Sonata; or, What Really Happened at Mordowar

Szewcy   *SEE*   The Shoemakers

They, 1965
  Wirth, Andrzej, "Brecht and Witkiewicz: Two Concepts of Revolution in the
    Drama of the Twenties", *Comparative Drama* (Fall 1969), 3:198-209

Wariat i Zakonnica, Czyli Nie ma Ztego, Co By Na Jeszcze Gorsze nie Wyszto
  SEE   The Madman and the Nun; or, There is Nothing Bad Which Could
  Not Turn Into Something Worse

The Water Hen, 1922
  Dukore, Bernard F. and Daniel C. Gerould, "Explosions and Implosions: Avant-Garde Drama Between World Wars", *Educational Theatre Drama* (Mar. 1969), 21:1-16
  Tarn, Adam, "Witkiewitz, Artaud, and the Theatre of Cruelty", *Comparative Drama* (Fall 1969), 3:162-67

WILLIAM WYCHERLEY

The Country Wife, 1675
  Berman, Ronald, "The Ethic of 'The Country Wife'", *Texas Studies in Language and Literature* (1967), 9:47-55
  Catholic World, 186:383, Feb., 1958
  Christian Century, 74:1515, Dec. 18, 1957
  Commonweal, 13:721, April 29, 1931, and 67:408, Jan. 17, 1958 and 67:431-32, Jan. 24, 1958
  "The Country Wife—No Place to Hide", *Notes and Queries*, 5:250-51, 1958
  Craik, T. W., "Some Aspects of Satire in Wycherley's Plays", *English Studies* (1960), 41:168-79
  Cunningham, John E., *Restoration Drama*. 1966. Pp. 83-89
  Edgley, R., "The Object of Literary Criticism", *Essays in Criticism* (1964), 14:221-36
  Elwin, Malcolm, *Handbook to Restoration Drama*. 1966. Pp. 75-79
  Fox, James H., "The Actor-Audience Relationship in Restoration Comedy, With Particular Reference to the Aside", *Dissertation Abstracts International* (1973), 33:6308A
  Gassner, John, *Dramatic Soundings; Evaluations and Retractions Culled from Thirty Years of Dramatic Criticism*. 1968. Pp. 553-54
  Greedman, William, "Impotence and Self-Destruction in 'The Country Wife'", *English Studies* (1972), 53:421-31
  Hallett, Charles A., "The Hobbesian Substructure of 'The Country Wife'", *Papers on Language and Literature* (1973), 9:380-95
  Holland, Norman N., *The First Modern Comedies*. 1959. Pp. 73-85
  Jackson, Wallace, "'The Country Wife': The Premises of Love and Lust", *South Atlantic Quarterly* (1973), 72:540-46
  Kaul, A. N., *The Action of English Comedy; Studies in the Encounter of Abstraction and Experience from Shakespeare to Shaw*. 1970. Pp. 122-30
  Klein, H. M., "'Where Are Your Maskers?': Queries About the 'Finale' in Wycherley's 'The Country Wife'", *Archiv für das Studium der Neueren Sprachen und Literaturen* (1974), 211:66-68
  Lagarde, Fernand, "L'Art de Wycherley créatur de Personnages dans 'The Country Wife'", *Caliban* (1970), 7:3-21
  Loftis, John Clyde, ed., *Restoration Drama; Modern Essays in Criticism*. 1966. Pp. 82-96
  London Mercury, 35:51, Nov., 1936
  Malekin, Peter, "Wycherley's Dramatic Skills and the Interpretation of 'The Country Wife'", *Durham University Journal* (Dec. 1969), 62:32-40
  Martia, Dominic F., "The Restoration Love Ethos and the Representation of Love in the Plays of William Wycherely", *Dissertation Abstracts International* (1972), 32:6987A

Matlock, Cynthia, "Parody and Burlesque of Heroic Ideals in Wycherley's Comedies; A Critical Reinterpretation of Contemporary Evidence", *Papers on Language and Literature* (1972), 8:273-86

Milburn, Daniel Judson, *The Age of Wit, 1650-1750.* 1966. Pp. 225-67

Miner, Earl, ed., *Restoration Dramatists; A Collection of Critical Essays.* 1966. Pp. 110-14

Morris, David B., "Language and Honour in 'The Country Wife'", *South Atlantic Bulletin* (1972), 37:3-10

Morrissey, L. J., "Wycherley's Country Dance", *Studies in English Literature, 1500-1900* (Summer 1968), 8:415-29

Mukherjee, Sujit, "Marriage as Punishment in the Plays of Wycherley", *Review of English Studies* (1966), 7:61-64

Nation, 141:62, July 17, 1935 and 143:714, Dec. 12, 1936 and 185:463, Dec. 14, 1957 and 201:538-39, Dec. 27, 1965

Nation (London), 40:421-22, Dec. 18, 1926

New Republic, 89:245-46, Dec. 23, 1936 and 154:35, Jan. 1, 1966

New Statesman, 22:573, Feb. 23, 1924

New Statesman and Nation, 7:410, March 17, 1934 and 12:586-87, Oct. 7, 1936

New Yorker, 33:95-96, Dec. 7, 1957

Newsweek, 6:22, July 13, 1935 and 8:34, Dec. 12, 1936 and 66:92-93, Dec. 20, 1965

Nicol, Bernard de Bear, ed., *Varieties of Dramatic Experience.* 1969. Pp. 114-23

Outlook (London), 53:127, Feb. 23, 1924 and 58:609, Dec. 18, 1926

Palmer, John Leslie, *The Comedy of Manners.* 1962. Pp. 92-140

Reporter, 18:37-38, Jan. 9, 1958 and 34:44-45, Jan. 13, 1966

Research Studies, State College of Washington, 1942, Pp. 141-72

Ricks, Christopher, ed., *English Drama to 1710.* (History of Literature in the English Language) vol. 3. 1971. Pp. 387-93

Rogers, Katharine M., *William Wycherley.* 1972. Pp. 57-75

Saturday Review, 142:767-68, Dec. 18, 1926 and 47:28, Aug. 15, 1964 and 48:41, Dec. 25, 1965

Sharma, Ram Chandra, *Themes and Conventions in the Comedy of Manners.* 1965. Pp. 62-63

Sharp, William L., "Restoration Comedy; An Approach to Modern Production", *Drama Survey* (Winter 1968/69), 7:69-86

Spectator, 152:370, March 9, 1934

Theatre Arts, 21:12, Jan., 1937 and 41:27-28, May, 1957 and 42:23, Feb., 1958

Time, 28:66-67, Dec. 14, 1936 and 70:74, Dec. 9, 1957 and 86:40, Dec. 17, 1965

Vernon, P. F., "Marriage of Convenience and the Moral Code of Restoration Comedy", *Essays in Criticism* (1962), 12:370-87

Vieth, David M., "Wycherley's 'The Country Wife': An Anatomy of Masculinity", *Papers on Language and Literature* (Fall 1966), 2:335-50

Vogue, 147:99, Feb. 1, 1966, 149:99, Feb. 1, 1966

Wolper, Roy S., "The Temper of 'The Country Wife'", *Humanities Association Bulletin* (Spring 1967), 18:69-74

Wooton, Carl, "'The Country Wife' and Contemporary Comedy; A World Apart", *Drama Survey*, 2:333-43, 1963

Young, Stark, *Immortal Shadows; A Book of Dramatic Criticism.* 1948. Pp. 181-84

The Gentleman Dancing Master, 1672
Elwin, Malcolm, *Handbook to Restoration Drama*. 1966. Pp. 74-75
Holland, Norman N., *The First Modern Comedies*. 1951. Pp. 64-72
Kaul, A. N., *The Action of English Comedy; Studies in the Encounter of Abstraction and Experience from Shakespeare to Shaw*. 1970. Pp. 123-30
Loftis, John, *The Spanish Plays of Neo-Classical England*. 1973. Pp. 97-130
Miner, Earl, ed., *Restoration Dramatists; A Collection of Critical Essays*. 1966. Pp. 107-10
New Statesman, 26:332, Dec. 26, 1925
Palmer, John Leslie, *The Comedy of Manners*. 1962. Pp. 92-140
Ricks, Christopher, ed., *English Drama to 1710*. (History of Literature in the English Language) vol. 3. 1971. Pp. 388-91
Rodes, David S., "William Wycherley's 'Love in a Wood' and 'The Gentleman Dancing Master'", *Dissertation Abstracts* (1969), 29:2277A
Sharma, Ram Chandra, *Themes and Conventions in the Comedy of Manners*. 1965. Pp. 61-62, 288-89
Ward, Adolphus William, *A History of English Dramatic Literature*, vol. 3, 1966. Pp. 463-64

Love in a Wood, or St. James Park, 1671
Elwin, Malcolm, *Handbook to Restoration Drama*. 1966. Pp. 70-74
Holland, Norman W., *The First Modern Comedies*. 1959. Pp. 38-44
Loftis, John, *The Spanish Plays of Neo-Classical England*. 1973. Pp. 97-130
Martia, Dominic F., "The Restoration Love Ethos and the Representation of Love in the Plays of William Wycherley", *Dissertation Abstracts International* (1972), 32:6987A
Matlock, Cynthia, "Parody and Burlesque of Heroic Ideals in Wycherley's Comedies; A Critical Reinterpretation of Contemporary Evidence", *Papers on Language and Literature* (1972), 8:273-86
Miner, Earl, ed., *Restoration Dramatists; A Collection of Critical Essays*. 1966. Pp. 106-07
Rodes, David S., "William Wycherley's 'Love in a Wood' and 'The Gentleman Dancing Master'", *Dissertation Abstracts* (1969), 29:2277A
Rump, Eric S., "Theme and Structure in Wycherley's 'Love in a Wood'", *English Studies* (1973), 54:326-33
Sharma, Ram Chandra, *Themes and Conventions in The Comedy of Manners*. 1965. Pp. 51-52, 60-61, 294-95, 299-300
Vernon, P. F., "Wycherley's First Comedy and Its Spanish Source", *Comparative Literature* (1966), 18:132-44
Ward, Adolphus William, *A History of English Dramatic Literature*, vol. 3. 1966. Pp. 463

The Plain Dealer, 1676
Auffret, J. M., "'The Man of Mode' and 'The Plain Dealer': Common Origins and Parallels", *Études Anglaises* (Jan.-Mar. 1966), 19:209-22
California University Dept. of English, *Essays Critical and Historical, Dedicated to Lily B. Campbell, by Members of the Dept. of English*. 1950. Pp. 161-69
Craik, T. W., "Some Aspects of Satire in Wycherley's Plays", *English Studies* (1960), 41:168-79
Cunningham, John E., *Restoration Drama*. 1966. Pp. 89-94

Donaldson, Ian, "Tables Turned; 'The Plain Dealer'", *Essays in Criticism* (1967), 17:304-21

—————————— , *The World Upside-Down; Comedy from Jonson to Fielding.* 1970. Pp. 99-118

Dorman, Peter J., "Wycherley's Adaptation of 'Le Misanthrope'", *Restoration and 18th Century Theatre Research* (Nov. 1969), 8:54-59

Elwin, Malcolm, *Handbook to Restoration Drama.* 1966. Pp. 79-83

Friedson, A. M., "Wycherley and Molière: Satirical Point of View in 'The Plain Dealer'", *Modern Philology* (1967), 64:189-97

Holland, Norman N., *The First Modern Comedies.* 1959. Pp. 96-113

McCarthy, B. Eugene, "Wycherley's 'The Plain Dealer' and the Limits of Wit", *English Miscellany* (1971), 22:47-92

Martia, Dominic F., "The Restoration Love Ethos and the Representation of Love in the Plays of William Wycherley", *Dissertation Abstracts International* (1972), 32:6987A

Matlock, Cynthia, "Parody and Burlesque of Heroic Ideals in Wycherley's Comedies; A Critical Reinterpretation of Contemporary Evidence", *Papers on Language and Literature* (1972), 8:273-86

Miner, Earl, ed., *Restoration Dramatists; A Collection of Critical Essays.* 1966. Pp. 123-38

Palmer, John Leslie, *The Comedy of Manners.* 1962. Pp. 92-140

Research Studies, State College of Washington, 1943, Pp. 234-56

Rogers, Katharine M., *William Wycherley.* 1972. Pp. 76-97

Shapherd, James L. III, "Molière and Wycherley's 'Plain Dealer'", *South Central Bulletin: Studies* (1963), 23:37-40

Sharma, Ram Chandra, *Themes and Conventions in the Comedy of Manners.* 1965. Pp. 63-64, 280-81

Ward, Adolphus William, *A History of English Dramatic Literature*, vol. 3. 1966. Pp. 464-66

Wolper, Roy S., "The Temper of the Country Wife", *Humanities Association Bulletin* (1967), 18 pt. 1:69-74

WILLIAM BUTLER YEATS

At the Hawk's Well, 1916

Baksi, Pronoti, "The Noh and the Yeatsian Synthesis", *Review of English Literature*, 6:34-43, 1965

Friedman, Barton, " 'On Baile's Strand' and 'At the Hawk's Well': Staging the Deeps of the Mind", *Journal of Modern Literature* (1975), 4:625-50

Gill, Stephen M., *Six Symbolist Plays of Yeats.* 1971. Pp. 44-49 and 77-79

Gorsky, Susan R., "A Ritual Drama; Yeats's Plays for Dancers", *Modern Drama* (1974), 17:165-78

Hoffmann, Gerhard, "Die Funktion der Lieder in Yeats Dramen", *Anglia; Zeitschrift für Englische Philologie* (1971), 89:87-116

Immoos, Thomas, "Kieta Izumi-Noh Butai ni Tojo Shita Yeats no 'Taka No I' ", *Sophia; Studies in Western Civilization and the Cultural Interaction of East and West* (1971), 20:176-80

Jochum, K. P. S., "Yeats' Last Play", *Journal of English and Germanic Philology* (Apr. 1971), 70:220-29

Linke, Hansjürgen, "Das Los des Menschen in den Cuchulain Drama; Zum 100. Geburtstag von W. B. Yeats", *Die Neueren Sprachen* (1965), 15:253-68

McGrath, Francis C. III, "Heroic Aestheticism: W. B. Yeats and the Heritage of Walter Pater", *Dissertation Abstracts International* (1974), 34:5981A

Menon, K. P. K., *Literary Studies; Homage to Dr. A. Sivaramasubramonia Aiyer*. 1973. Pp. 211-15

Moore, John Rees, *Masks of Love and Death; Yeats as Dramatist*. 1971. Pp. 201-10

Oppel, Horst, *Das Moderne Englische Drama; Interpretationen*. 1963. Pp. 149-65

Sandberg, Anna, "The Anti-Theatre of W. B. Yeats", *Modern Drama*, 4:131-37, 1961

Sharoni, Edna G., " 'At the Hawk's Well': Yeats's Unresolved Conflict Between Language and Silence", *Comparative Drama* (1973), 7:150-73

Sharp, William L., "W. B. Yeats: A Poet Not in the Theatre", *Tulane Drama Review*, 4:62-82, 1959

Tsukimura, Reiko, "A Comparison of Yeats' 'At the Hawk's Well' and Its Noh Version 'Taka No Izumi' ", *Literature East and West* (1967), 11:385-97

Vendler, Helen Hennessey, "Yeat's Changing Metaphors for the Otherworld", *Modern Drama*, 7:308-21, 1964

Vogt, Kathleen M., "Counter-Components in Yeats's 'At the Hawk's Well' ", *Modern Drama* (1974), 17:319-28

Wells, Henry W., *The Classical Drama of the Orient*. 1965. Pp. 310-14

Calvary, 1921

Baksi, Pronoti, "The Noh and the Yeatsian Synthesis", *Review of English Literature*, 6:34-43, 1965

Gorsky, Susan R., "A Ritual Drama: Yeats's Plays for Dancers", *Modern Drama* (1974), 17:165-78

Sharp, William L., "W. B. Yeats: A Poet Not in the Theatre, *Tulane Drama Review*, 4:62-82, 1959

Ure, Peter, "Yeats's Christian Mystery Plays", *Review of English Studies*, n. s. 11:171-82, 1960

The Cat and the Moon, 1931

Myung Whan Kim, "Dance and Rhythm; Their Meaning in Yeats and Noh", *Modern Drama* (1972), 15:195-208

Cathleen ni Houlihan, 1902

Firkins, O. W., "Cathleen ni Houlihan", *Review*, 3:76, July 21, 1920

Gwynn, S., "Cathleen ni Houlihan", *Fortnightly*, 78:1051-54, Dec., 1902

Holloway, John, "Yeats and the Penal Age", *Critical Quarterly* (1966), 8:58-66

Moore, John Rees, *Masks of Love and Death; Yeats as Dramatist*. 1971. Pp. 69-71

Countess Cathleen, 1899

Albright, Daniel, *The Myth Against Myth; A Study of Yeats's Imagination in Old Age*. 1972. Pp. 162-66

Atheneum, 101:16, Jan. 7, 1893

Baksi, Pronoti, "The Noh and the Yeatsian Synthesis", *Review of English Literature*, 6:34-43, 1965

Bookman (London), 3:25-26, October, 1892

Christian Science Monitor Magazine, Pp. 5, March 18, 1950

Clarke, Austin, "The Cardinal and the Countess", *Ariel: A Review of International English Literature* (1972), 3,iii:58-65

——————— , "W. B. Yeats and Verse Drama", *Threshold* (1965), #19:14-23

Gill, Stephen, *Six Symbolist Plays of Yeats*. 1971. Pp. 27-30 and 66-70

Haerdter, Von Michael, "William Butler Yeats—Irisches Theater Zwischen Symbolismus und Expressionismus", *Maske und Kothurn* (1965), 11:30-42

Heyes, Evelyn C. V., "A Theatre for Ideals; Yeats's Stagecraft in Context from 'The Countess Kathleen' (1892) to 'Cathleen ni Houlihan' (1902)", *Dissertation Abstracts International* (1973), 33:3651A

Hoffmann, Gerhard, "Die Funktion der Lieder in Yeats Dramen", *Anglia; Zeitschrift für Englische Philologie* (1971), 89:87-116

Krans, Horatio Sheafe, *William Butler Yeats and the Irish Revival*. 1905. Pp. 109-28

Malone, Andrew E., *The Irish Drama*. 1965. Pp. 134-35

Moore, John Rees, *Masks of Love and Death; Yeats as Dramatist*. 1971. Pp. 59-64

Oppel, Horst, *Das Moderne Englische Drama; Interpretationen*. 1963. Pp. 28-43

Orel, Harold, "Dramatic Values, Yeats and 'The Countess Cathleen'", *Modern Drama*, 2:8-16, 1959

Our Irish Theatre; A Chapter of Autobiography; by Lady Gregory. 1972. Pp. 190-93 and 267-70

Popkin, Henry, "Yeats as Dramatist", *Tulane Drama Review*, 3:73-82, 1959

Ranganathan, Sudha, "Rabindranath Tagore's 'Maline' and W. B. Yeats's 'The Countess Cathleen': A Study in 'Hominisation'", *Osmania Journal of English Studies* (1972), 9:51-54

Roll-Hansen, Diderik, "W. B. Yeats som Dramatiker", *Edda* (1965), 65:153-64

Storer, Edward, "Dramatists Today", *Living Age*, 281:329-32, 1914

Ure, Peter, "The Evolution of Yeats's 'The Countess Cathleen'", *Modern Language Review*, 57:12-24, 1962

Vendler, Helen Hennessy, "Yeats's Changing Metaphors for the Otherworld", *Modern Drama*, 7:308-21, 1964

Webster, Brenda S., *Yeats; A Psychoanalytic Study*. 1973. Pp. 40-47

Williams, Raymond, *Drama from Ibsen to Brecht*. 1968. Pp. 119-21

Death of Cuchulain, 1949

Baksi, Pronoto, "The Noh and the Yeatsian Synthesis," *Review of English Literature*, 6:34-43, 1965

Gill, Stephen M., *Six Symbolist Plays of Keats*. 1971. Pp. 54-57 and 83-85

Hoffmann, Gerhard, "Die Funktion der Lieder in Yeats Dramen", *Anglia* (1971), 89:87-116

Jochum, K. P. S., "Yeats' Last Play", *Journal of English and Germanic Philology* (Apr. 1971), 70:220-29

Linke, Hansjürgen, "Das Los des Menschen in den Cuchulain Drama; Sum 100. Geburtstag von W. B. Yeats", *Die Neueren Sprachen* (1965), 15:253-68

Marcus, Philip P., "Myth and Meaning in Yeats's 'Death of Cuchulain'", *Irish University Review* (1972), 2:133-48

Moore, J. R., "Cuchulain, Christ, and the Queen of Love, Aspects of Yeatsian Drama," *Tulane Drama Review*, 6:150-59, 1962

——————— , *Masks of Love and Death; Yeats as Dramatist*. 1971. Pp. 328-44

Pearce, Donald R., "Yeats' Last Plays: An Interpretation", *Journal of English Literary History* (ELH), 18:67-76, 1951

Sanesi, R., "Cuchulain Nella Terra Desolata", *L'Osservatore/Politico-Letterario* (Milano), 8:92-102, 1962

Dreaming of the Bones, 1931

Baksi, Pronoti, "The Noh and the Yeatsian Synthesis", *Review of English Literature*, 56:34-43, 1965

Brogunier, Joseph, "Expiation in Yeats's Late Plays", *Drama Survey* (1966), 5:24-38

Clark, David R., " 'Nichikigi' and Yeats's 'The Dreaming of the Bones' ", *Modern Drama* (1964), 7:111-25

———————— , "W. B. Yeats and the Drama of Perception", *Arizona Quarterly* (1964), 20:127-41

Gorsky, Susan R., "A Ritual Drama; Yeats's Plays for Dancers", *Modern Drama* (1974), 17:165-78

Moore, John Rees, *Masks of Love and Death; Yeats as Dramatist.* 1971. Pp. 226-35

Sharp, William L., "W. B. Yeats: A Poet Not in the Theatre", *Tulane Drama Review*, 4:62-82, 1959

Vendler, Helen Hennessey, "Yeats's Changing Metaphors for the Otherworld", *Modern Drama*, 7:308-21, 1964

Warschausky, Sidney, "Yeats's Purgatorial Plays", *Modern Drama*, 7:278-86, 1964

Wells, Henry W., *The Classical Drama of the Orient.* 1965. Pp. 316-17

Four Plays for Dancers, 1916

Sandberg, Anna, "The Anti-theatre of W. B. Yeats", *Modern Drama*, 4:131-37, 1961

Sharp, William L., "W. B. Yeats; A Poet Not in the Theatre", *Tulane Drama Review*, 4:67-82, 1959

Smith, Bobby L., "The Dimension of Quest in 'Four Plays for Dancers' ", *Arizona Quarterly* (1966), 22:197-208

A Full Moon in March, 1934

Baksi, Pronoti, "The Noh and the Yeatsian Synthesis", *Review of English Literature*, 6:34-43, 1965

Bentley, Eric, "Yeats as a Playwright", *Kenyon Review*, 10:196-208, 1948

Moore, John R., "Cuchulain, Christ and The Queen of Love: Aspects of Yeatsian Drama", *Tulane Drama Review* (1962), 6:150-59

Oates, Joyce Carol, *The Edge of Impossibility; Tragic Forms in Literature.* 1972. Pp. 163-87

———————— , "Tragic Rites in Yeats' 'A Full Moon in March' ", *Antioch Review* (Winter 1969/70), 29:547-60

Rose, Marilyn Gaddis, "The Daughters of Herodias in 'Herodiade', 'Salome', and 'A Full Moon in March' ", *Comparative Drama* (1967), 1:172-81

Wells, Henry W., *The Classical Drama of the Orient.* 1965. Pp. 317

The Green Helmet, 1910

Bushrui, S. B., *Yeats's Verse Plays; The Revisions, 1900-1910.* 1965. Pp. 168-208

Gill, Stephen M., *Six Symbolist Plays of Yeats.* 1971. Pp. 37-38 and 75-77

Jochum, K. P. S., "Yeats' Last Play", *Journal of English and Germanic Philology* (Apr. 1971), 70:220-29
Moore, John Rees, *Masks of Love and Death; Yeats as Dramatist.* 1971. Pp. 155-63

The Herne's Egg, 1937
Collins, James A., " 'Where All the Ladders Start': The Dramatic Verse of W. B. Yeats' 'The Herne's Egg' ", *Literary Half-Yearly* (1968), 9:105-14
Hoffmann, Gerhard, "Die Funktion der Lieder in Yeats Dramen", *Anglia; Zeitschrift für Englische Philologie* (1971), 89:87-116
Moore, John R., "Cold Passion; A Study of 'Herne's Egg' ", *Modern Drama*, 7:287-98, 1964
——————— , *Masks of Love and Death; Yeats as Dramatist.* 1971. Pp. 284-309
Murshid, K. S., "Yeats, Woman and God", *Venture* (1960), 1:166-77
Pearce, Donald R., "Yeats's Last Plays; An Interpretation", *Journal of English Literary History* (ELH), 18:67-76, 1951
Ure, Peter, "Yeats's Hero-Fool in 'The Herne's Egg' ", *Huntington Library Quarterly*, 24:125-36, 1961
Vendler, Helen Hennessey, "Yeats's Changing Metaphors for the Otherworld", *Modern Drama*, 7:308-21, 1964
Webster, Brenda S., *Yeats; A Psychoanalytic Study.* 1973. Pp. 144-57

The Hour Glass, 1903
Parker, J. Stewart, "Yeats' 'The Hour Glass' ", *Modern Drama* (1968), 10:356-63

The King of the Great Clock Tower, 1934
Myung Wham Kim, "Dance and Rhythm; Their Meaning in Yeats and Noh", *Modern Drama* (1972), 15:195-208
Webster, Brenda S., *Yeats; A Psychoanalytic Study.* 1973. Pp. 136-40
Wells, Henry W., *The Classical Drama of the Orient.* 1965. Pp. 317-18

Land of Heart's Desire, 1894
Bookman (London), 6:87, June, 1894
Chesterton, G. K., "Efficiency in Elfland", *Living Age*, 274:317-19, 1912
Critic, 25:4, July 7, 1894
Grierson, H., "Fairies—from Shakespeare to Mr. Yeats", *Living Age*, 269:651-58, 1911
Krans, Horatio Sheafe, *William Butler Yeats and the Irish Revival.* 1905. Pp. 119-128
Moore, John Rees, *Masks of Love and Death; Yeats as Dramatist.* 1971. Pp. 64-69
Roll-Hansen, Diderik, "W. B. Yeats Som Dramatiker", *Edda* (1965), 65:153-64
Storer, Edward, "Dramatists Today", *Living Age*, 281:329-32, 1914

The Only Jealousy of Emer, 1922
Baksi, Pronoti, "The Noh and the Yeatsian Synthesis", *Review of English Literature*, 6:34-43, 1965
Gill, Stephen M., *Six Symbolist Plays of Yeats.* 1971. Pp. 50-53 and 80-82
Gorsky, Susan R., "A Ritual Drama; Yeats's Plays for Dancers", *Modern Drama* (1974), 17:165-78

Jochum, K. P. S., "Yeats' Last Play", *Journal of English and Germanic Philology* (Apr. 1971), 70:220-29

Linke, Hansjürgen, "Das Los des Menschen in den Cuchulain Drama; Zum 100. Geburtstag von W. B. Yeats", *Die Neueren Sprachen* (1965), 15:253-68

Moore, John Rees, *Masks of Love and Death; Yeats as Dramatist*. 1971. Pp. 210-26

Popkin, Henry, "Yeats as a Dramatist", *Tulane Drama Review*, 3:73-82, 1959

Scanlon, Sister Aloyse, "The Sustained Metaphor in 'The Only Jealousy of Emer'", *Modern Drama*, 7:273-77, 1964

Sharp, William L., "W. B. Yeats: A Poet Not in the Theatre", *Tulane Drama Review*, 4:62-82, 1959

Vendler, Helen Hennessey, "Yeats's Changing Metaphors for the Otherworld", *Modern Drama*, 7:308-21, 1964

Wells, Henry W., *The Classical Drama of the Orient*. 1965. Pp. 315-16

Wilson, F. A. C., "Yeats and Hauptmann", *Southern Review* (Australia), 1:69-73, 1963

The Player Queen, 1919

Baumgarten M., "Body's Image; 'Yerma', 'The Player Queen' and the Upright Posture", *Comparative Drama* (1974), 8:290-99

Becker, William, "The Mask Mocked; Or Farce and the Dialectic of Self", *Sewanee Review*, 61:82-108, 1953

Hinden, Michael, "Yeats's Symbolic Farce: 'The Player Queen'", *Modern Drama* (1971), 14:441-48

Moore, John R., "The Janus Face; Yeats's Player Queen'", *Sewanee Review* (1968), 76:608-30

_____ , *Masks of Love and Death; Yeats as Dramatist*. 1971. Pp. 164-92

Newton, Norman, "Yeats as Dramatist: 'The Player Queen'", *Essays in Criticism* (Oxford), 8:269-84, 1958

Roy, Emil, *British Drama since Shaw*. 1972. Pp. 44-47

Vendler, Helen Hennessey, "Yeats's Changing Metaphors for the Otherworld", *Modern Drama*, 7:308-21, 1964

Webster, Brenda S., *Yeats; A Psychoanalytic Study*. 1973. Pp. 114-36

Young, Stark, "The Player Queen", *New Republic*, 36:257, Oct. 31, 1923

Purgatory, 1938

Baksi, Pronoti, "The Noh and the Yeatsian Synthesis", *Review of English Literature*, 6:34-43, 1965

Brogunier, Joseph, "Expiation in Yeats's Late Plays", *Drama Survey* (1966), 5:24-38

Clark, David R., "W. B. Yeats and the Drama of Perception", *Arizona Quarterly* (1964), 20:127-41

Collins, James A., "The Dramatic Verse in 'Purgatory'", *Literary Half-Yearly* (Jan. 1969), 10:91-98

Gaskell, Ronald, "Purgatory", *Modern Drama*, 4:397-401, 1962

McGrath, Francis C., III, "Heroic Aestheticism: W. B. Yeats and the Heritage of Walter Pater", *Dissertation Abstracts International* (1974), 34:5981A

Mercier, Vivian, "In Defense of Yeats as a Dramatist", *Modern Drama*, 8:161-66, 1965

Modern Drama, 7:351-56, 1964

Moore, John Rees, *Masks of Love and Death; Yeats as Dramatist.* 1971. Pp. 310-28

————— , "An Old Man's Tragedy—Yeats's 'Purgatory' ", *Modern Drama*, 5:440-50, 1963

Pearce, Donald R., "Yeats's Last Plays; An Interpretation", *Journal of English Literary History* (ELH), 18:67-76, 1951

Schmitt, Natalie C., "Curing Oneself of the Work of Time: W. B. Yeats's 'Purgatory' ", *Comparative Drama* (1973), 7:310-33

Vanderwerken, David L., " 'Purgatory': Yeats's Modern Tragedy", *Colby Library Quarterly* (1974), 10:259-69

Warschausky, Sidney, "Yeats's Purgatorial Plays", *Modern Drama*, 7:278-86, 1964

Webster, Brenda S., *Yeats; A Psychoanalytic Study.* 1973. Pp. 157-64

The Resurrection, 1934

Babu, M. Sathya, "Treatment of Christianity in William Butler Yeats' 'The Resurrection' ", *Wisconsin Studies in Literature* (1968), 5:53-63

Baird, Sister Mary Julian, "A Play on the Death of God: The Irony of Yeats's 'The Resurrection' ", *Modern Drama* (1967), 10:79-86

Baksi, Pronoti, "The Noh and the Yeatsian Synthesis", *Review of English Literature*, 6:34-43, 1965

Moore, John Rees, *Masks of Love and Death; Yeats as Dramatist.* 1971. Pp. 249-58

Ure, Peter, "Yeats's Christian Mystery Plays", *Review of English Studies*, n. s. 11:171-82, 1960

The Shadowy Waters, 1904

Bushrui, S. B., *Yeats's Verse Plays; The Revisions, 1900-1910.* 1965. Pp. 1-38

Krans, Horatio Sheafe, *William Butler Yeats and the Irish Revival.* 1905. Pp. 129-33

Malone, Andrew E., *The Irish Drama.* 1965. Pp. 140-41

Moore, John Rees, *Masks of Love and Death; Yeats as Dramatist.* 1971. Pp. 76-83

Parkinson, Thomas, "W. B. Yeats: A Poet's Stagecraft, 1899-1911", *Journal of English Literary History* (ELH), 17:136-160, 1950

Sidnell, M. J., "Manuscript Versions of Yeats's 'The Shadowy Water'; An Abbreviated Description and Chronology of the Papers Relating to the Play in the National Library of Ireland", *Papers of the Bibliographical Society of America* (1968), 62:39-57

Storer, Edward, "Dramatists Today", *Living Age*, 281:329-32, 1914

Webster, Brenda S. *Yeats; A Psychoanalytic Study.* 1973. Pp. 38-61

————— , "Yeats' 'The Shadowy Waters': Oral Motifs and Identity in the Drafts", *American Imago* (1971), 28:3-16

The Words Upon the Windowpane, 1930

Brogunier, Joseph, "Expiation in Yeats's Late Plays", *Drama Survey* (1966), 5:24-38

Clark, David R., "W. B. Yeats and the Drama of Perception", *Arizona Quarterly* (1964), 20:127-41

Haerdter, Von Michael, "William Butler Yeats—Irisches Theater Zwischen Symbolismus und Expressionismus", *Maske und Kothurn* (1965), 11:30-42

Moore, John Rees, *Masks of Love and Death; Yeats as Dramatist.* 1971. Pp. 258-67

Rogal, Samuel J., "Keble's Hymn and Yeats's 'The Words Upon the Window Pane'", *Modern Drama* (1973), 16:87-89

Roy, Emil, *British Drama since Shaw*. 1972. Pp. 47-49

Warschausky, Sidney, "Yeats's Purgatorial Plays", *Modern Drama*, 7:278-86, 1964

WILLIAM BUTLER YEATS AND LADY GREGORY

Deirdre, 1906

Baksi, Pronoti, "The Noh and the Yeatsian Synthesis", *Review of English Literature*, 6:34-43, 1965

Bushrui, S., B., *Yeats's Verse Plays; The Revisions, 1900-1910*. 1965. Pp. 120-58

Clark, David Ridgley, "W. B. Yeats's 'Deirdre': The Rigour of Logic", *Dublin Magazine*, 33:13-21, 1958

Fackler, Herbert V., "W. B. Yeats' 'Deirdre': Intensity by Condensation", *Forum* (Houston) (1968), 6 pt. 3:43-46

Haerdter, Von Michael, "William Butler Yeats—Irisches Theater Zwischen Symbolismus und Expressionismus", *Maske und Kothurn* (1965), 11:30-42

Hoffmann, Gerhard, "Die Funktion der Lieder in Yeats Dramen", *Anglia; Zeitschrift für Englische Philologie* (1971), 89:87-116

Oppel, Horst, *Das Moderne Englische Drama; Interpretationen*. 1963. Pp. 62-86

Popkin, Henry, "Yeats as Dramatist", *Tulane Drama Review*, 3:73-82, 1959

Reiman, Donald H., "Yeats's 'Deirdre'", *English Studies*, 42:218-32, 1961

Slattery, Margaret Price, "'Deirdre': The 'Mingling of Contraries' in Plot and Symbolism", *Modern Drama* (Feb. 1969), 11:400-03

Ure, Peter, "Yeats's 'Deirdre'", *English Studies*, 42:218-30, 1961

Vendler, Helen Hennessey, "Yeats's Changing Metaphors for the Otherworld", *Modern Drama*, 7:308-21, 1964

Wickstrom, Gordon M., "The Deirdre Plays of W. B. Yeats and Synge: Patterns of Irish Exile", *Dissertation Abstracts* (1969), 29:4027A

King Oedipus, 1926

Arts and Decoration, 38:58, March, 1933

Saturday Review of Literature, 9:402, Jan. 28, 1933

Grab, Frederic D., "Yeats's 'King Oedipus'", *Journal of English and Germanic Philology* (1972), 71:336-54

King's Threshold, 1903

Beerbohm, Max, *Around Theatres*. 1953. Pp. 314-19

Bushrui, S. B., *Yeats's Verse Plays; The Revisions, 1900-1910*. 1965. Pp. 73-105.

Byars, John A., "Yeats's Introduction of the Heroic Type", *Modern Drama*, 8:409-18, 1966

Friedman, Barton R., "Under a Leprous Moon: Action and Image in 'The King's Threshold'", *Arizona Quarterly* (1970), 26:39-53

Malone, Andrew E., *The Irish Drama*. 1965. Pp. 138-40

Moore, John Rees, *Masks of Love and Death; Yeats as Dramatist*. 1971. Pp. 88-103

Webster, Brenda S., *Yeats, A Psychoanalytic Study*. 1973. Pp. 62-72

On Baile's Strand, 1904

Bushrui, S. B., *Yeats's Verse Plays; The Revisions, 1900-1910.* 1965. Pp. 39-72

Byars, John A., "Yeats's Introduction of the Heroic Type", *Modern Drama*, 8:409-18, 1966

Friedman, Barton, "'On Baile's Strand' to 'At the Hawk's Well': Staging the Deeps of the Mind", *Journal of Modern Literature* (1975), 4:625-50

Gill, Stephen M., *Six Symbolist Plays of Yeats.* 1971. Pp. 33-36 and 71-73

Jochum, K. P. S., "Yeats' Last Play", *Journal of English and Germanic Philology* (Apr. 1971), 70:220-29

Krans, Horatio Sheafe. *William Butler Yeats and the Irish Revival.* 1905. Pp. 133-46

Linke, Hansjürgen, "Das Los des Menschen in den Cuchulain Drama; Zum 100. Geburtstag von W. B. Yeats", *Die Neueren Sprachen* (1965), 15:253-68

McGrath, Francis C., III, "Heroic Aestheticism: W. B. Yeats and the Heritage of Walter Pater", *Dissertation Abstracts International* (1974), 34:5981A

Moore, John Rees, *Masks of Love and Death; Yeats as Dramatist.* 1971. Pp. 104-27

Parkinson, Thomas, "W. B. Yeats: A Poet's Stagecraft, 1899-1911", *Journal of English Literary History* (ELH), 17:136-60, 1950

Schroeter, James, "Yeats and the Tragic Tradition", *Southern Review* (L. S. U.) (1965), 1:835-46

Storer, Edward, "Dramatists Today", *Living Age*, 281:329-32, 1914

Suss, Irving David, "Yeatsian Drama and the Dying Hero", *South Atlantic Quarterly*, 54:369-80, 1955

Webster, Brenda S., *Yeats; A Psychoanalytic Study.* 1973. Pp. 164-68

Unicorn from the Stars, 1908

Bryan, Robert A., Alton C. Morris, and A. A. Murphree and Aubrey L. Williams, eds., *All These to Teach; Essays in Honor of C. A. Robertson.* 1965. Pp. 224-36

New Statesman and Nation, 18:821, Dec. 9, 1939

Suss, Irving David, "Yeatsian Drama and the Dying Hero", *South Atlantic Quarterly*, 54:369-80, 1955

Webster, Brenda S., *Yeats; A Psychoanalytic Study.* 1973. Pp. 81-85

WILLIAM BUTLER YEATS, LADY GREGORY AND
DOUGLAS HYDE

Where There is Nothing, 1902

Thatcher, David S., "Yeats' Repudiation of 'Where There is Nothing'", *Modern Drama* (Sept. 1971), 14:127-36

Webster, Brenda S., *Yeats; A Psychoanalytic Study.* 1973. Pp. 71-81

YORK PLAYS

SEE

MIRACLE, MORALITY AND MYSTERY PLAYS

LIST OF BOOKS INDEXED

Abel, Lionel, *Metatheatre: A New View of Dramatic Form.* N.Y., Hill and Wang, 1963

Abraham, Claude, *Pierre Corneille.* N.Y., Twayne Pubs. 1972.

Actes du VI Congrès International de Langue et Littérature d'Oc et d'Etudes Franco-Provencales. Montpelier, Centre d'Estudis Occitans Revue des Langues Romanes. 1971.

Adams, Elsie B., *Bernard Shaw and the Aesthetes.* Ohio State Univ. Pr. 1971

Adams, Henry H. and Hathaway, Baxter, eds., *Dramatic Essays of the Neo-Classic Age.* N.Y., Columbia Univ. Pr. 1950

Adams, Henry H., *English Domestic or Homiletic Tragedy, 1575-1642, (Studies in English and Comparative Literature, #159).* N.Y., Columbia Univ. Pr. 1943

Adams, Robert M., *Strains of Discord: Studies in Literary Openness.* Ithaca, N.Y., Cornell Univ. Pr. 1958.

Agate, James Evershed, *Alarums and Excursions.* N.Y., Doran. 1922.

_____ , *English Dramatic Critics: An Anthology, 1660-1932.* N.Y., Hill and Wang. 1958.

Albright, Daniel, *The Myth Against Myth; A Study of Yeats's Imagination in Old Age.* London, Oxford Univ. Pr. 1972.

Aldrich, Richard, *Musical Discourse from the New York Times.* N.Y., Oxford Univ. Pr. 1928.

Aldrich, Thomas B., *Ponkapog Papers.* N.Y., Houghton. 1907.

Allen, Don Cameron, ed., *Studies in Honor of T. W. Baldwin.* Urbana, Univ. of Illinois Pr. 1958.

Allen, Rupert C., *Psyche and Symbol in the Theater of Federico Garcia Lorca.* Austin, Univ. of Texas Pr. 1974.

Allsop, Kenneth, *Angry Decade: A Survey of the Cultural Revolt of the 1950's.* N.Y., British Book Centre. 1959.

Alvarez, A., *Samuel Beckett.* N.Y., Viking Pub. Co. 1973.

Anderson, M. J., ed., *Classical Drama and Its Influence; Essays Presented to H. D. F. Kitto, B.A., D.-es-L., F.B.A., F.R.S.L., Pro. Emeritus of Greek at the University of Bristol.* Toronto, Canada, Methuen & Co., Ltd., 1965.

Anderson, Quenton, and Mazzeo, Joseph A., eds., *The Proper Study: Essays on Western Classics.* N.Y., St. Martin's Pr. 1962.

Angermeyer, Hans Christoph, *Zuschauer Im Drama.* Frankfurt Am Main, Athenäum. 1971.

Anniversary Papers, By Colleagues and Pupils of George Lyman Kittredge, Presented June, 1913. Boston, Ginn Pub. 1913.

Approaches: Essais sur la Poesie Moderne de Langue Francaise (Annales de la Faculte des Lettres et Sciences Humaines de Nice 15), Paris, Les Belles Lettres. 1971.

Aquila; Chestnut Hill Studies in Modern Languages and Literatures. vol. 1. The Hagues, M. Nijohoff Boekhandelen. 1968.

Armstrong, William A., ed., *Experimental Drama.* London, Bell & Son. 1963.

Ashley, Leonard R. N., *Colley Cibber.* N.Y., Twayne Pubs. 1965.

Atkins, J. W. H., *English Literary Criticism: Seventeenth and Eighteenth Centuries.* London, Methuen. 1951.

Auden, Wystan H., *The Dyer's Hand and Other Essays.* N.Y., Random House. 1962.

Bahner, Werner, ed., *Beiträge zum Französischen Aufklärung und zur Spanischen Literatur: Festgabe für Werner Krauss zum 70. Geburtstag.* Berlin, Akadamie. 1971.

Bailey, John Cann, *Continuity of Letters.* London, Oxford Univ. Pr. 1923.

Baker, Howard, *Introduction to Tragedy: A Study in a Development of Form in "Gorboduc", "The Spanish Tragedy", and "Titus Andronicus".* N.Y., Russell and Russell. 1965.

Baldini, Gabriele, *John Webster e il Linguaggio della Tragedia.* Rome, Edizioni dell 'Ateneo. 1953.

Baldry, H. C., *The Greek Tragic Theatre.* London, Chatto and Windus. 1971.

Banásević, Nikolas, ed., *Actes du V Congres d l'Association Internationale de Littérature Comparée, Belgrade, 1967.* Belgrade, Swets and Zeitlinger. 1969.

Baring, Maurice, *Punch and Judy and Other Essays.* N.Y., Heinemann. 1924.

Barker, Richard Hindry, *Thomas Middleton.* N.Y., Columbia Univ. Pr. 1958.

Barnard, G. C., *Samuel Beckett; A New Approach.* London, J. M. Dent & Sons. 1970.

Barnes, Hazel E., *Sartre.* London, Quartet Books. 1974.

Barr, Alan P., *Victorian Stage Pulpiteer; Bernard Shaw's Crusade.* Athens, Univ. of Georgia Pr. 1973.

Barthes, Roland, *Critical Essays.* Northwestern Univ. Pr. 1972.

Barzun, Jacques, *Energies of Art: Studies of Authors, Classic and Modern.* N.Y., Harper. 1956.

Bassan, Fernande and Sylvie Chevalley, *Alexandre Dumas, Père; et la Comédie Francaise.* Paris, Lettres Modernes. 1972.

Bauer, Gerhard and Sibylle, ed., *Gotthold Ephraim Lessing.* Darmstadt, Wissenschaftl. Buchgesellschaft. 1968.

Bauer, Sibylle, ed. *Hugo von Hoffmannsthall.* Darmstadt, Wissenschaftl. Buchgesellschaft. 1968

Bauland, Peter, *The Hooded Eagle: Modern German Drama on the New York Stage.* Syracuse, N.Y., Syracuse Univ. Pr. 1968.

Baxter, K. M., *Speak What We Feel: A Christian Looks at the Contemporary Theatre.* London, SCM Pr. 1964.

Bayerschmidt, Carl F. and Erik J. Friis, eds., *Scandinavian Studies; Essays Presented to Dr. Henry Goddard Leach on the Occasion of His 85th Birthday.* Seattle, Univ. of Washington Pr. 1965.

Beaty, John O. and others, eds., *Facts and Ideas for Students of English Composition.* Crofts. 1930.

Beck, Lily M. A., *The Gallants.* Boston, Little, Brown, Inc. 1924.

Beckerman, Bernard, *Dynamics of Drama; Theory and Method of Analysis.* N.Y., A. A. Knopf, Inc. 1970.

Beckermann, Thomas, *Uber Max Frisch.* Frankfurt am Main, Suhrkamp. 1971.

Beckett at 60: A Festschrift. Calder & Boyars, Ltd. 1967.

Beebe, Maurice, *Ivory Towers and Sacred Founts; The Artist as Hero in Fiction from Goethe to Joyce.* N.Y., New York Univ. Pr. 1964.

Beerbohm, Max, *Around Theatres.* Elmsford, N.Y., British Book Centre. 1953.

Behler, Ernst, *Die Europaische Romantik.* Frankfurt, Athenäum. 1972.

Belli, Angela, *Ancient Greek Myths and Modern Drama; A Study in Continuity.* N.Y., New York Univ. Pr. 1971.

Belloc, Hilaire, *On.* N.Y., Doran Pubs. 1923.

Bennett, Arnold, *Books and Persons: Being Comments on a Past Epoch.* London: Chatto. 1917.

Bennett, James O., *Much Loved Books: Best Sellers of the Ages.* N.Y., Liveright Pubs. 1927.

Bennett, Josephine W.; Cargill, O., Hale, Vernon, eds., *Studies in the English Renaissance Drama: In Memory of Karl Julius Holzknecht.* N.Y., New York Univ. Pr. 1959.

Benseler, Frank, ed., *Festschrift zum Achzigsten Geburtstag von Georg Lukács.* Neuwied, Luchterhand. 1965.

Bentley, Eric R., *Dramatic Event: An American Chronicle.* N.Y., Horizon Pr. 1954.

_____ , *In Search of Theatre.* N.Y., A. A. Knopf, Inc. 1953.

_____ , *The Theatre of Commitment and Other Essays on the Drama in Our Society.* N.Y., Atheneum Pubs. 1967.

_____ , *Theatre of War; Comments on Thirty-Two Occasions.* N.Y., Viking Pub. Co. 1972.

Bergonzi, Bernard, *T. S. Eliot.* N.Y., Macmillan Co. 1972.

Bergonzi, Bernard, ed., *The Twentieth Century.* (History of Literature in the English Language), Vol. 7. London, Barrie and Jenkins. 1970.

Bergstraesser, A., *Goethe and the Modern Age: The International Convocation at Aspen, Colorado, 1949.* Chicago, Ill., Regnery. 1950.

Berlin, Norman, *Thomas Sackville.* N.Y., Twayne Pub. Co. 1974.

Bermel, Albert, *Contradictory Characters; An Interpretation of Modern Theatre.* N.Y., Dutton Pub. Co. 1973.

Berry, Ralph, *The Art of John Webster.* London, Oxford Univ. Pr. 1972.

Berst, Charles A., *Bernard Shaw and the Art of Drama.* Urbana, Ill., Univ. of Illinois Pr. 1973.

Best, Otto F., *Peter Weiss; Vom Existentialischen Drama zum Maristischen Welttheater.* Munchen, Francke. 1971.

Besterman, Theodore, ed., *Studies on Voltaire and the 18th Century. Transactions of the Second International Congress on the Enlightenment.* 4 vols. Geneve: Droz. 1967.

Bevington, David, M., *From Mankind to Marlowe: Growth of Structure in the Popular Drama of Tudor England.* Cambridge, Mass., Harvard Univ. Pr. 1962.

Bhatti, Anil, ed., *Language and Literature in Society; Journal of the School of Languages.* New Delhi, Centre of German Studies, Jawaharlal Nehru Univ. 1973-74.

Bigsby, C. W. E., *Confrontation and Commitment; A Study of Contemporary American Drama, 1959-1966.* Columbia, Mo., Univ. of Missouri Pr. 1968.

Binger, Norman H. and A. Wayne Wonderley, eds., *Studies in Nineteenth Century and Early Twentieth Century German Literature; Essays in Honor of Paul K. Whitaker.* Lexington, Apra Pr. 1974.

Block, Anita C., *Changing Worlds in Plays and Theatre.* Boston, Little, Brown, Inc. 1939.

Block, Haskell M., Salinger, Herman, eds., *Creative Vision: Modern European Writers on Their Art.* N.Y., Grove. 1960.

Bluestone, Max and Norman Rabkin, eds., *Shakespeare's Contemporaries; Modern Studies in English Renaissance Drama*. 2nd ed. Englewood Cliffs, N.J., Prentice Hall. 1970.

Boas, Frederick S., *An Introduction to Stuart Drama*. N.Y., Oxford Univ. Pr. 1946.

——————— , *University Drama in the Tudor Age*. N.Y., Benjamin Blom, Inc. 1965.

Bogard, Travis and Oliver, William I., eds., *Modern Drama: Essays in Criticism*. London, Oxford Univ. Pr. 1965.

Bogard, Travis, *The Tragic Satire of John Webster*. Los Angeles, Univ. of California Pr. 1955.

Bonnard, A., *Greek Civilization: From Euripides to Alexandria*. N.Y., Macmillan. 1961.

Bourgeois, Maurice, *John Millington Synge and the Irish Theatre*. Bronx, N.Y., Blom. 1965.

Bowers, Fredson T., *Elizabethan Revenge Tragedy; 1587-1642*. Gloucester, Mass., Peter Smith. 1959.

Boyer, Clarence V., *The Villain as Hero in Elizabethan Tragedy*. N.Y., Russell & Russell. 1964.

Bradbrook, Muriel C., *The Growth and Structure of Elizabethan Comedy*. London, Chatto and Windus. 1955.

——————— , *Literature in Action; Studies in Continental and Commonwealth Society*. Barnes and Noble. 1972.

——————— , *Themes and Conventions of Elizabethan Tragedy*. London, Cambridge Univ. Pr. 1957.

Brahmer, Mieczyslav, Stanislav Helsztynski and Julian Krzyzanowski, *Studies in Language in Honour of Margaret Schlauch*. Warsaw, Polish Scientific Pub. 1966.

Brandes, George, *William Shakespeare: A Critical Study*, vol. 1. N.Y., Frederick Ungar Pub. Co., Inc. 1963.

Brandt, Per Aage, *Tekstens Teater; Bidrag til en Kritik af den Poetiske Økonomi*. Copenhagen, Borgen. 1972.

Bredvold, Louis I., et al, *Essays and Studies in English and Comparative Literature by Members of the English Department of the University of Michigan*. Ann Arbor: Univ. of Michigan Pr. 1932.

Bree, Germaine, *Literature and Society*. Lincoln, Neb., Univ. of Nebraska Pr. 1964.

Brereton, Geoffrey, *Principles of Tragedy; A Rational Examination of the Tragic Concept in Life and Literature*. Coral Gables, Univ. of Miami Pr. 1968.

Bridges-Adams, William, *Irresistible Theatre*. N.Y., World Pub. Co. 1957.

Brinkmann, Richard, et al, *Deutsche Literatur und Französische Revolution; Sieben Studien*. Gottingen, Vandenhoeck & Ruprecht. 1974.

Brinnin, John Malcolm, ed., *A Casebook on Dylan Thomas*. N.Y., Thomas Y. Crowell Co. 1960.

Brittin, Norman A., *Thomas Middleton*. N.Y., Twayne Pub., Inc. 1972.

Brockett, Oscar G., *Perspectives on Contemporary Theatre*. Baton Rouge, La., Louisiana State Univ. Pr. 1971.

Brockett, Oscar G., ed., *Studies in Theatre and Drama; Essays in Honor of Hubert C. Heffner*. N.Y., Humanities Pr. 1973.

Brockway, Wallace and Weinstock, Herbert, *Opera: A History of Its Creation and Performance*. N.Y., Simon and Schuster. 1941.

Bronwon, B. H., and others, *Studies in the Comic,* (Univ. of California Publications in English, vol. 8). Berkeley, Univ. of California Pr. 1941.

Brooke, Rupert, *John Webster and the Elizabethan Drama.* N.Y., John Lane Co. 1916

Brooks, Cleanth, *A Shaping Joy; Studies in the Writer's Craft.* Harcourt Pub. Co. 1972.

Brooks, Cleanth, ed., *Tragic Themes in Western Literature.* New Haven, Conn., Yale Univ. Pr. 1955.

Brother Gregory, F. S. C., *Catholicism in Schiller's Dramas.* N.Y., New York Univ. Pr. 1949.

Brower, Reuben, et al., *I. A. Richards; Essays in His Honor.* N.Y., Oxford Univ. Pr. 1973.

Brower, Reuben Arthur, *Mirror on Mirror; Translation, Imitation, Parody.* (Harvard Studies in Comparative Literature 33), Harvard Univ. Pr. 1974.

Brown, F. Andrew, *Gotthold Ephraim Lessing.* N.Y., Twayne Pub. Co. 1971.

Brown, John M., *Broadway in Review.* N.Y., W. W. Norton and Co., Inc. 1940.

—————— , *Dramatic Personae: A Retrospective Show.* N.Y., The Viking Pr., Inc. 1963.

—————— , *Seeing Things.* N.Y., McGraw-Hill Book Co. 1946.

—————— , *Two on the Aisle: Ten Years of the American Theatre in Performance.* N.Y., W. W. Norton and Co., Inc. 1938.

Brown, John Russell and Bernard Harris, ed., *Elizabethan Theatre.* (Stratford Upon Avon Studies, #9), London, Edward Arnold. 1966.

—————— , *Jacobean Theatre* (Stratford-on-Avon Studies). N.Y., St. Martin's Pr. 1960.

Brown, John Russell, ed., *Modern British Dramatists; A Collection of Critical Essays.* Englewood Cliffs, N.J., Prentice-Hall, Inc. 1968.

Brown, John Russell, *Theatre Language; A Study of Arden, Osborne, Pinter, and Wesker.* N.Y., Taplinger Co. 1972.

Browne, E. Martin, *The Making of T. S. Eliot's Plays.* London, Cambridge Univ. Pr. 1969.

Brustein, Robert, *The Culture Watch; Essays on Theatre and Society, 1969-1974.* N.Y., A. A. Knopf. 1975.

Brustein, Robert Sanford, *Seasons of Discontent; Dramatic Opinions, 1959-1965.* N.Y., Simon and Schuster. 1965.

—————— , *The Theatre of Revolt; An Approach to the Modern Drama.* Boston, Little, Brown & Co. 1964.

—————— , *The Third Theatre.* N.Y., A. A. Knopf, Inc. 1969.

Bryan, Robert A., Alton C. Morris, A. A. Murphree, and Aubrey L. Williams, eds., *All These to Teach; Essays in Honor of C. A. Robertson.* Gainesville, Fla., Univ. of Florida Pr. 1965.

Bryant, J. A., Jr., *The Compassionate Satirist; Ben Jonson and His Imperfect World.* Athens, Univ. of Georgia Pr. 1973.

Buehne, Sheema Z., James L. Hodge, and Lucille B. Pinto, eds., *Helen Adolf Festschrift.* N.Y., Frederick Ungar Pub. Co. 1968.

Burckhart, Sigurd, *The Drama of Language; Essays on Goethe and Kleist.* Baltimore, Johns Hopkins Univ. Pr. 1970.

Burdett, Osbert, *Critical Essays.* London, Faber and Faber, Ltd. 1925.

Burke, Kenneth, *Language as Symbolic Action; Essays on Life, Literature and Method.* Berkeley, Calif., Univ. of California Pr. 1966.

Burkman, Katherine H., *The Dramatic World of Harold Pinter; Its Basis in*

Ritual. Ohio State Univ. Pr. 1971.

Burnett, Anne Pippin, *Catastrophe Survived; Euripides' Plays of Mixed Reversals.* London, Oxford, Clarendon Pr. 1971.

Burnshaw, Stanley, ed., *Varieties of Literary Experience: Eighteen Essays in World Literature.* N.Y., New York Univ. Pr. 1962.

Burton, Richard, *Little Essays in Literature and Life.* N.Y., Appleton-Century-Crofts. 1914.

Burton, Thomas G., ed., *Essays in Memory of Christine Burleson in Language and Literature by former Colleagues and Students.* Johnson City, East Tennessee State Univ. Pr. 1969.

Bushrui, S. B., ed., *A Centenary Tribute to John Millington Synge, 1871-1909.* N.Y., Barnes and Noble. 1972.

——————— , *Yeats's Verse Plays: The Revisions, 1900-1910.* N.Y., Oxford Univ. Pr. 1965.

Cairns, Huntington and others, *Invitation to Learning.* N.Y., Random House. 1941.

California University, Dept. of English, *Essays Critical and Historical Dedicated to Lily B. Campbell, by Members of the Department of English.* Berkeley, Univ. of California Pr. 1950.

Cambon, Glauco, ed., *Pirandello; A Collection of Critical Essays.* Englewood Cliffs, N.J., Prentice-Hall, Inc. 1967.

Camille, Georgette, et al, *Le Théâtre Elizabethain.* Paris, Les Cahiers du Sud et Literairie, J. Corti. 1940.

Canfield, Mary C., *Grotesques and Other Reflections.* N.Y., Harper and Row Pubs. 1927.

Cargill, Oscar; Fagin, Nathan B., and Fisher, William, eds., *O'Neill and His Plays: Four Decades of Criticism.* N.Y., New York Univ. Pr. 1961.

Cargo, Robert T. and Emanuel J. Mickel, Jr., eds., *Studies in Honor of Alfred G. Engstrom.* Chapel Hill, Univ. of North Carolina Pr. 1972.

Carrere, Felix, *Le Théâtre de Thomas Kyd; Contributions à l'Etude du Drame Elizabethain.* Toulouse, E. Privat. 1951.

Carter, Alan, *John Osborne.* Edinburgh, Oliver and Boyd. 1969.

A Celebration of Ben Jonson; Papers Presented at the University of Toronto in October, 1972. Toronto, Univ. of Toronto Pr. 1973.

Chandler, Frank W., *Modern Continental Playwrights.* N.Y., Harper and Row Pubs. 1931.

Channing-Pearce, Melville, *Terrible Crystal: Studies in Kierkegaard and Modern Christianity.* London, Oxford Univ. Pr. 1941.

Chapman, John J., *Memories and Milestones.* Moffat Pub. 1915.

Chesterton, Gilbert K., *Miscellany of Men.* N.Y., Dodd, Mead & Co. 1912.

——————— , *Sidelights of New London and Newer New York and Other Essays.* N.Y., Dodd, Mead & Co. 1932.

——————— , *Uses of Diversity: A Book of Essays.* N.Y., Dodd, Mead & Co. 1921.

Chevigny, Bell J., *Twentieth Century Interpretations of "Endgame".* Englewood Cliffs, N.J., Prentice Hall. 1969.

Chiari, J., *Landmarks of Contemporary Drama.* London, Herbert Jenkins. 1965.

Chiari, Joseph, *T. S. Eliot; Poet and Dramatist.* N.Y., Barnes and Noble. 1972.

Chiarini, Paolo, et al, eds., *Miscellaneq di Studi in Onore di Bonaventura Tecchi.* 2 vols. Roma, Edizioni dell Ateneo. 1969.

Classical Studies in Honor of Charles Forster Smith. Madison, Univ. of Wisconsin Pr. 1919.

Classical Studies in Honor of W. A. Oldfather. Urbana, Univ. of Illinois Pr. 1943.

Clay, James H. and Daniel Krempel, *The Theatrical Image.* N.Y., McGraw-Hill Book Co. 1967.

Clurman, Harold, *The Divine Pastime; Theatre Essays.* Macmillan Pub. Co. 1974.

—————————, *Lies Like Truth: Theatre Reviews and Essays.* N.Y., Macmillan. 1958.

—————————, *The Naked Image: Observations on the Modern Theatre.* N.Y., Macmillan. 1966.

Clutton-Brock, Arthur, *Essays on Literature and Life.* N.Y., E. P. Dutton & Co. 1927.

Cobb, Carl W., *Federico Garcia Lorca.* N.Y., Twayne Pub. Co. 1967.

Coe, Richard N., *Ionesco; A Study of His Plays.* London, Methuen & Co. 1971.

—————————, *The Vision of Jean Genêt.* N.Y., Grove Pr., Inc. 1968.

Cohen, Robert, *Giraudoux; Three Faces of Destiny.* Chicago, Univ. of Chicago Pr. 1968.

Cohn, Ruby, *Currents in Contemporary Drama.* Bloomington, Indiana Univ. Pr. 1969.

Colby, Frank Moore, *Constrained Attitudes.* N.Y., Dodd, Mead & Co. 1910.

Cole, Douglas, *Suffering and Evil in the Plays of Christopher Marlowe.* Princeton, N.J., Princeton Univ. Pr. 1962.

Cole, Toby, and Chinoy, Helen K., eds., *Directing the Play: A Source Book of Stagecraft.* Indianapolis, Ind., Bobbs. 1953.

—————————, *Directors on Directing: A Source Book of the Modern Theatre,* Rev. ed., Indianapolis, Ind., Bobbs. 1963.

—————————, *Playwrights on Playwriting: The Meaning and Making of Modern Drama From Ibsen to Ionesco.* N.Y., Hill and Wang. 1960.

Colles, Henry C., *Essays and Lectures: With a Memoir of the Author H. J. C.* London, Oxford Univ. Pr. 1945.

Colleville, Maurice, et als, *Un Dialogue des Nations: Albert Fuchs zum 70. Geburtstag.* Paris, Klincksieck. 1967.

Cooper, Lane, ed., *Greek Genius and its Influences: Select Essays and Extracts.* New Haven, Conn., Yale Univ. Pr. 1917.

Cope, Jackson I., *The Theater and the Dream; From Metaphor to Form in Renaissance Drama.* Baltimore, Md., Johns Hopkins Univ. Pr. 1973.

Cordle, Thomas, *André Gide.* N.Y., Twayne Pub. Co. 1969.

Corrigan, Robert W. and James L. Rosenberg, eds., *The Art of the Theatre: A Critical Anthology of Drama.* San Francisco, Calif., Chandler Pub. Co. 1964.

Corrigan, Robert W., *The Theatre in Search of a Fix:* Delacorte Pr. 1973.

Corvin, Michel, *Le Theatre Nouveau en France.* Paris, Presses Universitaires de France. 1963.

Courthion, Pierre, *Romanticism.* Geneva, Switzerland, Skira. 1961.

Covatta, Anthony, *Thomas Middleton's City Comedies.* Lewisburg, Bucknell Univ. Pr. 1973.

Cowasjee, Saros, *Sean O'Casey, The Man Behind the Play.* Edinburgh, Scotland, Oliver and Boyd. 1963.

Cowell, Raymond, *Twelve Modern Dramatists.* Pergamon Press, Ltd. 1967.

Cox, C. B., ed., *Dylan Thomas: A Collection of Critical Essays.* Englewood Cliffs, N.J., Prentice-Hall.n 1966.

Cox, C. B. and A. E. Dyson, eds., *The Twentieth Century Mind; History, Ideas and Literature in Britain.* London, Oxford Univ. Pr. 1792.

Cox, Cynthia, *The Real Figaro: The Extraordinary Career of Caron De Beaumarchais.* London, Longmans. 1962.

Craig, Hardin, ed., *Essays in Dramatic Literature; The Parrott Presentation Volume.* Princeton, N.J., Princeton Univ. Pr. 1935.

Creed, Howard, ed., *Essays in Honor of Richebourg Gaillard McWilliams.* Birmingham, Ala., Birmingham-Southern College. 1970.

Crosby, Donald H. and George C. Schoolfield, eds., *Studies in German Drama; A Festschrift in Honor of Walter Silz.* Chapel Hill, Univ. of North Carolina Pr. 1974.

Cunningham, John E., *Elizabethan and Early Stuart Drama.* Evans Bros., Ltd. 1965.

————————— , *Restoration Drama.* London, Evans Bros., Ltd. 1966.

Daiches, David, *More Literary Essays.* Chicago, Univ. of Chicago Pr. 1968.

Daniel, George B., ed., *Renaissance and Other Studies in Honor of William Leon Wyley.* Chapel Hill, N.C., Univ. of North Carolina Pr. 1968.

The Darker Vision of the Renaissance; Beyond the Fields of Reason. (UCLA Center for Medieval and Renaissance Studies; Contribution 6), Univ. of California Pr. 1974.

Darlington, William A., *Literature in the Theatre and Other Essays.* N.Y., Holt. 1925.

Davies, Walford, ed., *Dylan Thomas; New Critical Essays.* London, J. M. Dent and Sons. 1972.

De Laura, David J., ed., *Victorian Prose; A Guide to Research.* N.Y., Modern Language Assn. 1973.

Delavenay, Emile, *D. H. Lawrence; The Man and His Work; The Formative Years, 1885-1919.* Carbondale, Southern Illinois Univ. Pr. 1972.

DeLuna, Barbara N., *Jonson's Romish Plot: A Study of "Catiline" and Its Historical Context.* Oxford, Clarendon Pr. 1967.

Demetz, Peter, ed., *Brecht, A Collection of Critical Essays.* Englewood Cliffs, N.J., Prentice-Hall. 1962.

Demorest, Jean-Jacques, ed., *Studies in Seventeenth Century French Literature Presented to Morris Bishop.* Ithaca, Cornell Univ. Pr. 1962.

Department de Francais, Recherches et Travaux. Supp. au Bull. d'Information du Service de Documentation. Grenoble, Univ. de Grenoble. 1968.

Dervin, Daniel, *Bernard Shaw; A Psychological Study.* Lewisburg, Bucknell Univ. Pr. 1975.

Descotes, Maurice, *Les Grands Rôles du Théâtre de Jean Racine.* Paris, Presses Universitaires de France. 1957.

deSelincourt, Aubrey, *Six Great Playwrights.* London, Hamilton. 1960.

Deutung und Bedeutung; Studies in German Comparative Literature Presented to Karl-Werner Maurer, ed. by Brigette Schludermann. (De Proprietatibus Literarum, Indiana Univ. Series Maior 25), Mouton Pub. 1973.

The Dial: A Dial Miscellany, ed. by William Wasserstrom. Syracuse, N.Y., Syracuse Univ. Pr. 1963.

Dickinson, Hugh, *Myth on the Modern Stage.* Urbana, Ill., Univ. of Illinois Pr. 1969.

Donaldson, Ian, *The World Upside-Down; Comedy from Jonson to Fielding.* Oxford Univ. Pr. 1970.

Donnelly, Francis P., *Literature the Leading Educator.* London, Longmans. 1938.

Donoghue, Denis, *The Ordinary Universe; Soundings in Modern Literature.* N.Y., The Macmillan Co. 1968.

——————, *Third Voice: Modern British and American Verse Drama.* Princeton, Princeton Univ. Pr. 1959.

Donohue, Joseph Walter, *Dramatic Character in the English Romantic Age.* Princeton, N.J., Princeton Univ. Pr. 1970.

Dorenkamp, John H., ed., *Literary Studies; Essays in Memory of Francis A. Drumm.* Worcester, Mass., College of the Holy Cross. 1974.

Dorey, T. A. and Donald Reynolds Dudley, eds., *Roman Drama.* (Studies in Latin Literature and Its Influence). N.Y., Basic Books, Inc., Pubs. 1965.

Dort, Bernard, *Théâtre Réel, 1967-1970.* Paris, Editions du Seuil. 1971.

Douglas, Mary, ed., *Witchcraft, Confessions and Accusations.* (A.S.A. Monograph 9), N.Y., Barnes and Noble. 1970.

Downer, Alan S., ed., *The American Theater Today.* N.Y., Basic Books, Inc., Pubs. 1967.

Downs, Brian Westerdale, *Modern Norwegian Literature, 1870-1918.* Cambridge Univ. Pr. 1966.

Downs, Robert B., *Famous Books, Ancient and Medieval.* N.Y., Barnes and Noble. 1964.

——————, *Molders of the Modern Mind: One Hundred and Eleven Books that Shaped Western Civilization.* N.Y., Barnes and Noble. 1961.

Driver, Tom F., *Sense of History in Greek and Shakespearean Drama.* Boulder, Colorado Univ. Pr. 1960.

Duprey, Richard A., *Just Off the Aisle; The Ramblings of a Catholic Critic.* Westminster, Md., Newman Pr. 1962.

Durzak, Manfred, *Dürrenmatt, Frisch, Weiss; Deutsches Drama der Gegenwart Zwischen Kritik und Utopie.* Stuttgart, Philipp Reclam. 1972.

Durzak, Manfred, Eberhard Reichmann, und Ulrich Weisstein, eds., *Texte und Kontexte; Studien zur Deutschen und Vergleichenden Literaturwissenschaft; Festschrift für Norbert Fuerst zum 65. Geburtstag.* Bern, Franck. 1973.

Duthie, G. I., ed., *English Studies Today, Third Series; Lectures and Papers Read at the 5th Conference of the International Association Professors of English Held at Edinburgh and Glasgow August 1962.* Edinburgh, Edinburgh Univ. Pr. 1964.

Dvoretzky, Edward, *The Enigma of "Emilia Galotti".* The Hague, Netherlands, Nijhoff. 1963.

Edgar, Irving I., *Essays in English Literature and History.* N.Y., Philosophical Library. 1972.

Egan, Michael, ed., *Ibsen, the Critical Heritage.* London, Routledge and Kegan Paul. 1972.

Eliot, George, *Essays*, ed. by Thomas Pinney. Boulder, Colorado Univ. Pr. 1963.

Eliot in Perspective; A Symposium; ed. Graham Martin. N.Y., Humanities Pr. 1970.

Eliot, Thomas S., *Sacred Wood: Essays on Poetry and Criticism.* N.Y., A. A.

Knopf, Inc. 1921.

_____ *Selected Essays*, 1917-1932. N.Y., Harcourt. 1932.

Eliot, Thomas Stearns, *Selected Essays*. N.Y., Harcourt, Brace & Co. 1950.

Elizabethan Studies and Other Essays in Honor of George F. Reynolds, (Univ. of Colorado Studies in the Humanities, Ser. 3, vol. 2, #4). Boulder, Univ. of Colorado Pr. 1945.

The Elizabethan Theatre, V; Papers Given at the 5th International Conference on Elizabethan Theatre Held at the University of Waterloo, Ontario, in July, 1973. Archon Books. 1974.

Elledge, Scott and Schier, Ronald S., eds., *The Continental Model: Selected French Critical Essays of the Seventeenth Century in English Translation*. Minneapolis, Univ. of Minnesota Pr. 1960.

Ellis, Havelock, *Views and Reviews: A Selection of Uncollected Articles, 1884-1932*. Boston, Houghton. 1932.

Ellis, J. R., ed., *Australasian Universities Language and Literature Association; Proceedings and Papers of the 13th Congress Held at Monash University, 12-18 August, 1970*. Melbourne, Q.U.L.L.A. and Monash Univ. Pr. 1971.

Ellis, Stewart, *Mainly Victorian*. London, Hutchinson. 1925.

Ellis-Fermor, Una, *Jacobean Drama*. 4th rev. ed. London, Methuen & Co., Ltd. 1958.

Elwin, Malcolm, *Handbook of Restoration Drama*. Port Washington, N.Y., Kennikat Pr., Inc. 1966.

Empson-Fermor, Una, *Jacobean Drama*. London, Chatto & Windus. 1935.

Emrich, Wilhelm, *The Literary Revolution and Modern Society and Other Essays*. N.Y., F. Ungar Pub. Co. 1971.

Engelberg, Edward, *The Unknown Distance; From Consciousness to Conscience; Goethe to Camus*. Cambridge, Mass., Harvard Univ. Pr. 1972.

English Association, London, *Essays and Studies by Members of the Association, vol. 10*. London, Oxford Univ. Pr. 1924.

English Association. London, *Essays and Studies by Members of the Association*. London, Oxford Univ. Pr. 1948.

English Association, *Essays and Studies, 1960, being Vol. 13 of the New Series of Essays and Studies Collected for the English Association by M. St. Clare Byrne*. 1960.

English Association. *Essays and Studies, 1967; Being Volume 20 of the New Series of Essays and Studies Collected for the English Association by Martin Holmes*. N.Y., Humanities Pr., Inc. 1967.

English Institute Essays, 1946-1952. Boulder, Colorado Univ. Pr.

The Era of Goethe: Essays Presented to James Boyd. Dufour. 1959.

Eriksen, Hans Peter Bonde, et al, *Tragedie og Tragik; Til Oparbejdelsen af en Teori om den Borgerlige Bevidsthed*. Aarhus. 1972.

Erskine, John, *Delight of Great Books*. Indianapolis, Ind., Bobbs. 1928.

Essays and Studies, 1971; Being Volume 24 of the New Series of Essays and Studies Collected for the English Association, ed. Bernard Harris. Humanities Pr. 1971.

Essays and Studies in Honor of Carleton Brown. N.Y., New York Univ. Pr. 1940.

Essays Contributed in Honor of President William Alan Neilson (Smith College Studies in Modern Language, vol. 21, #1-4). Northampton, Mass., Smith College Pr. 1939.

Essays in Dramatic Literature; The Parrott Presentation Volume by Pupils of Professor T. M. Parrott of Princeton University, Published in His Honor, edited by H. Craig. Princeton, N.J., Princeton Univ. Pr. 1935.

Essays in Honor of Walter Clyde Curry (Vanderbilt Studies in the Humanities). Nashville, Tenn., Vanderbilt Univ. Pr. 1954.

Esslin, Martin, *Brief Chronicles; Essays on Modern Theatre.* London, Temple Smith. 1970.

——————— , *The Peopled Wound; The Work of Harold Pinter.* Garden City, N.Y., Doubleday & Co. 1970.

——————— , *Reflections; Essays on Modern Theatre.* Garden City, N.Y., Doubleday & Co., Inc. 1969.

——————— , *The Theatre of the Absurd.* Garden City, N.Y., Doubleday. 1961.

Evans, Fareth L., *J. B. Priestley, The Dramatist.* N.Y., James H. Heinemann, Inc. 1964.

Evans, Ifor, *A Short History of English Drama.* Boston, Houghton Mifflin Co. 1965.

Ewing, S. Blaine, *Burtonian Melancholy in the Plays of John Ford.* Princeton, N.J., Princeton Univ. Pr. 1940.

Faber, Melvyn D., ed., *The Design Within; Psychoanalytic Approaches to Shakespeare.* Science House. 1970.

Falk, Eugene H., *Renunciation as a Tragic Focus: A Study of Five Plays.* Minneapolis, Univ. of Minnesota Pr. 1954.

Farnham, Willard, *The Medieval Heritage of Elizabethan Tragedy.* Berkeley, Cal., Univ. of California Pr. 1936.

Federman, Raymond, *Journey to Chaos: Samuel Beckett's Early Fiction.* Berkeley, Univ. of California Pr. 1965.

Fergusson, Francis, *Idea of a Theatre: A Study of Ten Plays: The Art of Drama in Changing Perspective.* Princeton, N.J., Princeton Univ. Pr. 1949.

Festschrift Ernst Kapp. Hamburg, M. Schroeder. 1958.

Fickert, Kurt J., *To Heaven and Back; The New Morality in the Plays of Friedrich Dürrenmatt.* Lexington, Univ. of Kentucky Pr. 1972.

Fiedler, Leslie Aaron, *The Collected Essays of Leslie Fiedler.* vol. 2, N.Y., Stein & Day. 1971.

Finley, John Huston, *Pindar and Aeschylus* (Martin Classical Lectures, V. 14). Cambridge, Mass., Harvard Univ. Pr. 1955.

Fjelde, Rolf, ed., *Ibsen; A Collection of Critical Essays.* Englewood Cliffs, N.J., Prentice-Hall. 1965.

Fleming, W., *Art and Ideas.* N.Y., Holt. 1955.

Fletcher, John and John Spurling, *Beckett; A Study of His Plays.* N.Y., Hill and Wang. 1972.

Ford, Boris, ed., *A Guide to English Literature.* vol. 2. Baltimore, Penguin Bks. 1955.

Forster, Edward M., *Two Cheers for Democracy.* N.Y., Harcourt. 1951.

Fowlie, Wallace, *Climate of Violence; The French Literary Tradition from Baudelaire to the Present.* N.Y., The Macmillan Co. 1967.

——————— , *Love in Literature; Studies in Symbolic Expression.* Freeport, Books for Libraries Pr. 1972.

The France of Claudel, ed. Henri Peyre. Jamaica, N.Y., St. John's Univ. Pr. 1973.

France, Peter, *Racine's Rhetoric*. N.Y., Oxford Univ. Pr. 1965.

Fraser, G. S., *Lawrence Durrell; A Critical Study*. N.Y., E. P. Dutton Co. 1968.

Freedman, Morris, *The Moral Impulse; Modern Drama from Ibsen to the Present*. Carbondale, Ill., Southern Illinois Univ. Pr. 1967.

Freeman, Arthur, *Thomas Kyd; Facts and Problems*. London, Oxford, Clarendon Pr. 1967.

Freeman, E., *The Theatre of Albert Camus; A Critical Study*. London, Methuen & Co. 1971.

French, Warren, ed., *The Thirties; Fiction, Poetry, Drama*. Deland, Fla., Everett/Edwards, Inc. 1967.

Fricke, Gerhard, *Studien und Interpretationen: Ausgewählte Schriften Zur Deutschen Dichtung*. Frankfort, Menck. 1956.

Friedman, Melvin J. and John B. Vickery, eds., *The Shaken Realist; Essays in Modern Literature in Honor of Friedrick J. Hoffman*. Baton Rouge, La., Louisiana State Univ. Pr. 1970.

From the N. R. F.: An Image of the Twentieth Century From the Pages of the "Nouvelle Revue Française", ed. by Justin O'Brien. N.Y., Farrar, Straus. 1958.

Fromm, Harold, *Bernard Shaw and the Theater in the Nineties; A Study of Shaw's Dramatic Criticism*. Lawrence, Kans., Univ. of Kansas Pr. 1967.

Fuchs, A. and H. Motekat, *Hans Heinrich Borcherdt zum 75. Geburtstag, 14. 8. 1962*. Munchen, Heuber. 1962.

Fuller, Edmund, *A Pageant of the Theatre*. N.Y., Thomas Y. Crowell Co. 1965.

Ganne, Gilbert, *Alfred de Musset; Sa Jeunesse et la Nôtre*. Paris, Librairie Academique Perrin. 1970.

Ganz, Arthur, ed., *Pinter; A Collection of Critical Essays*. Englewood Cliffs, N.J., Prentice-Hall Pub. Co. 1972.

Ganz, Peter F., ed., *The Discontinuous Tradition; Studies in German Literature in Honour of Ernest Ludwig Stahl*. Oxford, Oxford Univ. Pr. 1971.

Garland, H. B., *Schiller; The Dramatic Writer*. London, Oxford Univ. Pr. 1969.

Garland, Mary, *Kleist's "Prinz Friedrich von Hapsburg"; An Interpretation Through Word Patterns*. The Hague, Mouton & Co. 1968.

Garzilli, Enrico, *Circles Without Center; Paths to the Discovery and Creation of Self in Modern Literature*. Cambridge, Harvard Univ. Pr. 1972.

Gaskell, Ronald, *Drama and Reality; The European Theatre since Ibsen*. London, Routledge and Kegan Paul. 1972.

Gassner, John, *Directions in Modern Theatre and Drama*. N.Y., Holt, Rinehart and Winston, Inc. 1965.

——————— , *Dramatic Soundings; Evaluations and Retractions Culled from Thirty Years of Dramatic Criticism*. N.Y., Crown Pubs., Inc. 1968.

Gassner, John, ed., *O'Neill, A Collection of Critical Essays*. Englewood Cliffs, N.J., Prentice-Hall. 1964.

——————— , and Allen, Ralph G., eds., *Theatre and Drama in the Making*. Boston, Houghton. 1964.

——————— , *Theatre at the Crossroads: Plays and Playwrights of the Mid-century American Stage*. N.Y., Holt. 1960.

——————— , *Theatre in our Time: A Survey of the Men, Materials and Movements in the Modern Theatre*. N.Y., Thomas V. Crown Pubs., Inc. 1954.

Gay-Crosier, Raymond, *Le Theatre d'Albert Camus.* Paris, Minard. 1967.

Gayley, Charles Mills, *Representative English Comedies.* vol. 3. N.Y., Macmillan Co., 1912/14.

German Studies; Presented to Professor H. G. Fiedler by Pupils, Colleagues and Friends on His 75th Birthday, 28 April, 1937. London, Oxford Univ. Pr. 1938.

German Studies Presented to Walter H. Bruford on His Retirement by His Pupils, Colleagues and Friends. London, Geo. G. Harrap & Co. 1961.

Gill, Stephen M., *Six Symbolist Plays of Yeats.* New Delhi, S. Chand & Co. 1971.

Gilliatt, Penelope, *Unholy Fools; Wits, Comics, Disturbers of the Peace; Film and Theater.* Viking Pub. Co. 1973.

Gillie, Christopher, *Movements in English Literature, 1900-1940.* Cambridge Univ. Pr. 1975.

Gilman, Richard, *Common and Uncommon Masks; Writings on Theatre, 1961-1970.* N.Y., Random House, Inc. 1971.

Givens, Sean, ed., *James Joyce: Two Decades of Criticism.* N.Y., Vanguard Pr., Inc. 1948.

Glicksberg, Charles I., *The Tragic Vision in Twentieth Century Literature.* Carbondale, Ill., Southern Illinois Univ. Pr. 1963.

Goethe, Johann W., *Literary Essays, A Selection in English.* London, Oxford Univ. Pr. 1921.

Goldberg, S. L., *The Classical Temper; A Study of Joyce's "Ulysses".* London, Chatto and Windus. 1961.

Golding, Louis, *James Joyce.* London, Thornton Butterworth, Ltd. 1933.

Goldstein, Melvin, ed., *Metapsychological Literary Criticism; Theory and Practice; Essays in Honor of Leonard Falk Manheim.* Hartford, Conn., Univ. of Hartford Pr. 1973.

Goodell, Thomas Dwight, *Athenian Tragedy; A Study in Popular Art.* Port Washington, N.Y., Kennikat Pr., Inc. 1969.

Goodman, Paul, *The Structure of Literature.* Chicago, Univ. of Chicago Pr. 1954.

Goodman, Randolph, *Drama on Stage.* N.Y., Holt, Rinehart. 1961.

Goody, Jack, ed., *The Character of Kinship.* Cambridge Univ. Pr. 1974.

Gordon, Max, *Max Gordon Presents.* N.Y., Bernard Geis Asso. 1963.

Gorman, Herbert, *James Joyce; His First 40 Years.* N.Y., Huebsch Pub. Co. 1924.

Gossman, Lionel, *Men and Masks: A Study of Moliere.* Baltimore, Md., Johns Hopkins Univ. Pr. 1963.

Gottesman, Ronald and Scott Boyce, eds., *Art and Error; Modern Textual Edition.* Bloomington, Indiana Univ. Pr. 1970.

Graham, Ilse, *Schiller, Ein Meister der Tragischen Form.* Darmstadt, Wissenschaftliche Buchgesellschaft. 1974.

——————— , *Schiller's Drama; Talent and Integrity.* London, Methuen and Co. 1974.

Graves, Robert, *Food for Centaurs: Stories, Talks, Critical Studies, Poems.* Garden City, N.Y., Doubleday. 1960.

Gray, Ronald D., *The German Tradition in Literature, 1871-1945.* Cambridge Univ. Pr. 1965.

Grayburn, William F., ed., *Studies in the Humanities.* Bloomington, Indiana Univ. Pr. 1969.

Greek Poetry and Life; Essays Presented to G. Murray on His 70th Birthday. London, Oxford Univ. Pr. 1936.

Green, Paul, *Plough and Furrow: Some Essays and Papers on Life and the Theatre.* N.Y., Samuel French, Inc. 1963.

Greenwood, L. H. G., *Aspects of Euripidean Drama.* London, Cambridge Univ. Pr. 1953.

Grene D. and R. Lattimore, eds., *The Complete Greek Tragedies.* vol. 3. Chicago, Univ. of Chicago Pr. 1959.

Grene, David, *Reality and the Heroic Pattern; Last Plays of Ibsen, Shakespeare, and Sophocles.* Univ. of Chicago Pr. 1967.

Griffiths, Richard M., ed., *Claudel; A Reappraisal.* Chester Springs, Penna. Dufour Eds., Inc. 1970.

Grosshaus, Henry, ed., *To Find Something New; Studies in Contemporary Literature.* Pullman, Washington State Univ. Pr. 1969.

Grossvogel, David I., *Four Playwrights and a Postscript; Brecht, Ionesco, Beckett and Genêt.* Ithaca, N.Y., Cornell Univ. Pr. 1962.

Grube, G. M. A., *The Drama of Euripides.* London, Methuen. 1941.

Guicharnand, Jacques, ed., *Molière: A Collection of Critical Essays.* Englewood Cliffs, N.J., Prentice-Hall. 1964.

A Gunter Grass Symposium; ed. A. Leslie Willson. Austin, Univ. of Texas Pr. 1972.

Haac, Oscar A., *Marivaux.* N.Y., Twayne Pub. Co. 1973.

Haakonsen, Daniel et al, eds., *Ibsenforbundet; Arbok 1967.* Oslo Universitetsforlaget. 1968.

Haas, Gerhard, ed., *Kinder- und Jugendliteratur; Zur Typologie und Funktion einer Literarischen Gattung.* Stuttgart, Reclam. 1974.

Hackett, Francis, *Horizons: A Book of Criticism.* Munich, Germany, Huebsch. 1918.

———————————, *Invisible Censor.* N.Y., Viking. 1921.

Hamburger, Käte, *From Sophocles to Sartre; Figures From Greek Tragedy, Classical and Modern.* N.Y., F. Ungar Pub. Co. 1969.

Hamburger, Michel, *Art as Second Nature; Occasional Pieces, 1950-1974.* Carcanet New Pr. 1975.

Hamilton, Clayton M., *Seen on the Stage.* N.Y., Holt. 1920.

Hamilton, Edith, *The Ever-Present Past.* N.Y., W. W. Norton & Co., Inc. 1964.

Hammer, Carl, Jr., ed., *Studies in German Literature.* Baton Rouge: Louisiana State Univ. Pr. 1963.

Hampshire, Stuart N., *Modern Writers and Other Essays.* N.Y., A. A. Knopf, Inc. 1970.

Handelingen van het Eenendertigste Nederlands Filologncongres; Gehouden te Groningen op Woensdag 1, Donderdag 2 en Vrijdag 3 April 1970. Groningen, Wolters-Noordhoff. 1971.

Hardwick, Elizabeth, *Seduction and Betrayal; Women and Literature.* N.Y., Random House. 1974.

Harris, Frank, *Contemporary Portraits*, 4th ser. N.Y., Brentano Book Store. 1923.

Harrison, George Bagshawe, ed., *Major British Writers.* N.Y., Harcourt. 1954.

Harsh, Philip Whaley, *A Handbook of Classical Drama.* Stanford Univ. Pr. 1944.

Hartwig, Hellmut A., ed., *The Southern Illinois Celebration: A Collection of Nine Papers.* Carbondale, ill., Univ. of Southern Illinois Pr. 1950.

Harvard, T. B., ed., *European Patterns.* Dolman Pr. 1964.

Harward, Timothy Blake, ed., *European Patterns; Contemporary Patterns in European Writing.* Chester Springs, Pa., Dufour Editions, Inc. 1967.

Hastings, William Thomson, ed., *Contemporary Essays.* Boston, Houghton Mifflin, Inc. 1928.

Hathorn, Richmond, *Tragedy, Myth and Mystery.* Bloomington, Ind. Indiana Univ. Pr. 1962.

Havelock, Eric A., *Liberal Temper in Greek Politics.* N.Y., Yale Univ. Pr. 1957.

Hawkins, Harriett, *Likenesses of Truth in Elizabethan and Restoration Drama.* London, Oxford Univ. Pr. 1972.

Hayman, Ronald, *Arnold Wesker.* N.Y., Frederick Ungar. 1973.

——————— , *Eugene Ionesco.* London, Heinemann Pub., 1972.

——————— , *Harold Pinter.* London, Heinemann Pub., 1969.

——————— , *John Osborne.* London, Heinemann Pub., 1969.

Hein, Jürgen, ed., *Theater und Gesellschaft; Das Volksstück im 19. und 20. Jahrhundert.* Dusseldorf, Bertelsmann, 1973.

Heller, Erich, *The Disinherited Mind: Essays in Modern German Literature and Thought.* Dufour. 1952.

Heller, Otto, *"Faust" and "Faustus": A Study of Goethe's Relationship to Marlowe,* (Washington Univ. Studies in Language and Literature, n. s. #2). Seattle, Washington, 1931.

Henry, Stuart, *French Essays and Profiles.* N.Y., Dutton. 1921.

Henss, Rudolf and Hogo Moser, eds., *Germanistik in Forschung und Lehre. Vorträge und Diskussionen des Germanistentages in Essen, 21.-25. Oktober, 1964.* Berlin, Schmidt. 1965.

Herndl, George C., *The High Desire; English Renaissance Tragedy and the Natural Law.* Lexington, Univ. of Kentucky Pr. 1970.

The Hero in Scandinavian Literature; From Peer Gynt to the Present, ed. John M. Weinstock and Robert T. Rovinsky, Univ. of Texas Pr. 1975.

Hesse, Everett W., *Calderón de la Barca.* N.Y., Twayne Pub. Co. 1967.

Hewlett, Maurice Henry, *Extemporary Essays.* London: Oxford Univ. Pr. 1922.

——————— , *Last Essays.* N.Y., James H. Heinemann, Inc. 1924.

Heydebrand; Renate von and G. ust Klaus, eds., *Wissenshaft als Dialog; studien zur Literatur und Kunst Seit der Jahrhundert-wende.* Stuttgart, Metzler. 1969.

Hibbard, George R., ed., *The Elizabethan Theatre IV.* Hamden, Conn., Archon Pub. Co. 1974.

Hietsch, Otto, ed., *Österreich und die Angelsächsische Welt: Kulturbegegnungen und Vergleiche.* Wien, Braumuller. 1961.

Higginbotham, Virginia, *The Comic Spirit of Federico Garcia Lorca.* Austin, Univ. of Texas Pr. 1976.

Highet, Gilbert, *Explorations.* London, Oxford Univ. Pr. 1971.

——————— , *Powers of Poetry.* London: Oxford Univ. Pr. 1960.

Hill, Claude, *Bertolt Brecht.* Boston, Twayne Pub. 1975.

Hinchliffe, Arnold P., *Harold Pinter.* N.Y., Twayne Pub. Co., Inc. 1967.

Hodeige, Fritz and Rothe, Carl, eds., *Atlantische Begegnungen: Eine Freundesgabe für Arnold Bergstraesser.* Freiburg, Rombach. 1964.

Hofacker, Erich and Dieckmann, Lisolette, eds., *Studies in Germanic Languages and Literatures: In Memory of Fred O. Nolte.* Seattle, Washington Univ. Pr. 1963.

Hogan, Robert, *After the Irish Renaissance; A Critical History of the Irish Drama since "The Plough and the Stars"*. Minneapolis, Univ. of Minnesota Pr. 1967.

Hogg, James, ed., *Romantic Reassessment XI*. Salzburg, Inst. für Englische Sprache und Literatur, Univ. of Salzburg. 1973.

Holbrook, David, *Dylan Thomas; The Code of Night*. London, Univ. of London Pr. 1972.

Holland, Norman N., *The First Modern Comedies*. Cambridge, Mass., Harvard Univ. Pr. 1959.

Hollis, James R., *Harold Pinter; The Poetics of Silence*. Carbondale, Southern Illinois Univ. Pr. 1970.

Holmes, David M., *The Art of Thomas Middleton; A Critical Study*. London, Oxford Univ. Pr. 1970.

Holtan, Orley I., *Mythic Patterns in Ibsen's Last Plays*. Minneapolis, Univ. of Minnesota Pr. 1970.

Holtzhauer, Helmut, Bernhard Zeller and Hans Henning, eds., *Studien zur Goethezeit: Festschrift für Lieselotte Blumenthal*. Weimar, Bohlau. 1968.

Honig, Edwin, *Calderón and the Seizures of Honor*. Cambridge, Mass., Harvard Univ. Pr. 1972.

Horn, Francis H., ed., *Literary Masterpieces of the Western World*. Baltimore, Md., Johns Hopkins Univ. Pr. 1953.

Hosley, Richard, ed., *Essays on Shakespeare and Elizabethan Drama in Honor of Hardin Craig*. Columbia, Univ. of Missouri Pr. 1962.

Houston, John Porter, *Victor Hugo*. N.Y., Twayne Pub. 1975.

Howarth, W. D. and Merlin Thomas, eds., *Molière; Stage and Study; Essays in Honour of W. G. Moore*. Oxford, Clarendon Pr. 1973.

Howe, Irving, ed., *The Radical Imagination; An Anthology from "Dissent" Magazine*. N.Y.: New American Library, Inc. 1967.

Howells, William Dean, *Criticism and Fiction and Other Essays*. N.Y.: New York Univ. Pr. 1959.

Hudson, L. A., *Life and Theatre*. N.Y.: Roy Pubs., Inc. 1954.

Hughes, Catharine, *Plays, Politics, and Polemics*. Drama Book Specialists, 1973.

Hummert, Paul A., *Bernard Shaw's Marxian Romance*. Lincoln, Univ. of Nebraska Pr. 1973.

Huneker, James Gibbons, *Ivory Apes and Peacocks*. N.Y., Scribner. 1915.
————————— , *Variations*. N.Y., Scribner. 1921.

Hungerford, Edward B., *Shores of Darkness*. Boulder, Colorado Univ. Pr. 1941.

Hunningher-Schilling, Erica, ed., *Essays on Drama and Theatre; Liber Amicorum Benjamin Hunningher Presented to Professor Dr. B. Hunningher on the Occasion of His Retirement from the Chair of Drama and Theatre Arts in the University of Amsterdam*. Amsterdam, Moussanet's Uitgeverij. 1973.

Hunt, Leigh, *Leigh Hunt's Dramatic Criticism, 1808-1831*, ed. by L. H. Houtchens and C. W. Houtchens. N.Y., Columbia Univ. Pr. 1949.

Hunt, Mary Leland, *Thomas Dekker; A Study*. N.Y., Columbia Univ. Pr. 1911.

Hunter, G. K., and S. K., eds., *John Webster; A Critical Anthology*. Middlesex, Engl., Penguin Bks., Ltd. 1969.

Hurt, James, *Catiline's Dream; An Essay on Ibsen's Plays*. Urbana, Univ. of Illinois Pr. 1972.

Hyman, Stanley E., *Poetry and Criticism: Four Revolutions in Literary Taste.* N.Y., Atheneum. 1961.
Hyslop, Lois Boe, *Henry Becque.* N.Y., Twayne Pub. Co. 1972.
The Idiom of Drama. Ithaca, Cornell Univ. Pr. 1970.
Illinois Univ. English Dept., *Studies by Members of the English Department, Univ. of Illinois, in Memory of John Jay Parry.* Urbana, Univ. of Illinois Pr. 1955.
Institute for Religious and Social Studies, *Conflict of Loyalties: A Series of Addresses and Discussions.* N.Y., Harper. 1952.
——————— , *Great Moral Dilemmas in Literature, Past and Present,* ed. by R. M. MacIver, Pub. by the Institute. 1956.
Interpretationen zur Osterreichischen Literatur. Wien, Hirt, 1971.
The Isenberg Memorial Lecture Series, 1965-1966. East Lansing, Michigan State Univ. Pr. 1969.
Jackson, Robert Louis, *Chekhov; A Collection of Critical Essays.* Englewood Cliffs, N.J., Prentice-Hall, Inc. 1967.
Jacquot, Jean, ed., *Dramaturgie et Société; Rapports entre l'Oeuvre Théâtrale, Son Public aux XVI et XVII Siecles.* 2 vols. Paris, Eds. du Centre National de la Recherche Scientifique. 1968.
James, Henry, *Literary Reviews and Essays: On American, English and French Literature,* ed. by A. Mordell. N.Y., Twayne Pub., Inc. 1957.
——————— , *Scenic Art: Notes on Acting and the Drama, 1872-1901.* New Brunswick, N.J.: Rutgers Univ. Pr. 1948.
Jepson, Laura, *Ethical Aspects of Tragedy: A Comparison of Certain Tragedies by Aeschylus, Sophocles, Euripides, Seneca, and Shakespeare.* Gainsville, Univ. of Florida Pr. 1953.
Johnson, Robert B., *Henry de Montherlant.* N.Y., Twayne Pub. 1968.
Jolas, Maria, ed. *A James Joyce Yearbook.* Paris, Transition Pr. 1949.
Jonas, Klaus w., ed., *Deutsche Weltliteratur; Von Goethe bis Ingeborg Bachmann: Festgabe für J. Alan Pfeffer.* Tubingen, Niemeyer. 1972.
Jones, Henry J. F., *On Aristotle and Greek Tragedy.* London, Oxford Univ. Pr. 1962.
Jones-Davies, Marie Therese, *Un Peintre de la Vie Londonienne: Thomas Dekker (circa 1572-1632).* vol. 1, Paris, Didier. 1958.
Josai Jinbun Kenkyu, *Studies in the Humanities.* Sakado, Iruma-Gun, Saitama, Japan, Josai Univ. Keizai-Gaku-Kai. 1973.
Jost, Francois, ed., *Proceedings of the Fourth Congress of the International Comparative Literature Association, Fribourg, 1964.* The Hague, Mouton & Co., 1966.
Joyce, James, *Critical Writings of James Joyce,* ed. by Ellsworth Mason and Richard Ellmann. N.Y., Viking. 1959.
Kahn, Robert L., ed., *Studies in German; In Memory of Andrew Louis.* (Rice University Studies 55). Houston, Tex., Rice Univ. Pr. 1969.
Kauffmann, S., *Living Images; Film Comment and Criticism.* N.Y., Harper and Row. 1975.
Kaufmann, Ralph James, *Elizabethan Drama: Modern Essays in Criticism.* London, Oxford Univ. Pr. 1961.
——————— , ed., *G. B. Shaw; A Collection of Critical Essays.* Englewood Cliffs, N.J., Prentice-Hall, Inc. 1965.
Kaufmann, Stanley, *Figures of Light; Film Criticism and Comment.* N.Y., Harper and Row. 1971.

Kaufmann, Walter A., *From Shakespeare to Existentialism: Studies in Poetry, Religion, and Philosophy*. Boston, Beacon Pr. 1959.

Kaul, A. N., *The Action of English Comedy; Studies in the Encounter of Abstraction and Experience from Shakespeare to Shaw*. New Haven, Yale Univ. Pr. 1970.

Kaul, R. K., ed., *Essays Presented to Amy G. Stock, Professor of English, Rajasthan University, 1961-1965*. Jaipur, Rajasthan Univ. Pr. 1965.

Kayser, Wolfgang, Johannes, *The Grotesque in Art and Literature*. Bloomington, Indiana Univ. Pr. 1963.

Keeley, Edmund and Peter Adolph Bien, eds., *Modern Greek Writers; Solomos, Calvos, Matesis, Paferis, Cavafy, Kazantzakis, Seferis, Elytis*. Princeton Univ. Pr. 1972.

Kelman, John, *Among Famous Books*. London, Hodder. 1912.

Kennedy, Andrew K., *Six Dramatists in Search of a Language*. London, Cambridge Univ. Pr. 1975.

Kenner, Hugh, *Dublin's Joyce*. Bloomington, Indiana Univ. Pr. 1956.

——————— , *A Reader's Guide to Samuel Beckett*. London, Thames and Hudson. 1973.

——————— , *Samuel Beckett; A Critical Study*. Los Angeles, Univ. of California Pr. 1968.

Kermode, John Frank, *Shakespeare, Spenser and Donne; Renaissance Essays*. N.Y., Viking Pr., Inc. 1971.

Kern, Edith, ed., *Sartre: A Collection of Critical Essays*. Englewood Cliffs, N.J., Prentice-Hall. 1962.

Kernan, Alvin B., ed., *Ben Jonson: Volpone*. New Haven, Yale Univ. Pr. 1962.

Kernan, Alvin, *The Cankered Muse; Satire of the English Renaissance*. New Haven, Yale Univ. Pr. 1959.

Kernodle, George R., *Invitation to the Theatre*. N.Y., Holt, Rinehart and Winston, Inc. 1967.

Kerr, Walter, *The Theatre in Spite of Itself*. N.Y., Simon and Schuster. 1963.

——————— , *Thirty Plays Hath November; Pain and Pleasure in the Contemporary Theater*. N.Y., Simon and Schuster. 1969.

Kilian, Klaus, *Die Komödien Arthur Schnitzler*. Dusseldorf, Bertelsmann Univ. Pr. 1972.

Kilroy, Thomas, ed., *Sean O'Casey; A Collection of Critical Essays*. Englewood Cliffs, N.J., Prentice-Hall. 1975.

King, Bruce, *Dryden's Major Plays*. N.Y., Barnes and Noble, Inc. 1966.

Kinghorn, A. M., *Medieval Drama*. London, Evans Bros., Ltd., 1968.

Kirk, Russell, *Eliot and His Age; T. S. Eliot's Moral Imagination in the Twentieth Century*. N.Y., Random. 1971.

Kirsch, Arthur Clifford, *Jacobean Dramatic Perspectives*. Univ. Pr. of Virginia. 1972.

Kitto, Humphrey D., *Form and Meaning in Drama: A Study of Six Greek Plays and of "Hamlet"*. N.Y., Barnes and Noble. 1956.

Knapp, Bettina L., *Jean Cocteau*. N.Y., Twayne Pub. 1970.

——————— , *Jean Racine; Myths and Renewal in Modern Theater*. University, Ala., Univ. of Alabama Pr. 1971.

——————— , *Maurice Maeterlinck*, Boston, Twayne Pub. 1975.

Knauf, David, M., ed., *Papers in Dramatic Theory and Criticism*. Iowa, Univ. of Iowa Pr. 1969.

Knight, George W., *The Christian Renaissance*. N.Y., W. W. Norton and Co., Inc. 1962.

Knights, L. C., *Drama and Society in the Age of Jonson*. London, Chatto and Windus. 1962.

Knudsen, Nils L., Ole A. Olsen, and Erik Svejgaard, eds., *Subjekt og Tekst; Bidrag til Semiotikkens Teori*. (Nordisk Sommeruniversitets Skriftserie, 5), Kongerslev, GMT, 1974.

Kolb, Edward and Jorg Hasler, eds., *Festschrift Rudolf Stamm zu Seinem Sechzigsten Geburtstag*. Bern, Francke. 1969.

Kosok, Heinz, *Sean O'Casey; Das Dramatische Werk*. Berlin, Erich Schmidt. 1972.

Kossoff, A. David and José Amor y Vásquez, eds., *Homenaje a William L. Fichter; Estudios Sobre el Teatro Antigua Hispanico y Otros Ensayos*. Madrid, Castalia. 1971.

Kostelanetz, Richard, *On Contemporary Literature: An Anthology of Critical Essays on the Major Movements of Contemporary Literature*. New York, Avon Books. 1964.

Kott, Jan, *The Eating of the Gods; An Interpretation of Greek Tragedy*. Random House Pub. Co. 1973.

——————— , *Theatre Notebook: 1947-1967*. Garden City, N.Y., Doubleday & Co., Inc. 1968.

Kraft, Walter C., ed., *Proceedings; Pacific Northwest Conference on Foreign Languages. 23rd Annual Meeting, April 28-29, 1972*. Corvallis, Oregon State Univ. 1973.

——————— , *Proceedings; Pacific Northwest Conference on Foreign Languages*. Corvallis, Oregon State Univ. Pr. 1974.

Krans, Horatio Sheafe, *William Butler Yeats and the Irish Revival*. N.Y., James H. Heinemann, Inc. 1905.

Krause, David, *Sean O'Casey; The Man and His Work*. N.Y., Macmillan Pub. Co. 1975.

Kreiger, Murray, *The Classic Vision; The Retreat from Extremity in Modern Literature*. Baltimore, Md., Johns Hopkins Pr. 1971.

Kreuzer, Helmut and Käte Hamburger, eds., *Gestaltungsgeschichte und Gesellschaftsgeschichte. Literatur-, Kunst-und Musikwissenschaftliche Studien. Fritz Martini zum 60. Geburtstag*. Stuttgart, Metzler. 1969.

Kronenberger, Louis, *The Polished Surface; Essays in the Literature of Worldliness*. N.Y., A. A. Knopf Ltd. 1969.

——————— , *Republic of Letters: Essays on Various Writers*. N.Y., Knopf. 1955.

Kunkel, Francis L., *The Labyrinthine Way of Graham Greene*. Mamaroneck, N.Y. Paul P. Appel, 1973.

Lahr, John, *Up Against the Fourth Wall*. N.Y., Grove Pr. 1970.

Lamm, Martin, *August Strindberg;* Trans. and ed. Harry G. Carlson. N.Y., Benjamin Blom. 1971.

Lamont, Rosette C., ed., *Ionesco; A Collection of Critical Essays*. Englewood Cliffs, N.J., Prentice-Hall. 1973.

Lemaitre, Georges, *Jean Giraudoux; The Writer and His Work*. N.Y., Frederick Ungar Pub. Co. 1971.

Lancaster, Henry Carrington, *Adventures of a Literary Historian: A Collection of His Writings Presented to H. C. Lancaster by His Former Students and Other Friends in Anticipation of his 60th Birthday, Nov. 10, 1942*. Baltimore, Md., Johns Hopkins. 1942.

Lattimore, Richmond A., *Poetry of Greek Tragedy*. Baltimore, Md., Johns Hopkins Univ. Pr. 1958.

Laufe, Abe, *Anatomy of a Hit; Long-Run Plays on Broadway from 1900 to the Present Day*. N.Y., Hawthorn Books, Inc. 1966.

Lawrenson, T. E., F. E. Sutcliffe and G. F. A. Gadoffe, eds., *Modern Miscellany Presented to Eugene Vinaver by Pupils, Colleagues and Friends*. Manchester, Manchester Univ. Pr. 1970.

Lazarowicz, Klaus and Kron, Wolfgang, eds., *Unterscheidung und Bewahrung: Festschrift für Hermann Kunisch Zum 60 Geburtstag*. Berlin, deGruyter. 1961.

Lazenby, Walter, *Arthur Wing Pinero*. N.Y., Twayne Pubs. 1972.

Leech, Clifford, *John Webster; A Critical Study*. London, Hogarth Pr. 1951.

_____ , *Marlowe: A Collection of Critical Essays*. Englewood Cliffs, N.J., Prentice-Hall. 1964.

Lenski, B. A., *Jean Anouilh; Stages in Rebellion*. Atlantic Highlands, N.J., Humanities Pr. 1975.

Lerner, Laurence, *The Uses of Nostalgia; Studies in Pastoral Poetry*. Schocken Pub. Co. 1972.

Lerner, Max, *Actions and Passions: Notes on the Multiple Revolution of our Time*. N.Y., Simon and Schuster. 1949.

Lesky, Albin, *Greek Tragedy*. N.Y., Barnes and Noble, Inc. 1967.

Lever, Julius Walter, *The Tragedy of State*. Methuen and Co. 1971.

Levin, Dan, *Stormy Petrel: The Life and Work of Maxim Gorky*. N.Y., Appleton-Century. 1965.

Levin, Harry, *James Joyce; A Critical Introduction*. Norfolk, New Directions. 1941.

_____ , *Refractions; Essays in Comparative Literature*. Oxford Univ. Pr. 1966.

Levin, Harry, ed., *Veins of Humor*. Harvard Univ. Pr. 1972.

Levin, Richard, *The Multiple Plot in English Renaissance Drama*. Chicago, Univ. of Chicago Pr. 1971.

Levitt, Paul M., *A Structural Approach to the Analysis of Drama*. The Hague, Mouton & Co. 1971.

Lewis, Allan, *The Contemporary Theatre: The Significant Playwrights of our Time*. N.Y., Crown Pub., Inc. 1962.

Lewis, Allan, *Ionesco*. N.Y., Twayne Pubs. 1972.

Lewisohn, Ludwig, *Drama and Stage*. N.Y., Harcourt. 1922.

Ley-Piscator, Maria, *The Piscator Experiment: The Political Theatre*. James H. Heinemann, Inc. 1967.

Lindstrom, Thais S., *A Concise History of Russian Literature*. New York Univ. Pr. 1966.

Little Review Anthology, ed. by Margaret Anderson. Hermitage Pr. 1953.

Litz, Walton, *James Joyce*. N.Y., Twayne Pubs. 1966.

Lloyd-Jones, Hugh, ed., *The Greeks*. N.Y., World Pub. Co. 1962.

Locke, Louis G., Gibson, William M., and Arms, George W., eds, *Readings for a Liberal Education*, rev. ed., vol. 2. Rinehart. 1952.

Lockert, Lacy, *Studies in French Classical Tragedy*. Nashville, Tenn., Vanderbilt Univ. Pr. 1958.

Loftis, John Clyde, ed., *Restoration Drama; Modern Essays in Criticism*. Oxford Univ. Pr. 1966.

Loftis, John, *The Spanish Plays of Neoclassical England*. New Haven, Yale Univ. Pr. 1973.

Lorichs, Sonja, *The Unwomanly Woman in Bernard Shaw's Drama and Her Social and Political Background.* Stockholm, Uppsala Univ. Pr. 1973.

Lowell, Amy, *Poetry and Poets: Essays.* Boston, Houghton. 1930.

Lumley, Frederick, *New Trends in Twentieth Century Drama; A Survey Since Ibsen and Shaw.* Oxford Univ. Pr. 1967.

Lyons, Charles R., *Bertolt Brecht; The Despair and the Polemic.* Carbondale, Ill.: Southern Illinois Univ. Pr. 1968.

————————, *Henrik Ibsen; The Divided Consciousness.* London, Feffer and Simon. 1972.

Mabley, Edward, *Dramatic Construction; An Outline of Basic Principles.* Philadelphia, Chilton Bk. Co. 1972.

McCall, Dorothy, *The Theatre of Jean-Paul Sartre.* N.Y., Columbia Univ. Pr. 1969.

MacCarthy, Desmond, *Humanities.* London, Oxford Univ. Pr. 1954.

————————, *Shaw's Plays in Review.* Folcroft, Pa., Folcroft Pr. 1969.

————————, *Theatre.* London: Oxford Univ. Pr. 1955.

McCarthy, Mary T., *Sights and Spectacles, 1937-1956.* N.Y., Farrar, Straus. 1956.

McCollom, William G., *The Divine Average; A View of Comedy.* Cleveland, Ohio, Press of Case Western Reserve Univ. 1971.

McDonald, Charles Osborne, *The Rhetoric of Tragedy; Form in Stuart Drama.* Amherst, Mass., Univ. of Massachusetts Pr. 1966.

MacDowell, Edward A., *Critical and Historical Essays: Lectures Delivered at Colorado University,* ed. W. J. Baltzell. Schmidt Pub. 1912.

Mackenzie, W. Roy, *The English Moralities from the Point of View of Allegory.* Staten Island, N.Y.: Gordian Pr., Inc. 1966.

Macksey, Richard and Eugenio Donato, ed., *The Languages of Criticism and the Sciences of Man; The Structuralist Controversy.* Baltimore, Johns Hopkins Univ. Pr. 1969.

McNeir, Waldo F., *Studies in Comparative Literature.* Baton Rouge: Louisiana State Univ. Pr. 1962.

Magalaner, Marvin and Richard M. Kain, *Joyce; The Man, the Work the Reputation.* N.Y., New York Univ. Pr. 1956.

Magarshack, David, *The Real Chekhov; An Introduction to Chekhov's Last Plays.* London, George Allen & Unwin, Ltd. 1972.

Maguire, Robert A., ed., *Gogol from the Twentieth Century; Eleven Essays.* Princton Univ. Pr. 1975.

Mahal, Gunther, ed., *Ansichten zu Faust; Karl Theens zum 70. Geburtstag.* Stuttgart, Kohlhammer. 1973.

Mailer, Norman, *The Presidential Papers.* N.Y., G. P. Putnam's Sons. 1963.

Mais, Stuart Petre Brodie, *Some Modern Authors.* N.Y., Richards Co. 1923.

————————, *Why We Should Read.* N.Y., Richards Co. 1921.

Majault, Joseph, *James Joyce.* Paris, Editions Universitaires. 1963.

Malone, Andrew E., *The Irish Drama.* Bronx, N.Y., Benjamin Blom, Inc. 1965.

Mander, John, *The Writer and Commitment.* Dufour. 1962.

Manheim, Leonard Falk and Eleanor B. Manheim, eds., *Hidden Patterns; Studies in Psychoanalytic Literary Criticism.* N.Y., The Macmillan Co. 1966.

Mankin, Paul A., *Precious Irony; The Theatre of Jean Giraudoux.* The Hague, Mouton. 1971.

Manly Anniversary Studies in Language and Literature. Chicago, Univ. of Chicago Pr. 1923.

Mann, Thomas, *Essays of Three Decades.* N.Y., Knopf. 1947.

Marek, George R., *Front Seat at the Opera.* Allen, Towne and Heath. 1948.

——————— , *World Treasury of Grand Opera: Its Triumphs, Trials, and Great Personalities.* N.Y.: Harper. 1957.

Margolis, John D., *T. S. Eliot's Intellectual Development, 1922-1939.* Chicago, Univ. of Chicago Pr. 1972.

Martin, Edward S., *What's Ahead and Meanwhile.* New York, Harper. 1927.

Masinton, Charles G., *Christopher Marlowe's Tragic Vision; A Study in Damnation.* Athens, Ohio Univ. Pr. 1972.

Mattenklott, Gert and Klaus R. Scherpe, eds., *Demokratisch-Revolutionäre Literatur in Deutschland: Vormärz.* Kronberg/Taunus, Scriptor. 1974.

Matthaei, Renate, *Luigi Pirandello.* N.Y., Frederick Ungar Pub. Co. 1973.

Matthews, Honor, *The Primal Curse; The Myth of Cain and Abel in the Theatre.* N.Y., Schocken Books, Inc. 1967.

Mauriac, Francois, *Letters on Art and Literature.* N.Y., Philosophical Library, Inc. 1953.

Maxwell, Baldwin, *Studies in Beaumont, Fletcher and Massinger.* Chapel Hill, N.C., Univ. of North Carolina Pr. 1939.

May, Kurt, *Form und Bedeutung; Interpretationen Deutscher Dichtung des 18. und 19. Jahrhunderts.* Stuttgart, E. Klett. 1957.

Mayer, Hans, *Steppenwolf and Everyman.* Crowell Pub. Co. 1971.

Medievalia et Humanistica; Studies in Medieval and Renaissance Culture; New Series No. 5, ed. Paul Maurice Clogan. North Texas State Univ. Pr. 1974.

Mehl, Dieter, *The Elizabethan Dumb Show.* Cambridge, Harvard Univ. Pr. 1966.

Meier, Harri and Hans Sckommodau, *Wort und Text. Festschrift für Fritz Schalk.* Frankfort am Main, Vottorio Klostermann. 1963.

Melanges d'Histoire Littéraire (XVI-XVII Siecle): Offerts à Raymond Lebeques par Ses Collegues, Ses Élèves et Ses Amis. Paris, Nizet. 1969.

Melese, Pierre, *Samuel Beckett.* Paris, Editions Seghers. 1972.

Menon, K. P. K., *Literary Studies; Homage to Dr. A. Sivaramasubramonia Aiyer.* Trivandrum, St. Joseph Pr. 1973.

Mering, Otto von and Leonard Kasdan, eds., *Anthropology and the Behavioral and Health Sciences.* Pittsburgh, Univ. of Pittsburgh Pr. 1970

Merkel, Gottfried, ed. *On Romanticism and the Art of Translation: Studies in Honor of Edwin Hermann Zeydel.* Princeton, Princeton Univ. Pr. 1956.

Mews, Siegfried and Herbert Knust, eds., *Essays on Brecht; Theater and Politics* (Univ. of North Carolina Studies in Germanic Language and Literature #79), Univ. of North Carolina Pr. 1974.

Mews, Siegfried, ed., *Studies in German Literature of the 19th and 20th Centuries. Festschrift for Frederic E. Coenen.* Chapel Hill, N.C., Univ. of North Carolina Pr. 1970.

Meyer, Hans Georg, *Henrik Ibsen.* N.Y., Frederick Ungar Pub. Co. 1972.

Milburn, Daniel Judson, *The Age of Wit, 1650-1750.* New York, The Macmillan Co. 1966.

Miner, Earl Roy, ed., *English Criticism in Japan; Essays by Younger Japanese Scholars on English and American Literature.* Univ. of Tokyo Pr. 1972.

——————— , *Restoration Dramatists: A Collection of Critical Essays.* Englewood Cliffs, N.J., Prentice-Hall, Inc. 1966.

_____ , *Seventeenth Century Imagery; Essays on Uses of Figurative Language from Donne to Farquhar.* Berkeley, Univ. of California Pr. 1971.

Missions et Démarches de la Critique; Mélanges Offerts au Professeur J. A. Vier. Paris, Klincksieck. 1973.

Den Moderne Roman og Romanforskning i Norden. Innlegg ved den 8. Studiekonferanse Over Skandinavisk Literatur 10-14 August, 1970, Bergen. Bergen, Universitetsforlaget. 1971.

Moestrup, Jørn, *The Structural Patterns of Pirandello's Work.* Odense Univ. Pr. 1972.

Mony, G., ed., *Corneilla: Le Cid, La Chanson De Rodrigue: Explication and Compentaire.* Paris, Gabriel Mony. 1964.

Moore, Don D., *John Webster and His Critics, 1617-1964.* Baton Rouge, La., Louisiana State University Pr. 1966.

Moore, Harry T., *Twentieth Century French Literature to World War II.* Vols. I and II. Carbondale, Ill., Southern Illinois Univ. Pr. 1966.

Moore, John Rees, *Masks of Love and Death; Yeats as Dramatist.* Ithaca, Cornell Univ. Pr. 1971.

Moore, M., *Predilections.* N.Y., Viking. 1955.

Moore, Will G.; Sutherland, Rhoda; and Starkie, Enid, eds., *French Mind: Studies in Honour of Gustave Rudler.* London, Oxford Univ. Pr. 1952.

Mordaunt, Jerrold L., ed., *Proceedings: Pacific Northwest Conference on Foreign Languages. 19th Annual Meeting, April 19-20, 1968.* Univ. of Victoria Pr. 1968.

_____ , *Proceedings; Pacific Northwest Conference on Foreign Languages, 20th Annual Meeting, April 11-12, 1969.* vol. 20. Victoria, B.C., Univ. of Victoria Pr. 1969.

Morford, Mark, ed., *The Endless Fountain; Essays on Classical Humanism; Symposium in Honor of Clarence Allen Forbes,* Athens, Ohio State Univ. Pr. 1972.

Morgan, Margery M., *The Shavian Playground; An Exploration of the Art of Bernard Shaw.* London, Methuen & Co. 1972.

Moseley, Virginia, *Joyce and the Bible.* DeKalb, Northern Illinois Univ. Pr. 1967.

Moser, Hugh; Rudolf Schutzeichel and Karl Stackmann, eds., *Festschrift Josef Quint Anlässlich Seines 65. Geburtstages Uberreicht.* Bonn, Semmel. 1964.

Moses, Montrose Jonas and Brown, John M., eds., *American Theatre as Seen by its Critics, 1752-1934.* N.Y., W. W. Norton and Co. 1934.

Moskowitz, Samuel, *Explorers of the Infinite: Shapers of Science Fiction.* N.Y., World Pub. Co. 1963.

Moulton, Richard G., *World Literature and its Place in General Culture.* N.Y., Macmillan. 1911.

Muchnic, Helen, *Russian Writers; Notes and Essays.* Random House Pub. Co. 1971.

Mueller, Gustav E., *Philosophy of Literature.* N.Y., Philosophical Library, Inc. 1948.

Müller-Seidal, Walter, Hans Fromm, and Karl Richter, eds., *Historizität in Sprach und Literaturwissenschaft; Vorträge und Berichte der Stuttgarten Germanistentagung, 1972.* Munchen, Fink. 1974.

Müller-Seidel, Walter and Preisendanz, Wolfgang, eds., *Formenwandel: Festschrift Zum 65. Geburtstag Von Paul Böckmann.* Hamburg: Hoffmann und Campe. 1964.

Muller, Herbert Joseph, *In Pursuit of Relevance*. Indiana Univ. Pr. 1971.

Murray, Gilbert, *Tradition and Progress*. New York: Houghton. 1922.

Murray, Peter B., *A Study of Cyril Tourneur*. Philadelphia, Univ. of Pennsylvania Pr. 1964.

Myths, Dreams and Religion; ed. by Joseph Campbell. N.Y., E. P. Dutton Co. 1970.

Nassaar, Christopher S., *Into the Demon Universe; A Literary Exploration of Oscar Wilde*. New Haven, Yale Univ. Pr. 1974.

Nathan, George Jean, *Passing Judgments*. N.Y., A. A. Knopf, Inc. 1935.

—————— , *Theatre Book of the Year, 1942-1951*. N.Y., A. A. Knopf, Inc.

—————— , *Theatre in the Fifties*, Knopf. 1953.

—————— , *World of George Jean Nathan*, ed. by Charles Angoff, A. A. Knopf. 1952.

Nedden, Otto C. A., *Europäische Akzente; Ansprachen und Essays*. Wuppertal, Staats. 1968.

Neilson, Francis, *Cultural Tradition and Other Essays*. Schalkenbach. 1957.

Nevinson, Henry Woodd, *Books and Personalities*. Menlo Park, Calif., Land Magazine and Book Co. 1905.

—————— , *Essays in Freedom and Rebellion*. New Haven, Conn.: Yale Univ. Pr. 1921.

Newberry, Wilma, *The Pirandellian Mode in Spanish Literature from Cervantes to Sartre*. State Univ. of N.Y. Pr. 1973.

Nicol, Bernard de Bear, ed., *Varieties of Dramatic Experience*. London, Univ. of London Pr. 1969.

Nicoll, Allardyce, *World Drama from Aeschylus to Anouilh*. N.Y., Harcourt. 1949.

Northam, John, *Ibsen; A Critical Study*. Cambridge Univ. Pr. 1973.

Norwood, G., *Essays on Euripidean Drama*. Berkeley, Univ. of California Pr. 1954.

Novick, Julius, *Beyond Broadway; The Quest for Permanent Theatres*. Hill and Wang. 1968.

Nurse, Peter H., ed., *The Art of Criticism; Essays in French Literary Analysis*. Edinburgh, Edinburgh Univ. Pr. 1969.

Oates, Joyce Carol, *The Edge of Impossibility; Tragic Forms in Literature*. N.Y., Vanguard Pr. 1972.

O'Brien, Darcy, *The Conscience of James Joyce*. Princeton, N.J., Princeton Univ. Pr. 1967.

O'Brien, Justin, *Contemporary French Literature*. New Brunswick, N.J., Rutgers Univ. Pr. 1971.

—————— , *The French Literary Horizon*. New Brunswick: Rutgers Univ. Pr. 1967.

O'Casey, Eileen, *Sean*. N.Y., Coward, McCann and Geoghegan, Inc. 1972.

O'Driscoll, Robert, ed., *Theatre and Nationalism in 20th Century Ireland*. Toronto, Univ. of Toronto Pr. 1971.

Olson, Elder, *Tragedy and the Theory of Drama*. Detroit, Mich.: Wayne State Univ. Pr. 1966.

—————— , *The Theory of Comedy*. Bloomington, Ind.: Univ. of Indiana Pr. 1968.

O'Nan, Martha, *The Role of Mind in Hugo, Faulkner, Beckett and Grass*. N.Y., Philosophical Lib. 1969.

Oppel, Horst, *Das Moderne Englische Drama: Interpretationen.* Berlin: Erich Schmidt. 1963.

Ornstein, Robert, *The Moral Vision of Jacobean Tragedy.* Madison, Univ. of Wisconsin Pr. 1960.

Osborne, John, *The Naturalist Drama in Germany.* Manchester, Manchester Univ. Pr. 1971.

Our Irish Theatre; A Chapter of Autobiography; by Lady Gregory. N.Y., Oxford Univ. Pr. 1972.

Oxford and Asquith, Herbert H. Asquith, 1st Earl of, *Studies and Sketches.* Garden City, N.Y., Doran. 1924.

Palmer, John Leslie, *The Comedy of Manners.* Russell & Russel Pubs. 1962.

Papini, Giovanni, *Four and Twenty Minds.* New York: Thomas Y. Crowell Pub. Co. 1922.

Parr, Johnstone, *Tamburlaine's Malady and Other Essays on Astrology in Elizabethan Drama.* University, Univ. of Alabama Pr. 1953.

Parrott, Thomas M. and Ball, Robert H., *Short View of Elizabethan Drama, Together with Some Account of its Principal Playwrights and the Conditions Under Which it Was Produced.* Scribner. 1943.

Partisan Review, *New Partisan Reader, 1945-53.*

Pearson, L., *Popular Ethics in Ancient Greece.* Stanford, Stanford Univ. Pr. 1962.

Peckham, Morse, *The Triumph of Romanticism; Collected Essays.* Columbia, Univ. of South Carolina Pr. 1970.

The Persistent Voice; Essays on Hellenism in French Literature Since the Eighteenth Century in Honor of Professor Henri M. Peyre, ed. by Walter G. Langlois. N.Y., N.Y. Univ. Pr. 1971.

Peter, John Desmond, *Complaint and Satire in Early English Literature.* London, Oxford, Clarendon Pr. 1956.

Petit, Herbert H., ed., *Essays and Studies in Language and Literature.* Pittsburgh, Pa.: Duquesne Univ. Pr. 1964.

Pincus Sigele, Rizel and Gonzalo Sobejano, eds., *Homenaje a Casalduero: Critica y Poesia; Ofrecido por sus Amigos y Discipulos.* Madrid, Gredos. 1972.

Pocock, Guy Noel, *Little Room.* N.Y., E. P. Dutton and Co. 1926.

Poggioli, Renato, *The Oaten Fluke; Essays on Pastoral Poetry and the Pastoral Ideal.* Harvard Univ. Pr. 1975.

Pollmann, Leo, *Sartre and Camus; Literature and Existence.* N.Y., F. Ungar Pub. 1970.

Porter, Raymond J., *Brendan Behan.* N.Y., Columbia Univ. Pr. 1973.

Porter, Thomas E., *Myth and Modern American Drama.* Detroit, Wayne State Univ. Pr. 1969.

Pound, Ezra, *Pound/Joyce; The Letters of Ezra Pound to James Joyce, with Pound's Essays on Joyce*; ed. Forrest Read. N.Y., New Directions Pub. Co. 1967.

Price, Martin, *To the Palace of Wisdom: Studies in Order and Energy From Dryden to Blake.* Garden City, N.Y., Doubleday. 1964.

Prior, Moody Erasmus, *The Language of Tragedy.* N.Y., Columbia Univ. Pr. 1947.

Pronko, Leonard C., *The World of Jean Anouilh.* Berkeley, Univ. of California Pr. 1961.

Quiggiñ, E. C., ed., *Essays and Studies Presented to William Ridgeway on His 60th Birthday, August 6, 1913.* London, Cambridge Univ. Pr. 1913.

Rabkin, Norman, ed., *Reinterpretations of Elizabethan Drama.* N.Y., Columbia Univ. Pr. 1969.

————————————, *Twentieth Century Interpretations of the "Duchess of Malfi": A Collection of Critical Essays.* Englewood Cliffs, N.J., Prentice-Hall, Inc. 1968.

Rahv, Philip, *Literature and the Sixth Sense.* Houghton-Mifflin, 1969.

Rayfield, Donald, *Chekhov; The Evolution of His Art.* N.Y., Barnes and Noble. 1975.

Rees, Ennis, *The Tragedies of George Chapman; Renaissance Ethics in Action.* Cambridge, Mass., Harvard Univ. Pr. 1954.

Reid, Alec, *All I Can Manage, More Than I Could; An Approach to the Plays of Samuel Beckett.* Chester Springs, Pa., Dufour Eds. 1972.

Reinert, Otto, ed., *Strindberg; A Collection of Critical Essays.* Englewood Cliffs, N.J., Prentice-Hall. 1971.

Reiter, Seymour, *World Theater; The Structure and Meaning of Drama.* Horizon Pr. 1973.

Renaissance Drama; Essays Principally on Comedy, Ed. by S. Schoenbaum and Alan C. Dessen. Northwestern Univ. Pr. 1972.

Renaissance Drama, 1971; Essays Principally on the Playhouse and Staging, ed. S. Schoenbaum, Northwestern Univ. Pr. 1971.

Rexroth, Kenneth, *The Elastic Retort; Essays in Literature and Ideas.* Seabury. 1973.

Rhondda, Margaret H., *Notes on the Way.* N.Y., Macmillan. 1937.

Ribner, Irving, *The English History Play in the Age of Shakespeare.* Princeton, Univ. Pr. 1957.

Richards, Kenneth and Peter Thomson, eds., *Essays on 19th Century British Theatre; The Proceedings of a Symposium Sponsored by the Manchester University Department of Drama.* London, Methuen & Co. 1971.

Ricks, Christopher, ed., *English Drama to 1710.* (History of Literature in the English Language) vol. 3. London, Barrie & Jenkins. 1971.

Ridley, Maurice Roy, *Second Thoughts; More Studies in Literature.* London, J. M. Dent. 1965.

Riesner, Dieter and Helmut Gneuss, *Festschrift für Walter Hübner.* Berlin, Schmidt. 1964.

Ritchie, James MacPherson, ed., *Periods in German Literature.* Chester Springs, Pa., Dufour Eds. 1970.

Robinson, Lennox, ed., *Irish Theatre.* N.Y., Macmillan. 1939.

Roby, Kinley, *A Writer at War; Arnold Bennett, 1914-1918.* Baton Rouge, Louisiana State Univ. Pr. 1972.

Rogers, Katharine M., *William Wycherley.* N.Y., Twayne Pub. 1972.

Rohde, E., *Psyche*; tr. W. B. Hillis. London, Routledge and Kegan Paul. 1925.

Römer, Paul, *Molières "Amphytrion" und Sein Gesellschaftlicher Hintergrund.* Bonn, Romanisches Seminar der Univ. Bonn. 1967.

Rosenblood, Norman, ed., *Shaw; Seven Critical Essays; Seven Papers Presented at the Shaw Seminars, Niagra on the Lake, 1966-1968.* Toronto, Univ. of Toronto Pr. 1971.

Rosenmeyer, Thomas G., *The Masks of Tragedy: Essays on Six Greek Dramas.* Austin: Univ. of Texas Pr. 1963.

Rostvig, Maren-Sofie, et al, *The Hidden Sense and Other Essays*. New York: Humanities Pr., Inc. 1963.

Rothstein, Eric, *Restoration Tragedy; Form and the Process of Change*. Madison, Wis.: Univ. of Wisconsin Pr. 1967.

Rowe, William Woodin, *Through Gogol's Looking Glass; Reverse Vision, False Focus and Precarious Logic*. N.Y., N.Y. Univ. Pr. 1976.

Roy, Emil, *British Drama Since Shaw*. Carbondale, Southern Illinois Univ. Pr. 1972.

————————, *Christopher Fry*. Carbondale, Ill.: Southern Illinois Univ. Pr. 1968.

Royal Soc. of Literature of the United Kingdom, London, *Essays by Divers Hands, Being the Transactions of the Society*. London, Oxford Univ. Pr. 1928.

Rudd, Niall, ed., *Essays on Classical Literature*. N.Y., Barnes and Noble. 1972.

Ruitenbeek, Hendrik M., ed., *Psychoanalysis and Literature*. N.Y., E. P. Dutton and Co. 1964.

Saccio, Peter, *The Court Comedies of John Lyly; A Study in Allegorical Dramaturgy*. Princeton, N.J., Princeton Univ. Pr. 1969.

Sackville-West, Edward, *Inclinations*. Port Washington, N.Y., Kennikat Pr., Inc. 1967.

Sainte-Beuve, Charles A., *Selected Essays*. Garden City, N.Y., Doubleday. 1963.

Sammons, Jeffrey L. and Ernst Schurer, eds., *Lebendige form; Interpretationen zur Deutschen Literatur. Festschrift für Heinrich E. K. Henel*. Munchen, Fink. 1970.

Sanchez Romeralo, Jaime and Norbert Poulussen, eds., *Actas del Segundo Congreso International de Hispanistas. Celebrado en Nymegen del 20 al 25 de Agosto de 1965*. Nÿmegen, Holland, Inst. Espanol de la N. de Nimega. 1967.

Santayana, George, *Little Essays Drawn From the Writings of George Santayana by L. P. Smith*. N. Y., Scribner. 1920.

————————, *Three Philosophical Poets*, (Harvard Studies in Comparative Literature). Cambridge, Harvard Univ. Pr. 1910.

Sarkar, Subhas, *T. S. Eliot the Dramatist*. Calcutta, Minerva Asso. 1972.

Saurat, Denis, *Modern French Literature, 1870-1940*. N.Y., G. P. Putnam's Sons. 1946.

Sautermeister, Gert, *Idyllik und Dramatik im Werk Friedrich Schillers*. Berlin, W. Kohlhammer. 1971.

Savage, James E., *Ben Jonson's Basic Comic Characters and Other Essays*. Univ. and College Pr. of Mississippi. 1973.

Schau, Albrecht, *Max Frisch; Beiträge zur Wirkungsgeschichte*. Freiburg, Universtatsverlag Becksmann. 1971.

Schelling Anniversary Papers by His Former Students. N.Y., Appleton-Century. 1923.

Schelling, Felix E., *Elizabethan Drama, 1558-1642*. N.Y., Russell and Russell. 1959.

Schelling, Felix Emmanuel, *The English Chronicle Play; A Study in the Popular Historical Literature Environing Shakespeare*. N.Y., Macmillan Co. 1902.

Scheurwegns, Gustave, *Nicholas Udall's "Roister Doister"*, Librairie Universitaire. 1939.

Schiller, Ferdinand C. S., *Our Human Truths*. Boulder, Colorado Univ. Pr. 1935.

Schlesinger, Arthur Meier, *The Politics of Hope*. Boston, Houghton. 1963.

Schmidt, Ernst-Joachim, ed., *Kritische Bewahrung. Beiträge zur Deutschen Philologie. Festschrift für Werner Schroder zum 60. Geburtstag*. Berlin, Erich Schmidt. 1974.

Schmitt, Albert R., ed., *Festschrift für Detlev W. Schumann zum 70. Geburtstag*. Munchen, Delp. 1970.

Schoenbaum, Samuel, *Middleton's Tragedies; A Critical Study*. N.Y., Columbia Univ. Pr. 1955.

Schraibman, Jose, ed., *Homenaje a Sherman H. Eoff*. Madrid, Castalia, 1970.

Schröder, Jürgen, *Gotthold Ephraim Lessing; Sprache und Drama*. Munchen, Wilhelm Fink. 1972.

Schwartländer, Johannes and Michael ˚Landmann and Werner Loch, eds., *Verstehen und Vertrauen; Otto Friedrich Bollnow zum 65. Geburtstag*. Stuttgart, Kohlhammer. 1968.

Schwarz, Egon, Hunter G. Hannum and Edgar Lohner, eds., *Festschrift für Bernhard Blume; Aufsätze zur Deutschen und Europäischen Literatur*. Gottingen, Vanderhoeck and Ruprecht. 1967.

Scott, Kilvert, Ian, *John Webster*. London, Longmans, Green & Co. 1964.

Sedgewick, G. G., *Of Irony, Especially in Drama*. Univ. of Toronto Pr. 1967.

Segal, E., *Euripides*. Englewood Cliffs, N.J., Prentice-Hall. 1968.

Seidlin, Oskar, *Essays in German and Comparative Literature*. Chapel Hill, Univ. of N. Carolina. 1961.

Sells, A. Lytton, *Oliver Goldsmith; His Life and Works*. London, George Allen and Unwin. 1974.

Serreau, Genevieve, *Histoire du Nouveau Theatre*. Gallimard. 1966.

Sewall, R., *The Vision of Tragedy*. New Haven, Conn., Yale Univ. Pr. 1962.

The Shaken Realist; Essays in Modern Literature in Honor of Frederick J. Hoffman; ed. Malvin J. Friedman and John B. Vickery. Baton Rouge, La., Louisana State Univ. Pr. 1970.

Shalvi, Alice and A. A. Mendilow, eds., *Studies in English Language and Literature*. Jerusalem, Hebrew Univ. Pr. 1966.

Sharma, Ram Chandra, *Themes and Conventions in the Comedy of Manners*. Asia House. 1965.

Shaw, George Bernard, *Plays and Players: Essays on the Theatre*. London, Oxford Univ. Pr. 1952.

——————————— , *Selected Prose*, Sel. by Diarmid Russell. N.Y., Dodd. 1952.

——————————— , *Shaw on Theatre*, ed. by E. J. West. N.Y., Hill and Wang, Inc. 1958.

Shaw, Leroy Robert, *The Playwright and Historical Change; Dramatic Strategies in Brecht, Hauptmann, Kaiser and Wedekind*. Madison, Univ. of Wisconsin Pr. 1970.

Sheed, Wilfrid, *The Morning After; Selected Essays and Reviews*. N.Y., Farrar, Straus, and Giroux Inc. 1971.

Sherrell, Richard, *The Human Image; Avant-Garde and Christian*. Richmond, John Knox Pr. 1969.

Sices, David, *Theater of Solitude; The Drama of Alfred de Musset*. Hanover, N.H., Univ. Pr. of New England. 1973.

Sifakis, G. M., *Parabasis and Animal Choruses*. London, Univ. of London Pr. 1971.

Silz, Walter, *Heinrich von Kleist; Studies in His Works and Literary Character.* Philadelphia, Univ. of Pennsylvania Pr. 1961.

Simonson, Lee, *The Stage is Set.* N.Y., Dover Publications, Inc. 1946.

Simpson, Percy, *Studies in Elizabethan Drama.* London, Oxford Univ. Pr. 1955.

Skelton, Robin, *John Millington Synge.* Lewisburg, Bucknell Univ. Pr. 1972.

Slote, Bernice, ed., *Literature and Society.* Lincoln, Univ. of Nebraska. 1964.

Smiley, Sam, *Playwriting; The Structure of Action.* Englewood Cliffs, N. J., Prentice-Hall. 1971.

Smith, Hugh A., *Main Currents of Modern French Drama.* N.Y., Holt. 1925.

Smith, J. Percy, *The Unrepentant Pilgrim: A Study of the Development of Bernard Shaw.* N.Y., Houghton. 1965.

Snell, Bruno, *Scenes from Greek Drama.* Berkeley, Calif., Univ. of California Pr. 1964.

Solomont, Susan, *The Comic Effect of "The Playboy of the Western World".* Signalman Pr. 1962.

Sontag, Susan, *Against Interpretation and Other Essays.* N.Y., Farrar, Straus and Giroux, Inc. 1966.

Spanos, William V., *The Christian Tradition in Modern British Verse Drama; The Poetics of Sacramental Time.* New Brunswick, N.J., Rutgers Univ. Pr. 1967.

Spencer, Theodore, *Theodore Spencer; Selected Essays.* New Brunswick, N.J.: Rutgers Univ. Pr. 1966.

Spitzer, Leo, *Linguistics and Literary History: Essays in Stylistics.* Princeton, N.J., Princeton Univ. Pr. 1948.

Sprinchorn, Evert, ed., *The Genius of the Scandinavian Theater.* N.Y., New American Library. 1964.

Squire, John C., *Books Reviewed.* New York: James H. Heinemann, Inc. 1922.

Stallknecht, Newton Phelps and Horst Frenz, eds., *Comparative Literature; Method and Perspective.* Rev. ed. Carbondale, Southern Illinois Univ. Pr. 1971.

Stanford, W. B., *Ambiguity in Greek Literature.* London, Oxford Univ. Pr. 1939.

Stavig, Mark, *John Ford and the Traditional Moral Order.* Madison, Univ. of Wisconsin Pr. 1968.

Steane, J. B., ed., *The Shoemaker's Holiday.* Cambridge, Cambridge Univ. Pr. 1965.

Steene, Birgitta, *The Greatest Fire; A Study of August Strindberg.* Carbondale, Southern Illinois Univ. Pr. 1973.

Steffen, Hans, ed., *Das Deutsche Lustspiel.* II Göttingen, Vandenhoeck and Ruprecht. 1969.

Stevens, D. H., *Manly Anniversary Studies in Language and Literature.* Chicago: Univ. of Chicago Pr. 1923.

Sticca, Sandro, ed., *The Medieval Drama; Papers of the 3rd Annual Conference of the Center for Medieval and Early Renaissance Studies.* N.Y., State Univ. of New York, 1972.

Stoll, Elmer E., *Shakespeare and Other Masters.* Cambridge, Harvard Univ. Pr. 1940.

Studi in Memoria di Luigi Russo, Pisa, Nistri-Lischi. 1974.

Studia Iberica. Festschrift für Hans Flasche, hrsg. v. Karl-Hermann Körner und Klaus Rühl. Bern. 1973.

Studies for William A. Read: A Miscellany Presented by Some of His Colleagues and Friends, ed. by N. M. Caffee and T. A. Kirby. Baton Rouge, La.: Louisiana State Univ. Pr. 1940.

Studies in Bibliography: Papers of the Bibliographical Soc. of Virginia, ed. by Fredson Bowers, v. 14-17, The Society. 1961-64.

Studies in English in Honor of Raphael Dorman O'Leary and Selden Lincoln Whitcomb, by members of the English Dept. (Kansas Univ. Humanistic Studies, v. 6). Lawrence, Kan., Univ. of Kansas Pr. 1940.

Studies in French Language, Literature, and History Presented to R. L. Graeme Ritchie. London, Cambridge Univ. Pr. 1949.

Studies in German Literature of the 19th and 20th Centuries; Festschrift for Frederic E. Coenen. Chapel Hill, Univ. of North Carolina Pr. 1971.

Studies in Honor of Alfred G. Engstrom, ed. Robert T. Cargo and Emmanual Mickel, Jr. (Studies in Romance Languages and Literatures 124), Univ. of North Carolina Pr. 1972.

Studies in Honor of John Wilcox, by Members of the English Department, ed. by G. A. Doyle Wallace and Woodburn O. Ross. Detroit, Michigan, Wayne State Univ. Press. 1958.

Studies in Medieval Literature, in Honor of Albert Croll Baugh. Philadelphia: Univ. of Pennsylvania Pr. 1961.

Studies in Speech and Drama in Honor of Alexander M. Drummond. Ithaca, N.Y., Cornell Univ. Pr. 1944.

Sturgeon, May C., *Women of the Classics*. N.Y., Thomas Y. Crowell Pub. Co. 1914.

Styan, J. L., *The Eements of Drama*. London: Cambridge Univ. Pr. 1960.

Sullivan, Kevin, *Oscar Wilde*. N.Y., Columbia Univ. Pr. 1972.

Sullivan, Maurine, ed., *Colley Cibber; Three Sentimental Comedies*. New Haven, Yale Univ. Pr. 1973.

Sulton, Graham, *Some Contemporary Dramatists*. N. Y., Doran Pub. Co. 1925.

Swados, Harvey, *A Radical's America*. Boston: Little, Brown Pub. Co. 1962.

Swales, Martin, *Arthur Schnitzler; A Critical Study*. London, Oxford Univ. Pr. 1971.

Symons, James M., *Meyerhold's Theatre of the Grotesque; The Post-Revolutionary Productions, 1920-1932*. Coral Gables, Univ. of Miami Pr. 1971.

T. L. S., *Essays and Reviews from the Times Literary Supplement, 1963*, v. 2. London, Oxford Univ. Pr. 1964.

Talbert, Ernest William, *Elizabethan Drama and Shakespeare's Early Plays; An Essay in Historical Criticism*. Chapel Hill, N. C., Univ. of North Carolina Pr. 1963.

Tate, Allen, ed., *T. S. Eliot; The Man and His Work; A Critical Evaluation*. New York, Delacorte Pr. 1966.

Taylor, John Russell, *Anger and After; A Guide to the New British Drama*. London, Methuen & Co. 1962.

————————, *The Rise and Fall of the Well-Made Play*. New York, Hill and Wang. 1967.

————————, *The Second Wave; British Drama for the Seventies*. Hill and Wang. 1971.

Taylor, William E., ed., *Modern American Drama; Essays in Criticism*. Deland, Fla., Everett/Edwards. 1968.

Teatro di Pirandello Convegno di Studi ad Asti il 27 e 28 Maggio 1967 in Casa d'Alfieri. Asti, Centro Nazionale di Studi Alfieriani. 1968.

Texas Univ., *A Schiller Symposium: In Observance of the Bicentenary of Schiller's Birth.* Austin, Univ. of Texas Pr. 1960.

––––––––––––– , Dept. of English, *Studies in English.* Austin: Univ. of Texas Pr. 1948.

Thalheim, Hans-Gunther and Ursula Werthem, eds., *Studien zur Literaturgeschichte und Literaturtheorie. Gerhard Scholz Anlässlich Seines 65. Geburtstages Gewidmet von Seinen Schülern und Freunden.* Berlin, Rutten & Loening. 1970.

Theatre Arts Anthology: A Record and a Prophecy, ed. by Rosamond Gilder. Theatre Arts Books. 1950

Theatre at Work; Playwrights and Productions in Modern British Theatre, ed. Charles Marowitz and Simon Trussler. N.Y., Hill and Wang. 1968.

Thomas, Calvin, *Scholarship and Other Essays.* New York, Holt. 1924.

Thompson, Francis, *Literary Criticisms: Newly Discovered and Collected by Terence L. Connally.* New York, E. P. Dutton & Co., Inc. 1948.

Thomson, J. A. K., *Irony.* Cambridge, Mass., Harvard Univ. Pr. 1926.

Tillotson, Geoffrey, *Essays in Criticism and Research.* New York, Macmillan. 1942.

Time Was Away; The World of Louis MacNeice, ed. Terence Brown and Alec Reid. Humanities Pr. 1974.

Tindall, William York, *A Reader's Guide to James Joyce.* N.Y., Noonday Pr. 1959.

Tisch, J. H., *Proceedings of the Australian Goethe Society.* Melbourne, Monash Univ. 1966.

Todd Memorial Volumes: Philological Studies, ed. by J. D. Fitzgerald and P. Taylor, vol. 1, Boulder, Colorado Univ. Pr. 1930.

Tomlinson, Thomas Brian, *A Study of Elizabethan and Jacobean Tragedy.* Cambridge, Cambridge Univ. Pr. 1964.

Traditions and Transitions; Studies in Honor of Harold Jantz, ed. by Lieselotte E. Kurth et al. Munchen, Delp. 1972.

Trussler, Simon, *The Plays of John Osborne; An Assessment.* London, Victor Gollanz, Ltd. 1969.

Turnell, Martin, *Classical Moments: Studies of Corneille, Molière and Racine.* London, Hamilton. 1947.

––––––––––––– , *Graham Greene; A Critical Essay.* William Eerdmans Pub. 1976.

––––––––––––– , *Jean Racine, Dramatist.* N.Y., New Directions Pub. Co. 1972

Tynan, Kenneth, *Curtains; Selections from the Drama Criticism and Related Writings.* N.Y., Antheneum. 1961.

Tysdahl, Bjorn, *James Joyce and Ibsen; A Study in Literary Influence.* N.Y., Humanities Pr. 1968.

Untersuchungen zur Literatur als Geschichte. Festschrift für Benno von Wiese, hrsg. v. Vincent J. Gunther. Berlin. 1973.

Ure, Peter, *Elizabethan and Jacobean Drama; Critical Essays.* N.Y., Barnes and Noble. 1974.

Valency, Maurice, *The Cart and the Trumpet; The Plays of George Bernard Shaw.* N.Y., New York Univ. Pr. 1973.

––––––––––––– , *The Flower and the Castle; Introduction to Modern Drama.* N.Y., Macmillan Co. 1963.

Van Abbé, Derek, *Goethe; New Perspectives on a Writer and His Time.*
Lewisburg, Bucknell Univ. Pr. 1972.

Van Doren, Mark, ed., *New Invitation to Learning.* N.Y., Random House. 1942.

Van Nostrand, Albert D., ed., *Literary Criticism in America.* Liberal Arts Pr.
1957.

Vellacott, Philip, *Sophocles and Oedipus; A Study of "Oedipus Tyrannus".*
London, Macmillan & Co. 1971.

Vernois, Paul, ed., *l'Onirisme et l'Insolite dans le Théâtre Francais Contemporain.* Paris, Klincksieck. 1974.

Verrall, A. W., *The "Bacchants" of Euripides and Other Essays.* Cambridge,
Cambridge Univ. Pr. 1910.

————————— , *Essays on Four Plays of Euripides.* Cambridge, Cambridge
Univ. Pr. 1905.

Versenyi, Laszlo, *Man's Measure; A Study of the Greek Image of Man from
Homer to Sophocles.* State Univ. of New York Pr. 1974.

Vidal, Gore, *Homage to Daniel Shays; Collected Essays, 1952-1972.* Random
House Pr. 1972.

Viebrock, Helmut, ed., *Festschrift zum 75. Geburtstag von Theodor Spira.*
Heidelburg, C. Winter. 1961.

Von Arx, Paulette, *La Femme dans le Théâtre de Henry de Montherlant.* Paris,
Librairie A. G. Nizet. 1973.

Vos, Nelvin, *Eugene Ionesco and Edward Albee; A Critical Essay.* Grand
Rapids, Michigan, William B. Eerdmans. 1968.

Vossler, Karl, *Jean Racine.* N.Y., F. Ungar Pub. Co. 1972.

Wagenknecht, Edward C., ed., *Joan of Arc: An Anthology of History and
Literature.* Creative Age. 1948.

————————— , *Preface to Literature.* N.Y., Holt. 1954.

Wainwright, P., *The Burning Fountain.* Bloomington, Indiana Univ. Pr. 1954.

Waith, Eugene M., *The Herculean Hero in Marlowe, Chapman, Shakespeare,
and Dryden.* Boulder, Colorado Univ. Pr. 1962.

————————— , *Ideas of Greatness; Heroic Drama in England.* London,
Routledge & Kegan Paul. 1971.

Walker, Hallam, *Moliere.* N.Y., Twayne Pub. 1971.

Walkley, Arthur B., *Drama and Life.* N.Y., Brentano Book Store. 1908.

————————— , *More Prejudice.* N.Y., A. A. Knopf, Inc. 1923.

————————— , *Pastiche and Prejudice.* N.Y., A. A. Knopf, Inc. 1921.

————————— , *Still More Prejudice.* N.Y., A. A. Knopf, Inc. 1925.

Wallach, L., *Three Plays by Euripides.* Ithaca, Cornell Univ. Pr. 1966.

Wallis, Lawrence B., *Fletcher, Beaumont and Company, Entertainers to
Jacobean Gentry.* King's Crown Pr. 1947.

Ward, Adolphus W., *A History of English Dramatic Literature,* 3 vols. N.Y.,
Octagon Books. 1966.

Ward, Alfred Charles, ed., *Specimens of English Dramatic Criticism, 17th-
20th Centuries.* London, Oxford Univ. Pr. 1945.

Ward, David, *T. S. Eliot; Between Two Worlds.* London, Routledge and Kegan
Paul. 1973.

Wardropper, Druce W., ed., *Critical Essays on the Theatre of Calderon.* N.Y.,
New York Univ. Pr. 1964.

Waters, Harold A., *Paul Claudel.* N.Y., Twayne Pub. 1970.

Watt, H. A., *Elizabethan Studies and Other Essays in Honor of George F.
Reynolds,* (Univ. of Colorado Studies in Humanities, ser. B, vol. 2, #4).
Boulder, Univ. of Colorado Pr. 1945.

Weathers, Winston, *Pär Lagerkvist; A Critical Essay*. Grand Rapids, Michigan, William B. Eerdmans. 1968.

Webb, Eugene, *The Dark Dove; The Sacred and Secular in Modern Literature*. Univ. of Washington Pr. 1975.

————————— , *The Plays of Samuel Beckett*. Seattle, Univ. of Washington Pr. 1972.

Weber, Brom, ed., *Sense and Sensibility in Twentieth Century Writing; A Gathering in Memory of William Van O'Connor*. Carbondale, Southern Illinois Univ. Pr. 1970.

Webster, Brenda S., *Yeats; A Psychoanalytic Study*. Stanford Univ. Pr. 1973.

Webster, John, *The Duchess of Malfi*; ed. by F. L. Lucas. London, Chatto & Windus. 1958.

Weigand, Hermann John, *The Modern Ibsen; A Reconsideration*. E. P. Dutton & Co. 1960.

————————— , *Surveys and Soundings in European Literature*; edited by A. Leslie Willson. Princeton Univ. Pr. 1966.

Weimar, Karl S., ed., *Views and Reviews of Modern German Literature*; *Festschrift fur Adolf D. Klarmann*. Munchen, Delp. 1974.

Wilde, Alan, *Christopher Isherwood*. N.Y., Twayne Pub. 1971.

Weissman, Philip, *Creativity in the Theater; A Psychoanalytic Study*. N.Y., Basic Books, Inc. 1965.

Wellesz, Egon, *Essays on Opera*. N.Y., Roy Pubs., Inc. 1950.

Wells, Henry W., *The Classical Drama of the Orient*. N.Y., Asia Pub. House. 1965.

West, Ray B., ed., *Essays in Modern Literary Criticism*. N.Y., Rinehart. 1952.

West, Rebecca, *Ending in Earnest: A Library Log*. Garden City, N.Y., Doubleday. 1931.

Wiese, Benno von, *Das Deutsche Drama; Vom Barock bis zur Gegenwart*. vol. 1, Dusseldorf, A. Bagel. 1958.

Wiese, Benno von and Rudolf Henss, eds., *Nationalismus in Germanistik und Dichtung: Dokumentation des Germanistentages in Muchen vom 17 bis 22. Oktober 1966*. Berlin, E. Schmidt. 1967.

Williams, Raymond, *Drama from Ibsen to Brecht*. London, Chatto & Windus. 1968.

————————— , *Modern Tragedy*. Stanford, Calif., Stanford Univ. Pr. 1966.

Willig, Kurt, *Strena Anglica: Otto Ritter Zum 80. Geburtstag*. Leipzig, Germany, Niemeyer. 1956.

Wilson, Edmund, *American Earthquake: A Documentary of the Twenties and Thirties*. Garden City, N.Y., Doubleday. 1958.

————————— , *Shores of Light: A Library Chronicle of the Twenties and Thirties*. N.Y., Farrar, Straus. 1952.

————————— , *Wound and the Bow: Seven Studies in Literature*. N.Y., Houghton. 1941.

Wimmel, Walter, *Forschungen zur Römischen Literatur; Festschrift zum 60. Geburtstag von Karl Büchner*. Wiesbaden. 1970.

Wimsatt, William K., ed., *English Stage Comedy*. Boulder, Colorado Univ. Pr. 1955.

————————— , *Hateful Contraries; Studies in Literature and Criticism*. Lexington, Ky., Univ. of Kentucky Pr. 1965.

Wimsatt, William Kurtz, ed., *Literary Criticism; Idea and Act*. Univ. of California Pr. 1974.

Wisenthal, J. L., *The Marriage of Contraries; Bernard Shaw's Middle Plays.* Cambridge, Harvard Univ. Pr. 1974.

Die Wissenschaft von Deutscher Sprache und Dichtung; Methoden, Probleme, Aufgaben. Festschrift für Friedrich Maurer zum 65. Geburtstag am 5. Jan. 1963. Stuttgart, Klett. 1963.

Witte, William, *Schiller and Burns and Other Essays.* Oxford, England, Blackwell Pub. Co. 1959.

Woodard, Thomas, ed., *Sophocles: A Collection of Critical Essays.* Englewood Cliffs, N.J., Prentice-Hall. 1966.

Woolf, Virginia Stephen, *Collected Essays.* N.Y., Harcourt, Brace and World. 1967.

Woollcott, Alexander, *Portable Woollcott.* N.Y., Viking. 1946.

World Shakespeare Congress, 1st, Vancouver, B.C., *Shakespeare, 1971; Proceedings.* Univ. of Toronto Pr. 1972.

Worth, Katharine, *Beckett the Shape Changer.* London, Routledge and Kegan Paul. 1975.

Wright, Edward A. and Lenthiel H. Downs, *A Primer for Playgoers.* 2nd ed. Englewood Cliffs, N.J., Prentice-Hall, Inc. 1969.

Wynne, Arnold, *Growth of English Drama.* London, Oxford Univ. Pr. 1914.

Yates, W. E., *Grillparzer; A Critical Introduction.* Cambridge Univ. Pr. 1972.

Yearbook of Comparative and General Literature, 1961. Bloomington, Indiana Univ. Pr. 1962.

Yeats, William Butler, *Explorations.* N.Y., Macmillan. 1962.

Young, Stark, *Flower in Drama and Glamour: Theatre Essays and Criticism.* N.Y., Scribner. 1955.

——————— , *Glamour, Essays on the Art of the Theatre.* N.Y., Charles Scribner. 1925.

——————— , *Immortal Shadows: A Book of Dramatic Criticism.* N.Y., Scribner. 1948.

Zyla, Wolodymyr T. and Wendell M. Aycock, eds., *Joseph Conrad; Theory and World Fiction.* Lubbock, Inter. Dept. Comm. on Comparative Literature, Texas Tech Univ. Pr. 1974.

LIST OF JOURNALS INDEXED

Abhandlung der Preussichen Akademie der Wissenschaft. Berlin.
Abhandlungen zur Kunst, Musik-und Literaturwissenschaft. Bonn.
Abside, Revista de Cruz y Pensamiento. Ona, Spain.
Académie Royale de Belgique, Bull. de la Classe des Lettres. Brussels.
Acta Germanica. Cape Town, S. Africa.
Acta Litteraria Academiae Scientiarum Hungaricae. Budapest.
Acta Philologica. Rome.
Acta Psychotherapeutica, Psychosomatica et Orthopaedagogica.   Basel.
Adam: International Review. London.
Aegyptus. Milan, Italy.
America. New York.
American Academy of Religion. Chambersburg, Pa.
American Benedictine Review. Newark, N.J.
American-German Review. Philadelphia, Pa.
American Imago. Detroit, Mich., Wayne State Univ. Pr.
American Journal of Archeology.   New York.   Archeological Institute of
     America.
American Journal of Philology.   Baltimore, Md.   Johns Hopkins Univ. Pr.
American Notes and Queries. New Haven.
American Review. New York.
American-Scandinavian Review.   New York.   American-Scandinavian Founda-
     tion.
American Scholar. Washington, D.C.
American Society of Legion of Honor Magazine. New York.
Amsterdamer Beiträge zur Neueren Germanistik. Amsterdam.
Analele Stiintifice ale Universitatii Iasi. Bucharest.
Analele Universitatii, Bucuresti, Limbi Romanice. Bucharest.
Anales Cervantinos. Madrid.
Anglia: Zeitschrift für Englische Philologie.   Tübingen, Germany.
Anglo-Welsh Review. Pembroke Dock, Wales. Dock Leaves, Ltd.
Annales de la Faculté des Lettres de Bordeaux. Bulletin Hispanique. Bordeaux.
Annales de la Faculté des Lettres de Bordeaux. Revue des Etudes Anciennes.
     Bordeaux.
Annales de la Faculté des Lettres et Sciences Humaines.   Univ. of Yaounde,
     Cameroun.
Les Annales Politiques et Litteraires. Paris.
Annales Universitatis Turkuensis. Turku, Finland.
Annali della Scuola Normale Superiore di Pisa.   SEE   *Pisa. Scuola Normale
     Superiore. Annali. Lettere, Storia et Filosofia*.
Annali Institute Universitario Orientale, Napoli, Sezione Germanica.   Naples.
Antaios. Stuttgart.
Antigonish Review. St. Francis Xavier Univ. Antigonish.
Antike und Abenbland. Berlin, Germany.
Antioch Review. Yellow Springs, Ohio.
L'Antiquité Classique. Bruxelles.
*Anzeiger für die Altertumswissenschaft. von der Osterreichischen Humanis-
     tischen Gesellschaft*. Innsbruck.
Appalachian State Teachers College Faculty Publications.   Boone, N.C.
Arbor; Revista General de Investigación y Cultura. Madrid.

Arcadia. Zeitschrift für Vergleichen de Literaturwissenschaft. Berlin.
Archaeologia Classica. Rome, Italy.
Archiv für das Studium der Neueren Sprachen und Literaturen. Braunschweig, W. Germany.
Archivum. Oviedo.
Arethusa. Buffalo, N.Y. State Univ. of New York. Dept. of Classics.
Ariel; A Review of International English Literature. Alta, Can. Univ. of Calgary.
Arion; A Quarterly Journal of Classical Culture and the Humanities. Austin, Texas. Univ. of Texas Pr.
Arizona Quarterly. Tucson, Ariz. Univ. of Arizona.
Arlington Quarterly; A Journal of Literature, Comment and Opinion. Arlington, Tex. Univ. of Texas at Arlington.
Asociation Guillaume Bude. Boletin. Mexico.
Atene e Roma. Florence, Italy.
Atlantic Monthly. Boston, Mass.
Atlantida. Madrid.
Atlas. New York. The World Pr. Co.
Atti dell'Istituto Veneto di Scienze, Lettere, Arti. Classe di Scienze Morali e Lettere. Venezia.
Ausblick; Mitteilungsblatt der Deutschen Auslandgesellschaft. Lübeck.
Australian Journal of French Studies. Melbourne: Dept. of Modern Languages, Monash Univ. Pr.
Aylesford Review; A Literary Quarterly. Kent, Eng. St. Albert's Pr.
Ball State Teachers College Forum. Muncie, Ind. Ball State Univ.
Ball State Univ. Forum. Muncie, Ind. Ball State Univ.
Bamah; Educational Theatre Review. Jerusalem, Israel.
Basis; Jahrbuch für Deutsche Gegenwartsliteratur. Frankfort am Main.
Basler Studien zur Deutschen Sprache und Literatur. Bern.
Die Berufsbildende Schule. Wolfenbüttel.
Bibliographical Society of America. Papers. New York.
Boletin de Estudios Germánicos. San Luis, Argentina.
Boletin del Instituto de Filologia de la Univ. de Chile. Chile.
Bonniers Litterära Magasin. Stockholm.
Books Abroad; An International Literary Quarterly. Norman, Okla. Univ. of Oklahoma Pr.
Brecht Heute—Brecht Today; Jahrbuch de International Brecht-Gesellschaft. Frankfort am Main.
Bucknell Review. Lewisburg, Pa. Bucknell Univ.
Bulletin de l'Academie Royale de Langue et de Litterature Francaises. Brussels.
Bulletin de l'Association Guillaume Budé. SEE Asociation Guillaume Bude. Boletin.
Bulletin de la Faculté des Lettres de Strasbourg. Strasbourg.
Bulletin des Jeunes Romaniste. Strasbourg.
Bulletin Hispanique. Bordeaux, France.
Bulletin of Hispanic Studies. Liverpool, Engl. Liverpool Univ. Pr.
Bulletin of the Comediantes. Chapel Hill, N.C.
Bulletin of the Department of English. Calcutta Univ., India.
Bulletin of the Institute of Classical Studies of the University of London. London.
Bulletin of the New York Public Library. New York.
Bulletin of the Rocky Mountain Modern Language Assn. Albuquerque, N.M.
Bungaku. Tokyo.

Cahiers de l'Association Internationales des Etudes Francaises. Paris.
Cahiers de la Compagnie Madeleine Renaud-Jean-Louis Barrault SEE *Compagnie Madeleine Renaud-Jean-Louis Barrault. Cahiers.*
Cahiers de Linguistique Theorique et Appliquée. Bucharest.
Cahiers Elisabethans; Etudes sur la Pre-Renaissance et la Renaissance Anglaises. Montpelier, France.
Cahiers Internationaux de Symbolisme. Geneva.
Cahiers Raciniens. France.
Caliban. Toulouse.
Cambridge Journal. Cambridge, Engl.
Cambridge Philological Society. Proceedings. Cambridge, Engl.
Camp de l'Arpa; Revista de Literatura. Barcelona.
Canadian-American Slavic Studies. Pittsburgh, Pa.
Canadian Modern Language Review. Toronto, Can. Ontario Modern Lang. Teachers' Assn.
Canadian Review of Comparative Literature. Toronto.
Catholic World. New York.
CEA Critic. Shreveport, La.
The Centennial Review. East Lansing, Mich. Mich. State Univ. Pr.
Central States Speech Journal. Columbia, Mo. Univ. of Missouri.
Christ und Welt. Stuttgart.
Christengemeinschaft. Stuttgart.
Christian Century. Chicago, Ill.
Cithara; Essays in Judaeo-Christian Tradition. St. Bonaventure, N.Y. St. Bonaventure Univ. Pr.
CLA Journal. Baltimore, Md. Morgan State College.
Classica et Mediaevalia. Copenhagen.
Classical Bulletin. St. Louis, Mo. St. Louis Univ.
Classical Journal. Milwaukee, Wis. Univ. of Wisconsin.
Classical Philology. Chicago, Ill.
Classical Quarterly. London. Oxford Univ. Pr.
Classical Review. London. Oxford Univ. Pr.
Claudel Studies. Irving, Tex.
Clio; An Interdisciplinary Journal of Literature, History and the Philosophy of History. Univ. of Wisconsin.
Colby Library Quarterly. Waterville, Maine.
College English. Champagne, Ill. National Council of Teachers of English.
College Language Association. Journal. Baltimore, Morgan State College.
College Literature. West Chester, Pa.
Colliers, New York.
Colloquia Germanica, Internationale Zeitschrift für Germanische Sprach-und Literaturwissenschaft. Bern, Switzerland.
Columbia Essays on Modern Writers. N.Y., Columbia Univ. Pr.
Commentary. N.Y. American Jewish Committee.
Commonweal. New York.
Compagnie Madeleine Renaud, Jean-Louis Barrault Cahiers. Paris.
Comparative Drama. Kalamazoo, Mich. Dept. of English, Western Michigan Univ. Pr.
Comparative Literature. Eugene, Oregon. Univ. of Oregon.
Comparative Literature Studies. College Park, Md. Univ. of Maryland.
Concerning Poetry. W. Washington State College.

Conradiana. College Park, Md.
Contemporary Literature. Madison, Univ. of Wisconsin.
Contemporary Review. London.
Costerus; Essays in English and American Language and Literature. Amsterdam.
Criterion. Karachi, Pakistan.
Critic: A Catholic Review of Books and the Arts. Chicago, Ill.
Critical Quarterly. London. Oxford Univ. Pr.
Criticism. Detroit, Mich. Wayne State Univ. Pr.
Cuadernos Hispanoamericanos. Madrid.
Culture. Quebec, Canada.
D. H. Lawrence Review. Fayetteville, Ark. Univ. of Arkansas
Dalhousie Review; A Canadian Quarterly of Literature and Opinion. Halifax,
    N.S., Canada. Dalhousie Univ.
Degrés; Revue de Synthèse a Orientation Sémiologique. Brussels.
Delo. Belgrade, Yugoslavia.
Delos; A Journal on and of Translation. Austin, Univ. of Texas.
Deutsche Shakespeare-Gesellschaft West. Jahrbuch. SEE *Jahrbuch der
    Deutschen Shakespeare Gesellschaft West.*
Deutsche Vierteljahrsschrift für Literaturwissenschaft und Geistesgeschichte.
    W. Germany.
Der Deutschunterricht. Berlin, E. Germany
*Der Deutschunterrichter. Beiträge zu Seiner Praxis und Wissenschaftlichen
    Grundlegung.* Stuttgart.
Dialog. Warsaw.
Dialogi; Mesečnik za Vprašanja Kulturnega in Javnega Zivljenja. Mariboa.
Dietsche Warande en Belfort. Antwerp, Belgium.
Diliman Review. Quezon City, Philippines. Univ. of the Philippines.
Dioniso. Syracuse.
Discourse; A Review of the Liberal Arts. Moorhead, Minn. Concordia College.
Dissent. New York.
Dissertation Abstracts International. Ann Arbor, Mich. (Formerly *Dissertation
    Abstracts).*
Dix-Septieme Siecle. Paris.
Drama; The Quarterly Theatre Review. London.
Drama and Theatre. Fredonia, N.Y.
Drama Critique; A Critical Review of Theatre Arts and Literature. Washington,
    D.C.
Drama Review SEE *TDR; The Drama Review*
Drama Survey. Minneapolis, Minn.
Dramaforskning. Uppsala.
Die Drei. Stuttgart.
The Dubliner. Dublin: New Square Pub., Ltd.
Duquesne Hispanic Review. Pittsburgh. Duquesne Univ.
Durham Univ. Journal. Durham, Engl.
ELH; Journal of English Literary History. Baltimore, Md.
Edda. Oslo, Norway.
Das Edle Leben: Stuttgart.
Educational Theatre Journal. Washington, D.C. Amer. Educational Theatre
    Assn.
Eighteenth Century Studies. Berkeley, Calif.
Eigo Seinen. Tokyo

(Eire) Ireland; A Journal of Irish Studies. St. Paul, Minn.
Elizabethan Studies. Univ. of Salzburg, Austria.
Emerita; Revista de Linguistica y Filologia Classica. Madrid.
Emerson Society Quarterly. Hartford, Conn.
Emporia State Research Studies. Emporia, Kansas.
Encore. London
Encounter. London
English. London, Engl.
English Goethe Society. Publications. Leeds, Engl. Pub. for the Society by
    W. S. Maney and Son, Ltd.
English Journal. Urbana, Ill.
English Language Notes. Boulder, Col. Univ. of Colorado.
English Literary Renaissance. Amherst, Mass.
English Literature and Language. Tokyo.
English Literature in Transition (1880-1920). DeKalb, Ill. Northern Illinois
    Univ.
English Miscellany. Rome.
English Record. Binghamton, N.Y. N.Y. State English Council.
English Studies. Amsterdam.
English Studies in Africa. Johannesburg, S. Africa.
Epoca. Milan, Italy.
Eranos. Sweden.
Esprit. Paris, France.
L'Esprit Créateur. Lawrence, Kansas.
Esquire. New York.
Essays and Studies. London.
Essays and Studies by Members of the English Assn. SEE *Essays and Studies*
Essays by Divers Hands, Being the Transactions of the Royal Soc. of Literature.
    London.
Essays in Criticism; A Quarterly Journal of Literary Criticism. Oxford, Engl.
Essays in French Literature. Univ. of Western Australia.
Essays in Literature. Western Illinois Univ.
O Estado de São Paulo, Suplemento Literário. Sao Paulo.
Estudios Filologicos. Valdivia.
Etc; A Review of General Semantics. San Francisco, Calif.
Études. Paris, France.
Études Anglaises. Paris, France.
Études Classiques. Brussels.
Études de Linguistique Appliquée, New Series. Besarcon.
Études Francaises. Montreal, Canada.
Études Germaniques. Paris, France.
Études Slaves et Est-Europeennes. Montreal, Canada. Univ. of Montreal.
Euphorion. Zeitschrift für Literatur Geschichte. Heidelberg, Germany.
Europäische Begegnung. Koln.
Europe. Paris, France.
L'Europe Nouvelle. Paris.
Exil; Tidsskrift for Literatur og Semiologi. Oslo.
Explicator. Richmond, Va
Fabula. Zeitschrift für Erzahl Forschung. Berlin.
Far Western Forum; A Review of Ancient and Modern Letters. Berkeley, Cal.
Figaro Littéraire. Paris, France.

Filología Moderna. Madrid.
Filologiceskie Nauki. Moscow.
Filosofs'ka Dumka. Kiev.
Folktales Told of the World. Chicago.
Forschungen u. Fortschritte. Berlin.
Forskningsnytt. Oslo.
Forum. Houston.
Forum der Letteren. Leyden.
Forum for Modern Language Studies. Scotland: Univ. of St. Andrews.
FI: Forum Italicum. Buffalo, N.Y.
Four Quarters. Philadelphia.
Le Francais dans le Monde. Paris.
France Illustration. Paris.
Frankfurter Beiträge zur Germanistik. Bad Homburg.
Frankfurter Hefte. Zeitschrift für Kultur und Politik. Frankfurt, Main.
Freeman. New York.
French Review. Ypsilanti, Mich. Amer. Assn. of Teachers of French. Eastern
      Mich. Univ.
French Studies. Oxford, Engl.
French Studies in Southern Africa. Capetown.
Furman Studies. Greenville, S.C.
Garcia Lorca Review. Brockport, N.Y.
Gazetta del Mezzogiorno. Bari.
Gemini/Dialogue SEE *Gemini; The Oxford and Cambridge Magazine*
Gemini; The Oxford and Cambridge Magazine. London.
Genealogie. Deutsche Zeitschrift für Famielenkunde. Neustadt-Aisch.
Genre. Univ. of Illinois at Chicago Circle.
Georgetown Univ. French Review. Washington, D.C.
German Life and Letters. Oxford, England.
German Quarterly. Appleton, Wis.
Germanic Review. Columbia Univ. Pr. Irving-on-Hudson, N.Y.
Germanica Wratislaviensia. Wroclaw.
Germanisch-Romanische Monatsschrift. Heidelberg.
Germano-Slavica. Waterloo, Ontario.
Gewerkschaftliche Monatshefte. Köln.
Glaube und Gewissen. Eine Protestantische Monatschrift. Halle/Saale.
Glotta. Zeitschrift für Griechische und Lateinische Sprache. Gottingen.
Godisnjak Filozofskog Fakulteta u Novom Sadu.
Goethe; Neue Folge des Jahrbuchs der Goethe-Gesellschaft. Weimarer.
Goethe-Almanach. Berlin.
Goethe Jahrbuch. Weimar.
Gordon Review. Wenham, Mass.
Greece and Rome. London. Oxford Univ. Pr.
Greek, Roman and Byzantine Studies. Cambridge, Mass.
Greyfriar; Siena Studies in Literature. Londonville, N.Y. Siena College.
Grillparzer Forum Forchtenstein. Wien; Munchen.
Gruppenpsychotherapie und Gruppendynamik. Göttingen.
Guardian. Rangoon.
Harper's. New York
Harper's Weekly. New York.
Harvard Library Bulletin. Cambridge, Mass.

Hartford Studies in Literature; A Journal of Interdisciplinary Criticism. Hartford, Conn. Univ. of Hartford.
Harvard Studies in Classical Philology. Cambridge, Mass. Harvard Univ.
Harvard Theological Review. Cambridge, Mass. Harvard Univ.
Hasifrut; Quarterly for the Study of Literature. Tel-Aviv, Israel. Tel-Aviv Univ.
Heidelberger Jahrbucher. Heidelberg.
Helikon; Rivista di Tradizione e Cultura Classica dell Universita di Messina. Messina.
Helmantica. Revista de Humanidades Clásicas. Salamanca: Salamanca Univ.
Herder-Korrespondenz (Orbis Catholicus). Freiburg, Ger.
Hermathena. Dublin: Trinity College.
Hermes. Wiesbaden, Ger.
Hispania. Wichita, Kansas: Wichita State Univ.
Hispanic Review; A Quarterly Journal Devoted to Research in Hispanic Languages and Literatures. Philadelphia, Penna: Univ. of Penn. Romance Lang. Dept.
Hispanófila. Madrid.
Histoire des Sciences Médicales. Paris.
Hofmannsthal Blätter. Frankfurt am Main.
L'Homme et la Société. Revue Internationale de Recherche et de Synthèse Sociologique. Paris.
Hound and Horn. Portland, Maine.
Hudson Review. New York.
Humanistika Vetenskapssamfundet i Lund. Lund.
Humanties Association Bulletin. Canada: Univ. of Alberta, Dept. of English.
Huntington Library Quarterly. San Marino, Calif.
Ibero-Romania. Munchen.
Ibsenforbundet: Arbok. Oslo.
Icarus. Dublin. Univ. of Dublin.
Illustrated London News. London.
L'Illustration. Paris.
Independent Shavian. New York.
Indice. Madrid.
L'Information Littéraire. Paris.
Inostrannaya Literatura, Foreign Literature. Moscos.
International Journal of Comparative Sociology. Toronto, Canada. York Univ.
International Social Science Journal (UNESCO). New York.
Iowa English Bulletin Yearbook. Cedar Falls. Iowa Association of Teachers of English.
Italian Quarterly. Riverside, Calif. Univ. of California.
Italica. New York. Amer. Assn. of Teachers of Italian. Columbia Univ.
Interpretation; A Journal of Political Philosophy. The Hague.
Ireland; A Journal of Irish Studies. St. Paul.
Irish University Review. Shannon.
Jahrbuch der Deutschen Schiller-gesellschaft. Stuttgart.
Jahrbuch der Deutschen Shakespeare Gesellschaft West. Heidelberg.
Jahrbuch des Freien Deutschen Hochstifts. Frankfurt/Main.
Jahrbuch der Grillparzergesellschaft.
Jahrbuch der Wittheit zu Bremen. Bremen.
Jahrbuch des Wiener Goethe-Vereins. Vienna.
Jahrbuch für Amerikastudien. Heidelberg.

Jahrbuch. Literaturwissenschaftliches. Berlin.
James Joyce Quarterly. Tulsa, Okla. Univ. of Tulsa.
Jewish Quarterly. Philadelphia.
Journal of Aesthetics and Art Criticism. Detroit, Mich. Wayne State Univ.,
    Dept. of English.
Journal des Débats. Paris.
Journal of American Folklore. Philadelphia, Pa. Univ. of Pa.
Journal of Australasian Universities Language and Literature Assn. New
    Zealand.
Journal of Bible and Religion SEE *American Academy of Religion. Journal.*
Journal of English and Germanic Philology. Urbana, Ill. Univ. of Illinois.
Journal of English Literary History. SEE *ELH.*
Journal of European Studies. London.
Journal of Hellenic Studies. London.
Journal of Individual Psychology. Burlington, Vt. Univ. of Vermont.
Journal of Irish Literature. Newark, Delaware.
Journal of Modern Literature. Philadelphia. Temple Univ.
Journal of Popular Culture. Bowling Green State Univ.
Journal of the Warburg and Courtauld Institute. London.
Kentucky Romance Quarterly. Lexington. Univ. of Kentucky.
Kenyon Review. Gambier, Ohio. Kenyon College.
Kerygma. Stockholm.
Kirche. Dortmund.
Kirche in der Zeit. Dusseldorf.
Kirchenblatt für die Reformierte. Basel.
Kirke og Kultur. Oslo, Norway.
Die Kommenden. Freiburg.
Kommunität. Berlin.
Komos; A Quarterly of Drama and the Arts of the Theatre. Clayton, Australia.
    Monash Univ.
Kritik. Copenhagen.
Du. Kulturelle Monatsschrift. Zurich.
Kulturrleven. Leuven. Belgium.
Kunst en Cultur. Brussels.
Kwartalnik Neofilologiczny. Warsaw.
Language Quarterly. Tampa, Fla. Univ. of S. Florida.
Language Sciences. Bloomington, Ind.
Langues Modernes. Paris.
Laurel Review. Buckhannon, West Va. West Va. Wesleyan College.
Lessing Yearbook. Munich.
Les Lettres Nouvelles. Paris.
Les Lettres Romanes. Louvain. Universite Catholique.
Letture. Milan.
Liberal. Beiträge zur Entwicklung einer Freibeitlichen Ordnung. Bonn.
Liberté. Montreal.
Library. Birmingham, Engl. Univ. of Birmingham.
Library Review. Bucharest.
Life. Chicago, Ill.
LiLi; Zeitschrift für Literaturwissenschaft und Linguistik. Goettingen.
Listener. London.
Literary Digest. New York.

Literary Half-Yearly. Mysore, India.
Literatur in Wissenschaft und Unterricht. Kiel.
Literatur und Kritik. Salzburg.
Literatura: Lietuvos TSR Aukštuju Mokyklu Mokslo Darbai. Vilinius.
Literature and Ideology. Montreal.
Literature and Psychology. Hartford. Univ. of Hartford.
Literature East and West. Austin, Tex.
Literature/Film Quarterly. Salisbury, Md.
Literaturwissenschaftliches Jahrbuch der Görres-Gesellschaft. Berlin.
Littérature. Univ. of Paris.
Living Age. Boston.
London Magazine. London.
London Mercury. London.
Look. New York.
Louisburg College Journal of Arts and Science. Louisburg, N.C.
Lübeckische Blätter. Zeitschrift der Gesellschaft zu Förderung Gemeinnütziger Tätigkeit. Lübeck.
Luceafarul. Bucharest.
Lund Studies in English. Lund, Sweden.
Luther-Jahrbuch. Hamburg.
·*Luther. Zeitschrift der Luther-Gesellschaft.* Hamburg.
Maal og Minne. Oslo.
McNeese Review. Lake Charles, La. McNeese College.
A Magyar Tudományos Akadémia Nyelv-És Iroda Lom Tudományi Osztalyának Közlemenyei. Studia Slavica Academiae Scientiarum Hungaricae. Budapest.
Maia. Firenze.
Malahat Review. Victoria, B.C., Canada. Univ. of Victoria.
Mapocho. Santiago.
Marab: A Review. Heidelberg, Germany.
Marche Romane. Liege: Association des Romanistes de l'Universite de Liege.
Marginalien; Blätter der Pirckheimer-Gesellschaft. Berlin.
Maske und Kothern. Graz-Wien.
Massachusetts Review. Amherst, Mass. Univ. of Massachusetts.
Massachusetts Studies in English. Amherst, Mass. Dept. of English. Univ. of Mass.
Meander. Warsaw.
Meanjin Quarterly. Australia. Univ. of Melbourne.
Meddelanden fran Strindbergssallskapet.
Meddeleser fra Gymnasieskolernes Tyskloererforening. Copenhagen.
Medelingen de Koninklijke Nederlanse Akademie van Wetenschappen afd. Letterkunde. Amsterdam.
Médicine de France. Paris.
Medieval and Renaissance Studies. London.
Medieval Studies. Toronto, Canada.
Mélanges de Science Religieuse. Lille.
Melbourne Critical Review. Victoria, Australia. Dept. of English, Univ. of Melbourne.
Mercure de France. Paris.
Merkur. Koblenz. Stuttgart.
Michigan Acadamician. Ann Arbor, Mich.

Michigan Quarterly Review. Ann Arbor, Mich.
Midstream. New York.
Midwest Monographs. Dept. of English, Univ. of Illinois.
Midwest Quarterly. Pittsburg, Kansas. Kansas State College of Pittsburg.
Minerva. Oslo.
Mississippi Quarterly. State College, Miss.
Mnemosyne. Bibliotheca Classica Batava. Leiden.
Modern Age. Chicago.
Modern and Classical Languages Bulletin. Edmonton, Alta, Canada.
Modern Austrian Literature; Journal of the International Arthur Schnitzler Research Association. Pittsburgh, Pa.
Modern Drama. Lawrence, Kansas. Univ. of Kansas.
Modern Fiction Studies. Lafayette, Ind. Purdue Univ., Dept. of English.
Modern Language Association. Publications. New York.
Modern Language Forum. Los Angeles. Southern California Univ.
Modern Language Notes. Baltimore, Md. Johns Hopkins Univ.
Modern Language Quarterly. Seattle, Wash. Univ. of Wash.
Modern Language Review. London.
Modern Languages. London.
Modern Philology. Chicago. Univ. of Chicago.
Moderna Sprak. Stockholm.
Monatshefte SEE *Monatshefte für Deutsche Unterricht.*
Monatshefte für Deutsche Unterricht. Madison, Wis. Univ. of Wisconsin.
Monatsschrift. Heidelburg.
Month. London.
Moreana. Angers.
Mosaic. Manitoba, Can. Univ. of Manitoba.
Moskovsky Gosudarstvennyi Pedagogiceskij Institut Ucenye Zapiski.
Mundus Artium; A Journal of International Literature and the Arts. Athens, Ohio.
Musées Royaux des Beaux-Arts de Belgique. Brussels.
Museum Helveticum. Basel, Switzerland.
Musical America. New York.
Nassau Review. Nassau Community College, New York.
Nation. New York.
National Review. New York.
Natur und Kultur. Munchen-Solln.
Neohelicon; Acta Comparationis Litterarum Universarum. Budapest.
Neophilologus. Groningen, Netherlands.
Neue Deutsche Hefte. Berlin.
Neue Deutsche Literatur. Berlin.
Neue Rundschau. Berlin.
Die Neue Schau. Kassel.
Die Neueren Sprachen. Berlin.
Neuphilologische Mitteilungen. Helsinki, Finland.
Neusprachliche Mitteilungen aus Wissenschaft und Praxis. Berlin.
Neva. Moscow.
New German Studies. Hull, England.
New Leader. New York.
New Left Review. London.
New Republic. Washington, D.C.

New Society. London.
New Statesman. London.
New Statesman and Nation. London.
New Theatre Magazine. Bristol.
New York Folklore Quarterly. Cooperstown, New York.
New Yorker. New York.
Newsletter; Teaching Language Through Literature.
Newsweek. New York.
Nineteenth Century French Studies. New York.
Nordisk Tidskrift. Copenhagen.
Notes and Queries. London.
Notes on Contemporary Literature. West Georgia College, Carrollton.
La Nouvelle Critique; Revue du Marisme Militant. Paris.
Nouvelle Revue Francaise. Paris.
Neuva Revista de Filología Hispánica. Mexico.
Nuova Antologia. Rome.
Ochanomizu University Studies. Tokyo.
Ohio University Review. Athens, Ohio.
Onomastica Canadiana. Winnipeg.
Orbis Litterarum. Revue Internationale d'Études Littéraires. Kobenhavn.
Ord och Bild. Stockholm.
Orientierung. Zurich.
Osmania Journal of English Studies. Hyderabad, India.
Österreich in Geschichte und Literatur. Wien.
Outlook. London.
Oxford German Studies. London.
Pacific Coast Philology. Northridge, Cal. Philological Assn. of the Pacific Coast.
Panjab University Research Bulletin. India.
Papers of the Bibliographical Society of Ameria SEE *Bibliographical Society of Amer. Papers*.
Papers on English Language and Literature SEE *Papers on Language and Literature*.
Papers on Language and Literature. Edwardsville, Ill. Southern Illinois Univ.
Paragone. Florence.
La Parola del Passato. Rivista di Studi Antichi. Naples, Italy.
Partisan Review. New Brunswick, N.J. Rutgers Univ.
Pensée Catholique, Cahiers de Synthese. Paris.
Personalist; An International Review of Philosophy. Los Angeles. Univ. of Southern California.
Philobiblon. Eine Vierteljahrsschrift für Buch-und Graphik Sammler. Hamburg.
Philological Papers. West Virginia Univ. Pr.
Philological Pragensia. Academia Scientiarum Bohemo-Slovenico. Prague, Czechoslovakia.
Philological Quarterly. Iowa City, Iowa. Univ. of Iowa.
Philologus. Berlin, Germany.
Philosophisches Jahrbuch im Auftrag der Görres-Gesellschaft Herausgegeben. Munchen.
Phoenix. Toronto. Univ. of Toronto.
Pictorial Review. New York.
Pisa. Scoula Normale Superiore. Annali. Lettere, Storia, et Filosofia. Pisa.

Plays and Players. London.
Poet Lore. Boston.
Poetica. Zeitschrift für Sprach und Literaturwissenschaft. Munich.
Poetik. Copenhagen.
Poetry. Chicago, Ill.
Polish Review. New York.
Politics and Letters. London.
Il Ponte; Revista di Politica e Letteratura. Florence, Italy.
Poradnik Jezykowy. Warsaw.
Prairie Schooner. Lincoln. Univ. of Nebraska.
Praxis. Zagreb.
Présence Francophone. Sherbrooke, Quebec.
Preuves. Paris, France.
Primer Acto. Madrid.
Proceedings of the British Academy. London.
Proceedings and Transactions of the Royal Society of Canada. Ottawa, Canada.
Proceedings of the Cambridge Philological Society SEE *Cambridge Philological Soc. Pro.*
Prompt. London: Univ. College.
Provinz. Frankfurt/Main.
Psyche. Zeitschrift für Psychoanalyse und ihre Anwendungen. Stuttgart.
Psychoanalytic Quarterly. New York.
Psychoanalytic Review. New York.
Publications of the English Goethe Society. London.
Publications Universitaires. Lettres et Sciences Humaines de l'Université de Provence. Aix-en-Provence.
Quäker, Der. Monatshefte der Deutschen Freunde. Berlin.
Quarterly of Journal of Speech. New York.
Queen's Quarterly. Kingstone, Canada.
Quest. London.
Radius. Vierteljahresschrift der Engelischen Akademikerschaft in Deutschland. Stuttgart.
Rassegna della Letteratura Italiana. Florence.
Realismo Lirico. Florence.
Recherches Anglaises et Américaines. Strasbourg.
Recherches Germaniques. Strasbourg.
Reflexion II. Ottawa.
Regional. New York: New York Regional Group of the Shaw Society of London.
Religion in Life; A Christian Quarterly of Opinion and Discussion. Nashville, Tenn.
Renaissance and Modern Studies. Nottingham, Engl. Univ. of Nottingham.
Renaissance and Reformation. Toronto.
Renaissance Drama. Chicago, Ill. Northwestern Univ.
Renaissance Papers. Columbia, S.C.
Renaissance Quarterly. New York.
Renascence; A Critical Journal of Letters. Milwaukee, Wis.
Reporter; The Magazine of Facts and Ideas. New York.
Research Studies. Pullman, Wash. Washington State Univ.
Research Studies of the State College of Washington SEE *Research Studies.*
Response; A Contemporary Jewish Review. New York.
Restoration and Eighteenth Century Theatre Research. Chicago. Loyola Univ.

Review. Belgrade, Yugoslavia.
Review of English Literature. London.
Review of English Studies; A Quarterly Journal of English Literature and English Language. London. Oxford Univ. Pr.
Review of Reviews. New York.
Revista de Archivos, Bibliotecas y Museos. Madrid.
Revista de Estudios Hispánicos. Puerto Rico.
Revista de Estudios Hispánicos. University, Ala. Univ. of Alabama.
Revista de Filología Española. Madrid.
Revista de la Universidad de Costa Rica. Costa Rica.
Revista de Letras. Assis, Brazil.
Revista de Occidente. Madrid.
Revista Hispánica Moderna. New York.
Revista Signos de Valparaiso. Valparaiso.
Revue Belge de Philologie et d'Histoire. Brussels.
Revue de l'Histoire des Religions. Paris.
Revue de l'Institut de Sociologie. Brussels.
Revue de Littérature Comparée. Paris.
Revue de Paris. Paris.
Revue des Langues Vivantes. Brussels.
Revue de l'Université d'Ottawa. Ottawa.
Revue de Metaphysique et de Morale. Paris.
Revue de Philologie, de Littérature et d'Histoire Anciennes. Paris.
Revue des Deux Mondes. Paris.
Revue des Etudes Anciennes. Bordeaux.
Revue des Etudes Grecques. Paris.
Rue des Etudes Italiennes. Paris.
Revue des Langues Vivantes; Tijdschrift voor Levende Telen. Brussels, Bel.
Revue des Lettres Modernes; Histoire des Idees et des Littérature. Paris.
Revue d'Histoire du Théâtre. Paris.
Revue d'Histoire Littéraire de la France. Paris.
Revue des Sciences Humaines. Lille, France.
Revue Générale Belge. Brussels, Bel.
Revue Hispanique. New York.
Revue Politique et Littéraire. Paris.
Revue Romane. Copenhagen.
Rheinisches Museum für Philologie. Frankfurt/Main.
Rice University Studies; Writings in All Scholarly Disciplines. Houston, Tex.
Rivista di Filologia e di Istruzione Classica. Torino.
Rivista de Litterature Moderne and Comparate. Florence.
Romance Notes. Chapel Hill. Univ. of North Carolina.
Romanic Review. New York. Columbia Univ.
Romanische Forschungen. Frankfurt a. Main.
Romanistisches Jahrbuch. Hamburg, Germany.
Salzburg Studies in English Literature: Elizabethan Studies. Salzburg.
Samtiden; Tidsskrift for Politikk, Litteratur og Samfunnssporsmal. Oslo, Norway.
Saturday Review. New York.
Saturday Review of Literature. New York.
Sbornik Praci Filosofické Fakulty Brnenske Univ. Rady Archeology. Brno.
Scandinavian Studies. Menasha, Wis.

Scandinavica. London.
Schau. Kassel.
Scheidewege; Vierteljahrsschrift für Skeptisches Denken. Stuttgart.
School and Society. New York.
Schweizer Monatshefte für Politik, Wortschaft, Kultur. Zürich.
Schweizer Rundschau. Einsiedeln.
Science and Society. New York.
Scripta Hierosolymitana. Tel Aviv, Palestine.
Scrutiny; A Quarterly Review. Cambridge, Engl.
Seminar; A Journal of Germanic Studies. Toronto: Victoria College.
Serif. Kent, Ohio. Kent State Univ. Lib.
XVIIᵉ Siecle. Brussels.
Seventeenth Century News. New York Univ. New York.
Sewanee Reivew. Sewanee, Tenn. Univ. of the South.
Shakespeare Jahrbuch. Heidelburg.
Shakespeare Quarterly. New York.
Shakespeare Studies. Tokyo.
Shakespeare Survey. London.
Shavian. Kent, Engl.
Shaw Review. University Park, Pa. Pa. State Univ.
Siculorum Gymnasium. Catania. Univ. of Catania.
Sin Nombre. San Juan, Puerto Rico.
Sitzungberichte der Heidelberger Akademie der Wissenschaften. Mathematisch-Naturwissenschaftliche Klasse. Berlin.
Skandinavistik. Univ. Kiel.
Slavonic and East European Review. New York.
Social Science Information. The Hague, Netherlands. International Social Science Council.
Sophia; Studies in Western Civilization and the Cultural Interaction of East and West. Tokyo.
South Atlantic Bulletin. Chapel Hill, N.C.
South Atlantic Quarterly. Durham, N.C. Duke Univ.
South Central Bulletin. New Orleans, La.
Southern Humanities Review. Auburn, Alabama.
The Southern Quarterly; A Scholarly Journal in the Humanities and Social Sciences. Hattiesburg, Miss. Univ. of South Mississippi.
Southern Review. Adelaide, Australia.
Southern Review. Baton Rouge, La. Louisiana State Univ.
Southern Speech Journal. Tampa, Fla. Univ. of Southern Florida.
Spectator. London.
Speculum; A Journal of Medieval Studies. Cambridge, Mass.
Speech Monographs. New York.
Sprachkunst. Beitrage zur Literaturwissenschaft. Wien.
Stimmen der Zeit. Freiburg.
Studi Francesi; Rivista Dedicata all Cultura e al Civilta Letteraria della Francia. Turin, Italy.
Studi Germanici. Rome.
Studi Goldoniani. Venice.
Studi Urbinati di Storia, Filosofia e Letteratura. Urbino, Italy.
Studia Germanica Gandesia. Ghent.
Studien, Wiener. Zeitschrift für Klassische Philologie. Vienna.

Studies in Bibliography. Charlottesville, Va. Univ. of Virginia.
Studies in English and Comparative Literature. Columbia Univ.
Studies in English Literature, 1500-1900. Houston, Texas. Rice Univ.
Studies in English Literature. English Literature Society of Japan.
Studies in French Literature. The Hague.
Studies in Philology. Chapel Hill, Univ. of North Carolina.
Studies in Short Fiction. Newberry, S.C. Newberry College.
Studies in the Romance Languages and Literatures. Chapel Hill, N.C. Univ. of N.C.
Studies of Burke and His Time. Alfred, N.Y.
Symbolae Osloenses. Oslo.
Symposium; A Quarterly Journal in Modern Foreign Literatures. Syracuse, N.Y. Syracuse Univ.
Susquehanna University Studies. Selinsgrove, Pa.
TDR, The Drama Review. New York.
La Table Ronde. Paris.
Tamarack Review. Toronto, Canada.
Temps Modernes. Paris.
Tennessee Studies in Literature. Univ. of Tennessee.
Texas Quarterly. Austin, Tex. Univ. of Texas.
Texas Studies in Literature and Language; A Journal of the Humanities. Austin. Univ. of Texas.
Text und Kontext. Goettingen.
Theatre Annual. New York.
Theatre Arts. New York.
Theatre der Zeit. Berlin.
Theatre Heute. SEE *Theatre Heute. Zeitschrift für Schauspiel, Oper, Ballett.*
Theatre Heute. Zeitschrift für Schauspiel, Oper, Ballett. Hanover.
Theatre Notebook; Quarterly Journal of the History and Technique of the British Theatre. London.
Theatre Quarterly. London.
Theatre Survey. Waltham, Mass.
Theater und Zeit. (ceased).
Theatre Zeit. Germany.
Theoria; A Swedish Journal of Philosophy. Lund, Sweden.
Die Therapie des Monats. Mannheim.
Thoth. Syracuse, N.Y. Syracuse Univ.
Thought. Bronx, N.Y. Fordham Univ.
Threshold. Belfast, Ireland.
Time. N.Y.
Times Literary Supplement. London.
Trace. London.
Transactions and Proceedings of the American Philological Association. Cleveland, Ohio. Western Reserve Univ.
Travail Théâtral. Lausanne, Switzerland.
Travel, Floral Park, N.Y.
Tribune. Zeitschrift zum Verständnis des Judentums. Frankfort.
Tri-Quarterly. Evanston, Ill. Northwestern Univ.
Trivium. Oude Nederlandse Geschriften op het Gebied van Grammatica de Dialectica en de Rhetorica. Groningen.
Tulane Drama Review. New Orleans, La. Tulane Univ.

Tulane Studies in English. New Orleans, La. Tulane Univ.
Twentieth Century. London.
Twentieth Century Literature; A Scholarly and Critical Journal. Los Angeles, Calif.
Ultima. Florence.
Unisa English Studies. South Africa University.
Universitas; Zeitschrift für Wissenschaft, Kunst, Literatur. Stuttgart.
Universities and Left Review. London. Oxford Univ.
University of California Publications in Classical Philology. Los Angeles.
University of Dayton Review. Dayton, Ohio. Univ. of Dayton.
University of Kansas City Review SEE *University Review.*
University of Mississippi Studies in English. University, Miss.
University of North Carolina Studies in Romance Languages and Literatures. Chapel Hill, N.C.
University of Toronto Quarterly. Toronto, Canada.
University Review. Kansas City, Missouri.
Die Unterrichtspraxis. Philadelphia, Pa.
Valodas Un Literaturas Instituta Raksti. Riga.
Venture. Wheaton, Ill.
Vinduet; Gyldendals Tidsskrift for Literatur. Oslo, Norway.
Virginia Quarterly Review; A National Journal of Literature and Discussion. Charlottesville, Va. Univ. of Virginia.
De Vlaamse Gids. Brussels, Bel.
Vogue. New York.
Die Volksbühne. Hamburg.
Der Volkswirt. Wirtschafts und Finanzzeitung. Frankfort/Main.
Voprosy Literatury. Moscow.
Wascana Review. Regina, Saskatchewan, Canada.
Weimärer Beiträge; Zeitschrift für Literaturwissenschaft. Berlin.
Die Welt der Slaven. Wiesbaden.
Weltwoche. Zurich.
West Virginia University Philological Papers. Morgantown, W. Va.
Westerly. Nedlands, Western Aus. Univ. of Western Australia.
Westermanns Monatshefte. West Germany.
Wiener Beiträge Zur Englischen Philologie. Wien.
Wiener Studien; Zeitschrift für Klassiche Philologie. Wien.
The Wind and the Rain. London.
Wirkendes Wort. Dusseldorf.
Wisconsin Studies in Contemporary Literature. Madison. Univ. of Wisconsin.
Wisconsin Studies in Literature. Oshkosh, Wis. Council of Teachers of English.
Wissenschaftliche Zeitschrift der Friedrich Schiller-Universität Leipzig. Gesellschafts-u. Sprachwissenschaftliche Reihe. Leipzig.
Wissenschaftliche Zeitschrift der Humboldt-Universität zu Berlin. Gesellschafts-u. Sprachwissenschaftliche Reihe. Berlin.
Wissenschaftliche Zeitschrift der Pädagogischen Hochschule Potsdam. Gesselschafts-u. Sprachwissenschaftliche Reihe. Potsdam, Germany.
Wissenschaftliche Zeitschrift der U. Rostock. Rostock Univ.
World Literature; General Educational Journal. Quezon City.
World Theatre. New York.
Wort, Wirkendes. Deutsches Sprachschaffen in Lehre und Leben. SEE *Wirkendes Wort.*

Xavier University Studies. New Orleans, La.

Xenia.

Y Genhinen. Gamerian Pr., Llanysue Cards, Wales.

Yale Classical Studies. New Haven, Conn.

Yale French Studies. New Haven, Conn.

Yale Review. New Haven, Conn. Yale Univ.

Yale/Theatre. New Haven.

Yearbook of English Studies. Cambridge.

Yeats Studies. Shannon.

Zeichender Zeit. Berlin.

Die Zeit. Wochenzeitung für Politik, Wirtschaft, Handel und Kultur. Hamburg.

Zeitschrift für Anglistik und Amerikanistik. Berlin.

Zeitschrift für Deutsche Philologie. Berlin.

Zeitschrift für Französische Sprache und Literatur. Wiesbaden.

Zeitschrift für Papyrologie und Epigraphik. Bonn.

Zeitschrift für Religions-und Geistesgeschichte. Köln.

Zeitschrift für Romanische Philologie. Halle.

Zeitschrift für Slavische Philologie. Heidelberg.

Zeitschrift für Slawistik. Berlin.

Zeitschrift, Wissenschaftliche, der Humboldt Universität. Berlin.

Zeitschrift, Wissenschaftliche, der Martin Luther Universität. Halle-Wittenberg.

Zeitwende. Die Neue Furche. Hamburg.

AUTHOR / TITLE INDEX

l'Abbe Setubal, 321
ABELL, KJELD (1901-1961), 1
Der Abenteurer und die Sangerin, 250
Abraham and Isaac, 2
Absalom's Hair, 76
Accolade, 562
Ace of Clubs, 124
El Acero de Madrid, 540
The Acharnians, 24
Acque Turbate, 57
Act Without Words, 38
Acte, 146
Acte Sans Paroles, 38
Les Acteurs de Bonne Foi, 325
Actors in Good Faith, 325
ADAMOV, ARTHUR (1908-   ), 2
Adelphi, 530
Admiral Bashville, 478
The Admirable Crichton, 30
Adrienne Lecouvreur, 474
Advent, 517
Adventure Story, 447
The Adventurer and the Singer, 250
Die Aegyptische Helen, 250
AESCHYLUS (525 BC-456 BC), 3
Affairs of Anatol, 470
After the Dance, 447
After the Rain, 60
Agamemnon, (Aeschylus), 3
Agamemnon, (Seneca), 474
L'Age de Juliette, 134
Agesilas, 116
Aglavaine and Selysette, 321
Die Ahnfrau, 236
L'Aigle à Deux Tetes, 110
L'Aiglon, 451
Aiuola Bruciata, 57
Ajax, 505
El Alcalde de Su Mismo, 76
El Alcalde De Zalamea, 76
Alcestis (Euripides), 162
Alcestis (Hofmannsthal), 250
The Alchemist, 287
Alexander, Campaspe and Diogenes, 319
Alexander the Great, 436
Alexandre le Grand, 437
Alice Sit by the Fire, 30
The Alien Nest, 54
Alkestis, 163 and 250
All Against All, 2
All for Love; or, The World Well Lost, 136
All for the Best, 421
All That Fall, 38
All 'Uscita, 421

Alladine and Palomides, 321
Alma Triunfante, 54
L'Alouette, 13
Alphonsus, King of Arragon, 234
Als der Krieg zu Ende War, 179
l'Altro Figlio, 421
Amanecer, 345
Les Amants Magnifiques, 368
The Amazons, 405
The Ambitious Stepmother, 454
Amboyna, 137
Amédée; or, How to Get Rid of It, 278
Amédée; ou, Comment s'en Débarrasser,
    278
El Amor de Don Perlimplin con Belisa
    en Su Jardin, 189
The Amorous Quarrel, 368
L'Amour et la Verite, 325
Amphitryon, 38, 205
Amphitryon (Kleist), 301
Amphitryon (Plautus), 429
Amphitryon (Moliere), 369
Amphytryon, 138
The Anabaptists, 146
Anathema, 12
Ancestress, 236
And on the Seventh Day God Rested, 104
Andorra, 179
ANDREEV, LEONID, 12
ANDREYEV, LEONID (1871-1919), 12
Andria, 530
Androcles and the Lion, 478
Andromache, 163
Andromaque, 437
Andromeda, 116
An Angel Comes to Babylon, 146
Angel Street, 241
Angéle, 144
Angora Cat, 54
Anna Sophie Hedvig, 1
Annibal, 325
L'Annonce Faite à Marie, 105
The Anonymous Work, 564
ANOUILH, JEAN (1910-   ), 13
ANSKY, SOLOMON (pseud), 21
Antigone (Anouilh), 13
Antigone (Cocteau), 110
Antigone (Sophocles), 506
Antigone of Sophocles, 60
Antonio and Mellida, 342
Antonio's Revenge, 342
Antony, 144
Anything for a Quiet Life, 359
The Apple Cart, 478

Appollo of Bellac, 206
L'Appollon de Bellac, 206
L'Apollon de Marsac, 206
Arabella, 250
Arbitration, 352
ARBUSOV, ALEKSEL NIKOLAEVICH
(1908-   ), 21
ARCHER, WILLIAM (1856-1924), 22
L'Archipel Lenoir, 454
Ardele, 14
ARDEN, JOHN (1930-   ), 22
El Arenal de Sevilla, 540
The Argument, 325
Ariadne, 362
Ariadne and Bluebeard; or, The Useless
Deliverance, 321
Ariadne auf Naxos, 250
Ariadne in Naxos, 250
Ariane et Barbe-Bleu, 321
ARISTOPHANES (446 B. C.-388 B. C.),
24
Arlequin Poli par l'Amour, 326
Arms and the Man, 479
Armstrong's Last Goodnight, 22
As Before, Better than Before, 421
As You Desire Me, 421
Ascent of F6, 28
Así que Pasen Cinco Anos, 189
Asinaria, 430
Assignation; or, Love in a Nunnery, 138
El Astrologo Fingido, 76
At the Gate, 421
At the Hawk's Well, 568
Athalie, 438
The Atheist; or, The Second Part of the
Soldier's Fortune, 403
The Atheist's Tragedy; or, The Honest
Man's Revenge, 534
Atlas-Hotel, 454
Attila, 116
AUDEN, WYSTAN HUGH (1907-1973),
28
The Audience, 189
Der Aufhaltsame Aufstieg des Arturo Ui,
61
Aufstieg und Fall der Stadt Mahagonny, 61
Augustus Does His Bit, 480
Aulularia, 430
Aunt Edwina, 256
Aureng-Zebe, 138
L'Avare, 369
L'Aveu, 2
Les Aveugles, 321
L'Avenir Est Dans les Oeufs, ou, Il Faut de
Tout pour Faire un Monde, 278

Baal, 61
Bacchae, 163

Bacchides, 430
Bacchus, 110
Das Bacchusfest, 470
Back to Methuselah, 480
Bad Soldier Smith, 256
Das Badener Lehrstueck vom Einver-
staendnis, 61
Badger's Green, 503
BAGNOLD, ENID (1889-   ), 29
Bajazet, 439
Le Bal des Voleurs, 15
Le Balcon, 197
The Balcony, 197
The Bald Soprano, 278
The Ballygombeen Bequest, 24
Banbury Nose, 537
Banya, 324
Barabbas, 203
Barbara's Wedding, 30
Barber of Seville, 33
Barberine, 386
Le Barbier de Seville, 33
Barnavelt, 34
Barrabas, 309
Barretts of Wimpole Street, 56
Barricou, 134
BARRIE, JAMES MATTHEW (1860-
1937), 30
Bartholomew Fair, 289
Baruffe Chiozzotte, 227
The Basement, 409
Basta Callar, 76
Bataille de Dames, 474
The Bathhhhhuse, 324
Bathsheba, 134
Batrachoi, 24
The Battle of Arminius, 302
BAUM, VICKI (1888-1960), 32
The Bear, 95
Beatrice Cenci, 405
BEAUMARCHAIS, PIERRE AUGUS-
TIN CARON (1732-1799), 33
BEAUMONT, FRANCIS (1584-1616), 34
La Beaute du Diable, 134
Beautiful Sabine Women, 12
The Beaux' Stratagem, 173
The Beaver Coat, 242
Becket; or, The Honor of God, 15
Becket; ou, L'Honneur de Dieu, 15
BECKETT, SAMUEL (1906-   ), 38
BECQUE, HENRI FRANCOIS, 52
Bedbug, 324
Bedtime Story, 389
Beelzebub Sonata; or, What Really Hap-
pened at Mordowar, 564
Bees on the Boat Deck, 433
Before Sunrise, 242
Before Sunset, 242

Beggar's Bush, 34
Beggar's Opera, 194
BEHAN, BRENDAN (1923-1964), 52
Behind a Conspiracy; or, The Son of Black Donald, 144
Behind the Green Curtains, 390
Die Beiden Götter, 251
Believe as You List, 346
BENAVENTE Y MARTINEZ, JACINTO (1866-1954), 54
Benefit of the Doubt, 405
BENNETT, ARNOLD (1867-1931), 55
Bérénice, 439
Il Berretto a Sonagli, 421
BESIER, RUDOLF (1878-1942), 56
Bespridannitsa, 403
Der Besuch der Alten Dame, 146
Bethsabé, 204
Betrothal, 321
BETTI, UGO (1892-1953), 57
Bettine, 386
Beware of Smooth Water, 76
Bezimienne Dzieto, 564
Biberpelz, 242
Biedermann and the Firebugs, 179
Biedermann und die Brandstifter, 180
Bien Vengas, Mal, Si Vienes Solo, 76
The Big Drum, 405
Biografie, 180
Biography, 180
The Birds, 24
The Birth of Urson and Valentin, 540
Birthday Party, 409
Bishop's Bonfire, 390
Bit of Love, 187
Bittersweet, 124
Las Bizarrías de Belisa, 540
Den Blaa Pekingeser, 1
Black Comedy, 476
The Black Maskers, 12
The Blacks, 199
Blanca from Castile, 236
Blanka von Kastilien, 236
The Blind, 322
The Blind Beggar of Alexandria, 92
The Blind One, 146
Der Blinde, 147
Blithe Spirit, 124
The Blood of the Bambergs, 396
Blood Wedding, 190
Blow Your Own Trumpet, 537
The Blue Bird, 322
The Blunderer or The Mishaps, 369
Blurt, Master Constable; or, The Spaniard's Night Walk, 353
Blush of the Rose, 76
The Boars, 227
Bodas de Sangre, 191

Bödeln, 309
Body and Soul, 55
Le Boeuf sur le Toit, 110
BOLT, ROBERT (1924-   ), 58
The Bond, 517
A Bond Honoured, 396
Bondman, 347
Bonds of Interest, 54
Bonduca, 34
Les Bonnes, 200
Book of Christophe Colombus, 105
Die Bösen Köche, 231
La Bottega del Caffe, 227
Le Bourgeois de Gand; ou, Le Secrétaire du Duc d'Alba, 144
Bourgeois Gentilhomme, 369
Bourgeois Gentleman, 369
Le Bourgmestre de Stilemonde, 322
BOWEN, JOHN GRIFFITH (1924-   ), 60
Boy David, 30
Boy with a Cart, 182
Brand, 260
Brända Tomten, 517
Braut von Messina, 463
Breadwinner, 348
Break of Noon, 105
BRECHT, BERTOLT (1898-1956), 60
The Bridal Crown, 517
Bride of Messina, 463
Bridge of Europe, 455
Bright Island, 55
Britannicus, 440
Broceliande, 382
Broken Heart, 175
Broken Jug, 302
The Brothers, 530
Brott och Brott, 517
Browning Version, 447
Ein Bruderzweist in Habsburg, 236
BÜCHNER, GEORG (1813-1837), 73
La Buena Guarda, 540
The Buffoons, 52
Il Bugiardo, 227
Buoyant Billions, 481
Burgomaster of Stilemande, 322
Les Burgraves, 258
The Burned House, 517
The Burnt Flower-Bed, 57
Bussy d'Ambois, 92
But It Is Not a Serious Affair, 422
Bygmester Solness, 261

El Caballero de Milagro, 540
El Caballero de Olmedo, 540
Cabaret, 28
Los Cabellos de Absalon, 76
Cada Uno y Su Vida, 345

Caesar and Cleopatra, 481
Caesar's Wife, 348
CALDERON DE LA BARCA, PEDRO
  (1600-1681), 76
Caligula (Camus), 86
Caligula (Dumas), 144
Call of Life, 470
Calomnie, 474
Calvary, 569
Camel's Back, 349
L'Cameriera Brillante, 227
Camille, 143
Il Campiello, 227
CAMUS, ALBERT (1913-1960), 86
Candida, 482
The Candle Stick, 386
La Cantatrice Chauve, 279
Cantique de Cantiques, 206
Caps and Bells, 422
CAPEK, KAREL (1887-1945), 89
A Caprice, 386
Les Caprices de Marianne, 386
Captain Brassbound's Conversion, 483
The Captives; or, The Lost Recovered, 245
Captivi, 430
Cardinal d'Espagne, 382
Cardinal of Spain, 382
The Careless Husband, 103
The Caretaker, 411
Carmosine, 386
Carnival, 380
Caroline, 349
CARROLL, PAUL VINCENT (1900-
  ), 90
The Carthaginian, 430
Carving a Statue, 232
Casa Con Dos Puertas Mala es de Guardar,
  76
La Casa de Bernarda Alba, 191
La Casa Nova, 227
La Casa Sull'Acqua, 57
Cascando, 39
A Case of Mistaken Identity, 326
A Case of Sincerity, 326
Casina, 430
Caste, 451
El Castigo sin Venganza, 540
Castle of Perseverance, 91
The Cat and the Moon, 569
Catch as Catch Can, 15
Cathleen Listens In, 390
Cathleen ni Houlihan, 569
Cathy from Heilbronne; or, The Trial by
  Fire, 303
Catiline (Ibsen), 261
Catiline (Jonson), 290
The Caucasian Chalk Circle, 61
Los Cautivos de Argel, 540

Cavalcade, 125
The Cavalier of the Rose, 251
The Cavern, 15
Les Caves du Vatican, 204
Ce Soir à Samarcande, 134
Celles Qu 'On Prend dans Ses Bras, 383
Cendres, 39
Le Cercle, 349
El Cerco de Santa Fe, 540
Chabot, Admiral of France, 93
The Chairs, 279
Les Chaises, 281
The Chalk Garden, 29
A Challenge for Beauty, 245
The Chances, 34
Le Chandelier, 386
The Changeling, 359
Chantecler, 451
CHAPMAN, GEORGE (1539?-1634?),
  92
Charles VII and His Chief Vassals, 144
Charles VII Chez Ses Grands Vassaux, 144
A Chaste Maid in Cheapside, 353
Chayka, 95
CHEKHOV, ANTON PAVLOVICH
  (1860-1904), 95
Cher Antoine, 15
Cherry Orchard, 95
Chester Plays, 102
CHETTLE, HENRY (-d. 1607), 102
Chevaliers de la Table Ronde, 110
Chez Nous, 388
Chicken Soup with Barley, 557
Child Man, 405
Children of the Sun, 229
The Chinese Prime Minister, 29
The Chinese Wall, 180
Die Chinesische Mauer, 181
The Chioggian Brawls, 227
Chips with Everything, 557
Choephori, 4
CHRISTIE, AGATHA MILLER (1891-
  1976), 102
Christinas Heimreise, 251
Christina's Journey Home, 251
Christine à Fontainebleau, 144
The Chronicle Historie of Perkin War-
  beck, 176
Chyornye Maski, 12
Ciascuno à Suo Modo, 422
CIBBER, COLLEY (1671-1757), 103
The Cid, 117
Cinna; or, The Clemency of Augustus, 118
The Circle, 349
La Cisma de Ingleterra, 77
The City, 105
The City Madam, 347
The City Whose Prince Is a Child, 383

The Civil War, 383
CLAUDEL, PAUL LOUIS CHARLES (1868-1955), 104
Cleomenes, the Spartan Hero, 139
The Clever Lady's Maid, 227
Clitandre, 118
Clouds, 25
Cock-a-Doodle-Dandy, 390
The Cocktail Party, 151
COCTEAU, JEAN (1889-1963), 110
The Coffee House, 227
A Cold June, 405
The Collection, 413
A Collier's Friday Night, 311
Colombe, 15
La Colonie, 326
Colony, 326
Come and Go, 39
Come Prima, Meglio Di Prima, 422
Come Tu Mi Vuoi, 422
Comédie, 39
The Comedy of Seduction, 470
Los Comendadores de Cordoba, 540
The Comic Illusion, 118
The Comical Revenge; or, Love in a Tub, 161
The Commanders of Córdoba, 540
La Commère, 326
Complaisant Lover, 232
Comrades, 518
El Conde Lucanor, 77
The Condemned of Altona, 456
Confidential Clerk, 154
Conflagration, 242
CONGREVE, WILLIAM (1670-1729), 113
Conquest of Granada, 139
CONRAD, JOSEPH (1857-1924), 116
The Conspiracy and The Tragedy of Charles, Duke of Byron, 93
The Constant Couple, 174
The Constant Prince, 77
The Constant Wife, 349
Conversation Piece, 125
El Corazón Ciego, 345
Les Corbeaux, 52
Coriolan, 63
The Corn is Greene, 562
CORNEILLE, PIERRE (1606-1684), 116
Cornelia, 307
Cornelius, 433
La Corona de Hungria, 540
La Corona Merecida, 540
Corruption in the Palace of Justice, 57
Corruzione al Palazzo di Giustizia, 57
Cosí è (Se Vi Pare), 422
Count Lucanor, 77
Count Oderland, 181
Countess Cathleen, 569

Countess Mizzi; or, The Family Reunion, 470
Country People, 229
Country Wife, 565
La Coupe et les Levres, 386
COVENTRY PLAYS, 124
COWARD, NOEL PIERCE (1899-   ), 124
The Coxcomb, 34
Cradle Song, 346
The Creditors, 518
CREIGHTON, ANTHONY (n. d.), 130
Cresta Run, 504
Crime and Crime, 518
Crime on Goat Island, 57
Cristinas Heimreise, 251
Cristina's Journey Home, 251
The Critic; or, A Tragedy Rehearsed, 501
Cromwell, 258
Crown Bride, 518
Crusts, 106
Csoda a Hegyek Közt, 380
Cup and the Lip, 386
Cupid's Revenge, 34
Curculio, 430
Lo Cursi, 54
Curtmantle, 182
Curmudgeon, 352
Curtmantle, 182
The Custom of the Country, 34
Cyclops, 164
Cynthia's Revels, 291
Cyrano de Bergerac, 452

Dachniki, 230
Dage Paa en Sky, 1
La Dama Boba, 540
La Dame de Monsoreau, 144
La Dama Duende, 77
La Dame aux Camelias, 144
Damon and Phillida, 103
Dance of Death (Auden and Isherwood),
Dance of Death (Strindberg), 518
Dandy Dick, 405
Dangerous Corner, 433
Dans sa Candeur Naive, 134
Danton's Death, 73
Dantons Tod, 74
D'ARCY, MARGARETTA, 24
The Dark is Light Enough, 183
Dark Lady of the Sonnets, 484
Darkness, 242
Darlo Todo y No Dar Nada, 77
Daughter in Law, 311
Daughter of the Air, 77
The Daughter of the Cathedral, 242
DAVENANT, WILLIAM, (1606-1668), 130

David, 311
DAVISON, LAWRENCE H. (pseud), 131
Dawn, 345
A Day in the Death of Joe Egg, 388
The Days of the Commune, 63
Days on a Cloud, 1
Deadly Motorism, 432
Dear Antoine, 16
Dear Brutus, 30
Death and the Fool, 252
The Death of Cuchulain, 570
The Death of Dr. Faust, 203
Death of Pompey, 119
Death of Tarelkin, 525
The Death of Tintagiles, 322
The Death of Titian, 252
Death Without Burial; or, Men Without
   Shadows, 457
Deathwatch, 200
DESCASALIAS, JEANNE (n. d.), 115, 131
Deep Blue Sea, 447
Deirdre, 575
Deirdre of the Sorrows, 525
DEKKER, THOMAS (1570-1641), 131
DELANY, SHELAGH (1939-   ), 133
Delicate Story, 380
Delitto all Isola delle Capre, 57
Demain Il Fera Jour, 383
Demetrius, 463
Le Demoiselles de Saint Cyr, 144
Le Dénouement Imprévu, 326
Le Dépit Amoureux, 370
The Deputy, 247
La Dernière Bande, 39
La Dernière Nuit de Don Juan, 453
Desert Highway, 433
The Deserved Crown, 540
Design for Living, 125
Deti Solntsa, 230
Der Deutsche Hinkemann, 532
DEVAL, JACQUES (1890-   ), 134
Devil, 380
The Devil and the Good Lord, 458
Devil Came from Dublin, 90
Devil is an Ass, 291
The Devils, 558
Devil's Disciple, 484
The Devil's Lawcase; or, When Women
   Go to Law, the Devil is Full of Business,
   546
La Dévotión de la Cruz, 78 & 87
Devotion to the Cross, 78 & 87
Le Diable et le Bon Dieu, 458
Dial "M" for Murder, 306
Diana and Tuda, 422
The Didactic Play of Baden: On Consent,
   63
Dido, Queen of Carthage, 341

The Difficult Man, 252
Dinner with the Family, 16
The Direction of the March, 2
Dirty Hands, 458
La Dispute, 326
Dr. Faustus, 330
Dr. Harmer's Holidays, 405
The Doctor in Spite of Himself, 370
The Doctor's Dilemma, 484
The Doctor's Duty, 422
Dödsdansen, 519
The Dog Beneath the Skin; or, Where is
   Francis?, 28
The Dog in the Manger, 540
Dokhodnoye Mesto, 403
Doll's House, 261
Dom Garcie de Navarre; ou, Le Prince
   Jaloux, 370
Don Carlos, Infante of Spain, 463
Don Carlos, Prince of Spain, 403
Don Garcia of Navarre; or, The Jealous
   Prince, 370
Don Juan, 55 and 383
Don Juan oder die Liebe zur Geometrie,
   181
Don Juan; or, The Feast with the Statue,
   371
Don Juan; or, The Love of Geometry, 181
Don Juan; ou, Le Festin de Pierre, 372
Don Lope de Cardona, 540
Don Perlimplin, 192
Don Sanche d'Aragon, 119
Don Sebastian, 140
Doña Rosita la Soltera, 191
Doña Rosita the Spinster, 191
Los Donaires de Matico, 541
Don't Awaken Madame, 16
Dorothea Angermann, 242
Do   gaeff and the Others, 230
The Double Dealer, 113
The Double Gallant, 103
La Double Inconstance, 326
The Double Inconstancy, 326
Dover Road, 362
Il Dovere del Medico, 422
Dragon's Mouth, 436
Drayman Henschel, 242
A Dream (But Perhaps It Isn't), 422
A Dream Is Life, 236
Dreaming of the Bones, 571
Dream Play, 519
Dreigroschenoper, 63
Ett Drömspel, 520
Druga Vrata Levo, 432
Druid's Rest, 563
Drums in the Night, 63
Drums of Father Ned, 391
Drums Under the Window, 391

DRYDEN, JOHN (1631-1700), 136
Duchess of Malfi (Webster), 547
Duchess of Padua, 559
Duel of Angels, 206
Duenna, 501
Duke in Darkness, 241
The Duke of Guise, 143
The Duke of Viseo, 541
Et Dukkehjem, 262
DUMAS, ALEXNDRE, fils, (1824-1895), 143
DUMAS, ALEXANDRE, pere (1803-1870), 144
Dumbwaiter, 414
El Duque de Viseo, 541
DURRELL, LAWRENCE (1912-   ), 146
DURRENMATT, FRIEDRICH (1921-   ), 146
Dutch Courtesan, 343
The Dwarfs, 414
Dyadya Vanya, 97
DYER, CHARLES (1923-   ), 151
The Dybbuk, 446
Dyskolos, 352

Each in His Own Way, 422
The Eagle Has Two Heads, 110
East of Suez, 350
Easter, 520
Eastward Ho!, 344
Easy Virtue, 125
The Eccentric One, 471
Ecclesiazusae; or The Women in Council, 26
l'Echange, 106
Echo and Narcissus, 78
Eco y Narciso, 78
L'Ecole des Femmes, 372
l'Ecole des Maris, 372
l'Ecole des Mères, 326
Eden End, 433
Edward II (Brecht), 63
Edward II (Marlowe), 330
Egi ès Földi Szerelem, 380
Egmont, 212
Egor Bulychev and Others, 230
Egy, Kettö, Härom, 380
The Egyptian Helen, 253
Eh Joe, 39
Die Ehe des Herrn Mississippi, 147
Einsame Menschen, 242
Der Einsame Weg, 471
Ejemplo de Casadas, 541
Elder Statesman, 154
Electra (Euripides), 164
Electra (Giraudoux), 206
Electra (Hofmannsthal), 253

Electra (Sophocles), 509
Elektra, 242
ELIOT, THOMAS STARNES (1888-1965), 151
Embers, 39
Emilia Galotti, 312
Emperor and the Galilean, 262
The Emperor and the Witch, 253
The Emperor of the East, 347
En Attendant Godot, 40
En Esta Vida Todo es Verdad y Todo Mentira, 78
The Enchanted, 207
Enchanted Cottage, 405
The End of the Beginning, 391
End of the Party, 40
Endgame, 40
Endimion, the Man in the Moon, 319
Enemy of the People, 263
l'Enfant Prodigue, 52
Ein Engel Kommt Nach Babylon, 147
English Traveler, 245
Enrico IV, 422
Enter a Free Man, 516
Entertainer, 396
l'Envers d'Une Conspiration; ou, Le Fils de Donald le Noir, 144
Epicoene, or The Silent Woman, 291
Epidicus, 430
Epitaph for George Dillon, 402
Epitrepontes, 352
l'Epreuve, 326
Equus, 476
Ermine, 16
Die Ermittlung, 552
Errand for Bernice, 134
Es Steht Geschrieben, 147
Escape, 137
El Esclavo de Roma, 541
Escurial, 203
La Estatua de Promcteo, 78
Esther, 237 and 441
L'État de Siége, 87
ETHEREGE, GEORGE (1635-1691), 161
Etienne, 134
L'Etourdi, 372
L'Etre Invisible, 309
Eugenie, 33
The Eumenides, 4
Eunuch, 531
EURIPIDES (485 B. C.-406 B. C.), 162
Eurydice, 16
Eva Aftjener Sin Barnepligt, 1
Eva Serves Her Time as a Child, 1
An Evening's Love, 138 & 140
Ever Since Paradise, 433
Every Man in His Humor, 292
Every Man Out of His Humor, 293

Everyman (Hofmannsthal), 253
Everyman, 172
Evil Done to Us, 54
The Example for Married Women and the
    Test of Patience, 541
The Exchange, 106
L'Exil, 383
Exile, 383
Exiled, 188
Exiles, 299
Exit the King, 281
The Explorer, 350

Fadren, 520
Fair Game, 471
The Fair Penitent, 454
A Fair Quarrel, 361
The Fairs of Madrid, 541
The Fairy Lady, 78
The Fairy Tale, 471
A Faithful Servant of His Master, 237
The Faithful Shepherdess, 34
The Faithful Wife, 326
Fallen Angels, 126
False Astrologer, 79
False Confessions, 326
The False Servant, 327
Die Familie Schroffenstein, 303
Die Familie Selicke, 256
The Family of Love, 354
Family Man, 188
Family Reunion, 155
Family Strife in Hapsburg, 237
The Fan, 227
The Fancies, Chaste and Noble, 176
Fanny's First Play, 485
Fantasio, 386
Faraway Princess, 453
A Farkas, 380
FARQUHAR, GEORGE (1678-1707), 173
Farsang, 380
The Fatal Dowry, 348
The Father, 520
The Father of a Family, 227
A Father, Prudent and Just; or, Crispin,
    the Jolly Rogue, 327
Father Setubal, 322
La Fausse Suivante, 327
Les Fausses Confidences, 327
Faust, 212
The Feast at Solhaug, 263
Félicie, 327
La Femme Fidèle, 327
Un Femme Libre, 455
Les Femmes Savantes, 372
Las Ferias de Madrid, 541
The Festival of Bacchus, 471
The Festival of Our Lord of the Ship, 422

The Feud of the Schroffensteins, 303
Les Fiancailles, 322
Les Fiances du Havre, 455
La Fianza Satisfecha, 541
FIELD, NATHAN, 174
Fiesco; or, The Conspiracy of Genoa, 464
Fighting Cock, 16
Une Fille du Régent, 144
Fils de Personne, 383
Fin de Partie, 42
Film, 42
Lo Fingido Verdadero, 541
Fink und Fliederbusch, 471
Finnegan's Wake, 301
Die Finsternisse, 243
The Firstborn, 183
Five Finger Exercise, 476
Flare Path, 448
FLETCHER, JOHN (1579-1625), 34, 175
The Flies, 459
The Flood, 231
Florian Geyer, 243
Flowering Cherry, 58
La Foire d'Empoigne, 17
En Folkenfiende, 263
La Folla de Chaillot, 208
The Follies of Marianne, 387
Follow My Leader, 451
The Fop Reformed, 327
For Lucretia, 208
For Services Rendered, 350
For the Honour of Wales, 294
For the Time Being, 28
FORD, JOHN (1579-1625), 175
Fordringsägare, 521
The Forest, 188 and 403
Forget Me Not Lane, 389
Fortunas de Andromeda y Perseo, 79
The Fortunate Son, 541
Fortune by Land and Sea, 247
Fortunes of Andromeda and Perseus, 79
Four Plays for Dancers, 571
The Four Seasons, 557
Les Fourberies de Scapin, 372
Fourth Wall, 362
Frana allo Scalo Nord, 57
Frank der Fünfte, 147
Frank the Fifth, 147
Frau Carrars Gewehre, 64
Frau Ohne Schatten, 254
The Freaks, 406
The Free Thinker, 314
Free Woman, 455
Freeway, 389
Das Friedensfest, 243
Der Freigeist, 314
Freiwild, 471
French Without Tears, 448

Frenetiques, 455
Frenzied Ones, 455
Friar Bacon and Friar Bungay, 234
The Friends, 557
FRISCH, MAX (1911-   ), 179
The Frogs, 26
Fröken Julie, 521
From Bad to Worse, 79
Fru Inger til Ostraat, 263
Fruen fra Havet, 263
Fruits of Enlightenment, 533
FRY, CHRISTOPHER (1907-   ), 182
Fuente Ovejuna, 541
Fugitive, 188
Fuhrmann Henschel, 243
A Full Moon in March, 571
Furcht und Elend des Dritten Reiches, 64
The Future is in Eggs; or, It Takes All
    Sorts to Make a World, 281

El Gálan de la Membrilla, 542
Galathea, 320
La Galerie du Palais, 119
Galileo, 64
The Gallant of La Membrilla, 542
Gallantries of Belisa, 542
GALSWORTHY, JOHN (1867-1933), 187
The Gambler, 58
The Gamblers, 226
A Game at Chesse, 354
The Game of Love and Chance, 327
Gammer Gurton's Needle, 515
Der Gang zum Weiher, 471
GARCIA LORCA, FEDERICO (1898-
    1936), 189
La Gata de Angora, 54
GAY, JOHN (1685-1732), 194
Gay Lord Quex, 406
Die Gefährtin, 471
GÈNET, JEAN (1910-   ), 197
Geneva, 485
Gengangere, 263
Gente Conocido, 54
Gentle Jack, 59
Gentleman Dancing Master, 567
The Gentleman Usher, 94
Georges Dandin, 372
Germanen und Romer, 243
Das Gerettete Venedig, 254
Gertie, 29
Gesang vom Lusitanischen Papang, 552
Gestern, 254
Getting Married, 486
Die Gewehre der Frau Carrar, 64
GHELDERODE, MICHEL DE (1898-
    1962), 203
Ghost Sonata, 521
Ghosts, 264

GIDE, ANDRE (1869-1951), 204
I Giganti della Montagna, 422
Gildet Paa Solhaug, 265
Il Giocatore, 58
GIRAUDOUX, JEAN (1882-1944), 205
Girl from Samos, 352
Girl With No Dowry, 403
Girls and Boys, 406
Il Giuoco delle Parti, 422
Give Everything or Nothing, 79
Give Me Yesterday, 362
Gjengangere, 265
The Glass Cage, 433
Glass of Water; or, Causes and Effects, 474
GLAZER, BENJAMIN F. (n. d.), 33 & 212
GOETHE, JOHAN W. VON (1749-1832),
    212
Goetz Von Berlichingen, 222
GOGOL,   NIKOLAI   VASILYEVICH
    (1809-1852), 226
The Golden Fleece, 238
The Golden Harp, 243
Die Goldene Harfe, 243
Das Goldene Vliess, 238
GOLDONI, CARLO (1707-1793), 227
GOLDSMITH, OLIVER (1728-1774), 229
GOLDSMITH, PETER 229
The Goldwinged Duck, 432
El Golfo de las Sirenas, 79
Good Companions, 436
Good Custodian, 542
Good Fairy, 380
Good-Natured Man, 229
Good Woman of Setzuan, 65
Goodnight, Children, 434
Gorboduc, or Ferrex and Porrex, 389
GORKI, MAXIM (1868-1936), 229
The Gossip, 327
Graf Oderland, 181
Grafting, 422
El Gran Duque de Gandia, 79
Le Gran Duc de Moscou, 542
El Gran Teatro del Mundo, 79
Grand Duke of Gandia, 79
Grand Hotel, 32
La Grande et la Petite Manoeuvre, 2
GRANVILLE-BARKER, HARLEY
    GRANVILLE (1877-1946), 231
GRASS, GUNTER (1927-   ), 231
Great Adventure, 55
Great and Small Maneuver, 2
The Great Broxopp, 362
The Great Highway, 522
The Great Show, 471
The Great Theatre of the World, 80
Great World Theatre of Salzburg, 254
The Greatest Virtue of a King, 542
Greek Man Seeks Greek Maiden, 147

Green Cockatoo, 471
Green Goddess, 22
The Green Helmet, 571
Green Room, 325
GREENE, GRAHAM (1904-   ), 232
GREENE, ROBERT (1560-1592), 234
GREENWOOD, WALTER (1903-   ),
    235
Grieche Sucht Griechin, 147
GRILLPARZER, FRANZ SERAFIN
    (1791-1872), 236
Grossen Wurstel, 471
La Grotte, 17
The Grouch, 353
Der Grune Kakadu, 471
Guardate del Agua Mansa, 80
The Guardsman, 381
Guerillas, 249
La Guerra, 227
La Guerre Civile, 384
La Guerre de Troie n'Aura pas Lieu, 208
The Guilty Mother, 33
Gulf of the Sirens, 80
Gustav, III, 522
Der Gute Mensch von Sezuan, 66
Gypsies Metamorphosed, 294

Haermaendene Paa Helgeland, 265
Halbzwei, 471
Hall of Healing, 391
Halfway Up the Tree, 537
HAMILTON, PATRICK (1904-1962), 241
Hamlet, Prince of Denmark, 243 and 144
Hamlet in Wittenberg, 243
Han Som Fick Leva Oun Sitt Liv, 309
Hands Around, 471
The Hangman, 310
Hannibal, 327
Happy Days, 42
Happy Haven, 22
Harlequin Polished by Love, 327
Harlequinade, 448
Harold Muggins Is a Martyr, 22
Hats Off!, 432
A Hattyú, 381
HAUGHTON, WILLIAM (-d. 1605), 242
HAUPTMANN, GERHART J. R. (1862-
    1946), 242
Haute Surveillance, 201
HAWKES, J. H. (1910-   ), 245
Hay Fever, 126
He Was Born Gay, 563
He Who Gets Slapped, 12
Heart to Heart, 448
Hearbreak House, 486
Heautontimorumenos, 531
Hecuba, 165
Hecyra, 531

Hedda Gabler, 265
Die Heilage Johanna des Schlachthofe, 66
Hekabē, 165
Helen, 165
Henri III et Sa Cour, 145
Henry III and His Court, 145
Henry IV, 422
Hepta epi Thebas, 5
Her Cardboard Lover, 135
Heraclaidae, 166
Heracles, 166
Heraclius, 119
Hēraklēs, 166
Hercules and the Augean Stables, 147
Hercules Furens (Seneca), 474
Hercules Oetaeus, 475
l'Heritier du Village, 327
Die Hermannsschlacht, 303
La Hermosa Ester, 542
Hernani, 258
The Herne's Egg, 572
Hero and Leander, 238
The Hero Rises Up, 22
Herr Puntila und Sein Knecht Matti, 66
L'Heureux Stratageme, 327
HEYWOOD, THOMAS (1570-1641), 245
Hidden Horizons, 102
High Balcony, 537
La Hija del Aire, 80
El Hijo de Reduan, 542
El Hijo Venturoso, 542
Hiketides, 166
Himlens Hemlighet, 310
Himmelrikets Nycklar, Eller Sankte Per
    Vandrar Pâ Jorden, 522
Hinkemann, 532
Hippes, 26
Hippolytus, 166
His Helpmate, 472
His House in Order, 406
His Own Judge, 80
Histoire de Rire, 455
l'Histoire de Tobie et Sara, 106
The Historie of Orlando Furioso; One of
    The Twelve Peeres of France, 235
Historiomastix, 343
The Hobby Horse, 406
HOCHHUTH, ROLF (1931-   ), 247
Hochwasser, 231
HOFMANNSTHAL, HUGO VON (1874-
    1929), 250
Der Hofmeister, 66
HOLBERG, LUDVIG (1684-1754), 256
Hölderlin, 552
The Hole, 505
The Hollow, 102
The Holy Terrors, 111
HOLZ, ARNO (1863-1929), 256

El Hombre Pobre Todo Es Trazas, 80
Home at Seven, 503
Home Chat, 126
Home is Tomorrow, 434
HOME, WILLIAM DOUGLAS (1912-), 256
Homecoming, 415
Un Homme Comme les Autres, 455
Honest Whore, 131
Honeymoon, 56
Les Honnêtes Femmes, 52
The Honorable Historie of Friar Bacon and Friar Bungay, 235
Hop, Signor!, 203
Hoppla! Such is Life, 532
Hoppla! Wir Leben!, 532
Horace, 119
Horatius, 119
The Hostage (Behan), 52
The Hostage, (Claudel), 106
Hotel in Amsterdam, 397
The Hour Glass, 572
Hour of Recognition, 472
House of Bernarda Alba, 191
House of Regrets, 537
The House on the Water, 58
House with Two Doors Is Difficult to Guard, 80
HOUSMAN, LAURENCE (1865-1959), 257
HOWARD, ROBERT (n. d.), 257
HUGO, VICTOR MARIE, COMTE (1802-1885), 205-07, 258
Huis-Clos, 460
The Human Voice, 111
La Humildad y La Soberbia, 542
The Humiliation of the Father, 107
Humility and Pride, 542
The Humorous Lieutenant, 35
Hungarian Crown, 542
Hunger and Thirst, 281
L'Hurluberlu, 17
HYDE, DOUGLAS, 260

I Have Been Here Before, 434
I Knock at the Door, 391
IBSEN, HENRIK (1828-1906), 260
Ideal Husband, 559
Idiot Lady, 542
If Five Years Passes,
If Not So; or, Other People's Reasons, 423
Igroki, 226
Il Etait une Gare, 135
Il Ne Faut Jurer de Rien, 387
An Ill Beginning Has a Good End, 176
I'll Leave It to You, 126
Ill Met by Moonlight, 321
l'Ile de la Raison, 327

L'Ile des Esclaves, 328
L'Illusion Comique, 120
Im Dickicht der Staedte, 66
I'm Talking About Jerusalem, 557
The Imaginary Invalid, 373
The Imbecile, 424
Importance of Being Earnest, 560
L'Impromptu de Paris, 208
L'Impromptu de L'Alma, ou, Le Caméléon du Berger, 282
Improvisation, or, The Shepherd's Chameleon, 282
Imprudence, 406
In Chancery, 406
In Good King Charles's Golden Days, 488
In Praise of Love, 448
In the Jungle of the Cities, 66
In the Shadow of the Glen, 526
In This Life, Everything Is Both True and False, 80
Inadmissible Evidence, 397
Un Incompris, 384
L'Inconnue d'Arras, 455
The Inconstant; or, The Way to Win Him, 174
The Incorruptible Man, 254
Indian Emperor; or, The Conquest of Mexico by the Spaniards, 140
Indian Queen, 143
Infernal Machine, 111
The Inheritance, 328
The Inn of the Court, 543
l'Innesto, 424
Insect Play, 90
An Inspector Calls, 434
Inspector General, 226
Los Intereses Creados, 54
Interior, 322
Intermezzo, 208
Intimate Relations, 112
The Intruder, 323
L'Intruse, 323
L'Invasion, 2
Investigation, 552
The Invisible One, 310
L'Invitation au Chateau, 17
l'Invitation à la Valse, 145
Ion, 168
IONESCO, EUGENE (1912-), 278
Iphigeneia è en Aulidi, 168
Iphigeneia è en Taurois, 168
Iphigenia in Aulis, 168
Iphigenia in Delphi, 243
Iphigenia in Tauris (Goethe), 223
Iphigenia in Tauris (Euripides), 169
Iphigenie, 441
Iris, 406
An Irish Faustus, 146

The Irkutsk Story, 21
Irkutskaya Istoriya, 21
Iron Duchess, 256
Ironmaster, 406
ISHERWOOD, CHRISTOPHER (1904-), 286
Island Fling, 126
The Island of Reason, 328
The Island of Slaves, 328
Island of the Mighty, 22 & 24
The Island Princess, 35
Isle of the Dead, 522
L'Isola Meravigliosa, 58
It Is Enough to Keep Silent, 80
It is Written, 147
Ivanov, 97
Ivory Door, 362

Jack Drumm's Entertainment, 343
Jack or the Submission, 282
Jacob and Esau, 537
Jacques ou la Soumission, 282
James IV, 235
Játek a Kastélyban, 381
Jeanne d'Arc au Bùcher, 107
Jedermann, 254
JELLICOE, ANN (1927-   ), 286
Jeppe of the Hill, 256
Jeppe Paa Bjerget, 256
JEROME, JEROME KLAPKA, (1859-1928), 287
Le Jeu de l'Amour et du Hasard, 328
La Jeune Fille Violaine, 107
La Jeunesse de Louis XIV, 145
Jeux de Massacre, 282
Jews of Malta, 331
Jewess of Toledo, 239
The Jews, 314
Jezabel, 17
A Jó Tundér, 381
Joan of Arc at the Stake, 107
John Bull's Other Island, 488
John Gabriel Borkman, 268
Johnson Over Jordan, 434
La Joie Imprévue, 328
JONSON, BENJAMIN (1572-1637), 287
The Journalists, 557
Journey's End, 503
Joy Unforeseen, 328
JOYCE, JAMES (1882-1941), 299
Joyzelle, 323
Die Juden, 314
Judith (Abell), 1
Judith (Bennett), 56
Judith (Giraudoux), 208
Die Judin von Toledo, 239
Le Jugement Dernier, 323
Jumpers, 516

Der Junge Gelehrte, 314
Der Junge Medardus, 472
Die Jungfrau von Orleans, 464
Juno and the Paycock, 391
The Just Assassins, 88
Les Justes, 87
Justice, 188
Justice Without Revenge, 543

K Zvezdam, 12
Kabale und Liebe, 464
Der Kaiser und die Hexe, 254
Kameliadamen, 1
Kamraterna, 522
Kape Dole, 433
Das Kätchen von Heilbronn oder die Feuer-
    probe, 303
Katerina, 12
Katilina, 268
Der Kaukasische Kreidekreis, 67
Kean; or, Disorder and Genius, 460
Kean, ou, Désordre et Génie, 460
Keep the Widow Waking, 131
Kejser og Galilaeer, 269
Keys of Heaven; or, St. Peter Wanders on
    the Earth, 522
The Killer, 282
The Killing of Sister George, 325
The Kind Keeper; or, Mr. Limberham, 141
Kindred, 90
The King, 310
King and No King, 35
The King and the Farmer, 543
King Arthur; or, The British Worthy, 141
King Candaules, 204
King Edward the Fourth, 245
King Oedipus, 575
King Ottakar, His Rise and Fall, 239
The King of the Great Clock Tower, 572
King, the Greatest Alcalde, 543
The King Without a Kingdom, 543
Kingdom of God, 345
King's Threshold, 575
Kiss for Cinderella, 31
The Kitchen, 558
Kjaemphoien, 269
Kjoerlighedens Komedia, 269
Das Kleine Welttheater, 254
KLEIST, HEINRICH VON (1777-1811),
    301
Klop, 324
The Knack, 286
The Knight from Olmedo, 543
Knight of Malta, 35
Knight of The Burning Pestle, 35
Knights, 26
Knights of the Round Table, 112
KNOBLOCK, EDWARD (1874-1945), 56

KNOTT, FREDERICK (n. d.), 306
Komödie der Verführung, 472
Komtesse Mizzi; oder, Der Familientag, 472
König Ottakars Glück und Ende, 239
Kongs-Emnerne, 269
Krapp's Last Tape, 44
Kronbruden, 522
Kurka Wodna, 564
KYD, THOMAS (1557?-1595?), 307
Kyklōps, 169

Laburnum Grove, 434
Ladies of St. Cyr, 145
Lady Bountiful, 406
Lady Frederick, 350
The Lady from Belle Isle, 145
Lady from Monsoreau, 145
Lady from the Sea, 269
LADY GREGORY, 309
Lady Inger of Ostraat, 209
Lady Windermere's Fan, 561
The Lady with the Camelias, 144
The Lady's Last Stake, 103
Lady's Not For Burning, 184
Lady's Trial, 176
LAGERKVIST, PAR FABIAN (1891-1974), 309
Land of Heart's Desire, 572
The Land of Promise, 350
Landed Gentry, 350
Landscape, 417
Landslide at North Station, 58
Lark, 17
Last Joke, 29
Last Judgment, 323
The Last Man, 310
Last Masks, 472
The Last Night of Don Juan, 454
Låt Människan Leva, 310
Launzi, 381
El Laurel de Apolo, 80
LAWRENCE, DAVID HERBERT (1885-1930), 311
Lazarus, 424
The League of Youth, 269
The Learned Ladies, 373
Leben des Galilei, 67
Das Leben ein Traum, 254
La Leçon, 283
LEE, NATHANIEL (n. d.), 312
Left-Handed Liberty, 23
The Legacy, 472
Legend of Lovers, 18
LEGOUVE, ERNEST (1807-1903), 312
Le Legs, 328
Lenoir Archipelago; or, One Must Not Touch Immobile Things, 455

Léocadia, 18
Leonce and Lena, 75
La Lepra de Constantino, 80
Les, 403
Leshy, 97
LESSING, GOTTHOLD EPHRAIM (1729-1781), 312
The Lesson, 283
Let Man Live, 310
Letter, 351
Letty, 407
Die Letzten Masken, 472
The Liar (Corneille), 120
The Liar (Goldoni), 228
Libation Bearers, 5
Libussa, 239
Liebelei, 472
Life I Gave You, 424
Life in My Hands, 538
Life is a Dream, 80
The Life of Man, 13
The Life of St. Peter Nolasco, 544
Light of Heart, 563
Light of Love, 472
Liliom, 381
Lille Eyolf, 269
Linden Tree, 434
Liola, 424
The Lion in Love, 133
Literature, 472
The Litigants, 442
Little Eyolf, 269
Little Theater of the World, 254
Live Like Pigs, 23
Livet, 310
Living Corpse, 533
The Living Room, 233
Le Livre de Christophe Colomb, 107
Lo Que Ha De Ser, 544
La Locandiera, 228
Los Locos de Valencia, 544
London Life, 56
Lonely Lives, 243
The Lonely Way, 472
The Long Mirror, 435
Long Sunset, 504
Look After Lulu, 126
Look Back in Anger, 398
Lorelei, 135
Lorenzaccio, 387
Lorenzino, 145
Lost Ones, 45
Lottie Dundass, 30
Love and a Bottle, 174
Love and Intrigue, 464
Love and Truth, 328
Love for Love, 113
Love in a Wood; or, St. James Park, 567

Love in Idleness, 448
Love Makes a Man, 103
Love Match, 56
The Love of Don Perlimplin for Belisa in
  His Garden, 192
Love of Four Colonels, 538
Love Triumphant, 141
The Lover, 417
Lover's Melancholy, 176
Lover's Progress, 36
Love's Comedy, 270
Love's Cure; or The Martial Maid, 36
Love's Last Shift, 103
Love's Metamorphosis, 320
Love's Sacrifice, 176
The Lower Depths, 230
Loyalties, 188
Lucius Junius Brutus, 312
The Lucky One, 362
Lucky Per's Journey, 522
Lucky Strategem, 328
Lumié di Sicilia, 424
Luther, 400
Lycko-Pers Resa, 522
LYLY, JOHN (1554-1606), 319
Lysistrata, 26

Ma Non è Una Cosa Seria, 424
La Machine à Ecrire, 112
La Machine Infernale, 112
Machine Wreckers, 532
MACLIAMMOIR, MICHAEL (1899-
  ), 321
Mad Lover, 36
A Mad World, My Masters, 355
Madame Legros, 325
Madame Pepita, 345
Mademoiselle, 135
Mademoiselle de Belle Isle, 145
Mademoiselle Jaire, 203
The Madman and the Nun, 564
Madmen of Valencia, 544
The Madwoman of Chaillot, 208
MAETERLINCK, MAURICE (1862-
  1949), 321
The Magic of an Hour, 54
El Magico Prodigioso, 82
Magie Rouge, 203
The Magistrate, 407
The Magnetic Lady; or, Humours Recon-
  ciled, 294
Magnificent Lover, 373
MAIAKOVSKII, VLADIMIR VLAD-
  IMIROVICH (1894-1930), 324
The Maid in the Mill, 36
Maid of Andros, 531
The Maid of Honour, 347
The Maid of Orleans, 465

Maid Violaine, 107
A Maidenhead Well Lost, 246
The Maids, 201
Maid's Tragedy, 36
The Maidservant, 120
Les Mains Sales, 460
Le Maître de Santiago, 384
Major Barbara, 488
Make-Believe Becomes Truth, 544
Makropoulos Secret, 89
El Mal Que Nos Hacen, 55
La Malade Imaginaire, 374
Malatesta, 384
Malcontent, 343
Maleficio de la Mariposa, 192
Le Malentendu, 88
Le Malquerido, 55
Mama, 345
Man and Boy, 449
Man and Superman, 490
Man, Beast and Virtue, 424
A Man for all Seasons, 59
Man From Ghent, 145
Man in the Glass Booth, 500
Man in the Raincoat, 538
Man Like the Others, 455
Man of Destiny, 492
Man of Honour, 351
Man of Mode; or, Sir Fopling Flutter, 161
Man to Man, 449
The Man Who was Given His Life to Live
  Again, 310
The Man with a Flower in His Mouth, 424
The Man Without a Soul, 311
Mañanas de Abril y Mayo, 82
MANN, HEINRICH (1871-1950), 325
Mann ist Mann, 67
Mannen Utan Själ, 311
Man's a Man, 67
Marat/Sade, 553
Marauders, 523
Das Märchen, 472
Marching Song, 559
MARCUS, FRANK (1928-   ), 325
Le Mari de la Veuve, 145
Maria Stuart, 466
Le Mariage d'Argent, 474
Le Mariage de Figaro, 33
Un Mariage Sous Louis XV, 145
Mariana Pineda, 192
Les Maries de la Tour Eiffel, 112
Marion Delorme, 259
MARIVAUX, PIERRE CARLET DE
  CHAMBLAIN DE (1688-1763), 325
MARLOWE, CHRISTOPHER (1564-
  1593), 330
Marodörer, 523
MARQUINO, EDUARDO (1879-1946),

342
Marquise, 127
Marriage, 226
Marriage à la Mode, 141
Marriage for Money, 474
A Marriage of Convenience: Period Louis
    XV, 145
Marriage of Figaro, 33
Marriage of Mr. Mississippi, 147
Marriage Story, 135
Marriages Are Made in Heaven, 351
MARSTON, JOHN (1575?-1634), 342
MARTINEZ SIERRA, GREGORIO
    (1881-1947), 345
MARTINEZ SIERRA, MARIA (1880-
    ), 346
Mary Magdalene, 323
Mary Rosé, 31
Mary Tudor, 259
Maschinenstürmer, 533
The Masque of Augurs, 294
The Massacre at Paris, 333
Masse Mensch, 533
Masses and Man, 533
MASSINGER, PHILIP (1583-1640), 346
Die Massnahme, 68
Master Builder, 270
The Master of Santiago, 384
Master Olof, 523
Matka, 89
Die Matrone von Ephesus, 314
A Matter of Gravity, 30
MAUGHAM, W. SOMERSET (1874-
    1965), 348
MAURICE, ANTHONY (n. d.), 352
MAYAKOVSKY, VLADIMIR V., 352
Mayfair, 407
El Mayor Alcalde, el Rey, 544
El Mayor Impossible, 544
El Mayor Monstruo los Celos, 82
The Mayor of Quinborough; or, Hengist,
    King of Kent, 355
Mayor of Zalamea, 82
La Mayor Virtud de un Rey, 544
The Measures Taken, 68
Medea, 169
Médée (Anouilh), 18
Médée (Corneille), 120
Médée (Seneca), 475
Le Médecin Malgré Lui, 374
El Médico de su Honra, 83
Medved, 97
Des Meeres und der Liebe Wellen, 240
Meet the Prince, 362
Mélite, 121
MELMOTH, SEBASTIAN (pseud), 352
Melodien, der Blev Vaek, 1
The Melody that Got Lost, 1

The Menaechmi, 431
MENANDER (342 BC-291 BC), 352
Le Menteur, 121
La Méprise, 328
La Mère Confidente, 328
La Mère Coupable, 34
Merry Go Round, 52 and 312
El Meson de la Corte, 544
Mesyats v Derevne, 536
The Meteor, 148
Michael Kramer, 244
Michael and Mary, 362
Michaelmas Term, 355
Michel Pauper, 52
Midas, 320
Mid-Channel, 407
MIDDLETON, THOMAS (1580-1627),
    353
Midsummer, 523
Midsommardrom i Fattighuset, 311
Midsummer Night's Dream in the Work-
    house, 311
Miles Gloriosus, 431
Milestones, 56
Millionairess, 492
MILNE, ALAN ALEXANDER (1882-
    1956), 362
Mine Hostess, 228
Minna von Barnhelm; or, The Soldier's
    Fortune, 315
Miracle in the Mountains, 381
MIRACLE, MORALITY AND MYS-
    TERY PLAYS, 363
Misalliance, 492
Misanthrope, 374
The Miser, 376
Miss Julie, 533
Miss Mabel, 504
Miss Sara Sampson, 316
The Mistaken Husband, 141
Mr. Fox of Venice, 306
Mister, Mister, 231
Mr. Pim Passes By, 363
Mr. Prohack, 66
Mr. Puntila and His Hired Man, 68
Misteriya-Buff, 324
Mrs. Morli, One and Two, 424
Mrs. Mouse Are You Within?, 325
The Mistress of the Inn, 228
Mrs. Warren's Profession, 493
The Misunderstanding, 88
Misunderstood, 384
Mithradate, 442
The Mob, 189
The Mohocks, 196
Moi Bednyi Marat, 21
MOLIERE, JEAN BAPTISTE POQUE-
    LIN (1622-1673), 368

MOLNAR, FERENC(1878-1952), 380
Moment of Truth, 538
Monna Vanna, 323
Monsieur D'Olive, 94
Monsieur de Pourceaugnac, 376
Les Monstres Sacrés, 112
A Month in the Country, 536
MONTHELANT, HENRY DE (1896-1972), 382
MORAVIA, ALBERTO (pseud), 386
More Dissemblers Besides Women, 356
Morning Star, 563
Mornings in April and May, 83
La Morsa, 424
La Mort de Pompee, 121
La Mort de Tintagiles, 323
Mortimer, His Fall, 294
Morts Sans Sépulture, 460
Mostellaria, 431
Mother, 89
The Mother as a Confidante, 328
Mother Bombie, 320
Mother Courage and Her Children, 68
The Mother; Life of the Revolutionary Pelagea Vlassova from Tver, 68
Mother-in-Law, 531
Mots et Musique, 45
Les Mouches, 460
The Moutain Giants, 424
Mourning Bride, 114
Mousetrap, 102
La Moza de Cantaro, 544
A Murder Has Been Arranged, 563
Murder in the Cathedral, 157
Music at Night, 435
MUSSET, LOUIS CHARLES ALFRED DE (1810-1857), 386
Die Mutter; Leben der Revolutionären Pelegea Wlassove aus Twer, 70
Mutter Courage und Ihre Kinder, 70
My Son's My Son, 312
Mystery-Bouffe, 325

Na Bolshoy Doroge, 97
Na Dne, 230
Nachtasyl, 230
El Nacimiento de Urson y Valentin, 544
Naked; or, To Clothe the Naked, 425
Nannie's Night Out, 392
Nar Vi Döde Vagner, 271
Nathan der Weise, 316
Nathan the Wise, 316
The National Health, 389
The Natural Daughter, 225
Die Natürliche Tochter, 225
La Navette, 52
Ne Réveillez pas Madame, 18
Les Negres, 202

Nekrassov, 460
Nephelai, 27
The New Colony, 425
The New House, 228
The New Inn, 294
The New Tenant, 284
New Way to Pay Old Debts, 347
New Year's Night, 472
NICHOLS, PETER (1928-   ), 388
Nicomède, 121
El Nido Ajeno, 55
Night, 418
A Night in the Rich Man's House, 58
Night Lodging, 230
Night Must Fall, 563
A Night Out, 418
Night School, 418
Nights of Wrath, 455
No Exit, 461
No Hay Más Fortuna que Dios, 83
No Man's Land, 418
No Man's Son, 384
No Monster Like Jealousy, 83
No One Knows How, 425
No Trifling With Love, 388
No Sign of the Dove, 538
No Wit, No Help Like a Woman's, 356
Noble Gentleman, 36
La Noche del Sábado, 55
Non Si Sa Come, 425
The Non-Juror, 103
NORTON, THOMAS (1532-1584), 389
Not I, 45
Notorious Mrs. Ebbsmith, 407
Notte in Casa del Ricco, 58
Le Nouveau Locataire, 284
Now They Sing Again, 182
Nude with a Violin, 127
La Nuit Vénitienne; ou, Les Noces de Laurette, 388
Nuits de la Colére, 455
Nun Singen Sie Wieder, 182
La Nuova Colonia, 425

Oak Leaves and Lavender, 392
Oaths All Too Rashly Taken, 328
O'CASEY, SEAN (1884-1964), 389
The Ocean, 13
Octavia, 475
Oedipe (Corneille), 121
Oedipus (Gide), 204
Oedipus (Seneca), 475
Oedipus and the Sphinx, 255
Oedipus at Colonus, 510
Oedipus Rex (Cocteau), 112
Oedipus Rex, (Sophocles), 510
Oedipus und die Sphinx, 255
Off Limits, 2

Oh, Brother!, 135
Oh, Les Beaux Jours!, 45
Okean, 13
Olaf Liljekrans, 271
O Mistress Mine,
L'Oiseau Bleu, 323
The Old Bachelor, 114
Old English, 189
Old Foolishness, 90
Old Fortunatus, 131
The Old Law, 361
The Old Ones, 558
Old Times, 418
Ombre Chère, 135
On Baile's Strand, 576
On Ne Badine Pas Avec L'Amour, 388
On the Frontier, 29
On the High Road, 97
On the Rocks, 494
On with the Dance, 127
Ondine, 209
One Thirty, 473
One, Two, Three, 381
One Way Pendulum, 505
ONI, 564
Onkel, Onkel, 231
The Only Jealousy of Emer, 572
Le Onzième Commandement, 135
Operette, 127
Az Ordög, 382
Orestes, 170
Orestia, 5
Orlando Furioso, 235
Ornifle, ou le Courant d'Air, 18
Ornithes, 27
The Orphan; or, The Unhappy Marriage, 403
Orphée, 112
Orpheus, 112
OSBORNE, JOHN JAMES (1929-   ), 396
Den Osynlige, 311
OSTROVSKY, ALEXANDER NIKOLAI-VICH (1823-1886), 403
O'Otage, 107
Other People's Lives, 363
Other Son, 425
Othon, 121
Ottakar,
OTWAY, THOMAS (1652-1685), 403
Our Betters, 351
L'Ours et la Lune, 107
The Outrageous Saint, 544
Outward Bound, 539
Over-Ruled, 494
Overture, 539
The Ox on the Roof, 112

Las Paces de los Reyes y Judia de Toledo, 545
Il Padre di Famiglia, 228
Le Pain Dur, 107
The Painter of His Own Dishonor, 84
The Palace Corridor; or, The Rival Friend, 121
The Palace of Sadness, 345
El Palacio Triste, 345
Pantaglieze, 203
Paolo Paoli, 2
Paracelsus, 473
Parasitaster; or, The Fawn, 344
Les Paravents, 202
Les Parents Terribles, 113
The Pariah, 524
Paris Impromptu, 210
Paris Not So Gay, 538
La Parisienne, 52
La Parodie, 3
Partage de Midi, 107
Pasiphae, 384
Päsk, 524
The Passing of the Third Floor Back, 287
Passion Flower, 55
Patchouli, 455
Patient Grissil, 133
Patriot for Me, 401
Pauken und Trompeten, 70
Pauvre Bitos, ou Le Dinêr des Têtes, 18
Peace, 27
Peace in Our Time, 127
The Peace of Kings and the Jewess of Toledo, 545
Peer Gynt, 271
Pelléas et Mélisande, 323
Penny for a Song, 559
Pensaci, Giacomino!, 425
Penthesilea, 303
People at Sea, 435
People of Our Acquaintance, 55
Peor Está que Estaba, 83
Le Pere Humilié, 107
La Père Prudent et Equitable, 328
Perfect Alibi, 363
Peribanez y el Comendador de Ocana, 545
Perikeiromene, 353
Perkin Warbeck, 176
Perolla and Izadora, 104
El Perro del Hortelano, 545
Persa, 431
Persae, 7
Persecution and Assassination of Marat as Performed by the Inmates of the Asylum of Charenton under the Direction of the Marquis de Sade, 556
El Perseo, 545
Perséphone, 204

The Persians, 7
Persistence Until Death, 545
Pertharite, Roi des Lombards, 121
Pertharites, King of the Lombards, 121
Peter Pan, 31
Le Petit Maitre Corrige, 328
Phèdre (Racine), 443
Phèdre (Seneca), 475
Philanderer, 494
Philastre, 36
Philoctetes, 204 and 514
The Philosopher's Stone, 311
Philotas, 318
Phoenician Women, 170
The Phoenix, 185 and 356
A Phoenix Too Frequent, 185
Phoinissai, 171
Phormio, 531
Photo Finish, 538
The Physicists, 148
Die Physiker, 149
Il Piacere dell' Onesta, 425
The Picture (Ionesco), 284
The Picture (Massinger), 348
Pictures in the Hallway, 392
Pierette's Veil, 473
Le Piéton de l'Air, 284
Pietro Aretino, 75
Pillars of Society, 273
PINCHERLE, ALBERTO (1907-   ),
    405
PINERO, ARTHUR WING (1855-1934),
    405
Le Ping-Pong, 3
PINTER, HAROLD (1932-   ), 409
El Pintor de su Deshonra, 84
PIRANDELLO, LUIGI (1867-1936), 421
Pirette's Veil, 473
Pizarro, 501
La Place Royale, 121
Les Plaideurs, 446
The Plain Dealer, 567
Platanov; or, A Country Scandal, 97
PLAUTUS, TITUS MACCIUS (254 B. C.-
    184 B. C.), 429
Play, 45
Play Strindberg, 149
Playboy of the Western World, 526
Player Queen, 573
Playgoers, 407
Play's The Thing, 382
The Pleasure of Honesty, 425
Pleasure Reconciled to Virtue, 294
Die Plebejer Proben den Aufstand, 231
Plebians Rehearse the Uprising, 231
Los Pleitos de Ingalaterra, 545
Plody Prosveshcheniya, 533
Plough the Stars, 392

Pluto, 27
Plutus Triumphant, 328
Pobrecito Juan, 345
Poenulus, 431
The Poetaster; or, The Arraignment, 295
Point Valaine, 127
Les Polichinelles, 52
Polly, 196
Polyeycte, 122
Le Pont de l'Europe, 456
Poor Bitos, 18
Poor John, 345
Poor Judas, 30
POPOVIC, ALEKSANDAR (1929-   ),
    432
Porfiar Hasta Morir, 545
Port-Royal, 384
Portrait of a Planet, 149
Possessed, 88
Post Mortem, 127
The Potting Shed, 233
Pound on Demand, 393
Port Lucrèce, 210
Poverty Sharpens the Wits, 84
The Power of Darkness; or, "If a Claw is
    Caught, the Bird is Lost", 533
The Power of the Dead, 324
Prayer for the Living, 135
Les Précieuses Ridicules, 376
Le Préjuge Vaincu, 328
Prekrasnye Sabinyanki, 13
Present Laughter, 127
Preserving Mr. Panmure, 407
The Pretenders, 274
Prière Pour les Vivants, 135
PRIESTLEY, JOHN BOYNTON (1894-
    ), 433
The Prince in Disguise; or, The Illustrious
    Imposter, 328
Le Prince Travesti; ou, L'Illustre Aventur-
    ier, 329
La Princesa Bebe, 55
Princess and the Butterfly, 407
Princess Bebe, 55
La Princesse d'Elide, 376
La Princesse Lointaine, 454
La Princesse Maleine, 324
El Principe Constante, 84
Le Printemps, 3
The Prisoners of Altona,
Prinz Friedrich von Homburg, 304
The Private Ear and the Public Eye, 477
Private Life of the Master Race, 70
Private Lives, 128
The Private Tutor, 70
Prodigal Son, 52
Le Professeur Taranne, 3
Professor Bernhardi, 473

A Profitable Job, 403
The Profligate, 407
Prometheus Bound, 8
Prometheus' Statue, 84
The Promise, 21
The Phophetess, 37
Protée, 107
Proteus, 107
The Provincial Lady, 329
La Provinciale, 329
The Provok'd Husband, 104
Der Prozess der Jeanne d'Arc zu Rouen,
    1431, 70
Prunella; or, Love in a Garden, 257
Pseudolus, 431
Psyché, 124 and 380
The Public Square, 228
El Publico, 193
La Puissance des Morts, 324
Pulchérie, 123
The Puppet Play of Don Cristobal, 193
Purgatory, 573
Purple Dust, 393
La Purpura de la Rose, 84
La Putain Respectueuse, 462
Pygamalion, 494
Pyesa Bez Nazvaniya, 97

Quadrille, 128
Quality Street, 32
Quare Fellow, 53
Lo Que Ha de Ser, 544
The Queen, 177
Queen After Death, 385
The Queen of Corinth, 37
The Queen of the Rebels, 58
Queen Was in the Parlor, 129
Queen's Gambit; or, A Duel of Love, 474
Questa Sera si Recita a Soggetto, 425
QUINAULT, PHILIPPE, 436

RUR; Rossum's Universal Robots, 89
RACINE, JEAN BAPTISTE, (1639-1699),
    436
Ralph Roister Doister, 537
Rape of Lucrece, 246
RAPPOPORT,   SOLOMON,   (1863-
    1920), 446
Rat Trap, 129
The Rats, 244
Die Ratten, 244
RATTIGAN, TERRENCE (1911-   ),
    447
Die Räuber, 466
The Real Inspector Hound, 516
The Reconciliation, 244
The Recruiting Officer, 174
The Rector; The Story of Four Friends,
    408
Red Magic, 204
Red Roses for Me, 394
Reduan's Son, 546
The Refusal; or, The Ladies' Philosophy,
    104
The Regent's Daughter, 145
La Regina e Gli Insorti, 58
The Rehearsal, 18
Reigen, 473
La Reine Morte; ou, Comment on tue les
    Femmes, 385
El Reino de Dios, 346
Relative Values, 129
Reluctant Debutant, 257
Le Rendezvous de Senlis, 19
Renegado; or, The Gentleman of Venice,
    348
Le Repos du Septieme Jour,   107
Requiem for a Nun, 89
The Resistible Rise of Arturo Ui, 70
Resounding Tinkle, 505
The Respectful Prostitute, 462
The Restless Heart, 19
The Resurrection, 574
Retabillo de Don Cristobal, 193
Return Journey, 56
Return of A. J. Raffles, 234
La Reunion des Amours, 329
The Revenge of Bussy d'Ambois, 94
Revenger's Tragedy, 534
Revizor, 227
El Rey Sin Reino, 546
Rhesus, 171
Rhinoceros, 284
Richard's Cork-Leg, 54
Riders to the Sea, 528
The Ridiculous Snobs, 376
Right You Are, If You Think You Are, 425
Ring Round the Moon, 19
Rise and Fall of the City of Mahagonny, 71
The Rival Fools, 104
The Rival Ladies, 141
The Rival Queens, 104 and 312
The Rivals (Davenant), 130
The Rivals (Sheridan), 501
Road to Happiness, 346
The Roaring Girl; or, Moll Cut-Purse, 359
The Robbers, 466
Robert Guiskard, 306
Robert; ou, L'Intérêt Général, 204
ROBERTSON,   THOMAS   WILLIAM
    (1829-1871), 451
The Rock, 160
Rodogune, 123
The Rogueries of Scapin, 377
La Roi Candaule, 205
Le Roi Se Meurt, 285

Roma Abrasada, 546
The Roman Actor, 348
Les Romanesques, 454
Romanoff and Juliet, 538
Romantic Young Lady, 346
The Romantics, 454
Rome Burned, 546
Romeo et Jeanette, 19
Romulus, 145
Romulus der Grosse, 149
Romulus the Great, 149
La Ronde, 473
Roof, 189
Room, 418
Roots, 558
Rope's End, 241
Rosalind, 32
Rosas de Otono, 55
Rose Bernd, 244
La Rose de Septembre, 136
Rosencrantz and Guildenstern Are Dead, 516
Der Rosenkavalier, 255
Rosmersholm, 274
Ross, 449
ROSTAND, EDMOND (1864-1918), 451
Rosy Rapture, 32
Der Rote Hahn, 244
Roundabout, 435
The Roundheads and the Peakheads, 71
ROWE, NICHOLAS (1674-1718), 454
ROWLEY, WILLIAM (1585?-1642?), 454
The Royal Hunt of the Sun, 477
The Royal King and the Loyal Subject, 246
Rudens, 432
Der Ruf des Lebens, 473
Rule a Wife and Have a Wife, 37
Rules of the Game, 426
Die Rundköpfe und die Spitzköpfe, 71
Rusteghi, 228
Ruy Blas, 259

Sacred and Profane Love, 56
Sacred Flame, 351
SACKVILLE, THOMAS (1536-1608), 454
Sagra del Signore della Nave, 426
St. Helena, 504
St. Joan, 496
St. Joan of the Stockyards, 71
St. John's Eve, 275
Saint's Day, 559
SALACROU, ARMAND (1899-   ), 454
Salome, 561
Das Salzburger Grosse Welttheater, 255
La Samaritaine, 454
Samfundets Stotter, 275
Samia, 353

Samson in Chains, 13
Samson v Okovakh, 13
Sancthansnatten, 275
Santa Cruz, 182
Sappho (Durrell), 146
Sappho (Grillparzer), 240
Sapho and Phao, 320
Sarah Simple, 363
SARTRE, JEAN PAUL (1905-   ), 456
Satin Slipper, 107
Saturday Night, 55
Saul, 205
La Sauvage, 20
Savva (Ignis Sanat), 13
Savva; or, Fire Cures, 13
The Scandalous Affair of Mr. Kettle and Mrs. Moon, 435
Der Schatz, 319
SCHILLER, JOHANN CHRISTOPH FRIEDRICH VON (1759-1805), 463
Schism of England, 84
SCHLAF, JOHANNES, 470
Der Schleier der Pierrette, 473
SCHNITZLER, ARTHUR (1862-1931), 470
The School Boy, 104
The School for Husbands, 377
A School for Mothers, 329
School for Scandal, 502
School for Wives, 377
The School Mistress, 408
Die Schwestern; oder, Casanova in Spa, 473
Schweyk im Zweiten Weltkrieg, 72
Schweyk in the Second World War, 72
Der Schwierige, 255
Scornful Lady, 37
The Scottish Historie of James IV, 235
The Scream, 1
The Screens, 202
SCRIBE, AUGUSTIN EUGENE (1791-1861), 474
Se Non Cosi; o, La Ragione Degli Altri, 426
Sea Gull, 97
A Seat in the Park, 408
Second Door Left, 433
Second Maiden's Tragedy, 357
Second Mrs. Tanqueray, 408
The Second Surprise of Love, 329
La Seconde Surprise de l'Amour, 329
Secret Agent, 116
Secret Love; or, The Maiden Queen, 141
The Secret of Heaven, 311
Secret Vengeance for Secret Insult, 84
A Secreto Agravio, Secreta Venganza, 84
Sei Personaggi in Cerca d'Autore, 426
Sejanus, 295
Self-Tormentor, 531

SEMPLE, LORENZO, JR. (n. d.), 474
SENECA, LUCIUS ANNAEUS (3 B. C.-65 A. D.), 474
Señora Carrar's Rifles, 72
Le Sens de la Marche, 3
Separate Tables, 449
Les Sept Princesses, 324
Septem Contra Thebas, 10
Sequel to the Liar, 123
Les Séquestrés d'Altona, 462
Serjeant Musgrave's Dance, 23
Les Serments Indiscrets, 329
Sertorius, 123
Servant of Two Masters, 228
Il Servitore di Due Padroni, 228
Seven Against Thebes, 10
Seven Deadly Sins, 72
Seven Princesses, 324
Shadow and Substance, 90
Shadow of a Gunman, 394
The Shadowy Waters, 574
SHAFFER, PETER LEVIN (1926-   ), 476
Shall We Join the Ladies?, 32
SHAW, GEORGE BERNARD (1856-1950), 478
SHAW, ROBERT (1927-   ), 500
She Stoops to Conquer, 229
She Wou'd and She Wou'd Not, 104
She Would If She Could, 161
The Shearing of Glycera, 353
Sheppey, 351
SHERIDAN, RICHARD BRINSLEY BUTLER (1751-1816), 501
SHERRIFF, ROBERT CEDRIC (1896-   ), 503
Shewing Up of Blanco Posnet, 498
The Shoemakers, 564
The Shoemaker's Holiday, 132
The Shoemaker's Prodigious Wife, 193
Shore Leave, 456
Show, 189
Shred of Evidence, 504
La Sibila del Oriente, 84
Sibyl of the Orient, 84
Sicilian Limes, 426
Die Sieben Tödsünden, 72
The Siege of Rhodes, 131
Siege of Santa Fe, 546
Siegfried, 210
Sigh No More, 129
La Signora Morli, Una e Due, 426
Silence, 419
Silkeborg, 1
Silver Box, 189
The Silver Tassie, 395
The Simpleton of the Unexpected Isles, 498
SIMPSON, ALAN, 54

SIMPSON, NORMAN F. FREDERICK (1919-   ), 504
The Sincere Ones, 329
Les Sincères, 329
Sir Fopling Flutter, 162
Sir Harry Wildair, 174
Sir Martin Marall; or, The Feign'd Innocence, 142
Sir Miracle Comes a Cropper, 546
Sirocco, 129
Sista Mänskan, 311
Sister Beatrice, 324
The Sisters; or, Casanova in Spa, 473
Six Characters in Search of an Author, 426
Skin Game, 189
Slander, 474
Slave of Rome, 546
A Sleep of Prisoners, 186
Sleeping Prince, 450
Slight Ache, 420
Smert Tarelkin, 525
Smrtonosna Motoristika, 433
Sodom and Gomorrah, 210
Soeur Beatrice, 324
Sogno (Ma Forse No), 428
La Soif et al Faim, 285
Die Soldaten, 249
The Soldiers, 249
The Soldier's Fortune, 404
Someone Waiting, 563
Somov i Drugie, 230
Somov and Others, 230
Sonata Belzebuba, Czyli Prawdziwe Zdarzenie w Mordowarze, 564
A Song at Twilight, 129
Song of Songs, 210
Song of the Lusitanian Bogey, 556
Vor Sonnenuntergang, 244
SOPHOCLES (496 B. C.-406 B. C.), 505
Sophonisba, 312
Sophonisbe, 123
Soul Triumphant, 55
Le Soulier de Satin, 109
The Spanish Friar, 142
Spanish Gypsy, 361
Spanish Tragedy, 307
Spekes, 27
Splendors of Hell, 204
The Sport of My Mad Mother, 287
Spring, 71, 3
Spring, 1600, 563
Squire Jonathan, 24
Staircase, 151
The Staple of News, 296
The Star Turns Red, 395
Den Starkare, 524
Stasera Si Recita a Soggetto, 428
The State of Innocence, 142

State of Siege, 89
Stella, 225
Der Stellvertreter, 250
STEVENSON, WILLIAM (-d. 1575?), 515
Stichus, 432
STOPPARD, TOM (1937-   ), 516
Stora Landsvägen, 524
The Stranger, 503
STRINDBERG, AUGUST (1849-1912), 517
Strings, My Lord, Are False, 91
The Stroller in the Air, 285
The Stronger, 524
Stunde des Erkennens, 473
A Subject of Scandal and Concern, 402
Success, 363
Sueño de Una Noche de Agosto, 346
Sueños Hay que Verdad Son, 84
La Suite de Menteur, 123
La Suivante, 123
SUKHOVO - KOBYLIN, ALEXANDER VASILEIVICH (1817-1903), 525
Summer Day's Dream, 435
Summer Night, 33
Summerfolk, 231
Summertime, 58
Supplement au Voyage de Cook, 210
The Sunken Bell, 244
The Suppliants (Aeschylus), 11
The Suppliants (Euripides), 171
Surena, 123
Surgeon of his Honor, 84
La Surprise de l'Amour, 329
The Surprise of Love, 329
The Survivors, 231
Svadba, 99
Svanevit, 524
Den Svåra Stunden, 311
The Swan, 382
Swanwhite, 524
Sweeney Agonistes, 160
Sweet Lavender, 408
Sylvesternacht, 473
SYNGE, JOHN MILLINGTON (1871-1909), 525
Szewcy, 564

Le Tableau, 286
Der Tage der Commune, 72
Tamburlaine the Great, 333
Tartuffe; or, The Hypocrite, 378
A Taste of Honey, 133
TCHEKHOV, ANTON, 530
Tea Party, 420
The Tempest; or, The Enchanted Island, 143
Ten Little Indians, 102
The Tenth Man, 352

TERENCE (PUBLIUS TERENTIUS AFER) (195 B. C.-159 B. C.), 530
La Terre Est Ronde, 456
The Test, 329
La Testament de Cesar, 145
A Testör, 382
Tête d'Or, 109
La Thébaide; ou, Les Frères Ennemis, 446
The Thebans; or, The Enemy Brothers, 446
Their Very Own and Golden City, 558
Theodora, Virgin and Martyr, 123
Theodore, Vierge et Martyre, 123
There Are Dreams that Are True, 85
Thesmophoriazusae, 27
They, 564
They Came to a City, 435
They Don't Mean Any Harm, 363
Thierry and Theodoret, 37
Thieves' Carnival, 20
Things That are Caesar's, 91
Think It Over, Giacomino!, 428
Thirty-two Teeth, 232
This Happy Breed, 129
This Year of Grace, 129
THOMAS, DYLAN MARLAIS (1914-1953), 531
Thor, With Angels, 182
Thou Shalt Not Lie, 240
The Three Greatest Marvels, 85
Three Penny Opera, 72
Three Sisters, 99
Thunderbolt, 408
Thyestes, 475
The Tidings Brought to Mary, 109
Tiger and the Horse, 60
Tiger at the Gates, 210
Till Damaskus, 524
Time and the Conways, 435
Time of Vengeance, 58
Time Present, 402
Time Remembered, 20
Time to Go, 395
The Times, 408
Tinker's Wedding, 529
Tis Pity She's a Whore, 177
Tite et Bérénice, 123
The Title, 56
To Damascus, 524
To Find Oneself, 428
To Have the Honor, 363
To the Stars, 13
Tobias and Sara, 110
Die Tochter der Kathedrale, 244
Der Tod des Tizian, 255
TOLLER, ERNST (1893-1939), 532
TOLSTOY, LEV (LEO) NIKOLAEVICH (1828-1910), 533
Tomorrow the Dawn, 385

Tonight at 8:30, 130
Tonight in Samarkand, 136
Tonight We Improvise, 428
Too True to be Good, 499
Der Tor und der Tod, 255
Torquato Tasso, 225
La Torre de Babilonia, 85
Tot, Kto Poluchayet Poshchechiny, 13
Touch and Go, 312
Tour à Terre, 456
TOURNEUR, CYRIL (1575?-1626), 534
Tous Ceux Qui Tombent, 46
Tous Contre Tous, 3
Tovaritch, 136
Towards Zero, 102
The Tower, 255
Tower of Babylon, 85
TOWNLEY PLAYS, 536
Trachiniae, 515
The Tragedy of Caesar and Pompey, 94
Tragedy of Dido, Queen of Carthage, 341
Tragedy of Nero, Emperor of Rome, 312
Tragical History of Dr. Faustus, 336
The Tragical History of King Richard III, 104
Transfiguration, 533
The Transformation of Pierrot, 473
Der Traum ein Leben, 241
Traveller Without Luggage, 20
Travesties, 517
The Treasure, 319
Le Treizième Arbre, 205
Trelawny of the Wells, 408
Los Tres Mayores Prodigios, 85
Trespass, 563
Ein Treuer Diener seines Herrn, 241
Tri Sestry, 100
Trial of Joan of Arc at Rouen, 1431, 72
Trial of Lucullus, 72
A Trick to Catch the Old One, 357
Trinummus, 432
Le Triomphe de l'Amour, 329
Le Triomphe de Plutus, 329
The Triumph of Love, 329
Triumph of Plutus, 329
Troiades, 172
Troilus and Cressida; or, Truth Found Too Late, 142
The Trojan War Will not Take Place, 212
Trojan Women, 172
Trommeln in der Nacht, 73
Trotsky in Exile, 556
Troubled Waters, 58
Trovarsi, 429
Truculentus, 432
The True Friend, 228
True Lover, 546
Trumpets and Drums, 73

The Truth About Blayds, 363
The Trying Hour, 311
Tsar Golod, 13
Tsar Hunger, 13
Tueur Sans Gages, 286
Turandot oder der Kongress der Weisswaseher, 73
Turandot; or, The Congress of the White Washers, 73
Turandot, Princess of China, 467
TURGENEV, IVAN SERGEYVICH (1818-1883), 536
Der Turm, 255 and 556
Tutto per Bene, 429
Twin Rivals, 174
Two Kinds of Love Reconciled, 329
Two Noble Kinsmen, 37
Typewriter, 113
Tyrannick Love, 142

UDALL, NICHOLAS (1505-1556), 537
Die Überspannte Person, 473
Der Unbestechliche, 255
Uncle, Uncle, 232
Uncle Vanya, 100
Under Milk Wood, 531
Under Plain Cover, 402
Unexpected Guest, 102
The Unforeseen Solution, 329
De Unges Forbund, 275
Unicorn from the Stars, 576
Unknown, 352
Unknown Girl, 382
Unknown Soldier and His Wife, 539
Unknown Woman of Arras, 456
L'Uomo, la Bestia e la Virtu, 429
L'Uomo dal Fiore in Bocca, 429
USTINOV, PETER (1921-   ), 537
Utva Ptica Zlatorkrila, 433

Va-et-vient, 46
The Valencian Widow, 546
Valentinian, 38
La Valse des Toreadors, 20
Le Vampire, 145
VANE, SUTTON (1888-1963), 539
Variation on a Theme, 450
The Vatican Swindle, 205
Vec Makropulos, 70
VEGA CARPIO, LOPE FELIX DE (1562-1635), 540
Veland, 244
Venice Preserv'd (Hofmannsthal), 255
Venice Preserv'd (Otway), 404
A Venetian Night; or, Laurette's Wedding, 388
Il Ventaglio, 228
Ventôse, 136

Venus Observed, 187
Vera; or, The Nihilists, 562
El Verdadero Amante, 546
Die Verfolgung und Ermordung Jean Paul
  Marats Dargestellt Durch die Schau-
  spielgruppe des Hospizes zu Charenton
  unter Auleitung des Herrn de Sade, 557
Das Verhör des Lukullus, 73
Das Vermächtnis, 473
VERNER, GERALD (n. d.), 102
Il Vero Amico, 228
Verre d'Eau, 474
Die Verschwornung des Fiesco zu Genua,
  467
Die Versunkene Glöcke, 244
Die Verwandlungen des Pierrot, 473
A Very Woman, 348
Vessels Departing, 564
Vestire gli Egnudi, 429
Vetsera Blomster Ikke for Enhver, 2
La Veuve, 123
Victimes du Devoir, 286
Victims of Duty, 286
Victoria Regina, 257
The Victors, 462
Victory, 116
Victory Over Prejudice, 329
La Vida de San Pedro Nolasco, 546
La Vida es Sueño, 85
Vietnam Discourse, 557
Vikings of Helgeland, 275
Vildanden, 275
Village Heir, 330
Village Wooing, 499
El Villano en su Rincón, 546
La Ville, 110
La Ville Dont le Prince Est un Enfant, 386
The Viper and Her Brood, 357
The Virgin Martyr, 348
Virtuous Island, 212
Virtuous Women, 52
The Vise, 429
Den Vises Sten, 311
Vishnyovy Sad, 101
The Vision of Delight, 296
The Visit, 150
La Vita che ti Diedi, 429
La Viuda Valenciana, 546
Vivat! Vivat Regina!, 60
Vlast Tmy, Ili "Kogotok Wyaz, Vsey
  Pitchke Propast", 534
La Voix Humaine, 113
Volpone, or the Fox, 296
Vor Sennenaufgang, 244
Vortex, 130
Le Voyageur sans Bagage, 20
Vulgarity, 55
The Vultures, 52

Wait Until Dark, 306
Waiting for Godot, 46
Waiting in the Wings, 130
Walk to the Pond, 473
Wallenstein, 467
The Waltz of the Toreadors, 21
Die Wandlung, 533
The War, 228
Wariat i Zakonnica, Czyli Nie Ma Ztego Co
  By Na Jeszcze Gorsze Nie Wyszto, 564
Warrior's Barrow, 275
Wars of Pompey and Caesar, 94
The Wasps, 27
The Water Hen, 565
The Waters of Babylon, 24
Waters of Madrid, 546
Way of the World, 115
Wayward Saint, 91
The Weaker Sex, 409
The Weavers, 245
Die Weber, 245
WEBSTER, JOHN (1580?-1625), 546
Wedding, 101
Wedding on the Eiffel Tower, 113
Weh Dem, Der Lugt!, 241
WEISS, PETER (1916-   ), 552
Der Weisse Facher, 256
Das Weite Land, 473
Welcome, Trouble, If You Come Alone, 85
The Well of the Saints, 530
WESKER, ARNOLD (1932-   ), 557
West of Suez, 402
The What D'Ye Call It, 197
What Every Woman Knows, 32
What Must Be, Must Be, 546
What You Will, 344
When Five Years Passes, 193
When the Music Stops, 456
When the War Came to an End, 182
When We Are Married, 436
When We Dead Awaken, 275
Where Stars Walk, 321
Where There is Nothing, 576
While the Sun Shines, 450
White Carnation, 504
White Countess, 436
The White Devil, 549
The White Fan, 256
White Lies; White Liars, 478
White Steed, 91
WHITING, JOHN (1915-1963), 558
Who is Sylvia, 450
Whore of Babylon, 132
Who's Who in Hell, 539
The Wicked Cooks, 232
The Wide Country, 474
The Widow, 124 and 357
Widower's Houses, 499

The Widowing of Mrs. Holroyd, 312
The Widow's Husband, 146
The Widow's Tears, 95
Die Wiedertaufer, 151
A Wife for a Month, 38
The Wild Duck, 276
The Wild Gallant, 143
Wild Goose Chase, 38
WILDE, OSCAR FINGAL O'FLA-
HERTIE WILLS (1856-1900), 559
Wilhelm Tell, 468
William Tell, 468
WILLIAMS, EMLYN (1905-   ), 562
Wind of Heaven, 564
Windfall, 504
Windows, 189
The Winslow Boy, 450
Wipe-out Games, 286
Wise Have Not Spoken, 91
Wit at Several Weapons, 38
Wit Without Money, 38
The Witch, 357
The Witch of Edmonton, 133 & 178
The Witchery of the Butterfly, 193
Within the Gates, 395
WITKIEWICZ, STANISLAW IGNACY
(1885-1939), 564
Witness for the Prosecution, 102
The Wits, 131
Witty Sayings of Matico, 546
The Wolf, 382
The Woman Hater; or, The Hungry Court-
ier, 38
Woman in the Moon, 321
A Woman Killed with Kindness, 246
Woman of No Importance, 562
The Woman of Paris, 52
Woman of Samaria, 454
Woman Without a Shadow, 256
Woman's Wit; or, The Lady in Fashion,
104
Women Beware Women, 358
Women of Trachis, 515
Women One Takes in One's Arms, 386

The Wonder of Women; or, Sophronisba,
344
The Wonder Working Magician, 85
Wonderful Island, 58
The Wood Demon, 101
Words and Music (Beckett), 51
Words and Music (Coward), 130
The Words Upon the Windowpane, 574
The Workhouse Donkey, 24
World Is Round, 456
World of Paul Slickey, 402
World We Live In, 90
Woyzeck, 75
Write Me a Murder, 307
WYCHERLY, WILLIAM (1640-1716),
565

Xerxes, 104
Ximena, 104

YEATS, WILLIAM BUTLER (1865-1939),
568
Yegor Bulitchev and Others, 231
Yerma, 193
Yes, M'Lord, 257
Yesterday's Magic, 564
YORK PLAYS, 576
You Can't Be Sure of Anything, 388
You Never Can Tell, 500
Young Idea, 130
The Young Medardus, 474
The Young Scholar, 319
Your Five Gallants, 358
Youth of Louis XIV, 146

La Zapatera Prodigiosa, 194
Der Zerbrochene Krug, 306
Zhenitba; Sovershenno Neveroyatnoye
Sobytiye, 227
Zhivoy Trup, 534
Zhizn' Cheloveka, 13
Zweiunddreissig Zahne, 232
Zykovy, 231